Interviewing
and Change Strategies
for Helpers 8e

SHERRY CORMIER
West Virginia University

PAULA S. NURIUS
University of Washington

CYNTHIA J. OSBORN
Kent State University

CENGAGE
Learning®

Australia • Brazil • Mexico • Singapore • United Kingdom • United States

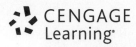

Interviewing and Change Strategies for Helpers, Eighth Edition

Sherry Cormier, Paula S. Nurius, Cynthia J. Osborn

Product Director: Jon David Hague

Product Manager: Julie Martinez

Content Developer: Elizabeth Momb

Product Assistant: Stephen Lagos

Marketing Manager: Margaux Cameron

Content Project Manager: Rita Jaramillo

Art Director: Vernon Boes

Manufacturing Planner: Judy Inouye

Production Service: Charu Khanna at MPS Limited

Text and Cover Designer: John Walker

Cover Image: Garry Gay/Getty Images

Compositor: MPS Limited

For product information and technology assistance, contact us at **Cengage Learning Customer & Sales Support, 1-800-354-9706**

For permission to use material from this text or product, submit all requests online at **www.cengage.com/permissions**
Further permissions questions can be e-mailed to **permissionrequest@cengage.com**

Library of Congress Control Number: 2015959070

Student Edition:

ISBN: 978-1-305-27145-6

Loose-leaf Edition:

ISBN: 978-1-305-86641-6

Cengage Learning
20 Channel Center Street
Boston, MA 02210
USA

Cengage Learning is a leading provider of customized learning solutions with employees residing in nearly 40 different countries and sales in more than 125 countries around the world. Find your local representative at **www.cengage.com**

Cengage Learning products are represented in Canada by Nelson Education, Ltd.

To learn more about Cengage Learning Solutions, visit **www.cengage.com**

Purchase any of our products at your local college store or at our preferred online store **www.cengagebrain.com**

Printed in the United States of America
Print Number: 01   Print Year: 2016

In memory of Sherry's parents, Bill and Edith Keucher,

Sherry's spouse, Jay H. Fast,

Paula's mother, Gwyndolyn Medley Garner,

and Cynthia's parents, Noel and Emma Ruth Osborn;

and in honor of Dick Mitchell, Cynthia's spouse, and Bill Garner,

Paula's brother, with grateful appreciation and affection.

About the Authors

Sherry Cormier is Professor Emerita in the Department of Counseling, Rehabilitation Counseling, and Counseling Psychology at West Virginia University in Morgantown, West Virginia. She is a licensed psychologist in the state of West Virginia. Her current research and practice interests are in counseling and psychology training and supervision models, health, wellness, stress management, and grief recovery. She is the mother of two 30-something daughters and the grandmother of a 10-year-old granddaughter. She enjoys yoga, walks on the beach, and kayaking in her Chesapeake Bay community.

Paula S. Nurius is the Grace Beals Ferguson Scholar, Professor, and Associate Dean in the School of Social Work at the University of Washington in Seattle. Dr. Nurius is a mental health specialist with research, practice, and teaching addressing perception and responding under conditions of stress and trauma. She brings particular concern for vulnerable, marginalized populations and toward fostering prevention and resilience-enhancing interventions. Her current scholarship focuses on childhood and cumulative life course stress, including impacts of maltreatment, nonviolent adversity, and poverty on physical, mental, and behavioral health disparities. She enjoys the outdoor life of the Pacific Northwest with her husband, daughter, and schnoodle pooch.

Cynthia J. Osborn is Professor of Counselor Education and Supervision at Kent State University in Kent, Ohio. She is a licensed professional clinical counselor and a licensed chemical dependency counselor in Ohio. Her research, clinical practice, and teaching have focused on addictive behaviors and counselor supervision from the perspectives of motivational interviewing and solution-focused therapy. Additional scholarship has addressed case conceptualization and treatment planning skills and stamina and resilience in behavioral health care. She enjoys reading character novels and practicing yoga, and she and her husband together enjoy exercising and the company of their Bichon Frisé dog, Jake.

Contents

CHAPTER 5

Influencing Responses 139

CHAPTER 6

Assessing and Conceptualizing Client Problems and Contexts 177

CHAPTER 7

Conducting an Interview Assessment with Clients 215

CHAPTER 8

Constructing, Contextualizing, and Evaluating Treatment Goals 251

CHAPTER 9

Clinical Decision-Making and Treatment Planning 302

CHAPTER 10

Models for Working with Resistance 336

CHAPTER 11

Cognitive Change Strategies 379

CHAPTER 12

Cognitive Approaches to Stress Management 425

CHAPTER 13

Self-Calming Approaches to Stress Management 460

CHAPTER 14

Exposure Therapy for Anxiety, Fear, and Trauma 491

CHAPTER 15

Self-Management Strategies 528

Preface

The eighth edition of *Interviewing and Change Strategies for Helpers* reflects a number of changes. The new edition represents a blending of our collective expertise in counseling, psychology, social work, and health and human services. Our partnership in these interdisciplinary areas augments the book's responsiveness to the unique perspectives of each discipline while also working at the interface or nexus, addressing cross-cutting issues and commitments. This book is intended to be used by *helpers* who are trained in a variety of health and helping-oriented disciplines, including counseling, social work, psychology, human services, and related professions. We recognize that terminology varies across settings. You will see the term *helper* as well as *practitioner, clinician, therapist,* and *service provider* used throughout the book. One of the fundamental changes we have made in this edition is in response to continued requests for a streamlined book that can be used with relative ease in the parameters of several quarters or a given semester.

Our Conceptual Foundation

Our conceptual foundation, which we describe in Chapters 1 and 2, reflects four critical areas for helpers from various disciplines: (1) core skills and attributes; (2) effectiveness and evidence-based practice; (3) diversity issues; and (4) critical commitments and ethical practice. The core skills that we present cut across all helping disciplines and in this edition we present them in Chapters 3, 4, and 5. Diversity issues and ecological models are presented in Chapters 2, 6, and 7, and also are integrated throughout the book. Evidence-based assessment and its implementation in the interviewing process are described in Chapters 6 and 7. Effectiveness and evidence-based practice is introduced in Chapter 1 and presented again in Chapters 8 and 9. Chapters 10 through 15 give special attention to research supporting the application of change strategies to diverse groups and the importance of culture and context in applying these and other helping strategies. Recognizing the enormous influence of evidence-based expectations on contemporary practice, we have incorporated current findings into each of our chapters on various change strategies (Chapters 10 through 15).

Layered across all of this is the fourth area of our conceptual model: critical thinking and ethical judgment. We focus on this area specifically in Chapters 1 and 2 and explore these topics again throughout the remainder of the book because they permeate all of the decisions that helpers face at each phase of the helping process, from establishing the helping relationship, to assessing client problems, setting treatment goals, and selecting, using, and evaluating change intervention strategies. Many users of the text have indicated that combining major stages of the helping process with specific change strategies facilitates integration within and across courses that aim for this bigger picture and is also beneficial for students.

Built-In and Supplemental Instructional Guides: Features of the Book

We have retained the specific features of the text that we have learned through feedback make it invaluable as a resource guide—and we have taken this emphasis a step further. We have worked to distinguish this teaching text by providing a rich array of built-in exercises, exemplars, and tools to promote and evaluate student comprehension. The book balances attention to conceptual and empirical foundations with an emphasis on real-life factors in practice settings and ample use of examples and how-to guidelines. In addition, consistent with the outcome emphasis of accreditation standards of counseling, psychology, social work, and human services, chapters are guided by learning outcomes and opportunities to practice with numerous learning activities and guided feedback. Model cases and dialogues are given in each chapter, as well as end-of-chapter evaluations (referred to as "Knowledge and Skill Builders") with feedback designed to help assess chapter competencies.

In addition, we have developed a range of supplementary materials to enrich the teaching experience. These include an instructor's manual, a bank of test questions (which can be used by instructors for course exams or by students in later preparing for accrediting exams), and PowerPoint slides for each chapter.

Brand new to this edition, MindTap® is the digital learning solution that helps instructors engage and transform today's students into critical thinkers. Through paths of dynamic assignments and applications that you can personalize, real-time course analytics, and an accessible reader, MindTap helps you turn your students into higher-level thinkers. Your students become practitioners of their own learning as they master practical skills and build professional confidence. Students will be engaged in a scaffolded learning experience designed to move their thinking skills from lower-order to higher-order by reinforcing learned skills and concepts through demonstrated application.

New to the Eighth Edition

With sensitivity to the value of using a book within a semester or two-quarter framework, we have worked for a more streamlined book in this edition. We have retained the same organizing structure and skill-building components that adopters have long valued, and provide some integrated and distilled content to provide an up-to-date compendium of interviewing and change practices applicable across a range of settings and clientele. Throughout, we aim to build on recent clinical evidence and to point to emerging developments relevant to instruction in clinical services.

1. In this edition we increased this book's enduring commitment to working with diverse groups. This includes further attention to working with youth, older adults, and sexual minorities, in addition to diversity implications related to gender, race/ethnicity, religion, immigration, and disability. Although this book is focused predominantly on individual change (e.g., strengthening problem-solving, adaptive coping, self-efficacy, management of long-term problems or conditions), we have aimed to strengthen attention to the importance of context and the frequent role of environmental sources of stress and injustices.

2. The longstanding commitment of this book to valuing human diversity is commensurate with its established commitment to consulting and incorporating scientific research. In many ways, this edition reflects a healthy dialectic or tension between science and innovation, empiricism, and improvisation. And it is this both/and approach, this practice of living and working in between polarities, that has spawned integrative therapies such as dialectical behavior therapy (DBT), an evidence-based practice that we draw from throughout the chapters.

3. Chapter 1 showcases the symbolism of the chambered nautilus featured on the cover of the book and introduces readers to the practice nexus featured on the inside cover of the book. In the first half of the chapter, the first component of the practice nexus is discussed. Specifically, four core skills and attributes (self-awareness and self-reflection, mindfulness, self-care, and self-compassion) are presented and discussed as a means of promoting helper stamina and resilience. In the second half of the chapter, the second component of the practice nexus, effectiveness, is highlighted. In this section extensive discussion is devoted to evidence-based practice (EBP). This discussion includes criticisms of EBP as well as continued efforts to adapt EBP to culturally diverse populations. A listing of culturally adaptive interventions to EBP is provided, along with examples of such adaptation.

4. The third and fourth components of the practice nexus are the focus of Chapter 2: critical commitments (including ethical practice) and diversity issues. We discuss four critical commitments professional helpers are encouraged to make to grow into clinical competence: commitment to lifelong learning; commitment to collaboration; commitment to values-based practice; and commitment to beneficence. The section on diversity issues includes prominent and newer frameworks for working with culturally diverse populations, such as the more idiosyncratic focus on the intersection of multiple identities proposed by feminist multicultural scholars. The ethical issues section includes updates from professional codes of ethics and a new section on telepractice, with a corresponding new learning activity.

5. Consideration of the therapeutic relationship has been expanded (Chapter 3) to include the ever-expanding empirical basis for various relationship conditions toward increasing effectiveness. New additions to this chapter include the additional evidence base for helper empathy, the working alliance, and relationship ruptures, as well as an expanded discussion of microaggressions and the therapeutic relationship and invalidating environments.

6. Chapter 4 includes an expanded discussion of the processes of listening as well as updated evidence-based literature on the listening responses, particularly reflection of feeling.

7. Chapter 5, Influencing Responses, includes an updated evidence base for the influencing responses, particularly self-disclosure. It also includes a new discussion of the effects of self-disclosure and environmental settings, technology, and information giving, and a new section integrated into the chapter and the Knowledge and Skill Builder on Skill Integration.

8. Chapter 6 focuses more broadly now on both clinical and evidence-based assessment. The material on the person-in-environment model has been updated and the functional assessment model has been expanded and includes new examples and new content regarding chain analysis, which is a component of dialectical behavior therapy. An entirely new section on the DSM-5 is also described in Chapter 6. This chapter also includes expanded coverage of conducting risk assessment in diagnostic interviewing and expanded coverage of mental status interviewing.

9. Chapter 7 describes the implementation of evidence-based assessment in the interviewing process. This chapter includes expanded coverage of clients' individual and environmental strengths and resources as well as functional analyses assessment queries. Case examples have been changed to reflect current DSM-5 diagnoses.

10. The purpose and process of developing treatment goals are described in Chapter 8, as are characteristics of well-constructed goals. Stage models (e.g., stages of change model) are introduced to assist with the sequential and collaborative task of treatment planning. The process of further refining—or contextualizing—treatment goals is likened to preparing for a journey and includes references to easy-to-use and evidence-based client assessment measures.

11. Chapter 9 is devoted to clinical decision-making and treatment planning. Updates include an expansion of client and helper factors contributing to client change, references to the newest addition of The ASAM Criteria used to match clients to levels of care, and resources for intentionally integrating cultural interventions.

12. Strategies of working through various forms of resistance, as well as client ambivalence, are found in Chapter 10. These strategies are informed by solution-focused therapy and motivational interviewing, two approaches whose respective research base has been expanded in this edition.

13. The science underlying cognitive therapies is demonstrating increasing complexity. In Chapter 11 we amplify the discussion of the multiple levels of processes involved in the development and operation of schemas involved in psychological disorders. This material illustrates ways that biological factors such as genetics, brain functioning, and physiology are systematically linked with cognitive and emotional factors, which then interplay with interpersonal, environmental, and behavioral factors in both the development of and intervention with psychological problems. Here we also update information about schema development and schema therapy, about new intervention findings for cognitive change strategies with diverse populations, and about developments of cognitive strategies with acceptance and commitment therapy (ACT) and DBT.

14. Stress is among the universally shared struggles of clients. Therefore, we have emphasized stress as a critical set of factors in the development of problems and in understanding ways that change strategies must address stress. In Chapter 12 we describe cultural, socioeconomic, and life course implications of stress. We update findings regarding neurophysiological pathways through which stress becomes embodied, leading to physical and mental health impairment. We update interventions applied with diverse groups, including attention to minority stress. We update development in stress inoculation and problem-solving therapies including incorporation of emotional mindfulness techniques.

15. In Chapter 13 we have expanded attention to the growing evidence support for stress management, particularly mindfulness-based practices. Here we provide an illustration of recent applications across a range of child and adult populations as well as settings (e.g., workplace) and contexts of helping. We also update ways that mindfulness constructs and meditation are being incorporated across a range of interventions, including mindfulness-based stress reduction, mindfulness-based cognitive therapy, DBT, and ACT.

16. In Chapter 14 we provide updates on extension learning and increased focus on prolonged exposure therapy, including applications with military veterans and cultural minority groups. This chapter also provides updates on virtual reality exposure therapies as well as additional coverage of clinical issues related to safety behaviors, return of fear, dropout, and fear tolerance.

17. In Chapter 15 we describe new uses of the Internet and technological devices to support longer-term self-management interventions, which are particularly valuable for clients with special needs, when people are more distant from services or support communities, or when access to immediate help is needed. This chapter includes numerous literature updates on each of the

categories of self-management, illustrating the rapid growth in populations and problem foci to which they are applied, including helping professionals managing complex and stressful work environments.

The instructor's manual is authored by Penny Minor, a PhD degree candidate in Counselor Education and Supervision at Kent State University and a licensed professional clinical counselor in Ohio. She also developed the test bank of questions for each chapter and the assessment that is available in MindTap. We also offer a resource that can be used for in-class or online teaching formats: a compendium of PowerPoint slides covering major points within each chapter. (These supplements are available to qualified adopters through the instructor section of the Cengage Learning website. Please consult your local sales representative for details.) This edition also features Cengage Helper Studio training videos in helping skills which Sherry Cormier and Cynthia Osborn developed and produced as a part of MindTap.

People We Acknowledge

Over the years, we have been asked, "What is it like to put together a book like this?" Our first response is always, "We require a lot of help." For this edition we are indebted to a number of people for their wonderful help: to Penny Minor, Kent State University PhD degree candidate in

Counselor Education and Supervision, for preparation of the instructor's manual, test bank, and PowerPoint slide resources; Kelly Martin-Vegue (University of Washington MSW student) for her invaluable insights, recommendations, and contributions from a consumer perspective; and to Dr. Daniel McNeil and Dr. Brandon Kyle for their collaborative authoring of Chapter 14 on exposure therapy.

We are very grateful to the staff at Cengage Learning, particularly to our current editor, Julie Martinez, for her commitment, enthusiasm, and wisdom. The final form of this book as you, the reader, now see it would not have been possible without the superb efforts of the entire Cengage Learning team, especially our content developers: Mary Noel, Stefanie Chase, and Elizabeth Momb. We also acknowledge with gratitude the contribution of our manuscript reviewers, who include the following:

Akira Otani, Ed.D, Spectrum Behavioral Health Center
Edward Keane, Ph.D., Housatonic Community College
Susan Adams, Ph.D., Texas Woman's University
Jacqueline Persons, Ph.D., University of California, Berkeley
Daniel W. McNeil, Ph.D., West Virginia University
Brandon N. Kyle, Ph.D., East Carolina University

To all of you: Many thanks! We could not have done this without your careful and detailed comments and suggestions.

Sherry Cormier, Paula S. Nurius, and Cynthia J. Osborn

Building Your Foundation as a Helper

Learning Outcomes

After completing this chapter, you will be able to

1. Recognize, in writing, using dialogue from a counseling supervision session, one example each of the need for developing the core helper skills of: (a) self-awareness and self-reflection; (b) mindfulness; and (c) self-care and self-compassion. You also will be able to identify one specific activity for developing each of these three skills to promote stamina and resilience as a professional helper.
2. Define evidence-based practice (EBP) from a list of descriptors provided (what it is and what it is not), identify two of its intended benefits and at least two of its criticisms, and identify at least six methods for adapting EBPs for culturally diverse populations.

The Chambered Nautilus

The story of the sea snail or mollusk that makes its home in the spiral-shaped nautilus shell is fascinating and compelling. It captures well the primary message of this book—change and growth. An inside and lateral, or "sliced," view of three empty nautilus shells is showcased on the cover of the book. We ask that you pause now to look at the designs of all three. Spend a few moments inspecting their shapes. Notice first the spiral formation of each shell, which has its beginning at the center. Also notice that the shell comprises successively larger compartments or chambers. Each chamber was where the mollusk lived at one time. As it grew, it created a new, larger living space. It is because of these chambers that this sea creature is often referred to as the chambered nautilus.

The chambered nautilus is in the family of cephalopods that also includes the octopus and squid. Unlike some of its close relatives, however, the nautilus does not discard an outgrown shell in search of a larger one. Rather, it retains its shell throughout its adult life. As the mollusk grows, it forms a new and larger chamber to accommodate its size. In other words, it builds on its foundation. In so doing, it seals off the last chamber. Its entire life is therefore dominated by the production of one new living chamber after another, each new chamber connected to earlier ones and a part of an ever-enlarging and stronger shell. How this is done remains a mystery. Nixon and Young (2003) state, "This process of forward movement is not understood but does involve the repositioning of the muscles that attach the animal to its shell" (p. 36). In other words, the growth and development of the chambered nautilus is ongoing and requires a firm foundation, strength, determination, perseverance, and flexibility.

The mollusk lives in only one chamber at a time—in the largest and last chamber of the shell. It firmly anchors itself to the shell by a pair of powerful muscles. It moves around the ocean depths entirely by jet propulsion and uses the empty chambers it once called home for buoyancy. Despite this buoyancy that allows it to move laterally with the ocean currents, the nautilus is able to travel vertical distances of up to 2,000 feet per day. This is made possible by the mollusk using the muscles in its body and tentacles to draw in and expel seawater. It is quite the strong, resilient, and versatile animal! This is one of the reasons the nautilus has been referred to as the "survivor" (Boyle & Rodhouse, 2005, p. 50). We encourage you to spend some time viewing some amazing videos on www.YouTube.com of living nautiluses. Simply search by using the key words "chambered nautilus."

As we have learned more about the chambered nautilus, we cannot help but make some comparisons to helping professionals, and to our helping professions. We believe skilled and effective helpers are part of a professional community yet are also one of a kind. Each helper is his or her own person, not a replica of a supervisor or someone working intently to be just like Carl Rogers, Aaron Beck, or Marsha Linehan. In addition, helpers make use of their buoyancy to "go with the flow" as needed, for example, by cooperating with clients and supervisors and by implementing a recently learned evidence-based practice (EBP). At the same time, however, skilled helpers also know when to "go against the current." This means that they stretch themselves by doing something uncustomary and perhaps uncomfortable at first, such as sitting in silence with a client or interrupting a client when needed. Like the chambered nautilus, the professional helper's vertical travel also suggests the deliberate use of clinically trained muscles in search of new ideas and better alternatives for clients, all the while remaining immersed in the necessity of ethical practice. An example of this is modifying an EBP to accommodate the cultural values, traditions, and needs of a particular client or client population, a practice consistent with the culturally affirmative services we discuss in Chapter 2.

Just as the chambered nautilus retains its shell and builds on its former living compartments, effective helpers use their life experiences and graduate training to build a strong foundation on which to grow and fashion a level of expertise in their work. In so doing, they remain resourceful and inventive. This parallels the forward movement of the nautilus, which involves the flexing and repositioning of its muscles to adapt to new living and work environments. Professional helpers can be like the strong and resilient nautilus by concentrating on the present moment and the current living environment while leaning into and preparing for the next stage of growth. This means that retreating to previous chambers is not possible—they no longer fit. Likewise, sticking to (or remaining stuck in) customary practice and "same-old, same-old" ways of thinking results in a stifling work environment, in addition to ethical vulnerability, burnout, and ineffective care. Just like the nautilus, we have no choice but to move on because change and growth are constant. The spiral shape of the nautilus shell suggests that the mollusk can keep growing forever. This also is true for professional helpers!

We hope the skills, strategies, and interventions described in this book will assist professional helpers to guide their clients step by step in the construction of new, more accommodating, and healthier living spaces using existing resources and strengths. Perhaps the maturing and determined

nautilus and its spiral-shaped shell can inspire helpers and clients alike in the process of change and growth.

A Practice Nexus for the Helping Professions

During the approximately 35-year history of this book, we have learned quite a bit from our readers and from the changing fields of practice, and our approach has evolved as a result. In Figure 1.1 we illustrate the unique nature of this text in terms of today's **practice nexus**—the interrelation, connections, and interfaces of our field. These might be likened to the interrelationships among the chambers of the nautilus shell. The figure depicts the relatedness and connection among the four major components of practice knowledge: (1) core skills and attributes; (2) effectiveness and accountability; (3) critical commitments; and (4) diversity. The components come together to define the central core of what you need for today's practice. So we focus on the interface—the area of overlap among the components of practice knowledge—to provide a coherent and unifying foundation. As the figure shows, each component contains specialized content that you will pursue to greater or lesser degrees, depending on the need. And as you specialize, you will certainly find other components of practice that you will need to master. The totality of it all will develop over years of practice, ongoing training, receiving feedback from clients and colleagues, and self-reflection. To begin, however, you need core content, an understanding of the interrelations, and practical as well as conceptual understanding.

Four Stages of Helping

The four components of today's practice nexus are addressed in the 15 chapters of this book and are part of four primary stages of helping:

1. Establishing an effective therapeutic relationship

2. Assessment and goal setting

3. Strategy selection and implementation

4. Evaluation and termination

The first stage of the helping process, **establishing an effective therapeutic relationship** with the client, is based primarily on client-centered or person-centered therapy (Rogers, 1951). We present skills for this stage in Chapters 3–5. The potential value of a sound relationship

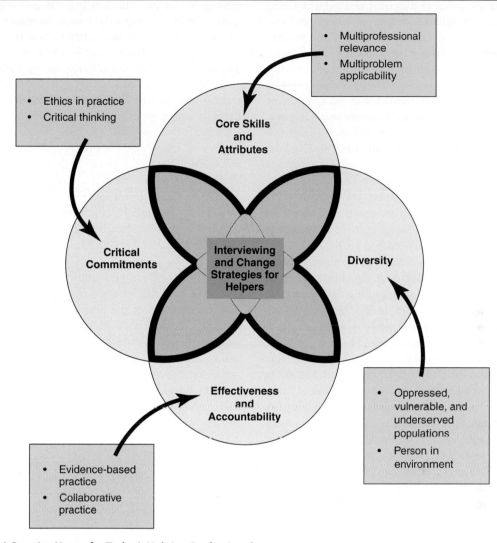

FIGURE 1.1 A Practice Nexus for Today's Helping Professional

base cannot be overlooked. Research has consistently noted that the therapeutic relationship accounts for a substantial amount of client change, approximately 30% (Lambert, 1992). This is understandable given that the relationship is the specific part of the process that conveys the helper's interest in and acceptance of the client as a unique and worthwhile person. It is the foundation for—or the container of—all subsequent therapeutic work. The helper's validation of the client can be empowering, generating hope the client may not have experienced in a very long time. For some clients, working with a professional helper who stays primarily in this stage of helping may be useful and sufficient. For other clients, the

relationship part of therapy is necessary but not sufficient to help them with the kinds of choices and changes they seek to make. These clients need additional kinds of action or intervention strategies.

The second stage of helping, **assessment and goal setting**, often begins with or soon after establishing a therapeutic relationship. In these first two stages, the practitioner is interested mainly in helping clients *explore* their concerns and wishes. Assessment is designed as a collaborative endeavor, a joint undertaking intended to help the clinician and client obtain a better picture, idea, or grasp of what is happening with the client and what prompted the client to seek the services of a helper at this time. Think of this stage as the client and helper locating the horizon for the client's journey of change and also determining the compass to be used to indicate progress toward reaching the client's preferred destination. The information gleaned from assessment is extremely valuable in planning strategies. It provides clarity and direction. It also can be used to manage resistance or occasions when client and helper do not agree or encounter an impasse. We describe assessment skills and strategies in Chapters 6 and 7. As the problems and issues are identified and defined, the practitioner and client also work through the process of developing outcome goals. The skill of treatment goal formulation is described in Chapter 8.

Strategy selection and implementation is the third stage of helping. The clinician's task at this point is to help with client understanding and related action. Insight can be useful, but insight alone is far less useful than insight accompanied by a supporting plan that helps the client translate new or different understandings into observable and specific actions or behaviors. Insight also is a Western and individualistic concept that may not apply or be useful to many culturally diverse clients. Think of this stage of helping as the skill-building phase when clients, like the chambered nautilus, are learning about and using new or reconfigured muscles to sustain a healthier living environment or to construct a new one. Toward this end, the helper and client select and sequence a plan of action: intervention strategies that are based on the assessment data and are designed to help the client achieve the designated goals. In developing action plans, it is important to select plans that relate to the identified concerns and goals and that are not in conflict with the client's primary beliefs and values (see Chapters 9–15).

The last stage of helping, **evaluation and termination**, involves assessing the effectiveness of interventions used—as well as the therapist's style in facilitating the process of change—and the progress the client has made toward the desired goals (see Chapters 8–10). This kind of evaluation assists you in knowing when to terminate the process or to revamp your initial action plans. Also, clients can easily become discouraged during the change process, realizing that transferring the skills learned in counseling to various aspects of their lives is a challenge. Social supports may not be in place, necessitating the development of new and healthier relationships. Clients often find observable and concrete signs of progress to be quite reinforcing.

Our listing of evaluation as the last stage of helping can inadvertently suggest that gauging effectiveness comes near the end of counseling. This is far from the truth. If we are not making effective progress in developing a collaborative, therapeutic relationship or in understanding the perspective of a client early on in our work, then we need to be aware of this right away. In reality, we need to be intentionally evaluating effectiveness throughout the helping process, sharing our observations with clients, soliciting their feedback, and negotiating a plan of care.

These four stages of helping are not discrete. Actually, there is quite a bit of flow and interrelationship among the four stages. In other words, elements of these stages are present throughout the helping process, with varying degrees of emphasis. Change rarely follows a predictable path. Clients encounter challenges and setbacks as they implement new behaviors. Symptoms may not abate quickly or respond well to preliminary interventions. A revision of the initial plan of care is not uncommon. The foci and tasks of each stage of helping thus are not confined to that stage. This also is true of the four components of the practice nexus. Their interrelationship is a constant throughout our work with clients.

We ask now that you return your gaze to Figure 1.1. Two components of the practice nexus—core skills and attributes and effectiveness and accountability—are the focus of this first chapter. The remaining two components—critical commitments (including ethical practice) and diversity—are addressed in Chapter 2. All four components, however, are woven throughout the book. To be more precise, the nexus of these components throughout the four stages of helping is the foundation of the book.

Core Skills and Attributes

Think back to when you knew you wanted to **LO1** become a professional helper. More than likely it was at a time when others had been telling you how good a listener you were. Even some might have said you offered helpful advice. It was not necessarily that you went out looking for people to help—they just seemed to migrate to you, asking if you could spare a moment, or, for others, not bothering to ask, but proceeding to divulge personal information and then waiting for your response. Your desire to become a professional helper also may have been propelled by witnessing the aftermath of tragedy in your school or hometown, or even experiencing first-hand debilitating fear, trauma, and injustices. Because of insufficient care provided to those in need or, by contrast, the helping hand you received that allowed you to breathe again and learn how to persist and be resilient, you vowed to be a part of a solution rather than to perpetuate a problem. "Never again," you may have said. "I want to help . . . and to do it right."

Maybe you cannot remember a specific time or event that crystallized your decision to become a professional helper. Perhaps it had to do with looking back over your life and realizing that some kind of change was in order, that remaining on the same life path did not portend much excitement or even any hope. "It's now or never," you may have said. "Something has to change . . . for the better."

Regardless of the circumstances that brought you to the entrance of your graduate training program, you're ready for something different. Although questioning how this may all work out for you (in terms of time, finances, and extent of community involvement), you are eager to get started and venture into this professional realm. You want to be a part of change—for others and for yourself. And you are ready to begin learning and to continue learning what it takes to be a change agent. "Bring it on," you may say. "Just give me the tools so that I can build my toolbox and get out there to help people."

The analogy of the toolbox is one we hear often from our graduate students. It brings to mind the work of a carpenter or an electrician, the professional who is equipped with various instruments to build something new or fix something that is broken. Although students and new professionals may take comfort in having a figurative toolbox that they can carry with them to each encounter with a client, we caution them to not allow this analogy to persist and remain prominent in their career. For one thing, a toolbox brings to mind something that is external to you, something like an appendage that is not you, that can be inauthentic. This is not to say that the "tools of the trade"—the strategies, interventions, guidelines, and practice principles of the profession—are not important. They are! They are critical! But when they are not understood and are not incorporated into the helper's overall practice style, their potential for misuse increases. This is when they are applied out of context, when the helper is faithfully implementing an assessment protocol, for example, but is not mindful of how some of the standard questions have offended a particular client. The open-ended question, "How do you feel?" is considered an important tool, as is the "miracle question" in solution-focused therapy. But when they are asked without understanding their purpose for a particular client at a particular time, they may be interpreted by the client as disrespectful and intrusive and may result in the client's early departure. Tools, therefore, are not intended to be used in a mechanical fashion, only applied because the instruction manual says so. Because of this, we do not want to encourage helpers to continue to rely on techniques they do not understand, have not yet practiced and received feedback on, and have not incorporated into their overall style. Doing so over the course of one's career would be disingenuous and inauthentic.

The analogy of a toolbox also suggests there is something that needs to be fixed or corrected and that it is the helper who must fix, correct, or straighten out what is wrong in clients. This is not a helpful perspective. Reference to tools also implies that it is the tools, the instruments themselves, that are responsible for client improvement. It is as if the tools are imbued with some kind of power to effect change and, regardless of the client or the therapist, each kind of tool will work in a particular way to fix what is broken. This is another example of using a tool out of context. Again, we do not find this comparison helpful. Thinking this way negates the contributions of the helper *and* the client!

Our fourth and final reason for not encouraging the toolbox analogy is that it can prevent a discussion of helper skills. Although some may liken tools or counseling techniques to helper skills, they are not quite the same. Tools and techniques are often regarded as external to the helper (especially when learning to use a new tool), whereas skills comprise the helper's qualities, traits, and learned behaviors. To speak of tools is to speak of something *other than* the helper; to speak of skills is to talk *about* the helper. The focus of the former is impersonal; the focus of the latter is the person of the helper and how he or she has learned to embody and demonstrate certain skills for the benefit of a client. A prime example of this distinction is found in what are referred to in person-centered therapy as the core conditions of the therapeutic environment: genuineness or congruence, unconditional positive regard, and empathic understanding. These are discussed in greater detail in Chapter 3. Notice that these are not impersonal "things" or tools—they are the qualities or attributes and skills *of the helper*, how he or she relates to another person to create the conditions for client change.

It may be more accurate, therefore, to talk about the skilled helper (Egan, 2014) or the helper who practices what is referred to in dialectical behavior therapy as **skillful means** (Linehan, 2015). Skills refer to and describe the way a helper practices and reflect how the helper has learned, made sense of, and integrated certain theories and techniques (or tools) of helping. In other words, skills reflect the person of the helper. A skilled and skillful helper is a professional, not a technician or what Skovholt and Jennings (2004) referred to as a "technique wizard" (p. 140). Whereas learning a technique can take only a few hours, becoming a skilled professional and a wise person takes many years (see Rønnestad & Skovholt, 2013). Our focus on core skills and attributes throughout this book is in effect a focus on you as the helping professional—your qualities, traits, and learned behaviors—so that clients derive maximum benefit from services provided. It is a learning and growth process:

from a mechanical and disjointed use of tools in the tool-box to practicing with skillful means. Like the way the chambered nautilus grows, this process can take place over many years, but its foundation begins now, with careful attention to matters of context and environment.

We dedicate the remainder of this section to a discussion of three core skills and attributes that are essential throughout the stages of helping: (1) self-awareness and self-reflection; (2) mindfulness; and (3) self-care and self-compassion. These make possible the promotion of stamina and resilience, concepts that also are addressed in this chapter. Think of these as core skills and attributes from which to start your journey of growth and change as a professional helper. Just as the chambered nautilus began its development at the core or center of the spiral shell, we believe these skills and attributes are the foundation of your own development as a professional helper.

Self-Awareness and Self-Reflection

Being drawn to uncertainty is one precondition for therapist development. According to Jennings, Skovholt, Goh, and Lian (2013), helpers who "thrive . . . are comfortable in the seemingly paradoxical reality of searching for clarity while enjoying the ambiguity and confusion of the human condition" (p. 239). This means that the terrain of helping is not clear and the journey cannot be predicted. It also means that there is no one-size-fits-all "answer book" to consult so that you know what to do with clients each step of the way. Rather than getting clearer as you move through your graduate studies, it may be that this work of professional helping seems to be getting murkier as you go along. Two of the 20 "hazards" of practicing as a professional helper that Skovholt and Trotter-Mathison (2011) listed illustrate this murkiness: lack of concrete results and closure in our work with clients, and not knowing how to measure improvement or even effectiveness.

What does uncertainty have to do with the core skills of self-awareness and self-reflection? Quite a bit! For one, it means that these skills are essential *because* there is no absolute "how to" manual out there for you to consult. In session with your clients, you are the one facilitating the conversation, establishing a connection with the client, assessing the case, and making decisions about client care. More often than not, no other professional is in the session to assume those responsibilities. You are the sole professional in the moment with clients. Understood in another way, you are the only active ingredient in that therapeutic encounter that you can control. More than likely other factors are beyond your control, such as client characteristics and the immediate treatment setting. Although you may be guided by a specific theoretical orientation or operating from an evidence-based treatment manual, that theory and those treatment protocols were not developed expressly for the client with whom you are working. Rather, you are the one in the immediacy of the moment to determine, adapt, and deliver services to each client. This is what it means to move beyond rote use of tools in a toolbox to developing skillful means. The tools are no longer disconnected from you; they now have become part of your routine functioning so that quality client care is maintained. This also is part of the professional development process, the forward movement similar to that of the growing chambered nautilus—developing from mere technician to a skilled and responsive professional. The instruction manual remains; its purpose is now understood.

Just as the chambered nautilus must navigate through the murky waters of the deep sea, so must practitioners make their way through the ambiguous terrain of clinical practice. The skills of self-awareness and self-reflection make this possible. These are practices intended to keep the practitioner in check and also to monitor the quality of services extended to his or her clients. High self-awareness and in-depth self-reflection are primary characteristics of highly skilled, effective, or "master" therapists in the United States and four other countries (Jennings et al., 2013). **Self-awareness** is being highly observant of oneself, and **self-reflection** is a form of self-monitoring or self-regulation. Rather than being self-absorbed in a narcissistic manner, self-awareness and self-reflection are skills of introspection that consider yourself from different dimensions (e.g., verbal expression, demeanor, values) as you learn new skills and are exposed to professional guidelines.

It might be helpful to think of self-awareness and self-reflection as consultation skills—that is, the ability to consult your inner compass as part of the clinical decision-making process. Your inner compass continues to be shaped as you learn more about theory, research, and professional standards. It could be said that your inner compass is what sits on the practitioner's stool, a stool Skovholt and Starkey (2010) described as having the three legs of practitioner experience, personal life, and academic research. These three legs are sources of knowledge for you to consult throughout your career. This must be done deliberately, such as setting aside time to read a self-help book and journal about what you have read, obtaining additional supervision, or attending an experiential professional growth workshop. Your compass requires routine calibration, just as your stool needs to be balanced and leveled. Self-awareness and self-reflection are the skills you use to calibrate your inner compass by consulting theory, research-informed practices, supervisory directives, and ethical and other professional guidelines. These skills also are used to maintain balance as you operate from your practitioner's stool.

Before reading further, we invite you to pause and participate in Learning Activity 1.1. This activity is intended to heighten your self-awareness and make use of your self-reflection skills. Specifically, this activity is designed to help you explore your reasons for entering the helping profession, as well as what you hope to gain from your work as a helping professional. Because this is demanding work that involves substantial personal commitment, routine self-reflection is essential to effective practice.

Mindfulness

Related to self-awareness and self-reflection is the core skill of **mindfulness**. Think of it as a specialized and disciplined form of self-awareness and self-reflection. It is an intentional practice that is central to dialectical behavior therapy (DBT; Linehan, 2015) and to acceptance and commitment therapy (ACT; Hayes, Strosahl, & Wilson, 2012). Mindfulness also is a core skill in at least four other approaches. Jon Kabat-Zinn's (1990) mindfulness-based stress reduction (MBSR) initially was developed for persons with chronic pain and is now intended for persons with a variety of psychological and medical issues.

It is group-based training conducted in 2.5-hour weekly sessions for 8 weeks, with an additional 1-day meditation retreat. Mindfulness-based cognitive therapy (MBCT) for depression (Segal, Williams, & Teasdale, 2002) and mindfulness-based relapse prevention (MBRP) for addictive behaviors (Bowen, Chawla, & Marlatt, 2011) are designed based on the work of Kabat-Zinn. A newer approach is mindful self-compassion (MSC; Germer & Neff, 2013) that teaches self-compassion skills to the general public and is fashioned according to MBSR's format.

Inspired by Eastern spiritual practices of meditation, namely Buddhism and Zen, mindfulness is understood as practicing focused attention, specifically, remaining aware of and deliberately attuned to the present moment. Although often confused with meditation, it is not. Rather than "zoning out" or retreating from the present moment, mindfulness is "a way of living awake, with your eyes wide open" (Dimidjian & Linehan, 2009, p. 425). This means that it is an attentional skill or a way of paying attention on purpose. It therefore is not "mindlessness." It is a heightened state of consciousness wherein the focus of attention is on in-the-moment perceptual experience, making use of as many senses as possible (e.g., sight, sound, smell)—and also attending to visceral functioning (e.g., breathing)—to be fully immersed in the textured detail of the concentrated now. In this way, mindfulness

Learning Activity 1.1

Survey of Helper Motives and Goals

This activity is designed to help you explore areas of yourself that in some fashion will affect your helping. Take some time to consider these questions at *different points* in your development as a helper. We offer no feedback for this activity, because the responses are yours and yours alone. You may wish to discuss your responses with a peer, a supervisor, or your own therapist.

1. What is it about the helping profession (e.g., social work, counseling, psychology) that is attractive to you or enticing for you?
2. What do you look forward to learning and doing over the next 5 years?
3. What is anxiety-provoking to you about the work or lifestyle of a professional helper?
4. What are you cautious or hesitant about as you continue in the profession?
5. If you had to select one event in your life or one personal experience that contributed to your decision to pursue the helping profession you are now in, what would that event or experience be?
6. What have you learned about yourself by having experienced tragedy, trauma, or types of personal pain and

injustices at some point in your life? What more do you still have to learn about yourself as a result of such pain?
7. Which of your personal qualities do you believe will serve you well as a helping professional? Why do you believe this?
8. What aspects of yourself (e.g., being "rough around the edges") do you still need to work on for you to be a helpful practitioner? How do you see yourself addressing these traits?
9. How do you handle being in conflict? Being confronted? Being evaluated? What defenses do you use in these situations?
10. How would someone who knows you well describe your style of helping or caring?
11. What client populations or client issues do you enjoy working with or look forward to working with? For what reasons?
12. What client populations or client issues are difficult for you to work with or do you foresee as being difficult for you to work with? For what reasons?
13. What are three primary factors that contribute to being an effective helper?
14. How will you know when *you* have been an effective helper?

is like stepping outside yourself, taking a meta-perspective on your own experience, so that you can consider your perception of the present moment with greater objectivity (Neff & Pommier, 2013).

Mindfulness is the means by which an individual makes direct contact to immediate experience, not to abstractions or concepts. Persons who practice mindfulness are able to control or focus their attention on the present moment. They do not control *what* is being attended to, such as deliberately trying to change their breathing or rid their mind of thoughts; rather, they control *how* they attend to what is happening in and around them in the here and now. In this way, mindfulness is unlike certain forms of prayer and is not to be confused with prayer. It is not a form of communicating with or connecting to a transcendent being. Furthermore, mindfulness does not seek to make something happen, such as relaxation or preventing certain kinds of behavior (e.g., fighting). Dimidjian and Linehan (2009) state, "Mindfulness has as its goal only mindfulness" (p. 425).

Mindfulness is the polar opposite of multitasking. It does not mean, however, doing nothing or being nonproductive. It does mean intently focusing on one thing at a time and doing so in the present moment. This requires effort! Although not intended to make something happen or to control that which is the focus of attention, research suggests that persons who consistently practice mindfulness experience a greater sense of control over their feelings and mood, their behaviors (e.g., not acting on impulses), and their attitudes (e.g., more hopeful). For example, primary care physicians trained over 1 year in mindfulness skills reported improved personal well-being, including decreased burnout and improved mood (Krasner et al., 2009). They also experienced greater changes in empathy, a finding that seems to fit Greason and Cashwell's (2009) survey of counseling student interns. They found that these students' high mindfulness scores predicted greater empathy and greater self-efficacy. Counseling students who had taken a graduate level course that focused on mindfulness and self-care reported similar benefits (Christopher & Maris, 2010) and also spoke of the positive effects of mindfulness specific to their work with clients, such as increased calm and comfort with silence and reduced fears of inadequacy and incompetence.

It appears that even though mindfulness is not practiced for the specific purpose of changing mood, behavior, or attitude, the practice of mindfulness results in positive changes in these areas of functioning. Think of these changes as positive side effects or the benefits of mindfulness. Davis and Hayes (2011) reviewed additional benefits of mindfulness from the research literature, including relationship satisfaction, improved physical functioning,

and increased patience. These and other benefits seem to support Carmody's (2009) contention that the overall goal of mindfulness is the reduction of human suffering (p. 272).

In both DBT and ACT, mindfulness is a skill taught to clients and is a skill practiced—and lived—by therapists. You do not have to be a religious or spiritual person to practice mindfulness. Consistent with our earlier discussion of skill and how it differs from technique, mindfulness is how the helper interacts with clients—or, more precisely, how the helper is present with clients. The premise of DBT and ACT is that helpers cannot teach skills to clients that therapists do not practice themselves. Manuals are available to teach clients mindfulness skills (e.g., Linehan, 2015), but mindfulness cannot be learned simply by talking about it or lecturing on it. Mindfulness must be practiced in session and modeled by the therapist. The therapist who is purposefully attentive to the client in the immediacy of the counseling session is modeling for the client the skill of mindfulness. The therapist who routinely practices mindfulness in and outside of therapy also is able to guide the client through the process of learning and continually practicing mindfulness.

Mindfulness Skills In DBT, there are six specific mindfulness skills divided into "what" and "how" skills. The three "what" skills are observing, describing, and participating; the three "how" skills are remaining nonjudgmental, focusing on one thing at a time in the present moment, and being effective. Observing is the act of noticing what is in your awareness, using your sight, hearing, or tactile senses, for example. It does not label or categorize what is observed; it is simply the act of paying attention to what is taking place around you and what is being experienced inside you in the here and now. The skill of describing requires a kind of stepping back from the experience to identify what has been observed. This may include naming the colors, sounds, and tactile sensations (e.g., soft, rough, warm temperature) observed and experienced. The third "what" skill is participating and refers to fully immersing yourself in the activity of the present moment. This has been described as throwing yourself into and becoming one with an activity or experience, and doing so without reservation or self-consciousness. This means that participating has the quality of spontaneity. Take, for example, the act of walking. When done mindfully, fully participating in walking means attending to your movements and the sensations as you walk, focusing on the act of walking, and immersing yourself in the activity.

As its name implies, the three "how" skills of mindfulness describe how the three "what" skills are used. First, observing, describing, and participating in the present moment is to be done nonjudgmentally. This means not evaluating the experience as either bad or good. This practice is similar to that of accepting, a core skill in ACT. It means assuming a noncritical or neutral stance by discarding the need to control what is, even that which has been experienced as unpleasant. To walk nonjudgmentally means to not ruminate on your movements or to experience them as "stupid," "difficult," or "painful." It does mean accepting your experience as is, and continuing to walk with your full attention on the present moment, the second "how" skill of mindfulness. This means not walking and thinking about your destination at the same time. This would be doing two things at once—a practice inconsistent with remaining in the present moment by doing one thing at a time. The third "how" skill of mindfulness is being effective, which is doing what works or what is helpful. Being mindful is not about doing what is right and avoiding what is wrong. It also is not about following orders or simply going through the motions (like pulling out tools from a toolbox!). It is about using

your attentional "muscles" so that you can tune in to your immediate experience, using your sensory resources. It's a way of becoming acquainted with you—with where you are and who you are in this present moment! Mindfulness that is effective becomes a welcome, inviting, and meaningful activity, not a scary, suspicious, or worthless one.

Each of the six mindfulness skills is not to be taken lightly. The skills also are to be used carefully with clients, not in a haphazard fashion or only because mindfulness may be regarded as a popular clinical perspective and practice. Again, mindfulness practice requires discernment and effort! To help you practice your mindfulness skills, we invite you to participate in Learning Activity 1.2. Even if you have learned about mindfulness prior to reading this book, we ask that you pause to "flex" and "tone" your mindfulness muscles. Think back to the mollusk that makes its home in the nautilus shell—to continue to grow and expand, it uses its muscles continuously. Doing otherwise would result in shriveling up or being swept away by the tide. If you are new to mindfulness practice, we ask

Learning Activity **1.2**

Mindfulness Practice

You can engage in this practice by yourself after reading through the activity. It can also be done in a group with one person volunteering to lead the practice, reading aloud the following activity.

Find a quiet spot where you know you will not be disturbed for approximately 10 minutes. Turn off or mute any mobile devices you may have around you. Sit down in a comfortable position, either on a chair or on the floor. Sit upright, with your feet firmly touching the floor (if sitting on a chair), or, if sitting on the floor, extend your legs, or cross them with one of your ankles resting comfortably on the knee or thigh of the other leg. Take three or four deep breaths in through your nose, noticing how it feels for the air to come in through your nostrils, and also noticing how your chest expands as it takes in new oxygen. As you breathe out through your nose, notice how your chest subsides and the motion of air in your throat and nostrils.

Now take your hands and rest them on your thighs, palms up. Keep them separate for now. Notice the palms of both of your hands, the lines or "creases" that make up the inside of your hands. Observe the length and the direction of these lines, notice how they change as you bend your fingers slightly and then extend your palms. See the detail of the lines, and how they criss-cross, as you move your hands slightly in the light. Pay attention to the detail across the surface of your palms. As you do, remind yourself that these palms and these fingerprints are yours and yours alone—unique and one of a kind. Now notice any other

visuals on your hands, such as the blood vessels below the skin, markings on the skin, or rings that appear on the inside of your fingers. Simply use your eyes to scan the open palms of your hands, the hands that have lifted objects for you, opened and closed doors, helped you write and type, and held the hand and cupped the face of a loved one.

Now take one of your hands and its fingers and touch the surface, the palm, of the other hand; notice how this feels. Glide your fingers and its palm across the palm and the fingers of the other hand. Simply notice the touch, how your open hand feels when gently touched by one or several fingers of the other hand. Describe this sensation without judging it as good or bad. Suspend any criticism. Hold off on assigning to the sensation any positive evaluation as well. Simply give a name to how the motion, the sensation, feels. Keep the motion of your fingers on the other palm slow, gentle, and deliberate so that you are able to notice the detail or the intricacies of the sensation. Continue doing this for a few moments, doing your best to remain focused on the activity in the here and now.

To close this activity, take three or four deep breaths, holding for just a moment each time before breathing out. As you gaze again at the palms of your hands and glide your fingers of one hand over the palm of the other, remind yourself of your uniqueness, that these hands are yours and one of a kind. Offer a word of gratitude to both hands, thanking them for being a part of you, making you unique, and for working for you. This might even include a warm shake between your two hands or a gentle clap.

that you enter into this exercise with an open mind, ready to try something new—a skill we believe is central to all forms of helping. You will have the opportunity to practice yet again your mindfulness skills in Chapter 4, so think of this activity as a warm-up!

Developing Skilled Intuition We believe the deliberate practice of mindfulness can assist new helpers in making the transition from relying on only intuitive judgments (decisions that are automatic, involuntary, and almost effortless) to incorporating deliberate judgments (decisions based on controlled, voluntary, and effortful activities). Although acting on your intuition or gut may have some appeal because it is thought of as genuine or authentic practice, it also suggests a dismissal of learned theory and skills. Think about it. If all it took to be an effective helper was the use of instinct and gut, why would graduate studies be necessary? The truth is that effective helping requires the application of genuine yet sophisticated skills—skills that have been learned, practiced, and revised over a period of time. If you hear a supervisor tell you to "just go with your gut," or "stop using your head and simply use your instinct," ask him or her to explain. It may be that your supervisor is encouraging you to integrate the skills you have learned ("head knowledge") into your natural style of interpersonal communication. His or her recommendation may be for you to practice what Kahneman and Klein (2009) described as **skilled intuition**, or the testing of your cue recognition skills. They proposed that skilled intuition develops only in an environment of regularity (e.g., meeting with clients on a routine basis and receiving supervision consistently) that makes it possible to validate your observational skills or cue recognition (e.g., discerning symptoms from client presentation).

We believe that mindfulness is a form of skilled intuition. In this case, what your supervisor may be trying to tell you is that in session with your clients, you must attend to the present moment in a more focused and deliberate manner, accepting what is without trying to force change. Now, *that* requires skill, doesn't it? Maybe that explains the practice of skillful means!

Self-Care

Another core skill for helpers is **self-care** (Norcross & Guy, 2007). Although mindfulness is a form of self-care (Wise, Hersh, & Gibson, 2012), self-care is a broader concept and practice and has been identified as an ethical imperative for counselors (American Counseling Association, 2014), psychologists (Wise et al., 2012), and social workers (Lee & Miller, 2013). This is true not

only in the United States but also in other countries. For example, the Canadian Code of Ethics for Psychologists (Canadian Psychological Association, 2000) regards self-care as an activity that fulfills the ethical principle of responsible caring. In its *Ethical Framework for Good Practice in Counselling and Psychotherapy*, the British Association for Counselling and Psychotherapy (2013) lists self-respect (the practice of "fostering self-knowledge and care for self") as one of six ethical principles. Professional associations and accrediting bodies based in the United States also have recognized the importance of professional self-care. For example, counseling programs accredited by the Council for Accreditation of Counseling and Related Educational Programs (CACREP, 2009) must include in their core curriculum "self-care strategies appropriate to the counselor role" (Standard G.1.D.). In addition, the National Association of Social Workers (NASW, 2008) has a policy statement supporting the practice of professional self-care, describing this practice as "a core essential component to social work practice" (p. 269).

That self-care is an ethical imperative for all professional helpers suggests four things: (1) it is not simply a personal matter or quality; (2) it is not an indulgence; (3) it is not optional; (4) it is not automatic; and (5) it is not to be practiced in a shallow or superficial manner. As a reflection of ethical conduct, self-care is a set of learned behaviors that must be demonstrated during graduate studies and throughout one's professional career. Just because you care for others does not automatically mean that you are able to care for yourself. More than likely, it is *because* you care for others that you are prone to not care for yourself adequately. It may be that for far too long you have prioritized the needs of others over your own, set aside your own goals to accommodate the goals of others, and sacrificed your own well-being to preserve your prize-worthy reputation as the devoted child, faithful spouse and partner, loving parent, generous friend, helpful neighbor, and dutiful employee. Although these are qualities many of us aspire to and would hope to have included in our eulogies and obituaries, they come with a price. And in the role of professional helper, you cannot afford what it costs to care for others while simultaneously ignoring caring for yourself.

Baker (2007) stated that "self-denial or self-abnegation is neglectful not only of our real self-needs, but ultimately of the well-being of our clients" (p. 607). In other words, self-care must become routine practice for helpers for the sake of client well-being and remaining effective as a clinician—and we believe this practice must begin during graduate studies. It is meant to prevent helper impairment and inadvertent client maltreatment. Its purpose also is to strengthen helper resilience and well-being. Self-care was identified by a group of 24 mental health practitioners from diverse ethnic backgrounds in the United States and Canada as an adaptive response and an essential practice to "detoxify from frequent forms of racial microaggressions they experience in their jobs" (Hernández, Carranza, & Almeida, 2010, p. 206). Self-care activities described by this group included physical exercise, meditation, visualizations, massage, acupuncture, chiropractic treatment, thinking positively and avoiding negative thoughts, and taking pride in their ethnic heritage. Self-care thus has a dual purpose: prevention of ineffective or even harmful client care (i.e., doing no harm, the ethical principle of nonmaleficence), and promotion of beneficial care (i.e., doing good, the ethical principle of beneficence).

In your work as a professional helper, you have no choice! You must practice self-care. And this is not self-indulgent, selfish, or narcissistic behavior. It also is not to be practiced in a shallow or superficial manner "'dumbed down' to socializing and recreational pursuits" (Putterbaugh, 2015, p. 54). Rather, as a stipulation for living and working as an effective professional helper, self-care is a deliberate, purposeful practice that involves quiet and deep reflection on our lives.

How do you practice self-care? In a recent study of psychology graduate students, Myers et al. (2012) found that three self-care behaviors predicted lower perceived stress: (1) engaging in better sleep hygiene; (2) having strong social support; and (3) regulating emotion through cognitive reappraisal (changing the meaning of an emotion-filled situation) and suppression (changing emotional expression, as in not acting on anger). Surprisingly, physical exercise and mindfulness practice did not predict reduced levels of perceived stress, which the researchers attributed to varying opinions on the benefit of these behaviors and lack disciplined engagement in these behaviors by graduate students. In Turner et al.'s (2005) study of psychology interns, engaging in pleasurable activities outside of the internship, using humor, getting a sufficient amount of sleep, and engaging in physical exercise were activities reported to be beneficial. When working at the internship, these same graduate interns reported that consulting with fellow interns, obtaining clinical supervision, diversifying internship activities, and setting realistic internship goals were beneficial self-care activities.

Turner and colleagues (2005) encouraged graduate interns to be intentional about participating in self-care strategies because "self-care is a life-long process and not limited to the internship year" (p. 679). Similarly, Jenaro, Flores, and Arias (2007) emphasized the importance of an appropriate balance between work and private life throughout one's career. Concentrating only on active coping strategies at work, they noted, may actually "exacerbate the psychological tiredness of the worker" (p. 85). Engaging in relaxing activities during one's leisure time is therefore important because these "off-the-clock" activities serve to address the emotional exhaustion that has been found to be the primary culprit of burnout (see Wallace & Brinkerhoff, 1991). It is assertive self-care over the career life-span that is essential (Skovholt & Trotter-Mathison, 2013).

Self-Compassion

A newer concept applied to professional helpers is that of **self-compassion**. It is a form of self-care, but it is a broader concept that encompasses self-care. Self-care refers to specified behaviors, whereas self-compassion is an overall, foundational, and transformational attitude or perspective (Patsiopoulos & Buchanan, 2011) that could be said to fuel self-care activities. Borrowing from Buddhist philosophy, Neff (2003a) proposed self-compassion as a healthier and more constructive self-attribution than self-esteem because, unlike self-esteem, self-compassion does not compare self to others and does not endorse the processes of separation and individuation in human development. Rather, self-compassion balances concern for self with concern for others, meaning that self-compassion fosters concern for others, and vice versa. In recent research, Neff and Pommier (2013) reported a significant association between self-compassion and concern for others.

There are three components of self-compassion (Neff, 2003a; Neff & Pommier, 2013):

1. self-kindness, or self-understanding rather than harsh judgment or self-criticism;

2. common humanity, the recognition that all humans are imperfect, that they fail and make mistakes, so that one feels connected to—rather than isolated from—others in the midst of personal struggles; and

3. mindfulness, referring to the acceptance of painful emotions and thoughts while not overly identifying with them.

Note the integral role of mindfulness in self-compassion. We contend that mindfulness sustains self-compassion, making it possible for persons to be kind to themselves because of their humanity. Said in another way, it is the heightened and concentrated awareness of one's self in the midst of current activity and surroundings (including people)—accepting what is without changing what is—that cultivates self-compassion.

Neff (2003a) defined self-compassion as being open to and moved by one's own suffering, assuming an understanding and nonjudgmental attitude toward one's own shortcomings and failures, and recognizing that one's own experience is part of the common human experience. This suggests that self-compassion promotes humility rather than self-centeredness or narcissism. At the same time, it also demonstrates resilience and a striving toward psychological well-being. These hypotheses were supported when Neff (2003b) first administered to undergraduate students the *Self-Compassion Scale* she developed. As expected, she found an inverse correlation between self-compassion and symptoms of depression and anxiety, as well as rigid perfectionism. From this same study, self-compassion was associated with greater life satisfaction. In subsequent studies, self-compassion was found to predict mental health among adolescents and young adults (Neff & McGehee, 2010; Neff, Kirkpatrick, & Rude, 2007), suggesting that self-compassion might be thought of as resilient humility or humble resilience.

Specific to professional helpers, Patsiopoulos and Buchanan (2011) identified six overlapping dimensions of self-compassion from their interviews with 15 Canadian counselors. With an average of 14 years of psychotherapy practice, these counselors defined self-compassion as: (1) being gentle with yourself; (2) being mindfully aware; (3) having a sense that as humans "we are all in this together"; (4) the importance of speaking the truth to yourself and others; (5) the development of spiritual awareness; and (6) having an ethic of professionalism. Specific practices of self-compassion used during therapy sessions included assuming a stance of acceptance (e.g., recognizing the limits of helping, making appropriate self-corrections), mindfulness (i.e., nonjudgmental in-the-moment attentiveness) and not knowing (i.e., counseling from a nonexpert stance), and participating in a caring and supportive work team as colleagues or supervisees. Counselors also described the importance of scheduling breaks in between therapy sessions and ending appointments on time as deliberate acts of self-compassion. According to the counselors in this study, these practices served to enhance their well-being, effectiveness in the work setting, and therapeutic relationships with clients.

The self-compassion website (http://self-compassion .org) established by Dr. Neff posts updates on self-compassion research, includes informational videos, and provides information on trainings and workshops. One of these is the 8-week Mindful Self-Compassion program (Germer & Neff, 2013).

Promoting Stamina and Resilience

Given the many facets of practicing as a professional helper, it is understandable how such a lifestyle can be exhausting at times. It is! Skovholt and Trotter-Mathison (2011) said this loud and clear in their listing and descriptions of not one but *20* hazards of practicing as a helping professional. Among these are: (1) providing constant empathy, interpersonal sensitivity, and one-way caring; (2) realizing that one's effectiveness is difficult to measure and thus remains elusive; and (3) working with clients who are not "honor students" and whose readiness to change lags behind our own hopes and desires for them. These and other consequences of "emotional labor" (Wharton, 1993) may lead to burnout and compassion fatigue, or what Stebnicki (2009) referred to as empathy fatigue. Counselors who volunteered to help victims of natural disasters were found to have twice the rate of compassion fatigue and vicarious traumatization compared to other counselors (Lambert & Lawson, 2013).

Burnout is a general term that describes emotional depletion, a lack of caring or empathy for clients, and a diminishing sense of personal accomplishment. The first two aspects of burnout describe what Skovholt and Trotter-Mathison (2011) termed *caring burnout*, whereas the third aspect of burnout, loss of meaning and purpose in one's work, is what they characterized as *meaning burnout*. In broad terms, burnout can be understood as a lack of resilience and constricted coping abilities. Jenaro and colleagues (2007) characterized burnout "as an answer to chronic labor stress that is composed of negative attitudes and feelings toward coworkers and one's job role, as well as feelings of emotional exhaustion" (p. 80). Compassion fatigue can signal the onset of burnout and is regarded as mental and physical exhaustion resulting from taking better care of others than you do of yourself. Empathy fatigue can also be a precursor to burnout and describes the practitioner's diminished capacity to listen and respond empathically to clients whose stories convey acute and cumulative psychosocial stress (Stebnicki, 2009, p. 804).

We may not have been fully briefed about the hazards of practicing as professional helpers before we submitted our own versions of informed consent and signed up for this career. It may not be until later in one's formal training (e.g., during practicum and internship) that a novice helper actually experiences some of the stresses and strains that are part of this work. But knowing about all the challenges may not have kept us away anyway, and perhaps some attraction to the challenge of this work spurred us to seek out this particular profession in the first place. It also may be that we are hardier than we realize and that it takes only a few reminders of our competence here and there—including some client success stories—to keep us going. Realizing that our experience of strain and exhaustion is not attributable to one thing or person but more than likely to an accumulation of factors over time, including ones beyond our control (e.g., vague and ambiguous expectations in the work setting), can ease our tendency to self-blame. Likewise, reframing our goals as helping clients manage or otherwise live with concerns rather than fixing, curing, or even solving difficulties may help us remain invested in this important work. There are additional and specific things we can do to help cultivate our resilience and stamina for providing professional care to others.

Osborn (2004) identified seven salutary suggestions for **stamina** for those who serve in the helping professions. These recommendations are intended to assist helpers not only remain vigilant about the hazards of professional helping, such as compassion fatigue, but also maintain their resolve for rewarding work. Based on a review of the scholarly literature and reflections on her clinical practice, Osborn's recommendations comprise a proactive rather than a reactive or preventive approach and are intended

to shift attention from a deficiency or pathological perspective (i.e., "burnout prevention") to a strengths-based or competency-based orientation (i.e., "stamina promotion"). Stamina is likened to resilience, endurance, and flourishing – not despite hardship but in the midst of challenges. Each suggestion for stamina corresponds to the seven letters in the word *stamina,* thus creating the acronym STAMINA. These are presented and described with examples in Table 1.1.

Although stamina and resilience are close cousins, we differentiate the two by thinking of stamina as the fuel for resilience. **Resilience** therefore refers to a set of specific skills that Tjeltveit and Gottlieb (2010) stated can be taught and then "marshaled when psychotherapists are faced with difficult situations" (p. 100). Specifically, resilience develops from social relationships and support networks (e.g., clinical supervision), but

TABLE 1.1 Seven Ingredients of Helper Stamina

Ingredients of Helper STAMINA	Definition	Examples
Selectivity	• Intentionally choosing and concentrating your efforts in only certain areas, such as limiting your areas of expertise • Undertaking daily activities and long-term endeavors with care and focused attention	• Setting limits on yourself and maintaining healthy boundaries with others (e.g., clients, family members) • Modifying high and perhaps unrealistic expectations you have of others and yourself • Not trying to "do it all" or be a "jack of all trades"
Temporal sensitivity	• Being mindful of the constraints on your time and working within these limits • Using time wisely • Focusing more on current resources and circumstances compared to past or even future challenges	• Joining with clients in the present moment • Beginning and ending counseling sessions on time • Engaging in mindfulness practice
Accountability	• Practicing according to justifiable, ethical, theoretically guided, and research-informed guidelines • Able to understand and to verbalize to others (e.g., clients, treatment team members) decisions made and actions taken • Credibility • Practicing self-regulation or operating from an internal locus of control within the parameters of professional standards	• Routinely consulting and learning from colleagues and supervisors • Attending quality workshops and professional conferences • Reading professional literature
Measurement and management	• Protecting and preserving those things that are important and valuable to you • Holding onto and accentuating the resources associated with choices you have made in your personal and professional life	• Engaging in routine self-care activities during the workday and your personal time • Engaging in personal therapy • Limiting the amount of your volunteer or pro bono services • Generating realistic goals with clients • Clarifying with your supervisor your exact role and responsibilities

(continued)

TABLE 1.1   Seven Ingredients of Helper Stamina (*continued*)

Ingredients of Helper STAMINA	Definition	Examples
Inquisitiveness	• Curiosity about other people and intrigue about how they function • Fascination with human development and change • Honoring client uniqueness and originality	• Practicing idiographic client care • Referring to diagnoses as conditions clients have, not who they are • Suspending judgment • Engaging in routine self-reflection • Routinely soliciting feedback from clients
Negotiation	• Flexibility and adaptation • Engaging in give-and-take without necessarily giving-in • Responding to and cooperating with others while simultaneously remaining steadfast to and upholding professional guidelines and standards	• Engaging in collaborative and coconstructive conversations with clients and colleagues • Remaining open to new ideas from colleagues • Revising over time long-held beliefs and practices that are no longer helpful • Becoming more assertive on a treatment team to advocate for a particular client's needs
Acknowledgment of agency	• Salutary or strengths-based orientation • Recognition and promotion of human instrumentality, intrinsic motivation, and resilience • Remaining confident in the undeniably persistent strength, resourcefulness, and will of the human spirit	• Assessing and promoting client strengths and resources • Conveying hope to clients • Living a life worth living • Implementing a recovery plan • Pursuing with diligence a new area of expertise • "Blooming where I'm planted"

Source: Osborn, C. J. (2004). Seven salutary suggestions for counselor stamina. Journal of Counseling & Development, 82, 319–328.

because it is multidimensional, Tjeltveit and Gottlieb (2010) also defined resilience as a set of relatively stable personal characteristics (e.g., virtues). Using the acronym DOVE, they identified four assets that enhance therapist resilience while decreasing therapist vulnerability to ethical misconduct. These therapist assets or dimensions of resilience are: having a Desire to help others, creating and making use of available Opportunities for personal enrichment and professional development, consulting and revising core Values, and approaching Education as lifelong learning. Among their eight recommendations for cultivating resilience to "move toward ethical excellence" (p. 108) are engaging in regular self-assessment and seeking psychotherapy and structured supervision.

The need for helper stamina and resilience is evident in the reflections of a bereaved father that Neimeyer (1998) shared and that are presented in Box 1.1 on page 15. This man's story underscores the importance of walking alongside and waiting with our clients rather than trying to "fix" them or "solve" their concerns. Before reading further, take a moment to read this father's reflections.

Having read this father's reflections, you may need to pause for a moment. Some of what he has to say is not easy to hear. His grief is quite evident.

Once you have paused to reflect on his words (perhaps rereading his reflections), what thoughts come to mind about your intended style of helping? What wisdom might he be conveying to you as you prepare for the work and lifestyle of a professional helper? How would you propose to offer help to this man at this time in his life? What would you tell him if you were working with him? In addition, what ingredients of stamina and resilience might you need to make use of intentionally as you work with this father? What aspects of temporal sensitivity or negotiation, for example, might be especially helpful to you? What further education would you need to pursue?

As we ourselves read and reflect on his words, it seems that this father's loss cannot be "fixed" and that he resents the well-meaning advice others have offered. As much as we'd like to think of ourselves as problem-solvers, we realize that some hurts and pains simply cannot be "solved." This father may experience living in the metaphoric three-sided house for some time, and no one can build a fourth wall for him—that is, his son will never be restored, will not be brought back to life. This father and all the clients we work with are in charge of constructing their own lives (the ethical value or principle of autonomy that we must honor when working with them); they are the carpenters. As professional helpers, we may be likened to their

BOX 1.1	Story of the Three-Sided House

Steve Ryan, a bereaved father, wrote the following metaphoric account of his life in the aftermath of the death of his 2-year-old son, Sean, from complications following a kidney transplant.

I am building a three-sided house.

It is not a good design. With one side open to the weather, it will never offer complete shelter from life's cold winds. Four sides would be much better, but there is no foundation on one side, and so three walls are all I have to work with.

I am building this place from the rubble of the house I used to own . . . It had four good walls and would, I thought, survive the most violent storm. It did not. A storm beyond my understanding tore my house apart and left the fragments lying on the ground around me . . . And so I must rebuild. Not, as so many onlookers would suggest, because

I need shelter once again. The storm now travels within me, and there is no shelter from the tempest behind doors or walls.

Who can show me how to build here now? There are no architects, no experts in designing three-sided houses. Why is it then that so many people seem to have advice for me? "Move on," they say, quite convinced that another house can replace the one I lost . . . I grow weary of consultations based on murky insight, delivered with such confidence.

. . . [And yet] among those who wish to see my house rise again[,] there are real heroes too. People who are not daunted by the wreckage. It is not a pleasant role for them to play because the dust clings to those who come to see and it will not wash off when they go home . . . Above all they know how difficult this task is, and no suggestion comes from them about how far along I ought to be.

Source: Neimeyer, 1998.

apprentices or at times consulting architects, but they themselves know best the constructed and reconstructed lives and houses that will fit them.

In addition, clients need helpers who are "not daunted by the wreckage," helpers who are able to deal with and make meaning from the "dust that clings" to them from the stories they (i.e., the helpers) have witnessed and indirectly participated in. Our clients deserve helpers who can demonstrate what Kenneth Minkoff characterized as "the courage to join them [clients] in the reality of their despair" (see Mental Illness Education Project, 2000).

Incorporating the seven ingredients of stamina (see Table 1.1) and the four dimensions of resilience (DOVE; see Tjeltveit & Gottlieb, 2010) may assist you in tempering the effects of this demanding work, work that is not for the faint of heart. Specifically, we encourage you to establish your own board of advisers with whom you can consult on a regular basis. These persons would include trusted friends, family members, a supervisor, respected colleagues, and your own therapist. Surrounding yourself with such a support system is essential.

As you read the next section of this chapter, you may understand our decision to discuss core skills and attributes—self-awareness and self-reflection, mindfulness, self-care, and self-compassion, as well as stamina and resilience—prior to discussing issues of effectiveness, accountability, and evidence-based practice (EBP). Just as clients need to be equipped with certain skills (e.g., mindfulness) before they can be expected to manage stressors and other symptoms effectively, professional helpers need to demonstrate core skills before they can be expected to deliver effective services. As we have already discussed, these core skills include self-care and self-compassion.

Think of your clinical skills and your self-care activities as the provisions needed for the arduous journey of service delivery in an age of accountability and EBP. Only by mobilizing learned skills will you be able to hold yourself accountable for the client care you provide.

Effectiveness and Accountability

Today's practice continues to be highly influenced by regulatory requirements and ethical expectations regarding accountability. Use of empirically supported practice and evidence-based decision-making has become part of training accreditation requirements as well as work site expectations, although certainly not without issue. It is expected that in the next 10 years helpers will need to demonstrate the evidence base of practice decisions and outcomes and use practice guidelines in standard therapy, while at the same time conducting short-term and brief therapy (Norcross, Pfund, & Prochaska, 2013). It is for this reason that Putterbaugh (2015) reinforces the importance of deliberate and purposeful practitioner self-care.

Recent health care reform in the United States stipulates that all practitioners will need to demonstrate increased accountability for their work. In effect, this means that we as clinicians need to demonstrate that our work is safe and makes a difference in the lives of our clients. Goodheart (2011) made clear that insurers are now making decisions about allocating funds for treatment services based on a review of client outcomes rather than what had been a utilization review. This means that helpers increasingly will need to provide evidence that clients have improved while in treatment for services to be reimbursed. This certainly raises ethical concerns, but it also suggests that, more than ever, professional helpers will need to deliver services that are consistent with current and established guidelines. No longer can personal experience suffice as the sole or primary standard for justifying treatment decisions (Beutler, 2009). Although the helper's personal experience influences how he or she makes treatment decisions, it is only one source of influence. As discussed earlier in the chapter, Skovholt and Starkey (2010) identified it as one of three sources of knowledge that inform clinical expertise, with the other two being professional experience and academic research. Together, these represent what they referred to as the three legs of the professional helper's learning stool. A one-legged stool will not suffice! All three must be securely in place to supply a firm foundation and a balance of practice.

Evidence-Based Practice

The delivery of evidence-based practice (EBP) or the **LO2** provision of empirically supported services is the expectation of contemporary clinical and behavioral practice, not only in the United States but also in many other countries. Thyer (2009; Thyer & Myers, 2011) noted that the major contributors to EBP, particularly in medicine and social work, were British and Canadian. Some might say it is only recently that U.S. health care providers are catching up with their Canadian, European, and Australian counterparts. This may be true in light of recent health care reforms in the United States, primarily the Patient Protection and Affordability Care Act signed into law in March 2010 by President Obama and upheld twice by the U.S. Supreme Court. This means that translating research findings into everyday clinical practice and substantiating treatment decisions made in the throes of an emergency or during routine work are now the global norm for health care providers.

Although psychologists have been at the forefront of EBP in the United States since the 1980s, what Thyer (2009) referred to as science-informed practice is not new to social work. He explained that it was this positivist focus that distinguished social work from its beginnings in the late 1880s as faith-based ministerial outreach and as a charitable organization. "Scientific charity" and "scientific philanthropy" actually were two of the original names for the social case work movement in the United States, leading Thyer (2009) to reinforce that "the principles of EBP are congruent with central core descriptions of social work dating back to the beginnings of our field" (p. 1117). Yet it has been the psychology profession in the United States that in many ways has framed the current conversation about EBP.

The Staying Power of EBP

It is evident that EBP is here to stay. The Evidence-based Behavioral Practice project (www.ebbp.org) claims that "all major health professions now endorse the policy of evidence-based practice." Many of these same organizations have developed what are known as evidence-based **clinical practice guidelines**, what Hollon et al. (2014) define as "a systematic approach to translating the best available research evidence into clear statements regarding treatments for people with various health conditions" (p. 214). The use of such guidelines in treatment planning is discussed in Chapter 9.

Many states have adopted the practice of evidence-based policymaking, which includes performance-based budgeting. This entails cost-benefit analysis so that only programs that have demonstrated effectiveness continue to receive state funding. These programs include child welfare and corrections. Fourteen states facing economic difficulties have partnered with the Results First Initiative, a project of the Pew Charitable Trusts and the MacArthur Foundation, to help them identify ineffective programs to budget only proven programs (see www.pewtrusts.org). One of these states is Illinois, whose governor established in February 2015 a criminal justice commission to reduce the state prison population by 25 percent by the year 2025. To do so, "evidence-based programming" will be pursued such as diversion programs (i.e., drug and specialty courts, intensive probation).

Straus, Richardson, Glasziou, and Haynes (2010) argued, however, that evidence-based medicine is not necessarily a cost-savings endeavor because "providing evidence-based care directed toward maximizing patients' quality of life often *increases* the costs of their care and raises the ire of health economists" (p. 8; emphasis added). This serves as a reminder that EBP should not be regarded as strictly or only a way to save money; rather, EBP should be used to provide quality care. In the context of economic realities, the point is to use limited resources wisely. As Miller, Zweben, and Johnson (2005) noted, "It makes good sense to give priority to [evidence-based treatments], particularly within this era of fiscal austerity. We owe it to our clients to provide the best treatment that we can offer them within available resources" (p. 274).

Discredited Therapies

Some have stated that rather than identifying so-called best practices or effective practices, EBP has helped to identify treatment interventions that are *not* effective (without effect or inert) or are potentially harmful. As Beutler (2009) indicated, "It appears to be easier to identify a bad treatment than a very good one" (p. 310). Although defining what exactly constitutes harm and what is directly responsible for harm in psychotherapy is a complicated endeavor (Dimidjian & Hollon, 2010), it seems that one contribution of EBPs is that they have been able to weed out certain practices—despite their recognition, appeal, and popularity—that actually have been found to be harmful to service recipients (i.e., clients are worse off after receiving these interventions than before). These practices include rebirthing therapy, boot camp interventions for juvenile offenders, critical incident stress debriefing, and drug abuse and resistance education (or DARE; see Lilienfeld, 2007, for a listing of additional potentially harmful treatments). Treatments such as these are regarded as discredited therapies (Norcross, Koocher, Fala, & Wexler, 2010; Norcross, Koocher, & Garofalo, 2006), therapies that have undergone testing over time and have been found not to make a difference or to exert a negative effect, in other words, to exert harm (e.g., exacerbated symptoms at follow-up, or even death as a direct result of treatment). It is thus important to recognize the reasons for EBP because helpers who do not "may fail to appreciate how readily they can be fooled by ineffective or harmful treatments" (Lilienfeld, Ritschel, Lynn, Cautin, & Latzman, 2013, p. 884).

Avoiding the use of discredited and harmful therapies or interventions actually is an ethical imperative. Section C.7. of the *ACA Code of Ethics* (2014) stipulates the types or quality of techniques, procedures, or modalities counselors are to use with clients. Specifically, only those practices "grounded in theory and/or have an empirical or scientific foundation" (Section C.7.a.) are to be considered. Furthermore, Section C.7.c. is explicit in its statement that "Counselors do not use techniques/procedures/modalities when substantial evidence suggests harm, even if such services are requested."

Discredited therapies must be differentiated from therapies that have yet to be tested or whose effects remain unknown or inconclusive—therapies that may be inert, beneficial, or detrimental but for which consistent and substantial evidence from methodologically sound investigations is absent. Solution-focused therapy (SFT) is one example. Although it is a popular therapy that has been practiced for more than 30 years, in many countries SFT has not been subjected to the rigorous testing that other therapies have undergone, such as motivational interviewing (MI). Unlike MI, SFT has not gained the recognition as an EBP. Recent efforts to examine the effects of SFT in more sophisticated ways are encouraging (see Franklin, Trepper, Gingerich, & McCollum, 2012), and we discuss these research findings—and those of MI—in Chapter 10.

Affirmative Therapies

As with SFT, affirmative therapies developed specifically for lesbian, gay, and bisexual (LGB) individuals (see Chernin & Johnson, 2003; Kort, 2008), transgender and gender nonconforming individuals, and lesbian, gay, bisexual, and transgender (LGBT) couples and families (see Bigler & Wetchler, 2012) have yet to establish a strong research base and to be recognized as an EBP (see Johnson, 2012). This has not thwarted their promotion by various professional associations (e.g., the American Psychological Association's 2009 *Resolution on Appropriate Affirmative Responses to Sexual Orientation Distress and Change Efforts*; see APA, 2011) and their depiction as synonymous with culturally competent therapy (Johnson, 2012). The APA (2012) also has developed *Guidelines for Psychological Practice with Lesbian, Gay, and Bisexual Clients* and guidelines for working with transgender persons are forthcoming.

It is because affirmative therapies endorse a strengths or empowerment perspective (see Boes & van Wormer, 2009) and represent a humanistic and nondiscriminatory practice that they are viewed today as the ethical alternative to so-called conversion therapies. Conversion or reparative therapies have been determined to cause more harm than benefit to LGB individuals and to society as a whole because they reinforce stigma and prejudice. The APA (2011) has referred to "the emerging knowledge on" culturally affirmative therapies as "a foundation for an appropriate evidence-based practice with children, adolescents, and adults who are distressed by or seek to change their sexual orientation."

The APA (2011) policy statement on affirmative therapies illustrates very well Thyer and Myers's (2011) contention that "EBP involves not just a consideration of research evidence but also of other factors...such as individual clinical expertise, patient preferences, values and circumstances, and no one of these elements is afforded primacy over the others" (p. 18). In other words, determining what constitutes the "evidence" for an EBP should not be confined to the outcomes of randomized clinical/control trials (RCTs). Perhaps this is what Goodheart (2011) meant in her statement that EBP does not privilege certain types of data. Although RCTs are considered the gold standard in medical research, the clinician's expertise, the client's culture and preferences, and ethical standards of professional associations must also serve prominent roles in determining the "evidence" of an EBP.

Defining EBP

It should be apparent by now that there are many ways to define EBP. Given our review of the research literature and the proceedings of professional associations, we endorse the APA definition: EBP is "the integration of the best available research with clinical expertise in the context of patient characteristics, culture, and preferences" (APA Presidential Task Force on Evidence-Based Practice, 2006, p. 273). Derived from the definition of evidence-based medicine (see Straus et al., 2010), this definition of EBP highlights the essential contributions of clinicians and clients to what is considered evidentiary practice. In other words, EBP is not—or *should not* be—a top-down mandate from researchers to clinicians, but rather is—or *should* be—a dynamic discourse among clients, clinicians, and researchers. This exemplifies the contention made by Thyer and Myers (2011) that EBP is a *process* and therefore is a verb, not a noun. This notion of process seems to be supported by Goodheart (2011) when she described EBP as that which incorporates new clinical phenomena, research, theory, and professional consensus (e.g., ethical codes) to provide clients with individualized and beneficial care. She and colleagues (Wampold, Goodheart, & Levant, 2007) also stipulated that EBP is not prescriptive but descriptive and serves as a guide in that EBP offers recommendations for the selection and implementation of treatment services. Lilienfeld et al. (2013) discussed other misconceptions of EBP. These are listed in Box 1.2.

Note that our discussion here is about evidence-based *practice, not* evidence-based *treatment*. This is a very important distinction (LaRoche & Christopher, 2009; Littell, 2010; Thyer & Pignotti, 2011; Westen, Novotny, & Thompson-Brenner, 2005). The former is inclusive of client and helper factors (e.g., client cultural diversity), treatment interventions and setting, and research findings (consistent with the 2006 APA definition); the latter is concerned only with interventions or techniques—the tools that we discussed earlier in this chapter that are external to the helper and therefore do not equate with helper skills. Furthermore, as Thyer and Myers (2011) noted, EBP is a dynamic process, a verb, whereas evidence-based treatment—or what have

been referred to as empirically supported treatments, or ESTs (Chambless & Hollon, 1998)—is a static noun. This implies that EBPs are fluid and susceptible to revision and cultural adaptation, whereas ESTs are absolute fixtures that are resistant to change and can be mistaken for the once-and-for-all solution for all clients.

Given these distinctions, it is extremely important that as an emerging professional helper you see yourself as an influential ingredient in the process of client change. This means that you not look to a specific treatment, technique, or tool as the sole answer to or the only source of healing for your clients. Thinking that all that is needed for client improvement is your selection of the best tool from your toolbox is thinking like a magician and investing power in a magic wand. In this era of EBP, magicians and magic have no place. Rather, the focus is on you as a skilled practitioner and your use of skillful means, which includes your ability to: (1) learn from and work in a collaborative fashion with each of your clients; (2) consult and critique empirical research findings; (3) understand the standards of professional ethics; (4) participate in and contribute to constructive dialogues with your clinical supervisor and other skilled practitioners in your profession and in related professions; and (5) adapt your therapeutic style over the course of your career based on what you have learned from these various constituents (i.e., clients, research literature, professional standards, supervisors and colleagues). It is this focus on skillful means—in the context of EBP—that we suspect contributed to Beutler's (2009) (re)definition of psychotherapy as "[t]he therapeutic management, control, and adaptation of patient factors, therapists' factors, relationship factors, and technique factors that are associated with benefit and helpful change" (p. 311).

Becoming Familiar with EBP

To help you develop and calibrate your skillful means—your therapeutic management, control, and adaptation

---

BOX 1.2	**Eight Misconceptions of Evidence-Based Practices**

Evidence-based practices (EBPs):

1. Stifle innovation and the development of new treatments and practices
2. Require "cookie-cutter" and "one-size-fits-all" approaches to treatment
3. Do not include nonspecific influences or common factors in therapy
4. Do not generalize to clients who have not participated in research studies, including randomized controlled trials (RCTs)

5. Neglect evidence other than that obtained from RCTs
6. Are unnecessary because all treatments are equally effective.
7. Are inherently limited because therapeutic changes cannot be measured or quantified
8. Are erroneous because human behavior defies prediction with certainty

Source: Lilienfeld et al., 2013

of various clinical factors—we encourage you to consult the lists, registries, and reviews of EBPs that are available currently from a number of professional organizations. Although EBP lists have been criticized (Beutler & Forrester, 2014; Thyer & Pignotti, 2011; Wachtel, 2010), we believe they offer professional helpers the opportunity to learn more about and to scrutinize approaches heard about only in passing. They also may provide helpers with information not offered to them by superiors during mandated training on a recently instituted EBP.

Seven online sources are presented in Table 1.2. These include reviews of EBPs. The contents of these electronic sources are updated periodically as new research findings are introduced or new selection criteria implemented, so it is best to check these sites every few months to determine what, if any, changes have been made. Bear in mind that none of these lists is exhaustive and that each site may use different criteria for what it deems to be an EBP. Therefore, we recommend that you use your critical thinking skills as you read the reviews of a selected intervention or practice on one of these lists. Read carefully the purported benefits as well as the criticisms. Look for how often and how recently each practice has been reviewed and updated. Take careful note of how the practices listed attend to cultural factors, such as the availability of treatment materials in languages other than English and the flexibility of extending or abbreviating services to accommodate specific client needs and preferences.

As you learn more about a specific practice and its interventions on one of these lists, you may wish to compare it against each of the nine ideal features of a mental health intervention proposed by Bond, Drake, and Becker (2010). According to their definition, the ideal features of a mental health intervention are that it should:

1. Be well defined

2. Reflect client goals

3. Be consistent with societal goals

4. Demonstrate effectiveness

5. Have minimum side effects

6. Have positive long-term outcomes

7. Have reasonable costs

8. Be relatively easy to implement

9. Be adaptable to diverse communities and client subgroups

In addition to consulting the lists, registries, and reviews of EBPs, professional helpers will soon be consulting evidence-based clinical treatment guidelines (see Hollon et al., 2014) mentioned earlier in this section. Described as recommendations for psychological interventions for specific disorders, Goodheart (2011) reported that these guidelines are intended to "facilitate

TABLE 1.2   Registries, Lists, and Reviews of EBPs

Registry Name	Sponsoring Group	Date Established	Website
National Registry of Evidence-Based Programs and Practices	Substance Abuse and Mental Health Services Administration	1997	www.nrepp.samhsa.gov
Cochrane Reviews	The Cochrane Collaboration	1995	www.cochrane.org/cochrane-reviews
Research-Supported Psychological Treatments	Society of Clinical Psychology, Division 12 of the American Psychological Association	2008	www.psychology.sunysb.edu/eklonsky-/division12
What Works Clearinghouse	U.S. Department of Education	2002	http://ies.ed.gov/ncee/wwc
Social Programs that Work	Coalition for Evidence-Based Policy	2001	http://evidencebasedprograms.org
The Campbell Collaboration Library of Systematic Reviews	The Campbell Collaboration	2000	www.campbellcollaboration.org/library
Results First Clearinghouse Database	Pew-MacArthur Results First Initiative	2015	www.pewtrusts.org/en/multimedia/data-visualizations/2015/results-first-clearinghouse-database

the integration of science into practice, offer a framework for clinical decision making, provide benchmarks for evaluating treatments, benefit patients by promoting quality improvements and discouraging harmful practices, identify gaps in research and care, and give clinicians flexible tools to support their work" (p. 341). She stipulated that these guidelines are decision aids and are not to be viewed as prescriptive protocols or a substitute for clinical judgment. Unlike practice guidelines that are practitioner-focused, these treatment guidelines are client-focused.

Concerns, Critiques, and Caveats of Evidence-Based Practice

EBP has become big business. You will likely find frequent references to practices or interventions that are "evidence-based" as you scan the issues of recent scholarly journals, peruse the titles of new books for professional helpers from a variety of publishing companies, and browse the listings of workshops offered at professional conferences. As we mentioned, this appeal of EBP is due in part to the belief that adopting an EBP will save time and money, apparent in the mandates of state legislative bodies in the United States. Morales and Norcross (2010) also discussed the trend among federal agencies that, to be considered for grant funding, applications must include an intention to implement one or more EBPs. Third-party payers and other funding sources—as well as accrediting bodies—thus have been known to latch onto certain evidence-based treatments because they are viewed as cost-effective and hence "successful." Short-term cognitive behavior therapy, for example, may be heralded by certain insurance companies as the "best" treatment for all their providers to practice because, in the long run, it is not as protracted or long-term (and hence expensive) as, say, certain types of expressive-supportive therapies. However, marketing EBPs as the solution to cash-strapped state and federal budgets exemplifies what Gambrill (2010) described as propaganda. In other words, it is misleading. It reflects a one-size-fits-all approach (see Bernal, Jiménez-Chafey, & Rodríguez, 2009) that Wachtel (2010) described as "the Walmart approach to mental health care" (p. 264). As we stated, Straus et al. (2010) noted that evidence-based medicine actually is *not* an effective cost-cutting tool. For certain interventions to be effective, they noted, longer and more intensive care may be necessary. We believe this is also true for mental health and addictions treatment.

The hype surrounding EBP therefore requires careful scrutiny and the EBP bandwagon must be approached with caution. Although EBP in social work is, according to Thyer (2009), differentiated from "impulsive altruism, the efforts of faith-based social missionaries, or unsystematic secular efforts aimed at helping others" (p. 1116), EBPs as a whole are not "magical answers for complex questions [or] over-simplistic approaches to complex problems" (Sexton & Kelley, 2010, p. 85). Healthy skepticism is in order. This includes inspecting what is meant by "evidence." For example, should only the findings from randomized clinical/control trials (RCTs) constitute the evidence for treatment practice? Or should findings from studies conducted in applied settings (e.g., a community mental health agency) following normal, routine clinical procedures also be included? The first type of research comprises studies conducted in the most ideal experimental conditions (e.g., controlled and manualized treatments, random assignment, selected clients and helpers), usually comparing one type of treatment to another or to a control group (e.g., clients on a wait list), or both. These are referred to as *efficacy* studies. The second type of research comprises *effectiveness* studies and does not adhere to the strict (or some might say "sterile") laboratory research standards of RCTs. Effectiveness studies exemplify what has been referred to as "pragmatic, utilitarian research" (Sanchez & Turner, 2003, p. 126) and may emphasize more idiographic than traditional nomothetic subject research. A concern about efficacy studies is that their findings may not easily transfer to actual, everyday practice (Beutler & Forrester, 2014). In a similar vein, a concern about effectiveness studies is that their findings may not be generalizable to other practitioners, treatment facilities, or clients. Hence, the evidence derived from the research question, "What works for whom under what conditions?" may have limited utility from either an efficacy or an effectiveness perspective.

In addition to the overreliance on RCTs (i.e., efficacy studies) as the gold standard for determining what constitutes an EBP, EBPs have been criticized for confining themselves to a single diagnostic category. It is true that many EBPs were developed for clients presenting with specified diagnostic disorders. For example, motivational interviewing (MI) is an EBP for persons with substance use disorders, and dialectical behavior therapy (DBT) is recognized as an EBP for persons with borderline personality disorder. According to Wachtel (2010), the solitary diagnostic confinement of EBPs dismisses the majority of persons with more than one disorder (i.e., comorbidity) and does not account for persons in therapy who do not fit the minimal criteria for any mental health or substance use disorder (i.e., at a subthreshold for a diagnosis). These are valid concerns. However, a greater number of EBPs now are being applied to persons presenting with a range of concerns. Seeking Safety (Najavits, 2002), for example, is intended for persons with a history of trauma and substance-related problems. Likewise, DBT now is considered appropriate for persons with multiple diagnoses (e.g., eating disorder, substance use disorder, and bipolar disorder) and concerns (e.g., chronically suicidal), and MI has expanded its application to include persons with a variety of health problems such as diabetes, high cholesterol, and obesity (Rollnick, Miller, & Butler, 2008).

EBPs also have been criticized for an overreliance on manuals. It is true that many if not most EBPs have a treatment manual and perhaps a separate training manual. To be included in the U.S. Substance Abuse and Mental Health Services Administration's (SAMHSA) National Registry of Evidence-Based Programs and Practices (NREPP), for example, recognized programs need to have developed training and support resources, implementation materials (e.g., treatment manual), and quality assurance procedures, all of which are ready for use by the public. The development and use of a treatment manual is an example of internal validity, allowing the intervention to be distinguished from and compared to other treatments in RCTs. Treatment adherence is referred to as fidelity and allows researchers to determine whether the intervention being tested was faithful to its design or purpose. The concern about treatment manuals is that the practice can become "manualized," resulting in an approach that is too rigid and objectifies clients (Littell, 2010). Clinicians themselves can feel "manualized"—that is, feel coerced and confined to one type of treatment—resulting in a restriction of their autonomy, flexibility, and creativity. According to Overholser (2010), adhering to a treatment manual can compromise clinical expertise, such as inhibiting clinical judgment/decision-making and complex reasoning skills. This is a valid concern and explains Barkham, Hardy, and Mellor-Clark's (2010) preference for *practice-based evidence* or the pursuit of effective care based on the "evidence" from routine clinical practice (consistent with effectiveness studies), whether or not a treatment manual is followed. This illustrates the practice of what Scott and Lewis (2015) refer to as *measurement-based care* wherein client feedback is routinely solicited.

A resolution to these criticisms and concerns of EBP is premature. We suspect that the controversies surrounding EBPs will continue for some time. Although it is frustrating for helpers and researchers alike (perhaps for different reasons), we believe there has been merit in this controversy over the past 20 to 25 years. For one thing, the debate has opened lines of communication between practitioners and researchers. Second, such conversations

perhaps have helped to keep the focus on what is in the best interest of the client, including prioritizing client experiences of treatment by soliciting their feedback (see Lambert, 2010). Third, discussions about evidence-based practices appear to have ushered in a more integrative or both/and perspective about client care, consistent with the APA (2006) definition of EBP. One example of an integrative approach to EBP is that of cultural adaptation, an overdue initiative given that racially and ethnically diverse participants historically have not been included in RCTs (Bernal & Sáez-Santiago, 2006; Comas-Díaz, 2006; Whaley & Davis, 2007). We discuss the role of culture in EBP in the following section.

Multiculturalism and Evidence-Based Practice

Traditional psychotherapy and EBPs for the most part have been developed, validated, and promoted by white European Americans for use with a predominantly white European American client population. The research to support these approaches has been conducted with a similarly privileged client population—that is, white European American, middle class, and heterosexual. The evidence to substantiate that these approaches are appropriate for culturally diverse and nondominant/minority group clients therefore is lacking, and implementing an EBP for clients for whom the EBP was not developed could potentially harm ethnic minority clients (Bernal et al., 2009). Thus, the challenge is to conduct methodologically sound research of culturally specific practices and interventions *and* adapt existing EBPs to fit the needs of culturally diverse clients. Doing both represents the inherent tension or dialectic of EBP: maintaining scientific soundness/rigor while ensuring clinical relevance. This dialectic is evident in Morales and Norcross's (2010) contention that "Multiculturalism without strong research risks becoming an empty political value, and EBP without cultural sensitivity risks irrelevancy" (p. 823).

Morales and Norcross (2010) describe the relationship between multiculturalism and EBP as transitioning from "strange bedfellows" to "fast friends." This suggests that cultural adaptation of EBPs or the integration of EBP and multicultural therapy is a promising initiative. However, Hwang (2009) noted that this focus must shift from simply being a set of abstract ideas about cultural competence to an emphasis on developing specific helper skills and strategies that can be implemented effectively with culturally diverse clients. This is not an easy task. It does not mean simply using existing EBPs with culturally diverse clients. And it involves more than a helper simply learning about a particular cultural group of which the client is a member or matching culturally diverse helpers with clients of their same cultural group (e.g., African American helpers working with African American clients). According to Helms (2015), EBPs must be culturally responsive by considering client and helper racial socialization (e.g., racism), client responses to EBPs, and client-helper cultural dynamics.

Culturally Adapted EBPs

Considerable attention has been given to what are referred to as culturally adapted EBPs. This involves systematically modifying, supplementing, or sequencing an intervention (e.g., thought-stopping technique) or intervention protocol (e.g., cognitive behavior therapy for anxiety) to accommodate or to be compatible with the client's cultural patterns, meanings, and values (Bernal et al., 2009; Morales & Norcross, 2010). According to Bernal and Sáez-Santiago (2006), this includes, among other things, a consideration of: (a) interdependent value systems (i.e., family system) rather than individualistic value systems; (b) spirituality in the healing process; and (c) poverty. Benish, Quintana, and Wampold (2011) emphasized understanding and explaining illness from the client's cultural milieu and adapting interventions to fit this illness explanation. Their research found that when helpers were able to do this, racial and ethnic minority clients benefitted more from culturally adapted EBPs than from conventional psychotherapy approaches. Aguilera, Garza, and Muñoz (2010) further noted that adaptation is a fluid process that must take into account not only broad ethnocultural values (e.g., family system) but also local and specific elements that are part of each client's social reality (e.g., level of acculturation, substance use, access to health care).

Culturally Adapted CBT

One EBP, cognitive behavior therapy (CBT), has been adapted to various cultural groups because of what Hays (2009) noted as the "remarkable number of assumptions" (p. 355) shared by CBT and multicultural therapy. These include the emphasis on: (a) tailoring treatment to the unique strengths and needs of each client; (b) empowerment; and (c) conscious processes (e.g., observed behaviors) that can be verbalized and assessed fairly easily. The latter emphasis, she stated, is suitable for persons whose primary language is not English or who do not share belief systems that are common among European Americans.

In their work with American Indians and Alaska Natives, BigFoot and Schmidt (2010) acknowledged that CBT principles complement many traditional tribal healing and cultural practices such as storytelling and expressing emotions in ceremonies. Bennett-Levy et al. (2014) reported that Aboriginal Australian counselors trained in CBT found CBT useful with their Aboriginal clients for several reasons. These included that CBT: (a) is pragmatic (simple interventions can be effective for complex problems); (b) highly adaptable and useful as a preventive measure (e.g., mental health hygiene); (c) provides structure that maintains focus; and (d) is empowering and promotes self-agency. One CBT method reported to be most useful with clients was the use of visual diagrams. Aboriginal counselors also found that CBT enhanced their skills and confidence, as well as their well-being (i.e., protecting from burnout).

Specific examples of culturally adapted EBPs based on CBT principles include: Aguilera et al.'s (2010) 16-week group CBT in Spanish for adults with depression; Nicolas, Arntz, Hirsch, and Schmiedigen's (2009) 8-week *adolescent Coping with Depression Course* for Haitian American adolescents; BigFoot and Schmidt's (2010) program for American Indian/Alaska Native children who have experienced trauma, *Honoring Children, Mending the Circle* (see www.icctc.org), an adaptation of trauma-focused CBT (Cohen, Mannarino, & Deblinger, 2006); and Cunningham, Foster, and Warner's (2010) adaptation of multisystemic therapy (MST; Henggeler, Schoenwald, Borduin, Rowland, & Cunningham, 2009) specifically for African American youth and their caregivers (e.g., parent, grandparent) to address the adolescents' delinquency and substance misuse. In all three of these culturally adapted programs, importance is placed on: (a) the use of culturally and clinically relevant language (e.g., reference to *proyecto personal* or "personal project" rather than "homework"); (b) maintaining a strength focus; (c) routinely soliciting feedback from clients and their caregivers or other family members about the helpfulness of therapy (including the formation of an advisory board comprising cultural experts to help develop a culturally relevant program before it is implemented); and (d) practicing reinforcement of positive behaviors, validation, and empathy among therapists as well as among clients (e.g., promoting *simpatía* or healthy social interactions among group members).

Evidence for Culturally Adapted EBPs

Evidence suggests that cultural adaptation of therapeutic approaches results in significant client improvement across a range of presenting concerns and conditions and according to a variety of outcome measures (Benish et al., 2011; Griner & Smith, 2006). But as Morales and Norcross (2010) contend, adaptation presumes that the helper "is competent in the cultural and linguistic aspects of the client and has experience in integrating these variables in a culturally competent and congruent manner" (p. 826). This means that a prerequisite for the cultural adaptation of any EBP is competence in multicultural counseling and therapy and, specifically, the ability to understand and empathize with the client's unique cultural identity and context. This means, for example, that helpers should not assume that all tribal and native people have similar traditions, a reminder offered by BigFoot and Schmidt (2010). This also means that helpers are able to appreciate the meaning each client has rendered to the intersection of his or her multiple identities, such as age, gender, sexual orientation, and race/ethnicity. These overlapping "selves" comprise the client's own cultural identity (a concept we discuss in more detail in Chapter 2), requiring the adaptation of any EBP to be tailored to that particular client. This constitutes an idiographic EBP adaptation rather than a nomothetic EBP adaptation. The former is tailored to a specific client, whereas the latter is considered applicable to persons who are members of a certain cultural group, such as lesbian, gay, bisexual, and transgender (LGBT) persons or persons of Latino/Hispanic descent. Duarté-Vélez, Bernal, and Bonilla (2010) provide a helpful clinical example of an idiographic adaptation of an EBP (in this case, CBT) for a gay Latino adolescent male who was raised in a Christian home.

Griner and Smith (2006) reviewed 76 studies published through 2004 to determine the effectiveness of culturally adapted treatment interventions. They identified 10 common types of cultural adaptations used in these studies. To their list we have added (number 11) the one recommended by Benish et al. (2011):

1. Explicitly incorporating cultural values/concepts into the intervention (e.g., storytelling of folk heroes to children)
2. Matching the client and helper according to race or ethnicity
3. Providing services in the client's native language (other than English)
4. Providing services in a treatment facility specifically targeting clients from culturally diverse backgrounds (e.g., Africentric programming for African American youth in a substance abuse treatment facility)
5. Collaborating/consulting with individuals familiar with the client's culture (e.g., family members, elders, tribal leaders)
6. Engaging in outreach efforts to recruit underserved clients
7. Providing extra services to increase client retention (e.g., child care, transportation)
8. Orally administering written materials for illiterate clients
9. Conducting cultural sensitivity training for professional staff
10. Providing referrals to external agencies for additional services
11. Understanding and explaining illness from the client's cultural beliefs and adapting interventions to this illness explanation

From their meta-analysis of outcomes reported in these studies, Griner and Smith (2006) found, overall, that clients improved significantly as a result of having received at least one culturally adapted intervention. One noteworthy finding was that groups of same-race clients who received services tailored specifically to their cultural group (e.g., older Cuban Americans seeking help for depression) improved considerably more than clients who were in mixed-race treatment groups (e.g., African American and Hispanic adolescents attending the same facility and receiving services for substance abuse). This reinforces the contention that optimal benefit is derived when services are tailored to a specific cultural context. Greater improvement was also found among older clients compared to younger clients (possibly due to the protective effects of lower acculturation levels among older clients) and when clients were matched with a therapist based on language (other than English) compared to clients who were not assigned to therapists who spoke their native language. An unexpected finding was that clients matched with therapists of their own race or ethnicity fared no better than clients who did not work with a therapist of their own race or ethnicity. The failure of client-therapist ethnic matching by itself to effect positive change in clients is consistent with previous studies, however (e.g., Knipscheer & Kleber, 2004), and suggests that therapist multicultural competence and organizational cultural competence (referred to as cultural congruence by Constantino, Malgady, & Primavera, 2009) is a multifaceted construct.

To investigate the effects of cultural adaptations of specific interventions and EBPs in general, research methods other than RCTs need to be used (Helms, 2015). One is the participatory action research method used with Aboriginal Australian counselors by Bennett-Levy et al. (2014) and praised by Hays (2014). Other research methods include naturalistic, quasi-experimental process-outcome studies (e.g., assessing in-session client-helper behaviors through audio or video recording or third-party live observation and rating) and single-case or $N = 1$ studies. As an example of practice-based evidence, McMillan and Morley (2010) described the process of conducting single-case quantitative research, which necessarily includes repeated measurement of client concerns and goals after baseline. We discuss these assessment practices in Chapters 7 and 8.

BigFoot and Schmidt (2010) described the cultural adaptation of EBPs as "the blending of science and indigenous cultures" (p. 855). They posited that the success of this blending or integration "is the translation of not just language but also core principles and treatment concepts so that they become meaningful to the culturally targeted group while still maintaining fidelity" (p. 855).

Adapting and Adopting Evidence-Based Practices

Most EBPs began as innovations in that they represent the integration of two or more therapies. For example, dialectical behavior therapy (DBT) is an adaptation of CBT in its incorporation of Eastern philosophy, namely Zen, and mindfulness practice. The balance of behavior change and acceptance—the fundamental tension or dialectic of DBT—is a treatment goal and reflects the innovative style of DBT. Although DBT is an EBP for borderline personality disorder, it must continue to undergo adaptation for it to be relevant and remain clinically useful for helpers and clients alike (see Dimeff & Koerner, 2007). This is true for all EBPs. If, as Thyer and Myers (2011) noted, EBP is a verb or a dynamic process rather than a static noun, and if, as Wampold et al. (2007) stipulated, EBPs are guidelines rather than absolutes and mandates, then EBPs must be subjected to ongoing modifications (e.g., cultural adaptations) that are able to demonstrate beneficial effects for clients and their families using a variety of sound measures. Only in so doing will EBPs shed their notoriety as reflections of what Wachtel (2010) termed "a poverty of imagination" (p. 254). It is from the (healthy) tension between science and clinical practice/expertise that innovations and future EBPs are born.

As innovations, adopting EBPs and implementing them into routine clinical practice (a process known as diffusion or technology transfer) is not a simple task. Klein and Knight (2005) discussed several reasons why innovations are difficult to implement. Among these are that many innovations are unreliable and imperfectly designed, a concern raised by De Los Reyes and Kazdin (2008) with respect to inconsistent findings among evidence-based interventions. They noted, however, that "some evidence, although inconsistent, is clearly better than none" (p. 50). Innovations also require prospective users to acquire new technical knowledge and skills—a time-consuming and often costly endeavor—and to change their roles, routines, and norms. Practitioners accustomed to meeting clients in an office setting, for example, would likely have difficulty transitioning to and adopting the EBP of multisystemic therapy (MST) because MST services are provided to adolescents and their caregivers in their natural environments, such as their school and their home. In addition, the decision to adopt an innovation is typically made by persons in authority. We discussed this earlier in the chapter with respect to state legislative bodies in the United States limiting funding only to those state-supported agencies that implement EBPs. The final reason innovations are difficult to implement, according to Klein and Knight, is that organizations (e.g., treatment facilities, schools, local communities) are a stabilizing force and therefore any change that disrupts stability, status quo, and homeostasis is not necessarily "welcomed with open arms." This might explain why certain discredited practices (e.g., DARE) continue to be popular despite the evidence that they are ineffective and potentially harmful. It also might explain why some in the scientific community remain skeptical of culturally adapted EBPs because they did not derive their evidence from RCTs.

The likelihood of adopting an innovation, such as an EBP, increases when it meets certain criteria. In his seminal book, *Diffusion of Innovations*, sociologist Everett Rogers (1995) identified five attributes of an innovation that, when perceived by members of a particular group (e.g., clinical team), determine whether or how quickly the innovation will be adopted and implemented into routine practice. The five attributes of an innovation are:

1. It must be perceived as having a relative advantage; that is, it must be viewed as being better than or an improvement on current practice. This advantage might be the perceived convenience, prestige, or cost of an EBP.

2. It must be perceived as being consistent with the adopter's experience, values, and goals; in other words, for a helper to use an EBP, it must be compatible or resonate with his or her own values and beliefs as well as previously introduced ideas and practices (e.g., theoretical orientation, cultural competence).

3. It must be easy to understand and use; it must be perceived as simple rather than as complex.

4. Potential users must be able to sample or try it out on a limited basis before making a decision. This is the innovation's attribute of trialability and can be likened to test-driving a car before making a purchase. A trial period is designed to dispel uncertainty about a new idea.

5. The benefits of adopting an innovation must be visible to others. This is the attribute of observability. In the case of EBPs, this is not limited to reading or hearing about research findings; it also includes—perhaps more so—helpers being able to directly witness and testify to the beneficial effects of the EBP for their clients. This appears to support the efforts of practice-based evidence.

Researchers and health care administrators cannot expect helpers to automatically and enthusiastically embrace EBPs simply because "the research says so." Rather, adopting and then implementing these practices is a process that requires time, involvement of and collaboration with clinical staff, provision of staff support (e.g., training, ongoing supervision, financial compensation), and evidence beyond research findings. Just as clients engage in a process of personal change—moving through various stages of readiness to change over time—practitioners also participate in a professional change process when introduced to new practices. Miller et al. (2006) likened this process to learning any new skill, which often entails three aids: ground school or basic training (e.g., graduate school, reading, attending workshops), practice with feedback, and coaching or supervision to reinforce correct practice and cultivate enhancement. We believe that researchers, clinical directors, and supervisors need to engage practitioners (as well as the systems or organizations they represent) in a similar stage of change process when attempting to disseminate innovative approaches.

As you learn more about EBPs in your coursework and in your clinical practice (e.g., from in-service training, professional workshops), we encourage you to consider each EBP you are introduced to according to the five attributes that Rogers (1995) identified. For example, be willing to ask, "How is this EBP intended to benefit clients in ways that that are currently not available?" and "Will I be able to explain this EBP to clients in a way they can understand, in a way that is simple and not confusing to them?"

Innovations with Integrity

Two therapies recognized as EBPs exemplify the benefit of a comprehensive and integrative perspective resulting from ongoing discussions between scientists and practitioners. They have become familiar practices in certain sectors, and the concepts that undergird and guide their respective approaches are not new. However, only in recent years have assertive community treatment (ACTx) and dialectical behavior therapy (DBT) gained wide prominence. An integration of ACTx and DBT also has been proposed (Reynolds, Wolbert, Abney-Cunningham, & Patterson, 2007). We discuss each of these EBPs briefly and encourage you to complete Learning Activity 1.3 on page 26 once you have familiarized yourself with ACTx and DBT.

Assertive Community Treatment

According to Bond, Drake, Mueser, and Latimer (2001), assertive community treatment was first developed in the 1970s as an intensive and holistic approach to the treatment of persons with severe and persistent mental illnesses (e.g., schizophrenia, bipolar disorder). (In this chapter we abbreviate assertive community treatment as ACTx to differentiate it from the acronym ACT that designates acceptance and commitment therapy mentioned earlier in the chapter.) Key features of ACTx (see Box 1.3 on page 26) are that integrated services (e.g., medication management, vocational rehabilitation) are provided not by one person but by a group of professionals (e.g., substance abuse counselor, case manager, nurse) who work as a team. All team members, therefore, share responsibility for caring for the same clients. It is highly unlikely that persons with severe and persistent mental illnesses initiate and maintain active involvement in formal services. Therefore, the majority (approximately 80%) of ACTx services are delivered in the field or *in vivo* (i.e., in the community rather than in a clinical setting) to engage and remain connected with persons challenged by a multiplicity of concerns and prone to frequent relapses and overall instability. In this manner, ACTx is regarded as a proactive, assertive, and persistent treatment approach. It is a "living-systems" alternative to hospital and residential care (see Ellenhorn, 2015) that often is described as "a hospital without walls."

Specific ACTx services target what some might consider basic client needs, such as obtaining housing, food, and medical care as well as managing finances. Although it resembles case management, ACTx is different from and far more comprehensive than intensive case management in that a range of services is delivered directly to the client (rather than linking the client to other service providers) by members of a team (rather than one case manager). In addition, ACTx services are tailored to the individual client, include individual counseling and crisis intervention, and are unlimited. The most encouraging and compelling aspects of ACTx are that it has been

Learning Activity 1.3

Compelling Evidence Exercise

This activity is intended to assess your own motivations for adopting and implementing an evidence-based practice. It can also be used as a classroom activity to generate discussion. As you complete the activity, consult the five attributes of an innovation identified by Everett Rogers (1995) that are listed and defined on pages 24–25.

Consider for a moment that you are on the clinical staff of a community-based mental health facility primarily serving a low-income population, many of whom have severe and persistent mental illnesses (e.g., schizophrenia, personality disorders). In response to the accrediting body's new policy that all accredited treatment facilities adopt and deliver evidence-based practices as standard service, you have been informed that you will soon become a member of a new assertive community treatment (ACTx) team and will need to attend training in dialectical behavior therapy (DBT). Given what you know about ACTx and DBT, what "evidence" will convince you that these two treatment approaches will be worth the investment of your time and energy? What information will compel you to adopt and begin implementing these two practices?

Check all of the following that apply, and add two of your own reasons, too.

1. ____ Learning about research findings from published clinical trials that justify both ACTx and DBT's designation as evidence-based practices.

2. ____ Knowing that I will be receiving close supervision and training tune-ups in the first few months of using these two approaches.

3. ____ Receiving training from seasoned practitioners who themselves have used both ACTx and DBT.

4. ____ Learning that my salary will remain the same and that I will have to pay for half of the DBT training costs.

5. ____ Knowing that I will be part of a team of other clinical staff who will meet at least once per week not only to review client cases but also to offer one another support.

6. ____ Learning that after 6 months of implementing ACTx and DBT, our facility saved the county mental health board several thousands of dollars due to our clients needing fewer psychiatric hospital bed stays.

7. ____ Hearing the stories of (and even being able to interact with) clients of other treatment facilities who have participated in ACTx and DBT and are now managing their symptoms fairly well.

8. ____ Receiving training from prominent researchers who have studied ACTx and DBT for a number of years.

9. ____ Learning that I will be provided with a mobile phone (at no expense to me) so that I can be on-call 24 hours once per week.

10. ____ Knowing that my current caseload will be reduced and that all members of the ACTx team (approximately six to eight) will assume responsibility for the same clients (approximately 50 to 60).

11. ____ Knowing that DBT is a highly structured approach that holds clients accountable for their behaviors while validating their experiences and circumstance in a nonjudgmental and empathic manner.

12. ____ Learning that after 6 months of implementing ACTx and DBT, approximately one-third of the clients our team serves have taken their medications as prescribed and have not been actively suicidal.

13. ____ Learning that client-helper collaboration is a priority in ACTx and DBT, and this resonates or fits with my own belief system of effective therapy.

14. ____ After 6 months of implementing ACTx and DBT, hearing one of my previously hostile and unstable clients describe a recent incident in which he was able to keep his cool after practicing one of his mindfulness exercises.

15. ____ _____

16. ____ _____

found to contribute to reduced psychiatric hospital stays, increased housing stability, and engaging and retaining clients in mental health services (Bond et al., 2001). Compared to case management or to a standard treatment, a review of research found that ACTx services specifically for homeless persons increased their engagement in medical, mental health, and substance use treatment services (Nelson, Aubry, & Lafrance, 2007). Early engagement and retention in ACTx also was found for older persons with severe mental illnesses (Stobbe et al., 2014). For helpers (specifically case managers), the benefits of ACTx participation include a decrease in burnout and an increase in job satisfaction (Boyer & Bond, 1999).

The Assertive Community Treatment Association (www.actassociation.org) was founded in the late 1990s and sponsors an annual conference.

Dialectical Behavior Therapy

Dialectical behavior therapy (DBT) was developed by Marsha Linehan (2015) as a highly structured, multimodal treatment program for suicidal clients meeting the criteria of borderline personality disorder (BPD). It is informed by cognitive behavior theory, biosocial theory (i.e., biological irregularities combined with certain dysfunctional environments), and Eastern philosophy, namely Zen. Although DBT is now regarded as an EBP

BOX 1.3	Key Principles and Practices of Assertive Community Treatment (ACTx)

- Multidisciplinary staffing
- Integration of services
- Team approach
- Low patient-to-staff ratios
- Locus of contact in the community
- Medication management

- Focus on everyday problems in living
- Rapid access
- Assertive outreach
- Individualized services
- Time-unlimited services

Source: Bond et al., 2001.

for the treatment of BPD, recent adaptations of DBT have expanded its application to persons with eating disorders (Wisniewski & Kelly, 2003; Wisniewski, Safer, & Chen, 2007), comorbid personality disorders (i.e., paranoid and obsessive-compulsive personality disorders; Lynch & Cheavens, 2008), and comorbid substance use disorders (i.e., substance use and borderline personality disorders; Lee, Cameron, & Jenner, 2015), whether or not BPD or suicidal intent is present. For adolescents with repeated suicidal and self-injurious behavior, DBT has been found to be effective in reducing those and depresssive behaviors (Mehlum et al., 2014). DBT also has been modified for deaf individuals (O'Hearn & Pollard, 2008), an example of a culturally adaptive EBP.

DBT is based on behavior theory and includes the principles of acceptance, mindfulness, and validation (Neacsiu, Ward-Ciesielski, & Linehan, 2012). Although it is highly structured and calls for the implementation of specific helper skills and client behaviors, DBT is not a rigid or prescriptive approach, and it fits well with the helper skill of flexibility discussed earlier in the chapter. Helpers are instructed to provide individualized care and therefore tailor specific practices to the needs of each client. For example, for persons with bulimia nervosa, Hill, Craighead, and Safer (2011) incorporated appetite awareness training into the first 4 weeks of DBT and modified the DBT diary card to include appetite monitoring.

A guiding premise of DBT is that a convergence or synthesis of what appear to be opposing forces is possible. This process of balancing and regulating conflicting feelings and behaviors is what is meant by *dialectical* in the name DBT. Take, for example, an adult woman with a history of sexual and physical abuse who has attempted suicide on several occasions (symptoms or characteristics often associated with BPD). Although she may interpret the violations she experienced as "proof" that she is "not fit to live," she also has a strong desire to experience an intimate connection with another human being, to be loved (a need that might be interpreted by some as an "attachment disorder" or traits of "dependency"). It is not that

one experience is "wrong" and the other is "right." Rather, both have validity, and in her work with a professional helper this woman would strive to acknowledge and accept both experiences, live with the tension or paradox (i.e., "not fit to live" vs. someone deserving of love), and arrive at a synthesis of the two polarities (e.g., "I have been violated *and* I am a survivor worthy of love").

As a comprehensive approach, DBT offers an array of behavioral strategies, including problem-solving, skills training, contingency management (e.g., behavioral contracting), exposure-based procedures, and cognitive modification. These are complemented by what Linehan (2015) refers to as acceptance-based procedures, such as validation, mindfulness, and distress tolerance. Validation and problem-solving strategies form the core of DBT, and all other strategies are built around them. Validation conveys to the client that the choices he or she has made and the behaviors he or she has engaged in make sense and are understandable, given the client's life situation (i.e., history, current circumstances). Problem-solving is undertaken only after validation has been conveyed (it may need to be repeatedly conveyed), and it includes clarifying the primary concern at hand and then generating alternative solutions. One such strategy, chain analysis, involves the development of "an exhaustive, step-by-step description of the chain of events leading up to and following the behavior . . . [so as to examine] a particular instance of a specific dysfunctional behavior in excruciating detail" (Linehan, 1993a, p. 258). This exercise not only informs the helper about the client's cognitive schema (e.g., the specific details that are remembered) but also teaches the client important self-observational and self-assessment skills, as well as the connections among many different variables, and it teaches that the client has the ability to exert control over those linkages and create new patterns of behavior.

We believe that both ACTx and DBT warrant further consideration by practitioners and scientists/researchers alike. They not only have compelling empirical evidence to justify their continued practice but they also have practical appeal (i.e., they make sense, can be implemented in everyday practice settings), and this is not always the case with evidence-based practices.

CHAPTER SUMMARY

We end this chapter as it began, with the story of the chambered nautilus. Before you complete the two activities at the end of the chapter, we ask once again that you pause to inspect the cover of the book. Think of this as another mindfulness activity! Once you have the book cover in sight, focus your gaze on the center of one of the three spirals, where the life of the mollusk began. Notice that as the mollusk grew and built new and bigger living spaces or compartments, those chambers remained connected to and wrapped themselves around its center, its beginning. It did not distance itself or grow away from its center—it embraced it.

Likening the story of the chambered nautilus to your own change and growth as a professional helper, consider the center of the shell's spiral as your own beginning and foundation as a professional helper, a foundation that includes the core skills and attributes we discussed in this chapter, the skills of self-awareness and self-reflection, mindfulness, and self-care and self-compassion. You will learn more skills and expand your repertoire as you continue in your career, but our wish for you is that you remain connected to these core skills—that you embrace and wrap yourself around these skills and build your practice on them.

As you return your gaze to the visual of the chambered nautilus on the cover of the book, also consider that the expansion of the shell, the ever-expanding and larger compartments, is symbolic of the growth and change of the helping profession. Specifically, think of the adaptations being made to evidence-based practices (EBPs) so that they will be relevant to a wider and more diverse client population. Our helping professions and our way of practice must expand! We cannot limit our work only to certain privileged groups of persons. This is not only disrespectful and discriminatory—an affront to persons who, by no fault of their own, are disadvantaged and have experienced disenfranchisement for perhaps their entire lives—but also stifling. By this we mean that helping professions that remain locked into "same-old, same-old" ways of thinking and practicing become irrelevant and obsolete. Choosing to remain in the same compartment or chamber almost guarantees one's demise. That is why—as with the chambered nautilus and individual professional helpers—helping professions must continually expand. This includes continuing to adapt EBPs to be culturally relevant to an ever-widening and more diverse population.

Our intent and hope is that the remainder of the chapters in this book will assist you in your efforts to grow and change as a helping professional, all the while remaining fastened to and informed by your firm foundation. Keep the story of the chambered nautilus front and center as you move through the book and through your career.

 Visit CengageBrain.com for a variety of study tools and useful resources such as video examples, case studies, interactive exercises, flashcards, and quizzes.

1 | Knowledge and Skill Builder

Part One

Part One is designed to help you recognize the need for the core helper skills of self-awareness and self-reflection, mindfulness, and self-care and self-compassion, consistent with Learning Outcome 1. It is also intended to highlight specific activities to develop each of these three skills to promote your stamina and resilience as a professional helper.

Read through the following dialogue between a counseling student and her practicum supervisor. In what the counseling student says or in what the supervisor says, identify one example (three examples total) of the supervisee's *need* for: (1) self-awareness and self-reflection; (2) mindfulness; and (3) self-care and self-compassion. For each of the three needs you identified, locate an example of a specific *activity* that either the supervisor mentioned or the counseling student verbalized. You can write the identified needs and the corresponding activities on a separate sheet of paper, or simply circle or underline the text in your book. Compare your responses to those provided on pages 33–34.

Jasmine is a full-time clinical mental health counseling student who also works part-time as a server at a popular fine dining restaurant in town. She is in her second semester of practicum and her clients are primarily traditional age college students seeking services at the university counseling center. Jasmine is directly supervised by Dr. Sarah Morton, a full-time professor in the counseling program who teaches practicum. Because it serves as a practicum site, the university counseling center is equipped with video recording equipment and Dr. Morton routinely views the video recordings of Jasmine's counseling sessions.

In a recent individual supervision session, Dr. Morton (Dr. M.) and Jasmine discuss specific skills Jasmine has demonstrated and skills she needs to improve. They also discuss how these skills are needed inside and outside the counseling room.

Dr. M.: You use your time well in session, Jasmine. You know how to begin a session and how to bring it to a close. You also provide your clients with a wealth of information related to resources on campus. You know this university pretty well!

Jasmine: Well, I did go to undergrad here, and being at the restaurant where I am, you have to be efficient. I mean, you can't be lazy, especially when the customers are paying top dollar for their meals.

Dr. M.: Sounds like you're kept on your toes at work. Now, in session with clients, I'd like to see you pace yourself a little better. Sometimes it seems like you're in a hurry to get the session over with. And I wonder, especially with the new client you saw last week, if he felt bombarded with all of the resources on campus you gave him—all in the first session. I noticed that he canceled for this week.

Jasmine: Hmm. I thought that session went fine. He really didn't seem bothered by what I had to say. And I just thought he canceled because he realized he got what he needed in that first session. We have been learning about brief therapy in my advanced theories class, you know, so I thought getting right to the issue and moving things along in the session was a good thing.

Dr. M.: But unless you asked the client directly at the end of the session, or followed up with him after he canceled, you don't really know whether he got what he needed.

Jasmine: Yeah, I guess that's true.

Dr. M.: Have you been able to watch your counseling sessions over the past 2 weeks?

Jasmine: Actually, no. I haven't had a chance. It's been real crazy at work and I've had to babysit my two nephews because my sister's work schedule changed. And on top of everything, I've been applying for an internship position for this fall. The deadline, you know, for getting a site is next week. And I need to graduate this December. My mom's counting on it!

Dr. M.: You have a lot going on right now. And you're trying to meet the expectations that others have for you. How are you managing everything?

Jasmine: Just doing what I need to do to get by. I'm pretty good at multitasking!

Dr. M.: Well, there's only so much that any one of us can handle at one time. Too many things on one plate—or a serving tray—can turn into a stumble or a fall. I imagine you know well from work that you can carry only so much on a tray at one time.

Jasmine: I've gotten pretty good at balancing heavy loads—even with one hand.

Dr. M.: It sounds to me, though, that things have gotten unbalanced for you recently, kind of lopsided. I have this image of you rushing around from one place to another. And in your last two or three counseling sessions, you've seemed distracted—sitting on the edge of your seat for most of the session, not allowing for silences, and providing quite a few suggestions—advice—to clients without first inviting them to come up with their own ideas. This is part of what I mean by needing to pace yourself better.

Jasmine: But they're obviously coming in for help. I mean, the two I saw last week actually asked me what they should do. How can I not tell them? And it just seems like a waste of time to sit there in silence, staring at each other. . .or the floor.

Dr. M.: Be careful that you're not doing all the work in session. This is one example of being lopsided. It really isn't our job as helpers to figure things out for clients—as much as they may want us to, you know, give them answers. It would be like you deciding for each of your customers what they should eat. No menus necessary! Not only does this go against the philosophy or ethic in counseling of a client-helper partnership and also helping clients make decisions for themselves—the idea of empowerment—it

(continued)

1   Knowledge and Skill Builder (*continued*)

also is draining on us. It would be like you having to decide for your customers what they should eat and then going into the kitchen to prepare it for each of them! You wouldn't be able to keep up, would you? And you'd be exhausted.

Jasmine: Yeah, I can see how I've been trying to do too much for my clients, you know, kind of wanting to spoon-feed them or rescue them. And…[pausing] I am tired.

Dr. M.: I'd be surprised if you weren't, especially with all that you have going on in your life right now. How *have* you been managing? I mean, are you getting enough sleep, eating properly, exercising?

Jasmine: No time, Dr. Morton. This is grad school, you know!

Dr. M.: Yes, it is, Jasmine. And grad school is also the time to learn ways of taking care of yourself so that you can endure and remain resilient—and do well—in this challenging work of counseling. If not now, I don't know when. It's not like you can be superwoman forever. You might need to set some time limits and possibly negotiate some of your responsibilities with family and people at work.

Jasmine: That really just seems so selfish, though. I mean, I want to help people.

Dr. M.: In this case, though, when clients are involved, it's not really selfishness; it's actually about self-care. A wise supervisor told me that one time. And it's a part of being a helping professional. When we're not taking care of ourselves, we're not taking care of our clients. Self-care is actually a standard for counselors in the ACA Code of Ethics.

Jasmine: Yeah, I guess we talked about it in my ethics class. It's just so different when you get to prac!

Dr. M.: Now's the time when you realize that you *are* practicing as a professional. And it's probably the time when students learn that they *can't* do everything—like "fixing" their clients, or giving them the so-called "answers." Maybe it's the time when we learn to accept ourselves as human, as not perfect. And, you know, this is what makes it possible to empathize with our clients.

Jasmine: Huh. I never thought about that before—that learning my limits makes me better able to empathize with clients.

Dr. M.: We're human helpers. And that means there's really only so much that any one of us can do. That's just part of being human. Now, speaking of setting limits, I don't know how much leeway you have at work and with your family.

Jasmine: Well, I have to work to pay for school, and with the holidays coming up, I really can't reduce my hours or ask for time off. That's the busiest time at the restaurant, you know, holiday parties and all. And I can't let my sister down. I promised her I'd help out. She's going through a rough time and being the big sister and all, my mom has expected me to take care of her.

Dr. M.: You're stretched to the limit, it seems.

Jasmine: Yeah, that's just how it is right now.

Dr. M.: Well, can I share something with you?

Jasmine: Sure.

Dr. M.: My concern is that all that you are trying to manage outside of counseling is having an effect inside of counseling—on the quality of care you're providing to your clients. I'm particularly concerned that you haven't been able to watch your counseling sessions. Taking the time—stepping outside the routine—to observe and critique yourself is really one of the best ways to improve your skills. Who knows? It might also help you better learn how to manage relationships outside of counseling. What do you think about what I just said?

Jasmine: Hmm. I never thought of it that way before.

Dr. M.: Yes, in many ways, who we are outside of counseling is who we are inside of counseling, and vice versa. And only by setting aside time to really pay attention to what's going on in session, in the present moment, can we really be genuine—with ourselves, and with our clients.

Jasmine: Kind of like doing therapy on yourself, I guess; you know, practicing what you preach.

Dr. M.: Yes, that's good awareness on your part.

Jasmine: But I have to graduate in December. I promised my mom.

Dr. M.: Is that promise set in stone? I mean, what will happen if you delay graduation until May and give yourself some time to do an extended internship, one that perhaps will be more effective in the long run, or at least healthier?

Jasmine: It's just that my mom has such high hopes for me, especially with my sister having problems right now. I've always been the high achiever—first one in my family to get a master's degree—and my mom's real proud of that.

Dr. M.: She has reason to be proud. I'm just wondering about the cost to you—and to your clients, both now in practicum and then in internship—of your rush to get done. I imagine that your customers at work would rather wait for a well-prepared meal—and one served by you when you're not out of breath or sweating from rushing around—than have a fast-food meal. I guess that's why they're paying, as you said, the top dollar that they are. They want attentive, quality service.

Jasmine: True. I'd never thought before about the connection between what I do at the restaurant and my work as a counselor.

Dr. M.: Well, they're both demanding positions because they're about working directly with people, and so you've developed some good people skills in your work at the restaurant that I can see you using here in your work with clients. But you will need to develop the skill of being able to engage clients more in session—working with them rather than leading them or pulling them along. And this means staying with them in the moment, sitting with silence from time to time, rather than rushing ahead just so you can clear the table and welcome a new customer. And brief therapy, if I may say, is not about just the number of sessions provided. It's really more about being purposeful and intentional in your work with clients. And to do this, you need to be fully alert or awake to what's going on with the client in each moment of the counseling session—facial expression, words used, gestures and mannerisms, voice inflection, and so forth. So, using your good observational skills—and not just with the client but also with yourself. For example, being sure that you're not spending more time thinking about what you need to get done *after* the session while you're *in* session with the client. Just being aware of being distracted is a start. It's then a matter of pulling yourself back to what's going on now, in the present moment. Well, I've gone on a bit here, but does any of this make some sense?

Jasmine: Yeah, it does. In fact, just sitting here and listening to you—and, just so you know, I *have* been listening to you—I've realized just how frantic I've been recently. And rushing around and being so concerned about getting my hours for practicum, getting an internship site, and graduating in December, I see that I *have* missed some important details right in front of me, right before my eyes. Like what you said earlier about the client who canceled this week. I had always thought I had a good eye for details, but maybe not in the past few weeks.

Dr. M.: You know, hearing you say that right now is encouraging. I mean, you've been able to catch yourself, so to speak, and to make some meaningful connections for yourself right now—connections between the kind of person and counselor you want to be and how what you're doing now is not making that happen. And you did that right here and now.

Jasmine: Yeah, this *has* been good, actually. I mean, it feels like supervision today has been the first breather I've had in a long time. Just being able to listen to you and talk about this stuff has been helpful, like I can breathe easier now, like I don't have to make things happen all at once. And that I really do have some options.

Dr. M.: Yeah, "breather breaks" are really essential for the kind of work we do. It's a way of being kind to yourself, too. [smiling] Something I can hear you saying to one of your clients!

Jasmine: [laughing] Yeah, you're right!

Dr. M.: So one thing we need to work on is making it possible for you to be okay with being still—inside and outside of counseling. You've done that here in supervision today, and you said it's been helpful.

Jasmine: Yeah, it's that whole time issue.

Dr. M.: But trying to do a whole lot at once—you know, multitasking—hasn't been working for you. In fact, some research suggests that multitasking is not any more productive than doing one thing at a time. It can actually make things worse.

Jasmine: Hmm. I hadn't heard that before. But now it makes sense to me.

Dr. M.: Okay, so I'm going to start by having you make time this week to watch your counseling sessions from last week.

Because the one client canceled, [smiling] you do have that hour already to be still in and to work on your good attending skills so that you don't miss important details—about clients and about yourself.

Jasmine: Thanks, Dr. Morton. I'll go ahead and schedule that hour for viewing now [smiling]...I mean, when we're done.

Part Two

Part Two addresses Learning Outcome 2 and is intended to help you define evidence-based practice (EBP)—what it is and what it is not. This activity is also designed to help you identify the intended benefits and criticisms of EBP as well as recent efforts to adapt EBPs for culturally diverse populations.

1. Imagine that you have been asked to give a brief presentation in class or at your internship site on the topic of evidence-based practice (EBP). Because of your graduate studies, you are regarded as someone who has received some training in EBP, specifically what it is, what it is not, its benefits and its criticisms.

   a. From the list of 18 descriptors below, select 10 that are consistent with the definition of EBP presented and discussed in this chapter. Place a check mark (☑) in the box next to each of the 10 descriptors selected. Place an X (☒) in the boxes (or simply strike out the text) that are not consistent with the definition of EBP provided in this chapter.

❏ Absolute truth	❏ Cost-saving measure	❏ Integration
❏ Best available research	❏ Noun	❏ Dynamic process
❏ Set of techniques	❏ Subject to revision	❏ Best practice
❏ Verb	❏ Superior treatment	❏ Client focused
❏ Prescriptive	❏ Clinical expertise	❏ Beneficial care
❏ Ethical standards	❏ Characteristics, culture, preferences	❏ One-size-fits-all

   b. Once you have selected 10 descriptors, use them to construct a **two-sentence definition** of EBP. This will be the definition you will use—and will be able to support and explain—during your presentation to classmates or to other professionals at your internship site. Write out this two-sentence definition using the 10 descriptors selected in the space below. **Evidence-based practice is. . .** _____

   _____

   _____

(continued)

Knowledge and Skill Builder (*continued*)

Knowledge and Skill Builder (*continued*)

1 Knowledge and Skill Builder (*continued*)

c. From the list below, select at least **two** intended **benefits** of EBP and also **two criticisms** of EBP. Add additional benefits and/or criticisms not on the list. Be prepared to explain each of your selections or additions.

- ❐ Identify potentially harmful therapies
- ❐ Adhering to a treatment manual may have the effect of helpers feeling "manualized"
- ❐ Limits helper creativity
- ❐ Research often not based on culturally diverse clinicians or clients
- ❐ Often mandated by persons in authority
- ❐ Engage practitioners and researchers in conversations about effective care
- ❐ Mistakenly promoted as a cost-saving measure

- ❐ Identify therapies that are most helpful to clients
- ❐ Often based on the "gold standard" of randomized/clinical control trials (RCTs)
- ❐ Holds clinicians more accountable for their decisions and practices
- ❐ Often misused as one-size-fits-all care
- ❐ Research often limited to single diagnostic categories, without consideration for complex client concerns

- ❐ _____
- ❐ _____
- ❐ _____
- ❐ _____

2. From the list below, identify at least **six** practices used to adapt EBP to culturally diverse populations. Place a check mark (☑) in the box next to each of the six practices selected. Place an X (☒) in the boxes (or simply strike out the text) that are not consistent with the practice of culturally adapting EBP described in this chapter. For each one selected, be prepared to explain how the practice is intended to provide beneficial care to a specific client or group of clients who share a similar cultural identity or background. Provide an example of how each one selected could be implemented.

- ❐ Explicitly incorporating cultural values/concepts (e.g., storytelling)
- ❐ Using materials (including a treatment manual) that are written only in English
- ❐ Providing services in the client's native language (other than English)
- ❐ Matching the client and helper according to race or ethnicity
- ❐ Providing services only in a treatment facility so that clients and their families are required to physically arrive for scheduled appointments
- ❐ Collaborating/consulting with family members
- ❐ Extending length and number of treatment sessions to accommodate specific needs of clients (e.g., use of American Sign Language for deaf clients in DBT skills groups)
- ❐ Understanding and explaining the client's presenting concern consistent with the client's cultural beliefs
- ❐ Conducting cultural sensitivity training for professional staff
- ❐ Limiting services only to talk therapy and discouraging other expressive means of communication (e.g., art, dance, singing) because the treatment manual does not include these
- ❐ Offering child care and transportation services to increase client retention
- ❐ Providing services in a treatment facility specifically targeting clients from culturally diverse backgrounds
- ❐ Discouraging social interaction among clients outside of group sessions because the treatment manual does not mention this activity
- ❐ Routinely soliciting feedback from clients about the helpfulness of services
- ❐ Engaging in outreach efforts to recruit underserved clients
- ❐ Establishing an advisory board of cultural experts to help develop a new program for persons in the community from a specific cultural group
- ❐ Maintaining a problem focus so that the core issue or the reason for the problem can be identified
- ❐ Orally administering written materials for illiterate clients
- ❐ Hiring only staff who live outside the local community to maintain clear boundaries between clients and professional staff
- ❐ Providing referrals to external agencies in the community (e.g., free health clinic, job skills training) for additional services

1 | Knowledge and Skill Builder **Feedback**

Part One

1. Examples of Jasmine's **need** for: (1) self-awareness and self-reflection; (2) mindfulness; and (3) self-care and self-compassion.

   a. Need for **self-awareness** and **self-reflection**:
   (1) She had not been watching her video recorded counseling sessions and so was not aware of her tendency to offer advice and too many suggestions to clients or of client reactions in session.
   (2) As a full-time student working part-time and trying to get an internship completed in one semester—while upholding family obligations (not letting her sister, nephews, or mother down)—she may not have the time or the space for honest self-reflection.

   b. Need for **mindfulness**:
   (1) She describes herself as a multitasker, someone who is efficient and not lazy, and one who has been rushing around recently—from school (and counseling center) to work to family commitments.
   (2) She describes brief therapy as "moving things along" in session.
   (3) She describes silence in session as being "a waste of time."
   (4) She has been more concerned about her future (e.g., accruing hours for practicum, getting an internship site by next week, graduating in December) than about her present.

   c. Need for **self-care** and **self-compassion**:
   (1) She describes herself as being tired.
   (2) She recognizes that she's been "trying to do too much" for her clients, wanting to "spoon-feed" them or "rescue them."
   (3) She appears to think that she cannot set limits on her responsibilities, that she must fulfill the expectations that others have for her, what Dr. Morton described as being "superwoman."

2. Examples of **specific activities** mentioned in the supervision session for Jasmine to engage in to meet her need for: (1) self-awareness and self-reflection; (2) mindfulness; and (3) self-care and self-compassion.

   a. Specific activities for **self-awareness** and **self-reflection**:
   (1) Watch the video recordings of her counseling sessions.
   (2) Realize that genuineness in counseling means "practicing what you preach" outside of counseling.
   (3) Recognize that being unbalanced or lopsided as a counselor is like carrying too much on the serving tray as a server in a restaurant.
   (4) Continue to be an active participant in supervision.

   b. Specific activities for **mindfulness**:
   (1) Allow for moments of silence in counseling sessions.
   (2) Remain alert and fully attentive to the present moment while in session.
   (3) Consider her work with clients as offering them a fine dining experience rather than a fast-food experience.
   (4) Elicit feedback from clients at the end of each session about their experience in counseling, and follow-up with clients when they have canceled.

   c. Specific activities for **self-care** and **self-compassion**:
   (1) Negotiate her work schedule, as needed.
   (2) Make time for additional "breather breaks."
   (3) Consider doing her internship over two semesters and graduating in May rather than doing it in one semester and graduating in December.
   (4) Accept that she is a human being, not "superwoman," and therefore has limits regarding what she can and cannot do, including not being able to "rescue" or "fix" clients. Also, realize that this self-acceptance will allow her to improve her empathy skills.
   (5) Reframe "selfishness" as "self-care" in her work as a counseling student and future counseling professional.

Part Two

1. a. Evidence-based practice (EBP) is defined using the 10 descriptors checked below and highlighted in bold font, and not using the descriptors that have an X in the box next to them (we have used the strike-out key to further clarify those descriptors not to be used in a definition of EBP).

☒ ~~Absolute truth~~	☒ ~~Cost-saving measure~~	☑ Integration/ Integrating
☑ **Best available research**	☒ Noun	☑ **Dynamic process**
☒ ~~Set of techniques~~	☑ **Subject to revision**	☒ ~~Best practice~~
☑ **Verb**	☒ ~~Superior treatment~~	☑ **Client-focused**
☒ ~~Prescriptive~~	☑ **Clinical expertise**	☑ **Beneficial care**
☑ **Ethical standards**	☑ **Characteristics, culture, and preferences**	☒ ~~One-size-fits-all~~

(continued)

1 | Knowledge and Skill Builder **Feedback** (*continued*)

b. Using the 10 descriptors selected above with a check mark (and in bold font above and underlined below), a two-sentence definition of EBP is: Evidence-based practice is the <u>dynamic process</u> of <u>integrating</u> the <u>best available research</u> with <u>clinical expertise</u> to provide <u>beneficial care</u> to clients. It is <u>client focused</u>, which means that it takes into consideration client <u>characteristics, culture, and preferences</u>, and is therefore a <u>verb</u>, or always <u>subject to revision</u> and innovation, while maintaining <u>ethical standards</u>.

2. The specific practices selected below with a checkmark (☑) are ones that should be considered as appropriate activities for adapting EBPs for culturally diverse persons. The practices that have been marked with an X (☒) are activities that are not considered appropriate as cultural adaptations. We do not recommend the ones marked with an X and this is emphasized by striking out the text.

☑ Explicitly incorporating cultural values/concepts (e.g., storytelling)

☒ ~~Using materials (including a treatment manual) that are written only in English~~

☑ Providing services in the client's native language (other than English)

☑ Matching the client and helper according to race or ethnicity

☒ ~~Providing services only in a treatment facility so that clients and their families are required to physically arrive for scheduled appointments~~

☑ Collaborating/consulting with family members

☑ Extending length and number of treatment sessions to accommodate specific needs of clients (e.g., use of American Sign Language for deaf clients in DBT skills groups)

☑ Understanding and explaining the client's presenting concern consistent with the client's cultural beliefs

☑ Conducting cultural sensitivity training for professional staff

☒ ~~Limiting services only to talk therapy and discouraging other expressive means of communication (e.g., art, dance, singing) because the treatment manual does not include these~~

☑ Offering childcare and transportation services to increase client retention

☑ Providing services in a treatment facility specifically targeting clients from culturally diverse backgrounds

☒ ~~Discouraging social interaction among clients outside of group sessions because the treatment manual does not mention this activity~~

☑ Routinely soliciting feedback from clients about the helpfulness of services

☑ Engaging in outreach efforts to recruit underserved clients

☑ Establishing an advisory board of cultural experts to help develop a new program for persons in the community from a specific cultural group

☒ ~~Maintaining a problem focus so that the core issue or the reason for the problem can be identified~~

☑ Orally administering written materials for illiterate clients

☒ ~~Hiring only staff who live outside the local community to maintain clear boundaries between clients and professional staff~~

☑ Providing referrals to external agencies in the community (e.g., free health clinic, job skills training) for additional services

Critical Commitments
▶ Diversity Issues and Ethical Practice for Helpers

Learning Outcomes

After completing this chapter, you will be able to

1. Identify values you hold as well as attitudes and behaviors that might aid in or interfere with establishing and maintaining a positive helping relationship.

2. Identify, in the context of contemporary service provision, issues related to values, diversity, and ethics that might affect the development of a helping relationship and the provision of appropriate services.

Toward Skillful Practice

Your decision to pursue a career in a helping profession (e.g., counseling, social work, psychology) suggests that you value and are committed to meaningful work. We suspect that working as a helping professional represents for you more than a job or a way to earn a living. More than likely it reflects your desire that your work become a way of living, a lifestyle. This means that it is important to you that who you are as a professional is consistent with who you are as a person. Being a genuine or authentic person is therefore a priority in the varied roles you serve, both on the job and off the job.

Although this chapter and the entire book present and describe strategies for practitioners, we realize that being a helping professional is not simply about implementing techniques. As we discussed in Chapter 1, there is more to this work, this lifestyle, than merely selecting and using "tools" from a "toolbox." In her review of the literature on the role and impact of the therapist in the work of psychotherapy, Reupert (2006) observed that "the 'self' or the 'person' of the counsellor is more important than the orientation chosen, or the interventions employed,

in both the process and outcome of therapy" (p. 97). She added that "counsellors bring to therapy more than their professional skills and knowledge" (p. 101).

Skills, however, clearly are essential to the work of helping professionals. Without the intentional use of theoretically informed and research-guided practices learned in formal training (e.g., graduate school) and at professional workshops, our work would be little more than shooting from the hip, relying more on gut and intuition than on discernible, reliable, and, ideally, tested and practiced skills.

We contend that a helper's skills are an integration of who the helper is as a person *and* his or her training in a behavioral health discipline. This is consistent with the contention made by Hoop, DiPasquale, Hernandez, and Roberts (2008) that "ethics and culture are intimately intertwined" (p. 353), and supports our decision to address diversity issues and ethical practice in the same chapter. Your skill as a practitioner is the product of your personal characteristics (e.g., the values you espouse, the cultural traditions you maintain, the decisions you make in your daily life) *and* your knowledge (e.g., what you have learned and what you are continuing to learn in your graduate studies). Who you are as a person and what you bring to this time of formal preparation inform the material you are learning (e.g., ethical practice) and, in turn, the theories and strategies you are learning help shape who you are as a person (e.g., your emerging cultural identity). This dynamic intersection constitutes what we regard as your **professional skills**—skills that are ever-evolving, influenced by past and current life experiences, and subject to ongoing refinement.

This chapter and the entire book are devoted to the skill of the helping professional, that dynamic intersection of person and professional as well as culture and ethics. Few professions rival the helping practice in the importance of understanding oneself and one's culture, the dynamics of human interaction, the ways in which diversity among us as people contextualizes both problems and solutions, and the complexity of implementing ethics into practice. These represent the issues and the critical commitments discussed in this chapter. Your personal work in sorting through these issues so that you can make the critical commitments essential to effective practice becomes a fundamental part of your professional identity and work. This is not an easy task, but it creates a strong foundation on which to build a resilient lifestyle as a helping professional.

Growing Into Professional Competence

If you attend professional conferences in the `LO1` `LO2` helping field today, pick up a current mental health journal and listen to conversations among faculty and researchers from the helping professions, you will no doubt hear and see numerous references to competence and specific competencies. The idea of professional competence is not new. For example, most state laws stipulate that a licensed helping professional maintain a self-disclosure statement describing his or her areas of competence. In recent years, however, professional competence has received quite a bit of press in academic institutions, accrediting bodies, and the scholarly literature.

Despite its liberal usage, the term **competence** often is not clearly defined and remains elusive. Does the word imply proficiency, effectiveness, having expertise, or simply meeting minimal standards of practice? Does earning a graduate degree, obtaining licensure as a professional helper, or completing certification in a specialized practice constitute competence? Is competence, once demonstrated, stable and here to stay? Is competence—like cultural identity—self-defined, or is it determined only by another person or group, such as a supervisor or licensure board?

These questions are not easily answered! They deserve our careful consideration. Growing into professional competence necessitates clarity about what it is we are growing into. Our own study of competence has revealed several of its key features. In a nutshell, competence . . .

1. is the demonstration of certain skills.

2. is a psychological need.

3. involves helper confidence or self-efficacy.

4. is always under construction.

5. is a commitment to personal and professional excellence.

6. requires self-awareness and self-exploration.

7. is not self-defined.

First, we regard competence as a practitioner's ability to demonstrate certain skills based on his or her knowledge and experience. As with Welfel (2016), our emphasis is on the actual *demonstration* or *performance* of skills, not simply the promise of or the capacity to mobilize learned skills into effective action. Welfel (p. 91) underscores that "[a]bility is a prerequisite for competence but is not identical with it." The skills for helpers to demonstrate must meet or exceed minimal standards of practice agreed upon or codified by a professional body of which the practitioner is a member, such as passing a state licensure exam. The British Association for Counselling and Psychotherapy (BACP; 2013) includes competence as one of the 10 personal moral qualities in its *Ethical Framework for Good Practice in Counselling and Psychotherapy* and defines it as "the effective deployment of the skills and knowledge needed to do what is required" (p. 03).

The second and third features of competence are informed by self-determination theory (Deci & Ryan, 2012), a theory of motivation. This theory posits that competence is one of three universal psychological needs or basic necessities for health (the other two are autonomy and relatedness). As a *psychological need*, competence is the hunger for *confidence or self-efficacy*. It propels people to seek challenges that will optimize their capacity for growth and well-being. This means that competence is never attained once and for all but instead is "an ongoing process . . . that . . . is in a constant state of flux and renewal" (Nagy, 2005, p. 29). Implied in this statement are the fourth and fifth features of competence: competence is *always under construction* because it reflects the practitioner's *pursuit of personal and professional excellence*. And it is this perpetual striving for excellence that differentiates competence from proficiency. Whereas competence assumes meeting minimal standards of practice, proficiency transcends these minimal standards by virtue of extended and rigorous study in a particular area that has been tested and refined in practice.

The pursuit of excellence requires *self-awareness* and *self-exploration*, the sixth feature of competence. To be self-aware is to be attentive to your idiosyncrasies in relation to others, such as how your learned beliefs and values are similar to, different from, and also influence others in your life. This infers attending to and exploring your own cultural identity and how it continues to be shaped. Think of self-awareness and self-exploration as the practice of humility, a personal moral quality that the BACP (2013) defines as "the ability to assess accurately and acknowledge one's own strengths and weaknesses" (p. 03). Improving your skills as a helper will involve this type of heightened awareness and self-monitoring, exposing yourself to new challenges and regulating your responses as you do so.

This is not done solo. Instructors and supervisors are charged with the task of promoting and evaluating your skills. Competence, therefore, is *not self-defined*. This seventh and last feature of competence means that competence is the product of incorporating feedback from others, including clients, who, from the perspective of motivational interviewing (Miller & Rollnick, 2013), are our best teachers. Our clients are the ones who determine whether or not we have established an empathic connection with them. They remain the final arbiters of effective helping.

Competence is a dynamic construct that resists repeated efforts to be tied down and operationalized once and for all. It is a mindset and a skill set that requires continued adjustment and refinement to be responsive and helpful to clients. Perhaps like ethical decision-making, competence is understood only in consultation with another person (e.g., supervisor) and in response to client feedback.

Four Critical Commitments

Kottler and Shepard (2015) state that becoming **LO1 LO2** a professional helper means making a commitment to a profession and to a lifestyle. Such a commitment is necessary to grow into professional competence and to continue striving for excellence. In this section we highlight four critical commitments that helpers are encouraged—if not expected—to make as part of growing into professional competence:

1. commitment to lifelong learning

2. commitment to collaboration

3. commitment to values-based practice

4. commitment to beneficence

These four commitments are essential throughout one's career and are established during formal training, including graduate studies.

Commitment to Lifelong Learning

The task of learning to be a professional helper is never done. Although you may be eager to have formal coursework completed and a graduate degree conferred, the process of professional learning and development has only begun. In your work with clients as a professional helper, you will realize that there are many things you don't know, things you believe you should have learned during your formal academic training. This is a common experience of practitioners early in their careers (Rønnestad & Skovholt, 2003, 2013; Skovholt & Trotter-Mathison, 2011). Attending professional workshops and conventions, reading scholarly journal articles and books, and participating in ongoing supervision or your own personal counseling will all serve as primary sources of learning and development beyond graduate school. In their study of psychotherapist development, Orlinsky and Rønnestad (2005) found that clinicians worldwide who reported high levels of professional progress were those who said, among other things, that they were committed to their professional development and were currently receiving specialty training or supervision as well as personal therapy.

Having a desire and being willing to continually learn is an essential disposition for all effective helpers. It also is central to developing clinical expertise (Overholser, 2010). Stretching one's clinical repertoire and flexing new helping skill muscles serve to prevent stagnation and boredom, ethical misconduct, burnout, and, most important, client deterioration. Skovholt (2001) very aptly described the choice practitioners have in their professional development: "The practitioner can have years of experience—rich, textured, illuminating, practice-changing professional experience in a helping, teaching, or health occupation. Or a person can have one year of experience repeated over and over" (p. 27). Assuming the role of perpetual student therefore contributes to the experience of a "rich, textured, illuminating, and practice-changing" career, one that requires of therapists the "courage to move outside their comfort zone" (Bridges, 2005, p. xiii).

As mentioned, a primary source of learning for practitioners is their clients. From their extensive interviews with approximately 100 therapists, Rønnestad and Skovholt (2003, 2013) found that a major theme for counselors who reflected on their professional development was that clients are a continuous source of influence and serve as primary teachers. What other opportunities would we have to sit and listen to an African American male who lives in Appalachia describe his method of pig farming? When else would we choose to sit in an emergency room and learn the details of her recent sexual assault from a 15-year-old female? If not for our role as professional helper, how else would we be able to witness a father's gradual acceptance of his son's decision to undergo gender reassignment surgery?

Living and working as professional helpers affords us the privilege of learning from others—"a delightful side effect" of being a professional helper (Kottler & Shepard,

2015, p. 6). Assuming the posture of lifelong learner not only enhances our helping skills but also can make us better people through reflection, consultation, supervision, and therapy. More than 90 percent of psychologists surveyed in one study (Radeke & Mahoney, 2000) reported that their work as clinicians had made them better and wiser persons.

Commitment to Collaboration

A second critical commitment in our work as professional helpers is a commitment to **collaboration**—collaboration with clients and their families, and collaboration with supervisors and other professionals. Collaboration is an interpersonal style, a specific philosophy, and an approach to working with another person or group of persons. Collaboration in therapy is the active and mutual involvement of client and helper. It is the process of the client and helper negotiating the goals and tasks of therapy (Tryon & Winograd, 2011) and also the therapist incorporating client preferences into therapy (Tompkins, Swift, & Callahan, 2013). This has been described in health care as **shared decision-making** (Adams & Drake, 2006). In dialectical behavior therapy (DBT; Linehan, 2015), collaboration is exemplified in the consultation-to-the-client strategy. This approach reflects the helper's belief in the client's capacity to learn how to effectively interact with and manage his or her own environment, including other people. The helper consults the client about how to skillfully manage stressors and build a life worth living, rather than the helper consulting other persons on behalf of the client, such as other professionals or family members. The client is considered the "responsible party" in DBT and therefore is the one the helper consults about solutions.

As helpers, we are clearly in a position of authority in relation to clients, and we are obligated by law in certain instances to exert influence over our clients even when they resist. This is true, for example, when we learn of suicidal or homicidal intentions or suspect child or elder abuse/neglect. In these instances, influencing the actions of our clients is done to protect their welfare and that of persons associated with them, such as family members. Clients often initiate contact with us in a state of vulnerability, and the decisions we make concerning client care can be life-changing. Because of this circumstance, there is an imbalance of power. The power vested in us as professional helpers—by virtue of our graduate training, license to practice, length of experience, and areas of expertise, to name a few—is not something to crave or to flaunt. Rather, the power afforded us should be handled with great care and practiced with respect and humility.

Thwarted Collaboration Even well-meaning helpers can miss the mark in their attempts to collaborate with clients and colleagues. Collaboration is thwarted when helpers misuse their power. This is evident in a helper's attempts to convince a new client that the assigned diagnosis is "right" and that interventions outlined in the preliminary treatment plan are "correct," sending the message that the client "should" participate in care or otherwise risk being viewed as "noncompliant." A helper also may mishandle power when others are not consulted in the event of a crisis or an ethical dilemma. This can happen with novice and experienced helpers alike when they think they should be able to handle complex client issues on their own. The seasoned and overly confident helper may say, "Heck, I've been doing this for many years. I know what to do. Besides, it'll take too much time to get others involved at this point." The novice helper may think, "I don't want to appear incompetent, so I'll figure this out on my own. Besides, my supervisor is in a meeting." As one clinical director once noted, "Because of the responsibility we assume, supervisors are meant to be interrupted."

The misapplication of power often is subtle and does not pertain exclusively to flagrant behavior such as entering into sexual relationships with clients. We misuse our power when we assume we know more things about a client's situation or experience than is possible. For example, saying with certitude that someone is "shy because she is Japanese American" assumes that this person's gender and ethnic/racial heritage is the direct cause of or fully explains a presumed or known interpersonal characteristic. Such an assumption may exemplify "all-knowing" thinking wherein the helper's frame of reference is considered central or true. We regard this kind of unchecked certainty as a subtle misuse of power. This type of thinking is evident in clinical decision-making errors, such as selective attention and confirmatory search strategies (Nezu, Nezu, & Lombardo, 2004). When helpers rely only on certain types of information (i.e., selective attention) and seek information that only confirms their initial impressions of clients, we believe they mismanage their power as professionals in their care of clients.

We also misuse our power and hence thwart collaboration when we assume a greater degree of intimacy with our clients than has been established. This is true, for example, when we use a nickname for a client when he or she has not given us permission to do so. Our power is further mishandled when we assure clients that their difficulties and challenges are manageable when we are not certain about this. Statements such as "Everything will be okay" or "You will get through" when there is little evidence to support them are a few examples. Offering a client glib or insincere reassurances might be associated with an expert stance or the belief that one has the ability to cure, fix, or solve a client's concerns. It can be experienced by the client as patronizing and invalidating. Such a helper may take unwarranted advantage—consciously or not—of his or her influence in a helping relationship by attempting to convince the client to believe or behave a certain way. A helper in recovery from alcoholism may earnestly believe that if her clients simply followed the same program she did to get sober, then they, too, would attain and sustain sobriety. Another helper may think that if his client would just take her medication as prescribed, then she would remain stable and not recycle back into the hospital. These examples are reminders that our power as helpers can be determined by our cultural identity. This includes being a member of a privileged class (e.g., heterosexual, white) and having certain societal advantages by virtue of having earned a graduate degree and possibly occupying a higher socioeconomic status than our clients.

Conversely, instead of exerting power, some helpers may be afraid of power or deny the degree of influence inherent in their professional role. These helpers unwittingly may attempt to escape from as much responsibility in counseling as possible. This might be the case when the helper explains to his or her supervisor, "Well, I didn't want to offend him [the client], so I didn't say anything, even though I didn't really think it would be in his best interest." Professional relationships between helping practitioners and clients have aspects of unequal power of various types. When helpers avoid acknowledging or dismiss this power differential, their ability to manage it productively is constrained and their collaboration with supervisors, peers, and clients is thwarted.

Enhancing Collaboration A commitment to collaborating with clients and other professionals is a commitment to making appropriate use of your power as a professional helper. Tryon and Winograd (2011) outlined several helper behaviors that reflect a commitment to client-helper collaboration. Among these are:

- Encourage clients' contributions throughout counseling by inviting their perspectives, elaborations, preferences, and feedback.
- Check in with clients frequently to ensure that you understand each other and are "on the same page."
- Inform clients about the importance of their contributions to the work of counseling, perhaps by referencing research linking client active participation in therapy to beneficial client outcomes.
- Encourage between-session home practice of skills (i.e., "homework") that relates to work done in session.
- Rarely push your own agenda. Listen to what your clients tell you.
- Modify your approach based on feedback from clients.

In your work with other professionals, a commitment to collaboration means remaining open to learning about and practicing from different approaches that demonstrate effective and valid care rather than believing that there is only one universal or correct way to care for clients. It also means seeing yourself as a member of a team of professionals caring for shared clients rather than seeing yourself as an individual client's only treatment provider. In this regard, we encourage helpers to discard the reference to "my client"—which connotes a sense of ownership as well as clinical isolation—and to refer instead to "our client."

Commitment to Values-Based Practice

The word **value** denotes something that we prize, regard highly, or prefer. Often it suggests something very personal and private and therefore not discussed openly on a routine basis. This explains the frequent reference to **personal values**. Although personal and private, they are expressed in how we go about our everyday lives: how we begin our day, what we eat, who we speak to, and how we interact with people. Just as "actions speak louder than words," so do our behaviors reflect our values. For example, if you say that you value spending time with friends but you hardly ever do this, then other activities and actions probably have more value for you.

Think of values as the guiding principles of life that organize your attitudes, emotions, and behaviors (Kasser, 2002). Because of this, there is an enduring quality to the values we hold, and thus they retain some consistency across time and different situations. This is not to say, however, that certain values we have held for a long time cannot be modified or reprioritized, or that new values cannot be developed. This can happen as a result of extended travel and cultural immersion experiences, personal tragedy and loss, or entering into a new relationship. Values are shaped over time and how they are expressed can vary as we encounter the values of others.

Aponte (1994) stated that "Values frame the entire process of therapy . . . All transactions between therapists and clients involve negotiations about the respective value systems that each party brings into the therapeutic process" (p. 170). Because the values of both clients and helpers permeate the entire helping process, we devote an extended discussion to values in this section of the chapter. This includes a discussion of what Fulford, Caroll, and Peile (2011) described as **values-based practice**, a multidisciplinary treatment team approach that respects different values. Specifically, values-based practice begins with prioritizing the values of the client, respects the diversity of values represented by other professionals on the treatment team, and is consistent with and is intended to complement evidence-based practice.

Three principles guide values-based practice:

1. All decisions rest on values as well as evidence. This is referred to as the "two feet" principle.

2. Often values are noticed only when they cause trouble, including those that prompt ethical conflicts. This is referred to as the "squeaky wheel" principle.

3. Advances in science should promote not only evidence-based practice but also values-based practice. This is the "science-driven" principle.

Personal Values in the Helping Process Our reference to values-based practice throughout this section highlights the helper's need to respect the values of the client while also upholding the standards of professional and ethical practice. These include consulting other professionals, providing culturally affirmative therapy, and substantiating counseling decisions and behavior based on available research.

To help you clarify and reflect on your own values and your reactions in different practice situations, we encourage you to engage in Learning Activity 2.1 before you read the remainder of this section. It is intended as a self-check exercise to gauge or evaluate your attitudes and anticipated behaviors in different situations.

When Helper and Client Values Collide Obviously, not all of our personal values will influence the helping process. The helper who is a pet lover can probably work without any difficulty with a client who has never had an interest in owning pets. The helper who does not smoke may be able to provide quality care to a client who smokes two packs of cigarettes per day. Even the clinician who is a strict vegetarian may say that maintaining a strong working alliance with a client who eats red meat on a regular basis is not impossible.

Learning Activity 2.1

Personal Values

This activity presents descriptions of six clients. If you work through this activity by yourself, we suggest that you imagine yourself counseling each of these clients. Try to generate a vivid picture of yourself and the client in your mind. If you do this activity with a partner, you can role-play the helper while your partner assumes the role of each client. As you imagine or role-play the helper, try to notice your feelings, attitudes, values, and behavior during the visualization or role-play process. After *each* example, stop to think about or discuss these questions:

1. What attitudes and beliefs did you have about the client?
2. Were your beliefs and attitudes based on actual or on presumed information about the client?
3. How did you behave with the client?
4. What values are portrayed by your behavior?
5. Could you work with this client effectively?

There are no right or wrong answers. Feedback to Learning Activity 2.1 is located on page 42.

Client 1

This client is a young white woman who has become addicted to heroin. She is the sole supporter of three young children and has worked as a nightclub dancer. She reports a history of childhood sexual abuse and recent incidents of unreported sexual assault from her so-called clients. She is primarily concerned about her finances but can't make enough money to support her kids.

Client 2

Your client is charged with rape and sexual assault. The client, a man, tells you that he is not to blame for the incident because the victim, a woman, was a "slut" who "asked for it."

Client 3

This client is concerned about general feelings of depression. Overweight and unkempt, the client is in poor physical condition, appears to lack proper hygiene practices, and acknowledges smoking on average two packs of cigarettes per day (and smells of tobacco smoke) during the interview.

Client 4

The client is a young white woman who comes to you at the college counseling center. She is in tears because her parents threatened to disown her when they learned that her boyfriend is African American.

Client 5

Your client, a gay man recently engaged to marry his male partner of 2 years, is angry and deeply hurt because he just found out from a mutual friend that his fiancé has been cheating on him.

Client 6

The client, an older man, confides in you that he is taking two kinds of medicine for seizures and "thought control." He states that occasionally he believes people are out to get him. He hasn't been employed for some time and is now thinking of returning to the workforce, and he wants your assistance and a letter of reference.

There are values we hold that may make it extremely difficult for us to generate or sustain empathy for certain clients. These might be values we would consider inviolate, values we might say comprise our essence or have shaped our identity—values such as the sanctity of human life, belief in a higher power, and the conviction that people create their own destiny, as in, "You only get out of life what you put into it." The helper whose family member recently died of lung cancer—a family member who never smoked—may find it difficult to remain nonjudgmental of a client who is a two-pack-per-day smoker and does not intend to quit. Likewise, the helper who is an ardent animal lover and a vegan may not be able to provide unconditional positive regard for a client who has a history of torturing and killing animals.

Although benevolence is a primary value of helpers (Kelly, 1995) and may provide the impetus for entering a helping profession, a referral may be necessary if the helper lacks the competence to be able to promote and respect a client's welfare (American Counseling Association, 2014; American Psychological Association, 2010; National Association of Social Workers, 2008). The decision to refer, however, is never automatic, is not that of helpers whose work is supervised (e.g., students in practicum or internship), and should never be done simply because the helper's personal values seem to differ from those of the client's. Kaplan (2014) reinforced that referral is an action of last resort, based on the helper's skill-based competency, not his or her personal values.

When Courts Intervene Four court cases in the past 15 years illustrate value conflicts in the helping relationship and when referral is not indicated. Two of the cases involve already licensed and practicing counselors; two involve former counseling students. All involve helpers who claimed their religious beliefs prevented them from providing services to gay or lesbian clients.

The first court case, *Bruff v. North Mississippi Health Services Inc.*, took place in 2001 and involved a professional counselor and her former employer. It is discussed by Hermann and Herlihy (2006) and then revisited by Herlihy, Hermann, and Greden (2014). The counselor in question, Ms. Bruff, was one of three counselors in an employee assistance program (EAP) and was dismissed from her position for refusing to continue counseling a client after the client disclosed that she was a lesbian and had requested help to improve her relationship with her partner. Ms. Bruff explained to the court that "a homosexual lifestyle" conflicted with her Christian beliefs and therefore she could not counsel a lesbian client on relationship issues with the client's significant other. The employer stated that refusing to provide services to this client had a discriminatory effect

and resulted in undue hardship on the counselor's two colleagues because additional referrals represented a disproportionate workload for them. Although Ms. Bruff appealed her termination and subsequently filed suit against her employer, an appeals court determined that making reasonable accommodations for the employee's religious beliefs did not extend to excusing the counselor from working with homosexual clients on relationship issues.

Herlihy et al. (2014) describe the second case, *Walden v. Centers for Disease Control and Prevention*, which has many parallels to the first case. Ms. Walden, another EAP counselor, was fired from her position with the Centers for Disease Control and Prevention (CDC) for informing a new client at intake that she would need to refer the client because Ms. Walden's "personal values" would "interfere" with the client-helper relationship. The client was a lesbian seeking counseling to address relationship concerns with her same-sex partner. Although Ms. Walden did not disclose to the client that it was specifically her Christian beliefs opposing same-sex relationships that prevented her from working with this client, the client later reported feeling "judged and condemned" by Ms. Walden. As with Ms. Bruff, Ms. Walden appealed her dismissal and filed suit against the CDC. The court sided with the CDC, stating that Ms. Walden's disclosure to the client of "personal values" conflict was contrary to the CDC's EAP providing a "welcoming environment" for any CDC employee seeking counseling services.

In 2010, two separate courts ruled that two different counseling students could not be excused from fulfilling academic requirements because of their religious beliefs. Although enrolled in two different graduate counseling programs at two different public universities in two different states, both students expressed strong disapproval about working with gay and lesbian clients because of their Christian values. In the case of *Keeton v. Anderson-Wiley et al.* (2010), Ms. Jennifer Keeton, a counseling student at Augusta State University in Georgia, had voiced in written assignments and in the classroom her condemnation of "the gay and lesbian lifestyle" based on her reading of the Bible, and also had expressed her support of conversion therapy (i.e., assisting clients in "returning to" a "normative" and heterosexual identity, a practice that lacks empirical support and has been discredited by major professional associations (see Cramer, Golom, & LoPresto, 2008). The faculty became concerned that Ms. Keeton would not be able to separate her personal values from her professional obligations (i.e., provide nondiscriminatory counseling services) and developed a remediation plan that the student subsequently refused to enter. Ms. Keeton was then dismissed from the program and lost her appeal in court.

2.1 Feedback

Personal Values

Did your visualizations or role plays reveal to you that you have certain biases and values related to substance use, socioeconomic status, impact of poverty, sexual behaviors, sexual orientation, age, cultures, race, physical appearance, healthy lifestyle and self-care, medical conditions, and mental health issues? Do any of your biases reflect your past experiences with a person or an incident? Most people in the helping professions agree that we communicate some of our values to our clients, often unintentionally. Try to identify any values or biases you hold now that could signal disapproval to a client or could keep you from promoting the welfare of your client. With yourself, a peer, or an instructor, work out a plan to re-evaluate your biases or to help you prevent yourself from imposing your values on clients.

In the case of *Ward v. Wilbanks et al.* (2010), Ms. Julea Ward, a counseling student at Eastern Michigan University, told her practicum supervisor that she could not meet with a new client because the client had identified as gay in counseling records from previous counseling and the counseling student could not affirm the client's homosexual behavior. Ms. Ward's faculty supervisor cancelled the scheduled client's appointment for that day and rescheduled the client for a later date with another counseling practicum student; Ms. Ward was not assigned any more clients. A remediation plan was developed by counseling faculty for Ms. Ward, which the student refused to enter, opting instead for a formal hearing with counseling faculty. It was after this formal hearing that Ms. Ward was informed that she had been dismissed from the program for refusing to fulfill an academic assignment (i.e., the remediation plan). Ms. Ward lost her initial appeal in court, but Eastern Michigan University settled the case out of court in December 2012 rather than continue to hear her appeal.

In response to these court cases, Kocet and Herlihy (2014) describe one strategy for addressing value conflicts in the helping relationship. *Ethical bracketing* is the helper's intentional practice of separating his or her personal values from his or her professional values as well as the "intentional setting aside of the counselor's personal values in order to provide ethical and appropriate counseling to all clients, especially those whose worldviews, values, belief systems, and decisions differ significantly from those of the counselor" (p. 182). This is accomplished by engaging in specific tasks, including helpers immersing themselves in self-reflection, seeking consultation and supervision, enlisting the services of a co-counselor or co-helper (only with client permission, of course), and seeking personal counseling.

Microaggressions toward LGBTQ Persons Making a client referral and excusing a counseling student from working with sexual and gender minority clients based simply on the helper or student's professed religious beliefs constitutes what we believe is further discrimination and marginalization of persons who identify as lesbian, gay, bisexual, transgender, and/or queer (LGBTQ), with queer defined as anyone who refuses to be constrained by socially accepted and binary categories of sex and gender (Levy & Johnson, 2011). For heterosexual helpers to think they can opt out of working with LGBTQ clients is an example of heterosexual privilege, a privilege or social advantage that affords access to decision-making power that sexual and gender minority individuals do not have. This also exemplifies what Pachankis and Goldfried (2013) define as heterocentrism, the individual and systemic bias against sexual minorities.

Acting on these biases, whether subtly or overtly, constitutes behavior that Sue (2010) refers to as a microaggression. **Microaggressions** are communications of prejudice and discrimination that are conveyed in seemingly meaningless or unharmful ways. Sexual-orientation microaggressions identified by Sue include *oversexualization*, or regarding sexual minority individuals (e.g., lesbian, gay, or bisexual persons) as mere sexual beings who "flaunt" their sexuality in Gay Pride parades. Another sexual-orientation microaggression is the *disavowal of individual heterosexism*, as in a straight person saying, "I don't have anything against gay people. God loves them, too." And a third sexual-orientation microaggression is the *endorsement of heteronormative culture and behaviors*, or the assumption that heterosexuality is the norm and that everyone is heterosexual.

Shelton and Delgado-Romero (2013) reported additional sexual-orientation microaggressions experienced by lesbian, gay, bisexual, or queer (LGBQ) clients when meeting with a mental health professional. These included therapists avoiding or minimizing the LGBQ clients' sexual orientation, assuming that sexual orientation was the cause of the clients' presenting concern(s), attempting to overidentify with their LGBQ clients, and warning about the dangers of identifying as LGBQ, as in, "Well, you should expect those sorts of things to happen with this lifestyle" (p. 65). As a result, these former clients felt misunderstood and invalidated by their former therapists, withheld information, and failed to discuss issues relevant to their sexual orientation.

Microaggressions also extend to gender minority persons, including transgender and transsexual individuals.

When left unchecked and not corrected, these and other microaggressions serve to dehumanize LGBTQ persons or at least characterize them as somehow inferior, and strengthen a culture of discrimination. The effects of discrimination may be partially responsible for a greater prevalence of mental health concerns among LGBTQ adults compared to heterosexual adults (Cochran, Sullivan, & Mays, 2003), and the higher rates of suicidal ideation and suicide attempts observed among gay, lesbian, and bisexual adolescents compared to heterosexual adolescents (Silenzio, Pena, Duberstein, Cerel, & Knox, 2007), especially in neighborhoods with high rates of hate crimes against LGBT persons (Duncan & Hatzenbuehler, 2014). The number of gay and lesbian youth suicides in the United States publicized by social media outlets in 2010 led to the creation of the *It Gets Better Project*™ (www.itgetsbetter.org) to support gay and lesbian youth. Stories of LGBTQ persons whose lives have gotten better also are available in the book entitled *It Gets Better* (Savage & Miller, 2012).

Generally, straight persons do not feel a need to hide their sexual orientation for fear of reprisal. The same is true for cis persons, those who are comfortable with the gender they were assigned at birth. For many LGBTQ persons, however, keeping silent about their sexual orientation and/or gender identity for fear of the consequences is a perpetual concern. This is particularly true of LGBTQ persons who were raised in devout Christian homes, including randy roberts potts (2012), the grandson of the late televangelist Oral Roberts. He describes his coming out process as "TERRIFYING," due in no small measure to the suicide of his uncle, Ronnie, the oldest son of Oral Roberts, who also was gay. He writes, "while the Evangelical community might not pull the trigger when one of their gay members commits suicide, they provide the ammunition" (p. 182). The coming-out stories of other LGBTQ persons who were raised in a Christian home are featured in the 2007 award-winning documentary entitled *For the Bible Tells Me So* (see www .forthebibletellsmeso.org).

Affirming LGBTQ Persons Because of what Greene (2009) described as the selective use and the literal interpretation of scripture and other religious writings, many LGBTQ persons experience discrimination and oppression within their religious communities. In their study on the intersection of religion and sexuality, Sherry, Adelman, Whilde, and Quick (2010) reported that 40 percent of their LGBT respondents either rejected religion or God or converted to a religious view more affirming of their sexual orientation. Although the professional helper's own professed religious beliefs are to be respected—as is true of clients and their own religious beliefs—Greene (2009) asserted that the professional helper's religious beliefs that do not support LGBTQ sexual orientation, gender identity, and expression may compromise client welfare and thus do harm.

Because more LGBTQ persons make use of the mental health system than do heterosexual persons (Cochran et al., 2003), we believe it is imperative for all helpers to practice what has been described as **affirmative therapy** for LGBTQ clients (Chernin & Johnson, 2003; Kort, 2008). Affirmative therapy is a form of culturally competent therapy (Johnson, 2012) and includes acknowledging the microaggressions you may have committed and addressing them with clients in a nondefensive and transparent manner (Shelton & Delgado-Romero, 2013). We also encourage helpers to follow the practice guidelines for working with LGBT clients developed by professional associations, such as the American Psychological Association's (APA, 2012) *Guidelines for Psychological Practice with Lesbian, Gay, and Bisexual Clients*.

Kort (2008) defined gay affirmative therapy as the practice of helping to repair the harm done to LGBTQ persons (through acts of discrimination and microaggression) and helping them move from shame to pride. This practice assumes that being a sexual minority is not an abnormality and therefore there is nothing wrong with being LGBTQ. What *is* wrong is how LGBTQ persons are treated by a nonaffirming society, including a nonaffirming professional treatment community. Gay affirmative therapy thus serves to enhance both helper and client awareness (e.g., by debunking myths about lesbians and gays, including the myth that homosexuality is attributed to childhood sexual abuse; see Kort, 2008, pp. 14–17), and to facilitate client empowerment and resilience. This is done by addressing several key issues with clients (Pachankis & Goldfried, 2013), such as identity development, intimate relationships and parenting, legal and workplace issues, and unique experiences of underrepresented sexual minority populations (e.g., ethnic minority, religious, older, and bisexual individuals).

We regard gay affirmative therapy as an example of values-based practice because it prioritizes the needs of the client to provide individualized care, seeks to enhance the values and beliefs of both client and helper, and follows ethical guidelines regarding standards of practice while eschewing the imposition of nonbeneficial interventions for each individual client following consultation with peers. This also resembles what Brown (2009) defined as culturally competent practice wherein helpers attend to the multiple identities of each client and seek to understand the intersection or integration—and meaning—of those identities for each client. In addition to sexual orientation, these identities include age, disability status, race and ethnicity, and gender. These particular identities, or cultural influences (Hays, 2008), exemplify minority groups, or *target groups* (Brown, 2008), in the United States today with histories of disempowerment and disenfranchisement. Learning about the challenges these persons continue to face promotes values-based helping, as well as culturally competent and culturally affirmative therapy.

Affirming Other Cultural Groups With respect to issues of race, Miller and Garran (2008) maintained that although no one person is responsible for racism's "long history and deep tentacles" (p. 3) in the United States, all helping professionals are responsible for responding to the racism that persists, because "[n]one of us *is a bystander* in a society structured by racism" (p. 2; emphasis theirs). Racism can be direct, overt, and intentional, or it can be indirect, covert, and unintentional, such as in microaggressions (Sue, 2010). Regardless of type, the experience of racism is associated with mental health concerns such as depression and anxiety (Nadal, Griffin, Wong, Hamit, & Rasmus, 2014). Racism exists at individual, group, institutional, and ideological levels; as Ridley (2005) indicated, anyone can be a racist, including members of racial minority groups.

Racial and ethnic disparities in the quality of mental health services have existed for quite some time in the United States (U.S. Department of Health and Human Services, 2001). They continue today for children and their families (Lê Cook, Barry, & Busch, 2013) and for older adults (Jimenez, Cook, Bartels, & Alegría, 2013), and are associated with worse client outcomes (Smedley, Stith, & Nelson, 2003). These disparities are not due to accessibility issues, clinical needs (e.g., severity level), or to client preferences, nor are they explained by socioeconomic factors only. Rather, these disparities are attributable to the race and/or ethnicity of the client and therefore exemplify one form of discrimination. Disparities include overdiagnosing or rendering inappropriate diagnoses and withholding services or providing unnecessary services.

With respect to closing the disparity gap between Hispanic and non-Hispanic clients who have mental health concerns, Blanco et al. (2007) recommended that non-Hispanic English-speaking helpers become more familiar with Hispanic culture, acquire specialized skills appropriate for Hispanic clients with mental health concerns (e.g., problem-focused and direct style when working with depression; see Kalibatseva & Leong, 2014), and learn Spanish. Language has been identified as the most significant barrier to quality mental health care among racial and ethnic minorities (Chen & Rizzo, 2010). Affirmative therapy for racial and ethnic minorities therefore necessitates ensuring that clients can be heard and understood in their preferred language.

According to Walsh, Olson, Ploeg, Lohfeld, and MacMillan (2011), older adults who are members of cultural groups with histories of discrimination and oppression are particularly vulnerable to abuse. These include persons with disabilities.

The Americans with Disabilities Act (ADA) of 1990 was intended to protect persons with documented disabilities, or who are regarded as having a disability, from discrimination and, when needed, to offer them reasonable accommodations and modifications so that they can participate fully in society, including having employment opportunities. Disability was defined at that time as physical or mental impairment that substantially limits one or more major life activities. Since then, however, U.S. Supreme Court rulings have consistently excluded from protection persons with serious diseases such as epilepsy, AIDS, cancer, and mental illness because of the Court's focus on a person's functioning at a given time rather than on his or her medical condition (Petrila, 2009; Thomas & Gostin, 2009). Furthermore, the Court's record has been to define "substantial limitation in a major life activity" according to the definition provided by the person or entity accused of discrimination rather than focusing on the discrimination itself. The effects of these rulings have been that persons with physical disabilities (e.g., multiple sclerosis), psychiatric disabilities (e.g., post-traumatic stress disorder), or other mental disabilities (e.g., traumatic brain injury) have experienced barriers to employment because of the stigmatizing attitudes of employers and coworkers (Scheid, 2005). This kind of discrimination has resulted in denied access to health care coverage (including medication) due to lack of employment and lower wages for employed persons with psychiatric disabilities who report stigmatizing experiences (Baldwin & Marcus, 2006).

The ADA Amendments Act was signed into law in 2008 and became effective in 2009 to address these gaps and the misapplication of the original law. The ADA Amendments Act expanded the list of "major life activities" that qualify for ADA review (including work or employment) and restored the broad coverage of disabilities intended in the original ADA, including conditions that are episodic (e.g., epilepsy) or in remission (e.g., cancer). It remains to be seen how the Court will rule on cases involving what Fox and Kim (2004) defined as **emerging disabilities**, or disabling conditions resulting from "newly recognized causes or diseases or expanded disability definitions" (p. 329), including environmental illnesses (e.g., asthma, Lyme disease), autoimmune deficiencies (e.g., lupus), and conditions related to poverty and violence (e.g., chronic pain from gunshot injury). Compared to persons with traditional or more socially recognizable disabilities (e.g., visual or hearing impairment), Fox and Kim reported that persons with emerging disabilities: (a) have less education; (b) experience greater difficulties with activities of daily living; (c) are insured more frequently with Medicaid (suggesting lower income); (d) are less likely to be working; and (e) seek medical assistance more frequently. Persons with emerging disabilities therefore may experience more widespread discrimination due to skepticism regarding the legitimacy of their condition (even from physicians) and the invisibility of their condition (e.g., fibromyalgia). For these and other persons with disabilities, a form of culturally affirmative therapy, disability-affirmative therapy (Olkin, 2009), is essential.

Summary of Values-Based Practice   Values-based practice is a commitment to learning from others—clients and other professionals—for the sake of providing quality care to a range of clients, many of whom present to counseling with the fresh or hardened scars of societal prejudice and discrimination. It is for this reason that we must not act in kind, that we not treat them in ways similar to how other persons (including their families) have treated them. We must not do (further) harm. Instead, we must do good.

Commitment to Beneficence

It should be evident that the values we hold about people, life, and the world around us impact our work as professional helpers. Our views on such things as same-sex partnerships and marriage equality, the death penalty, racial profiling, abortion and the time when human life begins, transitioning from one gender to another, illegal immigration, and various religious principles and practices (e.g., not ordaining women in the Roman Catholic Church) will more than likely filter into our conversations with clients and influence how we provide them with care.

Although certain values—and the intensity with which we and our clients ascribe to or endorse such values—may not be cause for concern, others are. As professionals, we are bound to certain codes of ethics that are founded on ethical principles. Two of these principles are beneficence and nonmaleficence. The BACP (2013) has defined beneficence as the commitment to acting in the client's best interests and promoting the client's well-being; in other words, doing good. Beneficence is implied in the value of service espoused by the National Association of Social Workers (NASW, 2008) in its Code of Ethics and used to inform the principle of elevating service to others above one's own needs.

For professional helpers it is not enough to simply do no harm, the ethical principle of nonmaleficence. However, nonmaleficence is a prerequisite to beneficence and often can be missed, minimized, or explained away.

In other words, professional helpers may not think they have done harm to a client when they have, or if they are made aware of this harm, they may minimize its effect on the client or explain, "I didn't mean it that way" or "You misinterpreted me." This might be the case when a helper engages in the unconscious gender microaggressions of inferring a female client's inferiority or traditional gender role (see Sue, 2010) by questioning the client's decision to join the military and "leave behind" her two young children to start basic training camp. Such questioning, even subtly, may add to this client's guilt about child abandonment as well as her lack of confidence in being able to measure up to the achievements of her older brother who also is in the military. Helpers likewise may engage in nonmaleficence when they refuse to continue working with a particular client once it is learned that the client's relationship status (e.g., in a same-sex relationship) is not consistent with the helper's value system. Even when the helper's religious values are cited as the conflict of interest (e.g., the religion-based assertion that marriage is limited to a man and a woman), the helper's decision to refer to another professional or withdraw care altogether may be experienced by the client as yet another form of discrimination. The importance of nonmaleficence is highlighted in Johnson and Buhrke's (2006) listing of the first of 15 recommendations for providing care to LGBT personnel in the U.S. military: first, do no harm (p. 94).

As persons committed to beneficence, we really cannot fake empathy or only pretend to really care about our clients' well-being. The life of a professional helper does require continuing education and perpetual learning; collaboration with clients, supervisors, and other professionals; and engaging in values-based practice and culturally affirmative therapy. It is not for the timid or faint of heart. Being a professional helper means that many of our values are continually challenged and that we need to critique and perhaps even change some long-held views to be able to effectively care for a variety of clients. Such views might include how we regard persons whose cultural identities, beliefs, and practices are different from our own.

Diversity Issues

Given the increasingly migratory and pluralistic **LO1** **LO2** world in which we live, we cannot expect to encounter only clients who share cultural backgrounds similar to ours or who look, sound, think, believe, and behave like us. Being able to provide quality services to a range of persons representing different backgrounds, professing different beliefs, and engaged in different customs is imperative for all helping professionals, regardless of the geographic location or setting of service delivery (e.g., private practice, rural hospital, suburban school). It must be emphasized that there are many forms of human diversity. The framework offered by Hays (2008, 2013) is quite informative and useful, and therefore we refer to it at various places in this book. Nine cultural influences comprise Hays's framework and each one is identified by a letter in the acronym ADDRESSING. (Although there are 10 letters in the ADDRESSING acronym, Developmental and other Disabilities is considered one cultural influence.) The ADDRESSING framework's nine cultural influences are listed in Box 2.1. Another way to refer to these is as experiences and expressions of culture.

Generally speaking, **culture** can be defined as a common heritage or a collection of beliefs and values that influence traditions, norms or standard practices, and social environments or institutions. Bryan (2007) contends that this collection of beliefs and behaviors or customs is "learned and reinforced through a socialization process" (p. 8), one that Bernal and Domenech Rodríguez (2012b) regard as "an intergenerationally transmitted system of meanings shared by a group or groups of people" (p. 4). Culture also is not static, but is constantly evolving (Falicov, 2014). That culture is learned and reinforced by interactions with others across generations, and that it is always evolving suggests that cultural identity is not inherited but develops over time.

The broad and inclusive term **multicultural** captures the array of human diversity; **multiethnic** is a narrower term focusing on specifically ethnographic characteristics, such as race and ethnicity. **Ethnicity** connotes a shared history, language, belief system, and rituals (perhaps by virtue of sharing the same or similar geographical place of origin, e.g., Latin America), and although **race** often is regarded as a biological category (i.e., identifying persons according to genetic traits such as skin color, shape of eyes and nose), it is not. According to the American Psychological Association (APA, 2003), "the definition of race is considered to be socially constructed rather than biologically determined" (p. 380). This means that race has more to do with how social groups "are separated, treated as inferior or superior, and given differential access to power and other valued resources" (U.S. Department of Health and Human Services, 2001, p. 9). Likewise, **gender** refers to a changing set of qualities culturally assigned to social categories such as masculine or feminine. This differs from the more biologically based understanding of *sex* (i.e., male or female), although the latter is not defined exclusively by genitalia or even by birth.

BOX 2.1	Cultural Influences: The ADDRESSING Framework

Age and generational influences

Developmental disabilities (e.g., disabilities related to Down syndrome, fetal alcohol syndrome, autism spectrum)

Disabilities acquired later in life

Religion and spiritual orientation

Ethnic and racial identity

Socioeconomic status (e.g., income, occupation, education)

Sexual orientation

Indigenous heritage (e.g., Aboriginal, Native, First Nations people)

National origin (e.g., birthplace, first or primary language, immigration experiences)

Gender (male or female or transgender, gender expression as masculine/feminine)

Source: Hays, 2008, 2013.

Many textbooks addressing diversity and multicultural considerations begin by presenting and discussing group characteristics. Learning about and understanding the commonalities of members of a particular cultural group (or "the ties that bind") are important. However, if this nomothetic or broad-brush approach to understanding diverse populations is the only one discussed, then it can promote overgeneralizations, stereotyping, gross misrepresentations (Bryan, 2007), and further divides by promoting "us versus them" kinds of thinking (Chisholm & Greene, 2008). As a result, helpers may be inclined to assess and make interpretations about an individual client based solely on his or her racial and/or ethnic group membership. This prevents a here-and-now focus in therapy (Chisholm & Greene, 2008) because the helper is distracted by the categorical and manualized definitions of diversity. This is evident in statements such as, "Amish people are healthy and hardy" and "Filipino Americans have strong family ties." Although these characterizations may apply to many individuals who identify as Amish and as Filipino American, respectively, they may not necessarily define the individual client who is seeking or in need of services, and therefore can represent "potentially misleading" information (Brown, 2009, p. 346). Assuming that clients who appear to represent a particular ethnic or racial group meet all of the stereotypical criteria of persons from that particular group "is actually one of the worst manifestations of prejudice" (Brems, 2000, p. 9).

Neufeldt et al. (2006) regarded a helper's consideration of individual or within-group differences as a "relatively advanced-level multicultural competence" (p. 474). This is similar to considering the **intersection of multiple identities** (Brown, 2009; Greene, 2009). In their study of case conceptualization practices—specifically, the incorporation of diversity issues—Neufeldt et al. found that only 3 of 17 therapists in training considered within-group differences when they were presented with the case of a female Chinese American client. The majority of these therapists in training did not consider ways in which this young woman differed from other members of her identified group, a practice that exemplifies the assumption of homogeneity. Similarly, Schomburg and Prieto (2011) found that an overwhelming majority of trainees in marriage and family therapy did not attend to racial factors when presented with a vignette of either an African American couple or a white couple attending therapy.

Attending to *both* the nomothetic, homogeneous, or general descriptions of a client's cultural group *and* his or her idiographic, idiosyncratic, or unique characterizations is essential in all cross-cultural interactions. This is the focus of multicultural counseling and therapy—the unique individual embedded in a cultural group or in multiple and overlapping/intertwined cultural contexts.

Multicultural Counseling and Therapy

Although all therapy could be thought of as cross- **LO1** **LO2** cultural therapy, multicultural counseling and therapy is a specific and very intentional approach that considers the cultural factors in *all* client-helper interactions. It operates from an idiographic *and* a nomothetic bifocal perspective that deliberately focuses on how culture influences counseling and therapy. It keeps culture front and center in the helping process to not dilute its significance. As Sue and Sue (2013, p. 83) emphasize, "Multicultural counseling and therapy is not for White helping professionals only!" It challenges *all* helpers to confront and work through their biases.

Multicultural counseling and therapy makes use of the tripartite framework of personal identity development that Sue (2001) developed. The three-level framework can be visualized as three concentric circles, each larger than the other and each corresponding to a level. As can be seen in Figure 2.1, the individual level is the center circle that depicts what is unique or idiosyncratic about the individual, such as genetic endowment and personal and private experiences. It is surrounded by or embedded in the second

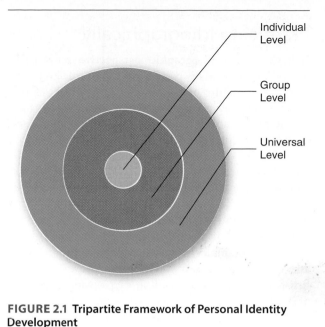

FIGURE 2.1 Tripartite Framework of Personal Identity Development
Source: Sue (2001) and Sue and Sue (2013).

and larger circle, the group level, which represents various cultural influences (e.g., the nine influences in Hays's ADDRESSING Framework, 2008, 2013) and the cultural groups the individual is similar to and different from. The third and largest circle, in which both the individual and group levels are embedded, is the universal level. This level represents what all human beings have in common—for example, the use of language, biological, and physical similarities, and experiences of birth and death.

The premise of multicultural counseling and therapy is that individuals cannot be understood from only one of the three levels of personal identity development—all three levels must be considered. And one of the major contributions of multicultural counseling and therapy is that level 2, the group level, is given prominence. That is, no two persons are alike *because of* cultural influences. The professional helper therefore must assess and appreciate the influence of age, race/ethnicity, and socioeconomic status, for example, on the client's past and current functioning, even if the client is not fully aware of these influences. The helper also participates with the client in learning more about the meaning for the client of the integration or intersection of these cultural influences or cultural identities (Brown, 2009; Chisholm & Greene, 2008; Greene, 2009). In other words, how is uniqueness (level 1) shaped over time by belonging to more than one group (level 2) as well as by challenging certain group norms? How am I similar to and how am I different from others?

Practicing Idiographically

Ridley's (2005) **idiographic perspective** remains [LO2] instructive for us. This perspective regards each client as unique, "a mixture of characteristics and qualities that make him or her unlike anyone else" (p. 85). It focuses on the person at the individual level, whose uniqueness is embedded in group level similarities and differences, as well as in universal level commonalities. Just like the focus on the intersection or matrix of multiple identities within each person (Brown, 2009; Chisholm & Greene, 2008; Greene, 2009), an idiographic perspective eschews broad-brush and potentially misleading categorical descriptions in favor of a kaleidoscopic description of each client. For example, an idiographic perspective would ask: "Who is this person who happens to be a 75-year-old first-generation Latina American widow who is a mother of six, grandmother of 10, and whose primary language is Spanish?" An idiographic perspective also seeks to understand what the convergence of multiple identities means for this and other clients. Certainly the helper will generate assumptions or hypotheses about individual clients. This is the practice of case conceptualization discussed in Chapter 8. By definition, hypotheses are tentative and remain so unless or until they are confirmed by the client. Cultural identity is always self-defined. An idiographic perspective therefore encourages clients to formulate and articulate their own cultural identity—or tapestry of cultural identities—prioritizing their own values and practices at particular times in their lives.

Ridley (2005) offered five principles of an idiographic perspective in mental health care, each of which is discussed briefly in this section. These principles assert that an idiographic perspective:

1. understands each client from the client's unique frame of reference.

2. considers nomothetic or general information, but recognizes that such broad information may not always fit particular individual clients.

3. considers each person to be a dynamic blend of multiple roles and identities.

4. is compatible with the biopsychosocial model of mental health.

5. is transtheoretical.

The first principle of an idiographic perspective is that practitioners should attempt to understand each client from the client's unique frame of reference. This might be similar to regarding each individual as "a self-contained universe with its own laws" (Shontz, 1965, cited in Cone, 2001, p. 14). Asking a light-skinned African American lesbian who lives in a fairly small town in the Midwest what she means by "passing" might be an example. Respecting and seeking to understand the reasons a young soldier has for requesting to return to the battlefront rather than remain at home after recovering from his physical wounds might be another example. Although the idiographic perspective appears to pertain only to working with individual clients, it does have application to families.

The second principle of an idiographic perspective (Ridley, 2005) is that nomothetic, normative information needs to be considered but may not always fit particular individual clients. For example, homelessness does not imply unemployment, drug addiction, or mental illness. One young African American man who spent nights and weekends in a San Francisco shelter and the subway restroom for several months did not "fit the mold" of a "down-and-out" "druggie" or "criminal." Christopher Gardner, whose true rags-to-riches story is featured in the motion picture *The Pursuit of Happyness* (Muccino, 2006), broke all the rules of such stereotypes. Although lacking a college education and providing the sole care for his young son, Mr. Gardner managed to succeed in a nonpaid internship at a top brokerage firm, pass the licensing exam on the first try, get hired by the firm, proceed to establish his own brokerage firm, and eventually become a millionaire. This one example underscores the importance of an idiographic perspective and is consistent with the adage "Don't judge a book by its cover."

Ridley's (2005) third principle of an idiographic perspective in the helping process is that people are a dynamic blend of multiple roles and identities. This is certainly true for multiracial or multiple heritage persons (Kenney & Kenney, 2012). It also matches the concept of multiple identities and the intersection of those identities (Brown, 2009; Greene, 2009), which is a more pronounced focus in social work (see Lee, 2010). From this perspective, it is impossible to understand and fully appreciate a client's experience if the client's race or ethnicity, for example, is thought to develop and operate in isolation from his or her gender or sex.

The intersection of multiple identities is evident in more than 9 million people, or 2.9 percent of the U.S. population, reporting two or more races in the 2010 census (U.S. Census Bureau, 2011). An astute helper, therefore, will not assume that a new client's racial identity is either black or white, for example. Rather, the helper may inquire about the intersection of racial/ethnic identities—or, more broadly, about cultural identities—and will elicit the client's own meaning of such an intersection or blending, what Lee (2010) referred to as internalized culture. For example, how might the son of a black African father and a white European American mother describe his cultural identity, particularly when influenced by his being raised in Indonesia?

According to Ridley (2005), the idiographic perspective is compatible with the biopsychosocial model of mental health. This fourth principle reinforces a comprehensive or holistic view of individuals. Rather than understanding someone from only one perspective (e.g., medical model), the biopsychosocial model challenges helpers to formulate their understanding of clients from a variety of perspectives.

The fifth and final principle of an idiographic perspective (Ridley, 2005) is that it is transtheoretical. This refers to the use of a variety of theoretical orientations and interventions with clients, not just one tried-and-true approach. A helper who identifies with the same general racial/ethnic group as one of his or her clients (e.g., both identify as Native American) may inadvertently assume that a particular therapeutic intervention (e.g., participating in a healing service) may be appropriate for the client based on the helper's own participation in such an activity. An idiographic perspective that is transtheoretical, however, would entertain several possible theories and strategies for the benefit of the individual client, even if such options did not fit the helper's own experience as a member of the same general racial/ethnic group.

Guidelines for Practicing Idiographically

To assist helpers in transferring principles to practice, Ridley (2005) developed 12 guidelines for providing idiographic care. These are listed in Box 2.2, and five of them are discussed in some detail.

Developing Cultural Self-Awareness

Providing idiographic care implies that helpers remain cognizant of the significance of cultural issues in their interactions with all clients. We believe that *all* conversations with clients are cross-cultural, that culture is embedded in all forms of professional helping. This means that cultural influences (e.g., sex, age, racial and ethnic identity, socioeconomic status, sexual orientation) are *always* pertinent and inform our work with *all* clients. If, as former U.S. Surgeon General Dr. David Satcher stated, "culture counts" (U.S. Department of Health and Human Services, 2001), then cultural factors should *always* be at the forefront of our awareness in our work with clients and our life as helpers.

Cultural self-awareness includes becoming aware of our own identities that are either privileged or disadvantaged (see Okun & Suyemoto, 2013; Hays, 2013). Privileged status means having access to power and decision-making in a particular society and being part of the dominant

BOX 2.2	**Guidelines for Practicing Idiographic Helping**

1. Develop cultural self-awareness.
2. Avoid imposing one's values on clients.
3. Accept one's naïveté regarding others.
4. Show cultural empathy.
5. Incorporate cultural considerations into counseling.
6. Avoid stereotyping.
7. Determine the relative importance of clients' primary cultural roles.
8. Avoid blaming the victim.
9. Remain flexible in the selection of interventions.
10. Examine counseling theories for bias.
11. Build on clients' strengths.
12. Avoid protecting clients from emotional pain.

Source: Ridley, 2005.

group in that society. Being socially disadvantaged means not having access to the benefits of power and decision-making in a society. Persons who are privileged are able to define societal norms, and persons who are disadvantaged are outside of those norms, prevented by those in power from enjoying the benefits of power. Regardless of numbers or population size, those who are privileged to power are in the majority, whereas those who are disadvantaged from power are in the minority.

Chisholm and Greene (2008) asserted that understanding the meaning of social privilege is a prerequisite to realizing whether or not one has it. Privilege essentially is a gift of advantage, a benefit that is not earned; it is an identity and a status that is not acquired through merit, such as working hard to earn a graduate degree. Josh, a white male born in the United States to a middle class or upper-middle class well-educated family, is privileged, even if he does not know it and even if he does not go to college. The meaning of privilege also can only be understood by comparison and in context; that is, someone is privileged only in comparison to someone else and only in the context of sociopolitical history and current circumstance. Once we learn that Josh was born deaf, came out as gay in high school, and has left home because his conservative Christian parents viewed him as a "pervert" and an "abomination" to their home, we realize that his privileged status is less compared to Evan, another white male who also was born in the United States to a middle class or upper-middle class well-educated family, who is heterosexual, and who since birth has not experienced any physical limitations.

The comparison of Josh and Evan illustrates well the concept of multiple identities and the focus on the intersection or the convergence of multiple identities and its meaning for each person (Brown, 2009; Greene, 2009). Although socially disadvantaged in terms of his sexual orientation and his physical limitation, Josh is part of a privileged group in terms of his sex, race/ethnicity, and family-of-origin socioeconomic status. Whereas Evan's sexual orientation and physical ability status are two

cultural identities that are privileged, these same cultural identities are disadvantages for Josh.

Developing and enhancing cultural self-awareness can be accomplished in many different ways. One way to do this is to use Hays's (2008, 2013) ADDRESSING Framework (see Box 2.1) and to consider the notion of multiple identities. We encourage you to pause at this time to engage in Learning Activity 2.2 before reading further.

Learning Activity 2.2

Cultural Self-Awareness: Tapestry of My Cultural Influences and Identity

This activity is intended to further enhance your own cultural self-awareness by considering the elements or ingredients of your cultural identity today. You will need a blank piece of paper and something to write with (having a selection of writing instruments of different colors may enhance the effect of this activity for you). We encourage you to find a quiet place where you will not be disturbed and to spend approximately 20 minutes on this activity. If done in the classroom, this could be done as an individual activity first, and then responses could be shared in student dyads or small groups.

Turn to the ADDRESSING Framework developed by Hays (2008, 2013) and presented in Box 2.1 on page 46 as you go through this activity. Follow the steps below. An example of another person's responses to step 4 is located on pages 53–54 (client Katrina, discussed in Learning Activity 2.3).

1. Read through the nine cultural influences in Hays's ADDRESSING Framework. These might also be considered multiple identities, as well as the elements, ingredients, or components of your cultural identity. (Although there are 10 letters in the word ADDRESSING, two of them focus on disabilities: Developmental and other Disabilities. Hays, 2013, thus refers to nine cultural influences.)
2. Consider who you are and where you are today in your personal and professional development. How does each of the nine cultural influences or multiple identities represent for you today either a social advantage/privilege or a social disadvantage? Do not skip any! Now, on a separate sheet of paper, create two columns, one with the heading *Privilege* and the other with the heading *Disadvantage*. One by one, place each of the nine cultural influences under the appropriate column based on whether you believe that it constitutes for you today a social advantage/privilege or a social disadvantage.
3. Think of a family member who was instrumental in your formative development. This could be a parent or grandparent who helped raise you as a child. How do your responses to Question 2 compare to the responses this family member might provide for himself or herself—when you were growing up *and* also today (if this person

is still living)? That is, how do your social advantages/privileges and social disadvantages today compare to those of your family member?

4. From Hays's list of cultural influences, select those you believe are prominent elements or ingredients in your cultural identity today. These may be all 10, or only four or five. You decide. Give a name to each cultural influence you selected, a name that makes sense and applies to you. Once you have made your selection of prominent elements or ingredients, on a blank sheet of paper draw a shape or symbol (e.g., circle, square, triangle, oval, octagon, free-flowing) for each cultural influence. The shape selected for each cultural influence, as well as the size, color, thickness of the lines used, and placement on the paper are up to you because only you can determine your cultural identity—no one else! You may wish to consult the sample tapestry of client Katrina's cultural identity located in Figure 2.2 on page 51. Although the shapes of Katrina's tapestry are not presented in multiple colors, this example might assist you in creating your own tapestry. Notice the shapes used for each cultural influence in the drawing, as well as which shapes have thicker outlines than the others. As you draw and create your own tapestry, consider the following questions:
   a. What shapes or symbols did you include? Were you aware of ascribing personal relevance to any of these?
   b. What do you notice about the relative size of each shape or symbol?
   c. Was your choice of color influenced by personal meaning attached to the color?
   d. How did you determine the thickness of the lines for each shape or symbol?
   e. Where did you locate each shape or symbol on the paper? Is there any overlap?
   f. Once you have illustrated your prominent cultural influences, step back to observe your drawing, a drawing that represents a tapestry of your cultural identity. If you were to name your tapestry, what title would you give it?
5. Guided by your comfort level and your desire to learn from another person, share your drawing, your tapestry, with a classmate.

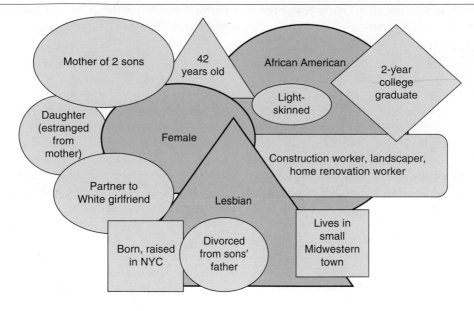

FIGURE 2.2 Sample of Katrina's Cultural Tapestry

After you have completed Learning Activity 2.2, we hope it has become evident that cultural self-awareness is enhanced by recognizing and naming the prominent identities or influences that comprise your own cultural tapestry. This is the first step. And remember, no one lacks a cultural identity or a mixture of cultural identities. It is simply more prominent or of a higher priority for some persons than for others. Persons with more traditional or visible physical disabilities (e.g., cerebral palsy), for example, may have developed a more pronounced cultural identity based in large part on their disability/ability status compared to able-bodied persons. This is particularly true if the disability is longstanding. Add to this the identity of race/ethnicity (e.g., black Hispanic), immigration status and level of acculturation (e.g., born and raised in Cuba, recent immigrant to the United States), and the identity of gender (e.g., female), and the resulting intersection is much more pronounced than would be the case for an able-bodied white male born and raised in the United States, for example.

The second step to enhance your cultural self-awareness is to assess your own stage of cultural identity development. Questions you may ask yourself include:

- "As a dark-skinned African American, have I adopted what Boyd-Franklin (2003) described as a 'blacker than thou' mentality by not trusting light-skinned African Americans?"
- "As a conservative Christian, have I secretly attributed severe mental illness and co-occurring alcohol dependence to a lack of morality and divine judgment?"

- "As an 'out' LGB helper, have I become intolerant of clients who continue to struggle with internalized shame that keeps them from coming out as LGB?"
- "As a bilingual second-generation Latina American, have I unknowingly become critical of recent immigrants who refuse to become proficient in English?"

The third step in the process of enhancing your cultural self-awareness is to evaluate the influences that have shaped you, and then to evaluate how your attitudes affect the helping process. Helpers are strongly encouraged to engage in activities that challenge long-held stereotypes and broaden their understanding of and appreciation for the experiences of others. Hays (2013) refers to stereotypes as the development of "hardening of the categories" (p. 25), believing that individuals can only or primarily be defined by rigid categories or overly broad generalizations. Activities that challenge rigid or "hardened categories" might include cultural immersion experiences, such as attending an international fair and worship services of a religious group different from one's own (e.g., visiting a mosque, temple, or synagogue). Processing these and other experiences is just as important as engaging in the activities. Ridley (2005) recommended seeking therapeutic services (i.e., assuming the role of client) from a professional of another race, someone whose ancestors have not held positions of sociopolitical power. Okun and Suyemoto (2013) include in Appendix B of their book several self-reflection activities intended to enhance helpers' understanding of their ethnic culture and also power and privilege.

Acknowledging and Accepting One's Naïveté about Others

Assuming a genuine posture of curiosity about clients is regarded as an essential skill for helpers in all cross-cultural conversations. Solution-focused and narrative therapies refer to the "not-knowing" (Anderson & Goolishian, 1992) approach wherein the helper conveys genuine interest and a sincere desire to be informed by the client without preconceived opinions and expectations about the client. Some might interpret this as helper ignorance and, indeed, it is! It is impossible for anyone to fully understand, let alone know, another's experience. Therefore, maintaining a stance that is naïve, curious, and genuinely open to being with clients actually represents a primary form of respect for the experiences of clients. To present otherwise would be disrespectful and insulting.

Acknowledging our naïveté about the experiences of culturally diverse clients means that we view clients as the experts on their self-defined cultural identity, regarding them as our "cultural consultants" (Vicary & Andrews, 2000). We are the students of our clients' cultural experiences, not the authorities. With that said, two very important points must be made:

1. It isn't the job of a client to educate the helper about the client's culture (Hays, 2014). It is our job as helpers to learn *about* our clients, not *from* them. We do this by engaging in activities outside of session (e.g., reading, attending cultural events) that expand our understanding of different cultural groups and provide us with a backdrop or a reference point for appreciating the nuances of each of our client's unique experiences and identity.

2. No client is the representative of or spokesperson for a cultural group (Falicov, 2014). The *primary* focus of an idiographic approach is on the individual, not the general cultural group(s) of which he or she is a member.

Learning about our clients may be possible only when we set aside or modify certain expectations (e.g., use of grammatically correct English), pause to consider a new or an alternative perspective, and flex our empathic muscles with each new client or family. As Ridley (2005) pointed out, "Only when counselors accept the limits of their own expertise are they likely to interpret their clients' problems and needs realistically" (p. 95). This exemplifies helper humility, which Hays (2013) regards as one of the most essential qualities for working across cultures. For one thing, humility may make it possible for the helper to envision more realistic goals for the client as well as offer culturally adaptive services (see Bernal & Rodriguez, 2012a).

Determining the Relative Importance of Clients' Primary Cultural Roles

Given the dynamic intersection of identities in the increasingly diverse United States and wider world, it seems important to explore with clients how these roles and identities intersect for them. For example, what meaning has a particular client constructed (or what meaning is still "under construction") about being a middle-aged white male veteran who was widowed 2 years ago, is now raising a 15-year-old daughter (the youngest of his three children), and is not able to secure full-time employment at this time because of a medical disability? From an idiographic perspective, this client might be asked about which of his roles and responsibilities is now most important to him. Such an inquiry also may assist in goal formulation and prioritization. For example, does he want to focus his energies during the helping process on how to be an effective single parent? Does he want to discuss what it is like to be a medically disabled war veteran and how such an identity represents a significant shift from his being a physically fit, mobile, and active man able to provide financially for his family? Promoting the client's right to determine the importance of his or her various roles and responsibilities is an opportunity for the helper to learn about the client's idiographic experience and unique cultural kaleidoscope.

Avoiding Blaming the Victim

Despite fulfilling multicultural competency, helpers may unwittingly blame their clients for the stressors and challenges they report having experienced. Such blame may be evident when the helper attributes a client's drug use, for example, to his being a young African American man who did not finish high school, grew up in subsidized housing, and was raised by a single mother. Although perhaps not verbalizing the idea, the helper might think to himself or herself, "Well, that explains it all. He's black and grew up poor. If he had just stayed in school, he could have stayed away from drugs." Unbeknownst to the helper, such thinking may exemplify in part what Ridley (2005) referred to as "unintentional racism," a practice he described as "the most insidious form of racial victimization" (p. 39).

Ridley (2005) contended that therapist inaction (e.g., not addressing the issue of race in session) perpetuates the victimization of racial minorities. This might be evident when a helper professes to be "color blind" or "culture blind," implying that the race, ethnicity, or other cultural identity (e.g., sexual orientation) of others really doesn't matter or is not important. Not only does this discredit Dr. David Satcher's (U.S. Department of Health and Human Services, 2001) admonition that "culture counts," but it dismisses the very identity of another human being. Indeed, such comments represent the ultimate form of insult. Ridley (2005) cautioned, however, that "white professionals are not the only ones guilty of therapist inaction" (p. 40). He stated that minority professionals can be said to engage in unintentional racism when they "assume they understand the dynamics of racism when they may not" and "posture as experts on treating minority clients" (p. 40) when they have avoided examining their own racism or have failed to become competent in dealing with minority issues.

Avoiding Protecting Clients from Emotional Pain

At the other end of the spectrum of blaming a racial or ethnic minority client's condition or circumstances on his or her status as a member of a racial or ethnic minority group is the practice of shielding the client from emotional pain. This protection may be a form of paternalism that the helper may initially justify as empathy, although others would regard it as condescension. Ridley (2005) termed it a "tactical error" to select "interventions that will cause the least pain rather than those that are most appropriate for helping" clients (p. 104). A multiracial college student may need to talk about feeling ostracized by mono-racial peers on campus, peers who are members of the racial groups that comprise this client's multiracial identity (see Kenney & Kenney, 2012). If a helper squelches exploring the issue in some way (e.g., "I'm sure they didn't mean to treat you that way")—all for the sake of protecting or rescuing the client from what may

be regarded as undue distress or pain—the client may interpret this response as not being taken seriously or as an indication that feeling ostracized is not acceptable, and the client's emotional pain may be prolonged.

As mentioned, helpers need to assume the role of learner or student by allowing their clients to teach them about what it's like to live the life of the client. Such helpers often will hear stories that are unsettling—accounts of discrimination and other forms of unfair treatment, for example—that cannot be tidied up for the client and removed from his or her experience. A significant challenge for helpers is to muster what Kenneth Minkoff eloquently phrased as "the courage to join [clients] in the reality of their despair" (featured in the Mental Illness Education Project, 2000). Doing so is intended not to "fix" or eradicate clients' pain but to provide clients with the company, companionship, and sense of safety that may assist them in becoming able to work through such difficulties. The work and process of healing or recovery not uncommonly is accompanied by pain, and helpers actually do their clients a disservice when they make the eradication of pain the primary purpose of helping (Ridley, 2005).

At this point we invite you to participate in Learning Activity 2.3. This is designed to help you apply Ridley's (2005) guidelines for idiographic helping (see Box 2.2) by also making use of Hays's (2008, 2013) ADDRESSING Framework (see Box 2.1). The case of "Katrina" is presented in Learning Activity 2.3 on pages 53–54 and a sample tapestry of her cultural identity (responding to Question 4 in the Learning Activity) is presented in Figure 2.2 on page 51.

Learning Activity 2.3

Idiographic Helping Applied

Read through the following case and then refer back to Hays's (2008, 2013) ADDRESSING Framework (Box 2.1) as well as Ridley's (2005) 12 guidelines for practicing idiographic counseling (Box 2.2). Once you have done so, respond as best you can (by yourself or with a classmate) to the eight questions related to Katrina's case, your assessment of her cultural intersection or integration, and your work with her. This also might be an activity for the entire class to engage in.

"Katrina" is a 42-year-old light-skinned African American female who moved from New York City approximately 15 years ago to the small midwestern town where she currently resides. She moved after a failed marriage to an African American man and a fallout with her mother, and out of a desire to raise her then 3- and 5-year-old sons in a "safer" place. Katrina seeks counseling at this time because of increased stressors at home and at work.

Her work history includes construction and she is proud of the marble inlay and columns she was responsible for erecting in a prominent building in downtown New York City. After earning an associate's degree in horticulture at a local community college, she now manages a landscaping business and also does home renovation during the off season.

Katrina discloses that she is a lesbian and that her white girlfriend, "Elaine," is planning to move out. They had a fight last week, and Katrina states she became enraged when Elaine proposed "cooling things" between the two of them and moving out of the apartment they have shared for 2 years. "Look, without her I have no one, not one person who really, I mean, really knows me and accepts me as I am. Even my sons, I know they think we're freaks . . . they haven't been around for a while . . . and I haven't heard from my mom since last Thanksgiving. She believes I've 'sinned' and 'gone astray,' and that I have 'brought on' my 'trials and

(continued)

tribulations.' Her words, not mine. This can be too small of a town, you know? Kind of suffocating. Don't get me wrong, there are times when I really like it here and there are some good people around. I get by, you know, I pass, but . . .'"

Questions to Consider

1. What are your initial impressions of Katrina?
2. Given the information presented and using your culturally empathic skills, what do you think life must be like for her?
3. What challenges has she likely encountered and experienced over at least the past 15 years?
4. How do these challenges correspond to the cultural influences that may be prominent in Katrina's cultural identity? To answer this question, consult Hays's (2008) ADDRESSING Framework in Box 2.1 and select any cultural influences that may apply to Katrina. Of the ones selected, which two or three might be more prominent for Katrina at this time? (A sample of Katrina's tapestry of her cultural

identity is presented in Figure 2.2 on page 51. Notice the influences represented and which ones appear to be more prominent for Katrina at this time, based on the thickness of lines used to draw the shapes.)

5. How would you begin a conversation with Katrina?
6. What questions might you ask or what things might you say that you believe would help you and Katrina establish initial rapport?
7. What additional information would you like for Katrina to share with you that would help you understand or resonate with her self-described cultural identity? How might the imparting of this information represent a risk for you?
8. Select at least three of Ridley's (2005) 12 guidelines for practicing idiographic counseling (listed in Box 2.2.) and apply them to your work with Katrina. For example, what things do you think would be helpful for *you* to do to enhance *your own* cultural self-awareness as you continue working with Katrina?

Beyond Multicultural Competencies to Cultural Attunement

For more than 25 years, educators in the helping **LO2** professions have emphasized the teaching and acquisition of specific competencies deemed essential to work effectively with diverse groups of clients. Several professional organizations have adopted **multicultural competencies**, including the American Psychological Association (APA, 2003), the National Association of Social Workers (2001), and the American Counseling Association (Sue, Arredondo, & McDavis, 1992).

First introduced by Sue et al. (1982), multicultural competencies have been conceptualized according to three domains: *beliefs and attitudes*, *knowledge*, and *skills*. In developing their set of multicultural counseling competencies, Sue et al. (1992) paired each domain with the three characteristics of a culturally skilled practitioner described by Sue and Sue (2013): (1) helper's *awareness* of his or her own assumptions, values, and biases; (2) understanding the *worldview* of the client; and (3) developing appropriate *intervention strategies and techniques*. This pairing resulted in nine competency areas. According to this matrix, the multiculturally competent helper is someone who, for example, is aware of his or her own attitudes toward persons of a different ethnic background, including stereotypes or instances of unintentional racism. Each

of the three helper characteristics can therefore be thought of as finding expression within each of the three domains.

Numerous studies have sought to determine the impact of multicultural competence on the helping process and client outcome (see Worthington, Soth-McNett, & Moreno, 2007, for a review of the research literature). For example, it appears that therapist multicultural competence impacts client ratings of therapist empathy and general competence (i.e., therapist attractiveness, expertness, and trustworthiness), suggesting an association between therapist multicultural and general competence (Fuertes et al., 2006; Owen, Leach, Wampold, & Rodolfa, 2011).

These and other research findings are complicated, however, by the lack of clarity as to how competence is defined and who determines competence, as discussed in this chapter. For example, therapists have been found to rate their multicultural competence significantly higher than do their clients (Fuertes et al., 2006). Therapists and those in training may therefore overestimate the extent of their multicultural competence, and neither level of racial identity development nor purported multicultural competence may translate into multicultural counseling skill.

An alternative to the term multicultural competence is that of **cultural attunement**. Roberts (2008) defined cultural attunement as "the dynamic nature of understanding diversity and cultures" involving "ongoing and active 'tuning in'" that exemplifies mindfulness and cultural humility. It is a practice adopted by behavioral health care workers in rural Alaska (Nelson, Hewell, Roberts, Kersey, &

Avey, 2012) who view routine consultation with elders as integral to the development of new trainings and practices. Elders are those persons who have earned the respect of their communities, can articulate the needs of their villages, and are the "wisdom keepers" of their culture. Helpers who thus practice cultural attunement are open to continuous learning, not only from clients but also from other members (and leaders) of the cultural groups with which the helper's clients identify.

We prefer the term cultural attunement (Roberts, 2008) to that of "achieving" multicultural "competence." Cultural attunement is consistent with Lee's (2007) depiction of multicultural "literacy," or what we regard as **multicultural fluency**. Lee described multicultural literacy as going "beyond mere competency to embracing a way of life that encourages maximum exposure to and understanding of the many-faceted realities of multiculturalism" (p. 261). Cultural attunement is a way of being with clients that suggests that we as helpers are always learning, remaining humble, and negotiating our way in a world of human diversity. This suggests that we cannot work effectively with all individuals and their families, but that we can learn and speak the language of **cultural empathy** (Brown, 2009), a language that we believe is an ethical imperative.

In the pursuit of cultural attunement, cultural fluency is fostered by working with and intentionally learning about persons who are different from me, persons whose values and customs are different from mine. This implies that conversations with one client may generate a different language or dialect than those conversations I have with other clients. The meaning or constructed realities of those conversations also are different from those with other clients. Furthermore, cultural attunement conveys that my beliefs and attitudes, knowledge, and skills about cultures and the persons who identify with such cultures are continuously in flux, never established, and open to reshaping. This suggests that my own values and behaviors may change as I learn from my clients, shifting me from being rigid, dogmatic, and absolutistic, for example, to being more accepting and affirmative of cultural differences. And because "ethics and culture are intimately intertwined" (Hoop et al., 2008, p. 353), we continue the chapter with a discussion of ethical practice.

Ethical Practice

We believe that ethical practice is the foundation, the **L02** cornerstone, of all helping professions, and therefore it is at the very heart of what we do as professionals. If we lack awareness of or if we don't adhere to the values, principles, and codes of professional ethics, then we are at the very least isolated practitioners, if not persons without a profession.

As mentioned in this chapter, professional helping is an intimate business: we are in close contact (both in proximity and at an affective level) with other persons and we engage other people during critical, life-changing moments, occasions when clients are vulnerable, impressionable, and susceptible to the potentially harmful consequences of their life situation or mental illness (e.g., trauma of intimate partner violence, a couple struggling with the suicide of their teenage daughter). How we conduct ourselves as professional helpers has a significant impact on the lives of our clients and their family members and can sometimes be a matter of life or death (e.g., ordering involuntary psychiatric hospitalization, reporting suspicion of child abuse). This work is definitely not for the faint of heart.

We believe that being a professional helper is not simply a matter of earning a graduate degree in mental health counseling or in another behavioral health discipline. It also is not restricted to passing a multiple-choice state licensure exam and being able to sign off on clinical documentation with your academic credentials (e.g., MA, MSW, or PhD) and your professional credentials (e.g., LISW, LPC, or LMFT). Credentials alone do not guarantee professional competence (Welfel, 2016). They signify a professional helper in name only, the bare minimum of what one needs to earn the legal right to practice as a professional helper.

The word *professional* in the phrase *professional helper* actually signifies or reflects who the helper is as a person, including such things as the helper's communication and interactional style, mannerisms, how he or she wrestles with and manages personal demands and dilemmas, and his or her own decision-making and problem-solving methods. This means that we cannot separate or segregate who we are as persons from who we are as professionals. Practicing as a professional helper—a practice conducted and lived out purposefully and authentically—demands the helper's whole self, not just a part or piece or slice of the helper. Who we are as helpers is therefore not simply determined by who we are "on the clock" or on the job, including how we conduct ourselves with clients and colleagues. Rather, being a professional helper requires the investment of a person's whole self—that is, the integration or intersection of (1) one's personal life and private self with (2) one's professional life and public self. In our opinion, this work is more of a lifestyle than a job, so being a professional helper is an identity we take with us wherever we go. Perhaps there is never a time when we are not professional helpers—it is an identity that defines both our personal and our professional conduct.

Ethical practice is therefore very much influenced by who we are as persons, what we believe, and what we sanction. Ethical practice consists of much more than knowing and having memorized ethical codes and guidelines or key vocabulary (the cognitive mechanics, if you will, of ethical practice). As some have described (e.g., Fisher, 2008), this is the "ethical floor" or the bare minimum of ethical practice. We believe that ethical practice represents the helper's behavior as a professional, the visible demonstration of his or her identity as a professional helper, and the meaning the helper ascribes to that identity. For such practice to be genuine and credible, the helper must understand the need or the rationale for such behavior. The explanation that a particular behavior is simply ethical or unethical bespeaks ignorance or a lack of appreciation for the necessity of certain professional behaviors.

For example, suppose that a client in your weekly therapy group informs you that he felt snubbed when you did not speak to him at the mall last weekend. Responding with any of the following statements would fail to explain the purpose of your behavior: "It's not ethical for me to initiate contact with you outside of counseling" or "I'm not allowed to meet with my clients outside the agency" or "My supervisor would be very upset with me if she knew I had talked with you in public." Any of these responses also would suggest a lack of ownership of or an identification with such practice (i.e., "I'm not allowed" insinuates involuntary behavior). A better explanation to the client for your behavior might be: "I respect your privacy enough that I would not want to publicize how I know you." Rather than referring to rules or mandatory codes, this response conveys an understanding of ethical practice as primarily that of protecting or enhancing the client's well-being. It also signals your adoption or integration of this behavior so that it is consistent with your own beliefs and values.

Returning to the notion of the connection or intersection of helper values with ethical conduct, Okun and Kantrowitz (2008) stated that

> those helpers whose behavior is consistent with their definition of helping, who are committed to examining their own behaviors and motives, and who seek consultation from others are less likely to function unethically than those who are closed to such reflections. (p. 292)

This suggests that values endorsed and prioritized by helpers—both on and off the job—do impact helper professional behavior. Bass and Quimby (2006) argued that "professional judgments are influenced by personal values" (p. 78). We believe, therefore, that when the personal values of helpers are consistent with professional standards of conduct, helpers are more likely to interact genuinely and credibly with clients and other professionals. According to the Preamble of the NASW (2008) Code of Ethics, such practice reflects the value of integrity (one of six core values listed). Put another way, consistency of personal values and professional conduct signals an authentic lifestyle of helping.

Ethics usually are understood as professional standards regarding what is deemed appropriate, proper, or acceptable behavior and what is deemed inappropriate, improper, or unacceptable professional behavior. Behaviors that comprise professional conduct typically are determined by a subgroup of members (e.g., ethics committee) charged with the task of outlining the behavioral expectations of all members of a particular organization or profession. Ethical codes are thus the product of a collective gathering and consensual validation by professional members of an organization or profession and are intended to guide professional conduct, discharge of duties, and the resolution of moral dilemmas. These codes include the American Counseling Association's (ACA; 2014) *ACA Code of Ethics*, the American Psychological Association's (APA; 2010) Ethical Principles of Psychologists and Code of Conduct (hereinafter referred to as APA's Ethics Code), and the NASW's (2008) *Code of Ethics*. Marriage and family therapists, rehabilitation counselors, school counselors, health care providers, and members of other helping professions have their own sets of ethical standards. Outside of the United States, the BACP's (2013) *Ethical Framework for Good Practice in Counselling and Psychotherapy* includes six ethical principles and outlines nine values and 10 personal moral qualities for its members. The *Canadian Code of Ethics for Psychologists* (Canadian Psychological Association, 2000) lists four principles, one of which is responsibility to society.

Ethical Values and Principles

All helping practitioners should be familiar with the ethical codes of their respective professions. As already mentioned, however, simply knowing the codes does not ensure ethical conduct. This is simply being on the ethical ground floor. It is the helper who reaches for the ethical ceiling by embracing, intentionally reflecting on, and honoring the values of helping (e.g., care and concern for the welfare of others, openness to learning) who is often more ethical than the one who simply memorized and can recite ethical codes.

As we emphasize throughout this chapter, our values about diversity, power, relationships, the helping process, religion and spirituality, and competence, to name a few, influence and guide our professional behavior. Simply practicing a certain way because "I have to" (insinuating a lack of agreement or at least an incongruence between values and actual practice) does not engender confidence in the helper's dedication to a lifestyle of helping. Considering the values and principles of ethical practice is therefore appropriate, and doing so in this chapter prior to discussing specific ethical issues is intended to inform and guide (perhaps even structure) the decision-making process of each issue.

Using extant data derived from in-depth interviews with 10 therapists (seven women, three men; all European American) who were nominated and deemed by their peers as "the best of the best," Jennings, Sovereign, Bottorff, Mussell, and Vye (2005) identified nine themes or ethical values held by these "master therapists." Because the original study (Jennings & Skovholt, 1999) did not focus specifically on ethics, transcripts of the therapist interviews were compared with ethical values embedded in ethical codes (e.g., APA's Ethics Code, 2010) and in the four ethical principles recognized by most helping professions: nonmaleficence, beneficence, respect for autonomy or self-determination, and justice or fairness (Beauchamp & Childress, 2013). Additional ethical principles often cited in professional codes of ethics include fidelity, veracity, and integrity.

The resulting nine ethical values of well-respected therapists from the study of Jennings et al. (2005) are presented in Box 2.3 and are referenced in the discussion of ethical issues highlighted in the remainder of the Ethical Practice section of the chapter. We should note that ethical values sometimes are referred to as morals, virtues, or moral virtues by different sources and can include the additional helper qualities or characteristics of truthfulness, courage, integrity, sincerity, discernment, resilience, acceptance of emotion, service, interdependence with the community, and social justice (BACP, 2013; Beauchamp & Childress, 2013; NASW, 2008).

Client Rights and Welfare

Jennings et al. (2005) grouped the first four ethical values of "master therapists" (i.e., relational connection, autonomy, beneficence, and nonmaleficence) into a category they labeled "building and maintaining interpersonal attachments." It is therefore clear that attending to the relational connection with clients is a primary ethical value. This is demonstrated in the listing of "The Counseling Relationship" as the first of eight sections in the *ACA Code of Ethics* (2014). Helpers are obligated to protect the welfare of their clients. In most instances, this means putting the client's needs first. It also means ensuring that you are intellectually and emotionally ready to give the best that you can to each client.

The helping relationship needs to be handled in such a way to protect and promote the client's well-being. Establishing an effective helping relationship entails being open with clients about their rights and options during the course of therapy. Nothing can be more damaging to trust and rapport than to have the client discover midstream that the practitioner is not qualified to help

BOX 2.3	Nine Ethical Values of "Master Therapists"

1. Relational connection
2. Autonomy
3. Beneficence
4. Nonmaleficence
5. Competence
6. Humility
7. Professional growth
8. Openness to complexity and ambiguity
9. Self-awareness

Source: Jennings et al., 2005.

with a particular issue, that the financial costs of therapy or other forms of helping are prohibitive, or that services involve certain limitations and that their outcome cannot be guaranteed. Any of these occurrences might help explain what Safran, Muran, and Eubanks-Carter (2011) described as therapeutic alliance "ruptures." At the outset, the practitioner should provide the client with enough information about therapy to help the client make informed choices (also called *empowered consent*; see Brown, 2010).

There appears to be consensus about what should be disclosed to prospective clients to inform their consent about participating in mental health care (Carlisle & Neulicht, 2010; Fisher & Oransky, 2008; Pomerantz, 2005; Wheeler & Bertram, 2015). Informed consent should include:

1. the kind of service, treatment, or testing being provided (including whether interventions are substantiated in research trials or are more exploratory or innovative in nature);

2. the risks and benefits of the service, treatment, or testing;

3. the logistics involved and the policies of the individual provider or facility regarding the length of appointments, number of sessions, missing appointments, fees, and payment methods;

4. information about the qualifications and practices of the helper (including whether the helper is being directly supervised and the involvement of other professionals who may comprise a multidisciplinary treatment team);

5. risks and benefits of alternatives to the treatment, service, or test or of forgoing it;

6. the meaning, extent, and limits of or exceptions to confidentiality;

7. records preservation and release policies, including risks associated with electronic communication (electronic health records, as well as electronic communication with the helper, such as texting and email);

8. involvement of an insurance company or third-party payer;

9. procedure for resolving disputes or complaints; and

10. emergency procedures.

Pomerantz (2005) emphasized that providing all clients with information about available interventions and resources is an ongoing process and that specific topics (e.g., fees, method of payment) should be introduced and discussed with clients sooner than other topics (e.g., total number of sessions anticipated). He characterized this type of sequencing as "increasingly informed consent."

An additional layer of consideration arises when children and adolescents or other vulnerable groups are involved. For example, particular care is needed regarding consent when working with children and adolescents (see Tan, Passerini, & Stewart, 2007). This is especially true for minors with limited cognitive functioning and for minors whose parents are involved in high-conflict divorce or separation (Shumaker & Medoff, 2013). Laws are often unclear about whether adolescents should be treated as adults or as children when it comes to consent issues (Koocher, 2008; Shumaker & Medoff, 2013). An example of this was the New Hampshire Supreme Court's 2005 ruling *In the Matter of Kathleen Quigley Berg and Eugene E. Berg* that the medical (including therapy) records of minor children could be sealed when one parent demands access to the records for the purpose of litigation (see Wolowitz & Papelian, 2007). As a result of this ruling, it appears that in certain circumstances there could be "mature minors" who would be able to consent to mental health treatment without also having parental consent and that these same children could also claim client-therapist privilege (i.e., deny parental access to therapy information, including therapy records). Professional helper consultation (e.g., state laws, codes of ethics) and discernment is essential in these matters because age is an arbitrary indication of maturity, children and youth reach developmental milestones at different rates, and mental health and substance use concerns can affect a young person's decisional capacity (Belitz & Bailey, 2009).

It is true that children and youth vary greatly in their capacity to provide truly informed consent. Soliciting a young person's **assent** or accepting the helper's invitation to participate in the therapeutic process (Belitz & Bailey, 2009) is encouraged by the American Medical Association

(AMA, 2008), and the *ACA Code of Ethics* (2014) stipulates this in Standard A.2.d. This means that although children and adolescents may not be able to provide legal consent, they are able to indicate whether or not they understand and agree to what is being proposed. Assent conveys that an individual is willing to accept recommended care after having the opportunity to express his or her own wishes, knowing that these wishes will be taken seriously although they will not be given the weight of full consent. Tan et al. (2007) explained that assent allows a young person to participate in decision-making without the burden or responsibility for making the choice alone. Koocher (2008) offered sample text that helpers may wish to consider for inclusion in an informed consent document when working with children and adolescents.

Confidentiality

Closely related to protecting client well-being is the issue of confidentiality. In many respects, **confidentiality**—or the promise to respect and honor another's privacy—is the foundation or cornerstone of all helping processes (Meer & VandeCreek, 2002). Donner, VandeCreek, Gonsiorek, and Fisher (2008) adamantly asserted that maintaining client confidentiality is our primary obligation as professional helpers and is of a higher priority than risk management or the threat of litigation. Therapy and other forms of professional helping could not be conducted without the infrastructure or buttress of confidentiality, the assurance that both the content and the process of client-helper interactions will be "contained" within established parameters or boundaries of privacy. Helpers who breach client confidences can do serious and often irreparable harm to the helping relationship.

Practitioners generally are not free to reveal or disclose information unless they have first received written permission from clients. Exceptions to confidentiality vary from state to state but generally include Merideth's (2007) "Five C's" mnemonic for remembering the five generally recognized exceptions to confidentiality:

Consent of client or legally authorized surrogate decision-maker (e.g., parent, guardian)

Court order, which is issued by a judge and should not be considered equivalent to a subpoena, unless the latter is also issued by a judge

Continued treatment that requires the clinician to communicate with other professionals and health care agencies (e.g., insurance company)

Comply with the law, which includes mandatory reporting (e.g., suspected child abuse or neglect)

Communicate a threat, or warn specifically identifiable potential victims of a clear and imminent danger

Confidentiality and the Duty to Protect The last of Merideth's (2007) "Five C's" of exceptions to confidentiality is commonly known as the helper's **duty to protect** (sometimes referred to as the **duty to warn**). The duty to protect is based on the case of *Tarasoff v. Regents of the University of California* (1976). There are at least 33 states that have adopted some type of duty to protect law (Bersoff, 2014) by which helping professionals in those states may not be subject to litigation if they take specific action when a client threatens to cause imminent bodily harm to an identified victim. Depending on the state, these helper actions may include implementing a risk management plan after consulting with a supervisor (e.g., prioritizing the goal of anger management in the treatment plan), involuntarily hospitalizing the client, encouraging the client to be hospitalized voluntarily, and/or notifying legal authorities of the client's threat and identity, as well as the potential victim's identity and location.

Notice that not all of these actions require the helper to breach client confidentiality, something Bersoff (2014, p. 465) contends is a helper's "last resort." He describes the dilemma between two forms of protective action: protecting the *client's privacy* and protecting *another person's safety* from the actions of the client. He writes:

> The therapist must tread a thin line between protecting confidentiality and protecting the potential victim. An error on either side of this line can lead to liability—either for malpractice in unreasonably breaching confidentiality or for wrongful death for failure to warn in the face of a real threat. (p. 466)

Prioritizing one form of protective action over the other requires consulting with a supervisor and possibly with legal counsel, as well as familiarizing yourself with your state's laws.

Confidentiality and Communicable Health Conditions A complex issue involving the limits to confidentiality is whether the client who tests positive for a contagious, communicable, and potentially life-threatening disease (e.g., human immunodeficiency virus or HIV) is regarded as a danger to others. Consider the case example adapted from Alghazo, Upton, and Cioe (2011):

> "Mark" is a 36-year-old married bisexual man recently diagnosed with HIV. He applies for life insurance at work and routine blood work identifies him as HIV-positive, which he chooses to keep private. Following this diagnosis, Mark begins missing an excessive amount of work (at least 2 days per week) and he has difficulty interacting with the public. Both of these behavior changes are problematic because he is a customer service representative for a media

provider. His supervisor notices these two work problems and suggests that Mark see a rehabilitation counselor. Mark agrees to remain employed and to address the grief process associated with his infection. While receiving services, Mark reports that he continues to have a sexual relationship with his wife and other unidentified male partners. He has not informed anyone about his recent diagnosis and does not intend to do so. He believes it is unnecessary because he says he is practicing safe sex (pp. 43–44).

Take a moment to reflect on the following questions about Mark's case:

1. What are the issues involved in this case?

2. If you had been seeing Mark and his wife in couples counseling and he disclosed this information to you outside of her presence, would you be able to keep this information from her?

3. Whether or not you were meeting with Mark in individual or couples counseling, what options are there for intervention?

4. What are your ethical obligations as a professional helper in your work with Mark?

Advances in science and technology have clearly influenced certain policies and professional recommendations. For example, the Centers for Disease Control and Prevention (CDC) now consider HIV and AIDS (acquired immunodeficiency syndrome, the late stage of HIV) to be chronic conditions that can be treated (although not cured) with therapies that were not available 10 to 15 years ago, namely antiretroviral therapy (ART). Because of this, the CDC now recommends routine testing for HIV/AIDS for adults, adolescents, and pregnant women seen in health care settings in the United States (see www.cdc.gov/hiv/topics/testing). This also is the recommendation of the U.S. Preventive Services Task Force, an affiliate of the U.S. Department of Health and Human Services (see www.uspreventiveservicestaskforce.org). Furthermore, President Obama (who was tested for HIV in 2009) issued an Executive Order in 2013 establishing the HIV Care Continuum Initiative to improve testing, care, and treatment outcomes for those living with HIV, their partners, and other family members.

Learning the results of a positive screen makes it possible for infected persons to then access available therapies and to receive valuable information so that they can take steps to manage their health and to protect their sex or drug-use partners from infection. These steps include learning about pre-exposure prophylaxis (or PrEP, a medication intended to prevent HIV infection among HIV-negative persons who are at risk for HIV exposure) and learning that ART can significantly reduce HIV infection in newborns (Ergin, Magnus, Ergin, & He, 2002).

Despite these treatments and recommendations, HIV and AIDS remain stigmatizing conditions. This may be due to the criminalization of certain behaviors of HIV-positive persons. Thirty-three states currently have one or more HIV-specific criminal laws, categorized as felonies in 28 of these states (Lehman et al., 2014). In 24 of the 33 states, persons who know they are HIV-positive are required to disclose their status to their sexual partners; in 27 states, criminal behaviors include those that pose a high-risk of HIV transmission (e.g., anal and vaginal sex, donation of blood). Although a majority of HIV-positive persons in two of these states (Michigan and New Jersey) who were aware of the disclosure law reported having disclosed their status to their sexual partners, Galletly and her colleagues (Galletly, Pinkerton, & DiFranceisco, 2012; Galletly, Glasman, Pinkerton, & DiFanceisco, 2012) found that awareness of the law in these two states was not associated with an increased disclosure to all prospective sex partners, increased use of condoms, or increased sexual abstinence. Rather than punishing persons for nondisclosure, Galletly and her colleagues recommend helping to increase the comfort level of HIV-positive persons to disclose their status or to remain abstinent.

Beauchamp and Childress (2013) refer to the American Medical Association's (AMA) guidelines to physicians for preventing HIV-positive individuals from infecting third parties as "a responsible, albeit demanding, strategy" (p. 322). The AMA's Council on Ethical and Judicial Affairs (2010) revised the AMA Code of Medical Ethics (Section E-2.23) so that physicians "honor their obligation to promote the public's health by working to prevent HIV-positive individuals from infecting third parties within the constraints of the law" (p. 5). Specifically, if a physician determines that "an HIV-positive individual poses a significant threat of infecting an identifiable third party, the physician should: (a) notify the public health authorities, if required by law; (b) attempt to persuade the infected patient to cease endangering the third party; and (c) if permitted by state law, notify the endangered third party without revealing the identity of the source person" (p. 5).

We believe it is essential for all helpers (not just physicians) to do all they can to enlist the cooperation of HIV-positive individuals to notify their sex partners of their infection. This includes becoming familiar with your state's law, remaining current about appropriate methods to protect against transmission of HIV, providing clients with information about medical interventions (e.g., ART, PrEP), processing with clients the meaning and implications of

their HIV-positive status (including their possible grief and anger), and engaging in specific skill-building practices, such as communication skills. Promoting *client* self-disclosure to partners is preferable to the helper doing so.

Based on this additional information, we encourage you to revisit the case of Mark mentioned earlier. What decisions would you make in his case given the information you now know?

Confidentiality in Addictions Treatment   Although not often mentioned in mental health practice, federal regulations exist in the United States that govern the confidentiality of client and patient records in alcohol and other drug treatment services. Known as **42 CFR** (42 Code of Federal Regulations, Part 2), these regulations (Code of Federal Regulations, 2002) were introduced in the early 1970s at a time when treatment for drug addiction was separate from alcohol addiction treatment so that someone contacting a drug treatment center would automatically be identified as having engaged in illegal activity. The intent of 42 CFR remains to protect the identity of persons inquiring about and receiving substance use treatment. Without such protections, law enforcement could use client records as a means of arresting clients (Manuel, Newville, Larios, & Sorensen, 2013). Geppert (2013, p. 625) claims that it is precisely because of the stigma attached to persons with addictive disorders that 42 CFR has the most "rigorous privacy protections" of all other types of health information, protections that Hughes and Goldstein (2015) describe as more stringent than the Health Insurance Portability and Accountability Act (HIPAA) of 1996, also known as 45 CFR.

Professional helpers may think that 42 CFR does not apply to them because they serve only those clients with mental health concerns. However, numerous studies indicate that the co-occurrence of mental illness and a substance use disorder is common worldwide (Jané-Llopis & Matytsina, 2006). From one study specific to the United States, 20 percent of those who sought treatment for a mood disorder also had a substance use disorder (Grant et al., 2004a) and approximately 29 to 48 percent of those with a personality disorder also had either an alcohol or a drug use disorder (Grant et al., 2004b). These prevalence data continue to support the view that "co-occurrence is the rule rather than the exception in psychiatric inpatient and substance abuse settings" (Brems & Johnson, 1997, p. 440). Therefore, 42 CFR confidentiality regulations are not restricted to chemical dependency treatment facilities; they potentially apply to all behavioral health care providers serving clients with substance use disorders. In an increasingly integrated U.S. health care service delivery system, 42 CFR may have a wider reach (Manuel et al., 2013).

Protecting the Confidentiality Rights of all Clients In an effort to "reach for the ethical ceiling" by reprioritizing confidentiality, Fisher (2008) outlined a six-step model for protecting the confidentiality rights of clients. Although it was developed for psychologists, we believe this model is appropriate for all professional helpers. First, as a helper you are exhorted to be prepared to have honest conversations with prospective clients about the meaning and implications of confidentiality, as well as the exceptions to confidentiality. This entails doing some of your own homework, such as reviewing the codes of ethics of your profession, understanding the policies and procedures of your treatment setting, and consulting with a supervisor about how to proceed if a prospective adult client refuses to sign a release of information form, for example. Second, it is up to you as a helper to explain to prospective clients up front, and in language they can understand, the nature and limits to confidentiality. Fisher (2008) described this step as *informing the consent* of a prospective client. This practice is particularly important for persons whose primary language is not English and persons who are mandated to counseling, such as by a court or judicial board or employer.

The third step in Fisher's (2008) model for maintaining client confidentiality is to obtain the client's truly informed consent, meaning that the client conveys to you an understanding of confidentiality and its limits and you are able to document the client's consent prior to disclosing client information. The fourth step is to respond ethically to legal demands for client information, such as when a subpoena or a court order is served, to know when to contest such demands and when not to make premature disclosures. Fifth, avoid the avoidable breaches of confidentiality, such as talking to your supervisor about a client in the public waiting area of the treatment facility. The sixth and final step is to talk with colleagues about confidentiality and its corollaries, which may include the need to confront a colleague's unethical practice.

Client Privilege A concept similar to confidentiality is that of **client privilege**. Privilege is the legal right that protects the client from the forced disclosure of personal and sensitive information in legal proceedings. Merideth (2007) cited a colleague's helpful method for differentiating confidentiality and client privilege: confidentiality is the *clinician's obligation* (or CO) not to disclose confidential information about a client, whereas privilege deals with the *patient's right* (or PR) to exclude from a legal proceeding communications made to a treating clinician. Sometimes referred to as testimonial privilege, client privilege defines how confidentiality can and cannot be used in the judicial arena (Younggren & Harris, 2008). As mentioned, in the New Hampshire Supreme Court ruling

in the 2005 *Berg* case (see Wolowitz & Papelian, 2007), this legal right may extend to certain "mature minors." In 1996, the U.S. Supreme Court ruled in the case of *Jaffee v. Redmond* that communications between a master's-level social worker and her client were privileged under federal law. Although the Court explained that important public and private interests are served by protecting confidential communications between "psychotherapists" and their clients, some see its practical impact as limited. For one thing, no state legislature licenses "psychotherapists," and the Jaffee court did not define its use of the term.

The ethical conflicts between duty to protect and duty to maintain confidentiality take many forms (see Werth, Welfel, & Benjamin, 2009). Because states vary regarding their laws about confidentiality, and because laws differ in what medical professionals and counseling or psychotherapy professionals are allowed, it is important to be informed about laws in your state. There are complex ethical, legal, and therapeutic issues surrounding confidentiality. These issues can vary based on treatment setting (e.g., school, hospital, correctional facility) and geographic location (e.g., rural) as well as client demographics (e.g., minors, older persons) and additional client information (e.g., sex offense history). Given this complexity, it is not uncommon to encounter conflicting positions about how to interpret and apply legal criteria and ethical codes.

Confidentiality and Cultural Values Meer and VandeCreek (2002) stated that the concept of confidentiality lends itself well to the Western value of individual rights to privacy and autonomy. Persons from cultural groups with a more collectivistic than individualistic orientation may struggle to fully grasp the meaning of this concept. Parents who recently immigrated to the United States from China, for example, may not understand why they cannot participate in all counseling sessions you will have with their 8-year-old son. Also, clients who have been victimized by persons they regard to be in positions of authority (e.g., women who have been repeatedly abused by their male partners), including members of minority or target groups who have experienced discrimination and trauma from members of the socially dominant group (e.g., a teen questioning his sexuality who has been bullied at school), may not be able to appreciate initially that they do have a voice in therapy and can make decisions for themselves. This includes not divulging to the therapist any information they choose not to, and limiting who the therapist can talk to about their case.

It is worth repeating that the helper must clearly explain to clients the nature of his or her professional obligations so that, for instance, not initiating contact outside of therapy (e.g., during an inadvertent meeting in the grocery store) does not signal the helper's lack of respect for the client. Rather, it actually represents the helper's highest respect for the client because it honors the client's right to acknowledge the counselor in public only if the client chooses to do so. See Chapter 7 for additional information on issues of confidentiality.

Multiple Relationships

Multiple relationships arise when the practitioner is in a professional helping relationship with the client and simultaneously or consecutively has one or more other kinds of relationships with that same person, such as an administrative, instructional, supervisory, social, sexual, or business relationship. Multiple role relationships can be subtle and are significant sources of ethical complaints. Such relationships are problematic because they can reduce the counselor's objectivity, confuse the issue, put the client in a position of diminished consent and potential abandonment, foster discomfort, and expose the client and practitioner to negative judgments or responses by others. Therefore, as much as possible, professional helpers should avoid becoming involved in dual or multiple relationships with clients.

There are occasions, however, when engaging in multiple relationships with clients is unavoidable. This is particularly true in smaller communities where professional helpers are more likely to know clients in other contexts and are less likely to be able to refer clients elsewhere. For example, a male client may be employed as a physical trainer at the local health club where his therapist is a member. The client and helper also may attend the same church, have children who attend the same elementary school, and/or attend the same support group or fellowship, such as Alcoholics Anonymous. These and other examples illustrate only a few of the many ways in which our lives intersect with others. Werth, Hastings, and Riding-Malon (2010) encouraged mental health professionals in rural areas to become actively involved in the community to promote others' trust in them and the work they do to lessen the stigma associated with mental health concerns that is common in low-density, isolated areas. To do otherwise would suggest a helper who does not appreciate and is out of touch with common, ordinary, and localized concerns, an insular, or at least a detached, professional who may not be able to establish meaningful connections with his or her clients. Interactions with clients outside of therapy, regardless of geographic setting, therefore may not only be inescapable but advisable. This makes the management of multiple relationships that much more sensitive and deliberate.

Take, for instance, the client who recently accomplished what for her was the monumental task of earning a 4-year college degree as a single parent. Because she regards you as someone who has provided her with helpful professional assistance over the past 2 years, offering support and encouragement to realize this goal, she invites you to her commencement ceremony and to her graduation party afterwards with family and friends. Declining her invitation on the grounds that such out-of-session contact would violate professional boundaries may actually strain the ongoing helping relationship you have with her. Any "nonprofessional interaction" with a client or former client must be initiated by the client, and the helper must document the rationale, potential benefit, and anticipated consequences of this interaction.

This nonprofessional interaction is what Bridges (2005) characterized as a "boundary crossing," an example of "enactments between the therapist and patient that may or may not be harmful to the therapeutic process" (p. 26). These types of interactions are differentiated from "boundary violations," defined as "egregious and potentially harmful transgression[s] of the therapeutic contract and treatment frame that involve a breach of the fiduciary contract and abuse of the therapist's power" (p. 29). Engaging in a romantic or sexual relationship with a current or former client would be an example of a boundary violation that would not uphold the ethical value of nonmaleficence (i.e., do no harm), and would result in the helper's being subject to ethical and legal sanctions (e.g., revocation of the helper's state license).

Obviously, sexual contact between practitioner and client is never warranted under any circumstance and is explicitly proscribed by all the professional codes of ethics and by state laws. In some states, initiating a romantic and sexual relationship with a client after therapy has concluded also is illegal. However, at least three professional associations allow for such relationships, but only after a required length of time elapses after termination and the therapist is able to document that the purpose of terminating services was not to initiate a post-therapy relationship. The APA's (2010) Ethics Code stipulates a 2-year interval after termination, whereas the *ACA Code of Ethics* (2014) and the CRCC's (2009) *Code of Professional Ethics for Rehabilitation Counselors* prohibit counselors and rehabilitation counselors, respectively, from engaging in a sexual or romantic relationship with a former client whose care was terminated or otherwise discontinued less than 5 years before the intimate relationship began. We strongly advise, however, that professional helpers *not* engage in such relationships with a former client at any time "because of the potential harm to the client," as the NASW (2008) *Code of Ethics* stipulates (see Ethical Standard 1.09(c)).

Telepractice

The ubiquitous use of many forms of communication technology in daily life explains the burgeoning use of diverse forms of technology in health care, specifically technology intended to enhance or make possible communication between clients and helpers, as well as among professionals. The increased sophistication of technology platforms in the past 20 years is reflected in the names assigned to this particular practice. Earlier references were to cybercounseling or cybertherapy, Internet-based or online counseling or online psychotherapy, e-therapy, or simply distance therapy. More recent references use the prefix tele-, as in telehealth, telecounseling, and telemental health. This signifies a broader scope of technological devices that can be used (e.g., smart phones), as well as practice formats (e.g., video teleconferencing).

The term **telepractice** captures this diversity and thus refers to any contact with a client (or patient) other than face-to-face or in the same room (Matthews, 2014). This includes synchronous (i.e., in real-time) and asynchronous (e.g., email, text) forms of communication. It is important to note, however, that as of this writing Medicare and Medicaid will only reimburse telehealth services that use real-time audio *and* video interactive telecommunications systems between the client and helper (see Centers for Medicaid & Medicare, www.cms.gov). Telephones, fax machines, and email therefore do not qualify as telehealth communication systems reimbursable by Medicaid or Medicare.

There are five important developments that explain the rapid and expansive application of telepractice, specifically telemental health (TMH), in the United States today (Turvey & Myers, 2013):

1. A growing shortage of mental health providers, specifically in socioeconomically disadvantaged geographic areas.

2. Advances in the quality and availability of desktop and Internet videoconferencing applications.

3. Reimbursement for TMH services from Medicaid, Medicare, and private insurance companies.

4. Research attesting to the benefits of treating mental health disorders through TMH, comparable to in-person or same-room care.

5. Health care reform in the United States, specifically the Patient Protection and Affordability Care Act signed into law in March 2010 by President Obama that, among other provisions, allows for certain telehealth services.

Onken and Shoham (2015) discuss several potential benefits of participating in TMH and other forms of technology-based interventions for clients and helpers. For clients, these include the increasing reach and availability of behavioral health care, affordability of treatment, and sense of anonymity that helps to alleviate stigma attached to having a mental health condition. For helpers, one benefit of conducting TMH is increasing the potency of treatment, particularly when technology-based interventions are used in conjunction with standard care, such as the computer-assisted delivery of cognitive-behavior therapy (CBT) for substance use disorders known as "CBT4CBT" (Carroll et al., 2008). Other potential benefits to helpers are the increasing reach and availability of online and other forms of technology-based training, affordability of training, and time available to invest in specific aspects of care (e.g., strengthening the therapeutic relationship) when skills-training, for example, is delivered via an interactive online program.

It is understandable that with telepractice comes a new set of ethical considerations. Taylor, McMinn, Bufford, and Chang (2010) predicted that ethics committees would be unlikely to establish formal guidelines on the use of specific technologies in the near future because of the accelerating rate of technological change. Indeed, being able to practice TMH has "outpaced" the enactment of regulatory reforms needed to address the modification of standards of practice to telepractice (Kramer, Mishkind, Luxton, & Shore, 2013).

In the past 5 years, however, professional associations have published guidelines and codes of ethics specific to telepractice. For example, the APA (2013) adopted *Guidelines for the Practice of Telepsychology*, and the most recent revision of the *ACA Code of Ethics* (2014) includes a new section (Section H) on *Distance Counseling, Technology, and Social Media*. In addition, the American Telemedicine Association (2013) developed *Guidelines for Video-based Online Mental Health Services* that encompass clinical, technical, and administrative guidelines. The TeleMental Health Institute (http://telehealth.org) maintains links to the guidelines and codes of conduct of other professional associations with respect to telepractice.

Three Ethical Considerations in Telepractice There are at least three ethical considerations addressed in professional association guidelines and codes of ethics with respect to telepractice: (1) helper competence using technology; (2) informed consent; and (3) protection of client confidentiality. Each of these is discussed briefly in this section.

It does not seem accidental that what is mentioned first in at least two professional association documents targeting telepractice is *helper competence*. Guideline 1 of the APA's (2013) eight *Guidelines for the Practice of Telepsychology* states that "psychologists who provide telepsychology services strive to take reasonable steps to ensure their competence with both the technologies used and the potential impact of the technologies on clients/patients, supervisees or other professionals" (p. 7). Similarly, Section H.1.A. of the *ACA Code of Ethics* (2014) stipulates that counselors who provide these services will develop knowledge and skills (i.e., competence) related to technology and ethical and legal considerations.

Helpers are advised to be trained in certain technologies, such as **video teleconferencing** (VTC), and then to initiate, explain, and coordinate their use; they must continuously evaluate the effectiveness of each method of telepractice. This includes attending to cultural factors and maintaining therapeutic boundaries. A TMH provider in Washington, DC, for example, who delivers primarily individual therapy to female U.S. military veterans on the east coast will need to adapt her method when asked to provide group-based TMH services to American Indian veterans in Alaska using VTC. In addition, it is recommended that helpers conduct VTC from a consistent environment, be mindful of what appears in the camera's view (from the client's as well as the helper's view), and always maintain professionalism (Drum & Littleton, 2014). With each new form of technology comes a unique set of communication challenges that may impact the development of the therapeutic relationship (Fitzgerald, Hunter, Hadjistavropoulos, & Koocher, 2010). Just because the technology is available (e.g., smart phones, tablet computers) doesn't mean it is appropriate for use in telepractice.

The second ethical consideration in telepractice is *informed consent.* This includes informing clients of the helper's physical location, any time zone differences, and the helper's credentials, including the state(s) in which he or she is licensed. Helpers are advised to contact their state licensing board and the licensing board of the state where the client is physically located prior to conducting TMH (American Telemedicine Association, 2013). Because licensure for a wide range of U.S. health care providers remains under the purview of the states and not the federal government, it is likely that TMH providers will need to obtain licensure in the state where the client is physically located (Kramer et al., 2013).

Additional aspects of informed consent in TMH include the helper clarifying methods for session cancellation and reviewing with the client procedures to follow in the event of a crisis (e.g., client suicidal thinking). This latter practice will require the helper to become familiar with resources in the client's location. Furthermore, the client will have to verify his or her age and establish means of payment for services. Adolescents have been found to easily engage in and also to benefit from various forms of TMH (Carlisle, 2013), but their participation in such services may remain contingent on a parent or guardian consent, as is true for same-room care.

The third ethical consideration in telepractice is *protection of client confidentiality.* This includes securing the transmission and storage of electronic records, and implementing encryption standards. Helpers who provide TMH must abide by a number of federal laws, including HIPAA (briefly described in this chapter), possibly 42 CFR (discussed previously), and also those of the Federal Communications Commission, which has established the mobile health (or mhealth) task force to offer recommendations for improving health care delivery using wireless health technologies (see Hughes & Goldstein, 2015). Laws governing the use and safety of consumer products (regulated by the Federal Trade Commission), such as mobile health apps and Web-based services, also will need to be consulted.

We invite you to place yourself in the shoes of a client who recently scheduled and then participated in an initial telemental health visit using video teleconferencing (VTC). This is Learning Activity 2.4 on pages 65-66. Please review the three ethical considerations in telepractice before you do this activity, as well as link to one of the professional association guidelines or code of ethics related to telepractice that are mentioned in this section. Feedback to Learning Activity 2.4 is provided on page 68.

Out-of-Session Client Communication

Zur (2009) noted that "the Internet has blurred the line between what is personal and what is professional, as well as between self-disclosure and transparency" (p. 24). This is particularly true of social networking, such as the use of *Facebook, Twitter, YouTube, LinkedIn,* and *Instagram.* Because the majority of young professional helpers and graduate students in a helping profession maintain a social networking site (Harris & Kurpius, 2014), it is highly likely that you will encounter clients or client information while online.

It is important to remember that, to your clients, you remain a professional helper whether in person/in the same room or online. Protecting your privacy and respecting their privacy remains essential, regardless of setting. Based on the *ACA Code of Ethics* (2014), this means that helpers clearly distinguish between their professional and personal virtual presence (Section H.6.a.), and that helpers do not view client information on social media without client consent (Section H.6.c.). Any contact with clients or encountering client information online must be documented. The APA (2010) *Ethical Principles* stipulate that "Psychologists have a primary obligation and take reasonable precautions to protect confidential information obtained through or stored in any medium" (p. 7). Conducting online searches of clients—especially out of personal curiosity—is likely an unethical action because it violates the fundamental right of clients to privacy (Harris & Kurpius, 2014).

Learning Activity 2.4

A Telemental Health Visit*

For this activity, place yourself as the client in the following scenario. Once you have read through the scenario, respond to the two questions posed at the end. Feedback to Learning Activity 2.4 is provided on page 68.

Imagine that you have begun to experience anxiety in almost all aspects of your life, especially at work. Dave, a coworker and friend, suggested going to Twin Rivers, the local community mental health center near your home town of Rupert. Dave shared that he went there approximately 1 year ago and the therapist he met with was very helpful. With some reluctance, you call Twin Rivers and schedule an appointment.

On the day and time of your appointment, you meet for approximately an hour with Jackie, an intake professional. Once the intake session is completed, you are somewhat surprised when Jackie explains that you will be served best by meeting with Dr. Brown, a licensed clinical counselor who specializes in anxiety disorders and is located in another state. She reassures you that you will not be traveling to where he is; Dr. Brown will come to you. She explains that given the rural nature of Rupert and its low population, Twin Rivers applied for and received funding to become a video teleconferencing (VTC) clinic earlier this year. This means that Twin Rivers now has state-of-the art technology to offer a greater variety and more specialized care at its facility delivered by behavioral health care specialists from around the country, like Dr. Brown, using VTC. Jackie explains that she is the VTC coordinator for Twin Rivers. She adds that although this treatment modality is different from traditional face-to-face or same-room counseling, current research indicates that telemental health counseling, including that delivered via VTC, can be equally effective.

After reviewing the informed consent material, you decide that VTC counseling is acceptable because it will make it possible for you to be seen by a specialist. You tell Jackie to go ahead and schedule the initial appointment with Dr. Brown. She proceeds to ask Marissa, the office manager in charge of scheduling, to make the appointment. After comparing your work schedule to Dr. Brown's availability, you schedule your appointment for 9:00 a.m. next Tuesday. As you leave, Marissa reminds you to arrive 15 minutes early to complete the additional paperwork required for telemental health counseling.

Fast-forward to Tuesday.

Eager to finally work with a specialist to get some relief from your anxiety, you arrive at Twin Rivers half an hour early. Your eagerness quickly turns to frustration when you learn that Marissa forgot to account for time zone differences. Dr. Brown is located in another time zone and is 1 hour behind your time zone, so he will not be available until 10:00 a.m. here in Rupert. Marissa apologizes profusely, explaining that Dr. Brown is a new provider for Twin Rivers, and offers to reschedule for another day, promising

that the mistake will not be made a second time. After taking a moment to consider rescheduling, you decide that because you are already here and took the morning off from work, you might as well wait for the appointment.

While waiting, you decide to re-read the informed consent material and VTC protocol sheets you were given by Jackie during your intake. This time you notice the protocols to follow if there is a technology failure during the session. Also included is a disclaimer about the risks and benefits of participating in VTC counseling. The disclaimer states that sessions will not be videorecorded or archived in any way without your consent. Also mentioned is that although Twin Rivers uses current legal standard encryption software, there is still a risk of unauthorized access to the session from an outside source. Despite some of the questions you still have about this VTC format, they don't prevent you from changing your mind. You're ready to get started.

After a long wait in the lobby, Marissa calls your name and guides you over to the counseling room, although to you it looks more like a room where you would file your taxes than receive counseling. There is only one chair and it is positioned in front of a computer monitor with an audio/video camera attached to it. As you sit in the chair, Marissa makes adjustments to the camera to ensure it is centered at your eye level. She explains how to move the device yourself in case Dr. Brown requests it be adjusted once the session begins. In the corner of the room is a printer/fax machine, which, as Marissa explains, can be used to deliver various materials that Dr. Brown deems appropriate once the session begins, such as assessments or therapy-related exercises. On the desk is a landline telephone that can be used in case there is a technical problem with the camera, or if the Internet connection is lost.

Before leaving the room, Marissa explains that the room is sound-proof and if you need her help with anything once the session starts, she or Jackie can be reached by dialing *1 on the telephone. As the door shuts, the blank computer screen is replaced by the image of an office. A moment later a smiling man appears on the screen who introduces himself as Dr. Brown. During his introduction, you notice someone moving around behind Dr. Brown, in what appears to be the corner of Dr. Brown's office. As if reacting to the concerned look on your face, Dr. Brown explains that his baby sitter is ill and therefore he had to work from home today. He adds that his children are too young to understand the conversation, so there is no need for you to worry. He also informs you that because he is working from home he does not have a copy of his credentials to show you, but refers you to the informed consent materials you signed earlier at Twin Rivers.

The session proceeds without any technical difficulties and it feels good to finally be able to talk with a specialist about your anxiety.

(continued)

Learning Activity 2.4 (*continued*)

When the session ends, though, you leave the counseling room still unnerved by the schedule time mistake, and also that Dr. Brown was working from home. As you approach the reception desk, Marissa asks if you would like to go ahead and schedule your next session. You respond by asking if it would be possible for you to remain at home for the next session. "If Dr. Brown can work from home," you explain, "why should I have to drive all the way here for each session?" You inform Marissa that you have Skype, you use it regularly to talk with family, and you think you could use it for any further counseling sessions with Dr. Brown. You add somewhat sarcastically, "If this video counseling is supposed to be convenient, it seems it's only convenient for the counselor."

Marissa apologizes again for the scheduling mistake, and politely informs you that to be accredited, their VTC software must meet encryption guidelines. She adds that not only does Skype not meet those encryption standards, the Internet connection at Twin Rivers must also meet encryption standards that most personal connections do not meet. With a reluctant grimace, you proceed to schedule the next appointment, but only after confirming that the scheduled time is correct for both you and Dr. Brown this time.

Questions to Consider

A. What ethical concerns are present in this vignette?
B. How could the ethical concerns present have been avoided?

*With thanks to Robert Bradley for his development of a draft of this Learning Activity.

Documentation, Electronic Records, and Federal Laws

Documenting or recording the provision of professional services and also carefully managing those documents and records are ethical issues that speak to helper competence. According to Mitchell (2007), helpers must keep timely and accurate records for three primary reasons: fiscal, clinical, and legal accountability. Entering and maintaining **electronic health records** or **electronic medical records** specifically has now become the standard tool for billing, keeping track of client progress, and easing the process of client transition from and to other providers.

Increasingly, for both government-funded agencies and private health maintenance organizations, Mitchell (2007) pointed out that if you don't have records to verify services rendered, both government-funded sources and insurance companies may not pay, or if they do, they may want their money returned until verification of services can be provided. Maintaining records for legal and ethical reasons therefore can help to resolve disputes regarding the nature of care provided, fee arrangements, or the effects of treatment (Drogin, Connell, Foote, & Sturme, 2010). The American Psychological Association's (2007) record-keeping guidelines can serve as a useful decision-making tool for all professionals concerning issues of documentation and record keeping.

Health Insurance Portability and Accountability Act (HIPAA)

Record-keeping gained prominence with the 1996 enactment of the Health Insurance Portability and Accountability Act (**HIPAA**) in the United States. It is the primary federal law protecting the privacy and security of health information (Hughes & Goldstein, 2015). Specific information about HIPAA is available at the website www.hhs.gov/ocr/hipaa, and most professional organizations also have HIPAA-related information on their websites. The U.S. Congress intended HIPAA to ensure the portability of health insurance between jobs for American workers (Robles, 2009). In a nutshell, HIPAA means that helpers must protect the confidentiality of health information they collect, maintain, use, or transmit about clients.

There are two basic components to HIPAA: the Privacy Rule and the Security Rule. The Privacy Rule relates to all protected information in any form—oral, written, and electronic. Under the Privacy Rule, clients are entitled to a written notice about the privacy practices of the helping setting, to review their record, to request a change of information in that record, and to be informed about to whom information has been disclosed. The Privacy Rule is designed to manage *intentional* releases of protected health information (referred to as PHI) by safeguarding and controlling when, under what circumstances, and to whom PHI is released.

The Security Rule, by contrast, is designed to manage electronic protected health information (referred to as EPHI) from *unintended* or unauthorized disclosure either through security breaches such as computer hackers or through unintended losses such as a natural disaster or a stolen laptop. The Security Rule means that service settings must develop policies and procedures to ensure that appropriate privacy procedures are followed and that potential risks to security are identified. Safeguards are to be implemented particularly in electronic client records and information transmitted or accessed on websites and by email, mobile or hand-held devices, pagers, and fax machines.

In March 2013, the U.S. Department of Health and Human Services (DHHS) issued further HIPAA mandates intended to strengthen the confidentiality, integrity, and security of patients' PHI in electronic health/medical records, including behavioral health information. Businesses that now must comply with HIPPA privacy and security rules include information technology firms such as cloud server providers and Amazon Web Services. Wang and Huang (2013) contend that these new rulings demonstrate that "a delicate balance between protecting patient privacy and unleashing the power of [technology] innovation" remains elusive. Because HIPAA is constantly evolving, we encourage you to consult the HIPAA website for updates.

Patient Protection and Affordable Care Act (PPACA) The Patient Protection and Affordable Care Act (**PPACA**) was passed by the U.S. Congress in March 2010 during President Obama's first term in office, and parts of it were upheld by the U.S. Supreme Court in October 2011. The PPACA has transformed health care in the United States. This includes the provision of mental health care and substance use services, collectively known as behavioral health care.

The fundamental goal of the PPACA is to ensure that all Americans have health care insurance (Nilsen & Pavel, 2015). This will involve curtailing the spiraling costs of health care and improving the overall quality of health care. To accomplish this, the PPACA has two priorities: preventive care and integrated care. Prevention practices include screening for the early detection of health conditions and the use of health information technology, such as self-monitoring of symptoms or behavioral targets (e.g., physical exercise) using Smartphone technology. Integrated care means that all health care professionals work collaboratively so that care is coordinated and comprehensive. This includes accessing shared electronic records.

Features and Content of Documentation It should go without saying that all forms of documentation must be completed in a timely and accurate manner, conform to confidentiality requirements and guidelines, and be clear and understandable. Swartz (2006) reminds us that documentation is "institutional memory for cases passed from one practitioner to another, and indeed as memory for practitioners needing to check detail with each returning client" (p. 429). Carefully worded reports are therefore essential to ensure ongoing and collaborative care. Furthermore, all signatures obtained must be authentic—that is, they cannot be forged. Although these are basic practices and should not require a reminder, it is not uncommon for helpers in the throes of hectic schedules, emergency situations, stress, and exhaustion to overlook adherence to some of these practices from time to time.

Mitchell (2007) likened record-keeping to a "logical, short story" (p. 13) that begins with an assessment, and then moves to a plan, notes, case reviews, and termination. Identifying data about the client are recorded initially, as well as appointment times, cancellations, and so on. The intake or the initial history-taking session is recorded next. When writing up an intake or a history, avoid labels, jargon, and inferences. If records were court-ordered, such statements could appear inflammatory or slanderous. Don't

make evaluative statements or professional judgments without supporting documentation. For example, instead of writing, "This client is homicidal," you might write, "This client reports engaging in frequent (at least twice daily) fantasies of killing an unidentified or anonymous victim." Instead of "The client is disoriented," consider writing, "The client could not remember where he was, why he was here, what day it was, and how old he was." The information collected in all of the assessment interviews is reflected in the intake report. Following the intake report, a written treatment plan is prepared. Although the specific format of this written plan can vary, it always includes the elements of treatment goals and objectives, interventions designed to achieve such objectives, and diagnostic codes. The process of constructing treatment goals is discussed in Chapter 9.

It is important to keep notes of subsequent treatment sessions and of client progress. These likely will be entered according to a standardized form or template of an electronic health records program. Generally, treatment notes are brief and highlight only the major activities of each session and client progress and improvement (or lack of it). These notes usually begin during intakes, and information from the assessment interviews is added. As the number of sessions increases, notations about goals, intervention strategies, and client progress are included. Again, labels and inferences always should be avoided in written notes and records. Remember that as long as you are being supervised, your supervisor needs to sign off on all progress notes and on treatment plans, too. If there are multiple clients, such as a parent and child, or two parents or partners, keep in mind that separate reports, treatment plans, and progress notes must be written for each person. If one party discusses a related party in the session, do not identify the discussed person by name in the progress note. For example, instead of writing "Kyle said he wants to break things off with Melissa," write "Client disclosed desire to end relationship with girlfriend." Notice the more formal and objective language used in this alternative statement.

The following list, adapted from the Quin Curtis Center for Psychological Service, Training, and Research of the West Virginia University's Department of Psychology, suggests a model for a **progress note** that we especially like:

- Session number, start and stop times, diagnostic and procedure codes
- Relevant assessment, current status, dangerousness, current stressors
- Progress toward treatment goals
- Interventions
- Plan
- Assignment
- Signature by clinician and supervisor
- Supervisor note/consultation

Notice that several key components of this kind of progress note are essential for quality control reviews and insurance company reviews. These include the session number, start and stop times, diagnostic and procedures codes, current assessment, and progress or lack of progress toward the achievement of the identified treatment goals. As Mitchell (2007) stated, the most helpful progress notes are ones that connect interventions to the treatment plan.

Under HIPAA, progress notes are defined as PHI (**protected health information**). PHI becomes part of the client's record or official clinical record. PHI includes

- Medication prescription and monitoring
- Counseling session start and stop times
- Modalities and frequencies of treatment provided
- Results of clinical tests
- Summaries of diagnosis, functional status, treatment plan, symptoms, prognosis, and progress to date

HIPAA also permits practitioners to keep a second set of notes (recorded in any medium) that are separate from the PHI or the clinical record. These are referred to as **psychotherapy notes** and are defined as **process notes** (*not* progress notes; see Robles, 2009) because they include the helper's impressions about clients and the therapeutic process (see DeLettre & Sobell, 2010) and *exclude* information contained in the PHI or the clinical record (as listed). DeLettre and Sobell (2010) found that 46 percent of the 464 psychologists they surveyed reported using psychotherapy notes, but another 21 percent reported not knowing about the option of keeping psychotherapy notes. HIPAA requires that clients have access to their PHI, but not to their helper's psychotherapy notes. There are provisions, however, for client access to psychotherapy notes, and these vary from state to state in the United States. Because psychotherapy notes may be ordered into a court of law, Mitchell (2007) and others have discouraged practitioners from keeping a separate set of psychotherapy notes. Whether or not to maintain psychotherapy or process notes is a topic of discussion for you and your supervisor or clinical director.

Feedback to Learning Activity 2.4

A Telemental Health Visit*

A. There are at least four ethical concerns evident in the telemental health visit scenario:
   1. You were given an incorrect time for your first visit with Dr. Brown, one that did not account for time zone differences.
   2. Because Dr. Brown was working from home, the security of his Internet connection is unclear. As Marissa explained, most home connections fail to meet proper encryption protocols.
   3. Dr. Brown did not inform you right at the start of the session that there was someone else in his office.
   4. Even though Dr. Brown's credentials were listed on the informed consent materials you received prior to your session, he did not show them to you during your session.

B. With reference to relevant practice guidelines and codes of ethics, these four ethical concerns could have been avoided by:
   1. According to the *ACA Code of Ethics* (2014), Section H.2.A., it is the responsibility of the provider to account for time zone variations. Although the time zone scheduling mistake was that of Twin Rivers office staff and likely due to Dr. Brown being a new provider for the agency, it is incumbent upon providers of telemental health services to ensure that time zone discrepancies are resolved. From this scenario, clients also may need to clarify times.
   2. Dr. Brown conducting the session from his regular counseling office where Internet connection security is established. This is addressed in Guideline 5 of APA's (2013), *Guidelines for the Practice of TelePsychology*.
   3. Dr. Brown should have announced at the very beginning of the session that there was someone else in his office, regardless of age. This type of information should be announced immediately and the client should not have to ask. See Guideline D of the American Telemedicine Association's (2013), *Practice Guidelines for Video-based Online Mental Health Services*.
   4. Most opening protocols for telehealth services recommend that professionals identify themselves, display their credentials, and state their geographic locations. When providing services across state lines, telemental health providers must verify that they are licensed in the state where they are located as well as the state where the client is receiving services. Section H.3. of the *ACA Code of Ethics* (2014) states that counselors who provide distance counseling are to take steps to verify client identify. This can include requesting some form of photo identification. Also see Guideline A of the American Telemedicine Association's (2013), *Practice Guidelines for Video-based Online Mental Health Services*.

*With thanks to Robert Bradley for developing a draft of this feedback.

BOX 2.4	Required Contents of a Standard Release-of-Information Form

- Name of program making the disclosure
- Name of individual or organization receiving the disclosure
- Name of client
- Purpose or need for the disclosure
- How much and what kind of information will be disclosed
- A statement that the client may revoke the disclosure at any time

- The date, event, or condition on which the disclosure expires
- Signature of client and/or authorized person
- Date the consent was signed
- Statement prohibiting redisclosure of information to any other party

Source: Fisher & Harrison, 2013.

It is important to document in detail anything that has ethical or legal implications, particularly facts about case management. For example, with a client who reports depression and suicidal thinking, it would be important to note that you conducted a suicide assessment and what its results were, that you consulted with your supervisor or another professional, and the outcome of consultations conducted, including whether or not you did anything else to manage the case differently, such as seeing the client more frequently or constructing a safety contract with the client.

The release of information pertaining to client involvement in therapy is possible only when the client has provided written consent. Obtaining client consent at times can be a challenge in itself, particularly when the client questions the need for a release of information and may be skeptical of your motives. Completing a detailed release-of-information form is therefore essential, and how it is explained to the client may determine whether the client will grant consent and invest in the process of helping. To be certain that necessary pieces of information have been addressed, Fisher and Harrison (2013) itemized the 10 "ingredients" of a standard release-of-information form, based on 42 CFR. These are presented in Box 2.4.

When the client terminates therapy, there also is a written record about termination. The termination or discharge report becomes the final piece in the written "short story" about the client. Such closing reports are very important in the event the client returns for additional services and in the event of any future litigation. A typical termination report includes the reason for termination, a summary of progress toward the treatment goals, a final diagnostic impression, and a follow-up plan (Mitchell, 2007, p. 75).

Practitioners also need to be concerned about *retention* of client records. All professional organizations, all states in the United States, and many other countries have regulations about the length of time that practitioners must retain client records. HIPAA requires that records be kept for a minimum of 6 years, many of the states in the United States specify 7 years or longer, and professional organizations often have longer lengths of record retention than these. Retention of records applies to electronically or digitally stored information as well as paper records.

The records we keep about clients are reviewed by a number of entities, including internal review boards, accrediting bodies, and insurance companies. Regardless of whether you keep electronic or written records, or both, bear in mind Mitchell's (2007) seven assumptions of record-keeping (p. 46):

1. The counseling record may be subpoenaed, and the court will need to be able to understand what occurred.

2. The client may present for treatment at a time when you are sick or on vacation and one of your colleagues will need to read your record.

3. The client may read your record.

4. The accuracy of your record is compromised if you wait more than a day to complete it.

5. The record should be the best possible reflection of your professional judgment.

6. Nothing you do with a client is considered a professional service until you enter it in the record.

7. Your record may be selected for an audit to verify a legally reimbursable service.

Referral

Referring a client to another practitioner may be necessary when, for one reason or another, you are not able to provide the service or care that the client requires or when the client requests another helper. If client symptoms persist and worsen, another level of care, such as hospitalization, may be indicated. Similarly, if a client's needs become increasingly complex and surpass your level of competence, then it will be necessary to refer the client to a practitioner whose expertise is likely to address the client's needs. Referrals are mandated when your services are interrupted by certain events in your life: illness, death, relocation, financial limitations, or any other form of unavailability on your part (ACA, 2014).

As discussed in this chapter, a **referral** is an act of last resort (Kaplan, 2014) and should not be made simply based on a conflict in personal values between helper and client (or a helper's *perceived* conflict in values). This is particularly important given that many clients may not follow through with a referral. For example, of the 25 percent of clients seen for at least two sessions in a university counseling center over 1 year and who were referred to another provider off campus, almost 42 percent were not successful in connecting with the referral, the majority of whom (57%) were clients of color (Owen, Devdas, & Rodolfa, 2007). With respect to the client's sexual orientation, Johnson and Buhrke (2006) indicated that the practitioner's "homonegative or heterosexist values and attitudes should never serve as an excuse for failing to render competent clinical services to [LGBTQ clients]" (p. 96). This form of discrimination could be especially debilitating to the client because its source is a professional helper viewed by the client as someone committed to caring for persons in distress.

Johnson and Buhrke (2006) recommended that all referrals be made "cautiously and collaboratively" (p. 96) to minimize the risk of perceived rejection or abandonment by the client. This underscores for us that referral is a process, and one that necessarily involves a supervisor or colleague. Indeed, the decision to refer is not that of the helper who is in training or who continues to receive clinical supervision (e.g., graduate working toward licensure). Walker and Prince (2010) developed a case study to assist counselor educators and supervisors in their supervision of counseling students who have been assigned a client who identifies as LGBTQ. They described a faculty supervisor who reassigned a gay client to another counseling student who was further along in her LGBTQ competency level so that the counseling student to whom the client was originally assigned and who claimed discomfort working with LGBTQ clients because of deeply held religious beliefs could improve her LGBTQ competency. The supervisor assigned reading to the first student and, despite this student's religious convictions, also required her to demonstrate her efforts in improving her LGBTQ competency before assigning her other LGBTQ clients.

Careful referral involves more than just giving the client the name of another person or agency. Ethical Standard 2.06 of the NASW (2008) *Code of Ethics* states that helpers who refer a client to another professional "should take appropriate steps to facilitate an orderly transfer of responsibility." "Appropriate steps" include explaining to the client the need for the referral, anticipated benefits to the client of such a referral, and providing the client with a choice of service providers who are competent and qualified to deal with the client's concerns and circumstances. In your recommendations and reasoning, you should respect your client's interest and self-determination. If a client declines your suggested referrals and you determine that you are no longer able to be of professional assistance to that client, the *ACA Code of Ethics* (2014) states that counselors are to discontinue the relationship (see Standard A.11.b.).

Additional steps to take in the referral process include obtaining written client permission before discussing the case with the new service provider. Meeting jointly or participating in a conference call with the client and the professional to whom you have referred the client is recommended, especially if a client is having difficulty understanding the need for the referral or is reluctant to follow through. Throughout the transfer process, the helper should be prepared to assume the role of advocate for the client and engage in the practice of *resource brokering* (Crimando, 2009). This means that because the client's welfare is the first priority, the helper may need to link the client to specific resources in the community (e.g., transportation, child care) to facilitate the client's access to the new professional's services. To protect against abandonment, the practitioner should follow-up with the client to determine if impediments were encountered and if assistance is needed for the client to meet with and establish a connection with the referral source.

Ethical Decision-Making Models

Professional codes of ethics provide one set of guidance about ethical expectations, roles, and responsibilities. When grappling with specific ethical dilemmas, however, they should not serve as "one-stop shopping" or the sole reference point. Said in another way, practitioners should not regard ethical codes as the only clearing house or the final answer to very specific and difficult ethical situations. The NASW (2008) stipulates that its *Code of Ethics* "does not provide a set of rules that prescribe how social workers should act in all situations" (p. 6). Furthermore, the *ACA Code of Ethics* (2014) directs counselors "to engage in a carefully considered ethical decision-making process" and "to use a credible model of decision making that can bear public scrutiny of its application" (p. 3). Several such models exist, including Welfel's (2016) 10-step model for ethical decision-making, and Garcia, Cartwright, Winston, and Borzuchowska's (2003) transcultural integrative model for ethical decision making. Garcia et al.'s (2003) model incorporates specific cultural strategies such as reviewing potential discriminatory laws or institutional regulations in processing an ethical dilemma, consulting with cultural experts if necessary, and ensuring that potential courses of action reflect the diverse perspectives of all parties involved.

Although there is not a "right" model for every practitioner and many ethical decision-making models share common steps, we have elected to highlight the Tarvydas integrative decision-making model of ethical behavior (Tarvydas, 2012). An earlier version of the Tarvydas model was used as the basis for Garcia et al.'s transcultural integrative model, and the current version of the Tarvydas model extends its application beyond the (micro) clinical counseling level to the levels of clinical multidisciplinary team, agency or institution, and society or public interest (the macro level). In this way, the **Tarvydas Integrative Model** can be applied to a range of ethical dilemmas and contexts. We feature it here because of its integrative foundation, wide applicability, emphasis on practitioner reflection and collaboration, and consistency with a multicultural approach.

The Tarvydas integrative decision-making model of ethical behavior (Tarvydas, 2012) is based on the work of several ethicists in the mental health and counseling communities. Summarized in Table 2.1, this model encourages practitioners to adopt four attitudes and corresponding behaviors: (1) reflection; (2) pursuing balance among issues, people, and perspectives; (3) attending to context; and (4) participating in collaboration. The model then offers four primary steps or stages, each with specific components, to help the practitioner carefully walk through the decision-making process with the best interests of the client in mind. Notice in particular the reflection that is called for once again in stage III, specifically with respect to the helper's personal values (e.g., social harmony, expediency) that might compete with the moral values or qualities of being a professional helper (e.g., autonomy, integrity). Engaging in deliberate reflection at this particular stage serves to guard against the helper acting on his or her blind spots or prejudicial views, such as cultural encapsulation or a privileged frame of reference. For example, the heterosexual helper may need to pause to consider whose values are being honored and whose interests are being served by discouraging a 16-year-old from coming out as gay to her conservative Christian parents—the client's? the parents'? the helper's? The course of action taken after this further reflection may uphold the ethical course of action selected at the end of stage III, or it may be a modified course of action, consistent with a culturally affirmative approach. At each stage, however, we recommend peer consultation, and for those helpers whose practice is supervised (e.g., counselor trainees), following supervisor directives is imperative.

Upon reviewing the Tarvydas integrative decision-making model of ethical behavior (Tarvydas, 2012), you may decide to return to the case of Mark (adapted from Alghazo et al., 2011, pp. 43–44) described previously in the chapter (see page 59). How might this model be used to further clarify the actions to be taken in his case? What additional considerations has this ethical decision-making model raised?

As has been emphasized throughout this chapter, a commitment to ethical practice is critical, complex, and difficult. It involves high levels of abstraction about values, principles, and duties. A proven how-to manual for resolving ethical dilemmas does not exist and often the process involves nonrational influences, such as intuition and cognitive errors or biases (e.g., maintaining initial impressions despite more recent information to the contrary; Rogerson, Gottlieb, Handelsman, Knapp, & Younggren, 2011). Because ethical decision-making and practice involves these and other nonrational influences, it is imperative that helpers consult colleagues and supervisors on a routine basis and also enlist the services of an ethics committee chairperson and/or legal counsel when questions remain on a specific dilemma. We hope that the Tarvydas integrative decision-making model of ethical behavior (Tarvydas, 2012) can serve as a helpful tool as you practice your critical decision-making skills and continue to develop and hone ethical competence.

Remaining attentive and responsive to these multiple considerations is not an easy task. Balancing our many roles and responsibilities is a perpetual challenge. Managing complexities and navigating our way through changes in our professional lives may not be too unlike the challenges faced by our clients in their personal lives. We can therefore gain further appreciation for what our clients experience and empathize with their circumstances. In addition, as persons who have selected a profession committed to human growth and development—that is, to change!—it is rather unlikely that we would be content with perpetual stability, predictability, and routine in the work that we do. Actually, being fascinated with change, attuned to its intricacies and the array of possibilities for evolution and transformation, is probably what attracted us to a helping profession in the first place. Living a life without encountering and responding to challenges to the status quo, therefore, would be mundane and boring for us.

CHAPTER SUMMARY

Part of being an effective helper is knowing your-   **LO2** **LO2**
self well so that you can engage as a creative, critical thinker who can work with clients toward meeting their goals. This self-awareness includes insight into your values, strengths, and challenges but also extends to a fuller awareness of how you as an individual helper and change

TABLE 2.1   The Tarvydas Integrative Decision-Making Model of Ethical Behavior

Themes or Attitudes

Maintain an attitude of *reflection*.

Address *balance* between issues and parties to the ethical dilemma.

Pay close attention to the *context(s)* of the situation.

Utilize a process of *collaboration* with all rightful parties to the situation.

Stages and Components

Stage I: Interpreting the Situation through Awareness and Fact Finding

Component 1	Enhance sensitivity and awareness.
Component 2	Determine the major stakeholders and their ethical claims in the situation.
Component 3	Engage in the fact-finding process.

Stage II: Formulating an Ethical Decision

Component 1	Review the problem or dilemma.
Component 2	Identify existing ethical codes, laws, ethical principles, and institutional policies and procedures that apply to the dilemma.
Component 3	Generate possible and probable courses of action.
Component 4	Consider potential positive and negative consequences for each course of action.
Component 5	Consult with supervisors and other knowledgeable professionals.
Component 6	Select the best ethical course of action.

Stage III: Selecting an Action by Weighing Competing Nonmoral Values, Personal Blind Spots, or Prejudices

Component 1	Engage in reflective recognition and analysis of competing nonmoral values, personal blind spots, or prejudices.
Component 2	Consider contextual influences on values selection at the collegial, team, institutional, and societal levels.
Component 3	Select the preferred course of action.

Stage IV: Planning and Executing the Selected Course of Action

Component 1	Ascertain a reasonable sequence of specific actions to be taken.
Component 2	Anticipate personal and contextual barriers to effective execution of the plan of action and establish effective countermeasures for them.
Component 3	Perform, document, and evaluate the course of action as planned.

*Source: **The Professional Practice of Rehabilitation Counseling**, Maki/Tarvydas, 2012, Springer Publishing Company, LLC. Used with permission.*

agent are part of the process of change for clients. Each of us brings a somewhat unique set of connections among knowledge, skills, commitments, diversity, and collaborative effectiveness. Ideally, awareness of these connections enables you to respond to each client as a unique person, to develop understanding of clients who have values different from yours, and to work in adaptive, collaborative ways with clients whose heritage may differ from your own in one or more significant ways. Finally, your self-awareness and context awareness should foster an appreciation of the balances to be struck in applying an ethical code of behavior and pursuing an active role as a lifelong learner to contemporize and strengthen practice.

When lived authentically and intentionally, the lifestyle of a professional helper can be extremely rewarding. This line of work affords us the privilege of being part of the lives of many different individuals and their families at a level of intimacy extended to few. We are in many ways

their guests; they extend to us an invitation to witness and share in their struggles and accomplishments. Participating in what may be characterized as sacred conversations with our clients is not something we should ever take for granted or otherwise minimize. It is something to always value and protect. We do this by learning from and with our many and diverse clients, honoring their experiences and stories, and upholding ethical guidelines as professional helpers. This critical work requires critical commitments on our part. We trust that as you continue to make and uphold your critical commitments to the helping profession and to your identity as a professional helper that you will be able to realize the many professional and personal benefits of this line of work.

 Visit CengageBrain.com for a variety of study tools and useful resources such as video examples, case studies, interactive exercises, flashcards, and quizzes.

2 | Knowledge and Skill Builder

Part One

According to Learning Outcome 1 listed at the beginning of this chapter, you will be able to identify attitudes and behaviors about yourself that could help or interfere with establishing a positive helping relationship. Here, we present a Self-Rating Checklist that refers to characteristics of effective helpers. Use the checklist to assess yourself *now* with respect to these attitudes and behaviors. If you haven't yet had any or much contact with actual clients, try to use the checklist to assess how you believe you would behave in actual interactions. Identify any issues or areas you may need to work on in your development as a helper. Discuss your self-assessment in small groups or with an instructor, colleague, or supervisor. There is no written feedback for this part of the Knowledge and Skill Builder.

Self-Rating Checklist

Check the items that are most descriptive of you.

A. Openness to Learning Assessment

___1. I already have learned a lot of life lessons, and I believe clients will benefit from hearing my own story of recovery.

___2. I invite clients to comment on their experiences in therapy and how my work has either helped or hindered the process.

___3. I am a member of a professional association that publishes a scholarly journal for its members.

___4. I think that taking notes in supervision is not necessary.

___5. I am considering participating in therapy as a client to learn more about my own developing style of helping.

___6. I routinely solicit feedback from my supervisor and trusted colleagues.

___7. I have attended a professional workshop or conference in the past 6 months.

___8. I think I've already learned what it is that I need to work on to provide good care to my clients. Reviewing audio or video recordings of my counseling sessions therefore is no longer necessary.

B Competence Assessment

___1. Constructive negative feedback about myself doesn't make me feel incompetent or uncertain.

___2. I tend to put myself down frequently.

___3. I feel fairly confident about myself as a helper.

___4. I am often preoccupied with thinking that I'm not going to be a competent helper.

___5. When I am involved in a conflict, I don't go out of my way to ignore or avoid it.

___6. When I get positive feedback about myself, I often don't believe it's true.

___7. I set realistic goals for myself as a helper, ones that are within reach.

___8. I believe that a confrontational, hostile client could make me feel uneasy or incompetent.

___9. I often find myself apologizing for myself or my behavior.

___10. I'm fairly confident I can or will be a successful helper.

___11. I find myself worrying a lot about "not making it" as a helper.

___12. I'm likely to be a little apprehensive about clients who idealize me.

___13. A lot of times I will set standards or goals for myself that are too difficult to attain.

___14. I tend to avoid negative feedback when I can.

___15. Doing well or being successful does not make me feel uneasy.

C. Power and Values Assessment

___1. If I'm really honest, I think my helping methods are a little superior to others.

___2. A lot of times I try to get people to do what I want. I might get pretty defensive or upset if the client disagrees with what I want to do or does not follow my direction in the interview.

___3. I believe there is (or will be) a balance in the interviews between my participation and the client's.

___4. I could feel angry when working with a resistant or stubborn client.

___5. I can see that I might be tempted to get some of my own ideology across to the client.

___6. Allowing the client to make certain decisions and not telling him or her what to do is a sign of weakness on the helper's part.

___7. Sometimes I feel impatient with clients who have a different way of looking at the world than I do.

___8. I know there are times when I would be reluctant to refer my client to someone else, especially if the other counselor's style differed from mine.

___9. Sometimes I feel rejecting or intolerant of clients whose values and lifestyles are very different from mine.

___10. It is difficult for me to avoid getting into a power struggle with some clients.

(continued)

2 | Knowledge and Skill Builder (*continued*)

Part Two

According to Learning Outcome 2 for this chapter, you will be able to identify issues related to values, diversity, and ethics that could affect the development of a therapeutic relationship. Here we present seven written case descriptions and a list of seven types of issues. Read each case description carefully; then, on the line preceding each case, write the letter of the major kinds of issue reflected in the case description. (More than one type of issue may be reflected in each case.) When you are finished, consult the feedback for this part of the Knowledge and Skill Builder.

Type of Issue
A. Values conflict
B. Values stereotyping
C. Ethics—breach of confidentiality
D. Ethics—client welfare and rights
E. Ethics—referral
F. Ethics—inappropriate disclosure
G. Diversity

Case Description

____ 1. You are counseling a client who is in danger of failing high school. The client states that he feels like a failure because all the other students are so smart. In an effort to make him feel better, you tell him about one of your former clients who also almost flunked out.

____ 2. During a break from the therapy group you co-facilitate, you overhear a member of the group describe you to another client as "really hot in a pink bikini." You immediately remember the photograph you recently posted on your boyfriend's social networking site of you in your new pink bikini.

____ 3. A 58-year-old man who is having difficulty adjusting to life without his wife of 36 years who recently died comes to you for counseling. He has difficulty discussing his concern with you, and he appears to not understand what your role is as a counselor and what counseling might do for him. He seems to feel that you can give him a tranquilizer. You tell him that you are not able to prescribe medication, and you recommend that he be evaluated by a physician.

____ 4. A fourth-grade girl is referred to you by her teacher. The teacher states that the girl is doing poorly in class yet seems motivated to learn. After working with the girl for several weeks, including giving a battery of tests, you conclude that she has a severe learning disability. After obtaining her permission to talk to her teacher, you inform her teacher of this and state that the teacher might as well not spend too much more time working on what you believe is an "unfortunate case."

____ 5. You are counseling a couple who are considering a trial separation because of constant marital problems. You tell them you don't believe separation or divorce is the answer to their problems.

____ 6. A Euro-American helper states in a staff meeting that "people are just people" and that he does not see the need for all this emphasis in your treatment facility on understanding how clients from diverse racial/ethnic/cultural backgrounds may be affected differently by the therapy process.

____ 7. A racial minority client comes into a mental health center and requests to meet with a helper of his own racial group. He also indicates that he would consider seeing a helper who is not a member of his racial group but who shares his values and perspective and also who has some idea of his cultural struggles. He is told that it shouldn't matter whom he sees because all the therapists on the staff are culturally sensitive.

2 | Knowledge and Skill Builder **Feedback**

Part Two

This feedback is to assist you in fulfilling Learning Outcome 2 for this chapter.

1. C: *Ethics—breach of confidentiality*. The helper broke the confidence of a former client by revealing his grade difficulties without his consent.

2. F: *Ethics—inappropriate disclosure*. The helper made what Zur (2009) might describe as an accidental self-disclosure that was inappropriate. To avoid further inappropriate self-disclosures on social networking sites or anywhere on the Internet, we strongly advise that helpers limit any self-disclosures to strictly professional information, select the highest level of security options on such sites, disguise their identity when engaging in online activities, or avoid participating altogether in social networking sites.

3. E: *Ethics—referral*. The helper did not refer in an ethical or responsible way, because of failure to give the

client names of at least several physicians or psychiatrists who might be competent to see the client.

4. B: *Values stereotyping*. The helper is obviously stereotyping all kids with learning disabilities as useless and hopeless (the "label" is neither helpful nor in the client's best interest).

5. A: *Values conflict*. Your values are showing. Although separation and divorce may not be your solution, be careful about persuading clients to pursue your views and answers to issues.

6. F: *Diversity*. The Euro-American helper is ignorant about the importance and influence of racial/ethnic/cultural factors and is not able to see beyond his white privilege of power.

7. B and G: *Values stereotyping and Diversity*. The helper ignores the client's racial identity status and also responds in a stereotypical way to his or her request.

Ingredients of an Effective Helping Relationship

Out beyond ideas of wrongdoing and rightdoing, there is a field. I'll meet you there. (Rumi)

Learning Outcomes

After completing this chapter, you will be able to

1. Communicate the three facilitative conditions (empathy, genu-ineness, and positive regard) to a client in a role-play situation.
2. Identify issues related to transference and countertransference that might affect the development of the helping relationship, given five written case descriptions.

The quality of the helping relationship remains the foundation on which all other therapeutic activities are built. Gelso and Samstag (2008) define a **helping relationship** as "the feelings and attitudes the therapy participants have toward one another and the manner in which these are expressed" (p. 268). The past several years have brought renewed acknowledgment of the significance of the most important components of that relationship. The components in the helping relationship that seem to be consistently related to positive therapeutic outcomes include the following and form the focus of this chapter:

1. *Facilitative conditions—empathy, genuineness, and positive regard.* These three therapist qualities, particularly empathy, represent conditions that, if present in the therapist and perceived by the client, contribute a great deal to the development of the relationship.

2. *A working alliance—a relationship in which helper and client collaborate and negotiate their work together toward particular goals and outcomes on an ongoing basis.* The working alliance is characterized by a cognitive component, in which both parties agree to the goals and tasks of counseling, and by an affective component, or emotional bond between the helper and client, characterized by mutual *regard* and *trust*. Regard

for the client involves acceptance and caring; trust includes principled behavior, credibility, and reliability.

3. *Transference and countertransference—issues of emotional intensity and objectivity felt by both client and helper.* These issues are usually related to unfinished business with one's family of origin, yet they are triggered by and felt as a real aspect of the therapy relationship. Transference and countertransference *enactments* form the basis of relationship *ruptures. A repair of these ruptures is* a central task of the helper.

The Importance of the Helping Relationship

The helping relationship is as important to the overall outcome of the helping process as any particular change or intervention treatment strategy. The power of the helping relationship is acknowledged in nearly all theoretical orientations of psychotherapy. What makes the helping relationship so powerful for clients? Many believe that the power lies in the helper's potential to be healing. **Healing** is a word derived from a term meaning "to make whole." Comas-Díaz (2006) speaks of the universality of healing, noting that "the archetype of the healer is present in many societies" (p. 95). It is through the helping relationship and the interpersonal interactions with the practitioner that clients learn to be whole or integrated. In the relationship clients can experience a healing of the brokenness that often leads them into the helping process in the first place. Yalom (2009) explains the healing process in the therapeutic relationship this way: connection is paramount, and because all human beings are hardwired for connection, the connection fostered by the therapeutic relationship helps to heal.

Empirical Support for the Helping Relationship

In recent years, there has been an explosion of empirical support for the helping relationship. Harmon, Hawkins, Lambert, Slade, and Whipple (2005) conclude that "empirical support for the importance of the therapeutic relationship in outcome spans more than four decades and hundreds of published research studies" (p. 178). Client ratings of the therapeutic relationship are significantly related to and good predictors of outcomes of therapy, leading these researchers to conclude that when clients respond to treatment negatively, "therapists need to be particularly alert to the client's level of comfort and satisfaction with the therapeutic relationship" (Harmon et al., 2005, p. 179).

In a qualitative study of what clients find helpful in therapy, the therapeutic relationship also emerged as an important component of effectiveness (Levitt, Butler, & Hill, 2006). In this study, clients spoke of their therapeutic relationship "in excess of any other factor" of perceived helpfulness (Levitt et al., 2006, p. 322). This finding was echoed in an outcome study with chronically depressed patients. In this study, the single best predictor of outcome was the overall degree of emphasis therapists placed on discussing the client-therapist relationship (Vocisano et al., 2004, p. 263). This study also highlighted the importance of the relationship as a key component of change in cognitive behavioral therapy (Vocisano et al., 2004).

Additional empirical support for the therapeutic relationship comes from the Interdivisional Task Force on Evidence-Based Therapy Relationships established by the American Psychological Association. The most recent findings of this task force are published in a book by Norcross (2011). In important ways, the evidentiary strength required for the research/evidence forming the basis of these conclusions is rigorous. In lieu of relying on only one or two studies, the evidence for relationship elements was drawn from comprehensive meta-analyses of many studies spanning various treatments and research groups (Norcross & Wampold, 2011).

Norcross and Wampold summarize the empirical support for the helping relationship (2011, p. 423):

1. The therapy relationship "makes substantial and consistent contributions to psychotherapy outcome" regardless of the specific type of treatment used.

2. The therapy relationship accounts for "why clients improve (or fail to improve)" as much as the particular treatment method being used.

3. Efforts to promulgate best practices or evidence-based practices (EBPs) without including the relationship "are seriously incomplete and potentially misleading."

4. The therapy relationship "acts in concert with treatment methods, patient characteristics, and practitioner qualities in determining effectiveness."

5. Adapting or tailoring the therapy relationship to specific patient (in addition to diagnosis) enhances the effectiveness of treatment.

In the helping relationship, there is no "one size fits all" approach. Data are increasingly showing that the therapeutic relationship needs to be adapted or tailored to the individual client. Using an identical therapy relationship (or, for that matter, an identical treatment intervention) for *all* clients is not supported by data, is inappropriate, and, in certain cases, is unethical (Norcross & Wampold, 2011). Tailoring the therapeutic relationship to each client is now the better standard of practice. A recent special issue of *Psychotherapy Research* (2014) explored various innovative practices in the therapeutic relationship.

What in the Helping Relationship Heals?

The results of the interdivisional task force point to specific elements of the helping relationship that are powerfully healing and that work. These include the following elements that we discuss in this chapter and are listed in order of the weight of the existing evidence base:

The alliance
Empathy
Positive regard
Congruence
Managing countertransference

In addition, the evidence points to adapting or tailoring the helping relationship to specific client characteristics that enhance the overall effectiveness of therapy. These client characteristics, again listed by weight of the evidence, include the following:

Reactance/Resistance level
Preferences
Culture
Religion and spirituality
Stage of change
Coping style

There is no single adaptation from any of these client characteristics that is best; many adaptations are possible, much like getting a multiflavor instead of a single-flavor ice cream cone. As an example of this, consider the data summarized by Smith, Rodriguez, and Bernal (2011) on the many possible adaptations of culture within the therapeutic relationship. These authors found that *multiple* cultural adaptations, such as the use of culturally relevant language, metaphors, content, tasks, and goals, were more effective than only one or two cultural adaptations.

What Does *Not* Heal/Help in the Relationship?

Just as there are helpful practitioner relational behaviors and practices, there are also ones that are not helpful, perhaps even damaging. Here are some of the main ones to *avoid* as cited by Norcross and Wampold (2011):

Confrontational Style   We include confrontation in Chapter 5 as an influencing response but add some caveats there. As an individual *response*, the confrontation or challenge response can be helpful when used judiciously and infrequently, but as a *style* this modus operandi is ineffective, especially when working with substance abuse and addiction issues. In these situations in particular, motivational interviewing, which we describe in Chapter 10, is a more helpful style.

Criticism, Blame, Attacks on Clients   It should go without saying that avoiding comments and behaviors that are judgmental, hostile, pejorative, critical, or demeaning is important in the helping process, but consider this a friendly reminder!

Rigidity   Inflexibility and excessive structuring of the helping process or "dogmatic reliance on particular relational or therapy methods" seem to damage the helping process and outcomes. Adhering to an identical therapy approach for all clients or using a singular matching treatment protocol for all clients are further examples of therapeutic rigidity. Again, customizing or tailoring the helping relationship to the individual client is a way to guard against rigidity.

Cultural Variables in the Helping Relationship

All helping relationships can be considered cross-cultural (Comas-Díaz, 2006, p. 82). Comas-Díaz asserts that an effective helping relationship is one that varies from culture to culture. In a ground-breaking article on cultural variations in the therapeutic relationship, she summarizes some of the ways in which the helping relationship is impacted by culture. For example, she notes that some clients from Eastern cultures often expect their helper to conform to a sort of "cultural hierarchy" and regard their helper as an "authority figure" (p. 90). As a result, the nondirective relationship approach of many practitioners can be unsettling to these clients, who prefer a relationship that is more hierarchical (p. 90).

Another way in which some ethnic/racial minority clients may be impacted by the therapeutic relationship has to do with notions of family and extended family. As Comas-Díaz (2006) points out, some clients expect the therapeutic relationship to extend beyond the therapy session and into the structure of the families or their extended support network. Further, clients from indigenous and collectivist cultures may rely on nonverbal communication and pay greater attention to contextual cues in the relationship to maintain a harmonious relationship with their helpers. Such clients may feel "put off" by an interpersonal style of relating that is "direct, explicit, and specific" (p. 93).

An important variable that shapes the helping relationship has to do with **microaggressions**—brief, common intentional and unintentional verbal, behavioral, and environmental indignities that convey derogatory slights and insults to the client—often based on some cultural dimension of difference such as race, sexual orientation, disability, and gender (Sue, 2010, p. 5). According to Sue, practitioners often are unaware of their microaggressions—characterized by this distinguished author as *microassaults*, *microinsults*, and *microinvalidations*—in their interactions with clients of color or with clients who differ on other cultural dimensions such as sexual orientation, gender, citizenship, religion, and disability. As a result, the helping relationship is likely to be impaired in some way(s) when microaggressions occur. Part of the surrounding distress and the resulting power of such microaggressions lies in their invisibility to the practitioner and sometimes to the recipient as well. For example, in the case of racial microaggressions, although the practitioner may find it hard to believe he or she has engaged in an act of racism, discrimination, or prejudice, the recipient of the microaggressive act faces loss of self-esteem, loss of psychic and spiritual energies, and increased levels of anger and mistrust (Sue, 2010). As Sue (2010) notes, any singular microaggression may be "minimally impactful, but when they occur continuously throughout a life-span, their cumulative nature can have major detrimental consequences" (p. 7). Sue and colleagues observe that a "failure to acknowledge the significance of racism within and outside of the therapy session contributes to the breakdown of the alliance between therapist and client. A therapist's willingness to discuss racial matters is of central importance in creating a therapeutic alliance with clients of color" (Sue et al., 2007, p. 281).

Comas-Díaz (2006) also emphasizes the importance of recognizing and validating sociopolitical factors to solidify the multicultural therapeutic relationship (p. 99). Additionally, she notes the ways in which the relationship conditions that we call "facilitative conditions" are also impacted by culture. We explore this topic in greater detail in the following section.

Facilitative Conditions

Facilitative conditions have roots in a counseling the- **LO1** ory developed by Rogers (1951) called *client-centered* or *person-centered* therapy. Because this theory is the basis of these fundamental skills, we describe it briefly here.

The first stage of this theory (Rogers, 1942) was known as the **nondirective** period. The helper essentially attended and listened to the client for the purpose of mirroring the client's communication. The second stage of this theory (Rogers, 1951) was known as the **client-centered** period. In this phase, the therapist not only mirrored the client's communication but also reflected underlying or implicit affects or feelings to help clients become more self-actualized or fully functioning people. (This is the basis of the current concept of empathy, discussed in the next section.) In the most recent stage, known as **person-centered therapy** (Meador & Rogers, 1984; Raskin & Rogers, 1995), therapy is construed as an active partnership between two persons. In this current stage, the emphasis is on client growth through *experiencing* himself or herself and *experiencing* the other person in the relationship. Evidence-based support for person-centered therapy in general is summarized in meta-analyses conducted by Elliott (2002) and Elliott and Freire (2008). Current descriptions of person-centered theory are described by Kirschenbaum and Jourdan (2005) and by Raskin, Rogers, and Witty (2014).

Although person-centered therapy has evolved and changed, certain fundamental tenets have remained the same. One of these is that all people have an inherent tendency to strive toward growth, self-actualization, and self-direction. This tendency is realized when individuals have access to conditions (both within and outside therapy) that nurture growth. In the context of person-centered therapy, client growth is associated with high levels of three core, or **facilitative**, **relationship conditions**: *empathy* (accurate understanding), *genuineness* (congruence), and *positive regard* (respect) (Rogers, Gendlin, Kiesler, & Truax, 1967). If these conditions are absent from the therapeutic relationship, then clients may fail to grow and may deteriorate (Carkhuff, 1969a, 1969b; Truax & Mitchell, 1971). Presumably, for these conditions to enhance the therapeutic relationship, they must be communicated by the helper *and* perceived by the client (Rogers, 1951, 1957). Clients have reported that these facilitative conditions are among the most helpful experiences for them in the overall helping process (Paulson, Truscott, & Stuart, 1999). It is important to note that although we (and other authors) discuss each of these three conditions separately, in reality they are not isolated phenomena but in fact interrelated ones (Wickman & Campbell, 2003).

In recent years, various persons have developed concrete skills associated with these three core conditions. This delineation of the core conditions into teachable skills has made it possible for people to learn how to communicate empathy, genuineness, and positive regard to clients. In the remainder of the Facilitative Conditions section, we describe these three important relationship conditions and associated skills.

Empathy or Accurate Understanding

Empathy may be described as the ability to understand people from their frame of reference rather than your own. Responding to a client empathically may be "an attempt to think *with,* rather than *for* or *about* the client" (Brammer, Abrego, & Shostrom, 1993, p. 98). For example, if a client says, "I've tried to get along with my father, but it doesn't work out. He's too hard on me," an empathic response would be something like, "You feel discouraged about your unsuccessful attempts to get along with your father." In contrast, if you say something like "You ought to try harder," you are responding from your frame of reference, not the client's. As described in the first Chapter Objective, our goal is to help you learn enough about empathy to be able to communicate this facilitative condition to clients.

The evidence base on empathy suggests that client perceptions of feeling understood by their helpers relate favorably to helping outcomes (Elliott, Bohart, Watson, & Greenberg, 2011; Watson, Steckley, & McMullen, 2014). Elliott et al (2011) conclude from their meta-analyses on empathy that it is a general predictor of helping outcomes across theoretical orientation of the helper, treatment formats, and severity levels of client problems. Moyers and Miller (2013) have found that empathy seems to exert an even larger effect on successful addiction treatment than in psychotherapy in general.

The Neuroscience of Empathy and Emerging Evidence

Empathy has received a great deal of attention from both researchers and practitioners over the years. We now know that there is even a brain connection with empathy! As Elliott and colleagues (2011) note, the emergence of active scientific research on the biological basis of empathy has been the most important development in the construct of empathy in the past two decades. In 1996, a team of neuroscientists discovered brain neurons called **mirror neurons**. Mirror neurons are tailor-made to mirror the emotions and bodily responses of another person. According to Siegel (2010), these mirror neurons help us create actual body sensations that allow us to resonate with the experiences of the other person. This forms the foundation of the empathic experience in therapy, which is based on the recognition of the self in the other. The resulting potential for empathic attunement with our clients is profound. This empathic mirroring helps clients feel understood, and ultimately it leads to brain changes in clients through the establishment of new neural firing patterns and increased neural integration (Cozolino, 2010; Pfeifer & Dapretto, 2009; Siegel, 2010).

Some recent research has postulated that empathic accuracy is associated with two specific areas of the brain: the inferior frontal gyrus (IFG) and the dorsomedialprefrontal cortex (dmPFC). Moreover, this research found that *training* individuals in compassion-oriented meditation not only increased brain activity in these two regions but also improved empathic accuracy in the meditation group of participants compared to the control group (Mascaro, Rilling, Negi, & Raison, 2012).

In addition to the discovery of the mirror neurons and their role in empathic communication, additional neuroscience research also points to a range of affective and perspective-taking components of empathy in people (Decety & Lamm, 2009). The results of this body of research suggest that empathy involves three interlinked processes with corresponding areas of brain activation (Decety & Ickes, 2009):

Affective simulation—the mirroring of emotional elements of the client's bodily experience with brain activation in the limbic system.

Perspective taking—understanding the client's experiences and how things feel and what they mean to the client with brain activation in both the prefrontal and temporal cortexes.

Self-regulation of one's own emotions—the ability to self-soothe one's own feelings or distress as the helper with brain activation in the frontal, prefrontal, and right inferior parietal cortexes.

Current concepts of empathy thus emphasize that it is far more than a single concept or skill. Empathy is believed to be a multistage process consisting of multiple elements, including affective and cognitive components (Bohart, Elliott, Greenberg, & Watson; 2002; Clark, 2010; Watson & Greenberg, 2011). The affective component refers to emotional connectedness between the practitioner and the client, and it involves the helper's ability to identify and contain the feelings and emotions or affective experience of the client. **Affective empathy** is based on emotional neural circuits activated by the client's expression of emotions and the helper's own understanding of specific situations that might stimulate various emotional

responses (Watson & Greenberg, 2009, p. 133). **Cognitive empathy** comprises a more intellectual or reasoned understanding of the client. Cognitive empathy is thought to operate independently of emotional neural networks and involves mirror neurons and the neural systems that facilitate perspective taking (Watson & Greenberg, 2009, p. 133). As Elliott and colleagues conclude, "empathy is best understood as a complex construct consisting of a variety of different acts used in different ways" (2011, p. 133). It is important to note, however, that most current constructs of empathy are based on Western culture because client perceptions of counselor empathy have rarely been explored with non-Western clients.

Cultural Empathy

Currently there are multiple explanations for what occurs in the empathic process between helper and client. Here we describe the cultural view of empathy, the person-centered view of empathy, and the self-psychology view of empathy. In our opinion, all three of these views are important for practitioners to be aware of and to incorporate into their therapeutic and relational style.

Ivey, Gluckstern, Packard, and Ivey (2007) distinguish between individual and multicultural empathy, saying that the concept of **multicultural empathy** requires that we understand different worldviews from our own. The culturally empathic helper responds not only to the client's verbal and nonverbal messages but also to her or his historical/cultural/ethnic background. Cultural empathy is important because it is considered one of the main foundations of prosocial behavior and of a justice orientation (Hoffmann, 2000). Moreover, empathy (and also positive regard) is an important component in culturally adapted therapies (Smith, Rodriguez, & Bernal, 2011).

Empathic accuracy is, to some extent, impacted by many aspects of social context. Recent research found that one contextual variable, that of social class, was associated with empathic accuracy (Kraus, Cote, & Keltner, 2010). In this study, lower-class individuals who were university students and employees obtained higher scores on a test of empathic accuracy and judged the emotions of an interaction partner more accurately than upper-class individuals (Kraus, Cote, & Keltner, 2010).

In an ethnographic study of empathy with Chinese clients, some evidence suggested that the clients in this study viewed empathy as a different phenomenon linguistically and conceptually (Ng & James, 2013). Using the literal Chinese translation, these clients described empathy as "having the heart to help" or "the heart of feeling the same." For the subjects in this qualitative study, this meant that helpers are responsible and are willing to engage in tasks beyond the prescribed duties, in other words, to "go the extra mile."

Comas-Díaz (2006) asserts that the practitioner in a multicultural helping relationship may be able to empathize cognitively or intellectually with the culturally diverse client but may not be able to empathize affectively or emotionally. As an example, consider a practitioner who encounters a client who is an African refugee. The helper may be able to study the client's culture and consult with others who have firsthand knowledge of the client's culture and historical experiences. However, the practitioner may not be able to relate emotionally either to the client's experiences as a refugee or to the practitioner's own emotions that are stirred up in working with this particular client. When affective empathy is missing, cultural misunderstandings abound.

Misunderstandings or breaches of empathy are often a function not just of miscommunications but also of differences in understanding styles, nuances, and subtleties of various cultural beliefs, values, and use of language (Sue & Sue, 2013). Smith and colleagues (2011) described the example of a U.S. mental health practitioner who volunteered in Haiti following the January 12, 2010, earthquake. The practitioner was working with a Haitian woman who, during the earthquake, had lost her child, her home, and one of her legs. While the client was most upset about losing her leg, the U.S. practitioner insisted that the client should be more upset about the loss of her child. In doing so, the U.S. practitioner privileged his or her own cultural understanding of what the client's traumatic experiences were instead of attempting to understand the client's frame of reference (Smith, Rodriguez, & Bernal, 2011). In an empathic misunderstanding, the helper should acknowledge it and take responsibility for it. Comas-Díaz (2006) concludes that misunderstandings or "missed empathetic opportunities" are prevalent but also subtle in cross-cultural relationships because clients from other cultures frequently communicate indirectly to test and assess the practitioner (p. 84).

Person-Centered and Self-Psychology Views of Empathy

Rogers's theory of person-centered therapy and his view of the role of empathy in the therapeutic process assume that at the beginning of counseling, a client has a distinct and already fairly complete sense of himself or herself—in Rogers's terms, a **self-structure**. This is often true of clients with more "neurotic" or everyday features of presenting problems—that is, they bring problems of living to the helper and at the outset have an intact sense of themselves. Rogers believed that clients come to the helping process as a complete person and become more whole through the unconditional acceptance of the helper.

In contrast to the Rogerian view of the function of empathy—which is to help actualize the potential of an already established self-structure—is the view of empathy offered by the **self-psychology theory** of Kohut (1971b). Self-psychology theory assumes that many clients do not come into therapy with an established sense of self, that they lack a self-structure, and that the function of empathy in particular and of therapy in general is to build on the structure of the client's sense of self by completing a developmental process that was arrested at some time, resulting in an incomplete sense of self. Kohut believes that the client comes to the helping process as an incomplete person who becomes whole through therapeutic corrective experiences such as empathic understanding.

Both Rogers (1951, 1957) and Kohut (1971b) have had an enormous impact on our understanding of the role that empathy plays in the development of a positive and authentic sense of self, not only in the normal developmental process but also in the helping relationship. Rogers's emphasis on understanding and acceptance helps clients learn that it is acceptable to be real, to be their true selves. Kohut's emphasis on empathy as a corrective emotional experience allows clients to discover parts of themselves that have been buried or split off and that in counseling can be integrated in a more holistic way. Both Rogers and Kohut stress the importance of a nonjudgmental stance on the part of the helper. It is our position that the views of both of these persons, even though disparate, can be used together in a pragmatic fashion to create and sustain a facilitative helping relationship. These views of empathy were corroborated in a recent empirical study in which clients' perceived therapist empathy decreased clients' negative views and treatment of themselves and increased their levels of secure attachment in interpersonal relationships, leading the authors to conclude that "therapist empathy is multifunctional in psychotherapy" (Watson, Steckley, & McMullen, 2014, p. 296).

We discussed the various *processes* involved in empathy. Similarly, there are different manners of *expression* of empathy to clients. For example, a study that validated a nine-item therapist empathy scale found expression of therapist empathy ranged from an expressive vocal tone, an attunement to the client's inner world, and an understanding and acceptance of the client's cognitive and affective experiences (Decker, Nich, Carroll, & Martino, 2014). We discuss two ways of expressing empathy to clients: *validating* responses and the provision of a *safe-holding environment*.

Empathy and Validation of Clients' Experiences: Kohut and Linehan

Both Rogers and Kohut developed their views on empathy from their work with various clients. For Kohut, the turning point was a client who came to each session with bitter accusations toward him. As he stopped trying to explain and interpret her behavior and started to listen, he realized these accusations were her attempts to show him the reality of her very early childhood living with incapacitated caregivers who had been unavailable to her. Kohut surmised that clients show us their needs through their behavior in therapy, giving us clues about what they did not receive from their primary caretakers to develop an adequate sense of self and also about what they need to receive from the helper.

It is important to remember that when a childhood need is not met or is blocked, it simply gets cut off but does not go away; it remains in the person in an often primitive form, which explains why some grown-up clients exhibit behaviors in therapy that can seem very childish. When these needs are chronically frustrated or repressed, the child grows up with poor self-esteem and an impaired self-structure. Also, the self is split into a **true self**, the capacity to relate to oneself and to others, and a **false self**, an accommodating self that exists mainly to deny one's true needs to comply with the needs of the primary caregivers (Winnicott, 1958).

Invalidating Environments

Linehan (1993a; 2015) has extended the work on the discussion about empathy and environments in her seminal work on dialectical behavior therapy in the treatment of individuals diagnosed with borderline personality disorder (BPD), a disorder characterized by emotional dysregulation. She notes that most persons with an initial temperamental vulnerability to emotion dysregulation do not go on to develop symptoms of BPD *unless* they are exposed to a particular developmental/social environment that she terms "invalidating." Neacsiu & Linehan (2014) note that **invalidating environments**, which can be immediate or extended family, school, work, or community, are characterized by the tendency to "negate, punish and/or respond erratically and inappropriately to private experiences, independent of the validity of the actual behavior. Private experiences, and especially emotional experiences and interpretations of events, are not taken as valid responses to events by others; are punished, trivialized, dismissed, or disregarded" (p. 414). In more optimal developmental environments, the individual's private, internal experiences are validated, giving rise to a stable identity and coherent sense of self. In invalidating environments, however, the individual "learns to mistrust his/her internal states, and instead scans the environment for cues about how to act, think, or feel. This general reliance on others results in the individual's failure to develop a coherent sense of self" (Neacsiu & Linehan, 2014, p. 415).

Corrective Emotional Experiences

Both Linehan (2015) and Kohut (1984) have discussed the role of empathy in response to the disrupted sense of self experienced by clients in these sorts of invalidating environments. Kohut (1984) believes that empathy—the therapist's acceptance of the client and his or her feelings—is at the core of providing a "**corrective emotional experience**" for clients. It means avoiding any sort of comment that may sound critical to clients. Because the lack of original empathic acceptance by caregivers has driven parts of the client's self underground, it is important not to repeat this process in helping interactions. Instead, the helper needs to create an opposite set of conditions in which these previously buried aspects of the self can emerge, be accepted, and be integrated (Kahn, 1991, pp. 96–97). The way to do this is to let clients know that the way they see themselves and their world "is not being judged but accepted as the most likely way for them to see it, given their individual history" (Kahn, 1991, p. 97). This is known as a validating response or an *empathic affirmation* (Elliott et al., 2011).

Validating Responses

Validating responses are usually verbal messages from the helper that mirror the client's *experience* (notice the emphasis on *experience* rather than on *words*) and validate the client's *perspective*. Validation can occur nonverbally as well through helper behaviors that communicate understanding and acceptance. This sounds remarkably easy to do but often becomes problematic because of our own woundedness. Too often we fail to validate the client because a button has been pushed in us, and we end up validating or defending ourselves instead. This reaction forms the basis of *countertransference,* which we discuss later in this chapter. The key to being able to provide validating responses is to be able to contain our own emotional reactions so that they do not get dumped out onto the client. Recall from our earlier discussion on the processes in empathy that one such process—that of *self-regulation of our own affective experiences*—is what helps us manage feelings that get stirred up in our work with clients. This is especially difficult to do when a client pushes your own buttons, and this is why working with yourself and your own "stuff" is so important.

For Linehan (1993a; 2015), validation is at the core of her dialectical behavior therapy (DBT) approach and forms the basis of acceptance. Linehan (1993b) describes validation in DBT in the following way:

The essence of validation is this: The therapist communicates to the client that her responses make sense and are understandable within her *current* life context or situation. The therapist actively accepts the client and communicates the acceptance to the client. The therapist takes the client's responses seriously and does not discount or trivialize them. Validation strategies require the therapist to search for, recognize, and reflect to the client the validity inherent in her response to events (p. 222).

Linehan further delineates six levels of empathic validating responses. Note that each level is more complete than the prior one and each level depends on one or more of the prior levels as well. Brief summaries of these six validation levels as described in Neacsiu and Linehan (2014) are as follows.

Level 1: Listening and Observing (V1)* The helper listens and pays attention to the client—not only the client's words but also the client's nonverbal behavior, expressions, and experiences. The key in Level 1 is that the helper is interested in the client and is showing that interest in both verbal and nonverbal responses. This occurs through helper behaviors such as verbal prompts of understanding ("Yes, I see," "Go on," "Tell me more about that") and also nonverbal activity, such as head nods, eye contact, and body posture, that shows the helper is *engaged with* the client. You probably can see that this level of empathic validation involves one of the processes of empathy we discussed previously, that of *affective simulation*, or mirroring of the emotional elements of the client's experience.

Level 2: Accurate Reflection (V2) Level 2 validation builds on Level 1 and extends it by accurately reflecting back to the client what the helper has heard and understood. "Validation at Level 2 sanctions, empowers, or authenticates that the individual is who he or she actually is" (Linehan, 2015, p. 89). For example, the client says, "I feel sure that my boss hates me." The helper responds at this level with an accurate reflection by saying something in response like, "Your experience tells you that your boss does not like you." Note that validation responses do not create "validity"—you do not have to agree or disagree with the client's perceptions. One way to do this is to remember that basically all realities are subjective anyway! We discuss reflections further in Chapters 4 and 10.

Level 3: Articulating the Unverbalized (V3) In Level 3 of validation, the helper extends levels one and two and "communicates understanding of aspects of the client's experience and response to events that have not been communicated directly by the client" (Neacsiu & Linehan, 2014, p. 433). In essence, in this level of validation, the helper articulates something about the emotions and meanings the client has not yet explicitly expressed but are inferred implicitly (Linehan, 2015). How does the helper accomplish this? It is accomplished by the use of *perspective taking* that we discussed in this section as one of the processes of empathy. In

the previous example about the client who feels like her boss hates her, the implicit assumption is that she wishes the boss wouldn't hate her. A validation response at Level 3 would be something like, "You don't think your boss likes you and you wish she (he) would. Then, you would have a different and more positive experience at work." Note that at Level 3 there is a fine balance between taking the perspective of the client and defining the client's subjective reality, so it is best to check out the accuracy of your validating response.

Level 4: Validation in Terms of Past Learning or Biological Dysfunction (V4) In Level 4, the client's *behavior* is validated in terms of its *causes*, As Neacsiu and Linehan suggest, "Validation here is based on the notion that all behavior is caused by events occurring in time; thus, in principle, it is understandable . . . even though information may not be available to determine all the relevant causes, the client's feelings, thoughts, and actions make perfect sense in the context of the client's current experience, physiology, and life to date" (2014, p. 433). In the example with the client, a Level 4 validation response might be something like this:

"Given the fact that this boss even reminds you of your last one, and that your last one was sort of a nightmare for you, I can see why you could feel the way you do about his (her) reactions to you."

Level 5: Validation in Terms of Present Context or Normative Functioning (V5) At this level of validation, the helper's task is to communicate that the client's behavior is "justifiable, reasonable, well grounded, meaningful, and/or efficacious in terms of current events, normative biological functioning, and/or the client's ultimate life goals" by looking for "the wisdom or validity of the client's response" (Neacsiu & Linehan, 2014, p. 433). Here the helper accomplishes this task by communicating understanding of the client's response and by finding relevant facts in the client's current context that support the client's behavior. In the example with the client, a sample validating response at Level 5 would be something like this one: "It makes sense to me that you would be feeling put off and discouraged by your boss's response to you given what is happening to you with this person at work."

Level 6: Radical Genuineness (V6) We describe genuineness in a later section in this chapter as one of the three core facilitative conditions described by Carl Rogers in person-centered therapy.

Linehan describes genuineness in her model in the following way: "In Level 6, the task is to recognize the person as he/she is, seeing and responding to his/her

*Source: From Linehan and Dexter Mazza, "Dialectical behavior therapy for borderline personality disorder," in Barlow, Clinical Handbook of Psychological Disorders, 4e. Copyright (c) 2009 by Guilford Press. Reproduced by permission of Guilford Press.

strengths and capacities, while keeping a firm empathic understanding of his/her actual difficulties and incapacities. The therapist believes in the client and his/her capacity to change and move toward ultimate life goals just as the therapist may believe in a friend or family member. The client is responded to as a person of equal status, due equal respect" (Neacsiu & Linehan, 2014, p. 434). At this highest level, the validation is, in essence, the validation of the client sitting in front of you "as is." Rather than being a specific response that builds on prior responses sequentially as we have seen in Levels 1–5, Level 6 is a sort of *stance*, an attitudinal response to clients that conveys your belief in them (see Learning Activity 3.1).

Teyber and McClure (2011) note that validating responses are especially important when working with clients of color, LGBT clients, low-income clients, physically challenged clients, and any other clients who may feel different. "These clients will bring issues of oppression, prejudice, and injustice into the therapeutic process, and their personal experiences have often been invalidated by the dominant culture. These clients in particular will not expect to be heard or understood by the therapist" (p. 65).

We believe that Linehan's six levels of validation can be extended to foster cultural empathy as well. Consider, for example, the scenario below.

Learning Activity 3.1

Validating Empathy

Part One

Consider the following case descriptions of clients. What might be the effect on you of hearing each client's issue? What might you try to defend about yourself? How could you work with this to give a validating response to the client instead? Provide an example of such a response. For our feedback on this activity, see page 86.

1. The client expresses a strong sexual interest in you and is mad and upset when she realizes you are not in love with her.
2. The client wants to be your favorite client and repeatedly wants to know how special he is to you.
3. The client is a man of Roman Catholic faith who wants to marry a Jewish woman. He is feeling a lot of pressure from his Latino parents, his priest, and his relatives to stop the relationship and find a woman of his own religious faith. He wants you to tell him what to do and is upset when you don't.

Part Two

In this part of Validating Empathy, match a client description/helper response with one of Neacsiu and Linehan's (2014) corresponding six levels of helper validation. Feedback is given on page 86.

Levels of Validation

V1 Listening and Observing
V2 Accurate Reflection
V3 Articulating the Unverbalized
V4 Validation in Terms of Past Learning
V5 Validation in Terms of Present Context
V6 Radical Genuineness

Client Descriptions/Helper Responses

_____ 1. The client thinks it is unfair that she does all the errands in her relationship with her partner. You say to the client, "You feel like it is unfair that you are shouldering all the responsibility for the errands in your relationship with your partner."

_____ 2. The client is very upset about the death of her beloved pet. The helper responds by listening attentively and being nonverbally engaged with the client.

_____ 3. The client believes that people do not like her at work because she is a lesbian. As the helper, you say something like, "Your experience at work tells you that your coworkers do not like you and you feel like this is because of your sexual orientation. Because you have been responded to quite negatively by others in the past due to your sexual orientation, I can see why you feel like this is happening to you once again."

_____ 4. The client had been expecting a bonus at work and is quite upset and angry that the expected bonus was not given to him. The helper says, "You are really angry about not getting that bonus you thought you would get. Given your existing workload, it sure makes sense that you would be feeling really upset about this situation."

_____ 5. The client is the only international student in a study group and feels constantly like she does not really fit into the group and that her participation is not that welcomed. As the helper, you acknowledge her experience of marginalization in this group and comment on her coping and resilience in response.

_____ 6. The client expresses sadness and frustration about her recent discovery that her partner in life has betrayed her. The helper responds by saying, "You are sad and upset about the discovery of your partner's betrayal; you wish this had not happened to your relationship and that things could just be the way they used to be with the two of you."

TABLE 3.1   Validation and Cultural Empathy

Level 1 (V1)	Sample Response
Listening/Observing	Helper nods head, looks at client, listens
Level 2 (V2)	"You feel upset about being taunted by the white kids because of your skin color."
Accurate Reflection	
Level 3 (V3)	Reflection above PLUS "You wish they would just leave you alone and let you be who
Articulating the Unverbalized	you are".
Level 4 (V4)	"I know this isn't the first time you've had to endure this. It gets too tiresome and I can
Validation of Past Learning	see why it would be so upsetting."
Level 5 (V5)	"It makes sense that being taunted for something so basic and so important to who
Validation of Present Context	you are, your identity, would feel so painful."
Level 6 (V6)	"It's so remarkable that in the face of all these taunts you always hold your head up
Radical Genuineness	high and don't back down."

Your client, Lettitia, who is a client of color, is crying about being taunted about her skin color on the bus. She is very upset about what has happened to her, and this is not the first time that she has had to endure taunts due to her race. Consider the possible ways in which a helper could facilitate cultural empathy via the use of these six levels of validation in Table 3.1.

Empathy and the Holding Environment

The empathic mirroring and limit-setting responses we have described are often referred to as the provision of a therapeutic **holding environment** (Winnicott, 1958). A holding environment means that the therapist conveys in words and/or behavior that he or she knows and understands the deepest feelings and experience of the client and provides a safe and supportive atmosphere in which the client can experience deeply felt emotions. As Cormier and Hackney (2012) note, it means "that the helper is able to allow and stay with or 'hold' the client's feelings instead of moving away or distancing from the feelings or the client. In doing this, the counselor acts as a **container**; that is, the counselor's comfort in exploring and allowing the emergence of client feelings provides the support to help the client contain or hold various feelings that are often viewed by the client as unsafe" (p. 114). The therapist as a container helps the client to manage what might otherwise be experienced as overwhelming feelings by providing a structure and safe space in having to do so.

Josselson (1992) points out that "of all the ways in which people need each other, holding is the most primary and the least evident," starting with the earliest sensations that infants experience—the sensation of being guarded by strong arms that keep them from falling and also help them to unfold as unique and separate

individuals (p. 29). A child is sufficiently nourished in such an environment and, just as important, the child also feels *real*. As Josselson notes in her affirmative work on adult human relationships, this need for holding or groundedness does not disappear as we grow up, although the form of holding for adults may be with institutions, ideas, and words as much as with touch. Individuals who do not experience this sense of holding as children often grow up without a sense of groundedness in their own bodies as well as without a sense of self as separate and unique persons. Often their energy or life force is bound up and/or groundless, and they may seek to escape their sense of nothingness by becoming attached to any number of addictions. Josselson (1992, p. 36) provides an excellent description of how the process of therapy can support clients' growth through the provision of this sort of holding environment:

People often come to psychotherapy because they need to be held while they do the work of emotionally growing. They need a structure within which they can experience frightening or warded-off aspects of themselves. They need to know that this structure will not "let them down." They also need to trust that they will not be impinged upon by unwanted advice or by a therapist's conflicts or difficulties. Psychotherapy, because of clinicians' efforts to analyze what takes place, is one of the best understood of holding environments. Therapists "hold" patients as patients confront aspects of their memory and affective life that would be too frightening or overwhelming to face alone. (One of my patients once described her experience of therapy as my sitting with her while she confronts the monsters inside) (p. 36.)

Keep in mind that in various cultures this sort of holding environment is supplied by indigenous healers as well.

Holding Environments and Family of Origin

Teyber and McClure (2011) have noted that the effective holding environment provided by a helper is usually dramatically different from what the young client is experiencing or what an adult client experienced while growing up. For example, if the child was sad, the parent may have responded by withdrawing, by denying the child's feelings, or by responding derisively (Teyber & McClure, 2011). In all these parental reactions, the child's feeling was not heard, validated, or "contained"; as a result, the child learned over time to deny or avoid these feelings (thus constituting the "false self" we described previously). Children are developmentally unable to experience and manage feelings on their own without the presence of another person who can be emotionally present for them and receive and even welcome their feelings. If the parent was unable to help the child hold feelings in this manner, then it will be up to the helper to do so. In this way, the helper allows clients to know that he or she can accept their painful feelings and still stay emotionally connected to them (Teyber & McClure, 2011). If the helper cannot do so, either because of discomfort with the client's pain or because of feelings that have been stirred

---

3.1 Feedback

Validating Empathy

Part One

Here are some examples of validating responses. Discuss your emotional reactions and your response with a partner or in a small group.

1. I realize you are disappointed and upset about wanting me to have the same sort of feelings for you that you say you have for me.

2. It is important to you to feel very special to me. I understand this as your way of telling me something about what has been missing for you in your life.

3. I realize you feel caught between two things—your religious and cultural history and your love for this woman. You wish I could tell you what to do, and you're upset with me that I won't.

Part Two

1. V2 Accurate Reflecting
2. V1 Listening and Observing
3. V4 Validation in Terms of Past Learning
4. V5 Validation in Terms of Present Context
5. V6 Radical Genuineness
6. V3 Articulating the Unverbalized

---

up in working with the client, then this constitutes a countertransferential reaction.

Holding Environments and Self-Object Relationships

Teyber's ideas reflect the work of Kohut (1971a, 1971b) on **self-object relationships**, in which the development of the child's sense of *self* depends greatly on the capacity of the child's caretakers, the "*self-objects*," to fulfill certain psychological functions that the child cannot yet provide for himself or herself. Support and empathy are two of the most important of these psychological functions that the caregiver provides for the developing child. These ongoing supportive and empathic exchanges (or lack thereof) form the basis of the child's psychic infrastructure and impact how the child will be able to relate to himself or herself as well as to others. Some relationship theorists consider this idea to be Kohut's most important contribution, not only because it explains much about an individual's capacity for relatedness but also because his notions about the relationship between the child and caregiver have many analogues in the therapeutic relationship between the helper and client. From this perspective, when misunderstandings or empathic breaches occur in counseling, the helper may gently inquire if the current empathic break feels similar in any way to something that occurred in the client's relationship with a caregiver. In fact, in this way, one could look at the healing that occurs in the therapeutic relationship as the result of giving the client "a second developmental chance" (Cashdan, 1988, p. 22).

Caveats and Adaptations in Empathic Responding

While empathic responding forms the basis for radical acceptance of clients, like other therapeutic responses it is not universally effective and the use of it needs to be adapted across clients. As Neacsiu and Linehan (2014) observe, impasses in helping can occur when the helping process is skewed either too much toward acceptance or too much toward problem-solving and a lack of balance ensues. Elliott and colleagues (2011) note that both "clinical and research experience suggest that the amount of therapist empathy varies as a function of the client" (p. 143). They assert that "certain fragile clients may find the usual expressions of empathy too intrusive, while hostile clients may find empathy too directive; still other clients may find an empathic focus on feelings too foreign." (p. 146). In some instances, helpers may be more empathic by not overtly expressing empathy with certain clients who do not respond favorably to empathic expressions. Because true empathy means therapeutic attunement with clients, the best expression of empathy is the one that best fits with the person sitting in front of us at a given moment in time. "When clients do not want therapists to be *explicitly* empathic, truly empathic therapists will use their perspective-taking skills to provide an optimal therapeutic distance in order to respect their clients' boundaries" (Elliott et al., 2011, p. 146).

Genuineness or Congruence

Genuineness—also referred to as **congruence**—is the art of being oneself without being phony or playing a role. Although most practitioners are trained to be professionals, a helper can convey genuineness by being human and by collaborating with the client. Genuineness contributes to an effective therapeutic relationship by reducing the emotional distance between the helper and client and by helping the client to identify with the helper, in other words, to perceive the helper as another person similar to the client. Congruence has a central place in the three facilitative conditions, in part because it supports empathy and positive regard and in part because Rogers saw the process of therapy as helping clients become more congruent (Kolden, Klein, Wang, & Austin, 2011). Empirical support for this facilitative condition of genuineness or congruence suggests that the contribution of congruence to client outcomes is mixed but leaning toward the positive and appears to be especially important in younger, less educated, and perhaps less psychologically sophisticated clients (Kolden et al., 2011). Genuineness has several components: supporting *nonverbal behaviors*, *role behavior, consistency*, and *spontaneity* (see also Egan, 2014; Kolden et al., 2011). Recent conceptualizations of genuineness also have extended the definition of it to include **therapeutic presence**, the notion of using oneself as a healer (Geller & Greenberg, 2002).

Supporting Nonverbal Behaviors

Genuineness is communicated by the helper's use of appropriate, or supporting, nonverbal behaviors. Nonverbal behaviors that convey genuineness include eye contact, smiling, and leaning toward the client while sitting. However, these three nonverbal behaviors should be used discreetly and gracefully. For example, direct yet intermittent eye contact is perceived as more indicative of genuineness than is persistent gazing, which clients may interpret as staring. Similarly, continual smiling or leaning forward may be viewed as phony and artificial rather than genuine and sincere. One way to convey genuineness with supporting nonverbal behaviors is to engage in nonverbal communication that parallels that of the client. This is called **synchrony**, which refers to the degree of harmony between a practitioner's and a client's nonverbal behavior. Synchrony, or mirroring of body posture and other client nonverbal behaviors, contributes to rapport and the facilitative conditions. Synchrony does not mean that the helper mimics every move or sound the client makes! It is more about matching the practitioner's overall nonverbal demeanor so that it is closely aligned with or very similar to the client's.

Role Behavior

Counselors who do not overemphasize their role, authority, or status are likely to be perceived as more genuine by clients. Too much emphasis on one's role and position can create excessive and unnecessary emotional distance in the relationship. Clients can feel intimidated or even resentful.

The genuine helper also is someone who is comfortable with himself or herself and with a variety of persons and situations and does not need to put on new or different roles to feel or behave comfortably and effectively. As Egan (2007) observes, genuine helpers "do not take refuge in the role of counselor. Ideally, relating at deeper levels to others and to the counseling they do is part of their lifestyle, not roles they put on or take off at will" (p. 56).

Consistency

Consistency exists when the helper's words, actions, and feelings match—when they are congruent. For example, when a therapist becomes uncomfortable because of a client's constant verbal assault, she acknowledges this feeling of discomfort, at least to herself, and does not try to cover up or feign comfort when it does not exist. Practitioners who are not aware of their feelings or of discrepancies among their feelings, words, and actions may send mixed, or incongruent, messages to clients— for example, saying, "Sure, go ahead and tell me how you feel about me," while fidgeting or tapping their feet or fingers. Clients are likely to find such messages very confusing and even irritating.

Spontaneity

Spontaneity is the capacity to express oneself naturally without contrived or artificial behaviors. Spontaneity also means being tactful without deliberating about everything you say or do. However, spontaneity does not mean that helpers need to verbalize every passing thought or feeling to clients, particularly negative feelings. Rogers (1957) suggests that helpers express negative feelings to clients only if the feelings are constant and persistent or if they interfere with the helper's ability to convey empathy and positive regard.

Therapeutic Presence

The word *presence* comes from the Latin word *praesentia,* meaning "to be present before others." Think of the opposite of the word presence and immediately the word *absence* will most likely come to your mind. In the simplest form, **therapeutic presence** means all that the Latin root conveys, *being there* for the client, not just in a physical sense, but in an emotional sense as well. Presence means bringing oneself into the room with the client, coexisting with the client for moments of time and space. (It remains unclear whether the quality of presence is conveyed in distance counseling or not.) When therapeutic presence exists, an unseen, unspoken connection exists between the helper and the client. Therapeutic presence is most commonly defined as the quality of self or way of being that helpers bring to the therapeutic encounter (Geller & Greenberg, 2002).

Therapeutic presence involves a giving of the self, emerging out of both qualities of accessibility and centeredness. Being **accessible** implies being available and being open to what is happening in the moment with the client, in a sense in an unedited fashion. Being **centered** involves the capacity to be so aware of and grounded in your own inner experience that your own energy remains stable and is not shaken even in the midst of strong client emotion. As Gehart and McCollum (2008) observe, from this perspective "the therapist must be able to fully encounter the client's experience while maintaining the ability to observe his or her own reactions and experiences and to act thoughtfully based on the confluence of these aspects of the relationship" (p. 178). Traditionally, it has been challenging to teach the concept and skills of therapeutic presence to trainees, yet emerging studies are using mindfulness training as a means for developing therapeutic presence (Geller & Greenberg, 2002; Gehart & McCollum, 2008). Research on mindfulness training indicates that such practice increases one's capacity to regulate mood and increases positive affect by increasing the ability of the prefrontal cortex in the brain to shut down stress responses from the brain's limbic system, allowing oneself to readily calm and self-soothe in moments of stress and crisis. Gehart and McCollum (2008) note that the parallels between mindfulness and therapeutic presence are remarkably similar. Some research has discovered that having clinicians who meditated prior to counseling sessions resulted in better treatment outcomes for clients (Grepmair et al., 2007).

Positive Regard

Positive regard, also called **respect**, is the ability to prize or value the client as a person with worth and dignity (Rogers, 1957). Communication of positive regard has a number of important functions in establishing an effective therapeutic relationship, including the communication of willingness to work with the client, interest in the client as a person, and acceptance of the client. Farber and Doolin (2011) conclude that "therapists' provision of positive regard is strongly indicated (by the research) in practice" (p. 183). In fact, these authors go on to say that "there is virtually no research-driven reason to withhold positive regard" from any client (p. 183). Their meta-analysis of positive regard found that this facilitative condition is especially important in situations wherein a nonminority helper is working with a minority client. Egan (2014) has identified several components of positive regard: having a sense of commitment to the client, suspending critical judgment, and showing competence and care. Positive regard also involves expressing warmth to clients (Rogers, 1957; Farber & Doolin, 2011).

Commitment

Commitment means you are willing to work with the client and are interested in doing so. It is translated into actions such as being on time for appointments, reserving time for the client's exclusive use, ensuring privacy during sessions, maintaining confidentiality, and applying skills to help the client. Lack of time and lack of concern are two major barriers to communicating a sense of commitment. Egan (2014) points out that commitment also involves a sense of being on the client's side. He states, "It is as if you are saying to the client, working with you is worth my time and energy" (p. 47).

Nonjudgmental Attitude

A **nonjudgmental attitude** is the helper's capacity to suspend judgment of the client's actions or motives and to avoid condemning or condoning the client's thoughts, feelings, or actions. It may also be described as the helper's acceptance of the client without conditions or reservations, although it does not mean that the helper supports or agrees with all the client says or does. A helper conveys a nonjudgmental attitude by warmly accepting the client's expressions and experiences without expressing disapproval or criticism. For example, suppose a client states, "I can't help cheating on my wife. I love her, but I've got this need to be with other women." The helper who responds with regard and respect might say something like, "You feel pulled between your feelings for your wife and your need for other women." This response neither condones nor criticizes the client's feelings and behaviors. In contrast, a helper who states, "What a mess! You got married because you love your wife. Now you're fooling around with other women," conveys criticism and lack of respect for the client as a unique human being.

The experience of having positive regard for clients can also be identified by the presence of certain (covert) thoughts and feelings, such as, "I feel good when I'm with this person," or "I don't feel bothered or uncomfortable with what this person is telling me."

Competence and Care

As helpers, we convey positive regard and respect by taking steps to ensure that we are competent and able to work with the clients who come to us for help. This means that we get supervision, consultation, and continuing education to maintain and improve our skills. It also means understanding that we are not know-it-alls and that we keep on learning and growing even after getting our degrees and working in the field. It also means that we act in principled ways with clients. When we are confronted with a client we cannot work with, we use an ethical referral process. Above all else, we do not use clients for our own needs, and we are careful not to behave in any way that would exploit clients. We also are careful to pursue agendas of the client rather than our own (Egan, 2014). Keeping the client's agenda in focus, as Egan (2014) states, is similar to not rushing to judgment about clients. Egan (2010) concludes that we are here to help clients pursue *their agendas* rather than pushing our own values and goals onto clients. *We need to recognize that the latter instance is an ethical violation of all of the professional codes for helping.*

Warmth

In his earliest writings, Rogers spoke of positive regard as **nonpossessive warmth**. Although warmth is hard to define operationally, we can connote the meaning of the term through the various kinds of interactions we have with other people. All of us know persons with whom we interact and feel some immediate connection from being in their presence. Also, we can recollect a chill that comes over a room or surrounds us when interacting with other folks who may be cold and distant in their approach.

A primary way in which warmth is communicated is by supporting nonverbal behaviors such as voice tone, eye contact, facial animation and expressions, gestures, and touch. Johnson (2014) describes some nonverbal cues that express warmth or coldness. For example, warmth is expressed with a soft tone of voice; a harsh tone of voice reflects coldness. Maintaining some eye contact, smiling, and using welcoming gestures also reflect warmth. Remember that these behaviors may be interpreted differently by clients from various ethnic, racial, and cultural groups. For example, in some cultures direct eye contact is considered disrespectful, particularly with a person of authority or an elder (Sue & Sue, 2013).

An important aspect of the nonverbal dimension of warmth is touch. In times of emotional stress, many clients welcome a well-intentioned touch. The difficulty with touch is that it may have a different meaning to the client than the one you intended to convey. In deciding whether to use touch, it is important to consider the level of trust between you and the client, whether the *client* may perceive the touch as sexual, the client's history associated with touch (occasionally a client will associate touch with punishment or abuse and will say, "I can't stand to be touched"), and the client's cultural group (whether touch is respectful and valued). Also, because of all the clients who present with trauma history, it is important to observe clear boundaries surrounding touch. Check with the client and discuss these boundaries first.

Warmth can also be expressed to clients through selected verbal responses. One way to express warmth is to use enhancing statements that portray some positive aspect or attribute about the client, such as, "It's great to see how well you're handling this situation," "You're really expressing yourself well," or "You've done a super job on this action plan." Enhancing statements offer positive reinforcement to clients and to be effective must be sincere, deserved, and accurate. Farber and Doolin (2011) conclude that it is probably insufficient for helpers to simply feel good about their clients. Instead, helpers need to communicate these positive feelings verbally when they are in the client's presence (though without gushing). The belief that one's helper "cares about me" serves a critical function in the helping relationship, especially as Farber and Doolin (2011) point out, in times of stress.

Caveats and Adaptations of Positive Regard

All three of the facilitative conditions, but especially positive regard, are related to the facilitation of the working alliance and the development of trust as well as to relationship ruptures in the helping relationship. Farber and Doolin (2011) recommend that helpers monitor and adjust their contribution of positive regard and adjust it as a function of particular client needs and characteristics. They conclude that "the research demonstrates that therapists vary in the extent to which they are able to convey positive regard to their patients, and clients vary in the extent to which they need, elicit, and/or benefit from a therapist's positive regard." (p. 184). These authors believe that the inevitable ruptures that do occur in the therapeutic alliance over the course of helping are not only the result of the helper's "technical errors" but also the helper's "occasional inability to demonstrate minimally facilitative levels of positive regard and support" (p. 184). In the next section, we explore how the working alliance is developed, tested, and sustained in the therapeutic process.

The Working Alliance

Horvath, Del Re, Fluckiger, and Symonds (2011) point out that the therapeutic alliance has a lengthy history in psychotherapy, beginning with the work of Freud, although all therapeutic approaches consider the alliance to be very important. The term **working alliance** was coined by Greenson (1967), who viewed the relationship as a sort of therapeutic collaboration and partnership in which counselor and client pull together in a joint venture, much like rowing a boat. It is important to note that the working alliance is related to but not synonymous with the therapeutic relationship. The working alliance can be thought of as what has been achieved between the helper and client as a result of the effective implementation of the therapeutic relationship elements. The working alliance is a way to think about *how* or in what ways the helper and client are working together (Muran and Barber, 2010).

Three Parts of the Alliance

Bordin (1994) expanded Greenson's work and noted specifically that this alliance comprises three parts:

1. Agreement on therapeutic *goals*

2. Agreement on therapeutic *tasks*

3. An *emotional bond* between client and therapist

Safran and Muran (2006) conceptualize the working alliance as an ongoing process of negotiation between the helper and the client that occurs at both conscious and unconscious levels. These more current conceptualizations of the working alliance emphasize the active collaboration between the helper and client, much like we emphasize in the practice nexus of this book. The alliance itself is not something that works independently of other processes in therapy. As Horvath et al. (2011) observe, the alliance is not really something the helper "builds," but rather something that is "forged," as it is "an essential and inseparable part of everything that happens in therapy" (p. 56). The alliance is also something that matters "in all forms of therapy, including treatments mediated through some media" such as the Internet, the telephone and so forth (Horvath et al., 2011, p. 56). Even when there is not face-to-face contact, as in distance counseling, the helper and client must establish a collaborative way to work together.

Empirical Support for the Working Alliance

Much research connects the quality of this working alliance to therapeutic outcomes. In fact, the quality and strength of the working alliance is one of the "strongest and most robust predictors of treatment success" (Horvath et al., 2011, p. 56). Overall, these data, summarized by Horvath et al. (2011), suggest that such an alliance needs to be founded early in therapy, may wax and wane over time, re-emerges during times of crisis, and may be especially influential with more severe client issues. Also, it may be more challenging for helpers to establish a sound working alliance with some kinds of clients, such as those who have high interpersonal anxiety or those diagnosed with personality disorders (Horvath et al., 2011).

The working alliance is also impacted by the skills of the helper, particularly negative behaviors such as exhibiting a take-charge attitude early in the helping process, displaying a lack of warmth, premature interpretation, and irritability. These data are underscored by interactional data suggesting that what is most important in establishing a positive working alliance is that the helper-client interactions are not hostile or negative (Horvath et al., 2011).

In addition, therapists appear to vary in their capacity to foster an effective working alliance with clients (Nissen-Lie, Monsen, & Ronnestad, 2010). A recent study found that one explanation for this might be the quality of therapists' personal lives (Nissen-Lie, Hoglend, Monsen, & Ronnestad, 2013). The results of this study suggest that therapists have a greater capacity to establish a strong working alliance with clients when they are not hindered or burdened by negative events in their own lives (Nissen-Lie et al., 2013).

Working Alliance and Client Feedback

The data on the working alliance highlight the importance of revisiting the strength of the alliance throughout the entire helping process, making sure that agreement on the therapeutic tasks and goals remains consistent and that the emotional connection between the helper and client remains strong. A critical element in the efficacy of the therapeutic alliance appears to involve *client feedback* to helpers about the way clients are experiencing the alliance. Miller, Duncan, Sorrell, and Brown (2005) found that when helpers get client feedback about the quality of the alliance, there is substantial improvement in the outcomes of treatment and in the retention of clients in treatment. These findings were especially true for mandated clients most at risk for treatment failure. Notably, the system developed by Miller, Duncan, Sorrell, and Brown (2005), called the Partners for Change Outcome Management System (PCOMS), involves a brief four-item adult or child Session Rating Scale (see www.-talkingcure.com) to assess the therapeutic alliance that can be used very easily and quickly by practitioners.

Learning Activity 3.2

Working Alliance

With a partner or in a small group, discuss how the working alliance may be affected by working with clients such as the following:

1. Children
2. Adolescents
3. Older adults

4. Persons with disabilities
5. Men
6. Women
7. Clients of color
8. LGBTQ clients
9. Clients living in poverty
10. Refugee clients
11. International clients

Helper Skills and the Working Alliance

What helper skills promote a strong working alliance? Clients report that feeling understood, supported, and hopeful is connected to the strength of the working alliance, particularly in the early part of the helping process. In addition, the working alliance is also impacted by the client's trust in the helper. As Safran and Muran (2006, p. 289) noted, the alliance highlights the fact that at the most basic level the client's ability to trust and have faith in the helper plays a pivotal role in the change process.

Practitioners obviously also need to pay attention to the ways in which this working alliance is formed with various clients, particularly clients from various cultural groups (see Learning Activity 3.2).

The emotional bond reflected in the working alliance between the helper and client is greatly impacted by the level of trust between the two participants. In the following section, we discuss ways helpers develop and nurture trust within the working alliance.

Trust

Trust has been described by clients as a "core trait" in the helping relationship (Levitt, Butler, & Hill, 2006, p. 218). Johnson (2014) points out that **trust** is a complex construct and consists of multiple elements, including behaving in an ethically and morally justifiable manner, making a good-faith effort to honor one's commitments, and being reliable (p. 99). In a qualitative study, clients deepened their trust in their practitioner after taking a risk by revealing some personal vulnerability and experiencing the therapist's response to the disclosure as caring and respectful (Levitt, Butler, & Hill, 2006). Like many other variables in the helping relationship, trust is an interactional and reciprocal process; the establishment and endurance of trust throughout the relationship can depend on the behaviors and responses of both helpers and clients. However, as with other relationship variables, the responsibility for creating and maintaining trust, especially initially, is in the hands of the helper because the therapeutic relationship is not a symmetrical one and the helper role has some unique responsibilities associated with it. One of these responsibilities is to behave in ways that are more likely to engender trust.

Establishing Trust with Clients

Many clients are likely to find helpers trustworthy, at least at first, because of the status of helpers' role in society. Clients also are more likely to perceive a helper as trustworthy if she or he has acquired a reputation for honesty and for ethical and professional behavior. Likewise, a negative reputation can erode early trust in a helper. Thus, many clients, particularly those from mainstream cultural groups, may put their faith in the helper initially on the basis of role and reputation and, over the course of time, continue to trust the helping professional unless the trust is in some way abused.

Clients who are not from a mainstream cultural group may view trustworthiness differently. For these and some other clients, helpers may have to earn initial trust and work hard to sustain trust, especially as helping progresses. Trust can be difficult to establish yet is easily destroyed. Initial trust based on external factors such as the helper's role and reputation must be solidified with appropriate actions and behaviors by the helper during successive interactions.

Johnson (2014) points out that many successive consistent behaviors are necessary to establish trust, but just one inconsistent behavior is all it takes to destroy it. Once destroyed or diminished, trust is extremely difficult to rebuild. Trust also can be damaged when the helper acts in any way that abuses the inherent power ascribed to the role as helper. For example, if the helper makes unilateral decisions about the client and the helping process and does not collaborate with the client, this abuse of power will diminish trust. Abuse of power may be particularly damaging when you are working with clients who are from nonmainstream cultural groups and who have been disempowered because of their race, ethnicity, income level, sexual orientation, religion, disability, or gender.

Whether the helper's trustworthiness becomes an issue may also depend on the age of the client, the client's history with other helpers, and the client's trauma history. Children often trust helpers very readily unless they have had a prior bad experience with a helper in which their trust was violated or unless they have a trauma history. Regardless of age, almost all clients who have trauma histories will have greater issues in trusting a helper than clients who do not.

The behaviors that contribute most importantly to trustworthiness include helper congruence or consistency of verbal and nonverbal behavior, nonverbal acceptance of client disclosures, nonverbal responsiveness and dynamism, dependability and consistency between talk and actions, confidentiality, openness and honesty, accurate and reliable information giving, and nondefensive reflections/interpretations of clients' "tests of trust." Incongruence, judgmental or evaluative reactions, and passivity quickly erode any trust that has developed.

Clients' Tests of Helper Trustworthiness

Trust between helpers and clients does not always develop automatically. Clients need to be assured that the helping process will be structured to meet their needs and that the helper will not take advantage of their vulnerability (Johnson, 2014). Usually clients develop trust after they first scrutinize the helper by engaging in subtle maneuvers to determine the helper's trustworthiness (Levitt, Butler, & Hill, 2006). Fong and Cox (1983) call these maneuvers "tests of trust" and liken them to small trial balloons sent up to see how they fly before the client decides whether to send up the big balloon. Practitioners may be insensitive to such tests of trust and fail to realize that trust is the client's real concern. Instead of responding to the trust issue or to the process level of the message, helpers may respond just to the content, the surface of the message.

Another perspective on client tests of trust is offered by **control-mastery theory** (Silberschatz, 2005; Weiss, 2002). According to **control-mastery theory**, clients are motivated to pursue life-enhancing goals but also are

afraid to do so because of "pathogenic beliefs" that tell them that in moving toward their goals, they will endanger themselves or others (Weiss, 2002, p. 2). Weiss (2002) asserts that these pathogenic beliefs are developed in early childhood, usually through traumatic experiences between the child and the caregivers and siblings. For example, if parents neglect a child, then the child may develop the pathogenic belief that he or she would be and even should be neglected by other people as well, including, of course, the therapist. During the counseling process, clients work to *disprove* these pathogenic beliefs, which are usually unconscious (out of awareness), by testing them in relationship to the helper, hoping that the helper will pass these tests. Typically this testing unfolds in a series of trial actions, usually verbal ones, which, according to the client's beliefs, should impact the helper in a particular way. If the helper does *not* respond in the predictable fashion, then the client will perceive the helper as passing the trust test and will feel safer to proceed.

Weiss (2002, p. 2) provides the following example of how this testing may occur in the actual practice process:

A female (client) who unconsciously believed that she had to comply with male authorities lest she hurt them, felt endangered by her therapy with a male therapist. She feared that she would have to accept poor interpretations or follow bad advice. Her plan for the opening days of therapy was to reassure herself against this danger. She tested her belief that she would hurt the therapist if she disagreed with him. First she tested indirectly, then progressively more directly. The therapist passed her tests; he was not upset, and after about 6 months' time the (client) had largely overcome her fear of complying with the therapist, and so became relatively comfortable and cooperative.

We hope that this example makes clear that the helper's task is to decipher what the test of trust is and to respond so that the client's belief is *not confirmed*. If a client believes the helper will be judgmental and

---

Learning Activity 3.3

Trust

With a partner or in a small group, develop responses to the following questions:

1. For clients belonging to a mainstream cultural group or from racial/cultural backgrounds similar to your own:
   a. How does trust develop during therapeutic interactions?
   b. How is trust violated during therapeutic interactions?

c. How does it feel to have your trust in someone else violated?
d. What are 10 things a helper can do (or 10 behaviors to engage in) to build trust? Of the 10, select 5 that are most important and rank these from 1 (*most critical or top priority to establish trust*) to 5 (*least critical or least priority to establish trust*).

2. Complete the same 4 questions listed for clients of color or from a racial/cultural background distinctly different from your own.

rejecting, then the helper will consistently show respect and acceptance. If a client believes that the helper will be domineering or autocratic, then the helper responds by being nonintrusive. Shilkret (2008) describes the use of control-mastery theory in the management of a long-term case in which she relates the client's test of trust via his pathogenic beliefs to the way in which he developed transference with her. She notes: "Clients in treatment will continuously, but unconsciously, assess the therapy relationship to determine if it is safe to recall traumatizing memories and the powerful affects associated with those memories. The client will do this by unconsciously testing the therapist in the transference and watching the therapist's response. But the greater the trauma, the more evidence the client will need to feel unconsciously reassured that it is safe" (p. 289). We discuss more about transference in the next major section of the chapter, as well as its "cousin," countertransference.

Tests of Trust in Cross-Cultural Helping

Tests of trust may occur more frequently and with more emotional intensity in cross-cultural helping, often because clients from nondominant groups experienced or are experiencing oppression, discrimination, and overt and covert racism. As a result, these clients may feel more vulnerable in interpersonal interactions such as helping ones, which involve self-disclosure and an unequal power base. During initial helping interactions, clients with diverse backgrounds are likely to behave in ways that minimize their vulnerability and maximize their self-protection (Sue & Sue, 2013). In U.S. culture, European American helpers may be viewed automatically as members of the power elite. We take the position that it may be particularly unwise for clients to trust a helper *initially* until the helper behaviorally *demonstrates* trustworthiness and credibility—specifically until the helper shows that he or she: (1) will not recreate an oppressive atmosphere of any kind in the helping interaction; (2) does not engage in discrimination, racist attitudes, and behaviors; and (3) has some understanding and awareness of the client's racial and cultural affiliation (see Learning Activity 3.3).

The communication of facilitative conditions, particularly positive regard, seems critical in the development of the level of trust necessary for the effective formation of a sound working alliance. Farber and Doolin (2011) found that the presence of this relational factor was especially salient when nonminority helpers worked with minority clients. They assert that potential client mistrust of the therapist stemming both from societal racial history and also neglect of minority clients by mental health communities may interfere with the formation of a working alliance. They conclude that "the possibility of such mistrust and of

related difficulties forging an effective therapeutic relationship may well be attenuated by clear indications of the therapist's positive regard, in turn facilitating the likelihood of a positive outcome" (Farber & Doolin, 2011, p. 182).

This assertion has been supported empirically in several studies of the impact of microaggressions in therapy (Owen, Tao, Imel, Wampold, & Rodolfa, 2014). In the most recent of these studies, the results echoed those of earlier studies that found that clients' perceptions of microaggressions are negatively associated with the working alliance in the helping process presumably because these offenses impact clients' levels of trust "conveying the message that therapy is not emotionally safe" (Owen et al., 2014, p. 289). An important finding in this study was that it was not only the presence of a microaggression that resulted in poorer alliance ratings but also whether the therapist discussed or ignored the cultural rupture. For clients who experienced a microaggression with no discussion, alliance ratings were lower compared to clients who either did not experience a microaggression or experienced such an offense but had discussion of it in the helping session, "illuminating the power of addressing missteps that can occur in therapy" (Owen et al. 2014, p. 288).

Transference and Countertransference

In addition to the facilitative conditions and the work- **LO2** ing alliance, the helping relationship includes elements of past relationships that both the client and the therapist bring to the current encounter. Historically, dynamically oriented helpers have referred to these components as *transference* and *countertransference* (see Learning Activity 3.4). Current interpretations of these two concepts are rooted in what is known as a **relational model** of helping. In a relational model, the emphasis is on the interaction between the two people—for example, the client and the helper—not just on the client. In the helping process, both the helper and the client are seen as participants cocreating enactments that represent configurations of transference and countertransference (Ornstein & Ganzer, 2005, p. 571). Relational models use the term *dysfunctional relational schemas* to describe transferential and countertransferential notions. Our goal, as illustrated in the second Chapter Learning Outcome, is to help you identify issues related to both transference and countertransference that impact the helping relationship and working alliance with clients.

Manifestations of Transference

Contemporary definitions of transference suggest that it has two components. One component is the client and the client's past. As Corey, Corey, Corey, and Callanan (2015) suggest, from this perspective **transference** is the client's projection of feelings and fantasies that are reactions to significant others in the client's past onto the helper (p. 47). The second component of transference is the interpersonal dynamic between the helper and client. As Ornstein and Ganzer (2005) observe, from this perspective transference involves the "here-and-now experience of the client with the therapist who has a role in eliciting and shaping the transference" (p. 567). As an example, a client may have been raised by a caregiver who was emotionally distant and unavailable to respond to the child's feelings. In therapy, the client may be reluctant to deal with feelings. When encouraged to do so by the helper, the client may react by becoming angry or withdrawn.

Transference tends to occur regardless of the gender of the helper (Kahn, 1991) and, according to Kohut (1984), may occur because old unmet needs of the client resurface in the presence of an empathic helper. In addition, clients' transferential reactions can include any significant other, not just parents—such as siblings or anyone involved in an earlier and traumatic situation. Transference can be positive, negative, or mixed. A positive transference can strengthen the helping relationship when the practitioner provides missing elements of understanding, impartiality, and reliability (Levitt, Butler, & Hill, 2006, p. 318).

Often the transference (positive or negative) is a form of re-enactment of the client's familiar and old pattern or template of relating. The value of it is that through the transference clients may be trying to show how they felt at an earlier time when treated in a particular way. Transference often occurs when the therapist (usually inadvertently) does or says something that triggers unfinished business with the client, often with members of the client's family of origin—parents and siblings or significant others. Helpers can make use of the transference, especially a negative one, by helping clients see that what they expect of us, they also may expect of other people in their lives. If, for example, a client wants to make the helper look bad, then that could be the client's intent with other individuals as well. One study (Hoglend et al., 2006) found that clients with troubled family-of-origin issues benefited more from therapy working with transference issues, lending support to the notion that transference is some form of re-enactment of impaired object relations.

Management of Transference

Gelso and colleagues (1999) found five consistent ways in which helpers worked with client transference: focusing, interpreting, questioning, teaching, and self-disclosing. These are summarized in Box 3.1.

Relational theorists also acknowledge a constructivist, narrative approach to working with client transference. Rather than responding to the client from an objective and detached position in which the client's reactions are analyzed and/or interpreted, the helper works collaboratively with the client to co-construct a number of different possible realities instead of one "true" interpretation of the client's experience (Ornstein & Ganzer, 2005). Also, as these authors note, what is potentially transformative in handling the transference is that the helper "must always view the client's perceptions as plausible given the client's history and lived experience" (p. 567). For example, Renata discloses that she felt disregarded by her mother when growing up and believed that her needs were not important to her mother. Although this statement represents some part of Renata's past experience, it would be wise to wonder aloud with Renata whether she has felt disregarded by the helper as well. Usually, as Teyber and McClure (2011) point out, there is "a kernel of truth" in the client's reactions toward the helper, which have in part been evoked by some aspect of the helper's behavior (p. 340). In this way, as Teyber and McClure (2011)

Learning Activity 3.4

Transference and Countertransference

In a small group or with a partner, discuss the likely transference and countertransference reactions you discover in these three cases. Feedback is provided on page 96.

1. The client is upset because you will not give her your home telephone number. She states that although you have a 24-hour on-call answering service, you are not really available to her unless you give her your home number.
2. You are an internship student, and your internship is coming to an end. You have been seeing a client for weekly sessions during your year-long internship. As termination approaches, the client becomes more and more anxious and angry with you and states that you are letting her down by forming this relationship with her and then leaving.
3. Your client has repeatedly invited you to his house for various social gatherings. Despite all you have said to him about "multiple nonprofessional relationships," he says he still feels that if you really cared about him you would be at his parties.

BOX 3.1	Ways of Working with Client Transference

1. *Focusing on the immediate relationship*: "I am aware that you seem to be feeling angry with me in today's session, and I am wondering what that means."

2. *Interpreting the meaning of the transference*: "Perhaps your feelings of anger toward me are related to the frustration of having your dad be so unavailable for you. And now I am telling you that I will be unavailable during the next month when I have surgery."

3. *Using questions to promote insight*: "Can you recall an earlier time in your life when you felt angry like you do now with me?"

4. *Teaching, advising, and educating about the transference*: "We all have times when we transfer emotional reactions from prior relationships onto other people who are significant to us. Sometimes this occurs in our helping relationship as well. When it does, it is usually useful for us to process this in the session. As I am saying this, are you aware of any particular reactions you are having about me?"

5. *Self-disclosing*: "Sure, there are times for me, too, when I react to someone in my current life with some unresolved reactions from my past. Sometimes my partner says something that triggers such a response in me. Is this something you have noticed with your partner?"

conclude, current management of transference means both comprehending and changing something about the current and real interaction between the helper and client (p. 341).

A final way in which helpers can work with transference issues is by empathically reflecting on the client's desire or wish—for example, the wish to be loved, the wish to be important, and the wish to control. (You may recall that this is, in fact, one of Neacsiu & Linehan's (2014) levels of empathic validation, articulating the unverbalized dimension of the client's communication and experience.) Often the transference acted out by the client not only includes a re-enactment of an earlier important relationship but also is a replay of how the client wishes it was (Kahn, 1991). With our client Renata in the example, the helper may say something such as the following: "Renata, I know how hard it was for you to feel overlooked by your mother. I can see that you wish you had been more important to her." Further, using a relational model, the helper may comment on what the client wishes or desires from the helper. With Renata, the helper may say something like, "Renata, I can see that in our work together it is important to you to be seen and heard and known accurately by me. Does this resonate with you as well?" Resolution of the transference process seems to occur with increased client insight, more realistic client expectations of the helper, and a more positive client view of himself or herself.

Ethnocultural Transference

Comas-Díaz (2014) has made an important contribution to the discussion of transference by her discussion of **ethnocultural transference**. She states that each therapeutic encounter involves potential projections of both "conscious and unconscious messages about the client's and the therapist's cultures" (p. 551). However, she goes on to point out that most mainstream helpers simply ignore transferential cultural issues. Alternatively, culturally sensitive helpers manage the ethnocultural transference by inquiring about similarities and differences between and among the client and helper. Comas-Díaz suggests inquiries such as, "How do you feel about my being from a different culture than you?" or "How do you feel about our being from similar cultures as we work together?" (p. 552)

Manifestations of Countertransference

Sheree, a beginning practicum student, finds herself working with Ronnie, a teenage boy who has been mandated to see a counselor. She has seen Ronnie for six sessions. She describes him as "nonresponsive." She states that he sits with his cap down over his eyes so he can't really look at her directly and that he responds with, "I don't know" to her inquiries. Sheree feels more and more frustrated. She states that she has tried so hard to establish a good relationship with Ronnie but feels that everything she tries is useless. It seems that Ronnie has succeeded in challenging her need to be helpful to him, and she is finding herself becoming more impatient with him in the sessions. This is an example of countertransference.

Countertransference includes feelings the therapist has about the client that are in some way atypical reactions either to a particular client or to clients in general (Nutt Williams, Hayes, & Fauth, 2008, p. 310). Such reactions may be covert and include thoughts, feelings, and visceral body sensations, or they may be overt behaviors (Gelso & Hayes, 2007). Nutt Williams, Hayes, and Fauth (2008) take the position, and we agree with it, that all helpers, "no matter how experienced, credentialed, or otherwise reputable, experience countertransference with some frequency" (p. 310). Hayes, Gelso, and Hummel (2011) believe that unresolved conflicts within the helper are at the heart of countertransference. The data on countertransference as summarized by Hayes and colleagues (2011) suggest that countertransference does adversely affect treatment outcomes in therapy. Hurtful countertransference that comes from our own woundedness occurs when: (1) we are blinded to an important area of exploration; (2) we focus on an issue more of our own than pertaining to the client; (3) we use the client for vicarious or real gratification; (4) we emit subtle cues that "lead" the client; (5) we make interventions not in the client's best interest; and, most importantly, (6) we adopt the roles the client wants us to play in his or her old script.

However, as contemporary relational theorists note, not all countertransferential reactions are damaging, unless they are acted out within the helping relationship. Countertransference can alert helpers to areas in which they feel stuck or puzzled and, as a result, helpers can begin to sort out what is going on rather than trying to "fix" the uncertainty (Ornstein & Ganzer, 2005). And in some situations it can even be helpful to self-disclose some of your countertransferential reactions in the client's presence as long as this is done without blame for the client and conveyed with respect and regard.

In the preceding example, Sheree might say something to Ronnie like the following:

> "You know, Ronnie, we have been working together now for approximately 6 weeks, and I feel like we are staying in the same place. I don't think we have moved backward, but I also don't think we have moved forward. I think we are just spinning our wheels in the same place, and I wish we could find some way to work together. I wish I could do or say something that would help you feel like coming to see me is worth it."

This is a situation that requires much discernment, and for the beginning helper the decision to self-disclose needs to be talked through with a supervisor.

Management of Countertransference

Hayes, Gelso, and Hummel (2011) and Rosenberger and Hayes (2002) reviewed the research on countertransference and concluded that uncontrolled countertransference has an adverse effect on therapy outcome. Moreover, the data they summarize indicate that countertransference management is effective in controlling the manifestation of negative helper reactions, and such management is also related somewhat to treatment outcome as well. Managing countertransference is an important clinical task for practitioners (Gelso, Latts, Gomez, & Fassinger, 2002). For us as helpers to manage our countertransference responses therapeutically, we must become aware of what they are and what they mean to us.

This self-awareness is depicted in what Gelso and Hayes (2007) refer to as the countertransference interaction hypothesis, simply meaning that countertransference is the result between client material or attributes known as *triggers* and therapist conflicts and vulnerabilities known as *origins*. Support for this view of countertransference has been provided by Tishby and Wiseman (2014), who concluded that "it is this interaction between the client's responses as perceived by the therapist and the unresolved conflicts which produces CT dynamics that are *unique* to a therapeutic dyad" (p. 371). Gaining awareness is a useful initial step in managing countertransference. When we are unaware of our responses, they may get projected onto or acted out in the therapy session. For example, if Tia is unaware of her covert feelings of aggressiveness surrounding "helpless females," when she encounters a needy, dependent female client she may behave in a way that conveys disrespect and dislike for the client.

Sometimes a sort of role reversal occurs, and the client is more aware of our own woundedness than we are. In these situations, the client unknowingly becomes the healer and the therapist inappropriately benefits, but the client's growth is stymied. For example, Ricardo may be unaware of his need to talk about himself, fueled by growing up with an inattentive and depressed caregiver. When his client Anna detects Ricardo's tendency to turn the focus onto himself during the session, she provides support for him to do so!

3.4 Feedback

Transference and Countertransference

1. The transference is the client's emotional reaction to not having you available to her at all times. Possible countertransference reactions by you include frustration, anger, and feelings of failure.
2. The transference is the client's feeling of abandonment as termination approaches. Potential countertransference includes sadness, irritation, and pressure.
3. The transference is the client's expectation for you to be socially involved with him. Possible countertransference includes feelings of letting him down, being upset, and impatience.

BOX 3.2	Interpersonal Process Notes

During sessions, jot down your thoughts, feelings, intuitions, sensations, and dreams.

How do feel when you're with this client?

How and where are you blocked with this client?

What is going on between the two of you?

What is going on inside of you when there is a blockage or an issue?

What keeps you from saying what you want to—what you feel?

What keeps you from sitting still and being silent?

How is your therapist activity maintaining the status quo—or moving the client?

What stops the flow in your session?

What disables you?

How is the client using you?

What are the client's expectations that force you into a certain mold or way of being with him or her?

What are you doing to the client—are you forcing him or her into a certain way of being with you?

What do your *imagination* and your *reveries* tell you about this client?

What symbols come to your mind to describe the process with this client? (Draw something.)

What about this client and session make you come alive? Make you go dead?

How are you afraid of disappointing the client?

What is lying behind the client's words?

How do you create reflective space in and around the session for both you and the client?

Where does play (in the best sense of the word) occur in this session?

Does the language you use reflect your own voice, or does it reflect more of a textbook voice?

What goes on in your body during this session with this client?

What do you do to be seen as an ideal person, to avoid carrying a shadow?

How are you taking care of yourself in this session with this client?

Source: Abridged from the presentation "The Person of the Analyst," by Mel Marshak, Ph.D., May 11, 1999, Pittsburgh, Jung Society. Used with permission of Mel Marshak, Ph.D.

Countertransference and Self-insight

Often a clue that we are having a countertransference reaction comes from our awareness of strong emotions such as those we described in the case involving Sheree. Awareness of countertransference is also dependent on *self-insight*—that is, intentional attention to what is going on inside us (Gelso & Hayes, 2002). One of the main reasons why, during and after training, helpers seek and receive individual and group consultation and supervision is that countertransference is inevitable and will occur throughout each helper's professional career. In Box 3.2 we present examples of interpersonal process notes derived from M. Marshak (personal communication, May 11, 1999) that you may find useful for developing awareness of your own reactions to clients. When consultation and supervision do not resolve a helper's reaction, a subsequent step in managing countertransference is to seek personal counseling. It is important for helpers in training to make a lifelong commitment to self-awareness. As Nutt Williams, Hayes, and Fauth (2008) note, experiencing countertransference is a fact of life for helpers: "To avoid countertransference reactions altogether, a therapist would either need to stop seeing clients or overcome the basic human condition"

(p. 310). Consultation, supervision, and personal counseling are important components of the self-awareness process. This is especially important in working with your own unresolved conflicts.

Countertransference and Conceptual Understanding

Being aware of our reactions is the important first step in managing countertransference. A second step is to develop what Gelso et al. (2002, p. 862) call *conceptual understanding*: hunches about what is occurring in the moment in the relationship with the client. This kind of understanding helps to prevent an automatic or reflexive response that may be counterproductive (Teyber & McClure, 2011). For instance, Tia, in the previous example, blurts out to a dependent female client, "Hannah, I am sure that you can figure this one out on your own." Alternatively, she may act out her covert aggression by terminating the session early or by being dismissive of the client's concerns. In acting or speaking thoughtlessly, she may inadvertently trigger a re-enactment of her client's history—that is, a relational pattern that is similar to an unproductive pattern with a significant person in Hannah's past or current life. In this way, the client's transference may become evoked. For example, the client may feel dismissed by Tia in same way in which the client felt dismissed by her primary caregiver and by her partner and other significant people in her life. (This is an example of the way in which transference and countertransference are often related in the helping relationship.) Self-insight without this second step of conceptual understanding is limited in preventing negative countertransferential reactions. By the same token, conceptual understanding without self-insight and awareness also seems ineffective at managing countertransference (Hofness & Tracey, 2010). As Nutt Williams, Hayes, and Fauth (2008) point out, to prevent negative countertransferential reactions from popping up, "therapists may need to have enough self-insight to know that they are experiencing countertransference feelings and also to have sufficient conceptualizing skills to know what to do with their reactions" (p. 311).

Countertransference and Helper Responsibility

This scenario points to a third step in the management of countertransference: the helper needs to be willing to examine and to take responsibility for his or her possible contributions to the issues that are emerging between the helper and client. At this point, Tia may say something to her client like the following: "Hannah, I feel like what I just said to you about your concern may have sounded dismissive. I am sorry if this is so. Can you tell me what you experienced when you heard me say that?" Obviously, such a response requires a great deal of *empathy* from the helper. Empathic attunement, both to oneself and to the client, is a fourth step in managing countertransference (Gelso et al., 2002). When the helper's anxiety and/or shame get triggered, however, the helper is likely to respond defensively to the client and to perpetuate the transferential-countertransferential conflict, thus masking any empathy the helper may feel.

An important consideration in managing our countertransferential reactions is to engage in practices that foster our self-awareness and self-insight such as self-care behaviors and reflective thinking. Meditation/mindfulness by helpers also has been found to be a great way to develop such self-awareness (Nutt Williams, Hayes, & Fauth, 2008). As these authors explain, "Mindfulness includes not just awareness but also acceptance of your experiences and acceptance may be a pivotal component in managing countertransference. When therapists are able to recognize, without judgment, their reactions to

clients, no matter how unpleasant or painful, several benefits may ensue. Therapists are less likely to act out on countertransference thoughts and feelings" (p. 312). In short, mindfulness is a skill that allows us as helpers to be less reactive, not only to clients but also to ourselves as well.

Countertransference and Boundaries

The final step in managing both transference and countertransference is to develop and use boundaries. Gelso and Hayes (2002) refer to this step as "*self-integration*" and say that in the helping process it "manifests itself as a recognition of ego boundaries or an ability to differentiate self from other" (p. 297). When we are without boundaries in the helping process, we either let too much in from the client's transference reactions or send out too much from ourselves to the client, causing the client discomfort and pain. In the first case, we fail to protect ourselves; in the second, we fail to protect the client.

Both scenarios can be managed with the use of internal **protective** and **containing boundaries** (Mellody, 2003). A protective boundary allows you to hold yourself in high esteem even when a client is saying something negative to you. When a client expresses a negative transferential reaction, you can establish a protective boundary for yourself by asking yourself whether the client's reaction is true for you and whether you contributed to the reaction. If you did, it is important to take the client's reaction in and be responsive to it while recognizing that it does not lessen your self-worth. Establishing a protective boundary is not the same as walling yourself off. If you withdraw behind a wall of anger, preoccupation, silence, worry, sadness, and so on, then nothing the client says or does reaches you (Mellody, 2003). Such a response is tantamount to being dismissive of the client's concern. Walling yourself off is appropriate only when a client is being clearly offensive to you, perhaps shouting an obscenity or a racial slur, and you cannot leave or you choose not to leave (Mellody, 2003).

Protective boundaries are also important to empathic understanding. They allow you to feel the client's feelings without reacting to the feelings as if they belong to you. The containing boundary is what helps us avoid leaking our countertransferential reactions onto the client. Tia, for example, lacked a containing boundary and leaked her feelings of impatience to her client. When we do not have good containing boundaries, it is difficult to provide the sort of holding environment that our clients need, because we have difficulty containing emotional reactions.

Ethnocultural Countertransference

Comas-Díaz (2014) also discusses ethnocultural countertransference. Recall from our discussion that she believes many clinicians, especially those from dominant cultural groups, simply ignore cultural manifestations of transference and countertransference. Yet, as she points out, both practitioners and clients imprint their ethnic, cultural, and racial experiences into the helping process. A very real part of self-awareness becomes cultural awareness. She describes some common **ethnocultural countertransferential** reactions in *interethnic* helping dyads. These include denial of cultural differences, excessive curiosity from the helper about some aspect of the client's culture, guilt, pity, aggression, and ambivalence. Comas-Díaz (2014) also points out that ethnocultural countertransference occurs within *intraethnic* cultural dyads as well. Forms of ethnocultural countertransference within intraethnic cultural dyads include: overidentification; shared victimization; distancing; survivor guilt; multicultural myopia; ambivalence; and anger.

Ruptures in the Alliance

At times, tears and ruptures occur in the course of the working alliance. These **relationship ruptures** are defined as tension or breakdown in the collaborative relationship between the helper and client (Safran & Muran, 2006). Ruptures can range from very minor tensions to something much more dramatic and are currently thought to revolve around disagreements about the tasks and/or goals of helping and strains in the helper-client bond (Safran, Muran, & Eubanks-Carter, 2011). Also, cross-racial tensions can result in relationship ruptures. As we mentioned, when clients experience racial or other kinds of microaggressions, relationship ruptures are likely to occur. As Owen et al. (2014) indicate, "(c)onceptually, microaggressions can be thought of as a special case of ruptures in therapy wherein experiences of discrimination and oppression from the larger society are recapitulated which places the therapeutic relationship under duress and strain" (p. 287).

Research on the effects of relationship ruptures is somewhat limited, but Safran et al. (2011) argue that because much data link the quality of the therapeutic alliance to outcome, the process of repairing relationship ruptures is important and is also supported by increasing evidence. Ruptures provide indicators about times when the strength of the working alliance may have waned or instances when agreement on the therapeutic tasks and goals may have drifted.

Safran and Muran (2000) originally viewed ruptures as windows that let helpers see something about the client's interpersonal relationships (p. 85). Safran and Muran (2006) now describe relationship ruptures as "transference–countertransference enactments" by both the client and the therapist (p. 288). As they explain, clients often re-enact an early, difficult, perhaps traumatic life experience and try to pull the helper into assuming a particular role that confirms the client's early experience (p. 85). When helpers allow themselves to get pulled into this role, ruptures result. When a rupture occurs, it can be repaired and begin to heal if the helper can recognize her or his contributions to the rupture and then acknowledge them directly to the client. This acknowledgment provides a new relational experience for the client and is a major way in which the therapeutic relationship becomes healing (Safran & Muran, 2000, p. 88).

Two Types of Relationship Ruptures

Safran and Muran (2006) distinguish between two types of ruptures in the therapeutic relationship: confrontation ruptures and withdrawal ruptures. In a **confrontation rupture**, the client deals directly with concerns about the relationship by confronting the helper. For example, Francine, the client, has been describing her history with her depressed and unavailable caregiver as well as current events with the same caregiver. Her helper emotionally retreats, shuts down, and does not validate her feelings about these experiences. As a result, Francine asks her practitioner directly why she seems so "nonresponsive." Safran, Muran, and Eubanks-Carter (2011) note that the type of rupture suggests differences in how the rupture is resolved. In the confrontation rupture described, the resolution "consists of moving through feelings of anger, to feelings of disappointment and hurt over having been failed by the therapist, to contacting vulnerability and the wish to be nurtured and taken care of" (Safran, Muran, & Eubanks-Carter, 2011, p. 234). In this example, healing of the rupture would move forward by having the practitioner help Francine express her feelings of anger and hurt over the helper's lack of responsiveness and also express her desire to be more nurtured by the helper.

In a **withdrawal rupture**, clients express their concern about the relationship by "withdrawing, deferring, or even complying" (Safran & Muran, 2006, p. 287). For example, the client, Tepe, has been describing his experiences of being sexually abused by a priest while growing up. Tepe's pain and sadness overwhelm his helper, who jumps in and tries to "fix" his feelings. Tepe's failure to show up for the next session signifies an intense withdrawal rupture. In a withdrawal rupture such as this instance, the resolution "consists of moving through increasingly clearer articulations of discontent to self-assertion, in which the need for agency is realized and validated by the therapist" (Safran, Muran, & Eubanks-Carter, 2011, p. 234). In this example, healing of the rupture would be assisted by having the practitioner help Tepe articulate and assert what he wants and needs from the helper in ensuing sessions.

Summarization of Steps for Repairing Ruptures

What do the helpers we described here do now about the ruptures? First, they examine their responses to their clients in their last session. This exploration may occur alone or in consultation with a colleague, a supervisor, or a personal therapist. When they realize their contribution to the rupture, they in some way take responsibility for it. When Francine confronts the helper about her lack of responsiveness, the helper addresses the experience directly, saying something like, "You know, it's true. When you were talking about all those times your parent was not there for you, I realized that I went away from you and shut down, and in doing so, I also was not there for you. I am sorry about this." Developing awareness about ways in which we may invalidate clients with cultural messages is particularly important and finding ways to directly address the cultural invalidation or misunderstanding is critical for the healing of rupture due to microaggressions (Owen et al., 2014). Helpers also can repair ruptures by empathizing with the client's experience of or reaction to the rupture (Safran & Muran, 2000, p. 102). For example, Tepe's helper could say, "I can understand that in our last session I failed to really communicate my acceptance of your pain and sadness about the abuse. Instead I tried to think of a solution. This must have felt like I, too, was not there for you in some fundamental way because I tuned in to myself then instead of you. I apologize for my lapse."

Other common rupture-repair interventions that Safran, Muran, and Eubanks-Carter (2011) recommend include the following:

Repeat the therapeutic rationale,
Change the therapeutic task or re-address the treatment goals,
Clarify misunderstandings at a surface level,
Explore relational themes associated with the rupture, and
Link the alliance rupture to common patterns in a client's life (p. 228).

To respond effectively to ruptures, we, as helpers, need to remain open to ourselves and to our own deepest feelings, both past and present, happy and difficult (Safran & Muran, 2000, p. 75). This process of staying open to ourselves requires us to find time or make space in our lives to stay attuned to ourselves and to feel our feelings. Activities such as meditating, deep breathing, and movement can assist in this process. For a list of additional ways to repair relationship ruptures, see Table 3.2. Learning Activity 3.5 presents guided imagery for working through relationship ruptures.

TABLE 3.2   Interventions for Repairing Relationship Ruptures

Discuss the here-and-now relationship with your client as it is occurring in the session.

Invite and provide feedback on the therapeutic relationship.

Intentionally explore the client's experiences in therapy.

Attend carefully to the agreement, explicit and implicit, that you and the client make regarding the outcomes of treatment and the strategies designed to achieve these outcomes.

Take responsibility for your contribution to the relationship rupture.

Attend carefully to informed consent; provide a careful rationale for everything you do in the helping process. Revisit the therapeutic rationale frequently.

Give the client time and space to express negative feelings about the relationship.

Allow the client an opportunity to reveal fears about expressing negative feelings to you.

Empathize with the client's experience and validate the client when he or she does express a disagreement or a negative feeling.

Provide more positive feedback to the client.

Process issues related to transference.

Be aware of your own countertransference reactions, and seek consultation and supervision to process them.

Source: Harmon et al., 2005, p. 175; Safran et al., 2002; Safran, Muran, & Eubanks-Carter, 2011.

Learning Activity 3.5

Relationship Ruptures

This activity uses guided imagery to deal with a rupture in a therapeutic relationship. To complete this activity, go through each step in your imagination, or have a partner read the steps to you and close your eyes and go through each step. Then, trade roles with your partner.

1. Bring your attention to yourself. What are you currently experiencing?
2. Bring your attention to your breath. Breathe in peace, and breathe out tension.
3. When you feel ready, picture the last client you saw with whom there was some kind of tension or some breakdown in communication. If you are not yet seeing clients, then picture some other person with whom you've had such an experience.
4. In your mind's eye, recall how you knew a rupture was going on in the relationship. What were the clues or cues?

5. In your mind's eye, focus on how you responded to the rupture.
6. What happened after your response? See and feel this.
7. Focus on anything you could have done or said to repair the rupture. See and feel this.
8. Bring your attention back to yourself and your breath, and notice how you are feeling now.
9. When you are ready, bring your energy back to the environment and the room, and open your eyes if they were closed.

If you are working with a partner, then we suggest you process this imagery with that person. Otherwise, you can process it with yourself. What did you learn from this imagery about ruptures? From this activity can you take something into another relationship to help you repair a rupture? If so, what would it be?

CHAPTER SUMMARY

This chapter describes three major components of the helping relationship: the facilitative conditions of empathy, genuineness, and positive regard; the working alliance; and transference and countertransference. None of these components operates independently from the others, and during the course of therapy they are connected to and influenced by one another. The three components also are, to some degree, affected by client variables such as type and severity of problem, gender, race, and cultural affiliation, because all helping relationships are also cross-cultural ones. These components contribute to both the effective process and the outcome of therapy and are considered important in all theoretical approaches to helping. In the past decade much empirical support for these aspects of

the therapeutic relationship has emerged. Whatever else may happen in the helping process, the relationship between therapist and client is always present. As Norcross and Wampold (2011) observe, "Psychotherapy is at root a human relationship. Even when 'delivered' via distance or on a computer, psychotherapy is an irreducibly human encounter. Both parties bring themselves—their origins, culture, personalities, psychopathology, expectations, biases, defenses, and strengths—to the human relationship. Some will judge the relationship as a precondition of change and others a process of change, but all agree that it is a relational enterprise" (p. 429).

Visit CengageBrain.com for a variety of study tools and useful resources such as video examples, case studies, interactive exercises, flashcards, and quizzes.

3 Knowledge and Skill Builder

Part One

According to Learning Outcome 1 for this chapter, you will be able to communicate the three facilitative conditions to a client, given a role-play situation. Complete this activity in triads, with one person assuming the role of the helper, another assuming the role of client, and the third assuming the role of the observer. The helper's task is to communicate the behavioral aspects of empathy, genuineness, and positive regard to the client. The client shares a concern with the helper. The observer monitors the interaction, using the accompanying Checklist for Facilitative Conditions as a guide, and provides feedback after completion of the session. Each role play can last 10–15 minutes. Switch roles so each person has an opportunity to play each of the three roles. If you do not have access to another person to serve as an observer, find someone with whom you can engage in a role-played helping interaction. Record your interaction and use the accompanying checklist as a guide to reviewing your tape.

Checklist for Facilitative Conditions

Helper _____

Observer _____

Instructions: Assess the helper's communication of the three facilitative conditions by circling the number and word that best represent the helper's overall behavior during this session.

Empathy

1. **Did the helper indicate a desire to comprehend the client?**

   1   2   3   4
   A little   Somewhat   A great deal   Almost always

2. **Did the helper refer to the client's feelings?**

   1   2   3   4
   A little   Somewhat   A great deal   Almost always

3. **Did the helper discuss what appeared to be important to the client?**

   1   2   3   4
   A little   Somewhat   A great deal   Almost always

4. **Did the helper pace (match) the client's nonverbal behavior?**

   1   2   3   4
   A little   Somewhat   A great deal   Almost always

5. **Did the helper show understanding of the client's historical/cultural/ethnic background?**

   1   2   3   4
   A little   Somewhat   A great deal   Almost always

6. **Did the helper validate the client's experience?**

   1   2   3   4
   A little   Somewhat   A great deal   Almost always

Genuineness

7. **Did the helper avoid overemphasizing her or his role, position, and status?**

   1   2   3   4
   A little   Somewhat   A great deal   Almost always

8. **Did the helper exhibit congruence, or consistency, among feelings, words, nonverbal behavior, and actions?**

   1   2   3   4
   A little   Somewhat   A great deal   Almost always

9. **Was the helper appropriately spontaneous (for example, also tactful)?**

   1   2   3   4
   A little   Somewhat   A great deal   Almost always

10. **Did the helper demonstrate supporting nonverbal behaviors appropriate to the client's culture?**

    1   2   3   4
    A little   Somewhat   A great deal   Almost always

Positive Regard

11. **Did the helper demonstrate behaviors related to commitment and willingness to see the client (for example, starting on time, responding with appropriate intensity)?**

    1   2   3   4
    A little   Somewhat   A great deal   Almost always

12. **Did the helper respond verbally and nonverbally to the client without judging or evaluating the client?**

    1   2   3   4
    A little   Somewhat   A great deal   Almost always

13. **Did the helper convey warmth to the client with supporting nonverbal behaviors (soft voice tone, smiling, eye contact, touch) and verbal responses (enhancing statements)?**

    1   2   3   4
    A little   Somewhat   A great deal   Almost always

Observer comments: _____
_____
_____

Part Two

Learning Outcome 2 asks you to identify issues related to transference and countertransference that might affect the development of the helping relationship, given five written case descriptions. Read each case carefully and then identify in writing the transference/countertransference issue that is reflected in the case description. Feedback follows below.

1. You are leading a problem-solving group in a high school. The members are spending a lot of time talking about the flak they get from their parents. After a while, they start to "get the leader" and complain about all the flak they get from you.

2. You are counseling a person of the other sex who is the same age as yourself. After several weeks of seeing the client, you feel extremely disappointed and let down when the client postpones the next session.

3. You find yourself needing to terminate with a client, but you are reluctant to do so. When the client presses you for a termination date, you find yourself overcome with sadness.

4. One of your clients is constantly writing you little notes and sending you cards basically saying what a wonderful person you are.

5. You are a straight, heterosexual helper working with a gay client. Your client indicates that he has experienced discrimination at his church, which he attributes to his being gay. You ignore this comment and steer the discussion back to his presenting concern of feeling conflicted about his career choice.

3 Knowledge and Skill Builder **Feedback**

Part Two

1. *Transference:* The group members seem to be transferring their angry feelings toward their parents onto you.
2. *Countertransference:* You are having an unusually intense emotional reaction to this client (disappointment), which suggests that you are developing some affectionate feelings for the client and countertransference is occurring.
3. *Countertransference:* Some emotional attachment on your part is making it hard for you to let go of this particular client (although termination usually does involve a little sadness for all parties).
4. *Transference:* The client is allowing herself to idealize you. At this point, the transference is positive, although it could change.
5. *Countertransference:* Your silence and omission of responding to the client's experience of discrimination about being gay indicate something has been triggered in you, resulting in silence and failure to respond to this stated concern.

Listening

The quieter you become, the more you are able to hear. (Rumi)

Learning Outcomes

After completing this chapter, you will be able to:

1. In an interview situation, identify nonverbal behaviors of the person with whom you are communicating. Describe the possible meanings associated with these behaviors. The nonverbal behaviors you identify may come from any one or a combination of these four categories: (a) kinesics, or body motion; (b) paralinguistics, or voice qualities; (c) proxemics, or spatial distance in interactions; and (d) the person's general appearance.

2. From a list of three client statements, write an example of each of the four listening responses for each client statement.

3. In a 15-minute helping interview in which you function as an observer, listen for and record five key aspects of client messages that the helper needs to attend to ensure effective listening.

4. In a 15-minute role-play interview or a conversation in which you function as a listener, demonstrate at least two accurate examples of each of the four listening responses.

When someone truly hears us, it is a special gift. We can all recall times when we felt wonderful simply because someone who means something to us stood or sat with us and really listened. Conversely, we also can remember instances in which we felt frustration because someone close to us was inattentive and distracted, perhaps checking their text messages! Nichols (2009) has referred to listening as a "lost art" because of time pressures that shorten our attention span and impoverish the quality of listening in our lives (p. 2). Lindahl (2003) observes that many of us, including high-powered executives, engage in a great deal of preparation prior to speaking but less than 5 percent of us do a similar amount of preparation prior to listening. This lack of listening can undermine our most prized relationships, contribute to interpersonal conflict, and leave us with a sense of loss. Nichols (2009) observes that this loss is most severe when lack of listening occurs in relationships in which we count on the listener to pay attention, such as in a helping relationship. From a neuroscience perspective, listening responses are critical

Lindahl (2003) observes that true listening involves our "whole being" (p. 29). The all-encompassing nature of listening is depicted in the Chinese symbol for *listening* shown in Figure 4.1. In the upper left side are squares that represent two ears. Squares in the upper right side represent two eyes. Underneath the "eye" squares is a line that represents "undivided attention," and in the lower right side of the symbol is a curved line that represents the heart. As Lindahl (2003) notes, this symbol "indicates that listening is more than hearing words; it encompasses our ears, eyes, undivided attention, and heart" (p. 29).

Ear — Eyes — Undivided attention — Heart

FIGURE 4.1 Chinese Symbol for *Listening*

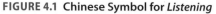

components of the helping process because these supportive kinds of helper responses activate both "clients executive networks and their self-reflective abilities" (Cozolino, 2010, p. 38).

Three Steps of Listening

Listening is a prerequisite for all other helping responses and strategies. Listening should precede whatever else is done. When a helper fails to listen, the client may be discouraged from self-exploring, the wrong issue may be discussed, or a strategy may be proposed prematurely.

Listening involves three steps: receiving a message, processing a message, and sending a message (see Figure 4.2). Each client message (verbal or nonverbal) is a stimulus to be received and processed by the helper. When a client sends a message, the helper receives it. Reception of a message is a covert process—that is, we cannot see how or what the helper receives. Failure to receive the entire message may occur when the helper stops attending. Reception of a message may be thought of as **contemplative listening** (Lindahl, 2003). A prerequisite for contemplative listening is the ability to be silent! Interestingly enough, the letters that spell listen also spell silent (Lindahl, 2003). When we are truly silent, we are not focused on what we are going to say next. Instead, we are creating space for ourselves to receive a message and for clients to send a message. Unfortunately, because our world is so noisy, true silence is uncomfortable for many of us and must be cultivated with daily practice. Turning off cell phones and pagers and sitting silently with oneself for a few minutes every day is a great way to develop contemplative listening skills.

Once a message is received, it must be processed in some way. Processing, like reception, is covert: it goes on within the helper's mind and is not visible to the outside world—except, perhaps, from the helper's nonverbal cues. Processing includes thinking about the message and pondering its meaning. Processing is important because a helper's cognitions, self-talk, and mental (covert) preparation and visualization set the stage for overt responding. Errors in message processing often occur when helpers' biases or blind spots prevent them from acknowledging

parts of a message or from interpreting a message without distortion. Helpers may hear what they want to hear instead of the actual message sent. Processing a message may be thought of as **reflective listening** (Lindahl, 2003). In reflective listening, we are listening to ourselves and focusing our attention inward to develop sensitivity to our internal voice. How do we cultivate reflective listening? Like achieving the silence of contemplative listening, reflective listening also requires practice. Lindahl (2003) recommends taking a few breaths before responding to a client's message and then, after the breaths, asking oneself, "What wants to be said next?" (instead of "What do *I* want to say?") (p. 32).

The third step of listening involves the verbal and nonverbal messages sent by a helper. Sometimes a helper may receive and process a message accurately but has difficulty sending a message because of lack of skills. Fortunately, you can learn to use listening responses to send messages. When sending messages back to our clients, we are engaging in listening that is **connective listening**—that is, listening that in some way connects us with our clients (Lindahl, 2003).

This chapter is designed to help you develop verbal and nonverbal communication skills to facilitate the listening process with clients. Part of the chapter will assist you in becoming more attuned and receptive to client nonverbal messages. The other part of the chapter is intended to help you acquire four verbal listening responses that you can use to send messages to a client: clarification, paraphrase, reflection, and summarization. Such responses convey that you are listening to and understanding client messages. Understanding what any client says can be difficult. When you are working with clients who are culturally different from you, understanding may be even more challenging because of cultural nuances in communication and expression. Sue and Sue (2013) illustrate the complexities in this process by noting that focusing on the *accuracy* of messages sent and received is incomplete without simultaneously also considering the *appropriateness* of the message (p. 213). They conclude that "effective multicultural counseling occurs when the counselor and client are able to send and receive both verbal and nonverbal messages appropriately and accurately" (p. 229).

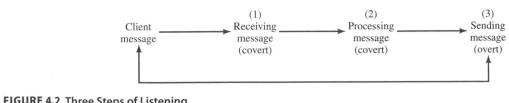

FIGURE 4.2 Three Steps of Listening

Listening to Clients' Stories

Ivey, D'Andrea, Ivey, and Simek-Morgan (2007) note that listening by the helper helps to bring out the client's story. Listening is healing because it encourages clients to tell their stories. **Clients' stories** are narratives about their lives and current experiences. From these narratives clients construct their identities and infuse their lives with meaning and purpose (White, 2007). A good therapist listens to these accounts to help clients recognize how they construct meaning and whether they help or hurt the development of client identity. Telling one's own story can also provide emotional relief to clients who have suffered trauma, even clients who are very young or old. Stories provide a way for clients who are suffering from loss—such as a separation or divorce, loss of a job, or death of a significant other—to make sense of the loss (Sedney, Baker, & Gross, 1994). For clients who are dying, stories can bring a sense of closure and also feelings of liberation. Healing is particularly evident if clients describe for the first time "hidden difficulties" or "shame" (Ostaseski, 1994). Each time a story is told, something new is learned, a wound is healed, another part of the story is remembered, or the story teller gains new insight (Lindahl, 2003).

Client narratives are stories that provide both historical and cohesive meaning to clients' lives, a link from the past to the present and the future, and a mechanism by which clients not only explain themselves to themselves but also introduce themselves to helpers (Arden & Linford, 2009, p. 111). Narratives also give clients a structure by which to organize their emotional experience. Generally speaking, the narrative approach moves away from negative themes in the story and helps clients reshape the story into more positive themes (White, 2007). Together, the client and helper can co-construct a new narrative, and it is this new narrative that actually strengthens new neural networks in the brain. Arden and Linford (2009) describe the process like this:

> Therapists utilize language and its associated left-hemispheric neural nets to co-construct positive and adaptive narratives. Originally, narratives are self-stories shaped by interactions with parents, peers, and the context of one's culture. When those narratives do not serve a person well in adolescence or adulthood, the therapist's job is to help the patient reconstruct those narratives so that he or she can live with diminished anxiety, depression, or other psychological problems. (p. 112)

Stories are almost universally present and relevant in various ethnic cultural groups. Helpers need to tune in to many aspects of clients' stories. Ivey and colleagues (2007) recommend listening for the *facts* of the story, for the client's *feelings* about the story, and for the way in which the client *organizes* the story. Sedney and colleagues (1994) recommend listening for how the story is started, for the sequences in the story, and for "hints of anger, regret, and what ifs," as well as for the client's understanding of the story and the role the client plays in it (p. 291). Significant omissions also may provide clues. Ostaseski (1994) comments that helpers must simply trust that some insight will arise for clients just from the telling of the story: "Often the story will deliver what is needed. So pay close attention to whatever you are presented with. Start with that. Take it. Believe it, and see where it leads you" (p. 11).

Listening to Clients' Nonverbal Behavior

Clients tell us stories in many different ways. As we noted, part of their story is expressed through words, language, and meaning. However, part of their story is expressed through nonverbal communication and body language. Even silence is often a powerful punctuation to a client narrative. Sometimes a client's story is so powerful that there are no real words to express what has happened. Anyone who witnessed the daring and successful October 2010 rescue of the 33 Chilean miners realizes that when they embraced their families after 70 days of being 2,300 feet underground, the initial communication was much more about body language than words. Hugs, tears, and embraces came first.

Nonverbal Communication, Culture, and Microaggressions

It is important to note that clients from some cultural groups place greater emphasis on nonverbal than on verbal behavior in themselves and their helper. In part, these clients have learned to rely more on nonverbal communication and less on verbal elaborations to explain something or to get a point across (Sue & Sue, 2013). Moreover, many racial/ethnic minority clients are very attuned to nonverbal behavior, particularly as a way to sense bias. As Sue and Sue observe (2013), often racial/ethnic minority clients feel that "nonverbal behaviors are more accurate reflections of what a white person is thinking or feeling than is what they say" (p. 221). No doubt this is because nonverbal cues often represent more "leakage" than verbal ones. Anyone who has seen the television show "Lie to Me," based on the work of nonverbal theorist Paul Ekman (Ekman and Rosenberg, 2005), can understand what we mean by this statement. **Leakage** is the communication of nonverbal messages that are valid yet are not sent intentionally.

Nonverbal leakages can also constitute subtle **micro-aggressions** that are likely to occur in cross-cultural counseling—such as dismissive looks, gestures, and tones—and are so pervasive and automatic that they are often ignored or denied (Sue & Sue, 2013; Sue, 2010). Some microaggressions may be directed toward race, such as when a white practitioner stammers and avoids eye contact when working with a client who is not white. Others may be directed toward other aspects of culture, such as gender, such as when a male practitioner says something to a female client that implies her opinion about an issue is not important. When a straight practitioner refuses to see a lesbian or gay client, a microaggression has been committed in the area of sexual orientation. Similar microaggressions occur when an able-bodied practitioner speaks more loudly when working with a client who has a visual impairment. This implies that because the client has an impairment in one sensory modality, the visual modality, it affects other sensory modalities and means that the client cannot hear well.

Neurobiology and Nonverbal Behavior

The brain is heavily involved in the communication of nonverbal behavior. This is true of the client who is sending nonverbal information all the time when communicating, and also of the helper who is using parts of the brain, particularly mirror neurons, to receive and process the nonverbal communications of the client. Generally speaking, we "read" nonverbal communication with the right hemisphere of our brains. Different areas of the brain become activated when we respond nonverbally, such as when we look directly at another person. Through the mirror neuron system we described in the prior chapter, clients often will unconsciously mimic the facial expressions of their helpers. Moreover, as Arden and Linford (2009) point out, some aspects of implicit racial bias that are demonstrated through nonverbal channels are linked to the brain, particularly the structure in the emotional brain area that is called the amygdala. This is probably why many racial/ethnic minority clients are so attuned to nonverbal communication and facial expressions of helpers—because they have learned that "actions speak louder than words."

Relationship of Nonverbal and Verbal Communication

Nonverbal behavior has been defined as "communication affected by means other than words, assuming words are the verbal element" (Knapp, Hall, & Horgan, 2014, p. 8). Nonverbal and verbal behavior are interrelated because each channel of communication supports the other. In reality, neither dimension, verbal or nonverbal, can be separated. (In current thinking, some scholars even use the term *face-to-face interaction* in lieu of nonverbal behavior because of this relationship between the two dimensions.) In the helping process, each channel of communication provides important information to helpers assuming we are attuned enough to receive and decode messages simultaneously from both channels. Like verbal behavior, nonverbal actions "may communicate more than one message at a time" (Knapp, Hall, & Horgan, 2014, p. 14). Identifying the relationship between the client's verbal and nonverbal communication may yield a more accurate picture of the client, the client's feelings, and the concerns that have led the client to seek help. In addition, the helper can detect the extent to which the client's nonverbal behavior and verbal behavior match or are congruent.

In the helping process, clients' early experiences that have been encoded in the brain often get played out in nonverbal communication but are "made sense of" through words and language. Note, for example, the way this interrelationship exists in the following short therapist–client dialogue described by Safran and Muran (2000):

T: It's like you're really struggling internally right now.
C: (sobbing in a controlled fashion and looking downward): Yeah, I guess, you know, I just think that for whatever reason this situation has brought out so much of my sadness and loss and disappointment, and that instead of me feeling like I'm going forward, I just feel like I keep on uncovering things that I'm not even aware of. I mean, I know you're there . . . but I don't know.
T: So a couple of things come to mind, but one is . . . you know . . . I'm very aware that in this moment *you're looking down . . . looking away from me*. Do you have a sense of that?
C: Well, yeah.
T: Yeah?
C: I mean I do . . . because I just . . . I want to push it back in, and it just feels so umm . . . I mean, I feel it's about nothing. It just seems like this endless self-pity or something and umm . . .
T: So what would happen if you didn't push your experience back in there? (p. 195)

In this dialogue, can you see the practitioner's sensitivity to the client's nonverbal cues? Arden and Linford (2009) comment on this vignette that "because so much of what we experience and respond to is based on implicit memories and nonverbal emotional experience, the patient here may be responding as much to the therapist noticing her *gaze* as anything that's said in the hour. On the other hand . . . this therapist uses the therapeutic dialogue . . . to enhance the patient's affect regulation . . . by putting nonverbal cues into language" (p. 117).

Three Categories of Nonverbal Behavior

There are three aspects of nonverbal behavior that **LO1** can aid us in listening to clients. These include kinesics, paralinguistics, and proxemics. (See also the Nonverbal Checklist on page 111.) **Kinesics**, or **body motion**, includes gestures, body movements, posture, touch, facial expressions, and eye behavior. In this area, helpers can listen to messages communicated by clients through nonverbal behaviors such as eye contact, facial expressions, and posture. For example, in talking about his reluctance to engage in counseling, the practitioner notes that the client, Roberto, looks away, sits sideways not facing the practitioner, and frequently frowns. In this instance, Roberto's nonverbal behavior seems to support his verbal message. **Paralinguistics** refers to the vocal cues—or the "how" of the communication. Paralinguistics includes vocal qualities, vocalizations, silent pauses, and speech errors, too. As Roberto continues to talk with his helper, James, at times his voice gets louder and higher in pitch. Occasionally, Roberto uses Spanish phrases to convey something with accentuated meaning. Also of interest to helpers is the area of **proxemics**—that is, one's use of personal and social space. In the context of the helping relationship, proxemics involves the size of the room, seating arrangements, the distance between helper and client, and the use of touch. Roberto sits down and pushes his chair farther away from James as he continues to reveal that he does not feel comfortable talking about his problems with a stranger.

In listening to these dimensions of client nonverbal behavior, it is important to note that the specific meanings of nonverbal behavior will vary with individuals, situations, and the meaning of the verbal messages. Further, the nonverbal behaviors of one culture may have different or even opposite meanings in another culture. For example, in some cultures, the avoidance of eye contact is regarded as an indication of respect. And, as Knapp et al. (2014) conclude, rarely does a nonverbal message have a *single* meaning. In the example with Roberto and James, an added dimension is the cultural difference in the helping dyad. For example, some of Roberto's nonverbal behavior may not be just about his reluctance to seek help in general, but his reluctance to seek help from a practitioner of a different culture, perhaps even one who is not bilingual and who does not understand his Spanish phrases. It would be interesting to see if and how Roberto's nonverbal behavior shifted with a Spanish-speaking helper or with a Latino male practitioner. Keep in mind that all communication, verbal and nonverbal, is contextual and, as helpers, we listen for the context embedded within each client's story.

Silence and Nonverbal Behavior

An important part of nonverbal communication involves silence. **Silence and pauses** are considered part of paralinguistics. Silence and pauses in communication are important in the helping process for several reasons. First, they help regulate the course of the conversation. When a helper and client are interacting, they are basically engaged in a dialogue (hopefully, anyway) in which silence and pauses help to regulate "turn taking"—that is, the exchange of who talks and who listens. Pauses and silence also give the helper important information about the client. Unfilled pauses, or periods of silence, serve various functions in a helping interview. The purpose of silence often depends on whether the pause is initiated by the helper or by the client. Clients use silence to express emotions, to reflect on an issue, to recall an idea or feeling, to avoid a topic, or to catch up on the progress of the moment.

Sue and Sue (2008) note that "there are complex rules regarding when to speak or yield to another person" and these rules vary with cultural groups. For example,

> U.S. Americans frequently feel uncomfortable with a pause or silent stretch in the conversation, feeling obligated to fill it in with more talk. Silence is not always a sign for the listener to take up the conversation. While it may be viewed negatively by many, other cultures interpret the use of silence differently. The British and Arabs use silence for privacy, while the Russians, French, and Spanish read it as agreement among the parties. In Asian cultures, silence is traditionally a sign of respect for elders. Furthermore, silence by many Chinese and Japanese is not a floor-yielding signal inviting others to pick up the conversation. Rather, it may indicate a desire to continue speaking after making a particular point. Often silence is a sign of politeness and respect rather than a lack of desire to continue speaking. (p. 166)

The *appropriateness* of silence and verbal expressiveness varies among cultures (Sue and Sue, 2013; Sue, 2010). Although people living in the United States often value a high degree of verbal expressiveness, it is essential not to assume this is the norm for all clients. This assumption in and of itself constitutes a kind of cultural microaggression because it devalues the experience of other cultural groups who are comfortable with more silence and less verbal expressiveness.

As you can see, like the other listening responses in this chapter, silence can have differential effects and purposes depending on the client. Many helpers, especially beginning ones, are so uncomfortable with this dimension of listening that their tendency is to fill in the conversation and prevent the client from elaborating or expressing something important or useful. Generally speaking, instead of jumping in and saying the first thing that comes to mind, the helper needs to keep in mind that it is important to allow silences to occur and to *develop* during a helping session. It is during the development of the silence that clients may reveal their innermost feelings, often conveyed nonverbally rather than with words. Helper-initiated silences are most effective when used with a particular purpose in mind, such as reducing the helper's level of activity, slowing the pace of the session, giving the *client* time to think, or transferring some responsibility to the client through turn-taking.

An occasion when silence would *not* be useful, even in the context of listening to clients, would be when a client discloses something very precious and significant, often revealing information that takes great vulnerability on the client's part. For example, Paul may share with you that he was recently diagnosed as HIV-positive, or Mariko may disclose something about the pain of being the only Japanese American student in her school. In instances like these, the helper's silence often makes the client feel ashamed of the revelation and misunderstood by the helper. Validation of the client's disclosure is essential. Particularly when clients self-disclose something that involves cultural vulnerabilities, being silent is the worst response a helper can make because it communicates invalidation and denial. In these instances, the verbal listening responses we describe later in the chapter such as paraphrasing and reflection are more useful because they tell clients you *have* heard something about their disclosure and you understand how much courage the disclosure represents for them. (See Learning Activity 4.1.)

Learning Activity 4.1

Nonverbal Communication

Part One

This activity will help you develop greater sensitivity to nonverbal behaviors of clients. It can be done in dyads or triads. Select one person to assume the role of the communicator and another to assume the role of the listener. A third person can act as observer. As the communicator, recall recent times when you felt: (1) very happy, (2) very sad, and (3) very angry. Your task is to retrieve that experience *nonverbally*. Do *not say* anything to the listener, and do *not* tell the listener in advance which of the three emotions you are going to recall. Simply decide which of the three you will recall; then tell the listener when to begin. The listener's task is to *observe* the communicator, to *note* nonverbal behaviors and changes during the recall, and from these to *guess* which of the three emotional experiences the person was retrieving. After approximately 3 to 4 minutes, stop the interaction to process it. Observers can add behaviors and changes they noted at this time. After the communicator retrieves one of the emotions, switch roles.

Part Two

In a role-play interaction or helping session in which you function as the helper, watch for some significant nonverbal behavior from the client, such as change in breathing, eye contact, voice tone, and proxemics. (Do not focus on a small nonverbal behavior out of context with the spoken words.) Focus on this behavior by asking the client whether she or he is aware of what is happening to her or his voice, body posture, eyes, or whatever. Do not interpret or assign meaning to the behavior for the client. Notice where your focus takes the client.

Part Three

Consider the aspects of culture that we have described in this chapter and also in Chapter 2—such as race, ethnicity, gender, sexual orientation, religious affiliation and faith heritage, social and economic class, ability/disability status, and so on.

Construct a list of potential microaggressions in these areas that have to do with the helper's nonverbal behavior toward the client.

Part Four

This activity is designed to help you develop a better comfort level with pauses and silences that occur during client sessions. Role-play a helping session with a classmate. One of you can be the helper first, and the other can be the client first. After engaging in a short role-play session, switch roles. During the role-play as the helper, your task is to desensitize yourself to the discomfort of having longer and longer periods of silence. After the client says something, wait about 5 seconds before responding the first time. The second time, wait about 10 seconds, and increase to 15 seconds for the third response. See if you can wait for up to 30 seconds before responding to the client. Note how you are feeling inside during the silences and also observe what the silences allow you to notice about the client.

Part Five

The purpose of this activity is to apply the material presented in this chapter in an interview setting. Using the Nonverbal Behavior Checklist that follows, observe a helper and determine how many behaviors listed on the checklist the helper demonstrates. In addition, see how much you can identify about the client's nonverbal behaviors in the role play. Finally, in your interview, look for mirroring, ways in which the helper and client's nonverbal communication mirrors each other.

Nonverbal Behavior Checklist

Name of Helper _____

Name of Observer _____

Instructions: During a recorded or a live interview, use the categories listed as guides for observing nonverbal behavior. You can use the checklist to observe the helper, the client, or both. Behaviors to be observed are listed in the first column. Check off a behavior when you observe it, and add descriptive comments about it—for example, "Blinking—excessive" or "Smiling—infrequently."

Kinesics   (✓)   Comments

1. *Eyes*

   Eyebrows raised, lowered, or drawn together _____ _____

   Staring or "glazed" quality _____ _____

   Blinking—excessive, moderate, or slight _____ _____

   Moisture, tears _____ _____

   Pupil dilation _____ _____

2. *Face, mouth, head*

   Continuity or changes in facial expression _____ _____

   Smiling _____ _____

   Swelling, tightening, or quivering lips _____ _____

   Changes in skin color _____ _____

   Flushing, rashes on upper neck, face _____ _____

   Appearance of sweat beads _____ _____

   Head nodding _____ _____

3. *Body movements, posture, gestures*

   Body posture—rigid or relaxed _____ _____

   Continuity or shifts in body posture _____ _____

Kinesics   (✓)   Comments

Frequency of body movements—excessive, moderate, or slight _____ _____

Gestures—open or closed _____ _____

Frequency of nonverbal adaptors (distracting mannerisms)— excessive, moderate, or slight _____ _____

Body orientation—direct (facing each other) or sideways _____ _____

Breathing—shallow or deep, fast or slow _____ _____

Continuity or changes in breathing depth and rate _____ _____

Crossed arms or legs _____ _____

Paralinguistics   (✓)   Comments

1. Continuity or changes in voice level, pitch, rate of speech _____ _____

2. Verbal underlining—voice emphasis of particular words/phrases _____ _____

3. Whispering, inaudibility _____ _____

4. Directness or lack of directness in speech _____ _____

5. Speech errors—excessive, moderate, or slight _____ _____

6. Pauses initiated by helper _____ _____

7. Pauses initiated by client _____ _____

Proxemics

1. Continuity or shifts in distance (closer, farther away) _____ _____

2. Position in room—behind or next to object or person _____ _____

Four Listening Responses

This chapter presents four listening responses: [LO2] [LO3] [LO4] clarification, paraphrase, reflection, and summarization. **Clarification** begins with a question, often posed after an ambiguous client message. It starts with "Do you mean that . . ." or "Are you saying that . . .", followed by a repetition or rephrasing of all or part of the client's previous message. A **paraphrase** is a rephrasing of the content part of a message—the part that describes a situation, event, person, or idea. **Reflection** is a rephrasing of the client's feelings, or the affect part of the message—the part that reveals the client's feelings about the content. For example, a client may feel discouraged (affect) about not doing well in a class (content). **Summarization** is an extension of the paraphrase and reflection responses; it is a tying together and rephrasing of two or more parts of a message or messages.

To illustrate these four listening responses, here is a client message followed by an example of each response:

Client, a 35-year-old Latina widow, mother of two young children (*says in a soft, halting voice, with downcast eyes, and corners of the mouth turned down, also accompanied by occasional tears*): My whole life fell apart when my husband died. I keep feeling so unsure about my ability to make it on my own and to support my kids. My husband always made all the decisions for me and brought home money every week. Now I haven't slept well for so long, and I'm drinking more heavily—I can't even think straight. My relatives help me as much as they can, but I still feel scared.

Helper clarification: Are you saying that one of the hardest things facing you now is to have enough confidence in yourself?

Helper paraphrase: Since your husband's death you have more responsibilities and decisions on your shoulders, even with the support of relatives.

Helper reflection: You feel worried about having to shoulder all the family responsibilities now.

Helper summarization: Now that your husband has died, you're facing some things that are very difficult for you right now . . . handling the family responsibilities, making the decisions, trying to take better care of yourself, and dealing with fears that have come up as a result.

Table 4.1 presents definitions and lists the *intended* or hypothesized purposes of the four listening responses. These responses may not produce the same results with all clients. For example, a practitioner may find that reflecting feelings prompts some clients to discuss feelings but that other clients do not even acknowledge the counselor's statement. Our point is that we are presenting some "modal" intentions for each listening response; there

TABLE 4.1   Definitions and Intended Purposes of Listening Responses

Response	Definition	Intended Purpose
Clarification	A question beginning with, for example, "Do you mean that . . ." or "Are you saying that . . ." followed by a rephrasing of the client's message	1. To encourage client elaboration 2. To check out the accuracy of what you think you heard the client say 3. To clear up vague, confusing messages
Paraphrase (responding to content)	A rephrasing of the content of the client's message	1. To help the client focus on the content of his or her message 2. To highlight content when attention to feelings is premature or self-defeating
Reflection (responding to feelings)	A rephrasing of the affect part of the client's message	1. To encourage the client to express more of his or her feelings 2. To help the client become more aware of the feelings that dominate him or her 3. To help the client acknowledge and manage feelings 4. To help the client discriminate accurately among feelings 5. To help the client feel understood
Summarization	Two or more paraphrases or reflections that condense the client's messages or the session	1. To tie together multiple elements of client messages 2. To identify a common theme or pattern 3. To interrupt excessive rambling 4. To review progress 5. To slow the pace of a session

are exceptions. The listening responses will achieve their intended purposes most of the time. However, other dynamics within an interview may give rise to different client outcomes. Moreover, the effects of these verbal messages may vary because of nonverbal cues that accompany the message. It is helpful to have some rationale in mind for using a response. However, always remember that the effect a response has on the client may not be what you intended to achieve. The guidelines in Table 4.1 should be used tentatively, *subject to modification, depending on particular client reactions.* Remember Sue and Sue's (2013) advice at the beginning of this chapter—consider not only the *accuracy* of responses but also the *appropriateness* of responses. The appropriateness of responses is most often determined by the client reactions to the message.

Sequencing of Listening Responses

It is not accidental that we have listed the four listening responses in the following particular order: clarification, paraphrase, reflection, and summarization. Because every helping session is different, and because every client is unique, it is not possible to predict an exact sequence to the listening responses. However, as Young (2013) points out, within these variations, there is sufficient predictability between helping sessions to estimate some sequencing of various listening responses. He refers to this as "the nonjudgmental listening cycle or NLC"—described as "a set of sequential procedures to be followed as each topic emerges, is discussed, and comes to closure" (p. 152). In essence, each new topic forms a circle beginning with clarifying questions and proceeding through to summarization. The clarifying response opens the topic, the paraphrasing and reflecting responses move the topic to deeper levels, and the summarization either makes a transition from one topic to another or ends the session. Think of this sequence, however, as a guide map and not as a prescription for what always occurs in sessions, because each session and each client are somewhat different.

In the next three sections we describe the listening responses and present model examples of each response. Opportunities for you to practice each one and receive feedback follow the examples.

The Clarification Response: Listening for Accuracy

Because most messages are expressed from the speaker's internal frame of reference, they may seem vague or confusing to the listener. Messages that are particularly likely to be confusing are those that include inclusive terms (*they*

and *them*), ambiguous phrases (*you know*), and words with a double meaning (*stoned, trip*). When you aren't sure of the meaning of a message, it is helpful to clarify it. A clarification asks the client to elaborate on a vague, ambiguous, or implied statement. The request for clarification is usually expressed as a question and may begin with phrases such as "Are you saying . . ." or "Could you try to describe . . ." or "Can you clarify . . .".

Purposes of Clarification

Clarification may be used to make the client's previous message explicit and to confirm the accuracy of your perceptions about the message. Clarification is appropriate whenever you aren't sure whether you understand the client's message and you need more elaboration. A second purpose of clarification is to check out what you heard of the client's message. Particularly in the beginning stages of helping, it is important to verify client messages instead of jumping to conclusions. This is a primary reason why the clarifying question is a good response with which to begin the nonjudgmental listening cycle described. The following example may help you see the value of the clarification response:

Client: Sometimes I just want to get away from it all.
Helper: It sounds like you have to split and be on your own.
Client: No, it's not that. I don't want to be alone. It's just that I wish I could get out from under all this work I have to do.

In that example, the helper drew a quick conclusion about the initial client message that turned out to be inaccurate.

The session might have gone more smoothly if the helper had requested clarification before assuming something about the client, as in this example:

Client: Sometimes I just want to get away from it all.
Helper: Could you describe for me what you mean by "getting away from it all?"
Client: Well, I just have so much work to do—I'm always feeling behind and overloaded. I'd like to get out from under that miserable feeling.

In that case, the clarification helped both persons to establish exactly what was being said and felt. Neither the client nor the helper had to rely on assumptions and inferences that were not explored and confirmed.

A skilled helper uses clarification responses to determine the accuracy of messages as they are received and processed. Otherwise, inaccurate information may not be corrected, and distorted assumptions may remain untested.

Steps in Clarifying

There are four steps in clarifying for accuracy. First, identify the content of the client's verbal and nonverbal messages. Ask yourself, "What has the client told me?" Pay attention not only to the client's words but also to the client's nonverbal messages. Second, identify any vague or confusing parts of the verbal or nonverbal message that you need to check out for accuracy or elaboration. Third, decide on an appropriate beginning, or sentence stem, for your clarification, such as "Could you describe . . .", "Could you clarify . . .", or "Are you saying . . .". In addition, use your voice to deliver the clarification as a question, not a statement. Fourth, remember to assess the effectiveness of your clarification by listening to and observing the client's response. If your clarification is useful, then the client will elaborate on the ambiguous or confusing part of the message. If it is not useful, then the client will clam up, ignore your request for clarification, and/or continue to reveal deletions or omissions. At this point, you can attempt a subsequent clarification or switch to an alternative response.

To decide whether to use clarification, to formulate this response, and to assess its effectiveness, consider the following cognitive learning strategy:

1. What has this client told me?

2. Are there any vague parts or missing pictures in the message that I need to check out? If so, what? If not, then I need to decide on another, more suitable response.

3. How can I hear, see, or grasp a way to start this response?

4. How will I know whether my clarification is useful?

Notice how the helper applies this cognitive learning strategy to clarify the client's message in the second example above:

Client *(says with downcast eyes, looking at the floor):* Sometimes I just want to get away from it all.
Helper *(asks and answers covertly):*

Self-question 1: What has this client told me?
That she wants to get away from something. Downcast eyes support the verbal idea.

Self-question 2: Are there any vague parts or missing pictures in her message? If so, what? (If not, then I'll decide on a more suitable response.)
Yes—I need to check out what she means by "getting away from it all."

Self-question 3: How can I begin a clarification response?
I can see the start of it, hear the start of it, or grasp the start of it. Something like "Well, could you tell me, or could you describe . . . ?"

Self-question 4: How will I know that the response will be helpful?
I'll have to see, hear, and grasp whether she elaborates or not. Let's try it . . .

At this juncture, the helper's covert visualization or self-talk ends, the helper addresses the client, and the client responds:

Helper clarification: Could you describe for me what you mean by "getting away from it all"?
Client response: Well, I just have so much work to do—I'm always feeling behind and overloaded. I'd like to get out from under that miserable feeling.

From the client's response, the helper can determine that the clarification was effective because the client elaborated and added the parts or pictures missing from her previous message. The helper can covertly congratulate himself or herself for not jumping ahead too quickly and for taking the time to check out the client's omission and the resulting ambiguity.

Learning Activity 4.2 gives you an opportunity to try this cognitive learning strategy to develop the skill of clarification.

Paraphrase and Reflection: Listening for Facts and Feelings

The practitioner needs to listen for information revealed in messages about significant situations and events in the client's life—and for the client's feelings about these events. Ivey and colleagues (2007) talk about this as listening for the main facts of the client's story and for the client's feelings about his or her story. Each client message expresses (directly or indirectly) some information about client situations or concerns and client feelings. The portion of the message that expresses information or describes a situation or event is called the **content**, or **cognitive part**, of the message. The **cognitive part** of a message includes references to a situation or event, people, objects, or ideas. Another portion of the message may reveal how the client feels about the content; the expression of feelings or emotional tone is called the **affective** part of the message (Cormier, 2016). Generally, the affective part of the verbal message is distinguished

Learning Activity 4.2

Clarification

In this activity, you are presented with three client practice messages. For each message, develop an example of a clarification response using the cognitive learning strategy described and outlined in the following example. To internalize this learning strategy, you may wish to talk through these self-questions overtly (aloud) and then covertly (silently to yourself). The end product will be a clarification response that you can say aloud or write down. An example precedes the three practice messages. Feedback is provided on page 118.

Example

Client, a 15-year-old high school student (*says in a slow, low voice tone while looking down at the floor*): My grades have really slipped. I don't know why; I just feel so down about everything.

Self-question 1: *What has this client told me?*
That she feels down and rather discouraged.

Self-question 2: *Are there any vague parts or missing pictures to the message that I need to check out? If so, what? If not, decide on a different response.*
Yes, several—one is what she feels so down about. Another is what this feeling of being down is like for her.

Self-question 3: *How can I hear, see, or grasp a way to start this response?*
"Are you saying there's something specific?" or "Can you describe this feeling . . .?"

Self-question 4: *How will I know whether my clarification is useful? Say aloud or write an actual clarification response:*
"Are you saying there is something specific you feel down about?" or "Could you describe what this feeling of being down is like for you?"

Client Practice Messages

Client 1, a fourth-grader (*says with a frown on the face and downcast corners of the mouth*): I don't want to do this dumb homework anyway. I don't care about learning these math problems. Girls don't need to know this anyway.

Self-question 1: *What has this client told me?*

Self-question 2: *Are there any vague parts or missing pictures I need to check out? If so, what?*

Self-question 3: *How can I hear, see, or grasp a way to start my response?*

Actual clarification response: _____
_____
_____

Client 2, a middle-aged man (*says with lowered eyes, looking away from helper, low, soft voice, corners of the mouth turned down*): I'm really discouraged with this physical disability now. I feel like I can't do anything the way I used to. It has affected me not only at my job but also at home. I just don't feel like I have anything good to offer anyone.

Self-question 1: *What has this client told me?*

Self-question 2: *Are there any vague parts or missing pictures I need to check out? If so, what?*

Self-question 3: *How can I hear, see, or grasp a way to start my response?*

Actual clarification response: _____
_____
_____

Client 3, an older person (*says with fast-paced, high-pitched voice, direct eye contact, excessive body motion*): Umm, well the company is going to make me retire even though I don't want to. What will I do with myself then? I find myself just thinking—thinking over the good times of the past, not wanting to face the future at all. Sometimes retirement makes me so nervous I can't sleep or eat. My family suggested I see someone about this.

Self-question 1: *What has this client told me?*

Self-question 2: *Are there any vague parts or missing pictures I need to check out? If so, what?*

Self-question 3: *How can I hear, see, or grasp a way to start my response?*

Actual clarification response: _____
_____
_____

by the client's use of an affect or feeling word, such as *happy, angry,* or *sad.*

However, clients may also express their feelings in less obvious ways, particularly via nonverbal behaviors. For example, "evidence of decreased general movement, decreased expressiveness, decreased speech, gestures, eye contact, and smiling; halting speech, have all been documented in depressed persons" (Knapp et al., 2014, p. 412). Facial cues from clients are important indicators of emotions and helpers can usually accurately infer

emotions from the clients' facial expressions, particularly the six basic emotions of happiness, anger, sadness, disgust, surprise, and fear (Knapp et al., 2014). Moreover, facial indicators of emotions are considered to be more universal rather than culture specific. Clients also reveal something about their feelings through their voice. And while there is no dictionary of emotion cues for the voice, we do rely on some consistent vocal indicators to identify client emotional states (Knapp et al., 2014, p. 341). For example, anxiety is often associated with speech disruptions or errors, happiness and joy are associated with a higher pitch of the voice, anger is conveyed by more intensity and a faster speech rate, and sadness is reflected in a quieter voice and slower speech (Knapp et al., 2014).

The following illustrations may help you distinguish between the content and affective parts of a client's verbal message:

> Client, a 6-year-old first-grader: I don't like school. It isn't much fun.

The first sentence ("I don't like school") is the affective part of the message. The client's feelings are suggested by the words "don't like." The second sentence ("It isn't much fun") is the content part of the message because it refers to a situation or an event in this child's life—not having fun at school.

Here is another example:

> **Client, a 20-year-old woman:** How can I tell my boyfriend I want to break off our relationship? He will be very upset. I guess I'm afraid to tell him.

In that example, the first two sentences are the content because they describe the situation of wanting to break off a relationship. The third sentence, the affective part, indicates the client's feelings about this situation—being *afraid* to tell the boyfriend of her intentions.

See whether you can distinguish between the content and affective parts of the next two client messages:

> **Client 1, a young man:** I can't satisfy my partner sexually. It's very frustrating for me.

In that example, the content part is "I can't satisfy my partner sexually." The affective part, or Client 1's feelings about the content, is "It's very *frustrating* for me."

> **Client 2, an institutionalized man:** This place is a trap. It seems like I've been here forever. I'd feel much better if I weren't here.

In that example, Client 2's statements referring to the institution as a trap and being there forever are the content parts of the message. The statement of "feeling better" is the affective part.

The skilled helper tries to listen for both the content and the affective parts of client messages because it is important to deal with significant situations or relationships and with the client's feelings about the situations. Responding to cognitive or affective messages will direct the focus of the session in different ways. At some points, the helper will respond to content by focusing on events, objects, people, or ideas. At other times, the helper will respond to affect by focusing on the client's feelings and emotions. Generally, the helper can respond to content by using a paraphrase and can respond to affect with a reflection. It is helpful to be able to use both of these responses skillfully because focusing on content can be important if the therapeutic relationship is not strong enough to process affect or if focusing on feelings may overwhelm the client. However, focusing on emotion is very important when clients are explaining their feelings away or exhibiting a lack of awareness of feelings, and the therapeutic relationship is strong enough to provide safety (Greenberg, 2010).

Paraphrasing

A paraphrase is a rephrasing of the client's primary words and thoughts. Paraphrasing requires selective attention to the content part of the message and translating the client's key ideas into *your own words*. An effective paraphrase does more than just parrot the words of the client. The rephrase should be carefully worded to lead to further discussion or to increased understanding by the client. It is helpful to stress the most important words and ideas expressed by the client.

Consider this example:

> **Client:** I know it doesn't help my depression to sit around or stay in bed all day.
> **Helper:** You know that to help your depression you need to avoid staying in bed or sitting around all day.

The helper merely parroted the client's message. The likely outcome is that the client may respond with a minimal answer such as, "I agree," or "That's right," and not elaborate further, or that the client may feel ridiculed by what seems to be an obvious or mimicking response. Here is a more effective paraphrase: "You are aware that you need to get up and move around to minimize being depressed."

Purposes of Paraphrasing The paraphrase serves several purposes in client interactions. First, the paraphrase tells clients that you have understood their communication. If your understanding is complete, then clients can expand or clarify their ideas. Second, paraphrasing can encourage client elaboration of a key idea or thought. Clients may talk about an important topic in greater depth. A third reason for using the paraphrase is to help the client focus on a particular situation or event, idea, or behavior. Sometimes, by increasing focus, paraphrasing can help get a client on track. For example, accurate paraphrasing can help stop a client from merely repeating a "story" (Ivey, Ivey, & Zalaquett, 2014). A fourth purpose is to help clients who need to make decisions. As Ivey and colleagues (2014) observe, paraphrasing is often helpful to clients who have a decision to make, because the repetition of key ideas and phrases clarifies the essence of the problem. Paraphrasing to emphasize content is also useful if attention to affect is likely to be premature or counterproductive.

Steps in Paraphrasing   There are five steps in paraphrasing content. First, attend to and recall the message by restating it to yourself covertly. Ask yourself, "What has the client told me?" Second, identify the content part of the message by asking yourself, "What situation, person, object, or idea is discussed in this message?" Third, select an appropriate beginning, or sentence stem, for your paraphrase. Paraphrases can begin with many possible sentence stems. See Table 4.2 for a list of phrases and sentence stems useful for beginning paraphrase and reflection responses.

Fourth, using the sentence stem you selected, translate the key content or constructs into your own words and express the key content in a paraphrase that you can say aloud. Remember to use your voice so that the paraphrase sounds like a statement, not a question. Fifth, assess the effectiveness of your paraphrase by listening to and observing the client's response. If your paraphrase is accurate, then the client will in some way—verbally and/or nonverbally—confirm its accuracy and usefulness.

TABLE 4.2   Phrases and Sentence Stems to Introduce Paraphrase and Reflection Responses

It seems like
It appears as though
From my perspective
As I see it
I see what you mean
It looks like
Sounds like
As I hear it
What you're saying is
I hear you saying
Something tells you
You're telling me that
You feel
From my standpoint
I sense that
I have the feeling that

Consider in the following example the way a helper uses the cognitive learning strategy to formulate a paraphrase:

Client, a 40-year-old Asian American woman *(says in a level, monotone voice)*: How can I tell my husband I want a divorce? He'll think I'm crazy. I guess I'm just afraid to tell him.

Helper *(asks and answers covertly)*:

Self-question 1: What has this client told me?
That she wants a divorce and she's afraid to tell her husband because he will think she's crazy.

Self-question 2: What is the content of this message—what person, object, idea, or situation is the client discussing?
She wants a divorce but hasn't told husband because husband will think she's crazy.

Self-question 3: What is an appropriate sentence stem?
I'll go with a stem such as "You think . . .," "I hear you saying . . .," or "It sounds like . . .".

Self-question 4: How can I translate the client's key content into my own words?
Want a divorce = break off, terminate the relationship, split.

Self-question 5: How will I know whether my paraphrase is helpful?
Listen and notice whether the client confirms its accuracy.

At this point the helper's self-talk stops, and the following dialogue ensues:

Helper paraphrase: It sounds like you haven't found a way to tell your husband you want to end the relationship because of his possible reaction. Is that right?

Client: Yeah—I've decided—I've even been to see a lawyer. But I just don't know how to approach him with this. He thinks things are wonderful, and I don't want to dishonor him by divorcing him.

That paraphrase encouraged both client elaboration and focus on a main issue.

Learning Activity 4.3 gives you an opportunity to develop your own paraphrase responses.

Reflection and Basic Empathy

The paraphrase is used to restate the *content* part of the message. Although paraphrase and reflection of feelings are not mutually exclusive responses, the reflection of feelings is used to rephrase the *affective* part of the message, the client's emotional tone. A reflection is similar to a paraphrase but different in that a reflection adds to the message an emotional tone or component that is lacking in a paraphrase.

4.2 Feedback

Clarification

Client 1

Question 1. *What did the client say?*
That she doesn't want to do her math homework—that she thinks it's not important for girls.

Question 2. *Are there any vague parts or missing pictures?*
Yes—whether she really doesn't care about math or whether she's had a bad experience with it and is denying her concern.

Question 3. *How can I see, hear, or grasp a way to start my response?*

Examples of Clarification Responses

"Are you saying that . . .?"
"Are you saying that you really dislike math or that it's not going as well as you would like?"
"Are you saying that math is not too important for you or that it is hard for you?"

Client 2

Question 1. *What did the client say?*
That he feels useless to himself and others.

Question 2. *Are there any vague parts or missing pictures?*
Yes—it's not clear exactly how things are different for him now and also whether it's the disability itself that's bothering him or its effects (inability to get around, reactions of others, and so on).

Question 3. *How can I see, hear, or grasp a way to start my response?*

Examples of Clarification Responses

"Could you clarify . . .?"
"Could you clarify exactly how things are different for you now from the way they used to be?"
"Are you saying you feel discouraged about having the disability—or about the effects and constraints from it?"
"Are you saying you feel differently about yourself now from the way you used to?"

Client 3

Question 1. *What did the client say?*
He is going to have to retire because of company policy. He doesn't want to retire now and feels upset about this. He's here at his family's suggestion.

Question 2. *Are there any vague parts or missing pictures?*
Yes—he says he feels nervous, although from his description of not eating and sleeping it may be sadness or depression. Also, is he here only because his family sent him or because he feels a need, too? Finally, what specifically bothers him about retirement?

Question 3. *How can I hear, see, or grasp a way to start my response?*

Examples of Clarification Responses

"Could you describe . . .?"
"Would you say you're feeling more nervous or more depressed about your upcoming retirement?"
"Are you saying you're here just because of your family's feelings or because of your feelings, too?"
"Could you describe what it is about retiring that worries you?"

Here are two examples that may illustrate the difference between a paraphrase and a reflection of feelings:

Client: Everything is humdrum. There's nothing new going on, nothing exciting. All my friends are away. I wish I had some money to do something different.

Helper paraphrase: With your friends gone and no money around, there is nothing for you to do right now.

Helper reflection: You feel bored with the way things are for you right now.

Notice the helper's use of the affect word *bored* in the reflection response to tune in to the feelings of the client created by the particular situation.

Purposes of Reflection The reflection of feelings has five intended purposes. First, reflection is used to encourage clients to express their feelings (both positive and negative) about a particular situation, person, or whatever. Some clients do not readily reveal feelings because they have never learned to do so; other clients hold back feelings until the helper

gives permission to focus on them. Expression of feelings is not usually an end in itself; rather, it is a means of helping clients and practitioners understand the scope of the issues or situation. Most, if not all, of the concerns presented by clients involve underlying emotional factors to be resolved. For example, in focusing on affect, the client may become more aware of lingering feelings about an unfinished situation or of intense feelings that seem to dominate his or her reaction to a situation.

Clients may also become aware of mixed, or conflicting, feelings. Clients often express ambivalence about problematic issues. Teyber and McClure (2011) identify two common affective constructions with mixed components: anger-sadness-shame and sadness-anger-guilt. In the first sequence, the primary feeling is often anger, but it is a negative response to hurt or sadness. Often, the experiencing of the anger and sadness provokes shame. In the second sequence, the predominant feeling is sadness, but it is often connected to anger that has been denied because the expression of it produces guilt. These two affective

Learning Activity 4.3

Paraphrase

In this activity, you are presented with three client practice messages. For each one, develop a paraphrase response using the cognitive learning strategy outlined in the following example. To internalize this learning strategy, you may wish to talk through these self-questions overtly (aloud) and then covertly (silently). The end product will be a paraphrase response that you can say aloud or write down. Feedback is given on page 121.

Example

Client, a middle-aged graduate student *(says in a level, monotone voice):* It's just a rough time for me—trying to work, keeping up with graduate school, and spending time with my family. I keep telling myself it will slow down someday.

Self-question 1: *What has this client told me?*
That it's hard to keep up with everything he has to do.

Self-question 2: *What is the content of this message—what person, object, idea, or situation is the client discussing?*
Trying to keep up with work, school, and family.

Self-question 3: *What is an appropriate sentence stem?*
I'll try a stem like "It sounds like . . ." or "There are . . ."

Actual paraphrase response: "It sounds like you're having a tough time balancing all your commitments" or "There are a lot of demands on your time right now."

Client Practice Statements

Client 1, a 30-year-old woman *(says in a level tone without much variation in pitch or tempo):* My husband and I argue all the time about how to manage our kids. He says I always interfere with his discipline. I think he is too harsh with them.

Self-question 1: *What has this client told me?*

Self-question 2: *What is the content of this message— what person, object, idea, or situation is the client discussing?*

Self-question 3: *What is an appropriate sentence stem?*

Actual paraphrase response: _____
_____
_____

Client 2, a 6-year-old boy *(says in slow, soft voice with downcast eyes):* I wish I didn't have a little sister. I know my parents love her more than me.

Self-question 1: *What has this client told me?*

Self-question 2: *What is the content of this message—what person, object, idea, or situation is this client discussing?*

Self-question 3: *What is an appropriate sentence stem?*

Actual paraphrase response: _____
_____
_____

Client 3, a college student *(says in a level tone with measured words and little change in pitch and inflection):* I've said to my family before, I just can't compete with the other students who aren't blind. There's no way I can keep up with this kind of handicap. I've told them it's natural to be behind and do more poorly.

Self-question 1: *What has this client told me?*

Self-question 2: *What is the content of this message— what person, object, idea, or situation is the client discussing?*

Self-question 3: *What is a useful sentence stem?*

Actual paraphrase response: _____
_____
_____

---

sequences are typically acquired in childhood and are a result of both the rules and the interactions of the family of origin. These affective elements are also strongly influenced by cultural affiliation. As Sue and Sue (2013) note, in Western cultures, which emphasize individualism, the predominant affective reaction following wrongful behavior is *guilt*. However, in some U.S. subcultures, such as Asian, Hispanic, and African American, where the psychosocial unit is the family, group, or collective society, the primary affective reaction to wrongful behavior is not guilt but *shame*.

A second purpose of reflection is to help clients manage feelings. Learning to deal with feelings is especially important when a client experiences an intense emotion such as fear, dependency, or anger. Strong emotions can interfere with a client's ability to produce a rational response

(cognitive or behavioral) to pressure. Also, when clients are given permission to reveal and release feelings, their energy and well-being are often increased. For example, during and after a crisis or disaster such as an earthquake, terrorist attack, plane crash, or bomb scare, people feel overwhelmed by the intensity of their emotions. This feeling can persist for months or even years after the event. Practitioners who help clients in these sorts of situations do so in part by encouraging them to name, validate, and express their emotions in a safe context (Halpern & Tramontin, 2007).

A third use of reflection is with clients who express negative feelings about therapy or about the helper. When a client becomes angry or upset with the helper or with the help being offered, there is a tendency for the helper to take the client's remarks personally and become defensive.

Using reflection in these instances helps to address and defuse inevitable misunderstandings that arise in the course of the helping process. This use of reflection lets clients know that the helper understands their feelings in such a way that the intensity of the anger is usually diminished. As anger subsides, the client may become more receptive, and the helper can again initiate action-oriented responses or intervention strategies. In this sense, reflection is used to defuse client resistance and is an important component of motivational interviewing (see also Chapter 10).

Reflection also helps clients discriminate accurately among various feelings. Clients often use feeling words like *anxious* or *nervous* that, on occasion, mask deeper or more intense feelings. Clients may also use an affect word that does not really portray their emotional state accurately. For instance, it is common for a client to say "It's my nerves" or "I'm nervous" to depict other feelings, such as resentment and depression. Other clients may reveal feelings through the use of metaphors. For example, a client may say "I feel like the person who plunged over Niagara Falls in a barrel" or "I feel like I just got hit by a Mack truck." **Metaphors** are important indicators of client emotion. As Ivey, Gluckstern Packard, and Ivey (2006) note, metaphors suggest that much more is going on with the client than just the "surface expression" (p. 73). Accurate reflections of feelings help clients to refine their understanding of various emotional moods.

Finally, reflection of feelings, if used effectively and accurately, helps clients to feel understood. Clients tend to communicate more freely with persons who they feel try to understand them. As Teyber and McClure (2011) observe, when understanding is present, "Clients feel that they have been seen and are no longer invisible or alone, different or defective, dismissed or unimportant, and so forth. At that moment, the client begins to perceive the therapist as someone who is different from many others in her life and possibly as someone who can help" (p. 72). The reflection-of-feelings response is the primary verbal tool used to convey basic empathy.

Verbal Means of Conveying Empathy Consider the following four verbal strategies for conveying empathy:

1. *Show desire to comprehend.* It is necessary not only to convey an accurate understanding from the client's perspective but also to convey your *desire* to comprehend from the client's frame of reference. Recall from our discussion of cultural empathy that this desire includes an understanding not only of the individual but also of the person's worldview: his or her environmental and sociopolitical context and cultural group.

McGill (1992) offers the idea of the **cultural story** as a way to open communication and develop understanding about the client's cultural group:

> The cultural story refers to an ethnic or cultural group's origin, migration, and identity. Within the family, it is used to tell where one's ancestors came from, what kind of people they were and that current members are, what issues are important to the family, what good and bad things have happened over time, and what lessons have been learned from their experiences. At the ethnic level, a cultural story tells the group's collective story of how to cope with life and how to respond to pain and trouble. It teaches people how to thrive in a multicultural society and what children should be taught so that they can sustain their ethnic and cultural story. (p. 340)

Your desire to comprehend is evidenced by statements indicating your attempts to make sense of the client's world and by clarification and questions about the client's experiences and feelings.

2. *Discuss what is important to the client.* Show by your questions and statements that you are aware of what is most important to the client. Respond in ways that relate to the client's basic problem or complaint. Formulate a brief statement that captures the thoughts and feelings of the client and that is directly related to the client's concerns.

3. Use verbal responses that *refer to client feelings.* One way to define verbal empathy is through the reflection-of-feelings response, which reflects the client's feelings and conveys your awareness of them. This response allows you to focus on the client's feelings by naming or labeling them. It is sometimes called **interchangeable** (Carkhuff, 1969), **basic** (Egan, 2014), or **reciprocal** (Hepworth, Rooney, Dewberry Rooney, & Strom-Gottfried, 2013) empathy. In motivational interviewing terms, these reflections are known as *simple reflections.*

4. Use verbal responses that bridge or *add on to implicit client messages.* Empathy also involves comprehension of the client's innermost thoughts and perspectives even when they are unspoken and implicit. According to Rogers (1977), "The therapist is so much inside the private world of the other that she can clarify not only the messages of which the client is aware but even those just below the level of awareness" (p. 11). The counselor bridges or adds to client messages by conveying understanding of what the client implies or infers to add to the client's frame of reference or to draw out implications of the issue. This is sometimes

4.3 Feedback

Paraphrase

Client 1

Question 1: *What has the client said?*
That she and her husband argue over child rearing.
Question 2: *What is the content of her message?*
As a couple, they have different ideas on who should discipline their kids and how.
Question 3: *What is a useful sentence stem?*
Try "It sounds like . . ." or "Your ideas about discipline are . . ."

Example of Paraphrase Responses

"It sounds like you and your husband disagree a great deal on which one of you should discipline your kids and how it should be done."
"Your ideas about discipline for your kids are really different from your husband's, and this creates disagreements between the two of you."

Client 2

Question 1: *What has this client said?*
He believes his little sister is loved more by his parents than he is, and he wishes she weren't around.
Question 2: *What is the content of this message?*
Client feels "dethroned"—wishes the new "princess" would go away.
Question 3: *What is an appropriate sentence stem?*
I'll try "It seems that . . ." or "I sense that . . ."

Examples of Paraphrase Responses

"It seems that you'd like to be 'number one' again in your family."
"I sense you are not sure of your place in your family since your little sister arrived."

Client 3

Question 1: *What has this client said?*
He is behind in school and is not doing as well as his peers because he is blind—a point he has emphasized to his family.
Question 2: *What is the content of this message?*
Client wants to impress on his family that to him his blindness is a handicap that interferes with his doing as much or as well as other students.
Question 3: *What is an appropriate sentence stem?*
"It sounds like . . .," "I hear you saying . . .," or "You'd like . . ."

Examples of Paraphrase Responses

"It sounds like it's very important to you for your family to realize how tough it is for you to do well in your studies here."
"You'd like your family to realize how difficult it is for you to keep up academically with people who don't have the added problem of being visually impaired."

called **additive** empathy (Carkhuff, 1969, Hepworth et al., 2013) or **advanced** empathy (Egan, 2014). At this level of empathy, the helper uses mild to moderate interpretations of the client's inferred feelings (Hepworth et al., 2013). In motivational interviewing, these reflections are known as *complex reflections.*

Carkhuff and Pierce (1975) developed a Discrimination Inventory that presents a scale for assessing both basic and additive empathy messages. Although this scale has been around for a number of years, it is still heavily used in training, especially as a way to help novice practitioners make discriminations about their level of empathic understanding. On this scale, helper responses are rated according to one of five levels. Level 3 is considered the *minimally* acceptable response. Level 3 responses on this scale correspond to Carkhuff and Pierce's concept of interchangeable empathy and to Egan's (2014) concept of basic-level empathy. Level 4 corresponds to additive empathy (Carkhuff, 1969) and to advanced empathy (Egan, 2014). Level 5 represents facilitating action.

Carkhuff and Pierce's Discrimination Inventory can be used to discriminate among levels of responses or to rate levels of helper communication. Here are examples of verbal empathic responses at each level:

Client: I've tried to get along with my father, but it doesn't work out. He's too hard on me.
Helper at Level 1: I'm sure it will all work out in time [reassurance and denial], *or* You should try harder to see his point of view [advice], *or* Why can't you two get along? [question].

The Level 1 response is a question, reassurance and denial, or advice.

Helper at Level 2: You're having a hard time getting along with your father.

At Level 2, the response is made to the *content* or cognitive portion of the message; feelings are ignored.

Helper at Level 3: You feel discouraged because your attempts to get along with your father have not been very successful.

The Level 3 response indicates understanding but provides no direction; it is a reflection of feeling and meaning based on the client's explicit message. In other words, a Level 3 response reflects both the feeling and the situation. In this example, "You feel discouraged" is the reflection of the feeling, and "because . . . not very successful" is the reflection of the situation.

Helper at Level 4: You feel discouraged because you can't seem to reach your father. You want him to let up on you.

The Level 4 response indicates understanding and provides some direction. A Level 4 response identifies not only the client's feelings but also the client's deficit that is implied. In a Level 4 response, the client's deficit is personalized—that is, the helper identifies the deficit, as in "you can't reach."

Helper at Level 5: You feel discouraged because you can't seem to reach your father. You want him to let up on you. One step could be to express your feelings about this to your father.

A Level 5 response contains all elements of a Level 4 response plus at least one action step that the client can take

to master the deficit and attain the goal. In this example, the action step is, "One step could be to express your feelings about this to your father."

Next, we present information about how to reflect feelings to convey *basic* empathy.

Steps in Reflection of Feelings Reflecting feelings can be a difficult skill to learn because feelings are often ignored or misunderstood. The reflection of feelings involves six steps, which include identifying the emotional tone of the communication and verbally reflecting the client's feelings in your own words.

1. Listen for feeling words, or affect words, in the client's messages. Positive, negative, and ambivalent feelings are expressed by affect words falling into one of five major categories: anger, fear, conflict, sadness, and happiness. Table 4.3 lists commonly used affect words at three levels of intensity. Becoming acquainted with such words may help you to recognize them in client communications and to expand your own vocabulary for describing emotions. Table 4.4 lists affect words to use with children and teens. With very young children,

TABLE 4.3   Words That Express Feelings

Relative intensity of words	Feeling category				
	Anger	Conflict	Fear	Happiness	Sadness
Mild feeling	Annoyed	Blocked	Apprehensive	Amused	Apathetic
	Bothered	Bound	Concerned	Anticipating	Bored
	Bugged	Caught	Tense	Comfortable	Confused
	Irked	Caught in a bind	Tight	Confident	Disappointed
	Irritated	Pulled	Uneasy	Contented	Discontented
	Peeved			Glad	Mixed up
	Ticked			Pleased	Resigned
				Relieved	Unsure
Moderate feeling	Disgusted	Locked	Afraid	Delighted	Abandoned
	Hacked	Pressured	Alarmed	Eager	Burdened
	Harassed	Strained	Anxious	Happy	Discouraged
	Mad	Torn	Fearful	Hopeful	Distressed
	Provoked		Frightened	Joyful	Down
	Put upon		Shook	Surprised	Drained
	Resentful		Threatened	Up	Empty
	Set up		Worried		Hurt
	Spiteful				Lonely
	Used				Lost
					Sad
					Unhappy
					Weighted

TABLE 4.3   Words That Express Feelings (*continued*)

Relative intensity of words	Anger	Conflict	Fear	Happiness	Sadness
Intense feeling	Angry	Coerced	Desperate	Bursting	Anguished
	Boiled	Ripped	Overwhelmed	Ecstatic	Crushed
	Burned	Wrenched	Panicky	Elated	Deadened
	Contemptuous		Petrified	Enthusiastic	Depressed
	Enraged		Scared	Enthralled	Despairing
	Fuming		Terrified	Excited	Helpless
	Furious		Terror-stricken	Free	Hopeless
	Hateful		Tortured	Fulfilled	Humiliated
	Hot			Moved	Miserable
	Infuriated			Proud	Overwhelmed
	Pissed			Terrific	Smothered
	Smoldering			Thrilled	Tortured
	Steamed			Turned on	

Source: From Hutchins & Cole. *Helping Relationships and Strategies,* 3e. Copyright © 1997 Wadsworth, a part of Cengage Learning, Inc. Reproduced by permission. www.cengage.com/permissions

TABLE 4.4   Affect Words and Phrases for Children and Teens

Anxious	Bored	Childish	Contented or fulfilled	Curious
Depressed	Determined	Disgusted	Doubtful	Embarrassed
Empty	Envious of others	Excited	Furious	Guilty
Hopeful	Humble	Hurt	Irritated	Jealous
Lovable	Mean and destructive	Nervous	Optimistic	Proud
Rebellious	Sad	Safe and secure	Scared or afraid	Silly
Sorry	Strong and capable	Terrified	Thrilled	Warm and cozy
Worried				

Source: Adapted from *Group Activities for Counselors,* by Eliot, Inner Choice Publishing, 1994.

we recommend using face symbols such as those depicted in Figure 4.3.

2. Watch the client's nonverbal behavior while he or she is delivering the verbal message. Recall our earlier discussion about the ways in which nonverbal cues such as body posture, facial expression, and voice quality are important indicators of client emotion. Observing nonverbal behavior is particularly important when the client's feelings are implied or expressed very subtly.

3. After the feelings reflected by the client's words and nonverbal behavior have been identified, reflect the feelings back to the client using different words. The choice of words is critical to the effectiveness of this response. Suppose a client feels "annoyed." Interchangeable affect words would be *bothered, irritated,* and *hassled.* Words such as *angry, mad,* and *outraged* probably would convey greater intensity than the client intends to express. With adult clients, it is important for the helper to select affect words that accurately match not only the type but also the intensity of feeling; otherwise, the helper produces an understatement, which can make a client feel ridiculed, or an overstatement, which can make a client feel put off or intimidated. Notice the three levels of feeling in Table 4.3: mild, moderate, and intense. You can also control the intensity of the expressed affect by your choice of a preceding adverb—for example, *somewhat* (weak), *quite* (moderate), or *very* (strong) *upset*. With children, use a word or a symbol that captures their feelings as closely as possible. Study Table 4.3 and Table 4.4 carefully so that you can develop an extensive vocabulary of affect words. If you overuse a few common affect words, then you will miss the nuances of clients' emotional experiences.

| Strong | Happy | Sad | Angry | Scared | Confused | Weak |

FIGURE 4.3 Feeling Symbols for Children

Source: From Henderson & Thompson. Counseling Children, 8e. Copyright © 2011 Cengage Learning. Reproduced with permission. www.cengage.com/permissions

4. Start your reflection statement with an appropriate sentence stem, such as one of the following:

> "It *appears* that you are *angry* now."
> "It *looks* like you are *angry* now."
> "It is *clear* to me that you are *angry* now."
> "It *sounds* like you are *angry* now."
> "I *hear* you saying you are *angry* now."
> "My *ears* tell me that you are *angry* now."
> "I can *grasp* your *anger*."
> "You are *feeling angry* now."
> "Let's get in *touch* with your *anger*."

For more sentence stems, refer to Table 4.2.

5. Add the context of the feelings or the situation in which they occur. This addition takes the form of a brief paraphrase. Usually the context can be determined from the content part of the client's message. For example, a client might say, "I just can't take tests. I get so anxious I never do well even though I study a lot." In this message, the affect is anxiety and the context is test-taking. The helper reflects both the affect ("You feel uptight") *and* the context ("whenever you have to take a test").

6. Assess the effectiveness of your reflection after delivering it. Usually, if your reflection accurately identifies the client's feelings, then the client will confirm your response by saying something like "Yes, that's right," or "Yes, that's exactly how I feel." If your response is off target, then the client may reply with "Well, it's not quite like that," "I don't feel exactly that way," or "No, I don't feel that way." When the client responds by denying feelings, it may mean your reflection was inaccurate or ill timed. It is very important for helpers to decide when to respond to emotions. Reflection of feelings may be too powerful to be used *frequently* in the very early stage of helping. At that time, overuse of this response may make the client feel uncomfortable, a situation that can result in denial rather than acknowledgment of emotions. But do not ignore the potential impact or usefulness of reflection later on,

when focusing on the client's feelings would promote the goals of the session.

In the following example, notice the way in which a helper uses a cognitive learning strategy (adapted from Richardson & Stone, 1981) to formulate a reflection of client feelings:

Client, a white middle-aged man *(says in loud, shrill, high-pitched voice, with clenched fists)*: You can't imagine what it was like when I found out my wife was cheating on me. I saw red! What should I do—get even, leave her? I'm not sure.

Helper *(asks and answers covertly)*:

Self-question 1: What overt feeling words has this client used?
None—except for the suggested affect phrase "saw red."

Self-question 2: What feelings are implied in the client's voice and nonverbal behavior?
Anger, outrage, hostility.

Self-question 3: What affect words accurately describe this client's feelings at a similar level of intensity?
"Furious," "angry," "vindictive," "outraged."

Self-question 4: What is an appropriate sentence stem?
Given the client's use of "imagine" and "saw red," I'll try sentence stems like "It seems," "It appears," and "It looks like."

Self-question 5: What is the context, or situation, surrounding his feelings that I'll paraphrase?
The client's discovery that his wife was unfaithful.

Self-question 6: How will I know whether my reflection is accurate and helpful?
Watch and listen for the client's response—whether he confirms or denies the feeling of being angry and vindictive.

Actual Examples of Reflection
> "It looks like you're very angry now about your wife's going out on you."
> "It appears that you're furious with your wife's actions."
> "It seems like you're both angry and vindictive now that you've discovered your wife has been going out with other men."

Learning Activity **4.4**

Reflection of Feelings

In this activity, you are presented with three client practice messages. For each message, develop a reflection-of-feelings response using the cognitive learning strategy (Richardson & Stone, 1981) described previously and outlined here. To internalize this learning strategy, you may wish to talk through the self-questions overtly (aloud) and then covertly (silently to yourself). The end product will be a reflection-of-feelings response that you can say aloud or write down. An example precedes the practice messages. Feedback is given on page 128.

Example

Client, a 50-year-old worker now laid off (*says in a loud, critical voice, staring at the ceiling, brow furrowed, eyes squinting*): Now look. What can I do? I've been laid off over a year. I've got no money, no job, and a family to take care of. We lost our house to foreclosure. It's also clear to me that my mind and skills are just wasting away.

Self-question 1: *What overt feeling words did the client use?* None.

Self-question 2: *What feelings are implied in the client's nonverbal behavior?*
Disgust, anger, upset, frustration, resentment, disillusionment, discouragement.

Self-question 3: *What affect words accurately describe the client's feelings at a similar level of intensity?*
There seem to be two feelings: anger and discouragement. Anger seems to be the stronger emotion of the two.

Self-question 4: *What is an appropriate sentence stem?*
Use stems like "I see you," or "It's clear to me that you," or "From where I'm looking, you." These are similar to the client phrases "Now look" and "It's also clear."

Self-question 5: *What is the context, or situation, surrounding his feelings that I'll paraphrase?*
Loss of job and home, no resources, no job prospects in sight.

Reflection-of-feelings response: "I can see you're angry about being out of work and discouraged about the future," or "It looks like you're very upset about having your job, home, and stability taken away from you."

Client Practice Statements

Client 1, an 8-year-old girl (*says in a level tone, with measured words, glancing from side to side, lips drawn tightly together, face flushed*): I'm telling you I don't like living at home anymore. I wish I could live with my friend and her parents. I told my mommy that one day I'm going to run away, but she doesn't listen to me.

Self-question 1: *What overt feeling words did the client use?*
Self-question 2: *What feelings are implied in the client's nonverbal behavior?*
Self-question 3: *What are accurate and similar interchangeable affect words?*
Self-question 4: *What is an appropriate sentence stem?*
Self-question 5: *What is the context, or situation, surrounding her feelings that I'll paraphrase?*
Actual reflection response: _____

Client 2, a middle-aged man in marital therapy (*says in a soft voice with eyes downcast*): As far as I'm concerned, our marriage turned sour last year when my wife went back to work. She's more in touch with her work than with me.

Self-question 1: *What overt feeling words did the client use?*
Self-question 2: *What feelings are implied in the client's nonverbal behavior?*
Self-question 3: *What are accurate and similar interchangeable affect words?*
Self-question 4: *What is an appropriate sentence stem?*
Self-question 5: *What is the context, or situation, surrounding his feelings that I'll paraphrase?*
Actual reflection response: _____

Client 3, an adolescent (*says in loud, harsh voice*): Now look, we have too damn many rules around this school. I'm getting the hell out of here. As far as I can see, this place is a dump.

Self-question 1: *What overt feeling words has this client used?*
Self-question 2: *What feelings are implied in the client's nonverbal behavior?*
Self-question 3: *What are accurate and similar interchangeable affect words?*
Self-question 4: *What is an appropriate sentence stem?*
Self-question 5: *What is the context, or situation, surrounding his feelings that I'll paraphrase?*
Actual reflection response: _____

Suppose that following the reflection, the client says, "Yes, I'm very angry, for sure. But I don't know about vindictive, although I guess I'd like to make her feel as awful as I do." The client has confirmed the helper's reflection of the feelings of anger and vindictiveness but also has given a clue that he finds the word *vindictive* too strong *at this time*. The helper picks up on the feelings, noting that the word *vindictive* might be used again later, after the client has sorted through his mixed feelings about his wife's behavior.

Learning Activity 4.4 gives you an opportunity to practice with reflection-of-feelings responses.

Summarization: Listening for Patterns and Themes

Usually, after a client expresses several messages or talks for a while, the helper is able to spot in the client's messages' certain consistencies or patterns, which we refer to as **themes**. The themes of a client's messages are evident in topics that the client continually refers to or brings up in some way. The helper can identify themes by listening to what the client repeats over and over and with the most intensity (Carkhuff, Pierce, & Cannon, 1977). The themes indicate what the client is trying to tell us and what the client needs to focus on in the helping sessions. Ivey and colleagues (2007) recommend listening to the *way* the client organizes his or her story. The counselor can respond to client themes by using a summarization response. Suppose that you have been working with a young man who, during the last three sessions, has made repeated references to relationships with gay men yet has not really identified this issue intentionally. You could use a summarization to identify the theme from his repeated references by saying something like, "I'm aware that during our last few sessions you've spoken consistently about relationships with gay men. Perhaps this could be an issue that we choose to focus on?"

Or suppose that in one session a client has given you several descriptions of different situations in which he feels concerned about how other people perceive him. You might discern that the theme common to all these situations is the client's need for approval from others, or "other-directedness." You could use a summarization such as this to identify this theme: "One thing I see in all three situations you've described is that you seem quite concerned about having the approval of other people. Is this accurate?"

A *summarization* can be defined as two or more paraphrases or reflections that condense the client's messages or the session. Summarization "involves listening to a client over a period of time (from 3 minutes to a complete session or more), picking out relationships among key issues, and restating them back accurately to the client" (Ivey et al., 2006, p. 94).

Purposes of Summarization

One purpose of summarization is to tie together multiple elements of client messages. In this case, by extracting meaning from vague and ambiguous messages, summarization can serve as a good feedback tool for the client. A second purpose of summarization is to identify a common theme or pattern that becomes apparent after several messages or sometimes after several sessions. Occasionally, a helper may summarize to interrupt a client's incessant rambling or "storytelling." At such times, summarization is an important focusing tool that brings direction to the interview.

A fourth use of summarization is to slow the pace of a session that is moving too quickly. In such instances, summaries provide psychological breathing space during the session. A final purpose of a summary is to review progress that has been made during one or more interviews. You can probably see from these purposes why summarization is the last response in the nonjudgmental listening cycle we described earlier in the chapter.

A summarization may represent collective rephrasings of either cognitive or affective data, but most summarization responses include references to both cognitive and affective messages, as in the following four examples.

Summarization to Tie Together Multiple Elements of a Client Message

Client, a Native American young medical student: All my life I thought I wanted to become a doctor and go back to work on my reservation. Now that I've left home, I'm not sure. I still feel strong ties there that are pulling me back. I hate to let my people down, yet I also feel like there's a lot out here I want to explore first.

Summarization: You're away from the reservation now and are finding so much in this place to explore. At the same time, you're feeling pulled by your lifelong ties to your people and your dream of returning as a doctor.

Summarization to Identify a Theme

Client, a 35-year-old European American male: One of the reasons we divorced was because she always pushed me. I could never say "no" to her; I always gave in. I guess it's hard for me just to say "no" to requests people make.

Summarization: You're discovering that you tend to give in or not do what you want in many of your significant relationships, not just with your ex-wife.

Summarization to Regulate the Pace of a Session and to Give Focus

Client, a young European American woman: What a terrible week I had! The water heater broke, the dog got lost, someone stole my wallet, my car ran out of gas, and to top it all off, I gained 5 pounds. I can't stand myself. It seems like it shows all over me.

Summarization: Let's stop for just a minute before we go on. It seems like you've encountered an unending series of bad events this week.

Summarization to Review Progress

Summarization: Monique, we've got about 5 minutes left today. It seems like most of the time we've been working on the ways you find to sabotage yourself from doing things you want to do but feel are out of your control. This week I'd like you to work on the following homework before our next session . . .

That type of summarization is often used as a termination strategy near the end of a session.

Steps in Summarizing

Summarizing requires careful attention to and concentration on the client's verbal and nonverbal messages. Accurate use of this listening response depends on good recall of client behavior, not only within a session but over time—across several sessions or even several months of therapy. Developing a summarization involves the following four steps:

1. Attend to and recall the message or series of messages by restating them to yourself covertly. What has the client been telling you, focusing on, working on? This is a key and difficult step because it requires you to be aware of many varying verbal and nonverbal messages you have processed *over time*.

2. Identify any apparent patterns, themes, or multiple elements of these messages by asking yourself questions like, "What has the client repeated over and over?" and "What are the different parts of this puzzle?"

3. Using the sentence stem you've selected, select words to describe the theme or to tie together multiple elements, and say this aloud as your summarization response. Remember to use your voice so that the summarization sounds like a statement, not a question.

4. Assess the effectiveness of your summarization by listening for and observing whether the client confirms or denies the theme or whether the summary adds to or detracts from the focus of the session.

To formulate a summarization, consider the following cognitive learning strategy (Learning Activity 4.5 gives you a chance to try this strategy):

1. What was the client telling me and working on today and over time—that is, what are the *key content* and *key affect?*

2. What has the client repeated over and over today and over time? What *patterns* or *themes* am I seeing?

3. How will I know whether my summarization is useful?

Notice how a helper applies this cognitive learning strategy when developing a summarization in the following example, where the client has told you for the past three sessions that his drinking is ruining his family life but he can't stop because it makes him feel better and helps him handle job stress:

Client, a white male fighting alcoholism *(says in low, soft voice, with downcast eyes and stooped shoulders)*: I know drinking doesn't really help me in the long run. And it sure doesn't help my family. My wife keeps threatening to leave. I know all this. But it's hard to stay away from the booze. Having a drink makes me feel relieved.

Helper *(asks and answers covertly):*

Self-question 1: What has the client been telling me today and over time?
Key content: Results of drinking aren't good for him or his family.
Key affect: Drinking makes him feel better, less anxious.
Self-question 2: What has the client repeated over and over today and over time? What patterns or themes am I seeing?
Despite adverse effects and family deterioration, he continues to drink for stress reduction and "medicating" of feelings. Stress reduction through alcohol seems worth more than losing his family.

Suppose that at this time the helper delivered one of the following summarizations to the client:

"Jerry, I sense that you feel it's worth having the hassle of family problems because of the good, calm feelings you get whenever you drink."

"Jerry, you feel that your persistent drinking is creating a lot of difficulties for you in your family, and I sense your reluctance to stop drinking despite these adverse effects."

"Jerry, I sense that despite everything, alcohol feels more satisfying (rewarding) to you than your own family."

If Jerry confirms the theme that alcohol is more important now than his family, the helper can conclude that the summarization was useful. If Jerry denies the theme or issue summarized, the helper can ask Jerry to clarify how the summarization was inaccurate, remembering that the summary may indeed be inaccurate or that Jerry may not be ready to acknowledge the issue at this time. (See Learning Activity 4.5 on page 130.)

4.4 Feedback

Reflection of Feelings

Client 1

Question 1: *What overt feeling words did the client use?*
"Don't like."
Question 2: *What feelings are implied in the client's nonverbal behavior?*
Upset, irritation, resentment.
Question 3: *What are interchangeable affect words?*
"Bothered," "perturbed," "irritated," "upset."
Question 4: *What sentence stem will I use?*
"Seems like," "It sounds like," or "I hear you saying that."
Question 5: *What is the context, or situation, surrounding her feelings?*
Living at home with her parents.

Actual examples of reflection

"It sounds like you're upset about some things going on at your home now."
"I hear you saying you're bothered about your parents."

Client 2

Question 1: *What overt feeling words did the client use?*
No obvious ones except for the phrases "turned sour" and "more in touch with."
Question 2: *What feelings are implied in the client's nonverbal behavior?*
Sadness, loneliness, hurt.
Question 3: *What are interchangeable affect words?*
"Hurt," "lonely," "left out," "unhappy."
Question 4: *What sentence stem is appropriate?*
"I sense" or "You feel."

Question 5: *What is the context, or situation, surrounding his feelings?*
Wife's return to work.

Actual examples of reflection

"You're feeling left out and lonely since your wife has gone back to work."
I sense you're feeling hurt and unhappy because your wife seems so interested in her work."

Client 3

Question 1: *What overt feeling words did the client use?*
No obvious ones, but words like "damn," "hell," and "dump" suggest intensity of emotions.
Question 2: *What feelings are implied in the client's nonverbal behavior?*
Anger, frustration.
Question 3: *What are interchangeable affect words?*
"Angry," "offended," "disgusted."
Question 4: *What sentence stem will I use?*
Stems such as "It seems," "It appears," "It looks like," and "I can see."
Question 5: *What is the context, or situation, surrounding the feelings?*
School rules.

Actual examples of reflection

"It looks like you're disgusted now because you see these rules restricting you."
"It seems like you're very angry about having all these rules here at school."

Listening to Diverse Groups of Clients

The listening process in a helping relationship is affected by factors such as the client's age, ethnicity, gender, sexual orientation, ability status, and languages. Active listening can be a useful way to establish rapport with children and adolescent clients (Henderson & Thompson, 2011). Elderly clients who lack social contacts often long for a good listener. Schoenbeck (2010) developed a project with elderly persons known as the Remembrance Project designed to help persons engage in conversations with elderly people about what they want to be remembered for in their lives and what was and is most important to them.

The listening process itself may conflict with the basic values of some clients of color. For example, client behaviors such as unresponsiveness to inquiries, minimal self-disclosure, lack of eye contact, and avoidance of feeling statements may not be an indication that the client is "resistant," "depressed," "unassertive," or "unemotional," but rather that the client is simply communicating in ways that are consistent with the client's culture. As an example of this, traditional Chinese culture "values restraint of strong feelings, and eye contact is avoided in the presence of higher-status individuals. Further . . . in many cultures similar to the Chinese, subtlety and indirectness in discussing delicate matters are highly valued attributes of communication. Discussion of personal and private matters is done indirectly rather than directly" (Sue & Sue, 2013, p. 212).

Sue and Sue (2013) note that those helping professionals reared in a European American middle-class society may assume "that certain behaviors or rules of speaking are universal and possess the same meaning"

(p. 213). This assumption violates the idiographic practice that we discussed in Chapter 2. In general, the practitioner needs to be able to be somewhat flexible to adapt one's communication style to the cultural frame of reference of the client. In nonverbal communication in particular, aspects of nonverbal attentiveness may need adaptations for various kinds of clients. With children, elderly clients, clients with hearing impairments, clients from contact cultures such as Latin Americans, Africans, African Americans, Arabs, French, South Americans, and so on, conversing with the client may dictate a much closer physical distance and space than the white helper may be comfortable with. Issues in listening and understanding can arise when cultural differences in proxemics are ignored. For example, the helper may view the client's physical closeness as intrusive or aggressive, whereas the client may view the helper's lack of physical closeness as arrogant or aloof. Because proxemics research concludes that conversational distances are a function of the ethnic and cultural background of the individual, "both the therapist and the culturally different client may benefit from understanding that their reactions and behaviors are attempts to create the spatial dimension to which they are culturally conditioned" (Sue & Sue, 2013, p. 215).

Kinesics also appears to be culturally conditioned to some degree. While some clients smile when they are happy, some Asian clients smile when they are embarrassed or experiencing apprehension. Other Asian clients have learned to have almost inscrutable facial expressions in recognition of the cultural value of restraint of strong feelings. Even something as simple as a handshake can be easily misunderstood. While most cultures use the right hand when shaking someone else's hand, in some Muslim and Asian countries extending the left hand could be a grave offense and insult because touching anyone with the left hand is considered an obscenity. Eye contact and head motion represent other parts of kinesics frequently misinterpreted in the listening process. Clients from some cultural groups avoid eye contact as a sign of respect. Some black clients may not nod their heads to indicate they are listening, but the absence of eye contact or head nodding should not be construed by the helper to mean the client is not paying attention!

In terms of paralinguistics, volume, pitch, intensity, and frequency of speech are influenced by culture. European Americans often speak more quickly and with more force than Asians do, for example, whereas many Arabs speak even more loudly than U.S. Americans.

Sue and Sue (2013, p. 218) conclude that a practitioner "working with clients would be well advised to be aware of possible cultural misinterpretations as a function of speech volume. Speaking loudly may not indicate anger and hostility, and speaking in a soft voice may not be a sign of weakness, shyness, or depression." Similarly, the directness of communication in a helping session also will vary a great deal among clients of various cultural groups. Sue and Sue (2013) observe that "since many minority groups may value indirectness, the U.S. emphasis on 'getting to the point' and 'not beating around the bush' may alienate others. Asian Americans, American Indians, and some Latino/Hispanic Americans may see this behavior as immature, rude, and lacking in finesse. However, clients from different cultures may be negatively labeled as evasive and afraid to confront the problem" (p. 219).

Gender differences also play a role. Gender has been linked to communication variables such as amount of talk time, swearing, interrupting, and use of silence. Some men tend to have a more directive style, asking more questions and doing more interrupting and problem-solving than some women, who may make more reflective statements (Ivey et al., 2007). Male clients may be viewed by practitioners as lacking in emotion compared to female clients, and so some forms of communication between genders in the helping process may not be male-friendly. However, practitioners may intentionally or unintentionally promote gender-based bias in power differentials by using language in listening to clients that conveys standards and expectations based on the norms of male experience (and privilege) rather than female experience.

Some practitioners will also experience challenges to listening and communication in working with gay clients. A common mistake that many practitioners make in listening to clients is to assume heterosexuality. The assumption of heterosexuality is often referred to as the **heterosexual privilege**. Even after listening to clients describe a prior or current relationship with someone of the opposite sex, it is biased to assume without self-identification of sexual orientation that the client is heterosexual (Lyons et al., 2010). Sue (2010) defines **heterosexism** as "a sexual orientation worldview that contains beliefs and attitudes that (a) all people are/or should be heterosexual, (b) it is more desirable to be heterosexual, and (c) it represents the norm of both gender identity and sexual attraction. By implication, then, nonheterosexuals do not exist or should become heterosexual, are undesirable, and are considered abnormal" (p. 190). As Sue (2010) notes, the implications of

Learning Activity 4.5

Summarization

In this activity you are presented with three client practice messages. For each message, develop a summarization response using the cognitive learning strategy described earlier and outlined here. To internalize this learning strategy, you may wish to talk through the self-questions overtly (aloud) and then covertly (silently to yourself). The end product will be a summarization response that you can say aloud or write down. An example precedes the practice messages. Feedback is given on page 132.

Example

Client, a 10-year-old girl, at the beginning of the session *(says in low, soft voice, with lowered, moist eyes):* I don't understand why my parents can't live together anymore. I'm not blaming anybody, but it just feels very confusing to me.

Same client, near the middle of the same session: I wish they could keep it together. I guess I feel like they can't because they fight about me so much. Maybe I'm the reason they don't want to live together anymore.

Self-question 1: *What has the client been telling me and working on today?*

Key content: She wants her parents to stay together.

Key affect: She feels sad, upset, and responsible.

Self-question 2: *What has the client repeated over and over today and over time? What patterns and themes am I seeing?* That she's the one who's responsible for her parents' breakup.

Examples of Summarization Response

"Joan, at the start of our talk today, you were feeling like no one person was responsible for your parents' separation. Now I sense you're saying that you feel responsible."

"Joan, earlier today you indicated you didn't feel like blaming anyone for what's happening to your folks. Now I'm sensing that you're feeling like you're responsible for their breakup."

Client Practice Messages

Client 1, a 30-year-old man who has been blaming himself for his wife's unhappiness *(says in low, soft voice with lowered eyes):* I really feel guilty about marrying her in the first place. It wasn't really for love. It was just a convenient thing to do. I feel like I've messed up her life really badly. I also feel obliged to her.

Self-question 1: *What has the client been telling me and working on today?*

*Key content:*_____

Key affect: _____

Self-question 2: *What has the client repeated over and over today? What patterns or themes am I seeing?*

Summarization response: _____
_____
_____

Client 2, a 35-year-old woman who focuses on how her life has improved since having children *(says with alertness and animation):* I never thought I would feel this great. I always thought being a parent would be boring and terribly difficult. It's not, for me. It's fascinating and easy. It makes everything worthwhile.

Self-question 1: *What has this client been telling me and working on today?*

Key content: _____

Key affect: _____

Self-question 2: *What has this client repeated over and over today or over time? What patterns or themes am I seeing?*

Summarization response: _____
_____

Client 3, a 27-year-old woman who has continually focused on her relationships with men and her needs for excitement and stability, at the first session *(says with bright eyes and facial animation and in a high-pitched voice):* I've been dating lots and lots of men for the past few years. Most of them have been married. That's great because there are no demands on me.

Same client, at the fourth session *(says in a soft voice, with lowered eyes):* It doesn't feel so good anymore. It's not so much fun. Now I guess I miss having some commitment and stability in my life.

Self-question 1: *What has the client been telling me and working on today?*

*Key content:*_____

Key affect: _____

Self-question 2: *What has the client repeated over and over today or over time. What patterns or themes am I seeing?*

Summarization response: _____
_____
_____

heterosexual privilege for LGBT clients constitute a large part of sexual orientation microaggressions.

Listening and understanding with LGBT clients are often absent when helpers use biased language to describe LGBT clients, such as referring to them as "homosexuals" or using terminology that is derogatory or demeaning (e.g., "That was so gay"). Practitioners contribute to this in very subtle ways in practice by using terms such as *boyfriend, girlfriend, wife, husband,* or *marriage* instead of *partner, spouse, significant other,* and so on. Asking a LGBT client about his or her "sexual preference" instead of asking about "sexual orientation" also constitutes a microaggression in the listening process because it communicates an underlying value that the LGBT client has *chosen* an alternative lifestyle. Lyons and colleagues (2010) note that listening and understanding are promoted when helpers are able to use language free of heterosexist bias and to have welcoming office environments for clients. Sue (2010) recommends that all practitioners should become aware of ethnocentric heterosexist language and vocabulary in our everyday use and be vigilant about our own words and those of others, too.

Persons with disabilities also present unique challenges for listening and empathy from practitioners who may be ill-prepared in the way of specialized training to respond appropriately. As Artman and Daniels (2010, p. 444) note, "most perceptions of disabilities are negative, and are frequently reflected in language." For example, they recommend the use of *person first* language to communicate with clients with disabilities, referring to the client as a person with schizophrenia, for example, rather than as a schizophrenic. Similarly, "people who use wheelchairs" is meant to replace phrases such as "confined to a wheelchair" or "wheelchair bound." These latter phrases represent the projections of able-bodied practitioners and are actually expressions of negativity toward clients with disabilities (Artman & Daniels, 2010, p. 444). Using negative language such as this in communicating with and listening to clients with disabilities simply perpetuates negative stereotyping that someone with a disability automatically is miserable, depressed, grief stricken, and so forth.

Another situation in which listening can pose special issues in the helping process arises when clients do not speak standard English, use English as a second language, or do not speak English at all. The helper may feel that he or she has more trouble listening to such clients, although it is really the clients who suffer. Sue and Sue (2013) note that the reliance on standard English in counseling and therapy can discriminate against clients from a bilingual or lower socioeconomic environment (p. 196). In other instances language may pose a listening challenge

for helpers when clients use words or phrases that are unknown to them. For example, a client who is French Canadian may exclaim, "Mon Dieu!" when expressing distress about a situation, while another client who is Jewish may use a Yiddish phrase to describe something like "this week I did a mitzvah for someone."

In general, listening to diverse groups of clients is facilitated when, as practitioners, we are both open and flexible in our approach to communicating with clients. We strive to listen to clients, and the worldviews and factors that make each client unique, by using listening responses and communication styles that consider all aspects of the client sitting in front of us at the moment. You can work with these concepts in Learning Activity 4.6 on page 134.

Distractions and Distractability: Listening to Yourself

Egan (2014) discusses what he calls the "**shadow side" of listening**—that is, ways in which the listening process may fail. As he notes, active listening sounds good in theory but in practice is not without "obstacles and distractions" (p. 100).

Egan (2014) points out that evaluations and filters can be obstacles to effective listening. Although it is not possible to suspend judgment completely, most clients have finely tuned antennae that detect evaluative responses—perhaps because they have heard judgment so often in their lives. Clients who experience individual or cultural shame are especially likely to shut down when they hear evaluative listening from counselors.

Labels and biases may cause **filtered listening** (Egan, 2014, pp. 100–101). For example, if you are required to give your client a diagnosis, you may run through possible labels in your head while you are simultaneously trying to listen to the client. Or perhaps someone already labeled the client you are seeing as the "borderline" client or the "dysthymic" client, or the "oppositional" kid. An obstacle to listening in each instance is the temptation to look for corroborative behaviors while listening to the client. All of us use filters to structure our worlds, but these filters, if very strong, can inject biased listening into the helping process and foster stereotyping (Egan, 2014, p. 101). Filters often come into play when we are listening to clients who are culturally different from ourselves in some way. Clients who detect "filtered listening" are likely to shut down, feeling it isn't safe to open their hearts and souls to us (Lindahl, 2003).

4.5 Feedback

Summarization

Client 1

Question 1: *What has the client told me?*
Key content: He married for convenience, not love.
Key affect: Now he feels both guilty and indebted.
Question 2: *What has the client repeated over and over? What patterns or themes do I see?*
Conflicting feelings—feels a strong desire to get out of the marriage yet feels a need to keep relationship going because he feels responsible for his wife's unhappiness.

Examples of Summarization Response

"I sense you're feeling pulled in two different directions. For yourself, you want out of the relationship. For her sake, you feel you should stay in the relationship."

"You're feeling like you've used her for your convenience and because of this you think you owe it to her to keep the relationship going."

"I can grasp how very much you want to pull yourself out of the marriage and also how responsible you feel for your wife's present unhappiness."

Client 2

Question 1: *What has the client told me?*
Key content: Children have made her life better, more worthwhile.
Key affect: Surprise and pleasure.
Question 2: *What has the client repeated over and over? What patterns or themes do I see?*
Being a parent is uplifting and rewarding even though she didn't expect it to be. In addition, her children are very important to her. To some extent, they define her worth and value as a person.

Examples of Summarization Response

"It seems like you're feeling surprise, satisfaction, and relief about finding parenting so much easier and more rewarding than you had expected it would be."

"I hear feelings of surprise and pleasure in your voice as you reveal how great it is to be a parent and how important your children are to you."

"You seem so happy about the way your life is going since you've had children—as if they make you and your life more worthwhile."

Client 3

Question 1: *What has the client told me?*
Key content: She has been dating lots of men who have their own commitments.
Key affect: It used to feel great; now she feels a sense of loss and emptiness.
Question 2: *What has the client repeated over and over? What patterns or themes do I see?*
At first she had feelings of pleasure and relief not to have demands in close relationships. Now, feelings are changing and she feels less satisfied; she wants more stability in close relationships.

Examples of Summarization Response

"Lee Ann, originally you said it was great to be going out with a lot of different men who didn't ask much of you. Now you're also feeling it's not so great—it's keeping you from finding some purpose and stability in your life."

"In our first session, you were feeling 'up' about all those relationships with noncommittal men. Now you're feeling like this is interfering with the stability you need and haven't yet found."

"At first it was great to have all this excitement and few demands. Now you're feeling some loss from lack of a more stable, involved relationship."

Sullivan (2004) describes three obstacles to deep listening. One is **playing tapes**—as he notes, like a jukebox, helpers often have prerecorded opinions on a variety of topics. Often beginning helpers do not realize that counseling is not a soapbox! True dialogue reverts to a monologue. As Sullivan (2004) states, "playing tapes requires minimal attention" and minimal presence (p. 190). A second obstacle Sullivan (2004) describes is **checklist listening**—outwardly we look like we are listening, but inwardly we are "checking" to see if we agree or disagree with what our clients say and believe rather than being really present to their communication and ideas. The third obstacle he mentions is **being oppositional**—listening that is clouded by our labels and judgments. Sullivan recommends the use of a mnemonic to help us identify when we move into oppositional listening—JUDABC—Justifying, Defending, Attacking, Blaming, and Complaining (p. 191).

Another obstacle to listening is *tension*. When we are tense as helpers, this tension diminishes our ability to listen to and feel with our clients. Think of the last time you sat with a client and felt the distraction of a tension headache in your neck. Or the last time you were with someone close to you and you felt tense about an upcoming test or work deadline. Physical and mental tension preclude deep listening. As the famous cellist Yo-Yo Ma put it, "With every year (of playing) you want to relax one more muscle. Why? Because the more tense you are, the less you can hear. So the more you can collect that energy and be unblocked and be totally present, the more you can say 'I'm here'" (Mermelstein, 2010, p. D8).

As an antidote to distractions and barriers to listening, consider slowing the pace of the session and even slowing the pace of your own mental activity as the helper. Resist the urge to "fix" the client, to rush in to problem-solve for the client.

A general guideline for deep listening is there is no rush to action. A metaphor for this is the idea of standing still for a few moments with the client instead of running forward with great speed. Sullivan (2004) points out that being too quick to offer suggestions is akin to what acupuncturists describe as "a rush to early ripening" (p. 189). As he notes, this quickness to discover solutions or to "fix" the client often encourages helpers to listen *only* to problems. Strengths and resources are then often overlooked or missed in the client's narrative.

In this chapter, we have described various listening responses that will help you become a good listener if you learn them. Truly effective listening, however, requires even more from you. It requires you to be fully present to the client and oblivious to distractions—both internal and external. It requires you to create a "holding environment" for clients. The helpers who listen best usually have developed this sort of "mindfulness." They are able to focus very intently on the client. Such mindfulness is especially well developed in Eastern cultures, where people rise at dawn to practice tai chi. Perhaps nowhere is this quality more evident than among helpers who work with dying persons. Frank Ostaseski (1994), director of the San Francisco Zen Hospice Project, discusses mindfulness in the following way:

We sit at the bedside and we listen. We try to listen with our whole body, not just with our ears. We must perpetually ask ourselves, "Am I fully here? Or am I checking my watch or looking out the window?"

At the heart of it, all we can really offer each other is our full attention. When people are dying, their tolerance for bullshit is minimal. They will quickly sniff out insincerity. Material may arise that we don't particularly like or even strongly dislike. Just as we do in meditation,

we need to sit still and listen, not knowing what will come next, to suspend judgment—at least for the moment—so that whatever needs to evolve will be able to do so (p. 11).

If you feel that mindfulness is a quality you need to develop further in yourself, we encourage you to practice Learning Activity 4.7 to learn to listen to yourself.

CHAPTER SUMMARY

We often hear these questions: "What good does all this listening do? How does just rephrasing client messages really help?" In response, let us reiterate the rationale for using listening responses in helping:

1. Listening to clients is a very powerful reinforcer and may strengthen clients' desire to talk about themselves and their concerns. Not listening may prevent clients from sharing relevant information.

2. Listening to a client first may mean a greater chance of responding accurately to the client in later stages of helping, such as problem-solving. By jumping to quick solutions without laying a foundation of listening, you may inadvertently ignore the primary issue or propose inadequate and ill-timed action steps (Sommers-Flanagan & Sommers-Flanagan, 2014).

3. Listening encourages the client to assume responsibility for selecting the topic and focus of an interview. Simply asking a series of questions or proposing a series of action steps in the initial phase of helping can cause the client to perceive you as the expert and can hinder proper development of client self-responsibility in the interview.

4. Good listening and attending skills model socially appropriate behavior for clients. Many clients have not yet learned to use the art of listening in their own relationships and social contacts. They are more likely to incorporate these skills to improve their interpersonal relationships when they experience them firsthand through their contact with a significant other, such as a skilled helper.

All these reasons take into account both the gender and the cultural affiliation of the client. Listening may have a differential effect depending on the client's gender and cultural affiliation.

Some helpers can articulate a clear rationale for listening but cannot listen during an interview because of blocks that inhibit effective listening. Some of the most common blocks to listening are these:

1. The tendency to judge and evaluate the client's messages.

2. The tendency to stop attending because of the topic, the time of day, or distractions such as noise.

3. The temptation to ask questions about "missing" pieces of information.

4. The temptation or the pressure that you put on yourself to solve problems, find answers, or somehow "fix" the situation.

5. Your preoccupation with yourself as you try to acquire the skills. Your preoccupation shifts the focus away from the client and actually reduces, rather than increases, your potential for listening. Preparation for effective listening is crucial, but being preoccupied with the technique of listening is not. Preoccupation with listening skills may lessen when you are able to engage

in what Lindahl (2003) refers to as contemplative listening, reflective listening, and connective listening.

Effective listening requires an involved yet contained sort of energy that allows you to be fully present to the client. Listening is a process that does not stop after the initial session but continues throughout the entire therapeutic relationship with each client. Listening is a process that not only impacts clients but also impacts ourselves as helpers. We as listeners can be nourished by the listening process and deepen our connectedness to ourselves and to our clients (Lindahl, 2003).

Nepo (2012) describes deep listening as a process that requires "*immersion, absorption,* and *presence*" (p. 99). He mentions that counters to deep listening are "noises of the modern world, where the tasks and passwords keep multiplying" (p. 152). Nepo (2012. p. 84) concludes that:

> Deep listening requires letting go of our internal argument with the world. Letting go of my internal argument with the world means not pushing off of everything that comes my way. It requires my looking at you as a sudden fish that has surfaced from the deep. It requires bringing you water rather than my judgments.

 Visit CengageBrain.com for a variety of study tools and useful resources such as video examples, case studies, interactive exercises, flashcards, and quizzes.

4 | Knowledge and Skill Builder

Part One

Conduct a short interview as a helper and see how many client nonverbal behaviors of kinesics (body motion), paralinguistics (voice qualities), and proxemics (space) you can identify by debriefing with an observer after the session (Learning Outcome 1). Describe the possible effects or meanings associated with each behavior you identify. Confer with the observer about which nonverbal client behaviors you identified and which you missed.

Part Two

For each of the following three client statements, Learning Outcome 2 asks you to write an example of each of the four listening responses. In developing these responses, you may find it helpful to use the cognitive learning strategy you practiced earlier for each response. Feedback is provided on page 138.

Client 1, a 28-year-old woman *(says in a high-pitched voice, with crossed legs and lots of nervous twitching in her hands and face)*: My life is a shambles. I lost my job. My friends never come around anymore. It's been months now, but I still can't seem to cut down. I can't see clearly. It seems hopeless.

Clarification: _____
Paraphrase: _____
Reflection: _____
Summarization: _____

Client 2, an African American high school sophomore: I can't seem to get along with my mom. She's always harassing me, telling me what to do. Sometimes I get so mad I feel like hitting her, but I don't because it would only make the situation worse.

Clarification: _____
Paraphrase: _____
Reflection: _____
Summarization: _____

Client 3, a 54-year-old man: Ever since my wife died 4 months ago, I can't get interested in anything. I don't want to eat or sleep. I'm losing weight. Sometimes I just tell myself I'd be better off if I were dead, too.

Clarification: _____
Paraphrase: _____
Reflection: _____
Summarization: _____

Part Three

Part Three gives you an opportunity to develop your ability to observe key aspects of client behavior that must be attended to if you are going to listen effectively:

1. **Vague or confusing phrases and messages**
2. **Expression of key content**
3. **Use of affect words**
4. **Nonverbal behavior illustrative of feeling or mood states**
5. **Presence of themes or patterns**

Learning Outcome 3 asks you to observe these five aspects of a client's behavior during a 15-minute interview conducted by someone else. Record your observations on the accompanying Client Observation Checklist. You can obtain feedback for this activity by having two or more persons observe and rate the same session and comparing your responses.

Client Observation Checklist

Name of Helper _____
Name(s) of Observer(s) _____
Instructions: **For each of the five categories of client behavior, write down key client words and descriptions of behavior as it occurs during a short helping interview. (If observers are not available, then record your sessions and complete the checklist while reviewing the tape.)**

1. **Vague or confusing phrases and messages**
   a. _____
   b. _____
   c. _____
   d. _____
   e. _____

2. **Expression of key content (situation, event, idea, person)**
   a. _____
   b. _____
   c. _____
   d. _____
   e. _____

3. **Affect words used**
   a. _____
   b. _____
   c. _____
   d. _____
   e. _____

4. **Nonverbal behavior indicative of certain feelings or mood states**
   a. _____
   b. _____
   c. _____
   d. _____
   e. _____

5. **Presence of themes or patterns**
   a. _____
   b. _____
   c. _____
   d. _____
   e. _____

Observer impressions and comments: _____
_____

Part Four

Part Four gives you a chance to demonstrate the four listening responses. Learning Outcome 4 asks you to conduct a 15-minute role-play interview in which you use at least two examples of each of the four listening responses. Someone can observe your performance, or you can assess yourself from a recording of the interview. You or the observer can classify your responses and judge their effectiveness by using the accompanying Listening Checklist. Try to select listening responses to achieve specific purposes. Remember, to listen effectively, it is helpful to

1. Refrain from making judgments
2. Resist distractions
3. Avoid asking questions
4. Avoid giving advice
5. Stay focused on the client

Obtain feedback for this activity by noting the categories of responses on the table and their judged effectiveness.

Listening Checklist

Name of Helper _____

Name of Observer _____

Instructions: In the "helper response" column of the table, jot down a few key words from each statement. In the "client responses" column, insert a brief notation of the client's verbal and nonverbal responses. Then, use a check (✓) to classify the helper response as a clarification, paraphrase, reflection of feeling, summarization, or other. Finally, rate the effectiveness of each helper response, using the following scale:

1. = Not effective. Client ignored helper's message or gave some verbal and nonverbal indication that helper's message was inaccurate, off target, or premature.
2. = Somewhat effective. Client gave some verbal or nonverbal indication that helper's message was partly accurate and on target.
3. = Very effective. Client's verbal and nonverbal behavior confirmed that helper's response was very accurate, on target, and well-timed.

Remember to watch and listen for the client's reaction to the response for your effectiveness rating.

Helper response (key words)	Client response (key words)	Type of helper listening response					Effectiveness of response (determined by client response) Rate from 1 to 3 (3 = high)
		Clarification	Paraphrase	Reflection of feelings	Summarization	Other	
1.							
2.							
3.							
4.							
5.							
6.							
7.							
8.							
9.							
10.							
11.							
12.							
13.							
14.							
15.							
16.							
17.							
18.							
19.							
20.							

Observer comments and general observations:

_____
_____
_____

4 | Knowledge and Skill Builder **Feedback**

Part One

Have the observer debrief you for feedback, or use the Nonverbal Behavior Checklist to recall which nonverbal behaviors you identified.

Part Two

Here are some examples of listening responses. See whether yours are similar.

Client Statement 1

Clarification: "Can you describe what you mean by 'cutting down'?"

Paraphrase: "You seem to realize that your life is not going the way you want it to."

Reflection: "You appear frightened about the chaos in your life, and you seem uncertain of what you can do to straighten it out."

Summarization: "Your whole life seems to be falling apart. Your friends are avoiding you, and now you don't even have a job to go to. Even though you've tried to solve the problem, you can't seem to handle it alone. Coming here to talk is a useful first step in 'clearing up the water' for you."

Client Statement 2

Clarification: "Can you describe what it's like when you don't get along with her?"

Paraphrase: "It appears that your relationship with your mom is deteriorating to the point that you feel you may lose control of yourself."

Reflection: "You feel frustrated and angry with your mom because she's always giving you orders."

Summarization: "It seems like the situation at home with your mom has become intolerable. You can't stand her badgering, and you feel afraid that you might do something you would later regret."

Client Statement 3

Clarification: "Are you saying that since the death of your wife, life has become so miserable that you think of taking your own life?"

Paraphrase: "Your life has lost much of its meaning since your wife's recent death."

Reflection: "It sounds like you're very lonely and depressed since your wife died."

Summarization: "Since your wife died, you've lost interest in living. There's no fun or excitement anymore and, further, you're telling yourself that it's not going to get any better."

Influencing Responses

Learning Outcomes

After completing this chapter, you will be able to

1. From a written list of 12 influencing responses, identify the six influencing responses by type, with at least nine accurate classifications.

2. With a written list of three client statements, write an example of each of the six influencing responses for each client statement.

3. In a 30-minute helping interview in which you are an observer, listen for and record six key aspects of client behavior that form the basis for influencing responses.

4. Conduct at least one 30-minute helping interview in which you integrate the core skills and knowledge you have acquired so far in the areas of ethics, multicultural competencies, relationship variables, nonverbal behavior, listening responses, and influencing responses.

Listening responses are responses to client messages made primarily from the client's point of view or frame of reference. At times in the helping process it is legitimate to move beyond the client's frame of reference and to use responses that include clinician-generated data and perceptions. These **influencing responses** are active rather than passive, and they reflect a helper-directed more than a client-centered style (Ivey, Ivey, & Zalaquett, 2014). Whereas listening responses from a helper influence the client indirectly, influencing responses from a helper exert a more direct influence on the client. Influencing responses are based as much on the helper's perceptions and hypotheses as on the client's messages and behavior. In this chapter, we present six influencing responses: questions, information giving, self-disclosure, immediacy, interpretations (also called additive or advanced empathy), and confrontation/challenge. The general purpose of influencing responses, according to Egan (2014), is to help clients see the need for change and action through a more objective frame of reference.

Social Influence In Helping

Underlying the six influencing responses is a helping relationship characterized by mutual and complementary influence processes. Over the past several decades the helping process has been described as a social influence process. Based on the work of Strong (1968) and Strong, Welsh, Corcoran, and Hoyt (1992), and drawing from social psychology literature, the **social influence model of counseling** presumes three factors at work in the helping process:

1. The practitioner establishes a base of influence with clients by the use of legitimate, expert, and referent power to effect attitude change with clients. **Legitimate power** is power that occurs as a result of the helper's role and trustworthiness. **Expert power** results from the helper's competence and expertness. **Referent power** is drawn from dimensions such as interpersonal attractiveness, friendliness, and similarity between helper and client (such as is found in "indigenous" helpers).

2. The practitioner actively uses this influence base to effect attitudinal and behavioral change in clients through the use of behaviors and tools that enhance the helper's trustworthiness, expertness, and interpersonal attractiveness with clients.

3. Clients are responsive to the ideas and recommendations set forth by the practitioners as a function of their sense of dependence on the helper. Dependence is considered to be a motivational factor in this model.

Influencing Responses and Timing

The most difficult part of using influencing responses is timing (deciding when to use these responses in the interview). Some helpers tend to jump into influencing responses before they listen and establish rapport with the client. Listening responses generally reflect clients' understanding of themselves. In contrast, influencing responses reflect the helper's understanding of the client. Influencing responses can be used moderately in the interview with most clients as long as the helper is careful to lay the foundation with attending and listening. The listening base can heighten the client's receptivity to an influencing message. If the helper voices his or her opinions and perceptions too quickly, then the client may respond with denial, with defensiveness, or even by dropping out of counseling. When this happens, often the helper needs to retreat to a less obtrusive level of influence and do more listening, at least until a strong base of client trust and confidence has been developed.

Influencing responses are considered more directive than listening responses, which are classified as indirective. The directiveness associated with influencing responses has varying effects on clients. Client-related variables that impact the timing and effects of influencing responses include *reactance* and *race and ethnicity*. **Reactance** has to do with the need to preserve a sense of freedom (J. W. Brehm, 1966; S. S. Brehm, 1976). More recent conceptualizations of reactance describe it as a "state" rather than a "trait," meaning that it is subject to change (Beutler, Harwood, Michelson, Song, & Holman, 2011). Clients may exhibit a great deal of reactance toward some things in counseling but not others, or around some issues but not others. When clients are high in reactance, they are generally oppositional and are motivated to do the opposite of whatever the helper suggests. (See also Chapter 10.) Thus, clients who are high in reactance are likely to be more allergic to influencing responses regardless of the point at which they are introduced in the helping process. With highly reactant behavior, usually less directive responses are associated with better therapeutic outcomes (Beutler & Harwood, 2000). A recent study found this to be true for clients with high alcohol use even across different counseling sessions (Karno & Longabaugh, 2005).

Some clients, however, may actually be more comfortable with an active and directive communication style because it is more consistent with their cultural values. Sue and Sue (2013) conclude that "the literature on multicultural counseling/therapy strongly suggests that American Indians, Asian Americans, Black Americans, and Hispanic Americans tend to prefer more active–directive forms of helping than nondirective ones" (p. 228). Some clients of color may feel more comfortable with the use of directive and active skills because these responses provide them with data about the practitioner's orientation. Moreover, the use of influencing responses connotes a locus of responsibility that is perhaps more systemic and less person-or individual-centered. This kind of focus is more consistent with the philosophy of many minority clients who have encountered societal discrimination and oppression.

Other clients may benefit more from a directive, influencing approach because of certain characteristics. For example, due to their limited personal-social development, children and adolescents as well as adults who are developmentally challenged may respond better to a more active influencing style than the passive attending style we described in the prior chapter.

What Does Influencing Require of Helpers?

Accurate and effective listening depends on the ability of helpers to listen to the client and to restrain some of their own energy and expressiveness. In contrast, influencing responses require the helper to be more expressive and more challenging. Egan (2014) describes the use of influencing responses as responding to "sour notes" present in the client's communication and behavior. To use influencing responses effectively, helpers must first provide a supportive and safe environment by listening carefully, and then they must feel comfortable enough with themselves to provide feedback or amplification to the client that the client may not like. Helpers who have esteem issues of their own may find the use of influencing responses difficult, because these responses carry the risk of upsetting a client by what is said or challenged. Ultimately, the use of effective influencing responses requires helpers to feel secure enough about themselves to have their own voice and to tolerate client disapproval and disagreement.

Some helpers prefer to stay in the safety net of a more passive attending style. This strategy may be acceptable to some clients, but it may also mean that the helper and client have entered into a covert collusion with each other not to say anything that expresses displeasure or disappointment.

Six Influencing Responses

We have selected six influencing responses **LO1** **LO2** **LO3** to describe in this chapter. *Questions* are open or closed queries that seek elaboration or information from clients. *Information giving* is the communication of data or facts about experiences, events, alternatives, or people. *Self-disclosure* involves sharing of personal information or experiences with the client. *Immediacy* is an extension of self-disclosure and is a verbal response that describes something while it is occurring within the helping interview. *Interpretations* are responses that identify themes and patterns, make implied client messages explicit, and often are based on the helper's ideas or hunches about the client. Interpretations are sometimes referred to as *advanced empathic responses* (Egan, 2014) or as *additive empathy* (Hepworth, Rooney, Dewberry Rooney, & Strom-Gottfried, 2013). *Confrontation,* also called *challenging,* describes patterns of discrepancies and inconsistencies in client behavior and communication.

Notice how these six influencing responses differ in the following example:

Client, a 35-year-old widow of a deployed soldier, mother of two young children: My whole life fell apart when my husband was killed in Afghanistan. I keep feeling so unsure about my ability to make it on my own and to support my kids. My husband always made all the decisions for me. Now, I haven't slept well for so long, and I'm drinking more heavily—I can't even think straight. My relatives help me as much as they can, but I still feel scared.

Helper questions: What sorts of experiences have you had in being on your own—if any—prior to your husband being deployed? What feels most scary about this?

Helper information giving: Perhaps you are still grieving over the loss of your husband. I'm wondering whether you have made use of grief support or recovery groups or used other military resources to help you cope with your loss.

Helper self-disclosure: I think I can really understand what you are facing and trying to cope with since your husband died. I also went through a period in my life when I was on my own and responsible for the well-being of my two children and me, and it was a tough time—lots to deal with at once. In your situation, I think it has got to be even tougher, because I know that losing a spouse in a war zone is very challenging on so many levels.

Helper immediacy: I can sense your vulnerability as you share this with me, and I'm glad you feel com-fortable enough with me to let me in on some of it. I think that might help ease some of the burden you are carrying.

Helper interpretation: When your husband was alive, before deployment, you relied on him to take care of you and your children. Now it's up to you, but taking on this role is uncomfortable and also unfamiliar. Perhaps your increased drinking is a way to keep from having to face this. What do you think?

Helper confrontation: It seems as if you're dealing with two things in this situation: first, the experience of being on your own for the first time, which feels so new and scary that you're unsure you can do it; and second, the reality that although your relatives help out, with your husband's passing the responsibility for you and your children does now rest on your shoulders.

Table 5.1 provides brief definitions and summarizes the intended purposes of those six influencing responses. The intended purposes are presented as tentative guidelines, not as the sole truth. In the remainder of this chapter we describe and present model examples of each response and provide opportunities for you to practice each one and receive feedback about your level of skill.

Sequencing of Influencing Responses In Interviews

Although there is no "set" or predefined sequence of influencing responses in interviews, there is some logical progression from certain influencing responses to others. For example, questions usually come earlier in the interview and in the initial stage of the helping process because they are used to begin interviews and to seek pertinent information from clients. And while information giving can be used at varying points in helping interviews, this response also is used early on to provide information to clients about the process at the outset of helping and also to guide key transition points during the process, too. Another influencing response that is used earlier in the process to create and build rapport is self-disclosure. Self-disclosure promotes universality and provides normalization and hope for clients. In this chapter we describe these three influencing responses first and in this order.

The other three influencing responses we describe in this chapter—immediacy, interpretation, and confrontation/challenge—are what we call more advanced influencing skills. These three responses are more difficult to use, require more judicious thinking about their use, and are used less frequently than the first three

TABLE 5.1   Definitions and Intended Purposes of Helper Influencing Responses

Response	Definition	Intended Purposes
Questions	Open-ended or closed query or inquiry	*Open-ended questions* 1. To begin an interview 2. To encourage client elaboration or to obtain information 3. To elicit specific examples of client's behaviors, feelings, or thoughts *Closed questions* 1. To narrow the topic of discussion 2. To obtain specific information 3. To elicit specific examples of client's behaviors, feelings, or thoughts 4. To motivate client to communicate
Information giving	Communication of data or facts	1. To identify alternatives 2. To evaluate alternatives 3. To dispel myths 4. To motivate clients to examine issues they may have been avoiding 5. To provide structure at the outset and major transition points in the helping process
Self-disclosure	Purposeful revelation of information about oneself through verbal and nonverbal behaviors	1. To build rapport, safety, and trust 2. To convey genuineness 3. To model self-disclosure for the client 4. To instill hope and promote feelings of universality 5. To help clients consider other alternatives and views
Immediacy	Description of feelings or process issues as they are occurring within the helping interview	1. To open up discussion about covert or unexpressed feelings or issues 2. To provide feedback about process or interactions as they occur 3. To help client self-disclosure
Interpretation (advanced or additive empathy)	Mirroring of client behaviors, patterns, and feelings, based on implied client messages and the helper's hunches	1. To identify the client's implicit messages 2. To examine client behavior from an alternative view 3. To add to client self-understanding and influence client action
Confrontation	Description of discrepancy/distortions	1. To identify client's mixed (incongruent) messages or distortions 2. To explore other ways of perceiving client's self or situation 3. To influence client to take action

described. They are powerful enough in their impact on clients that less frequent use is usually warranted. We begin the discussion of these more advanced influencing skills with immediacy, which may be thought of as an extension of self-disclosure, a special kind of self-disclosure in which the helper discloses something currently being experienced in the session. We follow this with discussion of interpretation and confrontation, two responses that are designed to promote insight and exploration and are usually used later in the helping process after a sound, therapeutic relationship has been established.

Questions

Questions are an indispensable part of the interview process. Their effectiveness depends on the types of questions asked and the frequency of their use. Questions have the potential for establishing desirable or undesirable patterns of interpersonal exchange, depending on the skill of the therapist. Beginning interviewers are prone to err by assuming that a helping interview is a series of questions and answers or by asking the wrong kind of question at a particular time. These practices are likely to make the client feel interrogated rather than understood. However, even experienced helpers overuse this potentially valuable influencing response. Although asking a question is all too easy to do during silence or when you are at a loss for words, you should not ask questions unless you have in mind a particular purpose for the question. For example, if you are using a question as an open invitation to talk, realize that you are in fact asking the client to initiate a dialogue, and be sure to allow the client to respond.

Open and Closed Questions

Most effective questions are **open-ended questions**; they begin with words such as *what, how, when, where,* or *who* and they encourage client elaboration. According to Ivey, D'Andrea, Ivey, and Simek-Morgan (2007), the particular word that is used to begin an open-ended question is important. Research has shown that *what* questions tend to elicit facts and information, *how* questions are associated with sequence and process or emotions, and *why* questions produce reasons. Similarly, *when* and *where* questions elicit information about time and place, and *who* questions are associated with information about people. Open-ended questions serve a number of purposes in different situations (Cormier, 2016; Ivey, Ivey, & Zalaquett, 2014):

1. Beginning an interview

2. Encouraging the client to convey more information

3. Eliciting examples of particular behaviors, thoughts, or feelings so that the helper can better understand the conditions contributing to the client's concerns

4. Developing client commitment to communicate by inviting the client to talk and guiding the client along a focused interaction

In contrast to open-ended questions, **closed (focused) questions** can be useful if the practitioner needs a particular fact or seeks a particular bit of information. These questions begin with words such as *is, are, do, did, can,* and *which,* and they can be answered with "yes," "no," or some other short response. Closed questions are a major tool for obtaining information during the assessment process. Here are three examples of closed questions:

1. Of all the issues we discussed, which bothers you the most?

2. Is there a history of depression in your family?

3. Are you planning to look for a job in the next few months?

Closed questions serve the following purposes:

1. Narrowing the area of discussion by asking the client for a specific response

2. Gathering specific information

3. Identifying parameters of concerns

4. Interrupting an overly talkative client who rambles or "storytells"

Closed questions must be used sparingly within an interview. Too many closed questions may discourage discussion and may subtly give the client permission to avoid sensitive or important topics. Hepworth and colleagues (2013), however, mention an exception to this general guideline. They note that it may be necessary to use more closed questions if the client is unresponsive, withholds information, or has limited "conceptual and mental abilities" (p. 143).

Guidelines for the Use of Questions

You will use questions more effectively and efficiently if you remember some important guidelines for their use. First, develop questions that center on the client's concerns. Effective questions arise from what the client has already said, not from the helper's curiosity or need for closure. Second, after a question, use a pause to give the client sufficient time to respond. Remember that the client may not have a ready response. The feeling of having to supply a quick answer may be threatening and may encourage the client to give a response that pleases the helper.

Third, ask only one question at a time. Some interviewers tend to ask multiple questions (two or more) before allowing the client time to respond. We call this tactic **stacking questions**. It confuses the client, who may respond only to the least important question in the series. This guideline is especially important when you are working with children, the elderly, and developmentally challenged persons, because these clients may need more information-processing time.

Fourth, avoid accusatory or antagonistic questions. These are questions that reflect antagonism either because of the helper's voice tone or because of use of the word *why*. You can obtain the same information by asking *what* instead of *why*. Young (2013) points out that "asking the client *why* they behaved or felt a particular way is very enticing because this inquiry seems very psychological and appears to be getting to the root of a problem" (p. 92). Yet, often, clients do not really know the reasons behind their feelings or behaviors, and accusatory questions like *why* ones can put the client on the defensive. As Ivey, Ivey, and Zalaquett (2014) note, *why* questions also are lacking in respect, empathy, and positive regard. This caution about *why* questions does not mean that exploring reasons for client behavior is unimportant, but as Young (2013) observes, such information is usually better extracted "from the whole of the client's story" (p. 93).

Finally, avoid relying on questions as a primary response mode during an interview (unless you are doing an intake, taking a history, or conducting an assessment session). Remember that some cultural groups may find questions offensive, intrusive, and lacking in respect. In any culture, consistent overuse of questions can create problems in the therapeutic relationship, such as fostering dependency, promoting the helper as an expert, reducing responsibility and involvement by the client, and creating resentment (Gazda et al., 2005). The feeling of being interrogated may be especially harmful with "reluctant" clients.

Questions are most effective when they provoke new insights and yield new information. To determine whether it is really necessary to use a question at any particular time during a session, ask the question covertly to yourself and see whether you can answer it for the client. If you can, then the question is probably unnecessary and a different response would be more productive.

Steps in the Use of Questions

There are four steps in formulating effective questions. First, determine the purpose of your question. Is it legitimate and therapeutically useful? Often, before you probe for information, it is of therapeutic value to demonstrate first that you actually heard the client's message. Listening before questioning is particularly important when clients reveal strong emotions. It also helps clients to feel understood rather than interrogated. For this reason, before each of our example questions we use a paraphrase or a reflection response. In actual practice,

this bridging of listening and influencing responses is very important because it balances the attending and action modes in the interview.

Second, decide what type of question would be most helpful. Open-ended questions foster client exploration. Closed or focused questions should be reserved for times when you want specific information or you need to narrow the area of discussion. Make sure that your question centers on concerns of the client, not issues of interest only to you.

Third, remember to assess the effectiveness of your questioning by determining whether its purpose was achieved. A question is not useful simply because the client answered or responded to it. Fourth, examine how the client responded and the overall explanation, inquiry, and dialogue that ensued as a result of particular questions.

Those four steps are summarized in the following cognitive learning strategy:

1. What is the purpose of my question, and is it therapeutically useful?

2. Can I anticipate the client's answer?

3. Given the purpose, how can I start the wording of my question to be most effective?

4. How will I know whether my question is effective?

Notice how the helper applies this cognitive learning strategy in the following example:

Client: I just don't know where to start. My marriage is falling apart. My mom recently died. And I've been having some difficulties at work.
Helper *(asks and answers covertly):*

Self-question 1: What is the purpose of my question—and is it therapeutically useful?
To get the client to focus more specifically on an issue of great concern to her.

Self-question 2: Can I anticipate the client's answer?
No.

Self-question 3: Given the purpose, how can I start the wording of my question to be most effective?
"Which one of these...?" "Do you want to discuss...?"

Self-question 4: How will I know whether my question is effective?
Examine the client's verbal and nonverbal response and the resulting dialogue, as well as whether the purpose

was achieved (whether the client starts to focus on the specific concern).

At this time the helper's covert visualization or self-talk ends, and the following dialogue ensues:

Helper question: Things must feel overwhelming to you right now [reflection]. Of the three concerns you just mentioned, which one is of most concern to you now? [question].

Client response *(accompanied by direct eye contact; body posture, which had been tense, now starts to relax):* My marriage. I want to keep it together, but I don't think my husband does.

From the client's verbal and nonverbal responses, the helper can conclude that the question was effective because the client focused on a specific concern and did not appear to be threatened by the question. The therapist can now covertly congratulate herself or himself for formulating an effective question with this client.

Learning Activity 5.1 gives you an opportunity to try out this cognitive learning strategy to develop effective questions.

Learning Activity 5.1

Questions

In this activity, you are given three client practice statements. For each client message, develop an example of a question using the cognitive learning strategy described previously and outlined here. To internalize this learning strategy, you may wish to talk through the self-questions overtly (aloud) and then covertly (silently). The end product will be a question that you can say aloud or write down. An example precedes the practice messages. Feedback is provided on page 147.

Example

Client 1, a middle-aged white woman: I get so nervous. I'm just a bunch of nerves.
Self-question 1: *What is the purpose of my question—and is it therapeutically useful?*
The purpose is to ask for examples of times when she is nervous. This is therapeutically useful because it contributes to increased understanding of the problem.
Self-question 2: *Can I anticipate the client's answer?*
No.
Self-question 3: *Given the purpose, how can I start the wording of my question to be most effective?*
"When . . . ?" or "What . . . ?"
Actual questions: You say you're feeling pretty upset [reflection]. When do you feel this way? *or* What are some times when you get this feeling? [question].

Client Practice Messages

The purpose of the question is given to you for each message. Try to develop questions that relate to the stated purposes. Remember to precede your question with a listening response such as a paraphrase or reflection.

Client 1, an older woman who is retired from the workforce: To be frank about it, it's been pure hell around my house the last year.

Self-question 1: *What is the purpose of my question?*
To encourage client to elaborate on how and what has been hell for her.
Self-question 2: *Can I anticipate the client's answer?*
Self-question 3: *Given the purpose, how can I start the wording of my question to be most effective?*
Actual questions: _____
_____

Client 2, a 40-year-old physically challenged man: Sometimes I feel kind of blue. It goes on for a while. Not every day but sometimes.
Self-question 1: *What is the purpose of my question?*
To find out whether client has noticed anything that makes the "blueness" better.
Self-question 2: *Can I anticipate the client's answer?*
Self-question 3: *Given the purpose, how can I start the wording of my question to be most effective?*
Actual questions: _____
_____

Client 3, a 35-year-old African American woman: I feel overwhelmed right now. Too many kids underfoot. Not enough time for me.
Self-question 1: *What is the purpose of my question?*
To find out how many kids are underfoot and in what capacity client is responsible for them.
Self-question 2: *Can I anticipate the client's answer?*
Self-question 3: *Given the purpose, how can I start the wording of my question to be most effective?*
Actual questions: _____
_____

Information Giving

There are many times in the helping interview when a client may have a legitimate need for information. A client who reports being abused by her partner may need information about her legal rights and alternatives. A client who has recently become physically challenged may need some information about employment and about lifestyle adaptations such as performing domestic chores or engaging in sexual relationships. Information giving is an important tool of feminist therapy approaches. Feminist therapists may give information to clients about gender role stereotyping, the impact of cultural conditioning on gender roles, strategies for empowerment, and social/political structures that contribute to disempowerment.

We define **information giving** as the communication of data or facts about experiences, events, alternatives, or people, and we identify five intended purposes of information giving (see Table 5.1 for a summary). First, information is necessary when clients do not know their options. Giving information is a way to help them identify possible alternatives. For example, you may be counseling a pregnant client who says she is going to have an abortion because it is her only choice. Although she may eventually decide to pursue this choice, she should be aware of other options before making a final decision.

Second, information giving is helpful when clients are not aware of the possible outcomes of a particular choice or plan of action. Giving information can help them evaluate different choices and actions. For example, if the client is a minor and is not aware that she may need her parents' consent for an abortion, then this information may influence her choice.

In the preceding two kinds of situations, information is given to counteract ignorance. Information giving can also be useful to correct invalid or unreliable data or to dispel a myth. In other words, information giving may be necessary when clients are misinformed about something. For example, a pregnant client may decide to have an abortion based on the erroneous assumption that an abortion is also a means of subsequent birth control.

A fourth purpose of information giving is to help clients examine issues they have been successfully avoiding. For example, a client who hasn't felt physically well for a year may be prompted to explore this problem when confronted with information about possible effects of neglected treatment for various illnesses.

A fifth purpose of information giving is to provide clients with structure at major transition points in the helping process such as beginnings and endings. At the outset of counseling, providing information fulfills the ethical

responsibility of helpers to inform clients of things such as the purposes, goals, techniques, and benefits and limitations of counseling. Another important component of information giving during the beginning stage of counseling has to do with therapeutic boundaries, confidentiality, limits of confidentiality, and HIPAA (the federal Health Insurance Portability and Accountability Act of 1996 and extensions thereafter). Provision of this kind of information at the outset helps to reduce potential ambiguity and anxiety that clients may feel as they approach a helper for the first time. A qualitative study found that clients experienced such structure as providing safety and empowerment (Levitt, Butler, & Hill, 2006). As counseling ensues, practitioners provide structure to clients through information giving at different points in the process. For example, helpers need to provide information about any assessment measures or standardized tests to be used as well as about potential treatment goals and treatment plans. Practitioners also are ethically obligated to provide structure and information to clients as termination of the helping process approaches and/or as referrals are needed to other practitioners.

Differences between Giving Information and Giving Advice

It is important to note that giving information differs from giving advice. A person giving advice usually recommends or prescribes a particular solution or course of action for the listener to follow. In contrast, information giving consists of presenting relevant information about an issue or problem. The decision concerning the final course of action—if any—is made by the client.

Consider the differences between the following two helper responses:

Client, a young mother: I find it so difficult to refuse requests made by my child—to say "no" to her—even when I know they are unreasonable requests or could even be dangerous to her.

Helper (advice giving): Why don't you start by saying "no" to her just on one request per day for now—anything that you feel comfortable with refusing—and then see what happens?

Helper (information giving): I think there are two things we could discuss that may be affecting the way you are handling this situation. First, we could talk about what you feel might happen if you say "no." We also need to examine how your requests were handled in your own family when you were a child. Very often as parents we repeat with our children the way we were parented in such an automatic way that we don't even realize it's happening.

In the first example, the practitioner recommends action that may or may not be successful. If it works, then the client may feel elated and expect the helper to have other magical solutions. If it fails, then the client may feel even more discouraged and question whether counseling can really help her resolve this problem. Appropriate and effective information giving indicates what the client *could* ponder or do, not what the client *should* do, and it indicates what the client *might* consider, not *must* consider.

Several dangers associated with advice giving make it a potential trap for helpers. First, the client may reject not only this piece of advice but also any other ideas presented by the helper in an effort to establish independence and thwart any conspicuous efforts by the helper to influence or coerce. Second, if the client accepts the advice and the advice leads to an unsatisfactory action, then the client is likely to blame the helper and may terminate therapy prematurely. Third, if the client follows the advice and is pleased with the action, then the client may become overly dependent on the practitioner and expect, if not demand, more advice in subsequent sessions. Finally, there is always the possibility that an occasional client may misinterpret the advice and may cause injury to himself or to herself or to others in trying to comply with it. Sommers-Flanagan and Sommers-Flanagan (2014) point out that in almost all cases, advice giving meets more of the needs of the helper than of the client.

Ground Rules for Giving Information

Information giving is generally considered appropriate when the need for information is directly related to the client's concerns and goals and when the presentation

---

5.1 Feedback

Questions

Client 1

Sample questions based on defined purpose: It sounds like things have gotten out of hand [paraphrase]. What exactly has been going on that's been so bad for you? *or* How has it been like hell for you? [question].

Client 2

Sample questions based on defined purpose: Now and then you feel kind of down [reflection]. What have you noticed that makes this feeling go away? *or* Have you noticed anything in particular that makes you feel better? [question].

Client 3

Sample questions based on defined purpose: With everyone else to take care of, there's not much time left for you [paraphrase]. Exactly how many kids are underfoot? *or* How many kids are you responsible for? [question].

---

and discussion of information are used to help the client achieve these goals. To use information giving appropriately, a helper should consider: (1) when to give information; (2) what information is needed; and (3) how the information should be delivered. Table 5.2 summarizes the *when*, *what*, and *how* guidelines for information giving in counseling.

The first guideline, the *when*, involves recognizing the client's need for information. If the client does not have all the data or has invalid data, then a need exists. To be effective, information giving also must be well timed. The client should indicate receptivity to the information

---

TABLE 5.2   The *When*, *What*, and *How* of Information Giving in Helping

When: Recognizing client's need for information	*What:* Identifying type of information	*How:* Delivery of information in an interview
1. Identify information presently available to client.	1. Identify kind of information useful to client.	1. Avoid jargon.
2. Evaluate client's present information. Is it valid? Data-based? Sufficient?	2. Identify reliable sources of information to validate accuracy of information, including computer sources.	2. Present all the relevant facts; don't protect client from negative information.
3. Wait for client cues of readiness to avoid giving information prematurely.	3. Identify any sequencing of information (option A before option B).	3. Limit amount of information given at one time; don't overload.
	4. Identify cultural relevance of information.	4. Ask for and discuss client's feelings and biases about information.
		5. Know when to stop giving information so action isn't avoided.
		6. Use paper and pencil to highlight key ideas or facts.

before it is delivered. A client may ignore information if it is introduced too early in the interaction.

The helper also needs to determine what information is useful and relevant to clients. Generally, information is useful if it is something clients are not likely to find on their own and if they have the resources to act on the information. The helper also needs to determine whether the information must be presented sequentially to make the most sense to the client. Because clients may remember initial information best, presenting the most significant information *first* may be a good rule of thumb in sequencing information. Finally, in selecting information to give, be careful not to impose information on clients who are ultimately responsible for deciding what information to use and act on. In other words, information giving should not be used as a forum for the helper to subtly push his or her own values on clients (Egan, 2014).

One of the critical facets of giving information has to do with the cultural appropriateness of the information being given. Lum (2011) observes that much cross-cultural contact involves communicating with people who do not share the same types of information. Also, people in different cultures vary in the types of information they attend to. For example, providing information to a sick client about a traditional physician and medical care setting may be useful if the client is European American. Many non-European American clients, however, may find such information so far removed from their own cultural practices regarding health and illness that the information is simply not useful.

Other cultural mismatches in information giving abound in family therapy. **Enmeshment**—the concept of a family system lacking clear boundaries between and among individuals—is a prime example. For some European American families, enmeshment is considered a sign of pathology because in enmeshed families the autonomy of individual members is considered hampered. However, for many Asian families and for some rural European American families, enmeshment is so completely the norm that any other structure of family living is foreign to them; in many of these families, the prevailing culture dictates that the good of the family comes before the individual members' needs and wishes (Sue & Sue, 2013). If the helper assumes that this behavior is pathological and gives the client information about becoming more "individuated" or "establishing clearer boundaries," then the client may feel misunderstood and greatly offended. Sue (2010) characterizes this kind of helper behavior as another example of a "**racial microaggression**"—that is, a brief and common yet derogatory indignity based on the notion that the values and communication styles of the

dominant/white culture are the ones that are the standard-bearer and hence are preferred. Therefore, the following important questions need to be addressed. Given the client's ethnic, racial, and cultural affiliations, what cultural biases are reflected in the information I will give the client? Is this information culturally relevant and appropriate? If you are not careful to assess the assumptions reflected in the information you share with clients, then your information may seem irrelevant and your credibility in the client's eyes may be diminished. Because of the effects of globalization, we cannot afford to be culturally obtuse about the kinds of information we make available to clients.

In the interview itself, the actual delivery of information, the "how" of information giving, is crucial. The information should be discussed in a way that makes it usable to the client and encourages the client to hear and apply the information. Moreover, information should be presented objectively. Don't leave out facts simply because they aren't pleasant. Watch out for information overload as well. Most people cannot assimilate a great deal of information at one time. Usually, the more information you give clients, the less they remember. Clients recall information best when you give no more than five or six pieces at one time.

Be aware that information differs in depth and may have an emotional impact on clients. Clients may not react emotionally to relatively simple or factual information such as information about a helping intervention, an occupation, or a résumé. However, clients may react with anger, anxiety, or relief to information that has more depth or far-reaching consequences, such as information about a biopsy or an HIV test. Ask about and discuss the client's reactions to the information you give. In addition, make an effort to promote client understanding of the information. Avoid jargon in offering explanations. Use paper and pencil as you're giving information to draw a picture or a diagram highlighting the most important points, or give clients paper and pencil so they can write down key ideas. Remember to ask clients to verify their impression of your information either by summarizing it or by repeating it to you. Also, try to determine when it's time to stop dealing with information. Continued information giving may reinforce a client's tendency to avoid taking action.

Information Giving through Technology

Information is given to clients not only during sessions but also by digital means. For example, a client who is struggling with having just learned about her malignant brain tumor can benefit from electronic information as well as from what the helper provides during the session.

We don't believe that all information should be given to clients in this way, but digital information is increasingly important in the helping process. Many useful websites are now available for clients; also, many community services, referral sources, and information services are now available online. In addition, many types of support groups are available online and may be especially useful for homebound clients. Currently, the Internet is developing rapidly with Google-targeted search engines for clients, social networking such as Facebook, video sharing via YouTube, and user-developed resource repositories such as Wikipedia.

A number of websites deal with information that may be especially pertinent to diverse groups of clients. However, many clients who are outside of mainstream groups, such as some rural, low-income clients, do not have ready access to computer technology. Across the globe, broadband coverage is uneven. In addition, there are also emerging ethical, legal, and regulatory issues related to providing information by means of computers. The quality and accuracy of web technology vary tremendously. Some sites may not be suitable for child clients, and many chat rooms contain offensive language. In addition, security issues often arise. Professional organizations in human services now provide standards on the use of information technology in the helping process, and the provision of Internet-based information is likely to be more regulated in the future. Many of these issues are summarized in a special issue of the *Journal of Technology in Human Services* (Finn and Schoech 2008).

We have found an excellent resource on online mental health resources at psychcentral.com/resources. These mental health resources are personally reviewed by Dr. John M. Grohol and are updated constantly. Other examples of online services include relationship help (http://thecoupleconnection.net/), information about PTSD (http://ptsd.va.gov), information about anxiety and panic (http://panicattacks.com.au/anxdis/index.html), information about moods (https://moodgym.anu.edu.au/welcome), and a variety of online support groups (e.g., http://www.mentalhealthamerica.net/find-supportgroups). There are also a number of mental health resources now available on smart phones and tablets. Some current examples of these include Mood 24/7, PTSD Coach, Personal Zen, Optimism, and Crisis Text Line.

Steps in Information Giving

There are six steps in formulating the *what, when,* and *how* of presenting information to clients. First, assess what information the client lacks about the issue. Second, determine the cultural relevance of any information you plan to share. Third, decide how the information can be sequenced in a way that aids client comprehension and retention. Fourth, consider how you can deliver the information in such a way that the client is likely to comprehend it. Keep in mind that in cross-cultural helping situations, effective delivery requires you to communicate in a language and style that the client can understand.

Fifth, assess the emotional impact the information is likely to have on the client. Sixth, determine whether your information giving was effective. Note client reactions to it, and follow-up on client use of the information in a subsequent session. Remember that some clients may store information and act on it at a much later date—often even after therapy has terminated. If you have provided information via technology, remember to follow-up on it and to ask for the client's reactions, questions, and concerns about it.

To help with your use of the strategy of information giving, we have put these six steps in the form of questions that you can use as a cognitive learning strategy:

1. What information does this client lack about the issue?

2. Given the client's ethnic, racial, and cultural affiliations, is this information relevant and appropriate?

3. How can I best sequence this information?

4. How can I deliver this information so that the client is likely to comprehend it?

5. What emotional impact is this information likely to have on this client?

6. How will I know whether my information giving has been effective?

Consider the way a helper uses this cognitive learning strategy in the first example of Learning Activity 5.2 on page 150.

Self-Disclosure

Self-disclosure can be defined in a variety of ways, but one useful definition is the revelation of personal information about the helper to the client. Generally, when a practitioner's disclosure "goes beyond the basic professional disclosure of name, credentials, fees, emergency contacts, cancellation polices, and similar information that appears in the office policies or informed consent to treatment, it is considered self-disclosure" (Zur, Williams, Lehavot, & Knapp, 2009, p. 22). Zur and colleagues (2009) also note that self-disclosure can be intentional or unintentional. For example, **unintentional disclosures** can occur when a client notices the practitioner has a cold,

Learning Activity 5.2

Information Giving

In this activity, three client situations are presented. For each situation, determine what information the client lacks and develop a suitable information-giving response using the cognitive learning strategy described previously and outlined here. To internalize this learning strategy, you may want to talk through these self-questions overtly (aloud) and then covertly. The end product will be an information-giving response that you can say aloud or write down. An example precedes the practice situations. Feedback follows on page 152.

Example

The clients are a married couple in their 30s. Gus is a European American man, and his wife, Asani, is an Asian American woman. They disagree about the way to handle their 4-year-old son. The father believes the boy is a "spoiled brat" and thinks the best way to keep him in line is to give him a spanking. The mother believes that her son is just a "typical boy" and that the best way to handle him is to be respectful. The couple admit that there is little consistency in the way the two of them deal with their son. The typical pattern is for the father to reprimand him and swat him while the mother watches, comforts him, and often intercedes on the child's behalf.

Self-question 1: *What information do these clients lack about this issue?*
Information about effective parenting and child-rearing skills.
Self-question 2: *Given the clients' ethnic, racial, and cultural affiliations, is this information relevant and appropriate?*
I have to recognize that the mother and father probably bring different cultural values to this parenting situation. I'm going to have to find information that is appropriate to both value systems, such as the following:
a. All children need some limits at some times.
b. There is a hierarchy in parent/child relationships; children are taught to respect parents, and vice versa.
c. Children function better when their parents work together on their behalf rather than disagreeing all the time, especially in front of the child.
Self-question 3: *How can I best sequence this information?*
Discuss item 3 first—working together on the child's behalf—and note how each parent's approach reflects his or her own cultural background. Stress that neither approach is right or wrong, but that the approaches are different. Highlight points of agreement.
Self-question 4: *How can I deliver this information so that the clients are likely to comprehend it?*
Present the information in such a way that it appeals to the values of both parents. The mother values understanding, support, and respect; the father values authority, respect, and control.

Self-question 5: *What emotional impact is this information likely to have on these clients?*
If I frame the information positively, it will appeal to both parents. I have to be careful not to take sides or to cause one parent to feel relieved while the other feels anxious, guilty, or put down.
Self-question 6: *How will I know whether my information giving has been effective?*
I'll watch and listen to their nonverbal and verbal reactions to it to see whether they support the idea. I'll also follow up on their use of the information in a later session.

Example of information-giving response: You know, Asani and Gus, I sense that you are in agreement on the fact that you love your child and want what is best for him. So, what I'm going to say next is based on this idea that you are both trying to find a way to do what is best for Timmy. In discussing how you feel about Timmy and his behavior—and this is most important—remember that Timmy will do better if you two can find a way to agree on parenting. I think part of your struggle is that you come from cultures where parenting is viewed in different ways. Perhaps we could talk first about these differences and then find areas where you can agree.

Client Practice Situations

Client 1 is a young Native American man whose driver's license was taken away because of several arrests for driving under the influence of alcohol. He is irate because he doesn't believe drinking a six-pack of beer can interfere with his driving ability. After all, as he says, he has never had an accident. Moreover, he has seen many of his male relatives drive drunk for years without any problem. He believes that losing his license is just another instance of the white man trying to take away something that justifiably belongs to him.
Information-giving response: _____
_____
_____

Client 2 is an African American male who has been ordered by the court to come in for treatment of heroin addiction. At one point in your treatment group, he talks about his drug use with several of his sexual partners. When you mention something about the risk of AIDS, his response is that it could never happen to him.
Information-giving response: _____
_____
_____

Client 3 is a 35-year-old European American woman with two teenage daughters. She is employed as an executive secretary in a large engineering firm. Her husband is a department store manager. She and her husband have had a stormy relationship for several years. She wants to get a divorce but is hesitant to do so for fear that she will be labeled a troublemaker and will lose her job. She is also afraid that she will not be able to support her daughters financially on her limited income.

However, she indicates that she believes getting a divorce will make her happy and will essentially solve all her own internal conflicts.

Information-giving response:_____

_____

_____

when the helper tells a client about a change in schedule due to surgery, when a practitioner sees a client at an event, perhaps with one or more significant others, or when a client reveals something they found out about the practitioner through an online search. Zur and colleagues (2009) observe that in the current Internet age, "with the click of a mouse, most psychotherapists' personal lives can be easily viewed" (p. 24). As a result, "clinicians must be aware that all their online postings, blogs, or chats may be viewed by their clients and will stay online, in some form, forever" (Zur et al., p. 25). Other examples of unintentional disclosures involve what the client notices in the office environment as well as spontaneous expressions or body language of the helper.

Environment, Clinical Settings, and Disclosure

Helping occurs in an environment and a particular setting—typically an office, although other indoor and outdoor environments can be used. The same environment and setting can impact clients in varying ways. Levitt, Butler, and Hill (2006) created a hierarchy of categories that represented what clients found important in therapy. One of the most important categories that emerged from this study was the office environment. Clients indicated that the office environment was a reflection of the care they experienced with the helper. Clients also noted that they viewed the therapy room as a "projection of the therapist," from objects in the room such as pictures, furniture, and background music (Levitt et al., 2006, p. 317). As Zur and colleagues (2009) note, most helping settings and environments foster unavoidable disclosure, particularly around issues of the helper's personal taste and perhaps even around family information and economic status.

Disclosure that occurs through helping environments and settings also has implications for working with culturally diverse clients. It is important to think about how suitable your helping environment and setting are for diverse kinds of clients. Cultural microaggressions can occur when clients are exposed to helping environments and settings that minimize or devalue the client's race such as the "exclusion of decorations or literature" that represent various aspects of cultural diversity (Sue et al., 2007,

p. 274). A recent study involving EuroAmerican college students and Latino community residents explored the impact of multicultural welcomeness through types and number of art objects displayed in a therapy office (Devlin, Borenstein, Finch, Hassan, Iannotti, & Koufopoulos, 2013). This study revealed that "a therapist whose office included art and artifacts from a variety of cultures was judged to be more open to multiculturalism than was the therapist whose office displayed objects from a tradition that could be categorized as more western" (pp. 173-174). Results from this study also suggested that the number of art objects is a factor because the therapy office with a larger number of multicultural art objects received higher ratings than the office with only a few items. The authors concluded, "it appears that the message communicated by the display of objects grows stronger with more items" (Devlin et al., 2013, p. 174). In addition, for clients with physical challenges, environments also need to be accessible and barrier-free.

Helper Nonverbal Behavior: Congruence and Disclosure

Nonverbal behavior of the helper represents another way in which unintentional and often unavoidable self-disclosures can occur in helping. Body language and spontaneous expressions such as a frown, a smile, and tapping of the hands or feet, all convey disclosures that "are neither always deliberate nor always under the psychotherapist's full control" (Zur et al., 2009, p. 23). Congruence between the helper's body language and verbal messages is important because incongruence conveys mixed messages to clients that are confusing. For example, suppose a practitioner says to a client, "I am really interested in how you feel about your parents," while looking away from the client and turning away as well. The client may respond to inconsistent or incongruent counselor messages such as these by increasing interpersonal distance and may view such messages as indicators of counselor deception. Further, when verbal and nonverbal messages are incongruent or contradict one another, usually the client believes the nonverbal disclosure more strongly than the verbal one.

5.2 Feedback

Information Giving

Client 1

Example of information-giving response: I realize this seems to you to be just another example of what white men do to people of your nation that is unjust and unfair. I also realize that you are following what you've seen many of your male relatives do. So I'm sure, based on all this, it does seem hard to believe that drinking a six-pack of beer can interfere with the way you drive. In fact, it can and does affect how you judge things and how quickly you react. Would you be willing to watch a short film clip with me or check out a website to get some additional information?

Client 2

Example of information-giving response: Kevin, when you say this could never happen to you, it makes me wonder what you know about HIV. Do you know any black men who have tested positive for HIV? And are you aware that the virus can be spread easily through shared needles and also through semen?

Client 3

Example of information-giving response: Leslie, in discussing your situation with you, there are a couple of things I want to mention. First, it might be useful for you to consider seeing a competent lawyer who specializes in divorce mediation. This person could give you detailed information about the legal effects and processes of a divorce. Usually, a person does not lose a job because of a divorce. In many instances, the husband is required to make support payments as long as the children are of minor age, depending on the custody arrangements. I would encourage you to express these same concerns to the lawyer. The other thing I'd like to spend some time discussing is your belief that you will feel very happy after the divorce. That might be very true. It is also important to remember, though, that just the process of ending a relationship—even a bad relationship—can be very unsettling and can bring not only relief but also some feelings of loss and maybe sadness for you and for your children.

Lack of congruence between helper verbal and nonverbal messages and resulting disclosures to clients can be especially detrimental in cross-cultural helping interactions. Sue and Sue (2013) observe that for many racial/ethnic minority clients, there is a sociopolitical facet to nonverbal communication. Minority clients may intentionally challenge a helper to discern the disclosure revealed by the helper's nonverbal message, because such disclosures often represent clues about bias on the part of the helper. For example, when topics related to a minority client's identity, such as race, are brought up in the session, what the helper says may often be negated by his or her nonverbal communication. If this is the case, then the minority client will quickly perceive the inconsistency and may conclude that the helper is incapable of dealing with cultural and racial diversity issues.

Intentional, Direct Self-Disclosure

Intentional self-disclosure, also called **direct self-disclosure**, is the form of self-disclosure that most practitioners define in their repertoire of responses with clients. Direct disclosure "refers to the intentional disclosure by the clinician of personal information and can be verbal or nonverbal" (Zur et al., 2009, p. 23).

Our focus in the remainder of this section is on the use of purposeful and direct self-disclosure as a verbal influencing response to achieve certain purposes in the helping process.

Direct self-disclosure is used with clients for several reasons. Conscious use of self-disclosure can build rapport and foster the working alliance by increasing the helper's authenticity, by promoting feelings of universality, and by increasing trust. This purpose of self-disclosure is important with all clients and is perhaps critical with clients from various racial and ethnic groups who may depend on some helper self-disclosure to feel safe. The whole idea of self-disclosing intimate aspects of one's life to a stranger such as a therapist may seem inappropriate to clients from some cultural groups who stress friendship as a precondition to self-disclosure (Sue & Sue, 2013).

Another purpose of self-disclosure is to instill hope in clients and to help clients who may feel alone. Also, self-disclosure can be used to help clients consider other and different alternatives and views, and it may be especially suitable to move clients who are stuck in a rut to take some action.

Empirical Evidence for Self-Disclosure

Henretty and Levitt (2010) have provided an exhaustive review of the empirical evidence surrounding the use of self-disclosure in psychotherapy. In general, their review of quantitative studies about this helper response found the following:

1. self-disclosure (versus nondisclosure) has positive effects on clients

2. clients liked helpers who self-disclosed more than those who did not disclose

3. clients perceived helpers who self-disclosed as warmer

4. client's level of self-disclosure increased with helpers who self-disclosed.

Also, the following variables did not impact or were not impacted by helper self-disclosure: helper's education, client's age, helper and client gender, and client's perceptions of helper's levels of trustworthiness, regard, empathy, congruence, and unconditionality. Although to date there are few studies exploring self-disclosure and ethnicity, the results of these few studies support the conclusion that culture does interact with self-disclosure in the helping process. Specifically, clients from some ethnic origins may prefer helper self-disclosure, whereas clients from other ethnic origins do not (Henretty & Levitt, 2010, p. 69). We discuss some of the clinical implications from these findings in the following section on Ground Rules and Client Reactions to Self-Disclosure.

Ground Rules and Client Reactions to Self-Disclosure

Self-disclosure is a complex skill. There are ethical issues surrounding the use of it. As Henretty and Levitt (2010) point out, the issues surrounding nondisclosure require as much scrutiny as self-disclosure, because both the "theoretical and empirical research suggests that nondisclosure has risks and benefits that need to be weighed" (p. 71). At the same time, intentional use of self-disclosure requires critical thinking and judicious adaptation, too. In part, this degree of forethought is necessary because it is often very tempting for helpers to disclose something about themselves that meets more of their own needs for expression and validation than the client's needs. Such disclosure constitutes a sort of role reversal. There is also the risk of a helper overidentifying with a client and projecting his or her own experiences and feelings onto the client in the self-disclosed material. For example, a client comes in and reports she is in a second marriage and comments, "Aren't second marriages great?" In response the helper self-discloses and says, "Yes, I think so, too. I have no regrets about having divorced my first husband. What about you?" The client looks sad and puzzled by this: "Well, my first husband died in a car wreck." In an example such as this, the thoughtless use of self-disclosure could get the helper into a lot of difficulty.

Here we provide some ground rules to help you think critically about self-disclosure. The first ground rule pertains to the timing or the decision about *when* to self-disclose to a client. Hepworth and colleagues (2013) suggest that self-disclosure in most instances is not useful until rapport has been established with the client. They note that "the danger in premature self-disclosure is that

such responses can threaten clients and lead to emotional retreat at the very time when it is vital to reduce threat and defensiveness" (p. 114). Remember that self-disclosure is an influencing response, so building a good preliminary base of listening responses with clients is usually a good idea. At the same time, though, low levels of self-disclosure can be useful in the early stages of helping as a way to build the alliance and relieve client apprehensions (Henretty & Levitt, 2010, p. 72). These authors recommend that a pragmatic way to deal with the timing of self-disclosure may simply be to inform clients at the beginning of the process that helpers will at times reveal their own thoughts, feelings, and information about themselves as appropriate (Henretty & Levitt, 2010, p. 72).

The second ground rule has to do with the breadth of the disclosure, or *how much* disclosure to provide: the amount of helper information shared. Most of the evidence indicates that a moderate amount of disclosure has more positive effects than no disclosure or too much disclosure (Levitt, Butler, & Hill, 2006; Henretty & Levitt, 2010). Some self-disclosure may indicate a desire for a close relationship and may increase the client's estimate of the helper's trustworthiness. Some self-disclosure can provide role modeling for clients from cultures with a low level of emotional expressiveness (Lum, 2011). Helpers who disclose very little could add to the role distance between themselves and their clients. At the other extreme, too much disclosure may be counterproductive. The helper who discloses too much may be perceived as lacking in discretion, being untrustworthy, seeming self-preoccupied, or needing assistance. A real danger in overdisclosing is the risk of being perceived as needing as much help as the client. This perception could undermine the client's confidence in the helper's ability to be helpful. Also, too much self-disclosure can lead clients who are from cultures unaccustomed to personal sharing to retreat (Lum, 2011).

Excessive self-disclosure may represent a blurring of good treatment boundaries. Greenberg, Rice, and Elliott (1993) refer to the process of too much helper self-disclosure and not enough attention to boundary issues as **promiscuous self-disclosure**. They note that effective use of self-disclosure is based on the helper's accurate awareness of his or her own inner experience (Greenberg et al., 1993). Also, excessive self-disclosure is the most common boundary violation that precedes unethical sexual contact between therapist and client (Smith & Fitzpatrick, 1995).

Another ground rule pertains to the *duration* of self-disclosure—the amount of time used to give information about yourself. Extended periods of helper disclosure will consume time that could be spent in client disclosure. As one person reveals more, the other person will necessarily reveal less. From this perspective, some conciseness in the length of self-disclosing statements seems warranted. Another consideration in duration of self-disclosure is the capacity of the client to use and benefit from the information shared. As Egan (2014) observes, helpers should avoid self-disclosing to the point of adding a burden to an already overwhelmed client. Of course, if the client doesn't seem to respond positively to the self-disclosure, then it is best not to use any more of it. And after the self-disclosure, it is wise to make sure that the focus doesn't stay on you but goes back to the client.

A fourth ground rule to consider in using self-disclosure concerns the *depth,* or intimacy, of the information revealed. You should try to make your statements similar in content and mood to the client's messages. Ivey, Gluckstern, and Ivey (1997) suggest that the practitioner's self-disclosure should be closely linked to the client's statements. For example:

Client: I feel so down on myself. My partner is so critical of me, and often I think she's right. I really can't do much of anything well.

Helper similar: There have been times when I've also felt down on myself, so I can sense how discouraged you are. Sometimes, too, criticism from someone close to me has made me feel even worse, although I'm learning how to value myself regardless of critical comments from those I care about.

Helper dissimilar: I've felt bummed out, too. Sometimes the day just doesn't go well.

Also, there is some evidence that disclosures of a *moderate* amount of intimacy are linked to more positive effects on the helping process (Kim et al., 2003). This same study found that to some degree counselors are able to determine how clients may perceive a particular disclosure and can therefore judge the appropriate amount of disclosure to make (Kim et al., 2003).

The final ground rule involves *with whom* self-disclosure may or may not be feasible. The nature of the client's problems, the client's ego strength, and any diagnoses are all relevant factors to consider. Hepworth and associates (2013) recommend very limited and concrete self-disclosure with clients who are psychotic or have severe and ongoing mental illness. Similarly, Henretty and Levitt (2010) found that self-disclosure is not used much with clients with poor boundaries or with those diagnosed with personality disorders. Self-disclosure is also used less with clients who have been diagnosed with disruptive, impulse control, and conduct disorders.

For some clients, however, the use of self-disclosure is highly indicated. These include clients who are adolescents and some clients of color, who may feel more comfortable and trusting of practitioners who self-disclose. Self-disclosure

is also a primary action tool in both individual and group counseling for clients with substance abuse problems.

Steps in Self-Disclosure

There are four steps in developing a self-disclosure response. First, assess the purpose of using self-disclosure at this time, and make sure that you're disclosing for the client's benefit and not your own. Simone and colleagues (1998) suggest a series of questions to help you think through the benefits and risks of self-disclosure with a client:

Will my disclosure pull the focus from the client?
Will it blur boundaries?
Will it make the client focus on my needs or feel frightened about my vulnerability?
Will my disclosure cause the client concern about my ability to help?
Will this disclosure improve or diminish our rapport?
Will it help the client look at different viewpoints, or will it confuse the client?
Will the disclosure help the client feel more hopeful and less alone, or could it demoralize the client?
Does this client need me to model disclosure behavior? (p. 182)

Second, assess whether you know enough about the client (and/or the client's diagnosis) to determine if this client can use your self-disclosure to add to insight and to take action. Consider the nature of the client's problems and diagnoses and how this situation may affect the client's ability to use your self-disclosure effectively. Third, assess the timing of the self-disclosure. Note what indicators you have that suggest whether the client is ready to accept your self-disclosure or be put off by it.

Fourth, remember to assess the effectiveness of your self-disclosure. You can follow-up on the client's reactions by paraphrasing and reflecting and by open questions. Observe whether the client is receptive to your self-disclosure or seems shut down by it. If the client seems uncomfortable with your self-disclosure or doesn't acknowledge any similarity with his or her own situation, then it is best not to make additional self-disclosures—at least in this session and perhaps not with this client.

To formulate an effective self-disclosure response, consider the following cognitive learning strategy:

1. What is my reason for disclosing now? Is it linked to the client's needs and statements rather than to my own needs and projections?

2. What do I know about this client and the nature of the client's problems and diagnoses? Can this client use the self-disclosure?

3. How do I know if the timing is right for using self-disclosure with this client?

4. How will I know if my self-disclosure is effective?

Notice how the practitioner uses this cognitive learning strategy for self-disclosure in the following example:

Client, a 45-year-old gay man whose partner recently left him: My partner of 20 years has recently left me for another man. I can't help but wonder if he didn't find me attractive anymore. I have been feeling so disgusted with myself. I keep wondering if I should have been doing things differently—if somehow it was entirely my fault. It just makes me feel that I must have done something wrong. I keep thinking if only I had done this or done that, he wouldn't have left.

Helper *(asks and answers covertly):*

Self-question 1: What is my reason for disclosing now?
My reason for disclosing now is to instill hope in this discouraged client. It is linked to his statements of feeling totally responsible for the breakup of his relationship.

Self-question 2: What do I know about this client and the nature of his problems? Can he effectively use the self-disclosure?

The client is not psychotic or severely mentally ill and does not appear to have an impulse or conduct disorder. I will keep my response short and get the focus back to the client after it.

Self-question 3: How do I know if the timing for self-disclosure is right?
The timing seems okay because the client seems very discouraged and stuck in his discouragement and self-blame.

Self-question 4: How will I know if my self-disclosure is effective?
I will follow-up my self-disclosure with a response that returns the focus to the client and checks out his reaction to the self-disclosure.

Helper self-disclosure: Rich, I have been in a similar situation, and it took me a long time to realize that it wasn't my fault, that no matter what or how much I did, my partner still would have left. Does my experience have any usefulness for you?

Rich's response seems to confirm the helper's intent of instilling hope and moving him out of his discouragement. In this situation, the use of self-disclosure seemed to be effective. Learning Activity 5.3 gives you the opportunity to develop and practice the skill of self-disclosure.

Learning Activity 5.3

Self-Disclosure

Respond to the following three client situations with a self-disclosing response using the cognitive learning strategy described previously and outlined here. Make sure you reveal something about yourself. It might help you to start your statements with "I." Also, try to make your statements concise and similar in content and depth to the client messages and situations. An example is given first, and feedback is provided on page 157.

Example

The client is having a hard time stating specific reasons for seeking counseling, and you have the feeling that a big part of this difficulty may be due to cultural differences between you and the client.

Client Practice Messages

Self-question 1: *What is my reason for disclosing now? Is it linked to the client's needs and statements rather than my own needs and projections?*
Self-question 2: *What do I know about this client and the nature of the client's problems? Can this client use the self-disclosure?*
Self-question 3: *How do I know if the timing is right for using self-disclosure with this client?*
Self-question 4: *How will I know if my self-disclosure is effective?*

Actual self-disclosure: I know it takes time to get started. I'm reluctant at times to share something that is personal about myself with someone I don't know, and we come from different ethnic groups. I'm wondering if you feel this way, too?

Client 1 is feeling like a failure because nothing seems to be going well. She states that she "works herself to death" but never feels as though she measures up.

Actual self-disclosure: _____

_____

_____

Client 2 is hinting that he has some concerns about sex but does not seem to know how to introduce this concern in the session.

Actual self-disclosure: _____

_____

_____

Client 3 has started to become aware of feelings of anger because of racist remarks being made at work and is questioning whether such feelings are legitimate or whether something is wrong with him.

Actual self-disclosure: _____

_____

_____

Immediacy

Immediacy is a characteristic of a helper verbal response that describes something as it occurs within a session. Immediacy involves self-disclosure but is limited to self-disclosure of *current* feelings or what is occurring at the present in the relationship or the session. When persons avoid being immediate with each other over the course of a developing relationship, distance sets in. Immediacy is a useful way to focus on the *here and now* in the helping relationship and, as Yalom (2009) advises, checking frequently on the here and now in the helping process is useful. He notes that he usually does one or more immediacy checks during any given session, at least at the very end of the session by saying the following to the client: "We are close to the end of the hour today and I want to focus a bit on how the two of us are working together today. How do you feel about the space between us today, or how well did we work together today?" (pp. 228–229). Sometimes Yalom (2009) adds observations, as in the following immediacy response example he provides: "I notice that we're circling the same things we talked about last week. Do you feel that way too?" (p. 229). As Yalom observes, sometimes nothing arises from this immediacy other than establishing a norm that both helper and client observe what happens between them in the helping relationship. At other times, the use of the here-and-now immediacy yields something very profound.

In using immediacy in counseling, the practitioner reflects on the current aspect of: (1) some thought, feeling, or behavior of the *counselor;* (2) some thought, feeling, or behavior of the *client;* or (3) some aspect of the *relationship*. Here are examples of these three categories of immediacy:

1. **Helper immediacy**. The helper reveals his or her own thoughts or feelings in the helping process as they occur in the moment:

   "I'm glad to see you today."
   "I'm sorry, I am having difficulty focusing. Let's go over that again."

2. **Client immediacy**. The practitioner provides feedback to the client about some client behavior or feeling as it occurs in the interview:

   "You're fidgeting and seem uncomfortable here right now."
   "You're really smiling now—you must be very pleased about it."

3. **Relationship immediacy**. The helper reveals feelings or thoughts about how he or she experiences the relationship:
   "I'm glad that you're able to share that with me."
   "It makes me feel good that we're getting somewhere today."

Relationship immediacy may include references to specific here-and-now transactions or to the overall pattern or development of the relationship. For example, "I'm aware that right now as I'm talking again, you are looking away and tapping your feet and fingers. I'm wondering if you're feeling impatient with me or if I'm talking too much" (specific transaction). Consider another example in which immediacy is used to focus on the development and pattern of the relationship: "This session feels so good to me. I remember when we first started a few months ago, and it seemed we were both being very careful and having trouble expressing what was on our minds. Today, I'm aware we're not measuring our words so carefully. It feels like there's more comfort between us."

Immediacy is not an end but rather a means of helping the practitioner and client work together better. If allowed to become a goal for its own sake, then immediacy can be distracting rather than helpful. It is primarily used to address issues in the relationship that, if left unresolved, would interfere with the helping relationship and the therapeutic alliance. Examples of instances in which immediacy might be useful include the following (Egan, 2010):

1. Hesitancy or "carefulness" in speech or behavior ("Juanita, I'm aware that you [or I] seem to be choosing words very carefully right now—as if you [or I] might say something wrong").

2. Feeling of being "stuck"—lack of focus or direction ("Right now I feel like our session is sort of a broken record. We're just like a needle tracking in the same groove without really making any music or going anywhere").

3. Tension and trust ("I'm aware there's some discomfort and tension we're both feeling now—about who we are as people and where this is going and what's going to happen") (p. 250).

Immediacy can also be used to deal with the issues of transference and countertransference we discussed in Chapter 3.

Immediacy has three purposes. One purpose is to bring out in the open something that you feel about yourself, about the client, or about the relationship that has not been expressed directly. Generally, it is assumed that covert (unexpressed) feelings about the relationship may inhibit effective communication or may prevent further development of the relationship unless the helper recognizes and responds to these feelings. This may be especially important for negative feelings. In this way, immediacy may reduce the distance that overshadows the relationship because of unacknowledged underlying issues.

5.3 Feedback

Self-Disclosure

Here are some possible examples of counselor self-disclosure for the three client situations. See whether your responses are similar. Your statements will probably reflect more of your own feelings and experiences. Are your statements fairly concise? Are they similar to the client messages in content and intensity?

To Client 1: I sense how difficult it is for you to work so hard and not feel successful. I have also struggled at times with my own high standards and gradually have learned to be more gentle and easier on myself. Is this something you can relate to?

To Client 2: Sometimes I find it hard to start talking about really personal things like sex. I wonder if this is what's happening to you right now.

To Client 3: I can remember times when it has been hard to admit I feel angry. I always used to control it by telling myself I really wasn't angry or that someone really didn't mean to say something offensive to me. Does this feel like what is happening with you?

A second purpose of immediacy is to generate discussion or to provide feedback about some aspects of the relationship or the interactions as they occur. This feedback may include verbal sharing of the helper's feelings or of something the helper sees going on in the interactive process. Immediacy is not used to describe every passing feeling or observation to the client. But when something happens in the process that influences the client's feelings toward counseling, as surmised by the helper, then dealing openly with this issue has high priority. Usually it is up to the helper to initiate discussion of unresolved feelings or issues. Immediacy can be a way to begin such discussion and, if used properly, can strengthen the working alliance.

A third purpose of immediacy is to help clients gain awareness of their relationships to other people and of issues that may be causing problems for them with other people. Teyber and McClure (2011) describe this as the client's *interpersonal style* and they identify three predominant kinds of interpersonal styles: moving toward others; moving away from others; and moving against others. The rationale for this use of immediacy is that clients usually respond to helpers the way they respond to other people in their lives. For example, if Butler is oppositional with the helper, then he is perhaps also oppositional with significant others in his life. If Catherina idealizes the helper, then she probably also idealizes other people in her life who are important to her. If Jorge goes out of his way to please the therapist, then he most likely works hard to please other people as well. Immediacy can provide a model for clients of how to address and resolve problems in their interpersonal relationships outside of therapy. Individual clients, as well as couples, families, and groups, usually follow the interpersonal model set by the practitioner (Hepworth et al., 2013). A naturalistic field study involving 16 cases of individual psychodynamic psychotherapy conducted by doctoral students with adult clients found that immediacy appeared to be an effective helping skill used to facilitate a corrective emotional experience for the clients, establish or negotiate boundaries, foster client disclosure, and promote client insight (Hill, Gelso, Chui, Spangler, Hummel, Huang, Jackson, Jones, Palma, Bhatia, Gupta, Ain, Klingaman, Lim, Liu, Hui, Jezzi, & Miles, 2013).

Ground Rules and Client Reactions to Immediacy

Several ground rules can help practitioners use immediacy effectively. First, the helper should describe what she or he sees *as it happens*. If the helper waits until later in the session or until the next interview to describe a feeling or experience, the impact is lost. In addition, feelings about the relationship that are discounted or ignored may build up and eventually be expressed in more intense or distorted ways. The helper who puts off using immediacy to initiate a needed discussion runs the risk of having unresolved feelings or issues damage the relationship.

Second, to reflect the here and now of the experience, any immediacy statement should be in the present tense—"I'm feeling confused now" rather than "I just felt confused." This models expression of current rather than past feelings for the client.

Further, when referring to your feelings and perceptions, take responsibility for them by using the personal pronoun *I, me,* or *mine,* as in "I'm feeling concerned about you now" instead of "You're making me feel concerned." Expressing your current feelings with "I" language communicates that you are responsible for your feelings and observations, and this may increase the client's receptivity to your immediacy expressions. Also, as in using all other responses, the helper should consider timing. Using a lot of immediacy in an early session may be overwhelming for some clients and can elicit anxiety in either the helper or client. Cultural differences also play a role in the decision to use immediacy. Some clients may feel awkward discussing personal feelings or be unwilling to give feedback if solicited by the helper.

As Gazda and associates (2005, p. 205) observe, "It is highly desirable that a strong base relationship exists before using the dimension of immediacy." If a helper uses immediacy and senses that this has threatened or scared the client, then the helper may discern that the client is not yet ready to handle these feelings or issues. And not every feeling or observation a helper has needs to be verbalized to a client. The session does not need to turn into a "heavy" discussion, nor should it resemble a confessional. Generally, immediacy is reserved for initiating exploration of the most significant or most influential feelings or issues. Of course, a helper who never expresses immediacy may be avoiding issues that have a significant effect on the relationship. Some preliminary research suggests that with fearfully/insecurely attached clients, helpers may need to tread more carefully in the use of immediacy, particularly in using this skill to discuss relationship issues or ruptures (Hill et al., 2013).

Finally, in using immediacy, even if it is well timed, helpers have to be careful that the immediacy response is based on what is actually happening in the relationship rather than being a reflection of their countertransference response to something occurring with the client. For example, Antony is a beginning helper who has just seen Marisa, one of his very first clients. Marisa is very depressed, so Antony suggests a consultation with the staff psychiatrist. Marisa is receptive to this idea, and Antony schedules this consultation for her after their session the following week. When the time arrives for the consultation, Antony takes Marisa over to the psychiatrist's waiting room, and Marisa is told that due to some scheduling problems she will have to wait at least an hour or longer before the consultation. Marisa becomes upset and lashes out at Antony, saying that she has taken extra time off from work for this consultation and is losing money because of it. Antony reacts on the basis of his first impulse: "Well, if that's the way you feel, you might as well not come back to see me next week." Fortunately, Antony has a safe and trusting relationship with his supervisor and discusses this situation in supervision. His supervisor helps Antony to see that what he blurted out was more a reflection of his countertransference and not truly based on what he really felt about Marisa and their relationship. In fact, he likes working with Marisa very much and she is important to him, but his response was based on his own feeling that he and the helping process were, in his eyes, not more important to her.

One way to prevent a situation like Antony's is to reach for feelings that underlie your immediate experiencing. For example, you may have a superficial level of a feeling such as dislike or boredom but, reaching underneath, discover curiosity or compassion. Or you may feel annoyed at the client for being late but, reaching deeper, feel

disappointment that the client isn't more committed to the helping process (Hepworth et al., 2013). Hill (2014) describes this process as recognizing when you are being "hooked" by the client's behavior and then learning how to pull out of being hooked.

Steps in Immediacy

The immediacy influencing response requires a complex set of skills applied in the context of both critical thinking and judicious adaptation. The first step toward immediacy—and an important prerequisite of the actual verbal response—calls for awareness, or the ability to sense what is happening in the interaction. To develop this awareness, you must monitor the flow of the interaction to process what is happening to you, to the client, and to your developing relationship. Awareness also implies that you can read the clues without a great number of decoding errors and without projecting your own biases and blind spots into the interaction.

After developing awareness, the next step is to formulate a verbal response that somehow shares your sense or picture of the process with the client. Sometimes this may include sharing more than one feeling or sharing conflicting feelings. The critical feature of immediacy is its emphasis on the here and now—the present.

The third step is to describe the situation or targeted behavior in neutral or descriptive rather than evaluative terms (Hepworth et al., 2013). The fourth step is to identify the specific effect of the problem situation, of the relationship issue, or of the client's behavior on others and on you (Hepworth et al., 2013). You help the client take action by authentically sharing how the client affects you instead of cajoling, pleading, or directing the client to change, which usually backfires. The last step is to get the client's reactions to your immediacy response. For example, you can ask the client something like, "What is your reaction to what I just shared?" If your response is not helpful, then the client will most likely shut down, retreat, or even lash out at you. If immediacy is helpful, then the client will provide feedback and engage in more exploration.

To formulate an effective immediacy response, consider the following cognitive learning strategy:

1. What is going on right now—in me, with the client, in the process and interaction between us—that needs to be addressed?

2. How can I formulate an immediacy response that addresses this issue in the here and now?

3. How can I describe the situation or behavior in a descriptive rather than an evaluative way?

4. How can I identify the specific effect of this situation or behavior?

5. How will I know if my immediacy response is useful to the client?

Notice how the helper uses this cognitive learning strategy for immediacy in the following example.

The client, Isabella, is struggling with a decision about whether to get a job or go back to school. She has been inundating you with e-mails and phone calls between your weekly sessions. This has gone on for several weeks. You are feeling put off by this. You decide during the session to use immediacy to respond because she is also talking about how much difficulty she seems to have in making connections with other people—who just don't seem to be responsive to her.

Helper *(asks and answers covertly):*

Self-question 1: What is going on right now that needs to be addressed?
With me—my feelings of moving away from Isabella. With her—her pattern of inundating me with e-mails and phone calls during the week, which I suspect may be happening with other people in her life. Underneath this are probably feelings of anxiety and uncertainty. With the interaction between us—as she increases her requests for my time and energy, I find myself pulling back and giving less.

Self-question 2: How can I formulate an immediacy response that addresses this issue in the here and now?
Use the present tense, and start first with what I'm aware of, such as, "I'm aware of some feelings that I'm having that might be related to your experiences in connecting with other people."

Self-question 3: How can I describe the situation or behavior in a descriptive rather than an evaluative way?
Take responsibility for my feelings by using an "I" message, describing her behaviors with the e-mails and phone calls without blaming her.

Self-question 4: How can I identify the specific effect of this situation or behavior?
Describe what I see happening in the process—as she requests more of my time and energy with the e-mails and phone calls, I find myself pulling back, giving less, and wondering if this is part of her difficulty in connecting with other people as well.

Self-question 5: How will I know if my immediacy response is useful to her?
I will ask for her feedback at the very end of my immediacy response.

Immediacy response: Isabella, I'm aware of some feelings I'm having that may relate to both your school and work decision and also to your feeling a lack of responsiveness from other people you try to connect with. If you feel willing to hear them, I'd like to share them with you now (*pause to get an indicator of her willingness, which often may be nonverbal*) . . . Okay. Well, I'm finding myself pulling back from you and giving you less of my time and energy as you are making more requests of me through daily e-mails and phone calls asking me what you should do. I'm guessing you're feeling a lot more anxious about this decision than I know. As a result, you are moving toward me with such intensity that I find myself moving back from you when this happens. I wonder if this might also be going on with some of the people in your life you are having trouble connecting with (*pause*). What's your reaction to this?

Isabella's response: Well, that's a lot to think about. I guess I never thought of myself in that way, and I didn't realize I would be having that effect on other people. But you are right in that I am feeling very uncertain and unsure about what step to take next and I have never had much confidence in my ability to make decisions, so getting tons of input from others is the way I deal with this.

Isabella's response suggests she has benefited from the helper's immediacy response in that she is able to begin to explore the idea of having trouble relying on herself for decisions. Although she did not respond to the part about the other people in her life, this may come at a later time in the session or in a subsequent session. Learning Activity 5.4 gives you the opportunity to develop and practice the skills for immediacy using the cognitive learning strategy described earlier.

Interpretations and Additive/Advanced Empathy

Interpretation is a response that calls for understanding and being able to communicate the meaning of a client's messages. In making interpretive statements, the helper uses her or his hunches or ideas to identify patterns and to make implied client messages more explicit. Interpretive responses can be defined in a variety of ways. We define an **interpretation** as a statement that—based on the helper's hunches—identifies behaviors, patterns, goals, wishes, and feelings that are suggested or implied by the client's communication.

Learning Activity 5.4

Immediacy

In this activity, you are given three client practice statements. For each client message, develop an example of an immediacy response. Apply the cognitive learning strategy and the five self-questions listed here to each client statement. Feedback follows on page 162.

Example

The client has come in late for the third time, and you have concerns about this behavior. One concern is that the client's lateness affects your whole schedule, and another is that you feel uncertainty about the client's commitment to the helping process.

Immediacy response: I'm aware that you're having difficulty getting here on time, and I'm feeling uncomfortable about this. I feel uncertain about when or whether to expect you for your session. I guess I'm also wondering about your commitment to being here. What is your take on this?

Apply the five self-questions to the following three client examples in formulating your immediacy response.

Self-question 1: *What is going on right now that needs to be addressed?*

Self-question 2: *How can I formulate an immediacy response that addresses this issue in the here-and-now?*

Self-question 3: *How can I describe the situation or behavior in a descriptive versus an evaluative way?*

Self-question 4: *How can I identify the specific effect of this situation or behavior?*

Self-question 5: *How will I know if my immediacy response is effective?*

Client Examples

Client 1 stops talking whenever you bring up the subject of her academic performance.

Your immediacy response: _____

_____

_____

Client 2 has asked you several questions about your competence and qualifications.

Your immediacy response: _____

_____

_____

Client 3 and you are experiencing a great deal of tension and caution; the two of you seem to be treating each other with kid gloves. You notice physical sensations of tension in your body, and signs of tension are also apparent in the client.

Your immediacy response: _____

_____

_____

Interpretation deals with the **implicit** part of a message—the part the client does not talk about explicitly or directly. As Brammer, Abrego, and Shostrom (1993) note, when interpreting, a helper will often verbalize issues that the client may have felt only vaguely. Our concept of interpretation is similar to what Egan (2014) calls *advanced accurate empathy*, because this response challenges clients to look deeper. Hepworth and associates (2013) refer to interpretive responses as *additive empathy*. They note that at this level of empathy the practitioner uses mild to moderate interpretive responses that accurately identify implicit underlying feelings and/or aspects of the problem, thus enabling the client to get in touch with somewhat deeper feelings and unexplained meanings and purposes of behavior. Further, these interpretive responses may also identify "implicit goals" or actions desired by but perhaps unacknowledged by the client (p. 523). These interpretive responses go beyond the expressed meaning of client messages to partially expressed and implied messages—hence, the term *additive* empathy. If these responses are accurate and well timed, clients will gain a new and fresh perspective.

There are many benefits and purposes for which interpretation can be used appropriately in a helping interview. First, effective interpretations can contribute to the development of a positive therapeutic relationship by reinforcing client self-disclosure, enhancing the credibility of the therapist, and communicating therapeutic attitudes to the client. Another purpose of interpretation is to identify patterns between clients' explicit and implicit messages and behaviors. A third purpose is to help clients examine their behavior from a different frame of reference to achieve a better understanding of the problem. Finally, almost all interpretations are offered to promote insight. Johnson (2014) observes that interpretation is useful for clients because it leads to insight, and insight is a key to better psychological living and a precursor to effective behavior change.

Here is an example that may help you understand the nature of the interpretation response more clearly:

Client 1, a young soldier after deployment: Well, I survived three deployments over there. I have seen it all, buddies killed, some so severely injured they will never really recover. So in light of this, my habit of porn doesn't seem so bad, given all I have been through in the past 10 years.

Interpretation: Tomas, I can tell from what you are saying and how you are saying it that you have really been through a lot—multiple deployments, witnessing the death and injuries of close friends and comrades. Could it be, though, that you are using this as a reason to justify continuing your porn habit?

Sometimes the implicit response may have to do with a cultural aspect of the client's message. Consider the voice of Thad, the only African American student in his communications class: "This is the first class I have ever had to stand up and give a real speech to. And I just feel like I can't do it, it won't be good enough, it won't meet standards, it won't be as good as the other speeches are . . . It just won't be good enough." The sensitive helper may hear the implied cultural aspect of Thad's message and give an interpretive response similar to the following: "Giving this speech is a first for you, and you feel gripped with doubt and fear about it—in part because this is a new experience for you and also perhaps because you're the only person of color in the room and you're holding yourself to a higher standard."

Ground Rules for Interpreting and Cautionary Notes

The overall quality of the therapeutic relationship affects the degree to which an interpretation is likely to be useful to the client. Interpretations need to be offered in the context of a safe and empathic contact with the client. For this reason, as Hepworth and associates (2013) note, interpretive responses are used "sparingly" with clients until a sound working alliance has been developed (p. 541). As you can imagine, interpretive responses are not used a great deal in brief therapy.

Another important aspect of the content of the interpretation is whether your interpretation is based on the client's actual message rather than on your own biases and values projected onto the client. You need to be aware of your own blind spots. For example, if you had a bad experience with marriage and are biased against people getting or staying married, you need to be aware of how this opinion could affect the way you interpret client statements about

marriage. If you aren't careful, you could easily advise all marital counseling clients away from marriage, a bias that might not be in the best interests of many of them.

A third guideline and cautionary note for the interpretation response is the way in which the helper phrases the interpretation and offers it to the client. In most cases, interpretations should be phrased tentatively. Tentative rather than absolute phrasing helps prevent the helper from engaging in one-upmanship and engendering client resistance or defensiveness to the interpretation. After responding with an interpretation, check out the accuracy of your interpretive response by asking the client whether your message fits. Returning to a clarification is always a useful way to determine whether you have interpreted the message accurately.

The content of an interpretation must be congruent with the client's cultural affiliations. Because many counseling theories are based on Eurocentric assumptions, achieving congruence can be a thought-provoking task. It is most important *not* to assume that an interpretation that makes sense to you will make the same sort of sense to a client whose racial, ethnic, and cultural backgrounds vary from your own. Also remember that a primary goal of the interpretive response is to promote client insight and that even the goal of promoting insight is a "culture bound value" (Sue & Sue, 2013, p. 188).

The *depth* of the interpretation you offer to the client is another factor related both to usage and caution regarding this influencing response. **Depth** is the degree of discrepancy between the viewpoint expressed by the helper and the client's beliefs. Presenting clients with a viewpoint discrepant from their own is believed to facilitate change by providing clients with a reconceptualization of the problem. An important question is to what extent the helper's communicated conceptualization of the issue should differ from the client's beliefs. Highly discrepant or very deep interpretations are more likely to be rejected by the client, possibly because they are unacceptable, seem too speculative, or evoke resistance. In contrast, interpretations that are either congruent with or only slightly discrepant from the client's viewpoint are most likely to prompt change. Hepworth and colleagues (2013) conclude that practitioners should avoid making any interpretive responses that are "far removed from the awareness of clients" (p. 542). Also, because interpretive responses can facilitate deeper self-exploration by clients, the quantity of these responses is also an important guideline. It is generally ill-advised to offer

5.4 Feedback

Immediacy

Here are some expressions of immediacy. See how they compare with yours.

To Client 1: Every time I mention academic performance, like now, you seem to back off from this topic. I'm aware that during this session, you stop talking when the topic of your grades comes up. Am I hitting a nerve there, or is there something else going on that would help me understand this better?

To Client 2: I'm aware that right now it seems very important to you to find out more about me and my background and qualifications. I'm sensing that you're concerned about how helpful I can be to you and how comfortable you're feeling with me. What's your reaction to this? Maybe you have something you want to share, and, if so, I'd like to hear it.

To Client 3: I'm aware of how physically tight I feel now and how tense you look to me. I'm sensing that we're just not too comfortable with each other yet. We seem to be treating each other in a very fragile and cautious way right now. I'm not sure what this is about. What reactions do you have to this?

too many interpretive responses in a single session, or for that matter even during the course of the helping process. It is far better to offer a few on-target, accurate interpretations that really create movement for the client from superficial to deep exploration than to try to push this movement by overinterpreting.

The depth of the interpretation also has some impact on the time at which an interpretation is offered—both within a session and within the overall context of treatment. The client should show some degree of readiness to explore or examine himself or herself before you use interpretation. Generally, an interpretation response is reserved for later, rather than initial, sessions because some data must be gathered as a basis for an interpretive response and because the typical client requires several sessions to become accustomed to the type of material discussed in counseling. The client may be more receptive to your interpretation if she or he is comfortable with the topics being explored and shows some readiness to accept the interpretive response. As Brammer and colleagues (1993, p. 181) note, a helper usually does not interpret until the time when the client can almost formulate the interpretation for herself or himself. Timing within a session is also important. If the helper suspects that the interpretation may produce anxiety or resistance or

break the client's "emotional dam," it may be a good idea to postpone it until the beginning of the next session (Brammer et al., 1993).

Client Reactions to Interpretation

Client reactions to interpretation may range from expression of greater self-understanding and release of emotions to less verbal expression and more silence and even more outright hostility and resentment of the helper. According to Cozolino (2010), these reactions occur because a number of things are occurring in the client's brain both during and after an interpretation, especially an accurate one. Specifically, both the cortical networks and subcortical networks in the brain are activated, ultimately allowing for "plasticity and new learning in prefrontal regions" (p. 295). In other words, of all the verbal responses, interpretive responses perhaps have the greatest potential to promote new neural networking and integration in the client's brain.

If your interpretation is met initially with defensiveness or hostility, it may be best to drop the issue temporarily and introduce it again later. However, don't push an interpretation on a resistant client without first re-examining the accuracy of your response. However, if the client responds to the interpretation affirmatively, as in venting feelings, confirming greater understanding, and bringing up additional related content, then the helper can proceed in the same direction. Remember that client reactions may be not only verbal responses but also nonverbal reactions. Clients may react simply by shutting down, becoming less verbally active, and even pulling their chair away from the helper. In a few extreme cases, clients may get up and walk out of the office, perhaps returning later or perhaps discontinuing therapy altogether. This is not necessarily a bad thing in the long term, because interpretations need time to be worked through by clients, but it is an indicator that your interpretation released some emotions in the client that he or she was unprepared to cope with at the time (Cozolino, 2010, p. 295).

Client reactions to interpretation also vary with cultural characteristics. Although the concept of promoting insight, a goal of interpretation, is compatible for some European American clients, insight may not be so valued by other clients. As Sue and Sue (2013) note, "When survival on a day-to-day basis is important, it seems inappropriate for the therapist to use insightful processes" (p. 188). Also, some cultural groups simply do not feel the need to engage in contemplative reflection. The very notion of thinking about oneself or one's issues too much is inconsistent for some clients, who may have been taught not to dwell on themselves and their thoughts. Other clients may have learned to gain insight in a solitary manner, as in a "vision quest," rather than with another person such as a helper. In actual practice, you can try to assess the client's receptivity by using a trial interpretation, bearing in mind that the client's initial reaction may change over time.

Steps in Interpreting

There are three steps in formulating effective interpretations. First, listen for and identify the *implicit* meaning of the client's communication—what the client conveys subtly and indirectly. Listen for behaviors, patterns, and feelings, as well as for implied goals, actions, and wishes. Be sure to take into account the client's nonverbal messages as well. Second, make sure that your view of the issue, your frame of reference, is relevant to the client's cultural background, keeping in mind some of the precautions we addressed earlier. Finally, examine the effectiveness of your interpretation by assessing the client's reaction to it. Look for nonverbal recognition signs such as a smile or contemplative look as well as verbal and behavioral cues that indicate the client is considering the issue from a different frame of reference or that the client may not understand or agree with you.

To formulate an effective interpretation and assess its usefulness, consider the following cognitive learning strategy:

1. What is the implicit part of the client's message?

2. Is my view of this issue culturally relevant for this client?

3. How will I know whether my interpretation is useful?

Notice how a therapist applies this cognitive learning strategy in the following example:

Client, a European American woman: I really don't understand it myself. I can always have good sex whenever we're not at home—even in the car. But at home it's never too good.

Helper (*asks and answers covertly*):

Self-question 1: *What is the implicit part of the client's message?* That sex is not good or fulfilling unless it occurs in special, out-of-the-ordinary circumstances or places. Also that the client doesn't understand what exactly is going on with her sexually and perhaps wishes she could have good sex at home as well as in other places.

Self-question 2: *Is my view of this issue culturally relevant for this client?* This client seems relatively comfortable in talking about and disclosing information about her sexual feelings and behaviors. However, be careful not to make any assumptions about the client's sexual orientation. At this point we do not know whether this person is lesbian, bisexual, or straight.

At this point the helper's covert visualization or self-talk ends, and the following dialogue ensues:

Helper interpretation: Ann, I might be wrong about this—it seems that you get psyched up for sex only when it occurs in out-of-the-ordinary places where you feel there's a lot of novelty and excitement. You don't quite understand this yet and perhaps wish you could have great sex at home, too. Does that sound accurate?

Client (*lips part, smiles slightly, eyes widen*): Well, I never thought about it quite that way. I guess I do need to feel like there are some thrills around when I do have sex—maybe it's that I find unusual places like the elevator a challenge.

At this point, the practitioner can conclude that the interpretation was effective because of the client's nonverbal recognition behavior and because of the client's verbal response suggesting the interpretation was on target. The therapist might continue to help the client explore whether she needs thrills and challenge to function satisfactorily in other areas of her life as well.

Learning Activity 5.5 gives you an opportunity to try out the interpretation response.

Confrontation/Challenge

Confrontation, also known as **challenge**, is an influencing response in which the helper describes discrepancies, conflicts, and mixed messages apparent in the client's feelings, thoughts, and actions. Hepworth and associates (2013) describe this response as follows: "Similar to interpretation and additive empathy it is a tool to enhance clients' self-awareness and to promote change. Confrontation however involves facing clients with some aspect of their thoughts, feelings, or behaviors that is contributing to or maintaining their difficulties" (pp. 542-543). Although some other authors prefer the term *challenge* over *confrontation*, we use these terms interchangeably because they both have the same function in the helping process, and that is to support and move the client forward simultaneously.

Confrontation/challenge has several purposes. One purpose is to help clients explore other ways of perceiving themselves or an issue, leading ultimately to different actions or behaviors. Egan (2014) refers to this purpose

Learning Activity 5.5

Interpretation

Three client practice statements are given in this activity. For each message, develop an example of an interpretation using the cognitive learning strategy described previously and outlined here. To internalize this learning strategy, you may want to talk through the self-questions overtly (aloud) and then covertly. The end product will be an interpretation that you can say aloud or write down. An example precedes the practice messages. Feedback follows on page 166.

Example

Client, a young Asian American woman: I don't know what to do. I guess I never thought I'd ever be asked to be a supervisor. I feel so content just being part of the group I work with.

Self-question 1: *What is the implicit part of the client's message?*

She feels uncertain and perhaps overwhelmed by the thought of this job transition—and perhaps is concerned about losing her place in the group if she moves out of it to become a supervisor.

Self-question 2: *Is my view of this issue culturally relevant for this client?*

With her Asian American background, the client may feel more comfortable working in and with a collective group of people.

Actual interpretation response: Despite your obvious success on the job, you seem to be reluctant to move up to a position that requires you to work by yourself. I'm wondering if you are responding in any part to your cultural background, which stresses belonging to a group,

and working for the good of the group rather than promoting yourself. Have I heard you accurately or not?

Client Practice Statements

Client 1, a young, Native American woman: I can't stand to be touched anymore by a man. And after I was raped, they wanted me to go see a doctor in this hospital. When I wouldn't, they thought I was crazy. I hope you don't think I'm crazy for that.

Actual interpretation response: _____

_____

_____

Client 2, a 50-year-old Jordanian man: Sure, I seemed upset when I got laid off several years ago. After all, I'd been an industrial engineer for almost 23 years. But I can support my family with my job supervising these custodial workers. So I should be very thankful. Then why do I seem so down?

Actual interpretation response: _____

_____

_____

Client 3, a young white man: I have a great time with Susie (his girlfriend), but I've told her I don't want to settle down. She's always so bossy and tries to tell me what to do. She always decides what we're going to do and when and where and so on. I get really upset at her.

Actual interpretation response: _____

_____

_____

as challenging the client's "blind spots," things the client fails to see or chooses to ignore (p. 172). This may involve challenging distortions as well as discrepancies. These distortions may be cognitive ones (often the result of inaccurate, incomplete, or erroneous beliefs and information) or affective ones, involving attributions made from inaccurate or erroneous perceptions (Hepworth et al., 2013).

A second purpose of the confrontation/challenge response is to help the client become more aware of discrepancies or incongruities in thoughts, feelings, and actions. This is important because discrepancies can be indicators of unresolved, contradictory, or suppressed feelings.

Many times during an interview a client may say or do something that is inconsistent. For example, a client says she doesn't want to talk to you because you are a male but then goes ahead and talks to you. In this case, the client's verbal message is inconsistent with her actual behavior. This is an example of an inconsistent, or mixed, message. The purpose of using a confrontation to deal with a mixed message is to describe the discrepancy or contradiction to the client. Often the client is unaware or only vaguely aware of the conflict before the helper points it out. In describing the discrepancy, you will find it helpful to use a confrontation that presents or connects *both* parts of the discrepancy. Motivational interviewing theory describes this as a *double-sided* reflection.

Six major types of mixed messages and accompanying descriptions of confrontations are presented as examples (see also Egan, 2014; Ivey, Ivey, & Zalaquett, 2014).

1. *Verbal and nonverbal behavior*
   a. Client says, "I feel comfortable" (verbal message) but at the same time is fidgeting and twisting her hands (nonverbal message).
   Helper confrontation: You say you feel comfortable, and you're also fidgeting and twisting your hands.
   b. Client says, "I feel happy about the relationship being over—it's better this way" (verbal message) but is talking in a slow, low-pitched voice (nonverbal message).
   Helper confrontation: You say you're happy it's over, and at the same time your voice suggests you have some other feelings too.

2. *Verbal messages and action steps or behaviors*
   a. Client says, "I'm going to call her" (verbal message) but reports the next week that he did not make the call (action step).
   Helper confrontation: You said you would call her, and as of now you are reporting that you haven't done so yet.
   b. Client says, "Counseling is very important to me" (verbal message) but calls off the next two sessions (behavior).
   Helper confrontation: Several weeks ago you said how important counseling is to you; now I'm also aware that you called off our last two meetings.

3. *Two verbal messages* (stated inconsistencies)
   a. Client says, "He's sleeping around with other people. I don't feel bothered (verbal message 1), but I think our relationship should mean more to him than it does" (verbal message 2).
   Helper confrontation: First you say you feel okay about his behavior; now you're feeling upset that your relationship is not as important to him as it is to you.
   b. Client says, "I really do love little Georgie (verbal message 1), although he often bugs the hell out of me" (verbal message 2).
   Helper confrontation: You seem to be aware that much of the time you love him, and at other times you feel very irritated toward him, too.

4. *Two nonverbal messages* (apparent inconsistencies)
   a. Client is smiling (nonverbal message 1) and crying (nonverbal message 2) at the same time.
   Helper confrontation: You're smiling and also crying at the same time.
   b. Client is looking directly at helper (nonverbal message 1) and has just moved chair back from helper (nonverbal message 2).
   Helper confrontation: You're looking at me while you say this, and at the same time you also moved away.

5. *Two persons* (helper/client, parent/child, teacher/student, spouse/spouse, and so on)
   a. Client's husband lost his job 2 years ago. Client wants to move; husband wants to stick around near his family.
   Helper confrontation: Edie, you'd like to move. Marshall, you're feeling family ties and want to stick around.
   b. A woman presents anxiety, depression, and memory loss. You suggest a medical workup to rule out any organic dysfunction, and the client refuses.
   Helper confrontation: Irene, I feel it's very important for us to have a medical workup so we know what to do that will be most helpful for you. You seem to feel very reluctant to have the workup done. How can we work this out?

6. *Verbal message and context or situation*
   a. A child deplores her parents' divorce and states that she wants to help her parents get back together.
   Helper confrontation: Sierra, you say you want to help your parents get back together. At the same time, you had no role in their breakup. How do you put these two things together?
   b. A young couple has had severe conflicts for the past 3 years, but still they want to have a baby to improve their relationship.
   Helper confrontation: The two of you have separated three times since I've been seeing you in therapy. Now you're saying you want to use a child to improve your relationship. Many couples indicate that stress increases from having a child and being parents. How do you put this together?

Ground Rules for Challenging

Confrontation needs to be offered in a way that helps clients examine the consequences of their behavior rather than defending their actions (Johnson, 2014). In other words, confrontation must be used carefully not to increase the very behavior or pattern that the helper feels may need to be diminished or modified. The following ground rules may assist you in using this response to help rather than to harm.

First, be aware of your own motives for challenging at any particular time. Although the word itself has a punitive or emotionally charged sound, confrontation/challenging in the helping process is not an attack on or

5.5 Feedback

Interpretation

Client 1

Interpretation example: I'm guessing that the rape affected your trust of other men—even doctors—and also that your cultural background is having some effect, too. I'm wondering if you would feel safe going to a traditional healer, one that you know, instead.

Client 2

Interpretation example: It sounds as though when you lost your job as an engineer, you also lost some parts of the role you have learned from your culture about being a man, a husband, and a father. Even though you're glad to have a job, you're sad about these losses and what they mean for you as a man, and as a husband, father, and provider for your family. Does that seem accurate?

Client 3

Interpretation example: You like spending time with Susie, but you feel pressured to settle down with her and are also put off by her bossiness. It sounds like you wish you had more of the control in the relationship. Does that fit with what you are saying?

---

an opportunity to badger the client (Welfel & Patterson, 2005). Confrontation also is not to be used as a way to ventilate or dump your frustration onto the client. It is a means of offering constructive, growth-directed feedback that is positive in context and intent, not disapproving or critical (Welfel & Patterson, 2005). Ivey, Ivey, and Zalaquett (2014) describe confrontation as a "supportive" kind of challenge and a "gentle skill that involves first listening to client stories carefully and respectfully, and then encouraging the client to examine self and/or situation more fully...it is not going against the client, it is going with the client" (p. 236).

To avoid blame, focus on the incongruity as the problem, not on the person, and make sure your supportive stance is reflected in your tone of voice and body language. In describing the distortion or discrepancy, the confrontation should cite a *specific example* of the behavior rather than make a vague inference. A poor confrontation might be, "You want people to like you, but your personality turns them off." In this case, the practitioner is making a general inference about the client's personality and also is implying that the client must undergo a major overhaul to get along with others. A more helpful confrontation would be, "You

want people to like you, and at the same time you make frequent remarks about yourself that seem to get in the way and turn people off."

Moreover, before a helper tries to confront a client, rapport and trust should be established. Confrontation probably should not be used unless you, the helper, are willing to maintain or increase your involvement in or commitment to the helping relationship (Johnson, 2014). The primary consideration is to judge what your level of involvement seems to be with each client and adapt accordingly. The stronger the relationship is, the more receptive the client may be to a confrontation.

The *timing* of a confrontation is very important. Because the purpose is to help the person engage in self-examination, try to offer the confrontation at a time when the client is likely to use it. The perceived ability of the client to act on the confrontation should be a major guideline in deciding when to challenge. In other words, before you jump in and confront, determine the person's attention level, anxiety level, desire to change, and ability to listen. A confrontation is most likely to be heard when the client feels safe with you; it is less likely to be heard when it occurs early in the relationship. An exception to this general ground rule is in instances of legal violations and danger to self or to others, when confrontation would be mandated earlier in the helping process (Hepworth et al., 2013).

Appropriate use of timing also means that the helper does not challenge clients on a "hit-and-run" basis (Johnson, 2014). Ample time should be given after the confrontation to allow the client to react to and discuss the effects of this response. For this reason, helpers should avoid confronting near the end of a session.

It is also a good idea not to overload the client with confrontations that make heavy demands in a short time. The rule of **successive approximations** suggests that gradual learning undertaken via small steps in implementing new behaviors is much easier than trying to make big changes overnight. Initially, you may want to challenge the person with something that can be managed fairly easily and with some success. Carkhuff (1987) suggests that two successive confrontations may be too intense and should be avoided. With clients who are fragile or clients who are experiencing severe stress or emotional strain, it is wise to avoid using confrontation altogether (Hepworth et al., 2013).

The gender and cultural affiliations of clients also have an impact on the usefulness of the confrontation/challenge response. This response may be more suitable for European American male clients, particularly manipulative and acting-out ones (Ivey, Ivey, & Zalaquett, 2014).

Some traditional Asian and Native American clients may view confrontation as disrespectful and insensitive (Sue & Sue, 2013). For *all* clients, it is important to use this response in such a way that the client views you as an *ally,* not an adversary (Welfel & Patterson, 2005).

Finally, acknowledge the limits of the confrontation/challenge response. Confrontation usually brings about client awareness of a discrepancy or conflict. Awareness of discrepancies is an initial step in resolving conflicts. Confrontation, as a single response, may not always bring about resolution of the discrepancy without additional discussion or intervention strategies. Genuine client awareness is often difficult to detect because it may be not an immediate reaction, but rather one that occurs over a period of time. According to Strong and Zeman (2010), the interactional process that occurs between helper and client when confrontation is used is more important than any other verbal skill because confrontation is part of a dialogic or relationally responsive way of communicating and interacting. They assert that "a skill such as confrontation tends to be inadequately depicted in the literature given that the counselor's utterance is only one part of a dialogic exchange between client and counselor. Thus, confrontation combines timing, perspicacity, careful delivery, equally careful responses to client responses when confronted, and talking until both client and counselor adequately accomplish the aim of the confrontation" (p. 332).

Client Reactions to Challenge

Sometimes helpers are afraid to challenge because they are uncertain how to handle the client's reactions to the confrontation. Even clients who hear and acknowledge the confrontation may be anxious or upset about the implications. Further, as Strong and Zeman (2010) note, clients will "do things with counselor confrontations, not simply receive them" (p. 333). From their dialogic perspective, what matters most is not only what the helper says in the challenge/confrontational response but also what the clients do with the challenge.

Hill and Nutt-Williams (2000) note that the empirical evidence surrounding client reactions to confrontation is mixed. A qualitative study also found mixed reviews for the effects of confrontation on clients (Levitt et al., 2006). In this study, many clients did not have a positive reaction to being challenged by their helper, but there were two notable exceptions: clients who were being manipulative and clients who were avoiding difficult material. These clients felt that being challenged was useful for them. One client noted that it was extremely helpful to have a therapist who was "stronger than her

eating disorder" (p. 320). For clients who have reasons (often cultural ones) to distrust helpers, or for clients such as some adolescents who may be oppositional, challenging can produce resistance and lead to poorer client outcomes. Some evidence suggests that in these cases, a process called *motivational interviewing,* which is based on the client-centered listening responses and basic empathy, may yield better client outcomes (Miller & Rollnick, 2013) (see Chapter 10).

Generally, a practitioner can expect four types of client reaction to a confrontation: denial, confusion, false acceptance, or genuine acceptance.

In denial of the confrontation, the client does not want to acknowledge or agree with the helper's message. Denial may indicate that the client is not ready or tolerant enough to face the discrepant or distorted behavior. Egan (2007) lists some specific ways in which the client might deny the confrontation:

1. Discrediting the helper (e.g., "How do you know when you don't even have kids?")

2. Persuading the helper that his or her views are wrong or based on misinterpretation (e.g., "I didn't mean it that way.")

3. Devaluing the importance of the topic (e.g., "This isn't worth all this time anyway.")

4. Seeking support elsewhere (e.g., "I told my friends about your comment last week, and none of them had ever noticed that.")

5. Agreeing with the challenger but not acting on the challenge (e.g., "I think you're right. I should speak up and tell how I feel, but I'm not sure I can do that.") (pp. 157–158).

At other times, the client may indicate confusion or uncertainty about the meaning of the challenge. In some cases, the client may be genuinely confused about what the practitioner is saying. This reaction may indicate that your confrontation was not concise and specific. At other times, the client may use a lack of understanding as a smoke screen—that is, as a way to avoid dealing with the impact of the confrontation.

Sometimes the client may seem to accept the confrontation. Acceptance is usually genuine if the client responds with a sincere desire to examine her or his behavior. Eventually such clients may be able to catch their own discrepancies and challenge themselves. But false acceptance also can occur. In this case, the client verbally agrees with the helper. However, instead of pursuing the confrontation, the client agrees only to get the helper to leave "well enough" alone. The risk of having confrontation rejected is greatest among clients who need to be challenged the most but, because they are less likely to engage in self-confrontation and may have lower self-esteem, are more likely to read criticism or blame into this response when none is intended (Hepworth et al., 2013).

There is no set way of dealing with client reactions to confrontation/challenge. However, a general guideline is to follow-up with basic empathy and go back to the client-oriented listening responses of paraphrase and reflection. As Strong and Zeman (2010) note, following a challenge response, returning to core listening skills is a critical part of the dialogic process that occurs surrounding the confrontation process in helping. A helper can use these responses to lay the foundation before the confrontation and return to this foundation after the challenge. The sequence might go something like this:

Helper: You seem to feel concerned about your parents' divorce. [reflection]

Client (says in a low, sad voice): Actually, I feel pretty happy. I'm glad for their sake they got a divorce. [mixed message]

Helper: You say you're happy, and at the same time, from your voice I sense that you feel unhappy. [confrontation]

Client: I don't know what you're talking about, really. [denial]

Helper: I feel that what I just said has upset you. [reflection]

Steps in Confronting/Challenging

There are four steps in developing effective confrontations or challenge responses.

1. Observe the client carefully to identify the type of discrepancy or distortions that the client presents. Listen for a period of time so that you can detect several inconsistencies before jumping in with a confrontation response.

2. Assess the purpose of your confrontation. Make sure that it is based on the client's need to be challenged in some way and not on your need to challenge. Assess whether the relationship is perceived to be sufficiently safe enough by the client for him or her to be able to benefit from the confrontation. Also assess whether the confrontation is appropriate based on the client's race and ethnicity, gender, and age.

3. Summarize the different elements of the discrepancy. In doing so, use a statement that *connects* the parts of the conflict rather than disputes any one part, because the overall aim of confrontation is to resolve conflicts

and to achieve integration. A useful summary is "On one hand, you ___, *and* on the other hand, ___." Notice that the elements are connected with the word *and* rather than with *but* or *yet*. This approach helps you present your confrontation in a descriptive rather than a judgmental way. Make sure that your tone of voice and nonverbal behavior convey concern and caring for the client as well.

4. Remember to assess the effectiveness of your confrontation. A confrontation is effective whenever the client acknowledges the existence of the incongruity or conflict. However, keep in mind that the effectiveness of your confrontation might not be immediate. Watch also for cues that the client may feel defensive or signs indicating indirect reactions to your confrontation. Remember that the client may be adept at masking an overt negative reaction but may subtly withdraw or shut down in the rest of the session if the confrontation has not been well received. Also, bear in mind that "confronting can bring with it breaches not only in the flow of conversation but also in the rapport established in the counselling relationship...What comes after a confrontation is, for us, analytically, a very interesting and often artful rhetorical improvisation by client and counsellor as they talk through where to go thereafter" (Strong & Zeman, 2010, p. 337).

To formulate a confrontation, consider the following cognitive learning strategy:

1. What discrepancy or distortion do I see, hear, or grasp in this client's communication?

2. What is my purpose in challenging the client, and is it useful for this client at this time?

3. How can I summarize the various elements of the discrepancy or distortion?

4. How will I know whether my confrontation is effective?

Notice how a helper uses this cognitive learning strategy for confrontation in the following example:

Client (says in low, soft voice): It's hard for me to discipline my son. I know I'm too indulgent. I know he needs limits. But I just don't give him any. I let him do basically whatever he feels like doing.

Helper (asks and answers covertly):

Self-question 1: What discrepancy or distortion do I see, hear, or grasp in this client's communication?

A discrepancy between two verbal messages and between verbal cues and behavior: client knows son needs limits but doesn't give him any.

Self-question 2: What is my purpose in challenging the client, and is it useful for this client at this time?

My purpose is to challenge the inconsistencies between what this parent actually does with his son and what he wants to do but has not yet been able to do, and to support him in engaging in the desired action. There doesn't appear to be anything about the client that would make him more defensive with the use of this response at this time.

Self-question 3: How can I summarize the various elements of the discrepancy or distortion?

Client believes limits would help son; at the same time, client doesn't follow through.

Self-question 4: How will I know whether my confrontation is effective?

Observe the client's response and see whether he acknowledges the discrepancy.

At this point the helper's self-talk or covert visualization ends, and the following dialogue occurs:

Helper confrontation: William, on one hand, you feel like having limits would really help your son, and at the same time he can do whatever he pleases with you. How do you put this together?

Client response: Well, I guess that's right. I do feel strongly that he would benefit from having limits. He gets away with a lot. He's going to become very spoiled, I know. But I just can't seem to put my foot down or make him do something.

From the client's response, which confirms the discrepancy, the helper can conclude that the confrontation was initially useful (further discussion of the discrepancy seems necessary to help the client resolve the conflict between feelings and actions).

Learning Activity 5.6 gives you an opportunity to apply this cognitive learning strategy to develop the skill of confrontation.

Learning Activity 5.6

Confrontation/Challenge

We give you three client practice statements in this activity. For each message, develop an example of a confrontation using the cognitive learning strategy described previously and outlined here. To internalize this learning strategy, you may wish to talk through these self-questions overtly (aloud) and then covertly. The end product will be a confrontation that you can say aloud or write down. An example precedes the practice messages. Feedback follows on page 170.

Example

Client, a Latino college student: I'd like to get through medical school with a flourish. I want to be at the top of my class and achieve a lot. All this partying is getting in my way and preventing me from doing my best work.

Self-question 1: *What discrepancy or distortions do I see, hear, or grasp in this client's communication?*

A discrepancy between verbal message and behavior. He says he wants to be at the top of his class and at the same time is doing a lot of partying.

Self-question 2: *What is my purpose in challenging the client, and is it useful for this client at this time?*

My purpose is to help him explore the two different messages in his communication and to do so with sensitivity and respect.

Self-question 3: *How can I summarize the various elements of the discrepancy or distortion?*

He wants to be at the top of his class and at the same time is doing a lot of partying, which is interfering with his goal.

Actual confrontation response: You're saying that you feel like achieving a lot and being at the top of your class and also that you're doing a lot of partying, which appears to

be interfering with this goal. *Or* Eduardo, you're saying that doing well in medical school is very important to you. You have also indicated you are partying instead of studying. How important is being at the top for you?

Client Practice Messages

Client 1, an Asian American graduate student: My wife and child are very important to me. They make me feel it's all worth it. It's just that I know I have to work all the time if I want to make it in my field, and right now I can't be with them as much as I'd like.

Actual confrontation response: _____
_____
_____

Client 2, a 13-year-old African American girl: Sure, it would be nice to have Mom at home when I get there after school. I don't feel lonely. It's just that it would feel so good to have someone close to me there and not have to spend a couple of hours every day by myself.

Actual confrontation response: _____
_____
_____

Client 3, a European American high school student: My dad thinks it's terribly important for me to get all As. He thinks I'm not working up to my potential if I get a B. I told him I'd much rather be well rounded and get a few Bs and also have time to talk to my friends and play basketball.

Actual confrontation response: _____
_____
_____

Skill Integration: Putting it all Together!

Up until this point in the book you have been exposed **LO4** to a number of elements and skills associated with the helping and interviewing process—including attention to ethical issues, development of multicultural competence, therapeutic relationship variables, nonverbal attending skills, and verbal listening and influencing responses. Of course there is something to be said for learning and applying these skills in a somewhat isolated fashion. When you're a novice helper, it's often easier to develop competence and acquire skills by learning them in a singular way to prevent being overwhelmed! Ultimately, however, your goal is to use all your developing competence and helping skills in combination and in concert with one another. This requires sufficient practice so that doing so becomes almost second nature to you and you experience "flow" rather than self-conscious awkwardness during your sessions. In Learning Outcome 4, and Part 4 of the Knowledge and Skill Builder, we give you an opportunity to integrate all of these developing skills by conducting an extended role-play interview. Of course we suggest doing this as many times as possible to "grow" your comfort level with all of these interviewing and helping skills you have learned so far on your journey to becoming a proficient professional helper!

Another way that you can integrate all of these skills into a cohesive pattern is to develop good observational skills. Seek out as many opportunities as you can to observe your colleagues' efforts at their integrative interviews. Watching others practice skill integration gives you additional ways to incorporate and internalize the repertoire of skills into your own style of working with clients!

5.6 Feedback

Confrontation/Challenge

Client 1

Examples of confrontation responses: "David, on one hand, you feel your family is very important, and on the other, you feel your work takes priority over them. How do you put this together?" or "You're saying that your family makes things feel worthwhile for you. At the same time you're indicating you must make it in your field to feel worthwhile. How do these two things fit for you?"

Client 2

Examples of confrontation responses: "Denise, you're saying that you don't feel lonely and also that you wish someone like your mom could be home with you. How do you put this together?" or "It seems as though you're trying to accept your mom's absence and at the same time still feeling like you'd rather have her home with you. I wonder if it does feel kind of lonely sometimes?"

Client 3

Examples of confrontation responses: "Gary, you're saying that doing a variety of things is more important than getting all As, whereas your father believes that all As should be your top priority." or "Gary, you're saying you value variety and balance in your life and your father believes high grades come first." or "Gary, you want to please your father and make good grades, and at the same time you want to spend time according to your priorities and values." (Note: Do not attempt to confront both discrepancies at once!)

CHAPTER SUMMARY

Listening responses reflect clients' perceptions of their world. Influencing responses provide alternative ways for clients to view themselves and their world. A change in the client's way of viewing and explaining things may be one indication of positive movement in counseling. According to Egan (2014), helper statements that move beyond the client's frame of reference are a bridge between listening responses and concrete change programs. To be used effectively, influencing responses require a great deal of helper concern and judgment.

Listening responses and influencing responses reflect two different sorts of helper communication styles. Part of the decision about the timing of these responses involves the helper's awareness of the client's cultural affiliations. As Sue and Sue (2013) note, it is important for helpers to be able to shift their communication style to meet the unique cultural dimensions of every client. For the most part, although with some exceptions, clients from some culturally diverse groups value influencing responses because they are more directive in nature than listening responses. However, for clients who are highly reactant, the directiveness reflected in influencing responses may thwart therapeutic progress. Part of the practitioner's task is to discern the effects of these responses on clients and to adjust his or her counseling style appropriately.

 Visit CengageBrain.com for a variety of study tools and useful resources such as video examples, case studies, interactive exercises, flashcards, and quizzes.

5 | Knowledge and Skill Builder

Part One

Part One is designed to help you assess your performance on Learning Outcome 1. Identify the type of influencing response—question, information giving, self-disclosure, immediacy, interpretation, confrontation—that is evident in each helper response. Each helper response may be an example of one type of influencing response. If you accurately label nine out of 12 responses, you will have met this objective. Check your answers against those provided in the feedback on page 176.

1. **Client** [talking rapidly, with pressured speech]: The pressure from my job is starting to get to me. I'm always in a constant rush, trying to hurry and get several things done at the same time. There's never enough time.
   a. Yeah, it sounds like that saying of "The hurrieder I go, the behinder I get." And in your situation, the more you rush, the more pressure you feel, and the more pressure you feel, the more you rush. So you're sort of caught in this ongoing process, and it barely feels tolerable. You'd like to find a way out of it.
   b. It's important you are aware of this. Continued anxiety and stress like this can lead to health problems if they go unchecked.
   c. Now that you are mentioning this, I'm noticing how pressured you seem with me, partly from how fast you're talking and also from how you seem to be hurrying through the session. Does that feel accurate to you?
2. **Client:** I'm tired of sitting home alone, but I feel so uptight when I ask a girl for a date.
   a. You seem to be saying that you feel lonely and also that you're not willing to risk asking a girl to go out with you.
   b. What makes you so anxious when you speak with girls?
   c. I can relate to what you are saying in that I, too, have had to deal with some fears of my own in meeting new people. One thing that helped me was to join a couple of social and community groups where everyone was new to each other. This helped me practice meeting new people in a low-risk situation—if they didn't like me, I didn't lose much. Although this example isn't specific to dating, I think some of the principles are similar. What do you think?
3. **Client:** I don't know why I tolerate his abuse. I really don't love him.
   a. On one hand you say that you don't love him, and on the other hand you remain in the house and allow him to beat you. How do you put these two things together?
   b. You may be caught up in a vicious cycle about whether your feelings for him, even though they're not love, outweigh your regard for yourself. Does this seem to fit you?
   c. It might be helpful for you to know the process that other women in your shoes go through before they finally get enough courage to leave for good. I'd like to give you the name of someone to talk to at our local domestic violence agency. Also, there are several websites I can give you if you have access to and would like to use the Internet.
4. **Client:** I don't know why we ever got married in the first place. Things were fine for a while, but since we moved, things have just started to fall apart in our marriage.
   a. What qualities attracted you to each other originally?
   b. You're having a difficult time right now, which has led you to question the entire marriage. I wonder whether you would react this way if this present problem wasn't causing such distress.
   c. I, too, have been in situations like this. When one thing goes wrong, it makes me feel like throwing the whole thing away. Is this something you can relate to in what you are experiencing now with your marriage?

Part Two

For each of the following three client statements, Learning Outcome 2 asks you to write an example of each of the six influencing responses. In developing these responses, you may find it helpful to use the cognitive learning strategy you practiced earlier for each response. Feedback is provided on page 176.

Client 1, a European American parent (says with loud sighs): My house looks like a mess. I can't seem to get anything done with these kids always under my feet. I'm afraid that I may lose my temper and hit them one of these days. I just feel so stressed out.
Question: _____
Information giving: _____
Self-disclosure: _____
Immediacy: _____
Interpretation: _____
Confrontation: _____

Client 2, an African American graduate student: I feel so overwhelmed. I've got books to read, papers to write.

(continued)

5 | Knowledge and Skill Builder (*continued*)

My money is running low, and I don't even have a job. Plus, my roommate is thinking of moving out. I just can't seem to get a break—no one goes out of their way to lift a finger to help me.

Question: _____

Information giving: _____

Self-disclosure: _____

Immediacy: _____

Interpretation: _____

Confrontation: _____

Client 3, a young, Native American man: I haven't gotten hooked on this stuff. It doesn't make me feel high, though, just good. All my bad thoughts and all the pain go away when I take it. So why should I give it up? You're not here to make me do it, are you?

Question: _____

Information giving: _____

Self-disclosure: _____

Immediacy: _____

Interpretation: _____

Confrontation: _____

Part Three

Part Three gives you an opportunity to develop your skills in observing six key aspects of client behavior that a helper must attend to in order to develop effective and accurate influencing responses.

1. Issues and messages that need more elaboration, information, or examples
2. Implicit messages and themes
3. Myths and inaccurate information
4. Feelings and process issues
5. Distorted perceptions and ideas
6. Discrepancies and incongruities

Learning Outcome 3 asks you to observe those six aspects of client behavior during a 30-minute interview. Record your observations on the Client Observation Checklist.

You can obtain feedback for this activity by having two or more persons observe and rate the same session and then compare your responses.

Client Observation Checklist

Name of helper _____

Name(s) of observer(s) _____

Instructions: Write down separate occurrences of each of the six categories of client behavior as they occur during a 30-minute helping interview. (If observers are not available, audiotape or videotape your sessions and complete the checklist while reviewing the tape.)

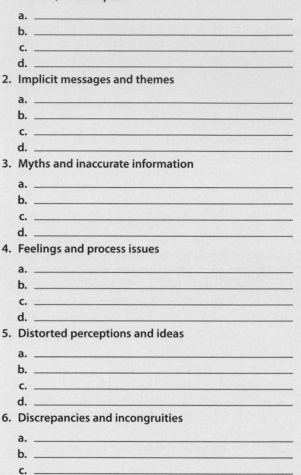

1. Issues and messages that need more elaboration, information, or examples
   a. _____
   b. _____
   c. _____
   d. _____
2. Implicit messages and themes
   a. _____
   b. _____
   c. _____
   d. _____
3. Myths and inaccurate information
   a. _____
   b. _____
   c. _____
   d. _____
4. Feelings and process issues
   a. _____
   b. _____
   c. _____
   d. _____
5. Distorted perceptions and ideas
   a. _____
   b. _____
   c. _____
   d. _____
6. Discrepancies and incongruities
   a. _____
   b. _____
   c. _____
   d. _____

Part Four

Learning Outcome 4 provides you with an opportunity to integrate the core skills and knowledge you have acquired so far from working with this book. To begin this process, conduct one 30-minute role-play interview. You may want to consider this an initial helping interview in which you are creating rapport and getting to know the "client." Here are the specific tasks for this integrative helping session:

1. **Be alert to ethical situations and issues that arise and how you resolve them.**
2. **Assess the degree to which you are able to conduct this interview in a culturally competent way. Be sensitive not only to cultural competencies but also to any communication and behavior that may be pejorative, biased, or insulting. Be especially alert to the possibilities of microaggressions.**

3. Assess the key aspects of your nonverbal behavior in the interview.
4. Pay attention to the quality of the helping relationship and specifically to your demonstration of the facilitative conditions of empathy, genuineness, and positive regard.
5. Use as many of the listening and influencing verbal responses as seem appropriate within the time span of this session.

Try to regard this interview as an opportunity to get involved with the person in front of you, not as just another practice. If you feel some discomfort, you may wish to do several more interviews with different kinds of clients. To assess the overall effectiveness of your interview, use the Interview Inventory, which follows. You may wish to make some copies of it.

This inventory has six parts. Ethical Issues assesses any ethical issues that arose during the interview and how these were resolved. Multicultural Competence assesses 10 aspects of culturally competent interview behaviors. Nonverbal Behavior evaluates your use of various nonverbal behaviors. Relationship Variables measures aspects of establishing and enhancing a therapeutic relationship. Verbal Behavior assesses listening and influencing responses. Overall Effectiveness summarizes these preceding parts. To use the inventory for rating, follow the instructions for each part.

Interview Inventory
Interview Number ___ Helper ___
Client ___ Rater ___ Date ___

Ethical Issues

Instructions: List any ethical issues that came up during the interview, and note how the helper responded to them.

Ethical Issue   Helper Response
1. _____   _____
2. _____   _____
3. _____   _____
4. _____   _____

Multicultural Competence

1. Was able to identify and discuss issues related to race/ethnicity/culture during the interview.

Not at All	Minimally	Somewhat	A Great Deal	Almost Always
1	2	3	4	5

2. Was aware of his or her own racial and cultural identity and the client's level of racial and cultural identity awareness and its impact on the helping process.

Not at All	Minimally	Somewhat	A Great Deal	Almost Always
1	2	3	4	5

3. Conveyed respect for and sensitivity to cultural differences among clients.

Not at All	Minimally	Somewhat	A Great Deal	Almost Always
1	2	3	4	5

4. Showed awareness of and sensitivity to the cultural values of each client as well as the uniqueness of each client within the client's racial and cultural group identification. Avoided language and responses that clashed with these cultural values.

Not at All	Minimally	Somewhat	A Great Deal	Almost Always
1	2	3	4	5

5. Was sensitive to nonverbal and paralanguage cross-cultural communication clues.

Not at All	Minimally	Somewhat	A Great Deal	Almost Always
1	2	3	4	5

6. Was able to use both nonverbal and verbal responses that conveyed acceptance of the client and the client's culture.

Not at All	Minimally	Somewhat	A Great Deal	Almost Always
1	2	3	4	5

7. Displayed an understanding of how race, ethnicity, and culture and sociopolitical influences can impinge on the life of clients.

Not at All	Minimally	Somewhat	A Great Deal	Almost Always
1	2	3	4	5

8. Was able to help the client sort out the degree to which the client's issues or problems are exacerbated by the larger society, racism, and/or biases of others.

Not at All	Minimally	Somewhat	A Great Deal	Almost Always
1	2	3	4	5

9. Was able to help the client deal with environmental frustration and oppression.

Not at All	Minimally	Somewhat	A Great Deal	Almost Always
1	2	3	4	5

10. Was alert to cultural biases, prejudices, discriminatory practices, and microaggressions.

Not at All	Minimally	Somewhat	A Great Deal	Almost Always
1	2	3	4	5

Nonverbal Behavior

Instructions: Listed below are significant dimensions of nonverbal behavior. Check (✓) any that you observe of the

(continued)

5 | Knowledge and Skill Builder (*continued*)

helper, and provide a brief description of the key aspects and appropriateness of the behavior. The first item serves as an example.

Behavior	Check (✓) if observed	Key aspects of behavior
1.	1. Body posture	Tense, rigid until last part of session, then relaxed
2.	Eye contact	
3.	Facial expression	
4.	Head nodding	
5.	Body movements	
6.	Body orientation	
7.	Gestures	
8.	Voice level and pitch	
9.	Rate of speech	
10.	Verbal underlining (voice emphasis)	
11.	Speech errors	
12.	Pauses, silence	
13.	Distance	
14.	Position in room	
15.	Autonomic response (e.g., breathing, sweat, skin flush, rash)	
16.	Congruence/incongruence between helper verbal and nonverbal behavior	
17.	Environmental sensitivity to diverse kinds of clients	

Relationship Variables

Instructions: Circle the number that best represents the helper's behavior during the observed interaction.

1. Conveyed accurate understanding of the client and the client's worldview.

Not at All	Minimally	Somewhat	A Great Deal	Almost Always
1	2	3	4	5

2. Conveyed support and warmth without approving or disapproving of the client.

Not at All	Minimally	Somewhat	A Great Deal	Almost Always
1	2	3	4	5

3. Focused on the person rather than on the procedure or on the helper's professional role.

Not at All	Minimally	Somewhat	A Great Deal	Almost Always
1	2	3	4	5

4. Conveyed spontaneity, was not mechanical when responding to the client.

Not at All	Minimally	Somewhat	A Great Deal	Almost Always
1	2	3	4	5

5. Responded to feelings and issues as they occurred within the session (i.e., in the here-and-now).

Not at All	Minimally	Somewhat	A Great Deal	Almost Always
1	2	3	4	5

6. Displayed comfort and confidence in working with the client.

Not at All	Minimally	Somewhat	A Great Deal	Almost Always
1	2	3	4	5

7. Responded with dynamism and frequency; was not passive.

Not at All	Minimally	Somewhat	A Great Deal	Almost Always
1	2	3	4	5

8. Displayed sincerity in intentions and responses.

Not at All	Minimally	Somewhat	A Great Deal	Almost Always
1	2	3	4	5

9. Conveyed friendliness and goodwill in interacting with the client.

Not at All	Minimally	Somewhat	A Great Deal	Almost Always
1	2	3	4	5

10. Informed the client about expectations and what would or would not happen in the session (i.e., structuring).

Not at All	Minimally	Somewhat	A Great Deal	Almost Always
1	2	3	4	5

11. Shared similar attitudes, opinions, and experiences with the client when appropriate (i.e., when such sharing added to and/or did not detract from the client focus).

Not at All	Minimally	Somewhat	A Great Deal	Almost Always
1	2	3	4	5

Observer comments: _____

_____

_____

Verbal Behavior

Instructions: Check (✓) the type of verbal response represented by each helper statement in the corresponding category on the rating form. At the end of the observation period, tally the total number of checks associated with each verbal response on the chart below.

	Listening responses				Influencing responses						
	Clarification	Paraphrase	Reflecting feeling (basic empathy)	Summarization	Open question	Closed question	Information giving	Self-disclosure	Immediacy	Interpretation	Confrontation
1.											
2.											
3.											
4.											
5.											
6.											
7.											
8.											
9.											
10.											
11.											
12.											
13.											
14.											
15.											
16.											
17.											
18.											
19.											
20.											
Total											

Overall Effectiveness

Instructions: After all the ratings are completed, look at your ratings in the light of these questions.

1. What ethical dilemmas arose for you, and how did you resolve them?
2. What aspects of multicultural competence do you feel most comfortable with? What parts are still hard for you?
3. Which nonverbal skills were easiest for you to demonstrate? Which ones did you find most difficult to use in the interview?
4. Which relationship variables were easiest for you to demonstrate? Hardest?
5. Examine the total number of verbal responses you used in each category. Did you use responses from each category with the same frequency? Did most of your responses come from one category? Did you seem to avoid using responses from one category? If so, for what reason?
6. What have you learned about the effectiveness of your interview behavior so far? What do you think you need to improve?

5   Knowledge and Skill Builder **Feedback**

Part One

1. a. Interpretation
   b. Information giving
   c. Immediacy and closed question
2. a. Confrontation
   b. Open question
   c. Self-disclosure and open question
3. a. Confrontation
   b. Interpretation and closed question
   c. Information giving
4. a. Open question
   b. Interpretation
   c. Self-disclosure and closed question

Part Two

Here are some examples of influencing responses. See whether yours are similar.

Client Statement 1

Question: "What exactly would you like to be able to accomplish during the day?" *or* "How could you keep the kids occupied while you do some of your housework?" *or* "When do you feel most like striking the children?" *or* "How could you control your anger?"

Information giving: "If you believe your problem would be solved by having more time alone, we could discuss some options that seemed to help other women in this situation—things to give you more time alone as well as ways to cope with your anger."

Self-disclosure: "I know what it is like to feel like your life is spinning out of control, and it's not a pleasant state to be in—for me, it's pretty stressful. How about for you?"

Immediacy: "I can tell from the way you're talking and breathing right now that this stress is very much with you—not just at home but even as we are working together here today."

Interpretation: "I wonder whether you would be able to accomplish what seems important to you even if the kids weren't always underfoot. Perhaps it's easy to use their presence to account for your lack of accomplishment."

Confrontation: "On the one hand, you seem to be saying the kids are responsible for your difficulties, and on the other, it appears as if you feel you are the one who is out of control."

Client Statement 2

Question: "How could you organize yourself better so that you wouldn't feel so overcome by your studies?"

or "What kind of work might you do that would fit in with your class schedule?" *or* "How might you cope with these feelings of being so over-whelmed?"

Information giving: "Perhaps it would be helpful if we talked about some ways to help you with your time and money problems."

Self-disclosure: "Wow. I think I know something about what you are saying, how it feels to have the whole world cave in on you at once. It's an awful lot to try to handle."

Immediacy: "I'm sensing how frustrated you're feeling right now as you talk, and I'm wondering if you're seeing me as someone unwilling to help you."

Interpretation: "You seem to feel so discouraged with everything that I imagine it would be easy now to feel justified in giving it all up, quitting grad school altogether."

Confrontation: "You've mentioned several reasons that you feel so overwhelmed now, and at the same time I don't think you mentioned anything you're doing to relieve these feelings."

Client Statement 3

Question: "What do you feel comfortable sharing with me about your pain?"

Information giving: "I'm wondering what you would think of the idea of our spending some time talking about other ways to deal with the pain—such as practices and rituals consistent with your own cultural and ethnic background."

Self-disclosure: "I went through a similar way of thinking when I gave up smoking. Cigarettes were always there for me—when nothing else was, they were. In that way, it was hard for me to see what could be so bad about continuing to smoke. Does this fit with what you're feeling in your situation?"

Immediacy: "I'm wondering if there is something I'm saying or doing to make you feel like I'm going to be policing your actions as we work together."

Interpretation: "Even though you don't feel hooked on this substance, it seems as if using it helps you avoid certain things. Do you think this is so?"

Confrontation: "You're telling me that you're pretty sure you're not hooked on this, and at the same time you recognize it seems to medicate your pain. How do you put these two things together?"

Assessing and Conceptualizing Client Problems and Contexts

After completing this chapter, you will be able to

1. Identify each of the following, in writing, using a client case description:
   a. The client's behaviors
   b. Whether the client's behaviors are overt or covert
   c. The client's individual and environmental strengths and resources
   d. Antecedent contributing conditions
   e. Consequences and secondary gains
   f. The way each consequence influences the behaviors
   g. The developmental context of the issue
   h. The sociopolitical and cultural context of the issue
2. Given a role-play interview, you will be able to conduct a history-taking session with the client.

Client Statements

Institutionalized patient: Why are people always out to get me?

Student: I can't even talk to my mom. What a hassle!

Physically challenged person: Ever since I had that automobile accident and had to change jobs, I don't seem to be able to get it together.

Older person: I didn't used to worry this much, but with our failing health and the skyrocketing medical costs, I am concerned now.

These client statements are representative of the types of concerns that clients bring to helpers every day. One thing these clients and others have in common is that their initial problem presentation is often vague. A helper can translate vague client concerns into specific problem statements by using certain skills associated with assessment. This chapter presents a conceptual framework that a helper can use to assess clients.

What Is Clinical Assessment?

Clinical assessment is about helping a client tell and develop a story. The story involves a number of details and plots, including why the client is coming to see you now, what the client wants from you, and how you can help the client get there. Haynes, Smith, & Hunsley (2011) define **clinical assessment** as a process "that provides essential information to help identify a client's behavior problems and treatment goals, to determine if the client's behavior problems are consistent with diagnostic criteria, and to specify the variables that affect those problems and goals…" (p. 1). Such information is used to design and subsequently evaluate the most effective intervention procedures for the client (Haynes et al., 2011).

Clinical assessment involves methods, procedures, and tools that are used to collect and process information from which the entire helping program is developed. Interviewing the client and having the client engage in other assessment procedures are only part of the overall assessment process in counseling and therapy. Equally important is the helper's own mental (covert) activity that goes on during the process. The helper typically gathers a great amount of information from clients during this stage of helping. Unless the helper can integrate and synthesize this information, it is of little value and use. The helper's tasks during the assessment process include identifying what information to obtain and how to obtain it, putting the information together in some meaningful way, and using it to generate clinical hunches, or hypotheses, about client issues, hunches that lead to tentative ideas for treatment planning. This mental activity of the helper is called **conceptualization** or **formulation**—which means the way the helper *thinks* about the client's presenting concerns. It is impossible to conceptualize or formulate hypotheses about client issues without a thorough assessment process. Similarly, it is impossible to develop outcome goals and treatment plans without a conceptualization process. Although these processes of assessment, conceptualization, goal setting, and treatment planning are described in this and the next three chapters, in practice they are not discrete processes. Moreover, in the best of helping environments, these activities occur in a collaborative manner between the helper and the client.

Hunsley and Mash (2010) note that in the past 15 years there have been some rather dramatic changes in the field of clinical assessment. The changes they describe include the following:

1. A decreasing emphasis on the use of complex, multi-dimensional instruments

2. A corresponding increasing emphasis on the use of brief, focused instruments

3. The development and use of appropriate instruments for a diverse range of clients including the availability of culturally appropriate norms and linguistic adaptations

4. The incorporation of behavioral assessment principles into most areas of clinical assessment

5. The use of information technology to facilitate the collection, scoring, and interpretation of assessment data (pp. 8–9).

As these authors indicate, for most helping professionals, the effect of these changes translates into "an enhanced focus on how scientifically sound assessment data can meaningfully inform treatment decisions, plans, and processes" (p. 9).

The assessment methods we describe later in this chapter, and our interview assessment model in particular (see Chapter 7), are based on an integrated model that we have used over the years in our teaching and in clinical practice. This chapter describes the concepts associated with our assessment model and the following chapter describes the implementation of the model in a clinical interview setting.

Our Assumptions About Clinical Assessment

Our model of assessment in helping rests on several assumptions about clients, issues, and behavior. This model integrates a number of theoretical approaches including learning theory, both operant and respondent, observational learning, cognitive theory, emotion theory, and developmental/ecological theory. Because both space and the purpose of the book preclude us from helping the reader learn about these various theories in depth, we suggest you consult Haynes, O'Brien, and Kaholokula (2011), Persons (2008), and Bronfenbrenner (1979, 2005) for more detailed information about these theories as well as additional citations in the rest of this chapter. Our major assumptions about therapeutic assessment are as follows.

The Role of Learning

Undesired (maladaptive) behavior is developed, maintained, and subject to alteration or modification in the same manner as normal (adaptive) behavior. Both prosocial and maladaptive behaviors are assumed to be developed and maintained by external environmental events or cues, by external reinforcers, and/or by internal processes such as cognition, mediation, and problem-solving. For the most part, maladaptive behavior is learned through operant conditioning, respondent conditioning, and social learning or modeling. This fundamental assumption means that we do not spend a great deal of time in sorting out or focusing on possible unresolved early conflicts or underlying pathological states in the client's story. However, this assumption does not mean that we rule out or overlook possible physiological conditions that can also impact undesired behavior. For example, clients who complain of "anxiety" and report *primarily* somatic (body-related) symptoms such as heart palpitations, stomach upset, chest pains, and breathlessness may be chronic hyperventilators or have mitral valve prolapse, hypoglycemia, or a thyroid or other endocrine disorder. This physiological response is usually not the primary cause of the anxiety disorder that is more likely created by anxiety sensitivity. However, these physiologic conditions can be an important contributing factor that may have bearing on the treatment and resolution of the presenting issue. Because learning can also influence behaviors that have biological or genetic components, we also consider the increasingly important role of neurobiology in assessing client concerns.

The Role of Neurobiology

Physiological variables should always be explored in the client's story, particularly when the results of the assessment do not suggest the presence of other specific stimuli associated with the problem behavior (Arden & Linford, 2009; Cozolino, 2010). Many psychological disorders have a biological component as well as a learning component. For example, the neurotransmitter serotonin is implicated in both depression and anxiety disorders. Further, the cycling rate of serotonin is affected by genetic markers. Some disorders such as alcoholism, schizophrenia, and autism spectrum disorders have both genetic and biochemical markers that can increase a person's vulnerability to such a disorder. This is one reason why medical history is assessed during an initial interview. In these situations, evaluation of the client by a physician is warranted.

It is also important to recognize the need for physiological management of psychological issues. For example, in the kinds of disorders mentioned, medications may be necessary *in addition to* psychological intervention. Antidepressants are often recommended for depression in conjunction with cognitive behavioral and interpersonal therapies.

Furthermore, a biological element seems to be present in many of the psychoses, such as schizophrenia, and these conditions usually require antipsychotic drugs to improve the client's overall level of functioning. Similarly, children with attention-deficit disorder may need a stimulant or other medication to optimize treatment response.

The field of neurobiology is rapidly expanding. As Cozolino (2010) points out, linkages between clinical disorders and symptomatic behaviors and changes in the relative metabolism of different areas of the brain are already being uncovered (p. 345). In addition, considerable evidence is accruing that supports the assumption "that reregulation of neural networks parallels some of the symptomatic changes we witness in psychotherapy" (Cozolino, 2010, p. 346). In the future, assessment and diagnoses aided by neural network activity could well improve the accuracy of assessment and conceptualization with clients.

The Role of Human Development

From infancy to old age, clients experience both change and constancy throughout the lifespan. Human development is lifelong, multidimensional and multidirectional,

highly plastic, and affected by multiple interacting forces (Berk, 2013). According to the lifespan model of human development, no single age period is more important in its impact on the course of one's life than another. As Berk (2013) notes, in each of the major periods of human development, ranging from infancy to late adulthood, events occur that can have a major impact on future change. Typically these changes occur in physical, cognitive, and emotional domains (Berk, 2013). Such changes can be described as developmental transitions and usually are triggered by physical growth, psychological maturation, social pressures, and life events (Ingram, 2012).

As Seabury, Seabury, and Garvin (2011) observe pragmatically, "development can be conceptualized as a long line drawn down a sheet of paper. On the top of the line is birth and on the bottom of the line is death. All along the life line, individuals are faced with transition after transition, from one role to another. Role transitions are a continuous process for individuals and later life has as many transitions as does infancy and childhood" (p. 252). All developmental and role transitions are potentially stressful and some, such as death of a child or spouse, divorce, and loss of job and income, are "particularly overwhelming and may create serious social dysfunction for the individual" (p. 254). Although we do not recommend spending a great deal of time in assessment and intervention on focusing on the client's past, some basic understanding of the client's developmental history and current developmental transitions are important factors in forming hypotheses and conceptualizing issues in sufficient depth to make well-informed treatment decisions. In part, this is because assumptions and core beliefs (or schemas) tend to persist across situations and time and are often learned through key developmental experiences (Kuyken, Padesky, & Dudley, 2009).

Beck (1995) places a great deal of importance on the client's developmental history to determine the etiology of cognitions and schemas. Beck recommends asking clients to recall the events in childhood associated with a particular target feeling and/or thought (feelings and beliefs about not being good enough when parents were constantly critical of one's efforts, for example). In addition to core beliefs and schemas, family history, parenting styles, and attachment history are all important influences on developmental processes.

Conditions for Healthy Development and Attachment
Ingram (2012) summarizes conditions for healthy development. She notes that the desired qualities and functions

of a *good enough* parent are similar to those provided by a good therapist. These include:

1. Being in tune with the child, experiencing the child as separate from the adult, accepting and labeling feelings, and not trying to shape the child into something she or he is not.

2. Being able to meet one's own needs as an adult, not expecting a reciprocal relationship with the child, and not looking to the child to meet one's adult needs.

3. Being able to adapt to the developing child's changing needs—particularly in the areas of dependence and autonomy. The adult does not feel threatened or rejected by the child's increasing sense of separateness and autonomy.

4. Being able to provide optimum levels of frustration that are tolerable and challenging rather than overwhelming and traumatic to support the child's capacity for increased independence and self-soothing (p. 316).

These characteristics of healthy parenting styles and healthy developmental environments form the basis of childhood attachment styles, that is, whether the child, and subsequently the child maturing into adulthood, is securely attached or whether the child (and later adult) exhibits anxious or disorganized attachment (Ainsworth, 1982; Main & Solomon, 1990).

Although we now know that these attachments are demonstrated in a wide variety of cultures, there also are cultural differences in attachment that are impacted by the environments in which the child–caretaker interactions and relationship occur (Gardiner & Kosmitzki, 2011). This underscores the fact that human development issues in general vary across cultures, and what may be considered normative human development in one culture is not necessarily the same in another culture. Although developmental transitions may vary in differing cultural environments, "the reality of continuous transitions is present in all cultural contexts" (Seabury, Seabury, & Garvin, 2011, p. 252). Furthermore, some individuals may find themselves in developmental, and specifically role, transitions that, in their cultural context, are stigmatized—for example, a formerly middle-class individual who has lost his job now finds himself standing in line for food bank supplies. As Seabury, Seabury, and Garvin (2011) note, the stigmatization of this developmental role transition compounds the natural stress arising from the transition itself.

Also, some developmental environments are more privileged than others. Theokas and Lerner (2006) describe

what they call "optimal contexts of development" (p. 62). In optimal contexts of development, clients have access to opportunities and resources and, as a result, may experience better mental and physical health than clients who are impacted by less privileged or less than optimal contexts of development.

The role of development provides information in the assessment process about both predisposing and protective factors that have contributed to presenting issues. **Predisposing factors** describe elements that make one client more likely to respond in a particular way to a life circumstance. **Protective factors** such as client strengths often have prevented the presenting issue from becoming worse or more intense. As Kuyken, Padesky, and Dudley (2009, p. 40) note, "protective factors interact with predisposing factors in complex ways to affect vulnerability and resilience."

A final way in which development plays a role in the assessment of client concerns is the consideration that there are certain risk factors, cultural issues, and system variables that are associated with the later development of mental health disorders. Jones (2010) lists a number of known child and adolescent risk factors associated with the subsequent development of mental health disorders in adulthood. These areas to assess include the following:

Behavior problems in childhood
Poor school performance (including failed grades)
Childhood diagnosis of attention deficit/hyperactivity disorder (ADHD)
Childhood depression
Child abuse
Trauma and/or losses during childhood. (p. 223)

The Role of Social Context and Culture: Ecological/Person in Environment

Client problems usually do not occur in a vacuum but are related to observable events (verbal, nonverbal, and motoric responses) and to less visible covert or indirect events (thoughts, images, moods and feelings, body sensations) that precipitate and maintain the problem. Simply put, in assessing a client's story it is crucial to note how the client's behavior affects the environment and vice versa—how the environment impacts the client's behavior. This functional relationship of the individual and the environment reflects an **ecological** view; it was articulated as early as 1979 and again in 2005 by Bronfenbrenner, as well as by Walsh, Craik, and Price (2000). In an **ecological** view, the individual client and his or her environment are linked together, so assessment includes not only an individual focus but also a contextual focus, including key social settings, events, and resources. Practitioners need to examine the social and cultural contexts of relationships among these key social settings, events, and resources. Whereas the ecological context of issues is important to consider for all clients, the sociopolitical context surrounding the client is especially important for clients who feel marginalized, such as clients of color and clients from minority and oppressed groups.

This **ecological systems theory**, articulated by Bronfenbrenner (1979; 2005) and now characterized as **bioecological** (Bronfenbrenner & Evans, 2000), delineates the varying kinds of systems that appear in and impact client lives. There are four systems or levels within Bronfenbrenner's approach; each level has an effect on human development. Changes in one level also impact the other levels as well. The first level, the **microsystem**, the innermost level, consists of activities and interaction patterns in the person's immediate surroundings. Structures within the microsystem include family, school, work, neighborhood, or child-care environments. More recently, Bronfenbrenner and Evans (2000) also included the biological context as a contributing factor in development. The second level, the **mesosystem**, comprises two or more microsystems; this level focuses on the interrelationships or connections between the microsystems. With a child client, examples of the mesosystem might be the involvement of the parents and the home in the child's academic progress at school. For an adult client, an example of a mesosystem could be the interaction between the adult's role in the home environment as a spouse and the adult's role as a teacher in the school or work environment. The third layer, the **exosystem**, is defined as the larger social system that impacts the person more indirectly than directly. This may include formal organizations, extended family, and community services. The fourth layer, the **macrosystem**, the outermost layer, is not considered a specific context but rather an overarching system comprising customs, cultural values, laws, and resources considered important in the individual's culture. An example of this would be the way an adolescent client's culture views education. All four of these levels within an environment exert influence on the development of the individual.

Assessing for Contextual and Relational Dimensions of the Problem

In our model of assessment, we refer to environmental and cultural variables that affect client issues as **contextual and relational dimensions** associated with the problem. It is important to assess the impact of these dimensions because "the reason for the client's problems may lie in the *context* rather than with the client" (Summers, 2012,

p. 75). The larger social context also may have affected the client's presenting concerns For example, one client may have experienced loss of employment, disenfranchisement in voting, a poor health care system, and a barely adequate school system. Another client may have experienced a boom in the stock market, preferential political treatment, a first-rate health care system, and a private school (Summers, 2012).

In assessing for **contextual and relational dimensions** of the client's issues, we look for areas of environmental supports and stressors, risks, and protective factors, including places, settings, events, and people who are sources of empowerment and disempowerment (Ungar, 2011). For example, one might ask about the strengths and assets and the weaknesses and barriers of the client's environment, and about the extent and availability of family and community resources. If the client is an immigrant or refugee, then one might ask how his or her status has been affected by the move. Are there ways to maximize the client's strengths within the environmental context? We cannot overemphasize the importance of assessing the contribution of these environmental variables to identified issues. This sort of assessment helps determine, for example, whether an issue may stem from racism and prejudice in *other persons* so that clients or helpers do not inappropriately personalize their concerns.

Another aspect of assessing the context includes a *cultural analysis* of client issues. Assessing for cultural data directly from clients is an ethical responsibility of helpers. And, further, if it is necessary to ask clients to clarify cultural data for your own understanding, then it is important to do so in a way that doesn't burden the client. A model to conduct a thorough and culturally sensitive assessment has been developed by White Kress, Eriksen, Rayle, and Ford (2005). In this model, the following areas are explored by the clinician with the client:

- Assessment of the client's worldview—that is, how the client sees the world and through what perspectives and lenses.
- Assessment of the client's cultural identity—that is, how the client makes sense of himself or herself culturally and what the client's understanding is (as well as your own understanding) of his or her own level or stage of cultural identity awareness.
- Assessment of the client's level of acculturation—that is, how the client identifies with both former and current cultures and how the client moves through these cultures with resources and/or barriers.
- Assessment of the cultural meaning of the client's issues and presenting symptoms—that is, what the presenting problem means to the client and how the

client views it, and what cultural context surrounds the client's concerns.

- Assessment of sources of cultural information available to the client—that is, what information the client reports about areas of his or her life related to both cultural history and current culture.
- Assessment of any stigmas associated with the client's concern—that is, what the cultural meaning of the concern is to the client and to his or her cultural community, how the client views seeking help for such concerns, and what the client's experiences are with stigma, prejudice, and discrimination.

Some literature also describes the ecological view as a *person-in-environment approach*. Moscript (2011) defines the **person-in-environment approach** as a "holistic, interactional model that stresses the impact of *both* environment and biology on an individual's social and psychological processes" (p. 47). The person-in-environment approach is a central feature of the growing edge of practice today (Neufeld et al., 2006). In the following section, we describe an assessment tool based on the ecological/person-in-environment model called the PIE (Person-In-Environment) Classification System.

The Person-in-Environment (PIE) Classification System

The **person-in-environment (PIE) classification system**, developed by Karls and Wandrei (1994), is an assessment/classification system that helps practitioners understand the interrelationships between individual clients and the system or environment in which clients reside. The PIE is a tool that practitioners use to collect relevant assessment information about the client and the client's environment for the express purpose of facilitating the planning of successful treatment interventions. The updated edition of the PIE (Karls & O'Keefe, 2008) also includes a strengths assessment. Overall, the PIE is used in a variety of practice settings and with a variety of theoretical orientations to assess the social functioning problems and strengths experienced by adult clients.

The PIE assesses these four factors for adult clients (Karls & O'Keefe, 2008):

Factor I: Social Functioning Problems and Strengths
Factor II: Environmental Problems and Strengths
Factor III: Mental Health Problems and Strengths
Factor IV: Physical Health Problems and Strengths

Factors I and II constitute the bulk of the PIE classification. Factor I comprises identification of social role problems and identification of the type of interactional difficulty with social role. Factor II comprises identification of type of environmental problem area. (See Table 6.1

for a listing of the dimensions assessed by Factors I and II.) Factor III borrows from the *DSM-IV* by using Axes I and II of the *DSM-IV*, and Factor IV lists physical health problems using the International Classification of Diseases and is the equivalent of Axis III of the *DSM-IV*. In addition, for all four factors there are four additional assessment indices: severity, duration, coping, and strengths.

Several considerations are worth noting when contemplating the use of the PIE classification system. One is that this system avoids classifying social roles in a culturally specific context. As a result, Factor I in particular is somewhat limited in clarifying some problems faced by certain culturally diverse groups of people (Appleby, Colon, & Hamilton, 2011). However, Factor II does consider culturally relevant dimensions of environmental problems by assessing the discrimination status of each. Second, the judgments involved in the classification and coding are based on the practitioner's perception rather than the client's perceptions. Third, the delineation of the types of problems is based on the person presenting for treatment—that is, the identified client—and not on other persons who may be contributing to the client's difficulties. Finally, the current PIE manual is not consistent with the latest diagnostic manual of clinical disorders, the *DSM-5*, which we present later in this chapter. The PIE is used around the globe and has been translated into a number of languages. We illustrate the use of the PIE in our model case of Isabella near the end of this chapter. To fully learn how to apply the PIE system with clients, you would need to consult the conceptual book (Karls & Wandrei, 1994) and the manual (Karls & O'Keefe, 2008). The manual contains both non-copyrighted, reproducible printed worksheets for PIE analysis that practitioners can complete following an assessment interview and also a CD called the CompuPIE©, which is a copyrighted software program for recording assessments based on the PIE system.

When assessment is conducted at the levels of both the individual client and the client's environment, practitioners obtain a more balanced and comprehensive story or picture about what is going on in terms of the presenting issues and concerns. The person-in-environment approach is based on the following two notions:

1. Client concerns do not reside solely within an individual but are embedded within cultural, environmental, developmental, and social systems or contexts.

2. There is a movement to incorporate a focus on strengths, resources, and coping skills of clients into the assessment and treatment process. This movement is also known as a strengths perspective (Saleebey, 2012), which is affiliated with the positive psychology movement (Seligman & Csikszentmihalyi, 2000).

TABLE 6.1   Summary of Factor I and Factor II of the PIE Classification System

Factor I: Social Role Problem Identification

Type of Problem

Family roles (parent, spouse, child, sibling, other family member, significant other)

Interpersonal roles (lover, friend, neighbor, member, other)

Occupational roles (worker–paid economy, worker–home, worker–volunteer, student, other)

Special life situation roles (consumer, caretaker, inpatient/client, outpatient/client, probationer/parolee/prisoner, immigrant–legal, immigrant–undocumented, immigrant–refugee, other)

Type of Interactional Difficulty

Power, ambivalence, responsibility, dependency, loss, isolation, oppression, mixed, undetermined, other

Level of Severity: 1 to 5 scale

1 = low, 2 = moderate, 3 = high, 4 = very high, 5 = catastrophic

Duration Index: 1 to 5 scale

1 = more than 5 years, 2 = 1 to 5 years, 3 = 6 months to 1 year, 4 = 1 to 6 months, 5 = 1 week to 1 month

Coping Index: 1 to 6 scale

1 = outstanding, 2 = above average, 3 = adequate, 4 = somewhat inadequate, 5 = inadequate, and 6 = unable to judge at this time

Strength Index: 1 to 2 scale

1 = notable strengths, 2 = possible strengths

Factor II: Environmental Problem Identification

Type of Environmental Problem Area

Economic/basic needs system, education and training system, judicial and legal system, health, safety, and social services system, voluntary association system, and affectional support system

Discrimination codes for any of these types of environmental problems

Coded by age, ethnicity, color, language, religion, gender, sexual orientation, lifestyle, noncitizen, veteran, dependency status, disability status, marital status, body size, political affiliation

Severity, Duration, and Strengths Indices:

Identical to Factor I.

Source: Karls & O'Keefe (2008).

These two assumptions are consistent with current and emerging policy guides on psychology, social work, counseling, and human services curricula as well as multicultural competencies.

The Role of Strengths

Clients and also their communities and environments can be assessed and conceptualized with a strengths-based model (Jones-Smith, 2014; Snyder, Lopez, & Pedrotti, 2014). Saleebey (2013) discusses a number of features of **strength-based assessment**. Among these features are:

1. Listening for hints and harbingers of strength, resilience, and rebound in the client's narrative of problems; naming and inquiring about the client's areas of competence and resourcefulness; and utilizing a vocabulary of strengths-based talk in the assessment process.

2. Assessing both natural and formal resources that may be available to the client and exploring to what extent they are adequate and acceptable to the client. As Ungar (2011) asserts, "people need resources, provided in ways that are meaningful to them, that are relevant to the context in which they live and the culture with which they identify themselves" (p. 44). In research that Ungar and his colleagues conducted internationally, they identified seven common categories of resources related specifically to well-being. These include:

   a. Access to material resources
   b. Relationships
   c. Identity
   d. Power and control
   e. Cultural adherence

f. Social justice

g. Cohesion

Levels of resources can be assessed for an individual client, for a family, and for a community and cultural group as well.

Jones-Smith (2014) comments that a strength-based assessment is founded on the premise that most clients are not that aware of their strengths but are acutely aware of their deficits! If a client is hesitant to discuss or identify strengths, then the practitioner may introduce a strengths assessment checklist such as the Clifton Strengths Finder (Rath 2007), the VIA Signature Strengths Survey (Peterson & Seligman, 2004), or the Behavioral and Emotional Rating Scale (BERS-2) for children and teenagers (Epstein and Sharma, 1998).

Anderson, Cowger, and Snively (2009) also discuss the process of assessing strengths. Their model is one that encourages practitioners to help clients identify acts of resistance to both violence and oppression as part of a strength-based assessment process. They contend that the current practice of assessing client "deficits" results in a number of issues, including generating obstacles to the "exercise of personal and social power," reinforcing "social structures that generate and regulate the unequal power relationship," fostering a "victimization model" of assessment, targeting the help seeker as the "problem" since "the context of oppression is stripped," and reinforcing the status quo "in a manner that is incongruent with the promotion of social and economic justice" (p. 182). Their model broadens the more traditional definition of resiliency from competency despite enduring adversity to focusing on individuals' survival strengths that develop as a means to protect themselves from oppression.

They suggest that to anchor a problem definition within a strengths perspective, "it is particularly important at the beginning of the assessment to acknowledge that the person seeking help is in charge of telling his or her story" so that the meaning of the client's narrative is not displaced by the practitioner's perspective (p. 189). A second step in their strengths-based model of assessment is to help the client uncover strengths and to make strengths more accessible to the client in some useful way. As Anderson and colleagues note, "since individuals often internalize shame and blame about their victimization experiences, providing a view of themselves as resourceful gives credit to their ability to persevere despite insurmountable odds. Consequently, they may view themselves differently, particularly their strengths, by recognizing how they actively responded to

adversity in the past and may now channel their survival strategies into confronting present struggles" (p. 189). Finally, during the assessment process, these authors recommend that practitioners "merge an understanding of individual issues with an awareness of power relationships that are embedded in the larger social environment" (p. 191).

The evidence base surrounding the strengths-based model is promising but mixed. In part, this may be due to the lack of consistent definitions of the meaning and function of strengths-based constructs (Oko, 2006). Taylor (2006) notes that the strengths perspective should not be an "end in and of itself," nor should it be used to argue against the neuroscience of mental illness. He advocates for the judicious use of strengths-oriented assessment and treatment in a differential manner. Saleebey (2013) argues that both quantitative and qualitative research shows that the strengths perspective has a degree of power that supports its usefulness (p. 293). Although empirical data are still accumulating, there is some support to suggest that when used in helping, the strengths perspective consistently achieves a reduction in symptoms and improved social functioning of clients.

The Role of Evidence

In prior chapters, we have discussed evidence-based helping relationships and also evidence-based treatments (EBTs). Equally important is the degree to which the assessment instruments used in studies of evidence-based relationships and treatments are valid and reliable since practitioners rely on the accuracy of these measures for diagnostic and conceptualization purposes. In general, though, the literature base for evidence-based assessment (EBA) has lagged behind the literature base for EBTs. This gap between scientifically sound assessment data and empirically supported treatments has put the evidence-based practice movement in some jeopardy, because an inaccurate or incomplete assessment can lead to the inappropriate or ineffective use of an EBT (Hunsley & Mash, 2010).

Hunsley and Lee (2014) define **evidence-based assessment** as an approach that uses research and theory to guide

1. the selection of variables to be assessed for a specific assessment purpose

2. the methods and measure to be used in the assessment

3. the manner in which the assessment process unfolds (p. 159)

EBA recognizes that assessment involves decision-making in which the practitioner conceptualizes, develops, and tests hunches or hypotheses using data obtained during the assessment process (Hunsley & Mash, 2007).

Reliability and Validity Hunsley and Mash (2008) have developed a rating system for various instruments used for specific assessment purposes and for specific clinical disorders. Their rating system requires the demonstration of predetermined psychometric levels in the areas of reliability, validity, and norms across published studies. Haynes, Smith, and Hunsley (2011) have also described issues related to evidence-based assessment. **Reliability** refers to stability and replicability, or whether an assessment measure or procedure produces the same results consistently. It generally is agreed that a measure must be reliable for it to also have validity, meaning that it is correct or accurate in what it measures. However, reliability does not guarantee validity! **Validity** has to do with the representativeness of the measure, or how well something measures what it is supposed to measure. Validity can vary across clients. For example, an assessment measure may be valid with clients from one ethnic group but not automatically with clients from another ethnic group. Further, as Haynes (2006) points out, an assessment measure can be valid in one domain but not in another. For example, a practitioner may use an assessment in a session to assess a couple's level and kind of marital conflict and may also use the same assessment to assess their conflict in the home domain. The validity of the same measure across the two domains of the clinic setting and the home setting may vary. As Haynes (2006) concludes, validity "is not an unconditional trait of a measure" but rather something that can vary across a number of dimensions (p. 27).

While there are many different kinds of validity, in assessment the concept of incremental validity is an important one. It refers to the extent to which one measure adds information above and beyond what is already available through other measures. Haynes (2006) defines **incremental validity** in this way: "the degree to which additional assessment data increase the power, sensitivity, specificity, and predictive efficacy of judgments" (p. 19). For this reason, we recommend supplementing the interview assessment process with other kinds of assessment tools, such as self-observation and monitoring and self-report measures such as behavior checklists, used on a *selective* basis; *more for the sake of more* is not necessarily better! Without incremental validity, the practitioner may be wasting time and money administering and using

multiple assessment strategies that, however, do not add any predictive power.

Sound clinical assessment relies on assessment tools that are both accurate and efficient and that involve both idiographic and nomothetic instruments (Hunsley & Mash, 2008, p. 7). **Idiographic measures** are those such as self-monitoring and goal attainment scaling that measure the unique aspects of an individual's experience. **Nomothetic measures** are those that allow for comparisons between groups of individuals. The psychometric properties of reliability and validity in the nomothetic measures are very important. Also important is whether the measure has either appropriate norms or replicated supporting evidence for the accuracy of cutoff scores (Hunsley & Mash, 2014). Moreover, there needs to be supporting evidence that the EBA is suitable for the client being assessed, particularly on demographic characteristics such as age, gender, and ethnicity. As Hunsley and Mash (2010) point out, this means that "careful consideration must be given to the characteristics of the samples on which the supporting scientific evidence was derived" (p. 8). Haynes (2006) points out that even in idiographic assessment, the consideration of reliability and validity is important, particularly content validity. **Content validity** involves "the degree to which the behaviors and events sampled by the instrument are those most relevant to the client" (Haynes, 2006, p. 38). Practically, this means ensuring that the assessment measures things most germane to the individual client.

Self-Monitoring We describe the use of self-observation and self-monitoring as an idiographic data collection tool in Chapter 8. (We also describe the use of idiographic goal attainment scaling in Chapter 8.) Briefly, **self-monitoring** (also referred to as self-observation or self-assessment) represents strategies that clients use outside of the clinical sessions to observe things about themselves and then to make written notations or recording about these observations that they bring back to the following session. For example, Neacsiu and Linehan (2014) use structured diary cards as a self-monitoring strategy with clients for many purposes, including with clients who engage in self-harm or suicidal ideation and behaviors. These diary cards are used each week by clients to record daily instances of suicidal and nonsuicidal self-injurious behaviors, urges to self-harm or engage in suicide behaviors (on a point rating scale of 0–5), feelings of "misery," use of substances (legal and illegal), and use of certain behavioral skills (Neacsiu & Linehan, 2014). The cards are reviewed with the helper at the beginning of each session to help assess suicide and self-harm risk. In addition to the use of the diary cards for self-harm, these cards are also used to monitor a variety of other kinds of behaviors, including coping skills, wise mind or mindfulness, self-soothing, and acceptance.

Electronic diaries and smart phone apps are being used now more frequently, both to provide a cue for recording something and also as a tool for entering the self-monitored or observed data (Piasecki, Hufford, Solhan, & Trull, 2007). To enhance the reliability of self-monitoring, clients can be coached on the process (see Watson & Tharp, 2014).

We also describe the use of a number of different kinds of self-report measures in Chapter 8. Although there are many of these available, we recommend judicious screening of such measures before they are chosen for use. Consider, for example, these three guidelines offered by Hunsley and Lee (2014):

1. Is the measure likely to be useful for clinical practitioners?

2. Is there replicated evidence that the measurement data provide reliable and valid information?

3. Does the use of the measure and its resulting data improve upon typical clinical decision making and treatment outcome? (p. 235)

For examples of measures utilized in empirical studies that have demonstrated adequate validity and reliability, consult the Assessment Instrument Index in Hunsley and Mash (2008). This index lists all of the instruments that met their rated criteria for sound psychometric properties. Finally, a description of various evidence-based assessment measures for selected clinical disorders has been made available by Antony and Barlow (2010).

An additional assessment tool that is a generic model with a considerable amount of research support across a wide range of client problems is the functional assessment (Hunsley & Mash, 2008; Haynes et al., 2011). (See also Learning Activity 6.1 on page 187.)

Functional Assessment: The ABC Model and Chain Analysis

Conducting a functional assessment involves **LO1** obtaining information about the client's story in a very specific way. It means assessing and conceptualizing clinically relevant behaviors within their historical and current context. It involves an analysis of both past and present learning experiences that may be responsible for current presenting issues (Thyer & Myers, 2000). Haynes,

O'Brien, and Kahokula (2011) describe a **functional assessment** as the clinician's hypothesized and dynamic working model of a client's behavior problem. The functional assessment helps both clinician and client determine the *functions* of the client's problem behaviors. This information is quite important for subsequent treatment planning. For example, consider a child who has a bad experience at school. The next day the child develops a tummy ache and his mom allows him to stay home from school. This continues for several days until the mom takes him to the doctor who can find nothing wrong. The mom sends him back to school but receives a call in late morning from the school indicating that her son has gone to the office and is reporting that he is sick and wants to go home! It doesn't take a rocket scientist to figure out that the function of the child's aches and illness is to avoid school! (However it is entirely possible that the school personnel and/or the parent may miss this). Once this information is gleaned, it becomes easier to develop an intervention plan that targets the identified problem and function of the client's behaviour, in this case, school avoidance.

The overall goal of functional assessment is to generate causal hunches or hypotheses from information about client behavior problems and causal variables known as antecedents and consequences. This type of assessment is referred to as the ABC model and is based on principles of learning. Although there are many classes of causal variables that are modifiable and could be of interest to the clinician, it is the *contiguous* antecedents, environmental events, situations, contexts, response contingencies, and cognitive antecedent and consequent variables that are most useful to determine, as research shows that they "exert important triggering or maintaining effects on behaviour problems" of clients (Haynes et al., 2011, p. 57).

The **ABC model** of behavior suggests that the **behavior** (B), something a client does, is influenced by certain events that precede it, called **antecedents** (A), and by some types of events that follow behavior, called **consequences** (C). An antecedent (A) event can tell a person when to behave in a situation. **Antecedents** are responsible for the behavior being performed in the first place because they "call the behavior up" or stimulate it in some way (Watson & Tharp, 2014, p. 138). A **consequence** (C) is defined as an event that strengthens or weakens a behavior and determines whether the behavior will occur again (Spiegler & Guevremont, 2010). Notice that these definitions of antecedents and consequences suggest that an individual's behavior is directly related to or influenced by certain stimuli such as the presence of another

Learning Activity **6.1**

Clinical Assessment Influences

After reading the case of Mrs. Oliverio, respond to the following:

1. Based on the case and on your clinical hunches or hypotheses, list what you think are the major issues for Mrs. Oliverio.
2. Examine the issues you named. Do they reflect something about Mrs. Oliverio as an individual, something about Mrs. Oliverio's environment, or both? If both, how do you see the issues as related?
3. Speculate about the following aspects to explore in your clinical assessment with Mrs. Oliverio:
   a. Learning components of the case
   b. Neurobiological components of the case
   c. Developmental components of the case
   d. Environmental/cultural components of the case
   e. Levels of environmental and individual strengths and resources in the case
4. Discuss your responses with a classmate or your instructor.

The Case of Mrs. Oliverio

Mrs. Oliverio is a 28-year-old married woman who reports that an excessive fear that her husband will die has led her to seek therapy. She further states that because this is her second marriage, it is important for her to work out her problem so that it doesn't ultimately interfere with her relationship with her husband. Her husband is a sales representative and occasionally has to attend out-of-town meetings. According to Mrs. Oliverio, whenever he has gone away on a trip during the 2 years of their marriage, she "goes to pieces" and feels "utterly devastated" because of recurring thoughts that he will die and not return. She states that this is a very intense fear and occurs even when he is gone on short trips, such as a half day or a day. She is not aware of any coping thoughts or behaviors she uses at these times. She indicates that she feels great as soon as her husband gets home. She states that this was also a problem for her in her first marriage, which ended in divorce 5 years ago. She believes the thoughts occur because her father died unexpectedly when she was 11 years old. Whenever her husband tells her he has to leave or actually does leave, she re-experiences the pain of being told her father has died. She feels plagued with thoughts that her husband will not return and then feels intense

anxiety. She is constantly thinking about never seeing her husband again during these anxiety episodes. According to Mrs. Oliverio, her husband has been very supportive and patient and has spent a considerable amount of time trying to reassure her and to convince her, through reasoning, that he will return from a trip. She states that this has not helped her to stop worrying excessively that he will die and not return. She also states that in the past few months her husband has canceled several business trips just to avoid putting her through all this pain.

Mrs. Oliverio also reports that this anxiety has resulted in some insomnia during the past 2 years. She states that as soon as her husband informs her that he must leave town, she has difficulty going to sleep that evening. When he has to be gone on an overnight trip, she doesn't sleep at all. She simply lies in bed and worries about her husband dying and also feels very frustrated that it is getting later and later and that she is still awake. She reports sleeping fairly well as long as her husband is home and a trip is not impending.

Mrs. Oliverio reports that she feels very satisfied with her present marriage except for some occasional times when she finds herself thinking that her husband does not fulfill all her expectations. She is not sure exactly what her expectations are, but she is aware of feeling anger toward him after this happens. When she gets angry, she just "explodes" and feels as though she lashes out at her husband for no apparent reason. She reports that she doesn't like to explode at her husband like this but feels relieved after it happens. She indicates that her husband continues to be very supportive and protective despite her occasional outbursts. She suspects the anger may be her way of getting back at him for going away on a trip and leaving her alone. She also expresses feelings of hurt and anger since her father's death in being unable to find a "father substitute." She also reports feeling intense anger toward her ex-husband after the divorce—anger she still sometimes experiences.

Mrs. Oliverio has no children. She is employed in a responsible position as an administrative assistant and makes $38,500 per year. She reports that she enjoys her work, although she constantly worries that her boss might not be pleased with her and that she could lose her job even though her work evaluations have been satisfactory. She reports that another event she has been worried about is the health of her brother, who was injured in a car accident this past year. She further reports that she has an excellent relationship with her brother and strong ties to her church.

individual or a particular setting. For example, a behavior that appears to be controlled by antecedent events such as anger may also be maintained or strengthened by consequences such as reactions from other people. Generally speaking, once the ABCs are identified, change

is maximized by identifying and using change intervention strategies that alter as many of the ABCs as possible (Watson & Tharp, 2014).

As a very simple example of the ABC model, consider a behavior (B) that most of us engage in frequently:

talking. Our talking behavior is usually occasioned by certain antecedent events, such as being asked a question or being in the presence of a friend. Antecedents that might decrease the likelihood that we will talk may include worry about getting approval for what we say or how we answer the question or being in a hurry to get somewhere. Our talking behavior may be maintained by the verbal and nonverbal attention we receive from another person, which is a very powerful consequence, or reinforcer. Other positive consequences that might maintain our talking behavior may be that we are feeling good or happy and engaging in positive self-statements or evaluations about the usefulness or relevance of what we are saying. We may talk less when the other person's eye contact wanders, although the meaning of eye contact varies across cultures, or when the other person tells us more explicitly that we've talked enough. These are negative consequences (C) or punishments that decrease our talking behavior. Other negative consequences that may decrease our talking behavior could include bodily sensations of fatigue or vocal hoarseness that occur after we talk for a while, or thoughts and images that what we are saying is of little value to attract the interest of others. As you will see, behavior often varies among clients, and what functions as an antecedent or consequence for one person in one environment is often very different for someone else in a different environment.

Behavior: External and Internal

Behavior can be both overt and covert. **Overt behavior** is behavior that is visible or could be detected by an observer, such as verbal behavior (talking), nonverbal behavior (for example, gesturing or smiling), or motoric behavior (engaging in some action such as walking). **Covert behavior** includes events that are usually internal— inside the client—and are not so readily visible to an observer, who must rely on client self-report and nonverbal behavior to detect them. Examples of covert behavior include thoughts, beliefs, images, feelings, moods, and body sensations. We include the role of cognition, primarily represented as internal speech, as well as its effect on emotion in our model. This model assumes that client behaviors are also influenced by the cognitive schemas and internal dialogues or self-talk of the individual. Cognitive schemas and self-talk can comprise part of the identifying behavioral issues or can also function as either an antecedent or a consequence to the identified problem behaviors. These cognitive schemas and self-talk exert effects on client feelings or emotions. As Haynes et al. (2011) point out, most client problem

behaviors have multiple response modes. And, over the course of therapy, these response modes may change. For instance, at the beginning of counseling, for the school-avoidant child with the stomach aches, the stomach pain might be the most relevant response mode while later in counseling the more relevant response mode for this child might shift to emotional reactivity concerning bullying at school.

These various overt and covert response modes are typically not independent of each other, but overlap, too (Haynes et al., 2011). As we indicated, behavior that clients report rarely occurs in isolated fashion. Most undesired behaviors are typically part of a larger chain or set of behaviors (see also our discussion of chain analysis). Moreover, each behavior mentioned usually has more than one component. For example, a client who complains of anxiety or depression is most likely using the label to refer to an experience consisting of an **affective** component (feelings and mood states), a **somatic** component (physiological and body-related sensation), a **behavioral** component (what the client does or doesn't do), and a **cognitive** component (thoughts, beliefs, images, schemas, and internal dialogue). Additionally, the experience of anxiety or depression may vary for the client, depending on **contextual** factors (time, place, concurrent events, developmental transitions, gender, culture, sociopolitical climate, and environmental events), and on **relational** factors such as the presence or absence of other people. All these components may or may not be related to a particular reported concern.

> As an example, suppose the client who reports "anxiety" is afraid to venture out in public places except for work because of heightened anxiety and/or panic attacks. She is an adult single woman in her 40s who still lives at her parental home, and she provides care to her elderly mother, whom she also describes as dependent and helpless. She has lived all of her life in a small, rural community. She reports mistrust of strangers, especially those whom she did not know while growing up. She states she would like to leave and be out on her own and move away, but she is too afraid. Her reported concern of anxiety seems to be part of a chain that starts with a cognitive component in which she thinks worried thoughts and produces images in which she sees herself alone and unable to cope or to get the assistance of others if necessary. These thoughts and images support her underlying cognitive schema or structure of limited autonomy, despite her chronological age and developmental stage of middle adulthood.
>
> The cognitive component leads to somatic discomfort and tension and to feelings of apprehension and dread,

which she rates at a high level of intensity (90 on a 100-point scale). These three components work together to influence her overt behavior. For the past few years, she has successfully avoided almost all public places. She states that, on average, she has left the house to go somewhere by herself several times per year, pointing to a low response rate of this behavior. Consequently, she depends on the support of friends to help her on the few occasions when she attends public activities. These people form her relational network. This support, although no doubt useful to her, also has helped to maintain her avoidance of venturing out to public places alone without being accompanied by other persons.

At the same time that you see these apparent behaviors and their concomitant dimensions (intensity of apprehension, rate of leaving the house alone), bear in mind this client will also demonstrate both overt and covert behaviors that represent strengths, resources, and coping skills. The very act of courage it takes to come and see you is an overt behavioral strength and action of initiative. Her recognition of some conflicting feelings and beliefs about her life choices is a covert behavioral strength. Her network of friends and her steady work situation are examples of environmental strengths; being a part of a small, close-knit community can be a cultural strength.

It is important to determine the relative importance of each component of the reported behavior to select appropriate intervention strategies. It is often valuable to list, in writing, the various components identified for any given behavior.

Causal Variables Once the problem behaviors have been defined, it is time to identify the causal variables and their relationship to the problem behaviors. In the functional analysis we define these **causal variables** as antecedents and consequences. Like behavior problems, antecedents and consequences can also have multiple components or attributes. In addition, for most client behavior problems, there are usually multiple causal variables. Haynes et al. (2011, p. 167) list the most useful types of causal variables to identify in the functional analysis assessment:

Antecedent stimuli and settings
Cognitive events (beliefs and self-statements)
Emotional states
Psychophysiologcal context (medication state, fatigue, pain, substance status)
Psychosocial context (recent history of social networks)
Early learning history
Genetic makeup
Neurophysiologic factors
Impairments and limitations (cognitive, neuropsychological, neurophysiological, physical)

Conditioned responses (such as fear)
Response contingencies (avoidance, positive and negative reinforcement, escape)

These types of causal variables must be defined concretely for each client behavior problem and should not include elements of the behavior problem itself (Haynes et al., 2011, p. 168). Further as these authors indicate, the causal variables need sufficient delineation to be measureable, because without measurability it is hard to obtain good baseline data for outcome evaluation (see also Chapter 8).

In the following two sections, you will see how antecedents and consequences are defined for the client example described.

Antecedents

According to Mischel (1973), behavior is situationally determined. This means that given behaviors tend to occur only in certain situations. For example, most of us brush our teeth in a public or private bathroom rather than during a concert or a spiritual service. Antecedents may elicit emotional and physiological reactions such as anger, fear, joy, headaches, or elevated blood pressure. Antecedents influence behavior by either increasing or decreasing its likelihood of occurrence. For example, a child in a first-grade class may behave differently at school than at home, or differently with a substitute than with the regular teacher.

Antecedent events that occur immediately before a specific behavior exert influence on it. Events that are not in temporal proximity to the behavior can similarly increase or decrease the probability that the behavior will occur. Antecedents that occur in immediate temporal proximity to the specified behavior are technically called **stimulus events** (Bijou & Baer, 1976) and include any external or internal event or condition that either cues the behavior or makes it more or less likely to occur under that condition. Antecedents that are temporally distant from the specified behavior are called **setting events** (Kantor, 1970). Setting events may end well before the behavior yet, like stimulus events, still aid or inhibit its occurrence. Examples of setting events to consider in assessing client issues are: the client's age, developmental stage, and physiological state; characteristics of the client's work, home, or school setting; multicultural factors; and behaviors that emerge to affect subsequent behaviors. Both stimulus and setting antecedent conditions must be identified and defined individually for each client. Further, as Haynes et al. (2011) suggest, contemporary or proximal antecedents usually have more clinical usefulness than historical or distal antecedents. This is because the distal ones have more to do with the emergence of the behavior problem while the proximal ones have more to do with the day-to-day aspects of the client's behavior (Haynes et al., 2011, p. 169).

Categories of Antecedents Antecedents also usually involve more than one category or type of event. Categories of antecedents may be **affective** (feelings, mood states), **somatic** (physiological and body-related sensations), **behavioral** (verbal, nonverbal, and motoric responses), **cognitive** (schemas, thoughts, beliefs, images, internal dialogue), **contextual** (time, place, multicultural factors, concurrent environmental events), and **relational** (presence or absence of other people). For example, for our client who reported "anxiety," a variety of antecedents may cue or occasion each aspect of the reported behavior—for example, fear of losing control (cognitive/affective), negative self-statements about autonomy and self-efficacy (cognitive), awareness of apprehension-related body sensations, fatigue, and hypoglycemic tendencies (somatic), staying up late and skipping meals (behavioral), being in public places (contextual), absence of significant others such as friends and siblings, and the demands of her elderly mother (relational).

There also are antecedents that make components of the client's anxiety less likely to occur. These include feeling relaxed (affective), being rested (somatic), eating regularly (behavioral), decreased dependence on her friends (behavioral), decreased fear of separation from mother (affective), positive appraisal of self and others (cognitive), expectation of being able to handle situations (cognitive), absence of need to go to public places or functions (contextual), and being accompanied to a public place by a significant other (relational).

During the assessment phase of the helping process, it is important to identify those antecedent sources that prompt desirable behaviors and those that are related to inappropriate responses. The reason is that during the intervention (treatment) phase it is important to select strategies that not only aid the occurrence of desirable behavior but also decrease the presence of cues for unwanted behavior.

Consequences

The consequences of a behavior are events that follow a behavior and exert some influence on the behavior, or are functionally related to the behavior. In other words, not everything that follows a behavior is automatically considered a consequence.

Suppose you are counseling a woman who occasionally embarks on drinking binges. She reports that after a binge she feels guilty, regards herself as a bad person, and tends to suffer from insomnia. Although these events are *results* of her binge behavior, they are not consequences unless in some way they directly influence her binges by maintaining, increasing, or decreasing them. In this case, other events that follow the drinking binges may be the real consequences. For instance, perhaps the client's binges are maintained by the feelings she gets from drinking; perhaps they are temporarily decreased when someone else, such as her partner, notices her behavior and reprimands her for it or refuses to go out with her.

Like antecedents, the things that function as consequences will always vary with clients. By definition, **rewarding or reinforcing events** will maintain or increase the behavior. Such consequences often maintain or strengthen behavior through positive reinforcement, which involves the presentation of an overt or covert event following the behavior that increases the likelihood that the behavior will occur again in the future. People tend to repeat behaviors that result in pleasurable effects. Also, response contingencies can be more immediate or delayed. Those consequences that more immediately follow a problem behavior are more likely to exert a stronger effect.

People also tend to engage in behaviors that have some payoffs, or value, even if the behavior is very dysfunctional (such payoffs are called **secondary gains**). For example, a client may abuse alcohol and continue to do so even after she loses her job or her family because she likes the feelings she gets while drinking and because the drinking helps her to avoid responsibility. Another client may continue to verbally abuse his wife despite the strain it causes in their relationship because the abusive behavior gives him a feeling of power and control. In these two examples, the behavior is often hard to change because the immediate consequences make the person feel better in some way. As a result, the behavior is reinforced, even if its delayed or long-term effects are unpleasant. In other words, in these examples, the client "values" the behavior that he or she is trying to eliminate. Often the secondary gain, the payoff derived from a manifest problem, is a cover for more severe issues that are not always readily presented by the client. For example, the husband who verbally abuses his wife may be lacking in self-esteem and may be feeling deeply depressed after the birth of their first child, feeling as if he has somehow "lost" his wife and is no longer the special person in her life. Clients may not always know why they engage in a behavior. Sometimes this knowledge is outside of the client's conscious awareness. Part of performing a good assessment involves making reasons or secondary gains more explicit in the client's story.

Consequences also can maintain behavior by **negative reinforcement**—removal of an unpleasant event following the behavior, thereby increasing the likelihood that the behavior will occur again. People tend to repeat behaviors that bring an end to or get rid of annoying or painful events or effects. They also use negative reinforcement to establish *avoidance* and *escape* behaviors. **Avoidance behavior** is maintained when an *expected* unpleasant event is removed. For example, avoidance of public places is maintained by removal of the expected anxiety associated with public places. **Escape behavior** is maintained when a negative (unpleasant) event *already occurring* is removed or terminated. For example, punitive behavior toward a child temporarily stops the child's annoying or aversive behaviors. Termination of the unpleasant child behaviors maintains the parental escape behavior.

Some consequences can weaken or eliminate the behavior. A behavior is typically decreased or weakened (at least temporarily) if it is followed by an unpleasant stimulus or event (**punishment**), if a positive, or reinforcing, event is removed or terminated (**response cost**), or if the behavior is no longer followed by reinforcing events (**operant extinction**). For example, an overweight man may maintain his eating binges because of the feelings of pleasure he receives from eating (a positive reinforcing consequence) or because they allow him to escape from a boring work situation (negative reinforcing consequence). In contrast, his wife's reprimands or sarcasm or refusal to go out with him may, at least temporarily, reduce his binges (punishing consequence). Although using negative contingencies to modify behavior has many disadvantages, in real-life settings, such as home, work, and school, punishment is widely used to influence the behavior of others. Helpers must be alert to the presence of negative consequences in a client's life and to the accompanying effects on the client. Helpers also must be careful to avoid the use of any verbal or nonverbal behavior that may seem punitive to a client, because such behavior may contribute to unnecessary problems in the therapeutic relationship and to subsequent client termination of (escape from) therapy.

Categories of Consequences Consequences also usually involve more than one source or type of event. Like antecedents, categories of consequences may be *affective, somatic, behavioral, cognitive, contextual,* and/or *relational.* For example, for our client who reports "anxiety," the avoidance of public places results in a reduction of anxious feelings (affective), body tension (somatic), and worry about more autonomy (cognitive). Additional consequences that may help to maintain the problem include avoidance of being in public (behavioral) and increased attention from family and friends (relational). Contextual consequences may include reinforcement of cultural and gender values of being tied to her family of origin, being the family caregiver, and being able to "stay in the nest." It would be inaccurate to simply ask about whatever follows the specified behavior and to automatically classify it as a consequence without determining its particular effect on the behavior. As Cullen (1983, p. 137) notes, "If variables are supposed to be functionally related to behavior when, in fact, they are not, then manipulation of those variables by the client or therapist will, at best, have no effect on the presenting difficulties or, at worst, create even more difficulties."

During the assessment phase of helping, it is important to identify those consequences that maintain, increase, or decrease both desirable and undesirable behaviors related to the client's concern. In the intervention (treatment) phase, this information will help you select change strategies that will maintain and increase desirable behaviors and weaken and decrease undesirable behaviors such as behavioral excesses and deficits. Information about consequences also is useful in planning treatment approaches that rely directly on the use of consequences to help with behavior change, such as self-reward. As Haynes et al. (2011) suggest, because interventions are selected that target the defined causes of client problems, identifying these causal variables and describing their relationship to the client's behavior problems is very important in the functional analysis. Ultimately, as these authors explain, the question for clinicians is: "*What is it about the causal variable that is exerting the most important effects on the behavior problem for this particular client?*" (p. 152). Identification of specific antecedents and consequences helps to answer this question very concretely so that helpers can identify the contexts under which antecedents and consequences have the most direct and strongest effect on the client's problem behavior (Haynes et al., 2011, p. 153).

It is important to reiterate that problem behaviors, antecedents, consequences, and components must be assessed and identified for each particular client. Two clients might complain of anxiety or "nerves," and the assessments might reveal very different components of the behavior and different antecedents and consequences. A multi-cultural focus also is important here: the behaviors, antecedents, and consequences can be affected by the client's cultural affiliations and sociopolitical context. Also remember that there is often some overlap among antecedents, behavior, and consequences. For example, negative self-statements or irrational beliefs might function in some instances as both antecedents and consequences for a given component of the identified concern.

Consider a college student who reports depression after situations with less than desired outcomes, such as asking a girl out and being turned down, getting a test back with a B or C on it, and interviewing for a job and not receiving a subsequent offer of employment. Irrational beliefs may function as an antecedent by cuing, or setting off, the resulting feelings of depression—for example, "Here is a situation that didn't turn out the way I wanted. It's awful; now I feel lousy." Irrational beliefs in the form of self-deprecatory thoughts may function as a consequence by maintaining the feelings of depression for some time even after the situation itself is over—for example, "When things don't turn out the way they should, I'm a failure." At the same time, keep in mind that this client has rational and coping beliefs as well as irrational ones and behavioral, environmental, and cultural strengths as well. These may be less obvious to him than the presenting issues, but part of your task is to help him uncover what they are. For additional information about the functional analysis assessment process, we urge you to consult the primer on this process developed by Yoman (2008).

Chain Analysis

It also is important to note that most issues presented by clients involve both multiple and complex chains of behavior sequences, so an ABC analysis is conducted on more than one factor. Neacsiu and Linehan (2014) refer to this as a **chain analysis**, defined as a "blow-by-blow description of the chain of events leading up to and following the behavior. In a chain analysis the therapist constructs a general road map of how the client arrives at dysfunctional responses, including where the road actually starts, and notes possible alternative adaptive pathways or junctions along the way...The overall goal is to determine the function of the behavior or, from another perspective, the problem the behavior was instrumental in solving" (p. 435). As Haynes et al. (2011) suggest, chain analyses are important because "they can point to several possible intervention points" (p. 58). We list the specific steps involved in Linehan's (2015a. 2015b) chain analysis that she uses in assessment within her dialectical behavior therapy (DBT) integrated approach:

Step One: Describe the specific problem behaviors. Be careful to operationalize the behaviors; that is, be specific and describe exactly what the client, did, said, or felt as well as the intensity of the behavior. Example: "I lost my temper when on the phone with my mom and gave her a lecture in a very stern voice."

Step Two: Describe the specific prompting event that started the whole chain of behavior. This helps to determine the specific event that precipitated the start of the chain reaction. Begin with some event in the environment that started the chain of behavior identified in step one. Example: "I felt mad that my mom told my stepdad about my problem at school without asking me first."

Step Three: Describe vulnerability factors happening before the prompting event. These are factors that made the client more susceptible to the problematic chain, such as illness, injury, substance use, stressful environmental events, and intense emotions. Example: "I hadn't gone to the gym that day to release my tensions that had built up from school."

Step Four: Describe in excruciating detail the chain of events that led up to the problem behavior. This step asks the client to imagine how the problem behavior is chained to the prompting event listed in step two. Questions such as, "How long is the chain?" "Where does the chain go next?" and "What are the links in the chain?" are useful for step four. The links can be overt behaviors, thoughts, emotions, somatic sensations, and so forth. The clinician can facilitate this step by continuing to ask the client, "What happened next?" and "What then?". Linehan (2015a) suggests having the client actually write out all the links in the chain no matter how inconsequential they seem, as if writing a script for a play (p. 22). Example:

1. I felt wired from not working out.

2. I felt hungry and short tempered from not eating enough during the day.

3. I heard my mom's voice on the phone telling me she told my stepdad about my school situation.

4. I thought "She had no right to do that without my permission."

5. I got mad and frustrated with her right away.

6. I wanted to teach her a lesson and so I lectured her like she was a child or student of mine.

Step Five: Describe the consequences of the problem behavior. Here the client needs to identify very specifically the effect the behavior had on her or him, the client's environment, and how the client felt both immediately after the behavior and later on. Additionally, reactions of other people both immediately after and later are identified. As with precipitating events or antecedents, the helper assesses both environmental and behavioral consequences by obtaining "detailed descriptions of the client's emotions, somatic sensations, actions, thoughts, and assumptions" (Neacsiu & Linehan , 2014, p. 435). Example:

Results in the environment: My mom had hurt feelings because she was just trying to be helpful.

Results for me: I felt immature. I missed an opportunity to have a great phone conversation with someone I love very much.

We illustrate the functional assessment model later in the chapter in our sample case of Isabella. We also suggest that you work with the material presented in this summary by consulting the visual summary in Figure 6.1 and by working with Learning Activities 6.2 and 6.4. In conclusion, although we believe that functional analysis provides useful information to clinicians for subsequent treatment planning, we also agree with the caveats

observed by Haynes et al. (2011). Functional analysis can be time-consuming, imprecise, and not always comprehensive enough to include all of the factors necessary for a useful treatment plan. As such, we discuss some additional factors necessary for treatment planning in Chapter 9.

Diagnostic Classification of Client Issues

Our emphasis throughout this chapter is on the need to conduct a thorough and precise assessment with each client to be able to define client issues in very concrete ways. In addition, helpers need to be aware that client behaviors

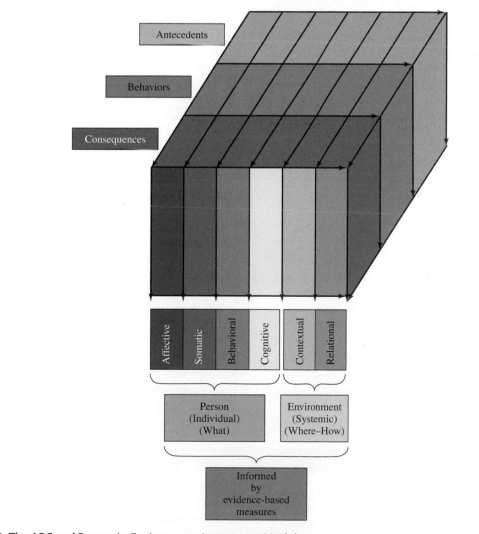

FIGURE 6.1 The ABC and Person-in-Environment Assessment Model

can be organized in some form of diagnostic taxonomy (classification). While the assessment model we have described in this chapter is based on cognitive, learning, and emotion theories, it is also possible to assess clients, develop clinical hypotheses, and plan treatment based on a clinical disorder using a diagnostic anchoring system (Persons, 2008). As Hunsley and Mash (2010) point out, while there has been much debate about the strengths and weaknesses of such a diagnostic classification system, "the reality is that much of what we know about psychological conditions is dependent on these diagnostic systems" (p. 10). The diagnostic system most frequently used in the United States is found in the 5th edition of the American Psychiatric Association's (APA) *Diagnostic and Statistical Manual of Mental Disorders* (*DSM-5*, 2013).

Our interest in this chapter is simply to summarize the basic information found in the *DSM-5* to help students understand how this system is used in assessing clients. With the Health Insurance Portability and Accountability Act (HIPAA) of 1996, providers in the United States are required to use diagnostic codes based on the ***ICD-CM***, or the ninth revision of the *International Classification of Diseases and Related Health Problems* of the World Health Organization (WHO) for electronic billing and reimbursement. In 2015, diagnostic codes from the 10th edition of the *ICD-CM* will be used and the *ICD-CM* 11 is already in process! The *DSM-5* is more consistent with the *ICD-CM* than prior editions of this diagnostic manual and clinical disorders are described both by a *ICD-9* numerical code in **BOLD** and an *ICD-10* code in parentheses.

The *DSM-5* and Clinical Disorders

DSM-5 consists largely of descriptions of various mental and psychological disorders broken down into 20 major diagnostic classes, with additional subcategories within these major categories. These 20 major diagnostic classes are listed in Table 6.2. Specific diagnostic criteria are provided for each category. These criteria are intended to provide the practitioner with a way to evaluate and classify the client's concerns. The *DSM-5* describes mental disorders as "syndromes characterized by clinically significant

TABLE 6.2   List of 20 Diagnostic Categories in the *DSM-5*
Neurodevelopmental Disorders
Schizophrenia Spectrum and Other Psychotic Disorders
Bipolar and Related Disorders
Depressive Disorders
Anxiety Disorders
Obsessive-Compulsive and Related Disorders
Trauma and Stressor-Related Disorders
Dissociative Disorders
Somatic Symptom and Related Disorders
Feeding and Eating Disorders
Elimination Disorders
Sleep–Wake Disorders
Sexual Dysfunctions
Gender Dysphoria
Disruptive, Impulse-Control, and Conduct Disorders
Substance-Related and Addictive Disorders
Neurocognitive Disorders
Personality Disorders
Medication-Induced Movement Disorders and Other Adverse Effects of Medication
Other Conditions that May be a Focus of Clinical Attention

disturbance in an individual's cognition, emotion regulation, or behavior that reflects a dysfunction in the psychological, biological, or developmental processes underlying mental functioning" (p. 20).

In perusing this list perhaps you can note a couple of things. First, the placement of the disorders within this list is not accidental! The disorders have been placed in a system based on their relatedness to each other and to their similarities in characteristics as well. Also, the order of the disorders reflects a developmental focus across the lifespan, beginning with the neurodevelopmental disorders that represent conditions developing earlier in life and ending with neurocognitive disorders that represent conditions developing in later life. In between these two anchors are disorders that are more commonly first manifested in adolescence and young adulthood. Within the discussion of each of these 20 disorders, there is also a

Learning Activity 6.2

Functional Assessment

In this learning activity, refer back to the case of Mrs. Oliverio found in Learning Activity 6.1 on page 187. Go through the case again. Then, complete as much of the grid in Figure 6.1 as you can from the information you have about the client. You may wish to complete this in dyads or small groups to brainstorm possible responses.

description of any criteria and specifiers relate to childhood manifestations and onset. Also, in the *DSM-5*, disorders have been arranged and classified according to clusters of disorders based on the factor of an internalizing or an externalizing disorders. **Internalizing disorders** are those such as anxiety and depression, whereas **externalizing disorders** involve conduct and impulse control issues and substance use.

The classification system in the *DSM-5* differs from prior editions of the *DSM* in that it is a nonaxial system. The clinician lists the principal diagnosis first and this diagnosis represents the focus of treatment. Secondary diagnoses that may also be present for a given client are listed underneath the principal one. Any other conditions that are not considered mental disorders but rather psychosocial and environmental problems that may impact the client's diagnosis and treatment are listed third. These include relational issues, abuse, educational and occupational problems, housing and economic issues, and so on.

Case Example of a *DSM-5* Diagnosis

As an example, consider the case of a 64-year-old white male who presents with the issue of having difficulty maintaining erections with his partner. He also mentions that he is 2 years away from retirement but his company is downsizing and has been laying off people in his age bracket and he has some concerns this will happen to him in the near future.

Assuming nothing else materialized in the assessment interviews, his *DSM-5* diagnosis would look like this:

302.72 (F52.21) Erectile Disorder
V62.29 (Z56.9) Other Problem Related to Employment

In our example with the 64-year-old client, for erectile disorder there are no subtypes but there are three possible specifiers: (1) whether the condition is lifelong or acquired; (2) whether the condition is generalized or situational; and (3) the current severity—if it is currently mild, moderate, or severe. Because he has indicated the issue began approximately 1 year ago and has not been lifelong, we would add the specifier Acquired. And because he also has suggested that it is present under conditions of sexual intercourse but not under masturbation, we would add the specifier Situational. And we would also, based on his self-report, add the specifier Moderate for current severity. Thus, his final diagnosis would look like this:

307.72, (F 52.21), Erectile Disorder, Acquired, Situational, Moderate Severity
V62.29 (Z 59.6) Problems related to Employment

Dimensional Classification, Specifiers, and Subtypes

One of the new features in the *DSM-5* is the approach to diagnosis reflected in this new edition that is dimensional rather than categorical. In other words, instead of a diagnosis being viewed as the presence or absence of a symptom as in a categorical approach, the *DSM-5* recognizes that separate disorders are often related conditions on a continuum, with some conditions being mild and other conditions being more severe; this is referred to as a **dimensional** diagnostic approach. Diagnostic categories such as bipolar disorders, autism, substance abuse, and schizophrenia are examples of disorders that are on a spectrum.

As part of this dimensional approach to assessment, many of the clinical disorders listed have what are called **specifiers**—these represent additional information about the diagnostic criteria that help with treatment planning.

The type of **specifiers** listed in the DSM-5 include the following:

Course: (partial or full remission)
Severity: (mild, moderate, severe)
Frequency (such as four episodes per week)
Duration (such as minimum duration of 6 months)
Descriptive features (such as poor insight)

Because these are not mutually exclusive, the practitioner may have more than one specifier listed in the diagnosis. For example, with delusional disorder, the practitioner might list if the delusions represent bizarre content as one specifier, and might also list whether this represents an initial episode or multiple episodes that are acute or are in partial or full remission. An additional specifier would be the severity of the delusions on a 5-point scale.

In addition, for some clinical disorders there are also **subtypes** of the disorder listed. **Subtypes** represent mutually exclusive descriptions within a diagnosis so the practitioner chooses one. For example, delusional disorders lists six possible subtypes of the primary disorder a practitioner chooses from to further describe the principal diagnosis.

Steps Involved in Making a Clinical Diagnosis with the *DSM-5*

A five-step process involved in making a clinical diagnosis using the *DSM-5* to do so is presented:

1. Identify the disorder that meets criteria in the DSM-5 manual.

2. Specify the name of the disorder, such as Hoarding Disorder

3. Next, add any subtype or specifiers that fit with the client's presentation (for hoarding disorder the specifiers include "with excessive acquisition" and "with absent, poor, or good insight")

4. Add the code number (located either at the top of the criteria set or within the subtypes or specifiers). In the *DSM-5* there is a **Bold** code and a code in parentheses. Recall that the **Bold** code refers to the *ICD-9 CM* and the code in parentheses refers to the *ICD-10 CM*.

In the event of multiple diagnoses, the focus of treatment or principal diagnosis is listed first, followed by other diagnoses in descending order of importance. For example, if hoarding is the primary disorder, and a secondary disorder is dependent personality disorder, then this would be listed and coded as follows:

300.3 (F42) Hoarding Disorder
301.6 (F60.7) Dependent Personality Disorder

5. If, in addition to the clinical diagnoses, there are other conditions that are also a focus in the clinical sessions, or are impacting the clinical disorder, recall that these would also be included and listed as a **V** (*ICD-9*) code or **Z** (*ICD -10*) code. For example, if a contributing condition to the client with the hoarding disorder was related to living alone, then we could add: **V60.3** (Z60.2) *Problem related to living alone* to this diagnosis. Also, while not required for a clinical diagnosis, if a particular client presented with a disability or an impairment, the *DSM-5* uses the World Health Organization Disability Assessment Schedule 2/0 (WHODAS 2.0), Section III, to note a disability or an impairment.

Despite apparent conceptual and practical limitations of diagnosis, the process can aid helpers in assessing target behaviors and in selecting appropriate interventions for treatment. For instance, knowledge about selected features of various types of clinical pathology, such as the usual age of the patient at the onset of some disorder or whether the disorder is more common in men or in women, can aid in assessment. An addition to the *DSM-5* is its routine inclusion of discussions of age, gender, and cultural implications of the various disorders. For example, it notes under panic attacks that fears about anxiety vary across cultures and it reports under agoraphobia that in some cultural or ethnic groups the participation of women in public life is restricted (APA, 2013).

Limitations of Diagnosis: Categories, Labels, and Gender/ Multicultural Biases

Diagnostic classification presents certain limitations, and these are most apparent when a client is given a diagnostic classification without the benefit of a thorough and complete assessment. The most common criticisms of diagnosis are that it places labels on clients—often meaningless ones—and that the labels themselves are not well defined and do not describe what the clients do or don't do that makes them "delusional" or "a conduct disorder" and so on. Some proponents of the strengths perspective we discussed earlier in the chapter question whether formulating diagnoses is in a client's best interest because of potential stigmatization associated with such labels.

In addition to these limitations, the process of making diagnoses using the current edition of the *Diagnostic and Statistical Manual* has come under sharp criticism from members of feminist therapy groups, from persons of color, and from those who are advocates for clients of color (Zalaquett et al., 2008, Paniagua & Yamada, 2013). For example, feminist therapists assert that the development of clinical disorders in women almost always involves a lack of both real and perceived power in their lives (Ballou & Brown, 2002). These therapists have noted that the concept of "distress," which permeates the traditional diagnostic classification system, reflects a "highly individualized phenomenon" and overlooks distress as "a manifestation of larger social and cultural forces" (Brown, 1992, p. 113). A feminist conception of diagnosis includes cultural relativity and ascertains what is normal for *this* individual at *this* particular time and place (Brown, 1992, p. 113). Thus, feminist practitioners would ask a client, "What has happened to you?" rather than, "What is wrong with you?" Similar concerns about bias in diagnosis have been raised by cross-cultural researchers and practitioners.

White Kress and colleagues (2005) note that "research and literature on cross-cultural assessment, diagnosis, and treatment continue to expose the inaccuracy of the DSM system with underrepresented and marginalized groups" (p. 98). Clients from these groups tend to be overdiagnosed, underdiagnosed, or misdiagnosed by clinicians. Misdiagnoses can easily occur when the languages between clinician and client are different and when the services of translators are not available or utilized. Sue and Sue (2013) point out that the history of oppression (described earlier by Brown for women) also affects resulting diagnoses made for clients of color who, because of this history, may be reluctant to self-disclose and, as a result, may be labeled *paranoid.* Sue and Sue (2013), like Brown, argue that diagnosis of clients of color must be understood from a larger social-political perspective. Otherwise, these clients may receive a diagnosis that overlooks the survival and protective value of their behaviors in a racist society. Further, the way in which disorders are experienced by clients varies with things like ethnicity, race, and age. For example, in many parts of Chinese society the experience of depression is more physical than psychological, and Latino/Latina clients as well as refugees may report symptoms of depressive disorders very differently than European Americans (Kleinman, 2004). Older clients may have more unique presentations of depression as well that impact clinical diagnoses (Gould, Edelstein, & Ciliberti, 2009).

In the *DSM-5,* in addition to very brief discussions of age, gender, and cultural features of many of the clinical disorders, there is an appendix that includes a glossary of nine various cultural concepts of distress—that is, what the *DSM-5* (APA, 2013) defines as "ways that cultural groups experience, understand, and communicate suffering, behavioral problems, or troubling thoughts and emotions" (p. 758). Paniagua (2013) has expanded this into a list of 19 culture-bound syndromes.

In addition to this glossary, the *DSM-5* appendix also includes an outline for a supplemental "**cultural formulation interview**" or CFI that, as they note, has been "field-tested for diagnostic usefulness among clinicians and for acceptability among patients" (p. 749). The CFI emphasizes four domains of assessment: Cultural Definitions of the Problem, Cultural Perceptions of Cause, Context, and Support, Cultural Factors Affecting Self-Coping, and Past Help Seeking and Cultural Factors Affecting Current Help Seeking. The manual includes both an interview outline that can be used with clients and informants, that is, family members or caregivers of the client. According to the *DSM-5,* "the boundaries between normality and pathology vary across cultures for specific types of behaviors" (p. 14).

One of the supplemental assessment tools in a diagnostic assessment that is used with some (but not all) clients is known as a mental status examination. We discuss this assessment tool in the next section.

Mental Status Examination

After conducting an initial interview, you may wish to conduct (or refer the client for) a mental status examination. A **mental status examination** is a model that allows the interviewer to assess current mental functioning of the client. It is not the same assessment tool as a diagnostic interview, although information gathered from the mental status examination may be linked to particular clinical disorders. As Sommers-Flanagan and Sommers-Flanagan (2014) point out, a formal mental status evaluation is not used with all clients. Their recommendation is that this assessment tool is used as the client's suspected level of psychopathology increases (Sommers-Flanagan & Sommers-Flanagan, 2014). Moreover, some clinicians believe the mental status examination has skewed results with culturally diverse clients because of the possibility of potentially invalid conclusions (Sommers-Flanagan & Sommers-Flanagan, 2014). Immigrant/refugee status, language differences, trust issues, cultural beliefs, cultural values, and norms can all affect the validity of the mental status examination with culturally diverse clients.

The major categories covered in a mental status exam include general *description and appearance of the client; mood and affect; perception; thought processes; level of consciousness; orientation to time, place, and people; memory; and impulse control.* Additionally, the examiner may note the degree to which the client appeared to report the information accurately and reliably. Of these categories, disturbances in **consciousness** (which involves ability to perform mental tasks, degree of effort, and degree of fluency/hesitation in task performance) and **orientation** (whether or not clients know when, where, and who they are and who other people are) are usually indicative of brain impairment or cognitive disorders and require neurological assessment and follow-up as well.

It is important for practitioners to know enough about the functions and content of a mental status exam to refer clients who might benefit from this additional assessment procedure. A summary of the content of a generic brief mental status exam is given in Table 6.3.

Although a mental status exam can provide a quick memory screening, it does not result in specific information about cognitive and memory impairments. To assess for dementia and cognitive impairment, an additional screening tool called the Mini-Mental Status exam (currently the MMSE-2) is used. (Note, do not confuse the two assessment tools because they share some of the same language in their titles!). The MMSE-2 is considered quite sensitive at detecting deficits in cognitive impairment. Zuckerman (2010) believes that two newer mental status tools, the St. Louis University Mental Status exam (available at aging.slu.edu) and the Montreal Cognitive Assessment (available at www.mocatest.org), are even more sensitive for detecting mild cognitive impairment than the MMSE-2. Also, a very new brief mental status exam that is available for use as a rapid assessment of

---

TABLE 6.3   Summary of Brief Mental Status Exam

Note the client's physical appearance, including dress, posture, gestures, and facial expressions.

Note the client's attitude and response to you, including alertness, motivation, passivity, distance, and warmth.

Note whether there were any client sensory or perceptual behaviors that interfered with the interaction.

Note the general level of information displayed by the client, including vocabulary, judgment, and abstraction abilities.

Note whether the client's stream of thought and rate of talking were logical and connected.

Note the client's orientation to four issues: people, place, time, and reason for being there (sometimes this is described as "orientation by four").

Note the client's ability to recall immediate, recent, and past information.

---

cognitive status in older adults is the Sweet 16 (Fong et al., 2011). This instrument is available as open access because it is not copyrighted. Mental status checklists suitable for child and adolescent clients can also be found at www4.parinc.com. For additional information about mental status examinations and neurophysiologic assessment, see Morrison (2014) and Zuckerman (2010).

Diagnostic Interviewing

In clinical settings, the interview(s) used to assess clinical disorders is known as the **diagnostic interview** (Segal & Hersen, 2009). Jones (2010) observes that once the task of only medically trained psychiatrists, now diagnostic interviewing is in the scope of practice of many master's level–trained practitioners. Accreditation standards in clinical kinds of programs such as counseling, social work, and psychology also require that trainees become familiar with diagnostic interviewing.

Diagnostic interviews may be unstructured, semistructured, or structured. As Jones (2010) notes, unstructured diagnostic interviews consist of "questions posed by the counselor with the client responses and counselor observations recorded by the counselor. This type of interview is considered unstructured because there is no standardization of questioning or recording of client responses" (p. 220). Jones (2010) describes a comprehensive general interview outline that practitioners can use to engage in an unstructured diagnostic interview with adult clients. We have integrated some of her suggestions into our discussion of the components of intake and history interviews.

Summerfeldt, Kloosterman, and Antony (2010) note that in the past three decades we have witnessed the development and use of a variety of both semistructured and structured diagnostic clinical interview protocols that are designed to minimize the sources of variability that make diagnosis unreliable (p. 95). Moreover, some new research has found that across inpatient, outpatient, and research settings, these kinds of more structured diagnostic

interviews are rated positively by both consumers and helpers (Suppiger et al., 2009).

Structured diagnostic interview schedules are available that consist of a standardized list of questions, a standardized sequence of questioning, including follow-up questions, as well as a systematic rating of client responses (Bagby, Wild, & Turner, 2003; Jones, 2010). The Anxiety Disorders Interview Schedule for *DSM-IV* (ADIS-IV) (Brown, DiNardo, & Barlow, 1994), the ADIS-IV: C for children (Silverman & Albano, 1996), the Diagnostic Interview for Borderline Patients (DIB-R) (Zanarini, Frankenburg, & Vujanovic, 2002), and the Depression Interview and Structured Hamilton (DISH) (Freedland et al., 2002) are all examples of structured diagnostic interview schedules.

Semistructured diagnostic interviews are still somewhat structured in the use of specific questions but allow the clinician more flexibility in the use of follow-up questions (Jones, 2010). A semistructured diagnostic interview compatible with the *DSM-5* is the SCID-5, which is published by the American Psychiatric Publishing group and available at www.appi.org. For examples and information of additional structured and semistructured clinical interview protocols, consult Summerfeldt, Kloosterman, and Antony (2010).

Generally, both structured and semistructured interviews have better reliability than unstructured interviews, meaning that different interviewers would be more likely to arrive at the same diagnosis for a particular client. However, as Summerfeldt, Kloosterman, and Antony (2010) point out, the reliability of a diagnostic interview is determined by many factors, including the clarity and nature of the questions asked, the degree and consistency of training of interviewers, the conditions in which the interview is conducted, the type of reliability assessed, and so on.

Sommers-Flanagan and Sommers-Flanagan (2014) summarize a number of issues about diagnostic interviewing from the research-based literature. They note that diagnostic interviews can produce more reliable results in diagnosis if the practitioner sticks with the *DSM* diagnostic criteria rather closely. They also note that training in diagnostic interviewing enhances the reliability of the process. Finally, they suggest that while structured diagnostic interviews that deemphasize contextual factors are more likely to produce reliable diagnoses, they are also more likely to overlook individual difference (p. 341). As an example of the latter issue, consider that most of the screening and diagnostic tools were developed for use with younger rather than older adults (Edelstein et al., 2008).

Sensitive Subjects and Risk Assessment in Diagnostic Interviewing

Morrison (2014) has pointed out that some important subjects that come up in intake and assessment interviews can be sensitive for both helpers and clients. This potential sensitivity does not mean that such subjects should be overlooked or discarded. However, it does mean that the helper should proceed with good judgment and seek consultation about when it is appropriate to assess these areas. On one hand, it may be seen as voyeuristic if a male counselor asks a young female presenting with an academic/career issue about her sexual practices and activity. On the other hand, if a client comes in and discusses problems in dating persons of the opposite sex and feelings of attraction to same-sex people, not pursuing this subject would be an important omission.

Specific subjects that may fall into the category of sensitive topics include questions about (1) suicidal thoughts and behavior; (2) homicidal ideas and violent behavior; (3) substance use, including alcohol, street drugs, and prescribed medications; (4) sexual issues, including sexual orientation, sexual practices, and sexual problems; and (5) physical, emotional, and sexual abuse, both past and current. Zuckerman (2010) has developed some structured interview questions to utilize for sensitive subjects such as these topics. In general, we should point out that omitting questions about sensitive topics is not considered optional! Each and every client should be asked about potential harm to self and others and substance use, and also should be screened for sexual, physical, and emotional abuse. Koven, Shreve-Neiger, and Edelstein (2007) recommend an interviewing strategy for handling sensitive subjects called the "plus minus approach." In this approach, the clinician balances difficult questions with those that are less threatening so that if a client reacts

emotionally to a difficult question, the interviewer follows up with a question that is more benign.

Risk Assessment: Violence or Harm to Others

A particular category of sensitive subjects has to do with potential **lethality or danger to self or others**. Interest in this sensitive area has mushroomed with recent events such as suicide bombings and school shootings. Domestic violence is another area that may be very relevant for mental health inquiries and assessment. Although an in-depth discussion of the assessment of lethality and risk is beyond the scope of this book, we include some brief comments about this topic and recommend additional resources.

The MacArthur study of high-risk clients for violence (excluding verbal threats for violence) identified more than 100 potential risk factors for violence but found no "magic bullet" predictor of future violence. The findings from this study suggest that a person's propensity for violence is the accumulation and interaction of a number of risk factors, including criminological factors (such as history of violence and criminality), childhood experiences (such as physical abuse), environmental conditions (such as poverty and unemployment), and clinical risk factors (such as substance abuse, antisocial personality disorder, persistent violent thoughts and fantasies, and anger control issues). The findings of the MacArthur risk assessment study are summarized by Monahan and colleagues (2001). The American Psychiatric Association recently published a task force report on psychiatric violence risk assessment (Buchanan, Binder, Norko, & Swartz, 2012). They note that crimes of violence are often committed by younger males with prior offenses and abuse of substances. This report also summarizes a number of risk factors but, like the MacArthur study, notes no magic bullet predictors of future violence. This report also delineates between the important distinction between predicting violence and managing violence.

Interview Leads/Questions for Harm to Others/Violence In the intake or history interview, questions about violence can be raised if the client discusses "arrests or time in confinement" (Morrison, 2014, p. 101). If clients do not indicate any legal difficulties such as these, you can raise the topic by asking questions such as those recommended by Morrison (2014, p. 102) and Zuckerman (2010, p. 78):

> "Have you ever had any thoughts of harming others? If so, how far ahead have you planned it?"
> "Have you ever had any trouble controlling your impulses?" "Lost your temper?"
> "Threatened to harm someone else or an animal?"

"Have you ever had feelings of uncontrollable rage?"
"Have you ever broken things, raised your fist, gotten into someone's face, grabbed, pinched, kicked someone?"
"Have you ever used a weapon of any kind such as a knife or something else?"

Affirmative responses to these questions need to be explored with follow-up queries such as exploration of the circumstances of the violence, whether substance use was involved, and the consequences.

While there are a number of structured risk assessment measures for assessing violence, a recent review and meta-analysis of these tools found low to moderate predictive values, depending primarily on how the instrument is used (Fazel, Singh, Doll, & Grann 2012). These authors conclude that "even after 30 years of development the view that violence, sexual, or criminal risk can be predicted in most cases is not evidence-based" (p. 9). These authors also warn that using structured risk assessment tools on their own is not sufficient for the purposes of risk assessment of violence.

If you are interviewing a client with the potential for or history of violence, it is crucial to become very aware of your own safety in the session. As Morrison (2014) notes, practically speaking, this means holding a session where others are nearby, seating yourself closer to the door than the client in case you should have to make an emergency exit, and having available some sort of easily triggered emergency alert system such as an alarm bell. Many practitioners have been stalked (either in person or in cyberspace), threatened, and/or physically attacked by at least one client. There is insufficient literature and training available to prepare practitioners to deal with potentially violent clients and to support helpers in the aftermath of attack. Consultation with colleagues and supervisors about this issue is very important, especially when dealing with a client who has a history of harassment, stalking, and aggression.

Risk Assessment: Harm to Self

Helping professionals are responsible for conducting suicide risk assessments or **harm to self** with all clients. In the United States, deaths from suicide now exceed those from vehicular crashes. There are a number of potential risk factors associated with suicidality in clients, although as Sommers-Flanagan and Sommers-Flanagan (2014) assert, "an absence of these factors in an individual client is no guarantee that he or she is safe from suicidal impulses" (p. 292). Among these factors, depression, particularly hopelessness, perceived burdensomeness, substance abuse, history of trauma *and* victimization, and prior attempts are key risk factors. For older adults, risk factors

include current mood disorders, psychiatric hospital admission within the previous year, limited social network, and negatively perceived health status and sleep quality (Gould, Edelstein, & Ciliberti, 2009). Warning signs of suicide include suicidal thoughts (also known technically as "ideation"), having a plan and the means to carry it out, expressions of meaninglessness or lack of purpose, relationship losses, notable changes in behaviors, and giving away of possessions (Sommers-Flanagan & Sommers-Flanagan, 2014). The top three warning signs include a threat to hurt or kill oneself, an attempt to find a means to hurt or kill oneself, and talking or writing about hurting or killing oneself.

Stuctured Clinical Interview Guides for Harm to Self and Suicide Assessment   In the area of suicide risk assessment, there are several useful structured clinical interview guides to assess potential danger to self. Chief among these are the Adolescent Suicide Assessment Protocol-20 (Fremouw, Strunk, Tyner, & Musick, 2005) and the Suicidal Adult Assessment Protocol (Fremouw, Tyner, Strunk, & Musick, 2008). These two protocols present a brief, user-friendly, structured clinical interview designed for practitioners to obtain an initial objective measure of adolescent and adult suicidal risk (Fremouw et al., 2005, p. 207). Both interview protocols include assessment of client demographic factors (such as gender, age, and marital status), historical factors (such as prior attempts and childhood abuse), clinical items (such as depression and hopelessness, impulsivity, and substance abuse), specific suicidal risk questions (such as thoughts, plans, and intentions), contextual factors (such as firearm access, recent loss, stressors, and social isolation), and protective factors (such as family responsibilities, spiritual and/or religious beliefs, and social support). At the completion of the structured interview, each client is classified according to level of risk; depending on that level of risk, the interviewer will identify various forms of action and intervention such as consultation, increased monitoring, contracting, notification, referrals to other forms of treatment, and elimination of the method of suicide. A brief, structured suicide assessment interview protocol suitable for use as a basic screening tool across many kinds of settings has been developed by Bryan, Corso, Neil-Walden, and Rudd (2009). Two specific suicide risk assessment instruments have been developed specifically for older adults (Edelstein, Woodhead, Segal, Heisel, Bower, Lowery, 2008).

These interview protocols help practitioners use a more systematic approach to suicide risk assessment, underscoring the fact that suicide risk assessment is a must, not an option, in a history-taking or intake interview, even if this subject is not raised by the client. Some clients may be at a serious risk for suicide but feel too embarrassed or despondent to share their concerns about it with the helper. Moreover, it is a myth that mentioning the topic could plant this idea in a client's mind! (Morrison, 2014). In fact, talking about suicide in appropriate ways actually seems to decrease the risk, because most suicidal individuals do not really want to die as much as they simply want to find a way to end their psychic pain (Shallcross, 2010).

Interview Leads/Questions for Harm to Self and Suicide Risk Assessment At the most basic level, including the question, "Have you ever had any thoughts of hurting or killing yourself?" in any intake or history interview is essential. We like the way that Zuckerman (2010, p. 76) approaches this initial question in the interview:

> You have told me about some very painful experiences. They must have been hard to bear, and perhaps you sometimes thought of quitting the struggle or harming yourself in some way—or perhaps ending your life. Is this true for you?

Follow-up queries, depending on the client's response, include things such as whether there have been prior attempts, methods used for such attempts, whether the client has a plan in place for a future attempt, whether the client possesses firearms, current stressors in the client's life, influence of substances, current social support or lack thereof in the client's life, reasons to live, things the client cares about (including animals, as well as people, values, projects, and so on), and the client's level of depression, hopelessness, and feelings of burdensomeness.

Hunsley and Lee (2014) provide a list of empirically supported questions to use in conducing suicide risk assessments with clients:

Have you had any thoughts of suicide recently?

When you think about suicide, what exactly do you think about?

Have you ever attempted suicide?

Have you made any plans for taking your life, such as obtaining the means to commit suicide?

Do you think you could follow through on a suicide attempt?

What are the reasons that you would consider suicide as an option?

Have you ever hurt yourself intentionally, such as by cutting or burning yourself?

Tell me about your family and friends. Do you feel supported and are you able to talk to them about your problems?

Do you think that anything can be done about your problems? (p. 182).

Cultural sensitivity is important in suicide risk assessment. When working with immigrants and refugees, some direct questions about suicidality may be met with silence or minimal responses. It is also important to realize that suicide risk can be both acute and chronic. Anyone who has two or more prior attempts is probably considered a chronic risk. As Pope and Vasquez (2011) note, remaining alert to the issue of suicide risk assessment throughout the therapeutic process is extremely important. In other words, suicide risk assessment is not just a "one shot" assessment.

In the following section, we describe ways in which sensitive topics and risk assessments are integrated into intake/history interviews with clients.

Intake Interviews and History

Part of assessment involves eliciting information [L02] about the client's background, especially as it may relate to *current* concerns. Past, or historical, information is not sought as an end in itself or because the helper is necessarily interested in exploring or focusing on the client's past during treatment. Rather, it is used as a part of the overall assessment process that helps the practitioner fit the pieces of the puzzle together concerning the client's presenting issues and current life context. Often a client's current issues are precipitated by events found in the client's history. In no case is this more valid than with clients who have suffered trauma of one kind or another. For example, a 37-year-old woman came to a crisis center because of the sudden onset of extreme anxiety. The interviewer noticed that she was talking in a little girl voice and was using gestures that appeared to be very childlike. The clinician commented on this behavior and asked the client how old she felt right now. The client replied, "I'm 7 years old," and went on to reveal spontaneously an incident in which she had walked into a room in an aunt's house and found her uncle fondling her cousin. No one had seen her, and she had forgotten this event until the present time. In cases such as this one, history may serve as a retrospective baseline measure for the client and may help to identify cognitive or historical conditions that still exert influence on the current issue and might otherwise be overlooked.

The process of gathering information about the client's background is called **history taking**. In many agency settings, history taking occurs during an initial interview called an **intake interview**. An intake interview is viewed as informational rather than therapeutic and, to underscore this point, is often conducted by someone other than the practitioner assigned to see the client. In these situations, someone else, such as an intake worker, sees the client for an interview, summarizes the information in writing, and passes the information along to the helper.

Various kinds of information can be solicited during history taking, but the most important areas are the following:

1. *Identifying information about the client.* Jones (2010) notes that the diagnostic clues provided by this information include both gender, race, and referral source.

2. *Presenting problems/symptoms, including history related to the presenting concerns.* Jones (2010) suggests that helpers listen especially for psychological symptoms, behavioral patterns, stressors, and interpersonal conflicts (p. 221).

3. *Psychiatric and/or counseling history/treatment and previous diagnosis.* Jones (2010) suggests that practitioners inquire not only about prior counseling but also about prior hospitalizations.

4. *Educational and job history.* Jones (2010) suggests that problems in academic achievement have been linked to substance abuse problems and the onset of early mental illness. Similarly, issues in work history may be indicative of disabling clinical disorders (p. 223).

5. *Health and medical history.* Some clients, such as indigent clients, older adults, and clients with disabling clinical disorders, may be at increased risk for medical conditions (Jones, 2010, p. 224). Jones (2010) lists a number of common medical conditions associated with psychological symptoms, including thyroid disorders, cardiac disorders, head trauma, neurological disorders, circulatory disorders, hepatitis, seizure disorder, lupus, electrolyte disturbances, and B-vitamin deficiencies (p. 224). Zuckerman (2010) describes the situation in which a client presents with psychological symptoms caused by a medical condition that is not immediately (and often never) recognized as "psychiatric masquerade" (p. 359). In his clinical thesaurus, he describes a number of specific medical conditions that may masquerade as psychological symptoms.

6. *Social/developmental history,* including religious, spiritual, and cultural background and affiliations, predominant values, chronological/developmental events, military background, social/leisure activities, present social situation, legal problems, and substance use history. Hunsley and Mash (2010) point out that awareness of what constitutes normative developmental tasks and age-related functioning throughout the lifespan is helpful in assessing history (p. 12). Knowledge of key developmental transitions is also useful (Ingram, 2006). Jones (2010) asserts that identifying known childhood and adolescent risk factors helps to establish information about clinical disorders in adulthood (p. 223).

7. *Family, marital, relationship, sexual history,* including any abuse history, partner status, and sexual orientation information. Jones (2010) recognizes that clinical disorders are often associated with family history and the client's current or prior interactions with family members (p. 222). Relationship history is useful in determining if the client has demonstrated the ability to initiate and sustain intimate relationships (Jones, 2010, p. 222). Changes in relationship status as well as violence in relationship or marital history also provide important diagnostic clues.

8. *Substance use and legal history.* Screening for alcohol and drug use is considered important regardless of the client's presenting issues; this can begin with less threatening subjects such as caffeine and tobacco use, followed by alcohol and other drug use. For some clients, substance abuse and legal history are connected.

9. *Military history.* In these times, it is not uncommon to encounter clients who are serving or have served in the military (often with multiple tours of duty), or who are members of a soldier's or veteran's family. Military history provides clues about possible posttraumatic stress.

10. *Suicidal and/or homicidal ideation.* Assess for ideation, plans, prior attempts, impulse control, reasons for living

11. *Behavioral observations,* including assessment of client communication patterns and appearance and demeanor; mental status assessment would be included here if applicable.

12. *Goals for counseling and therapy/treatment.*

13. *Diagnostic (DSM) summary.*

14. *Person-in-environment (PIE) classification.*

Table 6.4 presents specific questions or content areas to cover for each of these 14 areas.

TABLE 6.4 History-Taking Interview Content

1. Identifying information:
   Client's name, address, home and work telephone number; name of another person to contact in case of emergency

   Age

Gender	Disabilities
Ethnicity and indigenous heritage	Occupation
Race	Citizenship status
Languages	Referral source

2. Presenting concerns:
   Note the presenting concern (quote the client directly). Do this for *each* concern that the client presents.

   When did it start? What other events were occurring at that time?

   How often does it occur?

   What thoughts, feelings, and observable behaviors are associated with it?

   Where and when does it occur most? Least often?

   Are there any events or persons that precipitate it? Any specific stressors associated with it? Make it better? Make it worse?

   What chain of events led up to it?

   How much does it interfere with the client's daily functioning?

   What previous solutions/plans have been tried and with what result?

   What made the client decide to seek help at this time (or, if referred, what influenced the referring party to refer the client at this time)?

3. Psychiatric/counseling history:
   Previous counseling and/or psychological/psychiatric treatment

   Type of treatment

   Length of treatment

   Treatment place or person

   Presenting concern

   Outcome of treatment and reason for termination

   Previous hospitalization

   Prescription drugs for emotional and or psychological issues

   Nonprescription supplements used for emotional and psychological issues

4. Educational/job history:
   Trace academic progress (strengths and weaknesses) from grade school through last level of education completed

   Relationships with teachers and peers

   Types of jobs held by client and socioeconomic history, current employment, and socioeconomic status

   Length of jobs

   Reason for termination or change

   Relationships with coworkers

   Aspects of work that are most stressful or anxiety producing

   Aspects of work that are least stressful or most enjoyable

   Overall degree of current job satisfaction

5. Health/medical history:
   Childhood diseases, prior significant illnesses, previous surgeries

   Current health-related complaints or illnesses (e.g., headache, hypertension)

   Treatment received for current complaints: what type and by whom

   Date of last physical examination and results

   Significant health problems in client's family of origin (parents, grandparents, siblings)

   Significant health problems in client

   Client's sleep patterns

   Client's appetite level

(*continued*)

TABLE 6.4   History-Taking Interview Content (*continued*)

Current medications (e.g., aspirin, vitamins, birth control pills, recreational substance use, prescription medications)

Drug and nondrug allergies

Disability history

Client's typical daily diet, including caffeine-containing beverages/food, alcoholic beverages, and use of nicotine or tobacco products

Exercise patterns

6. Social/developmental/ history:

Current life situation (typical day/week, living arrangements, occupation and economic situation, contact with other people)

Social/leisure time activities, hobbies

Religious affiliation, childhood and current

Spiritual beliefs and concerns

Contacts with people (support systems, family, and friends) and notations about whether such contacts are acquaintances or close, personal friends

Community and cultural affiliations

Significant events reported for the following developmental periods: (note especially behavior problems, school problems, child/adolescent depression, ADHD symptoms, child abuse, traumas, losses as delineated by Jones (2010, p. 223)

Preschool (0–6 years)

Childhood (6–13 years)

Adolescence (13–21 years)

Young adulthood (21–30 years)

Middle adulthood (30–65 years)

Late adulthood (65 years and over)

7. Family, marital, relationship, sexual history:

Presence of physical, sexual, and/or emotional abuse from parent, sibling, or someone else

Composition of the family while client was living at home

Identifying information of client's parents and siblings (age, occupation, education, birth order of siblings)

How well parents got along with each other

Which sibling appeared to be most favored by mother? By father? Least favored by mother? By father?

Which sibling did client get along with best? Worst?

History of previous psychiatric illness/hospitalization among members of client's family of origin

Child abuse, domestic violence, other traumas in the family, including family history of suicide

Use of substances in family of origin

Dating history, prior relationships

Engagement/marital history, reason for termination of relationship

Current relationship with intimate partner (how well they get along, problems, stresses, enjoyment, satisfaction, and so on)

Prior and/or current violence in relationships

Number and ages of client's children

Other people living with or visiting family frequently

Description of previous sexual experience, including first one (note whether heterosexual, homosexual, or bisexual experiences are reported)

Present sexual activity

Any present concerns or complaints about sexual attitudes or behaviors

Current sexual orientation

8. Substance use and legal history:

Assess for tobacco use, including cigarettes, cigars, pipe, snuff

Assess for caffeine use, including coffees, teas, soft drinks, caffeine tablets, chocolate, and energy drinks like Red Bull

Assess for prescription and legal drug use, such as sedatives, hypnotics, anxiolytics, and central nervous system depressants. Note combinations of drugs and issues indicating intoxication and withdrawal.

Assess for alcohol use.

Assess for nonlegal drug use, including stimulants, opioids, hallucinogens, MDMA, dissociative anesthetics, inhalants, and cannabis. Zuckerman (2010) suggests beginning this assessment with the question: *What is/are your drugs of choice/preference?* (p. 71).

Detailed information also should be obtained in these categories about both history and consumption of the listed substances.

Ask about whether substance use has ever resulted in any legal issues.

Inquire about other legal issues such as tickets, detentions, warrants, convictions, probation, parole, evictions, bankruptcies, conflicts with others, abuse issues, protection from abuse orders (Zuckerman, 2010).

9. Military history:

Assess for reserve or active duty

Branch of service

Duration of duty, number of tours of duty

Combat or war zone duty

Type of discharge

Prior and current consequences of service for client and family

10. Suicidal and homicidal ideation:

Presence or absence of suicidal thoughts; if present, explore onset, frequency, antecedent events, duration, and intensity of such thoughts—ranging from *almost never*, to *occasional*, *weekly*, and/or *daily*.

Presence or absence of suicidal plan; if present, explore details of plan, including method, lethality, availability of method, and timeline of plan.

Prior suicide threats and attempts by the client and also attempts/completions by family members

Prior and/or current intentional self-harm or self-injurious behaviors such as cutting, burning

Overall suicidal intent—nonexistent, low, moderate, severe

Presence or absence of homicidal ideation; client attitudes that support or contribute to violence

Presence or absence of homicidal plan; if present, explore details of plan, including method, means, availability of means, timeline of means, intended victim(s)

Prior homicidal threats and acts—instances and patterns

Overall homicidal intent—nonexistent, low, moderate, severe

11. Behavioral observations (also include mental status results if administered):

General appearance and demeanor

Client communication patterns

12. Goals for counseling and therapy:

Client's desired results for treatment

Client's motivation for getting help at this time

13. Diagnostic summary (if applicable) and *DSM-5/ICD* codes:

14. PIE classification (Karls & Wandrei, 1994):

Factor I: Social Role Problem Identification: severity, duration, coping and strength indices, type of social role problem, type of interactional difficulty

Factor II: Environmental Problem Identification: severity, duration, and strength indices, type of environmental problem area and associated discrimination code

---

The sequence of obtaining this information in a history or an intake interview is important. Generally, the interviewer begins with the least threatening topics and saves more sensitive topics until near the end of the session, when a greater degree of rapport has been established and the client feels more at ease about revealing personal information to a total stranger. Not all of this information may be required for all clients. Obviously, this guide will have to be adapted for use with different clients—especially those of varying ages, such as children, adolescents, and the elderly, who may need a simpler way to provide such information and in a shorter amount of time.

Cultural Issues in Intake and Assessment Interviews

It is important to note and account for sources of cultural bias within a traditional intake interview and within assessment interviews in general. Canino and Spurlock (2000) point out that "in some cultures disturbed behavior may be viewed as related to a physical disorder or willfulness"; therefore, talking about the behavior is not expected to help (p. 75). In some cultural groups, there is a sanction against revealing personal information to someone outside the family or extended family circle. Also, clients' perceptions of what is socially desirable and undesirable behavior as well as their perceptions of psychological distress may reflect values different from the ones held by the practitioner: "Certain cultural factors must be considered in determining the normalcy or pathology of a response. For example, 'hearing the Lord speak' may be a culture-specific impression and therefore nonpathological for some religious groups. An inner-city African American adolescent's statement 'All whites are out to get us' may actually represent the thinking of the community in which he lives rather than qualify as a sign of paranoia" (Canino & Spurlock, 2000, p. 80).

In interpreting the information received from an intake interview and mental status exam, remember that some information can have cultural meanings that are unknown to you. For example, some cultures view the child as 1 year old at the time of birth; other cultures may favor the use of culturally sanctioned healing remedies instead of traditional Western medical or psychological treatment. Also, cultures have different practices regarding discipline of children and adolescents, so what you may view as either indulgent or harsh may not be seen that way by the client and the client's collective community. What constitutes a "family" also varies among cultures; in assessing for family history, it is important to ask about extended family members who may live outside the household as well as about a parent's significant other. Clients might also report religious and spiritual beliefs that are unfamiliar to the helper, and these can affect the client's help-seeking behavior and perceptions of distress.

Microaggressions in Intake and Assessment Interviews

Another issue pertaining to cultural dimensions of clients in intake and assessment interviews has to do with **microaggressions**—verbal comments or queries that communicate a derogatory slight or insult to the client (Sue, 2010). For example, a culturally insensitive interviewer may actually demonstrate some form of racial or ethnic profiling in an intake interview by assuming something pejorative about the client based solely on the client's race or ethnicity. An example of this would be a practitioner posing more questions about substance use with Native American clients than with other clients and viewing their reports of a nonexistent history with substances as "suspicious" (Sue, 2010). Another example provided by Sue and colleagues (2007) of a microaggressive act in an intake interview would be acting on the assumption that Asian Americans and Latino Americans are "foreign born." As Sue and his colleagues (2007) explain, "A female Asian American client arrives for

her first therapy session. Her therapist asks her where she is from, and when told 'Philadelphia,' the therapist further probes by asking where she was born. In this case, the therapist has assumed that the Asian American client is not from the United States and has imposed through the use of the second question the idea that she must be a foreigner" (p. 281). Microaggressions in interviews also can occur with clients who are older and/or have some kind of disability. For example, a practitioner may assume that an older adult cannot hear well and consequently the practitioner speaks to the client in a very loud voice. Or a clinician may assume that because a client has a visible disability that the client is not smart enough to process something that the clinician would assess with a nondisabled client. (See Learning Activity 6.3.)

Another challenge faced by practitioners in conducting intake and assessment interviews involves clients who do not speak English as their primary language. In these instances, when alternative helpers are not available, translators and interpreters may be brought in. The use of ancillary persons, while a culturally sensitive option, presents new issues in terms of confidentiality and privacy (Hunsley & Lee, 2010).

Additional guidelines for conducting cross-cultural clinical interviews have been provided by Martinez (2013). He observes that with clients from marginalized cultural groups that there may be "other layers of complexity" in ascertaining the client's presenting issues as some clients may describe presenting symptoms in words and phrases that are not understood to the practitioner.

There are several examples of culturally sensitive interview protocols. One such protocol, developed by Tanaka-Matsumi, Seiden, and Lam (1996), is the Culturally Informed Functional Assessment (CIFA) Interview. Designed to define client issues in a culturally sensitive manner, this interview protocol includes a variety of steps such as assessing the cultural identity and acculturation status of the client, assessing the client's presenting issues with reference to the client's cultural norms, probing explanations of the client's issue and possible solutions to avoid pathologizing seemingly unusual but yet culturally normative responses, conducting a functional assessment of the client's problem behaviors, and determining

Learning Activity 6.3

Cultural Issues in Assessment

In a dyad or a small group, identify examples of both potential and actual microaggressions that could easily occur in intake and history-taking sessions with clients.

whether the client's reactions to controlling variables are similar to or different from customary reactions of one's cultural referent group(s).

History taking (and mental status exams, if applicable) usually occur near the very beginning of the helping process. After obtaining this sort of preliminary information about the client as well as an idea of the range of presenting complaints, you are ready to do some direct assessment interviewing with the client to define the parameters of concerns more specifically. Direct assessment interviewing is the focus of our following chapter.

Putting it all Together: Evidence-Based Assessment and Conceptualization

At the beginning of our chapter, we stated that assessment is about helping our clients tell and develop their story. As helpers, we facilitate this process through many of the interviewing skills we have described in earlier chapters. We also use the lens of the assessment models and tools described in this chapter to help clients develop the narrative. Then, we have the task of integrating all the parts of the story into a cohesive whole, into a narrative that helps to answer questions and to make sense of varying parts. This includes a descriptive account of the client's prior and current life situation, the clinical disorders and potential diagnoses, the client's overall level of functioning including strengths and adaptive functioning, cultural factors, problem behaviors, and maintaining conditions. In short, **conceptualization** requires synthesis of a wide range of information and data obtained during assessment for the purpose of generating answers to questions about how the client can best be helped. The conceptualization process helps us figure out possible explanations for the development and maintenance of the client's problems and concerns. Helpers of almost all theoretical orientations engage in this sort of conceptualization process, although varying theoretical orientations are likely to develop different kinds of hunches and hypotheses about clients. As Hunsley and Mash (2008) observe, "the assessment process is inherently a decision-making task" in which practitioners formulate and test hypotheses by integrating data that are incomplete or inconsistent (p. 7).

Ingram (2012) asserts that developing and applying hypotheses about client cases is one of the most complex tasks facing practitioners. As she notes, it involves a number of processes including a search for the best-fit hypotheses that are compatible with the assessment data

for the individual client, testing the fit of the hypothesis by gathering data to rule it in or out and combining hypotheses that are efficient and accurate enough to lead to a good treatment plan (p. 12). Unfortunately, therapeutic bias can lead to errors in clinical decision-making; awareness of bias may help to minimize the impact of clinical decision-making errors in our conceptualization process (Hunsley & Lee, 2010). We can also enhance our clinical decision-making with practice of assessment and conceptualization processes as illustrated in the following model case and learning activities.

Model Case: Conceptualizing

To assist you in conceptualizing client concerns with the models from this chapter, we provide a case illustration followed by two practice cases for you to analyze in Learning Activity 6.4. The conceptual understanding you should acquire from this chapter will help you actually define and conceptualize client issues with a clinical interview assessment, which is the focus of our next chapter!

The Case

Isabella is a 15-year-old student completing her sophomore year of high school and presently taking a college preparatory curriculum. Her initial statement in the first counseling session is that she is "unhappy" and anxious at school, except when she is socializing with her friends. On further clarification, Isabella reveals that she is unhappy and worried because she doesn't think she is measuring up to her classmates and that she dislikes being with these "top" kids in her classes, who are very competitive. She reports feeling "on edge" at school, having difficulty focusing or concentrating, and trouble falling asleep due to staying awake at night and worrying about school the following day, particularly her "performance" in school. Her teachers have noticed her lapses in concentration and suggested she speak with you, the school counselor.

She reports particular concern in one math class, which she says is composed largely of "guys" who are much smarter than she is. She states that she thinks about the fact that "girls are so dumb in math" rather frequently during the class and she feels intimidated. She reports that as soon as she is in this class, she gets anxious and "withdraws." She states that she sometimes gets anxious just thinking about the class, and she says that when this happens she gets "butterflies" in her stomach, her palms get sweaty and cold, and her heart beats faster. When asked what she means by "withdrawing," she says she sits by herself, doesn't talk to her classmates, and doesn't

Learning Activity 6.4

Assessment Models

To help you in conceptualizing a client's issue, we provide two cases. We suggest that you work through the first case completely before going on to the second. After reading each case, respond to the questions following the case by yourself or with a partner. Then, compare your responses with the feedback on page 211.

The Case of Ms. Weare and Freddie

Ms. Weare and her 9-year-old son, Freddie, have come to Family Services after Ms. Weare said she had reached her limit with her son and needed to talk to another adult about it. Their initial complaint is that they don't get along with each other. Ms. Weare complains that Freddie doesn't get himself ready in the morning, and this makes her mad. Freddie complains that his mother yells and screams at him frequently. Ms. Weare agrees that she does, especially when it is time for Freddie to leave for school and he isn't ready yet. Freddie agrees that he doesn't get himself ready and points out that he does this just to "get Mom mad."

Ms. Weare says this has been going on as long as she can remember. She states that Freddie gets up and usually comes down to breakfast not dressed. After breakfast, Ms. Weare always reminds him to get ready and threatens that she'll yell or hit him if he doesn't. Freddie usually goes back to his room, where, he reports, he just sits around until his mother comes up. Ms. Weare waits until 5 minutes before the bus comes and then calls Freddie. After he doesn't come down, she goes upstairs and sees that he's not ready. She reports that she gets very mad and yells, "You're dumb! Why do you just sit there? Why can't you dress yourself? You're going to be late for school! Your teacher will blame me because I'm your mother." She also helps Freddie get ready. So far, he has not been late, but Ms. Weare says she "knows" he will be if she doesn't "nag" him and help him get ready. When asked about the option of removing her help and letting Freddie get ready on his own, she says that he is a smart kid who is doing well in school and that she doesn't want this factor to change. She never finished high school herself, and she doesn't want that to happen to Freddie. She also says that if he didn't have her help, he would probably just stay at home that day and she wouldn't get any of her own work done.

On further questioning, Ms. Weare says this behavior does not occur on weekends, only on school days. She states that as a result of this situation, although she's never punished him physically, she feels very nervous and edgy after Freddie leaves for school, often not doing some necessary work because of this feeling. Asked what she means by "nervous" and "edgy," she reports that her body feels tense and jittery all over. She indicates that this reaction does not help her high blood pressure. She reports that Freddie's father is not currently living at home because they recently separated, so all the child rearing is on her shoulders. Ms. Weare also states that she doesn't spend much time with Freddie after school; she does extra work at home at night because she and Freddie "don't have much money."

DSM-5 Diagnosis for Ms. Weare
V61.20 (Z62.820) Parent–child relational problem
V60.2 (Z59.6) Low Income

Respond to these questions.

1. What behaviors does Freddie demonstrate in this situation?
2. Is each behavior you have listed overt or covert?
3. What individual and environmental strengths and resources do you see for Freddie?
4. What behaviors does Ms. Weare exhibit in this situation?
5. Is each behavior you have listed overt or covert?
6. What individual and environmental strengths and resources do you see for Ms. Weare?
7. List one or more antecedent conditions that seem to bring about each of Freddie's behaviors.
8. List one or more antecedent conditions that seem to bring about each of Ms. Weare's behaviors.
9. List one or more consequences (including any secondary gains) that influence each of Freddie's behaviors. After each consequence listed, identify how the consequence seems to influence Freddie's behavior.
10. List one or more consequences that seem to influence each of Ms. Weare's behaviors. After each consequence listed, identify how the consequence seems to influence her behavior.
11. Identify aspects of the developmental context of the case that impact Freddie and Ms. Weare's situation.
12. Identify aspects of the sociopolitical/cultural context that appear to affect Ms. Weare's behavior.

The Case of Mrs. Rodriguez

Mrs. Rodriguez is a 34-year-old Mexican American woman who was a legal immigrant to the United States when she was 10 years old. She was brought to the emergency room by the police after her bizarre behavior in a local supermarket. According to the police report, Mrs. Rodriguez became very aggressive toward another shopper, accusing the man of "following me around and spying on me." When confronted by employees of the store about her charges, she stated, "God speaks to me. I can hear his voice guiding me in my mission." On mental status examination, the counselor initially notes Mrs. Rodriguez's unkempt appearance. She appears unclean. Her clothing is somewhat disheveled. She seems underweight and looks older than her stated age. Her tense posture seems indicative of her anxious state, and she smiles inappropriately throughout the interview. Her speech is loud and fast, often incoherent, and she constantly glances suspiciously around the room. Her affect is labile, fluctuating from anger to euphoria. On occasion, she looks at the ceiling and spontaneously starts talking. When the helper asks to whom she is speaking, she replies, "Can't you hear him? He's come to save me!"

Mrs. Rodriguez is alert and appears to be of average general intelligence. Her attention span is short. She reports no suicidal ideation and denies any past attempts. However, she does express some homicidal feelings for those who "continue to secretly follow me around." When the family members arrive, the helper is able to ascertain that Mrs. Rodriguez has been in psychiatric treatment on and off for the past 10 years. She has been hospitalized several times in the past 10 years during similar episodes of unusual behavior. In addition, she has been treated with several antipsychotic medicines. There is no evidence of any physical disorder or any indication of alcohol or drug abuse. Her husband indicates that she recently stopped taking her medicine after the death of her sister and up until then had been functioning adequately during the past year without a great deal of impairment, although she was not capable of holding regular paid employment outside of the home.

DSM-5 Diagnosis for Mrs. Rodriguez

295.90 (F20.9) Schizophrenia, Multiple episodes, currently in acute episode; Severity: 4 (present and severe)

V15.81 (Z91.19) Nonadherence to medical treatment

Respond to these questions. See page 211 for feedback.

1. List several of the behaviors that Mrs. Rodriguez demonstrates.
2. Is each behavior you have listed overt or covert?
3. List any individual and environmental strengths and resources you observe.
4. List one or more antecedents that seem to elicit Mrs. Rodriguez's behaviors.
5. List one or more consequences that appear to influence the behaviors, including any secondary gains. Describe how each consequence seems to influence the behavior.
6. Identify aspects of the developmental context of the case that affect her behavior.
7. Identify aspects of the sociopolitical and cultural context that affect her behavior.

volunteer answers or go to the board. Often, when called on, she says nothing. As a result, she reports, her grades are dropping. She also states that her math teacher has spoken to her several times about her behavior and has tried to help her do better.

However, Isabella's nervousness in the class has resulted in her cutting the class whenever she can find any reason to do so, and also faking illness or oversleeping to stay home from school whenever she can. As a result, she has almost used up her number of excused absences from school. She states that her fear of competitive academic situations has been there since she started high school a year ago, when her parents started to compare her with other students and put "pressure" on her to do well in school so she could go to college. When asked how they pressure her, she says they constantly talk to her about getting good grades and how success is tied to a college degree.

Isabella reports a strong network of girlfriends with whom she "hangs out a lot." She reports that during this year, since the classes are tougher and more competitive, school is more of a problem to her and she feels increasingly anxious. Isabella reports that all this has made her dissatisfied with school, and she has questioned whether she wants to stay in a college prep curriculum. She has toyed with the idea of going to culinary school instead of going to college. However, she says she is a very indecisive person and does not know what she should do. In addition, she is afraid to decide this because if she changed her curriculum, her parents' response would be very negative. Isabella states that she cannot recall ever having made a decision without her parents' assistance. She feels they often have made decisions for her. She says her parents have never encouraged her to make decisions on her own because they say she might not make the right decision without their help. Isabella is an only child. She indicates that she is constantly anxious about making a bad or wrong choice so that when she is confronted with decisions she feels worried and lacks confidence in her choices.

Analysis of the Case

There are two related problems for Isabella and these are reflected in our *DSM-5* diagnosis. The first is anxiety. Because she reports anxiety about school and about decision-making issues, and because she reports being on edge, lapses in concentration, and sleep disturbances, occurring on more days than not in the last 6 months, as well as other indicators, she shows evidence of a generalized anxiety disorder. In addition, there is clearly an academic/educational problem that is a focus of attention and in fact the setting where she is seeking help. (Note how these are coded below on the *DSM-5* diagnostic classification system).

Next, we use the functional assessment/ABC model (Figure 6.1) presented earlier in the chapter to analyze these two issues.

Analysis of the Anxiety Issue

Relevant Behaviors

1. Feeling "on edge"

2. Lapses in concentration

3. Trouble falling asleep

Isabella's feelings of edginess are a covert behavior, whereas the lapses in concentration and trouble falling asleep are overt behaviors.

Individual and Environmental Strengths These include Isabella's help-seeking behavior and teacher and peer support.

Context of Issue

Antecedent Conditions Isabella's anxiety (feeling on edge, lapses in concentration) regarding school is cued by being in a competitive, college prep curriculum as well as her self-deprecating beliefs about her performance compared to her peers. Her trouble falling asleep is also cued by internal worry and beliefs about her school performance, that is, her "not measuring up."

Consequences Isabella's anxiety (feeling edgy, lapses in concentration, trouble falling asleep) is maintained by increased teacher attention and avoidance of the school situation (faking illness and oversleeping to stay home).

Analysis of the School Issue

Relevant Behaviors Isabella's behaviors at school include:

1. Self-defeating labeling of her math class as "competitive" and of herself as "not as smart as the guys."

2. Sitting alone, not volunteering answers in math class, not answering the teacher's questions or going to the board, and cutting class.

Isabella's self-defeating labels are a covert behavior; her sitting alone, not volunteering answers, and cutting class are overt behaviors.

Individual and Environmental Strengths These include Isabella's help-seeking behavior and the support of her math teacher.

Context of Issue

Antecedent Conditions Isabella's behaviors at school are cued by certain "competitive" classes, particularly math. Previous antecedent conditions include verbal comparisons about Isabella and her peers made by her parents and verbal pressure for good grades and withholding of privileges for bad grades by her parents. Notice that these

antecedent conditions do not occur at the same time. The antecedent of the anxiety in the competitive class occurs in proximity to Isabella's problem behaviors and is a *stimulus event*. However, the verbal comparisons and parental pressure began approximately 1 year ago and probably function as a *setting event*.

Consequences Isabella's behaviors at school are maintained by:

1. An increased level of attention to her by her math teacher.

2. Feeling relieved of anxiety through avoidance of the situation that elicits anxiety. By not participating in class and by cutting class, Isabella can avoid putting herself in an anxiety-provoking situation.

3. Her poorer grades, possibly because of two payoffs, or secondary gains. First, if her grades get too low, then she may not qualify to continue in the college prep curriculum. This would be the ultimate way to avoid putting herself in competitive academic situations that elicit anxiety.

Developmental Context This part of the assessment addresses the developmental context of the case. In this case, Isabella is 15 and a teenager. Developmentally speaking, teenagers are in the business of identifying with their peer group and separating from the influence of their family, parents, and other caregivers to establish an increased sense of independence. In Isabella's case, you also can see the effects of her being an only child and the parenting style, which appears to be overprotective and authoritarian.

Social-Political /Cultural Context This part of the assessment addresses the question of how Isabella's presenting issues are a manifestation of the social-political context and cultural structure in which she lives. Isabella's concerns appear to be shaped by a context in which she has been reinforced (and punished) for what she does (or doesn't do). This pattern has led to a devaluing and uncertainty of who she is and what she wants and needs. She appears to feel powerless in her current environment—partly, we suspect, because of the power her parents have exerted over her, partly because of the power exerted by a school system and academic culture that emphasizes college prep values, and partly because of lessons she has learned from her cultural groups about men, women, and achievement. In her math classroom, the gender context plays a big role. She is literally in the gender minority. She compares herself negatively to the boys in the classroom, who hold the power, and she is shut down by her negative comparison. The relevant

6.4 Feedback

Assessment Models

The Case of Ms. Weare and Freddie

1. Freddie's behavior is sitting in his room and not getting ready for school.
2. This is an overt behavior because it is visible to someone else.
3. Strengths and resources for Freddie include his being smart, doing well in school, and having a mom who believes in him and wants to see him do well academically.
4. Ms. Weare's behaviors are (a) feeling mad and (b) yelling at Freddie.
5. Feeling mad is a covert behavior, as feelings can only be inferred. Yelling is an overt behavior that is visible to someone else.
6. Strengths and resources for Ms. Weare include her decision to seek help and her decision not to try to cope with this situation alone anymore.
7. Receiving a verbal reminder and threat from his mother at breakfast elicits Freddie's behavior.
8. Ms. Weare's behavior seems to be cued by a 5-minute period before the bus arrives on school days.
9. Two consequences seem to influence Freddie's behavior of not getting ready for school: (a) he gets help in dressing himself, and this interaction influences his behavior by providing special benefits; and (b) he gets some satisfaction from seeing that his mother is upset and is attending to him. These consequences seem to maintain his behavior because of the attention he gets from his mother in these instances. A possible secondary gain is the control he exerts over his mother at these times. According to the case description, he doesn't feel that he gets much attention at other times from his mother.
10. The major consequence that influences Ms. Weare's behavior is that she gets Freddie ready on time and he is not late. This result appears to influence her behavior by helping her avoid being considered a poor mother by herself or by someone else and by helping him succeed in school.
11. The developmental context impacting this parent–child relational issue involves the recent separation between Ms. Weare and Freddie's father, Ms. Weare's apparent stress about single parenting, and her parenting style.
12. This parent–child relational issue is undoubtedly affected by the fact that Ms. Weare is raising her son alone and appears to be living in a fairly isolated social climate with little social support. She also is the sole economic provider for Freddie, and her behavior and her child rearing are affected by her lack of financial resources. Overall, she appears to feel disempowered in her ability to handle her parental and financial responsibilities.

The Case of Mrs. Rodriguez

1. There are various behaviors for Mrs. Rodriguez: (a) disheveled appearance; (b) inappropriate affect; (c) delusional beliefs; (d) auditory hallucinations; (e) homicidal ideation; and (f) noncompliance with treatment (medicine).
2. Disheveled appearance, inappropriate affect, and noncompliance with treatment are overt behaviors—they are observable by others. Delusions, hallucinations, and homicidal ideation are covert behaviors as long as they are not expressed by the client and therefore not visible to someone else. However, when expressed or demonstrated by the client, they become overt behaviors as well.
3. Strengths and resources include a lack of reported suicide ideation and support and care from her extended family.
4. In this case, Mrs. Rodriguez's behaviors appear to be elicited by the cessation of her medication, which is the major antecedent. Apparently, when she stops taking her medicine, an acute psychotic episode results.
5. This periodic discontinuation of her medicine and the subsequent psychotic reaction may be influenced by the attention she receives from the mental health profession, from her family, and even from strangers when she behaves in a psychotic, helpless fashion. Additional possible secondary gains include avoidance of responsibility and of being in control.
6. The developmental context of the case that affects her behavior includes the fact that she was an immigrant to the United States when she was 10 years old, her diagnosis and subsequent psychiatric treatment that began when she was in her early 20s, and the developmental transition of the recent death of her sister.
7. With respect to the sociopolitical/cultural context of the issue, it is important in this case to note the potential influence of the cultural/ethnic affiliations of Mrs. Rodriguez. Ideas that may seem delusional in one culture may represent a common belief held by many persons in another culture. Delusions with a religious thread may be considered a more typical part of religious experience in a particular culture, such as a sign of "divine favor." The skilled helper would take this into consideration in the assessment before settling on a final diagnosis.

overt and the covert behaviors that we describe appear to be tools Isabella is using to cope with this loss and sense of powerlessness as well as ways to attempt to increase the power she has and decrease the power held by other sources of authority.

The *DSM-5* diagnoses for Isabella follow:

DSM-5 Diagnosis for Isabella
300.02 (F41.1) Generalized Anxiety Disorder
V62.3 (Z55.9) Academic or Educational Problem

CHAPTER SUMMARY

Assessment is the basis for development of the entire helping program. Assessment has important informational, educational, and motivational functions in therapy. Although the major part of assessment occurs early in the helping process, to some extent assessment, or identification of client concerns, goes on constantly throughout the process. As the assessment unfolds, the client's story unfolds as well. An important part of assessment is the helper's ability to conceptualize client concerns. Conceptualization models help the practitioner think clearly about the complexity of client issues.

The assessment model described in this chapter is based on several assumptions, including these:

1. Most behavior is learned, although some psychological issues may have biological causes.

2. Neurobiology is an increasingly important consideration in clinical assessment.

3. Client issues need to be viewed within a developmental context that includes things such as life stage, developmental transitions, family history, parenting style, and attachment.

4. Issues occur in a social and cultural context and include levels or systems and cultural variables impacting individuals' lives. This ecological perspective of clinical assessment, also known as the person-in-environment model, uses an assessment tool known as the PIE classification system.

5. In addition to assessment of client issues, a focus on clients' individual and environmental resources and strengths is also important.

6. Increasingly, clinical assessment is informed by evidence and the use of evidence-based assessment tools that have good reliability, validity, and norms or cutoff scores. Such measures also need to be valid for diverse clients.

7. The functional assessment, based on the ABC model, has a considerable amount of empirical support. It involves an analysis of the antecedents, behaviors, and consequences of a client's presenting issue and the functional relationships among these three components.

Another part of assessment may involve a clinical diagnosis of the client. Current diagnosis is based on the *Diagnostic and Statistical Manual of Mental Disorders,* fifth edition, and involves classifying clinical disorders using a dimensional process that reflects the *International Classification of Diseases* or *ICD* numerical codes. Diagnosis can be a useful part of assessment. For example, knowledge about selected features of various types of clinical syndromes can add to the understanding of a client's concern. However, diagnosis is not an adequate *substitute* for other assessment approaches and is not an effective basis for specifying goals and selecting intervention strategies unless it is part of a comprehensive treatment approach in which issues are identified in a concrete, or operational, manner for each client. Additional diagnostic assessment tools include the mental status exam and structured and semistructured diagnostic interviews.

An important part of assessment and diagnosis also involves risk assessment of clients, particularly risk or danger to self and others as well as obtaining information about the client's history. Research has shown that both assessment and diagnosis are subject to gender and cultural bias. The skilled practitioner conducts a multidimensional assessment process that includes an awareness of the current and historical sociopolitical context in which the client lives and also the client's gender and cultural referent groups.

 Visit CengageBrain.com for a variety of study tools and useful resources such as video examples, case studies, interactive exercises, flashcards, and quizzes.

6 | Knowledge and Skill Builder

Part One

For Learning Outcome 1, read the case descriptions of Mr. Huang and then answer the following questions:

1. **What are the client's behaviors?**
2. **Are the behaviors overt or covert?**
3. **What are the client's individual and environmental strengths and resources?**
4. **What are the antecedent conditions of the client's concern?**
5. **What are the consequences of the behaviors? Secondary gains?**
6. **In what way do the consequences influence the behaviors?**
7. **How does the developmental context of the issue impact the client's behaviors?**
8. **In what ways are the behaviors manifestations of the social-political and cultural context?**

Answers to these questions are provided in the Feedback section on page 214.

The Case of Mr. Huang

A 69-year-old Asian American man, Mr. Huang, came to counseling because he felt his performance on the job was "slipping." Mr. Huang had a job in a large automobile company. He was responsible for producing new car designs. Mr. Huang revealed that he noticed he had started having trouble approximately 6 months previously, when the personnel director came in to ask him to fill out retirement papers. Mr. Huang, at the time he sought help, was due to retire in 9 months. (The company's policy made it mandatory to retire at age 70.) Until this incident with the personnel director and the completion of the papers, Mr. Huang reported, everything seemed to be "okay." He also reported that nothing seemed to be changed in his relationship with his family. However, on some days at work, he reported, he had a great deal of trouble completing any work on his car designs. When asked what he did instead of working on designs, he said, "Worrying." The "worrying" turned out to mean that he was engaging in constant repetitive thoughts about his approaching retirement, such as, "I won't be here when this car comes out" and "What will I be without having this job?"

Mr. Huang stated that there were times when he spent almost an entire morning or afternoon "dwelling" on these things and that this seemed to occur mostly when he was alone in his office actually working on a car design. As a result, he was not turning in his designs by the specified deadlines. Not meeting his deadlines made him feel more worried. He was especially concerned that he would "bring shame both to his company and to his family who had always been proud of his work record." He was afraid that his present behavior would jeopardize the opinion others had of him, although he didn't report any other possible "costs" to himself. In fact, Mr. Huang said that it was his immediate boss who had suggested, after several talks and lunches, that he use the employee assistance program. Mr. Huang said that his boss had not had any noticeable reactions to his missing deadlines, other than reminding him and being solicitous, as evidenced in the talks and lunches. Mr. Huang reported that he enjoyed this interaction with his boss and often wished he could ask his boss to go out to lunch with him. However, he stated that these meetings had all been at his boss's request. Mr. Huang felt somewhat hesitant about making the request himself. In the past 6 months, Mr. Huang had never received any sort of reprimand for missing deadlines on his drawings. Still, he was concerned with maintaining his own sense of pride about his work, which he felt might be jeopardized since he'd been having this trouble.

DSM-5 Diagnosis for Mr. Huang

309.24 (F43.22) Adjustment disorder with anxiety

V62.89 (Z60.0) Phase of life problem (impending retirement)

Part Two

Learning Outcome 2 asks you to conduct a role-play history-taking interview with a client. We suggest you complete this part of the knowledge and skill builder by forming triads in your class, with one person being the helper, one being the role-play client, and a third being the observer. Conduct a 30-minute session with one person serving as the helper and the other taking the client's role; the observer should use the outline in Table 6.4 to provide feedback to the helper at the end of the interview. Switch roles two times so that each person functions as the helper, client, and observer one time each.

6 | Knowledge and Skill Builder Feedback

Part One

Learning Outcome 1 asks you to identify a series of responses for a designated client case. See if your responses are similar to those provided in the following feedback section.

The Case of Mr. Huang

1. Mr. Huang's self-reported behaviors include worry about retirement and not doing work on his automobile designs.
2. Worrying about retirement is a covert behavior. Not doing work on designs is an overt behavior.
3. Individual and environmental strengths and resources include Mr. Huang's prior job success and the support of his boss and family.
4. One antecedent condition occurred 6 months ago, when the personnel director conferred with Mr. Huang about retirement and papers were filled out. This is an overt antecedent in the form of a setting event. The personnel director's visit seemed to elicit Mr. Huang's worry about retirement and his not doing his designs. A covert antecedent is Mr. Huang's repetitive thoughts about retirement, getting older, and so on. This is a stimulus event.
5. The consequences include Mr. Huang's being excused from meeting his deadlines and receiving extra attention from his boss.
6. Mr. Huang's behaviors appear to be maintained by the consequence of being excused from not meeting his deadlines with only a "reminder." He is receiving some extra attention and concern from his boss, whom he values highly. He may also be missing deadlines and therefore not completing required car designs as a way to avoid or postpone retirement—that is, he may expect that if his designs aren't done, he'll be asked to stay longer until they are completed.
7. The anxiety that Mr. Huang is experiencing surrounding the transition from full-time employment to retirement is a fairly universal reaction to a major life change and developmental transition and is an important developmental factor impacting Mr. Huang's behavior.
8. Mr. Huang is also affected by his cultural/ethnic affiliation in that he is concerned about maintaining pride and honor and not losing face or shaming the two groups he belongs to—his family and his company.

Part Two

Learning Outcome 2 asked you to conduct a role-play history-taking interview with a client. Your observer used Table 6.4 to provide feedback to your on your role play. What can you conclude about your skills in conducting history-taking interviews? What are your strong suits? What parts were more challenging for you? What parts did you avoid?

Conducting an Interview Assessment with Clients

After completing this chapter, you will be able to

1. When given a written description of a selected client, outline in writing at least two interview leads for each of the 11 assessment categories that you would explore during an assessment interview with this person.

2. In a 30-minute role-play interview, demonstrate leads and responses associated with nine out of 11 categories for assessing the client.

Assessment is a way of identifying and defining a client's concerns to make decisions about therapeutic treatment. Various methods are available to help the practitioner identify and define the range and parameters of client issues. These methods include standardized tests, such as interest and personality inventories; psychophysiological assessment, such as monitoring of muscle tension with chronic headaches with an electromyograph (EMG) machine; self-report checklists, such as assertiveness scales and anxiety inventories; observation by others, including observation by the helper or by a significant person in the client's environment; self-observation, in which the client observes and records some aspect of the issue; imagery, in which the client uses fantasy and directed imagery to vicariously experience some aspect of the issue; role playing, in which the client may demonstrate some part of the issue in an *in vivo* yet simulated enactment; and direct interviewing, in which the client and helper identify concerns through verbal and nonverbal exchanges. All these methods are also used to evaluate client progress during the helping process in addition to their use in assessment for the purpose of collecting information about clients.

In this chapter we concentrate on direct interviewing, not only because it is the focus of the book but also because it is the one method readily available to all helpers without additional cost in time or money. It is also a method of assessment that allows the practitioner to observe the client(s) (Hunsley & Lee, 2014). For example, in interviewing a client you can note things like demeanor, grooming (or lack thereof), activity level, attention span, speech, and other nonverbal behaviors (Gould, Edelstein, & Ciliberti, 2009). In actual practice, it is important not to rely solely on the interview for assessment data but rather to use several methods of obtaining information about clients. Recall from Chapter 6 that **evidence-based assessment** involves a decision-making process that targets data from multiple measures with sound psychometric properties (Hunsley & Mash, 2008).

Assessment Interviewing

According to cognitive-behavioral literature, the interview is the first step in a comprehensive assessment of client issues (Sayers & Tomcho, 2006). As Sayers and Tomcho point out, although there are many assessment tools now available to practitioners, the **assessment interview** is the first step in identifying client problems. They note that guided by the client's concerns, the assessment interview "attempts to discover the relationship between the person's environment and his/her individual responses to it" (p. 63). Despite the overwhelming evidence confirming the popularity of the interview as an assessment tool, some persons believe it is the most difficult assessment approach for the helper to enact. Successful assessment interviews require specific guidelines and training to obtain accurate and valid information from clients that will make a difference in treatment planning (Koven, Shreve Neiger, & Edelstein, 2007; Sayers & Tomcho, 2006).

In this chapter we describe a structure and provide some guidelines to apply in assessment interviews to identify and define client issues. This chapter describes interview leads that in applied settings are likely to elicit certain kinds of client information. However, as Sayers and Tomcho (2006) observe, little research on the effects of interview procedures has been conducted. The leads that we suggest are supported more by practical and conceptual considerations than by empirical data. As a result, you will need to be attentive to the effects of using them with each client. Remember, too, that because the clinical assessment interview relies on client self-report, its accuracy and reliability are very much dependent on the accuracy and veracity of what the client says to the clinician.

Eleven Categories for Assessing Clients

To help you acquire the skills associated with **LO1** **LO2** assessment interviews, we describe 11 categories of information you need to seek from each client. These 11 categories are illustrated and defined in the following list and subsections. These categories are based on the conceptual models of assessment we described in Chapter 6.

They reflect the influences of learning, neurobiology, human development, social context and culture, strengths, and evidence. We have interwoven these influences on assessment into our assessment interviewing approach, which is conceptually based on the functional assessment and person-in-environment models of assessment we discussed in Chapter 6. These 11 categories are also summarized in the Interview Checklist at the end of the chapter (page 243) and in Box 7.1.

The first three categories—explanation of the purpose of assessment, identification of the range of concerns, and prioritization and selection of issues—are a logical starting place. First, it is helpful to give the client a rationale, a reason for conducting an assessment interview, before gathering information. Next, some time must be spent in helping the client explore all the relevant issues and prioritize issues to work on in order of importance, annoyance, and so on.

The other eight categories follow prioritization and selection. After the helper and client have identified and selected the issues to work on, these eight categories of interviewing leads are used to define and analyze parameters of the issue. The helper will find that the order of the assessment leads varies among clients. A natural sequence will evolve in each interview, and the helper will want to use the leads associated with these content categories in a pattern that fits the flow of the interview and follows the lead of the client. It is important in assessment interviews not to impose your structure at the expense of the client. The amount of time and number of sessions required to obtain this information

---

BOX 7.1   11 Categories of Assessing Clients

1. Explanation of *purpose* of assessment—presenting rationale for assessment interview to the client

2. Identification of *range* of concerns—using leads to help the client identify all the relevant primary and secondary issues to get the big picture

3. *Prioritization* and *selection* of issues—using leads to help the client prioritize issues and select the initial area of focus

4. Identification of *present behaviors*—using leads to help the client identify the six components of current behavior(s): affective, somatic, behavioral, cognitive, contextual, and relational

5. Identification of *antecedents*—using leads to help the client identify categories of antecedents and their effect on the current issue

6. Identification of *consequences*—using leads to help the client identify categories of consequences and their influence on the current issue

7. Identification of *secondary gains*—using leads to help the client identify underlying controlling variables that serve as payoffs to maintain the issue

8. Identification of *previous solutions*—using leads to help the client identify previous solutions or attempts to solve the issue and their subsequent effect on the issue

9. Identification of *client individual* and *environmental strengths* and *coping skills*—using leads to help the client identify past and present coping or adaptive behavior and how such skills might be used in working with the present issue

10. Identification of the *client's perceptions* of the concern—using leads to help the client describe her or his understanding of the concern

11. Identification of *intensity*—using leads and/or client self-monitoring to identify the impact of the concern on the client's life, including (a) degree of severity and (b) frequency and/or duration of current behaviors

will vary with the concerns and with clients. It is possible to complete the assessment in one session, but with some clients an additional interview may be necessary. Although the practitioner may devote several interviews to assessment, the information gathering and hypothesis testing that go on do not automatically stop after these few sessions. Some degree of assessment continues throughout the entire helping process just as the importance of the helping relationship continues throughout this time as well.

Category 1. Explaining the Purpose of Assessment

In explaining the **purpose of assessment**, the helper gives the client a rationale for conducting an assessment interview. The intent of this first category of assessment is to give the client a *set*, or an expectation, of what will occur during the interview and why assessment is important to both client and helper. Explaining the purpose of the interview assessment is especially important in cross-cultural helping because culturally based attitudes weigh heavily in a person's expectations about assessment.

Here is one way the helper can communicate the purpose of the assessment interview: *"Today I'd like to focus on some concerns that are bothering you most. To find out exactly what you're concerned about, I'll be asking you for some specific kinds of information. This information will help both of us identify what you'd like to work on. How does this sound [or appear] to you?"* After presenting the rationale, the helper looks for some confirmation or indication that the client understands the importance of assessing issues.

Also, depending on whether or not this is the initial helping interview (in some places the intake or history interview occurs initially and specific assessment interviews follow that), the practitioner must obtain informed consent and provide the client with information about privacy and confidentiality and the limits to confidentiality. **Informed consent** is usually accompanied by a written document given to the client at the outset of the helping process and provides information about you, your training, the kinds of services provided, the likely benefits and risks associated with therapy, the Privacy Act and implications for clients, and confidentiality and limits to it. However, the provision of a written informed consent document is not complete without addressing this issue directly with the client in the interview setting. The practitioner might say something like the following:

Juanita, I know that you read the agreement that we provided to you when you came in today and I wanted to take a few minutes to talk about that before we go further in the session. I wanted to see if you have any questions and I wanted to make sure to emphasize several things in the agreement about confidentiality. Generally speaking, the commitment to maintaining confidentiality means that I do not share what you tell me with anyone outside of the session. However, there are a couple of exceptions to this. If you told me that a child or an elder was being abused, I would need to break confidentiality and report this to the proper authorities. Similarly, if you indicated you were in danger of hurting yourself or hurting someone else, I would also need to break confidentiality and take steps to protect you and/or the other person, which would mean not being able to keep this information between us. Also, if there was ever some kind of a court case, a judge could order me to give testimony or to provide my records. Finally, if you would want me to give information to someone else about yourself, such as another provider, I can do that, but you would need to sign a written authorization form. I know this is a lot to absorb at once, so take a minute to reflect on what I said and what you read and let's make sure you feel clear about this.

Here is a sample of what a practicum student could say in the initial interview with a first-time client. This sample was provided by Barry Edelstein, Ph.D. and William Fremouw, Ph.D., who are affiliated with the Quin Curtis Training Center in the Department of Psychology at West Virginia University,

Hi (name of client). My name is _____. I am a student who is being supervised by Dr. _____, who is a licensed health care provider. Before we begin discussing your reasons for coming here today, I need to go over a few important points. First, everything you say during our sessions will be held in confidence. However, there are a few exceptions.

If I have reason to believe that you are abusing a child, vulnerable adult, or older adult, I am mandated to report that to the Office of Child Protective Services or the Office of Adult Protective Services, respectively. If I have reason to believe that you are at risk for taking your life, I have a duty to protect you. If I have reason to believe that you intend to harm someone else, I have a duty to warn that individual or to ensure that the person is not harmed. My clinical records for you can be subpoenaed by a court to discuss the content of our meetings. This would be rare, but it is important for you to know that it is a possibility. For example, if you were involved in a custody dispute and your fitness as a parent were questioned, then a court could subpoena your records or me. I am also required to submit information about you and your progress to your insurance company if your sessions are being paid for by your insurance company. My supervisor will be informed of your progress and have input into my work with you. If necessary, I may need to solicit a professional consultation to assist in your treatment, but I would discuss this with you. I know this is a lot of information to take in at once, so I am wondering if you have any questions or concerns I can address before we move on.

Category 2. Identifying the Range of Concerns

In this **range of concerns** category, the practitioner uses open-ended leads to help clients identify all the major issues and concerns in their life now. Often clients will initially describe only one concern, and on further inquiry and discussion the helper discovers a host of other ones, some of which may be more severe or stressful or have greater significance than the one the client originally described. If the helper does not try to get the big picture, then the client may reveal additional concerns either much later in the helping process or not at all. Here are examples of range-of-concerns leads:

"What are your concerns in your life now?"
"Please describe some of the things that seem to be bothering you."
"What are some present stresses in your life?"
"What situations are not going well for you?"
"Tell me about anything else that concerns you now."

After using range-of-concerns leads, the practitioner should look for the client's indication of some general areas of concern or things that are troublesome. An occasional client may not respond affirmatively to these leads. Some clients may be uncertain about what information to share, or clients may be from a cultural group in which it is considered inappropriate to reveal personal information to a stranger. In such cases, the helper may need to use an approach different from verbal questioning. For example, Lazarus (1989) has recommended the use of an **Inner Circle strategy** to help a client disclose concerns. The client is given a picture like this:

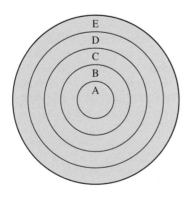

The helper points out that topics in circle A are very personal, whereas topics in circle E are more or less public information. The helper can provide examples of types of topics likely to be in the A circle, such as sexual concerns, feelings of hostility, intimacy problems, and dishonesty. These examples may encourage the client to disclose personal concerns more readily. The helper also emphasizes that progress

takes place in the A and B circles and may say things like, "I feel we are staying in circle C," or, "Do you think you've let me into circle A or B yet?" Sometimes the helper may be able to obtain more specific descriptions from a client by having the client role-play a typical situation.

Exploring the range of concerns is also a way to establish who the appropriate client is. A client may attribute the concern to an event or to another person. For instance, a student may say, "That teacher always picks on me. I can never do anything right in her class." Because most clients seem to have trouble initially owning their role in the issue or tend to describe it in a way that minimizes their own contribution, the helper will need to determine who is most invested in having it resolved and who is the real person requesting assistance. Often it is helpful to ask clients who feels that it is most important for the concern to be resolved—the client or someone else. It is important for practitioners not to assume that the person who arrives at their office is always the client. The client is the person who wants a change and who seeks assistance for it. In this example, if the student had desired a change and had requested assistance, then the student would be the client; if it were the teacher who wanted a change and requested assistance, then the teacher would be the client. Sometimes, however, the helper gets stuck in a situation in which a family or a client wants a change and the person whose behavior is to be changed is sent as the client. Determining who the appropriate client is can be very important in working with these mandated clients, who are required to see a helper but have little investment in being helped! One strategy that can be useful with clients in these situations is to establish a win-win contract where they agree to talk about what you want to discuss for half the session in exchange for talking (or not talking) about what they want to for the other half of the session.

The question of who is the appropriate client is also tricky when the issue involves two or more persons, such as a relationship, partnership, or family issue. In rehabilitation counseling, for example, the client may be not only the individual with a disability but also the client's employer. Many family therapists view family issues as devices for maintaining the status quo of the family and recommend that either the couple or the entire family be involved, rather than one individual.

Category 3. Prioritizing and Selecting Issues

Rarely do clients or the results of assessment suggest only one area or issue that needs modification or resolution. Typically, a presenting concern turns out to be one of several unresolved issues in the client's life. For example, the assessment of a client who reports depression may also reveal that the client is troubled by her relationship with her teenage daughter. History may reveal that this adult woman was also physically abused as a child. After a client describes all of her or his concerns, the practitioner and client will need to select the issues that best represent the client's purpose for seeking help. The primary question to be answered by these leads is, "What is the specific situation the client chooses to start working on?"

Prioritizing issues is an important part of assessment and goal-setting. If clients try to tackle too many issues simultaneously, then they are likely to soon feel overwhelmed and anxious and may not experience enough success to stay in therapy. Selection of the issue(s) to address in the current helping context is the client's responsibility, although the helper may help with formulating the client's choice.

The following guidelines form a framework to help clients select and prioritize issues to work on:

1. Start with the presenting issue, the one that best represents the reason the client sought help. Leads to use to help determine the initial or presenting issue include, "Which issue best represents the reason you are here?" and, "Out of all these concerns you've mentioned, identify the one that best reflects your need for assistance."

2. Start with the issue that is primary or most important to the client to resolve. Often this is the one that causes the client the most pain or discomfort or annoyance or is most interfering to the client. Modifying the more important issues seems to lead to lasting change in that area, which may then generalize to other areas. Here are some responses to use to determine the client's most important priority: "How much happiness or relief would you experience if this issue were resolved?" "Of these concerns, which is the most stressful or painful for you?" "Rank order these concerns, starting with the one that is most important for you to resolve to the one least important." "How much distress or loss would you experience if you were unable to resolve this issue?"

3. Start with the concern or behavior that has the best chance of being resolved successfully and with the least effort. Some issues/behaviors are more resistant to change than others and require more time and energy to modify. Initially, it is important for the client to be reinforced for seeking help. One significant way to do this is to help the client resolve something that makes a difference without much cost to the client. Responses to determine what issues might be resolved most successfully include, "Do you believe there would be any unhappiness or discomfort if you were successful at resolving this concern?" or "How likely do you think

we are to succeed in resolving this issue or that one?" or "Tell me which of these situations you believe you could learn to manage most easily with the greatest success."

4. Start with the issue that needs resolution before other issues can be resolved or mastered. Sometimes the presence of one issue sets off a chain of other ones; when this issue is resolved or eliminated, the other ones either improve or at least move into a position to be explored and modified. Often this concern is one that is central or prominent in the range of elicited ones.

5. Giving mandated clients the responsibility for prioritization of concerns is particularly important. This choice allows them to set the agenda and may foster greater cooperation than clinician-directed prioritization of concerns.

Category 4. Understanding the Present Behaviors

After selecting the initial area of focus, it is important to determine the **components of the present behavior**. For example, if the identified behavior is "not getting along very well with people at work," with an expected outcome of "improving my relationships with people at work," we would want to identify the client's *feelings* (**affect**), *body sensations* (**somatic phenomena**), *actions* (**overt behavior**), and *thoughts and beliefs* (**cognitions**) that occur during the situations at work. We would also explore whether these feelings, sensations, actions, and thoughts occurred with *all* people at work or only with *some* people (relationships) and whether they occurred only at work or in *other* settings, at what *times,* and under what *conditions* or with what *concurrent events* (context). Without this sort of exploration, it is impossible to define the behavior operationally (concretely). Furthermore, it is difficult to know whether the client's work concerns result from the client's actions or observable behaviors, from covert emotional responses such as feelings of anger or jealousy, from cognitions and beliefs such as, "When I make a mistake at work, it's terrible," from the client's transactions with significant others that suggest an "I'm not okay—they're okay" position, from particular events that occur in certain times or situations during work, as during a team meeting or when working under a supervisor, or from toxic people or environmental conditions in the workplace. Recall from Haynes et al. (2011) that problem behaviors have multiple response modes and that these modes or components may shift over the course of therapy. This underscores the fact that assessment is an ongoing rather than a one-shot process!

The advantage of viewing the problem this way is that vague phenomena are translated into specific and observable experiences. When this occurs, we not only get a better idea of what is happening with the client but also have made the issue potentially measurable, allowing us to define potential outcomes and monitor treatment progress toward the outcomes. The end result of this kind of specificity is that the behavior is defined or stated in terms such that two or more persons can agree on when it exists. We next describe specific things to explore for each of these six components, and we suggest some leads and responses to further this exploration with clients.

a. Affect and Mood States **Affective components of behavior** include self-reported feelings or mood states, such as "depression," "anxiety," and "happiness." Feelings are generally the result of complex interactions among behavioral, physiological, and cognitive systems rather than unitary experiential processes. Clients often seek help because of this component—that is, they feel bad, uptight, sad, angry, confused, and so on, and they want to get rid of such unpleasant feelings.

One category of things to ask the client about to get a handle on feelings or mood states is feelings about the present behavior. After eliciting feelings, note the content (pleasant/unpleasant) and level of intensity. Remember that positive feelings are as important to identify as negative ones, because they build resources, enhance creative problem-solving, increase coping skills, and enhance health (Lopez, Pedrotti, & Snyder, 2014). Although there are many ways to assess for content and level of intensity of affect, one simple way is to use a rating scale, such as the **Subjective Units of Distress Scale** (SUDS; Wolpe, 1990), with a 1–10 or a 0–100 range to assess intensity. The SUDS asks clients to provide a numerical rating ranging from no distress (1 or 0) to the most distress possible (10 or 100).

Example interview leads to assess positive and negative effects include the following:

"How do you feel about this?"

"What kinds of feelings do you have when you do this or when this happens?"

"Describe the kinds of feelings you are aware of when this happens."

"Describe the positive feelings you have associated with this. Also, describe the negative ones."

"On a 10-point scale, with 1 being low and 10 being high, how intense is this feeling?"

"If the number 0 represented no distress, and the number 100 represented severe distress, how would you rate the feeling on this scale of 0 to 100 in terms of intensity?"

A second category is **concealed or distorted feelings**— that is, feelings that the client seems to be hiding from, such as anger, or a feeling like anger that has been distorted into hurt. The following are example responses:

"You seem to get headaches every time your husband criticizes you. Describe what feelings these headaches may be masking."

"When you talk about your son, you raise your voice and get a very serious look on your face. What feelings do you have—deep down—about him?"

"You've said you feel hurt and you cry whenever you think about your family. Tune in to any other feelings you have besides hurt."

"You've indicated you feel a little guilty whenever your friends ask you to do something and you don't agree to do it. Try on resentment instead of guilt. Try to get in touch with those feelings now."

The practitioner can always be on the lookout for concealed anger, which is the one emotion that tends to get shoved under the rug more easily than most. In exploring concealed feelings, the clinician needs to pay attention to any discrepancies between the client's verbal and nonverbal expressions of affect. Distorted feelings that are common include reporting the feeling of hurt or anxiety for anger, guilt for resentment, and sometimes anxiety for depression, or vice versa. Remember that clients from some cultures may be reluctant to share feelings, especially vulnerable ones, with someone they don't yet know well or trust.

b. Somatic Sensations Closely tied to feelings are **body sensations**. Some clients are very aware of "internal experiencing"; others are not. Some persons are so tuned in to every body sensation that they become somatizers, whereas others seem to be switched off below the head (Lazarus, 1989). Neither extreme is desirable. Some persons may describe complaints in terms of body sensations rather than as feelings or thoughts—that is, as headaches, dizzy spells, back pain, and so on. Older adults with anxiety issues, for example, may present with more somatic symptoms than younger adults (Gould, Edelstein, & Ciliberti, 2009). Behavior can also be affected by other physiological processes, such as nutrition and diet, exercise and lifestyle, substance use, hormone levels, and physical illness. The helper will want to elicit information about physiological complaints, about lifestyle and nutrition, exercise, substance use, and so on, and about other body sensations relating to the behavior. Some of this information is gathered routinely during the health history portion of the intake interview, but bear in mind that the information obtained from a health history may vary depending on the client's cultural affiliation. Helpers can ask clients who have trouble reporting somatic sensations to focus on their nonverbal behavior or to engage in a period of slow, deep breathing and then to conduct a **body scan**, that is, a visualization from head to toe of where they may be experiencing sensations or discomfort in the body. Useful leads to elicit this component of the present behavior include:

"What goes on inside you when you do this or when this happens?"
"What are you aware of when this occurs?"
"Notice any sensations you experience in your body when this happens."
"When this happens, describe anything that feels bad or uncomfortable inside you—aches, pains, dizziness, and so on."

c. Overt Behaviors or Motoric Responses Clients often describe a behavior in very nonbehavioral terms. In other words, they describe a situation or a process without describing their actions or specific behaviors within that event or process. For example, clients may say, "I'm not getting along with my partner" or "I feel lousy" or "I have a hard time relating to authority figures," without specifying what they do to get along or not get along or to relate or not relate.

When inquiring about the behavioral domain, the helper will want to elicit descriptions of both the presence and the absence of concrete **overt behaviors** connected to the issue—that is, what the client does and doesn't do. The helper also needs to be alert to the presence of **behavioral excesses and deficits**. Excesses are things that the person does too much or too often or that are too extreme, such as binge eating, excessive crying, or assaultive behavior. Deficits are responses that occur too infrequently or are not in the client's repertoire or do not occur in the expected context or conditions, such as failure to initiate requests on one's behalf, inability to talk to one's partner about sexual concerns and desires, or lack of physical exercise and body conditioning programs. Again, it is important to keep a cultural context in mind here: what might be considered a behavioral excess or deficit in one culture may be different in another. The helper may also wish to inquire about "**behavioral opposites**" (Lazarus, 1989) by asking about times when the person does *not* behave that way. This is important because you are balancing the assessment interview by focusing on what the client does well, not just on the problematic behaviors. Prosocial behaviors are as important to assess

as nonsocial ones. Here are examples of leads to elicit information about overt behaviors and actions:

"Describe what happens in this situation."
"What do you mean when you say you're 'having trouble at work'?"
"What are you doing when this occurs?"
"What do you do when this happens?"
"What effect does this situation have on your behavior?"
"Describe what you did the past few times this occurred."
"If I was recording this scene, what actions and dialogue would the camera pick up?"

Occasionally the practitioner may want to supplement the information gleaned about behavior from the client's oral self-report with more objective assessment approaches, such as role plays and behavioral observations. These additional assessment devices will help practitioners improve their knowledge of how the client does and doesn't act in the situation and in the environmental setting.

d. Cognitions, Beliefs, and Internal Dialogue In the past few years, helpers of almost all orientations have emphasized the relative importance of **cognitions or symbolic processes** in contributing to, exacerbating, or improving situations that clients report. Unrealistic expectations of oneself and of others are often related to presenting issues, as are disturbing images, self-labeling and self-statements, and cognitive distortions. When the cognitive component is a very strong element of the concern, part of the resulting treatment is usually directed toward this component and involves altering unrealistic ideas and beliefs, cognitive distortions and misconceptions, and dichotomous thinking.

Assessment of the cognitive component is accordingly directed toward exploring the presence of both irrational *and* rational beliefs and images related to the identified issue. Irrational beliefs will need to be altered later. Rational beliefs are also useful during intervention. Remember, though, that cognitions and belief systems may be quite culturally specific.

Irrational beliefs take many forms, and the most damaging ones seem to be related to automatic thoughts or self-statements and maladaptive assumptions such as "shoulds" about oneself, others, relationships, work, and so on, "awfulizing" or "catastrophizing" about things that don't turn out as we expect, "perfectionistic standards" about ourselves that often are projected onto others, and "externalization," the tendency to think that outside events are responsible for our feelings and problems. The practitioner will also want to be alert for the presence of cognitive distortions and misperceptions, such as overgeneralization, exaggeration, and drawing conclusions without supporting data. Underlying these automatic thoughts and assumptions are cognitive **schemas**. A schema is a deep-seated belief about oneself, others, and the world that takes shape in the client's early developmental history and confirms the client's core beliefs about himself or herself, others, and the world. For example, depressed or anxious clients often focus selectively on cognitive schemas that reinforce their vulnerabilities (Leahy, Holland, & McGinn, 2011).

Although clients may have difficulty verbalizing specific cognitions and beliefs, their nonverbal cues may be important indicators that core beliefs and schemas are being activated in the assessment process. Linscott and DiGiuseppe (1998) note that

> when the therapist has touched on a core-disturbed belief system, the client will frequently exhibit emotional and behavioral reactions. The client who was previously actively engaged in the conversation with the therapist may abruptly begin to avoid the therapist's questions, make little eye contact, evidence disturbed facial expressions, and work to change the subject. Or the client may become enlivened, as if a light bulb has been illuminated by the therapist's inquiries…In addition, the client's sudden anger and confrontational arguments with the therapist may also signal that a core belief has been elicited. (p. 117)

Leads to use to assess the cognitive component include the following:

"What beliefs [or images] do you hold that contribute to this concern? Make it worse? Make it better?"

"When something doesn't turn out the way you want or expect, how do you usually feel?"

"What data do you have to support these beliefs or assumptions?"

"What are you thinking about or dwelling on when this [issue] happens?"

"Please describe what kinds of thoughts or images go through your mind when this occurs."

"Notice what you say to yourself when this happens."

"What do you say to yourself when it doesn't happen [or when you feel better, and so on]?"

"Let's set up a scene. You imagine that you're starting to feel a little upset with yourself. Now run through the scene and relate the images or pictures that come through your mind. Tell me how the scene changes [or relate the thoughts or dialogue—what you say to yourself as the scene ensues]."

"What are your mental commentaries on this situation?"

"What's going through your mind when _____ occurs? Can you recall what you were thinking then?"

e. Context: Time, Place, Concurrent Events, and Environment
Behaviors occur in a social context, not in a vacuum. What often makes a behavior a "problem" is the context surrounding it or the way it is linked to various situations, places, and events. This is at the heart of the person-in-context or person-in-environment assessment approach. For example, it is not a problem to undress in your home, but the same behavior on a public street in many countries would be called "exhibitionism." In some other cultures, this same behavior might be more commonplace and would not be considered abnormal or maladaptive. Looking at the context surrounding the issue has implications not only for assessment but also for intervention, because a client's cultural background, lifestyle, and values can affect how the client views the issue and also the treatment approach to resolve it.

Assessing the context surrounding the issue is also important because most issues are **situation-specific**—that is, they are linked to certain events and situations, and they occur at certain times and places. For example, clients who say, "I'm uptight" or "I'm not assertive" usually do not mean they are *always* uptight or nonassertive, but rather in particular situations or at particular times. It is important that the helper does not reinforce the notion or belief in the client that the feeling, cognition, or behavior is pervasive. Otherwise, clients are even more likely to adopt the identity of the "problem" and begin to regard themselves as possessing a particular trait such as "nervousness," "social anxiety," or "nonassertiveness." They are also more likely to incorporate this trait into their lifestyles and daily functioning.

In assessing **contextual factors** associated with the issue, you are interested in discovering:

1. **Situations *or* places** in which the issue usually occurs and situations in which it does not occur (*where* the issue occurs and where it does not).

2. **Times** during which the issue usually occurs and times during which it does not occur (*when* the issue occurs and when it does not).

3. **Concurrent events**—events that typically occur at or near the same time as the issue. This information is important because sometimes it suggests a pattern or a significant chain of events related to the issue that clients might not be aware of or may not report on their own.

4. Any **cultural, ethnic, and racial affiliations**, any particular **values** associated with these affiliations, and how

these values affect the client's perception of the issue, the client's worldview, and the client's view of change.

5. **Sociopolitical factors**—that is, the overall zeitgeist of the society in which the client lives, the predominant social and political structures of this society, the major values of these structures, who holds power in these structures, and how all this affects the client.

Here are example responses to elicit information about contextual components of the issue—time, place, and concurrent events:

"Describe some recent situations in which this issue occurred. What are the similarities in these situations? In what situations does this usually occur? Where does this usually occur?"

"Describe some situations when this issue does not occur."

"Can you identify certain times of the day [week, month, and year] when this is more likely to happen? Less likely?"

"Does the same thing happen at other times or in other places?"

"What else is going on when this problem occurs?"

"Describe a typical day for me when you feel 'uptight.'"

"Are you aware of any other events that normally occur at the same time as this issue?"

Assessing the context surrounding the client's problems includes exploring not only the client's immediate psychosocial environment but also wider environmental contexts such as cultural affiliation and community (Ungar, 2011). Part of your intervention approach often involves helping clients to feel more empowered to act on their own behalf in their environment. Typically, the kinds of environmental systems you assess for during the interview include ones such as neighborhood and community, institutions and organizations, socio-cultural-political systems, and person-family support networks. The last one—social networks—is discussed in the next section on relational aspects of the issue. Within each system, it is important to assess the extent to which the system adds to the client's concerns—as well as the availability of resources within the system to help the client resolve the concerns. Remember that environments can be for better *and* for worse.

A frequently used tool for assessing context and environment is the **ecomap** (see Figure 7.1). The ecomap was originally developed by Hartman as a paper-and-pencil assessment tool to map the ecological system of an individual client or a family (Hartman, 1979; 1994). Preliminary data on the ecomap as an evidence-based assessment tool are provided by Calix (2004). An ecomap is a useful visual tool used to supplement the interview leads in a way that helps assess and define the

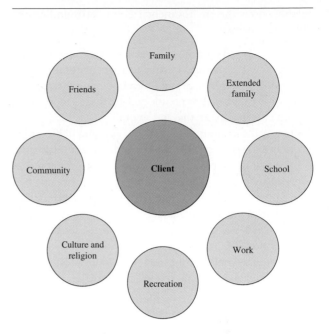

FIGURE 7.1 Sample Ecomap

Source: From Hepworth, Rooney, Rooney, & Strom-Gottfried, *Brooks/Cole Empowerment Series: Direct Social Work Practice*, 9 ed. Copyright 2013 by Cengage Learning. Reproduced by permission. www.cengage.com/permissions

interrelationships between individual clients and their families and other systems (Hepworth et al., 2013). An advantage of the ecomap is that it can be used with individuals, families, groups, and even organizations (Seabury, Seabury, & Garvin, 2011).

To complete an ecomap, the client writes his or her name or "me" in a circle in the center of a piece of paper. Then, the client identifies and encircles the people, groups, and organizations that are part of his or her current environment—work, day care, family, friends, community groups, religion, school, cultural groups, and so on. These circles can be drawn in any size, and the size may indicate the influence or lack of influence of that environmental system in the client's life. Next, the client draws a series of lines to connect his or her personal circle to the other circles. The type of line that the client draws indicates the client's view of the quality of the relationship with each system. Typically a client is instructed to use solid lines to link his or her own circle to the circles that represent something positive or a strong connection, and to use broken lines to link to circles that represent something negative or a stressful connection. Finally, the client draws wavy lines to the circles that represent something that he or she needs but is not available.

After completing the ecomap, the practitioner can use interview leads like the following ones to complete the picture about the environmental events surrounding the client's concerns:

"Describe the relationship between yourself and all these systems and structures in your current environment."

"How do you experience your current environment? How has this experience been affected by your gender, race, ethnicity, income status, and so on?"

"What is the relationship between you and these larger systems in your ecomap? What has this relationship been like so far in your life? How has this affected your current concerns?"

"Do you feel that you need stronger or closer relationships with any of these larger systems in your ecomap? If so, what has made it difficult for these relationships to develop?"

"How would you describe the sociopolitical and socioeconomic environment you are in? How has it affected your concerns?"

"How much has your concern been affected by oppression, prejudice, and discrimination in your environment?"

"How has your environment fostered empowerment? Or disempowerment? How has this affected the concerns you are bringing to me?"

"Does your environment have a primary story associated with it? If so, could you give this story a title, and what would it be?"*

To familiarize yourself with assessing an individual in relationship to her or his environment, complete Learning Activity 7.1.

f. Relationships, Significant Others, and Social Support Just as issues are often linked to particular times, places, events, and environmental conditions, they are also often connected to the presence or absence of other people.

People around the client can bring about or exacerbate a concern. Someone temporarily or permanently absent from the client's life can have the same effect. Assessing the client's relationships with others is a significant part of many theoretical orientations to counseling, including dynamic theories, Adlerian theory, family systems theory, and behavioral theory.

Interpersonal issues may occur because of a lack of significant others in the client's life, because of the way the client relates to others, or because of the way significant others respond to the client. Consider the role of other people in the development of Mario's school phobia:

Mario, a 9-year-old new arrival from Central America, had moved with his family to a homogeneous neighborhood in which they were the first Spanish-speaking family. Consequently, Mario was one of the few Latino children in his classroom. He soon developed symptoms of school phobia and was referred to an outpatient mental health clinic.

A clinician sensitive to cultural issues chose to work very closely with the school, a decision that facilitated access for Mario to a bicultural, bilingual program. The clinician also realized that Mario was a target of racial slurs and physical attacks by other children on his way to and from school. The school responded to the clinician's request to address these issues at the next parent–teacher conference. With the ongoing support of a dedicated principal, Mario's symptoms abated, and he was able to adjust to his new environment (Canino & Spurlock, 2000, p. 74).

Other persons involved in the issue often tend to discount their role in it. It is helpful if the practitioner can get a handle on what other persons are involved in the issue, how they perceive the issue, and what they might have to

---

Learning Activity 7.1

Ecomaps

1. Using the ecomap format in Figure 7.1, draw a circle representing yourself in the middle of a piece of paper, and around that circle list the systems that are part of your current environment—for example, work, school, family, friends, religion and cultural groups, community groups, recreation, and extended family.

2. Around each system draw circles of varying sizes to indicate the degree of influence of that environmental system in your life.

3. Draw a solid line from your circle to any circles that represent systems with which your connection is positive or strong.

4. Draw a broken line from your circle to any circles that represent systems with which your relationship is stressful or negative.

5. Draw a wavy line from your circle to any circles that represent systems that you need but are not available to you.

6. Look over your ecomap. What conclusions can you draw? You may wish to share your conclusions with a classmate.

---

*Adapted from Kemp, Whittaker, & Tracy, 1997, pp. 103–106 and Ungar, 2011, p. 206.

gain or lose from a change in the issue or the client. As Gambrill (2012) observes, such persons may anticipate negative effects of improvement in an issue and covertly try to sabotage the client's best efforts. For example, a husband may preach "equal pay and opportunity" yet secretly sabotage his wife's efforts to move up the career ladder for fear that she will make more money than he does or that she will find her new job opportunities more interesting and rewarding than her relationship with him. Other people can also influence a client's behavior by serving as role models. People whom clients view as significant to them can often have a great motivational effect on clients in this respect.

An important aspect of the **relational context** of the client's concern has to do with availability and access to resources in the client's social and interpersonal environment, including support from immediate and extended family, friends, neighbors, and people affiliated with the client in work, school, and community organizations. Remember that purposeful, positive relationships are just as important to identify as problematic ones (Lopez, Pedrotti, & Snyder, 2014). As Hepworth and colleagues (2013) point out, social support systems are being recognized increasingly as having a critical role in a client's level of functioning by meeting a variety of client needs such as attachment, belonging, nurturing, physical care, validation, and so on. These authors contend that certain kinds of clients are in particular need of social and relational support: the elderly, abused or neglected children, teenage parents, persons with AIDS, widows and widowers, persons and families with severe mental illness, the terminally ill and their caregivers, persons with disabilities, and persons who experience dislocation as refugees and immigrants (p. 239).

One specific tool that can supplement the interview leads to understanding about a client's social support system is the genogram. Similar to the ecomap tool, the genogram is a useful visual tool to use in the assessment of interactional patterns with clients and those in their environments. The genogram originated with Bowen's (1961) family therapy approach and has been further developed by McGoldrick (2011) and McGoldrick, Gerson, and colleagues (McGoldrick, Gerson, & Shellenberger, 1999; Gerson, McGoldrick, & Petry, 2008). The genogram shows in a visual way the kinds of relationships and patterns of relationships within a client's family system. It is a tool to help clients obtain better information about the relationships and interactional patterns in their families across generations (usually three generations), especially repetitive patterns that are emotional in nature. The point of the genogram, however, is not to draw a work of art that necessarily follows a standardized format but to obtain and assess information about interactional patterns within the client's family history that will shed light on assessing relational aspects of the client's current issues. (Specialized genograms that focus on additional areas of interest such as attachment, spirituality, and culture are also available). In typical genogram diagramming, symbols for males are drawn with squares and symbols for females are drawn with circles. Computer software for both genograms and ecomaps is available at www. genogramanalytics.com. We present a sample genogram with basic instructions in Figure 7.2. (For more detailed information about genograms, consult the sources we list and see also Learning Activity 7.2).

Example leads for assessing the relational component of the issue include the following:

"Tell me about the effects this issue has on your relationships with significant others in your life."

"What effects do these significant others have on this concern?"

"Who else is involved in this issue besides you? How are these persons involved? What would their reaction be if you resolved this issue?"

"From whom do you think you learned to act or think in this way?"

"Describe the persons *present* in your life now who have the greatest positive impact on you. Negative impact?"

"Describe the persons *absent* from your life who have the greatest positive impact on you. Negative impact?"

"What types of social support do you have available in your life right now—too much support or too little?"

"Who do you think you need in your life right now that isn't available to you?"

"Who are the main people in this social support system?"

"Which of these people are there for you? Which of these people are critical of you?"

"What people and social support systems in your life empower you? Disempower you?"

"What things get in your way of using these social support systems and the effective people in them?"

"What people in your life are nourishing to you? Toxic or depleting to you?"

"What people in your life do you look up to? What qualities do they have that help you in your current situation?"

Category 5. Identifying Antecedents

Antecedents are certain events that happen before and contribute to an issue. Much of the assessment process consists of exploring contributing variables that precede and cue the issue (antecedents) and things that happen after the issue (consequences) that in some way influence or maintain it. Recall that antecedents have to be identified for each behavioral issue the client presents (Haynes et al., 2011).

1. List the names of the client's family members for at least three generations with dates of birth and death (if applicable), cause of death, occupations, significant illness, and any substance abuse issues.
2. List important cultural/environment/contextual issues including ethnic identity, race, religion, economic, and social class factors. List significant developmental transitions and roles and life events such as divorce, trauma, loss, and so on.
3. Basic relationship symbols are shown as well as a sample genogram diagram.

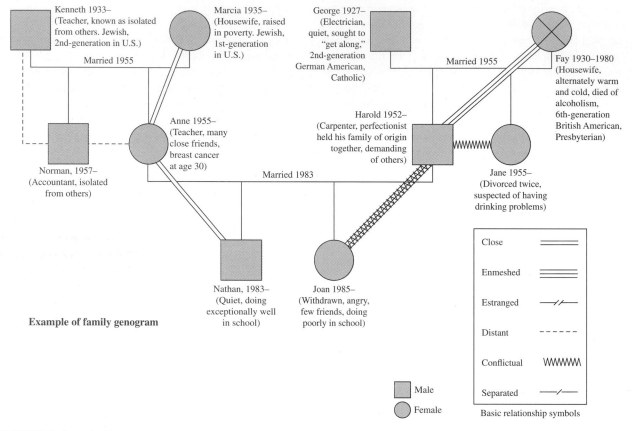

FIGURE 7.2 Sample Genogram

Adapted from *Intentional Interviewing and Counseling: Facilitating Client Development in a Multicultural Society*, 7 ed., by A. E. Ivey, M. B. Ivey, & C. P. Zalaquett, p. 276. Copyright 2010 by Cengage Learning. Reprinted by permission.

Remember that, like behaviors, antecedents (and consequences) are varied and may be affective, somatic, behavioral, cognitive, contextual, or relational. Further, antecedents (and consequences) are likely to differ for each client. Antecedents are both external and internal events that occasion or cue the behaviors and make them more or less likely to occur. Some antecedents occur immediately before (stimulus events); other antecedents (setting events) may have taken place a long time ago, but it is identification of the contiguous antecedents that is most useful because these are more likely to exert important triggering effects on the client's problem behaviors (Haynes et al., 2011).

In helping clients explore antecedents, you are particularly interested in discovering: (1) what *current* conditions (covert and overt) exist *before* the issue that make it

more likely to occur; (2) what *current* conditions (covert and overt) exist that occur *before* the issue that make it *less likely* to occur; and (3) what *previous* conditions, or setting events, exist that *still* influence the issue.

Example leads for identifying antecedents follow and are grouped by category:

Affective

"What are you usually feeling before this happens?"
"When do you recall the first time you felt this way?"
"Describe the feelings that occur before the issue and make it stronger or more constant."
"Identify the feelings that occur before the issue that make it weaker or less intense."
"Tell me about any holdover feelings or unfinished feelings from past events in your life that still affect this issue. For

---

Learning Activity 7.2

Genograms

1. Using the genogram format found in Figure 7.2, list the names of your family members for three generations. Include ages, dates of birth, and dates of death. List cause of death if known. List occupations, notable illnesses, and any substance abuse issues.

2. List important relational and contextual issues as well as significant life events.

3. Using the symbols displayed in Figure 7.2, draw the genogram to reflect males and females and the kinds of relationships among the family members ranging from close to separated.

4. Examine your genogram and, perhaps with a partner or in a small group, explore the following questions:

What behavioral patterns have occurred and recurred in your family system that have persisted throughout several generations? For example, do you see recurring patterns of victimization, domestic violence, suicide, substance abuse, discrimination?

What are the predominant cultural and spiritual beliefs that have persisted in your family system throughout generations?

Can you determine any patterns of coping used in various generations to deal with tragedies, developmental transitions, and stressful life events?

Adapted from Ivey, Ivey, and Zalaquett (2014) and Seabury, Seabury, and Garvin (2011).

---

example, can you recall events in your childhood associated with this particular feeling?"

Somatic

"Notice what goes on inside you just before this happens."

"Are you aware of any particular sensations in your body before this happens?"

"Describe any body sensations that occur right before this issue that make it weaker or less intense. Stronger or more intense?"

"Is there anything going on with you physically—an illness or physical condition—or anything about the way you eat, smoke, exercise, and so on, that affects or leads to this issue?"

Behavioral

"If I were recording this, describe the actions and dialogue the camera would see before this happens."

"Identify any particular behavior patterns that occur right before this happens."

"What do you typically do before this happens?"

"Can you think of anything you do that makes this more likely to occur? Less likely to occur?"

"What was the very first specific thing that happened that started this whole chain of events for you?"

Cognitive

"What kinds of pictures or images do you have before this happens?"

"What are your thoughts before this happens?"

"What are you telling yourself before this happens?"

"Identify any particular beliefs that seem to set the issue off. Now recall the events in your childhood associated with that particular belief."

"Describe what you think about [see or tell yourself] before the issue occurs that makes it stronger or more likely to occur. Weaker or less likely to occur?"

Contextual

"Has this ever occurred at any other time in your life? If so, describe that."

"How long ago did this happen?"

"Where and when did this occur the first time?"

"Describe how you see those events related to your concern."

"Tell me about anything that happened that seemed to lead up to this."

"When did the issue start—what else was going on in your life at that time?"

"What were the circumstances under which the issue first occurred?"

"What was happening in your life when you first noticed this?"

"Are you aware of any events that occurred before this issue that in some way still influence it or set it off?"

Relational

"Can you identify any particular people who seem to bring on this issue?"

"Who are you usually with right before or when this occurs?"

"Are there any people or relationships from the past that still influence or set off or lead to this issue in some way?"

Category 6. Identifying Consequences

Consequences are external or internal events that influence the current problem by maintaining it, strengthening or increasing it, or weakening or decreasing it. Consequences occur after the problem and are distinguished from results or effects by the fact that they have direct influence by either maintaining or decreasing the problem behaviors in some way. As Haynes et al. (2011) remind us, it is the contiguous consequences that are more likely to exert maintaining effects on the client's problem behaviors. Remember, too, that consequences need to be identified for each behavioral issue the client presents (Haynes et al., 2011).

In helping clients explore consequences, you are interested in discovering both internal and external events that maintain and strengthen the undesired behavior and also events that weaken or decrease it. Example leads for identifying consequences follow and are grouped by category:

Affective

"How do you feel after _____?"
"How does this feeling affect the issue (for example, keep it going, stop it)?"
"Describe any particular feelings or emotions that you have after it that strengthen or weaken it."

Somatic

"What are you aware of inside you just after this happens? How does this affect you?"
"Note any body sensations that seem to occur after the issue that strengthen or weaken it."
"Is there anything you can think of about yourself physically—illnesses, diet, exercise, and so on—that seems to occur after this? How does this affect it?"

Behavioral

"What do you do after this happens, and how does this make the issue worse? Better?"
"How do you usually react after this is over? In what ways does your reaction keep the issue going? Weaken it or stop it?"
"Identify any particular behavior patterns that occur after this. How do these patterns keep the issue going? Stop it?"
"What happens afterward that helps you avoid or escape from the problem?"

Cognitive

"What do you usually think about afterward? How does this affect the issue?"
"What do you picture after this happens?"
"What do you tell yourself after this occurs?"
"Identify any particular thoughts [or beliefs or self-talk] during or after the issue that make it better. Worse?"
"Tell me about any certain thoughts or images you have afterward that either strengthen or weaken the issue."

Contextual

"What happened after this?"
"When does the issue usually stop or go away? Get worse? Get better?"
"Where are you when the issue stops? Gets worse? Gets better?"
"Identify any particular times, places, or events that seem to keep the issue going. Make it worse or better?"

Relational

"Can you identify any particular people who can make the issue worse? Better? Stop it? Keep it going?"
"Can you identify any particular reactions from other people that occur after the issue? In what ways do these reactions affect the issue?"

Category 7. Identifying Secondary Gains: A Special Case of Consequences

Occasionally clients have a vested interest in maintaining the status quo of the concern because of the payoffs that the issue produces. For example, a client who is overweight may find it difficult to lose weight, not because of unalterable eating and exercise habits but because the extra weight has allowed him to avoid or escape such things as new social situations or sexual relationships and has produced a safe and secure lifestyle that he is reluctant to give up. A child who is constantly disrupting her school classroom may be similarly reluctant to give up such disruptive behavior even though it results in loss of privileges because it has given her the status of "class clown," resulting in a great deal of peer attention and support.

It is always extremely important to explore with clients the payoffs, or **secondary gains**, they may be getting from having the issue, because often during the intervention phase such clients seem resistant. In these cases, the resistance is a sign the payoffs are being threatened. The most common payoffs include money, attention from significant others, immediate gratification of needs, security, control, and avoidance of responsibility.

Questions you can use to help clients identify possible secondary gains include these:

"The good thing about _____ is . . ."
"What happened afterward that was pleasant?"
"What was unpleasant about what happened?"
"Has your concern ever produced any special advantages or considerations for you?"
"As a consequence of your concern, have you gotten out of or avoided things or events?"
"Please describe the reactions of others when you do this."
"How does this issue help you?"

"What do you get out of this situation that you don't get out of other situations?"

"Do you notice anything that happens afterward that you try to prolong or to produce?"

"Do you notice anything that occurs afterward that you try to stop or avoid?"

Category 8. Exploring Previous Solutions

Another important part of the assessment interview is to explore **previous solutions**, or what things the client has already attempted to resolve the concern and with what effect. This information is important for two reasons. First, it helps you to avoid recommendations for resolutions that amount to more of the same. Second, in many instances, solutions attempted by the client either create new concerns or make the existing concern worse. Leads to hep the client identify previous solutions include the following:

"How have you dealt with this or other concerns before? What was the effect? What made it work or not work?"

"Tell me about how you have tried to resolve this concern."

"What kinds of things have you done to improve this situation?"

"Describe what you have done that has made the concern better. Worse? Kept it the same?"

"What have others done to help you with this?"

"What has kept the issue from getting worse?"

Category 9. Identifying the Client's Coping Skills, Individual and Environmental Strengths, and Resources

When clients come to helpers, they usually are in touch with their pain and often only with their pain. Consequently, they are short-sighted and find it hard to believe that they have any internal or external **coping skills**, **strengths**, and **resources** that can help them deal with the pain more effectively. In the assessment interview, it is useful to focus not only on the issues and pains but also on the person's positive assets and resources that the pain may mask (Sayers & Tomcho, 2006). This sort of focus is the primary one used by the strengths-based assessment approach we described in Chapter 6. Recent cognitive therapists have also placed increasing emphasis on the client's **self-efficacy**—the sense of personal agency and the degree of confidence the client has that she or he can do something (see also Chapter 15). Positive cognitive processes such as self-efficacy, learned optimism, and hope reflect ways of thinking that can impact therapeutic outcomes (Lopez, Pedrotti, & Snyder, 2014). Additionally, helpers should remember that, like many variables, coping skills are culture- and gender-specific; some men and women may not

report using the same coping strategies, just as "effective coping" defined in one cultural system may be different in another one. Coping styles that you consider maladaptive may be adaptive for the client as a way to survive his or her environment (Canino & Spurlock, 2000, p. 66).

Focusing on the client's positive assets achieves several purposes. First, it helps convey to clients that despite the psychological pain, they do have internal resources available that they can muster to produce a different outcome. Second, it emphasizes wholeness—the client is *more* than just his or her "problem." Third, it gives you information on potential problems that may crop up during an intervention. Finally, information about the client's past success stories may be applicable to current concerns. Such information is extremely useful in planning intervention strategies that are geared to using the kind of problem-solving and coping skills already available in the client's repertoire. As Neacsiu and Linehan (2014) point out, clients can learn to prevent future issues by identifying coping strategies they could implement to prevent the problem from occurring another time or with the same intensity. Narratives with particular sources of adversity can be revised with the practitioner's help. For example, clients who have experienced trauma can help to heal themselves by telling or drawing the story of the trauma and its key events. It is also important for these clients to put an ending on the story. Clients with trauma histories usually feel helpless in the face of the trauma. As these clients co-construct their stories, they can also narrate strengths and resources they used to help cope with the trauma. Images of strength are especially important in healing stories of adult survivors.

Information to be assessed in this area includes:

1. *Protective factors associated with the client's history and development.* What about the client's background and history is associated with particular protective factors for the client?

2. *Behavioral assets and problem-solving skills.* When does the client display adaptive behavior instead of problematic behavior? Often this information can be obtained by inquiring about opposites—for example, "When don't you act that way?"

3. *Cognitive coping skills,* such as rational appraisal of a situation, ability to discriminate between rational and irrational thinking, selective attention and feedback from distractions, and the presence of coping or calming self-talk.

4. *Self-control and self-management skills,* including the client's overall ability to withstand frustration, to assume responsibility for self, to be self-directed, to control undesired behavior by either self-reinforcing or self-punishing consequences, and to perceive the self as

being in control rather than being a victim of external circumstances.

5. *Environmental strengths and resources.* In addition to the three individual client strengths described, it is increasingly important to assess the strengths and resources available within the client's environment. These include not only the support network we mentioned earlier but also things such as availability of adequate employment, housing, transportation, and health care. Environmental strengths also include cultural strengths of belonging to a collective community, such as community cohesiveness, community racial identity, and community resources, groups, and organizations (Jones-Smith, 2014; Ungar, 2011). Cultural affiliations can give clients certain protective factors that serve as sources of strength when clients experience adversity. Factors such as racial and ethnic pride, spirituality and religion, and interconnectedness of mind, body, and spirit are other examples of culturally protective factors for clients from marginalized groups (Sue, 2010).

To assess these kinds of individual and environmental strengths and resources, Saleebey (2013) has developed some assessment questions that recognize and build on strengths in eight specific domains. (Note that these strength-building assessment questions are quite compatible with a solution-focused behavior therapy (SFBT) approach, which we discuss in great detail in Chapter 10.).

Examples of these strength-based queries identified by Saleebey (2013, pp. 107–108) are shown in Box 7.2.

Other useful leads to identify these kinds of individual and environmental strengths and resources include the following:

"When you think about where you are in your life now and where you started from, what kinds of things in your background and development have been protective and helpful for you?"

"What strengths do you have as a member of your particular ethnic or cultural group?"

"What skills or things do you have going for you that might help you with this concern?"

"Describe your strengths or assets that you can use to help resolve this concern."

"What tools have you used in the past to help you overcome adversity?"

"When don't you act this way?"

"What kinds of thoughts or self-talk help you handle this better?"

"Notice when you don't think in self-defeating ways."

"What do you say to yourself to cope with a difficult situation?"

"Identify the steps you take in a situation you handle well. What do you think about and what do you do? How could these steps be applied to the present issue?"

"In what situations is it fairly easy for you to manage or control this reaction or behavior?"

"What kinds of coping strategies could you use the next time this happens to either prevent the problem or make it less intense?"

"Rate the degree of confidence you have in your capabilities when you are immersed in this situation." (self-efficacy query)

"When you think about this situation, is your expectancy that it will go well or go poorly?" (optimism query)

"Tell me about what kind of resources in any aspect of your community or environment you are currently using."

"What aspects of your community and overall environment do you find helpful?"

"What kinds of things in your community and environment would you describe as strengths or assets?"

"Describe what strengths and resources in your community and environment are available that you need to use more often."

BOX 7.2	Examples of Strength Questions

Survival questions: "How have you managed to get this far, given all the challenges you have described to me—what and who has helped you?"

Support questions: "Where have you found support in meeting these challenges? What people, groups, associations, organizations have helped you?"

Exception questions: "Recall times in your life when you believe things were going very well for you and tell me what was different then from now?"

Possibility questions: "What do you hope for now in this situation? What possibilities do you see arising for you from these challenging circumstances?"

Esteem questions: "In thinking about your life in general, and about these issues specifically, what gives you pride? What do you and can you feel good about?"

Perspective questions: "How are you making sense of these current struggles?"

Change questions: "What are your ideas about how things might change—about the potential for things being different for you?"

Meaning questions: "What does the current challenging situation you find yourself in mean to you?"

Adapted from Saleebey, 2013.

Category 10. Exploring the Client's Perception of the Concern: Patient Position

Most clients have their own perceptions of and explanations for their concerns. It is important to elicit this information during an assessment session for several reasons. First, it adds to your understanding of the concern. The helper can note which aspects of the concern are stressed and which are ignored during the client's assessment of the issue. Second, this process gives you valuable information about **patient position**, the client's strongly held beliefs and values—in this case, about the nature of the issue. Clients usually allude to such positions in the course of presenting their perceptions of concerns. Ignoring the client's position may cause the practitioner to develop a counseling strategy that the client resists because it is incompatible with this position. You can get a client to describe his or her view of the concern very concisely simply by asking the client to give the concern a one-line title as if it were a movie, play, or book. Another way to elicit the client's perception of the concern is to describe the concern in only one word and then to use the selected word in a sentence. For example, a client may say, "Guilt," and then, "I have a lot of guilt about having an affair." The same client might title the concern "Caught between Two Lovers." This technique works extremely well with children, who typically are quick to think of titles and words without a lot of deliberation. It is also important to recognize the impact of culture, ethnicity, and race on clients' perceptions and reports of concerns. For example, clients from some cultural groups may report the cause of concerns in terms of external factors, supernatural forces, or both. Helpers must not minimize or ridicule such explanations; also, they should incorporate such explanations into the assessment and treatment process.

In the change phase of helping, successful interventions often depend on recognizing and validating the client's "perception of the problem." This emphasis on the client's perspective has made a dramatic impact on the care of older adult clients, but the principle extends to all clients. When clients speak out about their perspectives, there is more collaboration and shared investment in the change process.

Leads to help clients identify and describe their views of concerns include:

"What is your understanding of this issue?"
"Tell me how you explain this concern to yourself."
"What does the issue mean to you?"
"What is your interpretation [analysis] of this concern?"
"What else is important to you about the concern that we haven't mentioned?"
"Give the issue a title."
"Describe the issue with just one word."

Category 11. Ascertaining the Intensity of the Concern

It is useful to determine the **intensity** of the concern. You want to check out how much the concern is affecting the client and the client's daily functioning. If, for example, a client says, "I feel anxious," does the client mean a little anxious or very anxious? Is this person anxious all the time or only some of the time? And does this anxiety affect any of the person's daily activities, such as eating, sleeping, or working? There are two kinds of intensity to assess: the degree or severity and the frequency (how often) and/or duration (how long) of it.

a. Degree of Intensity Often it is useful to obtain a client's subjective rating of the degree of discomfort, stress, or **intensity** of the concern. The helper can use this information to determine how much the concern affects the client and whether the client seems to be incapacitated or immobilized by it. To assess the degree of intensity, the helper can use leads similar to these:

"You say you feel anxious. On a scale from 1 to 10, with 1 being very calm and 10 being extremely anxious, where would you be now?"
"How strong is your feeling when this happens?"
"How has this interfered with your daily activities?"
"How would your life be affected if this issue were not resolved in a year?"
"On a scale from 0 to 100, with 0 being no distress and 100 being extreme distress, where would you place your distress now?"

In assessing degree of intensity, you are looking for a client response that indicates how strong, interfering, or pervasive the concern seems to be.

b. Frequency and/or Duration In asking about frequency and duration, your purpose is to have the client identify how often (**frequency**) and/or how long (**duration**) the current behaviors occur. Data about how often or how long they occur *before* a change strategy is applied are called *baseline data*. Baseline data provide information about the *present* extent of the problem. They can be used later to compare the extent of the problem before and after a treatment strategy has been used. Leads to assess the frequency and duration of the current behavior include the following:

"How often does this happen?"
"How many times does this occur?"
"How long does this feeling usually stay with you?"
"How much does this go on, say, in an average day?"

Some clients can discuss the severity, frequency, or duration of the behavior during the interview rather

BOX 7.3	Review of 11 assessment categories

1. Purpose of assessment
2. Range of concerns
3. Prioritization of issues
4. Identification of behaviors
5. Identification of antecedents
6. Identification of consequences

7. Identification of secondary gains (payoffs)
8. Previous solutions
9. Coping skills and individual and environmental strengths
10. Client perceptions of issue
11. Severity, frequency, and duration of issue

(4) Behaviors	(5) Antecedents	(6) Consequences and (7) Secondary gains (payoffs)
Affective	Affective	Affective
Somatic	Somatic	Somatic
Behavioral	Behavioral	Behavioral
Cognitive	Cognitive	Cognitive
Contextual	Contextual	Contextual
Relational	Relational	Relational

easily. However, many clients may be unaware of the number of times the behavior occurs, how much time it occupies, or how intense it is. As we described in Chapter 6, most clients can give the helper more accurate information about frequency and duration by engaging in self-monitoring of the behaviors with a written log. Use of logs to supplement the interview data is illustrated later in the model dialogue. Another useful supplement to obtain information about the intensity of the problem is the **TLFB or Timeline Follow-Back Assessment** (Sayers & Tomcho, 2006). This method is described as follows.

The key aspects of the TLFB method include the use of a calendar as well as a systematic review of each time period on the calendar, working backward to stimulate recall. First, the interviewer establishes the time period, such as 1 month, 6 months, and so on, depending on the predicted frequency and the clinical consideration regarding the type of behavior involved. The therapist then asks about key events in the patient's life during this period or holidays as marked on the calendar to relate these events to the behavior in question. Then, starting with the most current time period, the interviewer asks about the frequency of behavior for that period . . . Working backward, 1 week (or 1 month, depending on the context) at a time, the interviewer asks for the patient's estimate of the behavior for that period. If the patient has a calendar or appointment book of his or her own, then the patient is asked to use this as a cue for better recall (p. 73).

Box 7.3 provides a review of the 11 categories of client assessment. This table may help you conceptualize and summarize the types of information you will seek during assessment interviews.

Limitations of Interview Leads in Assessment

The leads we present in this chapter are simply tools that the helper can use to elicit certain kinds of client information. They are designed to be used as a road map to provide some direction for assessment interviews. However, the leads alone are an insufficient basis for assessment because they represent only approximately half of the process at most—the helper responses. The other part of the process is reflected by the responses these leads generate from the client. A complete interview assessment includes not only asking the right questions but also synthesizing and integrating the client responses.

Think of it this way: In an assessment interview, you are simply *supplementing* your basic skills with some specific leads designed to obtain certain kinds of information. While many of your leads will consist of open-ended questions, even *assessment* interviews should not disintegrate into a question-and-answer or interrogation session. You can obtain information and give the information some meaning through other verbal responses, such as summarization, clarification, confrontation, and reflection. Demonstrating sensitivity is especially important because sometimes during assessment, a client may reveal or even re-experience very traumatic events and memories. The quality of the helping relationship remains very important during assessment interviews. Handling the assessment interview in an understanding and empathic way becomes critical. It is also extremely important to clarify and reflect the information the client gives you before jumping ahead to another question. The model dialogue that follows after Learning Activity 7.3 illustrates this process. (See also Learning Activity 7.3.)

Learning Activity 7.3

Interview Assessment

Part One

This activity is designed to assist you in identifying assessment leads in an interview. You are given a helper/client dialogue that consists of an interview with a mother, Ms. Weare, about her relationship with her son Freddie (Chapter 6). For each helper response, your task is to identify and write down the type of assessment lead used by the helper. You may find it helpful to use the Interview Checklist at the end of this chapter as a guide for this activity. There may be more than one example of any given type of lead. Also, identify the listening and influencing responses used by the helper. Feedback follows on page 236.

Dialogue between Ms. Weare and the Helper

1. **Helper:** Hello, Ms. Weare. Could you tell me about some things going on now that are concerning you?

   Client: Not too much. Family Services sent me here.

2. **Helper:** So you're here just because they sent you—or is there something bothering you?

   Client: Well, they don't think my kid and I get along too well. My kid is Freddie.

3. **Helper:** What do you think about the way you and Freddie get along?

   Client: Well, I yell at him a lot. I don't like to do that, but sometimes he gets me so mad. I don't like to, but he needs to learn.

4. **Helper:** So there are times when you get real mad at Freddie and then you yell at him. You don't like to do this, but you see it as a way to help him learn right and wrong.

   Client: That's it. I don't like to, but there are times when he needs to know something. Like yesterday, I bought him new pants, and he came home from school with a big hole in them. Now, I just don't have money to keep buying him new pants.

5. **Helper:** You just mentioned the incident with Freddie's pants. What are some other times that you get mad at Freddie?

   Client: Every morning. Freddie's in third grade now. But he still doesn't dress himself in the morning. I want to be a good mother and get him to school on time, and he tries to be late. He waits around not getting dressed.

6. **Helper:** Any other times you can remember getting mad?

   Client: Well, not too long ago he was playing outside and broke a window. I got mad then. But that doesn't happen every day like his not getting dressed does.

7. **Helper:** So one thing that really bothers you is what goes on in the mornings. Tell me exactly what does happen each morning at your house.

   Client: Well, I call Freddie to get up and tell him to dress before he comes down for breakfast. He comes down all right—in his pajamas. I warn him after breakfast to get ready. Usually about 5 minutes before the bus comes, I'll go up. He'll just be sitting in his room! He's still not dressed. I'll yell at him and then dress him so he's not late.

8. **Helper:** And your main feeling at this point is that you're mad. Anything else you feel?

   Client: No, just very mad.

9. **Helper:** And what exactly do you do when you go upstairs and he's not dressed?

   Client: I yell at him. Then I help dress him.

10. **Helper:** What kinds of things do you usually say to him?

    Client: I tell him he's dumb and he's going to be late for school, and that I have to make sure he won't be.

11. **Helper:** You mentioned this happens in the morning. Does this situation go on every morning or only some mornings?

    Client: Just about every morning except weekends.

12. **Helper:** When did these incidents seem to begin?

    Client: Ever since Freddie started going to school.

13. **Helper:** So it appears that this has been going on for about 3 years, then?

    Client: Yes, I guess so.

14. **Helper:** Okay, now let's go back over this situation. You told me you remind Freddie every morning to get dressed. He never dresses by breakfast. You remind him again. Then, about 5 minutes before the bus comes, you go upstairs to check on him. When do you notice that you start to feel mad?

    Client: I think about it as soon as I realize it's almost time for the bus to come and Freddie isn't down yet. Then I feel mad.

15. **Helper:** And what exactly do you think about right then?

    Client: Well, that he's probably not dressed and that if I don't go up and help him, he'll be late. Then I'll look like a bad mother if I can't get my son to school on time.

16. **Helper:** So in a sense you actually go help him out so he won't be late. How many times has Freddie ever been late?

    Client: Never.

17. **Helper:** You believe that helping Freddie may prevent him from being late. However, your help also excuses Freddie from having to help himself. What do you think would happen if you stopped going upstairs to check on Freddie in the morning?

    Client: Well, I don't know, but I'm his only parent now. Freddie's father and I are separated now. It's up to me, all by myself, to keep Freddie in line. If I didn't go up and if Freddie was late all the time, his teachers might blame me. I wouldn't be a good mother.

(continued)

18. **Helper:** Of course, we don't *really* know what would happen if you didn't go up and yell at him or help him dress. It might be so different for Freddie after the first day or two he would dress himself. It could be that he thinks it's easier to wait and get your help than to dress himself. He might think that by sitting up there and waiting for you to help, he's getting a special advantage or attention from you.
    Client: You mean like he's getting a favor from me?

19. **Helper:** Sure. And when we find a way to get a favor from someone, we usually do as much as we can to keep getting the favor. Ms. Weare, I'd like to ask you about something else. Do you think maybe that you see helping Freddie out as a way to avoid having Freddie be late and then not having someone blame you for this?
    Client: Sure. I'd rather help him than get myself in hot water.

20. **Helper:** Okay, so you're concerned about what you think might happen to you if he's late. You see getting him ready on time as a way to prevent you from getting the heat for him.
    Client: Yes.

21. **Helper:** How do you usually feel after these incidents in the morning are over?
    Client: Well, it upsets me.

22. **Helper:** Okay, you feel upset. Do these feelings seem to make you want to continue or to stop helping Freddie?
    Client: Probably to stop. I get worn out. Also, sometimes I don't get my work done then.

23. **Helper:** So helping Freddie so he won't be late and you won't be blamed sort of makes you want to keep on helping him. Yet when you feel upset and worn out afterward, you're tempted to stop helping. Have I heard you accurately?
    Client: I guess that could be true.

24. **Helper:** Gee, I imagine that all the responsibility for a 9-year-old boy would start to feel like a pretty heavy burden after a while.
    Client: Yeah. I guess a lot of the time it does.

25. **Helper:** Those may be feelings we'll want to talk about more. I'm also wondering whether there are any other things in your life causing you any concern now?
    Client: No, this is about it.

26. **Helper:** Ms. Weare, we've been talking a lot about some problem situations you've had with Freddie. Describe some times when the two of you get along okay.
    Client: Well, on weekends we do. Freddie dresses himself whenever he gets up. I sleep later.

27. **Helper:** What happens on weekends when the two of you get along better?
    Client: Sometimes I'll take him to a movie or a game. And we eat all our meals together. Usually, weekends are pleasant. He can be a good boy, and I don't scream all the time at him.

28. **Helper:** So you realize it is possible for the two of you to get along. How do you feel about my talking with Freddie and then with both of you together?
    Client: That's okay.

Part Two

To incorporate the interview leads into your verbal repertory, we suggest that you try a role-play interview of the case of Ms. Weare (Chapter 6) or the case of Mr. Huang (Chapter 6) with a triad. One person can take the role of the client (Ms. Weare or Mr. Huang); another can be the helper. Your task is to assess the client's concerns using the interview leads described in this chapter. The third person can be the observer, providing feedback to the helper during or following the role play, using the Interview Checklist at the end of this chapter as a guide.

Model Dialogue: Interview Assessment

To see how these assessment leads are used in an interview, read the following dialogue in the case of Isabella. An explanation of the helper's response and the helper's rationale for using it appears before the responses. Note the *variety* of responses used by the helper.

Helper response 1 is a *rationale* to explain to the client, Isabella, the *purpose* of the assessment interview.

1. **Helper:** Isabella, last week you dropped by to schedule today's appointment, and you mentioned you were feeling unhappy and anxious at school. It might be helpful today to take some time just to explore exactly what is going on with you and school and anything else that concerns you. I'm sure there are ways we can work with this, but first I think it would be helpful to both of us to get a better idea of what all the issues are for you now. Also, I know I gave you an explanation and consent form to take home and review with your parents. I wanted to go over that as well and also highlight what we mean about the word in it called confidentiality. It basically means that what you tell me I keep to myself except in a few situations like if I find out about child abuse that has happened or is happening, or if you were planning to hurt yourself or someone else—I would have to tell someone else in these situations. Does this make sense to you?

Client: Yeah. I don't really have any questions about that or the form I took home (hands it to the counselor). Cause one time when my grandpa died and my grandma came to stay with us for a while we went to see a counselor for a couple times and she talked about this stuff, too. The main thing I want to talk to you about today is with school. It's really bugging me.

Helper response 2 is a lead to help Isabella identify the *range* of her concerns.

2. **Helper:** Okay, you just said school is the *main* concern. From the way you said that and the way you look right now, I have the feeling school isn't the *only* thing you're concerned about in your life.

Client: Well, you're right about that. I'm also kind of not getting along too well with my parents. But that's kind of related to this school thing, too.

In the next response, the helper simply *listens* to Isabella and synthesizes what she's saying by using a *paraphrase* response.

3. **Helper:** So from your point of view, the school thing and the issue with your parents are connected.

Client: Yeah, because I'm having trouble in some of my classes. There's too much competition. I feel the other kids are better than I am. I've thought about changing from this college prep program to the work-study program, but I don't know what to do. I don't like to make decisions anyway. At the same time, my parents put a lot of pressure on me to perform well, to make top grades. They have a lot of influence with me. I used to want to do well, but now I'm kind of tired of it all.

In the next response, the helper continues to listen to Isabella and *reflect her feelings*.

4. **Helper:** It seems like you're feeling pretty overwhelmed and discouraged right now.

Client (*lowers head, eyes, and voice tone*): Yeah, I am. I've started to have trouble sleeping at night cause I worry about all this stuff now when I try to sleep.

Helper senses Isabella has strong feelings about these issues and doesn't want to cut them off initially. Helper *instructs* Isabella to continue focusing on the feelings.

5. **Helper** (*Pause*): Let's stay with these feelings for a few minutes and see where they take you.

6. **Client** (*Pause—eyes fill with tears*): I guess I just feel like all this stuff is coming down on me at once. I feel edgy at school and worried about how I am doing there. I've been having more trouble concentrating, which just makes things worse for me. And honestly cause school is difficult for me now except when I'm hanging out with my friend like at lunch, sometimes I oversleep or fake illness so I can stay home.

Helper continues to *attend,* to *listen,* and to *reflect* the client's current experience.

7. **Helper:** It seems like you feel you're carrying a big load on your shoulders—

Client: Yeah.

In response 8, the helper *summarizes* Isabella's concerns and then uses a lead to determine whether Isabella has *prioritized* her concerns.

8. **Helper:** I think before we're finished I'd like to come back to these feelings, which seem pretty strong for you now. Before we do, it might help you to think about not having to tackle everything all at once. You know you mentioned several things that are bothering you—feeling unhappy and anxious at school, having trouble making decisions, having trouble sleeping and concentrating, and not getting along with your parents. Which of these bothers you most?

Client: I'm not really sure. I'm concerned right now about having trouble in my classes. But sometimes I think if I were in another type of curriculum, I wouldn't be so tense about these classes. But I'm sort of worried about deciding to do this.

Helper response 9 is a *clarification*. The helper wants to see whether the client's interest in work-study is real or is a way to avoid the present issue.

9. **Helper:** Do you see getting in the work-study program as a way to get out of your present problem classes, or is it a program that really interests you?

Client: It's a program that interests me. I think sometimes I'd like to get a job after high school instead of going to college, or maybe just go to culinary school. *But* I've been thinking about this for a year, and I can't decide what to do. I'm not very good at making decisions on my own.

Helper response 10 is a *summarization* and *instruction*. The helper goes back to the areas of concern. Note that the helper does not draw explicit attention to the client's last self-deprecating statement.

10. **Helper:** Well, your concerns about your present class problems and about making this and other decisions are somewhat related. Your parents tie into this, too. Maybe you could explore all concerns and then decide later about what you want to work on first.

Client: That's fine with me.

Helper response 11 is a lead to *identify some present behaviors* related to Isabella's concern about competitive classes. Asking the client for examples can elicit specificity about what does or does not occur during the situation of concern.

7.3 Feedback

Interview Assessment

Part One

Identification of the responses in the dialogue between Ms. Weare and the helper are as follows:

1. Open-ended question
2. Clarification response
3. Open-ended question
4. Summarization response
5. Paraphrase response and behavior lead: exploration of context
6. Behavior lead: exploration of context
7. Paraphrase response and behavior lead: exploration of overt behavior
8. Reflection-of-feelings response and behavior lead: exploration of affect
9. Behavior lead: exploration of overt behavior
10. Behavior lead: exploration of overt behavior
11. Paraphrase and behavior lead: exploration of context
12. Antecedent lead: context
13. Clarification response
14. Summarization response and antecedent lead: affect
15. Behavior lead: exploration of cognitions
16. Paraphrase and open question responses
17. Consequences: overt behavior
18. Consequences: secondary gains for Freddie
19. Consequences: secondary gains for Ms. Weare
20. Summarization response and exploration of secondary gains for Ms. Weare
21. Consequences: affect
22. Consequences: affect
23. Summarization (of consequences)
24. Reflection-of-feelings response
25. Range-of-concerns lead
26. Coping skills
27. Coping skills
28. Paraphrase and open-ended question

11. **Helper:** Okay, give me an example of some trouble you've been having in your most competitive class.

Client: Well, I guess I shut down in these classes. Also, I've been cutting my math classes. It's the worst. My grades are dropping, especially in math class. It's hardest for me to focus in that class in particular.

Helper response 12 is a *behavior* lead regarding the *context* of the concern to see whether the client's concern occurs at other *times* or other *places*.

12. **Helper:** Where else do you have trouble—in any other classes, or at other times or places outside school?

Client: Well, to some degree, I always feel anxious in any class because of the pressures my parents put on me to get good grades. But my math class is really the worst.

And then it bothers me at night when I try to go to sleep, too.

Helper response 13 is a lead to help the client identify *overt behaviors* in math class (*behavioral* component of concern).

13. **Helper:** Describe what happens in your math class that makes it troublesome for you. [The helper could also use imagery assessment at this point.]

Client: Well, to start with, it's a harder class for me. I have to work harder to do okay. In this class I get nervous whenever I go in it. So I withdraw.

Client's statement "I withdraw" is vague. So helper response 14 is another *overt behavior* lead to help the client specify what she means by "withdrawing." Note that since the helper did not get a complete answer to this, the same type of lead is used again.

14. **Helper:** What do you do when you withdraw? [This is also an ideal place for a role-play assessment.]

Client: Well, I sit by myself; I don't talk or volunteer answers. Sometimes I don't go to the board or answer when the teacher calls on me.

Now that the client has identified certain overt behaviors associated with the concern, the helper will use a *covert behavior* lead to find out whether there are any predominant *thoughts* the client has during the math class (*cognitive* component of issue).

15. **Helper:** What are you generally thinking about in this class?

Client: What do you mean—am I thinking about math?

The client's response indicated some confusion. The helper will have to use a more specific *covert behavior* lead to assess cognition, along with some *self-disclosure,* to help the client respond more specifically.

16. **Helper:** Well, sometimes when I'm in a situation like a class, there are times when my mind is on the class and other times I'm thinking about myself or about something else I'm going to do. So I'm wondering what you've noticed you're thinking about during the class.

Client: Well, some of the time I'm thinking about the math problems. Other times I'm thinking about the fact that I'd rather not be in the class and that I'm not as good as the other kids, especially all the guys in it.

The client has started to be more specific, and the helper thinks perhaps there are still other thoughts going on. To explore this possibility, the helper uses another *covert behavior* lead in response 17 to assess *cognition*.

17. **Helper:** What else do you recall that you tell yourself when you're thinking you're not as good as other people?

Client: Well, I think that I don't get grades that are as good as some other students'. My parents have been pointing this out to me since junior high. And in the math class I'm one of four girls. The guys in there are really smart. I just keep thinking how can a girl ever be as smart as a guy in math class? No way. It just doesn't happen.

The client identifies more specific thoughts and also suggests two possible antecedents—parental comparison of her grades and cultural stereotyping (girls shouldn't be as good in math as boys). The helper's records show that the client's test scores and previous grades indicate that she is definitely not "dumb" in math. The helper will *summarize* this and then, in the next few responses, will focus on these and on other possible *antecedents,* such as the nervousness the client mentioned earlier.

18. **Helper:** So what you're telling me is that you believe most of what you've heard from others about yourself and about the fact that girls automatically are not supposed to do too well in math.

Client: Yeah, I guess so, now that you put it like that. I've never given it much thought.

19. **Helper:** Yes. It doesn't sound like you've ever thought about whether *you, Isabella*, really feel this way or whether these feelings are just adopted from things you've heard others tell you.

Client: No, I never have.

20. **Helper:** That's something we'll also probably want to come back to later.

Client: Okay.

21. **Helper:** You know, Isabella, earlier you mentioned that you get anxious about this class. When do you notice that you feel this way—before the class, during the class, or at other times?

Client: Well, right before the class is the worst. About 10 minutes before my English class ends—it's right before math—I start thinking about the math class. Then, I get nervous and feel like I wish I didn't have to go. Recently, I've tried to find ways to cut math class.

The helper still needs more information about how and when the nervousness affects the client, so response 22 is another *antecedent* lead.

22. **Helper:** Tell me more about when you feel most nervous and when you don't feel nervous about this class.

Client: Well, I feel worst when I'm actually walking to the class and the class is starting. Once the class starts, I feel better. I don't feel nervous about it when I cut it or at other times. However, once in a while, if someone talks about it or I think about it, I feel a little nervous. And recently I've started feeling anxious and nervous at night when I try to go to sleep cause I find myself worrying about school the next day.

The helper realizes at this point that the words *nervous/anxious* have not been defined and goes back in the next response to a *covert behavior* lead to find out what Isabella means by *nervous* (affective component).

23. **Helper:** Tell me what you mean by the word *nervous and anxious*—what goes on with you when you're feeling like this?

Client: Well, I get sort of a sick feeling in my stomach, and my hands get all sweaty. My heart starts to pound. I feel on edge. And I have trouble concentrating at school now a lot of the time. And when this happens to me at night, I have trouble going to sleep.

In the next response, the helper continues to *listen* and *paraphrase* to clarify whether the nervousness is experienced somatically.

24. **Helper:** So your nervousness really consists of things you feel going on inside you like a pit in your stomach, sweaty hands, heart pounding, and so on.

Client: Yeah.

Next, the helper will use an *intensity* lead to determine the *severity* of nervousness.

25. **Helper:** How strong is this feeling—a little or very? Can you rate it on a 1 to 10 scale with 1 being low and 10 being extremely strong?

Client: Before class, very strong—like a 7 especially before math class. At other times, just a little, maybe a 3, but some nights it goes back up to maybe a 6.

The client has established that the nervousness seems mainly to be exhibited in somatic forms and is more intense before class. The helper will use an *antecedent* lead is used next.

26. **Helper:** Which seems to come first—feeling nervous, not speaking up in class, or thinking about other people being smarter than you?

Client: Well, thinking about the other kids and that I don't measure up to them cause they are so much smarter than I am. Because that starts before I get in the class and even sometimes starts the night before.

The helper has a clue from the client's previous comments that there are other antecedents that have to do with the client's concern—such as the role of her parents. The helper will pursue this in the next response, using an *antecedent* lead.

27. **Helper:** Isabella, you mentioned earlier that you have been thinking about not being as smart as some of your friends ever since you started high school. When do you recall you really started to dwell on this?

Client: Well, that's right, when I started high school a year ago.

The helper didn't get sufficient information about what happened to the client then, so another *antecedent* lead will be used to identify this possible *setting event*.

28. **Helper:** What do you recall happened then?

Client: Well, my parents said when you start high school, your grades become really important in order to go to college. So, for the last year they have been telling me some of my grades aren't as good as other students'. Also, if I get a B, they will take something away, like going out with my friends.

The helper has no evidence of actual parental reaction but will work with the client's report at this time, because this is how the client perceives parental input. If possible, a parent conference could be arranged later with the client's permission. The parents *seem* to be using negative rather than positive consequences with Isabella to influence her behavior. The helper wants to pursue the relationship between the parents' input and the client's present behavior to determine whether parental reaction is eliciting part of Isabella's present concerns. The helper will use a lead to identify this as a possible *antecedent*.

29. **Helper:** How do you think this reaction of your parents relates to your present problems?

Client: Well, since I started high school, they have talked more about needing to get better grades for college. And I have to work harder in school and especially in math class to do this. I guess I feel a lot of pressure to perform—which makes me withdraw and just want to hang it up. Now, of course, my grades are getting worse, not better.

The helper, in the next lead, will *paraphrase* Isabella's previous comment.

30. **Helper:** So, the expectations you feel from your parents seem to draw out pressure in you.

Client: Yes, that happens.

In response 31, the helper will explore another possible *antecedent* that Isabella mentioned before—thinking that girls aren't as good as boys in math.

31. **Helper:** Isabella, I'd like to ask you about something else you mentioned earlier that I said we would come back to. You said one thing that you think about in your math class is that you're only one of four girls and that, as a girl, you're not as smart in math as a boy. Do you know what makes you think this way?

Client: I'm not sure. Everyone knows or says that girls have more trouble in math than boys. Even my teacher. He's gone out of his way to try to help me because he knows it's tough for me.

The client has identified a possible consequence of her behavior as teacher attention. The helper will return to this later. First, the helper is going to respond to the client's response that "everyone" has told her this thought. Helpers have a responsibility to point out things that clients have learned from stereotypes or irrational beliefs rather than actual data, as is evident in this case from Isabella's academic record. The helper will use *confrontation/challenge* in the next response.

32. **Helper:** You know, studies have shown that when young women drop out of math, science, and engineering programs, they do so not because they're doing poorly but because they don't believe they can do well.* It is evident to me from your records that you have a lot of potential for math.

Client: Really?

Helper response 33 is an *interpretation* to help the client see the relation between overt and covert behaviors.

33. **Helper:** I don't see why not. But lots of times the way someone acts or performs in a situation is affected by how the person thinks about the situation. I think some of the reason you're having more trouble in your math class is that your performance is hindered a little by your nervousness and anxiety and by the way you put yourself down and compare yourself constantly to your peers.

In the next response, the helper *checks out* and *clarifies* the client's reaction to the previous interpretation.

34. **Helper:** I'm wondering now from the way you're looking at me whether this makes any sense or whether what I just said muddies the waters more for you?

*From studies conducted at Wellesley College's Center for Research on Women.

Client: No, I guess I was just thinking about things. But I guess it's not just that my parents expect too much of me. I guess in a way I expect too little of myself. I've never really thought of that before.

35. **Helper:** That's a great observation. In a way the two sets of expectations are probably connected. These are some of the kinds of issues we may want to work on if this track we're on seems to fit for you.

Client: Yeah. Okay, it's a problem.

The helper is going to go back now to pursue possible consequences that are influencing the client's behavior. The next response is a lead to identify *consequences*.

36. **Helper:** Isabella, I'd like to go back to some things you mentioned earlier. For one thing, you said your teacher has gone out of his way to help you. Would you say that your behavior in his class has got you any extra attention or special consideration from him?

Client: Certainly extra attention. He talks to me more frequently. And he doesn't get upset when I don't go to the board.

Helper response 37 will continue to explore the teacher's behavior as a possible *consequence*.

37. **Helper:** Do you mean he may excuse you from board work?

Client: For sure, and I think he, too, almost expects me *not* to come up with the answer. Just like I don't expect myself to.

The teacher's behavior may be maintaining the client's overt behaviors in class by giving extra attention to her and by excusing her from some kinds of work. A teacher conference may be necessary at some later point. The helper, in the next two responses, will continue to use other leads to identify possible *consequences*.

38. **Helper:** What do you see you're doing right now that helps you get out of putting yourself through the stress of going to math class?

Client: Do you mean something like cutting class?

39. **Helper:** I think that's perhaps one thing you do to get out of the class. What else?

Client: Well, let's see—I guess staying home from school cause then I don't even have to be in class!

The client has identified cutting class and staying home as ways to avoid the math class. The helper, in the next response, will suggest another *consequence* that the client

mentioned earlier, though not as a way to get out of the stress associated with the class. The helper will suggest that this consequence functions as a *secondary gain,* or *payoff,* in a tentative *interpretation* that is checked out with the client in the next three responses:

40. **Helper:** Also, Isabella, you told me earlier that your grades were dropping in math class. Is it possible that if these grades—and others—drop too much, you'll automatically be dropped from these college prep classes?

Client: That's right.

41. **Helper:** I'm wondering whether one possible reason for letting your grades slide is that it is almost an automatic way for you to get out of these competitive classes.

Client: How so?

42. **Helper:** Well, if you became ineligible for these classes because of your grades, you'd automatically be out of this class and others that you consider competitive and feel nervous about. What do you think about that?

Client: I guess that's true. Since I can't decide if I want to stay in these college prep classes or switch to the work-study program.

In the next response, the helper uses *summarization* and ties together the effects of "dropping grades" to math class and to the previously expressed concern of a curriculum-change decision.

43. **Helper:** Right. And letting your grades get too bad will automatically mean that decision is made for you, so you can take yourself off the hook for making that choice. In other words, it's sort of a way that part of you has rather creatively come up with to get yourself out of the hassle of having to decide something you don't really want to be responsible for deciding about.

Client: Wow! Gosh, I guess that might be happening.

44. **Helper:** That's something you can think about. We didn't really spend that much time today exploring the other things you were concerned about, so that will probably be something to discuss the next time we get together. I know you have a class coming up in about 10 minutes, so there are just a couple more things we might look at.

Client: Okay—what next?

In the next several responses (45–51), the helper continues to demonstrate *listening responses* and to help Isabella explore *solutions* she's tried already to resolve the issue. They look together at the *effects* of the use of the solutions Isabella identifies.

45. **Helper:** Okay, starting with the nervousness and pressure you feel in math class—is there anything you've attempted to do to get a handle on this concern?

Client: Not really—other than talking to you about it and, of course, cutting class and playing hooky.

46. **Helper:** How do you think these solutions have helped you?

Client: Well, like I said before—it helps mainly because on the days I don't go, I don't feel uptight.

47. **Helper:** So you see it as a way to get rid of these feelings you don't like.

Client: Yeah, I guess that's it.

48. **Helper:** Can you think of any ways in which these solutions have not helped?

Client: Gee, I don't know. Maybe I'm not sure what you're asking.

49. **Helper:** Okay, good point! Sometimes when I try to do something to resolve a concern, it can make the issue better or worse. So I guess what I'm really asking is whether you've noticed that your "solutions" of cutting class and playing hooky have in any way made the problem worse or in any way have even contributed to the whole issue?

Client *(Pause):* I suppose maybe in a way. *(Pause)* In that, by cutting class or staying home, I miss out on the work, and then I don't have all the input I need for tests and homework, and that doesn't help my poor grades.

50. **Helper:** Okay. That's an interesting idea. You're saying that when you look deeper, your solution also has had some negative effects on one of the issues you're trying to deal with and eliminate.

Client: Yeah. But I guess I'm not sure what else I could do.

51. **Helper:** At this point, you probably are feeling a little bit stuck, like you don't know which other direction or road to take.

Client: Yeah.

At this point, the helper shifts the focus a little to exploration of Isabella's *assets, strengths, and resources.*

52. **Helper:** Well, one thing I sense is that your feelings of being anxious are sort of covering up the resources and assets you have within you to handle the issue

and work it out. For example, can you identify any particular skills or things you have going for you that might help you deal with this issue?

Client: Well, I am pretty responsible. I'm usually fairly loyal and dependable. It's hard to make decisions for myself, but when I say I'm going to do something, I usually do it.

53. **Helper:** Okay, great. So what you're telling me is you're good on follow-through once you decide something is important to you.

Client: That sounds hopeful!

Isabella and the helper have been talking about *individual strengths.* Next (in responses 54–57), the helper will explore any *environmental and cultural strengths and resources* that can help Isabella in this situation.

54. **Helper:** So far we've been talking about your own individual assets. Can you think of any assets or resources—including people—in your immediate environment that could be useful to you in dealing with these concerns?

Client: Well, I mentioned my math teacher. He does go out of his way to help me. He even has given all of us his e-mail address to use if we get stuck on a homework problem, and he has a tutoring session after school every Thursday, too. But I haven't used his help too much outside of class.

55. **Helper:** So you rely on him more during class?

Client: Yup.

56. **Helper:** Are there any other people or resources available to you that you may or may not be using?

Client: Hmm. Not really sure about this one.

57. **Helper:** Earlier you mentioned your friends. Do you ever do homework with them or have study groups with them?

Client: No—we mainly just go out on weekends to do things. But I think that might be a good idea, and I think my parents would be in favor of that one, too.

In the next few responses, the helper tries to elicit *Isabella's perception and assessment of the main issue.*

58. **Helper:** Just a couple more things. Changing the focus a little now, think about the issues that you came in with today—and describe the main issue in one word.

Client: Ooh—that's a hard question!

59. **Helper:** I guess it could be. Take your time. You don't have to rush.

Client *(Pause):* Well, how about *can't?*

60. **Helper:** Okay, now, to help me get an idea of what that word means to you, use it in a sentence.

Client: Any sentence?

61. **Helper:** Yeah. Make one up. Maybe the first thing that comes in your head.

Client: Well, "I can't do a lot of things I think I want to or should be able to do."

Next, the helper uses a *confrontation* to depict the incongruity revealed in the sentence Isabella made up about her concern.

62. **Helper:** Okay, that's interesting too, because on one hand you're saying there are some things you *want* to do that aren't happening and, on the other hand you're also saying there are some things that aren't happening that you think you *should* be doing. Now, these are two pretty different things mixed together in the same sentence.

Client: Yeah. [Clarifies.] I think the wanting stuff to happen is from me and the should things are from my parents and my teachers.

63. **Helper:** Okay, so you're identifying part of the whole issue as wanting to please yourself and others at the same time.

Client: Mm-hmm.

In the next two responses, the helper explores the *context* related to these issues and sets up some *self-monitoring* homework to obtain additional information. Note that this is a task likely to appeal to the client's dependability, which she revealed during exploration of *coping skills*.

64. **Helper:** That's something we'll be coming back to, I'm sure. One last thing before you have to go to your next class. Earlier we talked about some specific times and places connected to some of these issues—like where and when you feel anxious and also where and when you put yourself down and think you're not as smart as other people. What I'd like to do is give you sort of a diary to write in this week to collect some more information about these kinds of problems. Sometimes writing these kinds of things down can help you start making changes and sorting out the issues. You've said that you're pretty dependable. Would doing this appeal to your dependability?

Client: Sure. That's something that wouldn't be too hard for me to do.

65. **Helper:** Okay, let me tell you specifically what to keep track of, and then I'll see you next week—bring this back with you. *(Goes over instructions for self-monitoring homework.)* (See Isabella's behavior log in Figure 7.3.)

For Isabella
Week of Nov. 6–13

Behavior	Date	Time	Place	Frequency/duration or Severity
Thinking of self as not as smart as other students	Mon., Nov. 6	10:00 A.M.	Math class: taking test	IIII
	Tues., Nov. 7	10:15 A.M.	Math class: got B on test	IIII IIII
	Tues., Nov. 7	5:30 P.M.	Home: parents didn't like test grade	IIII II
	Thurs., Nov. 9	9:30 A.M.	English class: thinking math is next	II
	Sun., Nov. 12	9:30 P.M.	Home: dread about school tomorrow	III
Feeling anxious and nervous	Mon., Nov. 6	10:00 A.M.	Math class: test	8 (on 1 to 10 SUDS Scale)
	Tues., Nov. 7	10:15 P.M.	Thinking about poor test grade	7 (on 1 to 10 SUDS Scale)

FIGURE 7.3 Example of a Behavior Log

At this time, the helper also has the option of giving Isabella a history questionnaire to complete and/or a brief self-report inventory to complete, such as an anxiety inventory or checklist.

CHAPTER SUMMARY

This chapter focuses on the use of interviewing to assess client concerns. The interview is one of the primary ways that practitioners assess clients, supplemented by other measures that are valid and reliable for clients, such as self-assessment and monitoring, observation, self-report measures, and so on.

The assessment interview approach presented in this chapter has been developed by incorporating aspects of both functional assessment and ecological assessment. The **functional assessment** is based on principles of learning while the **ecological assessment** is based on the **person-in-environment** approach. In the interview approach described in this chapter, practitioners focus on defining six components of behavior: affective, somatic, behavioral, cognitive, contextual, and relational. They also seek to identify antecedent events that occur before the issue and cue it and consequent events that follow the issue and in some way influence it or maintain it. Consequences may include payoffs, or secondary gains, that give value to the dysfunctional behavior and thus keep the issue going. Antecedents and consequences may also be affective, somatic, behavioral, cognitive, contextual, and relational. Contextual and relational ABCs form the basis of an environmental assessment to determine the ways in which clients' social network (or lack thereof) and environmental barriers and resources affect the issue. Other important components of assessment interviewing include identifying previous solutions the client has tried for resolving the issue, exploring individual and environmental strengths, exploring the client's perceptions of the issue, and identifying the frequency, duration, or severity of the concern.

The assessment interview approach described in this chapter yields important information to helpers about the etiology and maintenance of client issues and concerns. Such information forms the basis of outcome goals and treatment planning.

 Visit CengageBrain.com for a variety of study tools and useful resources such as video examples, case studies, interactive exercises, flashcards, and quizzes.

7 | Knowledge and Skill Builder

Part One

A client is referred to you with a presenting concern of free-floating, or generalized (pervasive), anxiety. Outline the specific interview leads you would ask during an assessment interview with this client that pertain directly to her presenting component. Your objective (Learning Outcome 1) is to identify at least two interview leads for each of the 11 assessment categories described in this chapter and summarized in Box 7.3. Feedback follows on page 250.

Part Two

Using the description of the client in Part One, conduct a 30-minute role-play assessment interview in which your objective is to demonstrate leads and responses associated with at least nine out of the 11 categories described for assessment (Learning Outcome 2). You can do this activity in a triad in which one person assumes the role of helper, another is an anxious client, and the third person plays the role of observer; trade roles two times. If groups are not available, audiotape or videotape to record your interview.

Use the Interview Checklist below as a guide to assess your performance and to obtain feedback.

After completing your interview, develop some hypotheses, or hunches, about the client. In particular, try to develop guesses about:

1. **Antecedents that cue or set off the anxiety, making its occurrence more likely**
2. **Consequences that maintain the anxiety, keep it going, or make it worse**
3. **Consequences that diminish or weaken the anxiety**
4. **Secondary gains, or payoffs, attached to the anxiety**
5. **Ways in which the client's previous solutions may contribute to the anxiety or make it worse**
6. **Particular individual and environmental strengths, resources, and coping skills of the client and how these might be best used during treatment/intervention**
7. **How the client's gender, culture, and environment affect the problem**

You may wish to continue this part of the activity in a triad or do it by yourself, jotting down ideas as you proceed. At some point, it may be helpful to share your ideas with your group or your instructor.

Interview Checklist for Assessing Clients

Scoring Yes / No	Category of information	Examples of helper leads or responses	Client response
___ ___	1. Explain purpose of assessment interview; obtain informed consent; explain limits to confidentiality	"I am going to be asking you more questions than usual so that we can get an idea of what is going on. Getting an accurate picture about your concern will help us to decide what we can do about it. Your input is important. Also, I want to go over the consent document you read. I want to make sure you understand about what confidentiality means and the exceptions to confidentiality, too."	_____ (check if client confirmed understanding of purpose)
___ ___	2. Identify range of concerns (if you don't have this information from history)	"What would you like to talk about today?" "What specifically led you to come to see someone now?" "Describe any other issues you haven't mentioned."	_____ (check if client described additional concerns)
___ ___	3. Prioritize and select primary or most immediate issue to work on	"What issue best represents the reason you are here?" "Of all these concerns, which one is most stressful (or painful) for you?" "Rank order these concerns, starting with the one that is most important for you to resolve to the one least important." "Tell me which of these issues you believe you could learn to deal with most easily and with the most success."	_____ (check if client selected issue to focus on)

(continued)

7   Knowledge and Skill Builder (*continued*)

Scoring	Category of information	Examples of helper leads or responses	Client response
		"Which one of the things we discussed do you see as having the best chance of being solved?"	
		"Out of all the things we've discussed, describe the one that, when resolved, would have the greatest impact on the rest of the issues."	
___ ___	4.0. Present behavior		_____ (check if client identified the following components)
___ ___	a. *Affective* aspects: feelings, emotions, mood states	"What are your feeling when this happens?" "How does this make you feel when this occurs?" "What other feelings do you have when this occurs?" "What feelings is this issue hiding or covering up?" "What positive feelings do you have surrounding this issue?" "Negative ones?"	_____ (check if client identified positive and negative feelings)
___ ___	b. *Somatic* aspects: body sensations, physiological responses, organic dysfunction and illness, medications	"What goes on inside you then?" "What do you notice in your body when this happens?" "When this happens, are you aware of anything that goes on in your body that feels bad or uncomfortable—aches, pains, and so on?"	_____ (check if client identified body sensations)
___ ___	c. *Behavioral* aspects: overt behaviors/actions	"In recording this scene, what actions and dialogue would the camera pick up?" "What are you doing when this occurs?" "What do you mean by 'not communicating'?" "Describe what you did the last few times this occurred."	_____ (check if client identified overt behaviors)
___ ___	d. *Cognitive* aspects: automatic, helpful, unhelpful, rational, irrational thoughts and beliefs; internal dialogue; perceptions and misperceptions	"What do you say to yourself when this happens?" "What are you usually thinking about during this problem?" "What was going through your mind then?" "What kinds of thoughts can make you feel _____?" "What beliefs [or images] do you hold that affect this issue?" Sentence completions: I should _____, people should _____, it would be awful if _____, _____ makes me feel bad.	_____ (check if client identified thoughts, beliefs)
___ ___	e. *Contextual* aspects: time, place, or setting events	"Describe some recent situations in which the issue occurred. Where were you? When was it?" "Does this go on all the time or only sometimes?" "Does the same thing happen at other times or places?" "At what time does this not occur? Places? Situations?" "What effect does your cultural/ethnic background have on this issue?" "What effects do the sociopolitical structures of the society in which you live have on this issue?" "Describe the relationship between yourself, your concerns, and your current environment. We could draw this relationship if you want to see it [using an ecomap]."	_____ (check if client identified time, places, other events)

"To what extent is your concern affected by oppression and discrimination that you experience in your environment?"
"To what extent does your environment give or deny you access to power, privilege, and resources?"
"What opportunities do you have in your environment for sharing spiritual and cultural values and activities?"

____ ____ f. *Relational* aspects: other people

"What effects does this concern have on significant others in your life?"
"What effects do significant others have on this concern?"
"Who else is involved in the concern? How?"
"What persons *present* in your life now have the greatest positive impact on this concern? Negative impact?"
"What about persons *absent* from your life?"
"Who in your life empowers you? Disempowers you? Nourishes you? Feels toxic to you?"

_____ (check if client identified people)

____ ____ 5.0. Antecedents—past or current conditions that cue, or set off, the behavior

_____ (check if client identified following antecedent categories)

____ ____ a. *Affective* antecedents

"What are you usually feeling before this?"
"When do you recall the first time you felt this way?"
"What are the feelings that occur before the issue and make it more likely to happen? Less likely?"
"Describe any holdover or unfinished feelings from past events in your life that still affect this issue. How?"

_____ (feelings, mood states)

____ ____ b. *Somatic* antecedents

"What goes on inside you just before this happens?"
"Are you aware of any particular sensations or discomfort just before the issue occurs or gets worse?"
"Are there any body sensations that seem to occur before the issue or when it starts that make it more likely to occur? Less likely?"
"Is there anything going on with you physically—like illness or a physical condition or in the way you eat or drink—that leads up to this issue?"

_____ (body sensations, physiological responses)

____ ____ c. *Behavioral* antecedents

"If I were recording this, what actions and dialogue would I pick up before this happens?"
"Identify any particular behavior patterns that occur right before this happens."
"What do you typically do before this happens?"
"What seems to start this entire chain of events?"

_____ (overt behavior)

____ ____ d. *Cognitive* antecedents

"What are your thoughts before this happens?"
"What are you telling yourself before this happens?"
"Can you identify any particular beliefs that seem to set the issue off?"
"What do you think about [or tell yourself] before the issue occurs that makes it more likely to happen? Less likely?"

_____ (thoughts, beliefs, internal dialogue, cognitive schemas)

(continued)

7 | Knowledge and Skill Builder (*continued*)

Scoring	Category of information	Examples of helper leads or responses	Client response
___ ___	e. *Contextual* antecedents	"How long ago did this happen?" "Has this ever occurred at any other time in your life? If so, describe that." "Where and when did this occur the first time?" "What things happened that seemed to lead up to this?" "What was happening in your life when you first noticed the issue?" "How were things different before you had this concern?" "What do you mean, this started 'recently'?"	_____ (time, places, other events)
___ ___	f. *Relational* antecedents	"Are there any people or relationships from past events in your life that still affect this concern? How?" "Identify any particular people that seem to bring on this concern." "Are you usually with certain people right before or when this issue starts?" "Are there any people or relationships from the past that trigger this issue in some way? Who? How?" "How do the people who hold power in your life trigger this issue?"	_____ (other people)
___ ___	6.0. Identify consequences that maintain and strengthen issue or weaken or diminish it		_____ (check if client identified following sources of consequences)
___ ___	a. *Affective* consequences	"How do you feel after this happens?" "When did you stop feeling this way?" "Are you aware of any particular feelings or reactions you have after the issue that strengthen it? Weaken it?"	_____ (feelings, mood states)
___ ___	b. *Somatic* consequences	"What are you aware of inside you—sensations in your body—just after this happens?" "How does this affect the issue?" "Are there any sensations inside you that seem to occur after the issue that strengthen or weaken it?" "Is there any physical condition, illness, and so on about yourself that seems to occur after the issue? If so, how does it affect the issue?"	_____ (body or internal sensations)
___ ___	c. *Behavioral* consequences	"What do you do after this happens, and how does this make the issue better? Worse?" "How do you usually react after this is over?" "In what ways does your reaction keep the issue going? Weaken it or stop it?"	_____ (overt responses)

"Identify any particular behavior patterns that occur after this."
"How do these patterns keep the problem going? Stop it?"

___ ___	d. *Cognitive* consequences	"What do you usually think about afterward?" "How does this affect the issue?" "What do you picture after this happens?" "What do you tell yourself after this occurs?" "Identify any particular thoughts [beliefs, self-talk] that make the issue better. Worse?" "Are there certain thoughts or images you have afterward that either strengthen or weaken the issue?"	_____ (thoughts, beliefs, internal dialogue)
___ ___	e. *Contextual* consequences	"When does this issue usually stop or go away? Get worse? Get better?" "Where are you when the issue stops? Get worse? Get better?" "Identify any particular times, places, or events that seem to keep the issue going. Make it worse or better?"	_____ (time, places, other events)
___ ___	f. *Relational* consequences	"Can you identify any particular reactions from other people that occur following the issue?" "In what ways do their reactions affect the issue?" "Identify any particular people who can make the issue worse. Better? Stop it? Keep it going?" "How do the people who have power in your life situation perpetuate this concern?"	_____ (other people)
___ ___	7. Identify possible secondary gains	"Has your concern ever produced any special advantages or considerations for you?" "As a consequence of your concern, have you gotten out of or avoided things or events?" "What do you get out of this situation that you don't get out of other situations?" "Do you notice anything that happens afterward that you try to prolong or to produce?" "Do you notice anything that occurs after the problem that you try to stop or avoid?" "Are there certain feelings or thoughts that go on after the issue that you try to prolong?" "Are there certain feelings or thoughts that go on after the issue that you try to stop or avoid?" "The good thing about _____ [issue] is . . ."	_____ (check if client identified gains from issue)
___ ___	8. Identify solutions already tried to solve the issue	"How have you dealt with this or other issues before? What was the effect? What made it work or not work?" "How have you tried to resolve this concern?" "What have you done that has made the issue better? Worse? Kept it the same?" "What have others done to help you with this?"	_____ (check if client identified prior solutions)
___ ___	9. Identify client coping skills, strengths, resources	"What skills or things do you have going for you that might help you with this concern?" "Describe a situation when this concern is not interfering."	_____ (check if client identified assets, coping skills,

(continued)

7   Knowledge and Skill Builder (*continued*)

Scoring	Category of information	Examples of helper leads or responses	Client response
		"What strengths or assets can you use to help resolve this?" "When don't you act this way?" "What kinds of thoughts or self-talk help you handle this better?" "When don't you think in self-defeating ways?" "What do you say to yourself to cope with a difficult situation?" "Identify the steps you take in a situation you handle well—what do you think about and what do you do? How could these steps be applied to the present issue? How could these prevent the issue from recurring in the future?" "What resources are available to you from your community and your environment?"	individual and environmental strengths, resources)
		"What kinds of things in your community and environment do you consider to be strengths and assets?" "What sorts of positive, purposeful relationships do you have now that help you with this issue?" "What do you find meaning in from particular aspects of your culture?"	
____ ____	10. Identify client's description/assessment of the issue (note which aspects of issue are stressed and which are ignored)	"What is your understanding of this issue?" "How do you explain this concern to yourself?" "Tell me about what the issue means to you." "What is your interpretation [analysis] of the concern?" "Sum up the issue in just one word." "Give the concern a title."	_____ (check if client explained issue)
____ ____	11. Estimate intensity of behavior/symptoms (assign self-monitoring homework, if useful) a. *Degree of Intensity* b. *Frequency/Duration*	"On a scale of 1 to 10, with 1 being very calm and 10 being very anxious, rate the intensity of the anxiety you feel." "How often do you feel this way?" How long does this persist when it occurs?"	_____ (check if client estimated intensity)

Yes	No	Other skills
____	____	12. The helper listened attentively and recalled accurately the information given by the client.
		13. The helper used basic listening responses to clarify and synthesize the information shared by the client.

14. The helper followed the client's lead in determining the sequence or order of the information obtained.

Observer comments: _____
_____
_____
_____
_____
_____
_____
_____
_____
_____
_____
_____
_____
_____
_____
_____

7   Knowledge and Skill Builder Feedback

Part One

See whether the interview leads that you generated are similar to the following ones:

"Is this the only issue you're concerned about now in your life, or are there other issues you haven't mentioned yet?" (Range of concerns)

"When you say you feel anxious, what exactly do you mean?" (Behavior–affective component)

"When you feel anxious, what do you experience inside your body?" (Behavior–somatic component)

"When you feel anxious, what exactly are you usually doing?" (Behavior–behavioral component)

"When you feel anxious, what are you typically thinking about [or saying to yourself]?" (Behavior–cognitive component)

"Try to pinpoint exactly what times the anxiety occurs or when it is worse." (Behavior–contextual component)

"Describe where you are or in what situations you find yourself when you get anxious." (Behavior–contextual component)

"Describe what other things are usually going on when you have these feelings." (Behavior—contextual component)

"How would you describe the relationship between yourself and these concerns and your current environment?" (Behavior–contextual component)

"Can you tell me what persons are usually around when you feel this way?" (Behavior–relational component)

"How would you describe your support in your life right now?" (Behavior–relational component)

"Who in your life now empowers you? Disempowers you?" (Behavior–relational component)

"Are there any feelings that lead up to this?" (Antecedent– affective)

"What about body sensations that might occur right before these feelings?" (Antecedent–somatic)

"Have you noticed any particular behavioral reactions or patterns that seem to occur right before these feelings?" (Antecedent–behavioral)

"Are there any kinds of thoughts—things you're dwelling on—that seem to lead up to these feelings?" (Antecedent–cognitive)

"When was the first time you noticed these feelings? Where were you?" (Antecedent–contextual)

"Can you recall any other events or times that seem to be related to these feelings?" (Antecedent–contextual)

"Does the presence of any particular people in any way set these feelings off?" (Antecedent–relational)

"Are you aware of any particular other feelings that make the anxiety better or worse?" (Consequence–affective)

"Are you aware of any body sensations or physiological responses that make these feelings better or worse?" (Consequence–somatic)

"Is there anything you can do specifically to make these feelings stronger or weaker?" (Consequence–behavioral)

"Can you identify anything you can think about or focus on that seems to make these feelings better or worse?" (Consequence–cognitive)

"At what times do these feelings diminish or go away? Get worse? In what places? In what situations?" (Consequence–contextual)

"Do certain people you know seem to react in ways that keep these feelings going or make them less intense? If so, how?" (Consequence–relational)

"As a result of this anxiety, have you ever gotten out of or avoided things you dislike?" (Consequence–secondary gain)

"Has this problem with your nerves ever resulted in any special advantages or considerations for you?" (Consequence–secondary gain)

"What have you tried to do to resolve this issue? How have your attempted solutions worked out?" (Previous solutions)

"Describe some times and situations when you don't have these feelings or you feel calm and relaxed. What goes on that is different in these instances?" (Coping skills)

"How have you typically coped with other difficult situations or feelings in your life before?" (Coping skills)

"What resources are available to you from your culture and community that you can use to help with this problem?" (Individual and environmental strengths–coping)

"What kinds of things in your community and environment do you feel are strengths and assets?" (Individual and environmental strengths–coping)

"If you could give this problem a title—as if it were a movie or a book—what would that title be?" (Client perceptions of issue)

"How do you explain these feelings to yourself?" (Client perceptions of issue)

"How many times do these feelings crop up during a given day?" (Frequency of issue)

"How long do these feelings stay with you?" (Duration of issue)

"On a scale from 1 to 10, with 1 being not intense and 10 being very intense, how strong would you say these feelings usually are?" (Severity of issue)

Constructing, Contextualizing, and Evaluating Treatment Goals

After completing this chapter, you will be able to

1. Identify a situation about you or your life that you would like to change. Construct, contextualize, and evaluate one desired outcome for this issue, using the Goal-Setting Worksheet in the Knowledge and Skill Builder section as a guide.

2. Apply at least 10 of the 13 categories reviewed in this chapter and listed in the Interview Checklist in the Knowledge and Skill Builder section to a written client case. In doing so, you will be able to describe the steps you would use with this client to construct, contextualize, and evaluate desired outcome goals.

3. Demonstrate during a role play with two colleagues at least 10 of the 13 categories reviewed in this chapter and listed in the Interview Checklist in the Knowledge and Skill Builder section. These are categories associated with constructing, contextualizing, and evaluating outcome goals.

4. With yourself or another person or client, conduct an outcome evaluation of a real or a hypothetical counseling goal, specifying *when, what,* and *how* you would measure the outcome.

3. What would be the payoffs or benefits to you if you made this change?

4. What would be some of the risks—to you or others—if you made this change?

5. Looking at where you are now and where you'd like to be, what are the steps along the way to get from here to there?

6. Identify anticipated interferences or obstacles (people, feelings, ideas, situations) that might interfere with the attainment of your goal.

7. Identify resources (skills, people, knowledge) that you would need to use or acquire to attain your goal.

8. How would you evaluate progress toward this outcome?

These questions reflect the process of constructing and evaluating goals for counseling. Goals represent desired outcomes and they function as benchmarks of client progress. In this chapter we describe and model concrete guidelines to help you and your clients construct, define, and evaluate goals for counseling.

Personal Reflection Activity

Pause for a few minutes to answer the following **LO1** questions by yourself or with someone else:

1. What is one thing you would like to change about yourself?

2. Suppose you succeeded in accomplishing this change. How would things be different for you? What would you be doing, thinking, or feeling as a result of this change?

Where Are We Headed?

Imagine a recent adventure in unfamiliar territory. **LO1** Because the place was new to you, you may have felt disoriented and lost. You may remember asking yourself, "Where am I?" and then asking your companion, "Where is it we want to go?" More than likely you consulted a map—one mounted on a wall or a post nearby, or a map on your mobile device. Whichever type of map you consulted, you more than likely saw the words, "You are here" accompanied by an arrow pointing to your current location or a blue circle or a pin drop on your mobile device. Simply figuring out your current location and orienting yourself geographically can be an accomplishment, especially when you feel lost. Isn't this the function of a global positioning system or GPS? In the helping professions, this is the purpose of client assessment—to determine where the client is at the start of therapy and to help orient the client to his or her current situation. "You are here" allows the adventure of therapy to begin in a meaningful and purposeful way. The next task, as in any voyage, is to determine where to go. In the helping professions, this is the task of goal formulation.

Beginning With The End in Mind

In general, **treatment goals** represent the destination **LO1** or the end point of therapy described by clients. This is the *telic* or purposeful nature of therapy. Goals are the direct response to one or more of the following questions:

"Where do I hope to be?"
"Where do I need to be?"
"Where do I want to be?"

Goals serve to facilitate client movement from the client's current circumstance to a destination the client values, an envisioned end point that is worth it. In this way, treatment goals represent a **vision of client improvement**—first and foremost, improvement envisioned by the client, and, secondarily, improvement endorsed or supported by the helper. Think about it: you are much more likely to move from here to there if *you* are clear about and can understand where "there" is. Not being able to see the desired end point on your GPS makes it much more difficult to invest the time, energy, and money needed to travel from your current location. And movement is much more likely when the traveler can see for himself or herself the destination in the distance or view the end point on the map rather than taking someone else's word for it.

Purposes of Treatment Goals

Goals have been defined as "cognitive representations that serve a directional function for behavior by focusing the individual on more specific possibilities" (Elliot, McGregor, & Thrash, 2002, p. 373). This definition captures the features of visualization and movement described thus far, and it also highlights important purposes of treatment goals. We highlight six.

1. Provide Direction

The first purpose of treatment goals is to provide direction for helping. Treatment goals are the signposts or the mile markers that serve to keep the work of therapy on track or on target. Without them, therapy would be analogous to "wandering in the wilderness" and would likely diminish into a futile and frustrating exercise. Just as in any journey, once the destination has been established, the direction (e.g., north, south) for travel—as well as the actual route and map—can be determined. Goals therefore serve as the structure or the framework for helping, identifying when the work of client and helper has been accomplished.

Although each theoretical orientation and evidence-based practice (EBP) has its own direction, constructing goals that are tailored to the person who is the client helps to ensure that helping is structured specifically to meet the needs of *that person*. This is what is referred to as an individualized or *idiographic* approach to goal formulation, an approach that focuses on the client's unique needs and preferences. It differs from a *nomothetic* approach to goal formulation, which follows general laws or guidelines and pertains to all individuals or groups of individuals (e.g., cultural groups, persons who share a primary diagnosis). A general or nomothetic treatment goal for a female college student who is experiencing depression and is meeting with a therapist trained in the EBP of acceptance and commitment therapy (ACT; Hayes, Strosahl, & Wilson, 2012) might be engaging in the standard practice of cognitive defusion so that she is able to decrease the believability of, or the attachment to, her long-held thought that she is worthless and subsequently experience behavioral flexibility. An idiographic goal for this same female client would be shaped by the particularities of her case (e.g., recent events in her life, familial history of depression, sexual orientation, ethnic identity) and would require further contextualization. Persons and Tompkins (2007) explain that "evidence-based *nomothetic* formulations [are] the foundation for the development of *idiographic* formulations" (p. 292). This means that both approaches are needed, that both must work in concert in service of the client. Once the foundation of care has been established, we believe that clients are much more likely to launch on a journey of change and travel to a specified destination if the plan or map that has been developed has been tailored or customized to them—their very own personalized itinerary.

2. Provide Focus

Treatment goals also provide a focus for helper and client activities, which is consistent with goal-setting theory in organizational psychology (Locke & Latham, 2002). According to this theory, goals serve to focus attention on goal-relevant activities and away from goal-irrelevant activities. This is quite evident in the performance of successful athletes, who set goals for themselves and then use the goals not only as motivating devices but also as standards against which they rehearse their performance over and over, often cognitively or with imagery. For example, running backs in football constantly see themselves getting the ball and running downfield and into the end zone. Champion snow skiers are often seen closing their eyes and bobbing their heads in the direction of the course before the race. Gymnasts and divers are known to engage in similar behaviors prior to competition. Goals therefore help with successful performance and problem resolution because they are usually rehearsed in our working memory and because they direct our attention to the resources and components in our environment that are most likely to help with devising a solution. In the case of treatment goals, clients must be able to picture or "taste" or somehow experience first-hand the target behaviors or end results reflected in their goals.

3. Foster Expectation and Hope for Improvement

Goals are intended to foster in clients an expectation and hope for improvement. As Lee, Uken, and Sebold (2007) noted, "The use of goals shifts the focus of attention from what cannot be done to what can be accomplished; it moves clients away from blaming others or themselves and holds them accountable for developing a better, different future" (p. 30). Clients who are able to envision a relief or a lifting of their current level of distress are likely to invest in the helping process, and informing clients that being able to resolve or at least to manage a long-held dilemma not only is possible but also is probably likely to engender hope. Hope is a major component of a strengths-based helping perspective (Lopez, Pedrotti, & Snyder, 2015) and, along with expectations of positive outcomes, has been identified as a significant factor in client change (Anderson, Lunnen, & Ogles, 2010; Wampold, 2007).

4. Determine Helper Qualifications

Treatment goals also make it possible for helpers to determine whether they have the necessary skills, competencies, and interests to work with a particular client toward a particular outcome. Given the client's choice of goals and the helper's areas of competence, the helper decides whether to continue working with the client or to consult with a supervisor or colleague about possibly referring the client to someone else who may be in a better position to render services.

There are at least three caveats about the practice of referral. First, the decision to refer is never that of the practitioner in training or someone who continues to receive training and clinical supervision. That decision belongs to the supervisor. Second, often helpers do not have the luxury of selecting the clients they want to work with or of simply opting out of helping based on the helper's personal values or preferences, or even skill level or expertise. For example, helpers providing services in a public school located in a large metropolitan area will need to be prepared to work with students, their families, and also school personnel who are affiliated with different religions and practice a range of customs. Third, hand-picking clients based on the helper's comfort level or how well the client's values match those of the helper's personal values is simply unethical (American Counseling Association's *ACA Code of Ethics*, 2014). As discussed in Chapter 2, client referrals are to be based on helper skill level, not personal values. Because of this, referring a client to another helper is as an action of last resort (Kaplan, 2014). A client whose presenting concerns may warrant specialized services may be unable to travel to or afford the recommended services of a specialty clinic. In this latter case, the helper may need to continue to provide routine services while pursuing specialized training and enlist the assistance of a qualified supervisor.

5. Justify Recommended Services

Treatment goals are a basis for the helper's recommendation to use particular change strategies and interventions. The changes that the client desires will, to some degree, determine the kinds of action plans and treatment strategies that can be used with some likelihood of success. Without clarifying what the client needs and wants, it is almost impossible to explain and defend one's choice to move in a certain direction or to use one or more change strategies. Without goals, the helper may use a particular approach without any justifiable basis. Whether the approach will be helpful is left to chance rather than choice.

6. Evaluate Outcomes

The sixth and final purpose of treatment goals is to determine whether or the extent to which services have been effective. If clients have not made progress toward an

BOX 8.1	Eight Characteristics of Well-Constructed Treatment Goals

1. Salutary, not remedial: Describe the presence of something positive, not the absence of something negative
2. New and different
3. Process-oriented, not static: Describe a regular and an ongoing process, not a once-and-for-all accomplishment

4. Realistic and achievable: Within the client's control
5. Specific and comprehensible
6. Compelling and useful: Personally meaningful
7. Interpersonally related: Noticed by and benefitting others
8. Involve hard work: Challenging for the client

Source: Berg & Miller, 1992; De Jong & Berg, 2013; Lee, Sebold, & Uken, 2003; Persons, 2008; Walter & Peller, 1992, 2000.

identified endpoint or goal after a certain time in counseling, it might be said that services have not been helpful. In this sense, treatment goals signify the consequence of treatment and its interventions. Keeping the ultimate goal in mind, the helper and client can monitor progress toward the goal and measure the effectiveness of a change intervention. These data provide continuous feedback to both helper and client.

One method for systematically collecting and using real-time outcome data from clients over the course of therapy has proven to enhance overall client outcomes in five large randomized controlled studies. Conceived by Michael J. Lambert (2010a, 2010b), this method entails alerting therapists to immediate client feedback about things such as symptom management and the therapeutic relationship, so that therapists can then make alterations in their plan for therapy, including the focus of the next session and specific interventions. Client feedback is obtained from brief standardized measures, such as versions of the Outcome Questionnaire (OQ) developed by Lambert and colleagues (available at www.oqmeasures.com), and then reported immediately to therapists on a mobile device. This client feedback can be used to assess the feasibility of the established outcome goals and also the effectiveness of interventions already applied. This type of system illustrates the interrelatedness of the processes of constructing and evaluating outcome goals.

Characteristics of Well-Constructed Treatment Goals

Think of the process of determining an **LO1** **LO2** **LO3** outcome goal with a client as similar to helping the client paint a picture of the life he or she wants to be living and the type of person he or she wants to be as a result of participating in counseling. The painting takes shape as the visual depiction meets certain criteria and develops certain characteristics. We discuss eight characteristics of well-constructed treatment goals in this section. They are listed in Box. 8.1.

1. Salutary, Not Remedial

If goals represent a vision of client improvement, then a primary characteristic of well-constructed treatment goals is that they represent the *presence of something positive*, not the absence of something negative. This feature is prominent in solution-focused therapy (Berg & Miller, 1992; De Jong & Berg, 2013; Macdonald, 2007; Walter & Peller, 2000) and other forms of strengths-based helping, such as person-centered care (Adams & Grieder, 2014), as well as in cognitive-behavior therapies (Persons, 2008). This means, in part, that treatment goals identify and describe what the client *will* be doing rather than what the client will *not* be doing. Consider this: What comes to mind when you are asked to describe not being angry or a decrease in anxiety? Can you picture an absence of anger or a decrease in anxiety? More than likely what is envisioned is what is in place of this absence and this decrease, that is, behavior associated with the alternative or the opposite of anger and anxiety, such as speaking calmly or remaining quiet, smiling faintly, engaging in deep breathing exercises, or counting down slowly from 10 to 1 or from 10 to 0. These are behaviors that can be seen and described and are therefore present. Envisioning the absence, decrease, or loss of something is really not possible because we cannot see what is no longer there! What is possible is seeing the replacement or the alternative to this absence or void—what is referred to as *instead* behaviors.

For the client who responds to the question, "What do you want to have happen as a result of being in counseling?" with, "I don't want to be all stressed out and feel panicky all the time," the helper can then ask, "What do you want to be feeling *instead of* stressed out and panicky?" The client's response to this question will then represent the goal for therapy, the alternative to "not stressed out" and "not panicky." If the client is not able to picture this right away—which is very common—then the helper can inquire further about preferred alternatives that the client can envision and identify with, such as "confident" and "self-assured." This process may take some time because the person who is steeped in anxiety and other stressors may not be able to see outside of or beyond the confines of this difficulty, especially if the symptoms have been present for a long time. With patience, skillful questioning, and coaching on the helper's part, specific behaviors associated with the preferred alternative, the "instead" (e.g., confidence and self-assurance), can be identified little by little, things for the client to do now, even in small measure, to achieve the goal and arrive at the preferred destination.

It is worth repeating that well-constructed treatment goals are preferred end points that can be seen, not descriptions of what cannot be seen. They represent the increase of desired behaviors, rather than the mere decrease or absence of undesired behaviors. As Persons (2008) explained, clients can limit their involvement in unwanted behaviors (e.g., avoiding a particular bully at school), but this does not automatically translate to an increase in desired behaviors (e.g., sleeping soundly through the night). One can do less of something undesirable, but this does not mean that what is desirable will increase as a result. In dialectical behavior therapy (DBT), the overarching goal is to help clients establish a life worth living, not just to prevent clients from killing themselves. In the words of DBT developer Marsha Linehan, DBT is "a life worth living program, not a suicide prevention program" (personal communication, October 1, 2009). Because treatment goals represent the vision of client improvement, helpers must be persistent in assisting clients to envision the instead, the presence of what they want and what is worth it to them, not simply describing what they hope will diminish or vanish.

Goals that describe the presence of something positive are what we refer to as **salutary goals**, whereas goals that mention the absence of something negative are **remedial goals**. As their name suggests, salutary goals are health-promoting, they provide sustenance, and they signify the addition or promotion of something good and beneficial. By contrast, remedial goals are corrections; they are the result of interventions designed to correct or calibrate a deficiency. The distinction between salutary goals and remedial goals is similar to the distinction made between approach goals and avoidance goals. Whereas **approach goals** focus on a positive end state and thus imply movement toward a desired outcome, **avoidance goals** focus on negative end states and therefore suggest moving or staying away from them.

Although Persons (2008) described good treatment goals as those that focus on increasing desired behaviors and also focus on reducing symptoms and problems (i.e., salutary *and* remedial, as well as approach *and* avoidance),

we contend that helpers must prioritize salutary and approach goals in their work with clients—particularly as therapy progresses—if therapy is to be effective. Research supports this strategy. Clients in a university counseling center who identified more avoidance goals at the beginning of counseling were less likely to report overall life satisfaction at the end of counseling compared to clients who identified fewer avoidance goals (Elliot & Church, 2002). In addition, Wollburg and Braukhaus (2010) found that patients participating in a cognitive behavioral therapy program for depression who developed only approach goals at the beginning of treatment reported significantly lower scores on the Beck Depression Inventory at the end of treatment than those patients in the same program who had developed at least one avoidance goal.

It is difficult for us to imagine therapy ending successfully when only remedial or avoidance goals and not salutary or approach goals have been met. This would be the equivalent in medicine of discharging patients from the hospital once they have been medically stabilized or terminating psychiatric services without a referral to talk therapy once the patient has responded well to a medication regimen. For persons assessed with severe alcohol use disorder, detoxification may be necessary (i.e., medically managed withdrawal), but it is not considered a specific form of treatment by itself; rather, it is a prelude to treatment and the recovery process (Doweiko, 2015). In the addictions field, persons who have been detoxed but who have yet to begin a plan of recovery are sometimes referred to as "dry drunks." For them, the remedial or avoidance goal would have been met (i.e., stopped drinking), but the salutary or approach goal (i.e., active and ongoing recovery) is unmet.

Intervening to avert and contain crises such as suicidal intent and drug overdose is certainly necessary, but we do not consider crisis intervention in itself to be sufficient for effective mental health care. In many ways, remedial treatment goals can be likened to intermediate goals or subgoals that we discuss later in the chapter—they are intended to be met along the way, fulfilled during active treatment; but they are not considered the end point of therapy or the equivalent of outcome goals. Again, reducing symptoms of anxiety denotes progress but does not justify terminating treatment if the client is not able to institute positive, instead behaviors.

2. New and Different

Goals that represent the presence of something positive, not just the absence of something negative, imply that new and different behaviors are intended. In their work with domestic violence offenders, Lee and colleagues (Lee, Sebold, & Uken, 2003; Lee, Uken, & Sebold, 2007, 2012) stipulated that treatment goals must describe behaviors that clients have not generally engaged in before. The expectation that clients develop new and different behaviors is understandable given that most persons seek counseling because their typical or routine behaviors are not working. Goals therefore must be geared to break the repetitive and failed attempts at coping and usher in more functional patterns.

3. Process Oriented, Not Static

Goals that are process-oriented reflect the continuity or maintenance of preferred outcomes, rather than a once-and-for-all achievement. Egan (2014) refers to these as sustainable goals. This characteristic exemplifies the assumption in systems theory and solution-focused therapy that change is constant (Lee et al., 2003). Examples of process-oriented goals include remaining gainfully employed rather than simply getting a job, consistently implementing specific parenting skills learned in treatment rather than enforcing appropriate discipline for the first time, continuing to excel in school rather than making the dean's list one semester, and managing symptoms of anxiety rather than becoming symptom-free.

There are two aspects of treatment goals that we hope are evident in these examples. First, well-constructed goals depict a destination that is ever present, that is nonending, suggesting that the benefits of therapy are meant to be enduring, extending beyond the completion of a treatment program. This is similar to how graduation and commencement are understood at various academic institutions. Whereas graduation signifies the successful completion and ending of a degree program, commencement signifies the beginning of a new venture. Earning the degree is not necessarily an ultimate outcome or end-all, be-all goal; it is actually the stepping stone or the intermediate goal to another destination.

Second, process-oriented treatment goals also make evident that the purpose of therapy is to help clients manage and cope with ongoing challenges, not to eliminate challenges entirely. An expectation and misconception that many clients may have when they enter counseling is that something can be done to take away or wipe out their concern and dilemma. "Fix my child," they may say, or "I want to be cured." This is understandable when clients are experiencing acute emotional distress and perhaps even physical pain. Medication may be targeted as the answer, but even medication cannot eliminate unwelcome and debilitating symptoms altogether.

As helpers in behavioral health who are not medical professionals and whose expertise is in the process of talk therapy, we would do well to not use static, fixed, or permanent language when constructing treatment goals. Process language is recommended. "Recovery" can be used instead of "recovered," "taking medication as prescribed" can be used instead of "medication adherent" or "medication compliant," and "detaching from emotional pain" or "grounding" can be used instead of "avoid triggers." (The practice of "grounding" is used in the treatment of women struggling with problematic substance use and post-traumatic stress disorder or PTSD to focus on, remain grounded in, and maintain connection with the external world. It is part of the evidence-based practice called Seeking Safety developed by Najavits, 2002.) Again, if change is constant, then our role as helpers is to help clients continue to manage difficulties by routinely practicing skills intended to promote and sustain well-being, not eradicate problems altogether.

4. Realistic and Achievable

It is not uncommon for clients to speak of preferred destinations that are too ambitious and therefore too distant and far off. This is particularly true at the beginning of therapy for all age groups and suggests limited understanding of, or investment in, the process of change. Goals may also be proposed that are simply impossible. Clients experiencing a great deal of distress, for example, are prone to grandiose thinking and may demand miraculous intervention. When this happens, it is important for helpers not to squelch the client's wishful thinking or to immediately and brusquely correct irrational or illogical proposals. Rather, helpers are advised to validate the client's need and then redirect the client's energies. This means bringing into focus what it is the client wants to be, have happen, or accomplish. Again, well-formulated goals are those destinations that can be seen by the client and therefore they must be in view and in focus, and thus attainable.

Well-constructed treatment goals that are realistic and achievable are also *within the client's control*. This means that goals must be fashioned according to what the *client* can accomplish rather than what can be accomplished *for* the client. According to self-determination theory (Deci & Ryan, 2012), this defines autonomy, one of three basic and universal psychological needs essential for human growth and well-being (the other two are competence and relatedness). Autonomy refers to self-governance or the need to view oneself as the source of decision-making. Behaving in an autonomous fashion means acting according to self-endorsed and integrated values and beliefs (i.e., what I believe is what I do, and vice versa) rather than being extrinsically motivated or coerced by others or acting in a certain way only to avoid shame and embarrassment. There is a volitional quality to autonomous behavior, which distinguishes it from independence. One can be forced by others to become independent, but one cannot be forced to become autonomous.

Autonomous behavior also is closely aligned with authenticity. This means that someone who is behaving autonomously is one whose behaviors are congruent with his or her values. This type of behavior is more likely to be maintained because it is intrinsically motivated and personally endorsed as valuable. Clients involved in outpatient therapy who identified personal goals for autonomous rather than extrinsically motivated or coerced reasons demonstrated lower levels of depression and anxiety, demoralization, and interpersonal problems, and higher levels of sense of coherence or meaning in life (Michalek, Klappheck, & Kosfelder, 2004). This suggests that treatment goals endorsed by clients as realistic and achievable are more likely to be enacted and maintained. Garvin (2009) noted that helpers should not support clients in their efforts to attain illegal or immoral goals.

5. Specific and Comprehensible

Goal specificity refers to clarity. Without a clear focus, forward movement cannot be expected. Constructing specific goals also means that forward movement can be traced and measured, allowing the client, helper, and others in the client's life to determine progress. Goals that are specific are often behaviorally defined, describing what the client will be doing when therapy has been successful. When treatment goals are described with specificity, they are thus detailed and clear, and the behaviors that comprise or fulfill each goal are evident.

When treatment goals are specific, they are also much more likely to be understood and endorsed by the client, thus supporting client autonomy. The practice of constructing goals in a way the client can comprehend is referred to in solution-focused therapy as "language matching." This means that the helper is deliberate in using words the client can relate to, words that are part of the client's lexicon, and, as recommended by Adams and Grieder (2014), written in the client's primary language. Clinical verbiage is relinquished for the sake of client discernment. These skills are particularly important in cross-cultural counseling.

6. Compelling and Useful

Although our formal training as helpers does not include sales and marketing, our work with clients may often feel like we are "selling" a new perspective and "marketing" a more functional and rewarding way of living. This is the product of our care, concern, and empathy for clients. We didn't enter the profession to watch clients persist in destructive behaviors, stumble, and fail. Nonetheless, it is imperative that we not impose our recommendations onto clients. As much as we believe a particular goal will benefit a client, buying into that goal is not our decision—it is the client's. It is the goal that he or she will be living, not us. And for clients to fully endorse a treatment outcome, it must be worth it to them—it must be what Persons (2008) describes as emotionally compelling, and it also must be seen by clients as useful.

Implied in this characteristic of compelling and useful treatment goals is that clients not only have choices but also have preferences, and these are paramount. Eliciting and incorporating client preferences have become essential features of evidence-based practice (Tompkins, Swift, & Callahan, 2013), and research indicates that clients who receive their preferred treatment are significantly less likely to end treatment prematurely and more likely to benefit from treatment than clients who receive nonpreferred treatments or whose preferences are ignored (Swift, Callahan, & Vollmer, 2011). Goal construction must therefore attend to what the *client* values, regards as important, and deems worthy of investment—again, supporting the client's autonomy. And for this to occur, the client must be able to see himself or herself as a full partner in the process of therapy, someone whose views are recognized, validated, and respected. As Lee and colleagues (2003) state, "People who set their own goals, in their own terms, are more likely to work on them and maintain investment in them" (p. 152).

7. Interpersonally Related

Well-constructed treatment goals also describe client behaviors that will be noticed by and will benefit others. Another way to say this is that client improvement should not be sequestered or hidden from view. Rather, it should be on full display for others to see and appreciate. The client should not be the only one to reap the benefits of effective therapy. Many persons enter therapy at the behest of someone else, because their behavior has negatively affected others or at least has been a concern for others. It is therefore logical to devise treatment goals that, when achieved, will have a positive impact on persons in the client's life. This is particularly true for clients from more collectivistic than individualistic cultures who view improvement as the betterment of their primary cultural group, be it family, neighborhood, or community. Although the client must be the primary beneficiary of treatment goals, client improvement must also have a positive side effect on others, or provide second-hand benefits.

One helpful way to construct treatment goals that are interpersonally related is to query, with the client's permission, the client's referral source or a family member or friend. Informed by solution-focused therapy, the questions posed might be:

"What does [client] need to do differently for you to know that therapy was helpful?"
"What will be some of the small signs to you that [client] is trying?"
"What will convince you that [client's] change is legitimate and lasting and not just a fluke?"

Responses would then be shared with the client and used to construct a treatment goal that will be beneficial not only to the client but also to others. Further questions to query the client directly about goals that would benefit others might be:

"How will others know that coming to counseling has been helpful for you?"
"What will you be doing that will convince [family member, friend, referral source] that you have changed for the better?"
"What do you hope others will notice first that will tell them that your hard work in counseling has paid off?"
"In what ways will your hard work make a positive and lasting difference for your family (or team, neighborhood, community)?"

8. Involve Hard Work

If change were easy, then therapy would not be necessary. Treatment goals must therefore be a challenge to clients and reflect the investment and hard work needed from clients for positive change to be realized. Of course, these should remain realistic accomplishments, with outcomes that are within the client's control and possible with support from the helper and other persons in the client's life, such as family members. But treatment goals should not simply describe what the client is already doing or what the client can easily accomplish. Constructing such goals would make a mockery of the treatment process and render therapy inconsequential. When persons are able to remain invested in a project that yields early and lasting benefits, their own self-efficacy is strengthened—the collective efficacy of their cultural group may also be strengthened—and this portends further and ongoing exertion toward subsequent goals. It is the client, however, who must be able to see the direct connection between his or her efforts and a positive outcome.

Support for Goal Characteristics

Lee and colleagues (2007) found that treatment goal characteristics predicted lower recidivism among domestic violence offenders. Specifically, clients who developed treatment goals that were behaviorally described, positively stated, stated as a small step, and stated in process form had lower recidivism rates after they completed treatment. In another study of adults with diabetes (Miller, Headings, Peyrot, & Nagarja, 2012), greater goal specificity was associated with attaining the goal of an improved diet. These and other studies (e.g., Wollburg & Braukhaus, 2010) highlight the importance of well-constructed treatment goals to mobilize client change.

Before reading further, we encourage you to review the eight characteristics of well-constructed treatment goals and then participate in Learning Activity 8.1. This activity is intended to test your ability to recognize well-constructed goals when you witness them in action.

Cultural Considerations

Clients from different cultural groups may require different counseling processes and goals. To gain an appreciation for another's cultural identity and values, Okun and Suyemoto (2013) recommend assessing sociocultural and sociostructural factors, such as age, ethnic and racial background, gender, sexual orientation, socioeconomic status, and violence history. As discussed in Chapters 2 and 6, Hays (2008, 2013) uses an expanded list of cultural influences that include developmental disabilities, disabilities acquired later in life, and indigenous heritage. These are organized according to the acronym ADDRESSING, which captures only a few of the vast elements that comprise the complexities of identity and the human experience and therefore influences the content and process of developing appropriate treatment goals.

It is worth repeating that treatment goals represent the vision of client improvement and that it is the client—more so than the helper—who must envision improvement for progress to be made. This means that helpers must privilege the experience and ideas of their clients (Bohart & Tallman, 2010), including their cultural identity and practices. Treatment goal formulation should therefore take into consideration the specific values, customs, and traditions of the client's culture (Bernal & Sáez-Santiago, 2006), even if these do not match those of the helper. Take, for example, the white Protestant clinician who thought her Arab Muslim college student would be able

Learning Activity 8.1

Goal Characteristics in Action

The centerpiece of Lee and colleagues' (2003) solution-focused group treatment for domestic violence offenders is the construction of treatment goals. Clients are the ones to identify their own treatment goal, a goal that, for them, represents a present and future behavior they are interested in. This goal-setting focus of treatment is intended to convey to clients that they are accountable for changing their behavior.

Although Lee and colleagues' (2003) goal-setting task (p. 56) incorporates most of the eight characteristics of well-constructed treatment goals listed in Box 8.1 and discussed thus far in the chapter, we have modified their goal-setting task in this Learning Activity so that all eight characteristics are represented. Can you spot them? We invite you to read through the following task that could be presented to clients in group therapy (consistent with Lee et al.'s treatment program) or to individual clients (and therefore the helper would use "I" language instead). Once you have read through the task, refer back to Box 8.1, and then respond to the following questions:

How many characteristics of well-constructed goals can you identify in the goal-setting task?

On a separate sheet of paper, write down each of the characteristics that you identified and, for each one, write down how it was illustrated in the goal-setting task. That is, what is the example provided in the task? Write down the specific words in the example that illustrate each characteristic. Also, develop an alternative or an additional example, one that is your own creation.

*Adapted from Lee, Sebold, and Uken, 2003, p. 56.

For each characteristic that you identified in the goal-setting task, explain to a classmate how the example in the task reflects the characteristic of well-constructed goals that you selected. Also share with your classmate your own example and explain how it reflects the specific characteristic of well-constructed goals. Compare your responses.

Feedback to Learning Activity 8.1 is provided on page 260.

Goal-Setting Task*

We want you to create a goal for yourself that will be useful to you in improving your life. Picture something that you *will* be doing rather than what you *won't* be doing. It's actually impossible to picture a behavior that's not in motion, something that's not being done! The goal should be interpersonal in nature, that is to say, that when you work on the goal, another person will be able to notice the changes you've made, and potentially that person could be affected by the change in how you behave. Another way to think about this is that if you brought us a videotape of yourself working on your goal, you would be able to point out the different things you were doing and maybe even note how these changes affected the other people on the tape. The goal needs to be something different, a behavior that you have not generally done before. This means it will reflect your diligence and hard work. It will also represent something positive and beneficial, something you're working toward instead of avoiding. Keep in mind that because you will be expected to report on your goal work every time we meet, it is important that your goal be a behavior you can do at least a few times per week.

to resolve her depression and anxiety by further "distancing" herself from her "overly protective" and "demanding" family back in the Middle East. The client, however, has made the decision to forgo a full scholarship for graduate studies in the United States so that she can return home and fulfill her "duty" to her family as the caretaker to her ailing grandmother. For her, this means a return to traditional dress and the inevitability of an arranged marriage.

This one example highlights the importance of assessing clients' collectivist and individualist orientation and, for ethnic minority clients, acculturation (extent of adopting values and practices of the majority culture) and enculturation (extent of identifying with one's own ethnic minority culture; Blume & García de la Cruz, 2005). Treatment goals for certain clients might also hinge on their experiences of being on the receiving end of microaggressions, what Sue (2010) defined as brief, common, and

daily verbal, behavioral, and environmental indignities (whether or not intentional) that communicate hostile, derogatory, or negative racial, gender, sexual orientation, and religious slights and insults to a target person or group. The helper's failure to consider a client's experience of microaggressions and how these have impacted the client over time might affect the client's decision not to return to counseling or the client's lack of improvement during counseling.

In using cultural awareness to develop goals, the important point for helpers is to be aware of their own values and biases, to remain perpetual learners of cultures of which they are not a member (Hays, 2008, 2013), and to avoid deliberately or inadvertently steering the client toward goals that may reflect their own cultural norms rather than the client's expressed wishes. The emphasis is on *adapting* therapy and *customizing* treatment goals

Goal Characteristics in Action

Goal Characteristic	Example in Goal-Setting Task	Explanation
Salutary, not remedial	What you *will* be doing rather than what you *won't* be doing Something positive and beneficial, something you're working *toward* instead of avoiding	A behavior that can be visualized rather than one that can't be seen Focus on encouraging purposeful behavior that for the client is rewarding and worth the effort Emphasis on advancing, or forward movement, rather than on retreat; approaching the goal rather than avoiding the problem
New and different	Something different, a behavior not generally done before	What good is therapy if the client continues as before, doing the "same-old, same-old"? Doing something new and different can serve as the evidence that participating in therapy made a positive difference
Process-oriented, not static	What you will be *doing* Something you're *working* toward	Verbs are stated in process form (i.e., do*ing*, work*ing*) rather than in static or end-state form (e.g., would have done or accomplished)
Realistic and achievable	A behavior you can do at least a few times per week	Something that with practice is not too difficult and can become routine or customary Something the client can take credit for enacting because it originated from the client, not from someone else (demonstrates the client's autonomy and self-regulation)
Specific and comprehensible	On a video segment, you can point out the different things you were doing	Client can detect specific behaviors that he or she has demonstrated Client can explain the purpose of these behaviors to another person
Compelling and useful	Meaningful and useful to you in improving your life	Something that convinces the client that the effort was worth it A behavior that makes a positive difference in the client's daily life
Interpersonally related	Another person will be able to notice the changes you've made Point out how these changes affected other people on a video segment	A new behavior that makes a positive difference for others, not just for the client Secondhand benefit of client's treatment gains May be viewed as a form of restitution or making amends so that client's good standing is reinstated by others
Involve hard work	Reflect your diligence and hard work	"*You* earned it!" or "You *earned* it!" Something done with effort, with purpose, is likely to have a lasting benefit than something done easily or casually

to the needs and preferences of each individual client because effective treatments are those that are culturally focused and adapted to the needs and circumstances of the client (Hays, 2014; Smith, Rodriguez, & Bernal, 2011).

The Process of Change

Treatment goals identify the content of change: *what* needs to change or *what* will be different when positive change has occurred. The process of change is concerned with the *how* of change: *how* change can and does occur for clients.

In nonclinical and clinical samples, there are accounts of quantum change, or the experience of sudden, surprising, and permanent personal transformation (Miller, 2004; Miller & C'de Baca, 2001). Most change, however, experienced in and outside of therapy, is gradual and ongoing and cannot be achieved instantaneously. As Bien (2004) remarked, "Deep and lasting change in psychotherapy occurs through [a] process—a process of sustained attention to a fundamental life dilemma" (p. 497). And dilemmas, by definition, are not simple to understand, much less work through. This explains our recommendation that helpers eliminate from their clinical vocabulary and from conversations with clients words that imply that change is automatic or even permanent, words such as "fix" or "cure" or even "recovered." Alternative or instead language to use would include "working on," "managing," or "recovering." Remember that one of the characteristics of well-formulated goals is that goals are stated in process form, meaning that they describe behaviors that are regular and ongoing. Determining what these ongoing behaviors will be is aided by the use of stage models. We discuss three, one prominently.

Transtheoretical Model and Stages of Change

Prochaska and colleagues (Prochaska & DiClemente, 1982; Prochaska, DiClemente, & Norcross, 1992) developed the *transtheoretical model of change*. The transtheoretical model (TTM) depicts a temporal sequence of change and suggests common activities that propel behavior change from one time period to another. It is transtheoretical because it "cuts across" and transcends or rises above existing theories of psychotherapy by offering something new. That something new is a theory of when and how people change. In this way, the TTM is an integrative model—integrating theories and practices and offering a new perspective.

The TTM has three dimensions: processes, levels, and stages of change. Processes of change in the TTM are

defined as 10 common activities or tasks that correspond to and mobilize change. Among these are consciousness- or awareness-raising (promoted by education and feedback), self-re-evaluation, dramatic relief or emotional arousal, stimulus control or regulating exposure to certain places or people, and counterconditioning or response substitution. This latter process is similar to the practice of opposite action in DBT (Linehan, 2015), whereby persons are coached to express an emotion in a manner inconsistent with a felt emotion, such as smiling in a relaxed manner when thinking of someone you argued with recently and still feel angry toward. Levels of change in TTM are the prioritization of five distinct but related problems addressed in psychotherapy: symptom/situational problems, maladaptive cognitions, current interpersonal conflicts, family/systems conflicts, and intrapersonal conflicts.

The TTM is best known for its third dimension: the outline of five time periods or stages in the change process, referred to as the **stages of change**. They are depicted in Figure 8.1. Each stage represents a step toward a particular outcome goal, and certain characteristics are prominent in each stage. Taken together, the stages signify different attitudes, intentions, and behaviors regarding changing a target behavior (Connors, DiClemente, Velasquez, & Donovan, 2013). The five stages of change and their corresponding characteristics are:

1. **Precontemplation:** Persons in precontemplation are unaware of or are oblivious to a need to change their behavior, are underaware or do not fully comprehend the need to change, or simply do not intend to change their behavior in the near future. They may be resigned to continuing as is or are adamant about not sacrificing something that is just too important to them at this point. When they enter treatment, it is because they have been mandated or otherwise coerced to do so by someone else because their behavior has become problematic for others.

2. **Contemplation:** Persons in contemplation are aware that a change in their behavior is needed, but they are not able to do so (e.g., they lack certain skills or confidence) or they do not want to make the change just yet. They know that change would offer benefits, but they also are well aware of the costs involved. Clients in this stage of change are torn between changing and remaining the same; they feel stuck and confused and are ambivalent about change. Because of this, contemplation may be considered the behavioral procrastination stage of change, and persons—whether or not they are in treatment—can remain in this stage of change for months or even years.

3. **Preparation:** Persons in preparation have made a decision to change their behavior in the near future (e.g., next month) because the negative consequences of change are not as great as before. They have resolved their ambivalence about changing a target behavior by convincing themselves that change is needed and will be beneficial. This may be considered the dress rehearsal stage of change in that clients are practicing their new behavior in baby steps, but they have yet to break out and engage fully in the new behavior. They are still planning, strategizing, and getting ready for their behavioral debut.

4. **Action:** Persons in the action stage of change are actively and deliberately engaged in changing their overt behavior. Their commitment to making a change is clear and firm and their efforts are noticeable to others. They have debuted their new behavior and are investing considerable time and energy into making this behavioral change routine and permanent; they intend to make this new behavior stick.

5. **Maintenance:** Persons who have continued to engage in the new behavior for more than 6 months and have realized the early benefits of change are considered to be in the maintenance stage of change. Because of their success, they are sold on this new behavior and want the benefits to keep on coming. They are intent on consolidating the gains made and preventing relapse.

Box 8.2 on page 263 provides a case example of the stages of change process applied to Corinne. We recommend that you read through her case now while inspecting Figure 8.1 more closely. As you do so, notice the sequence of stages in Figure 8.1. Four of them form a circle, and relapse and recycling are a part of this process. Notice that the precontemplation stage is not actually part of the cycle of change. It precedes the start of the cycle. This means that persons such as Corinne enter the change process when they move into the contemplation stage of change. It also means that no one can relapse to precontemplation; this would be the equivalent of going back to ignorance, which actually is impossible to do.

The relapse and recycling component of the stages of change model reinforces the cyclical and recursive aspect of change, that change is not linear. It also means that change is difficult, that change is a back-and-forth process and therefore requires trial and error over time, and that back steps in the process of change (e.g., back to contemplation) represent opportunities for enhanced learning and the practice of different skills. Corinne, featured in Box 8.2, likely did not make changes easily or smoothly. Her doubts about breaking up with Logan are not uncommon and signify a relapse to contemplation once she had moved into preparation. Clients and their family members should be alerted to the not uncommon phenomenon of relapse and recycling (but not back to precontemplation), and helpers should be ready to select effective interventions—appropriate for or matched to the lapsed stage of change—when this occurs.

The three dimensions of the TTM work together when the helper selects one process or a specific intervention

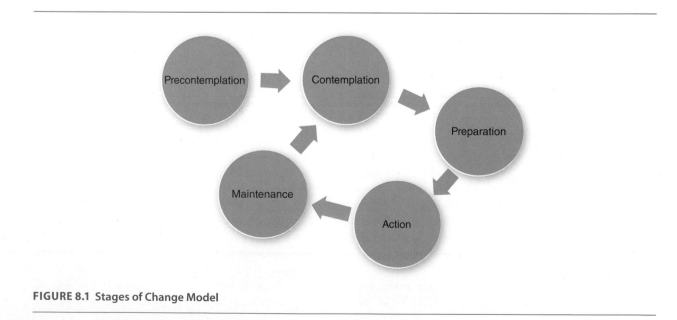

FIGURE 8.1 Stages of Change Model

BOX 8.2	Case Example of Stages of Change Process

To conceptualize the stages of change dimension of the TTM, consider Corinne, a young woman in a controlling relationship with her male partner, Logan. It is Corinne's sister and one of Corinne's long-time friends who have expressed their concern about Logan's seemingly tight control over Corinne's life, such as calling and texting her frequently during the day, recommending what she should wear, and expecting her to spend almost every evening and all weekend with him and no one else. During their nearly 1-year relationship, Corinne has obliged his requests, describing Logan as a "romantic" who really cares about her.

In the *precontemplation* stage of change, Corinne doesn't understand the concern about Logan expressed by her sister and friend, explaining to them that Logan is just "needy" and that she's glad to be able to care for him. She believes their concern is unfounded and she says she's happy in their relationship, even though she doesn't get to see her family or some of her friends as much as she used to. She doesn't see a need to change anything about her relationship with Logan. However, as Corinne learns more about the concern that her sister and friend have about Logan, and as she ponders further what her life is like now with Logan versus what it used to be like before she met him, she realizes why others might be concerned. Awareness of some of the downsides of being with him signifies a move into the *contemplation* stage of change. It is during this stage that Corinne struggles with wanting to please and care for Logan while at the same time wanting some of her old freedom back. "He does so much for me," she explains, "but I really do want to make more decisions for myself once again." The "but" is a tip-off that ambivalence has surfaced, representing a tension between these two polarities. She now asks herself: "Do I keep going as is or do I begin to make some changes for myself?"

Only after considerable time weighing the pros and cons of making changes in her relationship with Logan does Corinne realize the need to make a change. She becomes convinced that staying as is will not be in her best interest and, in fact, will become debilitating for her. She also realizes that there will actually be more advantages to changing her relationship with Logan than staying as is, and that the costs of changing won't be as considerable as earlier thought. This realization is the tipping point into the *preparation* stage of change. Time is now spent devising ways to change her behavior, including practicing new behaviors in small ways, such as not returning all of his calls right away, doing things with her sister, and using new communication skills, such as not apologizing to Logan unnecessarily.

As Corinne gains confidence and increased skill in her interactions with Logan (as well as time spent with her sister and friend), she "goes public" with her new behavior, thereby moving into the *action* stage of change. This entails breaking up with Logan, staying at her sister's place temporarily, getting a new phone, and enrolling in a self-defense class. This takes considerable effort because these alternative behaviors are still new for her and there is occasional doubt about ending things with Logan. After a period of time of experiencing an increasing number of benefits of being on her own and not being under his control, Corinne gains further confidence in her own decision-making and lifestyle. She remains committed to improving her own self. The focus now shifts to protecting and building on these benefits and not sliding back to her old ways of thinking that she needs to care for Logan or that she needs to be in a relationship right now. This is the *maintenance* stage of change wherein the new self and the new behaviors have been integrated into daily living.

based on its appropriate match with a particular client's stage of change or readiness to change so that it addresses one of the levels or problems of change. In this way, the TTM helps clinicians assist their clients in *how* (processes), *when* (stages), and *what* (levels) to intentionally change (Prochaska & Norcross, 2010). Given this method of integrating the three TTM dimensions, it is evident that the client's stage of change (SOC) is assessed first to determine an intervention that targets a specific level or presenting problem. Perhaps this explains the popularity of the SOC dimension of the TTM.

Stage of Change Assessment

Norcross, Krebs, and Prochaska (2011) emphasized that SOC assessment "has vital implications for guiding

treatment method and promoting therapy progress" (p. 151). This is true for several reasons. First, as practitioners, we need to have an understanding of what it means to change if we are to promote change in clients. Second, SOC assessment allows the helper to start where the client is. This "client-first" mentality exemplifies the client's defining role in therapy that research over many years has identified as one of the most important— if not *the* most important—variable to explain client change in therapy (Bohart & Tallman, 2010). Third, SOC assessment allows practitioners to formulate relevant treatment goals and to select appropriate interventions. These are presented in Table 8.1 and a few examples are used to explain.

Clients in the **precontemplation** stage of change come to counseling at someone else's request or under some sort of pressure. This is actually quite common and may be

TABLE 8.1   Stages of Change and Corresponding Interventions

Stage of Change	Interventions	Role of Helper
Precontemplation	Remain optimistic Provide rationale for interventions and change Convey respect and use active listening skills Increase the pros of change	Nurturing parent
Contemplation	Validate client's ambivalence about change Explore both sides of client's ambivalence: advantages and disadvantages of change Educate client about change process Decrease the disadvantages or costs of change while helping to increase the client's perception of the advantages of change	Socratic teacher
Preparation	Define, work toward, and evaluate selected outcomes Present all alternatives Encourage brief experiments with change	Experienced coach
Action	Develop cognitions and skills to prevent relapse/setbacks prior to termination Review action plan	Consultant
Maintenance	Provide emotional support	Consultant

the norm. Indeed, research suggests that approximately 40 percent of clients enter treatment in the precontemplation stage of change (Norcross et al., 2011). Clients in this stage can be difficult to engage, and therefore the helper's role is described as that of a nurturing parent. This role entails acknowledging the client's experience of feeling coerced, building a relationship, and increasing the client's awareness of the consequences of his or her behavior. One of the principles of change outlined by Prochaska (1999) is that for clients to move out of precontemplation and into effective action, the benefits of change must outweigh the shortcomings of change by 100 percent. That is, "therapists should place twice as much emphasis on the benefits of changing than on the costs" (p. 241).

Clients in the **contemplation** stage of change are aware of a concern but not able to see themselves as part of the solution, at least initially. Approximately 40 percent of clients enter treatment in the contemplation stage of change. It is important to recognize the experience of vacillation in these clients and to remember that ambivalence about change is common. All of us experience what Jungians refer to as "tension of the opposites"—the need to hold on to what is familiar while testing out what is new. During the contemplation stage of change, the helper's role is that of a Socratic teacher and appropriate interventions include validating the client's ambivalence, exploring the client's concerns or reasons for not changing

(or disadvantages of changing), and helping to raise the client's awareness of the potential benefits or advantages of changing, which might become apparent as the costs of change decrease. Indeed, Prochaska (1999) proposed that for persons to move out of contemplation into effective action, the costs of changing must decrease.

Clients in the **preparation** and **action** stages of change acknowledge that there is a problem, see themselves as part of the solution, and are committed to working toward specific outcomes. Only 20 percent of clients enter treatment in the preparation stage of change. Clients in this stage intend to take some action soon, may have already tried something, and may have a plan. The helper's role is that of an experienced coach and his or her primary task is to develop a plan of action with the client and to enhance the client's commitment to the change plan. It is an error to think that simply because the client has made a commitment to change, action will follow automatically. The helper as coach must craft a very specific plan of action with the client, remain vigilant in guiding the client through the process of testing the waters, and provide the client with detailed feedback. Strategies for helpers to use during the preparation stage of change include identifying specific behaviors to implement on a trial basis, teaching and demonstrating specific skills associated with the target behavior, rehearsing or role-playing those skills, correcting skill deficits, tracking progress, and remaining supportive and helpful for the client. These same helper strategies are then used when the client has moved into the action stage. In both the preparation and action stages of change, continuous evaluation of client progress is essential. This makes it possible to modify the plan, identify and replicate effective skills, and maintain momentum for change.

Clients in the **maintenance** stage of change often face difficulties holding on to the gains made in prior stages. It is often easier to prepare for and initiate new behaviors than it is to maintain new behaviors. Think of this stage as the period after the honeymoon, when the focus shifts from the wedding and being newly married to maintaining a healthy marriage. What was once new is now part of the person's daily routine and, as a result, the person's self-identity likely has changed. To continue to benefit from the newly acquired self-image and lifestyle, ongoing focus and deliberate action are needed. Maintenance can therefore be understood as a time of perpetual adjustment and is not an occasion for clients to sit back and hit the cruise control. Doing so would reflect a laissez faire attitude and a devaluing of the change process, and it could signal a person's propensity to relapse and cycle back into earlier stages of change. Maintenance goals and skills are especially important in the areas of problematic substance use, mood disorders such as depression, and chronic mental health problems such as schizophrenia. For clients in the maintenance stage of change, the helper is in the role of a consultant (Norcross et al., 2011).

An approach that seems particularly useful in working with clients in the maintenance stage of change is the **relapse prevention model** developed by Marlatt (see Marlatt & Donovan, 2005). This model is frequently used for relapse prevention in addictive behaviors and recently has expanded to highlight the importance of mindfulness practice in recovery (Bowen, Chawla, & Marlatt, 2011). Because relapse is a dynamic process involving intrapersonal and interpersonal determinants (Marlatt & Witkiewitz, 2005; Witkiewitz & Marlatt, 2004), relapse prevention is an ongoing process designed to help persons (1) identify high-risk situations for relapse, (2) acquire behavioral and cognitive coping skills (e.g., mindfulness), and (3) attend to issues of balance in lifestyle. Recent research suggests that mindfulness-based relapse prevention helps to lessen substance use and craving among culturally diverse persons experiencing substance use problems and symptoms of depression (Bowen et al., 2009; Witkiewitz & Bowen, 2010). Mindfulness skills also have been found to facilitate client movement toward treatment outcome goals, specifically approach or salutary goals (Crane, Barnhofer, Hargus, Amarasinghe, & Winder, 2010).

Stage of change assessment is invaluable, specifically in determining treatment goals. For a treatment goal to be realistic and achievable, it should clearly represent the *next* stage of change. Two examples may help explain. For a young client who is in the precontemplation stage of change about his participation in the vandalism of school property following his high school football team's loss in the division championship game, an appropriate treatment goal for him would be acknowledging that his behavior was wrong and realizing that he will likely have to change the group of friends he's been hanging out with if he wants to remain out of trouble, graduate on time, and be eligible for a college athletic scholarship. "Yeah, maybe I'll just do the tutoring after school instead," he says, "but I don't know what I'll tell them [his old friends] or if I can really stick with it [the tutoring]." Even though he voices uncertainty about being able to make a behavioral change, his use of the word "maybe" signals his movement out of precontemplation and into contemplation. In this case, a new perspective or heightened awareness that brings with it ambivalence actually represents improvement. And improvement is measured as transitioning into the *next* stage of change, not necessarily the action stage of change.

West and Brown (2013) criticize the stages of change model for its "arbitrary" differentiation between stages, its failure to predict behavior change, and its focus on conscious decision-making and planning processes. We believe, however, that because of its focus on decision-making and planning, it is a useful tool in treatment planning. Practitioners who are familiar with the stages of change can actively use it by first identifying the stage a client is in with respect to a target or change behavior, and then applying the appropriate interventions to facilitate the client's movement to the *next* stage. Referring back to Table 8.1 may be helpful at this point.

Two Other Stage Models

Other stage models exist to help assess client needs and determine the direction and sequencing of treatment. As opposed to the stages of change dimension of the TTM that conceptualizes a person's stage of change, these other models depict **stages of treatment** for persons presenting with specific disorders. These are discussed in the following two stage models.

For persons with co-occurring disorders (e.g., mental illness and substance use disorder), Osher and Kofoed (1989) identified four stages of treatment that continue to be promoted today in the provision of integrated treatment for co-occurring disorders (Mueser, Noordsy, Drake, & Fox, 2003). These stages are engagement, persuasion, active treatment, and relapse prevention. The focus of the engagement stage is to establish a therapeutic alliance by maintaining regular contact with the client, offering support, practical assistance (e.g., food, clothing), and crisis intervention. Once a connection has been made and the client has become engaged in treatment, the focus of treatment shifts to increasing the client's awareness about his or her substance use and facilitating motivation to change. It is in this persuasion stage of treatment that information is provided to the client (e.g., education about the effects of substances on mood, skills training) in the style of motivational interviewing (Miller & Rollnick, 2013) so that the client becomes empowered to make a decision about change. When the client has significantly reduced his or her substance use for more than 1 month and is actively seeking to maintain those reductions, he or she is considered to be in the stage of active treatment. The focus now is on more structured counseling and skills training. Similar to the maintenance stage of change in the TTM, the relapse prevention stage of treatment for persons with co-occurring disorders is concerned with helping the client develop a meaningful recovery process. The focus shifts from giving up substances to working toward a healthy life. Table 8.2 illustrates the goals of

treatment at each stage, along with sample interventions. Overlap with the stages of change in the TTM is also presented.

Dialectical behavior therapy (DBT; Linehan, 2015) structures treatment according to five stages or, more precisely, pretreatment and four stages of treatment. Each stage addresses a specific target or treatment need. Pretreatment orients and prepares a client for treatment. The target is for the client and therapist to agree to treatment goals and to commit to work together. Treatment cannot proceed unless and until both client and therapist commit to treatment and DBT requires voluntary rather than coerced treatment. This pretreatment stage underscores the importance of client-helper collaboration. Stage 1 of treatment targets life-threatening behaviors, therapy-interfering behaviors, behaviors that interfere with living a quality life, and behavioral skills needed to achieve these ends. Stage 2 targets post-traumatic stress responses and emotion dysregulation or duration of emotions, such as shame, anger, and emptiness. Stage 3 targets problems in living, such as employment difficulties, relationship/marital distress, and difficulties with problem-solving. Stage 4 of treatment targets a client's sense of incompleteness, such as the desire for spiritual fulfilment and managing boredom. It is in this

TABLE 8.2   Stages of Treatment and Corresponding Goals and Interventions for Persons with Co-occurring Disorders

Stage of Treatment	Goal	Interventions	Corresponding Stage of Change
Engagement	Establish working alliance	Outreach Practical assistance Crisis intervention Help in avoiding legal penalties	Precontemplation
Persuasion	Enhance client awareness of problematic nature of substance use and increase motivation to change	Individual and family education Motivational interviewing Social skills training Use of medications to treat mental illness	Contemplation Preparation
Active treatment	Help client further reduce substance use and, if possible, attain abstinence	Individual and family problem-solving Self-help groups Individual cognitive behavioral counseling	Action
Relapse prevention	Maintain awareness that relapses can happen and to extend recovery to other areas (e.g., social relationships)	Independent housing Involvement in supported or independent living Becoming role model for others	Maintenance

final stage of treatment that clients focus on achieving a sense of freedom and feeling joy.

Using a Stage Model

Use of any of the three stage models presented in this section helps clinicians and clients know how to determine what's next—how to identify suitable and realistic treatment goals based on the client's current functioning and preferences. Rather than thinking too ambitiously and thereby priming for potential failure or at least disappointment, stage models serve to keep both client and helper in check so that the process of change in therapy remains somewhat predictable and manageable.

Collaborative Construction of Treatment Goals

Kuyken, Padesky, and Dudley (2009) maintain that **LO3** **LO4** case conceptualization is a collaborative process, and that "the client must be integrally and explicitly involved at every stage of the conceptualization process" (p. 28). We believe this is also true during the construction of treatment goals. They and others (e.g., Persons, Beckner, & Tompkins, 2013) describe the principle of **collaborative empiricism**, which refers to the client and helper's shared commitment to therapy and their active style of partnership wherein each checks with the other about information collected from formal and informal assessments, such as the client's own observations and ideas. This pragmatic focus and systematic method suggests that the helper does not have the answer; rather, both client and helper serve as detectives, formulating hypotheses, and then testing out strategies that may be helpful to the client. Each is expected to provide evidence for what works.

Although client-helper collaboration in the construction of treatment goals is not a new concept, it has garnered explicit focus in most evidence-based practices (EBPs), specifically EBPs that incorporate principles of cognitive-behavior therapy (CBT). These include DBT and ACT, which make use of highly experiential strategies such as mindfulness activities and exposure-based acceptance exercises. Treatment goals thus are derived from client-helper transactions, specifically from the helper's focus on ensuring mutual understanding about what would be most useful for the client. In DBT, a lack of collaboration or progress is considered first a failure in dialectical assessment; that is to say, the therapist missed something in conceptualizing the client case and the focus of treatment

(Koerner, 2007, p. 337). The helper thus bears the responsibility for developing and maintaining client-helper collaboration in most EBPs.

Collaboration implies a joint effort. We therefore describe the helper's task of learning from and connecting with the client, and also leading the way. Returning to our earlier travel analogy, we think of this as the helper's dual role as fellow traveler and tour guide. This means that for collaboration to be taking place, the helper must learn from the client's previous travels, understand where the client wants to travel next, and then guide the way toward that preferred destination.

Situated in Relationship

Persons (2008) described the therapeutic relationship as a collaboration, or working together, that makes the enactment of treatment interventions possible, and also as an intervention in itself. She proposed a synthesis of these two perspectives that we believe applies to the process of goal formulation.

Collaborating to construct treatment goals cannot be done prior to or in lieu of a therapeutic relationship. Collaboration presumes that a relational connection has been established. As discussed in Chapter 3, Bordin (1979) defined the therapeutic alliance, a component of the therapeutic relationship, as the extent to which the therapist and helper agree on treatment goals and tasks, and also as the strength of the emotional bond between them. Defining the quality of the therapeutic connection in large part according to the client and helper's agreement on goals and tasks reinforces for us the prominence of the goal construction process. It also means that the two are inextricably linked: agreement on treatment goals cannot be accomplished outside the boundaries of an established and trusting partnership, and such a therapeutic partnership cannot be sustained if both partners do not agree on goals. Without investing time in deliberating goals that are mutually acceptable—and constantly staying in step with clients about the intent and direction of therapy—the bond between client and helper is likely to weaken or even rupture.

Collaborative goal construction itself is an intervention. This means that it is the helper's responsibility to be deliberate in using specific skills. It also means that client-helper agreement on the goal itself is a goal of treatment and that goal construction indeed is a process. Furthermore, goal construction as an intervention situates it—as with other interventions—in a therapeutic relationship. Prominent pronouns used are *we* and *us,* signifying a partnership and a team effort.

Mutual Cooperation

Having established a safe and trusting relationship—an emotional bond—with clients does not mean that collaborative goal construction is smooth sailing. The client-helper partnership simply means that the vehicle is in place for the work of counseling to continue. This work requires mutual cooperation, which we define as each partner consulting the expertise of the other in a dynamic and recursive way. In medicine, this practice is referred to as **shared decision-making** (Drake, Deegan, & Rapp, 2010) and is situated in between clinician paternalism (one who knows best) and client informed choice (I alone will decide). The partner or team shares with the other as much information at his or her disposal (e.g., client describes symptoms in detail, clinician explains all available treatment options) in an open manner so that treatment decisions result from mutual influence and not clinician unilateralism, or winning over the client on predetermined recommendations. The constant back-and-forth between client (or client and family members) and helper (or team of professional helpers) includes an ongoing assessment of the advantages and disadvantages of proposed goals, similar to exploring both sides of client ambivalence about change for clients in the contemplation stage of change.

Shared decision-making and mutual cooperation may require more effort on the helper's part than on the client's. In a professional helping relationship, clinicians hold more of the power than clients and, therefore, for the sake of expediency or prestige or both, may revert to a more persuasive and prescriptive approach when making decisions on treatment goals. Research with physicians has found that shared decision-making remains more a philosophy or value than actual practice (Karnieli-Miller & Eisikovits, 2009). Challenges of implementing shared decision-making include finding time, improving communication, and increasing access to relevant and evidence-based information so that good choices can be made (Torrey & Drake, 2010). To address these challenges, helpers are encouraged to become proficient in the use of electronic medical records so that information is readily accessible during a counseling session. It also is recommended that helpers are prepared to offer clients a menu of options, routinely solicit feedback from clients, and constantly check for clarity (see Osborn, West, Kindsvatter, & Paez, 2008). During treatment goal formulation, the helper cooperates with the client's ideas about goals rather than the other way around, a practice that can have an empowering effect on clients.

In their solution-focused group treatment for domestic violence offenders, Lee and colleagues (2007) found that when there was greater agreement between clients and helpers about the usefulness of clients' *self-generated* goals. At the end of the 3-month treatment clients had greater confidence in their ability to continue working toward their goals, and this (along with goal specificity) predicted a lower rate of recidivism. In an earlier description of this practice, Lee and colleagues (2003) stated that "the focus of treatment is not so much on determining the goal content but on facilitating the process of goal development and goal accomplishment in participants" (p. 33).

Referral and Collateral Consultation

Collaborative construction of treatment goals is aided by consulting persons external to the client-helper relationship, specifically persons who have an interest in the client's outcome. These persons are referred to as collaterals. Of course this consultation can only occur with the client's permission and therefore implies that it is the client-helper team—and not simply the helper—conducting the consultation. Persons to consult include the client's referral source and collaterals or family members and friends. Questions to pose include those listed earlier in this chapter in the discussion of the interpersonally related characteristic of treatment goals.

Not only can the referral source and collaterals help in the process of treatment goal construction, they can also provide feedback on progress made toward goals. This implies that the helper will periodically check in with a client's family member, for example, over the course of therapy. From a solution-focused approach, this might include coaching family members to be on the lookout for positive change behaviors. From a DBT approach, this might include the helper "commissioning" the client to consult key informants about their observations of change and then reporting back to the helper the client's findings. This would be a variant of the consultation-to-the-client strategy in DBT (Linehan, 2015) wherein the client is viewed as the key informant on his or her condition, not anyone else.

Commitment to Treatment Goals

Constructing treatment goals that the client and helper agree on does not necessarily mean that the client is committed to work toward those goals. The stages of change and the stages of treatment discussed earlier in this chapter remind us that change is a process and that it is, for the most part, a gradual process. Helpers must therefore engage in the constant process of assessing their clients' investment in working toward identified goals.

In motivational interviewing (MI; Miller & Rollnick, 2013), *commitment talk* is a form of change talk that signifies the client's intention to put his or her plans into action. Words that declare commitment are the same ones used when taking an oath of office or declaring one's vow to a beloved, words such as "I am" and "I will." In ACT (Hayes et al., 2012), commitment is understood specifically as committed action, engaging in overt behaviors to sustain a valued direction. Helpers operating from an integration of MI and ACT would therefore listen for and promote client change talk with respect to an identified treatment goal and then assist the client to "walk the talk" by acting on his or her commitment to that treatment goal. This involves mobilizing the client's self-efficacy, the belief in one's capacity to enact persistent yet flexible change.

In DBT, commitment is understood as both an agreement and a behavior and is not confined to the pretreatment stage. Recommitment to treatment goals is a constant goal of therapy and in DBT it is explicitly a shared enterprise. Helpers must therefore continually reassess their responsiveness to clients, adjusting their style and therapeutic commitment to accommodate client needs. A shared commitment to treatment goals might be likened to Bandura's (1997) concept of *collective efficacy*, defined as "a group's shared belief in its conjoint capabilities to organize and execute the courses of action required to produce given levels of attainments" (p. 477). The collective efficacy of certain communities (e.g., African American neighborhoods) has been found to mobilize community engagement to address depression in their community (Chung et al., 2009), reduce suicide attempts among adolescents in Chicago neighborhoods (Maimon, Browning, & Brooks-Gunn, 2010), and promote postdisaster mental health and general well-being following the damaging effects of a hurricane (Lowe, Joshi, Pietrzak, Galea, & Cerdá, 2015). Applied to the client-helper collaboration, collective efficacy may facilitate the realization of treatment goals.

Model Dialogue: Goal Formulation

To illustrate the process of goal formulation LO2 LO3 LO4 in treatment, the case of Isabella is continued here as a dialogue in an interviewing session directed toward goal construction. Helper responses are prefaced by an explanation. Note the italicized words that illustrate key principles and practices of goal formulation discussed thus far in this chapter.

In response 1, the helper starts out with a *review* of the last session.

1. **Helper:** Isabella, last week we talked about some of the things that are going on with you right now that you're concerned about. What do you remember about what we talked about?

Client: Well, we talked a lot about my problems in school—like my trouble in math class. Also about the fact that I can't decide whether or not to switch over to a vocational curriculum—and if I did, my parents would be upset.

2. **Helper:** That all fits with my memory, too. You summed it up well. We also talked about the pressure and anxiety you feel in competitive situations like your math class and your difficulty in making decisions. I believe we also mentioned that you tend to go out of your way to please others, like your parents, or to avoid making a decision they might not like.

Client: Mm-hmm. I tend to not want to create a hassle. I also just have never made many decisions by myself.

In the helper's next response, response 3, the helper moves from problem definition to goal selection. Response 3 consists of an *explanation* about goals and their *purpose*. Notice the helper's use of *first-person plural pronouns* that reinforce goal formulation as a *collaborative* effort, fueled perhaps by *collective efficacy*.

3. **Helper:** Yes, I remember you said that last week. I've been thinking that since we've kind of got a handle on the main issues you're concerned about, today it might be helpful to talk about things you might want to happen—or how you'd like things to be different. This way, we know exactly what we can be talking about and working on that's most helpful to you. How does that sound?

Client: That's okay. I mean, do you really think there are some things I can do about these problems?

The client has indicated some uncertainty about possible change. The helper will pursue this in response 4 and indicate more about the *purpose* of goals and possible effects of counseling for Isabella. Again, notice the helper's reference to a therapeutic *partnership*. Also notice that arriving at Isabella's preferred goal will take some *hard work* on her part.

4. **Helper:** You seem a little uncertain about whether things can be different. To the extent that you have some control over a situation, it is possible to make some changes. Depending on what kind of changes you want to make, there are some ways we can work together on this. It will take some work on your part, too. How do you feel about this?

Client: Okay. I'd like to get out of the rut I'm in.

In the helper's next response, the helper explores the ways in which the client would like to change. Because "get out of the rut I'm in" is a goal that cannot be visualized—a *remedial goal* rather than a *salutary goal*—the helper probes for *behaviorally specific* descriptors. This will allow Isabella to begin to paint the picture of her desired destination, a preferred outcome that she can actually see.

5. **Helper:** So you're saying that you don't want to continue to feel stuck. Exactly how would you like things to be different—say, in 3 months from now—from the way things are now?

Client: I'd like to feel less pressured in school, especially in my math class.

The client has identified one possible goal, although it is a *remedial goal*, stated in negative terms. In the helper's next response, the helper helps the client identify a *salutary goal*. This also means helping Isabella *approach* a desired alternative rather than *avoid* a problem.

6. **Helper:** Okay, that's something you *don't* want to do. Can you think of another way to say it that would describe what you *do* want to do?

Client: I guess I'd like to feel confident about my ability to handle tough situations like math class.

In the next response, the helper paraphrases Isabella's goal and *solicits feedback* to *clarify* whether she restated it accurately.

7. **Helper:** So you're saying you'd like to feel more positively about yourself in different situations—is that it?

Client: Yeah, I don't know if that is possible, but that's what I would like to have happen.

In responses 8–14, the helper continues to help Isabella *explore and identify desired outcomes*. Again, notice her consistent use of *first-person plural pronouns*.

8. **Helper:** In a little while we'll take some time to explore just how feasible that might be. Before we do that, let's make sure we don't overlook anything else you'd like to work on. In what other areas is it important to you to make a change or to turn things around for yourself?

Client: I'd like to start making some decisions for myself for a change, but I don't know exactly how to start.

9. **Helper:** Okay, that's part of what we'll do together. We'll look at how you can get started on some of these things. So far, then, you've mentioned two things you'd like to work toward—increasing your confidence in

your ability to handle tough situations like math and starting to make some decisions by yourself without relying on help from someone else. Is that about it, or can you think of any other things you'd like to work on?

Client: I guess it's related to making my own decisions, but I'd like to decide whether to stay in this program or switch to the vocational one.

10. **Helper:** So you're concerned also about making a special type of decision about school that affects you now.

Client: Yeah. But I'm sort of afraid to, because I know if I switch, my parents would have a terrible reaction when they found out.

11. **Helper:** You've mentioned another situation we might need to try to get a different handle on. As you told me last week, in certain situations, like math class or with your parents, you tend to back off and let other people take over for you.

Client: Yeah, I do, and I guess this school thing, math class, is an example. I mean a lot of times I do know what I want to do or say but I just don't follow through. Like not telling my parents about what I think about this whole college prep curriculum. Or not telling them how their harping on me about grades makes me feel. Or even in math class, just sitting there and sort of letting the teacher do a lot of the work for me when I really do probably know the answer or could go to the board.

12. **Helper:** So in certain situations, with your parents or in math class, you may have an idea or an opinion or a feeling, but you usually don't express it.

Client: Mm-hmm. Usually I don't because sometimes I'm afraid it might be wrong or I'm afraid my parents would get upset.

13. **Helper:** So anticipating that you might make a mistake or that your parents might not like it keeps you from expressing yourself in these situations.

Client: Yeah, I guess so. I hadn't thought of it that way before, really.

14. **Helper:** Then is this another thing that you'd like to work on? I mean, changing your expectations about how other people will respond?

Client: Sure. I can't keep on not doing things, running away from things, or withdrawing into my own little world forever.

Because Isabella has again stated the outcome in negative terms, in the next four responses (15–18) the helper helps

Isabella *restate the goal in positive terms* to make it a *salutary goal* rather than a *remedial goal*. Notice how the helper encourages this restatement by describing a goal as something that can be *visualized*, and also using the word *instead*.

15. **Helper:** Okay, now again you're sort of suggesting a way that you *don't* want to handle the situation. You don't want to withdraw. Can you describe something you *do* want to do in these situations in a way that you could see, hear, or grasp yourself doing it each time the situation occurs?

Client: I don't know exactly what you mean.

16. **Helper:** Well, for instance, suppose I need to lose weight to improve my health. I could say, "I don't want to eat so much, and I don't want to be fat." But that just describes not doing certain things and I can't really visualize a "not." So it would be more helpful to describe something I'm going to do instead, something I can picture or visualize doing, like "Instead of eating between meals, I'm going to go out for a walk, or talk on the phone, or create a picture of myself in my head as a healthier person."

Client: Okay, I see what you mean now. So I guess instead of withdrawing, I—well, what is the opposite of that? I guess I think it would be better if I volunteered the answers or gave my ideas or opinions—things like that.

17. **Helper:** Okay, so you're saying that you want to express yourself instead of holding back. Things like expressing opinions and feelings.

Client: Yeah.

18. **Helper:** Okay, so there are three things you want to work on. Anything else?

Client: No, I can't think of anything.

In the next response, the helper asks Isabella to *select one of the goals* to work on initially. This is also part of *specifying* the goal and making sure Isabella understands it. Tackling all three outcomes simultaneously could be overwhelming to a client.

19. **Helper:** Okay, as time goes on and we start working on some of these things, you may think of something else—or something we've talked about today may change. What might be helpful now is to decide which of these three things you'd like to work on first.

Client: Gee, that's a hard decision.

In the previous response, Isabella demonstrated one of her problems: difficulty in making decisions. In the next

response, the helper provides guidelines to help Isabella make a choice but is careful not to make the decision for her. She honors Isabella's *autonomy* and indicates her willingness to *cooperate* with Isabella.

20. **Helper:** Well, it's not a decision I can make for you. I'd encourage you to start with the area you think is most important to you now—and also maybe one that you feel you could work with successfully.

Client *(Long pause):* Can this change too?

21. **Helper:** Sure—we'll start with one thing, and if later on it doesn't feel right, we'll move on.

Client: Okay. Well, I guess it would be the last thing we talked about—starting to express myself in situations where I usually don't.

In the next response, the helper discusses the degree to which Isabella believes the *change represents something she will do* rather than something someone else will do.

22. **Helper:** Okay, sticking with this one area, it seems like these are things that you could make happen without the help of anyone else or without requiring anyone else to change too. Think about that for a minute and see whether that's the way it feels to you.

Client *(Pause):* I guess so. You're saying that I don't need to depend on someone else; it's something I can start doing.

In the next response, the helper shifts to exploring *possible advantages* of goal achievement as part of the process of *mutual cooperation*. This is similar to exploring both sides of *client ambivalence* about change for clients in the *contemplation stage of change*. Notice that the helper asks Isabella first to express her opinion about advantages, a strengths-based approach; the helper also is giving her *in vivo* practice in one of the skills related to her goal.

23. **Helper:** One thing I'm wondering about—and this will probably sound silly because in a way it's obvious—but exactly how will making this change help you or benefit you?

Client: Hmm. *(Pause)* I'm thinking. Well, what do you think?

In the previous response, the client shifted responsibility to the helper and "withdrew," as she does in other anxiety-producing situations such as math class and interactions with her parents. In the next response, the helper *summarizes* this behavior pattern. The helper also provides feedback to Isabella to *raise awareness* of her behavior that for Isabella has become a concern, a practice appropriate for clients in either the *precontemplation stage of change* or the *contemplation stage of change*.

24. **Helper:** You know, it's interesting; I just asked you for your opinion about something, and instead of sharing it, you asked me to sort of handle it instead. Are you aware of this?

Client: Now that you mention it, yeah, I can see that. But I guess that's what I do so often that it's sort of automatic.

In the next three responses (25–27), the helper assesses Isabella's problems, which results in information that can be used later for *planning of subgoals and action steps.*

25. **Helper:** Can you run through exactly what you were thinking and feeling just then?

Client: Just that I had a couple of ideas, but then I didn't think they were important enough to mention.

26. **Helper:** I'm wondering if you also may have felt a little concerned about what I would think of your ideas.

Client *(Face flushes):* Well, yeah. I guess it's silly, but yeah.

27. **Helper:** So is this sort of the same thing that happens to you in math class or around your parents?

Client: Yeah—only in those two situations I feel much more uptight than I do here.

In the next four responses, the helper continues to explore *potential advantages* for Isabella of attaining this goal. This exploration exemplifies *mutual cooperation* and *collaborative empiricism* in treatment goal construction and resembles the exploration of both sides of *client ambivalence* for clients in the *contemplation stage of change.*

28. **Helper:** Okay, that's really helpful because that information gives us some clues on what we'll need to do first to help you reach this result. Before we explore that, let's go back and see whether you can think of any ways in which making this change will help you.

Client: I think sometimes I'm like a doormat. I just sit there and let people impose on me. Sometimes I get taken advantage of.

29. **Helper:** So you're saying that at times you feel used as a result.

Client: Yeah. That's a good way to put it. Like with my girlfriends I told you about. Usually we do what they want to do on weekends, not necessarily what I want to do, because even with them I withdraw and don't express myself.

30. **Helper:** So you are noticing some patterns here. Okay, other advantages or benefits to you?

Client: I'd become less dependent and more self-reliant. More sure of myself.

31. **Helper:** Okay, that's a good thought. Any other ways that this change would be worthwhile for you, Isabella?

Client: Hmm...I can't think of any. That's honest. But if I do, I'll mention them.

In the next responses (32–35), the helper initiates exploration of *possible disadvantages* of this goal. This balances the exploration of possible advantages of this goal and is a strategy used for clients in either the *precontemplation* or the *contemplation stage of change.*

32. **Helper:** Okay, great! And the ones you've mentioned I think are really important ones. Now, I'd like you to flip the coin, so to speak, and see whether you can think of any disadvantages that could result from moving in this direction.

Client: I can't think of any in math. Well, in a way I can. I guess it's sort of the thing to do there. If I start expressing myself more, people might wonder what's going on.

33. **Helper:** So you're concerned about the reaction from other students.

Client: Yeah, in a way. But there are a couple of girls in there who are pretty popular...but they did make the honor roll, too. So I guess I wouldn't be like a geek or anything. And actually, with my girlfriends, I don't think they'd mind that I spoke up; it just hasn't been how I've acted with them. They might be surprised, but I think they'd be okay with that.

34. **Helper:** It sounds, then, like you believe that is one disadvantage you could live with. Any other ways in which doing this could affect your life in a less good way—or could create another problem for you?

Client: I think a real issue there is how my parents would react if I started to do some of these things. I don't know. Maybe they'd welcome it. But I sort of think they'd consider it a revolt or something on my part and would want to squelch it right away.

35. **Helper:** Are you saying you believe your parents have a stake in keeping you somewhat dependent on them?

Client: Yeah, I do.

This is a difficult issue. Without observing her family, it would be impossible to say whether this is Isabella's perception (and an unhelpful one) or whether the parents do play a role in this problem. Goal formulation at this point reflects the *interpersonal nature of treatment goals* and enhancing the *collective efficacy* of the family. The helper thus *reflects both possibilities* (similar to weighing advantages and disadvantages as part of *heightening awareness* for persons in the *precontemplation stage of change*) in the next response and also suggests *collateral consultation*.

36. **Helper:** That may or may not be true. It could be that you see the situation that way and an outsider like me might not see it the same way. However, it's possible your parents might subtly wish to keep you from growing up too quickly. This could potentially be a serious enough disadvantage that the four of us may need to sit down and talk together.

Client: Do you think that would help?

In the next two responses, the helper and Isabella continue to discuss potential *disadvantages* related to this goal. Notice that in the next response, instead of answering the client's previous question directly, the helper shifts the responsibility to Isabella and solicits her opinion (similar to DBT's *consultation-to-the-client* strategy), again giving her *in vivo* opportunities to demonstrate one skill related to the goal.

37. **Helper:** What do you think?

Client: I'm not sure. They are sometimes hard to talk to.

38. **Helper:** How would you feel about having them meet with us one time?

Client: Right now it seems okay. How could it help exactly?

In the following response, the helper changes from an *individual focus* to an *interpersonal or systemic focus,* because the parents may have an investment in keeping Isabella dependent on them or may have given Isabella an injunction: "Don't grow up." The systemic focus avoids blaming any one person.

39. **Helper:** I think you mentioned it earlier. Sometimes when one person in a family changes the way she or he reacts to the rest of the family, it has a boomerang effect, causing ripples throughout the rest of the family. If that's going to happen in your case, it might be helpful to sit down and talk about it and anticipate the effects, rather than letting you get in the middle of a situation that starts to feel too hard to handle. It could be helpful to your parents, too, to explore their role in this whole issue.

Client: I see. Well, where do we go from here?

40. **Helper:** Because our time is about up for today, that's what we will focus on first when we meet next week, okay? We'll map out a plan of action then.

(*Note:* The same process of goal formulation would also be carried out in subsequent sessions for the other two outcome goals that Isabella identified earlier in this session.)

Contextualizing Treatment Goals

Treatment with most clients involves **LO2** **LO3** **LO4** working toward more than one goal. This is particularly true for complex client cases, such as persons with co-occurring substance use and mental health disorders. It is useful to have the client specify one or more desired goals for each separate concern, but to tackle several outcome goals at one time would be unrealistic. The helper should ask the client to choose and specify one of the outcome goals to pursue first. Once this is done, the helper and client can then determine intermediate goals or subgoals and action steps.

In this section we present several methods for contextualizing treatment goals. By **contextualizing** we mean the helper's initiative to further define treatment goals for and with the client so that each goal can be understood in the context of corresponding **behaviors**, under certain **conditions** (settings, circumstances), and at particular **levels** (frequency, duration, and intensity). This process includes identifying intermediate goals or subgoals that correspond to each outcome goal, and then prioritizing or sequencing goals. We also discuss obstacles or interferences to goal attainment and resources to facilitate the achievement of goals.

Contextualizing treatment goals can be likened to preparations made for a long-awaited trip. Based on the location of the targeted destination, decisions are made about apparel and other belongings to pack, luggage to take, means of transportation, travel itinerary, and traveling companions. These decisions help to clarify the action plan; with greater texture or detail, the vision of client improvement is more apparent and realistic, and the map constructed is much more likely to help the client reach his or her final destination successfully.

Behaviors Related to Goals

Contextualizing goals involves specifying in operational or behavioral terms what the client (whether an individual, group member, or organization) is to *do* as a result of counseling. This part of an outcome goal defines the particular behavior the client is to perform and answers the question "*What* will the client do, think, or feel differently?" Examples of behavior outcome goals include exercising more frequently, asking for help from a teacher, verbal sharing of positive feelings about oneself, and thinking about oneself in positive ways. As you can see, both overt and covert behaviors, including thoughts and feelings, can be included in this part of the outcome goal as long as the behavior is defined by what it means for each client. Defining goals behaviorally makes the goal-setting process specific, and specifically defined goals are more likely than vaguely stated intentions to create incentives and guide performance. When goals are behaviorally or operationally defined, it is easier to evaluate the effects of your intervention strategy.

Specific methods the helper can use to identify the action part of a goal include:

"When you say you want to, what do you see yourself doing?"
"What could I see you doing, thinking, or feeling as a result of this change?"
"You say you want to be more self-confident. Describe the things you would be thinking and doing as a self-confident person."
"Describe for me an example of this goal."
"When you are no longer ___, what will you be doing *instead*?"
"What will it look like when you are doing this?"

It is important for the helper to use methods such as these until the client can picture and describe in detail the overt and covert behaviors associated with the goal. This is not an easy task because many clients, especially those in the early stages of change (e.g., contemplation), can only describe change in vague or abstract terms. If the client has trouble specifying behaviors, then the practitioner can provide further instructions, information, or examples. The practitioner can also encourage the client to use action verbs to describe what will be happening when the goal is attained. As we mentioned earlier, it is important for clients to specify what they *want* to do (salutary goal), not what they don't want to do or what they want to stop (remedial goal). This is also the difference between describing approach behavior rather than avoidance behavior. The goal is usually defined sufficiently when both client and helper can visualize and describe in detail the vision of client improvement.

Conditions of Treatment Goals

The second part of contextualizing an outcome goal is to determine certain conditions of the realized goal, namely the setting and the accompanying circumstances. These conditions include **where**, **when**, and **with whom** the behaviors associated with the goal will occur. Specifying the conditions of a behavior establishes boundaries and helps ensure that the behavior will occur only in desired settings or with desired people and will not generalize to undesired settings. For example, a woman may wish to increase the number of positive verbal and nonverbal responses she makes toward her partner. In this case, time spent with her

partner would be the condition or circumstances in which the behavior occurs. However, if this behavior generalized to all persons with whom she interacts, then it might have negative effects on the very relationship that she is trying to improve.

Methods used to determine the conditions of the outcome goal include:

"Where would you like to do this?"
"In what situations do you want to be able to do this?"
"When do you want to do this?"
"Who would you be with when you do this?"

The helper is looking for a response that indicates where or with whom the client will make the change or perform the desired behavior. If the client gives a non-committal response, then the helper may suggest client self-monitoring to obtain these data, such as completing a diary card consistent with dialectical behavior therapy. The helper also can use self-disclosure and personal examples to demonstrate that a desired behavior may not be appropriate in all situations or with all people.

Levels of Change

The third part of contextualizing an outcome goal is determining the **level** or **amount** of the behavioral change. In other words, this part answers the question "*How much is the client to do or to complete to reach the desired goal?*" The level of an outcome goal serves as a barometer that measures the extent to which the client will be able to perform the desired behavior. For example, a man may state that he wants to improve his overall health (a salutary goal) by decreasing his cigarette smoking (a remedial goal). The following week, he may report that he did a pretty good job of cutting down on cigarettes. However, unless he can specify how much he actually decreased smoking, both he and the helper will have difficulty in determining how much the client really completed toward the goal. In this case, the client's level of performance is ambiguous. In contrast, if he had reported that he reduced cigarette smoking by two cigarettes per day in 1 week, his level of performance could be determined easily. If his goal were to decrease cigarette smoking by eight cigarettes per day, then this information would help to determine progress toward the goal. Setting the level of amount of behavior change reflected in the outcome goal is the part of the goal that enables both the client and the practitioner to determine when the action has been accomplished or the behavior has been changed.

As with the behavior and condition parts of an outcome goal, the level of change should always be established individually for each client, whether the client is an individual, couple, group, or organization. The amount of satisfaction derived from goal attainment often depends on the level of performance established. A suitable level of change will depend on factors such as the present level of the undesired behavior, the present level of the desired behavior, the resources available for change, the client's readiness to change, and the degree to which other conditions or people are maintaining the present level of undesired behavior.

One way to set the level of a goal that is manageable is to use a scale that identifies a series of *increasingly desired* outcomes for each given area. This practice, known as **goal attainment scaling**, was introduced by Kiresuk and Sherman (1968) and has been used by a wide range of professionals (Kiresuk, Smith, & Cardillo, 1994) who work with diverse client and patient populations, including sex offenders (Hogue, 1994), violent offenders in inpatient treatment (Izycky, Braham, Williams, & Hogue, 2010), and patients in geriatric day hospitals (Stolee et al., 2012). Goal attainment scaling enhances client-helper collaboration, exemplifies individualized or idiographic treatment planning, and is appropriate when there are multiple goals to consider. In goal attainment scaling, the helper and client devise five outcomes for a given issue and arrange these outcomes by level or extent of change on a scale in the following numerical order: much less than expected or most unfavorable outcome (−2); less than expected outcome (−1); expected outcome (0); more or better than expected outcome (+1); and much more than or best possible expected outcome (+2).

Table 8.3 shows an example of a goal attainment scale (GAS). This example reflects Turner-Stokes' (2010) recommended alternative rating wherein a −0.5 is added to indicate partial achievement of the expected level. Using these numerical scores, you can quantify levels of change in outcome goals by transforming the scores to

standardized *T* scores (see Turner-Stokes, 2010). What is important is to ensure that both client and helper understand and agree on the meaning of each of the five levels on the GAS they construct. The primary purpose of goal attainment scaling is to assess the amount of client change on an identified target behavior, but because of its versatility it can also function as a therapeutic tool (Marson, Wei, & Wasserman, 2009). We introduce goal attainment scaling at this point to help make outcome goals more explicit; we return to this model later in the chapter when discussing various outcome measures.

The purpose of establishing a targeted level of change in the treatment goal is to determine present and future levels of the desired behavior. The level of an outcome goal can be expressed by the number of times, or **frequency**, the client wants to be able to do something. Occasionally, the frequency of an appropriate level may be only one, as when a client's outcome goal is to make one decision about a job change. In this instance, the *occurrence or lack thereof* is the level of change. In other instances, the level of an outcome goal is expressed by the amount of time, or **duration**, the client wants to be able to do something. And in other instances, particularly when the goal behavior reflects a change in emotions, the level is expressed as a rating or scaling, referred to as **intensity**.

Here are some ways to establish the level of change:

"How much would you like to be able to do this compared with how much you're doing it now?" (duration)
"How often do you want to do this?" (frequency)
"From the information you obtained during self-monitoring, you seem to be studying only approximately 1 hour per week now. What is a reasonable amount for you to increase this without getting bogged down?" (duration)
"If your feelings are very distressing, say about a 10 on a 0-to-10 scale, where would you like them to be after our work together using this 0-to-10 rating?" (intensity)

The practitioner can help the client establish an appropriate level of change by referring to the self-monitoring data collected during assessment. If the client has not engaged in self-monitoring, then it is almost imperative to have the client observe and record present amounts of the undesired behavior and the goal behavior. This information will give some idea of the present level of behavior—that is, the base rate or baseline level. This information is important because the *desired* level should be contrasted with the *present* level of the overt or covert behaviors. A client's data-gathering is very useful for defining issues and goals and for monitoring progress toward the goals. This is another example of the way in which goal

---

TABLE 8.3   Alternative Goal Attainment Scale

Verbal Description of Achievement	Corresponding Weight/Score
A lot more	+2
A little more	+1
As expected	0
Partially achieved	−0.5
Same as baseline	−1
Worse	−2

Source: Turner-Stokes, 2010.

definition and goal evaluation occur simultaneously in actual practice.

First Things First: Prioritizing and Sequencing Goals

In the tradition of cognitive behavioral therapies, LO2 LO3 Nezu and his colleagues (Nezu & Nezu, 2010; Nezu, Nezu, & Cos, 2007; Nezu, Nezu, & Lombardo, 2004) differentiate between **ultimate outcome goals** and **intermediate or instrumental outcome goals** in treatment. Ultimate outcome goals describe the end point of therapy, are directly related to the reason therapy was initiated, and reflect the overall purpose or point of therapy. They constitute the conditions for determining when treatment can be terminated and considered a success. They are the final *destination* of therapy. Instrumental or intermediate outcome goals, however, are goals that are achieved along the way, goals that lead to and are instrumental in eventually arriving at the ultimate goal. They are the stepping stones or stair-steps leading to the intended end point. In many ways they represent the preconditions or the prerequisites for fulfilling the ultimate outcome and arriving at the final destination. Although Nezu and colleagues refer to both types of goals as outcome goals, for our purposes we refer to **outcome goals** and **intermediate goals** or **subgoals**.

One way to explain the relationship between outcome goals and intermediate goals or subgoals is to entertain once again our travel or voyage analogy. To arrive at the final destination (the outcome goal) on one's itinerary, several stops along the way (the intermediate or subgoals) must be made. Destinations that are quite distant or are very difficult to reach will require several intermediate stops. And depending on certain conditions (e.g., weather, time changes, traveler's health, traffic, road conditions, or water conditions), changes may need to be made along the way, necessitating alternative stops or extra way stations, intermediate or subgoals that weren't in the original plan but are instrumental in arriving at the final destination.

To begin the journey and launch the process of change, the final destination or outcome goal must be broken down into a series of smaller and more manageable goals. These are the *intermediate or instrumental goals* or *subgoals* that are *action steps*. The subgoals are usually arranged in a hierarchy, and the client tackles the subgoals at the bottom of the ranked list before attempting the ones near the top. Although an outcome goal can serve as a compass

or general directive for change, the specific subgoals may determine a person's immediate activities and degree of effort in making changes. It may be helpful to think of subgoals as activities the client can do *now*, whereas the outcome goal remains a distant *not-yet* reality.

Once a primary outcome goal has been identified, the client and helper work together to identify several subgoals. The subgoals are then ordered as a series of tasks according to their *complexity* and *degree of difficulty and immediacy.* Because some clients are put off by the word *hierarchy*, we refer to **stair steps** that can be drawn on a piece of paper, similar to the stair steps depicted in Figure 8.2.

The first criterion for ranking subgoals is the complexity and degree of difficulty of the task. A series of tasks may represent either increasing requirements of the same (overt or covert) behavior or demonstrations of different behaviors, with simpler and easier responses sequenced *before* more complex and difficult ones. Although one of the characteristics of well-formulated treatment goals is that they involve hard work (see Box 8.1), clients need to experience success early on as an incentive for further change. As Lee and colleagues (2003) reason, "keeping the goal simple in the beginning allows for early success and room to expand it later on in the process" (p. 66). The second criterion for ranking is immediacy. For this criterion, the client ranks subgoals according to prerequisite tasks—that is, the tasks that must be done before others can be achieved.

The sequencing of subgoals in order of complexity is based on learning principles called shaping and successive approximations. **Shaping** helps someone learn a small amount at a time, with reinforcement or encouragement for each task completed successfully. Gradually, the person learns the entire amount or achieves the overall result through these day-to-day learning experiences that **successively approximate** the overall outcome.

After all the steps have been identified and sequenced, the client begins to carry out or *mobilize* the actions represented by the subgoals, beginning with the initial step and moving on. Usually, it is wise not to attempt a new subgoal until the client successfully completes the task at hand. Progress made on initial and subsequent steps provides useful information about whether the gaps between steps are too large or just right and whether the sequencing of steps is appropriate. As the subgoals are met, they become part of the client's current repertoire that can be used in additional change efforts toward the outcome goals.

The ultimate outcome goal for one client is stated at the top of Figure 8.2. The stair steps in Figure 8.2 illustrate how she intends to arrive at the destination of being healthy in 12 months. Think of each stair step as

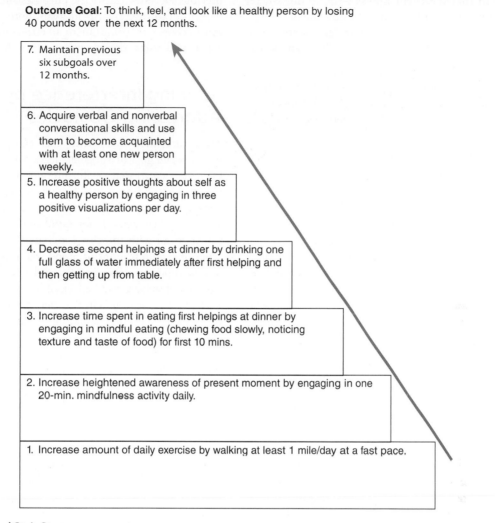

Outcome Goal: To think, feel, and look like a healthy person by losing 40 pounds over the next 12 months.

7. Maintain previous six subgoals over 12 months.

6. Acquire verbal and nonverbal conversational skills and use them to become acquainted with at least one new person weekly.

5. Increase positive thoughts about self as a healthy person by engaging in three positive visualizations per day.

4. Decrease second helpings at dinner by drinking one full glass of water immediately after first helping and then getting up from table.

3. Increase time spent in eating first helpings at dinner by engaging in mindful eating (chewing food slowly, noticing texture and taste of food) for first 10 mins.

2. Increase heightened awareness of present moment by engaging in one 20-min. mindfulness activity daily.

1. Increase amount of daily exercise by walking at least 1 mile/day at a fast pace.

FIGURE 8.2 Goal Stair Steps

an intermediate goal or a subgoal toward the ultimate outcome goal. This client's rationale is that if she increases exercise and relaxation first (stair steps 1 and 2), it will be easier for her to alter her eating habits (stair steps 3 and 4). For her, more difficult and also less immediate subgoals include restructuring her thoughts about herself as a healthier person (stair step 5) and developing social skills necessary to initiate new relationships (stair step 6). For her, stair step 6 will be the most difficult one because her weight serves partly to protect her from social distress situations. Once she arrives at stair step 6, the final subgoal, stair step 7, is to keep these actions going for at least 12 months. At the top of a client's stair steps, it is

important for the helper to discuss with the client ways for her to maintain the subgoals for a longer period of time. This is the equivalent of working with clients in the *maintenance stage of change*.

Notice in this example that the outcome goal is stated in positive terms and therefore reflects a salutary goal—not "I don't want to be overweight and unhealthy," but "I do want to feel, think, and look like a healthy person." The subgoals represent actions the client will take to support this desired outcome. Also notice that all the subgoals point to and are stated in the same way as the outcome goal—with the definition of the behaviors to be changed, the level of change, and the conditions or circumstances of change so that the client knows what to do, where, when, with whom, and how much or how often.

To help the client identify appropriate intermediate goals or subgoals and action steps, the helper can use the following strategies:

"How will you go about doing [or thinking, feeling] this?"
"What exactly do you need to do to make this happen?"
"Let's brainstorm some actions you'll need to take to make your goal work for you."
"What have you done in the past to work toward this goal? How did it help?"
"Let's think of the steps you need to take to get from where you are now to where you want to be."

The helper is always trying to encourage and support client participation and responsibility in goal formulation, remembering that clients are more likely to carry out changes that they themselves originate. This explains Lee and colleagues' (2003) policy that clients create their own goals in their group treatment program. Because it is the client who is the primary agent of change (Bohart & Tallman, 2010), Lee and colleagues "steadfastly refuse to give in to [their] urges to offer examples of goals" to clients (p. 58), believing that such "interference" would distract clients from discovering their own goals that work for them. Furthermore, they state their contention that "filling any uncomfortable silences only displays a lack of confidence in the [client's] abilities to begin the process" (p. 58). Their belief is that some clients have difficulty determining goals because they want to use their time wisely, wanting to be sure the eventual goals will benefit them. When this happens, they applaud the client's commitment to finding a goal that is meaningful for them, saying, "Even when it seems impossible right now, you are determined to find a goal that really fits for you." To help clients select their own goals and tasks, Lee and colleagues describe their style as patient, supportive, and persistent, encouraging clients to consult other members of the treatment group as well as family members and friends. Questions they pose to clients include

"What do you think someone who knows you well might advise you to work on?"
"What is the smallest thing that you could do that would help with that?"
"On a scale from 1 to 10, with 1 being 'not important at all' and 10 being 'extremely important,' how important is it to you that you accomplish this goal?"
"When you start working on this goal, what would you actually be doing that someone else would notice?"

Throughout the goal task exercise, Lee and colleagues recommend that helpers capitalize on their clients' previous successes, clarify the purposes and characteristics of well-formulated treatment goals, notice the client's effort to cooperate, compliment all efforts made to develop a goal, and restate the goal when it is well defined.

Running Interference by Addressing Obstacles

To ensure that the client can complete each **LO1** intermediate goal or subgoal successfully, it is helpful to identify *obstacles* that could interfere. Obstacles may include overt and/or covert behaviors, and in dialectical behavior therapy (DBT) these are referred to as therapy-interfering behaviors. Potential obstacles or interferences to check out with the client include the presence or absence of certain feelings or mood states, thoughts, beliefs and perceptions, other people, and situations or events. Another obstacle could be lack of knowledge or skill. For example, a 72-year old client experiencing sleep difficulty may not have an understanding of circadian rhythms or the changes in sleep patterns with natural aging, and may not be aware of specific sleep hygiene practices (e.g., reduce alcohol use, sleep only in the bedroom, avoid viewing a computer or other LCD screen 1 hour prior to bedtime, return to bed only when sleepy; Milner & Belicki, 2010). Identifying lack of knowledge or skill is important if the client needs information or training before the subgoal action can be attempted. After such obstacles are identified, the client and practitioner can develop a plan that addresses the obstacles so they do not linger as stumbling blocks to change.

Clients often are not very aware of any factors that might interfere with completing a subgoal, and they may need prompts from the helper, such as the following, to identify obstacles:

"Describe some obstacles or stumbling blocks you might encounter when working toward this goal."
"What people [or feelings, ideas, situations] might get in the way of arriving at this destination?"
"What or who might prevent you from working on this activity?"
"In what ways might you have difficulty completing this task successfully?"
"Identify information or skills you need to complete this action effectively."

Occasionally, the helper may need to point out apparent obstacles that the client overlooks, such as long-held beliefs and routines. If significant obstacles are identified, then a *plan* to deal with or counteract the effects of these factors needs to be developed. Often this plan resembles an anti-sabotage plan in which helper and client try to predict ways in which the client might not do the desired activity and then work around the possible barriers. Suppose you explore obstacles with the client who is experiencing sleep difficulty and wants to obtain restful sleep. While you explore subgoals with him, he acknowledges his recent increased alcohol consumption, his belief that he must get the same number of hours of time sleep at night at age 72 as he did when he was in his 40s, and that he should not need to nap during the day. In developing an antisabotage plan, you would need to target specific behaviors (e.g., alcohol use) and belief systems (e.g., he is not immune to aging) to work through these obstacles. Doing so might include training in mindfulness skills to accept certain things as they are in the present moment rather than forcing change.

Identifying Resources to Facilitate Goal Achievement

The next step is to identify **resources**—factors that [LO1] will help the client complete intermediate goal or subgoal tasks effectively. Like obstacles, resources include overt and covert behaviors as well as environmental sources. Potential resources to explore include feelings, thoughts and belief systems, people, situations, information, and skills. The practitioner helps clients identify already present or developed resources that, if used, can make completion of the subgoal tasks more likely and more successful.

A specific resource involved in attaining desired outcomes is referred to by Bandura (1997) and others as **self-efficacy.** Self-efficacy involves two types of personal expectations that affect goal achievement: (1) an *outcome* expectation and (2) an *efficacy* expectation. The outcome expectation has to do with whether and how much a client believes that engaging in particular behaviors will in fact produce the desired results. For a female client with diabetes, the outcome expectation would be the extent to which she believes that the actions represented by the subgoals will help her become a healthier person. The efficacy expectation involves the client's level of confidence regarding how well she can complete the behaviors necessary to reach the desired results.

People in the client's environment, especially those who observe and lend support to the client's goals, are potent resources; they also contribute to *collective efficacy* discussed earlier. Resources may also be found in the client's cultural community—people, situations, events,

and so on. Skills of the client or of others in the client's environment—skills such as resilience, persistence, flexibility, and optimism—can also be used as resources.

Strategies to help the client identify and make use of resources include:

"Identify resources you have available to help you as you go through this activity [or action]."
"What specific feelings [or thoughts] are you aware of that might make it easier for you to ___?"
"Tell me about the support system you have from others that you can use to make it easier to ___."
"What skills [or information] do you possess that will help you do ___ more successfully?"
"How much confidence do you have that you can do ___?"
"To what extent do you believe that these actions will help you do ___?"
"Describe what resources are available to you in your environment and cultures that can help you take this action."

It is an important reminder that goal formulation is a joint enterprise between client and helper, and that change is more often than not a process. This means that identifying goals and intermediate goals or subgoals and action steps should not be done hastily, nor should the helper prescribe or unilaterally assign goals. Even when the client demands or expects the helper to "fix" or somehow instantaneously remedy the presenting concern, the helper is advised to assume a collaborative stance, enlist the client's expertise, and engage in shared decision-making.

Evaluating Treatment Process and Outcomes

Good ethical practice calls for helpers to evaluate [LO2] [LO3] client progress toward outcome goals. Professional codes of ethics specify that practitioners have a responsibility to provide the best and most effective treatments to their clients. The purpose of evaluation is not merely descriptive; it also is to improve services to clients. A large body of research suggests that tracking client progress—a practice known as **treatment monitoring**—can improve client outcomes (Lambert, 2010a, 2010b). As Haynes, Smith, and Hunsley (2011) stated: "Accurate and meaningful measurements are crucial for determining whether real changes are occurring and understanding the variables that might be hindering or facilitating that change" (p. 97).

Evaluating therapy process and outcome also guides treatment planning. Process evaluation refers to the assessment of ongoing aspects of care, such as the therapeutic alliance and client status from one session to the next. Outcome evaluation generally is specific to the measurement of client status or client response to treatment during the course of therapy or at discharge. Both types of evaluation have been instrumental in research conducted over 50 years that has demonstrated the overall effectiveness of psychotherapy, a claim the American Psychological Association (APA) made official in 2012 (see www.apa.org /about/policy/resolution-psychotherapy).

Several tools are available for helpers to conduct routine process and outcome evaluation in either print (completed by hand) or digital/online format. Two of these are the Outcome Questionnaire (OQ®-45.2), developed by Michael J. Lambert and designed to measure patient progress in therapy, and the OQ®-ASC, a clinical assessment tool used in conjunction with the OQ®-45.2 to help clinicians know how to respond to client change in therapy. A Youth Outcome Questionnaire (Y-OQ®-2.0) also is available in the self-report version and a version completed by a parent/guardian. All OQ versions are available at www .oqmeasures.com. Two other measures are the Outcome Rating Scale (ORS) and the Session Rating Scale (SRS), both developed by Scott D. Miller and Barry C. Duncan, and available at www.centerforclinicalexcellence.com. A majority (61%) of clients participating in couples therapy found the use of the ORS and SRS in each session to be useful/helpful (Anker, Sparks, Duncan, Owen, & Stapnes, 2011). The OQ measures, as well as the ORS and SRS, are listed on the Substance Abuse and Mental Health Services Administration's (SAMHSA) National Registry of Evidence-based Programs and Practices (NREPP; www .nrepp.samsha.gov). They also are relatively easy to use and are not time-consuming.

Despite ethical mandates to evaluate process and outcome goals, the availability of measures to do so, and client improvement and positive ratings as a result of participating in treatment monitoring, many practitioners resist evaluating client outcomes (Bufka & Camp, 2010; Lambert, 2010a, 2010b). Reasons include believing: (1) it is time-consuming; (2) the tools for measuring outcome are not appropriate for the type of treatment they provide; or (3) the benefits of outcome evaluation will not be immediately apparent to themselves or their clients. Furthermore, many therapists tend to overestimate their skills, as well as client improvement, while overlooking and therefore not responding to client deterioration (Hatfield, McCullough, Frantz, & Krieger, 2010; Walfish, McCalister, O'Donnell, & Lambert, 2012).

Because of these concerns, we describe in the following section what we believe are pragmatic and cost-effective ways to evaluate outcome goals. As Brown and Minami (2010) indicated, reimbursement from third-party

providers rests on the helper's ability to provide evidence of treatment outcomes. There are similar expectations for clinical mental health practice in the school setting (Bohnenkamp, Glascoe, Gracey, Epstein, & Benningfield, 2015). Regardless of funding source, routine evaluation of client progress is one component of clinical expertise, and clinical expertise is integral to evidence-based practice (APA Presidential Task Force on Evidence-Based Practice, 2006, p. 276).

What to Evaluate

Goal behaviors are evaluated by measuring the amount or level of the defined behaviors. Three dimensions commonly used to measure the direction and level of change in goal behaviors are frequency, duration, and intensity. You may recall that these three dimensions are reflected by the *level* of the client's outcome goal. Whether one or a combination of these response dimensions is measured depends on the nature of the goal, the method of assessment, and the feasibility of obtaining particular data. It is important to measure the targets of treatment, that is, what have been identified as the needs, problem areas, or dilemmas of treatment—essentially the focus of intervention or change strategies—so that the measures represent valid indicators of the effectiveness of the intervention (Bloom, Fischer, & Orme, 2009). The response dimensions should be individualized, particularly because they vary in the time and effort that they cost the client.

Dimension 1: Frequency

Frequency reflects the number (how many, how often) of overt or covert behaviors and is determined by obtaining measures of each occurrence of the goal behavior. Frequency counts are typically used when the goal behavior is discrete and of short duration. Panic episodes and headaches are examples of behaviors that can be monitored with frequency counts. Frequency data are typically collected during or immediately after the occurrence of specified behaviors and therefore in the client's natural environment. This practice of collecting repeated real-time data *in vivo* is known as **ecological momentary assessment** (Shiffman, Stone, & Huffard, 2008), and it allows clinicians and clients to collect and monitor a specified range of client information (e.g., mood, attitude, behavior) outside of therapy. Data can be captured in writing, such as completing the diary card that is standard practice in DBT, and also by using a computer, smartphone, or other mobile device. For example, clients can be "beeped" to respond at certain times of the day to *yes* or *no* questions such as, "Did you experience a binge episode?" or "Have you completed your exercise task?" Programs have been developed to monitor behaviors such as binge eating and substance use on devices the client already owns or on a device issued to the client. Clients can also enter frequency counts of specified behaviors, such as the number of positive (or negative) self-statements before and after a bingeing episode. Occasionally, frequency is simply the presence or absence of a particular behavior, and in this case the level of the goal is referred to as **occurrence**. Occurrence refers to the presence or absence of target behaviors. Checklists can be used to rate the occurrence of behaviors. For example, an older client who has trouble with self-care could use a checklist to rate occurrence of self-care behaviors such as brushing teeth, flossing teeth, taking medicine, washing oneself, and combing hair.

Sometimes, frequency counts should be converted to percentage data. For example, knowing the number of times a behavior occurred may not be meaningful unless data are also available on the number of *possible* occurrences of the behavior. For example, data about the number of times an overweight client consumes snacks might be more informative if converted to a percentage. In this example, the client would self-monitor both the number of opportunities to eat snacks and the number of times he or she actually did snack. After these data are collected, they would then be converted to a percentage. The advantage of percentage scores is that they indicate whether the change is a function of an actual increase or decrease in the number of times the response occurs or is merely a function of an increase or decrease in the number of opportunities to perform the behavior. Thus, a percentage score may give more accurate and more complete information than a simple frequency count. However, when it is hard to detect the available opportunities or when it is difficult for the client to collect data, percentage scores may not be useful.

Dimension 2: Duration

Duration reflects the length of time a particular response or collection of responses occurs. The measurement of duration is appropriate whenever the goal behavior is not discrete and lasts for varying periods. Time spent thinking about one's strengths, the amount of time spent on a task or with another person, the period of time consumed by depressive thoughts, and the amount of time that anxious feelings lasted, for example, can be measured with duration counts. Duration may also involve time *between* an urge and an undesired response, such as the time one holds off before lighting up a cigarette or before eating an unhealthy snack. It also can involve *elapsed* time between

a covert behavior such as a thought or intention and an actual response, such as the amount of time before a shy person speaks up in a discussion (sometimes elapsed time is referred to as *latency*).

Measures of both frequency and duration can be obtained in one of two ways: continuous recording or time sampling. Both fulfill the purpose of ecological momentary assessment discussed earlier. If the client obtains data *each time* he or she engages in the goal behavior, then the client is collecting data continuously. Continuous recording, however, is sometimes impossible, particularly when the goal behavior occurs very often or when its onset and termination are hard to detect. In these cases, a time-sampling procedure may be more practical.

In time sampling, a day is divided into equal time intervals, for example, 90 minutes, 2 hours, or 3 hours. The client keeps track of the frequency or duration of the goal behavior only during randomly selected intervals. When time sampling is used, data should be collected during at least three time intervals every day and during *different* time intervals every day so that representative and unbiased data are recorded. One variation of time sampling is to divide time into intervals and indicate the presence or absence of the target behavior in each interval. If the behavior occurs during the interval, a *yes* is recorded; if it does not occur, a *no* is noted. Time sampling is less precise than continuous recordings of frequency or duration of a behavior, yet it does provide an estimate of the behavior and may be a useful substitute in monitoring high-frequency or nondiscrete target responses.

Dimension 3: Intensity

Clients can report the **intensity** of a behavior or a feeling with some kind of numerical rating. These are generally referred to as **individualized rating scales** and are tailor-made for each client and situation to measure treatment targets (Bloom et al., 2009). Solution-focused therapists obtain client ratings of intensity by using **scaling questions**—for example, "On a 10-point scale, with 1 being low and 10 being high, rank the degree of anxiety you are experiencing." Another example of an intensity rating is called the SUDS scale, or the Subjective Units of Disturbance Scale. On this scale, zero represents *no distress* and 100 represents *severe distress*. These kinds of scales can be used in a helping session or assigned to clients for self-monitoring between sessions. In addition, practitioners can develop more formalized rating scales for clients to rate intensity. For example, intensity of anxious feelings can be measured with ratings from 0 (*not anxious*) to 5 (*panic*) on a self-anchored scale.

Cronbach (1990) suggested three ways to decrease sources of error frequently associated with rating scales.

First, the helper should be certain that what is to be rated is well defined and specified in the client's language. For example, if a client is to rate depressed thoughts, then helper and client need to specify, with examples, what constitutes depressed thoughts (such as, "Nothing is going right for me," "I can't do anything right"). These definitions should be customized to each client on the basis of an analysis of the client's target behavior and contributing conditions. Second, rating scales should include a description for each point on the scale. For example, episodes of anxious feelings in a particular setting can be rated on a 5-point scale on which 1 represents *no anxiety or little anxiety,* 2 equals *some anxiety,* 3 means *moderately anxious,* 4 refers to *strong anxious feelings,* and 5 indicates *very intense anxiety.* Third, rating scales should be unidirectional, starting with 0 or 1. Negative points (points below 0) should not be included—a key difference with goal attainment scaling. In using self-anchored unidirectional rating scales, it is also important to tell clients that the intervals on the scale are equal—that the difference between 1 and 2, for example, is the same as the difference between 3 and 4 or between 5 and 6 (Fischer & Corcoran, 2007, p. 25). One advantage of these sorts of individualized or self-anchored scales is that they can be used at multiple times during a day and the results can be averaged to get a daily single score that can then be plotted on a chart or graph for a visual sign of progress (Bloom et al., 2009).

How to Evaluate

Hopwood and Bornstein (2014) recommend a [LO1] multi-method approach to initial assessment as well as treatment monitoring. This means collecting information from a variety of sources, not just one. Doing so is intended to provide a more comprehensive impression of client concerns, needs, and resources so that planning care can proceed with greater clarity and perhaps precision. Relying solely on client self-report—even when a variety of measures are used—provides limited and perhaps skewed information when compared to obtaining information from other sources as well. These include consulting family and friends (known as *collateral contacts*), other professionals (e.g., teachers, school counselor), and records from any previous therapy involvement. Although more expensive, the use of *biomarkers* has become more popular in the assessment and treatment planning of persons with certain conditions, such as schizophrenia, dementia, and depression. Biomarkers are the biochemical, genetic, or molecular indicators of a particular biological condition or process (Mihura & Graceffo, 2014)

and are generally obtained using electro-mechanical measures, such as positron emission tomography (PET), functional magnetic resonance imaging (fMRI), and other neuroimaging tests used for persons with degenerative conditions such as dementia. In addictions treatment, routine or periodic urinalysis tests are conducted to verify or refute a client report of substance use, as well as to track decreases in substance over time.

Selecting any type of outcome measure is not an easy decision for most practitioners. It involves consideration of measures that are: (1) psychometrically sound (accurate, reliable, and valid); (2) pragmatic and easy to use; (3) relevant to the client's stated goals; (4) relevant to the client's level of functioning; (5) related to the client's resources and constraints; (6) relevant to the client's cultural influences (e.g., gender, age, race/ethnicity, language); and (7) sensitive to treatment effects, or what Haynes et al. (2011) refer to as a measure's clinical utility. Leibert (2006) identified additional issues involved in the selection of outcome measures in an attempt to improve measurement validity. His recommendations include:

1. Norms for both client and nonclient populations

2. Clear administrative and scoring procedures for before, during, and after treatment

3. Clear operational definition of what is being measured to allow for replication by others

4. Brief enough measures that allow for repeated measurements during the counseling process

In the rest of this section, we discuss ways practitioners can use goal-related outcome measures to facilitate the evaluation process. We highlight methods that obtain information directly from clients because of their ease of use. There are three general categories of goal-related outcome measures: (1) individualized outcome assessment such as goal attainment scaling discussed earlier in the chapter; (2) specific measures of outcome, which typically involve the use of a rapid assessment instrument (RAI) to assess a given problem area; and (3) global measures of outcome that tap into broad problem areas across populations. Practitioners can use any or all of them. It is important to remember that the accuracy of the evaluation process is enhanced when multiple measures of the same goal behavior are used.

Individualized Outcome Assessment

Individualized outcome assessment is the process of measuring outcomes that are specifically defined for the client. The best known individualized outcome assessment measure is the goal attainment scale (GAS; Kiresuk & Sherman, 1968) described earlier in this chapter. The GAS is constructed while the helper and client are developing outcome goals and prior to the beginning of any treatment protocol or change intervention. A particular advantage of this method is that the GAS can be constructed during rather than outside the helping situation and with the client's participation and assistance. Therefore, the GAS requires almost no extra time from the helper, reinforces the client's role in the change process, and provides a quantifiable method of assessing outcome. Multidisciplinary care providers who used the GAS with patients in a geriatric day hospital rated its usefulness as good and noted that its primary strength was that it gave patients a voice in their care (Stolee et al., 2012).

The GAS for Isabella found in Table 8.4 on p. 283 uses *frequency* as the measure of change, but you can also construct scales using *duration* and *intensity* as indicators of change, as is true for the GAS in Table 8.3 on page 275. A GAS can also be constructed to measure the *intensity or severity* of a client's panic attacks on a 100-point SUDS scale. Goal-attainment scaling is useful because each point on the rating scale is described in a quantifiable way, eliminating ambiguity. Another advantage of this system is its applicability to assessing change in couples, families, and organizations, as well as in individual clients (Marson et al., 2009). Although scoring the GAS may be more difficult than a standardized assessment tool, and therefore more difficult to interpret, assistance with scoring (and additional GAS examples for use with children and families) is available on the GAS website: www.marson-and-associates.com/GAS/GAS_index.html.

Another way that outcomes specific to individual clients are measured is self-monitoring by clients. **Self-monitoring** entails observing and recording aspects of one's own covert or overt behavior as close in time as possible to the occurrence of the behavior. In evaluating goal behaviors, a client uses self-monitoring to collect data about the number, amount, and severity (frequency, duration, intensity) of the goal behaviors. Self-monitoring is an excellent way to obtain a daily within-person measure of the behavior over days or weeks. This can be done by using *ecological momentary assessment* (Shiffman et al., 2008) mentioned earlier, whereby clients track and record their behaviors at specified intervals, often prompted by a handheld device, such as a smartphone, that emits a signal at certain times so that the client can record their activity and/or response. This method has been used with persons with schizophrenia to record their social interaction behaviors and corresponding affective response at four different times during the day and then evaluating behaviors (Granholm, Ben-Zeev, Fulford, & Swendsen, 2013).

Self-monitoring provides a picture of a client's everyday behaviors or feelings that might be considered trivial and therefore easily forgotten; because monitoring is taking place in the client's natural environment, data have ecological validity. Self-monitoring helps determine environmental and social influences or the contributing conditions to target behaviors and involves not only noticing occurrences of the goal behavior but also recording data using paper-based diaries, mechanical counters, or smartphones or other electronic devices.

Self-monitoring has many advantages, although sometimes the accuracy or reliability of it is doubtful. The accuracy of self-monitoring can be improved when clients are instructed to self-monitor *in vivo* when the behavior occurs, rather than self-recording at the end of the day, when they must rely on recall. Using hand-held mobile devices to prompt the client to self-record also may enhance the accuracy of self-monitored data, including record of the day and actual time of reporting.

TABLE 8.4 Goal Attainment Scale for Isabella's First Outcome Goal

Levels of Predicted Attainment of Verbal Initiating Skills	Frequency of Verbal Initiating Skills
(−2) Most unfavorable outcome	0 per week
(−1) Less than expected success	1 per week—either with parents or in math class
(0) Expected level	2 per week—at least one with parents and at least one in math class
(+1) More than expected success	4 per week—at least two with parents and two in math class
(+2) Best expected success	8 or more per week—at least four with parents and four in math class

Specific Measures of Outcome

In addition to the individualized outcome assessment measures such as the GAS and client self-monitoring, the helper should consider giving clients paper-based **rapid assessment instruments** (RAIs) that can provide self-report data about symptom reduction and level of improvement. These instruments focus on specific areas of concern such as anxiety or depression. For a comprehensive listing of such measures, see Fischer and Corcoran's (2013) compendiums that describe measures appropriate for couples, families, and children (volume 1), as well as with adults (volume 2). These include measures that obtain information about a client from another source (i.e., collateral), such as the Behavior Rating Index for Children (BRIC; Stiffman, Orme, Evans, Feldman, & Keeney, 1984) that measures the degree of a child's behavior problems and is completed by parents, teachers, other caretakers, as well as children themselves. Another source of RAIs specific to children and youth mental health is the Center for School Mental Health at the University of Maryland's School of Medicine that maintains a list and description of (and links to) free clinical assessments that measure global outcomes (e.g., response to treatment), specific outcomes (e.g., trauma, disordered eating), and academic outcomes. This source can be accessed at http://csmh.umaryland.edu/Resources/ClinicianTools/index.html.

It is important to choose a rapid-assessment instrument that has good psychometric properties, is easy to read, use, and score, and relates directly to the client's identified problems and symptoms at intake and to the stated outcome goals of counseling. For example, the Beck Depression Inventory II (BDI-II; Beck, Steer, & Brown, 1996) is frequently used with clients who are depressed at intake and want to become less depressed, but it would not be suitable for someone who presents with a different problem such as anxiety, anger control, or relationship dissatisfaction. Also, because many of the psychometric properties of RAIs have been normed in Caucasian clients—often middle-class college students—caution must be applied when some of these instruments are used with culturally diverse clients. If you cannot find a culturally relevant RAI, perhaps you should use goal attainment scaling instead.

Most RAIs can be used to assess outcomes at the beginning, midpoint, termination, and follow-up of treatment. Fischer and Corcoran (2013) noted that RAIs can be overused because they are easy to use and score; therefore, they recommend that sufficient time should elapse between RAI completions, such as once per week or minimally twice per week. They further advise that RAI scores not be accepted uncritically as truth but rather as estimates of some attribute. Clients are more likely to submit honest rather than socially desirable responses when they understand how the information will be used for their benefit. RAIs also make it possible for clients to disclose sensitive information (particularly at the beginning of therapy) that might otherwise be difficult to verbalize. Generally speaking, RAIs are efficient and allow access to information about the client that would be difficult to observe. They are but one means of assessment and therefore should be used in conjunction with other methods, such as supervision and global measures of outcome.

Global Measures of Outcome

In addition to RAIs such as the Beck Depression Inventory II (Beck et al., 1996) and the Beck Anxiety Inventory (Beck, 1993), there are RAIs that tap into general levels of client functioning and a range of symptoms. These measures are called **global outcome measures** because they are "designed to be used *across* client diagnoses" (Leibert, 2006, p. 111). RAIs that cover a wide range of symptoms and are thus applicable as global outcome measures include the Symptom Checklist (SCL-90-R; Derogatis, 1983), the Brief Symptom Inventory (BSI; Derogatis, 1993), and the Behavior and Symptom Identification Scale (BASIS-32 and BASIS-24; Eisen & Grob, 2008; Eisen, Grob, & Klein, 1986). The SCL-90-R and the BSI both have nine subscales and a primary global severity index as well as extensive normative data across a variety of client populations and age groups. The BASIS-32 has five subscales and the BASIS-24 has six subscales (including a self-harm subscale), and both scales compute an overall average score. Because the BASIS-32 has been used most extensively in inpatient rather than in outpatient settings, the BASIS-24 was designed to be used with more diverse populations (see the BASIS website for more information: www.basissurvey.org). An outcome measure suitable for evaluating the goals of child and adolescent clients is the Child and Adolescent Functional Assessment Scale (CAFAS; Hodges, 1997).

A limitation of global measures of outcome is that they do not directly measure the behaviors specified in the client's outcome goals. However, an advantage of these broader and multifaceted RAIs has to do with clinical significance. In the past 25 years, there has been a major movement in the evaluation of mental health services toward criteria that reflect *clinically* significant outcomes (Lambert 2010a, 2010b).

Clinical significance refers to the effect of a treatment intervention on a single client, and it denotes improvement in client symptoms and functioning at a level comparable to that of the client's healthy peers. For change to be considered clinically significant, Lambert (2010a, p. 52) indicated that two criteria must be met: (1) the magnitude of change must be considered reliable and (2) the improvement results in the client must be "indistinguishable" on the measure of interest from individuals functioning normally. Clinically significant criteria are applied to each psychotherapy case and address not only the question of the *degree* to which the client makes the specified changes but also the *relevance* of those changes to the client's overall functioning and lifestyle. As mentioned, it is now customary for third-party payers to expect clinicians to demonstrate clinically significant improvement in their clients for treatment to be justified and reimbursed.

When to Evaluate

The timing and frequency of evaluation are important considerations. Haynes et al. (2011) remind helpers of the phenomenon of **reactivity**, or the reactive effects of measuring a behavior. This refers to the act of participating in an evaluation—that is, being evaluated or engaging in self-evaluation—that can itself modify the behavior or condition being measured. For example, there is some evidence that simply completing the BDI II repeatedly can reduce symptoms of depression even when there has been no effort to change those symptoms. Becoming familiar with administration protocols for each measure used—including issues of timing and frequency—is therefore essential for helpers.

Treatment monitoring is a constant in the helping process. There are key times, however, when formal evaluation is recommended.

Measurement before Treatment: Baseline

Information about a client's presenting concern or situation collected prior to formal treatment is referred to as a **baseline** (Bloom et al., 2009) and serves to provide a reference point or a *benchmark* against which therapeutic change in the client's goal behavior can be compared during and after treatment. Baseline information can help identify the targets of concern, their conditions (e.g., setting, circumstance), and their frequency, duration, and extent. The length of the pretreatment assessment period can be 3 days, 1 week, 2 weeks, or longer. One criterion for the length of this period is that it should be long enough to contain sufficient data points to serve as a *representative sample* of the client's behavior. For example, the helper working with a client struggling with depression may ask the client to complete self-ratings on mood intensity at several different times over the next week or two. The helper also may ask the client to self-monitor

instances or periods of depression that occur during this time. This situation is graphed in Figure 8.3. Notice that several data points are gathered to provide information about the stability of the client's behavior.

Bloom and colleagues (2009) recommend at least 10 baseline points to prevent making a mistake in determining that an intervention has worked when it really has not or that it does not work when it really does. If the helper does not collect any pretreatment data, then determining the magnitude or amount of change that has occurred will be difficult because there are no pretreatment data for comparison. Bloom and colleagues noted, however, that the number or extent of baseline measures collected must follow ethical practice guidelines, and if collecting information even for 7 days is not possible, then at least 3 baseline points is advised.

Baseline measurement may not be possible, however. The client's concern may be too urgent or intense to allow you to take the time for gathering baseline data. Baseline measurement is often omitted in crisis situations. In a less urgent type of example, if a client reports "exam panic" and is faced with an immediate and very important test, the helper and client will need to start working to reduce the test anxiety at once. In such cases, the treatment or change strategy must be applied immediately. In these instances, a *retrospective* baseline may be better than nothing—meaning that the helper and the client establish a picture of what life was like during a relevant window of time prior to the intake. For alcohol use, the Timeline Followback (TLFB; Sobell & Sobell, 2008) is the most psychometrically supported retrospective self-report method for collecting estimates of daily drinking from 6 to 12 months prior to treatment. The TLFB uses a calendar approach, and personal (e.g., birthdays) and common (e.g., national and school holidays) days are

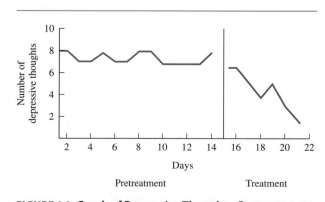

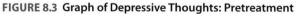

FIGURE 8.3 Graph of Depressive Thoughts: Pretreatment

noted to assist the client's recall of drinking patterns. Although usually administered in an interview, it can be self-administered, including by computer. The reliability and validity of the TLFB method has been supported in its use with adolescents to establish a baseline of their cigarette use (Lewis-Esquerre et al., 2005).

Measurement during Treatment

During the helping process, the helper and client monitor the effects of a designated treatment on the goal behaviors after collecting pretreatment data and selecting an intervention or treatment strategy. Monitoring during the treatment phase is conducted by the continued collection of data on the same behaviors and using the same measures as during the pretreatment period. For example, if the client self-monitored the frequency and duration of self-critical thoughts during the pretreatment period, this self-monitoring would continue during the application of a helping strategy. Or if self-report inventories of the client's social skills were used during the pretreatment period, then these same methods would be used to collect data during treatment.

Data collection during treatment is a feedback loop that gives both the helper and the client important information about the usefulness of the selected treatment strategy and the client's demonstration of the goal behavior. Both practitioners and clients alike benefit when feedback about progress is given to them immediately or in real-time (Lambert, 2010a, 2010b). Figure 8.4 shows the data of a client who self-monitored the number of depressed thoughts experienced during the application of two intervention or change strategies: cognitive restructuring and stimulus control. During this phase of data collection, it is important to specify the intervention as clearly as possible (Bloom et al., 2009). Collecting repeated measurements of the goal behavior(s) during treatment provides the most sensitive information about client improvement, or lack thereof.

From a practical standpoint, Lambert (2010a, 2010b) recommends that during treatment, practitioners are wise to administer any measure before counseling sessions rather than after sessions are over. Clients are more likely to complete measures prior to a session, and there is less of a risk that a client's responses given before counseling begins will have been biased or based on the immediate interactions with the practitioner. Lambert also asserts that client compliance with data collection is enhanced when practitioners take a minute or two during a session to review results and provide feedback to clients about any changes.

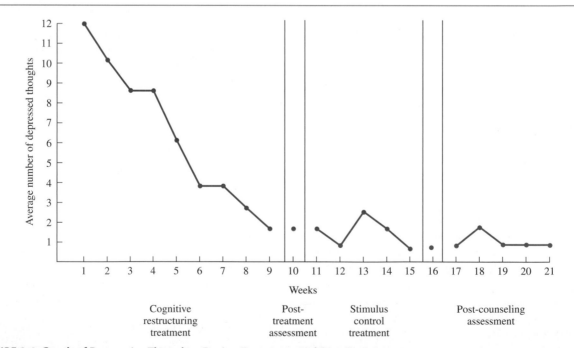

FIGURE 8.4 Graph of Depressive Thoughts: During Treatment and Post-Treatment

Although you cannot attribute client change directly to the intervention used, this concern has more to do with conducting research than practice evaluation (Bloom et al., 2009). If possible, it is recommended that data collection should continue immediately after a treatment has concluded (referred to as **post-treatment**) and also should extend beyond termination (referred to as **follow-up**). These added periods of evaluation of the client's goal behaviors help to determine if the observed changes maintain over time (Bloom et al., 2009). They also give us more information about whether the client's changes were achieved, at least in part, because of the treatment intervention used.

Post-treatment Measurement

At the conclusion of a treatment strategy and/or at the conclusion of counseling, the helper and client should conduct a post-treatment measurement to indicate how much the client has achieved the desired results. Specifically, the data collected during a post-treatment evaluation are used to compare the client's demonstration and level of the goal behavior after treatment with the data collected during the pretreatment period and during treatment.

The post-treatment assessment may occur at the conclusion of a change strategy or at the point when counseling is terminated—or both. For instance, if a helper is using cognitive restructuring to help a client reduce depressed thoughts, then the helper and client could collect data on the client's level of depressed thoughts after having finished working with the cognitive restructuring strategy. This assessment may or may not coincide with counseling termination. If the helper plans to use a second treatment strategy, then data would be collected at the conclusion of the cognitive restructuring strategy and prior to the use of another strategy.

Ideally, the same types of measures used to collect data before and during counseling should be used in the post-treatment evaluation. If the helper had also used questionnaires such as the Beck Depression Inventory II at pretreatment and during treatment, these measures would be used during post-treatment data collection as well. The overall purpose of a post-treatment evaluation is to assess the extent to which the effects of intervention have been maintained at the conclusion of a treatment strategy. Additional information about the maintenance of treatment effects can be gleaned from conducting a follow-up assessment.

Follow-up Assessment

After the helping relationship has terminated, some type of follow-up assessment should be conducted. This should be discussed with the client in the final counseling session, explaining its purpose and asking permission to contact the client at a later date. A helper can conduct both a short-term and a long-term follow-up. A short-term follow-up can occur 1 to 3 months after therapy. A long-term follow-up would occur from 3 months to 1 year (or more) after counseling has been terminated. Generally, the helper should allow sufficient time to elapse before conducting a follow-up to determine the extent to which the (former) client is maintaining desired changes without the helper's assistance.

There are several reasons for conducting follow-up assessments. First, a follow-up can indicate the helper's continued interest in the client's welfare. Second, a follow-up provides information that can be used to compare the client's performance of the goal behavior before and after counseling. Third, a follow-up can serve as an invitation to the client to re-engage in therapy as needed, similar to "leaving the light on" for subsequent and intermittent therapy. Fourth, a follow-up allows the helper to determine how well the client is able to perform the goal behaviors in his or her own environment without relying on the helper's support and assistance. It is this fourth reason that reflects one of the most important evaluative questions: Has counseling helped the client to maintain desired behaviors and to prevent the occurrence of undesired ones in some self-directed fashion? The response to this question is of paramount interest to third-party payers because it speaks to the effectiveness and durability therapeutic effects.

Both short-term and long-term follow-ups can take several forms, and can involve the client only, a family member (e.g., parent/guardian, spouse), or a combination of the two. In some cases, follow-up contact with the referral source (e.g., probation officer, child case worker) might be appropriate. The kind of follow-up that a practitioner conducts depends on the client's availability and the time demands of each situation. Also, any follow-up contact with the client, his or her legal guardian, and referral source must uphold ethical and legal practice, including the client's written permission. Here are some ways in which a follow-up can be conducted:

1. Invite the (former) client in for a follow-up interview. The purpose of the interview is to evaluate how the client is coping with respect to his or her former concern or issue. The interview may also involve client demonstrations of the goal behavior in simulated role plays.

2. Contact the (former) client via postal mail or email requesting that the client complete an inventory or questionnaire seeking information about her or his

current status in relation to the original problem or concern. The mailed questionnaire can be returned in a postage-paid envelope provided to the client. Former clients might also be provided a link to an online version of the inventory or questionnaire that is housed on a secure website.

3. Telephone the client for an oral report. The letter and telephone report could also incorporate the goal attainment scale rating if that was used earlier.

These examples represent one-shot follow-up procedures that take the form of a single contact. A more extensive (and sometimes more difficult to obtain) kind of follow-up involves the client self-monitoring or self-rating the goal behavior for a designated time period, such as 2 or 3 weeks. And, it is worth repeating that with any type of follow-up contact with former clients, helpers must abide by ethical codes and legal standards, including informed consent, confidentiality, and procedures compliant with HIPPA (the Health Insurance Portability and Accountability Act) that are discussed in Chapter 2.

Treatment Evaluation Pointers

It is important for helpers to partner with clients in the evaluation or treatment-monitoring process. The purpose of several evaluation tools—such as the SSR and the OQ®-ASC mentioned previously—is to enhance client-helper partnership. Collaborating with clients in the evaluation process includes the helper explaining the purpose of evaluation, what is being evaluated and how often, others who will be consulted only with client permission, how the information will be used, and the intended benefits to the client. It goes without saying that challenges to this process occur with clients who are cognitively impaired or literate in languages other than English, because few brief measures have been translated (Bufka & Camp, 2010). In all instances, evaluation strategies need to be tailored to the individual client and his or her circumstance.

Despite the challenges of evaluating outcome goals, it is an important practice worth pursuing. Haynes et al. (2011) do not mince words when they say that:

> …clinicians do a disservice to clients by not systematically monitoring their treatment process and outcome. Without frequently collecting valid, sensitive-to-change measures of treatment outcome and process with their clients, clinicians are more liable to use biased shortcuts in judging the effects of their intervention efforts. Doing so can result in harm to clients. (p. 119)

Model Dialogue: Evaluating Progress

In this section, we return to our client Isabella. The [LO4] model example and dialogue that follows illustrates the interconnected processes of defining and evaluating outcome goals.

Isabella's first outcome goal was contextualized as acquiring and demonstrating a minimum of four initiating skills, including four of the following: (1) asking questions or making reasonable requests; (2) expressing differences of opinion; (3) expressing positive feelings; (4) expressing negative feelings; and (5) volunteering answers or opinions in at least four situations in a week with her parents and in math class. This overall goal can be assessed on a goal attainment scale (GAS; Kiresuk & Sherman, 1968). See Table 8.4 on page 283 for Isabella's specific GAS. Additionally, a global outcome measure such as the Youth Outcome Questionnaire (Y-OQ®-2.0) described previously might be appropriate for Isabella to monitor progress.

Four intermediate goals or subgoals are associated with Isabella's first outcome goal:

1. To decrease anxiety associated with anticipation of failure in math class and rejection by parents from self-ratings of intensity of 70 to 50 on a 100-point scale during the next two weeks of treatment.

2. To increase positive self-talk and thoughts that "girls are capable" in math class and other competitive situations from zero or two times per week to four or five times per week over the next 2 weeks during treatment.

3. To increase attendance in math class from two or three times per week to four or five times per week during treatment.

4. To increase verbal participation and initiation in math class and with her parents from none or once per week to three or four times per week over the next two weeks during treatment. Verbal participation is defined as asking and answering questions with teacher or parents, volunteering answers or offering opinions, or going to the chalkboard. (For a summary of these subgoals, see Table 8.5 Isabella's goal chart, on page 289.)

The helper and Isabella need to establish the method of evaluating progress on each of the four intermediate goals or subgoals and to determine the response dimension for each one. For subgoal 1, Isabella could self-monitor intensity of anxiety associated with anticipated failure in math class and rejection from parents on a scale ranging from 0 to 100. For subgoal 2, we recommend that Isabella

TABLE 8.5   Isabella's Goal Chart

Outcome Goals	Related Subgoals
Goal 1 To acquire and demonstrate a minimum of four different initiating skills (asking a question or making a reasonable request, expressing differences of opinion, expressing positive feelings, expressing negative feelings, volunteering answers or opinions, going to the board in class) <u>in her math class and with her parents</u> *at least 4 situations in 1 week.*	1. To decrease anxiety associated with anticipation of failure <u>in math class or rejection by parents</u> *from a self-rated intensity of 70 to 50 on a 100-point scale during the next 2 weeks.* 2. To restructure thoughts or self-talk by replacing thoughts that "girls are dumb" with "girls are capable" <u>in math class and in other threatening or competitive situations</u> *from 0–2 per day to 4–5 per day.* 3. To increase attendance at math class from 2–3 times per week to 4–5 times per week. 4. To increase verbal participation skills (asking and answering questions, volunteering answers, or offering opinions) <u>in math class and with her parents</u> *from 0–1 times per day to 3–4 times per day.*
Goal 2 To increase positive perceptions about herself and her ability to function effectively <u>in competitive situations such as math class</u> *by 50% over the next 3 months.*	1. To eliminate conversations <u>with others in which she discusses her lack of ability</u> *from 2–3 per week to 0 per week.* 2. To increase self-visualizations in which she sees herself as competent and adequate to function independently <u>in competitive situations or with persons in authority</u> *from 0 per day to 1–2 per day.* 3. To identify negative thoughts and increase positive thoughts <u>about herself</u> *by 25% in the next 2 weeks.*
Goal 3 To acquire and use five different decision-making skills (identifying an issue, generating alternatives, evaluating alternatives, selecting the best alternative, and implementing action), at least one of which represents a situation when significant others have given her their opinion or advice on how to handle it *in at least two different situations during a month.*	1. To decrease thoughts and worry about making a bad choice or poor decision <u>in any decision-making situation</u> *by 25% in the next 2 weeks.* 2. To choose a course of action and implement it *in any* <u>decision-making situation</u> *at least once during the next 2 weeks.*

Key: Each of the three goals and related subgoals describe the target behavior (regular font), under certain conditions (underlined), and ***at a particular level*** (in italics).

self-monitor her self-talk during math class and in other competitive situations. She could be instructed to write (*in vivo*) her self-talk on note cards during baseline and treatment. Subgoal 3 is to increase her attendance in math class. Isabella could keep a record of the days she attended class, and these data could be verified from the teacher's attendance records, with Isabella's permission. Subgoal 4, verbal participation and initiation in math class and with her parents, also could be self-monitored (*in vivo*). Isabella could record each time she performed these verbal responses. Again, the same data would be collected before, during, and after an intervention. We illustrate this evaluation process in the following continuation of our model dialogue.

The helper starts by *summarizing* the previous session and by checking out whether Isabella's goals have changed in any way. Goal-setting is a flexible process subject to revisions along the way.

1. **Helper:** Okay, Isabella, just to recap from last week when we talked, you mentioned three areas you'd like to work on. Have you added anything or changed your thinking in any way about these since then?

Client: No. I still want to start with this whole issue of expressing myself and not worrying so much about what other people think. I've been doing a lot of thinking about it, and I think I'm really starting to see how much I let other people use me as a doormat and also control my reactions in a lot of ways.

2. **Helper:** You mentioned some of those things last week. They seem to be giving you some incentive to work on this.

Client: Yeah. I guess I'm finally waking up and starting to feel a little upset about it.

In the next response, the helper explains the *purpose* of the session and solicits Isabella's opinion, again giving her another opportunity to express her opinions. This is another example of *mutual cooperation* in the contextualization of treatment goals.

3. **Helper:** Last week I mentioned it might be helpful to map out a plan of action. How does that sound to you?

Client: Yeah, that's fine. I've been kind of gearing up for this all week.

In the next two responses, the helper helps Isabella contextualize the *behaviors* associated with the goal—what she will be doing, thinking, and feeling.

4. **Helper:** Okay, last week when we talked about this area of change, you described it as wanting to express yourself more without worrying so much about the reactions from other people. Could you tell me what you mean by expressing yourself—to make sure we're in sync about this?

Client: Well, like in math class, I need to volunteer the answers when I know them, and volunteer to go to the board. Also, I hesitate to ask questions. I need to be able to ask a question without worrying if it sounds foolish.

5. **Helper:** You've mentioned three specific ways in math class you want to express yourself [*makes a note*]. I'm going to jot them down in case we want to refer to them later. Anything else you can think of about math class?

Client: No, not really. The other thing I have trouble with is with my parents.

Note that "trouble" is not very specific. Again, a *behavioral contextualization* of the goal is sought in the next two responses.

6. **Helper:** Okay, "trouble." Describe exactly how you'd like to express yourself when interacting with them.

Client: Kind of the same stuff. Sometimes I would like to ask them a question. Or ask for help or something. But I don't. I almost never tell them my ideas or opinions, especially if I don't agree with their ideas. I just keep things to myself.

7. **Helper:** So you'd like to be able to make a request, ask a question, talk about your ideas with them, and express disagreement. Is that it?

Client: Yeah. [*pauses and sighs*] It just sounds hard.

In the following response, the helper prepares Isabella for the idea of working in *small steps* and also explores *conditions* (situations, people) associated with the goal.

8. **Helper:** It will take some time, and we won't try to do everything at once. Just one step at a time. Now, you mentioned two different situations where these things are important to you—math class and with your parents. I noticed last week there was a time when you seemed reluctant to tell me your opinion. Is this something you want to do in any other situation or with any other people?

Client: Well, sure—it does crop up now and then at different times or with different people, even friends. But it's worse in math and at home. I think if I could do it there, I could do it anywhere.

In the next response, the helper starts to explore the *level* or *desired extent of change*. The helper is attempting to establish a *current baseline* to know how much the client is doing now.

9. **Helper:** I'm making a note of this, too. Now could you guess at how often you express yourself in the ways you've just described *right now,* either in math class or with your parents, in a given week?

Client: You mean how many times do I do these things every week?

10. **Helper:** Yes.

Client: Probably almost never—at least not in math class or at home. Maybe once or twice at the most.

The helper continues to help Isabella identify a *useful* and *realistic level of change*.

11. **Helper:** If you express yourself in one of these ways once or twice per week now, then how often would you like to be doing this? Think of something that is also practical or realistic.

Client: Hmm. Well, I don't really know. Maybe four or five times per week—that's about once a day, and that would take a lot for me to do that in those kinds of situations.

At this point, the *behavior, conditions, and level of change* for this outcome goal are defined. The helper asks Isabella whether this definition is the way she wants it, an example of soliciting client input to ensure *client preferences* are honored.

12. **Helper:** I'll make a note of this. Here, check what I have written down—does it seem accurate? (*Isabella reads what is listed as the first outcome goal on her goal chart, Table 8.5, on page 289.*)

Client: Yeah. Wow, it seems so official!

This is the second time Isabella has expressed a little hesitation. So in the next response the helper checks out *her feelings* about the process.

13. **Helper:** Yeah? Tell me what you're feeling about all of this right now.

Client: Kind of good and a little scared, too. Like, do I really have what it takes to do this?

In the next response, the helper responds to and validates Isabella's concern. Isabella has already selected this goal, yet if she has difficulty later on moving toward it, they will need to explore what her present behavior is trying to protect.

14. **Helper:** I can understand that. One thing I'm sure of is that you do have the resources inside you to move in this direction as long as this is a direction that is important to you. If we move along and you feel stuck, then we'll come back to this and see how you keep getting stuck at this point.

Client: Okay.

Next, the helper introduces and *develops a goal attainment scale* for this particular goal (responses 15–20).

15. **Helper:** Let's spend a little time talking about this particular goal we've just nailed down. I'd like to set up some sort of a system with you for us to rank what you expect or would like to happen, but also the best possible and the least possible success we could have with this goal. This gives us both a concrete target to work toward. How does that sound?

Client: Okay. What exactly do we do?

16. **Helper:** Well, let's start with a range of numbers from −2 to +2. It will look like this [*Draws the following numbers on a sheet of paper*]:
    −2
    −1
     0
    +1
    +2
    Zero represents an acceptable and expected level, one you could live with. What do you think it would be in this case?

Client: I guess maybe doing this at least twice a week—at least once in math and once at home. That would be better than nothing.

17. **Helper:** We'll put that down for zero. If that's acceptable, would you say that the four per week you mentioned earlier is more than expected?

Client: Yes.

18. **Helper:** Okay, let's put that down for +1 and how about eight per week for −2. That's sort of in your wildest dreams. How is that?

Client: Let's go for it.

19. **Helper:** Now, if two per week is acceptable for you, what would be less than acceptable—one or zero?

Client: One is better than nothing—zero is just where I am now.

20. **Helper:** So let's put one per week with −1 and none per week with −2. Now we have a way to keep track of your overall progress on this goal. Do you have any questions about this? [*See Table 8.4 for the goal attainment scale for Isabella's first outcome goal.*]

Client: No, it seems pretty clear.

In the next response, the helper introduces the idea of *intermediate goals* or *subgoals,* which represent stepping stones and action steps toward the outcome goal, and asks Isabella to identify the *initial step,* which is subgoal 1 on Table 8.5.

21. **Helper:** Another thing I think might help with your apprehension is to map out a plan of action. What we've just done is to identify exactly where you want to get to—maybe over the course of the next few months. Instead of trying to get to this destination all at once, let's look at different steps you could take to get there, with the idea of taking just one step at a time, just like climbing a staircase. For instance, what do you think would be your first step—the first thing you would need to do to get started in a direction that goes right to where you want to end up?

Client: Well, the first thing that I can think of is that I don't want to be so uptight. I worry about what other people think when I do or say something.

In the next two responses, the helper helps Isabella contextualize the *behavior and conditions associated with this initial subgoal,* just as she did previously for the outcome goal.

22. **Helper:** So you want to be less uptight and worry less about what other people might think. When you say "other people," who do you have in mind?

Client: My parents, of course, and to some degree almost anyone that I don't know too well or anyone like my math teacher, who is in a position to evaluate me.

23. **Helper:** So you're talking mainly about lessening these feelings when you're around your parents, your

math teacher, or other people who you think are evaluating you.

Client: Yes, I think that's it.

In response 24 that follows, the helper is trying to establish the *current level of intensity* associated with Isabella's feelings of being uptight. The helper does this by using an *imagery assessment* in the interview. *Self-reported ratings of intensity* are used in conjunction with the imagery.

24. **Helper:** Now I'm going to ask you to close your eyes and imagine a couple of situations that I'll describe to you. Try to really get involved in the situation—put yourself there. If you start feeling nervous, signal by raising this finger. *(The helper shows Isabella the index finger of her right hand and describes three situations—one related to parents, one related to math class, and one related to a job interview with a prospective employer. In all three situations, Isabella raises her finger. After each situation, the helper stops and asks Isabella to rate the intensity of her anxiety on a SUDS 0-to-100-point scale, zero being complete calm and relaxation and 100 being total panic.)*

After the imagery assessment for base rate, the helper asks Isabella to *specify a desired level of change for this subgoal.*

25. **Helper:** Now, just taking a look at what happened here in terms of the intensity of your feelings, you rated the situation with your parents about 75, the one in math class 70, and the one with the employer 65. Where would you like to see this drop down to during the next couple of weeks?

Client: Oh, I guess about a 10.

It is understandable that someone with fairly intense anxiety wants to get rid of it, and it is possible to achieve that goal within the next few months. However, such goals are more effective when they are *immediate rather than distant.* In the next two responses, the helper asks Isabella to *specify a realistic level of change* for the immediate future.

26. **Helper:** That may be a number to shoot for in the next few months, but I'm thinking that in the next 3 or 4 weeks the jump from, say, 70 to 10 is pretty big. Does that gap feel realistic or feasible?

Client: Hmm. I guess I was getting ahead of myself.

27. **Helper:** It's important to think about where you want to be in the long run. I'm suggesting 3 or 4 weeks mainly so you can start to see some progress and lessening of intensity of these feelings in a fairly short time. What number seems reasonable to you to shoot for in the short run?

Client: Well, maybe a 45 or 50.

At this point, the helper and Isabella continue to *identify other intermediate goals* or *subgoals* between the initial subgoal and the outcome.

28. **Helper:** That seems real workable. Now, we've sort of mapped out the first step. Let's think of other steps between this first one and this result we've written down here.

The helper and client continue to generate possible action steps. Eventually they select and define the remaining three subgoals shown in Table 8.5. Assuming the remaining subgoals are selected and defined, the next step is to *rank order* or *sequence* the four subgoals and *list them in order on a goal staircase* like the one shown in Figure 8.2 on page 277.

29. **Helper:** We've got the first step, and now we've mapped out three more. Consider where you will be after this first step is completed. Which one of the three remaining steps comes next? Let's discuss it, and then we'll fill it in, along with this first step on the goal stair steps, which you can keep so you know exactly where on the goal stair steps you're on and when. *(The helper and Isabella continue to rank order subgoals, and Isabella lists them in sequenced order on a goal stair steps.)*

In response 30, the helper points out that *subgoals may change in type or sequence.* The helper then shifts the focus to exploration of potential *obstacles for the initial subgoal.*

30. **Helper:** Now we've got our overall plan mapped out. But this can change, too. You might find later on you want to add a step or reorder the steps. Let's go back to your first step—decreasing these feelings of nervousness and worrying less about the reactions of other people. Because this is what you want to start working on this week, describe anything or anybody who might get in your way or would make it difficult for you to work on this.

Client: It's mostly something inside me. In this case, I guess I'm my own worst enemy.

31. **Helper:** So you're saying there don't seem to be any people or situations outside yourself that may be obstacles. If anyone sets up an obstacle course, it will be you.

Client: Yeah. Mostly because I feel I don't have much control over those feelings.

The client has identified herself and her perceived lack of control over her feelings as *obstacles.* Later on, the helper will need to help Isabella select and work with one or two *intervention strategies.*

32. **Helper:** So one thing we need to do is to look at ways you can learn some skills to manage these feelings so they don't get the best of you.

Client: I think that would help.

In the next response, the helper explores *existing resources and support systems* that Isabella might use to help her work effectively with the subgoal.

33. **Helper:** That's where I'd like to start in just a minute. Before we do, can you identify any people who could help you with these feelings—or anything else you could think of that might help instead of hinder you?

Client: Well, coming to see you. It helps to know I can count on that. And I have a really good friend who is sort of the opposite of me, and she's really encouraging.

Social allies are an important factor in effecting change, and the helper uses this term in response 34 to underscore this point.

34. **Helper:** Okay, so you've got at least two allies.

Client: Yeah.

In response 35, the helper helps Isabella develop a way to continue the *self-ratings of the intensity* of her nervous feelings. This gives both of them a *benchmark to use in assessing progress and reviewing* the adequacy of the first subgoal selected.

35. **Helper:** The other thing I'd like to mention is a way for you to keep track of any progress you're making. You know how you rated these situations I described today? You could continue to do this by keeping track of when you feel uptight and worry about the reactions of others. Jot down a brief note about what happened and then a number on this 0-to-100 scale that best represents how intense your feelings were at the time. You could do this on your phone, if that's easier. Either way, I believe as you do this and bring it back, it will help both of us see exactly what's happening for you on this first step. This will also help us develop a plan of action and modify it if we need to. Does that sound like something you could do?

Client: Yeah...Do I need to do it in the moment, I mean when I'm worried, or after?

Clients are more likely to do *self-ratings or self-monitoring if it falls into their daily routine,* so this is explored in the next response.

36. **Helper:** What would be most practical for you?

Client: Probably after, because it's so hard to write or even put it on my phone in the middle of it.

The helper encourages Isabella to make her notes soon after the situation is over. *The longer the gap, the less accurate* the data might be.

37. **Helper:** That's fine. Try to get it down on paper or on your phone as soon as it ends or soon after, because the longer you wait, the harder it will be to remember. You might even want to prompt yourself on your phone, almost like beeping yourself at different times of the day. Also, to get an idea of your current level of anxiety, I'd like you to take a few minutes at the end of our session today to fill out a form that asks you some questions about what you may be feeling. There are no right or wrong answers on this, so it's not like a test. I'll be asking you to do this again several times during our work together. Would you feel comfortable doing this?

Before the session ends, they have to work on the *obstacle* Isabella identified earlier—that she is her "own worst enemy" because her feelings are in control of her.

38. **Helper:** Now, let's go back to that obstacle you mentioned earlier—that your feelings are in control of you…

Upon exploring this issue, the helper will select treatment interventions to use with Isabella.

CHAPTER SUMMARY

The primary purpose of constructing and evaluating treatment goals is to convey to the client the responsibility and role she or he has in contributing to the results of the helping process. Without active client participation, counseling may be doomed to failure. The construction of goals should reflect *client* choices, similar to Lee and colleagues' (2003, 2007, 2012) practice with domestic violence offenders. Effective goals are consistent with the *client's* cultural identity and belief systems. The helper's role is to assume a facilitative stance to guide the client in constructing his or her preferred therapeutic destination. Together, helper and client explore whether the goal is owned by the client, whether it is realistic, and what advantages and disadvantages are associated with it. This is done to support client autonomy. If helper and client commit to pursue the constructed goals, these goals must be contextualized, that is, defined clearly and specifically. Throughout this process the client moves along a change continuum ranging from contemplation to preparation and finally to action.

Treatment goals that are contextualized make it easier to note and assess progress and also aid in guiding the client toward the desired goal(s). A goal is contextualized with care when you are able to specify the overt and covert behaviors associated with the goal, the conditions, or context in which the goal is to be carried out or achieved, and the level of change. After the outcome goal is defined, helper and client work jointly to identify and sequence subgoals that represent intermediate action steps and lead directly to the goal. Obstacles or interferences that might hinder goal attainment and resources that may aid in goal attainment are also explored.

As outcome goals are constructed and contextualized, ways to evaluate progress toward these goals are also incorporated into the helping process. Treatment monitoring is an important component of the helping process. Without it, practitioners have no knowledge of how their interventions are working to help clients achieve their outcome

goals. Data related to client outcome goals are collected before, during, and after treatment. Individualized, specific, and global measures of goal-related outcomes are used in treatment monitoring as outcome indicators. A multi-method approach to treatment monitoring uses multiple measures (and sources for information) so that it is comprehensive. When used effectively, outcome measures represent a therapeutic tool that not only complements services but also enhances services to clients.

 Visit CengageBrain.com for a variety of study tools and useful resources such as video examples, case studies, interactive exercises, flashcards, and quizzes.

8 | Knowledge and Skill Builder

Part One

Learning Outcome 1 asks you to identify a problem for which you will construct, contextualize, and then evaluate an outcome goal. Use the Goal-Setting Worksheet for this process. You can obtain feedback by sharing your worksheet with a colleague, supervisor, or instructor.

Goal-Setting Worksheet

1. Identify a concern.
2. State the desired or preferred outcome of the concern.
3. Assess the desired or preferred outcome.
   a. Does it specify what you want to do? (If not, reword it so that you state what you want to do instead of what you don't want to do.)
   b. Is this something you can see (hear, grasp) yourself doing every time?
4. In what ways is achievement of this goal important to you? To others?
5. What will achieving this goal require of you? Of others?
6. To what extent is this goal something you want to do? Something you feel you should do or are expected to do?
7. Is this goal based on
   _____ Rational, logical ideas?
   _____ Realistic expectations and ideas?
   _____ Irrational ideas and beliefs?
   _____ Logical thinking?
   _____ Perfectionistic standards (for self or others)?
8. How will achieving this goal help *you?* Help significant others in your life?
9. What problems could achieving this goal create for you? For others?
10. If the goal requires someone else to change, is not realistic or feasible, is not worthwhile, or poses more disadvantages than advantages, rework the goal. Then move on to item 11.
11. As a result of achieving the goal, exactly what will you be
    a. Doing:_____
    b. Thinking:_____
    c. Feeling:_____
12. Contextualize (or put into context) your goal in item 11 by indicating
    a. *Where* this will occur: _____
    b. *When* this will occur: _____
    c. *With whom* this will occur: _____
    d. *How much or how often* this will occur: _____
13. Develop a plan that specifies *how* you will attain your goal by identifying the action steps to be taken.

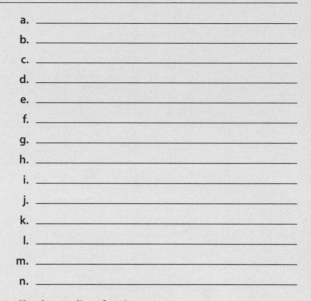

a. _____
b. _____
c. _____
d. _____
e. _____
f. _____
g. _____
h. _____
i. _____
j. _____
k. _____
l. _____
m. _____
n. _____

14. Check your list of action steps:
    a. Are the gaps between steps small? If not, add a step or two.
    b. Does each step represent only one major activity? Separate every step that does not into two or more steps.
    c. Does each step specify what, where, when, with whom, and how much or how often? If not, go back and define your action steps more concretely.
15. Use the goal stair steps on page 296 to prioritize or sequence your list of action steps. Start with the easiest, most immediate step at the bottom of the goal stair steps, and proceed to the most difficult, least immediate step at the top.
16. Starting with your first action step, brainstorm what could make each action step difficult to carry out or what could interfere with doing it successfully. Consider feelings, thoughts, places, people, and lack of knowledge or skills. List the *obstacles* in the space provided on page 296.
17. Starting with your first action step, identify for each action step existing resources such as feelings, thoughts, situations, people and support systems, information, skills, beliefs, and self-confidence that would make it more likely for you to carry out the action or complete it more successfully. List the *resources* in the space provided on page 296.
18. Identify a way to monitor your progress for completion of each action step.
19. Devise a plan to help yourself maintain the action steps after you attain them.

(continued)

8 Knowledge and Skill Builder (*continued*)

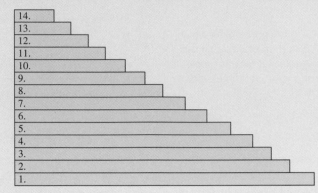

14-step Stair Steps

Goal Stair Steps

Obstacles	Resources
1.	
2.	
3.	
4.	
5.	
6.	
7.	
8.	
9.	
10.	
11.	
12.	
13.	
14.	

Part Two

In this part of the Knowledge and Skill Builder, we describe the case of Manuel. Assuming that Manuel is your client, describe the steps you would take to help him construct, contextualize, and evaluate desired actions, given his stated problem (Learning Outcome 2). Try to include at least 10 of the 13 steps or categories we described in this chapter for constructing, contextualizing, and evaluating outcome goals. These 13 steps or categories are listed in the second column (Category of Information) of the Interview Checklist for Constructing, Contextualizing, and Evaluating Goals found on pages 297–299 in this Knowledge and Skill Builder section. You can do this activity orally with a partner, in small groups, or by yourself. If you do it by yourself, you may want to jot down your ideas in writing for someone else to assess. Feedback follows on page 301.

The Case of Manuel

Manuel Tréjos is a 52-year-old Latino who is the manager of an advertising firm. He has been with the firm for 17 years and has another 12 years to go before drawing a rather lucrative retirement package. Over the past three years, however, Manuel has become increasingly dissatisfied with his job specifically and with work in general. He says he feels as if he wants nothing more than to quit, but he and his wife also want to build up a nest egg for their son's two young children, because their grandchildren are very important to them. Manuel realizes that if he leaves the firm now, he will lose many of his retirement benefits. Manuel defines his problem as feeling burned out with the 9-to-5 job routine. He wishes to have more free time, but as the head of his family he also feels a sense of great responsibility to provide financial security.

Part Three

According to Learning Outcome 3, you will be able to demonstrate, during a role play with two colleagues, at least 10 of the 13 categories for constructing, contextualizing, and evaluating client outcome goals described in this chapter. These are the same 13 steps or categories you consulted for completing Part Two and they are listed in the Interview Checklist for Constructing, Contextualizing, and Evaluating Goals found on pages 297–299 in this Knowledge and Skill Builder section. We suggest that you complete this part of the Knowledge and Skill Builder in triads. One person assumes the role of the helper and demonstrates helping the client with the goal-setting process in a 30-minute interview. The second person takes the role of the client.

You may wish to portray the role and problem described for Manuel Tréjos in Part Two (if you choose to present something unfamiliar to the helper, be sure to inform the helper of your identified problem or concern before you begin). The third person assumes the role of the observer. The observer may act as the helper's alter ego and cue the helper during the role play, if necessary. The observer also provides feedback to the helper after the interview, using as a guide the Interview Checklist for Constructing, Contextualizing, and Evaluating Goals. If you do not have access to an observer, audio or video record your interview so you can assess it yourself.

Interview Checklist for Constructing, Contextualizing, and Evaluating Goals

Instructions: Determine which of the following questions the helper demonstrated. Check each helper question demonstrated. Also check whether the client answered the content of the helper's question. Example questions are provided next to each item of the checklist. These are only suggestions; be alert to other responses used by the helper.

Scoring	Category of Information	Examples of Helper Responses	Client Response
___Yes ___No	1. Explain the purpose and importance of having goals or positive outcomes to the client.	"Let's talk about some areas you would like to work on during counseling. This will help us to do things that are related to what you want to accomplish."	___ identifies disadvantages
___Yes ___No	2. Determine *positive* changes desired by client ("I would like" versus "I can't").	"What would you like to be doing [thinking, feeling] differently?" "Suppose some distant relative you haven't seen for a while comes here in several months. What would be different then from the way things are now?" "Assuming we are successful, what do you want to be doing, or how would this change for you?" "In what ways do you want to benefit from counseling?"	___ identifies goal in positive and salutary terms
___Yes ___No	3. Determine whether the goal selected represents changes owned by the client rather than someone else ("I want to talk to my mom without yelling at her" rather than "I want my mom to stop yelling at me").	"How much control do you have to make this happen?" "Describe what changes this will require of you." "What changes will this require someone else to make?" "Can this be achieved without the help of anyone else?" "To whom is this change most important?"	___ identifies who owns the goal

(continued)

8 | Knowledge and Skill Builder (*continued*)

Scoring	Category of Information	Examples of Helper Responses	Client Response
___Yes ___No	4. Identify advantages (positive consequences) to client and others of goal achievement.	"In what ways is it worthwhile to you and others to achieve this?" "Describe how achieving this goal will help you." "What problems will continue for you if you don't pursue this goal?" "What are the advantages of achieving this change—for you? For others?" "Identify who will benefit from this change—and how."	___identifies advantages
___Yes ___No	5. Identify disadvantages (negative consequences) of goal achievement to client and others.	"Describe any new problems in living that achieving this goal might pose for you." "Identify any disadvantages to going in this direction." "How will achieving this change affect your life in adverse ways?" "How might this change limit or constrain you?"	___ identifies disadvantages
___Yes ___No	6. Identify what the client will be doing, thinking, or feeling in a concrete, observable way as a result of achieving this goal ("I want to be able to talk to my mom without yelling at her," rather than "I want to get along with my mom").	"What do you want to be able to do [think, feel] differently?" "What would I see you doing [thinking, feeling] after this change?" "Describe a good and a poor example of this goal."	___ specifies overt and covert behaviors
___Yes ___No	7. Contextualize (or put into context) the treatment goal by describing the conditions and what situations the goals will be achieved: when, where, and with whom ("I want to be able to talk to my mom at home during the next month without yelling at her").	"When do you want to accomplish this goal?" "Where do you want to do this?" "With whom?" "In what situations?"	___ specifies people and places
___Yes ___No	8. Specify how often or how much the client will do something to achieve goal ("I want to be able to talk to my mom at home during the next month without yelling at her at least once per day").	"How much [or how often] are you doing this [or feeling this way] now?" "What is a realistic increase or decrease?" "How much [or how often] do you want to be doing this to be successful at your goal?" "What amount of change is realistic, considering where you are right now?"	___specifies amount

Scoring	Category of Information	Examples of Helper Responses	Client Response
___Yes ___No	9. Identify and list small action steps the client will need to take to reach the goal (that is, break the big goal down into little subgoals). List of Action Steps 1. 2. 3. 4. 5.	"How will you go about doing [thinking, feeling] this?" "Identify exactly what you need to do to make this happen." "Let's brainstorm some actions you'll need to take to make your goal work for you." "What have you done in the past to work toward this goal?" "How did it help?" "Let's think of the steps you need to take to get from where you are now to where you want to be."	___ lists possible action steps
___Yes ___No	10. Prioritize and sequence the action steps on the goal stair steps in terms of: a. degree of difficulty b. immediacy (most to least immediate)	"Describe your first step. Your last step." "What is most important for you to do soon? Least important?" "How could we order these steps to maximize your (least to most difficult) success in reaching your goal?" "Let's think of the steps you need to take to get from where you are now to where you want to be and arrange them in an order from what seems easiest to you to the ones that seem hardest."	___assists in rank ordering
___Yes ___No	11. Identify any people, feelings, or situations that could prevent the client from taking action to reach the goal.	"Tell me about any obstacles you may encounter in trying to take this action." "What people [feelings, ideas, situations] might get in the way of getting this done?" "In what ways could you have difficulty completing this task successfully?"	___ identifies possible obstacles
___Yes ___No	12. Identify any resources (skill, knowledge, support) that client needs to take action to meet the goal.	"What resources do you have available to help you as you complete this activity?" "What particular thoughts or feelings are you aware of that might make it easier for you to ___?" "What kind of support system do you have from others that you can use to make it easier to ___?" "Describe what skills [or information] you possess that will help you do this more successfully."	___ identifies existing resources and supports
___Yes ___No	13. Develop a plan to evaluate progress toward the goal.	"Would it be practical for you to rate these feelings [count the times you do this] during the next 2 weeks? This information will help us determine the progress you are making." "Let's discuss a way you can keep track of how easy or hard it is for you to take these steps this week."	___ agrees to monitor in some fashion

(continued)

8 | Knowledge and Skill Builder (*continued*)

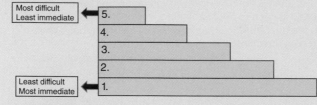

5-step Stair Steps

Part Four

Learning Outcome 4 asks you to conduct an outcome evaluation with yourself, another person, or a client, specifying *what* will be measured, *when* it will be measured, and *how*. Use the following guidelines:

1. Define and give examples of a desired goal behavior.
2. Specify what type of data you or the other person will collect (for example, verbal reports, frequency, duration, intensity, occurrence of the behavior).
3. a. Identify the methods to be used to collect these data (such as self-monitoring, goal attainment scaling, brief measures, and self-ratings).
   b. For *each* method to be used, describe very specifically the instructions you or the client would need to use this method.

4. Collect data on the goal behaviors at least several times before implementing any treatment (change) strategy (pretreatment).
5. Following pretreatment data collection, implement some treatment strategy for a designated time period. Continue to collect data during the implementation of this treatment strategy.
6. Collect data after treatment. Graph all of your data, or visually inspect them. What do your data suggest about changes in the goal behavior and the effectiveness of your treatment? Share your results with a partner, a colleague, or your instructor.

8 Knowledge and Skill Builder **Feedback**

Part Two

1. Explain to Manuel the *purpose and importance* of developing goals.

2. Help Manuel state the goal or desired change in *salutary* or *positive terms*.

3. Help Manuel determine whether the goal he is moving toward represents *changes owned by him* and whether such factors are under his control. This supports his autonomy. Probably, giving up his job or taking a leave of absence would be changes under his control.

4. Help Manuel identify *advantages* or *benefits* to be realized by achieving his goal. He seems to be thinking about increased leisure time as a major benefit. Are there others?

5. Help Manuel identify *disadvantages* or *possible costs* of making the desired change. He has mentioned loss of retirement benefits as one cost and subsequent loss of a nest egg for his grandchildren as another. Do the perceived benefits outweigh the costs? What effect would leaving his job have on his wife and family? Would this outcome be consistent with his cultural identity and beliefs?

6. Help Manuel *define his goal behaviorally* by specifying exactly what he will be doing, thinking, and feeling as a result of goal achievement.

7. Help Manuel specify *where, when,* and *with whom* this will occur.

8. Identify *how much* or *how often* the goal will occur. An option that might be useful for Manuel is to develop and scale five possible outcomes, ranging from *most unfavorable* to *most expected* to *best possible* outcome (goal-attainment scaling).

9. Help Manuel explore and *identify action steps or subgoals* that represent small approximations toward the overall goal. Help him choose action steps that are practical, are based on his resources, and support his values and culture.

10. Help Manuel sequence the action steps according to *immediacy and difficulty* so he knows what step he will take first and what step will be his last one.

11. Explore any *obstacles* that could impede progress toward the goal, such as the presence or absence of certain feelings, ideas, thoughts, situations, responses, people, knowledge, and skills.

12. Explore existing *resources* that could help Manuel complete the action steps more successfully. Like examination of obstacles, exploration of resources also includes assessing the presence or absence of certain feelings, ideas, thoughts, situations, responses, people, knowledge, skills, beliefs, and confidence in pursuing desired outcomes.

13. Help Manuel develop a *plan to review completion of the action steps* and *evaluate progress toward the goal*.

Clinical Decision-Making and Treatment Planning

After completing this chapter, you will be able to:

1. For the client case description of Karen (adapted from González-Prendes & Thomas, 2009) and the description of proposed treatment interventions, identify the following:
   a. Ways in which the selected treatment interventions used by the helper failed to address either contextual awareness or consciousness development.
   b. How the helper interpreted the client's distress (or what might be interpreted as resistance).
   c. Which of Lum's (2004) five interventions (see Box 9.4) the helper could have emphasized.
   d. The recommended type, duration, and mode of treatment you would follow as Karen's helper.
2. For the client case of Isabella, using a sample treatment planning form (see Figure 9.3), develop a written treatment plan that identifies the presenting concern, strengths and resources, goals, measures, and treatment interventions.

Treatment Planning Purpose and Benefits

Treatment planning is an essential therapeutic activity that includes case conceptualization/formulation, a construction of treatment goals, and the selection of the most appropriate interventions to help clients meet their goals. It is initiated after a comprehensive client assessment has been conducted (including assessing for client strengths and resources), a preliminary diagnosis assigned, and available services reviewed and identified. A treatment plan specifies the change interventions (type of treatment)

that will help clients reach their stated goals, the specific format or way in which the intervention will be delivered to clients (mode of treatment), activities clients will engage in to realize their goals (client implementation), prognosis, and the frequency and duration of services.

Treatment planning is not a discrete activity that occurs at one point in time. It is a continuous process: the initial plan is revised when new information about the client is received, when the service delivery setting changes or the types of available services are altered or disrupted (e.g., due to funding restrictions), or when the client-helper relationship is at an impasse or experiences what Safran, Muran, and Eubanks-Carter (2011) characterize as a "rupture." Therefore, the actual written treatment plan can be considered a living document—describing the client's current status as well as the services being rendered—always subject to modification.

Treatment planning is required by insurance companies and other managed care systems for third-party reimbursement. Its practice, however, should not be regarded as simply fulfilling a funding source's mandate. Furthermore, although helpers often are asked to complete a standard treatment plan form for each client, the task should not be undertaken expeditiously by simply checking boxes or hurriedly selecting goals and objectives from a pull-down menu. Treatment planning is a complex activity that requires helpers to have extensive knowledge and flexibility (Hunsley & Mash, 2010). Therefore, it must be practiced with great care in a thoughtful, comprehensive, and systematic manner. The most effective treatment plans are those that are idiographic or personalized and fit a specific client. This type of customization does take time.

There are quite a few benefits to treatment planning, whether or not an external entity has enforced its practice. For clients, Egan (2014) identifies six benefits for developing and carrying out treatment plans:

1. Helps clients develop needed discipline.

2. Keeps clients from being overwhelmed.

3. Helps clients search for more useful ways of accomplishing goals, that is, by selecting better strategies.

4. Provides clients an opportunity to evaluate the realism and adequacy of goals.

5. Makes clients aware of the resources they will need to implement their strategies.

6. Helps clients uncover unanticipated obstacles in the process of achieving goals.

For helpers, treatment planning stimulates critical thinking and helps to increase the likelihood that the best combination of interventions for a given client with particular outcome goals will be used. Developing a treatment plan is like constructing a road map. The plan itself is thus intended to keep the process on track—that is, it promotes a structure that ensures that client needs are considered and met as much as possible. This is true particularly of evidence-based practices wherein the treatment plan developed is consistent with—or faithful to—the specific practice being implemented. A final benefit of treatment planning is that it allows different professionals (e.g., members of a multidisciplinary treatment team) to coordinate care for a shared client, and the actual plan serves as the repository, concourse, or forum for their combined services.

Common Factors and Specific Ingredients of Treatment

A central question of treatment planning is, "What treatments or change intervention strategies are likely to be useful for this client?" This practical question is an extension of a general, more abstract (some might say existential), and all-encompassing question: "What contributes to or explains change in clients and in treatment outcomes?" Lambert's (1992) early and often-cited research suggests that client characteristics (or extratherapeutic factors, including social support and cultural composition) account for most (approximately 40 percent) of the client's improvement as a result of participating in the helping process. This is illustrated in Figure 9.1, along with the remaining three factors contributing to client change:

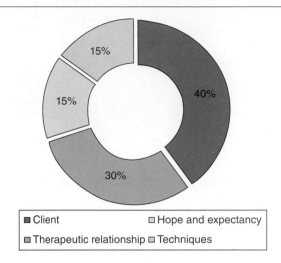

FIGURE 9.1 Factors Contributing to Client Change
Source: Lambert, 1992

the therapeutic relationship (approximately 30 percent), specific techniques used by the helper (15 percent), and hope and expectancy factors (15 percent). This means that client characteristics play a pivotal role in the outcomes of any change intervention strategy, regardless of its theoretical base. The quality of the helping relationship is also tremendously important in producing effective outcomes. These four broad contributions are referred to as **common factors** in facilitating change.

Lambert and Ogles (2004) proposed another set of common factors: support, learning, and action factors. Unlike the factors that Lambert identified in 1992, each factor in this newer research is attributable to the therapist, to therapy procedures, and to the client. In addition, Lambert and Ogles presented the three categories of common factors sequentially to indicate their developmental nature. They suggested that certain factors are emphasized at certain points in the helping process and that each factor builds on its predecessor. This explains the positioning of these three factors in the arrow in Figure 9.2. on page 304.

The developmental nature of the common factors of support, learning, and action appears to be similar to and corresponds with the three **phases of treatment** proposed by Howard and colleagues (Howard, Lueger, Maling, & Martinovich, 1993; Howard, Moras, Brill, Martinovich, & Lutz, 1996): remoralization, remediation, and rehabilitation. Notice that these are included in Figure 9.2 and correspond to the common factors. Support factors include things such as the client's experience of catharsis, identification with therapist, and therapeutic alliance, and they are intended to assist the client in experiencing greater

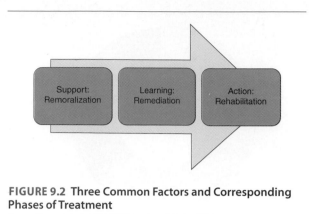

FIGURE 9.2 Three Common Factors and Corresponding Phases of Treatment
Source: Howard et al., 1993, 1996; Lambert & Ogles, 2004

well-being, or *remoralization,* in the early phase of treatment, including validation or normalization of his or her experiences (e.g., mitigation of isolation: "I'm not the only one who's experienced these symptoms before"). Learning factors include things such as cognitive learning, offering feedback, and providing a rationale for care, and they address the amelioration of symptoms, or *remediation,* the middle phase of treatment when the client is learning to cope with or actively manage stressors. And the intended outcome of action factors is *rehabilitation,* the third phase of treatment proposed by Howard et al. (1993, 1996). These include activities such as behavior regulation, taking risks, modeling, and practice. It is at this time that clients transfer what they've learned in therapy to several areas of their lives to improve their overall functioning.

According to Lambert (2013, p. 202), "common factors loom large as mediators of treatment outcome" (p. 202) and, when taken as a whole, are likely "more powerful than the contribution of specific techniques." Miller and Moyers (2015) contend, however, that clinician adherence to these common factors is not necessarily common in routine counseling practice. For example, levels of therapist empathic skill vary widely. Furthermore, Miller and Moyers criticize defining common factors as "nonspecific," stating that "we owe it to our clients to specify" effective practices (p. 407).

Factors Affecting Treatment Selection

We believe that clinical decision-making and treatment planning involve a consideration of common factors *and* differential interventions. This means that *skilled* helpers are helpers who can attend to both general and specific factors—one type does not take precedence over the other. Although considering both types of factors concurrently is often a challenging and ambiguous process, we believe it is natural, expected, and understandable given the complexities of human nature/behavior. There are no treatment planning recipes that, if followed exactly by the clinician, are guaranteed to result in effective care and treatment success. We would like to think that the allure of working as a professional helper is that we can work with a variety of persons (i.e., no two clients are alike), the helping process is not intended to be routine or boring, and there are no easy answers to the multiplicity of concerns that clients present.

Treatment planning can be likened to an adventure, one that the client and helper embark on together and one that requires the joint design and construction of a map rather than reliance on an existing or predetermined set of directions. There are certainly major thoroughfares that need to be traversed (e.g., standards of care, treatment guidelines) and signposts that need to be considered (e.g., assessment of symptoms that meet diagnostic criteria). However, because each client is unique, the methods of transportation and the routes taken to reach the intended destination (the treatment goal) will vary from client to client. Shifting the analogy, we may say that treatment planning requires the helper to be able to see the forest *and* the trees.

To embark on the journey of comprehensive treatment planning customized to each client, we need to consider several factors. These include client characteristics, helper characteristics, and practice and documentation guidelines. Although these and other factors (e.g., the therapeutic relationship) might be considered "inextricably intertwined" (Hill, 2005, p. 438), we believe it is helpful to discuss them separately to appreciate their interconnections.

Client Characteristics

Client contributions to the helping process are instrumental to therapeutic change. Refer back to Figure 9.1 and the 40 percent contribution clients make to therapeutic change. From their review of psychotherapy outcome research, Bohart and Wade (2013) concluded that "clients make the single strongest contribution to outcome" (p. 219). Rather than being passive recipients of counseling, clients are active learners and problem-solvers. Helpers who cultivate and make use of client proactivity are likely to enhance client outcomes.

The range of actual and potential client variables to consider in treatment planning is limitless. Characteristics include psychopathology (e.g., symptom severity), sociodemographic descriptors (e.g., gender, age), and personality traits (e.g., sociability, coping style) – all of which may be invariant (e.g., race and ethnic membership), relatively stable (e.g., socioeconomic status), or quite variable (e.g., motivation for change). Based on an accumulation of research conducted over a number of years, Beutler and his colleagues (Beutler, Clarkin, & Bongar, 2000; Beutler, Consoli, & Lane, 2005; Beutler & Harwood, 2000) identified six client characteristics or variables that affect the selection and implementation of treatment strategies. Clarkin and Levy (2004) grouped these six characteristics into three general categories: client impairment, symptom management, and interpersonal context. These three categories and the corresponding client characteristics are presented in Box 9.1. We discuss all six client characteristics in their corresponding category.

Category 1: Client Impairment

In general, impairment refers primarily to the type, level of severity, and chronicity of symptoms that clients present. The term **functional impairment** refers to the behavioral manifestation of these symptoms, that is, how these symptoms are expressed or made evident, along with their purpose or function for the client. Symptoms of impairment can be attributed to biological or genetic influences (e.g., family history of bipolar disorder), traumatic events (e.g., sexual abuse, natural disaster), learned behavior (e.g., specific phobias), social-cultural-economic-political influences (e.g., poverty, immigration, oppression), and a combination of two or more, which may add to the complexity of the case. From a cognitive behavioral perspective, Nezu and colleagues (Nezu & Nezu, 2010; Nezu, Nezu, & Cos, 2007; Nezu, Nezu, & Lombardo, 2004) differentiated between behavioral

deficits (e.g., poor social skills) and behavioral excesses (e.g., compulsive behavior, aggressive actions). They also noted differences between cognitive deficiencies and cognitive distortions. The former refer to the absence of certain thinking processes, such as the failure to realize the consequences of one's actions; the latter refer to errors in cognitive processing, such as irrational beliefs.

The assessment of client impairment is important because, according to Beutler and Harwood (2000), it determines the type, frequency, and intensity of treatment provided. The benefits of treatment directly correspond to treatment intensity among functionally impaired clients. In one recent study (McQuade & Gromova, 2015), persons with major depression, bipolar disorder, or schizophrenia who received frequent (16–30 sessions) and intensive outpatient services that included pharmacological interventions had reduced psychiatric hospitalization stays compared to clients who attended 15 or fewer outpatient sessions.

To help determine type and level of client impairment, family members and other collaterals should be consulted as well as professionals who were involved in previous treatment the client may have received. Medical records of previous mental health treatment should also be obtained. Depending on the complexity of the case, additional professionals should be included in the treatment planning process and the provision of comprehensive care. For certain presenting concerns and disorders, recommendations have been made for the delivery of services by multidisciplinary treatment teams. These include eating disorders (American Psychiatric Association, 2000b; Grave, 2005), chronic pain (Burns, 2010), victims of intimate partner violence (Miller, Veltkamp, Lane, Bilyeu,

---

BOX 9.1   Client Categories and their Corresponding Characteristics that Influence the Selection of Treatment Strategies

Categories of Client Characteristics

1. Client Impairment

2. Symptom Management: client's response(s) to impairment

3. Social Support: client's interpersonal context

Corresponding Client Characteristics

1. Functional Impairment

2. Problem Complexity/Chronicity

3. Subjective Distress

4. Coping Styles: internalizing or externalizing

5. Reactance/Resistance tendencies

6. Social Support

Source: Beutler, Clarkin, & Bongar, 2000; Beutler, Consoli, & Lane, 2005; Beutler & Harwood, 2000; Clarkin & Levy, 2004.

& Elzie, 2002), borderline personality disorder (Linehan, 2015), and co-occurring or comorbid disorders (i.e., substance use disorder and mental illness; Mueser, Noordsy, Drake, & Fox, 2003). Particularly when a client is struggling with a severe and persistent mental illness (e.g., schizophrenia), assertive community treatment (ACTx) conducted by a team of professionals has maintained its status as an evidence-based practice (Bond, Drake, Mueser, & Latimer, 2001; Salyers & Bond, 2009). We provided a brief description of ACTx in Chapter 1.

Category 2: Symptom Management

The ways in which clients experience and express their complaints (e.g., symptoms) and their response to treatment interventions also are important considerations in treatment planning. Three ways in which clients experience and manage their symptoms inside and outside of treatment are: subjective distress, coping styles, and reactance/resistance.

Subjective distress typically refers to an individual's internal state rather than his or her observable demonstration of that distress, and it thus is measured according to client report. In addition, Beutler and colleagues (2000) note that subjective distress is separate from specific diagnoses and represents transient states of well-being. This means that a client's level of internal distress can be modified and preferably alleviated, depending on the client's investment in the change process. Based on research findings, Beutler and colleagues (2000) offer three general guidelines for addressing or making use of the client's style of managing his or her own symptoms (p. 63):

1. Moderate distress may be important to sustain commitment and participation in treatment.

2. High initial distress may be an indicator for the use of supportive and self-directed therapy but bears no relationship to the effectiveness of active and therapist-guided interventions.

3. High distress may be an indicator for interpersonally focused interventions, perhaps including group or family formats.

Beutler, Harwood, Kimpara, Verdirame, and Blau (2011) define **coping styles** as "recurrent patterns of behavior that characterize the individual when confronting new or problematic situations" (p. 338). Two coping styles that persons use to respond to novelty are *externalizing* and *internalizing*. Beutler, Harwood, Kimpara, et al. (2011) describe persons whose predominant coping style is one or the other in this way:

> Internalizers/introverts are more easily overwhelmed by change and tend to become shy, withdrawn, and self-inspective, [whereas] externalizers/extroverts are more likely to act out, to seek stimulation and change, to directly escape or withdraw from conflict, and to be confrontational and gregarious in expressing problems. (p. 339)

It is important for helpers to recognize and differentiate between these two coping styles to select treatments that provide clients safe exposure to the experiences that are being avoided (Beutler & Harwood, 2000; Beutler, Harwood, Kimpara, et al., 2011; Ingram, Hayes, & Scott, 2000). In addition, an assessment of coping style may expand the helper's understanding of the client's cultural background and identity. Research has suggested, for example, that children in collectivist cultures may favor more internalized coping practices (e.g., respect for elders, academic diligence), whereas children in more individualist cultures may exhibit more externalized coping mechanisms (e.g., impulsive behaviors; see Caldwell-Harris & Ayçiçegi, 2006).

A third means by which clients manage their symptoms—and a client characteristic that affects treatment selection and planning—is **resistance or reactance**. Although grouped together here and often used interchangeably, there are important distinctions between the two (Beutler, Harwood, Michelson, Song, & Holman, 2011). As discussed in Chapter 10, resistance in psychotherapy often and unfortunately is attributed solely to the client. We understand it differently. Our view of resistance in psychotherapy parallels its definition in motivational interviewing (MI) (Miller & Rollnick, 2013): resistance is an interpersonal phenomenon characterized by disagreement and discord. Rather than the client being resistant to change, it is the helper-client interaction that is not conducive to client change. This means that certain client behaviors defined as resistant—such as missing appointments, questioning the helper's qualifications, and not following through on out-of-session practice of new skills—may be attributable to certain helper behaviors, including not being prepared for session, not soliciting client feedback, and continuing to implement a particular intervention despite the client's lack of responsiveness to it.

In feminist therapy (Brown, 2010), resistance is understood within a cultural context, including one's status as privileged or disadvantaged. Therefore, resistance strategies or efforts to manage distress are "attempts to solve the problems of powerlessness via whatever means are available" (Brown, 2010, p. 68). These may include a client's insistence that she "not get the run-around" from yet another helper in the health care system that, from the client's testimony, has only seen her as a "druggie" and not as someone who has experienced multiple traumas perpetrated by "johns" and other men in her life. This client's refusal to meet with a male intake worker, attend a mixed/co-ed psychoeducational group, or begin working on the 12 steps of Alcoholics Anonymous by "admitting" that she is "powerless over alcohol" and then "turning over" her "will" to a male entity (i.e., "God as we understood Him") could be understood in feminist therapy as healing and healthy—an act of resistance for a woman who repeatedly had been taken advantage of and mistreated by men.

Brehm (1966), a social psychologist and not a psychotherapist, coined the term *reactance* that today is understood as the need to preserve one's freedom. Clients who are high in reactance might be described by some as "oppositional" and often find ways to try to defeat or diffuse the helper, usually by saying or doing the opposite of whatever the helper says. Clients who are low in reactance potential are typically cooperative and comply with the helper's ideas. Helpers can assess this dimension early in the process by noticing whether the client consistently takes positions opposite or complementary to the helper's views and/or by assigning a straightforward task and noticing whether the client carries out or forgets the task.

Assessing resistance and reactance is important because clients with high or recurring levels of resistance or reactance benefit from a low level of helper directiveness provided in a safe context (Beutler & Harwood, 2000; Beutler, Harwood, Michelson et al., 2011). An emphasis on support factors with the goal of remoralization therefore is recommended (see Figure 9.2). Clients with low reactance levels are likely to benefit from more directive interventions such as information giving, interpretations, and structured homework assignments—all of which exemplify the learning and action factors described earlier. Beutler and colleagues (2011) caution helpers to avoid matching their level of directiveness in their work with clients to *their own* reactance level, a "common occurrence among neophyte therapists who unwittingly project their own personality structure onto their clients" (p. 276).

Category 3: Interpersonal Context

A primary client characteristic that influences the type and direction of proposed services is **social support**. As a characteristic that reflects a person's interpersonal context, social support may not always be under the client's direct control. Take, for instance, the teenager whose parents recently divorced and who, as a result, has been forced to change high schools mid-year because she is now living with her mother in another city. She may lack a ready-made social network, and in response to a number of stressors she may begin to act out in school, such as by

talking back to teachers and initiating fights with peers. Although this young woman may seem to lack control over the availability and quality of support networks, she might benefit from participating in a counseling group with other teenagers, a group assembled by the school counselor or by another helping professional in the community. The opportunities she is given to experiment with new and more socially acceptable behaviors in this group—and the positive feedback she receives from her fellow group members—may assist her in learning ways to interact appropriately and with beneficial effects at school. Her task might be to transfer what she has learned in group to her relationships at school, thus allowing her to realize that she does have some ownership over establishing and maintaining social support.

Access to and interaction with positive social support has been found to improve prognosis, predict treatment outcome, serve as a buffer against relapse, and maintain treatment gains (Beutler et al., 2000). Helpers therefore must assist clients in identifying positive support networks, help them acquire enhanced social skills to effectively interact with such persons, and rehearse behaviors to implement outside of treatment. As in the preceding example, the client's active participation in a counseling group may help her to establish a support outlet, or the helper providing individual care may use the therapeutic relationship to simulate interpersonal interactions outside of treatment (e.g., "So what have you learned about being able to trust me that you can put to use to identify a trustworthy friend?"). Furthermore, the helper can initiate contact with the client's family members and friends to assess the quality of existing social support and can offer psychoeducation, such as conflict resolution, to family members to involve them in the client's care. This might entail teaching family members to simply notice positive differences in their loved one's behavior and communicate their observations orally or in writing to the client. Family counseling also may be extended.

Summary of Client Characteristics

Although three categories of client characteristics were discussed separately in this section (i.e., impairment, symptom management, and interpersonal context), it is necessary for the helper to recognize the interconnections of these categories and the meaning of their patterns. Beutler and colleagues (2000) emphasized the importance of these connections when they stated that "general prognosis is a function of level of the patient's impairment, initial distress, and social support" (p. 112). As a helper, your clinical decision-making skills will be enhanced as you are able to recognize and interpret the unique configuration of characteristics that each of your clients represents.

Helper Characteristics

Client characteristics clearly are instrumental in the change process. However, helper characteristics also contribute to the process of change. Wampold (2001) notes that "the essence of therapy is embodied in the therapist" and that "the person of the therapist is a critical factor in the success of therapy" (p. 202). Like client characteristics, instrumental helper characteristics extend beyond mere sociodemographic characteristics such as age, sex, professional degree, and years of practice. Research suggests these therapist factors account for a minimal amount of client improvement. In individual outpatient therapy, these range from 5 percent (Wampold & Brown, 2005) and 8 percent (Kim, Wampold, & Bolt, 2006) to 17 percent (Lutz, Leon, Martinovich, Lyons, & Stiles, 2007). Therapist effects in couples therapy are comparable, explaining 8 percent of client outcomes (Owen, Duncan, Reese, Anker, & Sparks, 2014). In one study of inpatient therapy (Dinger, Strack, Leichsenring, Wilmers, & Schauenburg, 2008), only 3 percent of patient improvement (decrease in symptom distress) was attributed to the individual therapist.

Additional helper characteristics warrant further attention. These include the four therapist factors Miller and Moyers (2015) discuss that are linked to improved client outcomes in addictions treatment:

1. expecting client improvement (which corresponds to the hope and expectancy factor in Figure 9.1),

2. having strong interpersonal skills (namely empathy) that are essential to building and maintaining a therapeutic relationship (30 percent of the contribution to client change; see Figure 9.1),

3. having a strong belief in and a commitment to a particular approach (known as treatment allegiance), and

4. remaining faithful to or consist with a treatment approach (known as treatment fidelity).

Treatment allegiance and fidelity likely correspond to the techniques factor illustrated in Figure 9.1., a factor that accounts for 15 percent of client change.

Other helper characteristics are captured in the contextual and relational dimensions discussed by Okun and Suyemoto (2013), dimensions we have modified in Table 9.1. Each of the dimensions listed refers to the extent to which helpers focus on a particular area (e.g., client cognition, affect, or behavior) or engage in a specific interpersonal behavior (e.g., being confrontive, directive, structured) in their work with

TABLE 9.1   Dimensions of Focus for Helpers to Facilitate Change

Contextual Dimensions	
Location of Problem	Extent to which the presenting problem or concern is interpreted as residing primarily in the individual, in the family, or in the social structural environment, and (relatedly) whether the approach should focus on changing individual, family, or social structure or, if this cannot be changed, facilitating different means of negotiating or coping with a problem that is located outside the individual.
Focus of Change	Extent to which focus of change is on cognition, affect, or behavior.
Past/Present Focus	Extent to which emphasis is placed on therapeutic exploration of the past or the present.
Relational Dimensions	
Directive/Nondirective	Extent to which therapist directs the content of therapy to facilitate change.
Structured/Unstructured	Extent to which therapist structures the way in which content is explored (e.g., through activities, exercises).
Activity Level	Extent to which therapist is an active participant in the process (e.g., how much therapist talks, interjects, uses nonverbal expressions).
Level of Confrontiveness	Extent to which therapist calls the client's attention to contradictions, discrepancies, or things of which the client is unaware.
Significance of Relationship	Extent to which the therapeutic relationship is viewed as important for the facilitation of change: whether it is viewed as central and essential to *directly* facilitating change, or whether it is viewed as an important means to *other* mechanisms of change.
Real/Unreal Relationship	Extent to which a real or transferential relationship is emphasized.
Process Emphasis	Extent to which therapist attends to the process dynamics within therapy interactions, and the extent that the therapist uses this awareness to facilitate change.

Source: Adapted from Okun & Suyemoto, *Conceptualization and Treatment Planning for Effective Helping*, Table 2.1. Copyright 2013. Cengage Learning. Adapted and used by permission. www.cengage.com/permissions

clients. Because they are dimensions and not categories, each represents a continuum of helper attention and activity. This means, for example, that a helper's behavior is not structured or unstructured; rather, it's the extent to which the helper structures how content is explored with clients. In addition, the relational dimension of significance of relationship refers to the extent to which the helper views the therapeutic relationship as central to facilitating change. As such, it's not *if* the helper views it as significant; it's *how* essential the helper views the working relationship as instrumental to client change.

Okun and Suyemoto's (2013) relational dimensions for helper facilitation of client change are of particular importance. Baldwin, Wampold, and Imel (2007) found that therapists who formed strong working alliances with a variety of clients had better client outcomes. Similar findings have been reported in addictions treatment, with poor client outcomes (e.g., increase in drinking) linked to the absence of a strong working relationship between client and helper (Miller & Moyers, 2015). These and other findings represent the evidence base for the healing qualities of the therapeutic relationship (Norcross, 2011).

The American Psychological Association's (APA) Presidential Task Force on Evidence-Based Practice (2006) identified eight components of clinical expertise. They are presented in Box 9.2. Although they are intended to describe characteristics and skills of psychologists, we believe they apply to all professional helpers and directly impact treatment planning and clinical decision-making. Common across all eight components are the helper's ability to: (1) be flexible and receptive to feedback (specifically feedback received from clients and supervisors); (2) continually expand and enhance clinical skills; (3) articulate comprehensible clinical recommendations; and (4) be deliberate about identifying and incorporating idiosyncratic and cultural client characteristics throughout the helping process. Overholser (2010) added that clinical expertise also includes visibility within one's profession as well as in one's local community. We next discuss the first three of these four helper characteristics. Attentiveness to cultural considerations is addressed in a later section of this chapter.

Helper Characteristic 1: Flexibility and Receptivity to Feedback

An essential helper skill is flexibility in the selection of treatment interventions to accommodate client needs and preferences. Think of flexibility as the mid-point between the two extremes of rigidity and acquiescence or obliviousness. It is the balance of upholding standards or guidelines (e.g., a specific treatment manual) and at the same time modifying aspects of care to address the unique needs and preferences of the client. Such flexibility is commensurate with the practice of technical eclecticism wherein the practitioner carefully chooses several theoretical approaches to use in combination for the benefit of a particular client. The APA Presidential Task Force on Evidence-Based Practice (2006) further explicated the practice of clinician flexibility by stating that it is "manifested in tact, timing, pacing, and framing of interventions; maintaining an effective balance between consistency of interventions and responsiveness to patient feedback; and attention to acknowledged and unacknowledged meanings, beliefs, and emotions" (p. 276). In other words, flexibility is the helper's ability to adapt or adjust to client concerns and wishes, as well as to changes in the mechanisms of service delivery (e.g., philosophy of treatment setting, funding sources), "without sacrificing the empirical need for reliability and structure" (Beutler & Harwood, 2000, p. 23). This type of practice is what we have termed **informed improvisation**, or creative expression shaped and guided by established and evolving principles of research, theory, and practice.

It is widely held that supervision directly impacts helper skills (see Bernard & Goodyear, 2013). Indeed, supervision is required for most practitioners-in-training as they pursue licensure. Ethics committees and licensure boards also routinely prescribe supervision for licensed

BOX 9.2	Eight Components of Clinical Expertise
1. Assessment, diagnostic judgment, systematic case formulation, and treatment planning 2. Clinical decision-making, treatment implementation, and monitoring of client progress 3. Interpersonal expertise 4. Continual self-reflection and acquisition of skills	5. Appropriate evaluation and use of research evidence in both basic and applied psychological science 6. Understanding the influence of individual and cultural differences on treatment 7. Seeking available resources (e.g., consultation, adjunctive or alternative services) as needed 8. Having a cogent rationale for clinical strategies

Source: APA Presidential Task Force on Evidence-Based Practice, 2006.

practitioners who have violated ethical guidelines. Supervision, therefore, may be thought of as a corrective intervention. With respect to clinical decision-making and treatment planning, emerging research (viz., Lambert, 2010, 2013) suggests that the clients of helpers who receive specific, concrete, and timely feedback regarding their clients' status in treatment (e.g., functioning adequately or poorly) and are also provided with clear recommendations (e.g., consider termination, alter treatment plan, present client at case conference) demonstrate positive outcomes compared to clients whose helpers did not receive such feedback. It also appears that therapists who receive specific feedback about the progress made (or lack thereof) by their clients, and who heed the recommendations provided, make judicious use of the duration of therapy. This includes scheduling more therapy sessions when the client is not progressing and scheduling fewer when the client is on track or is progressing. In Lambert's (2010) review of research, clients identified early as nonresponders have been found to increase their attendance when their therapists followed through with specific feedback provided. Altogether, this research suggests that clients benefit when their helpers make use of supervisory interventions aimed at modifying care plans for individual clients.

Helper Characteristic 2: Commitment to Expanding and Enhancing Clinical Skills

Skovholt and Jennings (2004) describe master therapists as "voracious learners" who have an "appetite for knowledge [that] appears to be an intense source of development" (p. 33). In addition, master therapists value cognitive complexity and the ambiguity of the human condition and are likely to consider multiple criteria in clinical decision-making while realizing that clear, absolute, and definitive "answers" may never be determined. This description is similar to that of "intentional learning" reported by Miller (2007) in his study of "passionately committed psychotherapists" practicing in one state's public mental health system. From these depictions, it appears that an important helper characteristic is being committed to skill enhancement and ongoing professional development. This is discussed in Chapter 1.

Case conceptualization and treatment planning are specific skills that we believe benefit from constant refinement. Eells, Lombart, Kendjelic, Turner, and Lucas (2005) asked novice therapists (clinical psychology graduate students), experienced therapists (practicing for 10 or more years), and expert therapists (those who had published books or articles on the topic of case formulation) to "think aloud" for approximately 8 minutes about their conceptualizations of an individual client described

to them in writing. Therapists were also asked to talk out loud about how they would treat the client.

Eells and colleagues (2005) found that the treatment plans of expert therapists were more elaborate and rated as better-fitting to their case formulations compared with those of the novice and the experienced therapists. Furthermore, expert therapists were thought to make use of clinical principles, formulation guidelines, or "solution algorithms" as they made decisions of care rather than interpreting the client's presenting concerns according to their surface features alone. Eells and colleagues speculated that expert therapists appear to have strong self-monitoring skills, allowing them to detect potential deficits in their practice and make necessary changes or to calibrate their skills as a result.

Surprisingly, the case formulations of the novice therapists in the study by Eells and colleagues (2005) were rated *higher* in overall quality (e.g., comprehensiveness, complexity, precision of language, coherence) than those of the experienced therapists. This should be encouraging information to graduate students! Because of their current investment in formal studies, novice therapists were thought to be able to better calibrate their skills than experienced therapists. The skills of case conceptualization and treatment planning are therefore never set or finalized. We believe that helpers are more than likely to provide quality services to clients when they remain dedicated to expanding and enhancing their clinical skills. Your learning, therefore, is never finalized—even after graduation!

Helper Characteristic 3: Comprehensible Clinical Decision-Making

The goal of many students preparing for a career in the helping professions is to obtain a license to practice as a professional helper (e.g., social worker, psychologist, counselor). Newly licensed professionals may pursue independent licensure practice (e.g., diagnose and treat mental disorders) without being supervised. Although obtaining a professional license is a remarkable achievement, practicing as a licensed professional carries with it immense responsibilities. This is similar to the initiation of any new role, such as wife, husband, legally recognized domestic partner, or parent. The wedding day or the day of birth/adoption is cause for celebration. The responsibilities that accompany such roles (much like the "terrible twos" described by parents) often kick in after the honeymoon.

As a licensed professional, you will be making decisions that affect the lives of many people. As an independently licensed practitioner, you must be aware that your decision alone rather than that of a supervisor may determine whether a client is diagnosed with a personality disorder, involuntarily hospitalized, discharged from residential treatment, or deemed fit to assume legal custody of a child. Your ability to justify your clinical opinions and explain the decisions you have made is therefore critical. There may be no room for relying solely on intuition or on what some might interpret as "wishy-washy" thinking. Instead, you will need to be able to articulate a logical and cogent rationale for your treatment recommendations, and the expectation today is that these recommendations should be based on and informed by theory and research. The magnitude of this responsibility is probably apparent when you visualize yourself in the courtroom as an expert witness, providing testimony on a client's mental status. This is one of the reasons we recommend that clinicians substitute the word "believe" for "feel" when offering their clinical opinions to clients and to other professionals. As one of us routinely tells her students: "feelings do not have opinions."

Not only must your clinical opinions and treatment recommendations be comprehensible to other professionals, they must also make sense to your clients. Discussing the need for and the meaning of a diagnosis to a client, for example, may be time-consuming and perhaps frustrating, but it will likely engender certain benefits. One of these benefits may be that the client becomes more of an active participant in the helping process because he or she now has a better understanding of his or her symptoms and why certain activities need to take place in treatment.

Although we wholeheartedly endorse—indeed, insist on—a collaborative client-helper working relationship, we are clearly aware of the professional helper's responsibility for making treatment decisions. We believe that as much as possible, helpers should follow the "no surprises" rule when engaging clients in conversations about clinical assessment and treatment planning. This means that the client should not be surprised by the helper's recommendations because the client has been kept informed of the helper's thinking and reasoning, perhaps by the helper "thinking aloud" in session with his or her clients (the practice used in the Eells et al. 2005 study). The "no surprises" rule also has been recommended for clinical supervisors when evaluating the work of their supervisees (Osborn & Kelly, 2010). Now, just as the supervisee may not agree with the recommendations of his or her supervisor, it is true that the client may not agree with the helper's recommendations or directives—and this is the client's right. However, what the helper should strive for is to avoid hearing the client say, for example: "I really don't know why attending six weekly sessions of group therapy is

necessary" or "You never told me you'd need to speak with my partner! Why does she need to be involved in this?" An investment in the formulation and articulation of a clear and cogent rationale for your clinical decisions and treatment recommendations is a sign of an accountable practitioner.

Evidence-Based Practice and Treatment Planning

The APA Presidential Task Force on Evidence-Based Practice (2006) defines evidence-based practice (EBP) as "the integration of the best available research with clinical expertise in the context of patient characteristics, culture, and preferences" (p. 273). As discussed in Chapter 1, the intent of EBP has been to raise the bar by providing clients customized services that are responsive to client preferences and culture and that are supported by research.

Castonguay and Beutler's (2006a) promulgation of practice principles reflects the integrative priority of EBP. Their focus on the conditions, aspects, or qualities of treatment that appear to account for positive changes has resulted in guidelines (or flexible heuristics) that encompass not only prescribed interventions often found in treatment manuals but also client and helper factors, and factors related to the therapeutic relationship or alliance. The current focus, therefore, appears to be on effective treatment that is the product of a confluence of principles—principles that "are more general than a description of techniques and . . . more specific than theoretical formulations" (Beutler & Castonguay, 2006, p. 9). From their focus on four diagnostic dimensions (i.e., dysphoric, anxiety, personality, and substance disorders), Castonguay and Beutler's integrative efforts generated 61 principles of therapeutic change, 43 percent of which encompass at least two dimensions. Several principles related to client and therapist characteristics are inferred (e.g., "The benefits of therapy may be enhanced if the therapist is able to tolerate his/her own negative feelings regarding the patient and the treatment process," p. 358) in addition to those that have been observed (e.g., "Clients who have been diagnosed with a personality disorder are less likely to benefit from treatment than those who have not," p. 355). Please consult Castonguay and Beutler's (2006b) book for a comprehensive review of their practice principles.

Evidence-based Practice Guidelines

At least two major professional associations have developed practice guidelines to help practitioners in their clinical decision-making. Think of these practice guidelines as decision aids that help practitioners tailor treatment to specific clients (e.g., girls and women) presenting with certain conditions (e.g., autism spectrum disorders). The guidelines are recommendations for treatment structure, process, and strategies, and should not be considered directive or mandatory protocols.

To date, the American Psychological Association (APA) has developed 17 professional practice guidelines to assist psychologists (and other helpers as well) in navigating their work with client populations, such as older adults, and in contexts that include child custody evaluations and forensics. The full list of guidelines can be accessed at http://apa.org/practice /guidelines. The telepsychology and record-keeping guidelines are mentioned in Chapter 2. Practice guidelines specific to working with transgender and gender nonconforming persons are forthcoming, as are treatment guidelines for specific conditions.

Since 1991, the American Psychiatric Association (APrA) has published 14 practice guidelines specific to certain conditions such as bipolar disorder, HIV/AIDS, suicidal behaviors, and schizophrenia. They can be accessed at http://psychiatryonline.org/guidelines. New guidelines are undergoing development that will conform to standards of the Institute of Medicine.

Models of Treatment-Client Matching

The process of selecting specific practices or interventions to match client needs and preferences is referred to as client-treatment matching. This involves the use of a **decision rule** or a series of mental questions or heuristics that the helper constantly asks himself or herself during interviews to match interventions to clients and their identified concerns.

Several client-treatment matching models containing decision rules exist to help clinicians. Three of them are described in this section: (1) the problem-solving model of clinical decision-making developed by Nezu and colleagues (Nezu & Nezu, 2010; Nezu et al., 2004, 2007); (2) the integrative model known as systematic treatment selection developed by Beutler and colleagues (Beutler & Clarkin, 1990; Beutler et al., 2000, 2005; Beutler & Harwood, 2000; Beutler, Harwood, Kimpara et al., 2011; Beutler, Harwood, Michelson et al., 2011); and (3) the model for assessing and treating persons with addictive, substance-related, and co-occurring conditions developed by the American Society of Addiction Medicine (ASAM), known as *The ASAM Criteria* (Mee-Lee et al., 2013).

Problem-Solving Model

Nezu and colleagues (Nezu & Nezu, 2010; Nezu et al., 2004, 2007) describe a problem-solving model of clinical decision-making based on cognitive behavioral principles. Their two-part model consists of case formulation and treatment planning and is influenced by a multiple causality framework (i.e., client concerns have numerous and complex origins or explanations) and a systems perspective. The multiple causality framework suggests that disorders and their symptoms are characterized by either proximal features (i.e., immediate antecedent, such as the presence of a phobic object) or distal features (i.e., developmental history, such as the occurrence of a traumatic event several months or years ago). In planning care, attention is given to client-related variables and environment-related variables within the dimensions of time (i.e., client's current and past functioning) and functionality (i.e., how client and environmental characteristics are interrelated). And, consistent with cognitive behavioral practice, Nezu and colleagues (Nezu & Nezu, 2010; Nezu et al., 2004, 2007) recommended that the helper should evaluate the likelihood of potential solution alternatives (i.e., whether proposed goals and interventions will be achieved) by considering the following questions:

1. What is the likelihood that this particular intervention will achieve the specified goal(s)?

2. What is the likelihood that I as the therapist will be able to implement this intervention in its optimal form?

3. What is the likelihood that the client will be able to participate in, understand, and be able to carry out the strategy in its optimal form?

4. What is the likelihood that collaterals (e.g., caregivers, family members) or other health care providers will be able to implement a particular strategy in an optimal way?

5. How much time and effort are required to carry out this intervention?

6. What are the effects of resolving this problem on other client problem areas?

Strengths of the model presented by Nezu and colleagues (Nezu & Nezu, 2010; Nezu et al., 2004, 2007) include its foundation in and alignment with cognitive behavioral therapy (a therapeutic modality endorsed by third-party entities that often require treatment plans) and its comprehensiveness. Concerns about this model are that it may be too complex for a typical clinician to render it user-friendly and it does not specifically address cultural variables.

Systematic Treatment Selection Model

The systematic treatment selection model (Beutler & Clarkin, 1990; Beutler & Harwood, 2000; Beutler et al., 2000, 2005) is an integrated one that considers client predisposing qualities (i.e., problem, personality, and environment), context of treatment (i.e., setting, intensity, mode, and format), and therapist activity and relationship (i.e., therapeutic actions, alliance/relationship factors, and therapist-client matching). In formulating a treatment plan, the clinician selects features of client presentation or functioning (e.g., symptom severity and chronicity, readiness for change) to pair with certain treatment dimensions (e.g., therapist skill, level of directiveness) to identify the best client treatment match. Strengths of the model are that it has been revised over a period of time according to established and emerging psychotherapy process and outcome research, and that it has been applied specifically to clients with depressive disorders (Beutler et al., 2000).

The ASAM Criteria

Since 1991, the American Society of Addiction Medicine (ASAM) has published a clinical guide intended to enhance the use of multidimensional assessments in making decisions about matching patients/clients to appropriate levels of care. Although initially focused on clients with only substance-related concerns, the most recent edition, known as *The ASAM Criteria* (Mee-Lee et al., 2013), incorporates criteria that address a large subset of individuals with co-occurring conditions or disorders, that is, persons struggling with a substance use or addictive

behavior condition and one or more other conditions at the same time. This combination can include an alcohol use disorder and post-traumatic stress disorder (PTSD), as well as a gambling disorder and major depressive disorder. Mee-Lee and Gastfriend (2008) reported that these criteria have been adopted for use worldwide by the U.S. Department of Defense and by the U.S. Department of Veterans Affairs in its hospitals nationwide.

The ASAM Criteria assess all clients (both adults and adolescents) on six dimensions, after which clients are then assigned to one of four broad levels of service (and an early intervention level) that are on a continuum of increasing intensity. The six dimensions and the four levels of care (as well as the early intervention level) are presented in Box 9.3. Although presented as discrete levels, the four general levels of care (on the right side of Box 9.3) represent benchmarks that can be used to determine client progress. Notice also the levels of care within two of the broad levels, such as the Clinically Managed Low Intensity level within Level 3, Residential/Inpatient Services. The process of matching clients to treatment setting and level of service is based on the principle of "clinical appropriateness" rather than "medical necessity." The former emphasizes quality and efficiency, in contrast to the latter, which is often associated with restrictions on utilization.

Using the information presented thus far on client-treatment matching, review the case of Jane Wiggins presented in Learning Activity 9.1. To complete the activity, you may need to refer back to the three models just described.

BOX 9.3	The ASAM Criteria

Client Dimensions	**Levels of Care**
1. Acute Intoxication and/or Withdrawal Potential	0.5. Early Intervention
2. Biomedical Conditions/Complications	1. Outpatient Services
3. Emotional, Behavioral, and/or Cognitive Conditions/Complications	2. Intensive Outpatient/Partial Hospitalization
	a. Intensive Outpatient Services
	b. Partial Hospitalization Services
4. Readiness to Change	3. Residential/Inpatient Treatment
	a. Clinically Managed Low-Intensity Residential Services
	b. Clinically Managed Population-Specific High-Intensity Residential Services
	c. Clinically Managed High-Intensity Residential Services
	d. Medically Monitored Intensive Inpatient Services
5. Relapse, Continued Use, or Continued Problem Potential	4. Medically Managed Intensive Inpatient Treatment
6. Recovery/Living Environment	

Source: Mee-Lee et al., 2013.

Learning Activity 9.1

Factors Affecting Treatment Selection

Using the case of Jane Wiggins described here, respond to the following questions. You may wish to do this activity with a partner or in a small group.

1. What client characteristics do you see in Jane Wiggins that would affect your choice of treatment intervention strategies and also the overall therapeutic outcomes?
2. How would your training, your theoretical orientation to helping, and your practice setting affect your choice of change intervention strategies?
3. How aware are you of any evidence-based treatments that would be useful here?
4. What questions would you ask about these treatments?
5. If you are not aware of any evidence-based treatments, how could you find some?

The Case of Jane Wiggins

Jane Wiggins is a 34-year-old white American woman living in an isolated rural area. She has been referred to the nearest mental health center because she sought treatment at the local health care clinic following a rape.

She is very suspicious of the helper, who is a white man, and she talks reluctantly and without much eye contact. Gradually, she reveals that she is married, unemployed, has no children, and lives with her husband, who receives Social Security disability payments because of his very poor health. She has lived in this area all her life. She indicates that she has been followed for the past year by a white man

who also grew up in the area. She knows him by name and sight only. In addition to following her, he has sent her numerous letters and has made phone calls containing lewd and suggestive remarks. She indicates that she and her husband went to the sheriff's office several times to complain, but the complaints were never followed-up. It appears that this man may be related to a deputy in the sheriff's office.

Several weeks ago her husband went over the hill to a neighbor's house to visit and, as was their custom, left the door unlocked. The man who has been following her apparently was around, noticed the husband's departure, and came into her house and raped her. She says she told no one other than the neighbor and her husband because she feels so ashamed. She indicates she is a very religious person and has been reluctant to go to church or to confide in her minister for fear of what the church people may say. She also has been reluctant to tell her parents and sister, who live nearby, for the same reason. She sees no point in reporting the rape to the authorities because they dismissed her earlier reports.

She feels a lot of guilt about the rape because she thinks she should have been able to prevent it. She has been doing a lot of praying about this. As a few sessions go by, she gradually becomes more open with the helper and indicates she is willing to come back for a few more sessions to deal with her guilt and sadness; she would like to be able to feel happy again and not be so consumed by guilt. She finally discloses she would feel more comfortable talking these things out with another woman, as this is really a "female problem."

Planning for Type, Duration, and Mode of Treatment

Client-treatment matching is an ongoing process. **LO1** It may take time, patience, diligence, and a few mismatches to be able to identify one or more interventions that are suitable and effective for clients. Helpers may need to prepare clients for this. However, finding client-treatment matches ultimately is the helper's responsibility and depends on the helper's skill level. Clients may not have the resources necessary to stay the course with a particular helper who is unable to identify helpful interventions. Furthermore, helpers who remain unresponsive to client needs by insisting on one method of care to which the client has not responded positively may actually be doing their client harm.

There are at least three aspects of care to be considered in the process of client-treatment matching. These are the type, duration, and mode of treatment, and each is discussed in this section.

Care Consideration 1: Type of Treatment

It goes without saying that selecting appropriate types of treatment begins with the client or, more precisely, with determining "where the client is." This means assessing the client's current functioning, such as the nature of his or her symptoms (i.e., intensity or level of distress, chronicity, complexity), receptivity to treatment and readiness to change, and resources available (e.g., social support, financial status). Although some helpers may view assessing the client's ability to pay for services as counter to their practice as helpers, the financial information obtained is indeed critical to clinical decision-making.

Findings from the most recent national survey on mental health sponsored by the Substance Abuse and Mental Health Services Administration (SAMHSA, 2013) suggest that the principal reason given for persons not seeking treatment/counseling in the past year when mental health needs were present was cost/insurance issues (45.7 percent). This is followed by a belief in one's own ability to handle the problem without treatment

(28.2 percent) and not knowing where to go for services (22.8 percent). Somewhat similar reasons that follow have been given by those with substance use issues from 2010 to 2013 who knew they needed treatment but did not obtain treatment (see SAMHSA 2014): cost/insurance barriers (45.5 percent); not ready to stop using (24.5 percent); and did not know where to go for treatment (9.0 percent). Interventions should be selected that take these and other treatment concerns and barriers into consideration. This might mean, for example, recommending less costly services at the initiation of care, such as outpatient versus inpatient treatment.

When assessing the nature of the client's presenting concerns, recall that Nezu and colleagues (Nezu & Nezu, 2010; Nezu et al., 2004, 2007) recommend distinguishing between their *proximal* features (i.e., immediate antecedent, such as the presence of a phobic object) and their *distal* features (i.e., developmental history, such as the occurrence of a traumatic event several months or years ago). This differentiation appears to correspond with Beutler and Clarkin's (1990) assessment of client issues as those involving either symptom distress or symbolic conflicts, which can be determined by asking, "Are these problems simple habits maintained by the environment, or are they symbolized expressions of unresolved conflictual experiences?" (p. 226). For example, a teenage girl is referred to you by her mother, who explains that during the past few months her daughter has become more "distant and withdrawn" and has been spending a lot of time texting and on the computer. Although the mother claims to monitor her mobile phone and Internet use, she is concerned about her daughter's digital communications. The presenting concern in this case might be characterized as symptom distress with proximal features. Another teenage girl, however, is brought to you by her mother, who is concerned about her daughter's "distance and withdrawal" not only from her but also from her younger brother. However, the mother notes that this behavior is nothing new; it has been a pattern since she was adopted at age 2 along with her infant brother. In the latter case, the presenting concern might be characterized as more of a symbolic conflict with distal features.

For issues that are primarily symptom-based, have proximal features, and involve changes in altering behaviors and cognitions, recommended treatment strategies involve behavioral and cognitive interventions such as dialectical behavior therapy's (DBT) chain analysis, modeling, exposure and graded practice (e.g., systematic desensitization), cognitive restructuring, and self-monitoring, depending on the degree to which symptoms are overt or covert. Overt, external symptoms are more responsive

to behavioral strategies; covert symptoms are more responsive to cognitive therapies (Beutler & Clarkin, 1990; Beutler et al., 2005). Note that symptom distress or a behavioral type of treatment works best with clients who have predominantly externalizing coping styles, although beginning treatment with more direct, symptom-focused methods may work well with clients who have more internalizing coping styles (Beutler, Harwood, Kimpara, et al., 2011, p. 350). For problems that are primarily conflict-based, have distal features, and involve changes in altering feelings, recommended treatment strategies include interventions for enhancing emotional and sensory outcomes such as reflection of feelings, mindfulness, and play therapy. Recommended treatment strategies for resolving inner conflict include interpretation, confrontation with care (what DBT describes as "benevolently confrontational"; see McMain, Sayrs, Dimeff, & Linehan, 2007, p. 167), early recollections, genograms, and Gestalt two-chair work. In one of Neff, Kirkpatrick, and Rude's (2007) studies, undergraduate students who participated with a therapist in a Gestalt two-chair exercise to resolve an inner conflict experienced an increase in self-compassion. Note that these insight-focused treatments work best with clients who have predominantly internalizing coping styles (Beutler et al., 2011).

As further guidance for selecting these and other types of interventions, remember that from a developmental perspective, support factors would typically occur in the early phase of treatment and would address things such as concerns related to stigma and the client feeling demoralized (refer back to Figure 9.2). The goal for this phase would be what Howard and colleagues (1993, 1996) term *remoralization* and would include strategies such as role induction (i.e., client and helper discussing and agreeing on their mutual and distinct roles, responsibilities, and expectations), further exploration of the client's presenting concerns, and radically accepting or validating the client's experience (a core strategy in DBT). The next phase of treatment would focus on symptomatic relief (or remediation) by implementing learning (or cognitive modification) factors, such as skills training (e.g., emotion regulation in DBT) or psychoeducation (e.g., the ABC model of rational-emotive behavioral therapy, REBT), offering advice, and having the client engage in a structured self-assessment and family assessment. Building on what was learned in the second phase of treatment, the third phase would then be devoted to action factors— that is, rehearsing and implementing new behaviors to achieve Howard and colleagues' goal of rehabilitation (see Figure 9.2).

As discussed previously in this chapter, treatment planning is a continuous process, an adventure that client and helper undertake as a team. Because the treatment plan is tailored to the individual client, the routes taken to arrive at the client's destination cannot be predetermined. Rather, client and helper jointly construct a map, and the directions are subject to change with each new path traversed. Not all interventions can be identified at the beginning of care; what was thought to have been a beneficial activity during the last treatment plan review (or "rest stop") may now be discarded in favor of another approach in light of client progress or lack of progress, changes in the client's circumstances (e.g., securing employment), and the helper's knowledge and skill enhancement (e.g., completing training in DBT). What is key in selecting appropriate treatment strategies is to remain abreast of the client's case—and by this we mean maintaining a comprehensive understanding of the client, including history, assessment data, current status and context (e.g., environmental supports), response to treatment, and revised self-descriptions and aspirations. It is also important to adopt the practice of constant consultation when determining types of treatment. We believe that these clinical decisions are never done solo; rather, they are made in consultation with our clients, with their family members and other collaterals (e.g., referral source, community advocates), and with our colleagues (fellow practitioners, recognized theorists, and published scientists/researchers alike) within the parameters of ethical codes and legal requirements. Yet when we put our signature on the plan as licensed practitioners, it signifies the responsibility we have assumed for the client's professional care. However, that same signature should represent the culmination of conversations with clients, collaterals, and colleagues. Treatment decisions, therefore, are the product of consultative and continuous conversations with key constituents.

Care Consideration 2: Duration of Treatment

How many sessions are necessary for clients to improve in psychotherapy? This question was first introduced by Howard, Kopta, Krause, and Orlinsky (1986) and is referred to as the *dose-effect model*. Their meta-analysis of research studies conducted over a 30-year period and representing 2,431 patients indicated that the majority of patients improved in the first 8 sessions, and that by 26 sessions approximately 75 percent of patients had shown some improvement. Numerous studies since then (e.g., Kadera, Lambert, & Andrews, 1996; Kopta, Howard, Lowry, & Beutler, 1994; Lutz, Lowry, Kopta, Einstein, & Howard, 2001) upheld these findings for a variety of clients presenting with a range of concerns and receiving services in different treatment settings.

To explain the relationship between number of sessions attended and client improvement, Lambert (2013) recommends a more recent model. This model is known as the *good-enough level* (Barkham et al., 2006), and it suggests that clients end therapy when they have achieved a satisfactory level of change. Whereas a constant rate of change is implied in the dose-effect model, the good-enough level suggests a varied rate of change, one that is different for each client. How quickly clients change is dependent on the total number of psychotherapy sessions attended. Fewer sessions attended are related to faster rates of change, whereas more sessions attended correspond to slower change (Baldwin et al., 2009).

In their review of client length of stay in six different outpatient treatment settings, Hansen, Lambert, and Forman (2002) found that the average number of sessions utilized was 4.3 and the median number of sessions was 3. (It should be noted that these figures do not reflect the 33 percent of clients who remained in treatment for only one session.) The highest average (9.5 sessions) was in a university-supported training clinic, and the lowest average was in a local health maintenance organization (3.3 sessions) and in an employee assistance program (3.6 sessions). Hansen and colleagues (2002) describe these utilization numbers as "extremely low" and representing treatment "insufficient by most standards of care" (p. 338). Many health maintenance organizations, however, do limit mental health coverage to 20 sessions or fewer per year and assume that this number of visits represents a "safe harbor" for even those people needing more than the average amount of therapy. Obviously, some clients will need more sessions (e.g., those with severe and persistent mental illnesses), and, lacking their own resources or access to insurance coverage, they will be deprived of needed treatment (as is evident in the SAMHSA, 2013, 2014, survey data mentioned earlier). This is true for indigent clients and ethnically and racially diverse clients who have experienced unjust health care disparities for too long (Smedley, Stith, & Nelson, 2003).

It is difficult to make sweeping generalizations about an effective duration for *all* clients; indeed, this is why treatment plans are developed for each individual client. Time should be regarded as a commodity and used judiciously, but not at the expense of client need and care. It is recommended that clients with high levels of impairment be offered more frequent sessions spaced closer together than clients with low levels of impairment. Clients who present with transient situational concerns are good candidates for crisis intervention, but we cannot assume that all clients are automatically good candidates for brief or time-limited therapy. Brief therapy seems to be appropriate for clients who may drop out of therapy early, such as clients who are at the precontemplation stage of the transtheoretical model of change and who have unidimensional symptoms or conflictual issues. Brief therapy may serve as a stepping stone to more intensive services and may also fit the preferences and belief systems of some ethnically and racially diverse clients. Overall, we believe that duration of treatment should be a clinical rather than an economic decision. There are ethical issues in providing too little care due to cost containment and too much care under fee-for-service models of reimbursement.

Care Consideration 3: Mode of Treatment

Mode of treatment refers to the mechanism or format of service delivery and typically includes individual treatment, couples and/or family treatment, group treatment, and medication. All these modes have certain advantages (see Clarkin, 2005).

Individual therapy promotes greater privacy, self-disclosure, sharing, individualized attention, and identification with the helper than the other modes. *Couples therapy* allows for the direct observation of interaction between the partners, deals with both parties, including both sides of conflict, and allows for the development of mutual support, communication, and conflict-resolution resources. These same advantages are extended to *family therapy*. Participating in *group therapy* allows for extensive modeling, support, and feedback from others (particularly helpful for those with social anxiety disorder and others who could benefit from social skills training). Couples, group, and family interventions are good settings for providing education and skills training. Individual, couple/family, and group modes of treatment do not typically involve adverse side effects, although it goes without saying that not all clients improve with treatment.

Medication management or *psychopharmacology* involves the use of psychotropic drugs to help alleviate and/or manage the symptoms of psychological disorders for which there is a clear biochemical imbalance. Major drug classes used in treatment are antidepressants, antipsychotics, and stimulants intended for children (see Sparks, Duncan, Cohen, & Antonuccio, 2010). Their use has increased dramatically in the United States over the past 15 years, an increase that has surpassed the use of psychotherapy not involving psychotropic medications (Fullerton, Busch, Normand, McGuire, & Epstein, 2011; Olfson & Marcus, 2010). This increase has taken place at the same time that rates of psychotherapy use actually have decreased, suggesting that mental health care has become increasingly equated with only using psychotropic medications, and less so with "talk therapy" (i.e., counseling or psychotherapy).

The use of psychopharmacology to the exclusion of psychotherapy is unfortunate for at least three reasons. First, medications pose greater risks and there are adverse side effects to clients compared to other modes of treatment. Prescribing physicians (e.g., psychiatrists) often do not have or take the time to fully discuss these effects with clients (see Carlat, 2010). Nonmedical practitioners thus serve an important educational and supportive function. A second reason for concern is that clients rarely learn new ways of problem-solving and coping with *just* medication. This includes processing the meaning they ascribe to taking medication and how to talk to others (e.g., family members) about their medication. Third, as Comas-Días (2012) discusses, the use of pharmacological interventions with culturally diverse persons is little understood and has resulted in mistreatment to many persons of color (e.g., over prescribing or withholding medication). For example, Asians and African Americans tend to have slower metabolism rates of certain antipsychotic medications compared to whites, resulting in the need for prescribing physicians to "start low and go slow" in dosing these medications to their multicultural patients. This then calls for close and frequent monitoring. We recommend that clients prescribed psychotropic medications should also engage in some mode of psychotherapy and that the prescribing physician and nonmedical helper coordinate care.

The mode of treatment is often indicated by the nature of the client's issue. Although a helper trained primarily in couples/family/systems-based approaches may view all presenting issues and corresponding interventions as family-oriented, an individual format may be conducive for a client in the early phase of treatment (e.g., someone in the precontemplation stage of change). By the same token, another helper trained solely in individual interventions may miss or overlook important group and systemic parts of the issue as well as other nonindividual or collectivist-oriented interventions. The importance of having a multidimensional treatment perspective and remaining flexible cannot be overemphasized!

Given the information presented on the decision rules of planning for type, duration, and mode of treatment, we invite you to participate in Learning Activity 9.2. Two cases are presented (Antonio and Mr. Sharn) for you to apply several of the decision rules. Feedback is provided to help you evaluate the rules you selected.

Cultural Issues in Treatment Planning and Selection

It should go without saying that cultural considerations are an indisputable priority in clinical decision-making and treatment planning. Culture—broadly defined—is at the center of healing, not at its periphery (Comas-Días, 2012, 2014), and is integral to all aspects of the helping process. Race, ethnicity, gender and gender expression, socioeconomic status, and other cultural influences are woven into the very fabric of all helping practices. (Refer to Hays's [2008, 2013] ADDRESSING Framework in Chapter 2 for a refresher on cultural influences.) Helpers must therefore remain vigilant about the cultural background and identity of their clients, how their clients express their cultural identity (whether or not such expression is "obvious," as in client self-report, for example), and the meaning they and their clients attribute to the expression or manifestation of clients' cultural identity. This is true for all clients and helpers because all client-helper interactions are cross-cultural. Although clients and helpers may at times look alike (e.g., members of a similar racial/ethnic group) and may share similar backgrounds, identities, and values, there is no such thing as cultural sameness between clients and helpers. Borrowing from our earlier forest analogy, helpers need to recognize and incorporate into the step-by-step treatment planning process the idiosyncratic trees that make up the forest.

Many of the strategies described in this chapter are drawn from theoretical positions developed by white founding fathers. As a result, the most widely used therapeutic strategies often reflect the values of persons from dominant groups, which today in the United States include persons who were born in the United States of European descent, speak fluent English, are biologically male, heterosexual, express their gender in normative ways, are affiliated with some form of Protestant Christianity, belong to the middle or upper classes, are in the 25- to 49-year-old age group, have a college education or more, and do not have current disabilities (Brown, 2008, p. 26). Clients who do not have these characteristics are more likely to feel marginalized and may experience what Gary (2005) described as the "double stigma" of being a member of a cultural minority and having a mental illness. This type of stigma may be experienced as public stigma (e.g., institutional racism), self-stigma (e.g., diminished self-efficacy), or family and courtesy stigma (i.e., stigma generalized to a client's family members).

Learning Activity 9.2

Decision Rules in Treatment Planning

Use the following two case descriptions to identify some decision rules about treatment selection and planning. Respond orally or in writing to the five questions, which represent decision rules about treatment selection. Also review Table 9.1 on page 308 for assistance. You may want to do this activity with a partner or in a small group. Feedback follows on page 320.

1. What is this client's *level of functional impairment*? Present data to support your decision. Given the data, what would you recommend about treatment duration for this client?
2. What is this client's *predominant coping style*—externalizing or internalizing? Present data to support your decision. Given the information provided, what type of treatment would you select for this client—behavioral focus or insight-reflective focus?
3. What *mode of treatment* might work best for this client? Present data to support your choice.
4. How would you assess the *level of resistance* (low or high) that is apparent, as well as the nature of resistance expressed (e.g., culturally appropriate)? Present data to support your choice. Given the data, would you use directive or nondirective intervention strategies?
5. Consider how your training, practice setting, and theoretical orientation(s) to helping might affect your decision about treatment selection.

The Case of Antonio

Antonio is a 15-year-old boy who lives with his dad. His mother kicked him out because he stopped going to

school and got in trouble with the law for stealing. His parents are divorced. His dad owns a bar, and Antonio is now staying with his dad but says he doesn't see him much. He says he quit going to school because he didn't have any friends there, his teachers didn't seem to understand him, and he got into trouble all the time for fighting. He spends his time now playing videogames, although arrangements have been made for him to be home-schooled for the rest of the year. He denies any substance use. He doesn't understand why he has to see you.

The Case of Mr. Sharn

Mr. Sharn is a 72-year-old man who has come to see you because he has had trouble sleeping and has noticed problems with his memory, problems that he says are unusual. Also, his appetite is poor. He has been retired for 7 years and has really enjoyed himself until lately. He and his wife recently returned from visiting their son and grandchildren, who live in a town a few hours away. His other son lives in the same town as Mr. Sharn. Mr. Sharn says he has lots of friends, especially golfing buddies. He reports being close to both sons. He says they had a good visit, but ever since he has been back he has noticed some things about his sleep, memory, and appetite. He does report feeling lonely and kind of blue, but not overwhelmed by it, and he denies any suicidal thoughts. He is hoping you can help him. Although he has never consulted a professional helper before, he doesn't want to burden his wife or his sons with too many problems.

Discrimination and marginalization are particularly evident in the racial disparities that persist in behavioral health care. These include lower rates of medication management and outpatient utilization after inpatient discharge for racial and ethnic minorities compared to whites (Virnig et al., 2004), differences in diagnoses according to client race (irrespective of helper race; Neighbors, Trierweiler, Ford, & Muroff, 2003), and greater levels of psychological distress among African Americans, both before and after participating in treatment for co-occurring disorders compared to whites (Grella & Stein, 2006). Furthermore, although the majority (85 percent) of therapists reported having discussions about cultural differences with their clients, these discussions were reported to occur in less than half (43 percent) of cross-racial/ethnic therapy cases (Maxie, Arnold, & Stephenson, 2006). Helpers of various races and ethnicities may therefore be mindful of racial and ethnic issues, but they may choose not to address such issues directly with their clients (e.g., "She's lived here in the United States for so long and speaks fluent English—I didn't think the fact that she happened to be born in Haiti was really a major issue"), or they may not be able to provide specific culturally appropriate services (e.g., having a staff member who can speak a new client's preferred language).

Typically, traditional treatment planning and selection have not addressed issues of race/ethnicity, gender, and social class—particularly poverty and international perspectives (Hays, 2008). This might be due, in part, to the contention that racially and ethnically diverse participants have not been included in randomized clinical/control trials, the findings of which have supplied the evidence for evidence-based practice (Comas-Díaz, 2006, 2012; Whaley & Davis, 2007). Indeed, some traditional psychotherapeutic techniques found to be successful with white clients of European descent may be culturally contraindicated for clients who do not fit the dominant and mainstream social-political-economic culture. These might include certain expressive strategies associated with Gestalt therapy, group work (particularly in the early phase of the helping process), disputing what the helper might interpret as irrational thoughts, and identifying a "higher power" in one's recovery from substance dependence. Helpers accustomed to offering these and other strategies to their clients as part of their standard practice will need to expand their repertoire to include the diverse expressions of culture among their clients. Some of these practices are prayer and meditation, chanting, consultation with community elders/indigenous healers, drum work, and home-based or community-based visitation. Although some helpers might bristle at the idea of engaging in such practices, Ivey and Brooks-Harris (2005) contend that "Psychotherapy faces a time of major change . . .

[that includes] discarding the outmoded concept of self and replacing it with self-in-context, being-in-relation, and person-in-community" (p. 335). A more expansive understanding and practice of helping, therefore, is not only needed but also already at work. We believe it is time for such changes.

Intentional Integration of Cultural Interventions

Nezu (2005) described three barriers that prevent behavioral health care professions from fully incorporating issues of diversity in all aspects of practice: (1) excessive focus on internal psychological processes; (2) the "medicalization" of human behavior; and (3) the ubiquity of unconscious biases against out-group members—what Sue (2010) would define as microaggressions. Specific to race, Greene and Blitz (2012) proposed that many helpers may not address issues of race (including the experience of racism) with their clients because they believe that racial equity is a matter of being color-blind in their approach to persons. Furthermore, many helpers have been taught to follow the client's lead or to follow treatment manuals. The problem with either of these two approaches is that clients may not broach the topic of race for fear of being misunderstood or judged, and evidence-based treatment protocols have yet to be developed that address race and race-related stress.

Perhaps in an effort to address these and other impediments to adopting a cultural milieu of professional helping, Ivey and Brooks-Harris (2005) presented what we interpret as a preliminary portrait of mainstream multicultural helping. Their description derives from predictions Ivey and Ivey (2000) made about how cultural issues will change the very practice of psychotherapy in the next few decades, predictions Whaley and Davis (2007) would more than likely support. We delineate five features of Ivey and Brooks-Harris's portrait, and we discuss their relevance to clinical decision-making and treatment planning: (1) contextual awareness; (2) consciousness development; (3) diffusing distress and reframing resistance; (4) co-constructed, contextual-specific, and collaborative interventions; and (5) therapeutic proactivity. These five features of mainstream multicultural helping are not presented in any order of importance. Specific intervention strategies are discussed in each one.

Feature 1: Contextual Awareness

A multicultural focus in clinical decision-making and treatment planning must include a consideration of contextual issues, what Bernal and Sáez-Santiago (2006) describe as one of eight dimensions of culturally centered treatment. Such a perspective pertains to the client's past and current environment, especially his or her social system, including (but not limited to) acculturation stress and racism-related distress. Interventions might include conducting a comprehensive assessment of the client's living and working environment (both past and present), with particular attention given to social relationships. In addition to completing a genogram (and not necessarily restricted to biological relations or kin), for example, helpers might ask individual clients and each family member to draw a plan of their house or their current dwelling. In describing this activity, Rochkovski (2006) stated, "When we ask a family to 'draw the plan of their house,' previously invisible aspects of the family come to light" (p. 10), such as the types of space(s) involved, how each family member uses the space(s) in the depicted dwelling (as well as the space on the paper on which it is drawn), traffic patterns, furniture, and structure of the house (e.g., shanty, fortress, with/without windows).

Depicting a client's living environment and social system on paper as part of the helping process provides a glimpse into the client's interior and exterior cultural contexts, in some ways consistent with our trees (idiosyncratic or idiographic) *and* forest (nomothetic) analogy. A similar exercise can be undertaken for the client's neighborhood (e.g., "Draw the apartment building where you live" or "Map out the park you go to and the path you take to get there"), work environment (e.g., where offices are located and how office space is used), or school setting (e.g., "Draw your classroom for me," or "Draw a plan of your school cafeteria"). This same exercise can be adapted for clients who do not currently have a home, depicting the spaces they now occupy and how others may encroach on those spaces.

Contextual awareness also pertains to understanding the helper's context or, more precisely, the social system of the helping process. Ideally, this would constitute what Constantino, Malgady, and Primavera (2009) described as **cultural congruence**, or the matching of the cultural competence of the health care provider organization (or organizational cultural competence) to the cultural needs of the person seeking treatment. Organizational cultural competence includes encouraging staff training in cultural competence, hiring culturally diverse staff appropriate for the population served (including hiring staff from within the community it serves), and having an internal mission statement asserting a commitment to culturally appropriate services. Constantino and colleagues found that greater organizational cultural congruence was responsible for lower depression and increased physical

9.2 Feedback

Decision Rules in Treatment Planning

The Case of Antonio

1. Antonio's functional impairment seems high due to his family problems, his lack of social support, and his social isolation and withdrawal. As a result, treatment intensity would be increased, with more frequent sessions spaced closer together.

2. Antonio's coping style seems to be externalizing. He has been in trouble with the law for stealing and has been in trouble at school for fighting. As a result, your treatment focus would be behavioral.

3. Because of Antonio's family issues, social isolation, and lack of social support, family and group modes of treatment may be better than individual ones. Individual sessions may be needed at first, however, to establish your credibility and trustworthiness.

4. Antonio's level of resistance to meeting with you appears to be high, and he might be described as being in the precontemplation stage of change. His confusion and anger about having to see you might be understood from the context of his age, family disruption, and lack of stability within the home. Nondirective interventions would be more useful.

The Case of Mr. Sharn

1. Mr. Sharn's degree of impairment seems relatively low. He has a supportive and functional family and lots of friends, and he seems to have a good overall support system. So treatment intensity and duration would probably remain at once weekly. Of course, his level of depression would need to be carefully monitored to ensure he is not a danger to himself.

2. Mr. Sharn seems to have a more internalized coping style because he views himself as the cause of the problems, and he internalizes feelings of distress and sadness.

3. It would be useful to use individual sessions with Mr. Sharn; also, a possible evaluation with a physician may be necessary because of his sleep, appetite, and memory problems.

4. Mr. Sharn's level of resistance to meeting with you is low. He appears to be eager to accept your help and may be considered to be in the preparation stage of change. Using more directive interventions seems to be appropriate.

functioning in older Hispanic/Latino patients receiving services in specialty mental health clinics.

Within any health care treatment facility, culturally competent interventions might include informing clients about the helper's qualifications (e.g., providing them with a copy of one's professional disclosure statement), as well as disclosing to clients the helper's own cultural identity, background, or context (e.g., "I happen to be legally blind, but I can see the general outlines of faces. I'll probably be squinting quite a bit so I can see more of your facial expressions, and you'll probably see my eyes fluttering from time to time as they adjust to the light"). Contextual awareness of the helping process is also furthered by discussing with clients what they will do (i.e., client implementation) and what the helper will do (i.e., helper interventions), the goal being for clients to act on what Brown (2010) referred to as **empowered consent**. We prefer *empowered* consent to *informed* consent because the former suggests action on the client's part originating from more than simply knowledge given to the client by another or enlightenment. The client's empowered consent connotes an ownership of therapy—a client's readiness and resoluteness to actively participate in therapy.

We believe that the helper is acting in good faith to protect clients' rights and welfare by discussing with clients the following kinds of information about treatment strategies:

- A description of *all* relevant and potentially useful treatment approaches for this particular client with this particular problem
- A rationale for each procedure
- A description of the helper's role in each procedure
- A description of the client's role in each procedure
- Discomforts or risks that may occur as a result of the procedure
- Benefits expected to result from the procedure
- The estimated time and cost of each procedure

Empowered consent is designed to provide complete and meaningful disclosure in a way that supports the client's freedom of choice and may be considered the product of role induction. This practice, therefore, implies collaboration, which we believe is consistent with a mainstream multicultural milieu.

Feature 2: Consciousness Development

Consciousness development is the process of becoming increasingly aware of one's cultural identity and how it is expressed in varying contexts over time. Because "cultural identity is fluid and dynamic and may be differentially invoked, depending on the context and situation" (Lo &

Fung, 2003, p. 163), consciousness development is an ongoing activity and is relevant for both client and helper. The client may benefit from exploring internalized conflict/discrepancies that may arise, for example, when familiar surroundings change (e.g., relocation of residence), established relationships require reconfiguration (e.g., family member comes out as gay), or physical appearance and functioning or accustomed mobility are disrupted (e.g., loss of limbs in a freak accident). Validating the client's reactions to these and other changes may be the first step needed to relieve or at least ease what may be feelings of anger or guilt.

An Asian client who was the sole survivor of an automobile accident, for example, may experience survivor's guilt and believe that his ensuing depression that has resulted in his unemployment is simply his "bad luck" and "fate." In this instance, the culturally skilled helper may familiarize herself with certain folk beliefs in the client's specific Asian background that may have a salutary connotation and empowering effect. Lo and Fung (2003, p. 169) make reference to one such Chinese adage: "Survivors of great catastrophe will surely have good luck later on." The helper may thus offer this folk belief to the client and suggest that his survival is an example of his ability to withstand the "clutch of fate" and that gratitude for his life might be expressed to a particular deity by helping others (maybe even as a way to earn that deity's favor for future good luck).

The helper's own consciousness development can occur by conducting what Lo and Fung (2003) describe as a Cultural Analysis and what Ridley and Kelly (2007) described as the Multicultural Assessment Procedure (or MAP). Both of these practices are hypothesis-generating strategies for understanding how a client's culture influences self, relationships, and treatment. The goal of Cultural Analysis is to "achieve a more complete and culturally informed psychological understanding of the patient" (Lo & Fung, 2003, p. 166), and components of the analysis can include a sociopolitical history of the client's country of origin, current forces in the host country (e.g., discrimination), and particular dynamics and resources available in the client's local ethnic community. A focus of Ridley and Kelly's (2007) MAP is a consideration of both (1) group or nomothetic cultural data and (2) unique or idiosyncratic data (or, the forest *and* the trees). To differentiate the two, helpers can ask their clients about their personal meanings and experiences and then compare client responses to cultural norms. Helpers are also encouraged to determine client stressors that are dispositional in nature (i.e., originating from within the client) and those stressors that are environmental in nature (e.g., stress related to being a member of a cultural group with a history of disenfranchisement and discrimination in the United States, such as being gay, lesbian, bisexual, or transgender, or LGBT).

As a means of furthering an appreciation for each client's cultural context and consciousness, Comas-Díaz (2006) described the practice of cultural resonance, which she defined as "the ability to understand clients through clinical skill, cultural competence, and intuition" (p. 94). Integral to this helper skill is the focus on nonverbal communication: "Cultural resonance helps the clinician decipher the client's inner processes and provides information beyond messages that the client communicates verbally" (p. 94). Bernal and Sáez-Santiago (2006) also emphasized the importance of attending to metaphors and symbols (including idioms) that are part of a given client's culture and incorporating these, as much as possible, into the plan of care.

Feature 3: Diffusing Distress and Reframing Resistance

In their vision of a mainstream multicultural milieu, Ivey and Brooks-Harris (2005) state: "'Disorder' will cease to frame our consciousness about the deeply troubled. Rather, psychotherapy will engage serious client 'dis-stress' and not define it as 'dis-ease'" (p. 335). In addition, client issues and challenges will be understood "as a logical response to developmental history and external social conditions" (p. 335). This depiction implies a prioritization of client strengths, resources, and protective factors, in addition to a consideration of client challenges.

From a strengths-based perspective, we encourage helpers to develop treatment plans with clients that intentionally incorporate client assets and resources that, if you recall from Lambert's (1992) research, appear to significantly impact client outcome. In Figure 9.1, client factors account for 40 percent of client improvement during the helping process. The client's spirituality may play an important role in this regard; folk beliefs, mythology, and supernatural forces may all be significant factors. By embracing a "dis-stress" rather than a "dis-ease" perspective, and helping clients mobilize (indeed, positively exploit) the strengths and resources present in their cultural identity and community, helpers are in essence ushering in a new culture, one that resembles Ivey and Brooks-Harris's (2005) vision of what we have termed a mainstream multicultural milieu in professional helping.

Part of this milieu will be a reframing of resistance as it is traditionally understood and how it was described earlier in the chapter. Ridley (2005) defines resistance as "countertherapeutic behavior . . . directed toward one goal: the indiscriminate avoidance of the painful requirements of change" (p. 134). He emphasizes that resistance, like racism, is a "human motor activity . . . [that] can be observed, repeated, and measured" (p. 134). It "is not an attitude or a psychological state of the client, although resistant attitudes and psychological states are powerful motivators of client behavior" (p. 134). From a feminist perspective, resistance is viewed as positive functioning (Brown, 2010), that is, fighting against experiences of oppression and disempowerment. Promoting salutary resistance in clients requires helpers who, according to Brown (2010), invite clients "to perceive themselves as having been engaged in the struggle to be safe and well" (p. 71). At an individual level, this may mean helping the client resist an inequitable contract or workload agreement in her job that has been created without divergent voices and imposed by people who hold the power. Treatment strategies would be selected and implemented toward this act of resistance. At a systems level, both helper and client may need to resist system-wide practices that substitute compliance for difference and agreement for disagreement.

Feature 4: Co-constructed, Contextual-Specific, and Collaborative Interventions

Depending on the nature of their concerns (e.g., symptom intensity) and their cultural values, clients may present for mental health treatment with the expectation that a "cure" is possible (indeed, necessary), that the helper is the source of that "remedy," and that the "answer" to "fixing" the clients' concerns can (indeed, must) happen immediately. Such an orientation may be amenable to brief or time-limited cognitive behavioral interventions and some helpers may be eager to jump right in and accommodate what might be interpreted as the client's demands.

Although many clients of certain racial/ethnic backgrounds may wait a considerable amount of time before seeking professional help for mental health concerns and thus appear for the first session in a state of crisis (Paniagua, 2005), we would advise helpers not to assume a knee-jerk reaction of "doctor knows best" and proceed in what some might regard as a paternalistic manner of care. Extending treatment without an understanding of or a full appreciation for the client's cultural identity and context is, as we have discussed, inappropriate, inconsistent with professional guidelines (e.g., American Psychological Association, 2003), and potentially unethical (see the National Association of Social Workers' Code of Ethics, 2008, Standard 1.05: Cultural Competence and Social Diversity; also see the American Counseling Association's (ACA) *ACA Code of Ethics*, 2014, A.2.c.: Developmental and Cultural Sensitivity, and B.1.a.: Multicultural/Diversity Considerations).

Clients do need to have their presenting concerns taken seriously (e.g., physical symptoms, even if the helper suspects somatization or malingering). Indeed, when determining appropriate treatment goals, Lo and Fung (2003) emphasize that "the primary principle . . . should be the patient's subjective well-being, conducive to healthy functioning in the patient's environment" (p. 164). However, this does not mean that the helper should presume to know (particularly at the beginning of care) what is "best" for the client. Lo and Fung (2003) recommended a both/and principle of practice in this regard (consistent with the integrative—"trees *and* forest"—perspective emphasized throughout this chapter) in that helpers are able to "recognize and operate within the contrasting frameworks of therapeutic omniscience and naiveté" (p. 161). This means practicing according to one's training and scope of competence (e.g., crisis intervention) while remaining open to being instructed by cultural configurations and their meanings for each new, unique client.

Regardless of the client's cultural identity or context, the *ACA Code of Ethics* (2014; Section A.1.c.) stipulates that "counselors and their clients work jointly in devising integrated counseling plans" and also "regularly review counseling plans to assess their continued viability and effectiveness, respecting clients' freedom of choice." Selecting treatment goals and strategies therefore should be undertaken as a collaborative venture between client and helper. This is accomplished by learning more about the client's cultural identity and context (e.g., language preference, social network and family dynamics, acculturation status, experiences of discrimination), engaging in role induction and empowered consent, and possibly consulting with others involved in the client's life (e.g., family members, referral source, family physician). Indeed, the collaborative construction of a treatment plan may extend beyond the client-helper dyad to include the contributions of lay and professional consultants, all of whom would be involved only with the client's expressed permission, of course. When working with Asian American clients, Paniagua (2005) recommended collecting information gradually rather than all at once and planning on several sessions to obtain an adequate amount of necessary and relevant data.

Cognitive behavioral approaches, in particular, have potential strengths for use with culturally diverse clients (Hays, 2008, 2014). These approaches include the emphasis on the uniqueness of the individual and the adaptation of the helping process to meet this uniqueness, a focus on client empowerment, ongoing helper-client collaboration, use of a direct and pragmatic treatment focus, and an emphasis on conscious (versus unconscious) processes and specific (versus abstract) behaviors and treatment protocols (Hays, 2008). Lum (2004) describes five specific treatment strategies relevant to multicultural practice; they are described in Box 9.4. We believe each of these interventions operates within the framework of client-helper collaboration that includes the co-construction of a culturally appropriate treatment plan.

Feature 5: Therapeutic Proactivity

To realize the mainstream multicultural milieu that we emphasize here, mental health professionals will need to assume more of a proactive stance than in years past. We believe this is essential to address the prevalent and systemic issues of stigma and discrimination, and thus is consistent with social justice imperatives (see Lee, 2007). This proactive stance will entail engaging in more outreach services (resembling those of assertive community treatment discussed earlier in the chapter), "courting" (*not* coercing) clients once contact has been established to enhance help-seeking behaviors (e.g., easing into a system of care by gradually connecting clients with specialized service providers), providing more services in the community (e.g., home-based and mobile/ambulatory care) rather than exclusively in a professional clinic, and adopting a multicultural philosophy of care that is system-wide or institutional, the practice of cultural congruence (Costantino et al., 2009; e.g., the entire staff is trained in and committed to culturally appropriate services). Practices such as these exemplify the helper's role as advocate for societal conditions that unfairly impact clients, a role that will continue to take center stage as mental health care transitions into a multicultural milieu. Ivey and Brooks-Harris (2005) described their vision of this milieu:

> Psychotherapists will recognize the importance of directly attacking systemic issues that affect client development. We will move toward a proactive stance rather than our present reactive stance. We need not expect our clients to work alone. Psychotherapists have an ethical imperative to work toward positive societal change. (pp. 335–336)

Therapeutic proactivity (fueled by the principle of social justice) is needed in light of prevalence data suggesting that approximately 30 percent of the U.S. population meet criteria for a mental disorder in a given 12-month period, specifically anxiety, mood, and substance use disorders (Kessler et al., 2005) using *DSM-IV* criteria (American Psychiatric Association, 2000a, *Diagnostic and Statistical Manual of Mental Disorders, DSM-IV-TR*). Only a minority of those with a serious mental disorder, however, received treatment (24 to 40.5 percent). This is particularly true for Mexican American and African American adults who meet criteria for major depression (González et al., 2010). Kessler and colleagues argue for practices that increase access to and demand for treatment

BOX 9.4	Five Interventions Relevant In Multicultural Practice

Liberation (vs. oppression) is the client's experience of release or freedom from oppressive barriers and control when change occurs. For some, it accompanies personal growth and decision-making: the client has decided to no longer submit to oppression. In other cases, liberation occurs under the influence of environmental change, for example, the introduction of a job training program or the election of an ethnic mayor who makes policy, legislative, and program changes on behalf of people of color.

Empowerment (vs. powerlessness) is a process in which persons who belong to a stigmatized social category can be assisted to develop and increase skills in the exercise of interpersonal influence. Claiming the human right to resources and well-being in society, individuals experience power by mobilizing their resources and changing their situational predicament. The first step to empowerment is to obtain information about resources and rights. Second, by choosing an appropriate path of action, the client participates in a situation in which his or her exercise of power confers palpable benefits. Practical avenues of empowerment include voting, influencing policy, or initiating legislation on the local level.

Parity (vs. exploitation) refers to equality. For people of color, parity entails achieving equal power, value, and rank with others in society and being treated accordingly. Its focal theme is fairness and the entitlement to certain rights. Parity is expressed in terms of resources that guarantee an adequate standard of living, such as entitlement programs (Social Security, Medicare), income maintenance, and medical care.

Maintenance of culture (vs. acculturation) asserts the importance of the ideas, customs, skills, arts, and language of a people. By tracing the history of an ethnic group, helper and client can identify moments of crisis and challenge through which it survived and triumphed. Applying such lessons of history to the present inspires the client to overcome obstacles by drawing on the strength of his or her cultural heritage. Maintenance of culture secures the client's identity as an ethnic individual.

Unique personhood (vs. stereotyping) is an intervention strategy by which stereotypes are transcended. Functional casework maintains that each person is unique in the helping relationship and that there is something extraordinary in each individual. When people of color act to gain freedom from negative social or societal generalizations, they assert their unique personhood and collective ethnic worth.

Source: From D. Lum, *Social Work Practice and People of Color: A Process–Stage Approach* (5th ed.), pp. 254–262. Copyright 2004. Wadsworth, a part of Cengage Learning, Inc. Reproduced by permission. www.cengage .com/permissions

by providing care/services in targeted locations intended to reach traditionally underserved groups. In an ethnic-specific mental health program, however, Akutsu, Tsuru, and Chu (2004) reported a 30 percent client attrition rate from prescreening to scheduled intake. Based on their inspection of retained clients, they recommend that the prescreening interviewer be able to speak the client's native language and that this same practitioner continue as the client's intake therapist.

Recruitment and retention of culturally diverse clients can also be accomplished by offering a "gift" at the conclusion of the first session (and perhaps after each of the first few sessions). Although Smolar (2003) describes the use of intangible "gifts" (e.g., helper self-disclosure, time, presence), Paniagua (2005) emphasizes the extension of tangible gifts to clients—or, what we might refer to as more specific or concrete gifts. Examples of specific and concrete gifts include the helper's explanation about presenting concerns, reassurances, educational literature, and a copy of the helper's professional disclosure statement (to convey the helper's qualifications, which some clients might interpret as reasons to trust in the helper's credibility). These and other gifts may reinforce to the client the helper's genuine concern and investment in the process of care and may also encourage the client to "reciprocate" by investing in the process of change. The American Counseling Association's (2014) *ACA Code of Ethics* acknowledges that "in some cultures, small gifts are a token of respect and gratitude" (Section A.10.f.), and some clients may be inclined to offer helpers a tangible gift. Helpers may encourage these clients to instead offer a gift to the process of helping (e.g., implementing a new behavior that has been practiced in therapy with a family member), to another client's efforts to heal (e.g., offering an encouraging word in a group session), or to the treatment facility (e.g., a painting done by the client to be placed in the lobby). Reframing the purpose of such gifts and redirecting clients to offer a gift to another recipient (e.g., to themselves, to another client) may be described for clients as an investment in their or another person's "good fortune."

Therapeutic proactivity may also be evidenced in the helper's maintaining contact with clients between sessions (e.g., encouraging clients to telephone the helper at specific times, such as prior to any parasuicidal behavior, as is recommended in dialectical behavior therapy) as well as after the helping process has concluded for the time being. Lo and Fung (2003) refer to this latter practice as keeping the "door ajar"; it may include scheduling check-in sessions (possibly held at a community setting, such as the public library) and periodic telephone contact. Such practice resembles Cummings's (1995) description of mental health care as the provision of intermittent services across the life span. This means that care is always available and extended, that clients "re-enroll" in the helping process when needs arise (e.g., reactivation of symptoms, major life transitions), and that closure or termination is never permanent.

Summary of Intentional Integration of Cultural Interventions

That all client-helper interactions are cross-cultural encounters reinforces rather than minimizes the need for the intentional integration of cultural interventions. This is evident in the National Standards for Culturally and Linguistically Appropriate Services (or CLAS) in Health and Health Care developed by the U.S. Department of Health and Human Services Office of Minority Health (2013), which can be accessed at www.thinkculturalhealth.hhs .gov. These 15 standards are intended to address demographic changes in the United States, eliminate health disparities, improve quality of services and care, and meet legislative, regulatory, and accreditation mandates (e.g., the Affordable Care Act). Note that these are services and not simply techniques. Services encompass techniques and include helper style (e.g., focus on relationship-building), mode of treatment, and treatment setting and philosophy (e.g., cultural congruence). In this way services embrace common factors (see Figures 9.1 and 9.2) and are comparable to interventions, as we have described them in this section.

To help you intentionally integrate cultural interventions in your professional practice, we encourage you to participate in Learning Activity 9.3. Before doing so,

review the five features of a mainstream multicultural milieu described in this section as well as the decision rules in treatment planning presented in the preceding section.

The Process of Treatment Planning

The choice of appropriate helping strategies is a joint **LO2** decision in which both client and helper are actively involved. We realize this is an activity that is easier said than done, and the challenge might explain the abundance of what we have heard as lip service paid to client-helper collaboration by many treatment providers. Helpers may speak of establishing rapport with clients but inadvertently jump in and begin assigning homework before a client is ready or even willing to consider change. In addition, treatment plans may not always reflect therapeutic collaboration. This is evident when there is a listing of all that the client will do but there is no corresponding list of what the practitioner will do to help the client implement all that has been planned. A lack of client-helper collaboration is also suspected when, upon inspection of one helper's treatment plans for all clients on his or her roster, one standard plan applied to all clients is discovered. This one-size-fits-all approach to treatment planning overlooks clients' idiosyncratic concerns and resources and yields a predetermined, unilateral, "hand-me-down" plan of care. We believe it is a misuse of the inherent influence of the helping process for the practitioner to select a strategy or to implement a treatment plan independent of the client's input.

Shared Decision-Making

Health care professionals have prioritized the contributions of clients in their own health care decisions. Known in general as shared decision-making (Adams & Drake, 2006), this interactive process assumes that both client and helper have important information to contribute to the helping process: helpers have information about and skills in diagnostic assessment, treatment strategies, and interpersonal communication; clients have information about their symptoms, cultural identity and context, and what has been helpful in the past (e.g., coping mechanisms), as well as what they believe will be helpful at this time. Although certain aspects of shared decision-making are not without controversy (e.g., Are persons with severe mental illnesses able to participate rationally and effectively in discussions about their own mental health care?), the general principle on which it is based—client-centered care—cannot be disputed.

A primary activity in shared decision-making is negotiation. To accomplish this, clients are encouraged to be full participants in the process of change and are regarded as "coagents in a problem-solving context" (Young & Flower, 2001, p. 70) and equal members of the treatment or care team (see Adams & Grieder, 2014). This includes child and adolescent clients and their parents. Fiks and Jimenez (2010) discuss the promise and challenges of shared decision-making in pediatrics.

Applied to individualized treatment planning, shared decision-making means that treatment goals and objectives are not imposed on clients; rather, they are negotiated. If a client balks at the helper's initial recommendation, then the helper might provide a clearer and more detailed explanation about why he or she thinks this particular strategy would be helpful at this time. If a client remains adamantly opposed to seeing a psychiatrist to determine the appropriateness of psychotropic medication, for example (even after the helper has carefully explained his or her reasons for recommending this), the helper might propose an alternative strategy, such as having the client view a video that features persons who claim to have benefited from taking psychotropic medications, or having the client conduct a search on the Internet to determine the reported benefits and side effects of a particular medication. Certainly the helper needs to uphold professional ethics by not agreeing to substandard care that would knowingly place the client in certain danger. In the previous example, this might mean that the helper offer three options to the client—consult with a psychiatrist, watch the video, or conduct an Internet search—and indicate that the client will need to fulfill one of these to continue in this mode and at this level of care (e.g., individual outpatient therapy).

Documenting the Plan of Care

Many different formats are used to document the negotiated treatment plan, but we believe all must include the

following elements, which we have adapted from Maruish (2002, p. 133):

- Referral source and reason for referral
- Presenting complaint and additional/related concerns
- Client strengths and resources
- Client liabilities and potential barriers to treatment
- Diagnosis
- Goals negotiated by helper and client (vision of client improvement; destination)
- Treatment objectives (means or methods for achieving negotiated goals and arriving at envisioned destination)
- Helper interventions (i.e., specific activities and strategies that the helper will introduce, conduct, and facilitate)
- Client implementations (i.e., specific activities the client will engage in and fulfill, many of which will correspond to the helper interventions listed)
- Referral for evaluation
- Length, duration, and pace/frequency of treatment
- Criteria for treatment termination or transfer
- Treatment plan review date
- Prognosis (i.e., helper's prediction of client status/improvement by the review date)
- Responsible staff (individual helper, multidisciplinary treatment team members)

Figure 9.3 is a sample outpatient treatment planning form. It represents many forms currently used by practitioners in various human services settings. You can see that this form incorporates many of the elements listed above. It also serves a variety of functions and ties together the principles and practices emphasized in this chapter.

As we have emphasized, clinical decision-making and treatment planning constitute an ongoing, interactive process of care. However, a tangible document is necessary to record the nature and outcome of these client-helper interactions. Think of this document as a combination syllabus and grade/report card: it reminds client and helper about their joint decisions (e.g., "Okay, what are our respective assignments over the next 15 weeks of the semester?"), guides them on their adventure (i.e., serves as a map), and evaluates (i.e., grades) their progress along the way. Without such a document, both client and helper would likely get confused about the point of their meetings—not to say anything about getting lost!

To remain attentive to client needs and preferences, we recommend charting a direct route rather than a scenic route to the client's destination (i.e., treatment goals). Co-constructing and maintaining a written map (treatment plan) is more likely to ensure an expeditious route than is a protracted or long, drawn-out scenic route. The written plan is likely to keep the client and

9.3 Feedback

Gender and Multicultural Factors in Treatment Planning and Selection

Consider these guidelines about your plan for Ms. Wiggins:

1. To what extent does your treatment plan reflect a culturally attentive (or perhaps a *culturally resonant*) agreement? How might it even be an example of a mainstream multicultural milieu taking formation? In other words, how has the treatment plan been influenced by Ms. Wiggins's *contextual awareness* and *consciousness development,* or *therapeutic proactivity*? For example, have you considered that Ms. Wiggins is a low-income European American woman who has lived in the same rural community all her life surrounded by family and friends from church? She holds herself responsible for the rape and also feels powerless to get help from local authorities, who in fact have been unresponsive to her requests for assistance.

2. How has your plan addressed the impact of *contextual factors* or the client's *social system,* including oppressive conditions within that system? Have you noted that Ms. Wiggins is a poor white woman living with a husband on disability due to poor health in a rural area near a small town, that their complaints to local authorities have not been taken seriously, and that the man who raped her is related to a deputy in the sheriff's office? In essence, she feels disempowered and silenced by the system. Also, Ms. Wiggins views the rape at this time as a "female" problem and does not yet really see it as an act of social violence and misuse of power.

3. In what ways has your plan addressed any relevant *indigenous practices, supports,* and *resources*? Ms. Wiggins reports herself to be a very spiritual person who relies on the power of prayer to help her through tough times. How has your plan considered the role of important *subsystems* in the client's life? For this client, the most important subsystems are her family and her church. However, with the exception of her husband, who supports her, she feels cut off from both of these subsystems because of the nature of the issue, her own views about it, and her fears of her friends' and family's reactions.

4. Does your plan reflect the client's view of *health, recovery,* and *ways of solving problems*? For example, spirituality seems to play an important role in the way Ms. Wiggins solves problems. Gender also appears to

be an issue. She seems to feel that a female helper would be better equipped to help her with this issue (consider a referral to a woman helper and/or to a women's support group).

5. Have you considered the *level of acculturation* and any *language preferences* she has (also the use of culturally relevant themes, scripts, proverbs, and metaphors)? Implied in this framework are the following issues that should be considered: the role of the general history of Ms. Wiggins; the geographic location in which she lives and how long she has lived there; the type of setting; her socioeconomic status, age, gender, and role; and the specific effects of all of this on her language use and comprehension. Ms. Wiggins is a relatively young white woman on a limited and fixed income who has lived all her life in the same area—an isolated rural area near a small town. These demographics make for some interesting contradictions: she had felt safe living in this region—safe enough to keep doors unlocked—yet she has been raped. The area is small enough to know who lives in it and who is a stranger, yet she has no support from the local sheriff's office because the assailant in this case (rather than the victim) is a relative of a deputy.

   Influenced by the societal and cultural norms of the area, Ms. Wiggins feels ashamed about what has happened to her. All these things are likely to affect your plan. For example, she may not trust you because you are a male and an outsider. Also, she may view you as part of a social system that, in her eyes, is similar to the sheriff's office. The themes of cultural mistrust and gender-linked shame can be addressed in the types of treatment you use with Ms. Wiggins.

6. How does the proposed *length* of your plan meet the needs and the perspective of Ms. Wiggins? To what extent does her willingness to return for additional sessions depend on the gender of the helper? How will her income and her husband's disability status affect her ability to come in for more sessions? Does your agency offer free services or a sliding scale for low-income clients? If not, how can you be her advocate so she can receive the number of sessions she needs?

7. Did you list some or any of the following *oppressive forces* that Ms. Wiggins needs to name, validate, and resist, such as local authorities and people in her church and family who would shame her or make her feel guilty about being raped or who would not believe her?

helper on track. And, as we've noted in this chapter, clients presenting with acute symptoms and clients of various racial/ethnic groups prefer a direct, concrete, clear, and expeditious plan of care. The direct route is also consistent with evidence-based practice and makes judicious use of time and other resources. For these and other reasons, third-party payers (e.g., insurance companies) require a written and updated treatment plan.

TREATMENT PLAN

Client Name: _____   Client File No.: _____

Therapist: _____   Supervisor: _____

Treatment Start Date: _____   Treatment End Date (Est.): _____

Presenting Concerns	Strengths/Resources	Goals and Measures	Therapist Interventions and Client Implementations	Duration
1.				
2.				
3.				
4.				

_____   _____   _____   _____
Client   Parent (if client under 18)   Therapist   Supervisor

FIGURE 9.3 Sample Treatment Planning Form

Source: Adapted from Quin Curtis Center for Psychological Service, Training, and Research. Eberly College of Arts and Sciences, West Virginia University. Used with permission of William Fremouw, Ph.D., Director.

Can you imagine agreeing to pay for a trip for someone else without that person providing you with an itinerary? This could be likened to writing a blank check! Therefore, it makes sense that insurance companies want to see proof of how their money is being spent. This "proof" is the written treatment plan.

As you inspect the sample treatment plan form in Figure 9.3, notice that it serves to summarize information obtained from the assessment process in which the client's presenting concerns, as well as his or her strengths and resources, have been identified. The form also makes use of the methods of measuring and evaluating client status and progress toward arriving at the destination (or treatment goal). Notice that collaborative decision-making emphasized in this chapter is evident in the separation of treatment strategies into "therapist interventions" and "client implementations." The treatment plan form serves many functions and has a wider audience beyond the client and helper. This audience (all of whom have the right and the responsibility to inspect and approve the document once the client has given proper consent or assent) includes the client's parent/guardian (if the client is younger than 18 years of age), the helper's supervisor, and a third party who has been asked to pay the bill (e.g., insurance company representative, county mental health board director). Given these many different eyes reviewing the treatment plan form (now and possibly for years to come), we cannot emphasize enough the importance of accurate, timely, legible, and coherent documentation.

We believe that the process of treatment planning is most effective when the helper actively uses a form such as the one depicted in Figure 9.3 during the assessment, goal-setting, evaluation, and treatment selection sessions. In the spirit of shared decision-making, the client needs to be regarded as an active participant in and contributor to the completion of this form. We also recommend that the form should allow for client comments and that, without question, the client's signature and date of signing is documented. Although helpers would first need to consult agency and third-party payer policies, as well as state law, consideration may be given to supplying the client with a copy of the completed and signed treatment plan for ongoing reference.

When interventions in a treatment plan are reviewed, two questions are typically asked (Leahy, Holland, & McGinn, 2011, p. 7):

1. Does the level of care match the severity of the client's symptoms and issues? (Recall, for example, the six client dimensions and the five levels of care that comprise *The ASAM Criteria* for the treatment of substance use and other addictive disorders, discussed on page 313.)

2. Is the proposed treatment approach appropriate, given the client's symptoms and issues?

Most clients will present with complex problems necessitating a diverse set of outcome goals. Addressing these will require a set of interventions and a combination of strategies designed to work with all the major target areas of a person's functioning. Both helper and client should be active participants in developing a treatment plan and selecting treatment strategies that are appropriate for the client's concerns and desired outcomes. The strategies reflected in the overall treatment plan should be relevant to the client's gender and culture, sufficient to deal with all the important target areas of change, and matched, as well as possible, to the response components of the defined issue as well as to the client's level of impairment, resistance, and coping style. After the strategies have been selected, the helper and client will continue to work together to implement the procedures, to evaluate the results, and to work toward a planned termination process once the client's goals are achieved. These are all consistent with shared decision-making and collaborative cultural practice.

Model Dialogue: Exploring Treatment Strategies

In this dialogue, the helper explores and helps Isabella plan some of the treatment strategies that could help decrease her nervousness about math class and her anticipation of rejection from her parents. Note that all three strategies suggested are based on Isabella's diagnostic pattern of specific (focal) anxiety, as opposed to generalized anxiety.

In the initial part of the interview, the helper summarizes the previous session and introduces Isabella to the idea of *exploring treatment strategies*. Notice the helper's emphasis on Isabella's *preferences*.

1. **Helper:** Last week, Isabella, we talked about some of the things you would like to see happen as a result of counseling. One of the things you indicated as pretty important to you was being able to do more initiating. You mentioned things like wanting to be able to ask questions or make responses, express your opinions, and express your feelings. Together we decided that one thing that keeps you from doing these things more often is what we called the apprehension you feel in certain situations with your parents or in math class. There are several ways we might deal with this apprehension. I thought today we might explore some

activities that may help. These are things we can do together to help you get where you want to be. How does that sound?

Client: Okay. I just really need to find a way to feel less nervous and more comfortable with my parents, and in math.

In the next response, the helper tries to explain to Isabella the collaborative process of treatment planning (notice the helper's use of "we"), which necessitates *Isabella's input*—that is, Isabella being able to verbalize in session (*in vivo* practice of targeted goal) what will be helpful for her.

2. **Helper:** Yeah, it's gotten to the point for you that something has to change. One thing to keep in mind is that there are no easy answers and there is not necessarily one right way. What we can do today is explore some ways that are typically used to help people be less nervous in specific situations and try to come up with a way that *you* think works best for you. I'll give you some information about these activities to help you decide which ones you want to use.

Client: Okay.

In responses 3 and 4, the helper suggests possible strategies for Isabella to consider. The helper also explains how one intervention strategy, relaxation, *is related to Isabella's concerns and can help her achieve her goal*. Because there does not seem to be *resistance* between Isabella and the helper (i.e., they both seem to agree on the plan for this session), note throughout this process that the helper will be more directive and will offer guidance and suggestions.

3. **Helper:** From my experience, I believe there are a couple of things that might help you manage your nervousness to the point where you don't feel as if you have to avoid the situation. First of all, when you're nervous, you're tense. Sometimes when you're tense, you feel bad or sick or just out of control. One thing we could do is to teach you some relaxation skills. Relaxation can help you learn to identify when you're starting to feel nervous, and it can help you manage this before it gets so strong you just skip class or refuse to speak up. Does this make sense?

Client: Yeah, it does, because when I really let myself get nervous, I don't want to say anything. Sometimes I force myself to, but I'm still nervous, and I don't feel like it.

4. **Helper:** That's a good point. You don't have the energy or desire to do something you're apprehensive about.

Sometimes, for some people, just learning to relax and control your nervousness might be enough. If you want to try this first and it helps you be less nervous to the point where you can take more initiative, then that's fine. However, there are some other things we might do also, so I'd like you to know about these action plans, too.

Client: Like what?

The helper proposes an additional intervention strategy in response 5 and indicates how this procedure can help Isabella decrease her nervousness by *describing how it is also related to Isabella's concern and goal.*

5. **Helper:** Well, one procedure has a very interesting name—it's called "stress inoculation." You know when you get a shot like tetanus, the shot helps to prevent or inoculate you from getting tetanus. Well, this procedure helps you to prevent yourself from getting so overwhelmed in a stressful situation such as your math class or with your parents that you want to avoid the situation or don't want to say anything.

Client: Is it painful like a shot?

The helper provides more information about what stress inoculation would involve from Isabella in terms of the *time, advantages, and risks of the procedure;* this information should help Isabella assess her preferences and be able to make an *empowered consent.* The helper also alludes to one of Isabella's *strengths* and how this can be used to facilitate the implementation of one of the recommended strategies.

6. **Helper:** No, not like that, although it would involve some work on your part. In addition to learning the relaxation skills I mentioned earlier, you would learn how to cope with stressful situations—through relaxing your body and thinking some thoughts that would help you handle these difficult or competitive situations. You are a bright young woman and so I am confident that, with practice here, you will be able to do this successfully with me. We'll then work on how you can start to do it in your math class and with your folks. Once you learn the relaxation, it will probably take several sessions to learn the other parts to it. The advantage of stress management is that it helps you learn how to cope with rather than avoid a stressful situation. Of course, it does require you to practice the relaxation and coping skills on your own, and this takes some time each day, but you strike me as someone who is up to meeting challenges. And without

this sort of daily practice, this procedure may not be that helpful.

Client: It does sound interesting. Have you used it a lot?

The helper indicates some *information and advantages* about the strategy based on the helper's *experience,* training, and use of it with others in this setting. The helper also makes reference to *evidence-based practice* that it has been beneficial with a wide range of persons, adults *and* adolescents, male *and* female, racially and ethnically diverse persons (therefore, *culturally appropriate*).

7. **Helper:** I tend to use it, or portions of it, whenever I think people could benefit from learning to manage nervousness and not let stressful situations control them. I know other counselors have used it and found that people experiencing different kinds of stressors—including stress from racial discrimination—can benefit from it. Some research even suggests that it is helpful for a lot of people, younger and older persons, too. So it has a lot of potential if you're in a situation where your nervousness is getting the best of you and when you can learn to cope with the stress. Another advantage of this procedure is that it is pretty comprehensive. By that, I mean it deals with different parts of a nervous reaction—like the part of you that gets sweaty palms and butterflies in your stomach, the part of you that thinks girls are dumb in math or girls don't have much to say, and then the part of you that goes out of your way to avoid these sticky situations. It's kind of like going shopping and getting a whole outfit—jeans, shirt, and shoes—rather than just the shoes or just the shirt.

Client: Well, it sounds okay to me. It's something that might even help persons who've experienced racism. Knowing that is pretty important to me. I also like the idea of the relaxation that you mentioned earlier.

The helper moves on in response 8 to describe another possible treatment strategy, explaining what this involves and how it might help Isabella manage her nervousness, and *relates the use of the procedure to her concern and goal.*

8. **Helper:** There's also another procedure called "imaginal exposure" that is a pretty standard one to help decrease anxiety about situations. It's a way to help you desensitize yourself to the stress of your math class.

Client: What do you mean by desensitize?

9. **Helper:** It means to be less sensitive to. In some ways it is like the inoculation I mentioned. The goal is for you to respond with less nervousness to what have been

for you stressful situations, including thinking about those situations. Does that help?

Client: Yeah, okay. That makes sense. But how exactly does this "exposure" work? Do I face head-on what I'm afraid of?

The helper explains how this strategy can help Isabella decrease her nervousness and explains *elements, advantages, and risks* of this strategy (again, information provided so that Isabella can make an *empowered consent*).

10. **Helper:** Well, it works on the principle that you can't be relaxed and nervous at the same time. So, after learning how to relax, then you imagine situations involving your math class—or with your folks. However, you imagine a situation *only* when you're relaxed, so it's not like you're expected to throw yourself into a stressful situation without being ready or prepared for it. That would likely do more harm than good, actually, and so it's my responsibility to help you get prepared by teaching you how to practice. You practice the skill to the point where you can speak up in class or with your folks without feeling all the nervousness you do now. Most of this process is something we would do together in these sessions and is an advantage over something requiring a lot of outside work on your part.

Client: Does that take a long time?

The helper gives Isabella some information about the *time* or *duration* involved.

11. **Helper:** This may take a little longer than the other two procedures. This procedure has helped a great many people decrease their nervousness about specific situations—like taking a test or flying. Of course, keep in mind that any change plan takes some time.

Client: It sounds helpful.

The helper points out more of the *time factors* and the *mode (individual)* involved in these procedures. Also, notice the helper's continued reference to collaboration ("we" language).

12. **Helper:** We would be working together in these individual sessions for several months.

Client: That's okay. I have study hall during this period, and I usually just talk to my friends then anyway.

In response 13, the helper reinforces that this planning is *collaborative* (e.g., participation in *shared decision-making*) and again makes reference to *evidence-based practice.*

13. **Helper:** I'd like us to make the decision together. The procedures I've described have been found to be pretty effective for many people who are concerned about working on their nervousness in certain situations so that it isn't a handicap. In fact, for some of these procedures there are even guidelines I can give you so you can practice on your own.

Client: I'm wondering exactly how to decide where to go from here.

In response 14, the helper elicits information about *client preferences.* Also, the helper alludes to a written document (*treatment plan*) that the helper and Isabella will be reviewing together (client-helper *collaboration*), one that is subject to change and one that will help keep them on track.

14. **Helper:** Perhaps if we reviewed the action plans I've mentioned and go over them, you can see which one you feel might work best for you, at least for now. We can always change something at a later point. How does that sound?

Client: Good. There's a lot of information, and I don't know if I remember everything you mentioned.

In response 15, the helper itemizes and summarizes the possible change strategies (which are entered on the written *treatment plan*), which help map out the route both Isabella and the helper have agreed to take on this adventure. Note that the strategies are directed toward Isabella's predominant *coping style (internalizing)*, which also indicates the helper's attempt to *individualize care* by incorporating Isabella's *strengths and resources.*

15. **Helper:** Okay. We talked first about relaxation as something you could learn here and then do on your own to help you control the feelings and physical sensations of nervousness. Then we discussed stress inoculation, which involves giving you a lot of different skills to use to cope with the stressful situations in your math class. The third plan, imaginal exposure, involves using relaxation first but also involves having you imagine the scenes related to your math class and to interactions with your parents. This procedure is something we would work on together, although the relaxation requires daily practice from you. What do you think would be most helpful to you at this point?

Client: I think maybe the relaxation might help, because I can practice it on my own. It also sounds like it's really simple to do, not really time-wise, but in what's involved.

In response 16, the helper pursues the option that Isabella has been leaning toward during the session, thus building on *client preferences*. Because Isabella's *level of impairment* is low, the helper will suggest *weekly sessions*.

16. **Helper:** That's a good point. Of the three procedures I mentioned, relaxation training is probably the easiest and simplest to learn to use. You have also mentioned once or twice before in our session that you were intrigued with this idea, so it looks as if you've been mulling it over for a little while and it still sounds appealing and workable to you. If so, we can start working with it today. Then I would like to see you once every week during this time if that is possible for you.

CHAPTER SUMMARY

Throughout this chapter we have offered several analogies to the process of treatment plan construction, as well as to the actual written document (i.e., the treatment plan form):

- Treatment planning is a joint venture or *journey* undertaken by both client and helper.
- Treatment planning is an integrative process that takes into consideration the "forest *and* the trees."
- The treatment plan is a *map* constructed jointly by the client and helper: each treatment goal is a destination (or vision of client improvement), and each intervention is the route or the vehicle taken to arrive at that destination.
- The treatment plan is a combination of a *course syllabus* (i.e., outlining the helper's and the client's respective "assignments") and a *report/grade card* (i.e., an evaluation of progress made, conducted at different points in time).

To this list we now add a fifth analogy, that of a household *grocery list*. This analogy emphasizes the importance of individualized client care because just as no two households are alike, no two grocery lists are alike! If a family member loses the grocery list on the way to the grocery store, it won't make sense to borrow another customer's list. In addition, when a household consists of more than one person, each member of the household may have some say in what gets entered on the list. In a similar manner, treatment plans represent the "collection site" or the repository for the preferences of all persons involved in a particular client's care (e.g., referral source, parent/guardian, supervisor, members of a multidisciplinary treatment team). Furthermore, treatment plans, just like grocery lists, are time-sensitive. They are useful only for a specified period of time because they represent current client concerns, similar to current household needs. Now, unlike a grocery list, a new treatment plan is probably not needed every week! However, the treatment plan certainly needs to be reviewed and revised on a regular basis, and we suggest that it be updated with each client session and progress note completed.

There are clearly guidelines and decision rules to follow in the construction of a map, combined syllabus and grade/report card, and grocery list. These include information presented in this chapter on common factors and differential treatments, evidence-based practice, and models of treatment planning (e.g., matching client to levels and types of care), as well as information provided in previous chapters on assessment and the construction of treatment goals. Without these protocols, clients and helpers would be lost. There are also spectacles or other visual aids to use to view both general and idiosyncratic information in clinical decision-making and treatment planning. We have stated that this allows practitioners to be able to see both the "forest *and* the trees." These lenses include the vision proposed of a mainstream multicultural milieu, one that accounts for and prioritizes the cultural identities and contexts of all clients, and one that is realized in therapeutic proactivity and social justice efforts. Like any clinical activity conducted on behalf of another person's (or family's) wellbeing, clinical decision-making and treatment planning should be entered into humbly and handled with great care.

 Visit CengageBrain.com for a variety of study tools and useful resources such as video examples, case studies, interactive exercises, flashcards, and quizzes.

9 | Knowledge and Skill Builder

Part One

In this section we describe the case of Karen, adapted from González-Prendes and Thomas (2009), and discuss a preliminary treatment plan for her. After you read the case, identify the following: (1) ways in which the selected treatment interventions used by the helper failed to address either contextual awareness or consciousness development; (2) how the helper interpreted the client's distress (and perhaps resistance); (3) which of Lum's (2004) five interventions (see Box 9.4 on page 324) the helper could have emphasized; and (4) the recommended type, duration, and mode of treatment you would follow as Karen's helper. Feedback follows on page 000.

"Karen" is a 51-year-old single African American woman with one adult daughter and two grandchildren. She has a master's degree in education and has completed all coursework for a doctoral degree in counseling. She has been a public school teacher for nearly 30 years and is well liked and respected by her students and colleagues. Karen comes from a family in which women were viewed as strong, determined, self-reliant, and working to improve their lives by achieving their highest potential. She is the oldest of three children, raised in low-income housing by a single mother who worked full-time as an attorney after completing law school.

Karen has entered counseling on the advice of her primary care physician. She has been experiencing headaches, high blood pressure, poor sleep, and fatigue. She also acknowledges that over the past year she has struggled with periodic bouts of depression, crying spells, and anger. During the first counseling session, Karen also shares that she has experienced a number of losses in the past 18 months, including the deaths of three family members. Her daughter also was recently diagnosed with a malignant brain tumor and Karen is now serving as primary caregiver for her daughter, her two grandchildren, and her aging mother, who has her own health issues.

Upon further questioning, Karen describes the steady deterioration of the atmosphere at the public school where she teaches, including increased gang activity and violence inside the school and in the surrounding area. Karen says she and other teachers feel unsafe and believe they have not been provided with adequate resources to perform their duties and that the school administration does not seem to care about improving the educational environment.

Teaching has been Karen's passion, and so she is very frustrated with what she describes as a chaotic work environment and her diminishing ability to continue to advocate for students who are underprivileged. Karen acknowledges feeling angry while also blaming herself for being "weak" and "not strong enough" to do more for her students. She describes a pattern of experiencing a setback or adversity, followed by anger ("holding my tongue" more than expressing it) and then depression.

After completing the Brief Symptom Inventory (Derogatis, 1993), the helper reviews with Karen her elevated scores in the areas of depression, anxiety, and hostility. Karen also had been asked to rate the frequency and intensity of her anger episodes for the 4 weeks prior to entering counseling. Karen reported experiencing 2 to 3 anger episodes weekly with an average intensity of 8 or 9 on a scale from 0 (*no anger*) to 10 (*enraged*). After reviewing these ratings, the helper encourages Karen to maintain contact with her physician and to adhere to any medication regimen prescribed.

The helper proceeds to inquire about Karen's ability to take a leave of absence from work or even to begin a plan for retirement, given her recent family losses and her increased caregiving responsibilities. "You've already proven yourself to be a very capable woman," the helper tells her. "I'm sure your mother is very proud of you, following in her accomplished footsteps." Karen responds that she is committed to her teaching responsibilities and is not yet ready to retire. The helper then suggests that grief work should be the focus of treatment and recommends a grief support group in the community for Karen to attend. "I think this could also help you determine whether it's time for hospice to step in for your daughter," the helper states. Karen's participation in session at this point is very minimal—she provides only cursory responses and becomes increasingly quiet. Near the end of the session, the helper comments that Karen's quiet demeanor may actually represent the beginning of important grief work, which will help address her depression in subsequent sessions. "One thing at a time, you know," the helper states. "We don't want to move too quickly." When asked to assess their counseling session, Karen politely states that she really wanted to address her anger, not grief, and that she may not return.

Questions

1. How did the treatment interventions used by this helper not take into consideration Karen's cultural context and consciousness development?
2. How did the helper appear to interpret Karen's distress?
3. Which of Lum's (2004) five interventions (see Box 9.4 on page 324) could the helper have emphasized in working with Karen?
4. If you were Karen's helper, what type, duration, and mode of treatment would you use? Provide information to support your choices.

Part Two

Learning Outcome 2 asks you to develop in writing a treatment plan for a given client case using a sample treatment planning form modeled after the one in Figure 9.3 on page 328. Identify the presenting concern, strengths and resources, goals, measures, and treatment interventions. If

(*continued*)

9 | Knowledge and Skill Builder (*continued*)

you currently have a client caseload of your own, we suggest you do this for one of your actual clients and consult with your supervisor, a colleague, or your instructor after you and your client complete the treatment planning form. If you are a student and do not yet have clients, we suggest you use the case of Isabella based on the model dialogue that begins on page 329. After reviewing the dialogue between Isabella

and her helper, identify at least two of Isabella's presenting concerns. Once you have done so, identify goals and measures that correspond to each of the concerns you listed. Assess Isabella's strengths and resources and incorporate these into your formulation of therapist interventions and client implementations. Feedback for the case of Isabella follows on (Figure 9.4).

TREATMENT PLAN

Client Name: _Isabella_____   Client File No.: _____

Therapist: _____   Supervisor: _____

Treatment Start Date: _____   Treatment End Date (Est.): _____

Presenting Concerns	Strengths/Resources	Goals and Measures	Therapist Interventions and Client Implementations	Duration
1. Decreased academic performance, irregular class attendance	Expressed desire to do well academically	Consecutive class attendance, next 2 weeks	A. Math teacher consultation B. Client meets with teacher after class, twice per week	2 weeks
2. Math anxiety	Awareness of symptoms related to anxiety	Reduce anxiety from 70 to 50 on 100-point SUDS scale	A. Exposure therapy B. Client implement new self-talk (replace "girls are dumb" with "girls are capable")	4 weeks
3. Socially withdrawn, indecisive, acquiescent, inability to assert preferences and opinions	Self-perceptive, observant of others' behaviors, recognition of desired skills, openness to corrective feedback	Use of 4 initiating skills, at least 1–3 week	A. Collaborative construction of therapist-observed and client-reported values, opinions, preferences B. In-session role play of conversation with peers C. Client video record herself standing up and verbalizing opinion and preference to peers, view three times per week	4 weeks
4. Parental pressure to succeed	Parental concern, client willingness to involve parents in sessions	Parental clarification of concerns, family session in 1 week	A. Schedule family session B. Client verbalize directly to parents one thing most helpful and one thing least helpful in their communications with her over past week	1 week

_____   _____   _____   _____
Client   Parent (if client under 18)   Therapist   Supervisor

FIGURE 9.4 Treatment Planning Form Applied to the Case of Isabella

Source: Adapted from Quin Curtis Center for Psychological Service, Training, and Research, Eberly College of Arts and Sciences, West Virginia University. Used with permission of William Fremouw, Ph.D., Director.

9 | Knowledge and Skill Builder **Feedback**

Part One

1. It is not apparent that the helper engaged Karen in a discussion about Karen's contextual awareness or even oriented Karen to the helping process (e.g., helper's competencies and philosophy of professional care). Although standard assessment tools were administered and reviewed with Karen, the helper's focus on grief was not based on Karen's responses. Indeed, it appears that the helper dismissed relevant presenting symptoms and client concerns (e.g., anger) in favor of the helper's own preference and comfort level. Furthermore, no consideration seems to have been given to Karen's consciousness development, such as Karen's understanding of her cultural identity at this time in her life, the meaning for her of being raised by a strong-willed, determined, and accomplished African American mother, and her commitment to helping the underprivileged students in the school where she has taught for 30 years.

2. There is no indication that the helper took the time to understand Karen's symptoms and the meaning of her distress, including racism-related distress. It may be that Karen would have been more of an active participant in conversations with the helper if Karen's initial somatic complaints were taken seriously (i.e., validated). It appears that the helper "jumped right in" and made the unilateral decision that grief was Karen's prominent concern. Indeed, we would characterize the helper's manner with Karen as patronizing, condescending, and even demeaning— the helper seemed to suggest that Karen would not be able to address her concerns unless she took a leave of absence or even began planning for her retirement from work that has been fulfilling. The helper also insinuated that Karen's accomplishments were done to please her mother only and that Karen is at a time in her life when her family should receive more of Karen's care than her students.

3. We would have recommended that the helper use Lum's (2004) interventions of *liberation* (i.e., freeing herself from the immobilizing anger she has experienced),

empowerment (e.g., healthy expression and assertion of understandable anger), and *maintenance of culture* (e.g., collective strength of her African American female cultural heritage rather than strength as Karen's sole responsibility), and Karen may have been more amenable to the process of professional helping if various options had been explored with her, such as her involvement in the teachers' union at her school. This may have helped Karen feel empowered within her cultural context. Taking the time to conduct a Cultural Analysis would have supplied this valuable information.

4. As Karen's helper, it is important first to clarify Karen's preferences and expectations for the helping process because they may be different from your own. It is also important to select a type of treatment that honors and respects Karen's cultural values—perseverance and resisting oppression and other forms of limitation, and serving as a role model to others. Interventions that focus on cognitive reframing, enhanced cultural self-awareness that empowers rather than stifles, and behavioral skills that equip Karen to diffuse the stranglehold of anger and liberate herself from the immobilizing anger she has experienced may be more consistent with Karen's cultural identity and heritage than focusing exclusively on loss and grief at this point. Karen appears to have an *internalizing coping style* and therefore a structured yet supportive therapeutic approach is indicated, one that provides Karen with specific skills so that she is equipped to manage prominent symptoms. The *duration* of treatment may be short-term, but it may extend beyond six to eight sessions depending on Karen's need and preference for further assistance. Individual counseling is the recommended *mode* of treatment, but this may be complemented by one or two sessions of family therapy as well as Karen's involvement in a support group of her choosing.

Part Two

If you used the case of Isabella, check your responses with the ones in Figure 9.4 on p. 334.

Models for Working with Resistance
Solution-Focused Therapy and Motivational Interviewing

After completing this chapter, you will be able to identify, in writing, using a client case description and client-helper dialogue, at least three strategies to use from each of the following approaches:

1. Solution-focused therapy approaches
2. Motivational interviewing approaches
3. Combined solution-focused therapy and motivational interviewing approaches

Partnering with Client Experience

Think back to a time when you were annoyed by someone's suggestion that you do something different or change something about yourself. Perhaps a good friend advised you to make what you considered to be a drastic or an unnecessary change in your appearance (e.g., hairstyle, wardrobe). Maybe a family member strongly suggested that you change a certain habit or change the status of a relationship you were in with someone else (e.g., sever ties with a significant other). Although the suggestion may have been well intentioned, you may have been frustrated with what you interpreted as another's interference in your life.

This experience may not be unlike that of many clients when they first seek out a professional helper. A good number of clients arrive at the helper's office to appease someone else or to comply with a mandate. They may enter into a helping relationship feeling angry or fearful about what is to come; they may think they do not need to be talking to a helper, let alone making any significant changes in their lives. Although some type of change may be necessary (i.e., to ensure mental and physical health), it may not always be

welcomed with enthusiasm or embraced wholeheartedly. It may be stalled for a period of time, entered into begrudgingly, or defied altogether. This is very common.

In this chapter we discuss such responses to change as *resistance, reactance, reluctance,* and *ambivalence,* and we describe them as normal features of the change process. We view the helping relationship as a partnership between client and helper, and therefore both partners are involved in a process of change. We depict this change process as a type of dance between client and helper, wherein the helper works and moves *with* the client instead of *against* the client toward change. Rather than regarding resistance, reactance, reluctance, and ambivalence as missteps or stumbles, we see them as dance steps that clients and helpers use in their work together and how the helper uses them will determine how the client and helper dance together. Two helping styles that are conducive to working with and through resistance, reactance, reluctance, and ambivalence are offered and discussed here: solution-focused therapy and motivational interviewing. Specific strategies are described to assist helpers learn how to dance with their clients toward positive change.

Resistance, Reactance, Reluctance, and Ambivalence

Resistance, reactance, reluctance, and ambivalence comprise a range of human behaviors in response to change. It is not uncommon for one of them to be expressed when change is perceived as mandatory, threatening, urgent, or at least necessary; all four responses are influenced by personal characteristics of the client and helper (e.g., attitudes) and situations or contexts (e.g., helping relationship). Each of these four behaviors is not discrete. They are all highly interrelated and therefore can be thought of as a family of behaviors in response to change.

Resistance

Resistance in therapy is often and automatically associated with and descriptive of client behavior, in part because helpers typically are the ones to make an interpretation of resistance. Indeed, the noun *resistance* often is presented with the modifier *client,* and the adjective *resistant* commonly precedes *client.* Clients who pose particular challenges in session, who are thought of as "difficult," are often regarded as "resistant." This might be true for clients who habitually cancel or arrive late for sessions, appear unwilling to recognize problems and accept responsibility, do not follow through on tasks discussed and agreed upon in previous sessions, and contest the helper's expertise or integrity. These and other behaviors describe what is often referred to as *treatment resistance* and may be explained by the client's expectations about what therapy can or should accomplish (Leahy, 2010). Persons with certain anxiety disorders, for example, may resist helper recommendations to engage in an exposure intervention because they anticipate the activation of fear.

Westra and Arkowitz (2010) argue that resistance is one of the most challenging therapeutic issues to navigate successfully. One reason for this challenge is defining it. Resistance is not a unitary construct. It is a complex and ubiquitous phenomenon that defies a quick and simple definition (Arkowitz, 2002; Engle & Arkowitz, 2006). One early definition of resistance is any client statement that blocks or somehow impedes the helper's efforts toward change (Chamberlain, Patterson, Reid, Kavanagh, & Forgatch, 1984).

Newman (2002) suggested that resistance is difficult to define because it is linked to helpers' theoretical orientations. All major theories of psychotherapy address resistance. From a cognitive behavioral perspective, resistance is generally defined as the client's attempts to prevent or restore losses (e.g., sense of freedom, safety, integrity, power) anticipated during a personal change process such as therapy (Beutler & Harwood, 2000). Contemporary psychoanalytic thinking regards resistance as the client's in-therapy behavior that exemplifies transference and therefore is connected to the analyst or therapist (Wolitzky, 2011). The family of existential-humanistic therapies views resistance as internal and interpersonal blockage that serves as client self-protection (Schneider, 2011). Motivational interviewing also defines

resistance interpersonally, characterizing it as a disturbance in the client-counselor relationship, or simply as discord (W. R. Miller & Rollnick, 2013).

Reactance

A related concept is **reactance**, discussed in Chapter 5. Reactance is "a motivational state...[with] energizing properties that drive individuals to engage in freedom-restoration behaviors" (Miron & Brehm, 2006, p. 10). Reactance comprises the behaviors exhibited (e.g., opposition, defiance) and the feelings experienced (e.g., frustration, rage) when an individual's personal freedom (e.g., ability to choose among several options) has been threatened or eliminated (e.g., all but one option has been restricted). Reactance is therefore a specific type of resistance (see Beutler, Harwood, Michelson, Song, & Holman, 2011) that fluctuates depending on the situation at hand. In this way reactance is reactionary. Rather than being something ingrained in one's character, reactance is the behavioral and affective response to demands made by one's environment. Instances when persons might be expected to demonstrate reactance include the loss of driving privileges, custodial rights of a child, or employment. Clients informed that they will be involuntarily hospitalized in a psychiatric facility or that they will be imprisoned if they do not participate in counseling also are likely to exhibit some form of reactance.

Reactance is considered an expected response and a normal process intended to protect one's personal freedom against attack. This is true particularly when reactance is understood in the context of culture. Recent research has expanded the concept of reactance to include not only an individual's response to threats infringing on his or her *personal* freedom but also threats affecting the freedom or well-being of his or her *cultural group*—family, work associates, neighborhood, school, community, or other ingroup.

In a series of studies, Jonas and colleagues (2009) found that persons from collectivist rather than individualistic cultures—or persons whose values were more *inter*dependent than *in*dependent (i.e., values originating and embedded in group or collective identity rather than in self-identity)—demonstrated reactance behavior in the face of threats to collective freedom more so than threats to their individual freedom. This type of reactance would be apparent in 52-year-old Dominic's outrage expressed in a counseling session after recently learning that officials had decided to close the free health clinic and to discontinue public transportation in his part of the city. As someone with more of a collectivist identity and regarded as an elder in his community, Dominic might justify his anger because these changes represent another slight to his predominantly African American and impoverished neighborhood more than simply an inconvenience to him.

Reactance and other forms of resistance often have been equated with a lack of cooperation or with noncompliance. This is true in cognitive behavior therapy (CBT). Frequently cited examples of client noncompliance in CBT are not completing homework assignments, not adhering to a medication regimen, attempting to prolong therapy unnecessarily, or discontinuing therapy prematurely. Client demonstrations of noncompliance in session include interrupting and confronting helpers, placing unreasonable demands on helpers, presenting a negative attitude, repeatedly misinterpreting helpers' comments, and maintaining their own agendas (Newman, 2002; Patterson & Forgatch, 1985). Methods used to encourage client adherence to prescribed medication are part of compliance therapy (Kemp, David, & Hayward, 1996) and compliance enhancement therapy (see Heffner et al., 2010). Both are clinical programs that integrate cognitive therapy or CBT and motivational interviewing principles to increase insight and maintain medication adherence among patients with psychosis or a severe alcohol use disorder. Although the term *compliance* has been criticized for its connotation of client passivity and servitude (see Donohoe, 2006), its use and that of *noncompliance* likely will continue in medical and mental health practice until satisfactory alternatives are identified.

Reluctance

From another perspective, resistance can signify a reservation about change or a **reluctance** to change. Egan (2014) described reluctance as a hesitancy to participate in activities required in or associated with the helping process. This type of behavior is often passive and may be fueled by shame, a lack of trust, a loss of hope, or a fear of intimacy or therapeutic intensity. Good and Robertson (2010) attributed men's reluctance to seek professional help to such things as their allegiance to the conventional male gender role of independence and toughness, fear of embarrassment and powerlessness, and a belief that any therapeutic failure would be their sole responsibility. Reluctance may be evident in both male and female clients who only talk about peripheral or low-priority issues, seemingly agree with or acquiesce to all of the helper's recommendations, and set unrealistic goals in therapy that, when not achieved, are used to explain the lack of improvement. Egan (2014) distinguished between reluctance and resistance, defining the latter as the "'push-back' against any kind of helping at all or parts of the helping process" (p. 199). Cullari (1996) also differentiated the two concepts, with resistance representing a client's intrapsychic and unconscious process (consistent with a psychoanalytic perspective) and

reluctance being the "conscious ambivalence" (p. 4) that occurs between client and helper.

Ambivalence

Ambivalence has been characterized as fluctuating compliance (Westra & Dozois, 2006) and might be considered resistance to change. It closely resembles reluctance and is generally defined as feeling or thinking two ways about something. More specifically, ambivalence reflects a tension between two equally attractive yet opposing feelings or attitudes, resulting in indecision, confusion, and a sense of being stuck, indicative of behavioral procrastination. It is therefore a prime characteristic of persons who are aware of a need to make a lifestyle change (e.g., exercise, vocation/career, diet, intimate relationship, addictive behavior), are seriously considering or contemplating change within the next 6 months (Prochaska & DiClemente, 1982), but have not yet taken the steps necessary to change their current regimen or circumstance. The experience of ambivalence can be likened to the metaphor of being "in between a rock and a hard place," reflecting what Arkowitz (2002) described as "conflicts between desires and fears, and between 'shoulds' and oppositional attitudes toward change" (p. 221).

DiClemente (2003) suggested that ambivalence should be thought of as the opposite of impulsivity and therefore regarded as a necessary and welcome step in the process of change, particularly for persons prone to making hasty decisions and engaging in risk-taking and health-compromising behaviors (e.g., persons addicted to alcohol, other drugs, or gambling). From this perspective, ambivalence could signal a time-out or a rest stop from problematic behavior and therefore could represent a relief from the debilitating and exhausting consequences of a "problem-saturated" pattern of living. This alternative depiction of ambivalence appears to support Arkowitz's (2002) proposal for the term *ambivalence* to replace *resistance* because of the former's more neutral and less pejorative connotation. In motivational interviewing, the use of resistance is limited to describing dissonance in the helping relationship, whereas ambivalence is understood as the client's internal experience of struggling between changing and remaining the same (see W. R. Miller, Moyers, Amrhein, & Rollnick, 2006; Westra & Arkowitz, 2011). Ambivalence is therefore a normal and an expected stage in the process of change and represents a resource in the helping process.

Reframing Resistance

Although reactance, reluctance, and ambivalence represent varying gradations, or at least types, of client participation and cooperation in the helping process specifically and the change process more generally, we do not believe that as an overarching concept resistance is exclusively a client characteristic. This clarification is important because, as Arkowitz (2002) reminds helpers, "The way we conceptualize resistance clearly influences how we work with it" (p. 224). Resistance attributed solely to clients implies that resistance is something that resides in clients and is therefore entirely under their control. Such thinking absolves the helper of any responsibility for creating or contributing to resistance and can then be used by helpers as a convenient explanation for lack of therapeutic progress. De Jong and Berg (2013) contend that the concept of resistance is self-serving for helping professionals who ascribe to a medical model or expert model.

Take, for example, a client who refuses to give permission to his helper to contact his wife. The client may be labeled resistant until, upon reviewing his case in supervision, the supervisor learns that the helper failed to explain to the client her reasons for wanting to contact the wife or neglected to assure the client that she would not keep any of his wife's information a secret from him. Because the helper did not clarify her need to talk with the client's wife and did not carefully review with the client the contents of the release-of-information form—including what would be done with all information obtained from his wife—it is understandable that this client would question his helper's request to speak with his wife and thus withhold his consent. Rather than portraying this *client* as resistant, we would characterize the helping *interaction* as resistant or, more precisely, as generating resistance. The helper's failure to be direct and explicit more than likely contributed to the client's reluctance to give consent and to the subsequent resistance experienced in session.

Resistance is therefore not a one-person operation. Just as it takes two to tango, it takes two to resist. This perspective underscores a primary assumption of motivational interviewing (W. R. Miller & Rollnick, 2013)—namely, that the helper's style is a powerful determinant of resistance and change. Motivational interviewing interprets resistance in context, specifically the relational or interactional context of a helping relationship. Thus, resistance is an **interpersonal construct** that describes the dynamic between the client and helper. It also is a product of that interaction, such as when the client and helper do not agree on the goals for therapy. This implies that helpers contribute to resistance (e.g., fail to establish and maintain a healthy helping relationship) and clients should not be held entirely responsible for its occurrence (Norcross, 2010). This view also is shared in dialectical behavior therapy (Linehan, 2015) wherein therapy-interfering

behaviors include *therapist* behaviors that impede the process of therapeutic change, such as arriving late for sessions and making rigid demands of the client.

The helper's awareness of his or her role in resistance is critical in addressing what are referred to as therapeutic alliance ruptures (Safran, Muran, & Eubanks-Carter, 2011) and what we interpret as resistance gone awry. According to Leahy (2007), the helper's own internal schemas or core beliefs about the helping process can contribute to ruptures in the working relationship. These include a need for approval, demanding standards (e.g., "We should never waste time"), and fears of abandonment (e.g., "I'll be left with no clients"). A rupture can occur in any of what Hardy, Cahill, and Barkham (2007) described as the three components of an effective therapeutic relationship: affective bond and partnership, agreement on goals and tasks, and relationship history of client and helper. When resistance does occur, this indicates an issue has arisen that is important for the client, the helping relationship, or both, and it needs to be identified, addressed, respected, and understood (Arkowitz, 2002). More specifically, resistance is a signal to the helper that ineffective methods are being used (Beutler et al., 2011).

It is important for helpers to pick up on the subtle cues that the helping alliance is in trouble and then address those concerns with clients in a way that does not amplify anxiety, confusion, or frustration (Safran et al., 2011). Periodically saying, "I'm not sure if this makes sense" can signify the helper's attentiveness as well as his or her interest in understanding the client's perspective. Likewise, asking "How is this sitting with you so far?" can elicit valuable information from clients that they may not have offered on their own. These are but two examples of what Norcross (2010) referred to as helper "proactive monitoring" (p. 125), a practice that is recommended to prevent therapeutic misunderstandings and clients leaving therapy early.

It is worth noting that resistance can take many forms and may not always be amenable to change. As mentioned in Chapter 9, Beutler and Harwood (2000) discuss resistance *traits* (i.e., related to a stable, enduring disposition) and resistance *states* (i.e., varying reactions to situation-specific occurrences). The former is more descriptive of one's personality and thus is less subject to change, whereas the latter is depicted as fluid and transitory, and thus is more receptive to change, exemplifying reactance. Helpers must be able to distinguish between enduring and temporary forms of resistance and adapt their style of interaction accordingly.

Although Beutler and Harwood (2000) equate trait resistance with high client resistance and state resistance with low client resistance, there are occasions when situation-specific resistance can be quite acute and, likewise, when more stable, resistance that is consistent with one's personality can go unnoticed. For example, client cooperation may exemplify an acquiescent or people-pleasing personality style that, over time, may resist the helper's attempts to cultivate in the client greater autonomy and self-reliance. Resistance therefore may not be easily discernible. What the helper initially may have welcomed as client compliance actually may have been the client distancing himself or herself from the helper by shifting the topic or simply agreeing with the helper without any elaboration. Based on interviews with 14 clients about their first or second therapy session, Rennie (1994) defined client compliance as one form of client deference or negative politeness wherein the client felt pressure from the therapist's demands or apparent expectations and either submitted to them (i.e., complied) or rebelled against them (e.g., did not return for a subsequent session).

To more fully understand the concept of resistance to effectively work with and through it, the notion of **two-way resistance** is worth reinforcing. Resistance is an interactional phenomenon between the client and helper or, as Cullari (1996) offers: "Resistance is viewed as being due primarily to conflicts arising from simultaneous attempts at self-preservation and self-transformation both within the client and between the client, the therapist, and society" (p. 9). Trait and state resistance, therefore, must be interpreted and addressed relationally. A helper-client relationship characterized by trait or enduring resistance may require more structure and planning, more concrete and explicit parameters for interaction (e.g., written attendance agreement), consultation with other persons involved in the case (e.g., supervisor, referral source), and more objective measures of progress (e.g., specific behaviors to be implemented) than a relationship characterized by state or situation-specific resistance. The latter could be addressed through ongoing and deliberate client and helper conversations in which the helper initiates and facilitates in-the-moment discussion about observed disagreements and other indications of lack of therapeutic cohesion (see Safran et al., 2011 for further discussion).

Regardless of which type of resistance is present in the client-helper relationship, the helper must remain observant to both content (i.e., actual words spoken) and meta-communication (i.e., interpretation of content, as well as nonverbal expressions). Hara et al. (2015) strongly recommend video recording sessions and then reviewing them to enhance helper skills of recognizing the more subtle forms of resistance. When recognized in session, helpers are more able to address resistance appropriately, rather than simply ignoring its existence, and remain nonjudgmental and nonpunitive. Questions such as, "What do I need to hear from you that would help me better understand what you're going through?" and "What needs to change so that you are getting something out of our time together?" demonstrate the helper's interest in the client-helper interaction and can keep resistance to a minimum, use resistance productively (e.g., view it as signaling interest in and creating momentum for some type of change), and prevent alliance ruptures. Beutler and colleagues (Beutler et al., 2011; Beutler & Harwood, 2000) have identified several helper practices for addressing resistance (see Box 10.1). These and other strategies for working through trait and state types of resistance are discussed throughout the remainder of this chapter. These strategies are informed by solution-focused therapy, motivational interviewing, and an integration of the two approaches.

To better illustrate the helper's contribution to resistance and likewise to therapeutic rapport, we encourage you to participate in Learning Activity 10.1. You will need two other people to participate with you, with each one selecting the role of client, helper, or observer. If conducted in a classroom setting, this activity can help explain the occurrence of resistance between client and helper and highlight specific helper behavior to help manage and lessen resistance. The observer's feedback is critical in this particular activity.

BOX 10.1	Helper Practices for Addressing Resistance in Therapy

1. Regard resistance as a problem of therapy delivery and therefore a problem for the therapist to solve.
2. Acknowledge and reflect client's expressions of resistance (e.g., anger).
3. Avoid stimulating the client's level of resistance.
4. Discuss with client the therapeutic relationship.

5. Renegotiate the therapeutic contract regarding goals and therapeutic roles.
6. Match therapist's directiveness to client's level of reactance:
   a. high client reactance suggests less therapist directiveness.
   b. low client reactance suggests more directive interventions used by therapist.

Source: Beutler et al., 2011; Beutler & Harwood, 2000.

Learning Activity 10.1

The Helper's Role in Resistance

The purpose of this activity is to recognize the helper's role in both generating and managing resistance in the helping relationship. There are two parts or shifts for this activity: first shift and second shift. For both shifts, it is recommended that **three persons** participate in this activity:

- Person **A** to portray a **client**,
- Person **B** to be in the role of **helper**, and
- Person **C** to serve as an **observer** to the interaction between the client and helper.

Roles for Activity

Person **A**: Imagine that you have been given an ultimatum from someone in authority (e.g., school principal, boss, children's services case worker, judge) for something you have done or failed to do: either go to counseling or lose certain privileges. The privileges you might lose include your eligibility for graduation, employment, custody of your children, or driver's license. You have decided to attend counseling to not jeopardize what is important to you, such as maintaining custody of your children and keeping your job. You're not happy to be in counseling, though, and you don't think it will do any good.

Person **B**: You are the helper who has been assigned to work with Person A, the client. This is your first meeting. Knowing this client is not self-referred already has given you the impression that he or she will not be cooperative. You believe it is your responsibility to convince the client that he or she needs to be in counseling, needs to change his or her behavior now, and should take heed of all of your recommendations. Client excuses are not acceptable!

Person **C**: As the observer of the first meeting between client (Person A) and helper (Person B), consider the following questions:

- How is the client's displeasure or irritation at needing to be in counseling received by the helper?
- What does the helper say and do to convince the client of the need for immediate change, akin to an overhaul of the client's life?

- How does the client respond to the helper's definitive language (e.g., "You really need to change things around now or else something worse will happen")?
- What nonverbal communication is evident between the two of them?

Procedures for First Shift

Proceed with Person A, the client, and Person B, the helper, having a conversation, perhaps with the helper being the first one to start. As much as possible, stay in your assigned role, but do not take it to an extreme. Refrain from yelling, name-calling, and other disrespectful or inappropriate behavior for this exercise. Allow just 5 minutes for this first shift. Person C, the observer, keeps time and then provides his or her observations to both the client and the helper about their interaction.

Procedures for Second Shift

Staying in the same three-person group and using the same client scenario, Person C, the observer, and Person B, the helper, switch roles. The new helper's role is to acknowledge the client's aggravation about needing to be in counseling, affirm the client's decision to retain what is important to him or her (e.g., children, employment), emphasize that the client and helper will be working together to help the client reach his or her goals, and acknowledge that change may take some time. Convey a nonjudgmental and accepting attitude. The new observer is to notice how the client responds to the new helper's engagement. Again, after 5 minutes, the observer stops the interaction and asks the client these questions:

- What did this helper say that stood out for you (or was helpful for you)?
- What did you notice about this helper's interpersonal style (tone of voice, facial expression, posture, and other nonverbal expressions)?
- How did this helper's style compare to the first helper's style?
- Who would you be more willing to work with? Why?
- What specific aspects of these two helpers stood out to you?

Two Models for Working with Resistance

In their review of 12 studies investigating [LO1] [LO2] [LO3] resistance, Beutler and colleagues (2011) concluded that less directive therapeutic interventions generally work best for clients demonstrating high levels of resistance. Nondirective therapy has been defined as unstructured, void of

treatment-specific strategies (e.g., cognitive restructuring, role playing) aimed at teaching clients skills or providing solutions, and heavily focused on the helper's active listening skills, such as empathic reflection and encouragement (Cuijpers et al., 2012). It also often is equated with supportive therapy. Directive therapy, however, often is defined as highly structured and focused or directional. Most behavior therapies are in this category, with their purpose being to enhance behavior skills, such as assertive communication and emotion regulation. Directive therapies often make use of a curriculum and follow a manual.

To address and work through resistance in counseling, we recommend a helper style that blends support and direction. This means that helpers engage in purposeful conversations with clients, conversations that are directed toward resolving therapeutic resistance and client ambivalence, so that pragmatic solutions to clients' presenting concerns can be realized. And all the while these conversations are saturated in an atmosphere of therapeutic support.

Two models or helping styles that use a semi-structured, directive, or purposeful approach to the helping process are solution-focused therapy (SFT; often referred to as solution-focused brief therapy, or SFBT) and motivational interviewing (MI). These are brief interventions that reflect a supportive, humanistic, and client-helper collaborative philosophy, and therefore both are well suited for clients who are ambivalent about change and are less than eager to be in therapy. Both styles are strengths-based approaches that Lewis and Osborn (2004) recommended should be used together. The integration or combined use of SFT and MI has been recommended: (a) with cognitive behavior therapy (Corcoran, 2005); (b) specifically with African American women in drug treatment (Roberts & Nishimoto, 2006); and (c) with adolescents who have a history of school truancy (Enea & Dafinoiu, 2009). The combination of SFT and MI also has been used to address concerns such as diabetes management among adolescents (Viner, Christie, Taylor, & Hey, 2003) and to train medical residents (Hamada, Martin, & Batty, 2006).

Research on Solution-Focused Therapy (SFT) and Motivational Interviewing (MI)

The future of both SFT and MI remains very **LO1** **LO2** promising. The 70 experts in psychotherapy who participated in Norcross, Pfund, and Prochaska's (2013) Delphi study predicted that by the year 2022, the use or popularity of SFT would remain the same and the use or popularity of MI would increase. MI's wide appeal and increasing use are indicated in part by the extensive research that MI has generated, including more than 1,100 outcome studies (Lundahl, Kunz, Brownell, Tollefson, & Burke, 2010), and its recognition by the Substance Abuse and Mental Health Services Administration (SAMHSA, an agency of the U.S. Department of Health and Human Services) in December 2007 as an evidence-based practice for substance abuse treatment. MI's application has extended to practices in mental health, medicine (including nursing),

nutrition, and other health behaviors (e.g., physical exercise, safe water drinking, sustained breast feeding). In addition, more than 2,500 people have completed training as MI trainers, teaching in more than 45 languages (W. R. Miller & Rollnick, 2013). The Motivational Interviewing Network of Trainers (MINT) was incorporated in 2008 (www.motivationalinterviewing.org).

Although Corcoran and Pillai (2009, pp. 240–241) advised practitioners that SFBT has yet to establish a strong "evidence basis," Gingerich and Peterson (2012) later countered that there "is strong evidence that SFBT is an effective treatment for a wide variety of behavioral and psychological outcomes" (p. 281) based on their review of 43 studies. There has been a recent emergence of what we interpret as a serious commitment to conducting sound, rigorous research in SFBT (Franklin, Trepper, Gingerich, & McCollum, 2012; Kim, Smock, Trepper, McCollum, & Franklin, 2010). This includes the Helsinki Psychotherapy Study of mood and anxiety disorders in adults that has compared solution-focused therapy (SFT) to short-term and long-term psychodynamic therapies (Lindfors, Knekt, Virtala, Laaksonen, & the Helsinki Psychotherapy Study Group, 2012; Lindfors et al., 2015).

We regard the increased investment in sound SFBT research as an effort to explain SFBT's wide recognition and adoption, to substantiate perspectives held by practitioners that SFBT is effective (see Herbeck, Hser, & Teruya, 2008), and to prevent SFBT from being overlooked or dismissed altogether when compared to established evidence-based approaches that compete for resource allocation. This has been a focus of the Solution-Focused Brief Therapy Association (SFBTA; www.sfbta.org) established in 2002. SFBT was recognized in 2008 as a model program by the U.S. Department of Justice's Office of Juvenile Justice and Delinquency Prevention. Additionally, in 2010 the SFBTA Research Committee revised the SFBT treatment manual to help standardize the implementation of SFBT and therefore promote SFBT research (see Trepper et al., 2012), and a solution-focused fidelity instrument is currently undergoing development (Lehmann & Patton, 2012) to measure the extent to which therapies undergoing investigation are consistent with SFBT.

SFT Research

Kim and colleagues (2010, p. 301) referred to solution-focused brief therapy as one of the most popular and widely used models of therapy in the social work profession. Solution-focused therapy (SFT)—the designation we have selected to refer to this approach because it is essentially the same as SFBT—has earned a similar status in addictions treatment. From their survey of 30 program directors and 366 substance abuse treatment staff in California, Herbeck et al. (2008) found that SFT was frequently used and rated as somewhat effective, even though staff were not familiar with research evidence supporting SFT's effectiveness.

Despite its popularity, SFT still lacks a strong empirical research base. Corcoran and Pillai (2009, p. 235) attributed the "slow pace of empirical investigation" to SFT's assessment of strengths rather than problems, its brief focus, and its constructivist origins that do not allow for the positivist, quantitative measure of treatment outcomes. It also may be that because SFT was founded by persons who were primarily clinicians and not researchers or scientists affiliated with an academic institution or an established research institute, it was not deemed essential to subject SFT to scientific testing during its early years of development. The early research conducted was exploratory, practice-based, and qualitative in nature (Lipchik, Derks, LaCourt, & Nunnally, 2012).

As Corcoran and Pillai (2009) insinuate, empiricism was considered anathema to the postmodern paradigm that gave birth to SFT. SFT's pragmatic, "radically simple" (McKergow & Korman, 2009, p. 35), and strengths-based approach therefore seemed to speak for itself. Initial reports of its effectiveness (based primarily on the brevity and limited number of sessions needed) were promulgated by the founders of SFT and by clinicians who participated in intensive training beginning in the early 1980s at the Brief Family Therapy Center in Milwaukee, Wisconsin, the home of SFT. S. D. Miller (1994, p. 21) noted that these reports were "substantiated solely by reference to 'subjective clinical experience'" and often were presented in anecdotal form. As stated earlier, only recently has there been a call for rigorous SFT research. This effort has been led by SFT researchers at research universities and institutes, representing a shift in the evolution of this therapeutic approach. Without empirical evidence supporting its effectiveness, Kim and colleagues (2010) explain that SFT "will be marginalized and may not even be able to be practiced in settings that require the psychotherapy it offers to be demonstrated to be an [evidence-based practice] therapy model" (p. 301).

At least five reviews of SFT outcome research have been conducted and published in English. Gingerich and Eisengart (2000) were the first to do so and identified 15 studies published through 1999. Of these studies, only five met criteria as well controlled (e.g., focused on a specific disorder, used randomized group design or acceptable single-case design, and used treatment manual and procedures for monitoring treatment adherence). Four of the five studies found SFT to be significantly better than no treatment or than standard treatment services, and the remaining study reported that SFT demonstrated

equivalent outcomes when compared to another treatment intervention.

One of the five reviews of SFT outcome research is a meta-analysis (Kim, 2008). A meta-analysis combines and summarizes the quantitative results of studies that have a common focus and then calculates a standard metric of the overall effect of the treatment or intervention tested in all of the studies. The standard metric, or effect size, represents the magnitude of the effect or the strength of the intervention (e.g., SFT) when compared to another intervention (e.g., short-term psychodynamic therapy) or to a control condition on certain outcomes (e.g., school attendance, symptoms of depression and anxiety) across a variety of clinical populations and settings. Small, moderate, and large effect sizes are generally regarded as having the value of 0.20, 0.50, and 0.80, respectively.

Kim (2008) reported small but positive treatment effects favoring SFT for the 22 studies he reviewed that were conducted from 1988 to 2005. These studies examined externalizing behavior problems (e.g., hyperactivity, conduct disorder), internalizing behavior problems (e.g., depression, anxiety), and/or family and relationship problems, yielding effect sizes of 0.13, 0.26, and 0.26, respectively. Only the effect size for internalizing behavior problems was statistically significant ($p = 0.03$), suggesting that when compared to another treatment or control group, SFT's impact in ameliorating internalizing problems such as anxiety was small *and* meaningful.

Corcoran and Pillai (2009) reviewed 10 studies of SFT published from 1995 to 2006 that investigated SFT's effects on a range of areas, including child behavior problems and crisis stabilization. Overall effect sizes obtained immediately after SFT ranged from −1.07 to 3.03, although the statistical significance of these differences was not reported. The lack of rigorously designed SFT research led Corcoran and Pillai to characterize the effects of SFT as "equivocal" and to caution helpers about the lack of "a strong evidence basis for [SFT] at this point in time" (pp. 240–241). Kim and Franklin (2009) limited their review to seven SFT studies published from 2000 to 2008 that were conducted exclusively in school settings. Although SFT produced small to medium effect sizes on outcomes such as academic performance, classroom behavior, and self-esteem, these differences also were not statistically significant when compared to alternative interventions.

The most recent review of SFBT research was conducted by Gingerich and Peterson (2012), capturing 43 studies (including 17 dissertations) accessible through April 2012 and grouped into one of six categories: (1) child academic and behavior problems; (2) adult mental health;

(3) marriage and family; (4) occupational rehabilitation; (5) health and aging; and (6) crime and delinquency. As mentioned, their overall assessment of the effectiveness of SFBT is very positive, noting that 74 percent of the studies reviewed reported significant positive benefit of SFBT. However, SFBT fidelity in this collection of studies remains questionable (i.e., lack of assurance that the therapy delivered was an agreed upon or standard form of SFBT), and the effects of SFBT appear to be time-limited. For adults with a longstanding mood or anxiety disorder, for example, Lindfors et al. (2015) recommend a psychodynamic approach rather than "a purely supportive, solution-focused technique" (p. 35).

Despite the lack of methodologically sound SFT research, existing studies suggest that clients benefit when specific aspects of a solution-focused approach are incorporated into the helping process, such as inquiring about occasions when the presenting concern was nonproblematic. Solution-focused practitioners therefore are encouraged to reframe resistance as a useful resource in the helping process—that is, as an indication that the client is interested in or curious about and committed to some type of change. Helpers who adopt this perspective are then more inclined to solicit client preferences, offer genuine concern in the spirit of collaboration that supports client autonomy, and reinforce client steps toward change.

MI Research

Motivational interviewing (MI) has a more extensive and impressive record of well-conducted and compelling research than SFT. Numerous systematic reviews of MI studies have been conducted, including approximately 30 meta-analyses of MI effects on various client or patient outcomes (i.e., excluding analysis of MI training outcomes). Recent meta-analyses have been conducted on MI's effects on gambling behaviors (Yakovenko, Quigley, Hemmelgarn, Hodgins, & Ronksley, 2015), pediatric health behaviors (Gayes & Steele, 2014), conditions found in medical settings (Lundahl et al., 2013) and in primary care facilities (VanBuskirk & Wetherell, 2014), and increasing physical activity among persons with chronic health conditions (O'Halloran et al., 2014).

The earliest meta-analysis (Burke, Arkowitz, & Menchola, 2003) reviewed 30 studies of individually delivered adaptations of MI (or AMIs) for a wide range of behaviors, including alcohol use, drug use, and diet and exercise. In only 11 of these studies was there a statistically significant effect size for the AMI in addressing a specific problem when compared to another intervention or a control group for the treatment of drug addiction (0.56), diet and exercise (0.53), and alcohol use (0.25 to 0.53,

depending on the outcome measure). No effect was found when an AMI was used to treat smoking or HIV risk behaviors. Taken together, however, Burke and colleagues (2003) determined that clients receiving an AMI were 51 percent improved at follow-up compared to clients who received no treatment or participated in treatment as usual (37% improvement). Furthermore, AMIs appeared to have a convincingly beneficial effect (0.43 effect size) on a range of life issues (e.g., employment, legal involvement, physical health) beyond the target behavior, suggesting that the impact of AMIs extends beyond the issue identified as the primary focus of treatment.

Hettema, Steele, and Miller's (2005) often-cited meta-analysis of 72 studies identified a combined effect size of 0.77 for MI and adaptations of MI (AMIs) immediately after treatment, an affect size of 0.30 at 6 to 12 months post-treatment, and an effect size of 0.11 at 12 months or longer after treatment. These values suggest that the beneficial effects of MI diminish over time, although a subsequent meta-analysis of MI for smoking cessation (Hettema & Hendricks, 2010) yielded enduring beneficial outcomes (i.e., abstinence) for nonpregnant clients and for those with low levels of nicotine dependence. In studies in which MI had been added to another treatment, perhaps prior to cognitive behavior treatment, Hettema and colleagues (2005) found that significant change was maintained over time with an enduring effect size of 0.60.

The majority of studies (72%, $n = 51$) reviewed by Hettema and colleagues (2005) investigated MI or AMIs when applied to alcohol and other drug concerns. Other studies using MI addressed HIV/AIDS, treatment compliance, gambling, intimate relationships, water purification/safety, eating disorders, and diet and exercise. Hettema and colleagues concluded that 53 percent ($n = 38$) of the studies demonstrated a significant effect favoring MI. The strongest support for MI was found in studies focused on substance use, specifically alcohol abuse. This finding was corroborated in the meta-analysis conducted by Vasilaki, Hosier, and Cox (2006). They confined their review to studies that only investigated MI's performance in reducing alcohol consumption (15 studies published over a 20-year period). When compared to no-treatment control groups, the average effect size for MI was 0.18; when compared to other treatments (e.g., cognitive-behavioral, skill-based counseling), MI yielded an average effect size of 0.43. Both of these effect sizes are statistically significant.

The most recent and comprehensive meta-analysis of MI (Lundahl et al., 2010) encompassed 119 studies that reported the unique or direct effects of MI on a variety of outcomes (e.g., reduction in risk-taking behaviors, engagement in treatment). The average effect size across all outcomes was 0.22, representing a small but statistically meaningful effect of MI. Another way to explain this is that 75 percent of all participants improved somewhat from MI, and of those, 50 percent improved slightly but meaningfully and 25 percent improved moderately or strongly. Specific findings from this meta-analysis indicated that when compared to "weak" comparison groups (i.e., wait-list/control and nonspecific treatment-as-usual groups), MI performed better, particularly for African American participants, substance use–related outcomes, gambling, and longer treatment periods. When compared to "strong" comparison groups (e.g., specific treatments that included 12-step facilitation and cognitive behavior therapy), however, MI produced poorer outcomes (i.e., lower effect sizes) for African American participants and when MI studies were of higher methodological rigor. Contrary to earlier meta-analyses, Lundahl and colleagues reported lasting effects of MI, with statistically significant effect sizes of 0.29 and 0.24 up to 2 years beyond treatment.

The collection of meta-analyses to date depicts MI as exerting a small yet significantly positive effect across a wide variety of concerns. It has produced positive outcomes in individually delivered formats as a brief treatment, particularly in enhancing treatment engagement and reducing alcohol consumption, when delivered with targeted client feedback (i.e., as motivational enhancement therapy, MET), and when used with clients from ethnic minority groups as well as older participants. Group-only delivery of MI is not recommended, although its use in a group format recently has been described in some detail (Wagner & Ingersoll, 2013). Björk (2014) characterized MI as a fluid approach, meaning that it is adaptable to a wide variety of settings, populations, and client or patient conditions, and it can be integrated with other treatment approaches. He referred to this versatility as MI's greatest strength.

Despite the substantial scope of MI's research repository and findings that signal MI's presence in the treatment milieu for the foreseeable future, the exact mechanisms by which MI works remain unclear. This is attributed to a mix of research methods that do not all fulfill quality standards, such as not assessing for MI fidelity. There is some indication from recent meta-analyses, however, that client improvement is associated with helpers who demonstrate the "spirit" of MI (e.g., convey accurate empathy, promote client autonomy; Copeland et al., 2015; Pirlott, Kisbu-Sakarya, DeFrancesco, Elliot, & MacKinnon, 2012) and who also implement strategies consistent with MI (e.g., affirmation, reflections; Magill et al., 2014; Pirlott et al., 2012). Furthermore, clients whose therapists engage in behaviors *in*consistent with

MI (e.g., confronting, warning, and advising without permission) tend to exhibit higher levels of resistance in session than clients whose therapists do not engage in these behaviors, and this resistance has been found to be associated with poor outcomes (e.g., continued substance use; Apodaca & Longabaugh, 2009). Mechanisms of change in MI may thus include the absence of certain therapist-interfering or MI-inconsistent behaviors and also the presence of MI-consistent behaviors.

Further speculations about the beneficial components of MI include its usefulness as a precursor or adjunct to treatment, such as psychotherapy for depression (see Zuckoff, Swartz, & Grote, 2015). Specifically, MI appears to promote client commitment to and active involvement in therapy (Apodaca & Longabaugh, 2009). MI can assist ambivalent clients in preparing for cognitive behavior therapy (CBT; see Arkowitz & Westra, 2004; Westra & Arkowitz, 2011). Westra and Dozois (2006) found that when MI was used as a prelude to CBT for anxiety, clients were significantly more likely to expect positive results from CBT, complete CBT homework assignments, and effectively manage their anxiety symptoms than were clients who did not participate in MI prior to CBT. MI also can be incorporated throughout the helping process to cultivate client persistence in the face of more challenging aspects of treatment. It appears, therefore, that MI can assist clients in making a commitment to the helping process, thereby improving client engagement, adherence, and retention in CBT and other action-oriented therapies (see Westra & Arkowitz, 2011).

MI research continues to focus on the importance of client speech since Amrhein, Miller, Yahne, Palmer, and Fulcher's (2003) seminal study. As they explain, "Measuring strength of commitment language is a particularly appropriate way to assess the dynamic events in MI, given that strengthening client commitment to change is the stated primary goal of this approach" (p. 865). In their review of videotapes of counseling sessions with drug-abusing clients, Amrhein (2004) and his colleagues (Amrhein et al., 2003) found that it was not the *frequency* of client talk about committing to change that predicted eventual abstinence; rather it was the *strength* of such commitment talk that resulted in abstinence. For example, the statement "I'm not going to use" is much stronger than "I might stop using." Furthermore, commitment language expressed near the end of counseling sessions indicated eventual abstinence more than commitment language spoken earlier in sessions.

Findings from subsequent studies on the impact of therapist and client speech in MI sessions (e.g., Karno, Longabaugh, & Herbeck, 2010; Moyers et al., 2009;

Pirlott et al., 2012) have extended Amrhein and colleagues' (2003) initial findings and indicate that therapist behaviors directly influence not only client in-session speech but also behaviors in between sessions and once treatment has concluded. More specifically, clients whose therapists are able to cultivate and reinforce their sincere and convincing talk about change in session (by using skills consistent with MI and avoiding behaviors inconsistent with MI) are able to actually change their behavior, such as decreasing their alcohol use. This remains an exciting line of research that holds great promise for clinical practice and training.

Summary of SFT and MI Research

Both SFT and MI have evolved from intuitive and somewhat isolated practices (i.e., originating from their founders' reflections on their own therapeutic experiences and observations) to well-known approaches used today by a variety of helping professionals in a variety of settings with diverse populations. The ongoing development of both approaches has been strengthened by their fidelity to their theories of origin (i.e., social constructionism, family systems, person-centered therapy) and their adaptability or "willingness to play" with other treatment methods (e.g., cognitive behavior therapy). The scholarly scrutiny that both SFT and MI have undergone in research investigations also has bolstered their appeal and relevance; this is particularly true for MI. Although SFT and MI would benefit from continued and systematic inquiry concerning their respective and possibly shared "active ingredients," both have become well-established and well-respected methods for helping people through the process of change. Additional research on SFT and MI is discussed in the remainder of this chapter as it relates to specific helper strategies.

Working With Resistance, Reactance, Reluctance, and Ambivalence

Solution-focused therapy (SFT) and motivational interviewing (MI) offer slightly different perspectives on resistance. SFT historically has had an aversion to resistance, regarding its discussion as an unnecessary and unhelpful focus on the problem, and believing that even considering resistance percolates its existence. As O'Hanlon and Weiner-Davis (2003) noted, "If you are focused on finding resistance, you will almost certainly be able to find something that looks like it" (p. 29).

Resistance, therefore, was dismissed by some early solution-focused practitioners, even to the point of declaring it dead (de Shazer, 1984) and ceremoniously mourning its death (O'Hanlon & Weiner-Davis, 2003). The concept of resistance is considered moot by some solution-focused practitioners (e.g., Corcoran, 2005) when the helper gives his or her attention instead to honoring client preferences and collaborating with clients to achieve their goals. When this does not happen, it is because of practitioner resistance (De Jong & Berg, 2013). Other solution-focused practitioners (e.g., Shilts & Thomas, 2005) regard resistance as a form of curiosity. This suggests that both clients and helpers are intrigued by or at least interested in something and the task thus becomes identifying a shared interest (e.g., client regaining custody of her children; extending the client's time between psychiatric hospitalizations). Once a common curiosity has been established in session, therapeutic collaboration is underway.

Unlike some solution-focused practitioners, MI clinicians do not consider resistance to be uncommon. Noticeable discord in the client-helper relationship can occur when the helper does not practice MI consistently and drifts into what is known as the "righting reflex" of actively persuading or correcting a client's course of action. Asking, "Why would you want to do that?" might be interpreted as accusatory or at least judgmental and generate in the client a defensive stance. Likewise, imploring the client to engage in a particular task (e.g., "You really should take the medication as prescribed") might stir up resentment and prompt the client to push back. Although MI recommends that helpers "roll with resistance" or otherwise "sidestep resistance," this simply means that resistance should not be opposed or met with direct confrontation, but with reflection and appropriate reframing instead. In contrast to solution-focused practitioners, MI practitioners would declare resistance to be "alive and well" and therefore must be acknowledged, carefully handled and processed, and ultimately resolved. The importance of attending to resistance is reinforced by Arkowitz (2002) in his suggestion that resistance has meaning or signals that something is important to the client or helper, or both, and therefore serves a function or purpose in the helping process.

Both SFT and MI offer a framework from which helpers can work with clients through resistance. Both approaches regard client-helper cooperation and collaboration not simply as preferable by-products of therapy but also as essential ingredients to the helping process. Cooperation and collaboration between clients and helpers are intentionally established and monitored and are included as appropriate goals in treatment plans. It is safe to assume

BOX 10.2	Reframing and Working with Resistance

Three Reframes of Resistance:

1. **Therapeutic Discord**
   - Lack of agreement between client and helper about helping process and outcomes.
   - Alliance impasse or rupture.

2. **Ambivalence**
   - Uncertainty, confusion about change.
   - Tension between maintaining status quo and engaging in new and beneficial activities.
   - Normal, expected occurrence in the process of change.
   - Welcome time-out from impulsivity; opportunity for reflection.

3. **Curiosity**
   - Something is important to and has meaning for both helper and client.
   - Both helper and client are interested in some type of change.

Functional and Interactive Definition of Resistance:
- Resistance has meaning and serves a purpose in the helping process.
- Both helper and client contribute to the occurrence and resolution of resistance.

Working with Resistance in the Helping Process
- Helper and client playing doubles tennis.
- Helper and client learning to dance together.

---

that when clients and helpers have established a productive working alliance and are collaborating, resistance is nonexistent or at least minimal.

SFT and MI have extended refreshing and welcome characterizations of the client-helper relationship, and they do so with the assistance of analogies to two different types of physical activity, with each activity involving two people. SFT regards the helping relationship as a "multidisciplinary collaboration between experts" (Prochaska & Norcross, 2014, p. 411) in that the client and helper, according to de Shazer (1984), are not opponents but are like tennis partners playing on the same side of the net. Similarly, MI is "like dancing rather than wrestling. One moves with rather than against the person...A good MI conversation looks as smooth as a ballroom waltz" (W. R. Miller & Rollnick, 2013, p. 15).

It seems that for SFT and MI the focus is more on *how* helpers interact with clients rather than on *what* helpers do with or to clients. Helper style—and the interactional style that develops between client and helper over time—appears to be more important than specific and prescribed interventions (e.g., techniques) in working with and through resistance, reactance, reluctance, and ambivalence. Drawing on the analogies of two physical activities (i.e., tennis and dancing), it may be that the helping process is about the client and helper learning to (1) be successful tennis partners and together overcoming the client's presenting concern, or at least successfully managing the debilitating influence of such an opponent on the other side of the net; and (2) dance together and, in so doing, composing their own steps, rhythm, lyrics, and music that are helpful to the client. Box 10.2 presents a snapshot of alternative definitions of resistance and suggestions for how to work with it,

informed by and reflecting the philosophies of SFT and MI presented in this chapter.

Playing doubles tennis and learning to dance with a partner require that both participants learn and apply specific skills. When applied to the helping relationship for the purpose of establishing and maintaining an alliance and thereby working through resistance, reactance, reluctance, and ambivalence, it is the professional helper who is expected to take the lead and apply certain interpersonal skills integral to the practice of SFT and MI.

SFT and MI are discussed in more detail in the following sections with respect to applications with diverse populations and cultivating and maintaining a positive helping relationship. Specific helper strategies or "dance steps" intended to work with and through resistance, reactance, reluctance, and ambivalence are discussed.

Solution-Focused Therapy

As its name implies, **solution-focused therapy** (SFT) **LO1** is less interested in the origin and maintenance of a presenting concern than it is in constructing pathways through or around the concern that clients report. Rather than talking about resolving issues, SFT speaks of constructing solutions. As can be seen in Box 10.3, this is the first of nine tenets that inform SFT (Trepper et al., 2012). This perspective shifts the spotlight from deficiencies, liabilities, and seemingly insurmountable hurdles to strengths, resources, and possibilities. G. Miller and de Shazer (1998) stated that concerns, issues, or problems may be "unconnected" and even "irrelevant to the change process" (p. 370), the eighth tenet of SFT listed in Box 10.3. Presenting concerns might be likened to merely

BOX 10.3	Nine Tenets that Inform SFT*

1. Solution-focused therapy (SFT) is about building solutions rather than solving problems.
2. The helping process should focus on the client's desired future rather than on past problems or current conflicts.
3. Clients are encouraged to increase the frequency of current behaviors found to be useful.
4. There are exceptions to problems, times when the problem could have happened but didn't. These exceptions are the building blocks of solutions.
5. Helpers assist clients to identify alternatives to current undesired patterns of thinking and behavior that are in the client's repertoire, or that can be developed jointly by the client and helper.

6. Solution behaviors already exist for clients.
7. Small increments of change lead to large increments of change.
8. Clients' solutions are not necessarily directly related to a problem identified by the client or helper.
9. The conversational skills necessary for the helper to invite the client to build solutions are different from those needed to diagnose and treat client problems.

Source: Trepper et al., 2012
*Solution-focused therapy (SFT) is often referred to as solution-focused brief therapy (SFBT) in the literature, but the two are essentially the same.

an entry pass to an event—that is, they get persons in the therapy door, but a focus on the concern or issue doesn't help clients move through the helping process and out the therapy door. In SFT, helpers concentrate on **exceptions** to the presenting concern (the fourth tenet of SFT), occasions when it is not problematic (past or present), or times when the client has taken a break from—or can envision taking a vacation from—the concern. S. D. Miller (1992) referred to such occasions as "problem irregularit[ies]" (p. 2), times when the problem cycle was disrupted. Inquiring about and amplifying these exception times are parts of the process of solution construction, which can make problem clarification inconsequential.

SFT often is referred to as a nonpathological approach. However, rather than defining something by what it is not (and in so doing allowing the problem or concern to remain the protagonist), we prefer to speak of SFT as a **salutary** and strengths-based or competency-based approach to helping. The client's assets and resources are regarded as ingredients for building solutions, and the helper remains confident in the client's ability to make positive changes in his or her life by continually accessing and utilizing identified assets and resources. The client is regarded as the expert on what will be helpful and the helper is viewed as the client's student, learning from the client what are his or her preferences and what may and may not be useful. This notion is contrary to the expectation of a know-it-all therapist and explains, in part, SFT's characterization as "client-determined" (Berg & Miller, 1992b, p. 7).

The reversal of client and helper roles in SFT (compared to a traditional model of helper as expert and client as passive student) encourages cooperation and collaboration in the helping process, thus minimizing or

at least effectively managing resistance. Milton Erickson, whose work in hypnotherapy informed the early development of SFT, regarded resistance as client responsiveness and cooperation (Haley, 1967). For example, a client who voices her skepticism about the benefits of therapy is actually making her preferences known and, if she remains for the entire session, is at least demonstrating her willingness to hear the helper's perspective. Erickson also believed that resistance serves a purpose, such as the active engagement of both the client and helper. In addition, resistance can signal to the helper that a readjustment of treatment or the helping plan is necessary. Cooperation is possible when both client and helper are willing to acknowledge, work through, and understand the purpose of resistance. This is certainly necessary for tennis partners to be successful against their opponents! When the client is encouraged to voice his or her opinion and the helper conveys an interest in the client's perspective, resistance is addressed directly and cooperation is in motion.

Utilization of Resistance in SFT

An enduring assumption of SFT is that of **utilization**, a concept coined by Milton Erickson (1954) and defined as the helper's "acceptance of what the [client] represents and presents" (p. 127). This means that who the client is and what he or she brings to sessions is acknowledged, validated, prioritized, and factored into the helping process. Utilization also can be understood as intentionally incorporating into the helping process all resources represented and presented by the client *and* helper. Resources include resistance. This implies that resistance can serve a beneficial purpose, such as clarifying goals and objectives, establishing a strong and durable helping relationship, and demonstrating the client's ability to take action. In re-framing resistance as curiosity, Shilts and Thomas (2005) highlight the investment of both client and helper in the process of change, proposing that each person is interested in a positive outcome; therefore, momentum can be fostered and funnelled in productive ways.

Types of Helping Relationships

It is worth mentioning again that SFT refers to types of helping relationships rather than to types of clients or types of helpers. This speaks rather convincingly to SFT's prioritization of the client-helper relationship, a relationship that Lipchik (2002) argued must be different from the unhelpful professional relationships that clients (particularly mandated or involuntary clients) may have experienced. Berg and Miller (1992b) describe three types of client-helper relationships: (1) the customer-type relationship; (2) the complainant-type relationship; and (3) the visitor-type relationship. Each one is determined by both client and helper, is subject to change, and requires the helper to assume more responsibility for managing and making use of the relationship for the client's benefit.

A **customer-type relationship** characterizes the interaction of client and helper who have jointly identified and agreed on a workable goal. The helper has acknowledged and validated the client's needs and preferences and has agreed to serve in the role of ally and consultant in an effort to assist the client in constructing a realistic and relevant solution. In turn, the client recognizes the strengths and resources that he or she brings to the process and views himself or herself as an active participant in solution construction.

A **complainant-type relationship** describes the client and helper's agreement on preliminary goals, minus the identification of specific steps to be taken to realize a solution. The helper may be expecting the client to initiate or get moving with the process of change, and the client may be looking to the helper or to someone else (e.g., school principal) to make change happen. In other words, the client and helper "may not readily see themselves as part of the solution and, in fact, may believe that the only solution is for someone other than themselves to change" (Berg & Miller, 1992b, p. 23).

A **visitor-type relationship** occurs when the client and helper have neither jointly identified a need or concern nor agreed on a goal to work toward. This type of relationship may characterize the early phase of interaction when a client is perhaps vague about the purpose of professional care or may not even believe that such care is necessary. The helper in turn is unclear about what might be helpful for the client but remains willing to assist through the process.

Before proceeding to the next section, please participate in Learning Activity 10.2. This activity invites you to consider how four helper roles can facilitate the three client-helper relationships described in SFT. Feedback is provided on page 352.

Specific Strategies used in SFT

Holyoake and Golding (2012) noted that SFT "is often wrongly defined as a quick fix approach or a gimmicky and fashionable collection of skills" (p. 73). To counter this, they proposed a solution-focused philosophy or theory informed by 17 principles, including a systems orientation, a future orientation, the role of language in creating change, and the emphasis on social constructionism and not intrapsychic constructivism. These overlap with the nine tenets that inform SFBT (Trepper et al., 2012). Strategies or helper behaviors in SFT thus should

---

Learning Activity 10.2

Helper Roles in the Helping Relationship

The purpose of this activity is to consider further how helpers can work within the three client-helper relationships described in SFT. Feedback is provided on page 352.

Norcross, Krebs, and Prochaska (2011) have described four roles that helpers can assume in working with a variety of clients at various stages of change. The **nurturing parent** acknowledges and joins with the client's opposition or reluctance to change as well as the client's ambivalence about change. The **Socratic teacher** encourages clients to consider and achieve their own insights into their circumstance and options, and the **experienced coach** provides clients with a proposed plan of action and reviews clients' own proposals for solution construction.

Finally, the **consultant** provides helpful advice and support when the plan of action is not progressing as smoothly as anticipated.

Which of the four helper roles described by Norcross and colleagues (2011) would be helpful in managing and making use of the three client-helper relationships described by Berg and Miller (1992b): (1) **customer-type relationship**; (2) **complainant-type relationship**; and (3) **visitor-type relationship**? How would the helper know which role or stance to emulate or to operate from given the type of client-helper relationship? How would the helper know that a particular role had been beneficial for the client? How might the helper combine two of these roles in each of the client-helper relationships?

be guided by this belief system. A technique alone does not define a therapy.

Throughout the SFT session, the helper retains a posture of curiosity or wonderment, a keen interest in the client as a person, in his or her concerns and preferences, in his or her strengths and resources, and in the possibilities that can be cultivated and considered for the client's well-being. Lutz (2014) recommends that a solution-focused conversation should begin with problem-free talk, meaning that the helper explores the client or patient's strengths and resources. As a medical practitioner, she understands how difficult this is, particularly in medical settings. She argues, however, that just as money must be deposited in a bank before any withdrawals can be made, so must the client's resources be gathered and shored up before concerns can be mitigated.

Establishing, maintaining, and making full use of client and helper collaboration is a priority in SFT, and strategies are therefore viewed as joint activities and not solely in the helper's purview. Solutions are co-constructed between the client and helper. The practice of SFT is known for its creative use of questions (questions for both client and helper to consider, intended to stimulate *possibility* thinking) and for the attention given to the language used by both client and helper. The conversations between client and helper are therefore fluid, not scripted, and reflect a mutual inquisitiveness about alternative perspectives and realities.

Trepper et al.'s (2012) review of SFT research (Gingerich & Peterson, 2012; Kim, 2008; Kim & Franklin, 2009) identified 10 core components of SFT or techniques used in SFT:

1. Looking for exceptions to the problem, including pre-session change

2. Recognizing clients strengths, often in the form of "compliments"

3. Setting goals with clients

4. Asking the miracle question

5. Asking scaling questions

6. Asking relationship questions

7. Asking coping questions

8. Taking a consulting break

9. Assigning homework tasks

10. Focus on what is better

These are referenced in each of the five strategies we describe in this section, some more extensively than others.

SFT Strategy 1: Asking Constructive Questions

In SFT, encouraging client engagement and co-constructing realistic goals or solutions go hand-in-hand. This is most often done by the helper carefully crafting and then posing to the client unique questions for the specific purpose of engaging the client in the process of solution generation. Indeed, "Questions are perceived as better ways to create open space for clients to think about and evaluate situations and solutions for themselves" (Lee, 2003, p. 390). Known as **constructive questions** (McGee, Del Vento, & Bavelas, 2005), these questions introduce possibilities and new, more satisfactory, and beneficial realities, and they are intended to build solutions by developing "different enough differences" (Lipchik & de Shazer, 1986, p. 97). The purpose of constructive questions, therefore, is to "engage clients in conversation, while inviting consideration of extraordinary perspectives" such as client preferences (Strong, 2000, p. 29) "to prompt, promote, or elicit change or information about change" (Lipchik & de Shazer, 1986, p. 97).

Several types of questions are often used to invite client participation in the construction of solutions. Chief among these are **exception questions**. Exception questions presume that clients' lives are not always the same and that problems are neither pervasive nor permanent. Lipchik and de Shazer (1986) defined exceptions as any "behaviors, perceptions, thoughts and expectations that are outside the complaint's constraints...[which] can be used as building blocks for constructing a solution" (p. 89). Exceptions can be situated in the past or future, can be new, and can be recurring (Nunnally, 1993). For example, to assist a client who has assumed the full-time responsibility of caring for her ailing mother, the helper may say,: "Tell me about the last time you were able to take a break from your constant caretaking. How did you arrange that and how was that time helpful for you?" In posing this past-exception question, the helper is curious about the client's description of a nonproblem occasion, a time when the client benefited—even for a brief moment—from not having to be on-call. Once the client is able to identify an exception, the helper might encourage her to expand on the benefits and then envision a time in the future when similar benefits would be possible.

Another example of a past-exception question is the question asked in the first session of SFT when the helper is curious about pretreatment change. Weiner-Davis et al. (1987, p. 360) posed the following question to new clients: "Many times people notice in between the time they make the appointment for therapy and the first session that things already seem different. What have you noticed about your situation?" When clients responded in the affirmative, they were then asked: "Do these changes relate to the reason you came for therapy? Are these the kinds of changes you would like to continue to have happen?" In asking such questions, Lawson (1994) observed that "a counselor can significantly influence a client's expectation about a pre-existing solution to a problem by communicating a definite expectancy" (p. 247). And Weiner-Davis and colleagues (1987) emphasized that client depictions of pretreatment change are regarded not as "flights into health" but as "real change (although admittedly new and somewhat 'out of character')," and they described their subsequent work with clients as attempts "to 'keep 'em flying' by transforming these 'flights' into real lasting change" (p. 362). Helpers also can ask at the beginning of each subsequent session, "What's better?", which presumes and focuses on improvement rather than complaints.

To help construct a vision of client improvement in a complaintant-type relationship, the helper may ask: "Let's say that you and I have agreed on a goal for the use of our time together and our conversations are helpful to you. How will you know when this has occurred? What will tell you that we haven't been wasting our time?" This future-exception (or fast-forward) question presumes there will be a time when the client will derive benefit from the helping relationship. Fashioned in this way, exception questions resemble presuppositional questions (O'Hanlon & Weiner-Davis, 2003) or questions that presuppose the emergence of a positive or hopeful reality, as in "*When* you sense our conversations have been helpful for you…" as opposed to "*If* you think our conversations have been helpful for you…" Exception and presuppositional questions, therefore, are used to "amplify…exceptions, to convey the inevitability of change to clients, to elicit the client's outcome goal, and to co-create a future client reality without problems" (Selekman, 1993, p. 61).

The best-known exception question and perhaps the most distinctive feature of SFT is **the miracle question** (de Shazer, 1985). The client is invited to imagine that his

or her life has been changed "miraculously" (e.g., "Tonight, while you're asleep") in a desired direction (e.g., "the problem that brought you in to counseling is solved") and is then asked to describe how he or she will know that his or her life has changed (e.g., "When you wake up tomorrow morning, how will you know that a miracle has occurred while you were sleeping? What will be different that will clue you in?"). Benefits to the client of being asked the miracle question include being able to consider an unlimited range of possibilities and focusing on the future and away from current and past problems (De Jong & Berg, 2013).

Clients who initially respond to the miracle question with "I don't know" can be encouraged to "pretend" or give it your best shot to entertain the improbability of such a miracle actually occurring. "I know it may seem like a weird question, way out there in left field," the helper might say, "but use your imagination or put your magician's hat on." Whatever snippet of difference (i.e., exception) the client is able to provide (e.g., "Well, I would have gotten some sleep, actually") is intentionally deconstructed or clarified by the helper and then amplified to create the increasing likelihood of such a day actually occurring. For example, the helper may encourage the client to describe the feeling of waking up knowing that he or she had slept well the night before (e.g., "How will you know? How is that different?") and then inquire about client contributions to having slept well (e.g., "What would you have done the day or the night before to help make this happen? What would you be credited with doing?"). In asking such questions, the helper is assuming that such a miracle day is a possibility and is helping the client prepare for its arrival, engaging in a type of dress rehearsal. The focus is on client behavior to encourage and empower the client to summon forth positive change. De Jong and Berg (2013) offer six guidelines for asking the miracle question. These are listed in Box 10.4.

Coping questions, also referred to as "getting-by" questions (G. Miller, 1997), represent a third type of

---

BOX 10.4   Six Guidelines for Asking the Miracle Question

1. Speak slowly and gently, in a soft voice, to give your client time to shift from a problem focus to a solution focus.
2. Mark the beginning of the solution-building process clearly and dramatically by introducing the miracle question as unusual or strange.
3. Use frequent pauses, allowing the client time to absorb the question and process his or her experiences through its different parts.
4. Because the question asks for a description of the future, use future-directed words, such as "What

would be different" and "What *will be* signs of the miracle?"

5. When probing and asking follow-up questions, frequently repeat the phrase "a miracle happens and the problem that brought you here is solved," to reinforce the transition to solution talk.
6. When clients lapse back into problem talk, gently refocus their attention on what will be different in their lives when the miracle happens.

Source: De Jong & Berg, 2013, page 92.

10.2 Feedback

Helper Roles in the Helping Relationship

Helpers are encouraged to be intentional about the roles they assume and prioritize in a given type of client-helper relationship. Within the three client-helper relationships that Berg and Miller (1992b) described, one or more of Norcross and colleagues' (2011) helper roles are recommended. The diagram here depicts which helper role may be best suited for managing each of the three types of client-helper relationships. Notice that the Socratic teacher role may be beneficial for both the visitor-type relationship and the complainant-type relationship, and that the experienced coach role may likewise be beneficial for both the complainant-type relationship and the customer-type relationship.

The nurturing parent role, however, would be emphasized in the visitor-type relationship, given that this relationship often characterizes an early phase of the helping process wherein the helper would concentrate on establishing himself or herself as a caring companion for the client as the two determine how to proceed.

The consultant role would likely be prioritized in the customer-type relationship in light of the helper and client having established and agreed on a direction for change and having worked together over a certain period of time and having already experienced preliminary change.

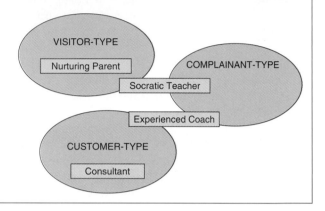

solution-focused question. These inquire about how clients are already managing the concerns they have raised in counseling and how they might build on current successes for the future, as in the query, "Given your recent struggle, how were you able to accomplish that?" Implicit in these questions are commendations of client strength, skill, and progress already at work. The client is asked about past or current successes and in so doing is complimented on being able to manage a difficult task. de Castro and Guterman (2008, p. 100) described Robert, an older man who had had thoughts of killing himself in the wake of his wife's suicide. When asked about a time when he had coped effectively with feeling suicidal, Robert responded, "I think to myself that this feeling will pass…and it passes." The therapist in turn further probed, "How did you make that happen? How did you make that feeling pass?" This question presumed that Robert was capable of managing his feelings, and this presumption may have been empowering for him. Robert replied, "I just remind myself that the feeling will pass because it always does." The therapist then proceeded to assign Robert and his adult daughter the task of observing occasions when Robert was effectively coping with his suicidal feelings. They were instructed to do this before the next session.

SFT's origins in family or systems therapy and social construction theory explain its use of **relationship questions**. These questions inquire about the social context of

solutions, by asking, for example, "Who in your life will be one of the first to recognize that things are different for you, that you have awakened to a 'miracle morning'?" With the client's permission, other persons in the client's life can be consulted and asked questions about their hopes and wishes for the client, responses that will be shared with the client. These questions to family members may be "What are you most proud of in your daughter?" and "What will convince you that your partner's change is for real and not a fluke?" Questions such as these are also helpful in couples and family therapy sessions.

Scaling questions encourage clients to quantify feelings and aspirations on a numerical scale (e.g., 0 to 10) anchored by diametrically opposed endpoints, such as 0 representing "no confidence at all" and 10 representing "as confident as you can be." They are self-anchored, meaning the client is the one to decide what a 3 or a 7 means (Lutz, 2014). Scaling questions are an important asset of the solution-focused helper (Macdonald, 2007) and have been described as the "work horses of solution-focused therapy because they are frequently asked…to achieve a variety of therapeutic ends" (G. Miller, 1997, p. 12). Their purpose is to help clients express previously unexplainable feelings, clarify the next desired steps for clients, and assess client progress (Davis & Osborn, 2000). Macdonald (2007) adds that scaling questions can also be used to clarify communication among other professionals (e.g., referral source) involved in the client's case.

In visitor-type helping relationships, scaling questions can be used to ascertain the degree of client investment in the process of change and to crystallize the direction needed to arrive at some realization of progress. For example, the helper may ask, "On a scale from 0 to 10, with 0 being 'clueless' and 10 being 'clear as a bell,' how clear are you about what needs to happen so that you don't feel like you're in a mess again?" If the client answers "1," the helper may respond with "Okay, so it's still cloudy or murky to you about what needs to happen. Let's fast-forward then to 2 weeks from now and let's say that your answer to the same question is a '2.' What would have happened in the next 2 weeks for you to have answered that question honestly?" Scaling questions can therefore be used to investigate exceptions for the purpose of constructing solutions.

Carefully constructed and purposeful questions in SFT not only address but also make use of client-helper resistance. This means that questions are regarded as not only an intervention in SFT but also the product of client-helper interaction. Said in another way, resistance—or what Shilts and Thomas (2005) regard as curiosity—is the intended recipient or target of constructive questions as well as the germination or yeast for such questions. The questions described are intended to engage clients in the helping process by tapping into client resources and strengths.

We encourage you to try your hand at developing constructive questions. Learning Activity 10.3 describes the case of Susan and asks you to formulate possible exception, coping, and scaling questions to pose to Susan. Review the material on these three types of questions before you participate in Learning Activity 10.3.

SFT Strategy 2: Offering Legitimate Commendations

Complimenting clients on managing or accomplishing difficult tasks is a core skill in SFT. Compliments—or our preferred term, **commendations**—acknowledge client strengths and competencies and are used to normalize a client's experience, help the client think differently about the problem or concern at hand, and exemplify the client's own ability to construct a solution. "Sounds like you did what you knew to do at the time" points out the client's use of his or her own decision-making skills and may serve to ease the client's concern about "not knowing what to do" or "not doing enough." In addition, a commendation such as, "You've been through a lot and have somehow managed to keep your head above water," conveys to the client that past and perhaps lingering challenges have not gotten the best of the client and that the client has been able to draw on and mobilize available resources to rise above difficulties. Hearing such an observation from a helper may offer the client a new perspective, one that may reinforce the client's ability to participate in his or her own solution-construction. This is certainly empowering.

Our concern about compliments (as well as SFT's reference to "cheerleading") is that they may be constructed and articulated rather hastily, and thus may be interpreted as superficial. Clients who are not yet engaged in and who are skeptical about the process of change may still be testing out the credibility and trustworthiness of the helper. Thus, they may construe early statements of praise (e.g., "You did great!") as disingenuous. Indeed, the client may regard the helper as ingratiating or being too eager to win over the client, which may actually result in the client's withdrawing from the helping process. Macdonald (2007) shares this concern and therefore situated compliments in the context of providing clients with feedback at the end of each SFT session, after a brief break to allow both the therapist and client to reflect on the session. He also recommends the use of compliments that are consistent with local custom and the client's culture. For example, he remarks that in the United Kingdom more than three compliments offered to one person would likely be regarded with suspicion.

We believe commendations connote the recognition of genuine or authentic material. We also believe that genuine feedback can be formulated during a time of reflection, perhaps when the helper has stepped out of the counseling room for a few minutes to consult with colleagues or to determine privately, outside of the client's presence, what information would be most useful to the client at the end of the session. Whereas compliments can be interpreted as flattery or showcasing rather shallow characteristics of the speaker (what some might think of as "feel-good warm fuzzies"), commendations are intended to draw out and place the spotlight on substantive client qualities—at the end of a SFT session and throughout. In addition, compliments may be ephemeral, whereas commendations are designed to be enduring. And when offered at the end of a session, a genuine commendation can be regarded as the helper's parting gift to the client. We believe that commendations are more respectful of clients and, in the long run, promote client engagement and investment in the change process.

SFT Strategy 3: Speaking the Client's Language

As a humanistic and client-directed approach, SFT is dedicated to recognizing, appreciating, and validating

Learning Activity 10.3

Formulating Constructive Questions

This activity gives you a chance to practice writing several SFT constructive questions using the case of Susan and following these four steps. Feedback follows on page 356.

1. Read through Susan's case and, consistent with SFT, identify or take an inventory of what you think are Susan's strengths and resources. These will constitute the ingredients for your constructive questions.

2. Formulate and write down three different *exception* questions: one intended to highlight past strengths and resources, another focused on current strengths and resources, and the third intended to elicit from Susan existing or anticipated strengths and resources for use in the future. This third exception question might be phrased as a miracle question.

3. Formulate and write down three different *coping* questions. How are these different from the exception questions?

4. Formulate and write down three different *scaling* questions. What are the endpoints or the anchors for each scaling question? In other words, what will be represented by 0 and what will be represented by 10 on each scale? Clients must always be provided with the numerical endpoints and what each one means when asking a scaling question. And we recommend that the lowest numerical rating on the scale be zero

(and *not* 1) to reflect the absence of something, such as "no confidence at all."

Susan is a 35-year-old Native American who has experienced faint tremors in her arms, hands, and face all of her life, a condition she says her father has as well. She quit her job as a waitress a year ago because the tremors were getting noticeably worse. She has entered counseling on the advice of her medical doctor and also because she wants to get back to work. She is very apprehensive, though, about talking with a counselor and is not sure what can be done that will be helpful to her. She is quiet, reserved, speaks softly and only when spoken to, and sits in a closed position with her hands clasped tightly in her lap, in part to control the tremors.

Susan has been divorced for 4 years after experiencing years of physical abuse. She says she finally left her ex-husband when he started hitting their son, Matt, now 14 years old. Matt currently lives with Susan's father some distance away, choosing to stay with his grandfather when Susan moved to her current residence a year and a half ago (Matt didn't want to leave his school and friends). Susan doesn't see Matt often because she and her current boyfriend, Sam, only have one car that he uses to drive 1 hour to and from his construction job 6 days per week, she hasn't been driving anyway, and Matt is busy with football and basketball at school. Susan tears up easily when she talks about Matt and says she hasn't been "very good at being a mom." She says that when she gets back to work, she'll be able to provide more for Matt and be more of the mother she says he deserves.

each client's unique experiences and perspectives. Furthermore, SFT has been informed by social constructionism, which postulates that reality is constructed in the moment through human interaction and dialogue. This means that reality is constantly changing and constructed, not static or discovered, and that client and helper together determine what is real or true and helpful for the client. Clients, therefore, do not meet with helpers to "get answers" or to "find solutions" (although some clients may expect this), as if some truth or recipe already exists and is simply waiting for the client's knock or access code. Rather, through their conversations, client and helper together create or construct a new, preferred reality for the client, one the client authors and the helper edits.

Therapy has been characterized as "a language system and a linguistic event" (Anderson, 1997, p. 2), and helpers have been described as "linguistic detectives" (Efran & Cook, 2000, p. 140) and "conversational artist[s]" (Lutz, 2014, p. 14). Solution-focused helpers, therefore, are perpetually tuning in to clients' expressions of their

unique experiences and perspectives. This requires a genuine and "focused curiosity" (Strong, 2002) on the helper's part, referred to in SFT as a position of "not knowing" (Anderson & Goolishian, 1992). This means that helpers do not presume to know what is helpful for their clients and do not try to impose their ideas or recommendations on clients. Rather, they assume the role of student of the client's subjectivity (e.g., "Tell me what it's been like for you" or "How would you describe what you're going through?"), attentive to the verbal and nonverbal expressions of that inner reality to fashion with the client—through conversation—a one-of-a-kind solution.

The process of solution construction is aided by the helper's ability to speak the client's language, which essentially means preserving and making use of the exact words uttered by the client. O'Hanlon and Weiner-Davis (2003) refer to this as "matching the client's language" (p. 61) or using the client's words to join with or stay connected to the client and his or her experience

(Macdonald, 2007). Rather than expecting the client to adopt the helper's understanding of panic disorder, for example, and the medical terminology associated with the condition, the helper remains inquisitive about how the client experiences what he or she is describing and uses the client's own words (e.g., "a fog," "stuck," "freeze frame") to discuss this reality. Client and helper discussions might then focus on what to use as "fog lights," how to get "unstuck," and what to do to "defrost" or "thaw out." In this example, it's the client's experience and the words he or she has used to describe that experience that are incorporated into ongoing client-helper conversations.

Speaking the client's language by preserving his or her exact words in responses made by the helper has been proposed as a distinctive practice of SFT. In a study of five different professionally produced training videos, Korman, Bevelas, and De Jong (2013) found that both solution-focused therapists preserved a higher percentage of their clients' exact words in their responses to the clients than the two therapists who demonstrated cognitive-behavior therapy (CBT) or the one therapist who demonstrated motivational interviewing (MI).

SFT Strategy 4: Exploring the Client's "Instead"

SFT assumes that clients do want to change, that they do not want things to remain as they are. The word **instead** is therefore a wonderful tool for helping clients envision and plan for change. It reflects SFT's proclivity for and adherence to finding exceptions to the problem. It also is consistent with one characteristic of well-formulated goals—namely, that goals describe what is desired or preferred rather than what is to be avoided or eliminated. Asking about a client's "instead" is therefore a means of eliciting client wants and preferences. For example, rather than being advised to "abstain from all mood/mind altering substances" (i.e., what to *avoid* or what *not* to do), clients would be encouraged to "initiate and actively participate in a sober lifestyle" (i.e., behaviors to engage in or what *to* do). The difference is that clients and helpers can envision the presence of positive behaviors (e.g., attending Alcoholics Anonymous meetings, taking medications as prescribed, engaging in physical exercise, journaling) more so than they can describe absent or even diminished problems. The absence of something can be fathomed only by what will take its place. Therefore, it is much more productive and promising to discuss what the client will be doing *instead of* drinking and in so doing to describe positive rather than problematic behaviors.

SFT Strategy 5: Honoring the Client's Preferences

Given that SFT is a client-directed form of helping, emphasis is placed on what the client wants to address, what the client wants to accomplish from talking with the helper. This can be thought of as a form of goal-setting and is a well-defined practice used by Lee and colleagues (Lee, Uken, & Sebold, 2012; Lee, Sebold, & Uken, 2003) in their solution-focused treatment for court-ordered domestic violence offenders. Inventory of the client's wants, desires, and preferences is therefore taken at the beginning of the helping process, and these are given full consideration throughout the process of helping. Walter and Peller (2000) refer to this practice as *preferencing*. Client preferences may be to talk through concerns and troubles, and Walter and Peller allow for this, stating that it may be more important to the client that he or she feels understood than to have the helper move the conversation (prematurely) toward solutions, a practice referred to as "solution-*forced* therapy" (Nylund & Corsiglia, 1994).

Eliciting client preferences and honoring what the client brings forth "invites a discussion of purpose, of what [the client] wants from coming to the consultation" (Walter & Peller, 2000, p. 65). This may be to "get my probation officer off my back" or "keep our family from falling apart," client preferences that may initially attribute the responsibility of constructing and implementing the solution to someone else or something else. Such utterances, however, should not be squelched. Rather, the solution-focused practitioner pursues discussion about how such an eventuality would be helpful and what the client could do to begin the journey to such an envisioned destination. Questions such as, "What will make it possible for your probation officer to be off your back?" and "What are some things you have already tried to keep your family from falling apart?" honor the client's preferences while considering client contributions to the solution under construction.

Model Dialogue: Deconstructing Solutions

Isabella and her helper have established a customer- **LO1** type relationship thus far, given Isabella's cooperation and investment in the change process. The helper has therefore assumed the role of consultant and in this dialogue is interested in identifying the pieces and parts of their co-constructed solutions. This process of deconstruction allows both Isabella and the helper to locate the active

10.3 Feedback

Formulating Constructive Questions

1. Susan's strengths and resources (reflecting the helper's observations and impressions)
   - Access to medical care.
   - Has followed medical doctor's recommendation to enter counseling, despite her apprehension about its benefits; is willing to give counseling a try.
   - Has desire and motivation to work again.
   - Wants to be a good mother to Matt.
   - Was able to leave an abusive marriage.
   - Other strengths and resources: _____

2. Examples of exception questions to ask Susan
   - **Past-exception question:** "Tell me about a time in your life that was special to you, a time that you still value and treasure. What made that time special? What about it set it apart from other times?"
   - **Present-exception question:** "Since the time you made the appointment to come in and talk with me, what have you noticed that's been going well in your life?"
   - **Future-exception question:** "Let's fast-forward to 3 months from now and imagine that things are going pretty well for you. Describe for me what that will be like. How will you know that things are going pretty well for you? What will be taking place that will tell you this?"
   - **Miracle question:** "Let's say that tonight, when you go to bed and you are fast asleep, a miracle happens, and the miracle is that the main concern that you brought in with you today, to our session, simply disappears. It vanishes or just evaporates. That's the miracle. But you don't know that a miracle has occurred right then and there because you're sound asleep. When you wake up tomorrow morning, what will be the first thing you will notice? What will indicate to you that something has changed, that something is different?"

3. Examples of coping questions to ask Susan
   - "What made it possible for you to come in and talk with me today despite not being convinced that counseling would help?"
   - "You say you've had these tremors all of your life. When was a time, even in the past week, that you were able to manage the tremors pretty well?"
   - "What made it possible for you to leave your abusive husband? How were you able to finally do that?"

   - "When you picture yourself being the good mother that you say Matt deserves, what do you see yourself doing? What are some of those things that you can say you're doing even now, maybe even in a small measure?"

   Notice that the coping questions make use of what the helper has already identified as some of Susan's strengths and resources (e.g., managing tremors, leaving an abusive husband), whereas the exception questions leave it up to Susan to determine what she regards as being different from, or the exception to, what some of her concerns are. The exception questions ask about differences in general (e.g., a special time in her life), whereas the coping questions inquire about specific instances that imply or presuppose that Susan is or will be doing something (or has already done something) to control, cope with, or manage some of her concerns. Both types of questions are intended to illustrate for the client that he or she is responsible and gets the credit for changes made.

4. Examples of scaling questions to ask Susan
   - "Let's say that 0 equals 'not helpful at all' and 10 equals 'extremely helpful.' How helpful would you say our conversation today, our session, has been for you?"
   - "On a scale from 10 to 0, with 10 being 'tremors out of control' and 0 being 'tremors not in the way at all,' tell me about how the tremors have been for you, on average, in the past week. What do you notice is responsible for a drop in a point, say, from a 6 to a 5, when the tremors are easing off a bit?"
   - "Given what you know about waitressing, how confident are you that in, say, 3 months you can return to that line of work and do well at it? On a scale from 0 to 10, with 0 being 'not confident at all' and 10 being 'very confident,' how confident are you right now about this?"
   - "If Matt were here today, what would he tell me about the kind of mother you have been to him? Let's say that 10 is 'the best mom ever!' and 0 is 'not a good mother at all.' How do you think Matt would rate you as a mom?"

ingredients of the solutions Isabella used so that specific behaviors within her control can be replicated once therapy has concluded. The helper is hopeful that Isabella will be able to recognize her (Isabella's) active role in the change process—that is, that the solutions realized weren't chance events but were the result of Isabella's own instrumentality. This realization can be very empowering for clients.

1. **Helper:** We've had several sessions together, Isabella, and I thought it might be helpful today to review the work we've done so far and for me to hear from you what's been helpful.

Client: Okay.

2. **Helper:** You really have worked hard and have made good progress at school with **your** math class. [Helper is *commending* Isabella for her progress, a commendation made possible from the helper's reflection on their previous sessions.] What would you say is the main thing that's made it possible for you to do well in school?

Client: Well, it hasn't been an all-at-once thing, you know? You broke things down for me so that speaking up in math class, for example, didn't seem overwhelming.

3. **Helper:** So doing things little by little, step by step, makes it possible for you to accomplish things that are important to you.

Client: Yeah. And you've been really patient with me. Respectful, too. I mean, you haven't been in my face demanding that I do certain things.

4. **Helper:** Ah. Patient, respectful, and not demanding. Good! That's good to hear! Those things have really been helpful for you. [Helper is *preserving* Isabella's own words, a form of "*speaking the client's language.*"]

Client: Yeah. I didn't get all nervous and hyped up in here. You always took your time explaining things to me in a way that wasn't talking down to me.

5. **Helper:** What do you think made it possible for you to cooperate in here, participate in all the practice sessions we had?

In response 5, the helper is attempting to redirect the conversation back to *Isabella's active role in solution construction and implementation*. The helper does not want to assume credit for Isabella's progress. Notice that in responses 3 and 4 the helper kept the verb tense in the present to counter Isabella's past-tense reference to the solution. Also notice in these responses that the helper kept the focus on Isabella's behaviors, not those of the helper. These are subtle attempts to reinforce Isabella's instrumentality—that is, *her* ability to continue to instigate positive change.

Client: I guess I had to.

6. **Helper:** You had to. I'm not sure what you mean. Help me with that. [Helper is consulting the client's expertise.]

Client: I mean if I didn't, I probably would have failed math and maybe even gotten kicked out of school for

pathetic grades. My parents would really have been upset with me then. So, I had to.

7. **Helper:** You wanted to stay in school and do well. The only alternative you saw was unacceptable to you. [Notice that the helper responds to the client's last three words, "I had to," and reframes these words as what is important to Isabella: to stay in school. The helper does not comment on the potentially negative consequences that Isabella identified.]

Client: I guess you could say it like that. I just didn't want to fail.

8. **Helper:** And you certainly haven't. In fact, you've done quite well grade-wise, from what you've told me. So let's fast-forward to the beginning of your junior year. What will be two or three things you'll catch yourself doing in advanced algebra that will tell you this time meeting with me, all the practice sessions we had, that this was all worth it?

Client: Wow. That's a great question!

In response 8, the helper asks a *future-oriented question* intended to help Isabella visualize her continued enactment of positive behaviors learned in therapy. The question *presupposes that positive change will endure* and will be done naturally, without too much effort (i.e., Isabella will catch herself maintaining positive behaviors).

9. **Helper:** It may take you a little while to think about it.

Client: Let's see. I guess I'll raise my hand in class when I have a question, and I'll ask to meet with the teacher after class if I'm still not clear on something.

10. **Helper:** That's great to hear! You didn't have to think too long on that, which tells me that one thing you'll be taking away from our work together is a lot of self-confidence and evidence of success from your work this year in math. [Helper *commending* Isabella's strength of increased self-confidence.] This is very encouraging!

Motivational Interviewing

It is important to emphasize that **motivational interviewing** (MI) is a style of helping and a method of communication, not a set of techniques. Beginning helpers often are eager to identify and try out specific interventions and then store them in their helper toolbox, as we discuss in Chapter 1. MI, however, is actually a belief system or a set of assumptions about human nature and the process of human change more so than simply a collection of helper strategies. This means that helpers themselves are influential participants in the change process and cannot attribute client progress or decline to an isolated technique brought out of storage and applied in session. Who the helper is (e.g., cultural identity), what he or she believes (e.g., theoretical orientation), and how he or she communicates and interacts in a consistent fashion with clients may have more of an impact on the change process than any specific intervention. Practicing MI therefore suggests embracing or identifying with a certain philosophy of helping rather than simply implementing a set of prescribed interventions.

MI "Spirit"

To highlight the intended contributions of motivational interviewing (MI), priority is given to the "spirit" of MI (W. R. Miller & Rollnick, 2013). This core or essence comprises the underlying perspective when practicing MI. Moyers and Rollnick (2002) likened this spirit to a song's melody rather than the lyrics: MI cannot be broken down into separate words or musical notes (e.g., techniques); it can be appreciated and dutifully practiced only as a gestalt, a composite belief system, or an entire musical score. In this way, the MI "spirit" is considered the relational aspect of MI compared to the technical aspect comprising MI-consistent strategies used by helpers.

The spirit of MI has four components: partnership, acceptance, compassion, and evocation. Think of each of these as descriptive of the MI helper and what the MI helper does. For example, the MI helper is a partner in the client's change process who actively engages the client in a conversation about change. Furthermore, the helper believes the client already has the wisdom and other resources to enact change (e.g., past accomplishments) and therefore the helper evokes, beckons, or calls forth the client's wisdom, almost like drawing up riches from the client's well. This is done from a position of genuine curiosity, inviting the client to enlighten the helper on the client's internal frame of reference or private logic. The helper remains compassionate and accepting of all the client represents and brings to the conversation.

Definitions of MI

There are three definitions of MI supplied by its founder, William R. Miller, and his long-time collaborator, Steven Rollnick (see W. R. Miller & Rollnick, 2013). The first definition is intended for laypersons or peer helpers, the second is geared toward professional helpers, and the third is technical and speaks to how MI works.

Motivational interviewing is a:

1. "collaborative conversation style for strengthening a person's own motivation and commitment to change" (p. 12).

2. "person-centered counseling style for addressing the common problem of ambivalence about change" (p. 21).

3. "collaborative, goal-oriented style of communication with particular attention to the language of change. It is designed to strengthen personal motivation for and commitment to a specific goal by eliciting and exploring the person's own reasons for change within an atmosphere of acceptance and compassion" (p. 29).

Notice in the first and third definitions that MI is a **collaborative** endeavor—a dance between client and helper—guided by the helper's intentional effort to promote the client's strength of motivation. Also notice the emphasis on this dance being a conversation, one focused on beneficial change for the client. Again, MI is not a set of techniques; it is a style, the helper's way of communicating with people, and is heavily influenced by person-centered counseling. Because of this influence, MI is a highly respectful approach, one that honors the client's autonomy or right to make decisions, including whether or not to dance or engage in therapy with the helper. The purpose of MI remains clear in all three definitions: to help persons move through ambivalence by making a commitment to change. It is this focus on helping persons make a *decision* to change that differentiates MI from other approaches (Moyers, 2014).

MI Themes

There are four guiding assumptions or themes of MI that continue to inform its practice. These are presented in Box 10.5 and discussed in this section.

First and foremost, MI is a **humanistic**, **client-centered helping style**, a testimonial to its roots in person-centered therapy. William R. Miller, the psychologist who developed MI, described (in Moyers, 2004) his early years of clinical practice as primarily listening to clients with alcohol use disorders because "I didn't know anything" (p. 292). His investment in purposeful listening without admonishing clients to change resulted in what Miller described as "an 'interesting and intense' learning experience... [and] an 'immediate chemistry' in talking with these clients" (Moyers, 2004, p. 292). He found he really enjoyed listening to and learning from his clients, and they seemed to appreciate and benefit from his attentive, listening stance.

1. Motivational interviewing is client-centered, deeply rooted in the humanistic philosophy of Carl Rogers. This implies that clients have an inherent drive for health and well-being. Emphasis is placed on the client's expertise and ability to make his or her own decisions about change.

2. Motivational interviewing is designed to evoke and explore the client's own motivation, which often includes ambivalence (or confusion, uncertainty, confliction, discrepancy) about change.

3. Motivational interviewing is directive or, more precisely, it has direction and is intentional. Its purpose is to elicit and strengthen or empower client motivation for positive change.

4. Motivational interviewing focuses on client speech, listening preferentially for and then reinforcing the client's own arguments for change (i.e., supporting and amplifying client change talk) while resisting the urge to argue for change by putting words in the client's mouth.

Source: W. R. Miller & Rollnick, 2004, 2009; Moyers, 2014; Rollnick, Miller, & Butler, 2008.

This same listening and learning posture is emphasized today in MI and is referred to as the **learning-to-learn** model (W. R. Miller & Moyers, 2006; W. R. Miller, Yahne, Moyers, Martinez, & Pirritano, 2004). In essence, helpers are trained to learn from their clients how to engage in MI. Implicit in this is that clients have a natural drive toward health and well-being (consistent with person-centered theory) and it is the helper's responsibility to "tap into" this resource. Specifically, helpers are encouraged to evoke or bring forth the client's strengths and resources for change, understood as consulting the client's expertise. Thus, the learning-to-learn model casts the helper in the role of student, the one who needs to be attentive to and learn from the client's spoken and unspoken expressions. This expands the meaning of the term *client-centered* in that the client is charged with teaching the helper about the helping process. It is the client's wisdom about beneficial and realistic change that is prioritized, not the helper's beliefs about change for the client.

Ambivalence is the second of four MI themes and, as defined in this chapter, refers to having simultaneous and conflicting or contradictory attitudes or feelings about something. An example might be relishing the learning of graduate school while also finding graduate studies to be taxing and draining and at times doubting one's decision to pursue a graduate degree. Ambivalence also is a defining characteristic of the contemplation stage of change (Prochaska & DiClemente, 1982). Although some persons are able to sort through and move beyond the confusion of ambivalence on their own, others can get stuck and remain entrenched in the tension and the push-pull of ambivalence for quite some time. The latter group may then require professional assistance. This is true of persons in abusive relationships, those engaged in addictive behaviors (e.g., nicotine smoking), and those experiencing other medically related concerns (e.g., eating disorders, diabetes, bipolar disorder). For these and other challenges that often include delayed action or behavioral procrastination, MI represents an appropriate intervention.

MI was originally intended as a practice to help clients move through ambivalence in the direction of positive change (W. R. Miller & Rollnick, 2013). It draws upon the helper's ability to elicit the client's own expressed reasons for and against change, with preferential attention given to the client's talk of change. Because of this, MI is not the same as conducting a decisional balance wherein equal attention is given to exploring the pros *and* cons of changing (W. R. Miller & Rose, 2015). MI is about helping persons get unstuck, and encouraging clients to voice their reasons for not changing can reinforce their sense of stuck-ness. Westra (2012; see also Westra & Aviram, 2015) argues, however, that MI is a form of conflict resolution and therefore exploring counter-change arguments (i.e., sustain talk) can be appropriate. She adds that a client whose helper does not discourage exploring the client's fears of change or what the client believes are the benefits of not changing can—with the helper's skillful assistance—develop more compassion and understanding for the part of him or her that resists change. This is one way that MI might cultivate the strength of client self-compassion, not just convey helper compassion.

A third theme of MI is that it is **directive**. This means that MI has direction and is intentional in its application. This is where MI veers off from its person-centered roots. MI's purpose is to evoke and strengthen client motivation for positive change. Although "directive" may be interpreted as confrontational or prescriptive, MI is far from that. As a humanistic and client-centered helper, the MI practitioner encourages the client to determine if change will occur and, if so, what that change will be. MI is directive in that the helper intentionally steers the conversation in the direction of considering change without imposing or forcing such change on the client. Indeed, W. R. Miller (2000, p. 12) harkens back to a core belief of Carl Rogers "that the therapist is not the author of change in clients so much as a witness to its emergence." The target of change is the client's perceptions—that is, changes once viewed as unacceptable or impossible by the client are now entertained and undertaken.

The fourth and final theme of MI is that it **focuses on client speech**. Specifically, the helper listens for and then reinforces the client's arguments for change, referred to as **change talk**. Because of ambivalence, it is to be expected that clients also will vocalize reasons against change or arguments for the status quo, referred to as **sustain talk**. As mentioned, it is the helper's selective or preferential listening for the client's arguments *for change* that is prioritized in MI (Miller & Rose, 2015). Sustain talk is acknowledged only for the sake of validating the client and helping the client to clarify his or her dilemma (W. R. Miller & Rollnick, 2009). What is emphasized in MI practice—and in effect what makes MI, MI—is remaining partial to and strategically reinforcing the client's expressed leanings toward change. Doing so is dancing for a purpose. It means that the helper is expressly guiding or steering the conversation toward change, using the client's own audible and visible arguments, and reasoning for change as the fuel.

Using open-ended questions, affirmations, reflective statements or empathic reflections, and summaries (referred to by the acronym **OARS**; W. R. Miller & Rollnick, 2013), the MI practitioner encourages clients to consider moving toward change by eliciting the client's own beliefs and feelings about change. More time and effort is spent on talking about the reasons for changing than on the reasons for not changing, and the helper specifically tunes into and amplifies the client's talk about change. All the while, the helper listens more than talks and evokes rather than installs a consideration of change by making use of the client's own resources (e.g., values) and undergirding or amplifying client strengths (e.g., motivation).

It is important for the client to utter words of commitment to positive behavior change because, as Amrhein (2004) noted, "by making a verbal commitment to change, the client is announcing that the current state of his or her emotions and beliefs justifies the risk of personal and public humiliation and disappointment that would result if change did not occur" (p. 325). Through such a process, W. R. Miller and Rollnick (2013) contend, the client can literally talk himself or herself into change because "we tend to believe what we hear ourselves say" (Rollnick et al., 2008, p. 8).

Cultivating Change Talk with OARS+2

As mentioned in this chapter, the types and strength of client speech remain a focus of MI research. Change talk is associated with and sometimes predicts the subsequent

implementation of change behavior, such as decreased alcohol use (Moyers, Martin, Houck, Christopher, & Tonigan, 2009) and eating more fruits and vegetables (Pirlott et al., 2012). Sustain talk, however, predicts an increase in the problem behavior, such as drinking among college students (Apodaca et al., 2014). These research findings reinforce the importance of helpers cultivating change talk and softening sustain talk in MI conversations.

Research also suggests that not only what the client says but also what the client *doesn't* say is important. For example, in a frequently cited study on problem drinkers, W. R. Miller, Benefield, and Tonigan (1993, p. 460) found that the *absence* of client resistant or uncooperative speech (i.e., interrupting, arguing, off-task responses such as silence or sidetracking, and negative responses such as disagreeing and blaming others) "was more strongly related to outcome than was the *presence* of client verbal responses ("positive") commonly thought to mark motivation for change (i.e., agreeing with the therapist and expressing concern, determination, or optimism)." This means that helpers should not be quick to latch onto what initially sounds like change talk, but they should be able to discern genuine change talk from yea-saying or acquiescence (i.e., a client saying only what he or she thinks the helper wants to hear). Genuine change talk will include reasons for change *without* resistance (i.e., conveying cooperation), whereas insincere change talk will evince remnants of resistance (e.g., compliance or withdrawal).

Recent anthropological research has noted a distinctive "**poetic pause**" in the style of seasoned MI practitioners. Carr and Smith (2014) define this is as a form of silence at specific junctures in an MI conversation (e.g., after a reflection) when the helper restrains himself or herself from saying anything else so that it is *the client* who "fills in" the "blank space." "By saying nothing," Carr and Smith explain, "the practitioner instigates the client to talk and perhaps therefore also to talk themselves into change" (p. 99). This intentional helper pause is one way to cultivate client change talk.

Distinction is made between two dimensions of change talk, namely **preparatory change talk** (desire, ability, reason, need, or **DARN**) and **mobilizing change talk** (commitment, activation, taking steps, or **CAT**). W. R. Miller and Rollnick (2013) recommend thinking of these two dimensions as being on opposite sides of the same hill: preparatory change talk (DARN) is on the incline of the hill, whereas mobilizing change talk (CAT) is on the decline. Getting up the hill can take a darn amount of energy, focus, and time; it's an effort to work toward

| BOX 10.6 | Preparatory Change Talk and Mobilizing Change Talk in Motivational Interviewing |

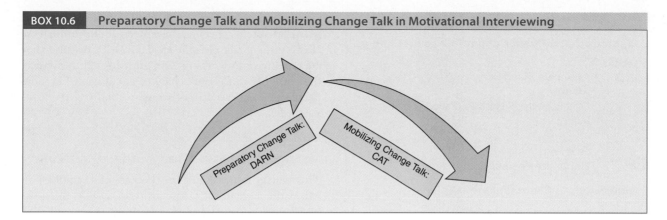

change. Once at the top, the climber is relieved, perhaps exhausted, but feels a sense of accomplishment. After a period of some rest, there is momentum to go down the hill. It's certainly not "free sailing" on the downward slope, but the energy and the motivation are different from that going up.

We have depicted these two dimensions of change talk as upward and downward arrows in Box 10.6. These also can resemble the ascent and descent of an airplane: taking off and landing both require a pilot's effort and concentration, but in different ways. Similarly, preparing for change (DARN) and putting change into action (CAT) are both types of change talk, but they sound different. Whereas DARN comprises quite a bit of internal conversation to convince oneself to change, CAT is more declarative and decisive about change. Compare the following two statements about weight management:

a. "I need to keep these pounds off or else I'll put my heart at risk again."
b. "I'm going to return to the gym and try to eat a piece of fruit after each workout."

Statement A is preparatory change talk: the upward arrow, going up the hill. It conveys urgency and also provides an explanation for making a change (need and reason in DARN). Statement B is mobilizing change talk (CAT): the downward arrow, descending the hill. It declares intent to engage in two specific behaviors. The first part of statement B is definitive ("I'm going to") and reflects commitment language (the C in CAT). The second part of statement B ("I'll try") is not as declarative as the first part, but it is tied to a specific behavior and a specific time and therefore exemplifies leaning into or activating change (the A in CAT). MI research (e.g., Amrhein et al., 2003; Karno et al., 2010) suggests that clients who have climbed the DARN hill and can be heard uttering CAT on their descent are more likely to follow

through on their change (to "walk the talk") than clients who remain stuck on the DARN hill (continue to "talk the talk"). Helpers are therefore encouraged to cultivate in their clients DARN language so that CAT language can eventually be heard.

To cultivate and reinforce in their clients both DARN and CAT change talk, helpers use several types of attending skills. Six of these are known by the acronym OARS+2 and are listed on the left side of Box 10.7. In many ways, these six methods reflect MI's philosophy that a directive or intentional helper stance, coupled with client-counselor collaboration, is curative or helpful. The specific types of client change talk corresponding to the two dimensions of preparatory change talk and mobilizing change talk (DARN CAT) are listed in Box 10.7 on page 362. The assumption is that by intentionally using OARS+2, helpers cultivate and reinforce DARN CAT in their clients that, when genuinely uttered, can lead to behavioral change. Said in another way, helpers who intentionally practice OARS+2 in the context of an empathic helping relationship will more than likely eventually hear their clients talk about change in one or more of its seven types (DARN CAT).

Learning Activity 10.4 on page 363 is designed to help you recognize client change talk and, when identified, to determine whether it is preparatory change talk (DARN) or mobilizing change talk (CAT). Before you participate in this activity, you may wish to review the case of Susan described in Learning Activity 10.3 on page 354.

Specific Strategies of MI that Strengthen Positive Change

Although MI is more of a helping style or a way of being with clients than it is a collection of techniques, there are specific strategies that MI practitioners engage in or postures they assume in their work with clients. Moyers,

| BOX 10.7 | Helper Contributions to Client Change Talk |

Methods that Influence Client Talk about Change

OARS+2

O	Ask **O**pen-ended Questions
A	**A**ffirm
R	Offer Empathic **R**eflections/**R**eflective Statements
S	**S**ummarize
+2	Seek Permission
	Emphasize Personal Control

Dimensions of Client Change Talk

DARN CAT

Preparatory Change Talk

Desire: preferences for change ("I want to")

Ability: perceived self-efficacy ("I think I can")

Reasons: benefits of change, what will be gained; "because…"

Need: sense of urgency; imperative ("I have to"); problems with status quo; what needs to be forfeited

Mobilizing Change Talk

Commitment: intention to change; change in action, ("I will," "I promise," "I am going to")

Activation: leaning into change ("I think I will," "I'll think about it")

Taking steps: already experimenting with change, spoken in past-tense ("I talked with my teacher," "I went to the gym")

Source: W. R. Miller & Rollnick, 2013; Rosengren, 2009.

been found to increase client change talk, whereas the MI-inconsistent behaviors have been found to increase client sustain talk (Magill et al., 2014). Because they are conducive to working with and through resistance, the seven MI-consistent behaviors are discussed in more detail and are viewed in contrast to the five MI-*in*consistent behaviors.

MI Strategy 1: Asking Open-Ended Questions

This strategy is mentioned here because of its emphasis in MI, particularly in working with resistance. As discussed in Chapter 5, **open-ended questions** are intended to open the door to further conversation by seeking information, inviting the client's perspective, or encouraging self-exploration. As opposed to closed-ended questions (which usually can be answered with a minimal response such as "yes," "no," or another single word or brief phrase), open-ended questions are designed to elicit many possible answers and in this manner are similar to the constructive questions in solution-focused therapy.

Open-ended questions usually begin with "What" (e.g., "What are your thoughts about being here and having to talk to me?") and "How" (e.g., "How would you like things to be different?"). Rather than interrogating (often implied when questions begin with "Why"), open-ended questions are designed to invite the client's opinion and encourage elaboration. Because of this intent, they need not always be in the form of a question. "Tell me about—" and "Say more about—" are both examples of invitational statements categorized as open-ended questions in MI because they are designed to elicit further information, including the client's thoughts and feelings, and to keep the client talking. By asking open-ended questions and posing invitational statements, the MI practitioner is able to do more listening than talking, an important goal when working with resistance.

Miller, and Hendrickson (2005) identified seven helper behaviors that reflect an MI-consistent style. These are listed in Box 10.8 below, along with five MI-*in*consistent helper behaviors. The MI-consistent behaviors have

| BOX 10.8 | Helper Behaviors Consistent and Inconsistent with MI |

MI-Consistent Behaviors	**MI-Inconsistent Behaviors**
1. Ask open-ended questions	1. Confront
2. Affirm	2. Direct
3. Reflect	3. Warn
4. Seek permission before offering advice, feedback, or information	4. Advise or persuade without permission
5. Emphasize personal choice and control/encourage client autonomy	5. Raise concern without permission
6. Reframe	
7. Support	

Source: Moyers, Miller, & Hendrickson, 2005.

Learning Activity 10.4

Detecting Dimensions of Client Change Talk

This activity is an opportunity to detect change talk, as defined in motivational interviewing, and when heard, to categorize it as either preparatory change talk or mobilizing change talk. The 12 client statements listed below were uttered by Susan, the client described in Learning Activity 10.3. The two areas of concern, or target behaviors, for Susan are (1) employment and (2) improving her relationship with her son, Matt. Knowing this will help you determine whether what she says is in the direction of change (change talk) or away from change (sustain talk or staying put). If you hear change talk, categorize it as either preparatory change talk (*desire, ability, reason,* and *need,* or DARN) or mobilizing change talk (*commitment, activation,* and *taking steps,* or *CAT*). Don't worry about identifying the type of preparatory change talk (e.g., desire or ability) or mobilizing change talk (e.g., taking steps). Simply categorize the change talk you hear as DARN or CAT. Feedback is on page 366.

1. "I only came in today because of Matt. He's a good kid and deserves a good mother."

   ❏ Change Talk   or   ❏ Sustain Talk?
   If change talk: ❏ DARN (preparatory) or ❏ CAT (mobilizing)?

2. "I can't keep going on like this. Something really has to change."

   ❏ Change Talk   or   ❏ Sustain Talk?
   If change talk: ❏ DARN (preparatory) or ❏ CAT (mobilizing)?

3. "My boyfriend, Sam, tells me I need to get back to work, but I'm not ready. Heck, I can't even write straight, you know, to take orders, let alone carry a tray or pour coffee without shaking."

   ❏ Change Talk   or   ❏ Sustain Talk?
   If change talk: ❏ DARN (preparatory) or ❏ CAT (mobilizing)?

4. "I did call and talk with Matt last night. It wasn't for long, but I told him I loved him, which I hadn't got to do for a while."

   ❏ Change Talk   or   ❏ Sustain Talk?
   If change talk: ❏ DARN (preparatory) or ❏ CAT (mobilizing)?

5. "I'm going to stop in that one restaurant tomorrow that has a 'hiring' sign out front."

   ❏ Change Talk   or   ❏ Sustain Talk?
   If change talk: ❏ DARN (preparatory) or ❏ CAT (mobilizing)?

6. "I wish I could drive again so I could go see Matt."

   ❏ Change Talk   or   ❏ Sustain Talk?
   If change talk: ❏ DARN (preparatory) or ❏ CAT (mobilizing)?

7. "I guess I've thought that if I could leave Matt's father, I should be able to stand up for myself in other ways, like telling Sam I want to go to Matt's football game next Friday."

   ❏ Change Talk   or   ❏ Sustain Talk?
   If change talk: ❏ DARN (preparatory) or ❏ CAT (mobilizing)?

8. "I need to find something soon because we can't continue to live off of Sam's pay much longer."

   ❏ Change Talk   or   ❏ Sustain Talk?
   If change talk: ❏ DARN (preparatory) or ❏ CAT (mobilizing)?

9. "Maybe I'll talk with my former boss. I guess it couldn't hurt."

   ❏ Change Talk   or   ❏ Sustain Talk?
   If change talk: ❏ DARN (preparatory) or ❏ CAT (mobilizing)?

10. "I'm tired of sitting around all day."

    ❏ Change Talk   or   ❏ Sustain Talk?
    If change talk: ❏ DARN (preparatory) or ❏ CAT (mobilizing)?

11. "I like my doctor, but I really don't know why she suggested I see a counselor. I mean, you can't get me a job or get me back with my son."

    ❏ Change Talk   or   ❏ Sustain Talk?
    If change talk: ❏ DARN (preparatory) or ❏ CAT (mobilizing)?

12. "I'm dependable and trustworthy; you know, I do what I say I'm gonna do. But those aren't really skills that'll get me a job."

    ❏ Change Talk   or   ❏ Sustain Talk?
    If change talk: ❏ DARN (preparatory) or ❏ CAT (mobilizing)?

Although asking open-ended questions may appear to be a simple or no-brainer activity, they do require the helper's vigilance. For one thing, the helper's tone of voice must convey genuine inquisitiveness and not incredulity. This can be monitored by paying attention to which words in the question are emphasized. In addition, an open-ended question may inadvertently turn into a closed-ended question, as in "Tell me about your smoking. Did you start in middle school?" Notice that what begins as a statement inviting a wealth of unlimited information quickly turns into a closed and fact-finding question. Such a detour is regarded as a "spoiled open question" (W. R. Miller et al., 2003). In their defense, closed-ended questions are useful when the helper knows what he or she is looking for (e.g., "Do you mean to say that…?"), to either confirm or disconfirm the helper's hypothesis, and to expedite the pace of gathering information. When the helper is facing resistance, however, open-ended questions are preferred, particularly in the beginning phases of the helping process, because they convey respect for the client's perspective, encourage participation and collaboration, and do not send the message that the practitioner knows best.

MI Strategy 2: Reflecting

Although reflective listening is described in Chapter 4, it is included here because of its indispensability in the practice of MI. Reflective listening has been characterized as "one of the most important and most challenging skills required for motivational interviewing" (W. R. Miller & Rollnick, 2002, p. 67). Moyers and colleagues (2009) found that therapists' use of reflections generated more client change talk than other MI-consistent behaviors such as affirmations.

Reflections—also known as *reflective* or *empathic* statements—capture and return to the client something that the client has said or has expressed nonverbally and in so doing verify that the client has been heard. The essence of reflective statements is that they make a guess as to what the speaker means (e.g., thoughts, feelings, intentions), but the guess is phrased as a statement, not a question, so the speaker's voice tone goes down at the end (i.e., ends with a period and not a question mark).

Practice for a moment saying out loud the statement: "You're confused about what to do next." Now say the same words again by intentionally placing a question mark at the end. Notice the difference? The question mark (i.e., voice tone going up at the end) makes the statement into a question, and a closed-ended question at that, resembling W. R. Miller and colleagues' (2003) "spoiled open question" mentioned earlier. Repeating the phrase and placing a period at the end (i.e., voice tone going down at the end) does not question the client's feeling or intention; instead, it leaves the door open for the client to agree or disagree and possibly elaborate. Helpers whose voice tone inadvertently and

repeatedly goes up at the end of a reflective statement—and thus makes a question out of an intended reflection—are encouraged to practice by repeating the statement with their chin pointing downward toward their chest or when looking at themselves in a mirror. These behaviors should quickly squelch your tendency to ask questions because it's difficult to do so with your head and chin bent down or while looking at yourself in a mirror.

Although several types of reflections are offered in MI, three basic reflective statements are discussed here and examples are provided in Box 10.9. **Simple reflections** mirror and acknowledge the client's emotion, opinion, or perception and thus repeat or rephrase what the client has said. **Complex reflections** go beyond simple reflections by adding substantial meaning or emphasis to what the client has said. They reflect the complexity of the client's meaning, feeling, or experience. One way helpers do this is to use metaphors or analogies (ones not used by the client). Another way is to exaggerate or amplify certain words to convey that the extent of the client's thinking or the intensity of his or her emotion has been heard. Responding in this way may encourage the client to cool down or back off a bit from the saturated feeling or the certainty of thought (i.e., serve as a space bar or a pause from the emotion or certainty). Inflecting one's voice and using overgeneralizations (e.g., "never," "only," "always," or "nothing") in a straightforward and empathic manner can help communicate to the client that his or her perspectives matter. Complex reflections, therefore, are designed to validate the client's experience and also offer an alternative perspective.

Double-sided reflections are categorized in MI as a specific type of complex reflection and are used when the client has voiced some ambivalence. The helper listens carefully for both sides of the ambivalence and then reflects both sides, not discounting or dismissing either one, and in so doing allows the client to wrestle with the tension. One signal that a double-sided reflection is in order is the client's use of the word *but,* suggesting that there are two conflicting or at least nonparallel views at work. In response, the helper may retain the *but,* although using *and*

BOX 10.9	Examples of Three Types of Reflective Statements

Client: Coming here is a bunch of crap. It's all political. I wouldn't mind getting some help to stay sober, but you know, the only reason I'm here is because that damn prosecutor is up for re-election! It's just not right.

Simple reflection: "You're frustrated about having to come here, especially when it's to help a politician get re-elected."

Complex reflection: "Coming here is a total waste of your time because you feel it doesn't have anything to do

with you. You're frustrated about being the guinea pig for someone else's career advancement, not your own well-being."

Double-sided reflection: "You'd like to get sober, but [or *and?*] you're also angry about being told to do it for the sole purpose of helping the prosecutor get re-elected."

to connect the two sides may initially help the client come face-to-face with the full weight or tension of both sides, resulting in a realization that "something's gotta give."

When used to shed light on both sides of a discrepancy or ambivalence, reflections can resemble a form of confrontation, which W. R. Miller (1999) reframed as an invitation for clarification. This means that clients are encouraged to come face to face "with a difficult and often threatening reality, to 'let in' rather than 'block it out,' and to allow this reality to change them. That makes confrontation a *goal* of counseling rather than a particular *style* or *technique*" (p. 10). Three helpful words that can be used as a preface to a reflective statement, one that confronts or invites clarification, are "Help me understand." The word *help* signals an invitation (or a request for permission), *me* personalizes the request, and *understand* indicates that the helper is intent on empathizing with the client's struggle. To practice using this preface, insert these three words at the beginning of the example of a double-sided reflection in Box 10.9. Notice how these words may catch the client's attention and then soften the effect of the double-sided reflection. We encourage you to periodically use "Help me understand" as a genuine request for shared clarity.

To help implement the practices of asking open-ended questions and reflective listening, W. R. Miller and Rollnick (2013, p. 326) offered these guidelines:

1. Offer more complex reflections than simple reflections.

2. Ask more open questions than closed questions.

3. Provide at least two reflections for every question.

MI Strategy 3: Affirming

A third MI practice is to affirm client efforts toward positive change. This practice dovetails nicely with solution-focused therapy's recommendation that helpers notice the difference (i.e., exceptions to client accounts of problem-saturated stories), or otherwise discern client strengths and resources, and then convey their observations or assessments to clients. As discussed in the chapter, we prefer **affirmations** or commendations to SFT's reference to "compliments" or "cheerleading." The former two terms imply genuine observations based on certain evidence (e.g., client's demonstration of a certain skill), whereas compliments could be construed as general or hollow accolades representing the helper's wishful thinking. Rosengren (2009) also explained that compliments can often convey evaluation and judgment. Notice the difference between "I think you've done a fantastic job" and "You persevered and accomplished a difficult task." The first statement is nonspecific and may be interpreted as overly

optimistic. Furthermore, because the first statement begins with "I," the focus is on the helper (the one offering the compliment) and not the client (the one intended as the recipient), and the message may be construed as evaluative and therefore patronizing. By contrast, the second statement identifies a specific client characteristic utilized (i.e., perseverance) that contributed to the client's positive outcome. The focus remains on the client. In this manner, affirmations are used to direct the client's attention to assets already in his or her possession, intrinsic or at least accessible resources that can be fostered and mobilized in future circumstances.

Rosengren (2009) offers six recommendations for using affirmations:

1. Focus on specific behaviors instead [of] attitudes, decisions, and goals.

2. Avoid using the word "I."

3. Focus on descriptions and not evaluations.

4. Attend to nonproblem areas rather than problem areas.

5. Think of affirmations as attributing interesting qualities to clients.

6. Nurture a competent instead of a deficit worldview of clients. (p. 62)

Helpers who are able to recognize and to accentuate client strengths, who remain hopeful about their client's ability to realize positive change, and who deliver affirmations that convey confidence in the client's abilities are practicing what W. R. Miller (2000) depicted as "other-efficacy." Whereas *self-efficacy* refers to confidence in oneself, *other-efficacy* is confidence in another person's abilities. Affirmations, therefore, are examples of the helper's other-efficacy.

MI Strategy 4: Seeking Permission

Obtaining the client's permission before providing him or her with information or advice exemplifies partnership in MI. Just as a good dance partner first asks another "May I have this dance?" before stepping on the dance floor, an MI helper gets the client's permission before offering feedback or a suggestion. Think of this as waiting for the client's "green light" before proceeding in a direction you believe might be helpful to the client.

The concept of offering clients advice may seem counterintuitive to the values of MI. Although described as a directive approach, the provision of advice in MI is not the same as telling the client what to do. Because of this, it may be more accurate to refer to providing clients with recommendations or suggestions than with advice. Recall that being directive in MI means that the helper is purposeful or intentional in promoting client discrepancy, acknowledging and working with ambivalence, and eliciting the client's own reasons for change. Offering clients recommendations is therefore directive insofar as it assists clients in decision-making and the process of change.

W. R. Miller and Rollnick (1991) developed three specific guidelines for offering advice or recommendations (pp. 118–119) that remain helpful today:

1. Helpers should not be too eager to give advice (and in so doing, play a bit "hard to get") and should wait for a direct invitation or request for information.

2. Helpers should qualify any suggestions made and present advice in a deliberately nonpersonal way. For example, the helper can say, "I don't know if this would work for you or not, but I can give you an idea of what has worked for some other people in your situation," or "You'll have to try it to see if it'll work for you."

3. Helpers should offer not one piece of advice but a cluster or a menu of options. Offering more than one option (and preferably three at the most rather than two) not only respects the client's autonomy but also

signifies the practitioner's effort to tailor care to the individual client. In addition, clients are more likely to feel empowered when given the opportunity to make choices about their care and may be more likely to adhere to a specific course of action when they are able to select it from among alternatives. The helper is following this third guideline when he or she states: "Let me describe a number of possibilities, and you tell me which of these makes the most sense to you."

After the helper has received the client's permission and has offered the client advice, feedback, or information, it is recommended that the helper elicit the client's perspective on what was provided. "What do you think?" is one example. Think of this as another way the helper stays in step with the client. A three-step rule of thumb is recommended in MI when providing advice, feedback, or any kind of information: elicit-provide-elicit or **E-P-E** (W. R. Miller & Rollnick, 2013). The first elicit is for the client's permission, and the second elicit is for the client's input on what was provided. These two elicits "bookend" the helper's input and remind the helper that the client's contributions are primary.

10.4 Feedback

Detecting Dimensions of Client Change Talk

1. Change talk: preparatory. Susan wants and has reasons to improve her relationship with Matt.

2. Change talk: preparatory. There is a sense of urgency in what she says, that something has to change, even though that change is not specified here.

3. Sustain talk. The impetus for change is coming from her boyfriend, not from Susan. She clearly states she's not ready to work again, giving reasons for not being able to waitress.

4. Change talk: mobilizing. Susan describes a recent interaction with Matt (telephone call) during which she engaged in a change behavior (told him she loves him) that exemplifies her efforts to improve their relationship.

5. Change talk: mobilizing. She is making an unwavering commitment to engage in a change behavior almost immediately ("tomorrow").

6. Change talk: preparatory. She describes what she wants for a specific purpose. That she uses "wish" here should not be discounted. Being able to drive is just one way to see Matt, and seeing Matt is the point of being able to drive.

7. Change talk: preparatory. She describes a skill or ability she was able to use at one time, one she doesn't think she has or is able to use now, but one she wants

and feels the need to use now. She's fairly specific about what that is.

8. Change talk: preparatory. Once again there is urgency in what she says.

9. Change talk: mobilizing. This exemplifies leaning into change, a consideration of a specific behavior (talking to her former boss) that she says has no drawbacks ("it can't hurt").

10. Change talk: preparatory. Although not tied to one of the two target or change behaviors (employment or improving relationship with Matt), she is voicing a reason for not remaining the same or staying put. She's tired of *not* changing!

11. Sustain talk. She is questioning her doctor's recommendation.

12. Change talk: preparatory. She has identified personal qualities that are important in almost any job. That she has described herself in this way is important. The "but" suggests ambivalence, that she's not convinced that these qualities alone will get her a job. She is probably correct. However, the presence of change talk before the "but" is significant, especially coming from someone with a low self-image. This change talk deserves recognition.

MI Strategy 5: Emphasizing Personal Choice and Control

Consistent with MI's humanistic philosophy is the practice of emphasizing to clients that they alone are the ones to decide how to invest in and make use of the helping process, including whether or not—or to what extent—they will make changes in their lives. This practice exemplifies the ethical principle of **autonomy** in the helping professions—that is, respecting the client's inherent right to make decisions about his or her care when the client is competent to do so.

Emphasizing the client's autonomy can be conveyed in a comment such as, "Well, it really is your choice what to do next. We've talked about several possibilities, but you alone are the one to say what's going to happen. I couldn't decide for you, let alone make you do anything." W. R. Miller and Rollnick (2002) contend that a reassuring statement such as this may be "the best antidote" (p. 106) for persons who feel threatened and are thus opposing the mandates or suggestions of others to behave differently. Furthermore, the helper is conveying the truth and that which respects the client's autonomy. This is best reflected in W. R. Miller's (1999) admonition to practitioners:

> In a motivational approach to counseling, it is not your task to *give* a client a choice—choice is not yours to give but the client's to make. You do not *allow* a client to choose because the choice is already and always belongs with the client. The *client* chooses. Your task is to help clients make choices that are in their best interests. (p. 90)

MI Strategy 6: Reframing

Although the skill of reframing is described in detail in Chapter 11, it is mentioned here because it is particularly useful in addressing and working with resistance. **Reframing** is similar to reflecting in the sense that both convey understanding. The difference is that reframes "also change the valence or emotional charge of a client statement" (W. R. Miller et al., 2003, p. 40) from a negative to a positive meaning or vice versa. Reframes offer a new meaning or interpretation and recast the client's information in a new light that is more likely to support change (W. R. Miller & Rollnick, 2002). Take, for example, a client who says, "I've reached my limit and I don't know if I can go on like this." A complex reflection might be something like, "You've hit a wall, or at least a stumbling block, and now you're wondering if you can keep going in the same direction or at the same pace." A reframe, however, might be phrased as, "You're at a crossroads and you're thinking you need to take another route." Whereas the reflection makes a guess as to the client's current circumstance or emotional state, the reframe offers new

meaning and introduces an alternative perspective (i.e., "at a crossroads" and "you need to take another route") that is more hopeful (i.e., the client has an opportunity to make a change, and another course of action is possible) than simply validating the client's feeling of hitting a wall.

Reframes can also alert clients to risks or dangers they were not aware of or heretofore considered advantageous or at least no big deal. For example, "holding one's liquor" may not necessarily be a source of pride when reframed as "tolerance" or the body's warning device that it is accommodating a toxin (W. R. Miller & Rollnick, 2002). In addition, being the "good daughter" may take its toll on being the "good wife and mother" if caring for an aging parent is depriving other family members of care and attention. Likewise, "keeping up with the Joneses" or pursuing the status of "super Mom" or "super Dad" may actually create a divide between parent and child valuing extraneous and transient things and modeling superficial characters. Additional examples of possible reframes are provided in Box 10.10.

MI Strategy 7: Supporting

Supportive statements are regarded in MI as expressions of agreement, concern, and compassion. "I'm here to help you with this" conveys an intention to lend comfort and reassurance, and "That must have been difficult" has an agreeing quality to it. In MI, supportive statements differ from affirmations in that supportive comments reflect more of the helper's concern for or investment in the client's well-being, whereas affirmations are intended to point out to the client strengths and resources already in his or her possession. Supportive statements may say more about the helper's qualities (e.g., compassionate, concerned) than about those of the client, whereas affirmations are intended to emphasize the client's qualities.

MI "Spirit" Encore

As has been emphasized throughout this chapter, MI is a style of helping, a way of being with and speaking with clients, rather than a collection of techniques applied to clients (W. R. Miller & Rollnick, 2013). MI is not about doing something to clients; it's about being with and partnering with clients on their journey toward change. Although we have reviewed seven specific strategies of MI (likened to individual musical notes within a song), none contains its essence or its "spirit." MI can be understood and appreciated only by stepping back to see the gestalt or to hear the entire musical score.

Prominent in MI is the theme, strand, or melody of client-centered humanism that emphasizes respect and empathy for others, particularly in the midst of resistance,

BOX 10.10 Examples of Possible Reframes

- Not making a decision right now = Being careful
- Stubborn = Determined
- Selfishness = Self-care
- "Do not resuscitate" = "Allow natural death"
- Compulsivity = Persistence
- Nagging = Concerned
- Failure = Learning opportunity
- Dinner leftovers = Extreme makeovers
- Aging = No more peer pressure

reactance, reluctance, and ambivalence. The centrality of this value to MI was made evident in a study of MI practitioners. Moyers and colleagues (2005) determined that therapist demonstration of both MI-preferred interpersonal characteristics and MI-consistent behaviors predicted client involvement in sessions, providing support for "particular clinician skills that can be expected to increase client collaboration, disclosure, and expression of affect" (p. 596). Surprisingly, however, MI-inconsistent behaviors did not decrease client involvement in session when clinicians demonstrated characteristics such as warmth, empathy, and acceptance. MI-inconsistent therapist behaviors (e.g., confrontation, directing clients, or giving advice without permission) that occur within an empathic, accepting, and egalitarian interpersonal context "may be consistent with a genuine and authentic stance that is well received by clients and therefore elicits cooperation and increased expression of affect and disclosure" (p. 59). Put another way, therapists who confront or direct clients within an atmosphere of empathy and acceptance may actually "convey a sense of honesty and transparency on the part of the clinician that may facilitate, rather than suppress, the alliance with the client" (p. 596). In general, however, MI helpers should avoid engaging in MI-inconsistent behaviors because Apodaca and Longabaugh (2009) found that these behaviors predict poor client outcomes.

To help you determine whether certain helper responses are MI-consistent or MI-inconsistent, we encourage you to participate in Learning Activity 10.5. This activity also challenges you to offer alternative and more appropriate helper responses in your effort to practice MI consistently. Feedback follows on page 371.

Model Dialogue: Affirming, Emphasizing Autonomy, and Advising only with Permission

Isabella has indicated that she wants to express herself **LO2** better in the classroom and with her parents. Specifically, she wants to express differences of opinion and positive feelings. From the work that Isabella has done so far with her helper, it appears that she has made progress toward

implementing these skills at school, specifically in her math class. Because of this, the helper now inquires about Isabella's readiness to implement some of these same skills at home with her parents. A motivational interviewing style seems appropriate here because Isabella is ambivalent about talking to her parents about changing her college preparation curriculum.

1. **Helper:** It's great to hear how well you've practiced and followed through on many of the skills we've worked on together. From what you've told me, it sounds like you've been able to participate more in math class and have been getting better grades on your assignments.

Client: Yeah, I'm kind a pleased with myself. It feels good to not feel all out of sorts and worried so much about things when I'm in school.

2. **Helper:** Wonderful! You've been very open to trying out all these exercises I've suggested. Your cooperation tells me that doing better at school is something that's very important to you. And it sounds like your diligence is now paying off in ways you can see first-hand. I'm sure it must feel good to be able to pat yourself on the back for a job well done.

Client: Yeah, I am kind of proud of myself. It feels good to know this is something I've done, that I can give myself credit for it, not something someone else did for me.

The helper has been intentional in offering Isabella several *affirmations* about the progress she has made thus far, with the focus remaining on Isabella's strengths.

3. **Helper:** I remember that in addition to being able to speak up in math class, you wanted to be able to talk with your parents more confidently about things. We haven't talked about that in a while. How is that going?

Client: Well, of course they're really happy about how I'm doing now in school. They've said, "See, we knew you could do it. You just had to put your mind to it." So now the pressure's on to continue to do well, to not disappoint them. It's like they've had in mind what I should be doing, what I should be studying, and they're pleased as punch that I've "come around" to finally see things their way. But I don't know if I want to do what they want me to do.

Learning Activity 10.5

Practicing MI Consistently

This activity lets you try your hand at detecting MI-consistent helper behaviors and offer alternative responses to those that are MI-inconsistent. Read through each of the following client statements, and then determine whether the helper responses *are* consistent with MI or not. If they are consistent, identify what *types* of helper responses they are from the seven presented in Box 10.7 on page 362. If the helper responses are *not* consistent with MI, identify what kinds they are (from the list of five presented in Box 10.7), then *rewrite* different responses that are MI consistent and explain what types of response they are. Feedback follows on page 371.

1. **Client:** Why are you giving me this booklet? Are you telling me I have to use condoms?
   a. "It's just information. What you do with it is up to you. Naturally, no one can make you use condoms."
   b. "I've thought that if you don't start wearing condoms, you're eventually going to have more than one child support payment to make."
   c. "I'm concerned about you and want you to have some information that you might find helpful."

2. **Client:** I was told I only had to come here for an evaluation. No one said anything to me about attending therapy. So you telling me I have to come back for some group therapy sessions is a load of crap!
   a. "You're not happy about my recommendation and believe you've been misinformed about—maybe even tricked into—coming here."
   b. "I do have another thought here. I could be off, but see what you think. Because you said you feel like no one's taking you seriously, I'm wondering if you at least attended one group session, just to try it out, I'm wondering if that might show that you are serious about doing something. Again, I could be wrong, but I'm thinking your attendance in at least one session would actually be in your favor. What do you think?"

   c. "Well, I do think it would be good for you to attend at least one group session."

3. **Client:** I really don't know what all the fuss is about. All of my friends drink and we have a good time. Isn't that what college is for? Yeah, my grades could be better, I'd have more money to spend on other things, and my parents would back off.
   a. "Sounds like you've given this a lot of thought, and you see some connection between your drinking and the hassles you've been dealing with."
   b. "You are young, though, and I wouldn't want to see you get into any more trouble."
   c. "Sounds like you've been having too much fun and not concentrating enough on your studies. I guess I think that *studying* is what college is for, not partying."

4. **Client:** My boss says *I'm* the one with the anger management problem. Hell, *he's* the guy who's always out of control!
   a. "Well, you're the one who's here, not your boss, so we'll need to focus on you in our conversations, not him."
   b. "What do you think are your boss's reasons for saying you needed to come to counseling?"
   c. "Yeah, it sounds like you got the short end of the stick. I'm thinking, though, that you actually might have some advantage here. Can I share what I'm thinking? [client gives permission] Who knows? You might just be able to model appropriate behavior to him as you learn more about anger management here. Just a thought. What do you think?"

5. **Client:** I have to drink or else I'll get sick.
   a. "Drinking keeps you from feeling sick."
   b. "Really? Seems like that's just another excuse for drinking."
   c. "It must be a terrible way to live to have to drink to not get sick."

4. **Helper:** You'd like to be able to make some of your own decisions about what to study.

In response 4, the helper offers a *simple reflection* that can serve to affirm Isabella, because its purpose is to convey that she has been heard and understood. In addition, the helper validates Isabella's desire to have some control over deciding what she wants to study.

Client: Exactly. Doing better in math has made me think that there are other things I can do well that I hadn't considered before. But I know my parents, especially my dad,

would go ballistic if he knew what I've been thinking I'd really like to study someday.

5. **Helper:** Your increased self-confidence has fueled your interest in other areas, areas that may not be in sync with those your parents have in mind for you.

Notice that in response 5, the helper does not ask Isabella what it is she'd like to study someday. Instead, the helper offers another reflection, one that we categorize as a *complex reflection* because it uses metaphors: "fuel" and "in sync." Recall that reflections should be at least twice the number of questions asked in motivational interviewing. The helper may be thinking that the specific area of study Isabella has in mind is secondary to Isabella's concern about her parents' reaction. Asking about the area of study may only satisfy the helper's curiosity. Isabella is free to disclose this information without being asked directly about it.

Client: Yeah. It's like they'll only support me if I'm studying what they want me to study.

6. **Helper:** And you want to have a little more control over what that is but not lose their support entirely.

In response 6, the helper uses a *double-sided reflection* that acknowledges both sides of Isabella's ambivalence—having more control on one hand and not losing her parents' support on the other.

Client: Maybe that's selfish, though. Maybe I should just give in and do what they want me to do, especially if I want them to pay for it—college, that is.

7. **Helper:** Well, I have some thoughts about this. Would you like to hear what they are? [Helper *asks for permission* before offering any observation, insight, or advice.]

Client: Sure.

8. **Helper:** I could be wrong, but I don't think you "just gave in" to your anxieties about math class. Seems to me you tackled them head on by using some of the relaxation, imagery, and coping thought skills we practiced together. So, I'm sitting here wondering how you cannot "just give in" to what you think are your parents' expectations and use some of the same skills in your conversation with your parents that you've used to help you in math class. What do you think? [Helper ends by inviting feedback from the client. The helper has followed the three-step method of elicit-provide-elicit (E-P-E) in responses 7 and 8.]

Client: You mean do some of the same things that have helped me in math with my parents?

9. **Helper:** Yes. I'm wondering if what's been helpful to you in math class might be helpful to you in your conversations with your parents. You've been able to speak up in class, for example. And it doesn't sound like you've done this inappropriately. So, I wonder how you can speak up or voice your own interests to your parents about what you really want to study and do this appropriately—in a calm, confident, and matter-of-fact manner. Does this make sense?

Client: I think so. Although I'm not sure I could do it.

10. **Helper:** You're not sure *right now* that you can. [Helper offers an *amplified reflection,* emphasizing the temporal aspect of Isabella's uncertainty. This opens up the possibility that she may not remain uncertain, that it may be just right now that she's not quite sure.]

Client *(sighs)*: I do want to be able to talk to my parents. And I would like to be able to study what I want to study.

11. **Helper:** Talking with your parents in a way you'd like to be able to is something we could practice in here, just like we practiced the skills you've used for school. You don't have to do this, though. It is your choice.

In response 11, the helper *emphasizes* Isabella's *personal choice* or *autonomy,* saying that it is her decision whether to practice initiating skills in her conversations with her parents.

Client: Well, maybe it's worth a try. I mean I didn't think a while ago that I'd be able to speak up in math class, and now I'm able to do it. So, maybe this is possible, too.

12. **Helper:** Step by step, right?

Client: Yep. That's one of the things I've learned—that change takes time and that it's definitely not a piece of cake!

Applications of SFT and MI with Diverse Groups

Both SFT and MI have been heralded as suitable and **LO2** helpful therapeutic approaches for diverse populations. This is particularly encouraging given the recent national data mentioned in Chapter 2 that racial and ethnic minorities in the United States receive significantly less mental health care than non-Latino whites. Gonzalez and colleagues (2010) found that compared to Puerto Ricans and Caribbean blacks, African Americans and Mexican Americans were the least likely to have received treatment for depression in the early 2000s despite similar prevalence rates of depression. Lack of health insurance coverage partially explained the disparities in service utilization of psychotherapy and/or psychopharmacology for Mexican Americans, but not for African Americans, suggesting other barriers to mental health care. Among these are societal stigma, intracultural group preferences for "taking care of our own business," clinicians' lack of awareness of cultural issues, and clients' fear and mistrust of professional help. Working with resistance may therefore allow SFT and MI to be particularly useful for clients from cultural backgrounds who are initially skeptical or suspicious of such care, given the clients' history and current

10.5 Feedback

Practicing MI Consistently

MI-Consistent or MI-Inconsistent?	Type of MI-Consistent Helper Behavior	Type of MI-Inconsistent Helper Behavior	Rewrite of MI-Inconsistent Helper Response or Alternative MI-Consistent Response
1. a. MI-consistent	Emphasize personal choice and control/ Encourage client autonomy		
1. b. MI-inconsistent		Warn	No, I'm not here to tell you what to do. [Emphasize personal choice and control] You're one who's committed to making his own decisions [Affirm], so I thought this booklet might help you in the process.
1. c. MI-consistent	Support		
2. a. MI-consistent	Reflect		
2. b. MI-consistent	Advise with permission		
2. c. MI-inconsistent		Advise without permission	It really is your choice whether or not you want to take me up on my recommendation. [Emphasize personal choice and control]
3. a. MI-consistent	Affirm		
3. b. MI-inconsistent		Raise concern without permission	On the one hand, you're having a good time drinking. On the other hand, you're able to see some specific benefits to you of not drinking. [Double-sided reflection]
3. c. MI-inconsistent		Direct	You're confused about why your drinking is such a concern. [Simple reflection]
4. a. MI-inconsistent		Confront	Sounds like you're perceptive about others and you have some insight about what could be helpful in our work together. [Affirm]
4. b. MI-consistent	Ask open-ended questions		
4. c. MI-consistent	Complex reflection, Asking permission before offering reframe, and Reframe		
5. a. MI-consistent	Simple reflection		
5. b. MI-inconsistent		Confront	Wow, it's gotten to that point, almost like drinking's become a sort of life-preserver for you, keeping you from getting really sick. [Complex reflection]
5. c. MI-consistent	Support		

experience of discrimination and oppression. The humanistic, semi-structured, supportive, and client-helper collaborative philosophy of both SFT and MI can therefore serve as a nonthreatening invitation to prospective and recent clients to engage in services.

SFT has been described as appropriate for use with ethnic minority (namely, African American, Mexican American, Asian American) families (Corcoran, 2000; Lee & Mjelde-Mossey, 2004) and individuals (Berg & Miller, 1992a), Appalachian individuals (Gunn, 2001), Hispanic children of incarcerated parents (Springer, Lynch, & Rubin, 2000), American Indians (Meyer & Cottone, 2013), and Muslim Americans (Chaudhry & Li, 2011). Given SFT's emphasis on the utilization of client (and community) strengths and resources, it certainly represents an empowerment approach typically recommended for working with diverse populations. This is supported in Hsu's (2009) research on the types of empowerment identified by nine married females in Taiwan who participated in one to ten sessions of SFT. The pragmatic features of SFT may also make it somewhat appealing (or contribute to professional care being perceived as less stigmatizing) to those from various cultural backgrounds. Indeed, Lee (2003) explains that "solution-focused therapy is goal-oriented and emphasizes clear indicators of progress, consistent with the pragmatic, problem-solving orientation shared by ethnic and racial groups that stress collectivism" (p. 390).

As the review of MI research earlier in this chapter indicated, MI and adaptations of MI appear to result in beneficial outcomes for minorities more so than for white clients. Although this differential has not been fully explained, Lundahl and Burke (2009) suggested that MI's client-centered, supportive, and nonconfrontational style may be regarded as a culturally respectful form of helping by some ethnic clients. This is particularly true for those who have experienced various forms of discrimination and oppression. It also may be that MI's primary focus on ambivalence renders it a suitable approach for persons who are quite familiar with a life of tension and struggling against opposing forces.

Roberts and Nishimoto (2006) recommended a combination of SFT and MI in working with African American women (specifically postpartum) in drug treatment. They described SFT as useful in providing hope by helping female clients focus more on "high-success" situations or "multiple episodes of sobriety" than on "high-risk" situations or "chronic relapses" (see Berg & Miller, 1992b; Mason, Chandler, & Grasso, 1995) and noted that MI is helpful in exploring with clients their internal motivation. Roberts and Nishimoto stated that "examining internal barriers may be associated with blaming the victim, but this is not necessarily so. Examining internal barriers provides opportunities for…practitioners to become competent in exploring and addressing issues of inner motivation, especially in light of the reality that a number of subjects are mandated to treatment" (p. 67).

CHAPTER SUMMARY

Perhaps resistance has been presented in a new or different light in this chapter, not as something to be attacked head-on or avoided but as something to be accepted and worked through in collaboration with clients. It may also be that understanding resistance as a two-person operation (i.e., something that client and helper generate and participate in together) rather than as solely a client characteristic and problem may open up more options for helpers.

Solution-focused therapy (SFT) and motivational interviewing (MI) represent what we believe are helpful ways to work with resistance with our clients. Their shared and complementary philosophies allow them to work in tandem for the benefit of clients and helpers. Lewis and Osborn (2004) identified seven similarities between SFT and MI and five differences, all of them listed in Box 10.11. They further described the integration of

BOX 10.11 Comparison of SFT and MI	
SFT and MI Similarities	**SFT and MI Differences**
1. Nonpathological, salutary focus	1. Social construction through language
2. Multiple perspectives	2. Concept of change
3. Anchored in change	3. Counselor focus and goals
4. Reframing the concept of resistance	4. Temporal focus
5. Cooperation is key	5. Reflectivity
6. Use of client strengths and resources	
7. Temporal sensitivity	*Source:* Lewis & Osborn, 2004.

SFT and MI as a constructive confluence and proposed three features of such a "synergistic emergence" (p. 45). First, they noted that *honoring client stories* bolsters the full participation of both client and helper in the helping process. Second, *motivation* and *ambivalence* are the *resources for change*, and third, *change occurs in relation*. They stated that when SFT and MI are intertwined, "change is understood in terms of conversational or relational movements or fluctuations over time, illustrating the systemic, holistic, dynamic or interactional, and recursive nature of counseling and the counseling process" (p. 46).

Lewis and Osborn (2004) conjectured that the confluence of SFT and MI can bolster the process of change by offering multiple passages through the challenges and impasses experienced during the change process. Client strengths and the resources present in the helping relationship itself can be mobilized to work with and through resistance, representing an example of solution construction.

As we have reflected on SFT and MI, a vivid and compelling image has emerged to describe their integrated approach to working with resistance: "dancing with curiosity." This image combines W. R. Miller and Rollnick's (2013) characterization of the helping relationship as a dance and Shilts and Thomas's (2005) reframe of resistance as curiosity. We believe that both clients and helpers benefit when they assume a posture of intrigue or curiosity during their collaborative effort (i.e., dance) to construct a more manageable and hopeful reality for the client.

Visit CengageBrain.com for a variety of study tools and useful resources such as video examples, case studies, interactive exercises, flashcards, and quizzes.

10 | Knowledge and Skill Builder

This activity is intended to address Learning Outcomes 1, 2, and 3. It is designed to assess your ability to identify solution-focused therapy (SFT) strategies and motivational interviewing (MI) strategies in a client-helper interaction.

Read through the case of Vince and the recent conversation he and his helper (a middle-aged white female) had in session. What three strategies of SFT did the helper use? What three strategies of MI did the helper use? What three strategies used by Vince's helper reflect a *combination* or *integration* of SFT and MI? For each response, provide a rationale for its use. For those intervention approaches that combine SFT and MI, describe how they illustrate a primary theme of this chapter—that "dancing with curiosity" is a recommended helping style for working with resistance. Feedback follows beginning on page 377.

Vince is a 25-year-old biracial (African American and white) male who is a high school graduate and currently a student in his first quarter at a local technical college. He is on parole for assault with a deadly weapon after serving a 4-year sentence in a prison in another state. As a condition of his parole, Vince is to obtain counseling at the local drug and alcohol treatment facility where you work. He states that "weed" (i.e., marijuana) is his drug of choice and that it's not going to be easy staying clean ("It helps calm me down") to pass the monthly urine screens his probation officer will administer. He last used 2 weeks ago right before his release from the local jail, where he was serving time for an alleged drug possession charge. The charges have been dropped. Vince acknowledges a 5-year "career" in cocaine trafficking, but he denies a history of cocaine use, stating that profits were used, in part, to support his use of marijuana. He says he started smoking cigarettes at age 8 and started smoking marijuana regularly at approximately age 10. He acknowledges occasional use of alcohol but states he really doesn't care for it.

Vince was adopted at age 2 by a white couple who already had two biological children of their own (6 and 8 years old at the time). Vince's dad is a college professor and his mother is a social worker. Vince says his parents continue to be concerned about him and want him to stay out of prison and finally get away from drugs. His relationship with them is estranged, and Vince acknowledges that he has never been able to trust anybody. He lives alone in his own apartment, just recently started working for a local trash collection company, and states he wants to get back to boxing, a talent he says won him a Golden Gloves competition when he was 19.

What follows is an excerpt from Vince and his helper's fifth individual counseling session.

Helper: You know, I'm really glad you decided to come in today. I wasn't sure you would because last week was the first time that we talked about you being adopted. I sensed you weren't too happy with me for bringing it up. You didn't say much at the end of our session and headed right out the main door without saying good-bye, and that was unusual for you. I could have been reading that all wrong.

Vince: Naw, I was a little pissed.

Helper: You were upset with me, then, for bringing up the adoption thing.

Vince: Yeah.

Helper: I appreciate you letting me know. I'm curious, though, what made you decide to come back in today, given that you were upset with me last week?

Vince (shrugging shoulders): I have to.

Helper: You have to.

Vince: Yeah.

Helper: Ah, so you don't want to break parole and have to go back to prison.

Vince: Yeah.

Helper: So you decided to do what you have to do to stay out of prison.

Vince: You got it.

Helper: I wonder, then, what you were thinking about, what you had in mind we'd be talking about, when you came in today.

Vince: Anything else but stuff back then. The past is the past, you know? I just want to keep movin' forward and not keep lookin' back all the time.

Helper: You've got your sights set on what's ahead, and looking back would trip you up or maybe even just be a waste of time.

Vince: Yeah. You know, I figure I've done my time. No use digging up stuff and going through what's already happened. What's done is done.

Helper: You're a man on a mission. You've probably been on a mission for most of your life.

Vince: Maybe.

Helper: Well, if so, what would you say that mission has been?

Vince (shrugging shoulders): I guess to be on my own. To not have to depend on anyone, you know? I guess just to be left alone.

Helper: Left alone.

Vince: (no response, looking down)

Helper: And that has its advantages and disadvantages.

Vince (looking up at the helper): What doesn't?

Helper: Most things in life have their up and down sides.

Vince: Yeah. You gotta take the bad with the good, the good with the bad, or whatever.

Helper: You know (pausing), do you mind if I share an impression with you?

Vince: (shrugs shoulders)

Helper: Yeah?

Vince: Go right ahead.

Helper: (leans forward slightly) One of the things that stands out about you, and one thing I think you have going for you, is that you're pretty realistic. I mean, you're not out there with your head in the clouds, your head filled with all these fancy, far-fetched ideas. You're down to earth. Pretty practical, getting done what you think needs to get done. I get the impression, though *(pauses)*, that this is fueled by some anger, that you're constantly fighting something, always on the attack. *(pauses)* What do you think? Am I on to something or did I just get it all wrong?

(silence)

Helper: *(pauses)* I guess I'm off the mark.

Vince *(hands tightly grasping his chair's arm rests):* Look, you'd be pissed, too, if you came from where I came from. And *(starting to get up from his chair)* I don't need you to try to get inside my head to try to figure me out. You're talkin' like my mom now and *(standing up now and walking to the office door)* I don't need another white woman telling me who I am and what I need to do. I should've known this would happen again today. *(hand holding the knob of the office door, pausing, not turning the doorknob)*

Helper *(still seated but turning to face Vince):* Um, you're free to go; you know that, Vince. No one's going to stop you. I just need to know what happened or what I just said that made you want to leave.

Vince *(still holding the doorknob):* Look, I thought this "treatment" stuff was about my smokin' weed, about helping me stay clean, not about this "psycho-talk" of my past and my anger.

Helper: This "psycho-talk" isn't relevant.

Vince: Naw, it's not that *(pauses)*, it's just, it just won't do no good.

Helper: Well, let me offer something, if I may *(pauses)*. And this may be way off, too, but it comes from what I've learned over the years from doing this work, and, and from what I've learned working with you. *(pause)* May I?

Vince: *(still standing holding, but hand dropping from doorknob; silence)*

Helper: I believe, in some way, they're all connected. I mean *(pauses)*, you weren't in prison for smoking pot, Vince.

(Silence)

Helper: Okay *(leaning back in chair)*, I guess I'm just not on my game today.

Vince: *(still in the room, facing the door)* Naw, it's not that.

Helper: Then help me, Vince. Help me understand.

Vince: This just won't do any good.

Helper: You're convinced of that.

(Silence)

Helper: Well, um, for what it's worth *(pauses)*, I'm sure convinced that you've been dealing with a lot of stuff for a long, long time; heck, for most of your life. It's still there, too—probably will be for a long time. I just want to help you deal with some of that. I'm not your mother; I don't want to be your mother. And I can't help it if I'm white. I just want to offer what help I can so that you can stay clean, stay out of prison, and do

some of the good things with your life that you've wanted to do for a long time. I want that for you, I really do.

(Silence)

Helper: What do you say? Will you stay in the ring for now so that we can box this out without using fists or gloves or any force? Can we talk this out without fighting?

Vince *(folding his arms across his chest, and leaning against the back of the door with his shoulder):* I just want to be left alone. I don't need anybody telling me what to do or how to live my life. I'm tired of all that.

Helper: You're able to do things on your own, figure things out on your own.

Vince: And no one seems to get it.

Helper: There's more for us to talk about, Vince. I wonder if we can keep talking with both of us sitting down. Would that be okay?

Vince *(standing up straight now, shrugging shoulders, and walking slowly back to his chair)*: Sure, whatever. *(sitting down)*

Helper: Thank you. *(pause)* Okay, so you tell me what about yourself you have figured out. I'm the student here. I have more to learn about you and you have more to teach me about you.

Vince: What do you want to know?

Helper: Well, for starters, I'm still curious about what keeps you going, what your fuel is. I threw out the notion of anger earlier, and that may have been the curveball. It was probably presumptuous on my part. I need to hear from you instead.

Vince: Naw, you're not off. There's a lot inside that's been burning. Anger, yeah, I guess.

Helper: Say more about that.

Vince: I don't know. It's been like that for as long as I can remember. *(pause)* It builds up, like a pressure cooker, and I have to get it out somehow.

Helper: Boxing helped, and so did smoking pot.

Vince: Yeah, and now I can't do either one.

Helper: You said you were "a little pissed" at me after last week's session. What did you do with that anger instead of smoking?

Vince: Oh, I don't know. I went to the gym, lifted weights, jumped rope.

Helper: Good. That's good. And how exactly did that help?

Vince: Release. Just working the muscles again, sweating, and doing it myself.

Helper: Something you could give yourself credit for. Not a joint.

Vince: Huh. Yeah, I guess so. Never thought of it that way before.

Helper: So there are some things you're *already* doing, even just last week, to help with that anger or tension or burning inside that you talk about. What else do you think could be helpful?

(continued)

Vince *(sighs):* Talking, I guess.
Helper: Talking in here, with me.
Vince: Yeah.
Helper: And you decided to do that today. You could have left, you know. But you stayed.
Vince: I was that close to leaving.
Helper: Yeah, it sure looked like you were. What made you decide to stay?
Vince: You gave me the choice. You didn't tell me what to do.
Helper: You were free to decide. What else?
Vince: You just said it straight. That I wasn't doing time for smoking pot.
Helper: And you didn't argue with me.
Vince: Naw. They're connected, I know. I just need to deal with it on my own.
Helper: Which has its advantages and disadvantages.
Vince: Huh?
Helper: Well, let's talk about some of the advantages of dealing with this stuff on your own—your anger, your attempt to stay clean, you staying in school. *(Vince identifies feeling in control, taking all the credit, pride, proving others wrong.)* Okay, so what are the disadvantages? What are the drawbacks of dealing with all of this stuff on your own? *(Vince talks about loneliness, sense of failure, getting tired, feeling depressed.)* Let's look at the other side. What would be the advantages of having others help you deal with all this stuff? What would be helpful about that?
Vince: Maybe it wouldn't seem so hard all the time.
Helper: Others would help carry the load. What else?
Vince: I wouldn't feel all alone all the time.
Helper: You'd have some company. Good. Now *(pauses)*, there probably would also be some drawbacks, some disadvantages, to having others help you with what you're dealing with. It won't always be smooth sailing.
Vince: You got that right. As you can see, I can get ticked off pretty easy.
Helper: So even having others help you deal with your anger, for instance, can get you angry.
Vince: I guess so. It sounds stupid when you say it like that, but I guess that's true.
Helper: You've got some insight about that, and that's good. The challenge, then, may be how to let others help you—at various times, in different ways, to certain degrees—without getting ticked off by them.
Vince: May not be possible.
Helper: It may be. You've stayed here today. You've worked with me on this advantages–disadvantages thing, and, I could be wrong, but it doesn't look like you're ticked off at me.
Vince: Naw, it's cool. I'm okay.

10 Knowledge and Skill Builder **Feedback**

Strategies of SFT

1. Asked *coping questions:* "What made you decide to come back in today, given that you were upset with me last week?"
   Rationale: Intended to draw out client's methods of managing concerns, behaviors that client is already implementing to address concerns or challenges.
2. Offered *legitimate commendations:* "You're down to earth. Pretty practical, getting done what you think needs to get done."
   Rationale: Highlights client's strengths and resources, capacities or abilities that are already in client's possession.
3. Engaged in "role switching": *helper as student, client as teacher:* "I'm the student here. I have more to learn about you, and you have more to teach me about you."
   Rationale: Emphasizes that the helping relationship is a partnership, that the helper is not a know-it-all, and that the client has valuable information to contribute.
4. Inquired about the *client's "instead":* "What did you do with that anger instead of smoking?"
   Rationale: Highlights client involvement in solution construction—that is, that Vince is already engaged in "exceptional behaviors" or positive behaviors that, when repeated, may "drown out" the presenting concern.
5. *Spoke the client's language:* In her responses, the helper preserved the client's own words to describe his experience or thinking, such as "burning inside," "ticked off," and "left alone."
   Rationale: Helper's attempt to convey that client has been understood, that his experiences are valid and accepted at face value.

Strategies of MI

1. Offered **reflective** or **empathic statements**: "You don't want to break parole and have to go back to prison" (simple reflection) and "You've got your sights set on what's ahead, and looking back would trip you up or maybe even just be a waste of time" (complex reflection).
   Rationale: Intended to verify that what the client was meaning to say has been heard and understood. The simple reflection was intended to mirror the client's experience, and the complex reflection offered an alternative perspective (e.g., "sights set on what's ahead" as opposed to "not keep looking back") or added meaning (e.g., "looking back" might be "a waste of time") to what the client had said.

2. Emphasized **personal choice and control**: "You're free to go…No one's going to stop you."
   Rationale: Reminded or reinforced for client what is already true: he has the right to decide whether or not to remain in session, to continue with counseling. This was particularly important for Vince to hear given that he values his freedom to choose, his right to make his own decisions. He says he stayed in session because "You gave me the choice. You didn't tell me what to do."
3. Provided **affirmations**: The client stated that "release" was a benefit of going to the gym and exercising. The helper's interpretation that this experienced benefit was something he could give himself credit for (i.e., a positive outcome that he was responsible for) appeared appealing to Vince ("Never thought of it that way before").
   Rationale: Like commendations in SFT, affirmations highlight the client's abilities and strengths.
4. Asked **open-ended questions**: "Say more about that." "What else?" "What made you decide to stay?"
   Rationale: Intended to solicit more information from client without being prescriptive.
5. Offered **support**: "I just want to offer what help I can so that you can stay clean, stay out of prison, and do some of the good things with your life that you've wanted to do for a long time."
   Rationale: Intended to convey to the client the helper's concern for his well-being and her commitment to stick with him through the helping and change process.
6. **Asked permission** before offering client feedback: "Do you mind if I share an impression with you?"
   Rationale: Partnership in action. The helper checks first before proceeding, although was not consistent in doing this at another point in the conversation.

Combined or Integrated Strategies of SFT and MI

1. **Client's preferences (or goals, ambitions) honored:** The helper does not push "back then" topics (e.g., client's adoption) because the client made it clear at the beginning of this session that he was "a little pissed" about "lookin' back" in the previous session. The helper instead inquires about the alternative perspective— that is, what's ahead. She does this by introducing the reframe "You're a man on a mission" and then inquiring about what his "mission" has been. The helper follows the client's lead (exemplifying the humanistic, person-centered philosophy of both SFT and MI) while introducing new territory to consider.

(continued)

10 | Knowledge and Skill Builder **Feedback** (*continued*)

2. **Ambivalence regarded as resource:** Although Vince acknowledges that talking with the helper has been helpful to him, he's still not sold on the idea of counseling (he explains that he returned to this session because "I have to"). He is therefore ambivalent about the helping process. He is also ambivalent about how to deal with his anger, wanting others to help him but also wanting to deal with it on his own. The helper uses this ambivalence as a resource in session by exploring with Vince both sides of the ambivalence in the form of a cost/benefit analysis (i.e., advantages/disadvantages of others helping, and the advantages/disadvantages of Vince dealing with his anger on his own). Although giving equal attention to both sides of the ambivalent seesaw is not recommended in MI (W. R. Miller & Rollnick, 2015), it can be used to help clients develop more compassion for the part of themselves that resists change (Westra, 2012; Westra & Aviram, 2015). In any respect, ambivalence was regarded as normal, and its consideration may have encouraged the client's participation in session, as a form of conflict resolution. Also notice the helper's use of the words "curious" and "Help me understand" as invitations for the client to offer his perspective. His ambivalence was regarded with intrigue and curiosity rather than dismissed or attacked head-on. The client may have experienced this approach as welcoming and encouraging his participation in session.

3. **Change in relation:** Throughout the session, the helper's style emphasized collaboration and that change was not experienced solo. This is particularly evident in the helper's frequent use of "I" statements, signifying her participation as a partner in the helping process. She also acknowledged that raising the issue of Vince's anger "fueling" his "practicality" and "mission" may have been a "curveball" and "presumptuous." Although raising this issue may have triggered Vince to get up and almost leave the session, it appears that the helper's observation was valid (Vince said her observation was not "off"). This may have been a time when she took the lead in their dance. Another occasion when she stepped out and took the lead was when she said, "You weren't in prison for smoking pot." This gentle confrontation, offered in an atmosphere of acceptance, may have contributed to Vince changing his mind about leaving the session. He intimated this when he said he decided to stay because the helper was "straight" with him. Although Vince doesn't like to be told what to do, it appears that he appreciates people being honest and up front with him, and he is open to help when it is offered to him rather than imposed or forced on him. Perhaps both client and helper are learning to work together as dance and doubles tennis partners to effectively manage the anger that Vince apparently has been struggling with for a long time.

Cognitive Change Strategies
Reframing, Cognitive Modeling, and Cognitive Restructuring

After completing this chapter, you will be able to:

1. Demonstrate 8 out of 11 steps of reframing in a role-play interview.
2. Describe how you would use the seven components of cognitive modeling and self-instructional training to help a fictitious client.
3. Identify and describe the six components of cognitive restructuring from a written case description.
4. Describe ways in which schemas are involved in cognitive functioning.

Cognitive change strategies are based on the findings that how clients perceive, interpret, and experience events significantly influence emotions and behaviors in both positive and negative ways. Elements of cognitive therapy are pivotal to all of the intervention chapters in this book. We separate out specific strategies in clusters that are well suited to various kinds of life problems. In subsequent chapters, for example, we focus on strategies to manage high stress. Some strategies focus on calming and regulating emotional and physical aspects of stress responding, whereas others target cognitive and behavioral skills or patterns helpful in stress management or problem-solving.

In this chapter we focus on three aspects of cognition believed to play a significant role in producing emotional and behavioral difficulties: (1) automatic thoughts; (2) **schemas** (the cognitive structures in which concepts or beliefs are stored in and activated from memory); and (3) cognitive distortions. Clinical improvement depends on various kinds of changes in one or more of these aspects. Specifically, we describe reframing, cognitive modeling,

and cognitive restructuring strategies. *Reframing* involves helping individuals revise how they perceive and interpret difficult situations or factors toward more constructive and workable directions. *Cognitive modeling* is a kind of self-instructional approach that individuals can use to structure and support their change efforts. Change is difficult, and this self-guidance tool can help people break down habits and bring stronger awareness and intentionality to their responding. *Cognitive restructuring* involves deeper kinds of changes. The goal is to help illuminate the nature of problematic thoughts and feelings (e.g., what is automatic, what feels like fact but is really an interpretation) and then to incrementally replace harmful patterns with constructive and positive alternatives.

Prochaska and Norcross (2013) characterize cognitive therapies as the fastest growing and most heavily researched system of psychotherapy. Features that underlie its growth include client collaboration, specification of how-to strategies to guide implementation, sensitivity to brevity and cost-effectiveness, commitment to empirical evaluation, openness to integration with other therapeutic techniques to augment effectiveness, and a steadily growing track record of effectiveness. Computer-administered cognitive treatments are on the rise, as are cognitive therapies in self-help and web-accessed formats.

Cognitive therapies tend to be approached in psycho-educationally oriented ways that can be consistent with collaborative practice. In addition to establishing a collaborative relationship, the client and therapeutic helper work together as an investigative team—for example, treating problematic automatic thoughts and schemas as hypotheses to be assessed rather than fact and thoughtfully weighing seemingly consistent or inconsistent evidence.

There are multiple processes specified in cognitive theory and, thus, a range of intervention tools aimed at various points where processing can become maladaptive. With reframing and cognitive modeling, we focus on broadly applicable strategies to interrupt problematic sequences of processing. Cognitive restructuring provides guidance for tapping less easily accessed core aspects of personal knowledge, the complexity of personal meaning systems, and the social embeddedness of people, problems, and meaning (see, for example, Dobson, 2010; O'Donohue & Fisher, 2012) that are pertinent to sustainably changing negative content and processing biases.

In this chapter we use the cognitive therapy as an umbrella term, focusing attention on the underpinnings of human cognition and how it works (in normative and problematic ways) and on strategies targeting cognitive change. We draw largely from the cognitive behavioral therapy (CBT) literature. However, cognitive behavioral models are evolving, resulting in extensions into related cognitive-oriented approaches that we note as part of the broader set of clinical resources.

An Overview of the Theoretical Framework

Advances in Cognitive Theory

The cognitive theory and therapeutic guidelines we draw upon stem from an evidence-based progression of work over multiple decades. The prime genesis of cognitive therapies is predominantly attributed to Albert Ellis and Aaron Beck, with defining publications emerging in the 1950s and 1960s for Ellis and Beck in the 1970s. The rapid dissemination, testing, and adaptation of these methods have involved many contributors, stymying efforts to attribute single developers to the strategies we describe here. And, as Marks (2012) reminds us in an historical overview, this clinical, research, and translational work has not all stemmed from the United States.

The term "generic" cognitive model has been applied by Beck to indicate the applicability of cognitive theory to a wide range of psychological disorders, specifying both pathways common across disorders as well as contexts, beliefs, and behaviors that distinguish development of different psychological disorders (Beck & Haigh, 2014). It is beyond the capacity of this chapter to fully review the complex cognitive model, although we encourage more in-depth reading (Beck, 2011; Hofmann, Asmundson, & Beck, 2013; Newman, 2013; Young, Rygh, Weinberger, & Beck, 2014) as well as applications across the life course regarding children and adolescents (Gosch,

Flannery-Schroeder, Mauro, & Compton, 2006; Mash & Barkley, 2006; Ronen, 2007; Weisz et al., 2006), couples and families (Belanger, Laporte, Sabourin, & Wright, 2014; Gingerich & Mueser, 2007; Granvold, 2007), older adults (Morimoto, Kanellopoulos, Manning, & Alexopoulos, 2015; Pinquart, Duberstein, & Lyness, 2007; Zahn & Zahn, 2007), and a wide range of specific problem areas (Beck, Davis, & Freeman, 2015; Ronen & Freeman, 2007) and culturally diverse groups (Boyd-Franklin, 2013; Lee, 2014; Muroff, 2007; Tang, 2014). We provide here a summary of central processes that the reader can bear in mind across the intervention chapters.

As Figure 11.1 illustrates, current cognitive theory recognizes multiple levels of factors involved in the development of cognitive schemas that generate and sustain psychological disorders, including ongoing transactions between an individual's cognitive and biological functioning and what they are being exposed to in their environments. Psychological problems are viewed as the result of exaggerated or distorted beliefs, expectancies, evaluations, and attributions (contained within schemas) that are negatively biasing interpretation as well as the prior attentional and memory activation steps involved in paying attention and making sense out of one's experiences (information processing). When information processing becomes distorted (characterized by persistently negative sensitivities, activations, and interpretations), other systems (e.g., emotional, motivational, behavioral) follow the cognitive distortion, reinforcing and deepening the psychological and interpersonal problems. This composite of maladaptive beliefs, affect, and problematic behaviors are continually interacting with the external environment, all of which can serve to intensify and solidify self-reinforcing cycles.

Faulty information processing can lead to a range of thinking errors—some of which we describe later in the chapter. Negative automatic thoughts or self-statements are, therefore, common targets of therapeutic change—redirecting maladaptive patterns in the direction of more adaptive patterns that incrementally support positive change throughout the cognitive, affective, behavioral, and environmental response systems. Dual information processing functions through two interacting subsystems (automatic and reflective) that are heavily involved in attention bias (e.g., what gets "paid attention to" and in what ways) and in memory bias (e.g., which schemas get activated from memory to function as primary drivers of subsequent contextual interpretation).

The automatic system processes stimuli rapidly and is sensitive to conditions that hold implications for threats, losses, or gains (e.g., survival or harm vulnerability), with

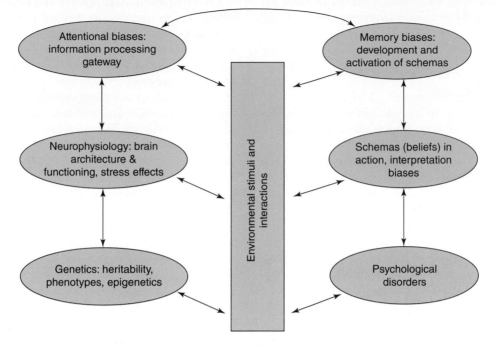

FIGURE 11.1 Multiple Levels of Contributors in Development of Problematic Cognitive Content, Processes, and Psychological Disorders

people often having little to no awareness of this cognition. Reflective system processing is more detailed, deliberate, and nuanced. This system is what is primarily being tapped in interventions that systematically work to augment self-awareness of how cognition works, to disrupt problematic habits, and to develop and strengthen more positive schemas and less extreme and negative information processing patterns. When new information that contradicts negatively biased beliefs is incorporated, schemas can be deactivated or at least rendered less powerful and absolute in processing, leading to reduction in troubling symptoms and outcomes.

Neuroscience investigations are proving valuable toward illuminating neurobiological mechanisms of change associated with cognitive change strategies. Reappraisal, for example, involves purposeful reframing or changing interpretation of stimuli (events, conditions) to modify its emotional impact, generally to change negative patterns of threat appraisal to more neutral or positive coping ones. Goldin and colleagues (2014) investigated whether gains in ability to use cognitive reappraisal would mediate the effects of cognitive-behavioral therapy for social anxiety disorder (SAD) on severity of social anxiety symptoms. They found that use of cognitive reappraisal was related to a range of brain responses that then lead to a cascade of subsequent neurophysiological sequences that contributed to their experiences of anxiety.

An inability to successfully use cognitive reappraisals in a timely manner was associated with less successful downregulation of amygdala (an emotion processing brain region) responses. This lack of downregulation, in turn, appears related to heightened levels of anxiety that can inhibit implementation of effective cognitive change strategies such as reappraisal. In short, in addition to cognitive and affective changes that individuals can more directly be aware of and report on, tools such as cognitive reappraisal can positively reshape patterns in brain and physiological responses to stress.

In addition to the aforementioned processes, evidence indicates that dysfunctional biases are influenced by combinations of genetic and environmental influences. Gibb, Beevers, and McGeary (2013) describe support for genetic influences wherein people who carry the 5-HTTLPR S allele exhibit an attentional bias toward negative stimuli and have difficulty disengaging attention from emotional stimuli. Also noted is support for genetic influences contributing to increased sensitivity or reactivity to environmental factors, which affects individuals' neurophysiological functioning (see Clark & Beck, 2010 for discussion of neurobiology), combining with other factors to increase risk for depression. Expanded detail regarding the interplay between biology, cognition, and the environment may increase understanding of some psychological disorders beyond what tools like the

Diagnostic and Statistical Manual of Mental Disorders can provide, potentially increasing treatment specificity and effectiveness.

Illustrating the Importance of Context and Personal Meaning

People who grow up in chaotic, abusive, rejecting, or neglectful environments are particularly vulnerable to distorted attribution processes. Such environments tend to foster appraisals that problems in living have no workable solution that will bring about emotional relief or meaningful change. For example, Al, a man who experienced rejection from his parents while growing up, may say, "I don't have the skills to work with people." From Al's frame of reference, his "lack of interpersonal skills" is unchangeable, and he feels a sense of hopelessness about working with people. His habitual view of himself leads to self-limiting patterns of feeling, thinking, and behaving with people. If Al continues this cycle of self-indictment, then he will experience a sense of despair and become regressive and withdrawn from social interactions. He feels stuck in his self-view, which was created at least in part by state-dependent memories associated with the learning and behaving that he experienced in his family. The meaning and emotions that he experiences in social interactions lock him in a tenacious cycle that only limits his perceptions, beliefs, and options for alternative ways of behaving.

We emphasize a contextualized and culturally sensitive approach to understanding variation not only in cognitive content (e.g., schemas, beliefs, and goals and whether we would evaluate these as "distorted" or "maladaptive") but also in the circumstances, norms, and power dynamics that constitute the surrounding environment and conventions of daily life. Keep in mind also that the notion of culture may usefully be applied to many collectives beyond those defined by national or racial heritage—for example, cultural dimensions related to disability, older age, sexual orientation, religion, and small town or rural life. Cognitive change strategies such as reframing (exploring how an event or situation is typically perceived and offering another view or "frame" for the situation) might be one intervention that could help Al revise his way of perceiving and modify his interpersonal skills. Cognitive change strategies go beyond an intellectual shift, more toward supporting a sense of agency or personal power. Fostering this window of hope of mutability is part of what makes tools like cognitive reframing, modeling, and restructuring effective when they are paired with change strategies that foster further insight, skill acquisition, and behavioral change.

It is important to note that the aim is not to discount feelings and worries that are very real to individuals, and also not to communicate a blithely, overly positive perspective or to ignore external realities of stress or injustice. Rather, cognitive change strategies can redirect energy to address a number of goals valued by clients. Reframing or restructuring what a client encodes and perceives can reduce defensiveness and mobilize the client's resources and forces for change. Second, it can shift the focus from overly simplistic trait attributions of behavior that clients are inclined to make (e.g., "I am lazy" or "I am not assertive") to analyses of important contextual and situational factors associated with the behavior. Finally, cognitive change strategies can be useful for helping bolster clients' self-efficacy—their confidence that they can actually accomplish something important to them.

Although cognitive therapy involves fundamental cognitive change, it is integrally inclusive of emotions, motivations, goals, and values. Recent work has advanced understanding of the profound interdependence not only of mind and environment (such as culture and dimensions of place) but also, as illustrated above, of critical interfaces among complex systems of brain and physiological functioning within environmental experiences, spawning notions such as the "embodied mind" and the embodiment of stress. Although we will not be describing these background developments in detail, it is becoming clearer that cognition is not limited to rationalistic or reductionistic attention to thoughts in one's head, but rather to much fuller and deeply rooted manifestations of meaning, purpose, and value.

Even though cognitive therapies may be clinically and empirically identified as a treatment of choice for problems like depression, it is becoming evident that some individuals' struggles will be ongoing or recurring. Thus, continuation treatment such as booster sessions subsequent to a more active course of treatment may be needed to curb relapse of problems such as depression (Vittengl, Clark, Dunn, & Jarrett, 2007). Mindfulness-based cognitive therapy, which integrates mindfulness-based stress reduction and cognitive behavioral therapy, has also demonstrated utility for preventing depressive relapse, particularly among people with a history of repeated major depressive episodes (Crane, 2009; Metcalf & Dimidjian, 2014).

Reframing

Reframing is an approach that modifies or restructures a client's perceptions of a difficult situation or a behavior. Efforts to reframe are implicitly constructivistic in that they reflect that a circumstance can have multiple meanings across individuals rather than a single truth. The aim is not self-deception but rather the search for *useful* ways to understand a circumstance relative to client goals and/or perspectives that impede efforts to achieve those goals. The emphasis is on reformulating problems or tasks in positive, growth-oriented terms.

In a sense, helpers reframe whenever they ask or encourage clients to see an issue from a different perspective. In this chapter, we propose a more systematic approach in helping clients reframe an issue. The most common method of reframing—and the one that we illustrate here—is to reframe the ***meaning*** of a problematic situation or behavior—the perception or interpretation of what events or conditions represent and of the implications that they hold through the eyes of the perceiver. When you reframe meaning, you are challenging the meaning that the client (or someone else) has assigned. Also, when meanings are attached to something over a long period of time, clients are more likely to develop ***functional fixity***—that is, they see things from only one perspective or become fixated on the idea that this particular situation, behavior pattern, or attribute is *the* issue.

Reframing helps by providing alternative ways to view the issue in question without directly challenging the behavior or situation itself. Once the *meaning* of a behavior or situation changes, the person's response to it usually changes also if the reframe is valid and acceptable to the client. This new meaning has a different connotation, and usually it is more positive or at least less troubling to the client. For example, "stubbornness" might be reframed as "independence," or "greediness" might be reframed as "ambition."

Reframing is used frequently in family therapy as a way to redefine presenting problems to shift the focus away from an identified patient or scapegoat and onto the family as a whole and as a system in which each member is an interdependent part. Used in this way, reframing changes the way in which a family encodes an issue or a conflict. Reframing can also help one person understand another's experience, which may make it easier for the client to behave differently toward the other person and thus disrupt the negative cycles in which the two have become ensnared (such as reframing what looks to one spouse like lack of caring to see the vulnerability and hurt behind withdrawing behaviors). Positive reframing can be applied to one's own perceptions, to the meaning a person is generating for what they are experiencing. It also can be used to help others consider a different view, as demonstrated by mothers of children with autistic spectrum disorder who worked to reframe others' perceptions of

their children's behaviors to influence the interpretations and responses of people unfamiliar with the disorder (Rocque, 2010). Reframing is often used as one part of a larger intervention to help clients come to grips with conflicts that are at the root of their issues.

Reframing Components

Reframing involves six components. In the skill-building **LO1** exercises at the end of the chapter, we will separate these into 11 steps because some of the components involve more than one activity. These 11 steps are also referred to in the learning outcomes at the beginning of the chapter.

1. Explanation of the treatment rationale: the purpose and an overview of the procedure

2. Identification of client perceptions and feelings in situations of concern

3. Deliberate enactment of selected perceptual features

4. Identification of alternative perceptions

5. Modification of perceptions in situations of concern

6. Homework and follow-up

A detailed description of the steps associated with these components is included in the Interview Checklist for Reframing at the end of this chapter and in Learning Activity 11.1.

Although the steps we propose for reframing involve reframing meaning, another strategy is to reframe the ***context*** of a concern. Reframing the context helps a client to explore and decide *when, where,* and *with whom* a given behavior, for example, is useful or appropriate. Context reframing is based on the assumption that many behaviors are useful in *some* but not all contexts or conditions. Thus, when a client states, "Sometimes I wonder if I'm too lazy," a context reframe could be "In what situations (or with what people) might it be OK or even helpful to be what you are calling lazy?" A mother may respond by noting that it is actually OK to be "lazy" when she wants to play with her children.

At this point, the practitioner can help the client sort out and contextualize a given behavior so that the person can see where and when she or he does and does not want the behavior to occur. Note that here the goal is to have the person be reflective about the nature of circumstances that may qualify how a given behavior or characteristics might be evaluated. This helps shift information

Learning Activity 11.1

Reframing

This activity is designed to help you use the reframing procedure with yourself.

1. Identify a situation that typically produces uncomfortable or distressing feelings for you—for example, you are about to initiate a new relationship with someone, or you are presenting a speech in front of a large audience.
2. Try to become aware of what you rather automatically attend to or focus on during this situation. Role-play it with another person, or pretend you're sitting in a movie theater and project the situation onto the screen in front of you. As you do so, ask yourself: "What am I aware of now?" and "What am I focusing on now?" Be sure to notice fleeting sounds, feelings, images, and sensations.
3. Establish a link between these encoded features of the situation and your resulting feelings. As you re-enact the situation, ask yourself: "What am I feeling at this moment?" "What am I experiencing now?"
4. After you have become aware of the most salient features of this situation, reenact it either in a role play or in your imagination. This time, deliberately attend to these selected features during the re-enactment. Repeat this process until you feel that you have awareness and control of the perceptual process you engage in during this situation.
5. Select other features of the session (previously ignored) that you could focus on or attend to during this situation that would allow you to view and handle the situation differently. Consider images, sounds, and feelings as well as people and objects. Ask yourself questions such as, "What other aspects aren't readily apparent to me that would provide me with a different way to view the situation?" You may wish to query another person for ideas. After you have identified alternative features, again re-enact the situation in a role play or your imagination—several times if necessary—to reinforce a more reflective, contextually aware perspective.
6. Construct a homework assignment for yourself that encourages you to apply this process during actual situations.

processing from automatic to a more reflective mode in which distinctions might be made. However, when perceptions reflect deeper, more enduringly problematic beliefs, cognitive restructuring approaches, described later in the chapter, may be appropriate. There the focus may shift to helping the client evaluate whether the cognition is indeed accurate or may involve distortions that need to be addressed.

Component 1: Treatment Rationale

Part of the function for providing a rationale for reframing is to strengthen the client's appreciation that perceptions or attributions about situations can cause emotional distress. Thus, revising in constructive ways how we are perceiving a situation plays a role in our emotions and our readiness to problem-solve. Here is a rationale that can be used to introduce reframing:

When we think about or are in a difficult situation, we automatically attend to selected features of the situation. As time goes on, we tend to get fixated on these same features of the situation and ignore other aspects of it. This fixation can lead to some uncomfortable emotions, such as the ones you're feeling now. In this procedure, I will help you identify what you are usually aware of during these situations. Then, we'll work on increasing your awareness of other aspects of the situation that you usually don't

notice. As this happens, you will observe that your feelings about and responses to this issue will start to change. Do you have any questions?

Component 2: Identification of Client Perceptions and Feelings

If the client accepts the rationale for reframing that the helper provides, the next step is to help the client become aware of what he or she automatically attends to in the problem situation. Clients are often unaware of what features or details they turn their attention to in a situation and what information about the situation they encode. For example, clients who have a fear of water may attend to how deep the water is because they cannot see the bottom, and they may encode the perception that they might drown. Clients who experience test anxiety may attend to the large size of the room or to how quickly the other people seem to be working. The encoding of these perceptions leads to feeling overwhelmed, anxious, and lacking in confidence. In turn, these feelings can lead to impaired performance in or avoidance of the situation.

During the interview, the helper assists clients in discovering what they typically attend to in problem situations. The helper can use imagery or role play to facilitate clients' re-enactment of situations to become aware of what they notice, interpret, and then do on the basis of that interpretation. While engaging clients in role play or in imagining the situation, the helper can foster clients' awareness of typical encoding patterns by asking questions like the following:

"What are you attending to now?"
"What are you aware of now?"
"What are you noticing about the situation?"

To link feelings to individual perceptions, these questions can be followed with further inquiries, such as these:

"What are you feeling at this moment?"
"What do you feel in your body?"

The helper may need to encourage clients to engage in role play or imagery several times so that they can reconstruct the situation and become more aware of salient encoded features. The helper may also suggest what clients might have felt and what the experience appears to mean to them to bring these automatic perceptions into awareness. The practitioner also helps clients notice *marginal impressions*—fleeting images, sounds, feelings, and sensations that were passively rather than deliberately processed, and yet affect their reactions to the situation.

Component 3: Deliberate Enactment of Selected Perceptual Features

After clients become aware of their rather automatic attending, they are asked to re-enact the situation and intentionally attend to the selected features that they have been processing automatically. For example, the water-phobic client re-enacts (through role play or imagery) approaching water and deliberately attends to the salient features, such as the depth of the water and his or her inability to see the bottom of the pool. By deliberately attending to these encoded features, the client is able to bring these habitual attentional processes fully into awareness and under direct control. This sort of "dramatization" seems to sharpen the client's awareness of existing perceptions. When these perceptions are uncovered and made more visible through this deliberate re-enactment, it is harder for the client to maintain prior response habits. This step may need to be repeated several times during the session or assigned as a homework task.

Component 4: Identification of Alternative Perceptions

The helper can help the client change his or her attentional focus by selecting other features of the target situation to attend to rather than overlook or ignore. For example, the water-phobic client who focuses on the depth of the water

might be instructed to focus on how clear, clean, and wet the water appears. For the test-anxious client who attends to the size of the room, the helper can redirect the client's attention to how roomy (nonconstricting) the testing place is or how comfortable the seats are. Both clients and practitioners can suggest other features of the situation that have a positive or at least a neutral connotation. The practitioner can ask the client which features provide a notably "felt" sense of relief.

For reframing to be effective, the alternative perceptions must be acceptable to the client. Reframes should be linked to difficulties that the client is having in moving forward and be perceived as just as valid of a way of looking at the world as the way the person sees things now. All reframes or alternative perceptions have to be tailored to the client's values, style, and sociocultural context, and they have to fit the client's experience and model of his or her world. The alternative perceptions or reframes also need to match the external reality of the situation closely enough to be plausible. If, for example, a man is feeling very angry with his partner or spouse because of an extramarital affair, reframing his anger as "loving concern" is probably not representative of the external situation, nor acceptable to the client. A more plausible reframe might be something like "frustration from the (marital) relationship not being safeguarded."

The delivery of a reframe is also important. When suggesting alternative perceptions to clients, it is essential that the practitioner's nonverbal behavior be congruent with the tone and content of the reframe. It is also important for the helper to use his or her voice effectively in delivering the reframe by emphasizing key words or phrases.

Component 5: Modification of Perceptions in Situations of Concern

Modifying what clients attend to can be helped with role play or imagery. The helper instructs the client to attend to other features of the situation during the role play or imagery enactment. This step may need to be repeated several times. Repetition is designed to embody new perceptual responses so that the client gradually experiences a felt sense of relief, strength, or optimism.

Component 6: Homework and Follow-up

The helper can suggest that during *in vivo* situations the client follow the same format as that used in their sessions. The client is instructed to become more aware of salient encoded features of a stressful or arousing situation, to link these to uncomfortable feelings, to engage in deliberate enactments or practice activities, and to try to make perceptual shifts during these situations to other features of the situation that previously were ignored.

As the client becomes more adept at this process, the helper will need to be alert to slight perceptual shifts and point these out to the client. Typically, clients are unskilled at detecting these shifts in encoding. Helping the client discriminate between old and new encodings of target situations can be very useful in promoting the overall goal of the reframing strategy: to modify encoding or perceptual errors and biases and alleviate the associated distress.

Reframing with Diverse Clients

For a reframe to be effective, it must be plausible and acceptable to the client. Client demographic factors such as age, gender, race or ethnicity, sexuality, and disability are important components to consider in developing reframes with diverse groups of clients. Religion and spirituality must also be considered given its influence on assigned meaning and purpose of life events, noted to be especially true for older adult African Americans (Hayward & Krause, 2013). Recent work illustrates a range of applications with culturally diverse people. Campbell and colleagues (2010), for example, found storytelling to assist Zimbabwean children in reframing the social stigma faced by their AIDS-affected peers, thereby achieving greater awareness and compassion. Chinese children affected by parental HIV/AIDS also demonstrated improved coping and decreased biomarkers of physical stress when using cognitive reframing (Slatcher et al., 2015). Hwang and Charnley (2010) similarly found that reframing strategies proved useful in work with South Korean children to reinterpret their experiences of living with autism from "strange" to "ordinary," thus helping to offset feelings of exclusion. Mothers of children with autism have also demonstrated improved adjustment and coping ability when using this technique (Benson, 2014). The importance of including reframing strategies in coping repertoires was again illustrated with adolescents whose use of reframing when interacting with depressed mothers significantly reduced symptoms of depression in the youths (Jaser et al., 2008).

Feelings are a common target of reframing, with the goal of offsetting unsettling emotions such as fear, abhorrence, or uncertainty about health conditions. Shifting from an initial stance of shock and resistant to one of engaged coping involves encouragement of different kinds of reframes. Varying belief systems regarding "the best way to cope," for example, involves individualizing reframing support for those who are more fighters (striving for certainty and agency) relative to those who are more followers (letting

the disease take its natural course). Adaptations in reframing strategies were investigated among Chinese women with breast cancer as a part of their process of coming to terms with their diagnosis (Ching, Martinson, & Wong, 2009). Ricci-Cabello and colleagues (2014) performed a large meta-analysis illustrating benefits of integrating reframing strategies into self-management programs for African American and Latino adults living with diabetes. Cognitive reframing strategies used by family caregivers to cope with the health–illness transitions they encounter daily with senior family members are also a valuable tool in multicomponent models of care—complementary to social support and problem-solving (Ducharme, 2009). Additionally, a group of first-time pregnant women found that a diary intervention regarding their negative thoughts about pregnancy resulted in enhanced positive thinking and increased comfort through guided strategies to re-examine thoughts and feelings from a positive perspective (Nakamura, 2010).

Research findings provide compelling portrayals of how internal tensions in one's perspective and emotions surrounding issues need to be understood for reframing to be meaningful. Kalichman and colleagues (2008) included cognitive reframing in programs undertaken with South African men to decrease HIV/AIDS transmission and rates of domestic violence with good result. These strategies have also proven successful in helping men who were sexually abused in their childhood see strength and positive growth arising from the survival of the abuse. Stressful and even traumatic experiences are arenas in which reframing strategies can be similarly effective. For example, positive reframing coping advice strategies proved to be beneficial in working with children who were survivors of Hurricane Katrina. In this case, reframing was more effective than other strategies, such as control attributions or caregiver warmth (Kilmer & Gil-Rivas, 2010). Qualitative research by Isakson and Jurkovic (2013) describes the positive role of reframing for individuals who attempt to heal and move on after suffering torture. O'Leary (2009) asserts that timing is not a critical factor in the application of this strategy; reframing can still be effective well beyond exposure to a stressor.

Cognitive Modeling Components

Cognitive modeling is a procedure in which [LO2] practitioners demonstrate to clients what to say to themselves while performing a task. Cognitive modeling has multiple applications useful in many new skill acquisitions, but our primary focus is its value in countering a person's negative self-talk that can impede change

BOX 11.1	Helper's Modeled Self-Guidance

1. Poses a question about the task: "Okay, what is it I have to do?"

2. Answers the question about what to do: "You want me to copy the picture with different lines."

3. Self-guidance and focused attention: "I have to go slow and be careful. Okay, draw the line down, down, good; then to the right, that's it; now down some more and to the left."

4. Positive coping observations with error correction options: "Now back up again. No, I was supposed to go down. That's okay. Just erase the line carefully."

5. Self-reinforcement: "Good. Even if I make an error I can go on slowly and carefully. Okay, I have to go down now…Finished. I did it."

efforts. Thus, the client is working to develop for herself or himself a new cognitive representation of being or doing the desired behavior—typically countering prior discouraging beliefs or patterns of responding that ran contrary to this goal.

This is a ***self-instructional strategy*** that starts out with active roles performed by the helper (to model the desired behavior, to prompt and reinforce), with the balance progressively shifting to the client to provide his or her own self-coaching and reinforcement. More deeply rooted problematic patterns of thinking may require more intensive strategies, such as those described under cognitive restructuring. However, cognitive modeling can often serve as a useful starting tool, helping to accomplish increments of success toward larger change goals.

We focus on seven components of cognitive modeling and self-instructional training. We list these here, followed by descriptions of the tasks and logic of each component. The Interview Checklist for Cognitive Modeling found at the end of the chapter provides illustrative detail regarding how to implement facets of each component.

Helper Groundwork

1. Treatment rationale

2. *Cognitive modeling of the task and of the self-verbalizations:* The helper serves as the model (or a symbolic model can be used) and first performs the task while talking aloud to himself or herself.

Client Practice

3. *Overt external guidance:* The client performs the same task (as modeled by the helper) while the helper instructs the client aloud.

4. *Overt self-guidance:* The client is instructed to perform the same task again while instructing himself or herself aloud.

5. *Faded overt self-guidance:* The client whispers the instructions while performing the task.

6. *Covert self-guidance:* The client performs the task while instructing himself or herself covertly.

7. Homework and follow-up

Component 1: Treatment Rationale

Here is an example of the practitioner's rationale for cognitive modeling:

It has been found that some people have difficulty in performing certain kinds of tasks. Often the difficulty is not because they don't have the ability to accomplish the task, but because of what they say or think to themselves while doing it. In other words, a person's "self-talk" can get in the way or interfere with performance. For instance, if you get up to give a speech and you're thinking, "What a flop I'll be," this sort of thought may affect how you deliver your talk. This procedure can help you perform something the way you want to by examining and coming up with some helpful planning or self-talk to use while performing (rationale). I'll demonstrate to you what I am saying to myself while performing the task. Then, I'll ask you to do the task while I guide or direct you through it. Next, you will do the task again and guide yourself by speaking aloud while doing it. This will be followed by you whispering to yourself as you again complete the task. The end result should be your performance of the task while thinking about and planning the task in your head (overview). How does this sound to you (client willingness)?

After the rationale has been presented and any uncertainty has been clarified, the helper begins by presenting the cognitive model.

Component 2: Model of Task and Self-Guidance

The helper's modeled self-guidance consists of five parts. Box 11.1 provides one illustration. The purposes of verbalizing the question about the nature and demands of the task are to compensate for a possible deficiency in comprehending what to do, to provide a general orientation, and to create a cognitive set. The second part of answering the question is designed to model cognitive rehearsal and planning to focus the client's attention on relevant task requirements. The purpose of deliberate verbalization (the third part) is to concentrate attention on the task and to inhibit any possible overt or covert distractions or task irrelevancies. Modeled verbalization contains coping self statements to handle errors and frustration is designed to maintain task perseverance. The model does make an error, but corrects it and does not give up. The last step is to be intentional in self-reinforcing reinforce effort and success—which can be flexibly matched to the nature of the circumstances and what feels most reinforcing in the moment. See whether you can identify these five elements of modeled self-guidance in Learning Activity 11.2.

Component 3: Overt External Guidance

After the helper models the verbalizations, the client is instructed to perform the task (as modeled by the helper) while the helper instructs or coaches. The helper coaches the client through the task or activity, substituting the personal pronoun *you* for *I* (for example, "What is it that *you*...; *you* have to wheel your chair...; *you* have to be careful"). The helper should make sure that the coaching contains the same five parts of self-guidance that were previously modeled: question, planning, focused attention, coping self-evaluation, and self-reinforcement. Sometimes in the client's real-life situation, other people may be watching when the client performs the task—as could be the case whenever the client in a wheelchair appears in public. If the presence of other people appears to interfere with the client's performance, then the helper might say, "Those people may be distracting you. Just pay attention to what you are doing." This type of coping statement can be included in the helper's verbalizations of overt external guidance to make this part of the procedure resemble what the client will actually encounter.

Component 4: Overt Self-Guidance

The helper next directs the client to perform the task while instructing or guiding himself or herself aloud. The purpose of this step is to have the client practice the kind of self-talk that will strengthen his or her attention to the demands of the task and minimize outside distractions. The practitioner should attend carefully to the content of the client's self-verbalizations. Again, as in the two preceding steps, these verbalizations should include the seven component parts, and the client should be encouraged to use his or her own words. If the client's self-guidance is incomplete or if the client gets stuck, then the practitioner can intervene and coach. If necessary, the practitioner can return to the previous steps—either modeling again or coaching the client while the client performs the task (overt external guidance). After the client completes this step, the practitioner should provide feedback about parts of the practice that the client completed successfully as well as identify any errors or omissions. Another practice might be necessary before moving on to the next step: faded overt self-guidance.

Component 5: Faded Overt Self-Guidance

The client next performs the task while whispering (lip movements accompany barely audible vocalization). This part of cognitive modeling serves as an intermediate step between having the client verbalize aloud, as in overt self-guidance, and having the client verbalize silently, as in covert selfguidance. In other words, whispering the self-guidance is a way for the client to approximate successively the last step of the procedure: thinking to himself or herself of the selfguidance steps while performing them. In our own experience, we have found that it is necessary to explain this rationale to an occasional client who seems hesitant or concerned about whispering. A client who finds whispering to be too awkward might prefer to repeat the overt self-guidance procedure several times and then

---

Learning Activity 11.2

Modeled Self-Guidance

The following helper verbalization is a cognitive model for a physically challenged rehabilitation client who is learning how to use a wheelchair. Identify the five elements of the message: (1) a question about what to do; (2) answers to the question in the form of planning; (3) self-guidance and focused attention; (4) coping self-evaluative statements; and (5) self-reinforcement.

Question: What do I have to do to get from the parking lot, over the curb, onto the sidewalk, and then to the building? Answers with Planning: I have to wheel my chair from the car to the curb, get over the curb and onto the sidewalk, and then wheel over to the building entrance. Self-Guidance and Focused Attention: Okay, wheeling the chair over to the curb is no problem. I have to be careful now that I am at the curb. Okay, now I've just got to get my front wheels up first. They're up now. So now I'll pull up hard to get my back wheels up. Coping Self-Evaluation and Error-Correction Option: Whoops, didn't quite make it. No big deal—I'll just pull up very hard again. Self-Reinforcement: Good. That's better, I've got my chair on the sidewalk now. I did it! I've got it made now.

move directly to covert self-guidance. If the client has difficulty performing the faded overt self-guidance step or leaves out any of the five parts, additional practice may be required before moving on.

Component 6: Covert Self-Guidance

Finally, clients perform the task while guiding or instructing themselves covertly, or in their heads, which is a very important step. When clients shift from practicing the self-instructions overtly to instructing themselves covertly, the practitioner might ask for a description of the covert self-instructions. If distracting or inhibiting self-talk has occurred, then the helper can offer suggestions for more appropriate verbalizations or self-talk and encourage the client to practice with these during additional practice. Otherwise, the client is ready to use the procedure outside the session.

Component 7: Homework and Follow-up

Assigning the client homework is essential for generalization from the interview to the client's environment. The helper should instruct the client to use the covert verbalizations while performing the desired behaviors alone, outside the helping session. A well-designed homework assignment will specify what the client is to do, including how much or how often, and when and where. The helper provides a way for the client to monitor and reward himself or herself for completion of homework. The helper should also schedule follow-up on the homework task.

These seven components of cognitive modeling are modeled for you in the following dialogue with our client Isabella. Again, this strategy is used as one way to help Isabella achieve her goal of increasing her verbal participation in math class.

Model Dialogue: Cognitive Modeling

In response 1, the helper introduces the possible use **LO2** of cognitive modeling to help Isabella achieve the goal of increasing initiating skills in her math class. The helper is giving a *rationale* about the strategy.

1. **Helper:** One of the goals we developed was to help you increase your participation level in your math class. One of the ways we might help you do that is to use a procedure in which I demonstrate the kinds of things you want to do—and also I will demonstrate a way to think or talk to yourself about these tasks. So this procedure will help you develop a plan for carrying out these tasks as well as showing you a way to participate. How does that sound?

Client: Okay. Is it hard to do?

In response 2, the helper provides an *overview* of the procedure, which is also a part of the rationale.

2. **Helper:** No, not really, because I'll go through it before you do. And I'll sort of guide you along. The procedure involves my showing you a participation method, and while I'm doing that I'm going to talk out loud to sort of guide myself. Then, you'll do that. Gradually, we'll go over the same participation method until you do it on your own and can think to yourself how to do it. We'll take one step at a time. Does that seem clear to you?

Client: Pretty much. I've never done anything like this, though.

In response 3, the helper determines Isabella's *willingness* to try out the procedure.

3. **Helper:** Would you like to give it a try?

Client: Sure.

In responses 4 and 5, the helper *sets the stage for modeling* **of the task and accompanying self-guidance and** *instructs the client in what will be done* and what to look for in this step.

4. **Helper:** We mentioned there were at least four things you could do to increase your initiating skills: asking Mr. Lamborne for an explanation only, answering more of Mr. Lamborne's questions, going to the board to do problems, and volunteering answers. Let's just pick one of these to start with. Which one would you like to work with first?

Client: Going to the board to work algebra problems. If I make a mistake there, it's visible to all the class.

5. **Helper:** Probably you're a little nervous when you do go to the board. This procedure will help you concentrate more on the task than on yourself. Now, in the first step, I'm going to pretend I'm going to the board. As I move out of my chair and up to the board, I'm going to tell you what I'm thinking that might help me do the problems. Just listen carefully to what I say, because I'm going to ask you to do the same type of thing afterward. Any questions?

Client: No, I'm just waiting to see how you handle this. I'll look like Mr. Lamborne. His glasses are always down on his nose, and he stares right at you. It's unnerving.

In responses 6 and 7, the helper *initiates and demonstrates* the task with accompanying *self-guidance.*

6. **Helper**: You do that. It will help set the scene. Why don't you start by calling on me to go to the board?

Client *(as teacher):* Isabella, go to the board now and work this problem.

7. **Helper** *(gets out of seat, moves to imaginary board on the wall, picks up the chalk, verbalizing aloud):* What is it I need to do? He wants me to find *y*. Okay, I need to just go slowly, be careful, and take my time. The problem here reads $4x + y = 10$, and *x* is 2.8. I can use *x* to find *y*. *(Helper asks question about task.)* I'm doing fine so far. Just remember to go slowly. *(Helper focuses attention and uses self-guidance.)* Let's see, $4 \times 2.8 = 10.2$. Oops, is this right? I hear someone laughing. Just keep on going. Let me refigure it. No, it's 11.2. Okay, good. If I keep on going slowly, I can catch any error and redo it. *(Helper uses coping self-evaluation and makes error correction.)* Now it's simple: $11.2 + y = 10$, so that makes the answer $y = -1.2$. Good, I did it, I'm done now, and I can go back to my seat. *(Helper reinforces self.)*

In responses 8 and 9, the helper initiates *overt external guidance.* The client performs the task while the helper continues to verbalize aloud the self-guidance, substituting *you* for *I,* as used in the previous sequence.

8. **Helper**: That's it. Now let's reverse roles. This time I'd like you to get up out of your seat, go to the board, and work through the problem. I will coach you about what to plan during the process. Okay?

Client: Do I say anything?

9. **Helper**: Not this time. You just concentrate on carrying out the task and thinking about the planning I give you. In other words, I'm just going to talk you through this the first time.

Client: Okay, I see.

In response 10, the *helper verbalizes self-guidance* while the *client performs* the problem.

10. **Helper**: I'll be Mr. Lamborne. I'll ask you to go to the board, and then you go and I'll start coaching you. Isabella, I want you to go to the board now and work out this problem: Solve for y if $2x + y = 8$ and $x = 2$. *(Isabella gets up from chair, walks to imaginary board, and picks up chalk.)* Okay, first you write the problem on the board. Now ask yourself, "What do I have to do with this problem?" Now answer yourself [question].

You can use *x* to find *y*. [answer to question]. Just go slowly, be careful, and concentrate on what you're doing. So, if $2(2) + y = 8$, you need to multiply and then subtract. You're doing fine—just keep going slowly [focuses attention and uses self-guidance].

If $4 + y = 8$, then you need to subtract 8 – 4. Someone is laughing at you. But you're doing fine; just keep thinking about what you're doing. That means $y = 4$ [coping self-evaluation]. Now you've got *y*. That's great. You did it. You can go back to your seat [self-reinforcement].

In response 11, the helper *assesses* the *client's reaction* before moving on to the next step.

11. **Helper**: Let's stop. How did you feel about that?

Client: Well, it's such a new thing for me. I can see how it can help. See, usually when I go up to the board I don't think about the problem. I'm usually thinking about feeling nervous or about Mr. Lamborne or the other kids watching me.

In response 12, the helper reiterates the *rationale* for the cognitive modeling procedure.

12. **Helper**: Yes, those kinds of thoughts distract you from concentrating on your math problems. That's why this kind of practice may help. It gives you a chance to work on concentrating on what you want to do.

Client: I can see that.

In responses 13 through 15, the helper instructs the client to perform the task while verbalizing to herself *(overt self-guidance).*

13. **Helper**: This time I'd like you to go through what we just did—only on your own. In other words, you should get up, go to the board, work out the math problem, and as you're doing that, plan what you're going to do and how you're going to do it. Tell yourself to take your time, concentrate on seeing what you're doing, and give yourself a pat on the back when you're done. How does that sound?

Client: I'm just going to say something similar to what you said the last time—is that it?

14. **Helper**: That's it. You don't have to use the same words. Just try to plan what you're doing. If you get stuck, I'll step in and give you a cue. Remember, you start by asking yourself what you're going to do in this situation and then answering yourself. This time let's ask you to solve for *y* if $5x + y = 10$ and $x = 2.5$.

Client *(gets out of seat, goes to board, writes problem):* What do I need to do? I need use *x* to solve for *y*. I know $x = 2.5$.

Just think about this problem. If $5(2.5) + y = 10$, my first step is to multiply and then subtract. Let's see, $12.5 + y = 10$, so I'll subtract $10 - 12.5$. *(Helper laughs; Isabella turns around.)* Is that wrong?

15. **Helper:** Check yourself but stay focused on the problem, not on my laughter.

Client: Well, $10 - 12.5 = -2.5$, so $y = -2.5$. Let's see if that's right: $(5 \times 2.5) + -2.5 = 10$. Yeah. I've got it.

In response 16, the helper *gives feedback* to Isabella about her practice.

16. **Helper:** That was really great. You only stumbled one time—when I laughed. I did that to see whether you would still concentrate. But after that, you went right back to your work and finished the problem. It seemed pretty easy for you to do this. How did you feel?

Client: It really was easier than I thought. I was surprised when you laughed. But then, like you said, I just tried to keep going.

In responses 17–19, the helper instructs Isabella on how to *perform the problem while whispering instructions* to herself [faded overt self-guidance].

17. **Helper:** This time we'll do another practice. It will be just like you did the last time, with one change. Instead of talking out your plan aloud, I just want you to whisper it. Now you probably aren't used to whispering to yourself, so it might be a little awkward at first.

Client *(laughs):* Whispering to myself? That seems sort of funny.

18. **Helper:** I can see how it does. But it is just another step in helping you practice this to the point where it becomes a part of you—something you can do naturally and easily.

Client: Well, I guess I can see that.

19. **Helper:** Let's try it. This time let's take a problem with more decimals, since you get those too. If it seems harder, just take more time to think and go slowly. Let's take $10.5x + y = 25$, with $x = 5.5$.

Client *(gets out of seat, goes to board, writes on board, whispers):* What do I need to do with this problem? I need to find y. This has more decimals, so I'm just going to go slowly. Let's see, 10.5×5.5 is what I do first. I think it's 52.75. [Helper laughs.] Let's see, just think about what I'm doing. I'll redo it. No, it's 57.75. Is that right? I'd better

check it again. Yes, it's okay. Keep going. So, $y = 25 - 57.75$, which means $y = 32.75$. I can check it. Yes, I got it!

The helper *gives feedback* in response 20.

20. **Helper:** That was great, Isabella—very smooth. When I laughed, you just re-did your arithmetic rather than turning around or letting your thoughts wander off the problem.

Client: It seems like it gets a little easier each time. Actually, this is a good way to practice math, too.

In responses 21 and 22, the helper gives Isabella instructions on how to *perform the problem while instructing herself covertly* [covert self-guidance].

21. **Helper:** That's right—not only for what we do in here, but even when you do your math homework. Now, let's just go through one more practice today. You're really doing this very well. This time I'd like you to do the same thing as before—only this time I'd like you to just think about the problem. In other words, instead of talking out loud or whispering these instructions to yourself, just go over them mentally. Is that clear?

Client: You just want me to think to myself what I've been saying?

22. **Helper:** Yes—just instruct yourself in your head. Let's take the problem $12x - y = 36$, with $x = 4$. Solve for y. *(Isabella gets up, goes to the board, and takes several minutes to work through this.)*

In response 23, the helper *asks the client to describe what happened during covert self-guidance practice*.

23. **Helper:** Can you tell me what you thought about while you did that?

Client: I thought about what I had to do, then what my first step in solving the problem would be. Then, I just went through each step of the problem, and after I checked it, I thought I was right.

In response 24, the helper *checks to see whether another practice is needed* or whether they can move on to homework.

24. **Helper:** So it seemed pretty easy. That is what we want you to be able to do in class—to instruct yourself mentally like this while you're working at the board. Would you like to go through this type of practice one more time, or would you rather do this on your own during the week?

Client: I think on my own during the week would be a big help.

In response 25, the helper sets up Isabella's *homework assignment* for the following week.

25. **Helper:** I think it would be helpful if you could do this type of practice on your own this week—where you instruct yourself as you work through math problems.

Client: You mean my math homework?

In response 26, the helper *instructs Isabella on how to do homework,* including what to do, where, and how much.

26. **Helper:** That would be a good way to start. Perhaps you could take seven problems per day. As you work through each problem, go through these self-instructions mentally. Do this at home. Does that seem clear?

Client: Yes, I'll just work out seven problems per day the way we did here for the last practice.

In response 27, the helper instructs Isabella *to track her homework completion* on log sheets and *arranges for a follow-up* of homework at their next session.

27. **Helper:** Right. One more thing. On these blank log sheets, keep a tally of the number of times you actually do this type of practice on math problems during the day. This will help you keep track of your practice. And then next week bring your log sheets with you, and we can go over your homework.

Now that you've seen an example, try the exercise in Learning Activity 11.3 applying cognitive modeling.

Cognitive Restructuring

Cognitive restructuring has its roots in the **LO3** elimination of distorted or invalid inferences, disputation of irrational thoughts or beliefs, and development of new, healthier cognitions and patterns of responding. Cognitive restructuring is considered an essential component of cognitive behavioral applications with a range of problems—such as depression (unipolar and bipolar), anxiety, panic disorders, trauma, social phobia, suicidality, obsessive compulsive disorder, schizophrenia, eating disorders, anger, pain, substance abuse, gambling, self-esteem, stress and coping, and relapse prevention, among others. Previously in the chapter we identified applications with varied age groups, types of problems, and populations with diverse characteristics or special needs. This arena of therapeutic care is complex and highly evolving. There is still much to be learned about the types of strategies that are most effective with specific problems, diverse populations, and differing conditions.

Cognitive Restructuring Components

Our presentation of cognitive restructuring is based **LO4** on a well-developed literature base as well as our own adaptations based on clinical implementation. We describe six components of cognitive restructuring:

1. Treatment preparation: rationale, overview, and basic concepts

2. Identifying client thoughts and schemas in problem situations

---

Learning Activity 11.3

Cognitive Modeling with Cognitive Self-Instructional Training

Ms. Weare wants to have a discussion with the tenant living in the apartment above her about his level of noise after midnight that is keeping her up late into the night. Ms. Weare is apprehensive about finding a way to discuss this with him and effectively communicate the current ground rules of shared tenancy in the building. She expects him to comply with the lease agreement that all tenants sign, which says there is to be no excessive noise after midnight. Ms. Weare would like to address the tenant first before alerting the property manager. Ms. Weare is afraid that after she tells the neighbor about the noise, he will react in a negative manner and will manifest opposition as she tries to discuss the issue. She is concerned that she will find it too challenging to confront the neighbor and to follow through with her plan to discuss the disregard he shows for his neighbors.

First, describe how you would use the seven components of cognitive modeling and self-instructional training to help Ms. Weare. Then, write out an example of a cognitive modeling dialogue that Ms. Weare could use to accomplish this task. Make sure that this dialogue contains the five necessary parts of the self-guidance process: question, answer, focused attention, self-evaluation, and self-reinforcement. Feedback on this learning activity follows on page 394.

3. Introduction and practice of coping thoughts

4. Shifting from self-defeating to coping thoughts

5. Introduction and practice of reinforcing self-statements

6. Homework and follow-up

Each of these six components is discussed in this section. For further detailed description, see the Interview Checklist for Cognitive Restructuring at the end of the chapter.

Component 1: Treatment Rationale

The rationale used in cognitive restructuring is designed to strengthen the client's belief that *self-talk* can influence perceptions, feelings, and performance. Self-talk includes a number of dimensions of problematic cognitions that the client will learn to look for and identify. Examples of these dimensions include whether certain kinds of thoughts tend to be repeated, seem to arise in an automatic fashion, tend to be negative or self-defeating, or include distortions that could reasonably be challenged. The conversation in which the client and helper explore the rationale for cognitive restructuring should be explicitly attentive to the client's age, gender, culture, and any other characteristics or features of his or her context related to values and sense of identity.

The following rationale addressing general performance anxiety can be used with clients confronted with various challenges or issues. You can tailor the rationale to the specific client concern.

> One of our goals is for you to become aware of your thoughts or what you say to yourself that seems to influence your level of anxiety when you are performing this activity. Once we have identified these automatic or habitual thoughts, we can modify or replace them. The thoughts about your performance are probably contributing to and/or maintaining your anxiety. The performance situation may trigger automatic thoughts, or perhaps the feelings you have about the situation leads to creation of these thoughts. In either case, your thoughts and feelings in turn generate physiological responses in your body, and the combination of these cognitive, affective, and physical responses influence your performance. When we become aware of these automatic thoughts, we can deal with them by changing what you think about.

Overview Here is an example of an overview of the procedure:

> We will learn how to deal with your automatic thoughts by becoming aware of when the thoughts occur and discovering what it is that you say to yourself, what these

internal self-statements are. Awareness of self-defeating automatic thoughts is one of the first steps in changing them to decrease the anxiety you experience while performing. Bringing these thoughts to a conscious level of awareness will allow you to consider them in a more objective light, for example, whether they represent distorted ways of thinking or contain negative messages you may have internalized from others. Once we know what the self-defeating statements are, you can recognize them as a red flag signaling you to stop and question those negative thoughts. Part of our work will involve understanding beliefs and feelings undergirding these self-statements. We then work to shift your self-talk to more self-enhancing performance statements. Together we will generate self-enhancing thoughts to replace the self-defeating thoughts. By shifting to the self-enhancing statements, your physiological and emotional responses also will become performance-facilitating, and this will help you reduce or eliminate self-defeating performance anxiety. We will learn how to activate self-enhancing statements before, during, and after your performances.

Basic Concept: Differentiating Self-Defeating and Self-Enhancing Thoughts In addition to providing a standard rationale such as the one just illustrated, the helper should preface the cognitive restructuring procedure by drawing some contrast between self-enhancing thoughts and self-defeating thoughts. In some of the literature, the contrast refers to distinctions between rational and irrational thinking. Our reading of cognitive behavioral principles tells us that the helper's goal is to help focus clients on the (lack of) available evidence for the automatic thoughts (e.g., noting contradictions between thoughts such as "I'm hopelessly incompetent" and evidence of achievement and effectiveness in various life roles) and to distinguish between self-enhancing and self-defeating thoughts in terms of how helpful or hurtful they are to the client and his or her goals. Many clients who could benefit from cognitive restructuring are all too aware of their self-defeating thoughts but are unaware of or unable to generate self-enhancing thoughts. Providing a contrast may help them see that they can develop more realistic thinking styles.

One way to contrast these two types of thinking is to model some examples of positive, enhancing self-talk and of negative, defeating self-talk. The examples can come out of your personal experiences or can relate to the client's problem situations. Again, providing culturally relevant examples is important. The examples might occur *before, during,* or *after* a problem situation. For instance, you might share with the client that when you are in a situation that makes you a little uptight, such as meeting

11.3 Feedback

Cognitive Modeling with Cognitive Self-Instructional Training

Description of the Seven Components

1. *Treatment rationale:* First, you would explain to Ms. Weare how cognitive modeling could help her in discussing excessive noise with her neighbor and what the procedure would involve. You might emphasize that the procedure would be helpful to her in both prior planning and practice.

2. *Model of task and self-guidance:* You would model a way for Ms. Weare to talk to the neighbor. You need to make sure that you use language that is relevant and acceptable to Ms. Weare. Your modeling would include both the task (what Ms. Weare could say) and the five parts of the self-guidance process.

3. *Overt external guidance:* Ms. Weare would practice giving her feedback to the neighbor while you coach her on the self-guidance process.

4. *Overt self-guidance:* Ms. Weare would perform the instructions while verbalizing aloud the five parts of the self-guidance process. If she gets stuck or if she leaves out any of the five parts, you can cue her. This step may need to be repeated.

5. *Faded overt self-guidance:* Assuming that Ms. Weare is willing to complete this step, she would perform the feedback to give her neighbor while whispering the self-guidance to herself.

6. *Covert self-guidance:* Ms. Weare would practice giving the feedback to her neighbor while covertly guiding herself. When she is able to do this comfortably, you would assign homework.

7. *Homework:* You would assign homework by asking Ms. Weare to practice the covert self-guidance daily and arranging for a follow-up after some portion had been completed.

Example of a Model Dialogue

"Okay, what is it I want to do in this situation [question]? I want to tell my neighbor that he is making too much noise after midnight and that I cannot sleep in the apartment below him [answer]. Okay, just remember to take a deep breath and talk firmly and slowly. Look at your neighbor. Say, 'I enjoy being your neighbor, but feel you are making too much excessive noise after midnight. This is not in accordance with the tenant agreement we sign for the building. I am unable to sleep due to the excessive noise from your apartment above me.' [focused attention and self-guidance]. Now, if he denies making noise or minimizes the impact in disregard of my shared tenancy rights, I will just stay calm and firm. I also have the option of talking to the property manager about this [coping self-evaluation]. That should be fine. I can handle it" [self-reinforcement].

---

a person for the first time, you could get caught up in very negative thoughts:

Before Meeting

"What if I don't come across very well?"

"What if this person doesn't like me?"

"I'll just blow this chance to establish a good relationship."

During Meeting

"I'm not making a good impression on this person."

"This person is probably wishing our meeting were over."

"I'd just like to leave and get this over with."

"I'm sure this person won't want to see me after this."

After Meeting

"Well, that's a lost cause."

"I never can talk intelligently to a stranger."

"I might as well never bother to set up this kind of meeting again."

"How stupid I must have sounded!"

In contrast, however, you might engage in positive, self-enhancing thoughts about the same situation as demonstrated in these examples:

Before Meeting

"I'm just going to try to get to know this person."

"I'm just going to be myself when I meet this person."

"I'll find something to talk about that I enjoy."

"This is only an initial meeting. We'll have to get together more to see how the relationship develops."

During Meeting

"I'm going to try to get something out of this conversation."

"This is a subject I know something about."

"This meeting is giving me a chance to talk about…"

"It will take some time for me to get to know this person, and vice versa."

After Meeting

"That went okay; it certainly wasn't a flop."

"I can remember how easy it was to discuss topics of interest to me."

"Each meeting with a new person gives me a chance to see someone else and explore new interests."

"I was able to just be myself then."

| BOX 11.2 | Examples of Distorted Automatic Thoughts |

1. *Mind reading:* Convinced that one knows what others are thinking, accompanied by assumption that those thoughts are negative.
2. *Fortune telling:* Foretelling the future in negative outcomes.
3. *Catastrophizing:* Anticipating the future in worst scenario terms.
4. *Labeling:* Attaching global traits to oneself and others that typically are negative.
5. *Discounting positives:* Minimizing or trivializing the positives (e.g., things you or others do, outcomes).
6. *Negative filtering:* Paying disproportionate attention to negative information, not allowing competing positive content to filter in.
7. *Overgeneralizing:* Jumping to conclusions based on a single experience; assumptions of a global negative pattern.
8. *Dichotomous thinking:* Categorizing events or people in overly simplistic, all-or-nothing, black-and-white terms.
9. *Shoulds:* Hyperfocus on what self, others, or situations should be or do.
10. *Personalizing:* Assigning disproportionate self-responsibility or self-blame for negative events; perceiving events as linked to oneself without evidence.
11. *Blaming:* Focusing on others as sources of one's negative feelings, externalizing causation, insufficiently accepting responsibility for changing oneself.
12. *Unfair comparisons:* Application of standards that are unrealistic, such as focusing on others who do better and seeing oneself inferior in comparison.
13. *Regret orientation:* Preoccupation with losses, missed opportunities, and the idea that one could have done better in the past.
14. *What if?:* Persistent worrying about possible negative outcomes, "yes, but" blocking of others' suggestions, failing to be satisfied with answers and explanations.
15. *Emotional reasoning:* Over-reliance on current feelings as global interpretations of reality; if one is feeling bad, then the situation must be bad.
16. *Inability to disconfirm:* Rejection of any evidence or arguments that might contradict one's negative thoughts; resistance to refutation of tenaciously held thoughts.
17. *Judgment focus:* Harshly viewing oneself, others, and events in terms of categorical evaluations; finding oneself and others to continually fall short.

Source: Adapted from Leahy & Holland, 2000.

Basic Concept: Influence of Self-Defeating Thoughts on Performance The last part of the rationale for cognitive restructuring should be an *explicit* attempt to point out how self-defeating thoughts or negative self-statements are unproductive and can influence emotions and behavior. You are trying to convey to the client that we are likely to believe and to act on whatever we tell ourselves. However, it is also useful to point out that in many situations people don't *literally* tell themselves something. Often, our thoughts are so well learned that they reflect our core beliefs or schemas and are not made explicit. For this reason, you might indicate that you will be asking the client to monitor or log what happens during actual situations between sessions.

The importance of providing an adequate rationale for cognitive restructuring cannot be overemphasized. If you begin implementing the procedure too quickly, or without the client's agreement, then the process can backfire. One way to prevent implementation difficulty is to enhance the client's self-efficacy. The helper can do this by practicing with the client in the session so that the client is comfortable with the shifting facets of the procedure. Repeated practice helps loosen the grip on self-defeating thoughts, enables the client to formulate experiences more realistically, and gain enough experience that the self-enhancing thoughts become almost as automatic as the self-defeating ones. Additionally, repeated practice can enhance the client's self-efficacy with the procedure. The helper should not move ahead until the client's commitment to work with the strategy is established.

Component 2: Identifying Client Thoughts and Schemas in Problem Situations

Assuming that the client accepts the rationale provided about cognitive restructuring, the next step involves an analysis of the client's thoughts and schemas in anxiety-provoking or otherwise difficult situations. Both the range of situations and the content of the client's thoughts in these situations should be explored. This includes identifying a number of dimensions, such as what automatic thoughts does the client tend to have, do these thoughts contain distortions, and, if so, do these distortions appear to be linked to broader conceptualizations of or beliefs about self or others (schemas)? We illustrate examples of these dimensions here.

Description of Thoughts in Problem Situations Within the interview, the practitioner should query the client about the particulars of distressing situations encountered and the things the client thinks about before, during, and after these situations. The practitioner might say something like, "Sit back and think about situations that are really upsetting to you. What are they? Can you identify exactly what you are thinking about or telling yourself when the situation first arises? What are you thinking during the situation? And afterward?"

In identifying negative or self-defeating thoughts, the client might be aided by a description of possible qualities or elements of a self-defeating thought. The practitioner can point out that a negative thought may have a worry quality, such as, "I'm afraid," or a self-oriented quality, such as, "I won't do well." Negative thoughts also may include elements of catastrophizing, such as, "If I fail, it will be awful," or exaggerating, as in "I *never* do well," or "I *always* blow it." Box 11.2 identifies several categories of thoughts that may become habitual or automatic for clients, particularly in problem situations, and that contribute to their difficulties. Each category is followed by a general description of the type of thought and an example. It may be useful to see if clients recognize their own thought patterns among these. Examine with the client what evidence may or may not be available to support such a thought and how helpful this type of thought pattern is or isn't, based on how it affects coping and distress. Clients can identify the extent to which such thoughts contribute to situational anxiety by asking themselves, "Do I (1) make unreasonable demands of myself, (2) feel that others are evaluating my performance or actions, and (3) forget that this is only one small part of my life?"

Modeling of Links Between Events and Emotions The therapist may need to point out that the thoughts are the link between the situation or event and the resulting emotion and ask the client to notice explicitly what this link seems to be. If the client is still unable to identify thoughts, then the practitioner can model this link using either the client's situations or situations from the practitioner's life. For example, the practitioner might say this:

> Here is one example that happened to me. I was a music major in college, and several times a year I had to present piano recitals that were graded by several faculty members and attended by faculty, friends, and strangers. Each approaching recital got worse—I got more nervous and more preoccupied with failure. Although I didn't realize it at the time, the link between the event of the recital and my resulting feelings of nervousness was the nature of the thoughts running through my mind, things I was thinking that I can remember now—like, "What if I get out there and blank out?" or "What if my arms get so stiff I can't perform the piece?" or "What if my shaking knees are visible?" Now can you try to recall the specific thoughts you had when you felt so upset about _____?

There is deepening recognition of the role of emotions and the effects of emotional processing within cognitive change approaches (Mennin & Farach, 2007). Thoma and McKay (2015) provide an overview of components and strategies related to working deeply with emotion in cognitive-behavioral therapy techniques. We incorporate some of these elements throughout the book, such as: 1) awareness and acceptance of emotions through mindfulness and acceptance-oriented change strategies; 2) exposure techniques to evoke and process difficult emotions; and 3) addressing emotional content captured, for example, within individuals' self-talk and schemas.

There are cognitive elements in emotion and certainly there are emotional elements in cognition. The validity of both emotions and cognitions can be evaluated. For example, the helper can ask the client to identify evidence supportive of, or unsupportive of feeling statements like, "I can't stand this," or "I will always be unhappy." Research and clinical exploration of therapeutic options for working with problematic emotions are increasing. Examples include overcoming nonproductive avoidance of feelings, identifying triggering links between emotions and cognitions, processing of emotional content, developing emotion regulation skills, and the cognitive evaluation of emotional experience (see Greenberg, 2011; Leahy, Tirch, & Napolitano, 2011; Thoma & McKay, 2015 for further depth in this area).

In working with the client to identify and even elicit automatic thoughts associated with problem situations, the practitioner can note and bring to the client's attention any emotional responses or changes during the session, such as increases in anxiety, anger, or sadness. Getting a working sense of the paired nature of certain types of activating events, thoughts, emotions, and behaviors can be a significant step toward self-observation and change efforts outside the helping session.

Identifying Client Schemas Underlying Distorted Thoughts

Underlying automatic thoughts are beliefs, expectancies, and assumptions that have, over time, become organized within the cognitive structure of schemas. Assumptions are the if–then understandings of how things work and the shoulds that we all carry with us but that can become maladaptive in their effects. For example, a heterosexual woman who finds social situations stressful may experience an automatic thought ("He'll reject me") based on a maladaptive assumption ("I need the approval of men to like myself") fueled by schemas of self and others ("I'm unlovable. Men are rejecting.") (Leahy & Holland, 2000).

Schemas contain and organize conceptually related elements to form complex constructs that are stored in memory and are activated to help us interpret new experiences. Rather than being passive repositories of information, schemas shape what we attend to, how we interpret ourselves and our world, and how we incorporate new information. For example, a client who has a schema of being inferior and abandoned will use selective attention to focus on information related to failure, isolation, and rejection, and will tend to overlook or dismiss information related to success, relational connection, and acceptance (Leahy, 2003). Thus, it is not enough to assess the cognitive content of a problematic schema; it also is necessary to identify the perceptual and interpretive habits the client may unwittingly be engaging in that are consistent with the schema and that tend to reinforce the schema's depiction of self, others, and what can be expected in the world.

Schemas contain emotional content as well as understandings about oneself and one's world, and they can be tenaciously resistant to challenge and change. By and large, this stability is a strength. It is part of what helps us all to retain a sense of coherence, understandability, and predictability of ourselves, others, and the world. However, it also means that a client and helper who are collaborating to reconstruct or replace long-standing schemas are working against the grain of cognitive functioning.

Figure 11.2 illustrates ways in which schemas can function. External situational events, such as the behavior of others, or internal ones, such as our own thoughts or

bodily sensations, activate schemas, drawing them out of memory storage and into an active state (although we may not be wholly aware that this is happening). These schemas become part of what is salient at the moment (making up "working memory") and influence our information processing and behavior at that particular point in time. Although schemas tend to drive immediate processing of situations, the double-headed arrows reflect that there is a continuous feedback loop.

This process works the same for adaptive and maladaptive schemas, but the outcomes from the two types are obviously different. Thus, it is important for helper and client to assess what types of situations tend to be problematic for the client, because problematic situations will trigger maladaptive schemas (e.g., "I'm incapable, undeserving"). These chains can be interrupted and replaced with more satisfying response sequences. It takes considerable repetition of these more favorable chains and outcomes to reinforce the change and really replace the prior patterns.

Tools for Identifying Schemas Schemas serve as foundations on which subsequent learning and memories take cognitive form, rendering the early schemas more and more elaborated and networked with other schemas,

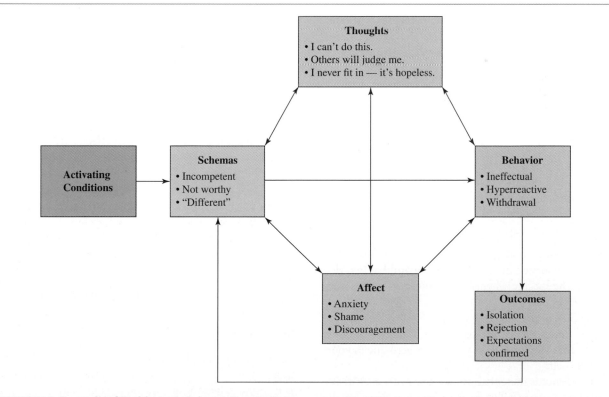

FIGURE 11.2 Example of Problematic Schema Functioning

sensory states (e.g., sights, smells, bodily sensations), and emotions. We are continually developing and accessing schemas, and problematic schemas are not necessarily rooted in childhood or in traumatic experiences. However, schemas that have become broad-based in their negative impact are generally those that the client has been living with and through for some time and that have become deeply integrated with multiple aspects of self, intensity of feeling, and a range of life situations. These ingrained schemas become so normative to our experience that it can be difficult to identify the underlying themes.

The cultural and sociopolitical contexts of a person's life are powerful environmental forces that can influence developing schemas. Schematic development is affected by factors related to language, traditions, and worldviews, and by experiences of marginalization, discrimination, and oppression. For example, children who experience or witness unfair, unjust, or traumatic events probably develop different schemas than children who live in a world of privilege and safety. Cognitive therapy must take lived differences into account as well as developmental considerations because individuals at different ages may require differing emphases, such as teaching emotional skills that better enable distressed youth to accomplish cognitive and behavioral change (Ronen, 2007).

Understanding development and processing of schemas is an important aspect of cognitive therapy. Fostering this understanding can be helpful in illuminating for clients the foundation underlying their perceptions of and responses to events, normalizing their current struggles as well as guiding their cognitive reconstruction efforts. An investigative approach is fundamental to cognitive therapy, whereby the practitioner helps the client to systematically gather data, evaluate evidence, draw conclusions, and generate alternatives. The self-observation skills honed during this process will be of benefit to the client well beyond the termination of the formal therapeutic endeavor. The following sample questions (Leahy, 1996) illustrate this investigative process:

How did your parents (siblings, peers, teachers) teach you that you are _____? (Fill in the word that best describes the specific schema being examined by the client and helper.)

When you learned this schema, you were 5 years old. What are some ways you have changed since that point in life that may make this schema less germane to your current self?

What evidence is there that you are not _____? Or that you are _____? (Fill in the word that best describes the client's schema.)

What is the consequence of demanding this of yourself? Is it ever okay to be helpless? To fail? To depend on others? To be disapproved of?

How would you challenge your mother and father, now that you are an adult, if they were to describe you as _____? (Fill in the word that best describes the client's schema.) (p. 194)

Young and colleagues (2001) describe a case example with a woman named Michelle whose problems included the inability to express herself and ask for things, especially with her husband, and recurrent thoughts that her husband had "one step out the door" of their marriage. The focused life review probed Michelle's childhood relative to the onset of her emotional difficulties and previous experiences with depression and counseling. One of the objectives was to determine if a series of experiences contributed to the development of schemas that were subsequently activated and reinforced, creating a vicious cycle. The review revealed themes of an absentee father, emotional isolation, anxiety about self-expression, and devaluation. The therapist hypothesized that these experiences generated thematic schemas of disconnection and rejection.

The Schema Questionnaire (Young & Brown, 2001; Young, Klosko, & Weishaar, 2003) is one tool to help clients assess the extent to which they see statements operationalizing schemas as representing them (Box 11.3 provides brief descriptions of 18 schema clusters based on this questionnaire). Through this activity and the focused life review, the helper and client, Michelle, identified four schemas that seemed most salient to her problems of concern. Experiential exercises can be profitably used in the helping session; by activating schemas, the client can more directly access their content and assess the intensity or degree of affect. After the helper provides a rationale for the exercise, strategies such as relaxation and guided imagery may be useful as calming strategies if emotionality runs high. An excerpt from the case of Michelle provides an illustration (Young, Weinberger & Beck, 2001, p. 299).

The practitioner and client were aiming to identify the origins of Michelle's abandonment schema:

T: Michelle, why don't you close your eyes now and see if you can get a visual image of anything that comes into your mind.

M: Do I have to see it?

T: Yes, it's not thoughts but pictures that we want. It could be a picture of a person, of a place, anything at all; almost as if you were looking at a movie in your head.

M: What is the point of all this again?

| BOX 11.3 | Examples of Maladaptive Themes and Schemas |

Disconnection and Rejection: Expectation that one's needs for security, stability, nurturance, empathy, acceptance, and respect will not be met in a predictable manner.

1. *Abandonment/Instability* (AB): Instability or unreliability of those available for support and connection; may be abandoned.
2. *Mistrust/Abuse* (MA): Others will hurt, abuse, cheat, lie, or take advantage—intentionally or through negligence.
3. *Emotional Deprivation* (ED): Normal degree of emotional support will not be adequately met; deprivation of nurturance, empathy, or protection.
4. *Defectiveness/Shame* (DS): One is defective, bad, unwanted, inferior, or invalid in important respects; feelings of shame and insecurity predominate.
5. *Social Isolation/Alienation* (SI): One is isolated from the rest of the world, different from other people, and/or not part of any group or community.

Impaired Autonomy and Performance: Expectations about oneself and the environment that interfere with one's perceived ability to separate, survive, function independently, or perform successfully.

6. *Dependence/Incompetence* (DI): One is unable to handle everyday responsibilities; requires considerable help from others; helpless.
7. *Vulnerability to Harm or Illness* (VH): Fear of imminent catastrophes—medical, emotional, or external—and one is powerless to control their onset or outcome.
8. *Enmeshment/Undeveloped Self* (EM): Excessive emotional involvement with one or more people at the expense of full individuation or normal social development.
9. *Failure* (FA): One has failed, will inevitably fail, or is fundamentally inadequate across areas of achievement (e.g., school, career, sports).

Impaired Limits: Deficiency in internal limits, responsibility to others, or long-term goal orientation; difficulty respecting the rights of others, cooperating, making commitments, or setting and meeting realistic personal goals.

10. *Entitlement/Grandiosity* (ET): One is superior, entitled to special rights and privileges, or not bound by the rules of reciprocity.

11. *Insufficient Self-Control/Self-Discipline* (IS): Difficulty/refusal to exercise self-control and frustration tolerance to achieve goals, or to restrain the excessive expression of one's emotions and impulses.

Other-Directedness: Focus on the desires, feelings, and responses of others, at the expense of one's own needs—to gain love and approval, maintain one's sense of connection, or avoid retaliation.

12. *Subjugation* (SB): Surrendering of control of needs and emotions to others because one feels coerced—to avoid anger, retaliation, or abandonment.
13. *Self-Sacrifice* (SS): Focus on voluntarily meeting the needs of others at the expense of one's own gratification; overlaps with concept of co-dependency.
14. *Approval Seeking/Recognition Seeking* (AS): Emphasis on gaining approval, recognition, attention, and fitting in at the expense of developing a secure sense of self.

Overvigilance and Inhibition: Emphasis on suppressing one's spontaneous feelings, impulses, and choices, or on meeting rigid, internalized expectations about performance and ethical behavior—often at the expense of happiness, self-expression, relaxation, close relationships, or health.

15. *Negativity/Pessimism* (NP): Focus on negative aspects of life (e.g., pain, loss, conflict, guilt) while minimizing or neglecting the positive or optimistic aspects.
16. *Emotional Inhibition* (EI): Inhibition of spontaneous action, feeling, or communication—usually to avoid disapproval by others, shame, or losing control.
17. *Unrelenting Standards/Hypercriticalness* (US): One must meet very high internalized standards of behavior and performance, usually to avoid criticism.
18. *Punitiveness* (PU): Belief that people should be harshly punished for making mistakes; angry, intolerant, punitive, and impatient with those (including oneself) who do not meet one's expectations or standards.

Adapted from Young, J. E. (1999). *Cognitive therapy for personality disorders: A schema-focused approach.* Professional Resource Exchange. Used by permission.

T: Well, the point is to try to discover feelings and themes, buttons if you like, that are getting pushed, but that you're not aware of right now. Like right now you told me you're feeling butterflies but you don't know why. We often find that when people close their eyes, they get pictures that tell them why they're feeling those butterflies, why they're nervous, so it's a way of sort of getting to the deeper issues without directly talking about them, but rather through picturing them...

M: I'm seeing something. I see my father leaving the house. He doesn't want to come in and be with me.

T: You're actually picturing him leaving the house?

M: Yeah, he's outside the house now leaving, and he knows I'm inside, he knows I want to be with him, but he just doesn't care to be with me. *(Cries.)*

The therapist continued to use guided imagery to assess whether there was a link between these childhood

Learning Activity 11.4

Self-Talk and Schema Implications

Learning Activity 11.4 provides exercises in distinguishing positive and negative self-statements and then considering ways that problematic schemas or themes may be underlying this self-talk. This will help you get familiar with these steps and some of the language before you work with a client.

Part One

Listed below are eight statements. Read each statement carefully and decide whether it is a self-defeating or a self-enhancing statement. A *self-defeating* thought is a negative, unproductive way to view a situation. A *self-enhancing* thought is a realistic, productive interpretation of a situation or of oneself. Write down your answers. Then compare your responses to those in Feedback Box 11.4 on page 402.

1. "Now that I've had this accident, I'll never be able to do anything I want to do again."
2. "How can I ever give a good speech when I don't know what I want to say?"
3. "Using a wheelchair is not as hard as it looks. I can get around wherever I want to go."
4. "I had to come to this country without my son and now that he is coming here, too, I know he won't want to have anything to do with me."
5. "What I need to think about is what I want to say, not what I think I should say."
6. "If I weren't a diabetic, then a lot more opportunities would be available to me."

7. "Why bother? She probably wouldn't want to go out with me anyway."
8. "Of course I would prefer that my daughter marries a man, but if she chooses to be single or be with another woman, I'm okay with that, too. It's her life, and I love her no matter what."

Part Two

Now, using the examples of distorted automatic thoughts in Box 11.2, see if you can find linkages between these categories and the statements that you believe to be self-defeating. Of the statements you found to be self-enhancing, how do those positive statements resist distortion?

Part Three

Now look at the maladaptive schemas listed in Box 11.3. Consider ways that these negative self-statements may have roots in themes or schemas that have become part of the person's self-concept. Alternatively, how might self-enhancing self-statements reflect adaptive, resilient schemas? We must note some caution in this exercise. This kind of assessment in reality takes a good bit of information about the client as well as dialogue with them regarding what resonates and makes sense. Be cautious about being too quick to jump to conclusions, particularly with limited or decontextualized information. Consider multiple possibilities that you would want to explore further.

---

experiences and the client's current problems with her husband.

T: Now, Michelle, please keep your eyes closed and see if you can get an image of Jim and tell me what you see.

M: Well, as you said that, what I saw Jim doing was just walking out the door and just slamming the door. He had his suitcase packed and with him, and he just walked out the door and there I was in the house all alone by myself.

T: Just like you were with your father, the same feeling that you had before?

M: Yeah, it feels exactly the same.

In sum, the practitioner develops a formulation with the client of the schemas that appear to be centrally involved in the most troubling issues and situations. This assessment then informs subsequent change efforts. More illustrations of assessment and interventions directed at schemas are available through Kienast and Foerster (2008), Nadort and colleagues (2009), and Rafaeli, Bernstein, & Young (2010). Within cognitive restructuring approaches, schema therapy (Young et al., 2003) focuses on the developmental context within which schemas evolved, unmet emotional needs, and use of experiential techniques such as imagery to identify schemas (Carter et al, 2013). Although largely equivalent to typical cognitive behavior therapy in outcomes, these differences in emphasis provide choices that may be more or less comfortable for some clients. If you would like to try out a schema identification exercise, see Learning Activity 11.4.

Client Monitoring of Thoughts The practitioner also can have the client monitor and record events and thoughts outside the interview in the form of homework. An initial homework assignment might be to have the client observe and record for 1 week on a daily log at least three self-defeating statements per day as well as the accompanying emotions when exposed to the stressful situation (see Figure 11.3). Later, more nuanced monitoring may be productive. Figure 11.4 on page 405 provides an illustration.

Using the client's data, the practitioner and client can determine which of the thoughts were self-enhancing

Date: _____ Week: _____

Situations	Emotions	Self-Defeating Statements
1. _____	1. _____	1. _____
2. _____	2. _____	2. _____
3. _____	3. _____	3. _____

FIGURE 11.3 Example of a Daily Log

and productive and which were self-defeating and unproductive. The practitioner should seek to have the *client* discriminate between the two types of statements and identify why the negative ones are unproductive. The identification serves several purposes. First, it is a way to determine whether the client's present repertory consists of both positive and negative self-statements or whether the client is generating or recalling only negative thoughts.

These data also may provide information about the client's degree of distress in a particular situation. If some self-enhancing thoughts are identified, the client becomes aware that alternatives are already present in his or her thinking style. Some specific attention may be needed in areas in which no self-enhancing thoughts are reported. The practitioner can demonstrate how the client's unproductive thoughts can be changed by showing how self-defeating thoughts can be restated more constructively.

Component 3: Introduction and Practice of Coping Thoughts

At this point in the procedure, the focus shifts from the client's self-defeating thoughts to other kinds of thoughts that are incompatible with the self-defeating ones. These incompatible thoughts may be called **coping thoughts**, **coping statements**, or **coping self-instructions**. They are developed for and with each client. Although it is common to challenge self-defeating thoughts (e.g., "What is the evidence for that conclusion?"), there is no attempt to have all clients accept a common core of rational beliefs.

Using terminology of coping is not inherent to cognitive restructuring. However, clients seeking help tend to be experiencing high levels of stress and most are familiar with coping language. You will see in later chapters ways that we extend the stress and coping framework to other intervention approaches.

Explanation and Examples of Coping Thoughts The helper should explain the purpose of coping thoughts clearly. The client needs to understand that it is difficult to think of failing at an experience (a self-defeating thought) while concentrating on doing one's best regardless of the outcome (a coping thought) that may also serve to calm some of the situational stress reactivity. Here's an example explaining the purpose and use of coping thoughts:

> So far we've worked at identifying some of the self-defeating things you think during ___. As long as you're thinking about those kinds of things, they can make you feel anxious. But as soon as you replace those self-defeating thoughts with coping thoughts, then the coping thoughts take over, because it is almost impossible to concentrate on both failing at something and coping with the situation at the same time. The coping thoughts help you to manage the situation and to cope if you start to feel overwhelmed.

The helper should also model some examples of coping thoughts so that the client can clearly differentiate between a self-defeating and a coping thought. Here are some examples of coping thoughts to use *before* a situation:

"I've done this before, and it is never as bad as I think."
"Stay calm in anticipating this."
"Do the best I can. I'm not going to worry how people will react."
"This is a situation that can be a positive form of challenge."
"Only a few people will be there and I can tolerate this discomfort."

Here are examples of coping thoughts to use *during* a situation:

"Focus on the task."
"Think about what I want to do or say."
"What is it I want to accomplish now?"
"Re-center so I can focus on the situation."
"Step back a minute, take a deep breath."
"Take one step at a time."
"Slow down, take my time, don't rush."
"Okay, don't get out of control. It's a signal to cope."

If you go back and read over these lists of coping examples, you may notice some subtle differences. There are four types of coping statements. **Situational coping statements** help the client reduce the potential level of perceived threat or the severity of the anticipated situation. Examples are "It won't be too bad," or "Only a few people

11.4 Feedback

Self-Talk and Schema Implications

Part One

1. Self-defeating: The word *never* indicates that the person is not giving himself or herself any chance for the future.

2. Self-defeating: The person is doubting his or her ability to give a good speech and his or her knowledge of the subject.

3. Self-enhancing: The person is realistically focusing on what she or he can do.

4. Self-defeating: The person is saying with absolute certainty, as evidenced by the word *know,* that there is no chance to regain a relationship with his or her son. This is asserted without supporting evidence.

5. Self-enhancing: The client is realistically focusing on his or her own opinion, not on the assessment of others.

6. Self-defeating: The person is viewing the situation only from a negative perspective.

7. Self-defeating: The person predicts a negative reaction without supporting evidence.

8. Self-enhancing: The person recognizes a preference yet focuses on her love for her daughter.

will be watching me." ***Task-oriented coping statements*** refer more to the plans, steps, or behaviors that the person will need to demonstrate during the situation, such as "Concentrate on what I want to say or do," "Think about the task," or "What do I want to accomplish?" ***Statements to cope with being overwhelmed*** are another type, such as "Keep cool," "Stay calm," or "Re-center and take a deep breath." ***Positive self-statements*** allow clients to reinforce themselves for having coped. Examples include "Great, I did it" or "I managed to get through that all right." Positive self-statements can be used during a stressful situation and especially after the situation. Later in this chapter we describe the use of positive self-statements in cognitive restructuring in more detail.

In explaining about and modeling potential coping thoughts, you may want to note with the client the difference between *coping* thoughts and *mastery* thoughts. Coping thoughts help an individual deal with or manage a situation, event, or person adequately. Mastery thoughts are directed toward helping a person conquer or respond to a situation in an almost flawless manner. For some clients, mastery self-instructions may function as perfectionistic standards that are, in reality, too difficult to attain. Use of mastery thoughts can make these clients feel more

pressured rather than more relieved. For these reasons, we recommend that helpers avoid modeling mastery self-statements and also remain alert to clients who may spontaneously use mastery self-instructions in subsequent practice sessions during the cognitive restructuring procedure.

Client Examples of Coping Thoughts After providing some examples, the practitioner should ask the client to think of additional coping statements. The client may identify self-enhancing or positive statements that she or he has used in other situations or noticed others using. Note that part of CBT cognitive restructuring includes logical analysis of negative cognitions to help the individual recognize when distortions are involved and to realign thinking with their sense of actual evidence. Clients may generate coping thoughts based on convincing counterarguments for their unrealistic thoughts. For example, "Now wait a minute. That absolute negative thought of mine seems distorted. I can think of several times it has not been the case." The helper should encourage the client to select coping statements that feel acceptable.

Client Practice Using client-selected coping statements, the practitioner should ask the client to practice verbalizing coping statements aloud. This recitation is useful because many clients are not accustomed to using coping statements. Such practice may reduce some of the client's initial discomfort and can strengthen confidence in being able to produce different self-talk. Like any new skill, the initial times may feel awkward, but explicit and repeated practice diminishes this. In addition, clients who are formally trained to practice coping statements systematically may use a greater variety and more specific coping thoughts, and may report more consistent use of coping thoughts *in vivo*.

At first, the client can practice simply verbalizing the individual coping statements that she or he selected to use before and during the targeted situation to break the ice of verbalizing practice. Gradually, as the client gets accustomed to making coping statements, these should be practiced in the natural sequence in which they would be used. First, the client would anticipate the situation and practice coping statements before the situation to prepare for it. Then, the client would practice coping thoughts during the situation—focusing on the task and coping with feeling overwhelmed.

It is important for the client to be actively involved in these practice sessions. Try to ensure that the client does not simply rehearse the coping statements in a rote manner. Instead, the client should use these practices to try to internalize the meaning of the coping statements. This challenge of distortions in one's patterned negative self-statements and process of reconstructing more accurate and positively adaptive alternatives is a large part of the work undertaken in sessions and extended through homework. One way to encourage more client involvement and self-assertion in these practice attempts is to suggest that the client pretend he or she is talking to an audience or a group of persons and needs to speak in a persuasive, convincing manner to get his or her point across.

Component 4: Shifting from Self-Defeating to Coping Thoughts

After the client has identified negative thoughts and has practiced alternative coping thoughts, the practitioner introduces the rehearsal of shifting from self-defeating to coping thoughts during stressful situations. Practice of this shift helps the client use a self-defeating thought as a cue for an immediate switch to challenging the veracity of the negative thoughts and deliberate use of positive self-statements. The importance of repeated and supported practice both within and outside of sessions, the latter being where most of the naturally occurring stressful situations will occur, cannot be overstated. New response patterns have to compete with older ones to gain salience and accessibility (ease of activating them) at times most needed, when emotional states and physiology can make this more difficult. Practice with support is essential to strengthening these new patterns.

Helper Demonstration of the Shift The helper should model this process before asking the client to try it. This gives the client an accurate idea of how to practice this shift. Here is an example of modeling for a high school student who constantly freezes up in competitive situations:

> Okay, I'm sitting here waiting for my turn to try out for cheerleader. Ooh, I can feel myself getting very nervous [anxious feeling]. Now, wait, what am I so nervous about? I'm afraid I'm going to make a fool of myself [self-defeating thought]. Hey, that doesn't help [cue to cope]. It will take only a few minutes, and it will be over before I know it. Besides, only the faculty sponsors are watching. I have done a lot of rehearsing of my routine and am ready to show it to them. [situation-oriented coping thoughts].

> Well, the person before me is just about finished. Oh, they're calling my name. Boy, do I feel tense [anxious feelings]. What if I don't execute my jumps [self-defeating thought]? Okay, don't think about what I'm not going to do. My jumps have been really good thus far. Okay, start out, it's my turn. Just think about my routine—the way I want it to go [task-oriented coping thoughts].

Client Practice of the Shift After the demonstration, the client should practice identifying and stopping self-defeating thoughts and replacing them with coping thoughts. The practitioner can monitor the client's progress and coach if necessary. Rehearsal of this shift involves four steps:

1. The client imagines the stressful situation or carries out his or her part in the situation by means of a role play.

2. The client is instructed to recognize the onset of any self-defeating thoughts and to signal this by raising a hand or finger.

3. The client is told to stop these thoughts or to reframe these thoughts. [This and the next step are predicated on time in sessions and homework wherein self-defeating thoughts and their underlying schemas have undergone realistic appraisal and alternative or adaptively modified alternatives have been identified.]

4. After the self-defeating thought is stopped, the client immediately replaces it with the coping thoughts. The client should be given some time to concentrate on the coping thoughts. Initially, it may be helpful for the client to verbalize coping thoughts; later, this can occur covertly.

When the client seems able to identify, stop, and replace the self-defeating thoughts, the practitioner can gradually decrease the amount of assistance. The goal is for the client to be able to practice and carry out this shift in the interview setting in a completely self-directed manner. Social support, such as friends or family members, can also support the client in this self-directed goal—for example, by anticipating stressful situations and walking through them, reviewing situations, and reinforcing use of the coping thoughts that have been identified with the helper. This kind of contextual support can be a powerful resource in situating clients' change efforts within their support systems and working realistically with their social environments.

Component 5: Introduction and Practice of Reinforcing Self-statements

The next-to-last part of cognitive restructuring involves teaching clients how to reinforce themselves for having coped. One way to accomplish this is through modeling by the practitioner—and possibly by others, if relevant—and by client practice of positive, or reinforcing, self-statements. Many clients who could benefit from cognitive restructuring report not only frequent self-defeating thoughts but also few or no positive or rewarding self-evaluations. Some clients may learn to replace self-defeating thoughts with task-oriented coping ones and feel better but not be satisfied with their progress. The purpose of including positive self-statements in cognitive restructuring is to help clients learn to praise or congratulate themselves for signs of progress. Although the helper can provide social reinforcement in the interview, as can others in the support network, the client cannot always be dependent on encouragement from someone else when confronted with a stressful situation.

Purpose and Examples of Positive Self-statements The helper should explain the purpose of reinforcing self-statements to the client and provide some examples. An explanation might sound like this:

> You know, Isabella, you've really done very well in handling these situations and learning to stop those self-defeating ideas and to use coping thoughts that contradict the negative and strengthen your positive beliefs. Now it's time to give yourself credit for your progress. I will help you learn to encourage yourself by using rewarding thoughts so that each time you're in this situation and you use these cognitive switching tools, you also give yourself a pat on the back for handling the situation and not getting overwhelmed by it. This kind of self-encouragement helps you to note your progress and prevents you from getting discouraged.

Then, the helper can give some examples of reinforcing self-statements:

Positive self-statements
"Gee, I did it."
"Hey, I handled that okay."
"I didn't let my emotions get the best of me."
"I made some progress and am getting more comfortable with these strategies."
"I can see some changes and that feels good."

Client Selection of Positive Self-Statements After the helper provides some examples, the client should be asked for additional positive statements. The client should select statements that feel suitable with respect to content and language. Client-selected statements are particularly important because the reinforcing value of a statement may be very idiosyncratic.

Helper Demonstration of Positive Self-Statements The helper should demonstrate how the client can use a positive self-statement in coping with a situation. Here is an example of modeling the use of positive self-statements during and after a stressful situation. In this case, the client was an institutionalized adolescent who was confronting her parents in a face-to-face meeting:

> Okay, I can feel them putting pressure on me. They want me to talk. I don't want to talk. I just want to get the hell out of here [self-defeating thought]. Slow down; wait a minute. Don't pressure yourself. Stay cool [coping with being overwhelmed]. This is the time to practice my reframes of this situation to help get me unstuck. [mentally walks through prepared reframe or challenge of negative appraisal.] Good. That's better [positive self-statement].
> Well, it's over. It wasn't too bad. I stuck it out. That's progress [positive self-statement].

Client Practice of Positive Self-Statements The client should be instructed to practice using positive self-statements during and after the stressful situation. The practice occurs first within the interview and gradually outside the interview with *in vivo* assignments. Learning Activity 11.5 provides illustrations of negative self-defeating and positive self-enhancing statements that you can use as models for those you identify or develop with clients.

Component 6: Homework and Follow-up

Although homework is an integral part of every step of the cognitive restructuring procedure, the client should ultimately be able to use cognitive restructuring whenever it is needed in actual distressing situations. The client should be instructed to use cognitive restructuring *in vivo* but be cautioned not to expect instant success. Clients can be reminded of the time they have spent playing the old tape over and over in their heads and of the need to make frequent substitutions with the new tape. The client can monitor and record the instances in which cognitive restructuring was used over several weeks.

The practitioner can help with the written recording by providing a homework log sheet that might look something like Figure 11.4. The client's log data can be reviewed at a follow-up session to determine the frequency with which the client is using cognitive restructuring and the amount of progress that has occurred. The helper can also use the follow-up session to encourage the client to apply the procedure to stressful situations that could arise in the future. This reminder may promote generalization of cognitive restructuring to situations other than those that are presently considered problematic. Learning Activity 11.5 provides you an opportunity to use Figure 11.4 in your own cognitive restructuring exercise.

Occasionally, a client's level of distress may not diminish even after repeated practice in restructuring self-defeating thoughts. In some cases, negative self-statements do not precede or contribute to the person's strong feelings. Some emotions may be classically conditioned and therefore may be better treated by a counter-conditioning procedure, such as exposure or systematic desensitization.

Learning Activity 11.5

Creating Adaptive Responses

Like Learning Activity 11.4, this activity focuses on particular aspects of cognitive restructuring—specifically, to prepare you to help clients build on their self-observations of problematic patterns toward brainstorming and trying out alternative ones.

Figure 11.4 provides an example of a homework log sheet to use with a client. Review that example. Notice that one part of the homework is to use questions at the bottom to compose an alternative response to a problematic automatic thought.

Use the six questions at the bottom of Figure 11.4 in your own cognitive restructuring exercise. Answer each question. Do these questions help you gain a new way of looking at yourself or at the situation that was unpleasant or distressing? Develop one or more alternative responses to the distressing situation that would be more adaptive. How readily can you do this? If generating adaptive alternatives is something of a struggle, consider what might be helpful (e.g., having a professional helper generate examples, playing either the client or the helper role, hearing examples from others who have made some gains with similar kinds of issues).

However, it bears noting that cognitive processes may play a role in maintaining or reducing strong emotions such as classically conditioned fears.

When cognitive restructuring does not reduce a client's level of distress (e.g., depression or anxiety), the practitioner and client may need to redefine the concern and goals. Perhaps treatment may need to focus more on external psychosocial stressors rather than or in addition to internal events. We have described here broadly applicable foundational components of cognitive restructuring. More advanced and intensive interventions may be more appropriate when more extensive or severe cognitive distortions and forms of psychopathology are involved. For examples of treatment resources for CBT methods, consider the following: Beck (2011), Barlow (2014), and Newman (2013).

The helper should consider the possibility that his or her assessment has been inaccurate and that there are, in

Date/Time	Situation	Emotion(s)	Problematic Thoughts	Reconstructed Responses	Outcomes
	1. What events or experiences led to the unpleasant emotions? 2. Did you notice any physical sensations (skin, breathing, heart)?	1. What feelings can you identify? 2. How strong was each emotion (rate 0 to 10)?	1. What thoughts or images did you have at this time? 2. How much did you believe or feel that thought made sense at the time (rate 0 to 10)?	1. In retrospect, would you say there was cognitive distortion and what type? 2. To "reconstruct" your initial response, write an alternative (the questions below may help).	1. Are your feelings different now? 2. Has your belief or sense of power that the problematic thought had over you changed? How so?

FIGURE 11.4 **Example of a Personalized Log of Problematic Thoughts and Feelings**

fact, no persistent thought patterns that are functionally tied to this particular client's issue. Remember that the initial assessment of issues in living may not always turn out to be valid, changes over the course of helping affect an intervention plan, and flexibility is needed to meet each client's unique needs.

If the helper believes that the original problem assessment is accurate, then perhaps a change in certain parts of the cognitive restructuring procedure is necessary. Here are some possible revisions:

1. The amount of time the client uses to shift from self-defeating to coping thoughts can be increased.

2. The coping statements selected by the client may not be very helpful. The practitioner may need to help the client change the type of coping statements.

3. Cognitive restructuring could be supplemented either with additional coping skills, such as deep breathing or relaxation, or with training in some behavioural skills that may be relevant to managing triggering situations.

Some Caveats

Although there is an exceptionally strong foundation of support for cognitive therapies (A. Beck, 2005; Butler, Chapman, Forman, & Beck, 2006), we encourage you to keep in mind that there is no one-size-fits-all or silver-bullet set of change strategies. Cognitively oriented interventions have their share of limitations. For example, although helpers can use cognitive therapies in a contextualized manner, attending to circumstances that may themselves be part of the problem, the emphasis tends to be inwardly directed—focusing on distorted, maladaptive, or otherwise nonproductive thinking and feeling. However, external social conditions that are unhealthy tend to be stressful, often fostering patterns of thought and feeling that will benefit from direct attention.

There may be some problems for which support-oriented cognitive therapies are not well suited, or at least not as sole change strategies. One meta-analytic review of 22 tests of treatment effectiveness (cognitive and other types) with previously arrested domestically violent men (Babcock, Green, & Robie, 2004), for example, found very limited impact on reducing recidivism. Although problematic thinking, such as entitlement attitudes regarding power and the use of aggression as a form of control, may well be a legitimate target of change, an effective treatment package will require additional change tools.

Moreover, significant and sustained cognitive change requires more than walking through rote exercises. Laboratory research with college students who were instructed to repeat broad-based positive self-statements such as "I am a loveable person" found that students with lower self-esteem tended to report feeling worse rather than better afterwards compared to those with higher self-esteem.(Wood, Perunovic, & Lee, 2009). These findings stand in contrast to clinical studies in which strategies such as use of self-statements to challenge negative self-schemas and to develop favorable self-schemas are embedded within psychoeducational training and individualized approaches that are meaningful and acceptable to the client. This highlights the importance of not approaching specific change techniques in a generic or isolated manner, which may introduce risk of negative reactions or outcomes.

We urge you to maintain your own critical consciousness in applying these or other interventions and to balance attention to environmental contributors, including sociopolitical and cultural factors that can easily be devalued or overlooked (Berlin, 2001).

Cognitive Change Strategies with Diverse Clients

Guidelines for Applications with Diverse Clients

Cognitive therapy and cognitive restructuring are **LO3** potentially quite applicable to diverse groups of clients, depending on the way the procedure is implemented and the therapist's sensitivity to diverse perspectives (Hays, 1995; Hays & Iwamasa 2006). We offer the following guidelines for using cognitive restructuring in a culturally sensitive manner.

First, be very careful about the language you use when describing client cognitions. Although we don't recommend the use of the terms *rational* and *irrational* with any client, we consider these terms—and others, such as *maladaptive* and *dysfunctional*—to be particularly inappropriate for women, gays, lesbians, clients of color, and all others who feel marginalized by the mainstream culture. These terms can further diminish a sense of self-efficacy and increase a sense of ostracization.

Second, present a rationale for cognitive restructuring that is educational rather than therapeutic to help remove the stigma that clients of some cultural groups may have associated with mental health treatment. A didactic approach that includes specific and direct homework assignments is useful.

Third, adapt the language presented in cognitive restructuring to the client's primary language, age, educational level, and hearing, seeing, and reading abilities. Avoid jargon. Consider streamlining the procedure, focusing on one or two steps rather than multistep processes such as challenging self-defeating thoughts. Provide examples of skills and coping thoughts that are bicultural and transcultural as appropriate.

Fourth, use and/or collaborate with bilingual, ethnically similar helpers and/or traditional healers who can help you address issues of psychosocial stressors, race, and discrimination. Remember that for clients who feel marginalized, addressing these issues is as important as addressing issues of internal cognition. Also consider the usefulness for some of these clients of cognitive restructuring offered in a group rather than an individual setting.

Finally, Comas-Díaz (2006) noted that ingredients of effective multicultural therapeutic relationships extend beyond cognitive and affective empathy to include cultural empathy. Cultural empathy involves perspective taking using a cultural framework as a guide for understanding the client from the outside in and an ability to gain and convey an understanding of the self-experience of clients from other cultures, informed by helpers' interpretations of cultural data (Ridley & Lingle, 1996).

Diversity Application Examples

In recent years, the use of cognitive therapy with diverse groups of clients has received increased attention (Lee, 2014; Strasser, 2015; Vera, Vila, & Alegria, 2003; Zane, Hall, Sue, Young, & Nunez, 2004; Huey, Tilley, Jones, & Smith, 2014). One caution is the need for attention to values implicit in some change-focused goals that may be reflective of mainstream culture and therefore not suited to certain individuals or populations. Emphasizing self-focus and self-control to increase personal agency or autonomy, for example, may be empowering for some clients but not for more collectivistic and interdependent cultural values of others. Similarly, focusing on changing cognitions and adapting to environments may inadequately acknowledge the powerful roles of oppression, racism, and structural inequality; conveying instead a view of personal responsibility for what are, in fact, societal influenced problems in living.

These concerns extend to issues of diversity in a range of ways. If applied in a highly narrow or rationalistic manner, cognitive change strategies may reinforce worldviews and cognitive processes that are stereotypically European American, masculine, and privileged—risking devaluation of more diverse worldviews and cognitive processing styles. Issues of misperception, stigma, and distrust constrain help-seeking, relationship building, and potential effectiveness of therapy, as illustrated by Gaston & Alleyne-Green, 2012, who examined adherence to retroviral therapy for African American men with HIV. Ascoli and colleagues (2011) note assessment of personality disorders to be particularly vulnerable to bias, given the extent to which what constitutes a "normal" or expectations for how a normal or aberrant person behaves is very considerably shaped by culture. Collaborative practice values, critical consciousness, and an informed person-in-environment perspective are essential to addressing these and related concerns in applying cognitive change strategies, particularly with vulnerable and diverse clients (Neal-Barnett, 2003; Boyd-Franklin, 2013).

When applied in a culturally sensitive manner that is mindful of the cautions outlined, change strategies can be applied to support empowerment, reflectiveness, and self-efficacy. There is growing attention to diversity factors in cognitive practice and promising evidence of their therapeutic benefit (Comas-Díaz, 2006). Practice scholars are recommending use of cognitive therapies infused with diversity awareness and adaptations (Ponterotto, Suzuki, Casas, & Alexan, 2010; Rebeta, 2015), including feminist perspectives (Goodman et al., 2007), Afrocentrism (Boyd-Franklin, 2013), recognition of heterosexist bias (Green, 2007), and other social justice dimensions (Aldarondo, 2007). Cognitive behavioral therapies have been implemented to assess and intervene with issues related to racism, oppression, coercion, loss, and stress. The versatility of cognitive approaches lends itself to integration with theories of minority stress, poverty, and gerontology (Comas-Díaz, 2007, Hatzenbuehler, 2009).

Recent literature provides illustrations. Malow, Rosenberg, and Devieux (2009) described the use of cognitive behavioral interventions with multiply challenged populations—ethnic minority, low-income, HIV-positive, and substance-abusing. St. Lawrence and colleagues (2005) evidenced a decrease in HIV risk-related behaviors by African American youth with use of education programming and cognitive restructuring. Such approaches reflected growing integration of cognitive change and stress management strategies, attentive to behavioral skill, emotion management, and social support dimensions that are complementary to cognitive targets of change. Miranda and colleagues (2003) targeted depression among predominantly low-income young minority women, and Peden, Rayens, and Hall (2005) reported promising outcomes in cognitive prevention interventions for depression. Sonderegger and Barrett (2004) described a similar approach targeting the prevention of mental health disorders, emotional distress, and impaired social functioning of immigrant and refugee children and adolescents. In this life skills program, cognitive behavioral treatment was integrated with family and interpersonal components. An emphasis was placed on the importance of understanding acculturation issues that were particularly relevant for those from non-English-speaking backgrounds.

Spirituality and religion have been integrated with cognitive interventions (Nielsen, Ridley, & Johnson, 2000; Tan & Brad, 2005; Oxhandler & Pargament, 2014). Naeem Waheed, Gobbi, Auub, & Kingdon (2011) illustrate the use of folk stories and examples drawn from the Quran within a CBT intervention to reduce symptoms of anxiety and depression in Pakistan. Successful use of culturally competent cognitive therapy has also been shown for Jewish women experiencing psychosis and religiously oriented delusions (Rosen, Rebeta, & Rothschild, 2014). Cognitive interventions can include myriad religious or spiritual elements or practices, such as meditations, readings, prayer, stories, and songs. Assessment of personal meaning that is important to treatment planning and devising cognitive change interventions can include spiritual dimensions. Considerations of spirituality and one's spiritual community may also be important for some clients in assessing their repertoire and support base.

Increasingly, cognitive restructuring is being used with the elderly, especially those with major depressive disorders (Morimoto, Kanellopoulos, Manning, & Alexopoulous, 2015). This use of the technique is especially important because many older people experience serious side effects and lack of therapeutic effect with some of the antidepressant medications. The most successful attempts have presented the intervention as an educational experience, with sensitivity to the older clients' fears and biases, and attention to relapse prevention following formal treatment (Laidlaw, Thompson, Dick-Siskin, & Gallagher-Thompson, 2003). Also, the delivery of the intervention may need to be modified depending on the client's auditory and visual acuities and medical risk factors known to be associated with later life depression such as hypertension, coronary heart disease, and diabetes (Delano-Wood & Abeles, 2005).

Cognitive restructuring also has been used with gay, lesbian, and bisexual clients, attending to special identity developmental challenges and ethical considerations (Martell, Safren, & Prince, 2004). Balsam, Martell, and Safren (2006) and Austin and Craig (2015) provided an overview of affirmative cognitive-behavioral therapy evidence and recommendations in work with lesbian, gay, bisexual, and transgender (LGBT) people. They observed evidence that LGBT people are more likely to participate in psychotherapy, possibly due to relative acceptance of counseling and self-exploration work within LGBT communities (Balsam, Beauchaine, Mickey, & Rothblum, 2005). This finding suggests that counselors are likely to encounter LGBT clients within their practice and for a range of concerns that may or may not be related to their sexual orientation. Emerging evidence is informing development of empirically grounded recommendations for working with this population (Martell, Safren, & Prince, 2004) as well as attention to effects of minority stress linked to mental health through higher levels of bias-related victimization and other forms of marginalization or trauma. Austin and Craig (2015) discuss transgender-affirming cognitive behavior therapy (TA-CBT) for transgender individuals suffering from depression and suicidality as a result of pervasive discrimination and targeted violence.

Organista (2006) and colleagues (Organista, Dwyer, & Azocar, 1993) offered several considerations for cognitive restructuring for Latino clients. Examples include: (1) ensuring a linguistic match between predominantly Spanish-speaking clients and their helpers; (2) recognizing cultural customs and concepts such as *guarda* (the value of holding in rather than expressing anger); and (3) streamlining cognitive restructuring by using "Yes, but" techniques to help frame problematic thoughts as half-truths that need to work closer to whole truths (thus sidestepping the framing thoughts as distorted or irrational).

It is beyond the scope of this chapter to provide exhaustive guidance on working with specific populations. However, the empirical base is growing, yielding more and more informed advice on best practice in working with diverse populations across a range of racial and cultural heritages. Sample resources include application with American Indian and Alaska Native people (Hays, 2006; McDonald & Gonzalez, 2006), African Americans (Kelly, 2006), Asian Americans (Iwamasa, Hsia, & Hinton, 2006), people of Arab heritage (Abudabbeh & Hays, 2006), and orthodox Jews (Paradis, Cukor, & Friedman, 2006), in addition to elders (Lau & Kinoshita, 2006) and people with disabilities (Mona, Romesser-Scehnet,

Cameron, & Cardenas, 2006). The need remains great for further research that will more fairly include representation of diverse populations. It will also be important to identify cultural-specific, population-specific, and developmentally specific considerations that will maximize the relevance, sensitivity, and effectiveness of cognitive change strategies.

Model Dialogue: Cognitive Restructuring

We demonstrate cognitive restructuring with [LO3] Isabella, who is having problems in math class. The interview is directed toward helping Isabella replace self-defeating thoughts with coping thoughts. This is the nuts and bolts of cognitive restructuring. After you review this demonstration, consider ways that being purposefully reflective and engaging in cognitive restructuring activities

yourself may help prepare you for work with clients. Learning Activity 11.6 provides an opportunity for this kind of exercise.

1. **Helper:** Good to see you again, Isabella. How did your week go?

Client: Pretty good. I did a lot of practice. I also tried to do this in math class. It helped some, but I still felt nervous. Here are my logs.

In response 2, the helper gives a *rationale* for cognitive restructuring, *explains the purpose of "coping" thoughts* to Isabella, and gives an *overview* of the strategy.

2. **Helper:** Today we're going to work on having you learn to use some more constructive thoughts. I call these coping thoughts. You can replace the negative thoughts with coping thoughts that will help you when you're anticipating your upcoming class, in

---

Learning Activity 11.6

Cognitive Restructuring

This Learning Activity is designed to enhance your understanding of the cognitive restructuring process by engaging in it and experiencing the benefits firsthand.

1. Identify a problem situation for yourself—a situation that you do not manage in the manner in which you'd like, not because you are unable, but because of your negative, self-defeating thoughts. Some examples include:
   a. You need to approach your boss about a raise, promotion, or change in duties. You know what to say, but you are keeping yourself from doing it because you aren't sure it would have any effect and you aren't sure how the person might respond.
   b. You have the skills to be an effective helper, yet you constantly think that you will be identified as an imposter who has not mastered the prerequisite competencies.
   c. You continue to get positive feedback about the way you handle a certain situation, yet you are constantly thinking you don't do this very well.
2. For approximately a week, every time this situation comes up, monitor all the thoughts you have before, during, and after the situation. Write these thoughts in a log. At the end of the week, do the following:
   a. Identify which of the thoughts are self-defeating.
   b. Identify which of the thoughts are self-enhancing.

c. Determine whether the greatest number of self-defeating thoughts occur before, during, or after the situation.
   d. Consider if the self-defeating thoughts are reflective of distorted automatic thoughts described in Box 11.2.
   e. Consider whether the self-defeating thoughts appear to have roots in any of the maladaptive themes of schemas outlined in Box 11.3.
3. In contrast to the self-defeating thoughts you have, identify some possible coping or self-enhancing thoughts you could use. On paper, list some you could use *before, during,* and *after* the situation, with particular attention to the time period when you tend to use almost all self-defeating thoughts. Make sure that you include in your list some positive or self-rewarding thoughts, too—for coping.
4. Imagine the situation—*before, during,* and *after.* As you do this, call a halt to any self-defeating thoughts and replace them with coping and self-rewarding thoughts. You can even practice this in a role play. Practice this step until you can feel your coping and self-rewarding thoughts taking hold.
5. Construct a homework assignment for yourself that encourages you to apply cognitive restructuring when self-defeating thoughts occur.

your class itself, and when things happen in your class that are especially hard for you—like taking a test or going to the board. What questions do you have about this?

Client: I don't think any—although I don't know if I know exactly what you mean by a coping thought.

The helper, in response 3, *explains and gives some examples of coping thoughts* and particular times when Isabella might need to use them.

3. **Helper:** Let me explain about these and give you some examples. Then, perhaps, you can think of your own examples. The first thing is that there are probably different times when you could use coping thoughts—like before math class, when you're anticipating it. Only instead of worrying about it, you can use this time to prepare to handle it. For example, some coping thoughts you might use before math class are "No need to get nervous. Just think about doing okay," or "You can manage this situation," or "Don't worry so much—you've got the ability to do okay." Then, during math class, you can use coping thoughts to get through the class and to concentrate on what you're doing, such as "Just psych yourself up to get through this," or "Look at this class as a stretch, not a threat," or "Keep your cool; you can control your nervousness." Then, if there are certain times during math class that are especially hard for you, like taking a test or going to the board, there are coping thoughts you can use to help you deal with really hard things, like "Think about staying very calm now," or "Relax, take a deep breath," or "Stay as relaxed as possible. This will be over soon." After math class, or after you cope with a hard situation, you can learn to reinforce yourself for having coped by thinking things like "You did it," or "You were able to control your negative thoughts," or "You're making progress." Do you get the idea?

Client: Yes, I think so.

In responses 4–7, the helper instructs Isabella *to select and practice coping thoughts at each critical phase,* starting with *preparing for class.*

4. **Helper:** Isabella, let's take one thing at a time. Let's work just with what you might think before your math class. Can you come up with some coping thoughts you could use when you're anticipating your class?

Client: Well *(Pause).* I could think about just working on my problems and not worrying about myself. I could think that when I work at it, I usually get it even if I'm slow.

5. **Helper:** Okay, good. Now just to get the feel for these, practice using them. Perhaps you could imagine you are anticipating your class—just say these thoughts aloud as you do so.

Client: I'm thinking that I could look at my class as a positive stretch. I can think about just doing my work. When I concentrate on my work, I usually do get the answers.

6. **Helper:** Good! How did that feel?

Client: Okay, I can see how this might help. Of course, I don't usually think these kinds of things.

7. **Helper:** I realize that, and later on today we'll practice actually having you use these thoughts. You'll get to the point where you can use your nervousness as a signal to cope. You can stop the self-defeating thoughts and use these coping thoughts instead. Let's practice this some more. *(Additional practice ensues.)*

In responses 8–10, the helper asks Isabella *to select and practice verbalizing coping thoughts* she can use *during class.*

8. **Helper:** Isabella, now you seem to have several kinds of coping thoughts that might help you when you're anticipating math class. What about some coping thoughts you could use during the class? Perhaps some of these could help you concentrate on your work instead of your tenseness.

Client: Well, I could tell myself to think about what I need to do—like to get the problems. Or I could think—just take one situation at a time. Just psych myself up 'cause I know I really can do well in math if I believe that.

9. **Helper:** It sounds like you've already thought of several coping things to use during class. This time, why don't you pretend you're sitting in your class? Try out some of these coping thoughts. Just say them aloud.

Client: Okay. I'm sitting at my desk; my work is in front of me. What steps do I need to take now? I could just think about one problem at a time, not worry about all of them. If I take it slowly, I can do okay.

10. **Helper:** That seemed pretty easy for you. Let's do some more practice like this just so these thoughts don't seem unfamiliar to you. As you practice, try hard to think about the meaning of what you're saying to yourself. *(More practice occurs.)*

Next, Isabella *selects and practices coping thoughts* to help her deal with especially *stressful or critical situations* that come up in math class (responses 11–13).

11. **Helper:** This time, let's think of some particular coping statements that might help you if you come up against some touchy situations in your math class—things that are really hard for you to deal with, like taking a test, going to the board, or being called on. What might you think at these times that would keep the lid on your nervousness?

Client: I could think about just doing what is required of me—maybe, as you said earlier, taking a deep breath and just thinking about staying calm, not letting my anxiety get the best of me.

12. **Helper:** Okay, great. Let's see—can you practice some of these aloud as if you were taking a test or had just been asked a question or were at the board in front of the class?

Client: Well, I'm at the board. I'm just going to think about doing this problem. If I start to get really nervous, I'm going to take a deep breath and just concentrate on being calm as I do this.

13. **Helper:** Let's practice this several times. Maybe this time you might use another tense moment, like being called on by your teacher. *(Further practice takes place.)*

Next, the helper *points out how Isabella may discourage or punish herself after class* (responses 14 and 15). Isabella selects and *practices encouraging or self-rewarding thoughts* (responses 16–18).

14. **Helper:** Isabella, there's one more thing I'd like you to practice. After math class, what do you usually think?

Client: I feel relieved. I think about how glad I am it's over. Sometimes I think about the fact that I didn't do well.

15. **Helper:** Well, those thoughts are sort of discouraging, too. What I believe might help is if you could learn to encourage yourself as you start to use these coping thoughts. In other words, instead of thinking

about not doing well, focus on your progress in coping. You can do this during class or after class is over. Can you find some more positive things you could think about to encourage yourself—like giving yourself a pat on the back?

Client: You mean like I didn't do as bad as I thought?

16. **Helper:** Yes, anything like that.

Client: Well, it's over, and it didn't go too badly. Actually I handled things okay. I can do this if I believe it. I can see progress.

17. **Helper:** Now let's assume you've just been at the board. You're back at your seat. Practice saying what you might think in that situation that would be encouraging to you.

Client: I've just sat down. I might think that it went fast and I did concentrate on the problem, so that was good.

18. **Helper:** Now let's assume class is over. What would be some positive, self-encouraging thoughts after class?

Client: I've just gotten out. Class wasn't that bad. I got something out of it. If I put my mind to it, I can do it. *(More practice of positive self-statements occurs.)*

In response 19, the helper instructs Isabella *to practice the entire sequence* of stopping a self-defeating thought and using a coping thought before, during, and after class. Usually the client practices this by *imagining the situation.*

19. **Helper:** So far we've been practicing these coping thoughts at the different times you might use them so you can get used to them. Now let's practice this in the sequence that it might actually occur—like before your class, during the class, coping with a tough situation, and encouraging yourself after class. If you imagine the situation and start to notice any self-defeating thoughts, you can practice stopping these. Then, switch immediately to the types of coping thoughts that you believe will help you most at that time. Concentrate on the coping thoughts. How does this sound?

Client: Okay, I think I know what you mean *(looks a little confused).*

Sometimes long instructions are confusing. Modeling may be better. In responses 20 and 21, the helper *demonstrates how Isabella can apply coping thoughts in practice.*

20. **Helper:** Well, I just said a lot, and it might make more sense if I showed this to you. First, I'm going to imagine I'm in English class. It's almost time for the bell; then it's math class. Wish I could get out of it. It's embarrassing. Stop! That's a signal to use my coping thoughts. I need to think about math class as a challenge. Something I can do okay if I work at it. *(Pause)* Isabella, do you get the idea?

Client: Yes, now I do.

21. **Helper:** Okay, I'll go on and imagine now I'm actually in the class. He's given us a worksheet to do in 30 minutes. Whew! How will dumb me ever do that! Wait a minute. I know I can do it, but I need to go slowly and concentrate on the work, not on me. Just take one problem at a time. Well, now he wants us to read our answers. What if he calls on me? I can feel my heart pounding. Oh well, if I get called on, just take a deep breath and answer. If it turns out to be wrong, it's not the end of the world.

Well, the bell rang. I am walking out. I'm glad it's over. Now, wait a minute—it didn't go that badly. Actually I handled it pretty well. Now, why don't you try this? *(Isabella practices the sequence of coping thoughts several times, first with the helper's assistance, and moving gradually to a completely self-directed manner.)*

Before terminating the session, the helper *assigns daily homework practice.*

22. **Helper:** This week I'd like you to practice this several times each day—just like you did now. Keep track of your practices on your log. And you can use this whenever you feel it would be helpful—such as before, during, or after math class. Jot these times down, too, and we'll go over this next week.

Integrative Interventions: Linkages of ACT and DBT with Cognitive Change Strategies

Cognitive behavioral therapy has systematically evolved over more than four decades to produce both evidence-supported changes strategies, as well as a foundation from which elaborations or integrations of other therapeutic components have developed. Some scholars have characterized these as third-generation developments—following behavior therapy first and cognitive therapies second (Hayes, Strosahl, Bunting, Twohig, & Wilson, 2004). Theoretical and clinical advancements in the arenas of mindfulness-based and acceptance-based treatments have been most prominent, emphasizing development of understanding and skills of attending to present-moment experiences toward promoting tolerance and acceptance and reducing problematic reactivity (Rector, 2013).

Rather than focusing on the *content, form,* or *frequency* of cognitions, emotions, sensations, and memories, these treatments focus more on the context and *function* of cognition and on fostering mindfulness and acceptance of cognitions and symptoms more so than eliminating symptoms per se. Here, emphasis is explicit around strengthening awareness of factors in the present moment and context, fostering openness to unwanted thoughts and feelings, and changing one's relationship to one's thoughts. Additionally, they emphasize concepts such as dialectics, spirituality, relationship, mindfulness, and acceptance.

Acceptance and commitment therapy (ACT), one of the treatments closely associated to CBT, encourages mindfulness tolerance and acceptance of disquieting thoughts and feelings, and cognitive defusion strategies such as watching thoughts go by as if in a stream without the need to stop or control them. These elements intend to foster psychological flexibility, reduce the sense of struggle, and cultivate behavior changes in the direction of valued goals. An ACT perspective considers that people can become "entangled" in cognition, relating to thoughts literally and persisting in problem-solving or control modes beyond, at times, what may be helpful (Hayes et al, 2013). The view is that efforts to control language and cognition can foster avoidance of distressing problems, feelings, and situations, which can often lead to worsening of conditions. Common ACT goals include assisting clients to increase their capacity: (1) to tolerate exposure to thoughts and feelings that are highly uncomfortable; (2) to cultivate mindfulness or awareness that allows observation of distressing events while maintaining a sense of neutrality; and (3) to change their own attitudes about their internal responding (negative emotions and thoughts), fostering greater acceptance, relaxation, and openness (Hayes, Follette, & Linehan, 2004).

ACT draws from theory and research—a core element being Relational Theory Frame (RFT)—on linkages between language, cognition, and subsequent psychological problems. Rather than specific intervention strategies

BOX 11.4	Six Core Clinical Processes of ACT

Acceptance: Fostering acceptance and willingness while reducing the prominence of attempts at emotional control and avoidance of difficult thoughts/feelings in clients' response habits

Defusion: Breaking down processes based on excessively literal language that causes private experiences (i.e., thoughts, feelings, sensations) to function as psychological barriers through unhelpful evaluations, fusion/confusion between what one directly experiences, and how one's use of language shapes interpretation of experience in negative ways

Getting in contact with the present moment: Living more in the moment, gaining skills in noticing what is being experienced in the present moment through the ongoing flow of experiences

The notion of self as context: Distinguishing between conceptualizations of self (one's life story, self-evaluations, the content of troubled thinking/feeling) and the context within which these conceptualizations occur; gaining experience with mindfulness that helps discriminate the thoughts from "I am the person having these thoughts"

Values: Focusing on valued outcomes, ways in which current patterns are blocking valued actions, clarifying values that legitimize confronting previously avoided psychological barriers

Committed action: Beginning and increasingly building larger patterns of committed action that are consistent with valued life goals and ends

Systematic clinical application of acceptance and commitment therapy is growing.

perse, ACT draws on six core clinical processes, which are implemented across a range of disorders in a contextually sensitive manner (Strosahl, Hayes, Wilson, & Gifford, 2004—see Box 11.4). Aiming to address some of the gaps noted in prior application of cognitive therapies, developers see ACT as part of a family of contextual cognitive behavioral therapies (Hayes, Villatte, Levin, & Hildebrandt, 2011).

Systematic clinical application of acceptance and commitment therapy is growing. Hayes & Strosahl (2004) provide practical guides for its application with anxiety, substance abuse, post-traumatic stress disorder, serious mental illness, stress, and pain; with varied populations such as children and adolescents; and in medical settings. Initial research in educational settings indicates promising outcomes for reducing stress in students as well as in teachers (Franco, Mañas, Cangas, Moreno, & Gallego, 2010). ACT is similarly being applied with positive outcomes in other workplace settings (Donaldson & Bond, 2004), for people at risk for disability (Dahl, Wilson, & Nilsson, 2004), and in medical care (Gregg, Callagham, Hayes, & Glenn-Lawson, 2007). ACT arguably holds potential to support effectiveness in prevention efforts spanning a range of problems and populations (Biglan, Hayes, & Pistorello, 2008).

As the evidence base for ACT grows, results are generally favorable (relative to control groups), although mixed. Meta-analytic review spanning multiple studies indicates that ACT is not yet solidly established as the intervention of choice for any given disorder. Ost's findings (2008, 2014), for example, suggest possible

efficaciousness for a range of disorders (e.g., depression, OCD, mixed anxiety), with results weaker with studies that involved multiple disorders or in studies that were methodologically weaker. More generally favorable findings were found by Ruiz (2012), although this may vary by disorder and specific outcomes The coming years will undoubtedly bring greater specification of intervention strategies, an understanding of how strategies are theorized to effect desired change, and stronger comparative analysis to discern for which problems and populations acceptance-based therapies are efficacious as well as their time and outcome effectiveness relative to other interventions such as cognitive-behavioral therapies (Nurius & Macy, 2007).

Similar emphasis on mindfulness and experiential acceptance can also be seen in dialectical behavior therapy (DBT) (Linehan, 1993), integrative behavioral couple therapy (Christensen et al., 2004), and mindfulness-based cognitive therapy (MBCT) (Segal, Williams, & Teasdale, 2013). Mindfulness as a core feature has considerable overlap with cognitive-behavioral strategies that strive to assist clients to move away from an "autopilot" mode of responding and toward greater awareness of their own thinking. Mindfulness espouses a decentered perspective that allows individuals to look at their own thoughts, feelings, and bodily sensations in a more removed manner—for example, simply as thoughts rather than being "you" or "reality."

In its simplest form, mindfulness involves "paying attention in a particular way,: on purpose, in the present moment, and nonjudgmentally" (Kabat-Zinn, 1994, p. 4); it is a central dimension in meditation and stress reduction. Augmenting the original focus on stress, mindfulness-based cognitive therapy has been applied to clients with problems such as depression within a relapse prevention framework, acknowledging that sad moods can activate thinking patterns associated with previous sad moods that, unexamined, can serve to intensify and maintain vicious cycles of depressive spirals (Crane, 2009; Segal et al., 2013). Many practitioners find it necessary to draw upon multiple treatment approaches, and we describe in this book many of those that are most commonly applied and empirically supported. In subsequent chapters you will find descriptions of cognitive stress management strategies, soothing strategies such as meditation and relaxation, emotional regulation techniques such as exposure therapy, self-management strategies, solution-focused treatment, and motivational interviewing.

Promising practices are reflecting a growing integrative trend in intervention theorizing and application. DBT, for example, incorporates behavioral principles, skills training, problem solving, exposure, cognitive therapy, mindfulness, and acceptance—typically blending individual and group modalities—often with telephone coaching, case management, and use of a consultation team. Yet there is nothing haphazard about the mix of methods. Rather, DBT is founded on a carefully formulated base of clinical theory, practice, and evidence (Dimeff & Koerner, 2007; Koerner, 2012; McKay, Wood, & Brantley, 2007). The notion of dialectical captures a worldview and approach that acknowledges that two seeming contradictions can both be true. A primary dialectic within the DBT approach is between acceptance and change—such as accepting oneself and reality while also working to achieve change, such as new skills and associated behaviors.

DBT has been used with a range of clients and problems, particularly those assessed with borderline personality disorder and suicide risk, including adapted models viable within college counseling centers treating distressed students within time-limited circumstances (Pistorello et al, 2012). Kliem, Kroger, and Kosfelder (2010) provided summaries of a number of reviews of DBT as well as their own meta-analysis of outcomes from a range of treatment outcome studies focused on borderline personality disorder. Rizvi, Steffel, and Carson-Wong (2013) summarize work over a broad range of applications, such as substance use, eating disorders, use with adolescents, treatment-resistant depression, and ADHD, and use in correctional and forensic settings. Comprehensive DBT is predicated on a set of intervention modalities that include individual therapy,

group work focused on skills training, availability of consultations or coaching from the therapist between sessions, and team consultations for DBT therapists. Most efficacy results involve this multimodal approach; therefore, evidence is not yet sufficient to determine the outcome benefits of offering certain components alone (Rizvi et al., 2013). The aforementioned summaries conclude that DBT overall is an effective, promising practice and has become a frontline treatment for borderline personality disorder and suicide risk in particular.

We discuss these integrative interventions further in other chapters. It is beyond the scope of this book to fully address them all, but we bring them to your attention so that you can monitor developments in the field, gauge their value for your clientele, and consider options for integrating effective change strategies in your practice.

CHAPTER SUMMARY

Various cognitive change procedures including reframing, cognitive modeling, and cognitive restructuring are used with considerable frequency in helping practice. A cognitive perspective likens an individual's construction of a particular situation to a photograph. The individual's emotional states and patterns of thinking and interacting can affect this picture—blurring, coloring, or distorting the images and what they represent in ways that do not serve the client well. Cognitive restructuring is akin to assisting clients to examine how their photographs take shape and to develop different pictures of themselves, others, or situations. Cognitive structural change can be more than modifying habitual cognitions, rules, expectancies, assumptions, and imperatives. It is also about providing emotional relief, fostering hopefulness, and supporting a view of options and agency in changing those aspects of a problem that are linked to one's own self and worldviews.

As with any intervention, adaptations need to be made depending on client characteristics and context. The challenges people are exposed to, the meaning these hold, and options for change or difference are deeply affected by sociodemographic status, including race, culture, gender, sexual orientation, religion, and other factors. Cognitive change techniques should be collaboratively applied with thoughtful attention to how diversity factors may bear on assessment and use of strategies. Moreover, conditions of inequality, marginalization, and other sources of stress and/or injustice argue for critical consciousness related to environmental contributors when assisting individuals to undertake cognitive changes in the service of their own goals and well-being. Finally, as research rapidly advances in illuminating the complex transactions among memories, thoughts, feelings, sensations, physical embodiment, and the social/material world, so, too, will clinical models need to

evolve. We anticipate important developments in the coming decade relevant to effective, appropriate, and culturally sensitive practice.

Visit CengageBrain.com for a variety of study tools and useful resources such as video examples, case studies, interactive exercises, flashcards, and quizzes.

11 Knowledge and Skill Builder

Part One

Learning Outcome 1 asks you to demonstrate eight out of 8 steps of the reframing procedure with a role-play client. Use the Interview Checklist for Reframing to assess your interview.

Interview Checklist for Reframing

Instructions: Determine whether the helper demonstrated the lead listed in the checklist. Check (☑) the leads that were used.

Treatment Rationale

___1. Helper explains purpose of reframing.

"Often when we think about a problem situation, our initial reaction can lead to emotional distress. For example, we focus only on the negative features of the situation and overlook other details. By focusing only on the selected negative features of a situation, we can become nervous or anxious about the situation."

___2. Helper provides overview of reframing.

"We'll identify what features you attend to when you think of the situation. Once you become aware of these features, we will look for other neutral or positive aspects of the situation that you may ignore or overlook. Then, we will work on incorporating these other things into your perceptions of the problem situation."

___3. Helper confirms client's willingness to use the strategy.

"How does this all sound? Are you ready to try this?"

Identification of Client Perceptions and Feelings in Problem Situations

___4. Helper has client identify features typically attended to during situation (may have to use imagery with some clients).

"When you think of the situation or one like it, what features do you notice or attend to? What is the first thing that pops into your head?"

___5. Helper has client identify typical feelings during situation.

"How do you usually feel?" "What do you experience [or are you experiencing] during this situation?"

Deliberate Enactment of Selected Perceptual Features

___6. Helper asks client to re-enact situation (through role play or imagery) and to deliberately attend to selected features. (This step may need to be repeated several times.)

"Let's set up a role play [or imagery] in which we act out this situation. This time I want you to deliberately focus on these aspects of the situation we just identified. Notice how you attend to ___."

Identification of Alternative Perceptions

___7. Helper instructs client to identify positive or neutral features of situation. The new reframes are plausible and acceptable to the client and fit the client's values and age, gender, race, and ethnicity.

"Now, I want us to identify other features of the situation that are neutral or positive. These are things you have forgotten about or ignored. Think of other features." "What other aspects of this situation aren't readily apparent to you could provide a different way to view the situation?"

Modification of Perceptions in Problem Situations

___8. Helper instructs client to modify perceptions of situation by focusing on or attending to the neutral or positive features. (Use of role play or imagery can help with this process for some clients. This step may need to be repeated several times.)

"When we act out the situation, I want you to change what you attend to in the situation by thinking of the positive features we just identified. Just focus on these features."

Homework and Follow-up

___9. Helper encourages client to practice modifying perceptions during *in vivo* situations.

"Practice is very important for modifying your perceptions. Every time you think about or encounter the situation, focus on the neutral or positive features of the situation."

___10. Helper instructs client to monitor aspects of the strategy on homework log sheet.

"I'd like you to use this log to keep track of the number of times you practice or use this. Also record your initial and resulting feelings before and after these kinds of situations."

___11. Helper arranges for a follow-up. (During follow-up, helper comments on client's log and points out small perceptual shifts.)

"Let's get together in 2 weeks. Bring your log sheet with you. Then, we can see how this is working for you."

Observer Comments: _____

Part Two

Describe how you would use the seven components of cognitive modeling and self-instructional training to help a fictional client we'll call Mr. Huang initiate social contacts with his boss (Learning Outcome 2). These are the seven components:

1. Rationale
2. Model of task and self-guidance
3. Overt external guidance
4. Overt self-guidance
5. Faded overt self-guidance
6. Covert self-guidance
7. Homework and follow-up

See Feedback section for answers. In addition, review the Interviewing Checklist for Cognitive Modeling for illustration of ways to implement facets of each of the seven components.

Interview Checklist for Cognitive Modeling

Instructions: Determine which of the following leads the helper used in the interview. Check (☑) the leads that were used.

Treatment Rationale

___1. Helper provides a rationale for the strategy.

"This strategy is a way to help you do this task and also plan how to do it. The planning will help you perform better and more easily."

___2. Helper provides overview of strategy.

"We will take it step by step. First, I'll show you how to do it, and I'll talk to myself aloud while I'm doing it so you can hear my planning. Then you'll do that. Gradually, you'll be able to perform the task while thinking through the planning to yourself at the same time."

___3. Helper checks client's willingness to use strategy.

"Would you like to go ahead with this now?"

Model of Task and Self-Guidance

___4. Helper instructs client in what to listen and look for during modeling.

"While I do this, I'm going to tell you orally my plans for doing it. Just listen closely to what I say as I go through this."

___5. Helper engages in modeling of task, verbalizing self-guidance aloud, using language relevant to the client.

"Okay, I'm walking in for the interview. [Helper walks in.] I'm getting ready to greet the interviewer and then wait for his cue to sit down" [sits down].

___6. Self-guidance demonstrated by helper includes five components:

___a. *Question* about demands of task:

"Now what is it I should be doing in this situation?"

___b. *Answer to* question mentions planning what to do:

"I just need to greet the person, sit down on cue, and answer the questions. I need to be sure to point out why they should take me."

___c. *Focused attention* to task and *self-guidance* during task:

"Okay, remember to take a deep breath, relax, and concentrate on the interview. Remember to discuss my particular qualifications and experiences and try to answer questions completely and directly."

___d. *Coping self-evaluation* and, if necessary, *error correction:*

"Okay, now, if I get a little nervous, just take a deep breath. Stay focused on the interview. If I don't respond too well to one question, I can always come back to it."

___e. *Self-reinforcement* for completion of task:

"Okay, doing fine. Things are going pretty smoothly."

Overt External Guidance

___7. Helper instructs client to perform task while helper coaches.

"This time you go through the interview yourself. I'll be coaching you on what to do and on your planning."

___8. Client performs task while helper coaches by verbalizing self-guidance, changing *I* to *you*.

"Now just remember you're going to walk in for the interview. When the interview begins, I'll coach you through it." Helper's verbalization includes the five components of self-guidance:

___a. Question about task:

"Okay, you're walking into the interview room. Now ask yourself what it is you're going to do."

___b. Answer to question:

"Okay, you're going to greet the interviewer. [Client does so.] Now he's cuing you to sit down." [Client sits.]

___c. Focused attention to task and self-guidance during task:

"Just concentrate on how you want to handle this situation. He's asking you about your background. You're going to respond directly and completely."

___d. Coping self-evaluation and error correction:

"If you feel a little nervous while you're being questioned, take a deep breath. If you don't respond to a question completely, you can initiate a second response. Try that now."

___e. Self-reinforcement:

"That's good. Now remember you want to convey why you should be chosen. Take your time to do that. [Client does so.] Great. Very thorough job."

Overt Self-Guidance

___9. Helper instructs client to perform task and instruct self aloud.

(continued)

"This time I'd like you to do both things. Talk to yourself as you go through the interview in the same way we have done before. Remember, there are five parts to your planning. If you get stuck, I'll help you."

___10. Client performs task while simultaneously verbalizing aloud self-guidance process. Client's verbalization includes five components of self-guidance:

___a. Question about task:

"Now what is it I need to do?"

___b. Answer to question:

"I'm going to greet the interviewer, wait for the cue to sit down, and then answer the questions directly and as completely as possible."

___c. Focused attention and self-guidance:

"Just concentrate on how I'm going to handle this situation. I'm going to describe why I should be chosen."

___d. Coping self-evaluation and error correction:

"If I get a little nervous, just take a deep breath. If I have trouble with one question, I can always come back to it."

___e. Self-reinforcement:

"Okay, things are going smoothly. I'm doing fine."

___11. If client's self-guidance is incomplete or if client gets stuck, helper

___a. Either intervenes and cues client:

"Let's stop here for a minute. You seem to be having trouble. Let's start again and try to…"

___b. Or recycles client back through step 10:

"That seemed pretty hard, so let's try it again. This time you go through the interview, and I'll coach you through it."

___12. Helper gives feedback to client about overt practice.

"That seemed pretty easy for you. You were able to go through the interview and coach yourself. The one place you seemed a little stuck was in the middle, when you had trouble describing yourself. But overall, it was something you handled well. What do you think?"

Faded Overt Self-Guidance

13. Counselor instructs client on how to perform task while whispering.

"This time I'd like you to go through the interview and whisper the instructions to yourself as you go along. The whispering may be a new thing for you, but I believe it will help you learn to do this."

14. Client performs task and whispers simultaneously.

"I'm going into the room now, waiting for the interviewer to greet me and to sit down. I'm going to answer the questions as completely as possible. Now I'm going to talk about my background."

15. Counselor checks to determine how well client performed.

a. If client stumbled or left out some of the five parts, client engages in faded overt practice again:

"You had some difficulty with ___. Let's try this type of practice again."

b. If client performed practice smoothly, then counselor moves on to next step:

"You seemed to do this easily and comfortably. The next thing is…"

Covert Self-Guidance

16. Counselor instructs client to perform task while covertly (thinking only) instructing self.

"This time while you practice, simply *think* about these instructions. In other words, instruct yourself mentally or in your head as you go along."

17. Client performs task while covertly instructing. Only the client's actions are visible at this point.

18. After practice (step 17), counselor asks client to describe covert instructions.

"Can you tell me what you thought about as you were doing this?"

19. On the basis of client report (step 18)

a. Counselor asks client to repeat covert self-guidance:

"It's hard sometimes to begin rehearsing instructions mentally. Let's try it again so you feel more comfortable with it."

b. Counselor moves on to homework:

"Okay, you seemed to do this very easily. I believe it would help if you could apply this to some things that you do on your own this week. For instance…"

Homework

20. Counselor instructs client on how to carry out homework.

"What I'd like you to do this week is to go through this type of mental practice on your own."

a. What to do:

"Specifically, go through a simulated interview where you mentally plan your responses as we've done today."

b. How much or how often to do the task:

"I believe it would help if you could do this two times each day."

c. When and where to do it:

"I believe it would be helpful to practice at home first, and then practice at school [or work]."

d. **A method for self-monitoring during completion of homework:**

"Each time you do this, make a check on this log sheet. Also, write down the five parts of the self-instructions you used."

21. **Counselor arranges for a face-to-face or telephone follow-up after completion of homework assignment.**

"Bring in your log sheets next week, or give me a call at the end of the week, and we'll go over your homework then."

Part Three

Learning Outcome 3 asks you to identify and describe the six components of cognitive restructuring in a client case. Using the case described here, explain briefly how you would use the steps and components of cognitive restructuring with *this* client, Doreen. You can use the six questions following the client case to describe your use of the procedure and compare your answers to the Feedback section.

Doreen is a junior in college; she is majoring in education and getting very good grades. She reports that she has an active social life and has some good close friendships with both males and females. Despite obvious pluses, the client reports constant feelings of being worthless and inadequate. Her standards for herself seem to be unrealistically high. Despite maintaining an almost straight A average, Doreen still chides herself that she does not have all As. Although she is attractive and has an active social life, she thinks that she should be more attractive and more talented. At the end of the initial session, Doreen adds that as an African American woman she always has felt as though she has to prove herself more than the average person.

1. How would you explain the rationale for cognitive restructuring to this client?
2. Give an example you might use with this client to point out the difference between a self-defeating and a self-enhancing thought. Try to base your example on the client's self-description.
3. How would you have the client identify her thoughts about herself—her grades, appearance, social life, and so on? How would you help her identify schemas underlying maladaptive ways of thinking?
4. What are some coping thoughts this client might use?
5. Explain how, in the session, you would help the client practice shifting from self-defeating to coping thoughts.
6. What kind of homework assignment would you use to help the client increase her use of coping thoughts about herself?

Part Four

Learning Outcome 5 asks you to describe ways in which schemas are involved in cognitive functioning. In client-accessible terms, briefly describe your understanding of how schemas are formed, how they are drawn into play in cognitive

operations, and why they can be difficult to change. Feedback follows the Knowledge and Skill Builder.

Interview Checklist for Cognitive Restructuring

Instructions: Determine whether the helper demonstrated the lead listed in the checklist. Check (☑) the leads that the helper used.

Treatment Rationale and Overview

___1. **Helper explains purpose and rationale of cognitive restructuring.**

"You've reported that you find yourself getting anxious and depressed during and after these conversations with the people who have to evaluate your work. This procedure can help you identify some things you might be thinking in this situation that are just beliefs, not facts, and are unproductive. You can learn more realistic ways to think about this situation that will help you cope with it in a way that you want to."

___2. **Helper provides brief overview of procedure.**

"There are several things we'll do in using this procedure. *First,* this will help you identify the kinds of things you're thinking before, during, and after these situations that are self-defeating. *Second,* we'll work to determine ways that these self-defeating beliefs (schemas) developed over time and what conditions tend to activate them. *Third,* this will help us develop cues and strategies for you to catch a self-defeating thought and replace it with a coping thought. *Fourth,* this will help you see ways to break long-standing patterns of responding and learn how to give yourself credit for changing these self-defeating thoughts."

___3. **Helper explains difference between self-enhancing thoughts and self-defeating thoughts and provides culturally relevant examples of both.**

"A self-defeating thought is one way to interpret the situation, but it is usually negative and unproductive, like thinking that the other person doesn't value you or what you say. In contrast, a self-enhancing thought is a more constructive and realistic way to interpret the situation—like thinking that what you are talking about has value to you."

___4. **Helper explains influence of irrational and self-defeating thoughts on emotions and performance.**

"When you're constantly preoccupied with yourself and worried about how the situation will turn out, this can affect your feelings and your behavior. Worrying about the situation can make you feel anxious and upset. Concentrating on the situation and not worrying about its outcome can help you feel more relaxed, which helps you handle the situation more easily."

___5. **Helper confirms client's willingness to use strategy.**

"Are you ready to try this now?"

(continued)

11 | Knowledge and Skill Builder (*continued*)

Identifying Client Thoughts in Problem Situations

___6. Helper asks client to describe problem situations and identify examples of self-enhancing thoughts and of self-defeating thoughts that client typically experiences in these situations.

"Think of the last time you were in this situation. Describe for me what you think before you have a conversation with your evaluator... What are you usually thinking during the conversation? What thoughts go through your mind after the conversation is over? Now let's see which of those thoughts are actual facts about the situation or are constructive ways to interpret the situation. Which ones are your beliefs about the situation that are unproductive or self-defeating?"

___7. If client is unable to complete step 6, then helper models examples of thoughts or "links" between event and client's emotional response.

"Okay, think of the thoughts that you have while you're in this conversation as a link between this event and your feelings afterward of being upset and depressed. What is the middle part? For instance, it might be something like 'I'll never have a good evaluation, and I'll lose this position' or 'I always blow this conversation and never make a good impression.' Can you recall thinking anything like this?"

___8. Helper instructs client to monitor and record content of thoughts *before, during,* and *after* stressful or upsetting situations before the next session.

"One way to help you identify this link or your thoughts is to keep track of what you're thinking in these situations as they happen. This week I'd like you to use this log each day. Try to identify and write down at least three specific thoughts you have in these situations each day, and bring this in with you next week."

___9. Using client's monitoring, helper and client identify client's self-defeating thoughts.

"Let's look at your log and go over the kinds of negative thoughts that seem to be predominant in these situations. We can explore how these thoughts affect your feelings and performance in this situation—and whether you feel there is any evidence or rational basis for these."

___10. Helper assesses client's schemas.

In some cases, more focal assessment of underlying schemas is needed. In-depth assessment of schemas (adaptive or maladaptive) can involve multiple tools such as a focused review of the client's history relative to the current problem, use of schema inventories, experiential exercises to trigger certain schemas, and client education about schemas (Young et al., 2014). As part of a case conceptualization, Leahy (1996, p. 194) suggests the following questions to get a better sense of how the client sees this. On each blank line, fill in the word that describes the schema in question.

"How did your (parents, other family members, peers, teachers, partner as relevant) teach you that you were ___? What evidence is there that you are not ___? How would you rate yourself on a continuum from ___ to (the opposite)? Does this depend on the situation or other factors? If so, how and why? What is the consequence of believing or demanding this of yourself? Is it ever okay to be ___? How would you challenge your (parent, teacher, others as appropriate) now that you are an adult, if they were to describe you as ___?"

Introduction and Practice of Coping Thoughts

___11. Helper explains purpose and potential use of coping thoughts and gives some examples of coping thoughts to be used:

___a. Before the situation—preparing for it

___b. During the situation

___ (1) Focusing on task___ (2) Dealing with feeling overwhelmed

"Up to this point, we've talked about the negative or unproductive thoughts you have in these situations and how they contribute to your feeling uncomfortable, upset, and depressed. Now we're going to look at some alternative, more constructive ways to think about the situation—using coping thoughts. These thoughts can help you prepare for the situation, handle the situation, and deal with feeling upset or overwhelmed in the situation. As long as you're using some coping thoughts, you avoid giving up control and letting the old self-defeating thoughts take over. Here are some examples of coping thoughts."

___12. Helper instructs client to think of additional coping thoughts that client could use or has used before.

"Try to think of your own coping thoughts—perhaps ones you can remember using successfully in other situations, ones that seem to work for you."

___13. Helper instructs client to practice verbalizing selected coping statements.

"At first you will feel a little awkward using coping statements. It's like learning to drive a stick shift after you've been used to driving an automatic. So one way to help you get used to this is for you to practice these statements aloud."

___a. Helper instructs client to begin by practicing coping statements individually. Coping statements to use before a situation are practiced first, followed by coping statements to use during a situation:

"First, just practice each coping statement separately. After you feel comfortable with saying these aloud, practice the ones you could use before this conversation. Okay, now practice the ones you could use during this conversation with your evaluator."

___b. Helper instructs client to practice sequence of coping statements as they would be used in actual situation:

"Now let's put it all together. Imagine it's an hour before your meeting. Practice the coping statements you could use then. Then we'll role-play the meeting. As you feel aroused or overwhelmed, stop and practice coping thoughts during the situation."

___c. Helper instructs client to become actively involved and to internalize meaning of coping statements during practice:

"Try to really put yourself into this practice. As you say these new things to yourself, try to think of what these thoughts really mean."

Shifting from Self-Defeating to Coping Thoughts

___14. Helper models shift from recognizing a self-defeating thought and stopping it to replacing it with a coping thought.

"Let me show you what we will practice today. First, I'm in this conversation. Everything is going okay. All of a sudden I can feel myself starting to tense up. I realize I'm starting to get overwhelmed about this whole evaluation process. I'm thinking that I'm going to blow it. No, I stop that thought at once. Now, I'm just going to concentrate on calming down, taking a deep breath, and thinking only about what I have to say."

___15. Helper helps client practice shift from self-defeating to coping thoughts. Practice consists of four steps:

"Now let's practice this. You will imagine the situation. As soon as you start to recognize the onset of a self-defeating thought, stop it. Verbalize the thought aloud, and tell yourself to stop. Then, verbalize a coping thought in place of it and imagine carrying on with the situation."

___a. Having client imagine situation or carry it out in a role play (behavior rehearsal)

___b. Recognizing self-defeating thought (which could be signaled by a hand or finger)

___c. Stopping self-defeating thought (which could be supplemented with a hand clap)

___d. Replacing thought with coping thought (possibly supplemented with deep breathing)

___16. Helper helps client practice using shift for each problem situation until anxiety or stress felt by client while practicing the situation is decreased to a reasonable or negligible level and client can carry

out practice and use coping thoughts in a self-directed manner.

"Let's keep working with this situation until you feel pretty comfortable with it and can shift from self-defeating to coping thoughts without my help."

Introduction and Practice of Reinforcing Self-Statements

___17. Helper explains purpose and use of positive self-statements and gives some examples of these to client.

"You have really made a lot of progress in learning to use coping statements before and during these situations. Now it's time to learn to reward or encourage yourself. After you've coped with a situation, you can pat yourself on the back for having done so by thinking a positive or rewarding thought like 'I did it' or 'I really managed that pretty well.'"

___18. Helper instructs client to think of additional positive self-statements and to select some to try out.

"Can you think of some things like this that you think of when you feel good about something or when you feel like you've accomplished something? Try to come up with some of these thoughts that seem to fit for you."

___19. Helper models application of positive self-statements as self-reinforcement for shift from self-defeating to coping thoughts.

"Okay, here is the way you reward yourself for having coped. You recognize the self-defeating thought. Now you're in the situation using coping thoughts, and you're thinking things like, 'Take a deep breath' or 'Just concentrate on this task.' Now the conversation is finished. You know you were able to use coping thoughts, and you reward yourself and positively reinforce your choices by thinking 'Yes, I did it' or 'I really was able to manage that.'"

___20. Helper instructs client to practice use of positive self-statements in interview following practice of shift from self-defeating to coping thoughts. This should be practiced in sequence (coping *before* and *during* situation and reinforcing oneself *after* situation).

"Okay, let's try this out. As you imagine the conversation, you're using the coping thoughts you will verbalize ... Now, imagine the situation is over, and verbalize several reinforcing thoughts for having coped."

Homework and Follow-up

___21. Helper instructs client to use cognitive restructuring procedure (identifying self-defeating thought, stopping it, shifting to coping thought, reinforcing with positive self-statement) in situations outside the

(continued)

interview. "Okay, now you're ready to use the entire procedure whenever you have these conversations in which you're being evaluated—or any other situation in which you recognize your negative interpretation of the event is affecting you. In these cases, you recognize and stop any self-defeating thoughts, use the coping thoughts before the situation to prepare for it, and use the coping thoughts during the situation to help focus on the task and deal with being overwhelmed. After the situation is over, use the positive self-thoughts to reward your efforts."

___22. Helper instructs client to monitor and record on log sheet the number of times client uses cognitive restructuring outside the interview.

"I'd like you to use this log to keep track of the number of times you use this procedure and to jot down the situation in which you're using it. Also, rate your tension level on a 1-to-5 scale before and after each time you use this."

___23. Helper arranges for follow-up.

"Do this recording for the next 2 weeks. Then let's get together for a follow-up session."

Observer Comments_____

_____

11 Knowledge and Skill Builder **Feedback**

Part One

Use the Interview Checklist for Reframing to assess your interview.

Part Two

1. *Rationale:* First, you would explain the steps of cognitive modeling and self-instructional training to Mr. Huang. Then, you would explain how this procedure could help him practice and plan the way he might approach his boss.

2. *Model of task and self-guidance:* You would model for Mr. Huang a way he could approach his boss to request a social contact. This would entail modeling the five parts of the self-guidance process: (a) the question about what he wants to do; (b) the answer to the question in the form of planning; (c) focused attention on the task and guiding himself through it; (d) evaluating himself and correcting errors or making adjustments in his behavior in a coping manner; and (e) reinforcing himself for adequate performance. In your modeling, it is important to use language that is relevant to Mr. Huang.

3. *Overt external guidance:* Mr. Huang would practice making an approach or contact while you coach him through the five parts of self-guidance as just described.

4. *Overt self-guidance:* Mr. Huang would practice making a social contact while verbalizing aloud the five parts of the self-guidance process. If he got stuck, you could prompt him, or you could have him repeat this step or recycle step 3.

5. *Faded overt self-guidance:* Mr. Huang would engage in another practice attempt, but this time he would whisper the five parts of the self-guidance process.

6. *Covert self-guidance:* Mr. Huang would make another practice attempt while using the five parts of the self-guidance process covertly. You would ask him afterward to describe what happened. Additional practice with covert self-guidance or recycling to step 4 or step 5 might be necessary.

7. *Homework:* You would instruct Mr. Huang to practice the self-guidance process daily before actually making a social contact with his boss.

   Now compare your notes regarding how you would operationalize each of these components with illustrations provided in the Interview Checklist for Cognitive Modeling.

Part Three

1. One overall goal may be for Doreen to feel more empowered about herself and to feel less pressure to have to constantly prove herself as an African American woman. You can explain that cognitive restructuring (CR) would help her identify some of her thoughts about herself that are beliefs, not inherent facts, and therefore contestable—perhaps unrealistic thoughts, leading to feelings of depression and worthlessness. In addition, CR would help her learn to think about herself in more realistic, self-enhancing ways in line with her values. See the Interview Checklist for Cognitive Restructuring for another example of the CR rationale.

2. A core issue for Doreen to challenge is her belief system about her race and gender—that as an African American and as a woman she must constantly prove herself to be a worthy person. Thinking that she is not good enough is self-defeating. Self-enhancing or positive thoughts about herself are more realistic interpretations of her experiences—good grades, close friends, active social life, and so on. Recognition that she is intelligent and attractive is a self-enhancing thought.

3. You could ask the client to describe different situations and the thoughts she has about herself in them. She could also observe this during the week. You could model some possible thoughts she might be having. See leads 6–9 in the Interview Checklist for Cognitive Restructuring. For schema identification, several tools and sample questions are listed in lead 10.

4. There are many possible coping thoughts that Doreen could use. Here are some examples: "Hey, I'm doing pretty well as it is." "Don't be so hard on myself. I don't have to be perfect." "That worthless feeling is a sign to cope—recognize my assets." "What's 'more' attractive, anyway? I am attractive." "Don't let that one B get me down. It's not the end of the world." "I'm an African American woman, and I'm proud of it. I feel okay about myself the way I am. I don't have to prove my worth to anyone."

5. See leads 14–16 on the Interview Checklist for Cognitive Restructuring.

6. Many possible homework assignments might help. Here are a few examples:
   a. Every time Doreen uses a coping thought, she could record it in her log.
   b. She could cue herself to use a coping thought by writing these down on note cards and reading a note before doing something else, like getting a drink or making a phone call, or by using a phone-answering device to report and verbalize coping thoughts.
   c. She could enlist the aid of a close friend or roommate. If the roommate notices that the client starts

(continued)

to put herself down, she could interrupt her. Doreen could then use a coping statement.

Part Four

You could explain that the word *schema* refers to how information gets organized and stored in memory. Schemas are built up over time and experience from input we get from others as well as from our own reflections and evaluations. Not all, but many, of the deeply problematic schemas have their beginnings in childhood and youth, when identity and attachment styles are being formed. Schemas are not passive file drawers of recorded information; they are more like complex filters that screen, direct, and shape what we notice, how we interpret ourselves and our world, and how we respond. We have too many schemas for them all to be actively working at any one time. Rather, because we tend to develop patterns and habits, some schemas get punched much like buttons under trigger situations. When these get punched, other schemas that are related get activated as well, and we are filled with the sense of them. This subset of active schemas influences our thoughts, feelings, and behaviors in the moment, and it is hard to access schemas that run counter to them. For example, when our schema of inadequacy is pushed, it brings with it related schemas such as shame and worthlessness, which make it difficult to access schemas about our talent, promise, and hope.

Cognitive Approaches to Stress Management

Stress Processes, Problem-Solving Therapy, and Stress Inoculation Training

Learning Outcomes

After completing this chapter, the student should be able to:

1. Describe the key components of the human stress response model.

2. Identify which step of the problem-solving strategy is reflected in each of 10 helper responses, accurately identifying at least 8 of the 10 examples.

3. Demonstrate 16 out of 19 steps of problem-solving in a role-play interview using the Interview Checklist for Problem-solving at the end of the chapter to assess your performance.

4. Demonstrate 17 out of 21 steps of stress inoculation in a role-play interview.

Feel anxious? Stressful? Wired?

Do you have tension headaches?

Do you abuse soft drugs—alcohol or tobacco?

Do you feel chronically fatigued?

Are you irritable, with low frustration tolerance?

Are you overwhelmed in certain situations or at certain times, making it hard to problem-solve?

Does your immune system seem to not be working well?

A great number of people would respond yes to one or more of these questions. Anxiety, agitation, and feeling taxed or overwhelmed are among the most common concerns reported by clients. Stress is related to physiological discomforts such as headaches, indigestion, and sleep dysregulation, as well as heart disease, cancer, and many other serious diseases. There has been a considerable amount of research exploring the relative strengths and weaknesses of stress management approaches, and a number of current guides are available that are applicable to children and adults (Contrada & Baum, 2011; Fink, 2007; Kahn,

2006; Lanius, Vermetten, & Pain, 2010; Lehrer, Woolfolk & Sime, 2007; Nurius & Hoy-Ellis, 2013; Rice, 2012; Weber, 2011; Wong & Wong, 2006).

As noted in the last chapter, people seeking professional counseling are inherently stressed. However, the nature and magnitude of their stress will suggest different kinds of strategies. This chapter provides an overview of clinical theory regarding key components of the stress response process, advances in understanding of linkages between biological and psychosocial process in stress and coping, factors related to socioeconomic and life course variations in how stress is experienced, and two sets of interventions: those that are oriented to problem-solving and those more oriented to coping and resilience (the latter under the rubric of stress inoculation). Both interventions are predicated on familiar cognitive theory—for example, that maladaptive emotions and thinking are influenced or mediated by beliefs, schemas, perceptions, and cognitions—and both have elements of cognitive restructuring as well as coping skills. Subsequent chapters provide complementary interventions, including, for example, strategies to calm one's physical stress through focus on breathing and meditation as well as strategies focused more on systematically assisting people to tolerate traumatizing experiences and strengthen their capacity to emotionally self-regulate under intense stress.

Stress and Coping

Stress, as applied to people's subjective sense of physical, mental, or emotional strain, has been widely studied in recent decades and has become a commonplace concept

| BOX 12.1 | Common Sources of Stress |

Stress is an inherent part of life, stemming from both fa-miliar and positive events (new jobs, adding new family members) as well as events that are clearly taxing or even traumatic. Review the following range of life domains and roles relative to some of the factors that can contribute to stress (Greenberg, 1996). What else would you include?

- *Educational attainment stress:* pressure regarding grades, performance, or competition; pressures related to obtain-ing a fulfilling education that leads to or enhances em-ployment and labor force access and success; necessary personal life compromises and sacrifices; debt; challenges to one's beliefs, values, and expectations; additional stressors for minority students (e.g., those for whom Eng-lish is not a first language, older students, students with disabilities, discriminatory assumptions or policies).
- *Relationship stress:* the changing definition and form of family (e.g., nuclear, extended, blended, family of choice, multigenerational, dual-career, single parent); financial concerns; separation/divorce; family planning; parenting;

relationship conflict or aggression; role overload or con-flict; loss of support relationships and the need to create new ones; peer pressures or mistreatment.
- *Aging and stress:* loss and adjustment in later years—for example, loss of valued roles, independence, health and physical strength, and mobility; loss of others and grief; the need to accept caregiving, role reversals, death and dying; loss of dignity; stereotyping or condescending attitudes or behavior from others.
- *Occupational stress:* stressors directly related to work, such as work overload or conflict, time pressures, poor working conditions, exposure to dangers of various kinds, lack of job security, thwarted goals or advancement, constraints on decision-making or options, poor relations with boss/ subordinate/co-workers, office politics, etc.
- *Traumatic stress:* exposure to and consequences of a wide range of significantly stressful experiences such as major accidents or illnesses, violence or other forms of criminality, war or other forms of conflict and oppression, victim of discrimination, natural disasters.

in our daily lives and language ("I am so stressed out!"). Stress essentially refers to experiences in which an indi-vidual perceives that demands of circumstances exceed one's capacity to mobilize resources or otherwise meet the demands. Stress can stem from what we might regard in largely positive terms (e.g., a desired job promotion, marriage or partnering, parenthood, a holiday, a move) as well as what we would regard in negative terms (e.g., significant losses; injuries or illnesses; serious financial, re-lationship, or mental health threats). Box 12.1 illustrates a range of stressors, many of them commonly encountered. Although challenges and adversities are inescapable parts of life, populations vary regarding the number, severity, and controllability of what they are likely to encounter. People vary also in how they respond to stressors (cogni-tively, affectively, biologically, behaviorally) and the extent to which they have coping resources available. Next we review some of the components of stress and coping rel-evant to assessment and intervention planning.

Stress Response Model Components

One's cognitive interpretations or **appraisals** of a life situ-ation and its implications are crucial components in how people construct the meaning that the situation holds to them; these appraisals greatly affect emotional reactions, neurological and physiological responding, perceptions of options and likely outcomes, and actions taken or not taken. Figure 12.1 illustrates key components in the process of cop-ing with stress. This depiction is rooted in a transactional, ecological view (Folkman, 2011; Lazarus & Folkman, 1984)

wherein both person and environmental characteristics are considered, as well as factors that are comparatively objective in nature (e.g., the mix of resources and demands in place, situational characteristics, one's own and others' behaviors) and how these factors are uniquely interpreted (perceived or appraised) and experienced by the people involved.

All these boxes and arrows make for a complex picture, but they are important for showing multiple points of help-ing toward improved outcomes or bolstering resiliency *if* one understands the relationships among these person and environmental factors relative to coping. For example, fo-cusing only on resources (including social "currency" and other types of resources) is unlikely to be sufficient if one does not take other coping, contextual, and sociocultural factors into account. Similarly, if one works only to change coping behaviors, then this alone is likely insufficient, given factors influencing these behaviors as well as outcomes sepa-rate from coping behaviors. Although health outcomes are used in Figure 12.1, the problematic or desired outcomes could take many forms, such as mental health, social or family well-being, or ability to accomplish valued outcomes (e.g., educational, work-related, life transitions).

Primary appraisals refer to whether the stressor itself is perceived as a threat of harm or loss or perceived in positive challenge terms. **Secondary appraisals** involve questions like the following: Who or what is responsible for this situation? Does the person have what is needed to handle this? What are the likely outcomes—positive and negative? Unpacking individuals' stress and coping patterns draws upon assessment skills addressed in several

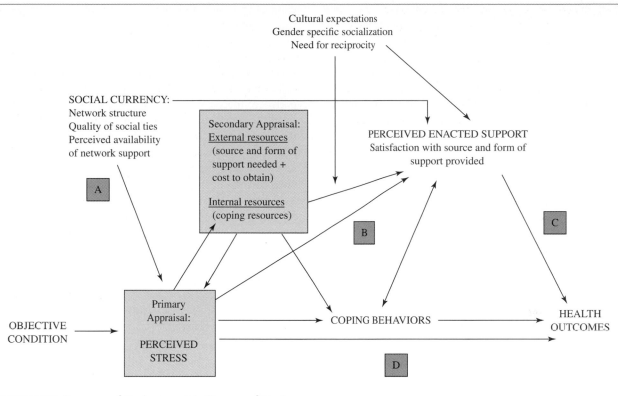

FIGURE 12.1 Person and Environment in Stress and Coping

Source: From "Social Support The Promise and the Reality," by P. W. Underwood. In V. H. Rice (Ed.), *Handbook of Stress, Coping, and Health: Implications for Nursing Research, Theory, and Practice,* pp. 355–380. Copyright © 2012 and is held by Patricia W. Underwood. Reprinted with permission of P. W. Underwood.

chapters to characterize the person and environmental strengths and vulnerabilities involved. How is the stressful situation being appraised or interpreted? Are there features of cognitive schemas or belief systems involved that need careful attention? What is the person's perceived social support relative to the stress and needs in question? What is their sense of self-efficacy relative to managing this stress? Appraisals set the stage for problem definitions and self-statements that clients develop about stressful problems that are targets of change in interventions such as problem-solving and stress inoculation training.

The nature of one's emotions can make a huge difference (e.g., feeling angry versus feeling guilty positions one very differently in terms of the likely response), and emotions stem in part from how the circumstances have been appraised and the meaning they hold for the individual (or their family, group, community) in question.

Coping is often separated into problem-focused (such as seeking information or new skills, evaluating pros/cons of options, taking action to remove or change the stressor) and emotion-focused approaches (such as reframing or reappraising the stressor in a different light, reducing problematic emotional responding, seeking comfort). Although

an oversimplification, these can be thought of as actions to manage the stressor as compared with actions to manage emotions associated with the stressor and surrounding context. Both types of coping have potentially productive roles. Problem-focused coping tends to be associated with more vigorous problem-solving and less depletion and burnout. Emotion-focused coping can be particularly important when the stressor is not changeable, for example.

Coping is not a one-shot step but rather an ongoing, constantly changing process that includes how people reappraise the stress context—does the situation seem as threatening, do I perceive changes (positive or negative) regarding my abilities to manage the situation or what I see to be the likely outcomes? These appraisal, emotion, and behavioral components mediate or filter the effects of stressors on the person's outcomes and well-being. How one perceives stressors will shape what coping behaviors they undertake. Stressors appraised as being threatening yet also, possibly with help, manageable are more likely to activate problem-focused coping than those perceived as threatening but also uncontrollable and with likely very negative outcomes arousing strong negative emotionality and greater likelihood of maladaptive coping behaviors.

And this whole set of experiences does not stop there; instead, it positions the individual—through increasing stress vulnerability or stress resilience—in a different place relative to encountering the next life stressor.

Social resources are pivotal to coping. Figure 12.1 shows a number of ways that social resources come into play—the notion of *social currency* being like resources "in the bank" that one sees themselves able to tap into as needed (Underwood, 2012). For example, a perception that one has different kinds of support people available tends to buffer the effect of stress (*A* in the model), and the stressor will feel less threatening from the outset. These resource people may vary in the types of support they provide—some may offer valuable information or expertise, others offer tangible or instrumental forms of help, and others may offer more socioemotional support and serve as confidants and sounding boards. Different types of support are needed in different circumstances. Secondary appraisals will tend to shape what kinds of external supports one perceives to be needed and seeks.

Enacted support refers to what types of support the person actually received and how much it cost them to get that help. How satisfied one is with the source and type of support will likely influence how much and in what ways that support affects outcomes (*C* in the model). Not all relationships or "support" turn out to be helpful and some can actually exacerbate a problem or undermine adaptive coping. Conversely, positive supports with which one feels reasonably satisfied can provide important benefits through enhancing health and other outcomes. Perceived social support may directly mediate the effects of stress (shown by the pathway *B* in the model). And, of course, there are many individual differences that people bring (personality, gender and cultural socialization, and beliefs or values) that can influence how social support is conceptualized and experienced (depicted by the arrow acting on *B* in the model). Finally, enacted supports—whether naturally occurring in the person's life or through helping interventions—can significantly shape what types of coping behaviors are undertaken and how long these are sustained toward improved outcomes (*D* in the model). Breaking the stress response into component parts helps us see multiple points of entry for intervention to slow or redirect problematic patterns that get in the way of effective stress management.

Neurophysiology and Stress Embodiment

Advances in a range of fields such as neuroscience, molecular biology, genomics, developmental sciences, and others are providing much more depth in our understanding of biological and psychosocial processes involved in the experience of stress, the accumulation of stress burden, and effects on well-being. As depicted in Figure 12.2, stress comes in multiple acute (e.g., abuse) and chronic (e.g., poverty-related) forms, with individual differences (e.g., genetic, prior experiences) shaping how these conditions are perceived and the pattern of physiological responses (chemical processes associated with the functioning of

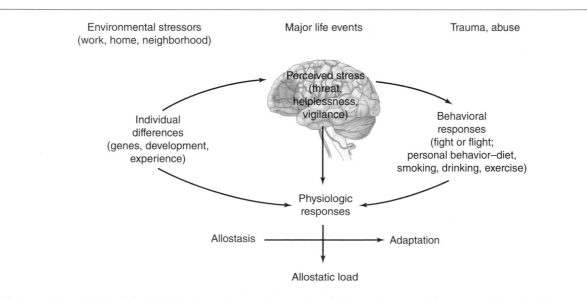

FIGURE 12.2 Central Role of the Brain in Stress Responding and Complex Pathways to Allostasis and Overload

Source: Juster, R. P., McEwen, B. S., & Lupien, S. J. (2010). Allostatic load biomarkers of chronic stress and impact on health and cognition. *Neuroscience & Biobehavioral Reviews, 35*(1), 2–16. Reprinted with permission.

organs) that are activated in the body. Appraisals and related perceptions of stress, like those described here, affect complex sequences of physiological responding as well as how people behaviorally respond, both of which go on to shape the efforts of the body and brain to adapt.

Some genetic predispositions, prior experiences, or points in lifespan development may sensitize people to certain kinds of stressors. Whereas some people, for example, have genes and/or histories that support a dandelion-type hardiness—able to root and weather tough conditions—others may be more fragile, like an orchid. With heightened stress sensitivity, these individuals experience biological sensitivity to environments that can foster especially negative effects in stressful conditions. However, within positive environments and resilience-fostering buffers, these individuals can thrive (Ellis & Boyce, 2008).

One might think of these biological levels of stress response as "surrounding" the more cognitive, emotional, and social processes depicted in Figure 12.1. Rather than operating independently "under the skin," these biological processes are interactive among themselves as well as with environmental, cognitive, and behavioral factors involved in stress responding. The environment has powerful effects on the brain and body through two important processes. The first is a biological embedding of earlier life experiences through which human biology and development are altered that, in turn, influence health, learning, behavior, and the effects of later experiences across the lifespan (Shonkoff, Boyce, & McEwen, 2009). A second set of processes involve the cumulative wear and tear effects of these interactions with the environment on the brain and body operating through neuroendocrine, autonomic, metabolic, and immune systems (McEwen, 2012).

Allostasis refers to processes of re-establishing physiological homeostasis or stability of functioning through change. As organisms undergo change, chemical processes to galvanize the person for fight or flight stress responding, for example, other chemical processes, are undertaken to accommodate for those prior changes, which catalyze interrelated changes through the various biological systems. Although this carries protective benefits as part of normal biological readjustment, it also carries the potential for damage in the long run.

Repeated stress exposure induces an erosive domino effect wherein these interlinked biological systems are repeatedly activated with insufficient opportunity for recovery, leading to overcompensation, exhaustion, and dysregulated (negatively imbalanced) patterns. Such stress-related overloads essentially serve to accelerate biological aging—referred to as **weathering** (excessive wear

and tear) and depletion of people's reserves that would typically help re-establish balance, leading to a wide range of physical and mental functioning disorders (McEwen & Gianaros, 2010). Ultimately, these adaptation efforts diminish the body's ability to cognitively process and physiologically respond to stressors, leaving the individual highly susceptible to stress-related disorders (Lupien, McEwen, Gunnar, & Heim, 2009).

Stress and allostatic load hold significant implications for brain development and function. There is potential for changeability or plasticity of brain development and health as a result of stress exposure that has myriad effects on cognitive functioning, learning, mood disorders, and self-regulatory capacity (McEwen, 2012). Effects of stressful experiences early in life are especially harmful in undermining brain development that has the potential for life-long impact. There is, however, considerable reversibility of acute and chronic stress-related plasticity in the young brain (Bloss, Janssen, McEwen, & Morrison, 2010). Although this ability to recover from stress-induced changes wanes with age, interventions such as promoting physical activity and positive social interaction appear to offer significant remedy. Stressful adversities in early life are high priorities to assess and address to support well-being in childhood as well as to reduce the erosive effects on well-being in later life (Anda et al., 2006; Cohen, Janicki-Deverts, Chen, & Matthews, 2010). The stress management, self-management, cognitive change, and exposure-oriented helping strategies described in this book offer a range of therapeutic tools to curb and offset negative stress-induced problems in living.

Stress Management and Growth Potential

By the time clients seek professional help, their level of stress and the salience of avoiding or minimizing negative outcomes may understandably be running very high. In conjunction with problem-specific interventions, **stress management** tools may also be useful in helping individuals understand their stress response experiences and better manage them. This may involve managing the symptoms or phenomenology of the stress itself (via relaxation, exercise, biofeedback, etc.), affecting factors that are creating the stress (through problem-solving, advocacy, conflict resolution, changing environmental stressors, etc.), fostering factors that will help buffer or otherwise weather or transform the stress (such as social supports, optimism, spirituality, reframing, meditation, etc.), and a range of methods for decreasing one's own stressful behavior, lifestyle characteristics, or ways of perceiving and responding to targeted stressors (Ramos & Liel, 2013).

Stress management research is suggesting the value of also looking at potential positive outcomes that may follow or come from coping with adversity or traumatic events. Calhoun and Tedeschi (2013; Calhoun, Tedeschi, & Tedeschi, 2014) provide resources on an array of features related to post-traumatic growth—including growth-related outcomes such as resilience, recovery, resistance, and reconfiguration, as well as measurement tools and linkages to cognitive-related theories such as schema change and constructive narrative applications. Illustrations also include specific contexts such as bereavement, disaster, life-threatening illness, major family loss, and special considerations with children. This and related work reminds us that stress, including significant crises and trauma, can include transcendent and transformative outcomes, building on new conceptions of self, meaning, and future. Clinical guidance related to growth in the face of stress reinforces the importance of carefully considering with clients the unique meaning that an adverse or traumatic experience holds for them, including perceived positive as well as negative possibilities or outcomes.

We may think of stress as something that happens to us, but we need to appreciate that how we approach stress and what we bring with us to the coping process can markedly affect what we experience and our outcomes. Interventions reflect growing attention to both clients' cognitive appraisals of their stress-provoking life situations as well as appraisal-related habits or patterns that become part of the stress cycle, such as triggered anxiety, anger, or sense of helplessness that are impeding desired actions. Stress inoculation training and problem-solving interventions build on understanding ways that our appraisals, emotions, and supports (or lack thereof) influence how we experience and respond to stress.

Cultural, Socioeconomic, and Discrimination Variations in Stress

The need to attend to cultural, historical, life course, and other forms of diversity is becoming increasingly apparent if we are to understand the stress experience and how different types of coping do or do not work well for people. Folk or other culturally specific resources or systems may be important components of helping, alone or combined with professional systems such as those that many of us work in or anticipate working in. In short, factors such as culture, socioeconomic status, and both personal and collective histories are infused throughout people's lives, shaping and coloring their encounters and experiences of

stress, and becoming integrated into biological and psychological functioning (Walters et al., 2011), all of which hold important implications for helping interventions.

People from differing cultural heritages may have presentations of anxiety and stress as well as differing views regarding whether stress and adversity are inherently problems or are legitimately brought to outside experts. People seeking relief may make offerings or undertake pilgrimages, access what would be referred to in the United States as alternative resources, such as faith healers, gurus, and homeopathic practitioners, or turn to self-healing forms of managing stress, such as meditation and yoga. Inquiring about cultural values or traditions will be important to understanding how stress is being experienced, what targets of change are likely to result in reduced stress, and what interventions and resources are likely to be most appropriate for clients' goals and contexts.

Cultural examinations of stress, coping, and implications for well-being need to be undertaken with structural conditions in mind. For example, factors such as poverty, toxin exposure, inaccessible or poor medical services, poor housing quality, and limited protection from injustices create contexts of adversity that may confound cultural dimensions. Recent research has shed considerable light on the biology of social and socioeconomic disadvantage—illustrating many layered ways through which "upstream" social determinant factors, such as economic resources, education, and discrimination, are associated with increased exposure to stressors, with multiple different forms of risk and stress, and with constraints on access to protective and health promoting resources (Adler & Stewart, 2010; Braveman, Egerter, & Williams, 2011).

Moreover, psychosocial and environmental stressors are socially patterned, with some groups more likely to be exposed to stressors such as discrimination. People who feel marginalized from the sociocultural and political mainstream, such as persons of color, gays and lesbians, older adults, and the physically and mentally challenged, are particularly vulnerable to experiencing greater numbers of stressful events in the form of discrimination, poverty, humiliation, and harassment, and thus are more susceptible to effects of minority stress (Baams, Grossman, & Russell, 2015; Pascoe & Richman, 2009).

Moreover, perceived discrimination, including that related to social class, contributes negatively to health above what stressors such as poverty itself accounted for (Fuller-Rowell, Evans, & Ong, 2012). Minority groups, particularly racial/ethnic minorities and those with multiple marginal statuses (such as LGBT people of color), are at substantially elevated risk for chronic exposure to cumulative forms of adversity. These chronic and multiple experiences of stress as outlined earlier in the chapter not only can have significant effects on the

Learning Activity 12.1

Cultural and Life Course Variations of Stress

In this learning activity, we ask you to reflect alone and with colleagues on ways that differences in culture and life course development can affect what is experienced as stressful and subsequent implications for stress management relevant to these differences.

First, on your own, think of two personally stressful times of life that are separated by at least a few years. Consider environmental context, language, and ethnohistory factors (e.g., education, economics, political and legal aspects, cultural values and lifestyle, kinship and social relations, religion and philosophy, technology) that you believe may have been shaping why and how that event or set of conditions was stressful. For example, were there values about responsibility, threats to something cherished, or external constraints that were prominent?

Repeat this exercise with the second stressful time of life. What are some differences you notice that may be partly the result of the different points of life—for example, differences due to experience, personal power or resources, or changed roles from one's youth to adulthood? What are some implications for these contextual differences in stress and coping for directions you would see as appropriate for stress management intervention?

In a group exercise, compare selected parts of your self-analysis with those of student colleagues. What differences do you notice in environmental, cultural, or life course development factors that may be related to how stress arose and was experienced, coping efforts, and what coping strategies or supports would be most useful?

---

manifestations of stress but also become embodied, affecting the body's neurophysiological ability to respond, resulting in significantly undermined health, functioning, and achievement (see Learning Activity 12.1).

Spirituality considerations

We use the term *spirituality* here to mean values, meanings, and personal experiences that may, but not necessarily, include a religious base. Whereas religion generally involves adherence to a belief system or practices associated with an established tradition or theology, spirituality can be defined as feelings of closeness to what is sacred, transcendental, or a sense of connection—such as to life, nature, humanity, or ultimate truths. We use spirituality quite broadly to signal the potential relevance of patterned ways in which clients' core values or meaning orientations may be affecting, positively or negatively, their experience of and response to stress.

Spiritual practices can serve as protective factors—reducing the risk of or reducing levels of physical and mental illnesses and bolstering resilience and adjustment (George, Larson, Koenig, & McCullough, 2000; Williams & Sternthal, 2007). Pursuit of spiritual comfort or guidance is commonly included as a component of coping repertoire assessment tools. Drawing upon values-oriented beliefs and activities (e.g., reading inspirational texts; meditation; participating in services, rituals, or traditions) and engaging in a community with shared values (e.g., for mutual assistance, social purposes, engagement with one's values) are examples of spirituality as a coping strategy.

Part of the clinical value of spirituality is that it generally taps into multiple health-linked factors, such as: (1) promoting healthy behaviors; (2) discouraging risky behavior; (3) fostering a sense of meaning or coherence; (4) locating people in support networks who tend to be responsive to need; and (5) encouraging hope and transcendent philosophy. Diversity has been notably apparent in research on spirituality, including factors relevant to gender, sexual minorities, religions, and specific cultural groups (e.g., Mofidi, DeVellis, Blazer, DeVellis, Panter, & Jordan, 2006; Simon, Crowther, & Higgerson, 2007). Increasingly, practitioners are encountering spiritual diversity among their clientele that may require some inquiry to assess whether these meaning orientations or practices should be part of an intervention plan.

It may be that spiritual values and activities foster situational appraisals or personal meanings that are emotionally comforting, help infuse ordinary events with positive meaning, and stimulate positive reframing and goal-directed problem-focused coping—important ingredients for adaptive stress management outcomes. Noted also have been populations such as gay and lesbian individuals who may be caught in the middle between their sexual orientations and religious beliefs that reject them. Roseborough (2006), for example, illustrates a developmental approach to integrating these intrinsic elements within oneself toward healthier outcomes, often framed as experiences of spiritual growth.

Research has generally used a lot of different ways of assessing spirituality—reducing our ability to generalize conclusions across studies—and we cannot yet sufficiently determine possible confounding or other

---

BOX 12.2   **Assessing Elements of Spirituality**

Orienting Questions about Beliefs and Behaviors

Do you consider yourself a religious or spiritual person? Has spirituality or religion been important to you in your life? Are there things in life that you see as sacred? Are you part of a spiritual or religious community? Are there religious or spiritual practices that are important to you?

The Relationship between the Client's Problems and Religion/Spirituality

Are spirituality or religion relevant to your current problem? Has your religion or spirituality been involved in your attempts to deal with this problem? Are you concerned about potential conflicts between your beliefs and what we

undertake in our work together? Is there anything I need to understand about your religion or spirituality in our work together?

Potential Resources

Do you see members of your religious or spiritual community as possible resources for you as you work with this problem? Is there someone you can turn to about religious or spiritual matters as these may relate to your problem? Is there anything I can do to help you access resource people in this regard? Do you believe it would be helpful for me to consult with, or for us to include, your spiritual leader or some other support person?

---

factors that may be responsible for outcomes. We need to learn more about components of spirituality other than Judeo-Christian traditions (Kier & Davenport, 2004). Richards and Worthington (2010) provide a summary of major findings of outcomes related to spiritually oriented psychotherapies, noting that although there is general support for efficacy of spiritually oriented intervention approaches, it remains a relatively small pool of studies with a need of continued commitment to develop a robust evidence base.

Box 12.2 provides examples of questions one may pose to clients toward assessing the relevance of spirituality to their concerns (Saunders, Miller, & Bright, 2010). There are also a number of measures of spirituality that may be useful to your practice. See Kapuscinski and Masters (2010) and Standard, Sandhu, and Painter (2000) for overviews of some assessment tools. Spirituality entails values on the part of the client, helper, and any others involved—values that may be in conflict with one another—that may not be well examined or understood and that may carry costs or challenges as well as benefits. The following resources provide guidance in this regard (Knapp, Lemoncelli, & VandeCreek, 2010; Meador & Koenig, 2000; Milstein, Manierre, & Yali, 2010; Worthington, Hook, Davis, & McDaniel, 2011).

Problem-Solving Therapy

Problem-solving therapy (**PST**) is a cognitive behavioral intervention through which an individual or group learns to systematically work through steps in analyzing a problem: identify new approaches, evaluate those approaches, and develop strategies for implementing those approaches, thereby generating more adaptive means of coping with stressful problems in living. It is based on a

relational/problem-solving model of stress in which real-life problem-solving stands between stressful life events (both major negative events as well as chronic, everyday stresses) and well-being. Effective problem-solving is expected to blunt the negative effect of stress on well-being and enhance positive functioning, whereas ineffective problem-solving is expected to have the reverse effect (Bell & D'Zurilla, 2009).

Problem-solving therapy (also referred to as problem-solving training) has been used with a wide range of issues across multiple disciplines (Chang, D'Zurilla, & Sanna, 2004; Nezu, Nezu, & D'Zurilla, 2010). Problem-solving therapy has been used with children, adolescents, adults, and elders as a treatment strategy, a treatment maintenance strategy, or a prevention strategy (Bell & D'Zurilla, 2009; Cuijpers, van Straten, & Warmerdam, 2007; Lee, Chiou, Chang, & Hayter, 2011; Malouff, Thorsteinsson, & Schutte, 2007 provide meta-analyses). It has been found useful across diverse groups and is explicitly collaborative in nature. Nezu, Nezu, and D'Zurilla (2007) provide a self-help guidebook for the layperson, emphasizing adaptiveness as illustrated in the acronym ADAPT (A = attitude, D = define, A = alternatives, P = predict, T = try out). As a treatment strategy, problem-solving has been used alone or in conjunction with other treatment strategies presented in this book.

We see problem-solving training as a potentially valuable tool for supporting critical thinking and locating persons within their environments. The stresses of a problematic situation may emanate to a greater or lesser degree from the environment (e.g., requirements, resource insufficiency, oppression) or the person (e.g., personal goals, patterns, limitations). Problem-solving therapy stems from a transactional view of problems in living attentive to imbalances and discrepancies in the person–environment relationship. The same conditions are not inherently or automatically problematic for all people, or and not all problems are of the same type or level.

Solutions must be situation-specific or context specific if they are to be a realistic match for that person in that set of environmental conditions.

A variety of assessment tools have been developed in the area of social problem-solving, with several attending not only to outcomes but also to process (e.g., attitudes, appraisals, skills), as well as illumination of clients' strengths and gaps as they undertake problem-solving efforts. Chang and colleagues (2004) provide a useful overview of these assessment tools, including a problem-solving self-monitoring tool that assists clients in assessing the problem, emotional impact and response, solution options, and outcomes. Eskin (2013) provides a detailed case example of problem-solving training including model scripts, and Nezu, Nezu, & D'Zurilla (2013) provide a detailed treatment manual including patient handout material and a range of very practical examples and guidelines.

Problem-Solving Therapy Components

Problem-solving therapy is a collaborative and educationally oriented intervention. As always, we start with a treatment rationale that helps the client understand the logic and components. We organize problem-solving into six components. Details on finer distinctions are provided by the developers (D'Zurilla & Nezu, 2007; 2010). Note also that we provide more detailed steps that operationalize these components in the Knowledge and Skill Builder exercises at the end of this chapter. Those detailed steps will provide you further guidance in assessing your learning outcomes.

1. *Treatment rationale and overview (initial structuring):* to discuss the goals, rationale, and general format of the training; to begin training in recognizing and labeling concerns, including use of problem-solving self-monitoring; to discuss the limited capacity of the conscious mind during problem-solving.

2. *Problem orientation:* to assess the clients' ways of thinking about problem-solving as a useful tool and about their own capacity as problem-solvers; what have been the clients' habits in the past, what have they tried thus far; to educate clients about maladaptive and facilitative problem-solving coping skills and foster a sense of self-efficacy; to determine cognitive and emotional obstacles to problem-solving with an eye to working from various vantage points to overcome these.

3. *Problem definition and formulation:* to help the client gather relevant and factual information for understanding the issues; to identify problem-focused and/or

emotion-focused components of the issues; and to identify problem-solving goals for each one.

4. *Generation of alternative solutions:* to instruct the client to think about different ways to handle each goal and to use the deferment of judgment, quantity, and variety principles.

5. *Decision-making:* to instruct the client to screen the list of alternative solutions; to evaluate (judge and compare) solution outcomes for each goal; and to select solution plans.

6. *Solution implementation and verification:* to encourage the client to carry out several alternative solutions simultaneously; to self-monitor, evaluate, and reinforce the implementation of the solutions; and to help the client troubleshoot and recycle the problem-solving strategy if the solutions do not work.

Each of these stages is described in this section. A detailed description of these six components is included in the Interview Checklist for Problem-Solving at the end of the chapter. In some cases, clients will bring skill deficits and will need a careful orientation to the steps. In other cases, clients may possess adequate problem-solving skills but are having difficulty implementing them effectively. Factors such as pessimism, lack of a sense of self-efficacy or lack of a positive problem orientation (e.g., appraising the problem as a solvable challenge, recognizing that problem-solving takes time and effort) can get in the way. Attention to emotions in problem-solving has grown, underscoring the importance of discussing the roles of emotions under stressful conditions, including ways emotion can be used to aid in problem-solving effectiveness and to provide instruction in the use of coping methods to manage disruptive emotions. Guided practice to develop proficiency in applying problem-solving attitudes and skills, planning for maintaining and generalizing effective problem-solving performance, and consolidating the training into rapid problem-solving guidelines are important parts of concluding therapeutic work.

Component 1: Treatment Rationale and Treatment Overview

Problem-solving therapy aims to strengthen clients' belief in problem-solving as an important coping skill and as well as to strengthen their ability to apply problem-solving strategies with problematic situations that create stress for them. The following is an example of the rationale for a problem-solving therapy approach to treatment:

Each of us is faced with both minor and important challenges. Some challenges are routine, such as trying to decide what to wear to a meeting or how to get the family out of the house more efficiently in the morning. Other challenges are more stressful, such as dealing with a difficult relationship. One way to enhance responsibility and self-control is to learn techniques for solving our difficulties. To take the time, energy, and commitment necessary to solve or deal with problems immediately may relieve future frustration and pain created by a concern.

Here is an example of an overview of the procedure. Keep in mind that this is a general statement that will need to be adapted. The rationale and treatment overview must be relevant to the client's culture, beliefs, and life circumstances.

> You will learn how to become aware of how you see an issue. You will look at how much control, time and effort, and commitment you feel you have for solving the issue. We will need to gather information to understand and define the key problem. Also, we'll need to look at what might prevent you from solving the problem. It is important that we explore a variety of solutions for solving the problem. After obtaining several solutions, you will decide which solutions feel most reasonable to implement simultaneously. Finally, you will implement the solution plans. I'm wondering what your thoughts and feelings are regarding what I have described. Do you have any questions?

Component 2: Problem Orientation

Problem orientation has to do with the person's general awareness of or attitudes regarding themselves as problem-solvers as well as their appraisals of their stress-related problems, which shape the motivational stance they bring to change. If these perceptions and attitudes are reasonably positive, then the client is more likely motivated to learn and engage in problem-solving behaviors. Clients who view the problem as a threat, who doubt their ability to effectively problem-solve, who become excessively emotionally upset with the problem, and/or who avoid dealing with issues have a negative problem orientation that will impede progress. In these cases, the helper will have to first help the client deal with problematic perceptions and attitudes, altering the client's problem orientation. The role of the helper is to help clients feel more hopeful and take more responsibility for solving problems within their means and committing to spending the time and energy needed to solve them, by changing the client's problem orientation. Changing clients' self-appraisals about the value of problem-solving and their ability to undertake problem-solving will have benefits complementary to the problem-solving activities themselves (Dixon, 2000).

As an initial step, the helper asks the client to describe how she or he typically solves problems. The aim is to determine whether the client has a maladaptive or helpful problem-solving style and then help the client distinguish between these coping styles. People with maladaptive styles may blame themselves or feel abnormal, hopeless, or unlucky. These styles may involve minimizing the benefits of problem-solving or exaggerating the losses that may occur from failure to solve the issue successfully, possibly doubting themselves and preferring others to produce a solution.

One role of the helper is to assist in reorienting problematic perceptions of this nature carefully, because there are differences in problem-solving styles across gender, age, race, ethnicity, and religious affiliation. Instead of viewing difficulties as a threat or a personal inadequacy, the helper offers a reorientation to see difficulties in more growth-oriented terms. Helpers need to help these clients to realize that if a problem is not solved, then it may very well persist or come back to haunt them later. Clients need to believe that there is a solution and that they have the capacity and self-control to find the solution independently and successfully. Problem-solving takes time and energy. People often respond to issues impulsively and emotionally, impeding their ability to think about viable solutions with an open, creative, and constructively critical mindset. The helper needs to assess the client's willingness to devote time and energy and to delay gratification, and the helper may have to motivate the client to generate the necessary level of commitment to solve the problem.

Clients may also be reluctant to work on the problem because of how they think about it. Problematic cognitions or self-talk, such as "it is their fault," "it will go away," or "I can't work on it," inhibits the motivation to work on an issue. The purpose of this change intervention is to instruct and to train the client in positive coping methods with the intent to overcome cognitive and/or emotional obstacles to problem-solving. Strategies such as cognitive restructuring, reframing, stress inoculation, meditation, muscle relaxation, exposure or systematic desensitization, breathing exercises, and self-management as well as environmental interventions may help a client deal with cognitive and/or emotional barriers to problem-solving. Once significant barriers have been minimized, the client is ready for the next phase of the problem-solving strategy.

Component 3: Problem Definition and Formulation

The purpose of the defining and formulating step in problem-solving is for the helper to assist the client in gathering as much objective information about the problem as possible. In cases where a client has a distorted cognitive view or perception of the problem, the helper may have to use rational-emotive therapy or cognitive restructuring. The helper explains that problem-solving is a skill and a practical approach whereby a person attempts to identify, explore, or create effective and adaptive ways of coping with everyday challenges (D'Zurilla & Nezu, 2007; 2010). A problem can be viewed as a discrepancy between how a present situation is being experienced and how that situation should or could be experienced. In a shorthand version, this can be thought of as questions that provide the client's view of

1. "What is"—what present conditions are unacceptable and to whom?

2. "What should be"—what conditions are demanded or desired and by whom?

3. What obstacles are influencing the availability of an effective response for reducing this discrepancy?

The client needs to identify obstacles that are creating any discrepancy or are preventing effective responses for reducing the discrepancy. It is also important to examine antecedent conditions or unresolved issues that may be contributing to or causing the present concern. These questions are then followed by goal-oriented "How can I...," or "What can I do to..." questions. These goals, as with any change goals, need to be realistic and stated in specific, concrete terms. In some cases, however, being too specific may miss the mark by being too narrowly defined. For example, D'Zurilla and Nezu (1999) cite the example of a small church with limited finances that hired a painter to repaint the church in time for an important event. It soon became apparent that the painter was very slow and that the quality of the work was very poor. The church committee initially framed their goal question as: How can we get the painter to improve the quality and efficiency of his work so that the church will be painted adequately in time for the celebration? A way to frame this question to make available a greater range of alternative solutions might look something like: How can we get the church painted adequately in time for the celebration at the lowest possible cost?

Problems that are changeable are appropriate for setting problem-solving goals with the purpose of changing the problem situation for the better. Problems that are not changeable and/or that have strong emotion-focused impediments might more profitably concentrate on changing the client's personal reactions to the problem. Things that initially look changeable may prove less so, and vice versa. It has been our experience that it is best to include both problem-focused and emotion-focused goals in defining the client's problem. Again, problem-focused and emotion-focused definitions of a problem and corresponding goals seem to have some gender and cultural variation.

After the concern has been identified and defined, the practitioner and the client set realistic emotion-focused and/or problem-focused goals. A **goal** is defined as what the client would like to have happen as a consequence of solving the problem. The goals should be realistic and attainable, and they should specify the type of behavior, level of behavior, and conditions under which the goal will aid in solving the problem. This process should include identification of obstacles that might interfere with problem-solving goals and thinking from different vantage points that may be relevant. Establishing problem-solving goals will help the client with the next step in the therapy: creating alternative solutions.

Component 4: Generation of Alternative Solutions

The purpose here is to have the client generate as many alternative solutions as possible. The helper instructs the client to think of *what* she or he could do, or *ways* to handle the situation. The helper also instructs the client not to worry about *how* to go about making a plan work or how to put the solution into effect; that will come later. The client is instructed to imagine a great variety of new and original solutions, no matter how ridiculous any given solution may seem. This is a generative process. Generally, greater quantity of alternative solutions that the client produces helps yield greater quality of solutions from among which to choose. Deferring judgment or critical evaluation of solutions similarly facilitates more creative and higher-caliber solutions.

This freewheeling or brainstorming process is intended to filter out functional fixity and premature emphasis on practicality and feasibility that might constrain or limit the range of solutions generated. If there are several goals, then the helper encourages the client to generate several alternative solutions for each problem goal, with the rationale being that most issues are complicated and a simple alternative is often inadequate.

Component 5: Decision-Making

The purpose of the decision-making step is to help the client decide on the best solution by judging and comparing all the alternatives. The client is first instructed to screen the list of available alternatives and to eliminate any solution that may be a risk or not feasible (D'Zurilla & Nezu, 2007; Nezu et al., 2013). The best solutions maximize benefits and minimize costs for the client's personal, immediate, and long-term welfare. The client is instructed to anticipate outcomes for each alternative and then is asked to evaluate each solution using the following four criteria: (1) Will the problem be solved? (2) What will be the status of the client's emotional well-being? (3) How much time and effort will be needed to solve the problem? and (4) What effect will the solution have on the client's overall personal and social well-being? When working with diverse groups of clients, it is important not to impose your own values and culture on this process.

After the client selects and evaluates the alternative solutions, it is time to weigh decision possibilities. For example, what solution or combination of solutions appears best suited to solve the problem? If the concern cannot be solved with one or more of the existing solutions, then the helper may have to help the client redefine the issue and/or gather more information about the problem. If the questions have been satisfactorily answered, then the client is ready to implement the solution, as long as the chosen solution is consistent with the goal of solving the concern as fully as possible.

During the first five components of the problem-solving strategy (including providing the rationale and overview), the helper assumes a directive role with the client to ensure a thorough application of the following steps: problem orientation, problem definition, generation of alternatives, and decision-making, often lessening the degree of directiveness with each step. The **therapeutic goal** is to support the client in becoming more agentic, confident, and responsible with each progressive step.

Component 6: Solution Implementation and Verification

The purpose of solution implementation and verification in problem-solving is to test the chosen solutions to the problem-solving goals and to verify whether these solutions solve the problem. The client simultaneously implements as many of the selected solutions as possible. There are four parts in verifying whether the solution plan is working. The first part is to implement the chosen solutions. There may be more than one approach or strategy useful to accomplishing any given solution. If there are obstacles (behavioral deficits, emotional concerns, or dysfunctional cognitions) to any given strategy to implement the solutions, alternative strategies might need to be generated. This is also a time to assess whether the client needs to acquire performance skills, defuse affective concerns, and restructure cognition to remove the obstacles.

Second, the client can use self-monitoring techniques to assess the effects of the chosen solutions for solving the problem. The helper instructs the client to keep a daily log or journal of the self-talk or emotional reactions to the chosen solutions. Some clients will prefer use of electronic devices that may used or adapted for this purpose (see Morris & Aguilera, 2012 for examples of applications). The self-talk or statements recorded in the journal can

be rated on a scale where $+5$ = extremely positive, 0 = neutral, and -5 = extremely negative. The accompanying emotional state also can be recorded, such as loved, depressed, frustrated, guilty, happy, or neutral. This step can increase the level of emotional awareness.

Third, the client assesses whether the chosen solution achieves the desired goals. This self-evaluation process is assessed in relationship to the solution in the following areas: (1) problem resolution; (2) emotional well-being; (3) time and effort exerted; and (4) the ratio of total benefit to cost (D'Zurilla & Nezu, 2007).

Finally, if the chosen solution meets all the criteria, the client engages in some form of self-reward for having successfully solved the problem. However, if the chosen solutions do not solve the concern, the helper and client try to pinpoint trouble areas and retrace the problem-solving steps. Some common trouble areas that clients encounter relate to emotional reactions to the problem, inadequate definition of the problem, unresolved antecedent issues to the problem, problem-focused instead of emotion-focused definition, and unsatisfactory solution choices.

Use and Control of Emotions in Problem-Solving

Problematic situations are typically stressful because they involve some difficulty, loss, conflict, or potential pain or harm. Emotions, positive or negative, inevitably are a part of problem-solving and can either impede or aid problem-solving performance. Emotions can arise from: (a) the problem situation itself; (b) clients' beliefs, appraisals, and expectancies about the problem and their ability to deal with it successfully; and/or (c) the problem-solving tasks used in attempting to solve the problem (D'Zurilla & Nezu, 2007; Nezu et al., 2013). Although low or moderate levels of emotional arousal can be helpful to motivate problem-solving efforts, sustained high levels of emotional stress are likely to impair problem-solving and can result in negative outcomes of their own, such as fatigue, depression, and inertia. In addition, unchecked emotional experience can influence problem-solving in ways not readily evident—for example, by narrowing or distorting how problems are labeled, how goals are set, and evaluations made along the way.

With these issues in mind, D'Zurilla and Nezu (2007) identify ways to increase problem-solving effectiveness by using one's emotional responses as:

1. A cue for problem recognition, such as using negative emotional feelings as a trigger to look for what may be eliciting them.

2. Motivation to galvanize problem-solving, such as purposefully using reframing to view the problem as a challenge rather than a threat.

Recent treatment guidelines have increased emphasis on emotion regulation when problem-solving under stress. Nezu, Nezu, and D'Zurilla (2013) provide the following SSTA acronym to assist clients in gaining emotional mindfulness of their stress responding and more effective ways of managing one's responding to support one's problem-solving. This involves:

1. "Stopping" when one becomes aware of negative emotional reactions that are or may become problematic,

2. "Slowing down" one's immediate emotional responding so it does not "go from 0 to 60."

3. "Thinking" more reflectively about what one's emotions are indicating and how to support a planful approach to reducing interfering emotionality and pursue problem-solving.

4. Taking "action" by taking a step-by-step approach to carrying out a solution or action plan suited to coping with the stressful conditions.

3. A problem-solving goal in its own right—if negative states such as anger or anxiety seem counterproductive, it is reasonable to set problem-solving goals to minimize these emotional responses and perhaps stimulate counterbalancing ones.

4. A possible consequence of some parts of problem-solving—for example, when evaluating solution alternatives, the emotions likely to be associated with various alternatives may be important to consider in decision-making.

5. A criterion for evaluating the solution outcome—expanding point 4, evaluating the effectiveness of a solution relative to a problem and goal may benefit from considering the emotional response to the outcome (e.g., sometimes a solution to one problem creates a new emotional outcome problem).

6. A reinforcer of effective problem-solving behavior—the counterpoint to point 5—achieving emotions such as hope, relief, and pride can be powerful outcomes of their own and reinforce subsequent problem-solving behavior.

In terms of controlling disruptive emotions, an assessment can determine what kinds of resources clients have for reducing and controlling emotional effects of stressful issues, such as social support, adaptive avenues for distraction, exercise, and informational or tangible resources. Some individuals may need specialized emotion-focused coping techniques whereas others may need training in how to: (a) recognize potentially disruptive feelings and thoughts; (b) identify triggers as well as resources they have for coping with these negative effects; and (c) use these resources when needed to reduce, manage, or prevent these effects. Feelings are also treated as potentially important sources of information. Increasing understanding of one's patterns of feelings under particular kinds of stress or problematic situations can guide consideration of strategies to manage versus avoid feelings, or redirect efforts toward soothing or otherwise getting emotional needs met in positive ways.

Nezu et al. (2013) incorporate increasing awareness of the complex layers in stress responding, including processes on neurophysiology that link stress, brain functioning, emotional responding, social problem-solving, and outcomes. Examples of strategies they recommend for slowing one's emotional reactivity in the moment include counting, deep breathing, guided imagery or visualization, "fake" smiling, "fake" yawning, mindful meditation, deep muscle relaxation, exercise, mindful walking, talking to someone, gum chewing, prayer or spiritual practices, or other techniques clients feel work well for them. They have also developed an acronym (SSTA—see Box 12.3) to help clients recall steps they can take in the moment to help slow down automatic emotional responding as a prelude to more intentional or deliberative steps of considering alternatives and problem-solving or related stress management actions. Note the overlap here with strategies related to stress inoculation training and calming approaches to stress, underscoring the value of drawing from multiple interventions to support effective emotion regulation, problem-focused coping, and sustainable planned change.

Maintenance and Generalization

Supporting clients' ability to take training out of the context of formal helping into their lives and futures is consistent with an empowering, collaborative approach to helping. D'Zurilla and Nezu (2007) suggest helping to consolidate maintenance and generalization of problem-solving training by: (a) continuing positive reinforcement and corrective feedback (identifying how and by whom this could be undertaken is one strategy); (b) reviewing positive problem orientation cognitions and strengthening them (for example, explicitly detailing significant gains made in learning how to generate these and in coping more effectively over the course of treatment); (c) directing attention to types of real-life issues that clients may well encounter to which their problem-solving skills can be applied; and (d) anticipating and preparing for obstacles to implementing clients' problem-solving agendas in ways consistent with the problem-solving approach.

Learning Activity 12.2

Rapid Problem-Solving

After initial problem-solving training, ongoing rapid practice can help form quick-response habits and enhance your ability to problem-solve in different kinds of situations. Give yourself very brief time limits for the following, literally 2 or 3 minutes. Think about a couple of relatively small dilemmas from your own life or something you can imagine (e.g., forgetting something important, an awkward situation, conflict about how to respond in a moment). Then, walk through the steps of rapid problem-solving either alone or with a student colleague. Try to stay within the time limits. Debrief afterwards—for example, did you draw a blank or get stuck at any step? It may help to write out some of your responses and review what might be effective. Repeat the practice with one or more training exercises until you have a good sense of the progression of steps and activities.

Step 1. Make the following self-statements:

"Take a deep breath and calm down."

"There is no immediate catastrophe."

"Think of this problem as a challenge."

"I can handle it."

"Stop and think."

Step 2. Ask yourself the following questions:

"What's the problem?" (State the discrepancy between "what is" and "what should be.")

"What do I want to accomplish?" (State a goal.)

"Why do I want to achieve this goal?" (Broaden the goal, if appropriate.)

Step 3. Think of a possible solution. Now think of several other alternative solutions (at least two or three).

Step 4. Think of the most important criteria for evaluating your solution ideas (at least two or three, such as "Will it achieve my goals?", "What effect will it have on others?", "How much time and effort will it take?", or some other important criterion). Decide quickly on the solution alternative that seems best. Think of one or two quick ways to improve the solution.

Step 5. Implement the solution. Are you satisfied with the outcome? If not, then try out your second choice if you still have time.

Source: D'Zurilla & Nezu, 2007.

Practice followed by reflection and feedback is one strategy to develop skills and help generalize their use across different types of problems, such as use of a rapid problem-solving framework in the final session(s). Learning Activity 12.2 presents an example of how to consolidate problem-solving training into a rapid problem-solving format. We suggest spending time with these exercises to achieve a working feel for applying the method. It's not that all problems can be handled in a 1- to 5-minute span—not at all! Rather, repetitions of problem-solving steps with tricky but delimited problems can help make the steps easier to recall and use with more cumbersome problems. For a more thorough overview of problem-solving intervention and learning exercises, see Learning Activity 12.3 and the Interview Checklist for Problem-Solving in the Knowledge and Skill Builder.

Some Caveats

Although evaluations have demonstrated problem-solving therapy to be equally effective as other psychosocial therapies and significantly more effective than no treatment or support/attention control groups, there are some factors to consider. One is the importance of adhering to the full PST package, particularly the inclusion and careful attention to problem orientation training. The various components of problem-solving skill are critical, but their utility is apparently undercut if clients do not develop positive problem orientation beliefs, bring a realistic understanding of the time and effort that change will take, and commit to the effort such as completion of out of session work (Bell & D'Zurilla, 2009; Malouff et al., 2007). However, the developers also note that the extensiveness of PST should be matched to the severity of the client's emotional distress and functional problems. Recent short-form classroom-like protocols have been developed, such as preparing military veterans for re-entry to civilian life (Tenhula et al., 2014), that may be applied or adapted for other populations or conditions.

Like other interventions, there are always concerns **LO2** about the appropriate match to the nature of the problem and the condition of the client. Clients with severe maladaptive behaviors or serious environmental factors that cannot realistically be managed through problem-solving will require other strategies. Similarly, developing rapport and a positive therapeutic relationship are important to successful application of any strategy; the problem-solving strategy is no exception. Problem-solving can sometimes be difficult for clients who are not accustomed to thinking of long-range effects, such as many adolescents and some clients with severe trauma

Learning Activity 12.3

Problem-Solving

This learning activity provides an opportunity to try out problem-solving. Think of a problem that you have and apply the problem-solving steps to your concern. Do this in a quiet place when you will not be interrupted.

1. Determine how you typically solve problems. How is your approach affected by your gender and culture?
2. Assess your problem-solving style. How does it reflect your world view(s)?
3. Use the following questions to define the underlying discrepancy and your goals: What is? What should be? What obstacle(s) might be barriers to solving this particular problem? What might need to change to overcome these obstacles?
4. How much time, energy, and commitment do you have for solving the problem?
5. Define your problem and determine whether your problem is problem-focused, emotion-focused, or both.
6. Generate potential solutions for solving the problem. Be sure to think of a variety of solution approaches that fit your culture.
7. Select the best solutions from among those you brainstormed, using the criteria in item 13 of the Interview Checklist for Problem-Solving.
8. Implement your solutions to the problem, or at least think about how to implement them. Choose a method for verifying the effectiveness of each solution.

histories who don't allow themselves to think much into the future. Careful assessment must guide how much it is the environment rather that the person that needs to change whether through problem-solving or other change strategies. The developers offer some broadly-applicable guidelines for implementing the problem-solving strategy, summarized in Table 12.1.

One role of the helper throughout the problem-solving process is to educate the client about the problem-solving strategy and to guide the client through the

---

TABLE 12.1   Problem-Solving Therapy: Do and Don't (See D'Zurilla & Nezu (2007) and Nezu et al. (2013) for more detail).

1. Training in problem-solving should *not* be presented in a mechanistic manner, but rather through interactive, engaging methods. Although a learning experience, "dryly" teaching will likely be poorly received.

2. The helper *should* attempt to individualize the training and make it relevant to the specific needs of a client or group. Incorporation of personal and relevant examples gleaned through assessment or other interactions is important, as is an atmosphere of respecting clients' values.

3. *Do* encourage practicing skills. Homework and *in vivo* practice of the problem-solving components as much as possible are important. Creative terms other than homework (assignments, opportunities to practice) may be more palatable and handouts can be useful during and beyond formal intervention.

4. The helper *should* be caring and sensitive to the client's concerns and feelings. Correct implementation of the intervention is important to effectiveness. Yet, clients need to experience themselves as the primary focus with their feelings and needs respected.

5. For the intervention to be most useful, the problems being targeted *should not* be superficial but should include those deemed most crucial for the given client. This will involve clinical decision-making skills regarding the core issue that is being addressed.

6. The helper *always needs* to undertake an accurate assessment of the problem and the client's problem-solving strengths and weaknesses, as well as how much control the client has over the problem situation.

7. The helper *should* emphasize that development of solid action plans are crucial to taking creative solution ideas forward to obtain feedback toward problem resolution or progress. Encourage the client to implement solution plans or parts thereof during training.

8. *Do* make active use of handouts as part of training (Nezu et al., 2013 provide many). These may need to be adapted to specific clients and have been found helpful by clients remembering and practicing skills within and beyond training.

9. *Do* be aware that, generally, both problem-focused coping and emotion-focused coping will be components of problem-solving coping. The helper must determine the forms or combination needed in the client's situation.

10. If conducting PST within a group format, *do* ensure that each participant's concerns are addressed. Group work often involves management of participation styles so that all are heard and benefit.

problem-solving steps. As mentioned before, the helper is less directive with the client during the last stage of the problem-solving process to help the client become more independent and take responsibility for applying the chosen problem solutions and verifying their effectiveness. The helper can help the client to maintain these problem-solving skills and to generalize them to other concerns. The helper also can assist the client in anticipating obstacles to solving strategies and prepare the client for coping with them. The client should be able to cope fairly well if he or she takes the time to *examine critically and carefully* her or his orientation to the problem, to carefully define the concern, to generate a variety of alternative solutions, and to make a decision about solution alternatives that are compatible with goals or desired outcomes. Solution implementation likely will be easier if the first four stages of the problem-solving process have been thoroughly processed. (See also Learning Activity 12.3.)

Problem-Solving with Diverse Clients

Examples of Applications

The value of problem-solving has been studied with **L03** diverse clients in several areas, such as academic achievement challenges, work-related problems, disabilities, problems associated with chronic conditions (e.g., obesity, diabetes, cancer, pain), and managing mental health risks such as depression, suicide, social anxiety, PTSD, and traumatic brain injury. It also has been incorporated as a component of various prevention programs, including HIV, tobacco use, substance abuse, and violence.

Problem-solving increasingly has been used with older adults. Late-life depression is often associated with executive dysfunction, which predicts slow, poor, and unstable response to medications such as antidepressants as well as other features such as behavioral disability and impaired planning, goal setting, and self-regulation. Interventions aimed to strengthen capacity to identify, focus on, and work to reduce specific problems can serve to mitigate disability, stress, and depression. Arean and colleagues (2010) note that PST has a very favorable track record with depression alone, and the benefits may be even greater for older clients with impaired executive function and recurring or severe depression. This finding is particularly important given the more limited value of psychopharmacology—providing more hopeful and acceptable alternatives to depressed elders and their families.

In a related vein, PST may be less cognitively demanding for older adults than other therapies, which appears particularly important for comorbid older populations such as those with both depression and substance use disorders (Rosen, Morse, & Reynolds, 2010) or significant behavioral problems (Ayalon, Bornfeld, Gum, & Arean, 2009). Problem-solving therapy is also proving promising within home-delivered contexts, such as the ***problem adaptation therapy model***, which blends PST with environmental adaptation and caregiver participation (Kiosses, Arean, Teri, & Alexopoulos, 2010), and through telehealth-delivered PST for homebound individuals, strengthening access to care (Choi et al., 2014). Ince and colleagues (2013) describe the effective use of an online delivery of PST for immigrants with depression who previously encountered barriers to care. Wade and colleagues (2012) delivered PST via telehealth for caregivers of teens with traumatic brain injuries, finding a reduction in global distress symptoms. Demiris and colleagues (2010) confirmed this positive result with family hospice caregivers.

Positive outcomes are also being achieved with young clients. Some of this research has focused on depression and suicidality among children and youth. Problem orientation has consistently emerged as a significant factor. For example, negative problem orientation and problem-solving styles characterized by avoidance or impulsiveness/carelessness play powerfully problematic roles, undermining treatment effectiveness (Becker-Weidman, Jacobs, Reinecke, Silva, & March, 2010). Similarly, development of active coping skills such as problem-solving, including maintaining positive thinking and a positive problem orientation, are important contributors to resilience in stressed youth (Pedro-Carroll, 2005).

The adaptability of PST across racial and cultural factors is yielding positive results. Kasckow and colleagues (2010) found equal willingness (receptivity) to participate in problem-solving therapy for depression by both African American and European American clients. Although African Americans in general tend to report coping styles more strongly inclusive of spirituality and seeking help from their own social networks, both racial groups appeared to benefit equally from the problem-solving process. For example, utilization of problem-solving therapy by older African Americans has been efficacious against episodes of major depression for individuals experiencing subsyndromal depressive symptoms (Reynolds et al., 2014).

Cultural factors also were directly assessed in a multi-site study of mothers with children recently diagnosed with cancer. In this highly stressful life experience, one question was whether cultural factors among monolingual Spanish-speaking mothers (predominantly of Mexican heritage) would lead to differences in outcomes. Findings indicated positive outcomes (stronger positive problem-solving skills and lower levels of negative distress) for both Spanish-speaking and English-speaking mothers, and Latina mothers benefited to a higher degree and younger, single mothers benefited most of all (Stahler et al., 2005). Emphasis on reducing negative problem orientation (e.g., a sense of helplessness), fostering optimism and efficacy, and promoting active engagement in problem-solving (and minimizing avoidant strategies) may be part of what accounted for Latina mothers—who may have been more isolated and overwhelmed as a function of language isolation—benefitting to a greater degree. Incorporating problem-solving therapy into collaborative care plans has also proven effective for low-income Hispanic populations with diabetes (Ell et al., 2010) and co-occurring conditions of cancer and depression (Ell et al., 2011).

Guidelines for Use with Diverse Groups

Problem-solving has been shown to be an effective intervention strategy with diverse groups of clients in various ways, but there are some guidelines to consider in enhancing its effectiveness. First, there is evidence that the specific nature of problem-solving skills varies according to gender, race, and ethnic group. It is unwise to assume that diverse groups of clients will solve issues in the same way. The traditional, individualistic Eurocentric and androcentric model of problem-solving is used widely by some male and Caucasian clients, whereas many females and clients of color prefer a more collaborative and cooperative approach. As a result, both intervention and prevention programs that incorporate problem-solving training must be adapted for client characteristics such as age, gender, race, and ethnic affiliation to make problem-solving both developmentally appropriate and culturally relevant.

Second, problem-solving training for clients from diverse cultures will be more effective for these clients when the training is conducted in a culturally sensitive manner—that is, in a way that respects the rituals and traditions of the client's culture—that promotes relevant cultural identity such as sexual and/or racial identity and also ethnic pride, which develops biracial and/or bicultural competence, and that helps these clients to acquire problem-solving skills without having to assimilate the norms of the mainstream culture. For example, Chu, Huynh, and Arean (2012) utilized the Formative Method for Adapting Psychotherapies (FMAP) to create Problem-Solving Therapy–Chinese Older Adult (PST-COA). This culturally adapted method of PST maintains core tenants of the therapy while remaining sensitive to cultural

variance in measurement procedures, expectations of the therapeutic relationship, and stigma associated with compromised mental health for this population. When PST-COA was utilized with elderly Chinese women experiencing clinical depression, the results indicated improved engagement in therapy and remission of depressive symptoms and improvements in mood (Chu & Huynh, 2012).

As always, it is important with problem-solving intervention to be aware of intersections among factors such as culture, socioeconomic status, and other issues that may marginalize some people from supportive services. Gammon's (2000) study of rural caregivers of adults with severe developmental disabilities emphasized the value of considering the broader context within which families are striving to cope and their experience with seeking services, such as relative inaccessibility or nonresponsiveness to needs. In addition to engaging family members as collaborators in developing programs, providers—particularly those in areas with limited resources—need to be inventive in pulling together problem-solving supports, such as partnering with churches to help provide respite care, transportation, and socialization, coordinating caregiving exchanges among rural families, and encouraging use of the Internet to access self-advocacy groups and legal information.

Model Example: Problem-Solving Therapy

In this model example, we present a narrative account [LO3] of how problem-solving therapy might be used with a 49-year-old male client. Yoshi, an air traffic controller, has reported that he would like to decrease the stress he experiences in his job. He believes that decreasing this stress will help his ulcer and help him cope better with his job. In addition to the physical signs of stress (insomnia), Yoshi also reports that he worries constantly about making mistakes in his job. He has also thought about taking early retirement, which would relieve him of the stress and worry.

Rationale

First, we explain to Yoshi that all of us face concerns and that sometimes we feel stuck because we don't know how to handle an issue. We tell Yoshi that solving problems as they occur can prevent future discomfort. We provide Yoshi with an overview of problem-solving therapy, telling him that we'll need to look at how he sees the problem and what obstacles there are to solving the problem. We tell him that we will need to define the concern, think of many different solutions, select several solutions, and try out the solutions and see how well the solutions solve the central concern. We emphasize that problem-solving is a collaborative, cooperative process. Finally, we confirm Yoshi's willingness to use a problem-solving strategy and answer any questions he may have about the procedure.

Problem Orientation

We determine how Yoshi typically solves problems. We ask him to give an example of a concern he has had in the past and how and what he did to solve it. Then, we describe for Yoshi the difference between maladaptive and helpful problem-solving. We explain to him that most people inherently have problem-solving ability but something blocks the use of it. We tell him that problem-solving therapy removes the blocks or obstacles that are maladaptive for good problem-solving. We explain that healthy problem-solving is the capacity to view issues as an opportunity. If Yoshi is encountering cognitive or emotional obstacles in his problem-solving attempts, then we would introduce appropriate strategies to help remove them. Finally, we assess how much time, energy, and commitment Yoshi has for solving the issue.

Problem Definition and Formulation

We briefly describe the problem-solving strategy for Yoshi. We explain to him that we need to gather information about the concern, such as his thoughts and feelings on the matter, what unresolved issues are contributing, how intense the issue is, what has been done to solve the issue, and when and where the issue occurs. We ask Yoshi what other information is needed to define the problem. If he has distorted views or perceptions of the issue, we would have to help him reframe his perception. We have to determine whether Yoshi's problem is problem-focused, emotion-focused, or both. For example, we can probably change his emotional and cognitive reaction to the work situation and help him reduce the stress, but he cannot change the job requirements unless he leaves or retires. We can help Yoshi identify problem-solving goals or what he would like to have happen so that the problem would be solved. For Yoshi, one of the most attainable and realistic goals might be to reduce job stress.

Generation of Alternative Solutions

Yoshi is instructed to generate as many alternative solutions as possible for solving the problem. We inform him not to worry about how to go about making the alternatives work or how to put the solution into effect. Also,

he is instructed to defer judgment about how good or feasible his ideas or solutions are until later, to generate as many alternatives as he can think of (because quantity produces quality), and to be creative and to think of non-traditional and unconventional solutions as well.

Decision-Making

We instruct Yoshi to screen the list of alternatives and to use the following criteria for evaluating each solution: Will the concern be solved with this solution? What will be the status of his emotional well-being? How much time and effort will be needed to use the alternative solutions? What will be his overall personal and social well-being using each of these alternative solutions? Yoshi is reminded that it is important to evaluate each solution by answering these four criteria questions. Finally, he is instructed to select the best solutions that are compatible with the problem-solving goals and that fit best with his own culture.

Solution Implementation and Verification

We instruct Yoshi to try his chosen solutions for solving the concern. We also instruct him to self-monitor the alternative solutions he chose to solve the problem to determine their effectiveness. Suppose that he chooses to reduce his stress in the workplace by using meditation as one solution. We suggest that Yoshi self-monitor by keeping a written log or journal of the effectiveness of meditation using the following criteria questions: How effective is meditation in reducing job stress? How well does he feel emotionally about the meditative experience? Are the time and effort spent with daily meditations worth it? Are there more benefits for using meditation than costs, and what are his thoughts, feelings, and behavior in relationship to the solution implementation? Yoshi is instructed to complete the self-monitoring log or journal each day just before bedtime. He is instructed to rate each of the criteria questions on a five-point scale, with descriptive words for each point on the scale. We tell him that he needs to reward himself after successfully solving the problem (reducing the stress) by selecting rewarding things or activities. Also, we encourage him to determine the best time to receive something or to engage in rewarding activity. Additionally, we ask Yoshi to reflect on any of the solution strategies that were not as effective as anticipated. If, for example, the meditation did not contribute to solving the issue, then we instruct Yoshi to look at trouble areas that might be obstacles to solving the problem, such as his emotional reactions, the fact that the issue may not be well defined, or unresolved issues that may be contributing.

Stress Inoculation Training: An Integrative Clinical Approach

Stress management can, and typically does, involve **LO4** change interventions that are integrated by the helper and the client into a tailored set appropriate to case-specific factors such as the nature of the stressors and goals. For example, Antoni and colleagues (2001) describe a stress management intervention for women diagnosed with breast cancer that includes didactic/educational material, experiential components, and between-session assignments (e.g., practicing relaxation techniques, monitoring stress responses). Content included problem-focused (e.g., active coping and planning, replacement of doubt appraisals with a sense of confidence via cognitive restructuring) as well as emotion-focused (e.g., relaxation training, emotional expression, and use of social support) coping strategies.

Notice that the aforementioned array of strategies spans several chapters in this book given our emphasis on recognizing stress contexts within which problems arise and helping practices are undertaken. The specific stress-management tools that are likely to be well suited will vary across different types of problems, circumstances, or client(s). We use stress inoculation training (SIT) as one way to illustrate a broad-based approach to stress-related problems (e.g., how to provide a psychoeducational orientation to clients) as well as to illustrate ways to select a range of specific strategies suited for your client. Intervention strategies, particularly from chapters 10–15, may well be integrated within an SIT approach.

Stress inoculation is an approach to teaching both physical and cognitive coping skills. As the name implies, the aim is to enhance resistance to stress by better preparing the client to respond more effectively when stressors are encountered. In psychosocial (and similar to medical) inoculations, a person's preventive or stress-resistance strength is enhanced by exposure to relevant stimuli sufficient to arouse defenses and coping processes without being overwhelmed. The strategies target several changes, such as increasing knowledge of how stress works, insights about one's own patterns, ability to analyze situations and oneself, introduction to new coping skills with opportunity to practice them, and bolstering of confidence and belief that one can be successful. This approach has evidence of effectiveness with a wide range of types of stress. It can be used with stressors that are more discrete and localized as well as those that are more frequently and enduringly encountered. See Box 12.4 for illustrations.

Stress inoculation training (SIT) builds on transactional models in viewing stress arising when the perceived demands of a circumstance meet or exceed the perceived capacities and resources of the person (or, by extension, a family or community) to handle these demands, especially when well-being or valued goals are believed to be at risk. This stress model closely attends to the roles of cognitive-affective processes and coping activities, whether these take adaptive or problematic forms. For example, stress is understood, at least in part, as a meaning making process. Events or experiences will vary regarding their stressfulness, what coping is evoked, partly on the basis of how these are perceived or appraised, and what meanings they hold for the person(s). As we have learned in earlier chapters, complex networks of cognitive representations (which include affective as well as sensory memory imprints) form the base of patterned reactions to anticipated and encountered stress.

Stress Inoculation Training Components

Stress inoculation training is a very flexible, multifac- **LO4** eted form of cognitive behavior therapy that allows considerable individual tailoring. We present here some of the foundational and organizing characteristics. SIT is made up of three overlapping phases: (1) a conceptual educational phase (helping the client better understand the nature of stress and stress effects); (2) a skill acquisition and skill consolidation phase (developing and practicing a repertoire of coping skills); and (3) an application and generalization phase (using coping skills in conditions approximating problem situations as well as those with potential stress effects).

We present a description of stress inoculation training organized under seven major components:

1. Treatment rationale (overview and purpose)
2. Information giving (psychoeducational component)
3. Learning and practice of direct-action coping skills
4. Learning and practice of cognitive coping skills
5. Application of coping skills to problem-related situations
6. Application of coping skills to potential problem situations
7. Homework and follow-up

A detailed description of each step associated with these seven parts is presented in the Interview Checklist for Stress Inoculation Training at the end of this chapter and Learning Activity 12.4. Meichenbaum's literature (2007; 2009) is a good source for additional detail.

Learning Activity 12.4

Stress Inoculation

Part One

Listed below are 12 examples of various direct-action coping skills. Using the coding system that precedes the examples, identify on paper the *type* of direct-action coping skill displayed in each example. Feedback follows in the Learning Feedback box.

Code

a. Information (I)
b. Escape route (ER)
c. Social support network (SSN)
d. Ventilation (V)
e. Perspective-taking (PT)
f. Attention diversion (AD)
g. Imagery manipulations (IM)
h. Muscle relaxation (MR)
i. Breathing techniques (B)

Direct-Action Coping Skills

____ 1. "Learn to take slow, deep breaths when you feel especially tense."
____ 2. "Instead of thinking just about the pain, try to concentrate very hard on one spot on the wall."
____ 3. "Imagine that it's a very warm day and the warmth makes you feel relaxed."
____ 4. "If it really gets to be too much, just do the first part only—leave the rest for a while."
____ 5. "You can expect some pain, but it is really only the result of the stitches. It doesn't mean that something is wrong."
____ 6. "Just tighten your left fist. Hold it and notice the tension. Now relax it—feel the difference."
____ 7. "Try to imagine a strong, normal cell attacking the weak, confused cancer cells when you feel the discomfort of your treatment."
____ 8. "When it gets very strong, distract yourself—listen hard to the music or study the picture on the wall."
____ 9. "If you talk about it and express your feelings about the pain, you might feel better."
____10. "Your initial or intuitive reaction might cause you to see only selected features of the situation. There are also some positive aspects we need to focus on."
____11. "It would be helpful to have your family and neighbors involved to provide you feedback and another perspective."
____12. "Social skills are important for you to learn to develop the support you need from other people. Others can lessen the effects of the aversive situation."

Part Two

Listed below are eight examples of cognitive coping skills used at four phases of cognitive coping. Match each coping skill with the letter of the appropriate phase. Feedback follows.

Phases

a. Preparing for a situation
b. Confronting or handling the situation
c. Dealing with critical moments in the situation
d. Self-encouragement for coping

Cognitive Coping Skills

____ 1. "By golly, I did it."
____ 2. "What will I need to do?"
____ 3. "Don't lose your cool even though it's tough now. Take a deep breath."
____ 4. "Think about what you want to say—not how people are reacting to you now."
____ 5. "Relax; it will be over soon. Just concentrate on getting through this rough moment now."
____ 6. "Can you feel this—the coping worked!"
____ 7. "When you get in there, just think about the situation, not your anxiety."
____ 8. "That's a signal to cope now. Just keep your mind on what you're doing."

Component 1: Treatment Rationale

Here is an example of a rationale that a helping practitioner might use for stress inoculation training.

Purpose   The helper might explain as follows the purpose of stress inoculation for a client having trouble with hostility:

> You find yourself confronted with situations in which your temper gets out of hand. You have trouble managing your anger, especially when you feel hassled or attacked. This procedure can help you learn to cope with provoking situations and can help you manage the intensity of your anger when you're in these situations so it doesn't control you.

Overview   Then, the helper can give the client a brief overview of the procedure:

> First, we will try to help you understand the nature of your feelings and how certain situations may provoke your feelings and lead from anger to hostility. Next, you will learn some ways to manage this and to cope with situations in which you feel this way. After you learn these coping skills, we will set up situations where you can practice using these skills to help you control your anger. How does this sound to you?

Component 2: Information Giving by the Helper

Before learning and applying various coping strategies, the client should be given some information about the nature of a stress reaction and how various coping strategies can help manage the stress. This education phase of stress inoculation helps the client conceptualize people's reactions to stressful events and builds a foundation for the components.

Conceptual Framework for Client's Reaction

In setting a framework, the helper works to identify and describe the nature of the client's reaction to a stressful situation. Although understanding one's reaction may not be sufficient for changing it, the conceptual framework lays some groundwork for beginning the change process. An explanation of some kind of stress (experienced in terms of anxiety, hostility, or pain) usually involves describing the stress as having two components: physiological arousal and covert self-statements or thoughts that provoke anxiety, hostility, or pain. This explanation may help the client realize that coping strategies must be directed toward the arousal behaviors *and* the cognitive processes. For example, to describe such a framework to

a client who has trouble controlling hostility, the helper could say something like this:

> Perhaps you could think about what happens when you get very angry. You might notice that certain things happen to you physically—perhaps your body feels tight, your face may feel warm, you may experience more rapid breathing, or your heart may pound. This is the physical part of your anger. However, there is another thing that probably goes on while your anger is escalating. When people become very angry, they may be unaware of or unable to access cognitions due to "hijacking by the amygdala." That is, the event may trigger an emotional sense of threat that swamps and overrides our logic and calmer reasoning. You might be thinking such things as, "He had no right to attack me," "I'll get back at him," "Boy, I'll show him who's boss," or "I'll teach her to keep her mouth shut." These kinds of thoughts only intensify your anger. So the way you interpret and think about an anger-provoking situation also contributes to arousing hostile feelings.

Note that in the case of this and related examples, we are differentiating between appropriate, legitimate feelings of anger and hostility that leads to abuse or damage.

Educating About Phases of Stress Reactions   After explaining a framework for emotional arousal, the helper should explore the kinds of times or conditions when the client's arousal level may be heightened. For example, phobic clients may view their anxiety as one massive panic reaction. Similarly, clients who are angry, depressed, or in pain may interpret their feelings as one large, continuous reaction that has no certain beginning or end. Clients who interpret their reactions this way may perceive the reaction as too difficult to change because it is so massive and overwhelming.

One way to help the client see the potential for coping with feelings is to describe the feelings by individual stages or phases of reacting to a situation. For example, the following distinctions can help clients conceptualize various critical points of a reaction: (1) *preparing* for a stressful, painful, or provoking situation; (2) *confronting* and handling the situation or the provocation; (3) *coping* with critical moments or with feelings of being overwhelmed or agitated during the situation; and (4) *rewarding* oneself after the stress for using coping skills in the first three phases. Note that the first phase concerns anticipatory coping skills *before* the situation, the second and third phases deal with coping *during* the situation, and the fourth phase concerns coping *after* the situation.

Explanation of these stages in the preliminary part of stress inoculation helps the client understand the

12.4 Feedback

Stress Inoculation

Part One

1. i. B	7. g. IM
2. f. AD	8. f. AD
3. g. IM	9. d. V
4. b. ER	10. e. PT
5. a. I	11. c. SSN
6. h. MR	12. c. SSN

If this exercise was difficult for you, you might want to review the information presented in the text on direct-action coping skills.

Part Two

1. d. Encouraging phase
2. a. Preparing for the situation
3. c. Dealing with a critical moment
4. b. Confronting the situation
5. c. Dealing with a critical moment
6. d. Encouragement for coping
7. a. Preparing for the situation
8. b. Confronting the situation

sequence of coping strategies to be learned. To explain the client's reaction as a series of phases, the helper might say something like this:

> When you think of being angry, you probably just think of being angry for a continuous period of time. However, you might find that your anger is probably not just one big reaction but comes and goes at different points during a provoking situation. The first critical point is when you anticipate the situation and start to get angry. At this point, you can learn to prepare yourself for handling the situation in a manageable way. The next point may come when you're in the middle of the situation and you're very angry. Here you can learn how to confront a provoking situation in a constructive way. There might also be times when your anger really gets intense and you can feel it starting to control you—and perhaps you feel yourself losing control. At this time, you can learn how to cope with intense feelings of agitation. Then, after the situation is over, instead of getting angry with yourself for the way you handled it, you can learn to encourage yourself for trying to cope with it. In this procedure, we'll practice using the coping skills at these especially stressful or arousing times.

Coping Skills and Strategies   The helper should provide some information about the kinds of coping skills and strategies that can be used at these critical points, emphasizing a *variety* of useful coping skills. This sets the stage for supporting clients in selecting and tailoring strategies for

themselves. In stress inoculation, both direct-action and cognitive coping skills are included. *Direct-action* coping strategies are designed to help the client use coping behaviors to handle the stress; *cognitive* coping skills are used to give the client coping thoughts (self-statements) to handle the stress. *Both* kinds of coping skills are important, serving different functions, although some clients may prefer to rely more on one type than another. To provide the client with information about the usefulness of these coping skills, the helper might explain them in this way:

> In the next phase of this procedure, you'll be learning a lot of different ways to prepare for and handle a provoking situation. Some of these coping skills will help you learn to cope with provoking situations through your actions and behaviors; others will help you handle these situations by the way you interpret and think about the situation. Not all the strategies you learn may be useful or necessary for you, so your input in selecting the ones you prefer to use is important.

Component 3: Learning and Practice of Direct-Action Coping Skills

The helper here discusses and models possible action strategies, and the client practices selected strategies with the helper's encouragement and assistance. Examples of commonly used direct-action coping strategies include:

1. Collecting objective or factual information about the stressful situation

2. Identifying short-circuit or escape routes or ways to decrease the stress

3. Palliative coping strategies

4. Mental relaxation methods

5. Physical relaxation methods

Information Collection   Collecting objective or factual information about a stressful situation may help the client evaluate the situation more realistically. Moreover, information about a situation may reduce the ambiguity for the client and indirectly reduce the level of threat. For example, for a client who may be confronted with physical pain, information about the source and expected timing of pain can reduce stress. This coping method is widely used in childbirth classes. The women and their labor coaches are taught and shown that the experienced pain is actually a uterine contraction. They are given information about the timing and stages of labor and the timing and intensity of contractions so that when labor occurs, their anxiety will not be increased by misunderstanding or a lack of information about what is happening in their bodies.

Collecting information about an anxiety- or anger-engendering situation serves the same purpose. For example, in using stress inoculation to help clients control anger, collecting information about the people who typically provoke them may help. Clients collect information that can help them view provocation as a *task* or a problem to be solved rather than as a *threat* or a personal attack.

Identification of Escape Routes   Identifying escape routes is a way to help clients cope with stress before it gets out of hand. The idea of an escape route is to short-circuit the stressful situation or to de-escalate the stress. This coping strategy may help, for example, clients with aggressive habits learn to identify cues that trigger them and to take some preventive action before striking out, similar to the stimulus-control self-management strategy. Although ultimate problem resolution is more complex, these escape or prevention routes tend to focus on very simple things that the client can *do* early in their change efforts and likely have success. An externalizing or anger-control client could, for example, work to avoid striking out by counting to 60, leaving the room, or talking about something humorous.

Palliative Coping Strategies   Palliative coping strategies may be particularly useful for aversive or stressful situations that cannot be substantially altered or avoided, such as chronic or life-threatening illnesses. Examples of strategies for dealing with unchangeable and uncontrollable stressors include perspective-taking, selective attention-diversion procedures, as in the case of chronic pain patients, and adaptive modes of affective expression such as humor, relaxation, and reframing the situation (Meichenbaum, 1993).

Mental Relaxation   Mental relaxation techniques may involve attentiondiversion tactics, which may build on early introduction of escape route strategies. Angry clients, for example, can increase control of their anger by concentrating on a problem to solve, counting floor tiles in the room, recalling a funny joke, or thinking about something positive about themselves. Attention-diversion tactics are commonly used to help people control pain. Instead of focusing on the pain, the person may concentrate very hard on an object in the room or on the repetition of a word (a mantra) or a number—redirecting attention away from the pain and the fear it evokes and fostering a less physically stressed state. Imagery can also prove useful. Instead of heightened attention to one's anxious thoughts and bodily sensations, a client might visualize lying on a warm beach, being on a sailboat, or savoring a favorite food. For pain control, the person can imagine different things about the pain—envisioning recurring pain as an ocean wave, for example, that washes over and moves on.

Physical Relaxation Methods   Physical relaxation methods may be useful for clients who report physiological components of anxiety and anger, such as sweaty palms, rapid breathing or heartbeat, or nausea. Physical relaxation can be supported by various strategies such as breathing techniques, muscle relaxation, meditation, and exercise. We more fully address a range of relaxation and soothing strategies in the next chapter. It is important to note, however, that the appropriateness of these methods will depend, in part, on the mechanisms causing the symptoms. If clients experiencing physiological symptoms also fear that these symptoms will spin out of control with catastrophic consequences, then relaxation methods may be premature or counterproductive, potentially fostering unintended outcomes like avoidance. In those circumstances, exposure-based methods may be better suited.

If relaxation methods appear well suited, then each direct-action strategy should first be explained to the client, with discussion of its purpose and procedure. Several sessions may be required to discuss and model various direct-action coping methods and make selections to work more deeply with. The number of direct-action strategies used by a client will depend on the intensity of the reaction, the nature of the stress, and the client's preferences. With the helper's assistance, the client should practice using each skill to be able to apply it in simulated and *in vivo* situations.

Component 4: Learning and Practice of Cognitive Coping Skills

The acquisition and practice of cognitive coping skills of SIT are very similar to cognitive restructuring. The helper models examples of coping thoughts that the client can use during stressful phases of problem situations. Then, the client selects and practices substituting coping thoughts for negative or self-defeating thoughts.

Helper Modeling Coping Thoughts   After explaining the four phases of stress reactions that provide different points in which to use cognitive coping skills (see previous section where these are described with an example), the helper models examples of coping statements that are especially useful for each of the four phases. Preparing for a stressor might include acknowledgments that this may be challenging, but reminders that the client has a plan, has learned new strategies, and can review planned coping steps as part of rehearsal and that calming exercises such as deep breathing are useful. Confronting or initially managing the stressor might focus more on staying focused, memory cues to follow planned steps, encouraging self-statements, and reminders to use negative sensations as coping cues. Coping with critical elements of the situation may benefit from focus on the particular feelings or thoughts that have been problematic in the past and may attend to different elements—for example, when one anticipates anger versus fear to be the prominent feelings in the moment. Modeling for this phase may include reminders to compartmentalize distracting physical or emotional sensations, to strive for reasonable coping rather than total mastery and perfection, and to maintain belief in one's ultimate aims and ability to attain them step by step. Finally, reinforcement should be generous. The focus is not on having the problem fixed per se, but in making steady progress. Modeling examples of reinforcement could acknowledge how difficult such situations are, congratulations for hanging in there, noting incremental gains and progress, and purposefully underscoring belief in one's potential and ultimate efficacy. (Also see Learning Activity 12.4 see page 444.)

Client Selection of Coping Thoughts The helper encourages the client to try on and adapt the thoughts in whatever way feels most natural. The client might look for coping statements that he or she has used in other stress-related situations. At this point in the procedure, the helper should be working to tailor a coping program *specifically* for this client. If the client's self-statements are too general, then they may lead only to rote repetition and not function as effective self-instructions. Also, specific coping statements are more likely to be culturally relevant. The helper might explain the importance of the client's participation like this:

> You know, your input in finding coping thoughts that work for you is very important. I've given you some examples. Some of these you might feel comfortable with, and there may be others you can think of, too. What we want to do now is to come up with some specific coping thoughts you can and will use during these four times that fit for *you,* not me or someone else.

Client Practice of Coping Thoughts After the client selects coping thoughts to use for each phase, the helper instructs the client to practice these self-statements by saying them aloud. This verbal practice is designed to help the client become familiar with the coping thoughts and accustomed to the words. After this practice, the client should also practice the selected coping thoughts in the sequence of the four phases. This practice helps the client learn the timing of the coping thoughts in the application phase of stress inoculation.

The helper can say something like this:

> First, I'd like you to practice using these coping thoughts just by saying them aloud to me. This will help you get used to the words and ideas of coping. Next, let's practice these coping thoughts in the sequence in which you would use them when applying them to a real situation. I'll show you. Okay, first I'm anticipating the situation, so I'm going to use coping statements that help me prepare for the situation, like "I know this type of situation usually upsets me, but I have a plan now to handle it" or "I'm going to be able to control my anger even if this situation is rough." Next, I'll pretend I'm actually into the situation. I'm going to cope so I can handle it. I might say something to myself like, "Just stay calm. Remember who I'm dealing with. This is her style. Don't take it personally" or "Don't overreact. Just relax."

> Now the person's harassment is continuing. I am going to cope with feeling more angry. I might think, "I can feel myself getting more upset. Just keep relaxed. Concentrate on this," or, "This is a challenging situation. How can I handle myself in a way I don't have to apologize for?" Okay, now afterward I realize I didn't get abusive or revengeful. So I'll think something to encourage myself, like, "I did it" or "Gee, I really kept my cool."

> Now you try it. Just verbalize your coping thoughts in the sequence of preparing for the situation, handling it, coping with getting really agitated, and then encouraging yourself.

Component 5: Application of Coping Skills to Problem-Related Situations

The next part of stress inoculation involves having the client apply both direct-action and cognitive coping skills in the face of stressful, provoking, or painful situations. Before the client is instructed to apply the coping skills *in vivo,* she or he practices applying coping skills under simulated conditions with the helper's assistance. The application phase of stress inoculation appears to be important for the overall efficacy of the procedure. Simply having a client rehearse coping skills *without* opportunities to apply them in stressful situations seems to result in an improved but limited ability to cope.

The application phase involves modeling and rehearsing to provide the client with exposure to simulations of problem-related situations. For example, the client who wanted to manage hostility would have opportunities to practice coping in a variety of hostility-provoking situations. During this application practice, the client needs to be faced with a stressful situation in which to practice the skills. In other words, the application should be arranged and conducted as realistically as possible. It is valuable to practice the feeling in question (anxiety) and to rehearse even starting to lose control, but then applying the coping skills to regain control. This type of application practice is viewed as the client's providing a self-model of how to behave in a stressful situation. In the application phase of stress inoculation, the client's anxiety, hostility, or distressful emotions are used as a cue or reminder to cope.

Helper Modeling of Application of Coping Skills The helper should first model how the client can apply the newly acquired skills when faced with a stressful situation. Here is an example of a helper demonstration of this process with a client who is working toward hostility control (in this case, with his family):

I'm going to imagine that the police have just called and told me that my 16-year-old son was just picked up again for breaking and entering. I can feel myself start to get really hot. Whoops, wait a minute. That's a signal [arousal cue for coping]. I'd better start thinking about using my relaxation methods to stay calm and using my coping thoughts to prepare myself for handling this situation constructively.

Okay, first of all, sit down and relax. Let those muscles loosen up. Count to 10. Breathe deeply [direct-action coping methods]. Now I'll be seeing my son soon. What is it I have to do? I know it won't help to lash out or to hit him. That won't solve anything. So I'll work out another plan. Let him do most of the talking. Give him the chance to make amends or find a solution [cognitive coping: preparing for the situation].

Now I can see him walking in the door. I feel sort of choked up. I can feel my fists getting tight. He's starting to explain. I want to interrupt and let him have it. But wait [arousal cue for coping]. Concentrate on counting and on breathing slowly [direct-action coping]. Now just tell myself—keep cool. Let him talk. It won't help now to blow up [cognitive coping: confronting situation].

Now I can imagine myself thinking back to the last time he got arrested. Why in the hell doesn't he learn? No son of mine is going to be a troublemaker [arousal]. Whew! I'm pretty angry. I've got to stay in control, especially now [cue for coping]. Just relax, muscles! Stay loose [direct-action coping]. I can't expect him to live up to my expectations. I can tell him I'm disappointed, but I'm not going to blow up and shout and hit [cognitive coping: feelings of greater agitation]. Okay, I'm doing a good job of keeping my lid on [cognitive coping: self-reinforcement].

Client Application of Coping Skills in Imaginary and Role-Play Practice After the helper modeling, the client should practice a similar sequence of both direct-action and cognitive coping skills. We find that it is often useful to have the client first practice the coping skills while imagining problem-related situations and then move to role-play. This practice can be repeated until the client feels very comfortable in applying the coping strategies to imagined situations. The role-play practice should be similar to the *in vivo* situations that the client encounters. For instance, our angry client could identify particular situations and people with whom he or she is most likely to blow up or lose control. The client can imagine each situation (starting with the most manageable one) and imagine using the coping skills. Then, with the helper taking the part of someone else such as a provoker, the client can practice the coping skills in a role play.

Component 6: Application of Coping Skills to Potential Problem Situations

Any therapeutic procedure should be designed both to help clients deal with current concerns and to help them anticipate constructive handling of potential concerns, helping prevent future problems. The prevention aspect of stress inoculation is achieved by having clients apply newly learned coping strategies to situations that are not problematic now but could be in the future. If this phase of stress inoculation is ignored, then the effects of the inoculation may be very short-lived. In other words, if clients do not have an opportunity to apply the coping skills to situations other than the current problem-related ones, then their coping skills may not generalize beyond the present problem situations.

The application of coping skills to other potentially stressful situations is accomplished in the same way as application to the present problem areas. First, after explaining the usefulness of coping skills in other areas of the client's life, the helper demonstrates the application of coping strategies to a potential, hypothetical stressor. The helper might select a situation the client has not yet encountered, one that would require active coping by anyone who might encounter it, such as not receiving a desired job promotion or raise, facing a family crisis, moving to a new place, anticipating retirement, or being very ill. After the helper has modeled application of coping skills to these sorts of situations, the client would practice applying the skills in these situations or in similar ones that she or he identifies. The practice can occur in imagination or in role-play enactments. A novel way to practice is to switch roles—the client plays the helper, and the helper plays the role of the client. The client helps or trains the helper to use the coping skills. Placing the client in the role of a helper or a trainer can provide another kind of application opportunity that may also have benefits for the client's acquisition of coping strategies and bolster the client's self-efficacy. Some version of Learning Activity 12.4 may be useful as part of training for clients as well as helpers.

Stress inoculation training is one of a number of cognitive-behavioral interventions for which computer-assisted programs have been developed and tested. Not surprisingly, one domain in which stress inoculation training is being pursued is with high-stress occupation populations, some of whom need to be reached remotely. Individuals involved in peacekeeping such as military personnel and police officers, for example, continuously face potentially life-threatening stress. Ways to strengthen both resistance to stress as well as healthy ways to regularly re-center and cope with stress are priorities for these populations. Virtual reality simulations and cyber interventions are emerging, in some cases paired with physiological monitoring (e.g., heart rate) to track and intervene with more precision emotional states and physiological manifestations associated with these emotions (Hourani et al, 2011; Serino et al. 2014). These technology-adapted interventions can assist in tailoring delivery of stressful stimuli and supporting individuals' effectiveness in managing their stress responding (Cosic, Popovic, Kukolja, Horvat, & Dropuljic, 2010; Spira, Johnston, McLay, Popovic, Russoniello, & Wood, 2010). Applications are pairing SIT with mindfulness training to prepare for and buffer against stress-related dysfunction such as deployment (Stanley, Schaldach, Kiyonaga, & Jha, 2011) with applications showing promise for preventing long-term psychological reactions to stress such as PTSD (Wiederhold & Wiederhold, 2008).

Similarly, medical treatment often involves ongoing exposure to stress and naturally occurring emotional and physical depletion. The next generation of stress inoculation training in this arena integrates medical science with SIT. Wiederhold and colleagues (2009), for example, describe use of prosthetics representing realistic wounds and tissue damage within stress inoculation training of trauma treatment to more closely approximate the stress arousal that could impair effective medical care. Use of mobile phones as part of SIT with oncology nurses who experience chronic stress reduces anxiety and supports coping skills acquisition (Vilani et al., 2013). Workplace applications also include stress inoculation training with police officers, targeting preparation for criticism management (both within and from outside the law enforcement agency). Findings indicate increased efficacy in dealing with interpersonal stress and reduced negative health-related consequences (Garner, 2008).

Component 7: Homework and Follow-Up

When the client has learned and used stress inoculation within the interviews, she or he is ready to use coping skills *in vivo*. The helper and client should discuss the potential application of coping strategies to actual situations. The helper might caution the client not to expect to cope beautifully with every problematic situation. The client should be encouraged to use a daily log to record the particular situations and the number of times that the coping strategies are used. The log data can be used in a later follow-up as one way to determine the client's progress.

Stress inoculation training is one of the more versatile therapeutic strategies. Teaching clients both direct-action and cognitive coping skills that can be used in current and potential problematic situations provides skills that are under the clients' control and are applicable to future as well as current situations.

Model Dialogue: Stress Inoculation

Session 1

In this session, the helper will teach Isabella some **LO4** direct-action coping skills for mental and physical relaxation to help her cope with her physical sensations of nervousness about her math class. Imagery manipulations and slow, deep breathing will be used.

1. **Helper:** Hi, Isabella. How was your week?

Client: Pretty good. You know, this, well, whatever you call it, it's starting to help. I took a test this week and got an 85—I usually get a 70 or 75.

The helper introduces the *idea of other coping skills to deal with Isabella's nervousness*.

2. **Helper:** That really is encouraging. And that's where the effects of this count—on how you do in class. Because what we did last week went well for you, I believe today we might work with some other coping skills that might help you decrease your nervous feelings.

Client: What would this be?

In responses 3 and 4, the helper explains and *models possible direct-action coping skills*.

3. **Helper:** One thing we might do is help you learn how to imagine something that gives you very calm feelings, and while you're doing this to take some slow, deep breaths—like this *(helper models closing eyes, breathing slowly and deeply)*. When I was doing that, I thought about curling up in a chair with my favorite book—but there are many different things you could think of. For instance, to use this in your math class, you might imagine that you are doing work for which you will receive some prize or award. Or you might imagine that you are learning problems so you'll be in a position to be a helper for someone else. Do you get the idea?

Client: I think so. I guess it's like trying to imagine or think about math in a pretend kind of way.

4. **Helper:** Yes—and in a way that reduces rather than increases the stress of it for you.

Client: I think I get the idea. It's sort of like when I imagine that I'm doing housework for some famous person instead of just at my house—it makes it more tolerable.

In response 5, the helper asks Isabella to *find some helpful imagery manipulations to promote calm feelings.*

5. **Helper:** That's a good example. You imagine that situation to prevent yourself from getting too bored. Here, you find a scene or scenes to think about to prevent yourself from getting too nervous. Can you take a few minutes to think about one or two things you could imagine—perhaps about math—that would help you feel calm instead of nervous?

Client *(pauses):* Well, maybe I could pretend that math class is part of something I need to do something exciting, like being an Olympic downhill skier.

In responses 6 and 7, the helper instructs Isabella to *practice these direct-action coping skills.*

6. **Helper:** OK, good. We can work with that, and if it doesn't help, then we can come up with something else. Why don't you try first to practice imagining this while you also breathe slowly and deeply, as I did a few minutes ago? [Isabella practices.]

7. **Helper:** How did that feel?

Client: OK—it was sort of fun.

In response 8, the helper gives *homework*—asks Isabella to engage in *self-directed practice* of these coping skills before the next session.

8. **Helper:** Good. Now, this week I'd like you to practice this in a quiet place two or three times each day. Keep track of your practice sessions in your log, and also rate your tension level before and after you practice. Next week we will go over this log and then work on a way you can apply what we did today—and the coping thoughts we learned in our two previous sessions. So I'll see you next week.

Session 2

In this session, the helper helps Isabella integrate the strategies of some previous sessions (coping thoughts, imagery, and breathing coping skills). Specifically, Isabella learns to apply all these coping skills in imagery and role-play practices of some stressful situations related to math class. Application of coping skills to problem-related situations is a part of stress inoculation and helps the client to generalize the newly acquired coping skills to *in vivo* situations as they occur.

In responses 1 and 2, the helper will *review Isabella's use of the direct-action skills homework.*

1. **Helper:** How are things going, Isabella?

Client: OK. I've had a hard week—one test and two pop quizzes in math. But I got 80s. I also did my imagination and breathing practice. You know, that takes a while to learn.

2. **Helper:** That's to be expected. It does take a lot of practice before you really get the feel of it. So it would be a good idea if you continued the daily practice again this week. How did it feel when you practiced?

Client: Okay—I think I felt less nervous than before.

The helper introduces the idea of *applying all the coping skills in practice situations and presents a rationale for this application phase.*

3. **Helper:** That's good. As time goes on, you will notice more effects from it. Up to this point, we've worked on some things to help you in your math class—stopping self-defeating thoughts and using imagination and slow breathing to help you cope and control your nervousness. What I think might help now is to give you a chance to use all these skills in practices of some of the stressful situations related to your math class. This will help you use the skills when you need to during the class or related situations. Then, we will soon be at a point where we can go through some of these same procedures for the other situations in which you want to express yourself differently and more frequently, such as with your folks. Does this sound OK?

Client: Yes.

Next, the helper *demonstrates (models) how Isabella can practice her skills in an imaginary practice.*

4. **Helper:** What I'd like you to do is to imagine some of the situations related to your math class and try to use your coping thoughts and the imagination scene and deep breathing to control your nervousness. Let me show you how you might do this. I'm imagining that it's almost time for math class. I'm going to concentrate on thinking about how this class will help me train for the Olympic downhill program. If I catch myself thinking I wish I didn't have to go, then I'm going to use some coping thoughts. Let's see—class will go pretty fast. I've been doing better. It can be a challenge. Now, as I'm in class, I'm going to stop thinking about not being able to do the work. I'm going to just take one problem at a time. One step at a time. Oops! Mr. Lamborne just called on me. Boy, I can feel myself getting nervous. Just take a deep breath... Do the best I can. It's only one moment anyway. Well, it went pretty well. I can feel myself starting to cope when I need to. Okay, Isabella, why don't you try this several times now?

(Isabella practices applying coping thoughts and direct action with different practice situations in imagination.)

In response 5, the helper *checks Isabella's reaction* to applying the skills in practice through imagination.

5. **Helper:** Are you able to really get into the situation as you practice this way?

Client: Yes, although I believe I'll have to work harder to use this when it really happens.

Sometimes *role play makes the practice more real.* The helper introduces this next. Note that the helper will add a stress element by calling on Isabella at unannounced times.

6. **Helper:** That's right. This kind of practice doesn't always have the same amount of stress as the real thing. Maybe it would help if we did some role-play practice. I'll be your teacher this time. Just pretend to be in class. I'll be talking, but at an unannounced time, I'm going to call on you to answer a question. Just use your coping thoughts and your slow breathing as you need to when this happens. *(Role-play practice of this and related scenarios occurs.)*

The helper *assesses Isabella's reaction* to role-play practice and *asks Isabella to rate her level of nervousness* during the practice.

7. **Helper:** How comfortable do you feel with these practices? Could you rate the nervousness you feel as you do this on a 1-to-5 scale, with 1 being not nervous and 5 being very nervous?

Client: Well, about a 2.

The helper encourages Isabella to *apply coping statements in the math-related problem situations* as they occur, assigns *homework,* and schedules a *follow-up.*

8. **Helper:** I think you are ready to use this as you need to during the week. Remember, any self-defeating thought or body tenseness is a cue to cope, using your coping thoughts and imagination and breathing skills. I'd like you to keep track of the number of times you use these on your log sheets. Also, rate your level of nervousness before, during, and after math class on the log sheet. How about coming back in 2 weeks to see how things are going?

Client: Fine.

CHAPTER SUMMARY

In this chapter, we examined various forms that stress takes, including cultural variations of stress as well as current models of factors that affect stress and coping.

We have seen ways that stress and its management relate to many other assessment and intervention strategies described in this book. Understanding current models of stress and coping should help guide you in developing an intervention plan appropriate to specific client needs, depending on the factors that appear most important either in how stress is being experienced or what types of stress management are likely to best achieve client goals.

We have focused in this chapter on two cognitively oriented sets of interventions that can be flexibly applied to stress: problem-solving and stress inoculation training. Both have demonstrated effectiveness, can be modified in a manner responsive to client characteristics or priorities, and can be used alone or in conjunction with other treatment strategies. Problem-solving training provides clients with a formalized system for viewing and managing issues more constructively. Problem-solving is often about changing aspects of one's environment—tangible, relational, power, sociocultural, or other dimensions—that are the root or at least a considerable part of the client's problem.

We also described stress inoculation as an approach to teaching both physical and cognitive coping strategies. Stress inoculation training pulls together a number of strategies to increase knowledge about stress and coping, self-monitoring, cognitive change, problem-solving, relaxation training, rehearsal preparation, and environmental change. SIT recognizes diversity in what individuals are exposed to, differential stress-related meanings these challenging exposures may entail, and the value of preventive as well as remedial approaches to managing stress and its negative effects on physical and mental health.

As with any intervention, you will need to assess the appropriateness of intervention philosophies and application components. For example, spirituality may be an important resource to consider for use in stress management intervention for some groups or individuals and not for others. Moreover, although consideration of cultural diversity is becoming much more common in practice involving stress and coping, much of the research and intervention development is rooted in a Western framework, for example, that stress is viewed as a problem requiring the assistance of an external source such as a professional helper and some training to be alleviated or managed. For some clients, stress may be viewed more as a part of life, and self-healing practices such as meditation, movement, or one or more forms of self-management (perhaps anchored within one's personal network or community) may be attractive and relevant.

 Visit CengageBrain.com for a variety of study tools and useful resources such as video examples, case studies, interactive exercises, flashcards, and quizzes.

12 | Knowledge and Skill Builder

Part One

Learning Outcome 1 asks you to describe the key components of the human stress model. Take a blank piece of paper and, without referring to the book, draw in diagram form the key components described in the chapter introduction (and portrayed in Figure 12.1). Below that diagram, provide descriptions of what is entailed in each of the key components, for example, what do primary appraisals involve?

Part Two

Learning Outcome 2 asks you to identify the steps of the problem-solving strategy represented by at least 8 out of 10 helper interview responses. Match each helper response with the letter of the step of the problem-solving procedure that is being used. More than one helper response may be associated with a step. See Feedback section for answers.

Steps of Problem-Solving

a. Rationale for problem-solving
b. Problem orientation
c. Problem definition and formulation
d. Generation of alternative solutions
e. Decision-making
f. Solution implementation and verification

Helper Responses

_____ 1. "Self-monitoring involves keeping a diary or log about your thoughts, feelings, and behaviors."

_____ 2. "To help you assess each solution, you can answer several questions about how effective the solution will be in solving the problem."

_____ 3. "Be creative and freewheeling. Let your imagination go. Write down whatever comes into your mind."

_____ 4. "What goals do you want to set for your emotional or personal reaction to the issue?"

_____ 5. "Think about when you are aware of concerns, and give me an example of a concern and describe how you typically solve it."

_____ 6. "Solving problems as they occur can prevent future discomfort."

_____ 7. "Most people have an ability to solve problems, but often they block the use of it and become poor problem-solvers."

_____ 8. "What unresolved issues may be contributing to the problem? When does the problem occur? Where does it occur?"

_____ 9. "Look over your list of solutions to see how much variety is on your list; think of new and original options for solving the problem."

_____10. "You need to think about what you can reward yourself with after you complete this step."

Part Three

Learning Outcome 3 asks you to demonstrate 16 out of 19 steps associated with the problem-solving strategy in a role-play interview. Note that these steps illustrate detail regarding how to operationalize the six components of problem-solving. You can audiotape your interview or have an observer rate it using the Interview Checklist for Problem-Solving.

Interview Checklist for Problem-Solving

Instructions: Determine whether the helper demonstrated each of the leads listed in the checklist. Check (☑) the leads that were used.

Treatment Rationale

_____ 1. **Helper explains purpose of problem-solving therapy in a way that is consistent with the client's culture.**

"All of us are faced with little and big concerns. Sometimes we feel stuck because we don't know how to handle a concern. This procedure can help you identify and define a difficulty and examine ways of solving it. You can be in charge of the issue instead of the issue being in charge of you. Solving difficulties as they occur can prevent future discomfort."

_____ 2. Helper provides brief overview of procedure in a way that is consistent with the client's culture.

"There are five steps we'll do in using this procedure. Most problems in living are complex, and achieving changes often requires many different perspectives. First, we'll need to look at how you see the problem. We'll examine what are unhelpful and helpful problem-solving skills. Another part of this step is to explore how to overcome thoughts and feelings that could be obstacles to achieving your goals. We'll also need to see how much time and energy you are willing to use to solve the problem. Second, we will define the problem by gathering information about it. Third, we'll want to see how many different solutions we can come up with for solving the problem. Next, we'll examine the solutions and decide which one to use. Finally, you will try out the chosen solutions and see how well they solve the problem. What are your thoughts about what I have described? Do you have any questions?"

Problem Orientation

_____ 3. Helper determines how the client solves problems.

"When you have concerns or problems, give me an example of the problem and describe how you typically solve it."

(continued)

12 | Knowledge and Skill Builder (*continued*)

___ 4. Helper describes the difference between maladaptive and helpful problem-solving, recognizing variations across gender, age, and culture and worldviews.

"Most people have the ability to solve problems, but often they block the use of it. Problem-solving therapy helps to remove blocks or obstacles and helps bring important issues into focus. Problem-solving therapy provides a formalized system for viewing problems differently. People who don't solve problems very well may feel inadequate or incompetent to solve their problem. Often these people want to avoid the problem or want someone else to solve it. People sometimes feel that it is easier not to solve the problem and assume that things will get better on their own. At times, poor problem-solvers feel hopeless, depressed, or unlucky. If you feel like a poor problem-solver, then we'll have to consider ways that make you feel like you are in charge. You can solve problems; they are a part of daily living. There are usually a variety of solutions to every problem, and you have the capacity to find the solution. It can be helpful to think of problems as an opportunity to seek worthwhile change."

___ 5. Helper determines what cognitive and emotional obstacles the client might have as barriers to solving the problem.

"When you think about your problem, what thoughts do you have concerning the problem? What are you usually thinking about during this problem? Do you have any 'shoulds' or other beliefs concerning the problem? What feelings do you experience when thinking about the problem? Are there any holdover or unfinished feelings from past events in your life that still affect the problem? How do your thoughts and feelings affect the problem and your ability to solve it? You may not be aware of these influences, but think about some past issues or unfinished business you may have as we engage in problem-solving." If there are any obstacles, then the helper introduces a strategy or strategies (for example, rational emotive therapy, cognitive restructuring, reframing, meditation, muscle relaxation) to help the client remove cognitive or emotional obstacles to problem-solving.

___ 6. Helper assesses the client's time, energy, and commitment to solving the problem.

"Any problem usually takes time, effort, and commitment to solve. But it is often important to solve the problem now rather than wait and solve it later—or not at all. It is important to know how committed you are to solving the problem. *(Wait for the answer.)* Also, solving a problem takes time. Do you feel you have enough time to work on the problem? *(Pause; wait for answer.)* Thinking about and working on a problem can take a lot of energy. How energized do you feel about working on this problem?" *(Pause for answer.)*

Problem Definition and Formulation

___ 7. Helper describes the problem-solving strategy for the client in a culturally relevant way.

"People have problems or concerns. Some concerns are minor, and some are major. Problem-solving is a skill and a practical approach. People use problem-solving to identify, explore, or create effective ways of dealing with everyday concerns or difficult situations."

___ 8. Helper helps the client gather information about the problem to define it.

"We want to gather as much information about the concern as we can. What type of issue or situation is it? What thoughts do you have when the difficulty occurs? What feelings do you experience? How often does the difficulty occur, or is it ongoing? What unresolved issues may be contributing? Who or what other people are involved? When does the problem occur? Where does it occur? How long has this been going on? How intense is the problem? What have you done to solve the problem? What obstacles can you identify that prevent you from making desired changes? Tell me, how do you see the issue or troubling situation? What other information do we need to define the problem? What is your definition of the problem?"

___ 9. Helper determines whether the client's problem is problem-focused, emotion-focused, or both.

"From the way you have defined the problem, how can the problem be changed? What aspects of the problem can be changed? What emotional reactions do you have about the problem? How would you like to change your personal/emotional reaction to the problem? There may be some things about the problem that you cannot change. Some problem situations are unchangeable. If there are aspects of the problem that are changeable, we will work on those things that can be changed. One thing we can change is your emotional or personal reaction to the problem."

____10. Helper helps the client identify culturally relevant problem-solving goals.

"Now that we have identified and defined the problem, we need to set some goals. A goal is what you would like to have happen so that the problem would be solved. The goals you choose should be things you can do or things that are attainable and realistic."

"How many obstacles are there that prevent you from setting problem-solving goals? How can you remove these obstacles? What goals do you want to set for your emotional or personal reaction to the problem? What behaviors do you want to change? How much or what level of behavior is going to change? Under what condition or circumstance will the behavior change occur? What goals do you want to set for things that are changeable in the problem situation? What behavioral goals do you want to set for yourself, the frequency of these behaviors, and in what problem conditions? These goals will help us in the next stage of problem-solving."

Generation of Alternative Solutions

____11. Helper presents guidelines for generating alternative solutions.

"We want to generate as many alternative solutions for solving the problem as possible. We do this because problems are often complicated and a single alternative is often inadequate. We need to generate several alternative solutions for each problem-solving goal."

____ a. What options:

"Think of what you could do or ways to handle the problem. Don't worry about how to go about making your plan work or how to put the solution into effect—you'll do that later."

____ b. Defer judgment:

"Defer judgment about your ideas or solutions until later. Be loose and open to any idea or solution. You can evaluate and criticize your solutions later."

____ c. Quantity:

"Quantity breeds quality. The more alternative solutions or ideas you can think of, the better. The more alternatives you produce, the more quality solutions you'll discover."

____ c. Variety:

"Be creative and freewheeling. Let your imagination go. Write down whatever comes into your mind. Allow yourself to think of a variety of unusual or unconventional solutions as well as more traditional or typical ones. Look over your list of solutions, and see how much variety there is. If there is little variety on your list, generate more and think of new and original solutions."

Decision-Making

____12. Helper instructs the client to screen the list of alternative solutions.

"Now you need to screen and look over your list of alternative solutions for solving the problem. You want to look for the *best* solutions. The best solutions are the ones that maximize benefits and minimize costs for your personal, social, immediate, and long-term welfare."

____13. Helper provides criteria for evaluating each solution.

"To help you assess *each* solution, answer the following four questions:

____ a. Will the problem be solved with this particular solution?

____ b. By using this solution, what will be the status of my emotional well-being?

____ c. If I use this solution, how much time and effort will be needed to solve the problem?

____ d. What will be my overall personal and social well-being if I use this solution?

Remember that it is important to evaluate *each* solution by answering the four questions."

____14. Helper instructs the client to make a decision and select the best solutions compatible with problem-solving goals and the client's culture.

"Select every solution that you think will work or solve the problem. Answer these questions:

____ a. Can the problem be solved reasonably well with these solutions?

____ b. Is more information about the problem needed before these solutions can be selected and implemented?

Decide whether the solutions fit with the problem-solving goals." If the answers to question a and question b are *yes* and *no*, respectively, then move on to step 15. Answers of *no* to question a and *yes* to question b may require recycling by redefining the problem, gathering more information, and determining problem obstacles.

Solution Implementation and Verification

____15. Helper instructs the client to carry out chosen solutions.

"For the last stage of problem-solving, try out the solutions you have chosen. If there are obstacles to trying out the solutions, then we'll have to remove

(continued)

12 | Knowledge and Skill Builder (*continued*)

them. You can use several alternative solutions at the same time. Use as many solutions as you can."

____16. Helper informs the client about self-monitoring strategy.

"We'll need to develop a technique for you to see whether the solutions you implement solve the problem. Self-monitoring involves keeping a diary or log about your thoughts, feelings, and behavior. You can record these behaviors as you implement your chosen solutions. We'll need to discuss what responses you'll record, when you'll record them, and the method of recording."

____17. Helper instructs the client to use certain criteria to assess whether the solutions achieve the desired goal for solving the problem.

"You'll need to determine whether your solutions solve the problem. One way to do this is to ask yourself the following:

____ a. Problem resolved:

"Did the solutions solve the problem?"

____ b. Emotional well-being:

"How is your emotional well-being after you used the solutions?"

____ c. Time and effort exerted:

"Was the time and effort you exerted worth it?"

____ d. Ratio of total benefits to total costs:

"Were there more benefits for using the solutions than costs?"

____18. Helper instructs the client about self-reward.

"You need to think about how you can reward yourself after successfully solving the problem. What types of things or activities are rewarding to you? When would be the best time to receive something or to engage in a rewarding activity?"

____19. Helper instructs the client on what to do if solutions do not solve the problem.

"When the solutions do not solve the problem, we need to look at some trouble areas that might be obstacles to solving the problem. What is your emotional reaction to the problem? The problem may not be defined well. There may be old unresolved problems that are contributing to the present problem."

Part Four

Learning Outcome 4 asks you to demonstrate 17 out of 21 steps of the stress inoculation procedure with a role-play client. Use the Interview Checklist for Stress Inoculation to assess your role-play interview.

Interview Checklist for Stress Inoculation

Instructions: Determine which steps the helper demonstrated in using stress inoculation with a client or in teaching stress inoculation to another person. Check (☑) any step the helper demonstrated in the application of the procedure.

Treatment Rationale

1. Helper explains purpose of stress inoculation.

"Stress inoculation is a way to help you cope with feeling anxious so that you can manage your reactions when you're confronted with these situations."

2. Helper provides brief overview of stress inoculation procedure.

"First, we'll try to understand how your anxious feelings affect you now. Then you'll learn some coping skills that will help you relax physically—and help you use coping thoughts instead of self-defeating thoughts. Then, you'll have a chance to test out your coping skills in stressful situations we'll set up."

3. Helper checks to see whether client is willing to use the strategy.

"How do you feel now about working with this procedure?"

Information Giving by Helper

4. Helper explains nature of client's emotional reaction to a stressful situation.

"Probably you realize that when you feel anxious, you are physically tense. Also, you may be thinking in a worried way—worrying about the situation and how to handle it. Both the physical tenseness and the negative or worry thoughts create stress for you."

5. Helper explains possible *phases* of reacting to a stressful situation.

"When you feel anxious, you probably tend to think of it as one giant reaction. Actually, you're probably anxious at certain times or phases. For example, you might feel very uptight just anticipating the situation. Then, you might feel uptight during the situation, especially if it starts to overwhelm you. After the situation is over, you may feel relieved—but down on yourself, too."

6. Helper explains specific kinds of coping skills to be learned in stress inoculation and the importance of client's input in tailoring coping strategies.

"We'll be learning some action kinds of coping strategies—like physical or muscle relaxation, mental relaxation, and just common sense ways to minimize the stress of the situation. Then, you'll also learn some different ways to view and think about the situation. Not all these coping strategies may seem best for you, so your input in selecting the ones you feel are best for you is important."

Client Learning and Practice of Direct-Action Coping Strategies

7. Helper discusses and models direct-action coping strategies (or uses a symbolic model).

"First, I'll explain and we can talk about each coping method. Then, I'll demonstrate how you can apply it when you're provoked."

  a. Collecting objective or factual information about a stressful situation:

"Sometimes it helps to get any information you can about things that provoke and anger you. Let's find out the types of situations that and people who can do this to you. Then, we can see whether there are other ways to view the provocation. For example, what if you looked at it as a situation to challenge your problem-solving ability rather than as a personal attack?"

  b. Identifying escape routes—alternative ways to de-escalate stress of situation:

"Suppose you're caught in a situation. You feel it's going to get out of hand. What are some ways to get out of it or to de-escalate it *before* you strike out? For example, little things like counting to 60, leaving the room, using humor, or something like that."

Mental Relaxation

  c. Attention diversion:

"Okay, one way to control your anger is to distract yourself—take your attention away from the person you feel angry with. If you have to stay in the same room, concentrate very hard on an object in the room. Think of all the questions about this object that you can."

  d. Imagery manipulations:

"Another way you can prevent yourself from striking out at someone is to use your imagination. Think of something very calming and very pleasurable, like listening to your favorite music or being on the beach with the hot sun."

Physical Relaxation

  e. Muscle relaxation:

"Muscle relaxation can help you cope whenever you start to feel aroused and feel your face getting flushed or your body tightening up. It can help you learn to relax your body, which, in turn, can help you control your anger."

  f. Breathing techniques:

"Breathing is also important in learning to relax physically. Sometimes, in a tight spot, taking slow, deep breaths can give you time to get yourself together before saying or doing something you might later regret."

Palliative Coping Strategies

  g. Perspective taking:

"Let's try to look at this situation from a different perspective. What else about the situation might you be overlooking?"

  h. Social support network:

"Let's put together some people and resources you could use as a support system."

  i. Ventilation of feelings:

"Perhaps it would be helpful just to spend some time getting your feelings out in the open."

8. Client selects most useful coping strategies and practices each strategy under helper's direction.

"We've gone over a lot of possible methods to help you control your anger so it doesn't result in abusive behavior. I'm sure that you have some preferences. Why don't you pick the methods that you think will work best for you? We'll practice with these so you can get a feel for them."

Client Learning and Practice of Cognitive Coping Strategies

9. Helper describes four phases of using cognitive coping strategies to deal with a stressful situation.

"As you may remember from our earlier discussion, we talked about learning to use coping procedures at important points during a stressful or provoking situation. Now, we will work on helping you learn to use coping thoughts during these four important times: preparing for the situation, handling the situation, dealing with critical moments during the situation, and encouraging yourself after the situation."

10. For each phase, helper models examples of coping statements.

"I'd like to give you some ideas of some possible coping thoughts you could use during each of these four important times. For instance, when I'm trying to psych myself up for a stressful situation, here are some things I think about."

11. For each phase, client selects the most natural coping statements.

"The examples I gave may not feel natural for you. I'd like you to pick or add ones that you could use comfortably, that wouldn't seem foreign to you."

(continued)

12   Knowledge and Skill Builder (*continued*)

12. Helper instructs client to practice using these coping statements for each phase.

   "Sometimes, because you aren't used to concentrating on coping thoughts at these important times, it feels a little awkward at first. So I'd like you to get a feel for these by practicing aloud the ones you selected. Let's work first on the ones for preparing for a provoking situation."

13. Helper models and instructs client to practice sequence of all four phases and verbalize accompanying coping statements.

   "Next, I'd like you to practice verbalizing the coping thoughts aloud in the sequence that you'll be using when you're in provoking situations. For example, *(helper models)*.
   Now you try it."

Application of All Coping Skills to Problem-Related Situations

14. Using coping strategies and skills selected by client, helper models how to apply these in a coping manner while imagining a stressful (problem-related) situation.

   "Now you can practice using all these coping strategies when confronted with a problem situation. For example, suppose I'm you and my boss comes up to me and gives me criticism based on misinformation. Here is how I might use my coping skills in that situation."

15. Client practices coping strategies while imagining problem-related stressful situations. (This step is repeated as necessary.)

   "This time, why don't you try it? Just imagine this situation—and imagine that each time you start to lose control, that is a signal to use some of your coping skills."

16. Client practices coping strategies in role play of problem-related situation. (This step is repeated as necessary.)

   "We could practice this in role play. I could take the part of your boss and initiate a meeting with you. Just be yourself and use your coping skills to prepare for the meeting. Then, during our meeting, practice your skills whenever you get tense or start to blow up."

Application of All Coping Skills to Potential Problem Situations

17. Helper models application of client-selected coping strategies to nonproblem-related or other potentially stressful situations.

"Let's work on some situations now that aren't problems for you but could become problems in the future. This will give you a chance to see how you can apply these coping skills to other situations you encounter in the future. For instance, suppose I just found out I didn't get a promotion that I believe I really deserved. Here is how I might cope with this."

18. Client practices, as often as needed, applying coping strategies to potentially stressful situations by

   a. Imagining a potentially stressful situation:
   "Why don't you imagine you've just found out you're being transferred to a new place? You are surprised by this. Imagine how you would cope."

   b. Taking part in a role-play practice:
   "This time let's role-play a situation. I'll be your husband and tell you I've just found out I am very ill. You practice your coping skills as we talk."

   c. Assuming the role of a teacher of coping strategies:
   "This time I'm going to pretend that I have chronic arthritis and am in constant pain. It's really getting to me. I'd like you to be my trainer or helper and teach me how I could learn to use some coping skills to deal with this chronic discomfort."

Homework and Follow-up

19. Helper and client discuss application of coping strategies to *in vivo* situations.

   "I believe now you could apply these coping skills to problem situations you encounter during a typical day or week. You may not find that they work as quickly as you'd like, but you should find yourself coping more and not losing control as much."

20. Helper shows client how to use log to record uses of stress inoculation for *in vivo* situations.

   "Each time you use the coping skills, mark it down on the log and briefly describe the situation in which you used them."

21. Helper arranges for a follow-up.

   "We could get together next week and go over your logs and see how you're doing."

Observer Comments _____
_____

12 | Knowledge and Skill Builder **Feedback**

Part One

Use Figure 11.2 to compare to your handwritten model of key components in the stress response process. Use definitions in the text explaining the components to compare to your definitions. Exchange figures and descriptions of components with a classmate to see if she or he understands your portrayal and finds it sufficiently captures the key components.

Part Two

1. f.   Solution implementation and verification
2. e.   Decision-making
3. d.   Generation of alternative solutions
4. c.   Problem definition and formulation
5. b.   Problem orientation

6. a.   Rationale for problem-solving
7. b.   Problem orientation
8. c.   Problem definition and formulation
9. d.   Generation of alternative solutions
10. f. Solution implementation and verification

Part Three

Rate an audiotape of your interview or have someone else rate it, using the Interview Checklist for Problem-Solving in the Knowledge and Skill Builder.

Part Four

Use the Interview Checklist for Stress Inoculation to assess your role-play interview.

Self-Calming Approaches to Stress Management

Breathing, Muscle Relaxation, and Mindfulness Meditation

Learning Outcomes

After completing this chapter, you will be able to:

1. Demonstrate five of the six steps for diaphragmatic breathing.
2. Describe how you would apply the seven components of the muscle relaxation procedure, given a simulated client case.
3. Explain and demonstrate the body scan technique with a role-play client.
4. Teach the basics of mindfulness meditation to another person.

We all know that it is difficult to focus, learn, be open to, and feel energized for change or take on the hard work involved in helping interventions when we are wound up, fragmented, overwhelmed, and exhausted from stress. Thus, strategies such as those described in this chapter are increasingly used in conjunction with the cognitively intensive strategies that are part of the cognitive behavioral repertoire. This pairing is especially true for stress management training and as adjuncts to other interventions when skills in self-calming, physical awareness, emotional regulation, and help with focus and presence are needed. It is also important for helpers to keep in mind the value of these strategies for themselves. We previously noted the importance of self-care, and it may be particularly important when we are relatively new to the helper role, anxious, and scrambling to juggle the multiple roles of student, professional helper, family member, and so forth.

First, we present approaches to **diaphragmatic breathing**, **muscle relaxation training**, and **body scan technique**. We then discuss **meditation** procedures and the state of relaxation response—with the latter being the counterpart to fight or flight responses to stress that, over

time, can seriously erode physical and mental health. These elements can be combined with one another or with other interventions.

Within meditation, we focus particularly on mindfulness. Mindfulness meditation is not about inducing relaxation per se; rather, it promotes nonjudgmental observation of current conditions, such as intrusive thoughts, physiological arousal, or muscle tension. Achieving a more calmly aware and nonjudgmental state is important to a number of therapeutic interventions that we describe elsewhere in this book and is a core component of mindfulness-based treatments that are gaining in evidence-based strength.

The Physiology of Breathing and Stress

An overview of the physiology of breathing is helpful in explaining what happens to the mind/body when breathing is disordered. Breathing supplies the body, including, of course, the brain, with oxygen. **Respiration** (inspiration) oxygenates body cells, and **ventilation** (expiration) removes excess carbon dioxide. Inhalation or respiration brings air into the lungs. The heart takes the oxygen-rich blood from the lungs and pumps the blood through the aorta to all parts of the body. The oxygen-poor returning blood—carrying carbon dioxide—is pumped to the lungs for the exchange of gases. From the lungs, some of the oxygen moves from the air into the bloodstream. At the same time, carbon dioxide moves from the blood into air and is breathed out (ventilation).

Metabolic activity provides oxygenation to the body, a process achieved by blood circulation or by the oxygen transport system that adjusts the amount of oxygen delivery needed. Two problematic conditions include hypoventilation and hyperventilation. **Hypoventilation** stems from insufficient lung functioning, for example, due to lung disease, and is manifest by a sensation of labored breathing and deficient levels of oxygen in the blood (*hypoxemia*). **Hyperventilation** is when ventilation is too great and carbon dioxide pressure drops, resulting in deficient levels of carbon dioxide in the blood, or **hypocapnia**. Both conditions pose a serious risk of impairment to all bodily systems. Thus, we see the danger of a vicious cycle in some patterns of stress responding that include disordered breathing leading to conditions of hypoxemia and hypocapnia that significantly impair the individual's capacity to reason and function effectively and that may lead to exacerbated stress and eroded health.

Hyperventilation is often associated with stress, particularly anxiety, fear, and extreme tension. Note the correspondence between symptoms of hyperventilation with symptoms commonly associated with stress: dizziness, faintness, feeling of tension/stiffness, shivering, fatigue, sweating, rapid heartbeat, chest tightness, unrest, apprehension or anxiety, feelings of uncertainty, difficulty concentrating, and coldness of hands/feet. Many of us have had experiences where we could not get our breath or breathe well and felt a rising sense of panic, or we have found that what may have started as low anxiety quickly accelerated when we could not effectively manage our physical responding, such as breathing and heart rate. Chest or shallow breathing created by stress or by learned breathing patterns is a common element of problematic stress responding. Tools such as diaphragmatic or abdominal breathing training can help an individual learn or re-establish effective breathing, thereby avoiding physiological dysregulation and helping to foster mental relaxation.

A Focus on Diaphragmatic Breathing

There are many approaches to and dimensions of **LO1** breathing and changing breathing habits or patterns. Promoting **diaphragmatic or abdominal breathing** (usually emphasized through slow, deep patterns) is among the most common, demonstrating effectiveness in helping people become or remain calm and reduce stress (see Hendricks, 1995; Hazlett-Stevens & Craskke, 2009; van

Dixhoorn, 2007 for more complete coverage of diaphragmatic and other breathing). This practice serves to balance the sympathetic and parasympathetic nervous systems, which affect vascular functioning, heart rate, blood pressure, unconscious breathing, and digestion. The **sympathetic nervous system** (SNS) activates stress responding, which often can include disordered breathing as a normal, self-protective reaction to threatening situations. The **parasympathetic nervous system** (PNS) is important to cultivating a relaxation response that carries homeostatic and balancing function, often supported by deep, abdominal breathing.

In assessing stress, consider posing the following questions to clients: Does your chest inflate when you take a deep breath? Is your breathing typically shallow? Do you often feel that you are not getting a full breath? Do you tend to sigh? Do you feel breathless fairly often? A client with a "yes" answer to any of these questions, or to symptoms noted as common to stress and hyperventilation, may benefit from diaphragmatic breathing exercises. The positive outcomes associated with conscious or mindful breathing exercises are wide-ranging and include benefits such as releasing stress and tension, reducing chronic fatigue and burnout, building energy and endurance, contributing to emotional mastery, preventing and healing physical problems, managing pain, contributing to graceful aging, enhancing mental concentration and physical performance, and reducing psychological problems such as anxiety, phobia, panic, and depression (Busch et al., 2012; Mourya, Mahajan, Singh, & Jain, 2009; van Dixhoorn, 2007). For healthy subjects, a relaxation breathing exercise was also shown to provide acute improvement in glucose plasma levels and increased insulin response after administration of an oral glucose challenge. This provides valuable insights regarding the effect of deep breathing exercises on postprandial interpretation of glycemic index measurements used by multidisciplinary clinicians (Wilson et al., 2013).

When you are teaching awareness orientation to breathing or breathing exercises, consider diversity factors such as the client's age, ethnicity or culture, and disability status in addition to any medical or physical condition that could render these breathing exercises inappropriate. If you or the client has any doubts, instruct the client to confer with his or her primary care physician and receive approval to engage in the exercise *before* you begin the instruction.

We also note interesting developments in stress and emotion regulation strategies that engage use of computer technology such as avatars and virtual environments. Particularly with younger populations, use of models with which a client can more readily identify (than an older helper, for example) can increase acceptance and effectiveness. Wrzesien et al. (2015) illustrate benefits of physically similar avatars in applying emotion regulation treatment (such as slow breathing). The results appear to indicate significantly greater impact of the intervention on specific brain regions related to emotional arousal as well as greater identification with the physically similar avatar that was associated with activation of a brain region involved in self-awareness.

These neurological and physiological results confirm Bandura's much earlier argument for the value of identification reinforcement in treatment, encouraging assessing the value of avatars and virtual environments to bolster treatment effectiveness.

Awareness of Breathing

There are various dimensions of breath and types of problems in breathing that can be explored and addressed in the context of a helping relationship. For example, the practitioner can: (1) observe the location of the client's breath—chest for problem breathing and belly for relaxed breathing; (2) bring awareness to the client of the depth of breath—shallow for problem breathing and deep for relaxed breathing; (3) determine the rate of breathing—fast for problem breathing and slow for relaxed breathing; (4) observe whether the client holds or has a rapid exhalation of the breath; and (5) observe whether the client's inhalation is choppy and shallow.

An **awareness-of-breathing orientation** can be used to help a person become more conscious of her or his breathing. Consistent with full diaphragmatic breathing training (described next), have the client get into a comfortable position with legs parted and feet relaxed; one arm is bent at the elbow and the hand is placed on the navel, with the other hand on the chest. Ask the client to notice the movement of the hands during inhalation and exhalation and to assess which hand moves more. If the hand on the upper chest moves more than the hand below the navel, it probably means the client is breathing from the chest rather than the abdomen, in which case the breathing is shallow and not as deep, relaxed, or effective as diaphragmatic or abdominal breathing.

For some clients, this exercise brings awareness of breathing that can be helpful when the rationale and training for diaphragmatic breathing are presented. Try Learning Activity 13.1 yourself. This can provide you a way to become comfortable with the method and more mindful of your own breathing. This activity also could be used as a homework exercise for clients for whom it appears useful.

Rationale and Overview for Breathing Training

The rationale and overview for breathing training could be presented like this:

A lot of people do not breathe deeply enough. Learning to breathe with greater use of your diaphragm or abdomen can increase your oxygen intake. Increased oxygen capacity can have many mental and physical benefits, like stimulating a relaxation response and calming the central nervous system. In the beginning you might experience a little discomfort or light-headedness, but these tend to resolve quickly. If you feel any pain or discomfort, then be certain to let me know and we will stop immediately and check in on what you are experiencing. The process will include training you in abdominal breathing, or breathing with your diaphragm. You can be trained to use the breathing exercises in one session, and then you can practice during the week, 5 minutes or so at a time. The great thing is that you can practice diaphragmatic breathing any time during the day—while you are waiting in a line at the grocery store or bank or while in your car stuck in traffic. Practice will help you incorporate deep breathing in your everyday life. You will learn to use deep breathing when you are in stressful situations, or when you need a break, or for a refreshing relief to re-energize yourself. How does that sound?

Learning Activity 13.1

Breathing Exercises

In this activity, you will practice breathing exercises that will help with your teaching of others.

1. Try both the breathing awareness exercise and the diaphragmatic breathing exercise presented in the chapter. Do each exercise for several days so that you become familiar with them and consciously experience their effects.

2. Try to use the diaphragmatic breathing in *in vivo* stressful situations—whenever you need to feel calmer, more in control, or energized.

3. During a 2-week period, keep a journal or log of each practice session, describing what you experienced in your practice. Record your overall degree of relaxation, sense of control, and level of energy subsequent to your practice with the breathing exercises.

Instruction in Diaphragmatic Breathing

It may be useful to start training either by describing how a diaphragm works or with a picture that illustrates the diaphragm as a wide, fan-shaped muscle below the lungs that contracts and relaxes, pulling air in or pushing it out, respectively. You can use the following steps as a guide in teaching this exercise:

1. Providing a description of the technique

2. Finding a comfortable body position while reclining or lying on the back

3. Breathing through the nose

4. Placement of hands and visualization

5. Simulating movement of the diaphragm

6. Regular practice

Here are sample instructions to implement training:

1. Provide the client with a *description*. You can say to the client, "Notice that at the start of each breath your stomach rises and the lower edge of your rib cage expands. If your breathing is too shallow, diaphragmatic breathing should help you acquire a deeper pattern of breathing." The helper explains to the client that when a person inhales, the muscle fibers of the diaphragm contract and are drawn downward toward the abdomen, making room for the inflating lungs. A picture may help the client to visualize the movement of the diaphragm at the beginning of diaphragmatic breathing training.

2. Instruct the client to get in a *comfortable position*. Reclining or lying on the back is particularly helpful to focus on the sensations. However, a seated position also works well (with erect posture) and may be more comfortable for some clients or realistic for some settings. Legs are comfortably apart, with feet relaxed and off to the side.

3. Instruct the client to *breathe through the nose*. The helper focuses the client on the bodily sensations of breathing in and out, noting movement in the abdomen. Diaphragmatic breathing is also called belly or abdominal breathing because of the outward movement of the abdomen during inhalation and inward movement during exhalation.

4. Demonstrate *placement of hands* and *visualization*. The client is told to bend the arms at the elbow and to place the thumbs gently below the rib cage; the rest of the hand and fingers are pointing toward each other and perpendicular to the body. As the client inhales, he or she is asked to visualize the muscular fibers of the diaphragm contracting and drawing downward. Upon exhalation, the helper invites the client to visualize the diaphragm being drawn upward to form a cone shape as the air is pushed out of the lungs. A balloon image may be helpful, representing the lungs: "As you inhale, allow your abdomen to extend outward (as a balloon inflates); as you exhale, allow your abdomen to come inward (consistent with the diaphragm lifting upward to press the air out of the lungs or 'balloon.' You may wish to exaggerate this movement. Always breathe through your nostrils in an even and smooth manner. When you start, it is helpful to focus on the rise and fall of your hand as you inhale and exhale. Focus on each inhalation; your belly rises and your hand goes up. On your exhalation, press in and back on your abdominal muscles (allowing the abdomen to draw inward toward the spine), and your hand goes down. Remember, the diaphragm is a muscle, and like any muscle it can be trained and strengthened."

5. Ask the client to *simulate the movement of the diaphragm* with the hands. The thumbs are just below the rib cage on the abdomen, and the fingers are slightly interlaced. As the client inhales, the interlaced fingers are flattened to simulate the diaphragm being drawn downward. On the exhalation, the client is instructed to curve the fingers so they are cone-shaped, simulating the movement of the diaphragm drawing upward, pushing air out of the lungs. On the inhalation, the muscle fibers of the diaphragm contract and are drawn downward. The diaphragm becomes less cone-shaped and almost flat. As the diaphragm descends, it presses on the stomach, liver, and other organs and gently massages and stimulates them. Try to visualize the diaphragm working and exercising smoothly and regularly in this way.

6. Instruct the client to *practice* diaphragmatic breathing for homework, initially at least twice each day, finding a time and location that will be free of distractions and interruptions. Also, instruct the client to use abdominal or diaphragmatic breathing when in a stressful situation or to re-energize the mind or body.

Caveats with Diaphragmatic Breathing

Although the practice is helpful for many individuals, there are a few considerations related to deep abdominal/diaphragmatic breathing. Some medical or physical conditions may warrant medical consultation prior to implementation or even may contraindicate its use. Examples include injury, malformation, recent surgery affecting muscle or other tissue, conditions causing metabolic acidosis in which hyperventilation may be compensatory, such as diabetes, kidney disease, heart disease, or severe hypoglycemia, low blood pressure or related conditions such as syncope/fainting, insulin-dependent diabetes, some cases of pregnancy, and conditions associated with heavy smoking (Fried, 1993). At times individuals identify unpleasant awareness of bodily functions that previously were not noted. Relaxation-induced anxiety or discomfort related to a fear of losing control also arises for some. Although these reactions tend to occur at mild levels in a minority of people, they can be unsettling.

Because breathing training often is used to address stress related to high anxiety or panic disorder, it is important to note that breathing interventions alone are unlikely to be sufficient to fully resolve these conditions. Moreover, helpers should be observant to ensure that breath regulation does not become a method of safety-seeking or avoidance of negative physical symptoms. Although breathing retraining can be a useful coping tool, tolerance of distressing feelings like fear or anxiety or more focal attention to underlying cognitive changes are likely to be important complementary interventions.

Finally, in some cases, slower but shallower breathing may be a better-suited intervention. Recent work focusing on symptoms of panic and hyperventilation has applied **capnometry**, or the measurement of carbon dioxide in the bloodstream. One such example, capnometry-assisted respiratory training (CART), provides ongoing feedback regarding carbon dioxide levels and is proving useful in reversing hyperventilation, with the goal of normalizing respiratory physiology. Although cognitive therapy was significantly contributive to reducing panic symptoms, CART was the component that resulted in physiological alterations through its focus on hyperventilation (Meuret, Rosenfield, Seidel, Bhaskara, & Hofmann, 2010).

Muscle Relaxation

There are a number of therapeutic relaxation **L02** techniques. Our focus here is on one of the most flexible and commonly used—progressive muscle relaxation. Muscle relaxation has been used with favorable outcomes for a variety of client concerns. Examples include depression, anxiety, anger and frustration tolerance, pain, fatigue, hypertension, sleep disturbance, and generalized stress reduction (Bernstein, Carlson, & Schmidt, 2007), and include a range of populations from those with severe psychological disturbance (Vancampfort et al., 2011) to

stressed out college students (Dolbier & Rush, 2012)! Muscle relaxation appears particularly efficacious for anxiety disorders, especially more generalized conditions, demonstrating equivalent treatment effects relative to cognitive behavior therapy in some instances (Dugas et al., 2010).

The procedure of **muscle relaxation** teaches a person to relax by becoming aware of the sensations of tensing and relaxing major muscle groups. Try a simple exercise. First, make a fist with your preferred (dominant) hand. Clench the fist of that hand. Clench it tightly, and study the tension in your hand and forearm. Feel the sensations of tightness and pulling. Now release the tension in your hand and forearm. Relax your hand and rest it. Notice the difference between tension and relaxation. Do the exercise once more, but this time close your eyes. Clench your fist tightly, become aware of the tension in your hand and forearm, and then relax your hand and let the tension flow away. Notice the different sensations associated with tensing and relaxing your fist.

Did you notice that your hand and forearm *cannot* be tense and relaxed at the same time? Tension is incompatible with relaxation. Here you sent messages from your brain to your hand to impose tension and then to create relaxation. You can cue any muscle group to perform or respond in a particular manner (tense up and relax). Probably this exercise was too brief for you to notice changes in other bodily functions that become involved. Tension and relaxation can affect blood pressure, heart rate, and respiration rate, and also can influence covert processes—how we think and feel—and the way a person performs or responds overtly. One goal of muscle relaxation is that of heightening sensitivity to our bodily experience "under our skins," learning to monitor our muscular signals, and use deliberate actions of tension and relaxation to rebalance our body's reactions to stress, relieving tensions that are beyond what is constructive and can lead to distress and poor health (McGuigan & Lehrer, 2007).

The effects of muscle relaxation, like those of any other strategy, are related to satisfactory problem assessment, client characteristics, and the helper's ability to apply the procedure competently and confidently. One caution that practitioners should heed is that they should not apply relaxation training indiscriminately without first exploring the underlying causes of the client's reported tension. Hopefully the practitioner made a reasonable determination of root causes during the assessment process to inform intervention decision-making and planning. For example, is muscle relaxation a logical strategy for alleviating the client's discomfort? Is it a meaningful component of a broader intervention plan? If the client is experiencing tension in a job situation, then the practitioner and client may need to deal first with the client's external situation (the job) and/or the client's thoughts and feelings about the job context. If the client is experiencing tension as a result of oppression and discrimination, this context will need to be targeted for exploration of change possibilities. Different kinds and levels of severity of problems will involve different sets of interventions.

As previously noted, body scanning is a technique for tuning into sensations of the body. The goal of body scan is to facilitate a gentle awareness of one's body. We see this as a broadly useful exercise that can be helpful within a range of activities such as mindfulness meditation, and this enhanced awareness can facilitate muscle relaxation. Thus, rather than set a section aside for body scanning, we discuss its incorporation across several activities in this chapter. Box 13.1, following description of the muscle relaxation procedures, provides a sample script for guiding a client through a body scan. After this initial body scan training, briefer versions of the prompts may be sufficient.

Muscle Relaxation Procedure

The muscle relaxation procedure we describe here **LO3** consists of the following seven components:

1. Treatment rationale

2. Instructions about client dress

3. Creation of a comfortable environment

4. Helper modeling of relaxation exercises

5. Instructions for muscle relaxation

6. Post-training assessment

7. Homework and follow-up

Each component is described in this section. We provide very detailed descriptions of the steps associated with each part in the Interview Checklist for Muscle Relaxation in the Knowledge Builder at the end of the chapter. These descriptions can be used in practice role plays with a colleague, as guides for use in practice, or as guides to provide clients.

Component 1: Treatment Rationale

Here is an example of one way a helper might explain the *purpose* of relaxation: "This process, if you practice it regularly, can help you become relaxed. The relaxation benefits you derive can help you address (*describe their problem*)." An *overview* of the procedure might be: "The procedure involves learning to tense and relax various muscle groups

in your body. By doing this, you can become aware of and compare the differences between tenseness and relaxation. This will help you to recognize tension so you can instruct yourself to relax."

In addition, the helper should explain that muscle relaxation is a *skill*. The process of learning will be gradual and will require regular practice. The helper might explain that some discomfort may occur during the relaxation process. If so, then the client can move his or her body into a more comfortable position. Finally, the client may experience some floating, warming, or heavy sensations. The helper should inform the client about these possible sensations. The explanation of the rationale for muscle relaxation should be concluded with probing of the client's willingness to try the procedure.

Component 2: Instructions about Client Dress

Before the actual training session, clients should be instructed about appropriate clothing. They should wear comfortable clothes that will not be distracting during the exercises. Clients who wear contact lenses might prefer to wear their regular glasses for the training (as these can easily be removed during the exercises).

Component 3: Creation of a Comfortable Environment

A comfortable environment is necessary for effective muscle relaxation training. The training environment should be quiet and free of distracting noises. A padded recliner chair should be used, if possible. Alternatively, an office chair with some form of ottoman or foot/leg rest could substitute. If relaxation training is applied to groups, yoga mats, foam camping pads, or blankets can be placed on the floor, with pillows to support each client's head. Clients can lie on the floor on their backs, with their legs stretched out and their arms along their sides with palms down.

Component 4: Helper Modeling of Relaxation Exercises

Just before the relaxation training begins, the helper should model briefly at least a few of the muscle exercises that will be used in training. The helper can start with either the right or the left hand (make a fist and then relax the hand, opening the fingers), tense and relax the other hand, bend the wrists of both arms and relax them, shrug the shoulders and relax them, and continue modeling as many of the rest of the exercises as seems appropriate to set the scene for the client. The helper should tell the client that the demonstration is going much faster than the speed at which the client will perform the exercises. The helper should also punctuate the demonstration with comments like, "When I clench my biceps like this, I feel the tension in my biceps muscles, and now, when I relax and drop my arms to my side, I notice the difference between the tension that was in my biceps and the relative relaxation I feel now." These comments are used to show clients how to become attuned to and to discriminate between tension and relaxation.

Component 5: Instructions for Muscle Relaxation

Muscle relaxation training can start after the helper gives the client the rationale for the procedure, answers any questions about relaxation training, instructs the client about what to wear, creates a comfortable environment for the training, and models some of the various muscle exercises. In delivering (or reading) the instructions for the relaxation training exercises, the helper's voice should be conversational, not dramatic. We recommend that the helper practice along with the client during the beginning exercises. Practicing initial relaxation exercises with the client can give the helper a sense of appropriate timing for delivering the directions for inducing tension and relaxation and may decrease any awkwardness that the client feels about doing body exercises.

In instructing clients to tense and relax muscles, remember that you do *not* want to instruct the client to tense up as tightly as possible. You do not want clients to strain muscles or otherwise hurt themselves. Be cautious in your selection of vocabulary when giving instructions. Do not use phrases like "as hard as you can," "sagging or drooping muscles," or "tense the muscles until they feel like they could snap." You might wish to supplement instructions to tense and relax with comments about the client's breathing or the experiencing of warm or heavy sensations.

The various muscles used for client training are often categorized into 16 groups. We provide here encapsulated groupings of seven and four muscle groups, which can be useful after clients have achieved mastery with the more specific groupings (see Table 13.1; Bernstein, Carlson, & Schmidt, 2007). Generally, in initial training sessions, the helper instructs the client to exercise all 16 muscle groups. This may help the client to discriminate sensations of tension and relaxation in different parts of the body. When the client can alternately tense and relax any of the 16 muscle groups on command, you may shorten the procedure by gradually reducing the number of muscle groups involved to seven. After learning this process, the client may practice relaxation using only four groups.

When the client gets to the point of using the relaxation procedure *in vivo,* exercising four muscle groups is much less unwieldy than exercising 16!

We next describe how you, as helper, can instruct the client in relaxation of all 16 muscle groups. First, ask the client to settle back as comfortably as possible—either in a recliner chair or on the floor with the client's head on a pillow. The arms can be alongside the body, resting on the arms of the chair or on the floor, with the palms facing down. Then, instruct the client to close her or his eyes. Some clients may not wish to do this, or helper and client may decide that it might be more therapeutic for the client's eyes to remain open during training. In such cases, the client can focus on some object in the room or on the ceiling. Tell the client to *listen* and to *focus* on your instructions. When presenting instructions for each muscle group, direct the client's attention to the tension, which is held for 5 to 7 seconds, and then to the feelings of relaxation that follow when the client is instructed to relax. Allow approximately 10 seconds for the client to enjoy the relaxation of each muscle group before you deliver another instruction. Intermittently throughout the instructions, make muscle group comparisons—for example, "Is your forehead as relaxed as your biceps?" While delivering the instructions, gradually lower your voice and slow the pace of delivery. Usually each muscle group is presented twice in initial training sessions.

Here is a way the helper might proceed with initial training in muscle relaxation using the 16 muscle groups listed in Table 13.1:

1. *Dominant hand and forearm:* "First think about your dominant arm, particularly your hand. Clench your fist tightly and note the tension in the hand and in the forearm. Study those sensations of tension. *(Pause)* Now let go. Just relax the hand and let it rest on the arm of the chair [or floor]. *(Pause)* And notice the difference between the tension and the relaxation." *(10-second pause)*

2. *Nondominant hand and forearm:* "Now we'll do the same with your other hand. Clench your other fist. Notice the tension *(5-second pause),* and now relax. Enjoy the difference between the tension and the relaxation." *(10-second pause)*

3. *Dominant upper arm:* "Now clench your dominant hand into a fist and bring that toward your shoulders. As you do this, tighten your biceps muscles, the ones in the upper part of your arm. Feel the tension in these muscles. *(Pause)* Now relax. Now try pressing your elbow firmly down against the arm of the chair [or floor] and hold. Let your arm drop down to your

TABLE 13.1   Relaxation Exercises for 16, 7, and 4 Muscle Groups

16 Muscle Groups	7 Muscle Groups	4 Muscle Groups
1. Dominant hand and forearm	1. Make a fist with dominant arm in front, elbow bent at an approximately 45-degree angle (hand, lower arm, biceps muscles).	1. Right and left hands, arms, and biceps (same as 1 and 2 in 7-muscle group).
2. Nondominant hand and forearm	2. Same exercise with nondominant arm.	2. Face and neck muscles. Tense all face muscles (same as 3 and 4 in 7-muscle group).
3. Dominant upper arm	3. Facial muscle groups. Wrinkle forehead, squint eyes, wrinkle nose, clench jaws, press lips or pull corners of mouth back.	3. Chest, shoulders, back, and stomach muscles (same as 5 in 7-muscle group).
4. Nondominant upper arm	4. Press or bury chin in chest (neck and throat).	4. Both left and right upper leg, calf, and foot (combines 6 and 7 in 7-muscle group).
5. Forehead	5. Chest, shoulders, upper back, and abdomen. Take and hold deep breath, pull shoulder blades back and together, while pulling stomach in.	
6. Upper cheeks, nose, eyes	6. Dominant thigh, calf, and foot. Lift foot off chair or floor while pointing toes and turning foot inward.	
7. Lower face (tongue, jaws, lips)	7. Same as 6, with nondominant thigh, calf, and foot.	
8. Neck		
9. Shoulders		
10. Back		
11. Chest muscles		
12. Abdomen		
13. Dominant upper leg		
14. Nondominant upper leg		
15. Dominant calf and foot		
16. Nondominant calf and foot		

Adapted from Bernstein and Borkovec, 1973; Bernstein, Carlson, and Schmidt, 2007.

sides. See the difference between the tension and the relaxation." *(10-second pause)*

4. *Nondominant upper arm:* "Now let's repeat that same exercise with the other arm." *(Repeat as per above.)*

5. *Forehead:* This and the next two exercises are for the facial muscles. Here are the instructions for the forehead:

"Now we'll work on relaxing the various muscles of the face. First, wrinkle up your forehead and brow. Do this until you feel your brow furrow. *(Pause)* Now relax. Smooth out the forehead. Let it loosen up." *(10-second pause)*

6. *Upper cheeks, nose, eyes:* "Now pull your lips back firmly and scrunch up your cheeks, wrinkling your

nose. Hold that. *(5-second pause)* Then release. Now close your eyes tightly. Can you feel tension all around your eyes? *(5-second pause)* Now relax those muscles, noticing the difference between the tension and the relaxation." *(10-second pause)*

7. *Lower face—tongue, jaws, lips:* "Now clench your jaw by biting your teeth together. Pull the corners of your mouth back. Study the tension in your jaw. *(5-second pause)* Relax your jaw now and focus on the contrast." *(10-second pause)* This exercise may be difficult for some clients who wear dentures. An alternative exercise is to instruct them to "Press your tongue into the roof of your mouth. Notice the tension within your mouth. *(5-second pause)* Relax your mouth and

tongue now." *(10-second pause)* "Now press your lips together tightly. As you do this, notice the tension all around the mouth. *(Pause)* Now relax those muscles around the mouth. Enjoy this relaxation in your mouth area and your entire face. *(Pause)* Is your face as relaxed as your biceps [intermuscle group comparison]?"

8. *Neck:* "Now we'll move to the neck muscles. Press your head back against your chair. Can you feel the tension in the back of your neck and in your upper back? Hold the tension. *(Pause)* Now let your head rest comfortably. Notice the difference. Keep relaxing." *(10-second pause)* "Now continue to concentrate on the neck area. Bring your head forward. See whether you can bury your chin into your chest. Notice the tension in the front of your neck. Now relax and let go." *(10-second pause)*

9. *Shoulders:* The client can shrug one shoulder at a time or both. "Now we'll move to the shoulder area. Shrug your shoulders. Bring them up to your ears. Feel and hold the tension in your shoulders. *(Pause)* Now, let both shoulders relax. Notice the contrast between the tension and the relaxation that's now in your shoulders." *(10-second pause)* "Now take a deep breath. Hold it and pull shoulder blades together—holding this for several seconds. Now relax and notice the contrast."

10. *Back:* Be careful here; you don't want the client to get a sore back. "Now direct your attention to your upper back area. Arch your back as if you were sticking out your chest and stomach. Can you feel tension in your back? Study that tension. *(Pause)* Now relax. Notice the difference between the tension and the relaxation." *(10-second pause)*

11. *Chest muscles:* Inhaling [filling the lungs] and holding the breath focuses the client's attention on the muscles in the chest and down into the stomach area. "Now take a deep breath, filling your lungs, and hold it. Feel the tension all through your chest and into your stomach area. Hold that tension. *(Pause)* Now relax and let go. Let your breath out naturally. Enjoy the pleasant sensations." *(10-second pause)*

12. *Abdomen:* "Now think about your abdomen or stomach area. Tighten up the muscles in your abdomen. Hold this tension. Make your stomach like a knot. Now relax. Loosen those muscles now. *(10-second pause)* Is your stomach as relaxed as your back and chest [muscle-group comparison]?" An alternative instruction is to tell the client to "pull in your stomach" or "suck in your stomach."

13. *Dominant upper leg:* "I'd like you now to focus on your dominant leg. Stretch that leg. Feel tension in your thigh. *(5-second pause)* Now relax. Study the difference again between tension in the thighs and the relaxation you feel now." *(10-second pause)*

14. *Nondominant upper leg:* (Repeat as per above.)

15. *Dominant calf and foot:* "Now concentrate on your dominant lower leg and foot. Tighten your calf muscle by pointing your toes toward your head. Pretend a string is pulling your toes up. Can you feel the pulling and the tension? Notice that tension. *(Pause)* Now relax. Now point your toes downward—turning your foot in and gently curling your toes. Hold that for several seconds. Now let your leg relax, enjoying the difference between tension and relaxation." *(10second pause)*

16. *Nondominant calf and foot:* (Repeat as noted.)

After each muscle group has been tensed and relaxed twice, the helper usually concludes relaxation training with a summary and review. The helper goes through the review by listing each muscle group and asking the client to dispel any tension that is noted as the helper names the muscle area. Here is an example:

> Now I'm going to once more go over the muscle groups that we've covered. As I name each group, try to notice whether there is any tension in those muscles. If there is any, try to concentrate on those muscles and tell them to relax. Think of draining any remaining tension out of your body as we do this. Now relax the muscles in your feet, ankles, and calves. *(Pause)* Get rid of tension in your knees and thighs. *(Pause)* Loosen your hips. *(Pause)* Let the muscles of your lower body go. *(Pause)* Relax your abdomen, waist, and lower back. *(Pause)* Drain the tension from your upper back, chest, and shoulders. *(Pause)* Relax your upper arms, forearms, and hands. *(Pause)* Loosen the muscles of your throat and neck. *(Pause)* Relax your face. *(Pause)* Let all the tension drain out of your body. *(Pause)* Now sit quietly with your eyes closed.

The practitioner can conclude the training session by evaluating the client's level of relaxation on a scale from 0 to 5 or by counting aloud to the client to instruct him or her to become successively more alert. For example:

> Now I'd like you to think of a scale from 0 to 5, where 0 is *complete relaxation* and 5 is *extreme tension*. Tell me where you would place yourself on that scale now. I'm going to count from 5 to 1. When I reach the count of 1, open your eyes. Five...four...three...two...one. Open your eyes now.

Component 6: Post-training Assessment

After the session of relaxation training, the helper asks the client about the experience: "What is your reaction to the procedure?" "How do you feel?" "What reaction did you have when you focused on the tension?" "What about relaxation?" "How did the contrast between the tension and relaxation feel?" The helper should be encouraging about the client's performance, offer sincere and specific praise to the client, and build positive expectations about the training and practice.

During the initial stages of relaxation training clients may report experiences such as unfamiliar sensations, inability to relax individual muscle groups, spasms or tics, cramps, intrusive thoughts, excessive laughter or talking, falling asleep, and holding the breath.

The occurrence of unfamiliar sensations includes perceptions of floating, warmth, and headiness. The helper should point out that these sensations are not at all unusual and that the client should not fear them. If the client has difficulty or is unable to relax a particular muscle group, then the helper and client might work out an alternative exercise for that muscle group. If spasms and tics occur in certain muscle groups, then the helper can mention that these occur commonly, often during one's sleep, and that possibly the reason the client is aware of them now is that he or she is awake. If a client experiences muscle cramps, then it is possible that too much tension is being created in the muscle group being exercised. In this case, the helper can instruct the client to decrease the amount of tension.

If intrusive client thoughts become too distracting, then the helper might suggest changing the focus of thought to something less distracting or to more positive or pleasant thoughts. It might be helpful for some clients to gaze at a picture of their choosing placed on the wall or ceiling throughout the training. Another strategy for dealing with interfering or distracting thoughts is to help the client use task-oriented coping statements or thoughts that would aid in focusing on the relaxation training.

Excessive laughter or talking are most likely to occur in group-administered relaxation training as participants attempt to address self-consciousness about engaging in new body work procedures in the company of others. These behaviors tend to self-resolve as participants become more comfortable with the process, and so the helper may choose to ignore such indicators of mild anxiety unless they prove to be too distracting to the group. Another common training issue is for clients to fall asleep during relaxation training. Clients should be informed that repeatedly falling asleep can impede the learning of skills associated with muscle relaxation. By watching clients

throughout training, the helper can confirm whether they remain awake. The helper also can remind clients to stay awake during the muscle relaxation process.

Finally, some clients have a tendency to hold their breath while tensing a muscle. The helper needs to observe clients' breathing patterns during muscle relaxation. If clients are holding their breath, then the helper can instruct them to breathe freely and easily.

Component 7: Homework and Follow-up

The last step in muscle relaxation is assigning homework. Some clients will find that one or two formal sessions followed by daily home practice is sufficient; for others, four or five training sessions with daily home practice sessions may be needed. They can practice the relaxation exercises using a tape recording of the relaxation instructions or from memory. Some practitioners have found that home-based relaxation training using manuals and audiotapes or videotapes with in-session consultation can be equally effective. Regardless of the amount of time or the number of training sessions with the client, the helper should inform the client that relaxation training, like learning any skill, requires consistent practice.

The more the client practices the procedure, the more proficient he or she will become in gaining control over tension, anxiety, or stress. The client should be instructed to select a quiet place for practice, free from distracting noise. The client should be encouraged to practice the muscle relaxation exercises approximately 15 to 20 minutes twice per day. The exercises should be done when there is no time pressure. Some clients may not feel that they can schedule practice twice per day. The practitioner can encourage these clients to practice several times or as often as they can during the week. The exercises can be done in a recliner chair or on the floor, with a pillow supporting the head. The client should be encouraged to complete a homework log after each practice. Clients can rate their reactions on a scale from 0 to 5, where 0 is *complete relaxation* and 5 is *extreme tension* before and after each practice. A simple journal log can be used. However, also consider incorporating these relaxation practices into a more formal weekly log such as the mindfulness practice log in Figure 13.1. For example, use one or more of the blank lines to incorporate muscle relaxation ratings and comments.

A practitioner can use several techniques to promote client use of relaxation homework assignments. One technique is to ask the client to demonstrate during the training session how the exercises for the muscles in the neck or the calf, for example, were done during last week's home practice. The helper can select randomly from four

BOX 13.1	Body Scan Script

Allow the body to begin to completely relax. Inhale and feel the breath flow from the soles of the feet to the crown of the head, like a gentle slow motion wave. With each exhalation allow tension to flow out of the body. Bring your awareness to the fingers of the left hand. Inhale breath and awareness through the fingers and up the left arm. Exhale, release the arm into the support of the earth. Allow relaxation to deepen with each exhalation. Now bring your awareness to the right fingertips and inhale the breath up the arm, exhale, and completely relax. As you relax the arms, become more aware of all the feelings and sensations. Focus all of your awareness into these sensations and then relax into them.

Now bring your awareness down to the toes of the left foot, drawing the wave of breath up to the top of the leg, and on exhalation relax the leg fully. Now bring your awareness into the right leg, and allow the wave of breath to flow up the right leg, and with the exhalation completely surrender the weight of the leg. Feel and see both legs now and with each breath become more aware of all the sensations in the legs; with each exhalation, relax even more deeply. Listen to the sound of the waves as the breath flows through the body.

Now bring the breath and your awareness up into the hips, pelvis, and buttocks. On the inhalation, feel the pelvis area naturally expand, and on exhaling allow it to rest down into the earth. With each inhalation feel the pelvic floor being drawn gently up into the abdomen and with each exhalation allow it to completely release. Feel the wave of breath rising up from the pelvis, filling the abdomen. Feel the abdomen rise and fall, and explore the abdomen with your awareness. With each exhalation the abdomen becomes softer and softer. Feel this softness touch the lower back and feel the breath there. Explore the sensations in the low back and then allow this area to soften into the earth.

Now allow breath and awareness to flow up the spine. With each inhalation, the spine fills with sensation. With each exhalation, the spine relaxes into the earth. Feel the breath now through the entire back. Inhaling, sensing; exhaling, completely relaxing.

Now bring your awareness again to the rising and falling of the abdomen. As you inhale, draw the breath up into the solar plexus, filling that area fully with breath and awareness. And as you exhale, relax into the center of that awareness. Now focus the breath up into the heart and lungs, and with each exhalation relax deeper and deeper into the center of the heart.

Draw the breath into the neck and throat. Exhale, allowing any tension to be released. Allow the breath to flow up through the head; with each inhalation, become more aware of the sensations, and with each exhalation, relax. Relax the jaw, the eyes, the forehead, and the back of the head, soften the inner ears, and relax into the earth.

Feel the entire body now washed by a gentle wave of breath from the soles of the feet and the tips of the fingers, all the way to the crown of the head. Feel the peace and complete relaxation as the breath becomes softer and softer. Feel the sensations in the body becoming softer and more subtle and relax into them.

Now allow the wave of breath to be felt a little more strongly, rising up through the soles of the feet, and rising and falling in the abdomen. As the breath becomes stronger, allow the sensations in the body to increase. Let the body gently begin to move with the breath. Move the toes and fingers... Allow the whole body to begin to gently stretch. Remaining with the eyes closed, begin to gently roll over onto the right side. Let every movement be an experience of awareness. Over the next minute come up into a seated position. And as you come to the seated position, feel the deep three-part breath and experience how the body, breath, and mind are in balance.

Source: Integrative Yoga Therapy Manual, by Joseph LePage, pp. 7.3–7.4. Copyright ©2007 by Integrative Yoga Therapy, Shelby, North Carolina. Used by permission.

or five muscle groups for the client to demonstrate. If the exercises are demonstrated accurately, then the client probably practiced.

Strategy to Foster Body Awareness—Body Scanning

As noted, the body scan is a broadly applicable strategy to assist the client in sensing each region of the body and, thus for the present purposes, each muscle group. One approach is to tune into sensations in narrow horizontal bands—as with a CAT scan, slowing moving one's focus down from head to feet. Listening to the helper's instructions, the client focuses each breath on a particular region of the body, inhaling into that region and exhaling out of the same region. If the client feels tension in one region, then the helper instructs the client to breathe the tension out on the exhalation. In Box 13.1 we offer a detailed script for body scanning using cues to focus on the breath throughout the instructions. The body scan is a particularly useful variation of the traditional method of muscle relaxation for clients who tend to hold their breath while tensing their muscles. Additional instructions for body scanning can be found in Shapiro and Carlson (2009); instructions for deep muscle relaxation with little focus on breathing can be found in Patel (1993).

Caveats with Muscle Relaxation

Generally, muscle relaxation is benign and pleasant. As with breathing and other relaxation-oriented experiences, for some people there can be unanticipated and/or adverse side effects—such as unease with sensations, anxiety-producing thoughts, or sexual arousal (Bernstein et al., 2007). In cases of anxiety or panic disorders, the helping practitioner can start with stress reduction breathing exercises such as diaphragmatic breathing (van Dixhoorn, 2007). If a client has difficulty with a particular muscle group, the helper can avoid that group or do a body scan. Although muscle relaxation is generally well tolerated and quite beneficial, it may be contraindicated, especially early on, for clients who present with severe trauma histories because of their need to maintain some degree of vigilance to feel safe. Similarly, Taylor's (2004) findings indicated that relaxation training alone is relatively ineffective in treatment of more severe stress—such as post-traumatic stress disorder. Exposure treatment (see Chapter 14) is likely to be better suited for these populations, although self-soothing skills, such as mantra meditation used with combat veterans, have shown impressive results and are discussed later in the chapter.

Clients with muscles or connective tissues that have been damaged or are chronically weak may experience difficulty in tensing and relaxing a particular muscle group. Also, some clients are incapable of exercising voluntary control over all muscles in the body because of a neuromuscular disability. Finally, a medical consultation may be necessary before beginning muscle relaxation training with clients who are taking certain types of medication. For example, some clients who are taking medications for diabetes or for hypertension may require a change in the amount of medication they need. Be sure to seek client permission to request a medical consultation if there is a question about medications.

Model Dialogue: Muscle Relaxation

In this dialogue, the helper demonstrates relaxation **LO2** training to help Isabella deal with her physical sensations of nervousness. First, the helper provides Isabella with a *rationale* for engaging in the relaxation process. The helper explains the *purpose* of muscle relaxation and provides a brief *overview* of the procedure.

1. **Helper:** Basically, we all learn to carry around some body tension. Some is okay. But under conditions of stress, usually your body becomes even more tense, although you may not realize this. If you can learn to recognize muscle tension and relax your muscles, this state of relaxation can help to decrease your nervousness or anxiety. What we'll do is help you recognize when your body is relaxed and when it is tense by deliberately tensing and relaxing different muscle groups in your body. We should get to the point where, later on, you can recognize the sensations that mean tension and use them as a signal to yourself to relax. Does this make sense?

Client: I think so. You'll sort of tell me how to do this?

Next, the helper *sets up* the relaxation by *attending to details about the room* and the *client's comfort.*

2. **Helper:** Yes. At first I'll show you so you can get the idea of it. One thing we need to do before we start is to get you as comfortable as possible. So that you won't be distracted by brightness, I'm going to turn off the overhead light. If you are wearing your contact lenses, feel free to take them out, because you may feel more comfortable if you go through this with your eyes closed. Also, I use a special chair for this. You know the straight-backed chair you're sitting on can seem like a rock after a time. That might be distracting, too. So, I have a padded chaise that you can use for this. *(Gets lounge chair out.)*

Client *(sits in chaise):* Umm. This really is comfortable.

Next, the helper begins *to model the muscle relaxation* for Isabella. This demonstration shows her how to do it and may alleviate any embarrassment on her part.

3. **Helper:** Good. That really helps. Now I'm going to show you how you can tense and then relax your muscles. I'll start first with my right arm. *(Clenches right fist, pauses and notes tension, relaxes fist, pauses and notes relaxation; models several other muscle groups.)* Does this give you an idea?

Client: Yes. You don't do your whole body?

The helper provides *further information about muscle relaxation, describes sensations* Isabella might feel, and checks to see whether she is completely clear about the procedure before going ahead.

4. **Helper:** Yes, you do. But we'll take each muscle group separately. By the time you tense and relax each muscle group, your whole body will feel relaxed. You will feel like you are letting go, which is very important when you tense up—to let go rather than to tense even more. Now you might not notice a lot of difference right away—but you might. You might even feel like you're

floating. This really depends on the person. The most important thing is to remain as comfortable as possible while I'm instructing you. Do you have any questions before we begin, anything you don't quite understand?

Client: I don't think so. I think that this is maybe a little like yoga.

The helper proceeds with *instructions to alternately tense and relax* each of 16 muscle groups.

5. **Helper:** Right. It's based on the same idea—learning to soothe away body tension. Okay, get very comfortable in your chair, and we'll begin. *(Gives Isabella a few minutes to get comfortable, and then uses the relaxation instructions. Most of the session is spent in instructing Isabella in muscle relaxation as described earlier in this chapter.)*

After the relaxation, the helper *queries Isabella* about her feelings during and after the relaxation. It is important to find out how the relaxation process affected the client.

6. **Helper:** Isabella, how do you feel now?

Client: Pretty relaxed.

7. **Helper:** How did the contrast between the tensed and relaxed muscles feel?

Client: It was pretty easy to tell. I guess sometimes my body is pretty tense, and I don't think about it.

The helper assigns *relaxation practice* to Isabella as *daily homework.*

8. **Helper:** As I mentioned before, this takes regular practice for you to use it when you need it—and to really notice the effects. I have put the instructions on this audiotape, and I'd like you to practice with the tape each day during the next week. It is best to do the practice in a quiet place at a time when you don't feel pressured, and to use a comfortable place when you do practice. Do you have any questions? Is this something that you feel is worthwhile and that you can commit to doing?

Client: No, I don't think I have any questions right now. I understand that it will be important to practice this and I think I'll be able to fit it into my schedule with no problem. I do feel that learning this relaxation routine would be really helpful in helping me deal with some of my other issues.

Helper *explains that use of a log* can help encourage practice and chart progress.

9. **Helper:** Also, I'd like you to use a log sheet with your practice. Mark down where you practice, how long you practice, what muscle groups you use, and your tension level before and after each practice on this

6-point scale. Remember, 0 means *complete relaxation,* and 5 means *extreme tension.* Let's go over an example of how you use the log. *(The helper completes a practice example with Isabella.)* Now, any questions?

Client: No. I can see this will take some practice.

Finally, the helper arranges a *follow-up.*

10. **Helper:** Right, it really is like learning any other skill. It doesn't just come automatically. Try this on your own for 2 weeks and then we'll schedule a check-in session. Sound okay?

Learning Activity 13.2 outlines exercises that can help familiarize you with muscle relaxation.

Meditation: Processes and Uses

The usefulness of **meditation** for attaining mental calmness and physical relaxation has long been recognized. Meditation and mindfulness practices more broadly are receiving increasing clinical and empirical support for use with a range of issues commonly encountered in direct service practice, with growing understanding of the underlying processes and use with other interventions (Brown, Creswell, & Ryan, 2015 provide an overview). There are various approaches to meditation, such as forms of mantra meditation (see Carrington, 2007, for a useful overview). Although all approaches to meditation are not inherently aimed at relaxation, the effects of meditation do tend to support maintaining or re-establishing a state of relaxation. Within a stress reduction framework, the notion of cultivating a relaxation response reflects an aim of experiencing one's mind and body, much as when one perceives a relative sense of safety and control. This involves fairly observable sensations such as heart rate, breathing, and muscular tension, and it also includes observable states such as cortisol and adrenalin production.

Because the term *meditation* is used colloquially to mean many different things, it is useful to distinguish the meaning we are using in this chapter. Meditation is not about falling asleep, going into a trance, becoming lost in thought, or shutting yourself off from reality. Rather, we refer to meditation more in terms of disciplined activities to augment awareness and to foster calming or stress relaxation responding. It involves activities intended to promote selective alertness, focus, and concentration. Some forms of meditation are classified as concentrative, wherein attention is drawn to single, repetitive, or unchanging stimuli such as a mantra, sound, rhythm, image, or an object. Other forms are classified as

Learning Activity 13.2

Muscle Relaxation

Because muscle relaxation involves the alternate tensing and relaxing of muscle groups, learning the procedure well enough to use it effectively with a client is sometimes difficult. The easiest way for you to learn muscle relaxation is to do it yourself. This not only helps you learn what is involved but also may bring indirect benefits for you—increased relaxation!

In this activity, you will apply the muscle relaxation procedure you've just read about to yourself. You can do this by yourself or with a partner. You may wish to try it out alone first and then with someone else.

By Yourself

1. Check to make sure that you are wearing loose clothing, consider removing your glasses or contact lenses, and get in a comfortable position, either in a reclining chair or lying on the floor with a pillow beneath your head.
2. Use the written instructions in this chapter to practice muscle relaxation. You can do this by putting the instructions on tape or by reading the instructions to yourself. Go through the procedure quickly to get a feel for the process; then do it again slowly without trying to rely too much on having to read the instructions. As you go through the procedure, study the differences between states of muscular tension and relaxation.

3. Try to assess your reactions after the relaxation. On a scale from 0 to 5 (with 0 being *very relaxed* and 5 being *very tense*), how relaxed do you feel? Were there any particular muscle groups that were hard for you to contract or relax?
4. One or two times through the muscle relaxation process likely is not enough to learn it or to notice any positive residual effects. Try to practice this procedure on yourself once or twice daily over the next several weeks.

With a Partner

One person takes the role of helper; the other person is the client learning relaxation. Switch roles so you can practice helping someone else through the procedure as well as try it out on yourself.

1. The helper provides you with an explanation, a rationale, and an overview of the instructions for muscle relaxation before beginning the procedure.
2. The helper then reads each step of the instructions on muscle relaxation to you. The helper should give you ample time to tense and relax each muscle group and should encourage you to notice the different sensations associated with the states of tension and relaxation.
3. After going through the process, the helper should query you about your relaxation level and your reactions to the process.

---

nonconcentrative in nature, where the aim is to expand the person's field of attention to include a broad spectrum of mental activities and/or sensations and, in some cases, external stimuli. In this sense mindfulness meditation is more closely aligned with nonconcentrative approaches.

Borysenko (1987) offered the following analogy:

> Meditation is any activity that keeps the attention pleasantly anchored in the present moment. To develop a state of inner awareness, to witness and to let go of the old dialogues, you need an observation point. If you went out in a boat to view offshore tides but neglected to put down an anchor, you would soon be carried off to sea. So it is with the mind. Without an anchor to keep the mind in place, it will be carried away by the torrent of thoughts. Your ability to watch what is happening will be lost. The practice of meditation, which calms the body through the relaxation response and fixes the mind through dropping the anchor of attention, is the most important tool of self-healing and self-regulation. (p. 36)

Previously we provided an overview of purposefully concentrative strategies, including breathing and muscle relaxation skills. **Mindfulness meditation**, in contrast, is less like a laser beam and more like a searchlight that illuminates a wide range of thoughts or sensations as they arise in awareness, fostering a relaxed awareness among the changing elements of experience (Germer, 2005). Davis and Hayes (2011) define mindfulness mediation as "a moment-to-moment awareness of one's experience without judgment" and point out that different styles of meditation seem to elicit varying brain benefits and results (pp. 198–199). Two main aspects of this form of meditation are a practical perspective of the fluid, changing nature of perceived reality and a capacity to self-monitor as a present-centered, nonevaluative observer. Desbordes et al. (2014) provide a thought recommendation for equanimity (defined as even-minded mental state or dispositional tendency toward object or experiences, irrespective of pleasant or unpleasant nature) as a meditation outcome goal that is complementary to yet distinct from mindfulness and, for some clients, may be a helpful construct with challenging elements such as emotion regulation under stress.

Neurobiological Effects of Mindfulness

Recent research models are able to more precisely specify mechanisms that govern mind-body connections associated with meditation. For example, although evidence has indicated cardiovascular benefit from long-term meditation, Steinhubl et al. (2015) found significant, immediate benefits (EEG changes and decrease in blood pressure, suggesting changes in the central nervous system) even among individuals just beginning a meditation practice. Davidson (2002) used both EEG and magnetic resonance imaging (MRI) to demonstrate the promotion of neuroplasticity and ability for neural networks to grow in response to training. Valiente-Barroso (2014) summarizes neuroanatomical changes in the brain associated with meditation (particularly extensive practice), irrespective of the meditation type. These patterns of neurofunction are associated with cognitive functions crucial to learning, awareness, decision-making, and related aspects of attention, perceptual sensitivity, and inhibitory control. Xu and colleagues (2014) have shown nondirective meditation techniques to activate the area of the brain associated with daydreaming known as the Default Mode Network (DMN), which has clinical significance for psychiatric conditions associated with hyperactivation in this region, such as schizophrenia. Meditating with more concentrated foci, such as mantra meditation, reduces activation of the DMN, which is beneficial for decreasing mind wandering and improved cognitive performance (Mrazek, Franklin, Phillips, Baird, & Schooler, 2013). The findings of Wells and colleagues (2013) show meditation's ability to decrease atrophy of the hippocampus, providing a possible new adjunct modality for treatment of Alzheimer disease.

Research also has been exploring the neurobiological mechanisms through which meditation may be producing ameliorative effects. One example involves specific brain regions related to emotions and emotional regulation, through which meditation appears to foster calming and more flexible regulation in addition to physiological effects such as reduced blood pressure and agitation (Chiesa & Serretti, 2010; Hanson & Mendius, 2009; Treadway & Lazar, 2009). Related results on pain reduction suggest a functional decoupling of the cognitive-evaluative and the sensory-discriminative dimensions of pain—possibly allowing meditators to view pain more neutrally. Specifically, the use of MRI has demonstrated that meditators, compared to people who were not meditating, had reduced activity in executive, evaluative, and emotion areas of the brain during pain episodes. Individuals with the most extensive meditation experience showed the greatest pain reductions (Grant, Courtemanche, & Rainville, 2011).

However, the neurological underpinnings of mindfulness meditation appear to be nuanced. Some research, for example, illustrates stronger functional coupling among regions of the brain implicated in self-monitoring and cognitive control among experienced meditators, which may be one basis for their lower levels of mind-wandering (Brewer et al., 2011). Evidence is revealing specific changes in the body associated with gene regulatory pathways. Following intensive mindfulness practice, meditators showed a range of genetic and molecular changes that differed from nonmeditators, including reduced levels of pro-inflammatory genes. These reduced levels were, in turn, correlated with faster physical recovery from stressful conditions, which encourage further clinical research regarding the value of meditation for treatment of chronic inflammatory disorders (Kaliman et al., 2014). Collectively, these findings provide productive challenges to some current concepts related to pain, emotion regulation, and cognitive control, suggesting particular benefits from the more "passive" methods of mindfulness.

Mindfulness Meditation Overview

We focus on mindfulness meditation because of its explicit linkage with thought and feeling processes, rapidly growing application in psychological practice, and promising evidence of effectiveness (Baer, 2003; Davis & Hayes, 2011). Although consistent with other cognitive behavioral methods described in this book, meditation therapy provides distinct and complementary tools. For example, whereas some cognitive interventions focus on changing the content of a client's problematic thoughts (e.g., "I am a failure"), mindfulness meditation therapy focuses more on altering the client's attitude or relationship to the thought. This approach may include regarding thoughts as similar to the five senses in that negative thoughts are noticed as "**thought stimuli**" (akin to smell or hearing stimuli) and accepted as natural behavior of the mind but not as inherently defining the self or dictating subsequent feelings or actions.

Focusing on mindfulness meditation in particular, Marlatt and Kristeller (1999) noted the element of being aware of the full range of experiences that exist in the here and now. They added that mindful awareness is based on an attitude of acceptance. Rather than judging one's experiences as good or bad, healthy or sick, worthy or unworthy, mindfulness accepts all personal experiences (e.g., thoughts, emotions, events) as just "what is" in the present moment (p. 68). One important clinical application of mindfulness is developing the capacity of an "**observing self**" that can see thoughts as "just thinking" rather than as facts or directives. The observing self is also described as "metacognitive awareness" and "metacognitive insight" in which emotions are viewed as passing events rather than inherent aspects of oneself (Teasdale, Moore, Hayhurst, Pope, Williams, & Segal, 2002, p. 285)

There are levels of mindfulness. We can periodically disengage from the tumble of our ongoing experiences to purposefully stop and deliberately focus our attention on what we are sensing, feeling, and thinking at the moment—to what is going on and how are we responding. Because you are likely to be using these techniques with clients for whom this is a new experience, we focus on beginning levels of mindfulness practice. Meditation is like other skills in that practice is needed to establish comfort, skill, and sustainable incorporation into one's life.

Examples of more intensive approaches can be found in Germer et al. (2005), Segal, Williams, and Teasdale (2013), and a practical workbook for practitioners by Teasdale, Williams, and Segal (2014). Kabat-Zinn (2003) provides an overview of the background of mindfulness practice, issues related to culture, and recommendations for training. Lee and colleagues (2009) present an extensive integrated description with case illustrations and practice guidelines. Hamilton, Kitzman, and Guyotte (2006) offer a summary of mechanisms through which mindfulness meditation is understood to help support stress reduction, cognitive change, and adaptive coping response patterns. Davis and Hayes (2011) provide a summary review of mindfulness with an eye toward specific evidence-based effects and benefits.

Mindfulness Meditation Procedure

The major components of mindfulness meditation include the following components:

1. Treatment rationale and overview

2. Inform client about attitudinal foundations for practice

3. Discuss commitment, self-discipline, and energy

4. Prepare for meditation

5. Perform a body scan to enhance bodily awareness

6. Provide instructions for breathing

7. Provide instructions for when the mind wanders

8. Instructions for beginning meditation

9. Postmeditation assessment of the experience

10. Provide homework and follow-up

Each component will be described in this section. In addition we also provide very detailed descriptions of the steps for mindfulness meditation in the form of an Interview Checklist included in the Knowledge and Skill Builder section at the end of the chapter. These descriptions can be used in practice role-plays with a colleague, in helping sessions, or as guides to provide to clients for home implementation.

Component 1: Treatment Rationale

Here is an example of how a helper might explain the *purpose* of meditation:

> "I would like to teach you mindfulness meditation. Meditation is an activity that can be used to root your attention into the present moment by sitting calmly with your eyes closed and focusing on your breath. Mindfulness meditation helps you to increase inner awareness while witnessing the abundance of thoughts that parade through the mind, and simultaneously letting them go through nonattachment. It may bring new insights about yourself and a new way of seeing and doing in your life."
>
> An overview of meditation might be: "First you select a quiet place in which to meditate. You will then get into a relaxed and comfortable position. With your eyes closed, you will allow your thoughts to flow freely. If your mind wanders off, you can bring it back by focusing on the breath. You will meditate for 10–20 minutes. Then, we will talk about the experience. How do you feel about taking part in a practice meditation?"

Component 2: Attitudinal Foundations for Practice

Mindfulness meditation is about letting go and watching or witnessing whatever comes up from one moment to the next. To enhance the practice of meditation, a participant needs definitions about core concepts of mindfulness (Kabat-Zinn, 2005). Experience suggests that understanding and valuing these concepts is essential to successful meditation. Moreover, it is not uncommon for people reared in North American culture to struggle with incorporating the underlying attitudes and "habits of mind" (Kabat-Zinn, 1991). see Box 13.2 on page 476. Attitudinal Foundations for Mindfulness Meditation for elaboration.

Component 3: Instruction about Commitment, Self-Discipline, and Energy

Mindfulness meditation is insight-oriented and is intended to enhance well-being and awareness and to discipline one's mind and emotions. The skills do not necessarily come easily, requiring a commitment similar

BOX 13.2	Attitudinal Foundations for Mindfulness Meditation

1. *Nonjudging* means that mindfulness is aided by being an impartial witness or observer to one's own experience. We have a habit of categorizing or judging our experiences, which locks us into unaware "knee-jerk" or mechanical reactions that often do not have an objective basis. For example, you can be practicing and think about all the things you have to do and how boring the practice is. These are judgments that take you away from observing whatever comes up. If you pursue these thoughts, it takes you away from moment-by-moment awareness. To remedy this, just watch your breathing.

2. *Patience* means that we often have to allow things to unfold in their own time. Practicing patience means that we don't have to fill our lives with moments of doing and activity.

3. *Expectations of the beginner's mind* are often based on our past experiences or cognitive schema, but they prevent us from seeing things as they really are. It is important for beginning meditators to be open to moment-by-moment experiences without framing the moment with expectations of how we think the moment will be.

4. *Trust* is about developing confidence in your feelings and intuition. Clients are instructed to trust their feelings and wisdom, not discount them. For example, if you are sitting in a particularly uncomfortable posture while meditating, change to another posture that feels better. If your intuition says to do this, follow what your intuition is telling you and experiment to find a way that matches your needs. The message is to obey and have faith in what your body or feelings are telling you.

5. *Nonstriving* means that mindfulness meditation is about the process of practice and not about striving to achieve something or get somewhere. Instruct clients to experience the moment; they do not have to get anywhere—just attend to or be with whatever comes up.

6. *Acceptance* means not worrying about results. Instruct the client to just focus on seeing and accepting things as they are, moment by moment, and in the present.

7. *Letting go* means nonattachment or not holding on to thoughts. If, for example, a client becomes judgmental, instruct the client to let go and just observe the judging mind (Kabat-Zinn, 1991; p. 33–40).

8. *Decentering* refers to a "view of emotions as impermanent entities with which we can engage, without avoiding or becoming entangled" (Hays & Feldmann, 2004; p. 257), which has increasingly become viewed as a principle mechanism underlying mindfulness (Feldman, Greeson, & Senville, 2010).

to that which would be required in athletic training. Clients should be reminded not to be discouraged if it feels difficult or awkward, instead reinforcing the importance of making a serious commitment to working on themselves, recognizing the importance of self-discipline, perseverance, and sustained energy. As with many health-promoting activities, we do not have to like it—we just have to do it. Recommend a realistic period of time—as one would with any new athletic skill—such as 6 to 8 weeks of practice. At this point the client will be better equipped to evaluate whether and in what the meditation has been useful. Hopefully, in addition to recognizing the benefits of meditation, clients will appreciate the gift they give themselves of a mini-vacation in which they focus simply on *being* rather than *doing*!

Component 4: Preparations for Meditation

The location should be comfortable and free of interruptions. The recommended pose for mindfulness meditation is a *sitting posture* on a chair or on the floor (with a cushion if on the floor). These guidelines provide detail regarding posture and comfort. Some people prefer to meditate while lying on their backs, but we find that some clients who meditate lying down fall asleep, especially early on in their training and practice. They associate relaxation with sleep and subsequently lose consciousness. After meditating for a couple of weeks, however, these clients start to maintain awareness and decrease their urge to sleep.

Component 5: Body Scan to Enhance Bodily Awareness

The helper often begins mindfulness mediation by introducing the body scan (described in this chapter in Box 13.1), which involves focusing on one's breath and systematically directing attention to each part of one's body—attending to sensations, whether of pleasure or discomfort, without judgment of these sensations. As previously noted, the body scan helps the client to enhance mind-body awareness to the moment and can be used in conjunction with a range of strategies.

Component 6: Breathing Instructions

The client is instructed to focus on the breath as it flows in and out. Ask the client to notice the difference in temperature of the inhaled breath and the exhaled breath and to feel the sensations of the air as it moves in and out of the nostrils. See the guidelines presented and the next section on breathing for more detail.

Component 7: Instructions about the Mind Wandering

Attention is often carried away by thoughts cascading through the mind. A common term to describe this phenomenon is the monkey mind—when the unfocused mind is compared to a monkey jumping from one tree branch to another. The opposite may be thought of as the donkey mind, referring to rigid fixation on a thought or image, like a donkey bound to a stake by its own leash (Hoffman, 2008). Instruct clients that when this happens, they are to return their attention to the flow of their breathing and to let go of the thoughts. Note that this level of meditation is designed to focus on breathing. Initially, what matters is whether you are aware of your thoughts and feelings during meditation and how you handle them.

Mindfulness meditation is not intended to stimulate thinking per se, or analysis of one's thinking. Rather, the intent is to make room for awareness—without reaction (**reactance** = response to perception of impingement on psychological freedom) or analysis—of one's thoughts, emotions, and sensations on a moment-to-moment basis. If the client feels cornered or trapped by a thought, feeling, sensation, sound, pain, or discomfort, encourage a return of attention to breathing and a focus on letting go by exhaling the distractions. As the client gains experience with meditation, a conscious and deliberate shift can be made to follow the stream of thoughts in the manner of just noticing—without judgment or attempt to control—what predominates in awareness.

Component 8: Instructions to Begin Meditation

The helper can now instruct the clients to sit quietly, close their eyes, be present in the moment, and to meditate for 10 to 20 minutes following the guidelines. The helper can be the timekeeper and assist the clients in knowing when to start and stop the meditation. After clients conclude the meditation, they may wish to sit quietly as they reconnect with their external environment, then gently move or stretch, and just relax for a few moments before opening their eyes.

Component 9: Postmeditation Assessment of the Experience

Once the client has returned full attention to the helping session, the helper should invite discussion of the

client's experience and reaction to meditation. Clients may be unsure of themselves because they are judging the process. The helper should model a nonjudgmental stance about what clients experience. For example, if clients say that most of their meditation session entailed chasing after thoughts, encourage them to continue meditating appreciating that meditation, especially early on, can feel like a battle for cognitive control. Every practice will be different, and it is the process of the experience that is important. The focused attention component is relatively familiar—bringing attention back to a particular object of focus such as one's breathing or a mantra or visual object. The open awareness component takes time. van Vugt (2015) refers to open awareness as the process of observing in a relatively detached manner what may be distracting. For example, rather than behaviorally respond to the thought "I want ice cream" (by going to the kitchen), watch the thought and allow it to pass. The development of this capacity for nonattached observing that may, in time, foster cognitive flexibility and less susceptibility to strong emotion.

Component 10: Homework and Follow-up

It is recommended that clients find a *special place* in their homes to meditate as well as set aside a particular *block of time* every day to practice meditation. We find that a 3-week period is minimally necessary for a practice to take hold, but ideally it would be at least 6 days per week for at least 6 to 8 consecutive weeks. There are practical considerations in planning meditation sessions as well, such as avoiding meditation within 1 hour after eating. If meditation is done in the evening, it is best not to engage in the process immediately before bedtime. Figure 13.1 provides an example of a practice log that can be used to prompt, keep up with, and reflect on one's mindfulness meditation experiences over time. Note that this could be modified a number of ways to reflect the schedule and priorities of the client, as well as incorporating other activities such as muscle relaxation. Chapter 15 on self-management also offers other examples of practice and monitoring approaches that can be used with calming or other self-change strategies. Finally, you can also encourage the client to seek mindful awareness throughout the day while, for example, eating, getting stuck in traffic, doing everyday tasks, and interacting with people. The mantra is "to be here now," "be in the moment," and "be present with what you are experiencing—in feeling and thought."

Name: _____

Week of: _____   Target No. of Days/Time: _____

Monday	Tuesday	Wednesday	Thursday	Friday	Saturday	Sunday
☐ 5 min ☐ 10 min ☐ 20 min ☐ ____ ☐ Day off	☐ 5 min ☐ 10 min ☐ 20 min ☐ ____ ☐ Day off	☐ 5 min ☐ 10 min ☐ 20 min ☐ ____ ☐ Day off	☐ 5 min ☐ 10 min ☐ 20 min ☐ ____ ☐ Day off	☐ 5 min ☐ 10 min ☐ 20 min ☐ ____ ☐ Day off	☐ 5 min ☐ 10 min ☐ 20 min ☐ ____ ☐ Day off	☐ 5 min ☐ 10 min ☐ 20 min ☐ ____ ☐ Day off
Note:	Note:	Note:	Note:	Note:	Note:	Note:

Getting to It: What strategies (time of day, place, timers, etc.) made it easiest to practice this week?

Quality of Practice: What strategies (type of focus, refocus technique, etc.) helped you to improve the quality of your practice?

Changes in Daily Life: Did you notice any benefits in your daily life (patience, calmer, etc.) from your practice this week?

Plans for Next Week: What is one thing you can do next week to improve practice and/or maximize benefits?

FIGURE 13.1 Mindfulness Practice Log: Weekly Version

Caveats with Meditation

Meditation does not come naturally for some people. Western predilections to *do* something, and to actively dig in to solve problems, present a potentially discordant starting point. Progress through meditation strategies often does not come quickly. It generally takes time to feel less self-conscious about use of the techniques and to slow down and reorient one's habits of responding to thoughts, emotions, physical sensations, and external phenomena to experience the benefits. Thus, it is important to alert clients to the incremental nature of change and to encourage discipline and persistence through the initial stages.

It also is important to be aware of cautions about using meditation and mindfulness. For example, although these strategies have demonstrated effectiveness for dealing with stress and a range of other difficulties and disorders, they are not intended to promote avoidance, but rather they are designed to support more effective responses to life challenges. A relaxed state is one potential outcome; however, meditation also increases awareness of the salience of one's internal entanglements and may present a challenge to attainment of a state of relaxed openness.

Meditative states can foster feelings that clients experience as contradictory to current perceptions of themselves, such as feelings of well-being or optimism for depressed or distrustful individuals. Similarly, pleasurable sensations that emerge during meditation may be experienced as frightening or inappropriate, thus evoking anxiety or reactivity in individuals who have high needs for a sense of control and discipline (Carrington, 2007). These, or other sensitivities, may argue for shorter periods of meditation than might be recommended for other clients.

Some clients may release emotional material that surprises them or that they find difficult to handle. This problem is especially relevant to clients with a trauma history, underscoring caution with these clinical groups. If counter-reactions arise, then the practitioner may determine that it is in the clients' best interests to use additional therapeutic tools such as reframing, cognitive restructuring, stress inoculation training, or acceptance-oriented strategies. Kristeller (2007), for example, noted feelings of "defenselessness" that can arise, potentially leading to emotionality manifesting in fear, anger, or despair. Clients' displays of such feelings often can provide important opportunities for inquiry and insights but must be handled sensitively.

Goleman (1988) pointed out that some clients with psychological conditions such as schizoid disorder may become overly absorbed in their inner experiencing and less connected with external reality if they meditate.

Additionally, although meditation is generally well suited for soothing stress, some individuals in acute emotional states may be too agitated to undertake meditation, whereas others may be grappling with conditions, such as obsessive-compulsive disorder, that predispose them to engaging in meditation in ways that defeat its purpose. Some clients may become disconcerted by sensations of dissociation (e.g., feelings of floating or of being in a trance, sometimes with disturbing thoughts flooding the mind), or may have heretofore repressed or forgotten experiences surface to awareness (Kristeller, 2007). Such reactions to meditation may contraindicate its use or suggest the need for modified approaches such as journaling following meditation or adjunctive treatment components.

Finally, the action of certain drugs may be affected by meditation. Helpers and clients are therefore reminded of the value of monitoring reactions when practicing meditation if anti-anxiety, antidepressive, antihypertensive, or thyroid-regulating drugs are being used (Carrington, 2007). The continued practice of meditation may result in lower dosages being required of some medications. This determination would, of course, be made in consultation with the client's primary care physician, prescribing psychiatrist, or other medical practitioner. To this end, it is crucial that the helping professional be aware of any medication the client is taking and possible interactions with helping processes such as meditation.

Integration of Mindfulness with Other Interventions

Meditation practices have deep roots in many cultures of the world. Chen (2006a, b) described aspects of meditative practices from Buddhist and Taoist traditions, illustrating integrative perspectives of mind-body connections. Although deriving from these Buddhist meditative traditions, mindfulness training and meditation largely have been pursued in a secularized form, often incorporated with other intervention strategies across both physical and psychological disorders, and spanning multiple theoretical orientations (Baer, 2003; Germer, Siegel, & Fulton, 2005). The use of meditation and mindfulness as treatment components has been well-illustrated across broadly ranging populations and problem targets (Baer, 2006; Lee, Ng, Leung, & Chan, 2009; Davis and Hayes, 2011).

Mindfulness-based stress reduction (MBSR) has been extensively studied, showing robust empirical support for conditions such as anxiety, depression, panic, and eating disorders, as well as fostering an increased sense of compassion and self-esteem (Kabat-Zinn, 1991; 2005;

Miller, Fletcher, & Kabat-Zinn, 1995; Birnie, Speca, & Carlson, 2010; Holzel-Lazar, Vago, Ott, 2011). Dutton et al. (2013) provide a detailed process-oriented account of applying MBSR with low income, predominantly African American women with PTSD and a history of intimate partner violence. This purposeful application with a highly vulnerable, underserved, difficult to reach, and clinically complex population surfaced useful insights, such as the need to emphasize the secular nature of mindfulness to minimize perceived conflict with religious values, the need for clear expectations and guidelines as well as continual feedback regarding practices and progress, and the potential for unintended effects such as body scanning triggering panic responses. They achieved overall positive findings regarding acceptability and feasibility informed by practical considerations regarding successful implementation and sustainability success with populations coming for service with both trauma histories and cumulative and enduring life stressors such as poverty, discrimination, and family instability factors that require services to be highly attentive to context.

Mindfulness-based cognitive therapy (MBCT) is a hybrid of major elements of MBSR and aspects of cognitive therapy designed to target relapse prevention for depression (for an overview see Irving, Farb, & Segal, 2015). Extended application has shown efficacy for diverse clinical conditions, such as improved emotional regulation in incarcerated youth (Leonard et al., 2013) and treatment of chronic fatigue and anxiety (Marchand, 2012). MBCT has proven sufficiently successful for treatment of Major Depressive Disorder, and it is now included as a group intervention in the American Psychiatric Association's Practice guidelines for treatment (Marchand, 2012; Piet & Hougaard, 2011). MBCT is increasingly being applied to a range of disorders with generally promising findings, particularly with anxiety-related and depression-related problems. Some of these applications do not, however, specify formal meditation, orienting more to mindfulness exercises and philosophy, which raises uncertainty regarding whether mindfulness is an active ingredient of MCBT or whether MCBT outperforms standard interventions such as cognitive behavioral therapy (Metcalf & Dimidjian, 2014).

Mindfulness meditation is a component in dialectical behavior therapy (DBT) where brief meditation is often taught (Dimidjian & Linehan, 2003; 2009) and has been used in the treatment of varying forms of chronic mental illness, such as borderline personality disorder (Bach, Gaudiano, Pankey, Herbert, & Hayes, 2006; Linehan, 1993a; Welch, Rizvi, & Dimidjian, 2006). DBT is designed for individuals with heightened sensitivity

to and intense experiencing of emotion, who often are at high risk for impulsivity and self-injury. The word *dialectical* refers to a balance or middle place that must be achieved between, for example, acceptance and change, in the service of balancing and regulating conflicting thoughts, feelings, and behaviors. A **wise mind** represents the middle ground, and most desirable state, between the extremes of a completely rational mind and the tumultuous currents of a wholly emotional mind. DBT comprises four foundational modules of coping strategy and skill development (Linehan, 1993a): (1) nonjudgmental mindfulness; (2) distress tolerance; (3) emotional regulation; and (4) interpersonal effectiveness.

Of these four skill modules, mindfulness skills, along with distress tolerance skills, have been found to be the most commonly practiced by the patients in standard DBT treatment (Lindenboim, Comtois, & Linehan, 2007). A similar study of skill usage found that mindfulness techniques were the most common skills used in everyday life by DBT clients (Stepp, Epler, Jahng, & Trull, 2008), underscoring the centrality of mindfulness in DBT skills training. DBT developer Linehan's conceptualization (1993b; Dimidjian & Linehan, 2003) differentiates three qualities when practicing mindfulness: (1) observing, noticing, bringing awareness; (2) describing, labeling, noting; and (3) participating, with an emphasis on a nonjudgmental approach and focus in the present moment. Targeting clients with borderline personality disorder—who demonstrate attention deficits and impulsivity—Soler et al. (2012) found positive effects, relative to a client comparison group, in both attention and impulsivity. Longer mindfulness practice was correlated with prominent reduction in depressive, confusion symptoms and reactivity to inner experiences. Although there may be variation in ways the mindfulness core is administered across therapists and settings and the extent to which meditative practice per se is emphasized, mindfulness skills have emerged as deeply important for vulnerable client populations for which DBT is designed (Rizvi, Steffel, & Carson-Wong, 2013).

The combination of acceptance and mindfulness-oriented procedures with interventive strategies such as behavioral contracting, exposure-based methods, and cognitive modification has proven highly effective and serves as an illustration of one of the integrated practice models that are becoming increasingly important in a helping professional's repertoire. Others modalities include acceptance and commitment therapy (Hayes & Strosahl, 2004), incorporation of mindfulness into extant treatments for generalized anxiety disorder (Borkovec, Alcaine, & Behar, 2004) and post-traumatic stress disorder (Orsillo & Batten, 2005), as well as addiction treatment (Witkiewitz, Marlatt, & Walker, 2005; Bowen, Chawla, & Marlatt, 2011). (see Learning Activity 13.3).

Model Example of Mindfulness Meditation

In this model example, we present a narrative **LO4** account of how mindfulness meditation might be used with a 49-year-old Japanese American male client. Yoshi, an air traffic controller, has reported that he would like to decrease the stress he experiences in his job. He believes that decreasing his stress will help to heal his ulcer and allow him to cope better with the demands of his job. In addition to describing the physical signs of stress (hypertension), Yoshi reports that he worries constantly about making mistakes at work. Note that, in addition to this example, Learning Activity 13.3 offers you an opportunity to rehearse skills related to providing meditation guidance as well as meditative practices yourself.

Treatment Rationale

First, we explain to Yoshi that mindfulness meditation can be used to assist people in coping with job-related stress. We tell him that the procedure also is used to help people with high blood pressure and anxiety as well as those who

want to feel more alert. We provide an overview of mindfulness meditation, informing Yoshi that the process is undertaken while seated in a quiet place, with eyes closed, allowing thoughts to flow freely. We recommend that he redirect his focus to his breathing if his thoughts become too distracting, and we advise him that most people using this technique meditate for 10 to 20 minutes per day. We illustrate the foundational attitudes that contribute to the building of a meditative practice. Finally, we confirm Yoshi's willingness to try meditation, and we answer any questions he has about the process.

Attitudinal Foundations for Practice

We describe to Yoshi the attitude frameworks that are conducive to mindfulness meditation. We advise him that mindfulness is facilitated if we avoid the human tendency to categorize experiences and instead endeavor to be nonjudgmental and impartial witnesses or observers of our experiences. We explain to Yoshi that we don't have to fill every moment of our lives with doing and activity. We ask him to be patient and to allow things to unfold in their own time while he is meditating. We tell him that beginners usually have expectations about what will happen while they are meditating, and we urge him simply to be open to the moment-by-moment experiences without injecting expectations based on past experience. We encourage Yoshi to trust his feelings and intuition; there

Learning Activity 13.3

Meditation Exposure

Part One

The teaching of meditation is a psychoeducational process. The helper provides the instructions, and the client engages in meditation in a self-directed manner. To practice giving instructions to someone about meditation, select a partner or a role-play client, and give instructions. This can focus on mindfulness techniques as described in the Interview Checklist for Mindfulness Meditation at the end of the chapter, or another type such as a more concentrative approach where one may focus on a sound or image. Then assess how well your partner was able to implement your instructions. If you wish, reverse roles so that you can experience being instructed by another person.

Part Two

This activity provides an opportunity to engage in a meditation session. Do this in a quiet, restful place where you will not be interrupted for 20 minutes. Do *not* do this within 1 hour after a meal or within 2 hours of going to sleep.

1. Get into a comfortable sitting position and close your eyes.
2. Relax your entire body. Think about all the tension draining out of your body.
3. Meditate for 10 to 20 minutes. The following are brief guidelines for a concentrative approach.
   a. Breathe easily and naturally through your nose.
      i. Focus on your breathing with the thought of a word or phrase. Say (or think) your word or phrase silently each time you inhale and exhale.
   b. If other thoughts or images appear, don't dwell on them, but don't force them away either. Just relax and focus on your selected word/phrase or your breathing.
4. Reflect on your reactions to your meditative experience:
   a. How did you feel about engaging in the meditative process?
   b. How did you feel after completing the meditation session?
   c. What sorts of thoughts or images came into your mind?
   d. How much difficulty did you have with distractions? How did you deal with this?
5. Practice twice daily for a week, if possible.

is no "right" or "correct" way to meditate. We ask him to experiment with the process to learn what best fits his needs, and to trust and obey what his feelings and intuition tell him. We explain that mindfulness meditation is about the process of practice and is not about striving to achieve something or to get somewhere. We talk to Yoshi about letting go and experiencing nonattachment—not holding on to thoughts and feelings. All Yoshi has to do is to be "in the moment," to attend to or be with whatever comes up. Finally, we speak about acceptance and encourage him not to worry about the outcome—to instead see and accept the way things are, in the present.

Instruction about Commitment, Self-Discipline, and Energy

We tell Yoshi to commit to practicing mindfulness in much the same way an athlete would commit to training. Yoshi understands that he must make a firm commitment, discipline himself to persevere, and generate enough energy so that he can develop a strong meditative practice.

Preparations for Meditation

We ask Yoshi to set aside a block of time each day and to meditate at least 6 days per week. We recommend that he find a quiet and special place where he can meditate without interruption, and note that meditation should be performed in a sitting position with the back straight. We encourage Yoshi to meditate for 8 weeks so that he can become adjusted to the process. We instruct him not to meditate within 1 hour after eating and to wear comfortable clothing during the practice time.

Body Scan to Enhance Bodily Awareness

We conduct a body scan with Yoshi and suggest he consider this scanning of different muscle groups of his body as a kind of purification process. We explain that this can bring mind-body awareness into the moment and, when joined with other techniques like breathing, may foster a more relaxed physical experience.

Breathing Instructions

Some recommend a deep breathing approach, encouraging clients to notice sensations such as how their belly expands on the inhaled breath and falls on the exhaled breath or the sensation of the air as it goes in and out of one's nostrils. Others, however, raise concern that this may distract from a peaceful mind and instead recommend natural, calm breathing. We are inclined to recommend the latter to Yoshi, but this option can be explored with the client.

Instructions about the Mind Wandering

Yoshi notes that his attention often is carried away by cascading thoughts. We tell him that there is nothing wrong with that; when it happens, he is just to return his attention to the flow of breathing and let the thoughts go. We encourage him to be aware of his thoughts and feelings during meditation. If he gets caught up with a thought, feeling, bodily sensation, sound, pain, or discomfort, then he is to bring his attention back to breathing and exhale those distractions.

Instructions for Meditating

We instruct Yoshi to sit quietly and get relaxed for approximately 1 minute. Then, he is to close his eyes and focus on his breathing. As the air comes in and goes out, he is to "ride" the tide of his breath. We tell Yoshi that mindfulness meditation is not an exercise and requires no effort; he can't force it. We mention to him that if distracting thoughts, feelings, sensations, or sounds occur, then he should allow them to come, and not try to influence them. He simply should observe them and then return to awareness of his breathing: "The air comes in and goes out." We tell Yoshi that he will meditate for 10 to 20 minutes. When the time is up, we ask him to come out of the meditation slowly by sitting with his eyes closed for approximately 1 minute and inform him that he may want to move and stretch. We instruct Yoshi to notice and absorb what he is experiencing and then to open his eyes slowly.

Inquiring about the Just-Completed Meditation Experience

We ask Yoshi a series of questions about his experience: "How did you feel about the experience? How did you handle distractions? What are your feelings right now?"

Homework

We instruct Yoshi to select a special time to meditate once per day, preferably in the morning soon after he wakes up. We advise him not to meditate within an hour after eating or within 2 hours of going to sleep. We remind Yoshi of the things to do to prepare: find a quiet environment, assume a comfortable sitting position, do a quick body scan, and remember the foundational attitudes and the requirements of commitment, discipline, and energy. Beyond the formal daily meditation session, we encourage Yoshi to try to be increasingly mindful and aware throughout the day, with an emphasis on present-centered, moment-by-moment openness to experience.

Applications of Meditation for Diverse Issues and with Diverse Clients

Although no one intervention strategy is a silver bullet or is appropriate for all people or circumstances, meditation is becoming a common tool in a variety of therapeutic and self-development contexts. Goyal and colleagues (2014), Carrington (2007), and Kristeller (2007) reviewed some of the symptoms or difficulties for which a person might benefit from meditation: tension and/or anxiety states; psychophysiological disorders; chronic fatigue states, insomnias, and hypersomnias; alcohol, drug, or tobacco abuse; depression, anger, and irritability; low frustration tolerance; difficulties with self-assertion and self-blame; pathological bereavement reactions; blocks to productivity or creativity; inadequate contact with affective life; breathing problems such as asthma; hypertension; stuttering; pain management; and adherence to dietetic treatment for diabetes or obesity.

Several reviews of the physical and psychological applications of meditation and mindfulness, such as the meta-analysis by Sedlmeier and colleagues (2012), illustrate the range of its uses (Baer, 2006; Germer, Siegel, & Fulton, 2005; Greeson, 2009; Roemer & Orsillo, 2009). Davis and Hayes (2011) summarize effects of mindfulness on therapists and helpers as well as clients. Meditation is increasingly used in health care settings across a range of problems and populations. Ott (2004) and colleagues illustrated the value of mindfulness meditation in pediatric medicine, with recent meta-analyses indicating particular promise for youth who suffer from high levels of symptomology, such as youth found in settings such as clinics, hospitals, homeless shelters, and child welfare and juvenile justice settings (Zoogman, Goldberg, Hoyt, & Miller, 2014). Curiati and colleagues (2005) reported positive outcomes with elderly patients. Gallegos and colleagues (2013) also demonstrated improved immune system function in older adults with use of mindfulness therapy. Williams and colleagues (2005) and Brazier, Mulkins, and Verhoef (2006) similarly evaluated findings as beneficial for patients with terminal or late-stage disease. Not surprisingly, mindfulness has been applied to reduce stress and pain among patients with difficult and potentially relapsing conditions such

as cancer (Kvillemo & Bränström, 2011; Matchim, Armer, & Stewart, 2011) and multiple sclerosis (Tavee & Stone, 2010), with robust support by meta-analytic evaluation across studies wherein improvement of emotional distress and mental health were found (Ledesma & Kumano, 2009). Hoge and colleagues (2013) and Carlson and colleagues (2014) have shown mindfulness practices alter gene expression through improved length of telomeres, holding clinical relevance for diseases associated with short telomeres such chronic stress, accelerated aging, and even cancer.

Addictions and relapse prevention is an arena in which mindfulness is rapidly advancing (Hsu, Grow, & Marlatt, 2009; Bowen et al., 2014), including intervention recommendations with difficult-to-reach populations such as incarcerated adults (Bowen et al., 2006). Youth involved in the juvenile justice system have also demonstrated improvement with impulse control and unwanted reactions to interpersonal conflicts after participating in an Internet-based mindfulness meditation program (Evans-Chase, 2013). Similarly, in a study examining violence and anger, Wongtongkam and colleagues (2014) reported an increased level of self-awareness and self-regulation in Thai youth after implementing a meditation program. Jennings and colleagues (2013), Razza and colleagues (2013), and Milligan and colleagues (2013) have shown evidence for improved learning environments, self-regulation, and resilience to childhood stress when mindfulness programs are implemented in schools. Abenavoli (2013) demonstrated teachers using mindfulness practices also reported protective effects against burnout through the use of mindfulness practices. When delivered in an online format within the workplace, mindfulness-based interventions have improved task performance, job satisfaction, and aided stress reduction in diverse occupational settings (Aikens, Astin, Pelletier, Levanovich, Baase, Park, Yeo, & Bodnar, 2014; Hulshegar, Alberts, Feinholdt, and Lang, 2013).

In general, reports of mindfulness and meditation interventions tend to be organized relative to problem topics or life stage groups such as children, adolescents, and older adults (Baer, 2006). Research with methods such as mindfulness-based stress reduction has been undertaken with largely middle-class and working-class populations with intrinsic diversity. Yet we do not yet find a clear body of evidence that explicitly addresses effectiveness across cultural groups in the United States. However, recent contributions such as the book by Lee, Ng, Leung, and Chan (2009) have provided theoretical and practice frameworks of integrative body-mind-spirit practice that include strong implementation detail and case illustrations, as well as empirical evidence. Roth and Calle-Mesa (2006) provide an overview of ways that factors such as socioeconomics and race are related to stress and health, and highlighted effective use of mindfulness and meditative interventions with low income, diverse populations. Dutton, Bermudez, Matas, Majid, & Myers (2013) found positive results using mindfulness-based stress reduction (Kabat-Zinn, 1991) with low-income, predominantly African American women with post-traumatic stress disorder and a history of intimate partner violence. The mindfulness therapy was shown to be feasible and accepted, although logistical factors such as childcare needs, transportation issues, lack of practice space, and scheduling conflicts were notable barriers to integrating the practice. Similar to Vallejo and Amaro (2009), who studied mindfulness-based stress reduction (MBSR) with ethnic minority groups overcoming addiction, Dutton et al. (2013) chose to not issue home practice logs to minimize stigma and shame in this population. Although there is a great density of meditation resources such as books, DVDs, and CDs that are now available (Siegel, 2010), this type of resource for home practice may not be appropriate for use with populations seeking a more discreet mindfulness practice. In this case, a helper may offer the option of a mobile phone application related to mindfulness and meditation, so the client can feel more comfortable or safe using the stress reduction programs.

Similarly, research with combat veterans has also demonstrated significant improvement in post-traumatic stress disorder and hyperarousal symptoms when practicing mantra meditation. This portable technique of using a self-calming phrase, or mantra, can be used discreetly in various locations identified by veterans to be triggers for debilitating stress responses, such as in crowds, supermarkets, or traffic. Traditional trauma-focused therapies can often potentiate the stigma of PTSD, making the portability and self-regulation aspects of mantra meditation more desirable (Bormann, Thorp, Wetherell, Golshan, & Lang, 2013; Bhatnagar, Phelps, Rietz, Juergens, Russell, Miller, & Ahearn, 2013). The Department of Defense National Center for Telehealth and Technology has also partnered with the Veterans Administration National Center for Post-traumatic Stress Disorder to create "Mobile App: Mindfulness Coach" to offer veterans a portable guide for practicing mindfulness-based techniques, such as meditation, to improve coping and resiliency during episodes of acute stress and anxiety (USDVA, 2015).

CHAPTER SUMMARY

In this chapter we address self-calming strategies. These strategies often are integrated in treatment plans to prevent or mitigate stress symptoms and to deal with a wide range of conditions that can be highly distressing. They can be implemented in a manner complementary to other stress management approaches, exposure therapies, and interventions such as cognitive change, self-management, or working with resistance in which additional aids for relaxation or mindfulness appear indicated.

Specific to stress management, we present breathing interventions to help address physiological dimensions of stress that can impede more cognitive or behaviorally oriented change efforts. Clients can achieve greater awareness of their breathing patterns and engage in breathing exercises that will help calm the central nervous system, reduce symptoms such as dizziness, and better prepare the clients to undertake additional steps in managing their stressful circumstances. The muscle relaxation training can be used in a thorough application (working through the 16 muscle groups) or a more abbreviated approach (with seven or four muscle groups). We conclude with attention to meditation strategies. Here we have focused on mindfulness meditation, but a variety or alternatives are available. We illustrate the ways that mindfulness perspectives and strategies are increasingly permeating well-established therapeutic interventions. All of these methods can be used *in vivo*. Despite their well-documented benefits, helpers should be aware that these techniques can have triggering effects and are contraindicated for some clients. Thus, self-calming approaches should be introduced only when a comprehensive assessment of client issues, strengths, and challenges identifies them as appropriate interventions.

 Visit CengageBrain.com for a variety of study tools and useful resources such as video examples, case studies, interactive exercises, flashcards, and quizzes.

13 Knowledge and Skill Builder

Part One

Learning Outcome 1 asks you to demonstrate five of the six steps for diaphragmatic breathing. Use the Checklist for Diaphragmatic Breathing to assess your performance.

Checklist for Diaphragmatic Breathing

1. **Provide a Description**

   Help the client visualize and pay close attention to the sensations of diaphragmatic breathing. Have a picture available if this seems helpful with visualization and understanding.

2. **Comfortable Position and Breathing Through the Nose**

   Get in a comfortable position that will permit you to experience and feel the movement of your abdomen.

3. **Breathe Through Your Nose.**

   Focus the client on noticing the bodily sensations. For example: "Just notice your breath. As you inhale, notice how cool the air feels, and how much warmer the air feels when you exhale."

4. **Placement of Hands and Visualization**

   Have the client bend his or her arms and place their thumbs below their rib cage. Have them place the rest of the fingers of each hand perpendicular to their body and focus using visualization on the abdominal movement. You might use the image of a balloon expanding and contracting as the lungs do. When exhaling, the diaphragm moves up to press against the lungs to help to move air out of the lungs (much like a balloon deflating). When inhaling, the diaphragm moves down to flatten and make room for the lungs (like a balloon) expanding.

5. **Simulate Movement of the Diaphragm**

   To simulate movement of the diaphragm, have the client interlace their fingers and place them on their abdomen, with thumbs just under their rib cage. You might say: "Straighten the fingers as you inhale (much like the diaphragm flattens down to make room for expansion of the lungs), and then curve the fingers outward as you exhale (much like the diaphragm lifting up to push air out of the lungs)."

6. **Regular Practice and Use in Stressful Situations**

   Reinforce the value of regular practice. Have them select a time and place to practice daily for a week. Note that when they are in a stressful situation they should start concentrating on breathing diaphragmatically.

Part Two

Learning Outcome 2 asks you to describe how you would apply the seven parts of the muscle relaxation procedure.

Using the client description here and the seven questions following it, describe how you would use the procedure with this person. You may wish to refer to the Interview Checklist for Muscle Relaxation (p. 470).

The client is a middle-aged man who is concerned about his inability to sleep at night. He has tried sleeping pills but does not want to rely on medication.

1. **Provide a rationale for the use of muscle relaxation. Include the purpose and an overview of the strategy.**
2. **What instructions would you give this client about appropriate dress for relaxation training?**
3. **List any special environmental factors that may affect the client's use of muscle relaxation.**
4. **Model some of the relaxation exercises for the client.**
5. **Describe some of the important muscle groups that you would instruct the client to tense and relax alternately.**
6. **Give two examples of probes you might use after relaxation to assess the client's use of and reactions to the strategy.**
7. **What instructions for homework would you give to this client?**

Part Three

Learning Outcome 3 asks you to demonstrate the body scan procedure with a role-play client. An observer can assess you, or you can record this activity using the script presented.

Part Four

Learning Outcome 4 asks you to teach basic elements of mindfulness meditation to another person. You may have an observer evaluate you, or you may audio-record your teaching session and rate yourself. The Interview Checklist for Mindfulness Meditation may be used to prepare for your role play. The following checklists incorporate sample scripts outlining how the various steps of the interventions presented in this chapter might be undertaken. The scripts can be used to prepare for role-plays with others, to guide your own practice, or as aids for clients.

Interview Checklist for Muscle Relaxation

Instructions: Indicate with a check (☑) each helper lead demonstrated in the interview.

Treatment Rationale

1. **Helper explains purpose of muscle relaxation.**

   "The name of the strategy that I believe will be helpful is *muscle relaxation*. Muscle relaxation has been used very effectively to benefit people who have a variety of concerns like insomnia, high blood pressure, anxiety, or stress, or people who are bothered by everyday tension. Muscle relaxation will be helpful in decreasing your tension. It will benefit you because you will

   (continued)

13 | Knowledge and Skill Builder (*continued*)

be able to control and to dispel tension that interferes with your daily activities."

2. Helper gives overview of how muscle relaxation works. "I will ask you to tense up and relax various muscle groups. All of us have some tension in our bodies—otherwise, we could not stand, sit, or move around. However, sometimes we have too much tension. By tensing and relaxing, you will become aware of and compare the feelings of tension and relaxation. Later we will train you to send a message to a particular muscle group to relax when nonessential tension creeps in. You will learn to control your tension and relax when you feel any tightness or rigidity."

3. Helper describes muscle relaxation as a skill. "Muscle relaxation is a skill. And, as with any skill, learning it well will take consistent practice. Training and repetition are needed to acquire muscle relaxation skill."

4. Helper instructs client about moving around if uncomfortable and informs client of sensations that may feel unusual. "At times during the training and muscle exercises, you may want to move while you are in the recliner [or on your back on the floor]. Feel free to do this so that you can get more comfortable. You may also feel heady sensations as we go through the exercise. These sensations are not unusual. Do you have any questions concerning what I just talked about? If not, do you want to try this now?"

Instructions about Client Dress

5. Helper instructs client about what to wear for a training session. "For the next session, wear comfortable clothing. You may wish to wear regular glasses instead of your contact lenses."

Creation of a Comfortable Environment

6. Helper provides a quiet environment, a padded recliner chair, or a pillow if the client lies on the floor. "During training, I'd like you to sit in this recliner chair. It will be more comfortable and less distracting than this wooden chair."

Helper Modeling of Relaxation Exercises

7. Helper models some exercises for specific muscle groups. "I would like to show you [some of] the exercises we will use in muscle relaxation. First, I make a fist to create tension in my right hand and forearm and then relax it."

Instructions for Muscle Relaxation

8. Helper reads or recites instructions from memory in a conversational tone and practices along with client.

9. Helper instructs client to get comfortable, close eyes, and listen to instructions. "Now, get as comfortable as you can, close your eyes, and listen to what I'm going to be telling you. I'm going to make you aware of certain sensations in your body and then show you how you can reduce these sensations to increase feelings of relaxation."

10. Helper instructs client to tense and relax alternately each of 16 muscle groups (*two* times for each muscle group in initial training). Also, helper occasionally makes muscle group comparisons.
    a. Fist of dominant hand:
       "First, think about your right arm, particularly your right hand. Clench your right fist. Clench it tightly and study the tension in the hand and in the forearm. Study those sensations of tension. *(Pause)* Now let go. Just relax the right hand and let it rest on the arm of the chair. *(Pause)* And notice the difference between the tension and the relaxation." *(10-second pause)*
    b. Fist of nondominant hand:
       "Now we'll do the same with your left hand. Clench your left fist. Notice the tension *(5-second pause)*, and now relax. Enjoy the difference between the tension and the relaxation." *(10-second pause)*
    c. One or both wrists:
       "Now bend both hands back at the wrists so that you tense the muscles in the back of the hand and in the forearm. Point your fingers toward the ceiling. Study the tension, and now relax. *(Pause)* Study the difference between tension and relaxation." *(10-second pause)*
    d. Biceps of one or both arms:
       "Now clench both your hands into fists and bring them toward your shoulders. As you do this, tighten your biceps muscles, the ones in the upper part of your arm. Feel the tension in these muscles. *(Pause)* Now relax. Let your arms drop down again to your sides. See the difference between the tension and the relaxation." *(10-second pause)*
    e. Shoulders:
       "Now we'll move to the shoulder area. Shrug your shoulders. Bring them up to your ears. Feel and hold the tension in your shoulders. *(Pause)* Now let both shoulders relax. Notice the contrast between

the tension and the relaxation that's now in your shoulders. *(10-second pause)* Are your shoulders as relaxed as your arms?"

f. Forehead:

"Now we'll work on relaxing the various muscles of the face. First, wrinkle up your forehead and brow. Do this until you feel your brow furrow. *(Pause)* Now relax. Smooth out the forehead. Let it loosen up." *(10-second pause)*

g. Eyes:

"Now close your eyes tightly. Can you feel tension all around your eyes? *(5-second pause)* Now relax those muscles, noticing the difference between the tension and the relaxation." *(10-second pause)*

h. Tongue or jaw:

"Now clench your jaw by biting your teeth together. Pull the corners of your mouth back. Study the tension in your jaw. *(5-second pause)* Relax your jaw now. Can you tell the difference between tension and relaxation in your jaw area?" *(10-second pause)*

i. Lips:

"Now press your lips together tightly. As you do this, notice the tension all around the mouth. *(Pause)* Now relax those muscles around the mouth. Just enjoy the relaxation in your mouth area and your entire face." *(Pause)*

j. Head:

"Now we'll move to the neck muscles. Press your head back against your chair. Can you feel the tension in the back of your neck and in your upper back? Hold the tension. *(Pause)* Now let your head rest comfortably. Notice the difference. Keep relaxing." *(10-second pause)*

k. Chin into chest:

"Now continue to concentrate on the neck area. Bring your head forward. See whether you can bury your chin into your chest. Notice the tension in the front of your neck. Now relax and let go." *(10-second pause)*

l. Back:

"Now direct your attention to your upper back area. Arch your back as if you were sticking out your chest and stomach. Can you feel tension in your back? Study that tension. *(Pause)* Now relax. Notice the difference between the tension and the relaxation." *(10-second pause)*

m. Chest muscles:

"Now take a deep breath, filling your lungs, and hold it. See the tension all through your chest and into your stomach area. Hold that tension. *(Pause)* Now relax and let go. Let your breath out naturally.

Enjoy the pleasant sensations. Is your chest as relaxed as your back and shoulders?" *(10-second pause)*

n. Stomach muscles:

"Now think about your stomach. Tighten up the muscles in your abdomen. Hold this tension. Make your stomach like a knot. Now relax. Loosen those muscles now." *(10-second pause)*

o. Legs:

"I'd like you now to focus on your legs. Stretch both legs. Feel tension in your thighs. *(5-second pause)* Now relax. Study the difference again between the tension in the thighs and the relaxation you feel now." *(10-second pause)*

p. Toes:

"Now concentrate on your lower legs and feet. Tighten both calf muscles by pointing your toes toward your head. Pretend a string is pulling your toes up. Can you feel the pulling and the tension? Notice that tension. *(Pause)* Now relax. Let your legs relax deeply. Enjoy the difference between tension and relaxation." *(10-second pause)*

11. Helper instructs client to review and relax all muscle groups.

"Now, I'm going to again go over the different muscle groups that we've covered. As I name each group, try to notice whether there is any tension in those muscles. If there is any, try to concentrate on those muscles and tell them to relax. Think of draining any remaining tension out of your body as we do this. Now relax the muscles in your feet, ankles, and calves. *(Pause)* Get rid of tension in your knees and thighs. *(Pause)* Loosen your hips. *(Pause)* Let the muscles of your lower body go. *(Pause)* Relax your abdomen, waist, and lower back. *(Pause)* Drain the tension from your upper back, chest, and shoulders. *(Pause)* Relax your upper arms, forearms, and hands. *(Pause)* Loosen the muscles of your throat and neck. *(Pause)* Relax your face. *(Pause)* Let all the tension drain out of your body. *(Pause)* Now sit quietly with your eyes closed."

12. Helper asks client to rate his or her relaxation level following training session.

"Now I'd like you to think of a scale from 0 to 5, where 0 is *complete relaxation* and 5 represents *extreme tension*. Tell me where you would place yourself on that scale now."

Post-training Assessment

13. Helper asks client about first session of relaxation training and discusses problems with training if client has any.

(continued)

13 | Knowledge and Skill Builder (*continued*)

"How do you feel?"

"What is your overall reaction to the procedure?"

"Think back about what we did. Did you have problems with any muscle group?"

"What reaction did you have when you focused on the tension?

What about relaxation?"

"How did the contrast between the tension and relaxation feel?"

Homework and Follow-up

14. Helper assigns homework and requests that client complete homework log for practice sessions.

"Relaxation training, like any skill, takes consistent practice. I would like you to practice what we've done today. It will be most helpful if you can do the exercises twice per day for 15 to 20 minutes each time. Do them in a quiet place in a reclining chair, on the floor with a pillow, or on your bed with a head pillow. Also, try to do the relaxation at a time when there is no time pressure—perhaps when you have first awoken in the morning, after school or work, or before dinner. Try to avoid any interruptions like phone calls and people wanting to see you. Complete the homework log I have given you. Make sure you fill it in for each practice session. Does this seem doable? Do you have any questions?"

15. Helper arranges for follow-up session.

"Why don't you practice with this over the next 2 weeks and come back then?"

Notations for Problems Encountered or Variations Used

Interview Checklist for Mindfulness Meditation

Instructions: Determine which of the following helper leads or questions were demonstrated in the interview. Check (☑) each of the leads that the helper used.

Treatment Rationale

1. Helper describes purpose of procedure.

"I would like to teach you mindfulness meditation. This type of meditation has been used to relieve fatigue caused by anxiety, to decrease stress that leads to high blood pressure, and to bring balance and focus into one's life. Meditation helps you become more relaxed and to deal more effectively with tension and stress. It may bring you new awareness about yourself and a new way of seeing and doing in your life."

2. Helper gives client an overview.

"First you will select a quiet place in which to meditate. You will then get into a relaxed and comfortable position. With your eyes closed, you will focus on your breathing and allow your thoughts to flow freely. If

your mind wanders off, then you can bring it back by focusing on the breath. You will meditate for 10 to 20 minutes. Then, we will talk about the experience."

3. Helper confirms client's willingness to use strategy.

"How do you feel about taking part in a practice meditation?"

Attitudinal Foundations for Practice

4. Helper instructs client about attitudes to help the practice of meditation.

"There are eight attitudes that will help with your practice of meditation."

5. Helper instructs the client about being nonjudging.

"First, it is best to be nonjudging. We have a tendency to categorize or judge people, things, or our experiences. These judgments take you away from observing whatever comes up while you are meditating. Judging steals energy from the moment-by-moment awareness. To remedy this, focus on your breathing."

6. Helper instructs the client about patience.

"Second, have patience, which means just allow things to unfold in their own time. We don't have to fill every moment of our lives with nonstop doing and activity."

7. Helper instructs the client about the beginner's mind and basing moment-by-moment awareness on past experiences.

"Third, as a beginner, what we experience in the moment is often based on our past experiences and ways of doing things. Just be open to moment-by-moment experience. Don't let past experiences judge and steal energy from moment-by-moment awareness."

8. Helper instructs client about trusting feelings and intuition.

"Fourth, trust your feelings and intuition while meditating. For example, if your body tells you that your posture for meditating is not comfortable, then change to another posture that feels better."

9. Helper instructs the client to be nonstriving.

"Fifth, try to be nonstriving, which means that mindfulness meditation is about the process of practice; every practice will be different. You don't want a mindset that requires you to achieve something or get somewhere. Just be in the moment, and attend to whatever comes up."

10. Helper instructs the client about acceptance.

"Sixth, just focus on seeing and accepting things as they are, moment by moment, and in the present."

11. Helper instructs the client about letting go.

"Seventh, just let go, which means nonattachment or not holding on to thoughts."

Instructions about Commitment, Self-Discipline, and Energy

12. Helper instructs client about commitment, self-discipline, and energy.
"You want to make the kind of commitment required in athletic training. This strong commitment is about working on yourself. You have to summon enough self-discipline to generate enough energy that you can develop a strong meditative practice and a high degree of mindfulness. You don't have to like it; you just have to do it. Then, at the end of 8 weeks of practice, we can see whether the practice was useful."

Preparations for Meditation

13. Helper instructs the client about time, place, and posture.
"Select a particular time every day to meditate. Meditate for at least 6 days per week, and for 8 weeks. Find a place to meditate that will be free of interruptions and that will be comfortable. When you meditate, sit erect in a chair or lie on the floor. Try to position your back so that it is self-supporting."

Body Scan Instructions

14. Helper instructs client to do a body scan.
"Allow the body to begin to relax completely. Inhale and feel the breath flow from the soles of the feet to the crown of the head, like a gentle slow motion wave. With each exhalation, allow tension to flow out of the body." (Continue from the script related to breathing presented earlier in the chapter.)

Breathing Instructions

15. Helper instructs the client about breathing.
"Observe your breathing as it flows in and flows out. Notice the difference in temperature of the out breath and in breath. Feel the sensation of the air as it goes in and out of the nostrils."

Instructions about the Mind Wandering

16. Helper instructs client about what to do with cascading thoughts, feelings, sensations, sounds, pain, or discomfort. "If you find yourself getting stuck in thoughts, feelings, sensations, sounds, pain, or discomfort, this is normal; just bring your attention to breathing, and let go by exhaling these distractions."

Instructions for Meditating

17. Helper instructs client about sitting quietly and relaxed for a minute. You can do a quick body scan to help with awareness and relaxation.
"Sit quietly for a while; just relax; focus on your breathing."
18. Helper instructs client to close eyes, focus on breathing, and get in a comfortable position.
"Close your eyes, get in a comfortable position, and focus on your breathing; the air comes in and flows out."
19. Helper instructs client to be in the moment, to have awareness and observe what comes up, and not give distractions any energy.
"Just be in the moment; be aware and observe whatever comes to mind. If distractions of thoughts, feelings, sounds, pain, or discomfort steal energy, just breathe them out and continue to observe and not move with the flow of these distractions."
20. Helper tells client that she or he will meditate for 10 to 20 minutes.
"Meditate for 10 to 20 minutes. I will keep time and tell you when to stop."
21. Helper instructs client to come out of meditation slowly.
"I want you to come out of the meditation slowly. Just sit there with your eyes closed for a while; take time to absorb what you experienced. You may wish to stretch and then open your eyes slowly."

Discussion of Client's Reaction to Mindfulness Meditation

22. Helper asks client about experience with mindfulness meditation.
"What was the experience like for you?"
"How did you handle distractions?"
"How did you feel about mindfulness?"

Homework

23. Helper instructs client to meditate at home once per day and reminds client about preparation for meditation.
"Practice mindfulness meditation once per day at least 5 days per week. Remember to select a quiet environment without distractions. Be aware that what you consume can affect your meditative states. Consider, for example, limiting use of alcoholic beverages or nonprescription drugs prior to meditating, and waiting for an hour after eating solid foods or drinking beverages containing caffeine. Be in the moment when you meditate; just observe what comes up without being carried away."
24. Helper instructs client about informal meditation.
"You can meditate informally when you are facing stressful situations that may occur daily. Just relax and focus on your breathing. Be aware and observe what is going on without giving energy to stress, and be peaceful in the situation."
Observer Comments _____

13 | Knowledge and Skill Builder **Feedback**

Part One

Use the Checklist for Diaphragmatic Breathing to assess how completely you covered each step in your demonstration.

Part Two

Use the Interview Checklist for Muscle Relaxation to assess your performance.

Part Three

Use the body scan script in Box 13.1 to assess the way you used the body scan with a role-play client.

Part Four

Use the Interview Checklist for Mindfulness Meditation as a guide to assess your teaching.

Exposure Therapy for Anxiety, Fear, and Trauma

By Daniel W. McNeil, West Virginia University and Brandon N. Kyle, East Carolina University

Learning Outcomes

After completing this chapter, you will be able to do the following:

1. Define exposure therapy and name at least three problems for which it may be used.

2. Describe one of the possible theoretical explanations for exposure and list at least two implications of that theory for exposure.

3. List and describe at least two of the three phases in preparing and planning for exposure as outlined in Table 14.2, as well as 8 of the 11 steps in implementing exposure therapy, as outlined in Figure 14.1.

4. Name and describe at least one gradual method and at least one intensive method for implementing exposure therapy.

5. Name at least three issues a helper should consider in choosing an exposure method with a client.

6. Articulate at least two issues of informed consent and be able to detail at least one caution in the use of exposure therapy.

7. Describe at least two important issues to consider when using exposure with a client who is from a cultural minority or vulnerable group.

Exposure has been well supported empirically and clinically in treating a broad spectrum of anxiety and fear-related client concerns and in addressing the extreme manifestations of these states observed in emotional disorders such as anxiety disorders, trauma-related and stress-related disorders, and obsessive-compulsive and related disorders. The genesis of anxiety and fear includes, but is not limited to, traumatic stress experiences. Exposure treatment almost invariably involves stressed populations—either those who have experienced disturbing events or those who suffer the burden of disabling maladaptive patterns of response to daily life challenges. There are many cognitive behaviorally oriented approaches that target stress, anxiety, and fear, several of which have been presented in previous chapters. These include aspects of cognitive therapy (Chapter 11) that aid clients in examining personal meaning associated with experiences and modifying ways of thinking that are contributing to distress and impeding recovery; stress management (Chapter 12) designed to help clients anticipate and prepare to respond more effectively in situations that evoke distress; and calming methods (Chapter 13) that encourage mindfulness, acceptance, and diaphragmatic breathing and physical relaxation. And, of course, combinations of these and other treatment components may be appropriate for use with given cases.

In this chapter, we illustrate several approaches to exposure that work to reduce learned fear and arousal responses associated with objects, events, traumatic memories, and the stimuli that elicit them. There are a number of choices in approach, such as whether exposure is gradual or intense, involves imaginal or actual stimuli, or involves short bursts or prolonged contact. We include definitions, theoretical mechanisms that may underlie exposure, and methods by which both gradual and intensive exposure can evoke change. Contemporary applications of exposure therapy are described, as are developing areas of treatment research. It is important to note that treatment of severe stress and trauma is a complex and extensive clinical topic. We need to focus here on selected intervention tools, but readers are encouraged to pursue a more expansive literature review. Examples of related practice resources that span a range of disorders include those authored by Abramowitz,

Deacon, and Whiteside (2011); Craske, Treanor, Conway, Zvozinek, and Vervliet (2014); Foa, Hembree, and Rothbaum (2007); Follette and Ruzek (2006); Hofmann and Otto (2008); and Richard and Lauterback (2007).

It also is important to note that exposure therapy has been utilized most commonly for the treatment of both fear and anxiety. Although these states are similar, they represent unique constructs: fear is more present-oriented toward specific proximal stimuli and psychophysiologically focused (as in a fight-flight reaction), whereas anxiety is more future-oriented toward distal stimuli and involved with worry and other cognitive processes (Barlow, 2002; Craske, 2003). Nevertheless, for the sake of simplicity and readability, these terms are used interchangeably in this chapter because exposure is an effective treatment for both pathological fear and anxiety.

What Is Exposure?

Exposure is a broad term that refers to a variety of **LO1** specific treatment strategies involving some form of contact between the client and what he or she finds anxiety-provoking, frightening, or otherwise distressing. Various modalities can be applied. Initially, exposure might be conducted using imagery or visualization. This might lead to *in vitro* exposure that would be conducted in the treatment setting under controlled conditions and involve simulated stimuli such as role play or virtual technology. Eventually, the client might be ready for *in vivo* methods that include actual exposure to objects, events, or situations that cause distress, either within the treatment setting or in the client's environment. The exposure is conducted in some organized fashion and may involve a **systematic desensitization** process in which fear-evoking stimuli are presented gradually, typically in an ascending hierarchy. Other treatment methods that are subsumed under *exposure* are **flooding** and **implosive therapy**; these are considered to be intensive exposure methods, typically involving repeated, long-lasting, or extremely emotionally evocative exposure. Along with the exposure, relaxation or some other coping response that is incompatible with fear may be taught and utilized before, during, and/or after the procedure.

If our client, Isabella, was fearful of going for a dental visit, for example, then a thorough, individualized assessment first would be conducted, followed by a rationale for exposure. Working collaboratively, Isabella and the helper would construct a hierarchy and descriptions of emotionally evocative situations ranging from least to most fear-provoking for Isabella. Over the course of a number of sessions, the helper would expose Isabella to these

situations in her imagination by reading the descriptions to her in a systematic way. Once the hierarchy was completed, or perhaps while it was in progress, Isabella would have homework assignments related to self-exposure to dental situations. The first assignment might be to simply call for information about dental services. Then, Isabella might visit a dental office without scheduling dental treatment. Next, she could meet the dentist or hygienist in the office, and later still she could actually receive dental services. Additionally, perhaps early in the process, the helper might assist Isabella in learning progressive muscle relaxation training. Up to several therapy sessions would be devoted to Isabella's learning to relax herself and to providing psychoeducational information. Isabella would have homework assignments that would include self-monitoring her relaxation practice so that she could develop that skill to be used to allow exposure to be conducted fully.

Both psychosocial and pharmacological treatments depend on the mechanism of exposure to help clients relearn adaptive responses to people, objects, and situations that trigger emotional arousal and distress. *Exposure therapy* has been defined as

> ...a form of behavior therapy that is effective in treating anxiety disorders. Exposure therapy involves systematic confrontation with a feared stimulus, either *in vivo* (live) or in the imagination. It works by (a) habituation, in which repeated exposure reduces anxiety over time by a process of extinction; (b) disconfirming fearful predictions; (c) deeper processing of the feared stimulus; and (d) increasing feelings of self-efficacy and mastery. Exposure therapy may encompass a number of behavioral interventions, including systematic desensitization, flooding, implosive therapy, and extinction-based techniques (VandenBos, 2007, p. 357).

When effective, the extinction of the arousal and distress response through exposure occurs after repeated or prolonged contact with the stimulus that evokes fear (be it a small animal like a snake, a place such as a glass elevator overlooking a large city, or a situation such as receiving dental treatment) without any aspects that would lead to aversive reactions, such as a snake bite, the elevator uncontrollably dropping a number of floors, or pain during dental care.

Types of Problems for Which Exposure May be Used

A variety of problems related to fear and anxiety are addressed by exposure, but a range of emotional issues including grief and depression also can be targeted with this strategy. There are elements of exposure in treatment for alcohol and other drug problems as well, such as cue desensitization, in which individuals are exposed to the sights, sounds, smells, and other aspects of alcohol and drug consumption situations without actual substance use, so that new associations can be learned in regard to those stimuli.

Anxiety disorders are among the diagnoses most commonly addressed by exposure, particularly **phobias**, which are marked, persistent, and disproportionate fears of specific situations or objects (e.g., heights, dogs, water, blood, driving, flying). In the *DSM-5*, various types of phobias are classified under the heading of specific phobia (APA, 2013). Additional anxiety disorders described by the DSM-5 (APA, 2013) that may be addressed by exposure include social anxiety disorder (i.e., fear of negative evaluation in one or more social situations), panic disorder (i.e., persistent concern for or maladaptive behavior changes related to recurrent and unexpected panic attacks), agoraphobia (i.e., fear or avoidance of being in public transportation, in open spaces, in enclosed spaces, in crowds, or outside the home alone because escaping or obtaining help would be difficult), and generalized anxiety disorder (i.e., excessive and uncontrollable worry about a variety of events or activities).

In addition, exposure is a preferred treatment for many trauma-related and stress-related disorders and obsessive-compulsive and related disorders. Post-traumatic stress disorder (PTSD) can develop when individuals are exposed to death, injury, or sexual violence, whether actual or threatened (APA, 2013); exposure is a "gold standard" for the treatment of PTSD (Gallagher, Thompson-Hollands, Bourgeois, & Bentley, 2015). Treatment of obsessive-compulsive disorder (OCD) also can include exposure for the obsessions (i.e., recurrent and persistent thoughts, urges, or images that are intrusive and unwanted) or compulsions (i.e., repetitive behavior or mental acts performed in response to obsessions or according to rigid rules) associated with it (APA, 2013). In the case of treatment for a client with hand-washing rituals, for example, there can be planned exposure to dirt or germs, followed by response prevention to restrict excessive hand-washing or other cleansing rituals. Evidence indicates that both individual and group modalities can be effective in exposure treatment of OCD (Jonsson & Hougaard, 2009).

Exposure also can be useful in cases of comorbidity, such as PTSD and panic disorder (Falsetti, Resnick, & Davis, 2008) or PTSD and alcohol use disorder (Coffey, Stasiewicz, Hughes, & Brimo, 2006). Additionally, exposure can be effective treatment when a client has a comorbid personality disorder (Becker, 2002), including the case of PTSD and personality disorder in female assault survivors (Hembree, Cahill, & Foa, 2004). In fact, a protocol for prolonged exposure has been found to be successful in work with women with borderline personality disorder who are suicidal and self-injuring (Harned, Korslund, Foa, & Linehan, 2012). Nevertheless, clients with personality disorders may have less treatment gains than clients without personality disorders (Feske, Perry, Chambless, Renneberg, & Goldstein, 1996; Hansen, Vogel, Stiles, & Götestman, 2007) or poorer post-treatment overall functioning (Hembree et al., 2004).

Successful exposure treatment leads to adaptive changes in an individual's responses to the objects, situations, and/or people that previously elicited fear or anxiety. Behavioral changes typically are emphasized over others, because actually performing the desired action (e.g., flying in an airplane, for someone with a flying phobia) is seen as the ultimate outcome. Moreover, there is some evidence that overt behavioral changes often precede physiological and cognitive changes in the treatment process; if a person can first outwardly behave in a certain way, then his or her frightening thoughts and physiological responses will diminish as well. Nevertheless, cognitive and psychophysiological changes are extremely important, too, and often are direct targets for change in the helping process; cognitive and somatic coping strategies can help clients tolerate exposure, but also may hinder progress at times (Meuret, Wolitsky-Taylor, Twolig, & Craske, 2012). During exposure, the duration of contact or interaction with the phobic stimulus is important and typically is associated with fear reduction, which argues for repeated and/or prolonged exposure. In general, the greater the duration of exposure, the more the fear tends to be reduced (Marks, 1975), allowing for greater stimulus and overall context variability, which can aid learning and generalization (Craske et al., 2014).

Case Illustrations with Isabella

Consider another illustration with our client Isabella. If during childhood Isabella had been a victim of a dog attack, then she may have developed a dog phobia. After completing an appropriate assessment and providing the client with a thorough rationale, the helper might assist Isabella in learning relaxation skills that she could implement to prevent or combat later anxious responses, if that seemed necessary for her "buy in" for treatment. Then, the helper might adopt a psychoeducational approach, providing information about different breeds and rules for interacting with dogs. Even this discussion about dogs would be a form of exposure, albeit a mild one.

Next in the sequence, **imaginal exposure** might be undertaken, first involving construction of a hierarchy of fearful events involving dogs, ranging from very mildly arousing situations (e.g., walking through the dog accessories section of a retail store) to situations that are highly fear-evoking (e.g., having a large, snarling dog break its chain and come running toward you with mouth agape and teeth flashing). The helper then would expose the client to these scenes in a systematic way for brief periods of time, vividly describing the scenes while the client imagines them with eyes closed to limit visual distraction. The relaxation skills could be used before and/or after imaginal exposure to help with the client's comfort and satisfaction with the treatment and her continued engagement with it.

Exposure to actual dog stimuli then would take place *in vivo*. Isabella may have homework assignments from the clinician to visit retail stores to spend time in the dog section, looking at and holding collars, leashes, and other dog-related items. Then, Isabella may be asked to visit pet stores and view dogs that are in cages. She also may be asked to go to a local dog park and view the dogs and owners from outside the fence. The clinician may open the possibility of Isabella's inviting a friend with a dog known to be friendly and gentle to a helping session so that the clinician could work directly with Isabella to interact with a dog in real life. In such a session, the clinician and/or friend may model how to interact with a dog, such as petting or scratching it. The friend might rub the dog, and Isabella would place her hand on top of the friend's hand with the knowledge that over time the friend would remove her hand, allowing Isabella to touch the dog directly.

Future hierarchy steps might include walking a friend's dog or going to a park where owners let their dogs run loose under close supervision. The client may be encouraged to maintain an exposure-based lifestyle involving dogs so that fear would be unlikely to return. For example, Isabella might be encouraged to offer to look after a dog for a friend on vacation or to get a puppy so that she could learn to enjoy it day in and day out.

From a developmental perspective, exposure can happen naturally in a person's life, providing the individual with opportunities to learn adaptive responses without ever having to go through the unlearning of an encapsulated anxiety response. For example, if when Isabella was a young child she had been exposed to dental care by a professional before any dental problems developed, then she may never have had an opportunity to directly learn a phobic response to dental situations. Note, however, that social learning from family members, peers, and others can lead to the indirect, vicarious acquisition of both

healthy and accepting attitudes as well as anxieties such as dental phobia. In pediatric dentistry, for example, children often are provided positive exposure such as having a ride up and down on the dental chair, tooth-counting by the dentist or hygienist, receiving a bright new toothbrush and balloon, and other fun activities that help the child to learn positive expectations of the dental experience and reduce the risk of strongly linked fear responses.

In other instances, life situations bring new opportunities, which actually may be challenges to which a person must respond (leading to exposure) or from which a person may choose to retreat (representing avoidance). For example, in the case of Isabella, if she is interested in running for student council at her high school but campaigning required her to speak publicly in front of a school assembly, then she may find herself experiencing fear or even phobia related to the possibility of the public speaking. The new demand poses both a challenge and an opportunity. Isabella may choose to attempt to get through the public speaking assignments with considerable dread and endure the unpleasant physiological and cognitive sequelae. Perhaps over time this kind of exposure would operate so that she feels more comfortable doing public speaking. (This outcome, however, is uncertain, because many times such phobias resist extinction, even with periodic exposure.) Alternately, she may choose to seek out professional treatment for her phobia. Or she may choose to decline the possibility of running for student council to avoid the phobic situation.

Theoretical Background for Exposure

Exposure therapy is an empirically supported treatment strategy (Abramowitz et al., 2011; Chambless et al., 1998; Hofmann & Smits, 2008; Institute of Medicine, 2008; Norton & Price, 2007), although there are varied perspectives regarding how exposure reduces distress and improves functioning (Abramowitz, 2013; Craske, Kirkanski, Zelikowsky, Mystkowski, Chowdhury, & Baker, 2008; Craske, Treanor, Conway, Zbozinek, Vervliet, 2014; Tryon, 2005). A full and thorough review of the various theories advanced to explain exposure therapy is beyond the scope of this chapter. Instead, we briefly describe several explanations of exposure treatment, with an emphasis on more contemporary theories.

As suggested by Abramowitz (2013), we believe it is vital for helpers to understand how and why exposure works if they are to properly apply exposure-based treatments to a wide variety of clients and in a multitude of situations. When helpers learn the "what" of exposure therapy without learning the "why," they are more likely to improperly use exposure, implementing it either incorrectly or with patients for whom exposure may not be beneficial (Abramowitz, 2013). In contrast, helpers well versed in the theoretical background of exposure have knowledge that can inform assessment, case conceptualization, and implementation. They also have the ability to provide clients with a rationale for exposure-based treatment.

Early Perspectives on Exposure

The roots of exposure therapy can be traced to research on learning and anxiety during the middle of the twentieth century, although several decades passed before the terms exposure or exposure therapy came into regular use (Schare & Wyatt, 2013). Some of the earliest work on exposure treatment (e.g., Wolpe, 1958) focused on training clients in relaxation before gradually exposing them to feared stimuli, often imaginal representations, while clients utilized relaxation strategies; terms used to label and explain treatment included *systematic desensitization*, *reciprocal inhibition*, and *counter-conditioning* (Tryon, 2005; Wolitzky-Taylor, Horowitz, Powers, & Telch, 2008). These treatments generally shared an emphasis on the use of a relaxation response to oppose fear-based and anxiety-based arousal, which clients learned to apply to increasingly challenging stimuli.

Although these treatments often were successful, several challenges to the assumptions underlying them arose (Tryon, 2005). People treated by repeated and/or prolonged exposure to feared stimuli without being taught relaxation skills have shown treatment gains comparable to the gains of people trained to relax in conjunction with exposure (e.g., Yates, 1975). Additionally, individuals exposed to stimuli in a random and variable order have similar, if not better, outcomes compared to individuals exposed to stimuli in increasing order of aversion (Craske et al., 2008; Lang & Craske, 2000).

Emotional Processing Theory

As evidence grew that relaxation might not be an essential component of exposure therapy, focus shifted to other possible mechanisms. Emotional processing theory proposes that exposure therapy accesses and modifies a client's *fear structure*, which is a set of propositions and behaviors that a person associates with a feared stimulus (Foa & Kozak, 1986; 1998). According to this theory, a client's fear structure is more fully accessed when exposure treatment elicits higher levels of initial fear activation.

Once accessed, the fear structure can be modified by incorporating new and incompatible information during exposure. Modification of the fear structure can be indexed by within-session habituation and between-session habituation, or a decrease in the physiological or verbal fear response due to decreased estimation of risk of harm and decreased negative valence associated with the feared stimulus (Craske et al., 2008).

Although emotional processing theory guided much of the research and clinical work with exposure treatment in subsequent decades, important aspects of emotional processing theory have not been supported consistently. More specifically, the evidence that initial fear activation or habituation (within- or between-session) predicts treatment outcomes of exposure therapy has been mixed at best, and weak or disconfirming at worst (Abramowitz, 2013; Baker, Mystkowski, Culver, Yi, Mortazavi, & Craske, 2010; Craske et al., 2008; Lang & Craske, 2000). Put another way, although decreased arousal and fear responding may occur during exposure therapy, these constructs do not appear sufficient for explaining long-term maintenance of treatment gains in exposure therapy.

Extinction and Inhibitory Learning

One of the simpler yet more comprehensive explanations for the effectiveness of exposure therapy has been *inhibitory learning* during *extinction* (Craske et al., 2008; Craske et al., 2014; Hazlett-Stevens & Craske, 2003). In a respondent conditioning model, a client might develop a fear of an initially neutral stimulus (a conditioned stimulus, or CS) when that neutral stimulus is paired with another stimulus (an unconditioned stimulus, or US) that naturally elicits an unpleasant response (an unconditioned response, or UR) that a client finds aversive, such as intense physiological arousal or pain. With repeated pairings of the US and CS (or perhaps with only one extremely aversive pairing), because the CS is associated with and predicts the US, the CS begins to elicit a conditioned response (CR) of fear that the client finds aversive.

Consider the example of a child and health care providers wearing white coats. The cues associated with health care providers (white coat, scrubs, stethoscope, etc.) are not inherently aversive. However, injections often are administered in health care settings by providers, which a child can experience as a painful and frightening US. Through the pairing of provider-related cues with injections, the stimuli associated with the provider, as well as the provider herself, may become a CS that is experienced as predictive of the US and that elicits fear and arousal in the child.

With extinction, the CS is repeatedly presented without the US, which decreases and can eliminate the CR. The mechanism through which extinction appears to exert its influence is inhibitory learning (Craske et al., 2008; Craske et al., 2014). Inhibitory learning means that, rather than *unlearning* the CS–US association during extinction, the original CS–US connection remains, but new learning that the CS no longer predicts the US (CS–no US) inhibits original excitatory responding (Craske et al., 2008; Craske et al., 2014). Returning to the aforementioned example, the child might be exposed to visits to the physician without injections, thus experiencing the CS without the US. Rather than erasing the original learning of physician-injection, the child learns a new association of health care provider and no injection that inhibits the excitatory fear responding of the original association; health care providers (and associated stimuli such as white coats) no longer reliably predict injections. Eventually the child should experience less fear related to health care providers, including less distress related to white coats, stethoscopes, and medical/dental instruments.

From basic to translational to clinical research, support for inhibitory learning continues to grow, increasing its role in helpers' understanding and use of exposure treatment (Abramowitz, 2013; Craske et al., 2008; Crasket et al., 2014). Additionally, as suggested by Craske and colleagues (Craske et al., 2008; Craske et al., 2014; Hazlett-Stevens & Craske, 2009; Mystkowski, Craske, & Echiverri, 2002), an extinction and learning-based conceptualization of exposure subsequently has several implications for enhancing delivery of exposure therapy through application of general principles of learning. learning (see Table 14.1).

First, exposure exercises should be designed to contradict a client's expectations to enhance the salience of and attention to the CS in the absence of the US. Rather than use a client's fear level during exposure to determine parameters of the exposure session (i.e., continue exposure until habituation occurs), exposure should be continued until the nonoccurrence of the client's predicted CS–US association. Such an approach also suggests that, during exposure, helpers should emphasize self-efficacy in

toleration of fear, rather than a possibly false sense of competence in fear reduction. If a child expects an injection to result within 5 minutes of a physician visit, then exposure to a physician would need to continue until at least 5 minutes had passed, without direct reference to the child's reduction of fear.

Second, after exposure to different CSs separately, clients can be exposed to CSs in combination to enhance learning and prevent the return of fear. A child could be exposed to a white coat, then a stethoscope, and then both in combination, which would decrease the likelihood of fear of health care providers returning at a later time.

Third, the removal or elimination of safety signals or safety behaviors during exposure should be emphasized. Such signals, although they may increase palatability of exposure, interfere with inhibitory learning. They decrease the salience of the CS, because clients may be distracted from the CS, may learn a safety signal–no US association instead of the CS–no US association, or may learn that the CS–no US inhibitory association is contingent on the presence of the safety signal. Fear may quickly return in the absence of the safety signal, suggesting inferior learning. For a child who undergoes exposure to physician-related stimuli while being allowed to hold a blanket or stuffed animal, fear of physicians may quickly return or be expressed if the child no longer has these safety signals present. For the military veteran with PTSD, positioning oneself so one's back is protected (e.g., not toward a door) may be a safety behavior that should be addressed clinically. The individual with agoraphobia may position herself so that she always sits on the edge of a row of chairs, so that she can leave the situation easily; this safety behavior may need to be addressed over the course of exposure therapy with encouragement by the helper to sit toward the front of a room, and toward the middle of a bench, pew, or row of chairs.

Fourth, variation in exposure sequence and context can enhance retention of inhibitory learning, presumably by increasing the salience of the CS–no US association and decreasing the likelihood that learning will be context-dependent. Rather than present a child with a less-feared stimulus of a stethoscope until extinction occurs before progressing to a more-feared stimulus of a white coat, all while in a helper's office, it may prove more effective to vary the order of presentation and conduct exposure in other settings, such as the home or the physician's office.

Additional Theoretical Considerations

Although much of the theoretical discussion of exposure therapy in the literature has emphasized extinction in the respondent conditioning sense of the term, it is important

---

TABLE 14.1   Implications of Inhibitory Learning and Extinction for Enhancing Exposure Therapy

1. Emphasize violation of CS–US expectation over habituation

2. Combine CSs

3. Remove or eliminate safety cues

4. Vary exposure sequence and context

Note: CS = conditioned stimulus; US = unconditioned stimulus

to note that extinction in an operant conditioning sense of the term also may be relevant for exposure. When clients escape or avoid a CS, their escape or avoidance may be negatively reinforced by eliminating or preventing the experience of the CR of fear or anxiety. Reinforcement makes the escape and avoidance behavior more likely to occur in the future, and exposure therapy can be conceptualized as extinguishing escape or avoidance behavior by preventing it from occurring and allowing for reinforcement for alternative responses. For example, if a client had a diagnosis of agoraphobia and left his child's school production of a theater play early because he feared having a panic attack, then the relief he felt upon exit could negatively reinforce his escape and avoidance. Exposure therapy focused on having him stay through the play could extinguish the negative reinforcement, as well as provide the opportunity for positive reinforcement through enjoyment of the play.

Additionally, in recent years, acceptance-oriented interventions have been applied to anxiety-related disorders and offered as an alternative to contemporary forms of cognitive behavioral therapy (Eifert & Forsyth, 2005; Hayes, Strosahl, & Wilson, 2012). One prominent approach, acceptance and commitment therapy, suggests that exposure therapy can work by teaching people to accept the aversive private events (e.g., distressing cognitions, private verbal behavior, or physiological states) they experience in the presence of their feared stimuli, thus allowing them to engage in valued tasks while experiencing such events. Whereas traditional cognitive behavioral therapy rationales for exposure tend to focus on altering the *form* of private events as the goal of therapy (e.g., decrease the experience of fear in the presence of feared stimuli; revising meaning and cognitive patterns), ACT rationales for exposure identify the therapeutic goal as altering the *function* of private events (e.g., not allowing fear to prevent a client with acrophobia from enjoying a beautiful but elevated scenic view). Clients purportedly learn new relations between their private events and their overt behavior without specific emphasis on decreasing or altering their private events.

On a final note, different theoretical explanations for the effectiveness of exposure therapy are not mutually exclusive and often are overlapping. Respondent extinction with inhibitory learning and operant extinction easily could occur simultaneously, the concepts of fear tolerance and self-efficacy may complement acceptance, and habituation may not be sufficient for exposure but may remain an additional benefit for many patients. For further reading regarding the theoretical issues underlying exposure, we recommend Abramowitz (2013), Craske et al. (2008), Craske et al. (2014), and Vervliet, Craske, and Hermans (2013). For a very practical and client-friendly guide to assessment and case conceptualization, we suggest Zayfert and Becker (2007).

Components and Processes of Exposure Therapy

The components of exposure therapy that we describe **LO3** include:

1. Treatment Rationale

2. Addressing Questions, Obtaining Informed Consent, and Psychoeducation

3. Identifying Fear-Provoking Stimuli

4. Constructing an Exposure Hierarchy

5. Relaxation Response Training (if appropriate)

6. Imagery Assessment and Training (if doing imaginal exposure)

7. Initial Exposure

8. Discussing the Experience and Disconfirming Maladaptive Cognitions

9. Identifying and Addressing Avoidance and Safety-Seeking Behaviors

10. Continuing Exposure through the Hierarchy

11. Homework

Gradual exposure therapies present increasingly fear-provoking or anxiety-provoking stimuli in a steady, incremental fashion over several or many shorter sessions, although some researchers suggest varying the order of stimuli presentation (Craske et al., 2014). In contrast, intensive exposure therapies place the client in contact with more intense fear- or anxiety-provoking stimuli almost immediately and for an extended period of time, sometimes during only one or very few sessions. Both clients and helpers tend to be more comfortable with gradual exposure. More caution is warranted in using intensive exposure, including greater focus on preparing the client, and even greater emphasis on informed consent. Gradual exposure is accepted more readily and may be more palatable to clients, thus increasing satisfaction, at least early in treatment, and perhaps with fewer dropouts. Nevertheless, the efficacy and efficiency of intensive methods are appealing to many clients, who may not have persisted with treatment if it seemed to plod along.

Component 1: Treatment Rationale

Regardless of the particular combination of gradual exposure approaches a helper chooses to utilize, the general sequence of therapy remains similar (see Figure 14.1). First, the helper explains the rationale for exposure, which will be influenced by the theoretical viewpoint the helper holds. Generally, it can be explained to the client that anxiety and fear are natural, normal, and sometimes helpful human emotions. For example, being scared of a bear in the woods prompts people to run away and escape harm. Sometimes, though, excessive fear and anxiety can become associated with a variety of stimuli or situations and impair daily functioning, for example, being afraid to go into a wooded city park for fear of bears. Simply put, a person learns to be afraid. Exposure therapy can be used to help clients break the pairing of fear and anxiety with certain stimuli or situations and learn an alternate response to fear and anxiety (or anticipation thereof) besides avoidance and escape. Even education about the physical manifestations of fear and anxiety can be therapeutic for clients, as knowledge of arousal as "understandable" or "expected" based on learning history can help clients alter beliefs about the meaning and implications of their symptoms.

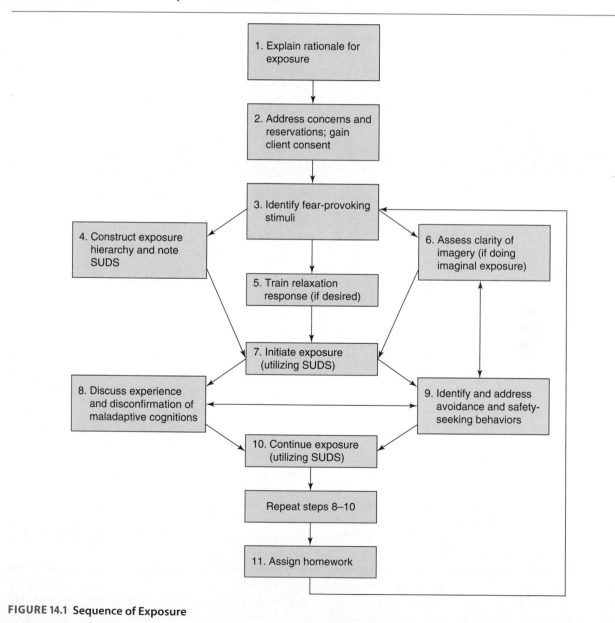

FIGURE 14.1 Sequence of Exposure

Component 2: Addressing Questions, Obtaining Informed Consent, and Psychoeducation

After explaining the rationale for exposure therapy, helpers should address questions and concerns and gain informed consent from clients before proceeding. Rushing into exposure therapy without adequately addressing reasonable client uncertainties can damage rapport and the therapeutic alliance and can potentially lead to premature termination of treatment. Some common concerns that clients might have are that exposure-based treatment will progress too quickly, make them feel worse, and fail to address the underlying or original cause of their problem. Concerns about the pacing of progress usually can be addressed by assuring the client that although the helper will challenge the client to push beyond his or her current comfort zone, treatment ultimately will move at the client's pace. In regard to concerns about feeling worse, clients can be informed that the effort they put forth in therapy now will lead to less anxiety in the future. As for the underlying or original cause of the client's fear, the helper can candidly explain that although information about the history of the client's problem will be gathered and should prove useful in augmenting client and helper understanding, treatment will focus more on the situations in the client's current environment that generate responses of fear and avoidance or escape. It can be communicated that while the past cannot be changed, one can gain at least some degree of control over one's current thoughts, feelings, and behaviors.

Essentially, exposure will not be easy for most clients, nor will it be perceived as a pleasant experience. Although the helper should not guarantee success, he or she can point to the empirical evidence supporting exposure treatments and suggest honestly that many clients receive great benefits from exposure therapy. An opportunity for you to practice explaining exposure therapy is presented in Learning Activity 14.1.

Learning Activity 14.1

Explaining Exposure Therapy

This activity is designed to give you some practice in explaining exposure therapy to a client. You can do this activity with a colleague, a fellow student, or a friend. Someone who is not a helping professional may be a good choice because that interaction may most closely resemble explaining exposure to a client.

Part One: *Developing a Script*

Create a sample script using bullet points so that you are not tempted to read the script word by word. Order the points from most to least important. Include several opportunities throughout the explanation for comments or questions from the client.

Part Two: *Practicing the Explanation*

You may wish to go through the explanation out loud several times in a private setting, hearing yourself and finding the best word combinations for your speaking style.

Part Three: *Delivering the Explanation*

Sit facing the person whom you have invited to participate in this role play. Deliver the explanation as if you are in a real situation with an actual client. (Do you realize that this role play is also a form of exposure for yourself?)

Part Four: *Getting Feedback*

This is the time to listen! Ask the person you involved in your practice what he or she understands exposure to be. Give him/her time and encouragement to think. Ask what questions about exposure remain unanswered. Is there anything else the person wants to know?

Part Five: *Feedback*

Here are some important aspects of exposure therapy to mention in your explanation (these may be written in bullet form on your cue sheet):

- Fear is learned.
- Because fear is learned, there must be new learning to replace inaccurate learning or learning that is no longer accurate in your current context.
- Exposure is a learning-based therapeutic approach that has been found to be very successful in treating fear, anxiety, and other problems.
- Exposure may be a good choice to help you with your problems.
- What are your thoughts so far?
- There are various types of exposure: imaginal, role play (also referred to as *in vitro*), real life (also known as *in vivo*).
- Exposure can be gradual or intensive.
- Do you have any comments and questions? What are your thoughts about the best way for you to use exposure?
- Homework assignments are very helpful and so we'll likely use them.
- Let's plan together a course of exposure to help you with your problems.

Component 3: Identifying Fear-Provoking Stimuli

After gaining informed consent for treatment, the helper begins the process by identifying precisely the fear-provoking stimuli, in some detail. Clients suffering from problems with anxiety generally can be grouped into diagnostic categories, but no two clients are exactly alike. Helpers should take care to discover just what it is that leads to a client's fear and avoidance. Although this sounds deceptively simple on the surface (e.g., "What are you afraid of?"), helpers must be aware of several barriers to information gathering. Many clients have engaged in avoidance behaviors for years and might no longer be certain of what frightens them most. Further, mere discussion of feared topics during therapy can be distressing for some clients. Verbal and cognitive representations of feared stimuli often are aversive, much like the actual situation (e.g., conversations about the traumatic event for a client with PTSD), or they are *the* aversive stimuli (e.g., the obsessive thoughts that a client with OCD finds disturbing). Specifying exactly which aspects of a situation are distressing also can be difficult for clients with more complex anxiety reactions. For example, a client might report a fear of elevators. A skilled helper must not let this statement stand on its own, though. Instead, it should be determined what specifically about the elevator distresses the client. Is it the enclosed space, or the height involved, or the motion of the elevator and subsequent physiological sensations, or an overwhelming sense of dread that the elevator will fall or get stuck for an extended period of time? Although eliciting such details can be time consuming, such information is vital for designing exposure exercises that will disconfirm client expectations regarding the CS and US.

Component 4: Constructing an Exposure Hierarchy

Although a helper must take care not to push the client for information too quickly, the preceding types of questions should be answered in detail to effectively conduct the next step of exposure: constructing an exposure hierarchy. In this step, the client and helper work together to delineate and rank or order the situations the client fears. A good tool for helping the client rank stimuli is the subjective units of discomfort (also labeled distress or disturbance) scale, or SUDS (Wolpe, 1990). SUDS ratings generally range from 0 to 100 and have verbal anchors at each end to assist the client in determining the appropriate ratings. Typical anchors used for the purposes of exposure therapy would be "No fear/anxiety" and "Most fear/anxiety possible" or "No

distress" and "Most distress possible." Most clients can quickly understand SUDS ratings, and these ratings can become a fast and simple tool for self-report of levels of fear and anxiety. Ideally, the client should be able to list at least 10 fear-provoking situations, with each no more than 10 units away from the next situation listed. For each situation, clients should attempt to be as specific as possible.

Other information important to gather for each situation on the hierarchy includes the client's typical thoughts related to the situation, the client's typical response to the situation (an especially important piece of information for particularly avoidant clients or clients with obsessive-compulsive disorder who engage in compulsive rituals), and the client's typical physiological reactions to the situation. Such data provide the helper with a clear vision of the client's experience and perspective and assist the client in rationally deciding which situations provoke the most fear or anxiety (e.g., "My palms sweat when I see a spider in the *basement*, but my palms sweat, my heart races, and I can't stop thinking 'It will get me while I sleep' when I see a spider in my *bedroom*"). Situations can be written in paper form for future reference or, better yet, may be recorded using a word processing program to allow future revisions and additions. Figure 14.2 provides an example of such a form. Once sufficient situations or stimuli have been identified and recorded, an exposure hierarchy can be made, and Figure 14.3 provides a sample hierarchy for a patient with dental phobia. Learning Activity 14.2 provides a chance to practice the development of scenes for exposure therapy.

Component 5: Relaxation Response Training

At this point in treatment, the helper has the option of training the client how to engage in a relaxation response to be used in conjunction with exposure. Many resources exist, including relaxation training exercises such as progressive muscle relaxation and breathing retraining (see Chapter 13; Ferguson & Sgambati, 2009). Other breathing exercises, based on emerging research on Capnometry-Assisted Respiratory Training (Meuret, Wilhelm, Ritz, & Roth, 2008), also might be used to train management of hyperventilation in clients particularly affected by that problem, thereby helping to maintain a relaxed state through slow breathing.

Contemporary literature suggests that relaxation training or similar methods are not necessary for exposure therapy to result in a reduction of fear and avoidance (Craske et al., 2008; Craske et al., 2014; Tryon, 2005). In fact, use of relaxation can be a "**safety behavior**" in

Scene Description Information

Brief description _____ SUDS _____

Describe the scene in detail using all senses (sight, sound, smell, taste, touch) _____
_____
_____

What are your typical behavioral responses? _____
_____

What are your thoughts? _____

What are your physiological responses? _____

(After the client spontaneously reports such responses, inquire about bodily systems not mentioned, and about potential physiological activation, such as increased heart rate, elevated muscle tension, rapid breathing, sweating, and blurry vision.)

FIGURE 14.2 Exposure Scene Description Information

Stimulus	SUDS
Lying reclined in a dental chair alone, with a dentist drilling my teeth	100
Lying reclined in a dental chair, alone, receiving an oral injection from a dentist	95
Lying reclined in a dental chair, with spouse in the room, with a hygienist cleaning my teeth	90
Lying reclined in a dental chair, alone, with a dentist examining my teeth	85
Lying reclined in a dental chair, with spouse in the room, with a dentist examining my teeth	80
Sitting upright in a dental chair, alone, as the dentist enters the room	75
Sitting upright in a dental chair, with spouse in the room, with a dentist in the room and answering the dentist's questions	70
Sitting upright in a dental chair, with spouse in the room, without a dentist in the room	65
Checking in alone at the reception desk for an appointment with a dentist	60
Sitting in the waiting room of a dentist's office alone	55
Checking in with spouse at the reception desk for an appointment with a dentist	50
Sitting in the waiting room of a dentist's office with spouse	45
Walking up to the door of a dentist's office and standing outside the door	40
Sitting in the parking lot of a dentist's office when the office is open	35
Sitting in the parking lot of a dentist's office when the office is closed	30
Calling a dentist's office and making an appointment for a routine visit	25
My spouse or partner reminding me that I have not been for a dental visit in a long time	20
Receiving an "appointment reminder card" from my dental office	15

FIGURE 14.3 Sample Exposure Hierarchy for a Client with a Dental Phobia

which clients avoid experiencing the full force of the anxiety response, instead focusing on performing some action that allows distraction, which may be counter-therapeutic. Nevertheless, we recommend training a relaxation or similar response for several reasons. First, the client may find the overall treatment more acceptable if learning calming skills is involved. To the degree that exposure works through the mechanism of learned self-efficacy, relaxation training can foster a client's sense of mastery and control during exposure. Next, relaxation exercises can help clients become more aware of their physiological and somatic sensations. Over time, mindful attunement to bodily sensations can promote awareness that arousal of the sympathetic nervous system typically does not lead to a permanently debilitating state. For example, the client who states, "If my heart keeps racing and my head keeps spinning, I'm gonna go crazy or have a heart attack," can be supported in noticing and accepting that both arousal and relaxation occur and cycle naturally. Many clients with anxiety problems also report stress from various sources in their lives. Encouraging the client to practice relaxation exercises on a daily basis can reduce

---

Learning Activity 14.2

Developing Scenes for Use in Exposure Therapy

This activity is designed to give you practice in detailing a situation that may be used in exposure. You can do this activity by yourself because almost everyone harbors at least some degree of fear or anxiety about something. It can be helpful to engage in the activities in which we ask our clients to participate and to experience the process from their perspective.

Part One: *Describing the General Situation*

Prepare a written description of a situation that you find anxiety-provoking, including any relevant parameters, such as time of day, weather, the presence or absence of others, and so on. It may be best not to choose a situation that is truly phobic for you, because the degree of emotionality may be counterproductive to this exercise.

Part Two: *Describing Your Behavioral Reactions*

Describe how you typically behave in this situation, such as asking others for reassurance, moving away from the glass wall of the elevator, or closing your eyes.

Part Three: *Describing Your Thoughts*

What thoughts do you have before, during, and after this situation? List anything you can remember regarding the situation, whether it appears rational or not. What are you worried that might happen? What do you believe actually would happen if you would remain in the situation?

Part Four: *Describing Your Physiological Reactions*

How does your body respond in this situation? Review your bodily systems, and list all of the reactions of which you are aware (e.g., cardiovascular, respiratory, gastrointestinal).

---

the overall level of stress, which in turn can have positive effects on anxiety. Finally, relaxation or similar methods can be phased out over the course of exposure treatment; their utilization earlier in treatment can promote client satisfaction, comfort, and adherence, and then can be faded as the client grows more comfortable and confident.

Component 6: Imagery Assessment and Training (if doing imaginal exposure)

In using imagery in therapy, it is important to know the imagery ability of the client. Imagery ability differs across individuals, likely along a continuum, ranging from those people who are quite proficient and able to elicit and control images with ease, to those who report little or no ability to "see pictures in the head" and who do not respond even to what are seemingly the most evocative prompts. The helper can assess imagery ability informally by taking a client through a brief trial of mildly evocative imagery and following-up with questions about the client's degree of engagement and ability to think and feel "as if" the situation actually were happening. There also are self-report instruments that assess imagery ability, such as the Questionnaire on Mental Imagery and the Vividness of Visual Imagery Questionnaire.

It is possible to perform imagery training with clients (Lang, 1977), although when imagery ability is low, other forms of exposure usually are better alternatives than devoting time to helping the client to learn imagery skills. Nevertheless, in certain instances when the actual stimuli are difficult to access for practical or ethical reasons, training in imagery may be a good choice. In such training, clients

are given brief instructions by the clinician, such as trying to act as if the situation actually was happening rather than being a passive, distant observer of an event. Clients also are encouraged to use the full range of sensory modalities, trying to recreate not only the sights but also the smells, tastes, sounds, and physical feelings associated with the situation. Imagery trials are conducted using emotionally positive scenes. The client is asked to imagine and then is asked to report on his or her experiences in imagery, particularly physiological responses. These responses are the focus of attention for the practitioner, who praises and encourages the client to accentuate such responses in future trials.

Component 7: Initial Exposure

With an exposure hierarchy constructed and a relaxation response trained (if desired), the client and helper are ready to begin exposure. It is our experience that given the option, clients generally will attempt to delay exposure as much as possible. This avoidance behavior can take the form of asking repeated questions about the exposure or bringing in a crisis to discuss at the beginning of the therapy session. Although extraordinary crises (e.g., a death in the family, job loss) warrant attention, the skilled helper begins exposure as soon as possible while politely and professionally curtailing avoidance ("I understand that you still have some questions about the process, but I really think that we've covered it enough and at this point the best way to answer any further questions you have is to begin," or, "That sounds like a topic really worth devoting some attention to, and we can discuss it more later, but for now I think we should move on to beginning exposure").

Exposure Record

Name _____ Day/Date _____ Time Start/Finish _____

Location _____ Persons Present _____

Stimulus/Situation _____

	SUDS	Thoughts	Physical Sensations
Start			
5 min			
10 min			
15 min			
20 min			
25 min			
30 min			
35 min			
40 min			
45 min			
50 min			
55 min			
60 min			
65 min			
70 min			
75 min			

FIGURE 14.4 Exposure Record Sheet

Exposure treatment usually begins with the selection of a situation from the client's exposure hierarchy that is sufficiently fear-evoking but not overwhelming (e.g., elicits a SUDS rating of 30 to 60, suggesting a situation that elicits significant anxiety, allowing for new learning to occur) (Craske et al., 2014). The intent is for an exposure that a client will be able to tolerate while still being challenging, allowing for some initial success. The situation may be one in which a client already self-exposes when necessary, but starting here with exposure therapy will allow the client to practice the methods of exposure therapy and experience any differences from how he or she normally endures the situation (e.g., deliberately noting thoughts, feelings, and sensations versus distracting oneself by counting down the minutes until it is over). The exact method by which the client can be exposed to the stimuli depends on the type of exposure being conducted. Constant across all methods of exposure, however, is the general formula of the client's

moving through his or her feared situations and being fully exposed to each situation until there is disconfirmation of the client's expectancy of a negative outcome (Craske et al., 2014), and either a learned toleration of the fear or fear reduction. As one alternative, one might focus on reduction of SUDS ratings; what constitutes an acceptable level depends on the goals and model of the exposure therapy. A model focused on *mastery* would emphasize a high level of proficiency in minimizing the anxiety response and would have as a goal a SUDS rating approaching 0. In contrast, a *coping* model of exposure would focus on reducing anxiety to a manageable level rather than complete anxiety reduction. For example, Foa et al. (2007) suggest a SUDS rating 50% less than the peak SUDS value might be an acceptable goal for each item. Regardless of the model, the helper and client should discuss and agree on what the goals of exposure therapy will be. Each exposure session should be recorded on a sheet similar to the example in Figure 14.4.

When a client's expectations have been disconfirmed, or when the SUDS ratings have been reduced to a pre-determined level, the stimuli can be presented again to reinforce the achievement and assess its stability. The helper should take care to encourage the client to remain in the exposure situation until he or she experiences a dis-confirmation of expected negative outcome or a reduction in anxiety and distress, depending on one's approach, even if this takes some time. If the client or the clinician termi-nates exposure prematurely, several negative outcomes are likely: the client will be reinforced for escape/avoidance behavior, the clinician will be reinforcing distorted cogni-tions that the stimulus is dangerous and worthy of fear and avoidance, new learning overriding the connection between fear and the stimulus will not occur, and client self-efficacy will be decreased even further.

Component 8: Discussing the Experience and Disconfirming Maladaptive Cognitions

In planning the exposure session, the helper should have a period set aside at the end to discuss the client's experience and to identify behaviors that may be helpful or detrimen-tal to progress. The helper and the client can benefit by reviewing the client's perspective of the session so that dis-confirmation of any problem thoughts and actions can be highlighted, as can adaptive responses. For example, a cli-ent with social anxiety disorder – performance only might have the belief that he will "go blank" or "say nonsensical things" if he stands up in front of a small audience in a clinic setting. Gradual exposure may be most appropriate here, first having the client stand in front of the group and looking at them for 30 seconds, then sitting down for 30 seconds, and repeating that cycle a few times. Then, the client gradually would introduce himself a few times with breaks, moving on to beginning a speech as exposure.

After exposure, the client and helper can discuss the experience and relate it to expectations beforehand with open-ended questions ("What did you expect would hap-pen during the exposure?" "What did you expect would happen if you stood in front of the group and said noth-ing?" "How did it feel to stand in front of the group and look at the audience?" "What happened after the expo-sure?" "What do you think will happen the next time you stand in front of a group?") followed by reflections. This discussion promotes the salience of "**expectancy viola-tion**," in which a client's negative beliefs and predictions about exposure to feared stimuli are disconfirmed.

It is important to facilitate the client drawing his or her own conclusions, rather than the helper first telling the client what seems to have happened. Exposure is *ex-periential* learning; it contradicts the spirit of the therapy to engage in a didactic component at the end instead of allowing the client to reach his or her own conclusions independently at his or her own pace, similar to principles of Motivational Interviewing reviewed in Chapter 10.

Component 9: Identifying and Addressing Avoidance and Safety-Seeking Behaviors

The helper also must be watchful for signs that the cli-ent is engaging in avoidance or **safety-seeking** behaviors during exposure (such as escaping by leaving a situation literally or attentionally). Such actions delay progress in therapy and reinforce behaviors detrimental to coping effectively with anxiety. Avoidance and safety-seeking behaviors manifest in multiple forms, and helpers are strongly encouraged to examine the function a given be-havior serves rather than to focus solely on the form of the behavior. Some clients with panic disorder, for example, keep benzodiazepine rescue medications with them at all times in case a panic attack should occur. Typically, it is best to work toward fading that behavior over time because having the pill present is a contextual safety cue upon which the client is dependent, disallowing true reso-lution of the client's problems. There are several red flags that warrant a helper's vigilance because they probably indicate that a client is not fully benefiting from exposure therapy. If during exposure a client's SUDS ratings do not rise near the anticipated level, then the client pos-sibly could be engaging in overt (e.g., looking away from the stimulus) or covert (e.g., thinking of something else) avoidance behaviors. Although some clients have learned to avoid a stimulus so proficiently that they overestimate their SUDS rating ahead of time, helpers will need to gently but firmly address the possibility of avoidance.

Freezing is a type of phobic reaction that is a form of avoidance. It sometimes occurs in public speaking or den-tal situations. Functionally, freezing allows the individual to temporarily avoid interaction and to insulate himself or herself from the ongoing situation. Camouflage is another form of avoidance in which clients, consciously or subconsciously, attempt to minimize their detection in feared situations. If an individual is less noticed, then there is reduced opportunity for social demand. Our cli-ent Isabella, for example, may choose to wear inconspicu-ous clothing at a school dance so that she is less noticed by potential dancing partners. Not being noticed allows her to avoid social encounters and to not have the social demand of accepting or declining invitations to dance. Actually, Isabella may avoid going to the dance altogether if she experiences social anxiety disorder. Alternately, she may escape the dance by leaving early, perhaps saying that "it was boring," a form of reason giving.

As human beings, we may avoid not only uncomfortable objects, situations, and events but also our own distressing physiological and cognitive reactions to them or to the prospect of them. From an ACT perspective, there can be experiential avoidance in which the client withdraws from experiencing negative cognitive and psychophysiological reactions (Hayes, Strosahl, & Wilson, 2012). This avoidance may be produced through processes of shutting down or psychological numbing or distancing, and it may be aided by the use of alcohol and other substances. Not allowing oneself to experience uncomfortable states, however, is a problem in that it serves to reinforce, maintain, and possibly exacerbate the fear.

A helper also should take note when clients talk excessively during exposure sessions or repeatedly ask questions such as, "Are you sure this is safe?" or, "You're sure that snake can't get out of the terrarium?" Excessive talking often acts as a form of distraction and indicates that the client is not fully experiencing the stimulus. Repeated questions, in contrast, often are an attempt to seek reassurance from the helper. Although it can be tempting to answer all questions to allay client fears, such behavior can have a detrimental effect by implicitly reinforcing the belief that the stimulus is unsafe and deserving of worry. Clients also could learn to become dependent on the helper to complete exposure exercises ("If it hadn't been for you letting me know it was safe, I don't think I could have done it"). Clients should be learning that they are capable of coping independently and effectively with the feared stimuli, not that exposure is possible only with the assistance of an expert.

Component 10: Continuing Exposure through the Hierarchy

After assessing the client's first exposure session and addressing any difficulties that arise, the helper typically utilizes exposure again and again, session after session. When the client gains competence with one stimulus from the hierarchy by showing a minimal SUDS rating and minimal avoidance, the client and helper should move on to the next item on the exposure hierarchy. After each session, the client and helper should take time to discuss the exposure and any insights the client had, as well as address any safety-seeking or avoidance behaviors. Gradual exposure therapy is an iterative process and evolves over time as new issues arise and are addressed.

This sequence of steps in exposure therapy allows helpers to gain an initial understanding of the how-to of exposure. No substitute exists, though, for supervised experiences. Just as exposure therapy rests on the assumption that several sessions of experiential learning can begin the process of reversing learned habits of fear and avoidance, learning and mastering exposure therapy skills also require learning by doing.

Component 11: Homework

As therapy progresses, the client should engage in independent, self-directed exposure exercises outside of the therapeutic context, which should be recorded on an exposure record (see Figure 14.3). Some protocols (e.g., Foa et al., 2007) request that clients engage in multiple exposure homework assignments between therapy sessions. Such homework assignments can include self-exposure to stimuli with which the client already has demonstrated some proficiency in session while still pushing the client out of his or her comfort zone; some researchers suggest introducing variability to exposure exercises (interspersing more challenging stimuli or situations from the hierarchy with less challenging situations) to enhance learning and long-term retention of treatment gains (Craske et al., 2014). These homework assignments allow the client to experience a decrease in anxiety in the presence of a fear-provoking stimulus and to violate CS–US expectations in multiple contexts. Such learning is vital to ensure that the client generalizes new associations made between stimuli and the absence of anxiety.

Gradual Exposure

Gradual exposure therapy (which historically has **LO4** been known as systematic desensitization) has been used efficaciously and effectively to reduce fear and anxiety for decades. Proper implementation of gradual exposure is vital to achieve the most success with clients exhibiting anxiety problems. Each disorder has its own nuances related to exposure therapy. It is our experience, however, that while the specifics of gradual exposure change with each client, the general principles remain the same across individuals and contexts. Therefore, we present the underlying principles, but the helper must determine how best to apply the corresponding strategies and techniques to assist a client in overcoming problem levels of fear and anxiety.

As previously noted, exposure can take one of three forms. First, clients can be exposed to *imaginal* stimuli (i.e., fear- or anxiety-provoking stimuli of which the client creates a mental image). Second, clients can engage in ***in vitro exposure*** in which the stimuli are more tangible but still simulated. For example, client and helper can roleplay an interaction with the client's boss that caused the client anxiety in the past or that the client worries about occurring in the future. Finally, clients can be exposed to the actual situations and stimuli that elicit fear and anxiety, a process referred to as *in vivo exposure*. A client who has a fear of spiders might first touch a spider, and later allow a spider to crawl over his or her hand, or even over his or her face. These three forms of gradual exposure therapy can be used sequentially, in tandem, or independently.

Gradual exposure involves development of a graduated list or hierarchy of anxiety-eliciting cues through which helper and client progressively work. An array of cognitive behavioral interventions often is paired with exposure therapy, depending on the nature of the problem and goals (McNally, 2007). Relaxation training commonly is paired with exposure to support a relaxed state in the face of distress-generating stimuli. Implementation details are provided here; see also Head and Gross (2009) for a useful overview.

Imaginal Exposure

The topics relevant to imaginal exposure we discuss include:

1. Description of imaginal exposure
2. Advantages of imaginal exposure
3. Limitations of imaginal exposure
4. Imagery ability
5. Eye movement desensitization and reprocessing

Topic 1: Description of Imaginal Exposure In this approach, the client is prompted to think about and otherwise experience scenes that provoke anxiety. Commonly, the client describes anxiety-provoking scenes in detail, and the helper or client records the information. Historically, note cards were used, but there are many advantages to typing and storing the information electronically, allowing for ongoing revisions. To make the image as realistic as possible, the client should attempt to explain the scene using as much sensory and response information as possible. A client who has suffered a motor vehicle accident and now fears driving might describe the scene of simply sitting behind the wheel of an automobile. In addition to being able to list all the visual cues present when behind the wheel (e.g., the color of the dashboard and upholstery, the different gauges behind the steering column, the view from the rearview mirror), the client also should attempt to recall smells (e.g., of leather upholstery), sounds (e.g., of the engine idling), tactile sensations (e.g., the softness of the seats), and even tastes when possible (e.g., of mint chewing gum if the client sometimes chews gum while driving). The ability to imagine a scene with great detail allows exposure to as many cues as possible to elicit

anxiety, which then allows for subsequent anxiety reduction and new learning.

Imaginal exposure can be especially potent for clients whose primary fear-provoking stimuli are cognitions. For example, someone who witnessed the traumatic event of a fatal car accident could be fearful about his or her memories of the accident. In these cases, special care should be taken to walk the client through imaginal exposure in a supportive environment while establishing evidence for the new belief and understanding that thoughts themselves cannot cause harm, nor must they necessarily lead to overt motor behaviors.

Imaginal exposure can entail direct and immediate relating of fear-evoking situations by the helper's auditory prompts in reading a script or suggesting cues or memories of an event. It also is possible to incorporate relaxing, positive, or neutral images that are incompatible with anxiety and fear. One possible sequence of such imaginal exposure is to establish a relaxing, positive, or neutral image selected by the client that elicits a SUDS rating of 0. Sitting back in a chair with eyes closed at the start of the exposure session, the client can imagine this scene to assist with relaxation. When the client is relaxed with a SUDS rating at or near 0, he or she should give some signal to the helper, preferably nonverbal (e.g., raise index finger) to minimize the strain on the client's attention. The helper then asks the client to imagine a scene from the exposure hierarchy. When the client signals that the scene is a clear image, the helper continues the exposure for a brief period of time (typically 15 to 30 seconds) before asking the client to erase the image. Following this step, the helper quickly asks for a SUDS rating before asking the client to imagine the neutral, relaxing, or positive scene again for a minute or two. When the client signals relaxation again, the helper asks the client to return to the scene from the hierarchy. This pattern continues until the SUDS rating that the scene elicits diminishes significantly and the neutral or positive scene has followed to induce relaxation. At this point, the helper and client move on to the next scene. It is best to end sessions with successful completion of an anxiety scene, followed by a neutral or relaxing scene. The next session should begin with the last scene from the previous session that elicited a minimal amount of anxiety.

For other uses of imaginal exposure (e.g., prolonged exposure for PTSD; Foa et al., 2007), the client takes the lead in describing the imagined scene for exposure, and the helper does not participate in story-telling beyond occasional prompts if the client's description lacks sufficient detail. With other imaginal exposure, much depends on the helper being a good storyteller, reading the scripts in an evocative manner to spark the client's imagination and elicit images. Whether the client or helper takes responsibility for describing the scene during exposure will depend on the treatment protocol being used and helper judgment. Client avoidance can take the form of refusal to clearly imagine an anxiety-provoking scene. The helper and client should discuss the client's concerns regarding clearly picturing the scene, and care should be taken to make sure the hierarchy is not ascended too quickly. Homework for imaginal exposure typically takes the form of practicing at home with items that have been completed successfully in therapy.

Imaginal exposure can be used either alone or in conjunction with (and generally before) *in vitro* or *in vivo* exposure. If all the client's fear-provoking stimuli are cognitive, then imaginal exposure as the primary method of exposure would make sense. As an example, a significant component of prolonged exposure for PTSD is imaginal exposure to the traumatic memory. Usually though, even for clients whose anxiety-provoking stimuli are primarily cognitive, real-world events tend to increase the likelihood of such cognitions. Clients with PTSD who experience anxiety and distress from memories of the trauma might experience distress more often in the context of stimuli that remind them of the event, for example, and exposure to these stimuli and situations also is incorporated into treatment. Usually, imaginal exposure should be used as a stepping stone to more realistic exposure so new learning can better generalize to the client's everyday life.

Topic 2: Advantages of imaginal exposure Imaginal exposure offers several advantages to helpers. It might be the only form of exposure that clients with severe cases of anxiety are willing to endure at first. Disconfirming negative expectations and building self-efficacy can occur through imaginal exposure, which then can allow for the client to progress to more reality-based exposure. Another benefit derives from the element of control that is present. Imagined scenes can be created to conform precisely to how the helper and client would like to see exposure progress. Unforeseen occurrences that could potentially hinder progress for some clients (e.g., a client with obsessive-compulsive disorder falling ill subsequent to a session involving touching a bathroom door handle, or a client with a specific phobia of dogs inadvertently being bitten) have much less likelihood of occurring with imaginal exposure. Imaginal exposure also presents the most direct form of exposure for fear-provoking stimuli that are primarily cognitive. Finally, imaginal exposure is more practically implemented because some situations are impossible to reliably produce (e.g., flying on an airplane with severe turbulence) or are ethically inappropriate to recreate (e.g., trauma in combat or physical assault) *in vivo*.

Topic 3: Limitations of imaginal exposure Although offering some distinct benefits, imaginal exposure certainly has limitations. Some clients less skilled in creating mental images might have a difficult time fully immersing themselves in anxiety-provoking scenes and may view the process as hokey or overly contrived. If the scene does not evoke a sufficient amount of anxiety or does not closely resemble the actual anxiety-provoking stimuli, then new learning capable of overriding old learning may not occur. Imagined scenes might be quite realistic for clients with vivid imaginations, but they still are symbols and representations of actual stimuli. The best (i.e., longest-lasting and most likely to generalize) learning likely occurs in the presence of real stimuli because research suggests that *in vivo* exposure may be the most effective (Davey, 1997; Zoellner, Abramowitz, Moore, & Slagle, 2009). Finally, although the helper can monitor a client's SUDS ratings and infer from self-report that the client is imagining certain scenes, the only person with complete access to precisely what the client is imagining is the client. With real stimuli, conversely, the clinician at the least can directly observe and quantify their presentation (e.g., timing how long a patient with dental phobia can tolerate having a dental instrument held in his or her mouth).

Topic 4: Imagery ability The efficacy of imaginal therapies depends at least in part on the client's ability to vividly imagine. What is in the imagination has the power to evoke emotions, including psychophysiological responses in the form of heart rate change, muscle tension, and sweat gland activity, among others. The use of imagery in therapy often takes the form of visualization, focusing on visual images, or "pictures in the head." Nevertheless, the act of seeing transcends all sensory modalities, including smell, taste, hearing, and touch. In the case of dental phobia, for example, the client not only may have memories of visual images of the dentist, dental chair, and instruments but also may remember the smell of the dental office, the taste in the mouth associated with different dental procedures, the sound of the dental drill, the feeling of the instruments on her teeth and gums, and the touch of the dentist's gloved fingers inside her mouth. These images may be distressing to the individual with dental phobia, but it is precisely this material that provides the basis for positive therapeutic change. These images actually are grist for the mill of imaginal exposure. In fact, the more psychophysiologically evocative such images are, the greater is the likelihood of successful imaginal exposure. It should be noted that these images are stored in the client's memory and may be based on actual experiences, but they may also originate from vicariously learned material, such as stories from friends, relatives, and media reports, or they may have been created from the client's own fearful anticipation of what might happen.

Peter Lang and colleagues had an early and lasting impact on our understanding of the value of imagery in therapy (Lang, 1977; Lang, Cuthbert, & Bradley, 1998). They found that the client's images, across sensory modalities, are powerful tools that can be used effectively in therapy. Images often are prompted by the clinician, who helps the client manage them so that they are evocative when therapeutically indicated but so that thinking about them does not spiral out of control. Typically, personally relevant imagined scenes are more evocative than generic ones. In fact, helpers should be aware that there is a great deal of personal relevance in imagery. Relaxing scenes, for example, are highly individual, and the clinician should elicit them from the client rather than assuming that what he or she considers relaxing would also be so for the client. An image of spending a lazy day lounging by a waterfall may seem relaxing to the helper, but not for a client who has a phobia of water or for a client who remembers a nasty breakup with a romantic partner after a day spent together at a waterfall. Learning Activity 14.3 provides an opportunity to practice an imaginal exposure session.

Topic 5: Eye movement desensitization and reprocessing Some might consider eye movement desensitization and reprocessing (EMDR) a form of imaginal exposure. Briefly, EMDR is a form of therapy primarily focused on traumatic memories (Shapiro, 2001) wherein the client recalls and attunes to a target image associated with a traumatic memory while the helper moves his or her fingers rapidly back and forth across the client's field of vision. EMDR procedures are implemented within and across sessions until the memories of the traumatic incident no longer evoke anxiety and fear.

At best, the empirical support for EMDR has been mixed. Although several organizations list EMDR as an effective or probably efficacious treatment for trauma populations (American Psychiatric Association, 2004; Chambless et al.,

1998; U.S. DoVA/DoD, 2004), an Institute of Medicine (2008) review suggested that evidence is insufficient to conclude treatment efficacy with PTSD in particular. Perhaps the strongest criticism of EMDR has been a lack of evidence that it represents a different mechanism of change than other exposure treatments (Davidson & Parker, 2001; Devilly, 2002) and that it has proven no more effective as a treatment for anxiety disorders than other established treatments, such as exposure (de Jongh & ten Broeke, 2009).

In Vitro Exposure (Simulated Situations)

The topics of *in vitro* exposure we describe here include:

1. Description of *in vitro* exposure

2. Advantages of *in vitro* exposure

3. Role play

4. Virtual reality

5. Limitations of *in vitro* exposure

Topic 1: Description of in vitro exposure Although *in vitro* literally means "in the test tube," we use that term to refer to exposure that happens in an office situation, using role plays, other simulated situations, or even technology in the form of **virtual reality exposure therapy** (VRET). *In vitro* exposure, which consists of exposure to stimuli and situations meant to simulate actual fear-provoking stimuli, lies between imaginal exposure and *in vivo* exposure in degree of realism. Role plays are used extensively in cognitive behavioral group therapy for social phobia (Hope et al., 2010), which uses exposure to simulated social situations in the safety of a group therapy session. The helper attempts to recreate the events that the client reports as eliciting an anxiety response. The complexity and degree of realism of these simulated situations can vary greatly. A helper who has a thorough understanding of the habits and mannerisms of an individual whom a client associates with anxiety

---

Learning Activity 14.3

Developing an Example Imaginal Exposure Session

This activity is designed to give you some practice in using imaginal exposure. Assume that Isabella, the model client, has a phobia about receiving a dental injection.

Part One: *Developing a Hierarchy of Situations*

Prepare a list of likely situations related to needles and oral injections that Isabella would find uncomfortable.

Part Two: *Develop the Scenes*

Use the sample form (see Figure 14.2) to help fully develop the description of each situation, including behavioral, cognitive, and physiological aspects of Isabella's response.

Part Three: *Conducting Exposure*

Read the situations out loud with appropriate feeling and a persuasive storytelling voice designed to engage the client. Use appropriate pauses to allow the hypothetical (but absent) client to think about and fully experience the scene.

can serve as an "actor/actress" to create a fairly realistic and anxiety-provoking stimulus. Similarly, a helper with the proper resources can create realistic faux vomit for a client with a fear of vomiting by others (e.g., one's child). Various CDs and clips from popular films can be used to simulate phobia situations as *in vitro* exposure.

One way to conduct *in vitro* exposure is to begin by examining the scenes and stimuli described by the client as part of his or her exposure hierarchy. The helper should decide which scenes are better suited for *in vitro* exposure and which scenes are better suited for *in vivo* exposure. Additionally, some scenes lend themselves well to both *in vitro* and *in vivo* exposure. For example, a client with social anxiety disorder might experience anxiety in relation to speaking with coworkers (SUDS = 40) and speaking with the boss (SUDS = 60). Most likely, *in vivo* exposure would be recommended as a homework assignment, perhaps later in therapy. *In vitro* exposure, through role plays in the therapy session, however, offers the chance to ease into *in vivo* exposure, to practice social skills, and to gain exposure to a variety of possible reactions from coworkers and the boss (warmth and support, indifference, hostility, etc.).

Because *in vitro* exposure is typically meant to imitate real-life scenes and stimuli that elicit anxiety, it is important to make the situations as real as possible for the client. Properly trained and ethically sanctioned confederates can be enlisted to simulate situations involving strangers or people of a different sex or age from the therapist. In addition, because *in vitro* exposure mirrors reality, it usually is important to have the goal of eventually moving on to *in vivo* exposure, although in other instances prolonged imaginal exposure is the most appropriate option (Foa et al., 2007). Sometimes, moving on to *in vivo* exposure will prove challenging. A helper using *in vitro* exposure with a client who has a fear of flying will most likely not move on to *in vivo* exposure until toward the end of therapy, whereas a helper using role plays to expose a client to social interactions might use a format in which situations for *in vivo* exposure homework are practiced first in session via *in vitro* exposure, and then practiced as *in vivo* homework prior to the next session.

In vitro exposure also can focus on *interoceptive* cues—that is, internal physiological sensations that the client fears. Interoceptive exposure involves clients engaging in physical exercises that produce bodily sensations (especially ones signaling negative arousal) such as dizziness, shortness of breath, or increased heart rate that are fearful to them and that mimic some of the symptoms of a panic attack. Activities include spinning in a chair or doing step-up exercises with a stool (Barlow, 2002). For example, a client with panic disorder might have

the belief that he will go crazy or suffer a heart attack if he experiences another panic attack. Interoceptive exposure may be appropriate here in that the client could be exposed to increased heart rate through doing step-up exercises. As we noted in Chapter 13, any physically exerting procedures should be undertaken only if assessed to be appropriate to the client's medical status. These exercises increase heart rate and can lead to client fear and anxiety that subsequently subside. Properly managed interoceptive exposure has a strong record of success (e.g., Forsyth, Fusé, & Acheson, 2009), including in cases with comorbidity (Wald, 2008).

It can be argued that interoceptive exposure actually is *in vivo*, but we classify it as *in vitro* because it typically takes place in the helper's office, under the helper's supervision, not in a naturalistic environment. Forsyth and colleagues (2009) provide a range of illustrations and exercises that can be useful in helping to simulate bodily sensations in the use of interoceptive exposure. The importance of establishing a trusting relationship and clear communication between helper and client is underscored. Interoceptive techniques are experiential strategies that evoke the very kinds of feelings that clients wish to avoid or about which they want to rid themselves.

Helpers should be vigilant against client attempts to avoid and escape *in vitro* exposure. A refusal by the client to attempt to immerse herself or himself in simulated situations could be related to a fear of the consequences of immersion. Clients might protest against repeated role plays of the same scenario, claiming not to understand why it is necessary to conduct the exercise again and again if it went well the first time. When using virtual reality technology, clients might protest that it gives them motion sickness. Although client concerns with interoceptive exposure may be legitimate, helpers also need to be prepared to deal with resistance and to support the client in holding the course and pushing through these challenges. Careful pacing, honest dialogue, and a collaborative helping style are essential.

Topic 2: Advantages of *in vitro* exposure *In vitro* exposure offers the skilled helper several distinct advantages. Clients can be exposed to situations and stimuli through *in vitro* exposure that would be very difficult to conduct using *in vivo* exposure. Unlike imaginal exposure, *in vitro* exposure allows the helper to directly observe the stimuli to which the client is exposed. Moreover, the helper can execute greater control during *in vitro* exposure than during most *in vivo* or imaginal exposure sessions. For example, the helper is limited only by his or her imagination as to how a role play can be directed. Initially, a positive and reinforcing experience can be crafted for the client;

later, a situation designed to challenge the client's ability to cope with adverse circumstances can be orchestrated. This element of control permits the helper to direct exposure with a degree of precision and certainty not possible with most *in vivo* exposure.

Topic 3: Role play Role plays are simulated interactions between two or more people meant to approximate interactions that have happened or will potentially happen in the future. The client typically plays himself or herself while the helper and confederates play other people in the client's everyday environment. Sometimes, especially for clients with skill deficits accompanying anxiety problems, the helper can assume the role of the client at first to model proficient social and coping skills. Role plays have proven useful in treatment for anxiety disorders (e.g., Foa, 1997).

Role plays can be conducted in several ways, based on the client's current skill level and the experience the helper wishes the client to have. If the client's skill level appears to be low, approximately less than 60 percent proficient, then it probably will be a better learning experience to watch the helper perform the task first. Similarly, if the client's anxiety level most likely will prevent a somewhat competent performance, the helper probably will want to perform the role play first to demonstrate the correct way to do it. But if the client appears to possess a minimum level of skill and likely will not be hindered too greatly by anxiety, then it might be best to have the client perform the task first without the helper modeling it.

An additional decision that helpers must face with role plays is the level of proficiency to expect during the role play. If the emphasis is on the client's being able to perform certain tasks while still experiencing some anxiety, then perfection certainly would not be a realistic goal for the role play. When modeling the role play, the helper also might portray himself or herself as coping with the situation despite dealing with anxiety. Alternatively, if the emphasis of treatment is on almost complete anxiety reduction, then role plays might be repeated until no anxiety seems apparent. Modeled role plays might be performed with greater mastery by the helper to create a higher standard.

Topic 4: Virtual reality A form of *in vitro* exposure gaining considerable attention in recent years has been *virtual reality exposure therapy*, or VRET (Diemer, Muhlberger, Pauli, & Zwanzger, 2014; Meehan, Razzaque, Insko, Whitton, & Brooks, 2005). Virtual reality exposure involves using electronic media equipment to create a realistic three-dimensional environment in which a person can be immersed. Either the helper or the client can control

the client's progress through the virtual reality environment. Depending on the level of technology being used, VRET can be an experience closely resembling real life for some clients. Even if the VRET environment does not precisely resemble a real-world setting, many clients still can experience significant anxiety and fear in response to VRET stimuli, thus creating the opportunity for new learning to occur.

VRET can be especially useful for exposing clients to situations and stimuli not easily accomplished through *in vivo* exposure. Further, it presents the opportunity to expose clients to a variety of situations without the need to leave the treatment setting. A helper assisting a client with a paralyzing fear of heights does not need to locate an appropriately tall building or another height-related stimulus in the surrounding area and arrange a field trip. Instead, the client can come to the helper's work setting, and suitable stimuli can be created with VRET equipment (e.g., a tall building with an observation deck, a bridge, a cliff, a glass elevator, a hot air balloon ride). The stimuli to which the client can gain exposure are limited only by imagination and technology, although the expense of developing programs and securing equipment are significant. VRET also is discussed later in this chapter as a contemporary development in the arena of exposure.

Topic 5: Limitations of *in vitro* exposure Perhaps one of the biggest disadvantages of *in vitro* exposure can be the time and resources sometimes required to properly conduct the exposure. Not all helpers have ready access to virtual reality equipment, nor can all helpers easily enlist the help of confederates to assist with the exposure. The amount of time and effort required to conduct *in vitro* exposure in addition to, or instead of, *in vivo* exposure might not seem to be worthwhile, especially because not all forms of *in vitro* exposure have received the same amount of empirical support as *in vivo* exposure. Finally, not all clients will engage seriously in *in vitro* exposure and fully immerse themselves in the experience, thus potentially not benefiting as much as they might from *in vivo* exposure. Ending our discussion of *in vitro* exposure, Learning Activity 14.4 focuses on practicing an *in vitro* exposure session.

In Vivo Exposure

The topics of *in vivo* exposure we discuss here include:

1. Description of *in vivo* exposure

2. Advantages of *in vivo* exposure

3. Limitations of *in vivo* exposure

Developing a Sample *In Vitro*

Exposure Session

This activity is designed to give you some practice in preparing to use *in vitro* exposure. Again, assume that Isabella, the model client, has a phobia about receiving a dental injection.

Part One: *Developing a Hierarchy of Situations*

Brainstorm a hierarchical list of situations related to needles and oral injections that Isabella likely would find uncomfortable. (This list may be the same one you constructed for Learning Activity 14.3.)

Part Two: *Develop the In Vitro Steps*

Prepare a list of vignettes that you could enact in an office environment to work through each of the items on the fear hierarchy that was developed in Part One above. Some possibilities include bringing in books or brochures with pictures of dental situations, accessing pictures of dental situations available on the Internet, showing the client a set of dental instruments borrowed from a dentist, showing the client one or more syringes of different sizes, showing pictures or video clips of injections other than oral ones, showing pictures or video clips of dental injections, having the client interact with a toy or modified syringe (with no needle), role-playing an injection in the arm with the therapist wearing a white lab coat, and bringing the toy syringe close to the client's mouth (but not inside, for sanitary reasons) while she is seated (as in a dental chair).

Topic 1: Description of *in vivo* exposure This approach involves exposure to the actual stimuli and situations that provoke anxiety and fear for a client. *In vivo* exposure can be conducted in or out of the therapy setting depending on the nature of the client's problem. It might be feasible to conduct *in vivo* exposure in session with a client who has a fear of spiders by bringing in different spider stimuli. With a client who has a fear of riding in a motor vehicle, *in vivo* exposure ultimately must take place outside of the therapy setting in an actual automobile. (In such instances, it generally is prudent for the exposure sessions to be guided by professionals from a driving school.)

In vivo exposure is conducted in much the same way as imaginal and *in vitro* exposure, and it generally follows the steps described (see Figure 14.1). When a client engages in *in vivo* exposure, it is important that the helper takes steps to ensure that the client remains physically and psychologically in the presence of the feared stimulus until his or her expectancies about negative outcomes are disconfirmed, or SUDS rating decreases. Often the helper is assisting the client in overcoming years of avoidance, and so ensuring that the client remains present with the fear-provoking stimuli for an extended period of time can require skilled application of the helper's clinical acumen. If the client is to break the association of avoidance or escape with anxiety reduction, then he or she should engage in new learning in which anxiety reduction occurs in the presence of the feared stimulus.

As with other forms of exposure, helpers must be on the lookout for avoidance, escape, and safety-seeking behaviors from the client. Clients might attempt to delay exposure by talking about it rather than doing it. During exposure, clients might not look directly at the stimulus, or they may engage in other sensory avoidance (e.g., not listening, thinking about something else). Clients with PTSD may position themselves so their backs are never exposed and so they can see the entire crowd or room, and clients with panic disorder and/or agoraphobia may only engage in exposure to crowds if they can remain at the periphery, near exits where escape will be easier. Clients also could engage in distraction by conversing with the helper. Helpers should note that clients can learn to escape *in vivo* exposure by reporting lower SUDS ratings despite minimal reduction in actual levels of fear and distress. If a helper notices a disparity between a client's self-reported distress and overt motor behavior (e.g., looking away from the stimulus) or physiological response (e.g., sweating profusely), the helper should attempt to bring this disparity to the client's attention in a nonaccusatory manner.

In vivo exposure has the additional advantage of lending itself well to homework assignments. A client who is being seen for a 1-hour therapy session once per week is living the other 167 hours of his or her life outside of the therapy session. With evidence suggesting that learning from exposure therapy has a strong contextual component (Mystkowski et al., 2002), it is essential for clients to engage in exposure exercises outside of the therapy context and in the settings in which they live their daily lives. Homework can be assigned to a client based on progress in therapy, and the client can complete exposure exercises with a particular stimulus for the first time outside of the therapy context. To create a palatable title for the exercise and to reduce unrealistic, all-or-none expectations of success, homework assignments might be referred to as behavioral experiments. Consider the example of a client with social anxiety disorder speaking with a colleague at work. The helper can present the exposure exercise of conversing with the colleague as a behavioral experiment to test the client's beliefs and assumptions. This way, the helper can create a situation in which the client seldom fails. If the exposure experience goes well, then the client builds self-efficacy and engages in new learning suggesting he or she can cope with social anxiety. If the conversation goes poorly, then the client and helper emphasize that it was an experiment to learn why the experience went poorly and what can be done differently in the future to create a more positive experience.

One consideration that is discussed in more detail later in the chapter is the presence or absence of the helper during *in vivo* exposure. The therapist's presence early in a course of *in vivo* therapy can help to make the exposure more gradual and palatable. In some instances, a team of two or more practitioners may be helpful, adding generalization to the situation so that the client's success completing an activity is not ascribed to the presence of a specific individual such as the primary helper. Variability in fear stimuli and overall context (and in fear levels) throughout the course of exposure is a strategy that is central to an inhibitory learning approach (Craske et al., 2014) that may help prevent later return of fear after treatment.

In vivo exposure can come after imaginal and/or *in vitro* exposure, or it can be the sole means of exposure used during treatment. As discussed, some clients might find it easier to engage initially in imagined or simulated forms of exposure before facing real-life versions of anxiety-provoking stimuli. At other times, the client's situation might lend itself quite well to *in vivo* exposure right from the beginning. The ultimate use of *in vivo* exposure methods will call upon the clinical judgment of the helper and the informed preference of the client.

Topic 2: Advantages of *in vivo* exposure Despite disagreement over the precise mechanism(s) through which exposure works, most researchers probably agree that the most effective learning during exposure likely occurs in the presence of the actual anxiety-provoking stimuli. As the goal of treatment typically involves improving the client's adaptive functioning and reducing his or her distress in daily living, it makes sense to engage in exposure to the stimuli from the client's day-to-day life that have resulted in impaired functioning and increased distress. Finally, *in vivo* exposure involves exposure to tangible stimuli that can objectively be quantified to document the client's treatment gains. For example, a helper utilizing *in vivo* exposure can note that a client who began therapy unable to remain in a room with a caged, common garden snake

1 foot in length was able nine sessions later to drape a python 6 feet in length over his or her shoulders for a period of 5 minutes.

Topic 3: Limitations of *in vivo* exposure Many clients have reservations about engaging in *in vivo* exposure, especially without any sort of preparation through imaginal or *in vitro* exposure. First, because the helper cannot exercise complete control over *in vivo* exposure exercises, the potential always exists that unforeseen events will cause a temporary setback in the client's progress. Second, behavioral experiment homework assignments can be an aversive experience for a client who meets with a high degree of perceived failure, and the helper might have to spend therapy time repairing the client's damaged self-confidence and faith in exposure treatment. Third, the primary anxiety-provoking stimuli for some clients can be imaginal in nature, and *in vivo* exposure might not be the best form of exposure therapy for eliciting the greatest amount of client anxiety to promote the most new learning. Fourth, there are practical and ethical limitations that sometimes prohibit use of *in vivo* exposure. As with imaginal and *in vitro* exposure, we present an opportunity to practice *in vivo* exposure in Learning Activity 14.5.

Intensive Exposure

In addition to the methods of gradual exposure **LO4** described, exposure can be conducted in a much more time-limited, intense fashion. Whereas gradual exposure procedures emphasize moving at a pace in which the client slowly pushes himself or herself (with the aid of the helper) beyond his or her zone of comfort, intensive exposure procedures present clients with fear or anxiety-provoking stimuli in a more compressed period of time. Rather than bringing the client in for approximately an hour per week for several weeks to ascend the exposure hierarchy, the clinician (with informed and voluntary consent from the client) can begin therapy with exposure to items the client reports as being the most fear-provoking. In fact, Öst (1997) has pioneered the one-session treatment of specific phobias, involving a prior comprehensive functional assessment and then, typically, an extended therapy session of 3 or more hours, which can be exhausting but exhilarating for both client and helper.

To date, much evidence indicates that intensive exposure seems to be effective in reducing fear and avoidance (Ollendick & Davis, 2013; Zoellner, Abramowitz, & Moore, 2003; Zoellner et al., 2009), with gains maintained over time. With evidence supporting various

Learning Activity 14.5

Developing an Example *In Vivo* Exposure Session

This activity is designed to give you some practice in using *in vivo* exposure. Again, assume that Isabella, the model client, has a phobia about receiving a dental injection.

Part One: *Developing a Hierarchy of Situations*

Brainstorm a hierarchical list of situations related to needles and oral injections that Isabella likely would find uncomfortable. (This list may be the same one you constructed for Learning Activity 14.3 or 14.4.)

Part Two: *Develop the In Vivo Steps*

Create a list of steps that Isabella likely would take to work through each of the items on the fear hierarchy that was developed in Part One. If Isabella is in need of dental treatment

that will require the use of a dental injection, then *in vivo* exposure involves actually visiting a dentist for the necessary treatment. Ideally, there would not be time pressure to complete the appointment immediately, although that sometimes is the case. Collaboration with Isabella's dentist is necessary, with the written permission of Isabella and her parents. Possible steps associated with *in vivo* exposure may include entering the dental office, talking to the dentist about the injection, receiving education about dental injections, injection safety, and how they are best completed, having a topical substance applied in the area of the mouth for the injection as a physically desensitizing agent, having the dentist touch the part of Isabella's mouth in which the injection will take place, having the dentist use good chair-side technique and not simply show Isabella the syringe and needle but bring them into her mouth for the length of time an injection would take place, and then actually performing the injection.

approaches to conducting exposure, the method selected for an individual client will be decided by several factors. First, and perhaps most important, it is our experience that gradual exposure techniques tend to be more palatable for many clients. Clients who have engaged in avoidance and worry for years predictably balk at the idea of immediately being exposed to the worst situations they can conceive. Yet some clients enter therapy so motivated to change that they are willing to do whatever is required to help that change occur as quickly as possible. Second, the timing of the different sessions required for the two general methods of exposure must be considered. Gradual exposure most likely will require one or two shorter (1 to 1.5 hours) sessions per week for several weeks, depending on the rate of client attendance and progress. Intensive exposure demands extended blocks of time (often a minimum of 3 hours per session), but usually fewer sessions are required. Third, some presenting problems lend themselves more readily to gradual or to intensive exposure. For example, a helper more skilled with *in vivo* exposure with access to a zoo or pet shop might readily consider intensive exposure for a client with a fear of snakes. But a helper who has a client with an intense fear of flying might not be able to conduct intensive exposure through flying on an airplane because of the implications of the client experiencing panic on a plane crowded with other passengers.

It remains, then, for the helper and client to decide together which form of exposure is most appropriate for the client's specific difficulties in living. The gradual exposure methods may be more acceptable to a broader range of clientele, but intensive exposure has its place, both

historically and presently. With clients who desire rapid change, intensive exposure methods such as flooding and implosive therapy may be more direct and efficient and provide relief much more quickly.

Flooding

Flooding essentially is an intensive form of *in vivo* exposure therapy. Clients are confronted with intensely fear-provoking stimuli for an extended period of time until they experience a reduction in anxiety and distress (Zoellner et al., 2003; 2009). Several important differences from the more gradual *in vivo* exposure therapy involve the nature and order of the stimuli presented, the lack of focus on training of a relaxation response, the length of the session, and the explanation of why the technique is presumed to work. Whereas *in vivo* exposure typically involves a gradual ascent up the exposure hierarchy beginning with the *least* fear-provoking stimuli, exposure in flooding commences with the stimuli that elicit the *most* fear from a client. Whereas a typical *in vivo* exposure session might last an hour and a half at most, a session of flooding often lasts for several hours, because the session continues until the client's fear reaction subsides almost completely. Finally, the assessment of treatment gains for *in vivo* exposure often focuses on a client's between-session reductions in physiological responses and SUDS ratings in response to fear-provoking stimuli, which suggests that extinction could be the method of learning. In contrast, helpers using flooding emphasize within-session reduction in SUDS ratings and physiological reaction.

Alternately, what may be most important is whether the client was able to tolerate fear during exposure, whether there was disconfirmation of beliefs (i.e., expectancy violation), and if stimuli were variable, among other possible factors (Craske et al., 2014).

One example of how *in vivo* exposure and flooding differ could be illustrated in the treatment of a fear of spiders. *In vivo* exposure might progress over several sessions from cartoon images of spiders, to photographs of spiders, to being in a room with a spider, to holding a spider. Flooding would more likely involve being in a room with a spider and ultimately touching it over the course of several hours during a single session.

Implosive Therapy

If flooding can be compared to *in vivo* exposure, then implosive therapy would probably best be contrasted with imaginal exposure. Implosive therapy utilizes prolonged and clinician-facilitated imagination of fear-eliciting scenes more intense than those of traditional imaginal exposure (Levis, 2009; Levis & Krantweiss, 2003). One advantage of implosive therapy is the client's ability to imagine distressing scenarios that a clinician would be incapable of recreating in real life. It bears considering, however, that the images can be quite horrific and the treatment can be extremely stressful for both client and helper.

Collaborative Considerations in Conducting Exposure

Conducting exposure treatment must be undertaken **L05** with adequate preparation by both helper and client, including plans for assessing progress over time. The most effective treatment is developed from a strong theoretical base, with a clear goal in place and plans for ongoing evaluation. The preparation phase should not be taken lightly, because adequate planning is necessary to ensure that this often stressful procedure is executed properly and sensitively. See Table 14.2 for phases in preparation for exposure.

1. First, the clinician must develop a preliminary plan for exposure that will address the client's problems.

TABLE 14.2   Phases in Preparing and Planning for Exposure

Phase 1	Helper develops preliminary plan
Phase 2	Helper obtains informed consent from client
Phase 3	Helper and client collaborate on further specifics of exposure plan

---

Consideration must be given to the client's type of problem and personal characteristics, including both strengths (e.g., strong verbal and imaginative abilities) and limitations (e.g., depression) that may affect treatment progress. The type of problem likely will dictate at least the initial approach to exposure. For example, in the case of flying phobia, our experience is that imaginal approaches are generally a good choice as an initial approach because they can be readily utilized within in-office sessions. Nevertheless, the availability of local resources, such as a nearby airport or airline programs aimed at helping (potential) customers to become more comfortable with flying, should be considered in this treatment planning. Also important is the timeline for the treatment. In our experience, clients with phobias sometimes present for treatment only when there is a looming real-life exposure requirement, such as an essential business trip necessitating travel by air or an upcoming speech that is unavoidable.

2. Perhaps the most important step is to obtain the expressed consent of the client: exposure must be conducted only with the client's fully informed agreement. Above and beyond any treatment contracts in writing, the client must understand the rationale for exposure and appreciate its potential for therapeutic success. It is necessary, too, for the client to be dedicated to the process of change. It may be helpful to view readiness for change from the perspective of the transtheoretical model of change, a theory describing the stages through which an individual progresses as he or she resolves ambivalence and commits to effecting behavior change (Prochaska, DiClemente, & Norcross, 1992). Motivational interviewing strategies may be useful with clients who are unsure about their readiness for exposure treatment, or who become reluctant the further up they move in their exposure hierarchy, to help them reduce ambivalence (Simpson, 2009; Simpson, Zuckoff, Page, Franklin, & Foa, 2008; Slagle & Gray, 2007). See Chapter 10 for additional information about working with clients expressing resistance to change. According to Hope and colleagues (Hope, Heimberg, & Turk, 2010), clients participating in exposure must willingly "invest anxiety in a calmer future" (p. 9). We find that adage quite useful, sharing it with clients and reminding them of it over the course of treatment. Over time, as exposure leads to improved functioning in a client's everyday life, we encourage the idea of an exposure-based lifestyle. For a client to sustain the progress made in regard to a phobia or other problem, there must be ongoing exposure at periodic intervals to lessen the possibility that problem

levels of the fear will reemerge. As a rule, reaching agreement about exposure requires the clinician to share the conceptual background and mention at least some of the research support for this treatment. Also, the clinician explains the general approach (e.g., imaginal exposure first, followed later by *in vivo* exposure).

3. After there is agreement between client and helper, working on the specifics of the exposure plan is the next step. Like other parts of this therapy, the process is best implemented as a collaborative one in which client and clinician work together rather than the clinician being highly directive and imposing specific steps. In many cases, depending on the client's verbal and writing abilities, the client is asked to do homework by bringing in a list of objects or situations that relate to the phobia or other clinical target problem. Often, we ask clients to construct a list that includes 10–15 stimuli or situations, in sequential order from least to most anxiety-provoking. If a client appears to be highly avoidant or to have less well-developed paper-and-pencil or verbal skills, then we co-construct this list in session. Typically, we first explain a SUDS rating system (e.g., 0–100; Wolpe, 1990), and we ask clients to have a representation of 10–15 objects or situations that fall across the range of possible scores, with no greater than 10 points between items.

As the helper and the client plan exposure, the following are several topics of particular importance to consider:

1. Individual Approach
2. Preparation and Flexibility of the Clinician
3. Repeated Exposure
4. Response Prevention
5. Re-emergence or Return of Fear
6. Sequencing of Stimuli Presentations

Topic 1: Individual Approach

Like other forms of psychotherapy, exposure almost always is best individualized to the particular client and his or her problems. Phobias that require clinical intervention often are highly idiosyncratic, such as in the case of a client who feared green snakes but not brown ones based on a belief about the relative danger they posed.

Topic 2: Preparation and Flexibility of the Clinician

As with any treatment, the clinician should be appropriately trained in exposure therapy and strategies prior to implementing them with a client. Supervision of a clinician's first cases, and of unusual or challenging cases, is recommended. Some degree of anxiety on the part of the clinician in conducting exposure therapy is normal and natural. Such anxiety may motivate the clinician in a manner that will foster reflective practice and professional growth through supervision, consultation, reading, careful treatment planning, behavioral rehearsal, and the like. It is not necessary for a helper to be a master of the situation confronting the client or to be fearless or a paragon of mental health vis-à-vis the client's problem. In fact, a therapist's sharing of his or her own mild discomfort about some aspects of the phobic situation may be helpful to the client, normalizing the client's reactions and leading the client to believe that he or she too may be able to develop successful coping strategies. There is suggestion in the literature that some clinicians may themselves be so uncomfortable with inducing temporary discomfort in clients that they do not utilize exposure, even though it has a tremendous amount of empirical support and is considered a best practice in most cases (Schare & Wyatt, 2013). Newer therapists may be even more vulnerable to this reluctance. Given their empathy, they do not want to cause distress, and perhaps have not yet internalized that some temporary distress can lead to long-lasting change and better quality of life. There is an argument that failure to use exposure therapy when appropriate can result in harm to clients (Jayawickreme et al., 2014).

The helper must be flexible in developing and implementing exposure treatments and be able to respond to changing information about the client's phobia or other problem. As treatment progresses, both client and clinician learn more about the client's problem, and that insight often indicates a need for modification in the way in which exposure is implemented. Often, the imagined scenes or actual *in vivo* stimuli must be altered somehow to more closely reflect what the client truly fears. For example, imagined scenes often are embellished over time as clients remember new details, ones that perhaps previously were cognitively unavailable to them because of anxiety and related avoidance processes.

Topic 3: Repeated Exposure

The research on the underlying mechanisms of exposure treatment (e.g., Craske et al., 2008; Craske et al., 2014; Hazlett-Stevens & Craske, 2003; Mystkowski et al., 2002) has frequently indicated that, to be effective, exposure must be of sufficient intensity, duration, and repetition. Gradually evolving the intensity of exposure is fine in many cases and may be more palatable to clients who wish to ease into this form of treatment. Nevertheless, ultimately the stimuli or situations that clients confront must be highly evocative to allow them to fully experience the maximum possible anxiety response (Forsyth et al., 2009). Only in doing so will they *learn* that they can survive and even conquer that which causes them the greatest fear or distress.

Length of exposure is a critical factor, both within sessions and across the entire course of treatment. Related to avoidance, some clients delay exposure by talking about it rather than doing it. This delay can take place before any exposures in a session or between exposures. This is not to say that clients' discourse about their thoughts and feelings should be ignored or discouraged. It is the case, however, that clinicians should be cognizant of the possibility of subtle avoidance behavior about which the client may be unaware. Avoidance also can result from clinicians' own discomfort or fear of doing exposure. Our experience with beginning clinicians is that they often are uncomfortable exposing clients to thoughts and tangible stimuli and situations that can be highly distressing. Sometimes, then, both client and helper conspire to approach exposure very gradually, through very brief exposures followed by considerable time spent discussing the exposure and its emotional sequelae. This situation is a trap, however, because the outcome is less exposure than would be ideal to help the client. Delaying or minimizing exposure to aversive stimuli during exposure treatment also may reinforce client beliefs that the stimuli are dangerous and worthy of the escape/avoidance in which they have been engaging. Most often, repeated and/or continuing exposures are recommended within single treatment sessions. Similarly, the client must experience the confrontation with the stimuli or distressing situation for a long enough time to allow an anxiety (or related) response to fully develop, manifest, and then dissipate through extinction or habituation.

Topic 4: Response Prevention

Particularly with OCD, but with other clinical problems as well, it is important for the client not to engage in anxiety-reducing activities during or after exposure (Franklin, Ledley, & Foa, 2009; Roth, Foa, & Franklin, 2003). A client with an obsession about germs accompanied by compulsive hand-washing behaviors, for example, should not wash his hands for some period of time after exposure to dirt or other "germy" stimuli during exposure. This response prevention allows the anxiety arising from exposure to be fully operative and not diminished by a potentially detrimental, although immediately and temporarily reinforcing, reaction to the anxiety by the client. Typically during exposure

clients also should not engage in activities that distract them from their experiencing of anxiety, such as counting or thinking about something else other than that which is causing them distress. To do so may ameliorate or eliminate the anxiety, which can be counterproductive. Early literature on distraction during exposure was complex and had mixed results (Rodriguez & Craske, 1993). In a review attempting to clarify divergent findings, Parrish, Radomsky, and Dugas (2008) suggest that distraction during exposure may not be detrimental if it does not demand significant attention (so as not to impair learning), enhances self-efficacy without facilitating misattribution of success to safety cues or other stimuli, and encourages more approach behavior and exposure.

Topic 5: Re-emergence or Return of Fear

Although exposure therapy has proven to be an effective treatment for many clients suffering from problems with anxiety, some clients experience a re-emergence of high levels of fear during or after treatment, which may even be considered a relapse (Arch & Craske, 2009). For example, consider a person with a phobia of flying on airplanes for whom exposure treatment was effective. If the client did not fly again for several years after treatment, then the phobia could return in response to newspaper and other media reports about airline disasters. Such relapses are an important clinical problem and are an active area of study in the animal and human literatures (e.g., Craske et al., 2006; Craske et al., 2008; Craske et al., 2014). Several possible factors contributing to return of fear have been identified, including repeated presentations of the US after extinction learning (Hermans et al., 2005). If a person experiences significant pain in several dental appointments after successful treatment for dental phobia, then high levels of fear nevertheless may well return. Fear also has returned for clients who were exposed to a fear-provoking stimulus in a context different from the context of exposure treatment (Mystkowski et al., 2002). A client who learns how to manage her fear in the presence of spiders in the helper's office might experience intense fear when encountering a spider during a picnic outdoors. Additionally, Tsao and Craske (2000) found that uniformly spaced sessions and *expanding-spaced* sessions—in which the time length between sessions increases over time—produce longer retention-of-treatment gains than do massed sessions that occur in close temporal proximity to one another, possibly because these schedules require more effort by the client to retrieve information learned between sessions and contextual cues can be more varied. In general, to prevent return of fear, helpers should encourage clients to engage in exposure exercises in a variety of contexts at various times with as much repetition as possible and to maintain an exposure-based lifestyle to increase the odds of greater learning and generalization to the greatest number of possible future contexts. Additionally, it is important for helpers to remember that exposure therapy likely involves the learning of new information incompatible with old information, not the unlearning of the previous fear response (Mystkowski et al., 2002). Therefore, the general rules of learning should apply, and helpers should make every attempt to take advantage of what is currently known about learning, particularly extinction learning, as well as anxiety and fear (e.g., Craske et al., 2006; Craske et al., 2008; Craske et al., 2014; Mineka & Zinbarg, 2006). Variability in presenting fear-evoking stimuli across multiple contexts, as well as asking clients to remove safety signals and to not engage in safety behaviors, among others, may be important in preventing renewal or reinstatement of fear, or its spontaneous recovery (Craske et al., 2008; Craske et al., 2014).

Topic 6: Sequencing of Stimuli Presentations

The traditional order of presentation of stimuli during gradual methods of exposure therapy has been from less fear-provoking to more fear-provoking stimuli. As discussed, part of the rationale for this sequencing has been to build client self-efficacy and to increase client acceptance of exposure therapy. Certainly, these considerations are important in developing an exposure-based treatment plan. Just as importantly, though, helpers should consider the empirical support for certain sequencing of stimuli. Although exposure therapy often utilizes graded hierarchies, the success of flooding treatments that begin with the most fear-provoking stimuli (e.g., Miller, 2002) serves as an indication that presenting less fear-provoking stimuli first is not always necessary for clients to overcome their fears. Similarly, other research has suggested that hierarchies adapted to the individual or to particular methods of presenting hierarchies do not necessarily influence the successful outcome of exposure treatments (Yates, 1975).

Some research has even suggested that fears *summate*—that is, when a stimulus eliciting less fear is followed by a stimulus eliciting more fear, the subsequent simultaneous presentation of both stimuli together results in a greater fear response (Rachman & Lopatka, 1986). A client reports a SUDS rating of 50 for a spider crawling on her hand and reports a SUDS rating of 90 for a spider crawling up her arm. When the client is exposed to a spider on her hand and then to a spider crawling up her arm, she might report an even higher SUDS rating (maybe 95) if during the next exposure the spider crawls from her hand up her arm.

Rachman and Lopatka also found that the opposite order of stimulus presentation (i.e., a stimulus eliciting more fear preceded a stimulus eliciting less fear) resulted in a lower fear level when the two stimuli were presented together. Although most helpers probably will continue to rely on graded exposure to stimuli from client hierarchies, they should consider the evidence supporting the importance of variation (Craske et al., 2014), including alternate orders of stimuli presentation, especially for clients who might not respond well to initial attempts at exposure therapy.

Caveats about Exposure

As with all psychotherapies, exposure treatment offers **L06** unique challenges that helpers must dutifully consider and address if treatment is to be respectful and humane, while still affecting change. Detailed here are some of the more common concerns helpers may encounter utilizing exposure treatment treatment (see Table 14.3 for a summary of concerns).

Caveat 1: Informed Consent

Any form of helping, including psychological treatment, requires the client to be fully informed and to consent to the treatment that is being provided (i.e., to give informed consent). This step may be particularly important in exposure treatment, which often is highly emotionally evocative and involves clients' behaving in ways that are directly antagonistic to what their cognitive or physiological state tells them to do (e.g., to immediately leave the situation as part of a fight-or-flight reaction so as not to encounter that which they most fear). At some level, then, exposure can feel counterintuitive to the client, so it is extremely important for the helper to provide a thorough rationale and to periodically remind the client of the rationale over the course of treatment. It is imperative to help the client understand that while avoidance may feel reinforcing in the short-term, it allows the phobia to be maintained. It should be emphasized that exposure therapy approaches, as noted, represent an investment of anxiety at the present time for greater calmness in the future (Hope et al., 2010).

TABLE 14.3 Caveats about Exposure

Caveat 1	Informed consent
Caveat 2	The client's right to choose
Caveat 3	When to push and when not to do so
Caveat 4	Presence or absence of the clinician
Caveat 5	Worsening symptoms, inappropriate coping, or dropout

Caveat 2: The Client's Right to Choose

When you are treating clients, it may be best to inform them that they are in control at all times and that you as the helper will not force them to do anything: "Not that I could, as you ultimately are in charge of your life and your actions. I am here as a guide, certainly to encourage you, but always to respect you and your right to your own decisions." At the same time, it may be wise to share with your clients that you will encourage them, often repeatedly, to touch (sometimes psychologically) that which they most fear, because that is the route to change and ultimately to greater comfort. Rather than trying to cajole or "guilt-trip" a client into a recommended action, it may be wise to break the action down into its component parts and to have the client gradually experience it.

Caveat 3: When to Push and When Not to Do So

When a helper should push (psychologically, not physically) and when the helper should be patient and allow the client to consolidate his or her gains are matters of individual client characteristics, helper style, and clinical judgment. Some clients depend on the clinician to provide this encouragement and consider it a valued part of treatment. Other clients want any movement to be of their own accord and therefore resist any clinician encouragement except prior to entering an evocative situation.

The ability of the client to cope with sensory and cognitive results of exposure to feared objects and situations is akin to *distress tolerance* (Zvolensky, Bernstein, & Vujanovic, 2011). Distress tolerance spans a range of possibilities— some more cognitively oriented like evaluating the pros/ cons of taking specific actions, very much akin to problem-solving strategies described previously in the book. Some are more oriented to relaxation, distraction, or focus on alternatives. Others, as we described elsewhere in the book, involve fostering of mindfulness. Twohig and Peterson (2009) provide guidance regarding ways to promote distress tolerance.

There simply is no getting around the fact that therapeutically utilizing exposure involves traversing palpably salient distress in clients. Pushing through challenges with the aid of the helper can take multiple and supportive forms. The warmth, genuineness, and support from the helper throughout the process can be essential. Helper affirmations (from Motivational Interviewing, as discussed in Chapter 10) of clients' courage and determination in engaging in exposure steps also can be quite helpful.

Caveat 4: Presence or Absence of the Clinician

The presence or absence of the clinician is a critical element in many exposure treatments. In the context of obsessive compulsive disorder, as well as agoraphobia and some other anxiety disorders, the presence of the clinician or another safe person can prevent the occurrence of any anxiety whatsoever and subverts the therapeutic aspects of exposure. Sometimes, however, the presence of the clinician can allow the client to take those baby steps necessary to begin the steps of exposure. One common dimension of hierarchies is the presence or absence of others, with the involvement of safe others being included early, during the period when the client is acclimatizing to the exposure process.

There certainly are ethical, legal, and safety issues involved in the presence of the clinician during *in vivo* exposure. In some instances, for safety reasons, two clinicians should be present. Also, merely being in the presence of the clinician in the community can cue others that the client is under the care of a helper, which compromises confidentiality. This is not to say that issues of confidentiality preclude such an approach, only that the client must be made aware of these added dimensions of *in vivo* practice and that the ramifications of this choice should be considered by both client and clinician. As a form of exposure, *in vivo* can be extremely powerful, and often the clinician's presence is necessary, particularly in the early stages of treatment.

The client's safety, as well as that of the public and the clinician, must be a paramount concern during *in vivo* exposure. A client with an elevator phobia who is encouraged to ride a few floors on an elevator in a five-story building has less potential for encountering safety concerns than an individual with agoraphobia who has not traveled alone for years and whose *in vivo* assignment involves driving by herself in a urban area. (In the latter case, the *in vivo* exposure likely would be best handled by a driving school, for such an organization provides expertise in the physical aspects of driving.) Clients sometimes ask (and even plead), for example, for clinicians to accompany them on airplane flights. Even if the clinician were to agree to the client's request, he or she may or may not be able to make it all right for the client during the exposure exercise, is on someone else's turf by virtue of supporting a client in another organization's venue (i.e., a commercial airplane), and is subject to the rules and regulations of that company (i.e., the airline). Prior permission for such therapeutic work may be necessary and/or appropriate from the company or entity that provides opportunity to engage in the exposure activity.

Caveat 5: Worsening Symptoms, Inappropriate Coping, or DropOut

Potentially worsening symptoms that the treatment was designed to ameliorate has been noted as a concern of some clinicians, particularly with PTSD. A corollary is concern about other psychologically related issues emerging, such as inappropriate coping via self-medication via alcohol or other drug use, or guilt that may worsen even if anxiety or trauma symptoms abate. In a review of findings related to the implementation of prolonged exposure with PTSD, however, Hembree et al. (2003) reported that rates of symptom exacerbation with exposure treatments are generally very low and are no more an issue than with other treatments. Waiting list controls, by contrast, from whom treatment was withheld, did report symptom deterioration. High dropout rates, perhaps due to the degree of emotional distress associated with exposure therapy, also is a concern. Nevertheless, Hembree et al. (2003) reviewed 25 studies and reported no difference in drop-out rates for exposure therapy when compared to other treatments (e.g., stress inoculation training or combination approaches). Drop-out rates, however, are higher with active treatment in comparison to those in control conditions who do not have to directly confront their fears. Thus, although the tolerance levels for exposure therapy appear comparable to other forms of treatment, rejection of the proposed treatment is possible, as are premature termination or drop-out, which should be anticipated and discussed in advance with the client. Nevertheless, even prolonged exposure therapy has been found to be regarded as an acceptable treatment by veterans with PTSD (Kehle-Forbes et al., 2014), and failure to use exposure therapy when appropriate may be an ethical issue associated with potential harm to clients (Jayawickreme et al., 2014).

Research with Diverse and Vulnerable Groups

In this section, we consider exposure related to the **L07** following topics:

1. Stress and Trauma in Various Cultural Groups
2. Children and Adolescents
3. Trauma and the Military

With its emphasis on basic learning processes and its practical, common sense foundation, exposure is appropriate for a broad range of groups. Comas-Díaz (2007) addressed the disproportionate stress exposure of racial minorities under both historical and contemporary conditions. She notes the value of interventions, such as guided imagery, stress inoculation training, and exposure therapies, that can be applied with cultural sensitivity and that are flexible in accommodating unique sociopolitical stressors such as

racism and racial trauma. Acute cultural awareness may be warranted, however, when the clinician is a member of a dominant cultural group and is using exposure therapy with a client who is a member of a cultural minority group, particularly when the issue being targeted potentially is related to intergroup social issues. For example, cultural consideration would be an essential treatment component when a European American helper uses exposure strategies aimed at increasing the assertive behavior of a client who is a member of an ethnic/racial minority group.

Topic 1: Stress and Trauma among Various Cultural Groups

The rate of experiencing traumatic events, possible development of PTSD, and psychological/psychiatric treatment utilization for that disorder differs among racial and ethnic groups in the United States (Roberts, Gilman, Breslau, Breslau, & Koenen, 2011) and presumably among cultural groups globally. Most profoundly, ethnic/racial minority individuals in the United States are less likely to seek treatment for PTSD than whites who have the disorder, with less than half of those from minority groups seeking treatment (Roberts et al., 2011).

The higher incidence of PTSD in many immigrant and refugee groups invites consideration of exposure as a treatment option. Research has demonstrated promising outcomes incorporating exposure in treating those who are refugees and have been traumatized, including the pairing of exposure and narrative therapies. Culturally adapted cognitive behavior therapy (CA-CBT) for traumatized refugees and ethnic/racial minority individuals emphasizes exposure to emotion as an important aspect of treatment (Hinton, Rivera, Hofmann, Barlow, Otto, 2012). In a small group of traumatized refugees, Paunovic and Ost (2001) found that exposure was associated with a large improvement over 16 to 20 weeks of individual treatment. Ruf and colleagues (2010) found that narrative exposure therapy contributed to clinically significant improvement in symptoms and functioning among refugee children, with effects remaining stable a year after treatment. Moreover, these effects were achieved in only eight treatment sessions. Robjant and Fazel (2010) reviewed research on narrative exposure therapy with cultural minority adults as well as children and discovered reduced distress and trauma symptoms in comparison with other therapeutic approaches and control groups, including sustained changes even in volatile and precarious environments. One-session exposure treatment has been culturally adapted (i.e., OST-CA) for use with phobic Asian Americans, with indications that it outperforms standard OST with this group (Pan, Huey, & Hernandez, 2012).

Similarly, prolonged exposure therapy has been culturally adapted for use with African Americans to prevent and treat PTSD; guidelines for use of appropriate exposures are provided in light of the need to consider incorporating race-related trauma topics (Williams et al., 2014). Exposure is appropriate not only for PTSD in cultural minority groups, but also for other anxiety disorders. In African Americans, for example, anxiety disorders have been a subject of interest due to their relative prevalence in this group and their culturally unique features (e.g., sleep paralysis). Exposure therapy has been explored in this demographic group, and it appears to be an effective therapeutic modality. There are, however, distinct challenges that face many African American clients (as well those who demonstrate other characteristics of cultural diversity related to race/ethnicity, religious affiliation, sexual orientation, etc.) in terms of historical trauma, discrimination, and treatment delivery barriers.

Care and caution are of paramount importance in understanding the ecological issues related to the clinician, as an authority figure, exposing survivors of traumatic events and ethnic/racial minority group members to emotionally evocative images and situations. A "phase approach" in which emotion regulation methods are taught and learned prior to exposure may be quite important in traumatized or highly stressed groups, along with using culturally adapted methods (Simos & Hofmann, 2013). The ethical imperative to provide the most effective and appropriate therapy, however, still remains, and in the case of PTSD and most anxiety disorders, that typically is exposure (Jayawickreeme et al., 2014). It is incumbent upon clinicians and public policy-makers to insure that exposure therapy is available to clients who would benefit from it, including ethnic/racial minority group members and refugees.

Topic 2: Children and Adolescents

Exposure, particularly using a gradual methodology, has been utilized effectively to treat phobias in children and adolescents (Beidel & Turner, 2005). Intensive exposure methods with children and youth must be carefully assessed regarding their suitability with respect to developmental stage and psychological stability. Nevertheless, Ollendick and colleagues (Davis, Ollendick, & Öst, 2009; Ollendick, Öst, Reuterskiöld, Costa, Cederlund et al., 2009) have utilized one-session treatment involving *in vivo* exposure and other elements of CBT with both children and adolescents; conclusions from a review in this area are that one-session exposure for children and adolescents is effective across varying types of phobias (Ollendick & Davis, 2013). Moreover, therapeutic

case examples are illustrated by Hunter (2010) in which the use of prolonged exposure treatment with traumatized juvenile sex offenders yielded marked abatement of symptoms, improvement in mood, and investment in offender treatment. A form of prolonged exposure has been adapted for traumatized adolescents and shows good efficacy (Foa, Chrestman, & Gilboa-Schechtman, 2009).

In vivo exposure can be effective with children and youth with developmental disabilities who do not have the language or conceptual abilities to benefit from imaginal approaches. Issues of informed consent and other ethical concerns must, of course, be carefully considered in such cases. Gradual exposure may be preferred in these instances because it allows the clinician to proceed slowly and carefully, and to assess the impact of exposure on an ongoing basis.

In recent years, we have become increasingly aware of the extent to which children and adolescents are exposed to potentially traumatizing experiences. Although most individuals who experience a single childhood trauma do not develop PTSD or other sustained behavioral or psychological problems, outcomes are far less favorable for children exposed to multiple traumatic events such as chronic maltreatment including neglect and abuse, serious accidents or illness, natural disasters, and domestic and community violence (Copeland, Keeler, Angold, & Costella, 2007; Gabbay, Oatis, Silva, & Hirsch, 2004). Adverse childhood experiences are indeed becoming recognized not only as significant risks for impaired physical and mental health outcomes in youth but also, as life course developmental effects suggest, as childhood roots of health disparities and sustained stress impacting adulthood (Shonkoff, Boyce, & McEwen, 2009). This persistent exposure to stress during development can then lead to a variety of impairments in brain, physiological, and psychosocial development (Anda et al., 2006; Ford, 2005).

Treating trauma in childhood and adolescence can be complex and multileveled with the added involvement of family members and, at times, child protective systems. Although in-depth coverage is beyond the scope of this chapter, a number of informative resources are available (Brom, Pat-Yorenczyuk, & Ford, 2009; Cohen, Mannarino & Deblinger, 2006; Cloitre, Cohen, & Koenen, 2006; Malchiodi, 2008; Weisz & Kazdin, 2010). Interventions often focus on fostering resilience, offering parenting/caregiver support via skill development, and attending to diminished resources at the individual, family, school, and/or community levels (Brom et al., 2009). For example, child-focused trauma interventions may enlist the assistance of social supports in the child's life, such as parents, teachers, other counselors, and peers with the goal of re-establishing and nurturing self-regulation in the affected child.

These interventions can be thought of as helping the child to gain greater conscious awareness and control over his or her neurobiological alarm systems that have been dysregulated and are now overly sensitized to cues and events. Therapeutic approaches that foster self-regulation include: developing skills of focused attention and calming techniques that can help with reduce hyperarousal; learning to identify stimuli that trigger reactions and to recognize what one's triggered stress reactions feel and look like; learning to identify and reframe or reconstruct problematic thoughts, emotions, and behaviors that have become patterned in negative ways; and fostering attitudes and perceptions of self-efficacy and personal worth (Ford, Albert, & Hawke, 2009).

Notice how many of these intervention guidelines link to specific strategies described in this book, such as cognitive change, problem-solving, stress inoculation training, self-calming, and self-management. In some cases, group interventions are well suited—particularly for older youth (DeRosa & Pelcovitz, 2009); in other cases, dyadic and family-based strategies are recommended (Van Horn & Lieberman, 2009; Saltzman, Babayan, Lester, Beardslee, & Pynoos, 2009). Whether and at what developmental point after trauma exposure therapy might be helpfully utilized with youth who have experienced multiple traumas are open questions and potential future research directions.

Topic 3: Trauma and the Military

The ever-increasing number of military service members in need of trauma-related mental health intervention has fueled considerable clinical research. A special issue of the journal *Cognitive and Behavioral Practice* (Renshaw, 2011) provides a number of valuable reports of trauma-related treatments, addressing topics such as suicide risk, violence, chronic pain, family reintegration challenges, conjoint therapy, brief exposure interventions, and the importance of further developing trauma treatments targeting military personnel. Prolonged exposure is regarded as an acceptable treatment by most U.S. Iraq War veterans (Kehle-Forbes et al., 2014) and is associated with decreased use of later psychotherapy (Meyers et al., 2013).

Steenkamp and colleagues (2011) describe a brief intervention known as *adaptive disclosure treatment*, including imaginal exposure and subsequent cognitive restructuring and meaning-making strategies, that is explicitly attentive to themes of traumatic loss and moral injury. As they noted, service members often are exposed to threats to their own lives and well-being as well as witnessing

intense human cruelty and suffering and traumatic loss of comrades. Some veterans especially may struggle with the "moral injury" of having had to injure or kill others during combat in the line of duty. Their trauma, then, may be different in nature from other types of trauma in that veterans may need to reconcile their past actions with their morality and sense of self. The range of combat experiences can be considerable but have in common haunting and deeply disturbing effects. Building on exposure therapy, adaptive disclosure treatment aims to foster clients' willingness to share and disclose (rather than conceal and avoid) traumatic experiences and to challenge rigid, maladaptive appraisals that otherwise would foster traumatic guilt, moral injury, and other maladjustment. One of the treatment goals is to promote adaptive ways of dealing with combat stress before avoidant and other maladaptive responses become entrenched and serve to evoke secondary problems. Clinical research, such as that reported by Steenkamp and colleagues (2011), demonstrates the value of integrative models of treatment that augment a foundation of empirically supported core methods with extensions and adaptations that increase relevance to history, context, and complex clinical dynamics. Ongoing clinical intervention developments are evolving to target heretofore underserved therapeutic needs, such as that of military sexual trauma (*Journal of Trauma & Dissociation,* 2011).

Virtual reality methods also have been used extensively with service members to treat trauma. Some of this work has targeted middle to later-age veterans of earlier conflicts (Gamito et al., 2010; Ready, Geradi, Backscheider, Mascaro, & Rothbaum, 2010), whereas a robust body of research targets currently or very recently active duty service members, including those who presently are in the combat theater. Wood, Widerhold, and Spira (2010) provide an overview of some elements of VR used in exposure treatment with PTSD, including the extent to which the virtual content is experienced as highly immersive and present or real, as well as the importance of intervention aids such biofeedback, meditation, and paced diaphragmatic breathing in conjunction with real-time SUDs monitoring. Speaking to the technological evolution of exposure therapy, veterans with PTSD have been successfully treated with exposure via "telehealth," in which they were in a community clinic working with a therapist present only on a visual monitor and speaker system (Gros, Yoder, Tuerk, Lozano, & Acierno, 2011). Finally, a special issue of *Professional Psychology: Research and Practice* (2011) offers a rich overview of treatments of military service members and their families reflecting many of the interventions described in this book, including mindfulness-based treatments, cognitive change strategies, problem-solving, reframing, stress reduction, and exposure, in addition to a range of supportive measures. Although work with military personnel involves exploration and treatment of unique professional and personal life conditions and experiences, these and related findings (such as the value of positive emotions in transcending traumatic conditions; Riolli, Savicki, & Spain, 2010) provide important guidance for other populations struggling with the challenges of acute and/or persistent high stress.

Virtual Reality

VRET has become a vigorous area of research in recent years, and investigation into its efficacy and effectiveness is growing (Diemer et al., 2014; Meehan et al., 2005). As an approach, it is well suited to specific phobias and other anxiety disorders (Parsons & Rizzo, 2008) and has indications that it performs as well as *in vivo* exposure (Opris et al., 2012), with large reductions in anxiety symptoms (Parsons & Rizzo, 2008). Nevertheless, the overall current quality of VRET randomized control trials generally is low (McCann et al., 2014). The use of virtual reality equipment has become more common in exposure therapy in recent years, and the literature on the efficacy of this approach is growing (e.g., Diemer et al., 2014; Meehan et al., 2005). VRET may be beneficial scientifically in providing controlled situations that will allow greater understanding of the underlying mechanisms of exposure techniques. Lang (1977) has indicated that any form of a feared object or situation may evoke fear, and thus should be capable of eliciting change. This potential exists even if it is a symbolic representation (e.g., a "degraded" stimulus) as in pictures, movies, or even stories, although the level of responsivity may vary depending on how close it is to the actual stimulus. Therefore, VRET offers the opportunity to present highly controlled fear-evoking stimuli that can allow clients to experience realistic "immersion" in the virtual environment, acting as if it were real by perceiving their own personal "presence" in it (Slater & Wilbur, 1997). Immersion also is possible with other exposure approaches, including provocative narratives, although VRET uniquely can provide virtual environments.

Virtual reality exposure offers several advantages to helpers, including the ability to create situations that would be impractical to replicate in reality, are of greater intensity than commonly found in real life, and can be directly controlled by the helper for manipulation of key variables (e.g., number of spiders present for a client with a phobia of spiders). VRET also carries disadvantages, including the cost for the initial purchase of equipment (although prices have decreased for certain types of devices), possible technical errors associated with utilization of electronic equipment, time and effort required to learn how to use the equipment, and potential difficulties in creating situations that are perceived as real enough by clients. Nevertheless, research in the area of VRET has proven promising in addressing clinical concerns such as fear of flying and fear of heights (Krijn, Emmelkamp, Olafsson, & Biemond, 2004), and has since been extended to a considerable range of phobia targets (Gorrindo & Groves, 2009). Additionally, through therapeutic pairing with methods such as stress inoculation training, VRET has been applied in prevention or attenuation of stress-related reactions, with efficacy demonstrated across diverse populations (Wiederhold & Wiederhold, 2008).

Journals such as the *Annual Review of Cyber Therapy and Telemedicine* have evolved in recent years and provide a useful resource for further exploration of the applications of VRET. Perez-Ara and colleagues (2010), for example, described virtual reality methods for interoceptive exposure. Virtual reality (VR) programs can simulate physical sensations, such as audible presentation of rapid heartbeat and panting as well as blurry or tunnel vision, in a controlled manner while the client is engaged in therapeutic VR environments. Results in areas such as panic disorder, agoraphobia, and social anxiety disorder (Anderson et al., 2013) favor continued development of these intervention approaches.

Pharmacotherapy to Enhance Exposure

One might wonder whether anti-anxiety medications such as benzodiazepines would help clients cope with the rigors of exposure treatment. The available evidence, however, suggests otherwise (Abramowitz et al., 2011). It seems likely that the medication has a context effect involving state-dependent learning, so what clients can do while on medication is different from when they are on their own. Nevertheless, some forms of exposure with particular patient groups are robust enough that they may still be effective, even when benzodiazepines are being administered (Rosen et al., 2013). Still, in most cases, anti-anxiety medications can inhibit clients from experiencing the physiological arousal inherent in much of exposure treatment. While that is temporarily reinforcing and makes exposure easier, it also makes the treatment less effective. Also, clients' self-efficacy can be compromised by using anti-anxiety medications because they may attribute their successes to the medications instead of their own efforts. Many patients who have disorders for which exposure will be a primary treatment already will be prescribed various medications, so it will be important for helpers to coordinate treatment with the client's physician or other prescribers (Abramowitz et al., 2011).

There is a burgeoning interest in medications that affect the neural circuitry involved in extinction learning during exposure. These medications are intended as cognitive enhancers, do not have an anti-anxiety effect on their own, and in fact typically have been used for other purposes in the past (e.g., tuberculosis treatment). The most prominent current example is the medication **D-cycloserine** (DCS). Initial translational research (e.g., Hofmann et al., 2006) examining the use of DCS in augmenting exposure proved promising, and now meta-analyses support its effectiveness (Bontempo, Panza, Bloch, 2012; Rodrigues et al., 2014). DCS has been used effectively in enhancing exposure treatment with specific phobia, social phobia, panic disorder, PTSD, and OCD.

DCS does not reduce anxiety; it appears to help in the consolidation of memory after extinction learning, such as that which happens during exposure treatment, and may specifically target automatic learning (Grillon, 2009). Participants who were administered DCS before exposure exercises recorded faster initial decreases in fear and anxiety (Chasson et al., 2010). The early gains made under the influence of DCS were maintained over time, although in several additional sessions participants who did not use DCS caught up with participants using DCS. Thus, the ongoing work in this area indicates DCS likely is useful for speeding up the process of extinction learning during exposure (Hofmann, 2014).

Several cautions about DCS should be mentioned, including the fact that it must be prescribed and monitored by a physician. It must be made explicitly clear to clients that DCS is not meant to replace exposure (unlike many anxiety reduction medications) and that DCS is still being studied; the long-term consequences of its use are not known. It has been suggested that DCS reconsolidates memories and what is learned doing exposure, whether it is positive or negative; therefore, it can make beneficial exposure better, but it also may make sensitizing exposure worse (Hoffman, 2014). It is essential, then, that learning takes place during exposure, with an ample amount of time for extinction and a concomitant decrease in fear by session's end.

Some researchers have concerns that DCS will detract from self-efficacy gains made during exposure and that research on DCS will detract from time potentially spent researching basic behavioral mechanisms of exposure. For psychologists, the potential utility of DCS may further fuel the debate over prescription authority. Still, many researchers see DCS and other medications that target neural processes involved in extinction learning as a ripe area of research, one that could well impact the way exposure therapy is conducted in the future.

Model Dialogue for Exposure Therapy

To get a sense of how a clinician might conduct exposure therapy, examine the following dialogue between a helper and Isabella, who experiences a specific phobia of spiders. First, the helper reminds Isabella of the process of *identifying fear-provoking stimuli and creating a hierarchy*. Additionally, the helper gives a brief overview of what to expect from the exposure exercise and asks about any questions Isabella might have.

1. **Helper:** Isabella, we've discussed your fear of spiders, and we've identified many different things related to spiders that lead to you feeling anxious. You rated these stimuli based on how much you fear them using the SUDS system I explained to you. So here's how we can proceed. We will start with the first item on your hierarchy, which we have prepared for today: holding a fake rubber spider for 5 minutes. I have a fake spider with me, and when we are ready to start, I will ask you to hold the spider for at least 5 minutes. As you hold the spider, I will occasionally ask you for your SUDS rating. After we have finished 5 minutes with the fake spider, we will discuss the experience, and then either repeat it, or possibly move on to another item on your hierarchy. How does all of this sound?

Isabella: How many items will we do today? We won't do the items at the top of my list today, will we? I'm really worried about a camping trip this coming weekend. There might be spiders!

Isabella's response here could be interpreted as an attempt to delay and avoid exposure. The helper takes care to briefly but adequately address Isabella's concerns while gently but firmly redirecting the session to exposure. The helper also creates expectancy for success.

2. **Helper:** You pose some good questions. I also understand that exposure brings up some anxiety as it causes us to think about the very thing that makes

us the most anxious and upset. We'll move through your hierarchy at a pace that is tolerable enough, but one that will allow you to make progress. You'll have a choice about continuing the entire time. The pace will be set by how quickly your fear decreases; I can't really say for sure how many items we'll get through, but I can say we won't move on to the next item until you're ready for it. I do suspect you'll move through the items faster than you might initially expect.

Isabella: Okay, I think I can handle that.

The helper verbally praises Isabella's willingness, and presents one last opportunity to address client concerns.

3. **Helper:** Excellent! I know this may not be easy for you, and I admire your willingness to experience anxiety in the service of being able to live your life more fully and perhaps do things like go on camping trips. I believe we are ready to begin exposure. You may have concerns about your ability to handle this, and we've discussed these fears and why engaging your fears in our work together can be beneficial to you in the long-term. Are you ready to begin?

Isabella: I'm still a bit worried about how this will go, but I also believe it could really help me overcome my fears. Let's do it.

The helper reinforces Isabella's positive attitude and moves through the steps of *in vivo* exposure with her. The spider is presented to Isabella, and she is asked to give a SUDS rating. With minimal talking to minimize distraction, the helper encourages Isabella to focus her attention on the experience, asking for a SUDS rating every 60 to 90 seconds.

4. **Helper:** Great. That's an attitude that should help you really succeed with exposure. Let's begin then. *(The helper removes a fake rubber spider from a box.)* Go ahead and take the spider from me when you are ready, and hold it in your lap. *(Isabella gingerly pinches the spider between her thumb and forefinger and holds it at arm's length from her body.)* You are doing a great job to take the spider, and I would like to ask you to fully make contact with it by holding it in your lap to really get the most benefit from this exposure. *(Isabella moves the spider to her lap.)* Good work. Please tell me your SUDS rating. *(Helper records Isabella's SUDS rating of 30.)* Thank you. Continue to hold the spider on your lap, looking at it and noticing what you are experiencing. *(The helper continues to ask her SUDS rating every 60–90 seconds, reminding her to continue focusing her attention on the exposure.*

After this item is finished, after a short break, the item is repeated, or another item from the hierarchy is presented, and this cycle continues until the end of the exposure therapy portion of the session.)

Afterwards, the helper and Isabella discuss the experience to make the CS–no US association and violation of her expectancy more salient, before assigning homework and talking about the next session.

The helper begins discussion in an open-ended manner to allow Isabella to reach her own conclusions, which begin with disconfirmation of her expectancies.

5. **Helper:** Well, Isabella, tell me a little bit about what your thoughts and feelings are about the session. What did you notice about your anxiety related to spiders?

Isabella: That wasn't as bad as I had imagined it was going to be. I thought it was going to be terrible and I might not be able to stand holding even a fake spider without fainting or losing it, but that didn't happen, and I stopped feeling anxious pretty quickly. The whole thing made me think that maybe I can deal with real spiders, if they are safely in a cage.

The helper reinforces Isabella's increased self-efficacy in response 6.

6. **Helper:** Wonderful! A lot of people feel the same way as you do after their first exposure session. Many times we've avoided something so much we anticipate more anxiety than we actually experience when we confront the situation. How does that fit with your experiences?

Isabella: Yeah, I think that really matches with how I feel about today's session.

The helper capitalizes on Isabella's success in session by proposing a homework exercise for more *in vivo* exposure.

7. **Helper:** Good, I'm glad you feel that way. I would like to propose an exercise to try this coming week. You say you normally avoid going in your basement because you saw a spider there last summer, and you are afraid if you stay down there for 10 minutes, you will get attacked by a black widow spider. I would like you to see what happens if you do just that and stay in your basement for 10 minutes. Do you think you could try that?

Isabella: I am a little scared to try that out. I know how important you said it was to practice things outside of therapy, though. Plus, maybe it'll be like today; how worried I am ahead of time will be worse than how it will actually be.

Once again, the helper praises Isabella's choice of an exposure-based lifestyle.

8. **Helper:** That's a wonderful attitude to have, Isabella. I can't say exactly how you'll feel while you are in the basement, but I encourage you to notice both what you expect before and what happens after. I'll see you next week.

CHAPTER SUMMARY

Exposure is a powerful therapeutic approach that can be of great benefit to clients suffering from phobias, post-traumatic stress disorder, OCD, and other clinical problems such as excessive and prolonged grief, and even illnesses such as chronic obstructive pulmonary disease. Exposure can be used in gradual or intensive ways, even in one session, depending on clients' presenting issues as well as their characteristics and preferences. We have reviewed here various approaches to exposure therapy. Two of these include focusing on imaginal presentation of stimuli, and *in vitro* exposure—typically involving a secure setting and controlled circumstances (perhaps even using a virtual reality apparatus), such as in role play or involving phobic stimuli that are introduced into a venue in which they typically are not found (e.g., viewing and touching dental instruments in a helper's office). Finally, exposure in its strongest forms is that which is conducted *in vivo* or in a prolonged fashion.

This real-life or extended exposure offers the greatest potential benefit when it is practical and when the client is ready for it.

Regardless of the type of exposure, systematic contact with the stimuli that cause arousal and emotional response (such as distress, anxiety, or fear), with a prompting of fear learning that leads to extinction, seems to be the operative factor. Exposure methods can be paired with additional interventions, such as relaxation and mindfulness techniques, although the literature has moved somewhat away from such approaches. Although such adjuncts to treatment may not directly lead to fear reduction, they may nonetheless be essential for client acceptance, active participation, and follow-through. Successful treatment must be followed by an exposure-based lifestyle to prevent the return of a fear response and to ensure that treatment gains are maintained. There are ethical and practical considerations that must be addressed in conducting exposure treatment, including issues of informed consent and therapist presence or absence. Nonetheless, there is an ethical imperative for helpers to provide the best possible care for their clients, and exposure, in most instances, seems to be the best practice for a number of clinical problems. With proper implementation and follow-through, exposure has great potential to expand clients' comfort in engaging in a range of previously avoided activities, to allow learning of new responses, and to enhance quality of life generally.

 Visit CengageBrain.com for a variety of study tools and useful resources such as video examples, case studies, interactive exercises, flashcards, and quizzes.

14   Knowledge and Skill Builder

Part One

Learning Outcome 1 asks you to define exposure therapy and to name at least three clinical problems to which it can be applied. How would you explain exposure to a client who is unfamiliar with it? What problems might you discuss as being relevant for this treatment?

Part Two

Learning Outcome 2 asks you to describe a theoretical background for exposure, and to list at least two implications of that theory. What theoretical basis would you choose as a basis for exposure, and how would you explain it to a client? How would you implement exposure with a client taking into account that theoretical basis? If you wish to use extinction learning as a theoretical background, then you may want to refer to Table 14.1.

Part Three

Learning Outcome 3 asks you to list and describe at least 2 of the 3 phases in preparing and planning for exposure, as well as 8 of the 11 steps in implementing exposure therapy with a client who identifies a fear of heights. Before referring to Table 14.2 and Figure 14.1, try to recall as many of the phases and steps that you can.

Part Four

Learning Outcome 4 asks you to name and describe at least one gradual method and at least one intensive method of exposure. Imagine that you are being asked about different forms of exposure therapy by a new client who has accessed a few Internet sources about treatment for a phobia about speaking in front of groups. Name and describe at least one gradual and one intensive method for exposure.

Part Five

Learning Outcome 5 asks you to name at least three issues that a helper should consider in choosing an exposure method with a client. Consider that you are trying to decide on an exposure method for a client with a fear of flying. What are some issues you would consider in choosing an exposure method with this client?

Part Six

Learning Outcome 6 asks you to articulate at least two issues of informed consent, as well as at least one caution in the use of exposure. What are issues of informed consent you should cover with your client in doing exposure therapy? What occurs to you as a caution you should consider in using this form of treatment? Before referring to Table 14.3, try to identify caveats about the use of exposure.

Part Seven

Learning Outcome 7 asks you to describe at least two issues to consider in using exposure with cultural minority clients or those who are from vulnerable groups. What considerations should you think about in working with an African American woman in her 30s who has fears about driving a car after a motor vehicle accident, or what issues would you reflect on in working with a military veteran who has PTSD?

14 Knowledge and Skill Builder **Feedback**

Part One

Your explanation would differ depending on the client's educational background and overall health literacy. One general explanation could be: "Exposure is a systematic way for you to learn how to encounter and interact with whatever it is that causes you distress. Over time, you learn new ways to cope, new ways to think about it, new ways that your body responds to it, and new ways to act in the situation. Exposure is an evidence-based treatment that can be used for specific phobias, other anxiety disorders, post-traumatic stress disorders, prolonged grief, and even anxiety issues that are related to medical disorders."

Part Two

In explaining possible theoretical accounts of exposure to a client, you again would consider his/her educational background and overall health literacy. If you chose extinction learning as a theory base, you might say: "One way to understand how exposure works is by considering learning, and particularly learning about dealing with whatever causes you distress, without having anything bad happen, at least at first. By continuing to expose yourself to whatever makes you anxious or fearful, you essentially are practicing, over and over, and learning that the bad outcomes you expected actually typically do not happen. Through this process, the fear or anxiety response is "extinguished" and new learning takes it place." In the therapy, you would focus on disconfirming or "violating" prior expectations of negative outcomes, you could combine different stimulus elements (e.g., not just exposure to a dental drill sound for someone with dental phobia, but dental instruments and a dental chair, too), ask the client to not engage in safety behaviors (e.g., having a Xanax pill in his/her pocket, "just in case"), and generally vary the sequencing and content of the exposures to promote generalization.

Part Three

Briefly, explain the rationale behind exposure therapy to the client and then address the client's concerns before gaining the client's informed consent to treatment. The next step will be to identify precisely what situations and stimuli involving heights evoke fear and anxiety for the client using the information to construct a hierarchy of feared items with the client. If appropriate, then you can train the client in relaxation skills to use in conjunction with exposure exercises. If you are using imaginal exposure, then the client's imaginal ability should be assessed. Exposure to the items identified by the client as fear-provoking should then begin. After exposures, encourage the client to discuss thoughts and feelings by emphasizing how maladaptive thoughts were disconfirmed and providing discussion time at the end of session to address client insights, avoidance, and safety-seeking behavior. Using information gained during initial exposure, you can continue and modify later exposure exercises, and homework exercises can be created.

Part Four

A gradual exposure method a helper might use is *in vivo* exposure, in which a client is progressively exposed to real stimuli (as opposed to imagined or simulated stimuli) that provoke fear and anxiety. Alternatively, a client can be treated with the intensive exposure method of flooding, in which a client is exposed for an extended period of time to his or her most fear-provoking stimuli until fear and arousal decrease.

Part Five

In choosing an exposure method to use with your client with a phobia about flying, you need to consider at least some of the following issues: practical considerations such as the availability of a local airport, access to virtual reality equipment, other resources such as flying-related DVDs, the motivation level of the client, the willingness of the client to engage in different forms of exposure therapy, and the client's health status.

Part Six

Three components of informed consent to remember when you are discussing exposure therapy with a client are ensuring that the client: (1) is competent to give consent; (2) has adequate information on which to base consent; and (3) gives consent voluntarily and is not feeling forced or coerced by the helper. One caution the helper should be aware of in using exposure treatment is that clients with certain health conditions, such as cardiac problems, may be at increased risk from the physiological activation sometimes observed in exposure therapy. Medical clearance is necessary for exposure treatment with such clients.

Part Seven

In working with an African American woman in her 30s who has fears about driving a car after a motor vehicle accident, you would consider your own ethnic/racial/cultural background and how that may interact with that of your client. You should consider your client's history, including other trauma and lifetime history of discrimination she may have encountered. You may wish to use a phased approach to exposure, and one that is culturally adapted to your client. Similarly, with a military veteran with PTSD, one would consider one's own military status, if any, and might consider prolonged exposure as an option. Considerations such as helping the veteran to reduce or eliminate safety behaviors (e.g., positioning oneself so one's back is never to a place where others might enter) over time would be a part of the treatment. For both these clients, one would consider the ethical imperative to offer the most effective, helpful treatment (e.g., exposure) for them, even if it may cause temporary distress.

Self-Management Strategies
Self-Monitoring, Stimulus Control, Self-Reward, and Self-Efficacy

Learning Outcomes

After completing this chapter, you will be able to

1. Given a written client case description, describe a use of self-monitoring and stimulus control suited to the client.
2. Teach another person how to engage in self-monitoring as a self-change strategy.
3. Teach another person how to use a self-monitoring, stimulus control, self-reward, or a self-efficacy enhancement method.
4. Given a written client case description, describe features of a culturally relevant self-management program for the client.

In this final chapter, we focus on knowledge and skills that can be powerful change supports in the context of formal helping and that are equally recognized as important self-directed change tools outside of formal services. **Self-management** is a particularly collaborative, teaching-oriented approach. It is oriented to breaking down the processes of goal setting, motivating, monitoring, managing self-impediments, self-reinforcers, and environmental impediments and reinforcers, and sustaining confidence and persistence in goal achievement. *During* formal sessions, the helper teaches clients about processes that are fueling problems and about processes that will lead to desired changes after clients undertake activities *outside* formal sessions to achieve sustainable changes. Thus, the client does most of the work *between* and *beyond* sessions.

You may recognize that this educational, collaborative, and practical orientation is indeed consistent with all the helping strategies that we have introduced in this book. In fact, self-management draws on a great many specific insight- or change-oriented strategies, depending on the nature of the problems, goals, context, and client. One of

the major underpinnings of self-management intervention is assisting clients in gaining a greater capacity for self-determined initiative, or "**agency**," relative to their goals as well as fostering optimism about success that is so important to persevering and achieving those goals.

We do urge caution because self-management strategies can be presented or approached in a decontextualized manner—inattentive, for example, to environmental inequities or stressors that are a part of life circumstances issues that the client is struggling with. We see the emphasis on self here to be valuable in empowering goal-achieving awareness, skill building, and confidence. The aim is to help develop client-centered goals, strategies, and tools to manage, over the long-term, the cognitive, emotional, social, or medical factors related to their needs. Because longer-term issues (such as diabetes, substance use, insomnia, autism, and many others) often entail different facets that need ongoing management, individualized self-management plans will vary regarding the self-management and adjunct strategies that the helper and client find appropriate.

Terminology and Areas of Focus

Definitions of self-management vary in part because of differing emphases regarding processes and strategies, and in part because of overlap among related terms that are sometimes used interchangeably and that therefore can be confusing. For example, self-directed change methods have been referred to as *self-control, self-regulation,* and *self-management.* We use *self-management* because it conveys the notion of handling one's life within a set of life conditions and because literature searches on this term are likely to identify applications of change techniques and less likely reports of basic research on underlying processes. Also, the term *self-management* is less reliant on the concepts of inhibition and restriction often associated with the words *control* and *regulation*—although these associations can be misleading.

Self-management approaches tend to be anchored in social learning and social cognitive theories underlying cognitive behavioral models. Abert Bandura (1986, 1997), for example, provided a perspective of people that acknowledges inner impulses and environmental forces, but emphasizes people as self-organizing, proactive, self-reflecting, and self-regulating creatures who are in continuous reciprocal interaction with their social worlds. Social cognitive theory and clinical research provided greater detail regarding the cognitive, affective, and neurobiological mechanisms that are involved in both perceiving and responding to the world. This includes the degree to which one develops a sense of **efficacy**—positive beliefs about and expectations of one's abilities such as completing tasks or achieving goals—which we also refer to as agency. Thus, self-management intervention is an umbrella term that encompasses a broad range of integrated strategies like the ones we describe here, with continuous attention to clients' sense of efficacy.

Increasingly, self-management applications are attentive to opening new options and building a strong base of empirical and clinical support. There are robust literatures under the rubric of self-regulation that can inform therapeutic self-management, spanning a wide range of intrapersonal and interpersonal problems with applications from infants to elders and identifying integrative linkages among physiology, psychology, and social phenomena (Schaie & Carstensen, 2006; Schunk & Zimmerman, 2008; Stroebe, 2008; Vohs & Baumeister, 2011; Vohs & Finkel, 2006). Self-management has been shown to improve self-care capabilities of adults living with multimorbidity and to positively affect mood, anxiety, and overall quality of life (Bratzke, Muehrer, Kehl, Lee, Ward, & Kwekkeboom, 2014; Turner, Anderson, Wallace, & Bourne, 2015). In a study examining how self-management is perceived by clients who have returned to the community after a stroke, Satink and colleagues (2014) found collaborative goal setting, meaningful activities, and delivery within the home were particularly beneficial. For those with interest in younger populations and in ways to foster development of emotion and behavior change from an early age, clinical readings related to effortful control will be of assistance (e.g., Eisenberg, Smith, & Spinrad, 2011).

Behavioral change is very often challenging, dealt with under stressful conditions, and frequently not particularly pleasant. Self-efficacy is very important in helping clients to persevere through the challenging and unpleasant parts. Thus, efforts to enhance clients' optimism and confidence along with knowledge and skills go hand-in-hand toward incrementally executing effective and sustainable self-management strategies. Of course, there also are real-world situation characteristics or difficulties that cannot be readily changed. Part of the aim, then, may be to assist clients in developing coping strategies to handle these intractable situational factors as effectively as is realistically possible while continuing to make headway toward valued goals.

Four Strategies of Client Self-Management

In this chapter, we focus on four broadly applicable and malleable strategies of self-management:

Self-monitoring: Observing and recording one's own particular behaviors (using *behavior* here to include thoughts and feelings as well as actions in relation to oneself and one's interactions with environmental events).

Stimulus control: Prearranging antecedents or cues to increase or decrease one's performance of a target behavior.

Self-reward: Giving oneself a positive reinforcement following a desired response.

Self-efficacy: Increasing one's positive beliefs and expectations of being able to perform certain actions under certain circumstances.

We describe each of these strategies, illustrating them with model examples of our case client Isabella. Of course, none of these strategies is entirely independent of the client's personal history, gender, age, culture, abilities, or environmental variables. In fact, because self-management treatment planning is so greatly dependent on careful assessment of concerns and needs, and also on the client's ability to take on a self-manager role, diversity and contextualizing factors are particularly important considerations. We first provide an overview of features of developing and maintaining effective client self-management programs, followed by detailed attention to our four focal strategies.

Steps in Developing Self-Management Programs

In Figure 15.1 we have summarized the steps associated with developing a self-management program. Universal characteristics of effective self-management reflected in

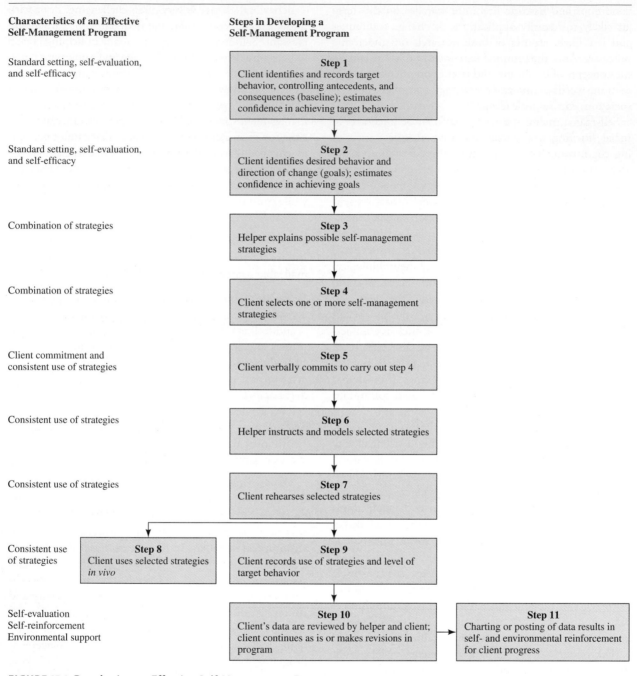

FIGURE 15.1 Developing an Effective Self-Management Program

these steps are noted in the left column of the figure. The steps are applicable to any program in which the client uses stimulus control, self-monitoring, self-reward, or engages self-efficacy.

For developing a self-management program, steps 1 and 2 both involve aspects of standard setting and self-evaluation. In step 1, the client identifies and records the target behavior and its antecedents and consequences. This step involves self-monitoring, in which the client collects baseline data about the behavior to be changed. Continuing self-monitoring provides clients the information they need to self-evaluate where they currently stand relative to their baseline and their own standard or goal for change. If baseline data have not been collected as part of assessment, then it is imperative that such data be collected now, before implementing any self-management strategies. In step 2, the client explicitly identifies the desired behavior, conditions, and level of change. The behavior, conditions, and level of change represent the three parts of a counseling outcome goal. Defining the goal is an important part of self-management because of the possible motivating effects of standard setting. The process of establishing goals may interact with some of the self-management procedures and contribute to desired effects.

Steps 3 and 4 are directed toward helping the client select a combination of self-management strategies to use. The helper will need to assist the client in identifying a range of possible self-management strategies (step 3). The helper should emphasize that the client is to select some strategies that involve prearrangement of the *antecedents* and some that involve manipulation and self-administration of *consequences*. Ultimately, the client is responsible for selecting which self-management strategies will be used (step 4). Client selection of the strategies is an important part of the overall *self-directed* nature of self-management, although at this step the client may benefit from assistance from the professional helper or supportive others in sorting through the options.

Steps 5–9 all involve procedural considerations that may strengthen client commitment and encourage consistent use of the strategies over time. First, the client commits himself or herself verbally by specifying what and how much change is desired and the action steps (strategies) the client will take to produce the change (step 5). Next, the helper instructs the client in how to perform the selected strategies (step 6). The helper can follow the guidelines listed later in the chapter for self-monitoring, stimulus control, and self-reward. Explicit instructions and modeling by the helper may enhance the client's ability to use a procedure accurately and effectively. Thus, the instructional set given by a helper may contribute to some degree to the overall treatment outcome. The client also may use the strategies more successfully if there is an opportunity to rehearse the procedures in the interview under the helper's direction (step 7). Finally, the client applies the strategies *in vivo* (step 8) and records (monitors) the frequency of use of each strategy and the level of the target behavior attained (step 9). It is important to be aware that some of the treatment effects of self-management may actually be a function of the client's self-recording.

Steps 10 and 11 involve aspects of self-evaluation, self-reinforcement, and environmental support. The client has an opportunity to evaluate progress toward the goal by reviewing the self-recorded data collected during strategy implementation (step 10). Review of the data may indicate that the program is progressing smoothly or that some adjustments are needed. When the data suggest that progress toward the goal is being made, the client's self-evaluation may set the occasion for self-reinforcement. Charting or posting the data (step 11) can enhance self-reinforcement and can elicit important environmental support for long-term maintenance of client change.

Characteristics of Effective Self-Management Programs

Well-constructed and well-executed self-management programs have some advantages over helper-administered procedures. For instance, the use of a self-management procedure may increase a person's perceived control over the environment and decrease a sense of dependence on the helper or others. Second, self-management approaches are practical—inexpensive, portable, and applicable to a wide range of life problems. Third, such strategies are usable. By this we mean that some people may not feel comfortable with the idea of going into therapy or formalized helping for a variety of reasons, but they may well be open to a more individually tailored set of self-administered instructions or tasks that a self-management program provides. This may be particularly advantageous with some clients who are mistrustful of therapy or related forms of professional helping. Finally, self-management strategies enhance generalization of learning—both from the interview to the environment and from one set of specific situations to a different set.

Although details will vary with case specifics, the following section discusses broadly applicable features of effective self-management programs.

Combination of Strategies We have mentioned that self-management typically combines a number of change strategies that, when well matched to problems and goals, tend to be more useful than a single strategy. Use of self-rewards/punishments can, for example, significantly enhance effects achieved through stimulus control or through self-monitoring, as we illustrate in later sections. Multicomponent intervention sets can be undertaken with self-management principles, drawing from interventions such as those in earlier chapters here or other interventions specifically suited to the needs. The literature offers examples such as integrating cognitive behavioral treatment of insomnia and relaxation training with use of self-management tools such as sleep diaries for monitoring and stimulus control of factors associated with sleep (Hood, Rogojanski, & Moss, 2014; Pigeon, 2010). Other clients or problem types may combine self-management strategies with other interventions such as mindfulness, relaxation methods, coping skill supports, reframing techniques, cognitive restructuring, education, and exercise.

Consistent and Regular Use of Strategies Seeming ineffectiveness may be partly attributable to sporadic or inconsistent use of self-management strategies. Monitoring for consistency and fidelity in application of the self-administered plan can offset this risk. Lack of positive outcomes in a self-management program may be due to lack of clarity about how best to use the procedures, or may reflect lack of efficacy even with consistent and reinforced application. Also, if self-management efforts are not used over a sufficient period of time, then their effectiveness may be too limited to produce sufficient change. Ongoing assessment of the fit of the particular techniques or the independence that self-management requires may be warranted. Those who have external supports and encouragement for consistency of use also are likely to have a more successful experience.

Self-Evaluation, Standard Setting, and Self-Efficacy Self-evaluation in a form of standard setting (or goal setting) and intention statements are important to sustaining focus and gauging achievement. Relatively stringent self-selected standards appear to support performance more positively than do lenient standards. Self-evaluation entails the client's willingness and capacity to be open and accurate in assessing on an ongoing basis how close he or she is to meeting self-set standards. We refer throughout the book to *self-monitoring,* the tools and skills used to implement systematic evaluation of one's progress relative to one's beginning baseline and one's short-term or longer-term goals or standards.

It is important in both goal setting and evaluation to distinguish *outcome* expectations (one's beliefs about whether a certain behavior or event will produce a particular outcome) from *self-efficacy* expectations (the belief or level of confidence a person has in his or her ability to develop intentions, set behavioral goals, and successfully execute the behaviors in question). A client may have confidence that she or he can manage a certain action but may not undertake it because of a belief that it will not accomplish the desired outcome (or that obstacles will intervene to prevent the desired outcome). This may well be a realistic assessment of a situation, underscoring the importance of careful assessment of a client's circumstances, taking into account other agents or factors

that may have significant roles in the desired outcome. Successful self-managers usually set higher goals and criteria for change than unsuccessful self-managers do—although in all cases standards set should be realistic and within reach.

Use of Overt, Covert, or Material Self-Reinforcement Self-reinforcement can be undertaken in covert, overt, and/or material form, depending on what the client will experience as genuinely reinforcing. Being able to praise oneself or to note positive improvement is associated with self-change, whereas self-criticism (whether covert or verbal) tends to mitigate against change. Some people may find that material self-reward (such as money or valued items) may be more effective than either self-monitoring or self-punishment; others may find various forms of social support or personal pride in accomplishment to be more effective.

External or Environmental Support External support is valuable to all significant change efforts. Although self-management programs often are accompanied by some degree of support from a formal helper, the proactive engagement of support people can be particularly important because of their contributions in the form of encouragement and reinforcement. For example, public display of self-monitoring data and the help of another person provide opportunities for social reinforcement that often augment behavior change. As with self-reinforcement, reinforcement from others that is liberal, enthusiastic, genuinely laudatory, and pleasurable helps to celebrate achievement and to extend positive emotional states. Support is something from which we all benefit; of course, its nature should be appropriate to the clients' cultural backgrounds, age cohorts, and life circumstances.

Self-Monitoring Overview

Self-monitoring is a process in which people observe **LO1** and record things about themselves and their interactions with environmental situations. Self-monitoring is a useful adjunct to assessment because the observational data can verify or identify the need to modify the client's verbal report about the target behavior. We recommend that clients record their daily self-observations over a designated time period on a behavior log. Usually the client observes and records the target behavior, the controlling antecedents, and the resulting consequences.

Self-monitoring is a core early step in any self-change or self-maintenance program. The client must be able to discover and acknowledge intrapersonal and interpersonal patterns *before* implementing a self-change strategy, just as the helper must have a clear sense of what has transpired before selecting a therapeutic procedure. In other words, a self-management strategy, like any other intervention, should be preceded by a baseline period of self-observation and recording. During this period, the client collects and records data about the behavior to be changed (B), the antecedents (A) of the behavior, and the consequences (C) of the behavior. In addition, the client may wish to note how much or how often the behavior occurs. For example, a client might record the daily amount of study time or the number of times he or she left the study time and place to do something else. Behavior logs used to collect assessment data also can be used by a client to collect baseline data before implementing a self-management program. Self-management strategies are sometimes introduced after other change methods, for example, in preparing for closure of formal treatment with the expectation that a client can continue his or her own self-directed change efforts. Thus, tools for self-monitoring may sometimes be introduced later in a helping process.

Self-monitoring also is very useful for evaluation of goals or outcomes. Monitoring target behavior, either before or during a treatment program, provides both baseline data as well as concrete ways to observe incremental change (or the lack thereof, which would suggest the need to modify the change plan). Moreover, the mere act of self-observation can produce change. As one collects data about oneself, the act of data collection itself often influences the behavior being observed, which can be a positive kind of reactivity. Thus, in several respects self-monitoring is useful not only to collect data but also to promote client change—engendering a more nuanced understanding of processes. (See Learning Activity 15.1.)

Clinical Uses of Self-Monitoring

A very wide range of research reports and clinical studies have identified self-monitoring as a major change strategy. An online search of the literature with key terms relevant to problem types you find in your practice will provide an array of examples that you may find appropriate to your practice. Self-monitoring has been used with many different

---

Learning Activity 15.1

Self-Monitoring

This activity is designed to help you use self-monitoring yourself. The instructions describe a self-monitoring plan for you to try out.

1. *Rationale* for self-monitoring: How would you describe the purpose and provide an overview?
2. *Discrimination of a target response:*
   a. Specify one target behavior you would like to change. Generally, it is best to monitor both the positive and the negative sides of the behavior to gather complete information (Am I increasing what I hope to? Decreasing what I hope to?).
   b. Write down a definition of this behavior. How clear is your definition?
   c. Can you provide some written examples of this behavior? If you had trouble with these, try to tighten up your definition—or contrast positive and negative instances of the behavior.
3. *Recording of the response:*
   a. Specify the *timing* of your self-recording. Remember the rules of thumb:
      1. Record immediately—don't wait.
      2. Record when there are no competing responses.
      3. Record on a regular basis, paying attention to what helps make this possible.
      4. Be aware of potential reactivity—and keep recording.

   b. Select a *method* of recording (frequency, duration, intensity). Remember:
      1. Frequency counts are used for clearly separate occurrences of the response.
      2. Duration or latency measures are for responses that occur for a period of time. For frequently occurring behaviors, time sampling may be more sustainable than continuous recording.
      3. Intensity measures are used to determine the severity of a response.
   c. Select a *device* to assist you in recording. Remember that the device should be
      1. portable
      2. accessible
      3. economical
      4. obtrusive enough to serve as a reminder to self-record
   d. After you have made these determinations, engage in self-monitoring for at least a week (preferably two). Then complete steps 4, 5, and 6.
4. *Charting of the response:* Take your daily self-recording data and chart them on a simple line graph for each day that you self-monitored.
5. *Displaying of data:* Select a location (with which you feel comfortable) to display your chart.
6. *Analysis of data:* Compare your chart with your stated behavior change goal. What has happened to the behavior? How do you interpret these data? Undertake self-evaluation and self-reinforcement?

populations, including people with a range of disabilities, people with chronic mental illness, children, elders, and care-givers, and across cultures. Attention to self-monitoring may help achieve a more nuanced understanding of processes—such as Kosic, Mannetti, and Sam's (2006) finding that self-monitoring plays a role in moderating between differing acculturation strategies and the sociocultural and psychological adaptation outcomes of immigrants. Ennis and Jolivette (2014) found targeted academic skills of children with or at risk for emotional and behavioral problems improved measurably with the use of goal setting, self-monitoring, self-instruction, and self-reinforcement strategies.

Factors Influencing Reactivity

Reactivity involves behavior change in response to the experience of monitoring, which may include reaction from the environment as well as from the target individual. Reactivity can be positive such that people begin changing their response patterns as an outcome of self-monitoring alone in ways that are consistent with their change goals. Reactivity can also be negative, including client unease, irritation, boredom, or various forms of push back. Although the reactivity within self-monitoring can be a dilemma in data collection, it can be an asset when self-monitoring is used intentionally as a helping strategy—when positive reactivity of self-monitoring reinforces clients' change efforts and motivation. The process of carefully monitoring one's habits, or the nature of one's interactions with others, raises self-awareness, which

in itself can support self-control strategies that change these habits (see Karoly, 2005, for examples).

This implies the potential benefits of purposefully trying to maximize the reactive effects of self-monitoring—at least to the point of producing desired behavioral changes. A number of factors seem to influence the reactivity of self-monitoring. A summary of these factors suggests that self-monitoring is most likely to produce positive behavioral changes when change-motivated individuals continuously monitor a limited number of discrete, positively valued target behaviors; when performance feedback and goals or standards are made available and are unambiguous; and when the monitoring act is both salient and closely related in time to the target behaviors. The factors summarized in Box 15.1 merit particular attention in that these seem to be related to reactive effects of self-monitoring.

Self-monitoring can be very simple methods like log sheets focused on single behaviors or can involve a range of more complex methods and/or multiple targets. The field of persuasive technology is generating persuasive personal monitoring systems that are being used in the management of a wide range of health-related conditions. These types of systems may involve a range of interconnected technologies (e.g., cell phone applications, sensor data from phone or wearable devices, Web-based tools or interfaces, as well as hard copy tracking devices). The aim is to help users by enabling them to monitor and visualize their behaviors, keeping them informed about their physical state, reminding them to perform specific tasks, providing feedback on the effectiveness of their behaviors, and recommending healthier behaviors or actions.

BOX 15.1   **Factors Related to the Occurrence, Intensity, and Direction of Reactive Effects of Self-monitoring**

1. *Motivation:* Clients who are interested in changing the self-monitored behavior are more likely to show positive reactive effects when they self-monitor.

2. *Valence (positivity or negativity) of target behaviors:* Behaviors that a person values positively are likely to increase with self-monitoring; negative behaviors are likely to decrease; neutral behaviors may not change.

3. *Type of target behaviors:* The nature of the behavior that is being monitored may affect the degree to which self-monitoring procedures affect change (e.g., some behaviors may be more appealing or aversive to a client).

4. *Standard setting (goals), reinforcement, and feedback:* Reactivity is enhanced for people who self-monitor in conjunction with goals and the availability of performance reinforcement or feedback.

5. *Timing of self-monitoring:* The time when the person self-records can influence the reactivity of self-monitoring. Results may differ depending on whether

self-monitoring occurs before or after the target response.

6. *Devices used for self-monitoring:* More obtrusive or visible recording devices seem to be more negatively reactive than unobtrusive devices. However, as technology is expanding devices and their social acceptability, reactivity is changing and needs to be assessed with the client.

7. *Number of target responses monitored:* Self-monitoring of only one response tends to increase reactivity to that target. As more responses are concurrently monitored, reactivity tends to decrease. However, as technology integrates multiple sources of monitoring, an overall more positive reactivity may be achieved.

8. *Schedule for self-monitoring:* The frequency with which a person self-monitors can affect reactivity. Continuous self-monitoring may result in more behavior change than intermittent self-recording.*

*Adapted from Nelson, 1977.

Bardram et al. (2012) provide a detailed example of the MONARCA Self-Assessment System designed in collaboration with patients for use by bipolar patients and their service provider teams. Aims of the monitoring and feedback systems are to help or "persuade" clients to align their behaviors with three central goals related to medication adherence, stable sleeping patterns, and staying both physically and socially active. We illustrate additional tools in the Devices for Self-Monitoring section.

Components of Self-Monitoring

Self-monitoring involves at least six important components:

1. rationale for the strategy,
2. discrimination of a response,
3. recording of a response (issues of timing, structure, instrument format, and devices used—physical, mobile, wearable),
4. charting of a response,
5. displaying of data, and
6. analysis of data.

Each of these six components is discussed here and is summarized in Learning Activity 15.1. Remember that the components are interactive and that the presence of all of them may be required for a person to use self-monitoring effectively. Also, remember that any or all of these components may need to be adapted depending on the client's age, gender, and culture.

Component 1: Treatment Rationale

First, the practitioner explains the rationale for self-monitoring. Before using the strategy, the client should be aware of what the self-monitoring procedure will involve and how the procedure will help with the client's concern. Consider this example:

> The purpose of self-monitoring is to increase your awareness of your sleep patterns. Research has demonstrated that people who have insomnia benefit from keeping a self-monitoring diary. Each morning for a week you will record: the time you went to bed the previous night; approximately how many minutes it took you to fall asleep; if you awakened during the night, how many minutes you were awake; the total number of hours you slept; and the time you got out of bed in the morning. Also, on a scale you will rate how well you think you

were functioning the previous day, your level of physical tension when you went to bed, your level of mental activity when you went to bed, how difficult it was to fall asleep, the quality of your sleep, and how rested you feel in the morning. The diary will help us evaluate your sleep experiences. This kind of awareness helps in identifying and correcting factors that might contribute to your insomnia. How does that sound? Adapted from Benson and Stuart, 1992.

Component 2: Discrimination of a Response

To self-monitor, one must first establish what aspect of responding to focus on. For example, a client who is monitoring fingernail biting or skin picking must be able to be aware of instances of biting or picking. Discrimination of a response requires this awareness, reflecting the client's ability to identify the presence or absence of the behavior and whether it is overt, like nail biting, or covert, like a positive self-thought.

Discrimination of a response involves identifying *what* to monitor. This decision often will require helper assistance. The type of the monitored response may affect the results of self-monitoring. For example, self-monitoring may produce greater weight loss for people who record their daily weight and daily caloric intake than for those who record only daily weight. What works for each individual may vary; the selection of target responses remains a pragmatic choice regarding what seems to work well. Moreover, self-monitoring of certain responses could be premature and/or detract from intervention effectiveness if, for example, a client feels overwhelmed or is acutely distressed.

The effects of self-monitoring also vary with the valence of the target response. There are always two sides of a behavior that could be monitored—the positive and the negative. There are also times when one side is more important for self-monitoring than the other. Unfortunately, there are very limited data to guide a decision about the exact type and valence of responses to monitor. Because the reactivity of self-monitoring is affected by the value assigned to a behavior (Watson & Tharp, 2014), one guideline might be to have the client monitor the behavior that she or he cares *most* about changing. Generally, it is a good idea to encourage the client to limit monitoring to one response, at least initially. If the client engages in self-monitoring of one behavior with no difficulties, then more items can be added. That said, technology is offering more devices that can automatically capture and track multiple forms of information (e.g., location, movement, various aspects of physical condition) that reduces monitoring burden and can offer more integrative characterizations.

Component 3: Recording a Response

After the client has learned to make discriminations about a response, the helper can provide instructions and examples of the method for recording the observed response. Most clients probably have never recorded their behavior *systematically*. Systematic recording is crucial to the success of self-monitoring, and so it is imperative that the client understand the importance and methods of recording. Recent clinical research on childhood obesity demonstrated, for example, that children who completed their journals on a regular basis lost more weight comparatively; these results are consistent with adult findings (Mockus, 2011). The client needs instructions about when and how to record and about devices for recording. The timing, method, and recording devices can all influence the effectiveness of self-monitoring.

Timing Self-Monitoring: When to Record Some circumstances may involve careful attention to timing issues, such as working around potential impediments. Overall, however, the guidelines are relatively straightforward:

1. Record immediately—don't wait.

2. Record when there are no competing responses.

3. Record on a regular basis, paying attention to what helps make this possible.

4. Be aware of potential reactivity—and keep recording.

A central factor is the amount of time between the response and the actual recording. There is general agreement that delayed recording of the behavior weakens the efficacy of the monitoring process. For example, the helper might suggest to the client, "Record *immediately* after you have the urge to smoke—or *immediately* after you have covertly praised yourself; do not wait even for a few minutes because the impact of recording may be lost." Second, the client should be encouraged to record the response when not distracted by the situation or by other competing responses. Both the accuracy and effects of self-monitoring are compromised if this is significantly competing for the person's attention at the time the response is recorded. As previously noted, relatively haphazard self-monitoring can be misleading given the incomplete picture the partial data creates.

The client should be instructed to record the behavior *in vivo* as it occurs rather than at the end of the day, when he or she is dependent on recall. *In vivo* recording may not always be feasible, however, and in some cases the client's self-recording may have to be performed later.

Structure of Self-Monitoring: How to Record There are a number of basic characteristics shared by effective recording methods. The recording should be easy to implement, provide a reasonably representative picture of the behavior in question, and be sensitive to changes so that increments of change can be discerned. The helper needs to help the client identify a suitably matched *structure or system* for recording the target responses and provide instruction in its implementation to ensure success.

Frequency, duration, and intensity can be recorded with either a continuous recording or a time-sampling method. Continuous means recording every instance of a behavior or event. Time sampling means to identify specific times (which may literally be specific times of day or more in terms of certain kind of situations) that are the only times that the client records. Selection of one of these methods will depend mainly on the type of target response and the frequency of its occurrence. To record the *number* of target responses, the client can use a frequency count. Continuous frequency counts are most useful for monitoring events or behaviors that are fairly discrete, that do not occur frequently, and are of relatively short duration. For instance, clients might record the total number of times that they praise or compliment themselves covertly (for those with low levels, aiming to increase). Time-sampling approaches are better suited to more frequent behaviors or those that are contextually elicited. Someone in a smoking cessation program may note the number and strength of urges to smoke under conditions that they identify as higher risk and that they want to foster greater mindfulness about their sensations and response patterns.

Other kinds of target responses are recorded more easily and accurately by duration. Anytime a client wants to record the amount or length of a response, a duration count can be used. Duration assessments are most appropriate when the target behavior is not discrete and varies in length. Self-management approaches to mood problems such as depression, for example, might use a duration scale to note the length of a happy or pleasant mood. Academic-focused interventions might measure the amount of time spent reading textbooks or engaging in a physical activity.

Sometimes a client may want to record two or more different responses and use both the frequency and the duration methods. For example, a client might use a frequency count to record each urge to smoke and a duration count to monitor the time spent smoking a cigarette. Additionally, clients may self-record the intensity of responses whenever data are desired about the relative severity of a response. For example, a client might record the intensity of happy, anxious, or depressed feelings or moods.

Format of Self-Monitoring Instruments There are many formats of self-monitoring instruments that a client can use to record the frequency, duration, and/or intensity of the target response as well as information about contributing variables. The particular format of the instrument can affect reactivity and level of client compliance with self-monitoring. Therefore, the format of the instrument should be tailored to the client, the situation, and the change goals. Figure 15.2 shows three formats for monitoring instruments. For each format a variety of self-recording devices may be used. Watson and Tharp (2014) provide a range of additional examples.

Example 1 displays a format useful for relatively frequent recordings—for example, couples self-monitoring the content and quality of their interactions. In this format, each person records the content of the interaction with the partner (e.g., having dinner together, talking about finances, discussing work, going to movies, dealing with a parenting issue) and rates the quality of that interaction. This format aims to capture all substantial interactions and characterize them. Other approaches may focus on certain types of interactions, such as discussing a sensitive topic or dealing with conflict, or may track aspects of interactions, such as the use of active listening skills.

Example 2 shows a format that is useful when more detail is needed and the client is likely to benefit from having her or his attention directed to components (e.g., What was I saying to myself just then?), to connections (e.g., the types of events that seem to systematically trigger certain reactions), and to the level of one's reaction and views about how it was handled. This example is designed for anxiety responses, but it could readily be modified for a range of other affective states, thinking patterns, or behaviors.

Example 3 illustrates a brief diary format. This directs attention to the triggering event but also includes the recording of coping efforts and self-administered praise or reinforcement as well as affective states before and after the coping efforts. The illustration uses headaches as a physical manifestation of stress, but, again, the general format could be applied to any number of targeted issues.

Physical Self-Monitoring Device Examples Clients often report that one of the most intriguing aspects of self-monitoring is the device or mechanism used for recording. A variety of devices have been used to help clients keep accurate records. Note cards, daily log sheets, and diaries are low-cost and simple devices to make written notations. Another popular self-recording device is a wrist counter, such as a golf counter that can be used to log counts of events or behaviors in a range of different settings. If several behaviors are being counted simultaneously, then the

client can wear several wrist counters, use knitting tallies, or use a tally counter application on a cell phone. A wrist counter with rows of beads permits the simultaneous recording of several behaviors. Toothpicks, pennies, small game tokens, or other small objects can be used as recording devices—transferring one object to another pocket each time a behavior occurs. Children can record frequencies by pasting stars on a chart or by using a prepared matrix that has pictures and numbers for three recording columns: "What do I do," "My count," and "What happens." Clocks, watches, and kitchen timers can be used for duration counts. The nature of the device depends, of course, on what kind of observations are most useful (e.g., notes about thoughts, feelings, circumstances, and reactions require different devices than those needed for frequency or duration).

Mobile and Wearable Devices Technology is rapidly expanding potential for mobile monitoring options. Many if not most paper-and-pencil formats can be transferred electronically across a range of devices for use when needed. Mobile (e.g., smart phones, tablets, laptops, personal digital assistants, specialized hand held devices) and wearable technologies allow individuals to measure themselves and their environments, and to integrate a range of forms of information, help, and engaging formats. There is growing evidence that these technological tools offer positive benefits, such as being viewed as more normative and less stigmatizing, more engaging with a resultant higher use, strengthening data accuracy as it is more real-time than recalled or objectively sensed such as temperature, sleep, or pulse, and integrating multiple forms of information in understandable formats (Morris & Aguilera, 2012).

Vilardaga, Bricker, and McDonell (2014) illustrate a range of ways in which mobile and sensory devices can be of substantial and adaptable benefit to self-monitoring, adding richness and precision to clients' and helpers' understanding and tracking of their behaviors (both struggles and successes) within their life circumstances. Social media present an additional technological resource, albeit one with both positive and negative potential, such as reducing a sense of loneliness (Burke, Kraut, & Marlow, 2011) coupled with privacy and exposure concerns. Magnezi and colleagues (2015) illustrate positive potential with clients obtaining interpersonal support and information regarding their health conditions, possibly leading to improved treatment compliance and self-managed care.

Technology often provides quicker and more accessible approaches to self-monitoring. Recording forms can be sent electronically, as can responses (aiding with communication between client and helper between sessions),

Example 1: Content and Quality of Partnered Interactions
(Record the type of interaction under "Content." For each interaction, circle one category that best represents the quality of that interaction.)

Time	Content of Interaction	Quality of Interaction				
		Very Pleasant	Pleasant	Neutral	Unpleasant	Very Unpleasant
___	___	+ +	+	0	–	– –
___	___	+ +	+	0	–	– –
___	___	+ +	+	0	–	– –
___	___	+ +	+	0	–	– –

Example 2: Self-Monitoring Log for Recording Anxiety Responses (This could be adapted for other feeling/thought/behavior targets.)

Date and Time	Situation Features	Internal Dialogue (Self-Statements)	Degree of Feeling	Behavioral Factors	Satisfaction in Handling Situation	Alternatives to Consider
	Describe each problematic situation; note what seemed to trigger anxiety	Note your thoughts or things you said to yourself when this occurred	Rate the intensity of the anxiety: (1) a little intense, (2) somewhat intense, (3) very intense, (4) extremely intense	Note how you responded—what you did	Rate how effectively you believe you handled the situation: (1) a little, (2) somewhat, (3) very, (4) extremely	What different thoughts or behaviors seem useful to try? What would help you prepare to try this next time?

Example 3: Brief Diary Format

Instructions: For each situation in which you experience a headache, record the following. After several episodes, reflect on what you see to be trends and what seems to be associated with reduced tension.

Headache Diary:

Stressful situation: _____

Negative thoughts: _____

Tension level rated   1   2   3   4   5   6   7   8   9   10

Coping strategies: _____

Praising self for coping: _____

Resulting tension level   1   2   3   4   5   6   7   8   9   10

FIGURE 15.2 Examples of Formats for Self-Monitoring Instruments

Source: Adapted from *Self-Directed Behavior* (10th ed.), by D. L. Watson & R. G. Tharp, p. 87. Copyright © 2007 Thomson.

and they are always available in a file or at a website. Technology-assisted therapy increases access to services and supports for people with health care access barriers (Patel, Park, Bonato, Chan, & Rodgers, 2012) as well as acceptability and efficacy among low-income client populations (Herring, Cruice, Bennett, Davey, & Foster, 2014). Newman, Przeworski, Consoli, and Taylor (2014) investigated the advantages and disadvantages of technology tools in this regard, including the use of palmtop computers that are sufficiently small to be carried at all times (and, thus, more likely to be available in target situations relevant to intervention) with comparable or more favorable outcomes. They also offer reviews of technology-assisted self-help and minimal contact therapies with technologies such as Skype, voiceover Internet protocols, ambulatory electrophysiological monitoring, and global positioning systems (Newman, Szkodny, Llera, & Przeworski, 2011).

Portable devices also are increasingly available to support behavioral self-monitoring, as illustrated by Gulchak (2008), using handheld computers to teach behaviorally disordered children to monitor and increase on-task behavior. Amato Zech, Hoff, and Doepke (2006) describe the use of an electronic, vibrating beeper as a tactile reminder to self-monitor attention in a special education classroom. Formal applications in mental health are emerging with, for example, anxiety (Dennis & O'Toole, 2014) and depression (Kauer et al., 2012), as are more informal auto-analytic applications, such as trackyourhappiness (https://www.trackyourhappiness.org/)

Mobile technology is being used more frequently in health self-management. Technology-based weight loss interventions increasingly use technology-related monitoring aids such as personal digital devices, electronic digital scales, and Internet applications. Spring et al. (2013) point to challenges of limited helper access within existing systems of care and the value of technology to augment goals like weight loss, particularly when paired with cost-effective helper contact such as biweekly coaching calls. Cell phone glucose monitoring for young diabetics (where data are automatically transmitted to a health care provider who can support the youth via phone by indicating needed adjustments) is one example of assisting youth in tracking and self-managing their behavior and health (Carroll, DiMeglio, Stein, & Marero, 2011). Although well accepted by youth, findings noted the importance of an integrated package of self-management tools, such as use of behavioral contracts with youth and support around family conflict, to enhance the self-monitoring technology's ability to improve health outcomes.

Guidelines for Self-Monitoring Devices In summary, the helper and client review and select a recording

device—whether it be coins, counters, or contemporary technology. Here is an opportunity to be inventive! There are several practical criteria to consider in helping a client. The device should be portable and accessible so that it is present whenever the behavior occurs. It should be easy, convenient, and economical. The obtrusiveness of the device also should be considered. For the recording device to function as a cue (discriminative stimulus) for the client to self-monitor, it should be noticeable enough to remind the client. However, a device that is too obtrusive may draw attention from others, with variable results. Others' awareness might lead them to reward (e.g., offer positive reinforcement in the form of praise) or punish (e.g., ostracize, stigmatize) the client for self-monitoring. Finally, the device should be capable of giving cumulative frequency data so that the client can chart daily totals of the behavior.

After the client has been instructed in the timing and method of recording, and once a recording device has been selected, the client should practice using the recording system. Breakdowns in self-monitoring often occur because a client does not understand the recording process clearly. Rehearsal of the recording procedures will help to ensure that the client records accurately. Generally, a client should engage in self-recording for 3 to 4 weeks because the effects of self-monitoring are often not apparent after only 1 or 2 weeks.

Component 4: Charting of a Response

The data recorded by the client should be translated into a more permanent storage record, such as a chart or graph, that will enable the client to inspect the self-monitored data visually. Some electronic devices will provide this, but in other cases the helper may need to create a visual aid.

These visual guides may provide the occasion for client self-reward or self-reinforcement, which, in turn, can influence the reactivity of self-monitoring. The data can be charted by days using a simple line graph. For example, a client counting the number of urges to smoke a cigarette could chart these by days, as in Figure 15.3. A client recording the amount of time spent studying each day could use the same sort of line graph to chart duration of study time. The vertical axis would be divided into time intervals such as 15 minutes, 30 minutes, 45 minutes, or 1 hour.

The client should receive either oral or written instructions on how to chart and graph the daily totals of the recorded response. The helper can assist the client in interpreting the chart in the sessions on data review and analysis. If a client is using self-monitoring to increase a behavior, then the line on the graph should climb gradually if the self-monitoring is having the desired effect. If the intent of self-monitoring is to influence an undesired

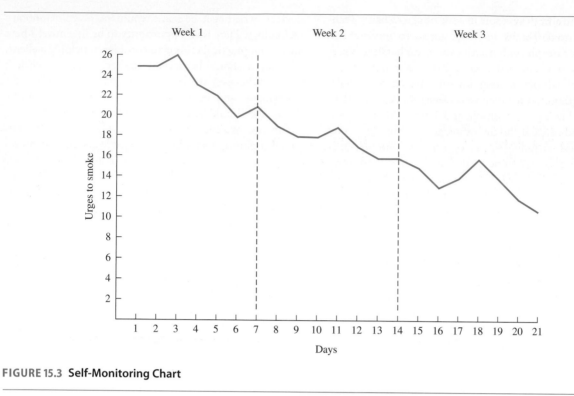

FIGURE 15.3 Self-Monitoring Chart

response to decrease, then the line on the graph should go down gradually.

Component 5: Displaying of Data

After the graph has been prepared, the client has the option of displaying the completed chart. If the chart is displayed in an area shared by others or displayed to a group within group treatment, then this display may prompt environmental reinforcement, a valuable part of an effective self-management program. The effects of self-monitoring usually are augmented when the data chart is displayed as a public referent—meaning shared selectively to others by the client. However, some clients may prefer not to make their data open for reasons of confidentiality or stigma avoidance.

Component 6: Analysis of Data

If the client's self-monitoring data are not reviewed and analyzed, then the client may soon feel as if he or she was told to make a graph just for practice in drawing straight lines! A very important facet of self-monitoring is the information that it can provide to the client. There is some evidence that people who receive feedback about their self-recording change more than those who do not. The recording and charting of data should be used *explicitly* to

provide the client with knowledge of results about behavior or performance. Specifically, the client should bring the data to weekly sessions for review and analysis. In these sessions, the helper can encourage the client to compare the data with the desired goals and standards. The client can use the recorded data for self-evaluation and determine whether the data indicate that the behavior is within or outside the desired limits. The helper also can aid in data analysis by helping the client to interpret the data correctly. Guidance on ways to meaningfully display and analyze client self-monitoring data has been growing in sophistication over the years. In general, many of the methods and guidelines used for identifying, defining, and evaluating outcome goals can be adapted for client self-monitoring.

Model Example: Self-Monitoring

Our case example, Isabella, indicated the goal of [LO2] increasing her positive thoughts (and simultaneously decreasing her negative thoughts) about her ability to do well with math. This goal lends itself to the application of self-management strategies for several reasons. First, the goal represents a covert behavior (positive thoughts), which is observable only by Isabella. Second, the flip side of the goal (negative thoughts) represents a very well-learned habit.

Probably most of these negative thoughts occur *outside* the helping sessions. To change this thought pattern, Isabella will benefit from the use of strategies that she can apply as needed *in vivo* and that she can administer herself.

Here is a description of the way in which Isabella could use self-monitoring to achieve the above goal:

1. *Treatment rationale:* The helper provides an explanation of what Isabella will self-monitor and why, emphasizing that this is a strategy she can apply herself, can use with a private behavior, and should use as frequently as possible in the actual setting.

2. *Discrimination of a response:* The helper needs to help Isabella define the target response explicitly. One definition could be: "Anytime I think about myself doing math or working with numbers successfully." The helper provides some possible examples of this response, such as, "Gee, I did well on my math homework today," or, "I was able to balance my check book today." The helper also encourages Isabella to identify some examples of the target response. Because Isabella wants to increase this behavior, the target response will be stated in positive terms.

3. *Recording of a response:* The helper instructs Isabella about timing, method, and a device for recording. Isabella is instructed to record *immediately* after a target thought occurs. She is interested in recording the *number* of such thoughts, so she will use a frequency count. A tally on a note card or a wrist counter can be selected as the device for recording. After these instructions, Isabella will practice recording before officially implementing the self-monitoring plan. The helper instructs her to engage in self-monitoring for approximately 4 consecutive weeks.

4. *Charting of a response:* After each week of self-monitoring, Isabella can add her daily frequency totals and chart them by days on a simple line graph, as shown in Figure 15.4. Isabella is using self-monitoring to increase a behavior; as a result, if the monitoring has the desired effect, then the line on her graph will gradually rise. It is just starting to do so here; additional data for the next few weeks will show a greater increase if the self-monitoring is influencing the target behavior in the desired direction.

5. *Displaying of data:* After Isabella makes a data chart, she may wish to post it in a place such as her room, although this is a very personal decision.

6. *Analysis of data:* During the period of self-monitoring, Isabella brings in her data for weekly review sessions

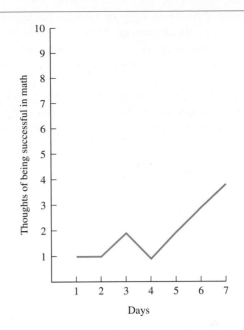

FIGURE 15.4 Simple Line Graph for Self-Monitoring

with the helper. The helper provides reinforcement and helps Isabella interpret the data accurately. Isabella can use the data for self-evaluation by comparing the story the data tell with her stated desired behavior and level of change.

Stimulus Control Components

Antecedents play pivotal roles in our patterns of behavior. They set the stage for and can greatly affect behavior in the sense of stimulating or triggering responses. Managing or controlling these response stimulants are therefore often key to developing and sustaining changed patterns. In many cases, changing behaviors—such as dietary and exercise for those with diabetes—involve changing engrained habits and can be very challenging indeed. The original behaviors that now need to be changed—such as smoking or eating sweet or fat-rich foods—may have comfort or coping functions, even if, in the long run, they are maladaptive. Thus, it may be useful to begin with a small step approach that breaks the ultimate change goal into interim steps to foster incremental progress. Other factors, such as withdrawal symptoms, may need to be clinically managed. Although beyond the scope of this chapter, resources such as Hogarth, Balleine, Corbit, and Killcross (2013) discuss learning mechanisms underlying shifts from early or recreational consumption habits to those that are more driven by dependence that hold implications for stimulus control.

Stimulus control can be understood as a purposeful arrangement of environmental conditions that serves to hamper engagement in undesired behavior (placing snack foods or alcohol in difficult-to-access locations to reduce consumption) or, conversely, that cue or prompt desired behaviors (such as leaving cue cards or objects in plain sight, e.g., to take medications). Recall that within the ABC model, a behavior often is guided by certain conditions or circumstances that precede it (antecedents) and is maintained by positive or negative events that follow it (consequences)—and both antecedents and consequences can be external and observable (overt) or internal and unobservable (covert). For example, an antecedent could be an object or situation, an emotion, a cognition, or an overt or covert verbal instruction.

The strategies and tools described for self-monitoring will be important to establishing conditions under and patterns of the triggering response for individuals. The notion of **ecological momentary assessment** has gained some prominence, referring to a collection of assessment information that characterizes emotions, behaviors, cognitions, sensations associated with various environments (e.g., using diaries, physiological sensors, and other devices that help to characterize the ABC components, for example). See aan het Rot, Hoheneist, and Schoevers (2012), Buckner et al. (2012), and Schüz, Bower, and Ferguson (2015) for illustrations with different types of target behaviors and circumstances.

How Antecedents Acquire Stimulus Control

When antecedents are consistently associated with a behavior that is reinforced in the *presence* (not the absence) of these antecedent stimuli, they gain control over the behavior. You might think of this as antecedents working as stimuli for a certain response. When antecedents gain stimulus control over the response, there is a high probability that the response will be emitted in the presence of these particular antecedent events. For example, most of us automatically slow down, put our foot on the brake, and stop the car when we see a red traffic light or the brake light of the car in front of us. The red light is a stimulus that has gained control over our stopping-the-car behavior. Generally, the fact that antecedents exert stimulus control is helpful, as it is in driving: we go when we see a green light and stop at the sight of a red light.

Inappropriate Stimulus Control in Troubling Behavior

Behaviors that trouble clients may occur because of *inappropriate* stimulus control. Inappropriate stimulus control includes behaviors that are triggered by multiple environmental cues. If a person not only eats something at the dining table but also experiences eating triggers when working in the kitchen, watching television, walking by the refrigerator, and stopping at a Dairy Queen, then the sheer number of eating responses could soon result in excess weight. Some lifestyle patterns, such as eating, result from a complex interplay of cultural, biological, and behavioral response factors that may need consideration in developing a well-suited self-management plan. Stimulus control techniques that target behaviors to decrease and/or to increase (such as food consumption and sedentary behaviors) are often paired with other components such as education, self-monitoring, cognitive restructuring, stress management, and self-support and social support strategies (Carter, Dyer, & Mikan, 2013; Epstein, Paluch, Kilanowski, & Raynor, 2004; Kumar, Cohen, Porter, & Jyothi, 2008).

Having too many environmental cues that stimulate undesired behaviors is often related to other client difficulties, particularly excesses such as substance use. In these cases, a primary aim of a self-management stimulus control method is to reduce the number of cues associated with the undesired response, such as eating or smoking. Werthwein (2009), for example, illustrated the use of stimulus control and coping strategies in a smoking cessation treatment, creating individualized hierarchies of smoking situations graduated from least to most cue-provoking. Brodbeck, Bachmann, and Znoj (2013) undertook a multicomponent smoking cessation relapse treatment combining different types of stress-coping and temptation-coping strategies distinguishing engagement from disengagement strategies. Engagement-oriented coping was more effective; within this, stimulus control (avoiding or removing oneself from high-risk situations or exposure to conditioned coping cues) was the only coping variable that predicted lower relapse risk and also lower urge levels.

Other behaviors involve excessively narrow stimulus control. Many of us recognize the limited number of environmental cues in everyday life that compellingly stimulate physical activity. In contrast to excess consumption are people who eat so little that their physical and psychological health suffers (e.g., anorexia nervosa). In these instances, there are often too few positive eating cues, among other elements involved with this issue. Insomnia is another example of needing to increase behaviors in which stimulus control is a core component. Fowler (2010) illustrated a clinical application that paired stimulus control over behaviors associated with sleep (that would inhibit or facilitate) and with sleep restriction—with favorable results that avoided use of pharmacological interventions and fostered self-efficacy. Noteworthy is the use of the Internet in delivering self-help interventions, insomnia being an example, that includes use of PDFs for education, multimedia clips, and a range of other presentation and data recording devices (Ritterband et al., 2010). In these types of problem areas, the primary aim of a stimulus control strategy is to increase the number of cues that will elicit the desired behavior and help to stabilize new behavioral patterns.

To summarize, stimulus control self-management involves reducing the number of antecedent stimuli associated with an undesirable behavior and simultaneously increasing the antecedent cues associated with a desirable response (Watson & Tharp, 2014). Table 15.1 illustrates the components and process of stimulus control strategies associated with each of the two primary goals of decreasing or increasing a target behavior.

Using Stimulus Control to Decrease Behavior

To decrease the rate of a behavior, the antecedent cues associated with the behavior should be reduced in frequency or altered in time and place of occurrence. When cues are separated from the habitual behavior by alteration or elimination, the old, undesired habit can be phased out and terminated (Watson & Tharp, 2014), particularly when embedded with complementary strategies such as self-reward, reframing, and social support. Existing cues can be prearranged to make the target behavior so difficult to execute that the person is unlikely to do it. An example would be altering the place of smoking by moving one's smoking chair to an inconvenient place like the basement or outside. A person can prearrange cues by placing control in the hands of someone else. Giving your pack of cigarettes to a friend is an example of this method. The friend should agree to help you reduce smoking and not to reinforce or punish any instances of your smoking behavior (the undesired response).

A behavior also can be reduced through stimulus control by interrupting the learned pattern or sequence that begins with one or more antecedent cues and results in the undesired response. This sequence may be called a *chain*. A troubling behavior is often the result of a long chain of events. For example, a variety of behaviors make up the sequence of smoking. Before puffing on a cigarette, a person has to go to a store, buy cigarettes, remove one cigarette from the pack, and light up.

TABLE 15.1 Components and Process of Stimulus Control Strategies

Change Goal	Components and Process
To decrease a behavior: Reduce or narrow the frequency of cues associated with eating behavior.	1. Prearrange or alter cues associated with the place of the behavior: a. Prearrange cues that make it hard to execute the behavior. Place fattening foods in high, hard-to-reach places. b. Prearrange cues so that they are controlled by others. Ask friends or family to serve you only one helping of food and to avoid serving fattening foods to you. 2. Alter the time or sequence (chain) between the antecedent cues and the resulting behaviors: a. Break up the sequence. Buy and prepare food only on a full stomach. b. Change the sequence. Substitute and engage in nonfood activities when you start to contemplate snacking (e.g., moving toward refrigerator, cupboard, or candy machine). c. Build pauses into the sequence. Delay second helpings of food or snacks for a predetermined amount of time.
To increase a behavior: Increase or prearrange the cues associated with the response of studying.	1. Seek out these cues deliberately to perform the desired behavior. Initially arrange only one room with a desk to study. When you need to study, go to this place. 2. Concentrate on the behavior when in the situation. Concentrate only on studying in the room. If you get distracted, get up and leave. Don't mix study with other activities, such as listening to music or talking. 3. Gradually extend the behavior to other situations. When you have control over studying in one room, extend the behavior to another room or place that is similarly conducive. 4. Promote the occurrence of helpful cues by other people or by self-generated reminders. Ask your roommate to remind you to leave the desk when you are talking or distracted. Remind yourself of good study procedures by posting a list over your study desk or by using verbal or covert self-instructions.

A chain might be interrupted in a number of ways—for example, by breaking or unlinking the chain of events, changing the chain, or building pauses into the chain (Watson & Tharp, 2014). A chain of events can be broken by interrupting an event early in the sequence or by scrambling the typical order of events. For example, the smoker could break the chain by not going to stores that sell cigarettes. Or if the smoker typically smokes at certain times, the usual order of events leading to smoking could be mixed up. People who start to light up a cigarette whenever they are bored, tensed, or lacking something to do with their hands could perform a different activity at this point, such as calling a friend when bored, relaxing when tensed, or knitting or playing cards to provide hand activity.

When antecedents exert strong control, a behavior can occur almost automatically. Thus, imposing pauses can interrupt this automaticity—for instance, building in a deliberate pause of 10 minutes before lighting up a cigarette in response to a stress cue. Gradually, this time interval can be increased. Deliberately building in pauses to record (in a journal, computer notebook, or using other monitoring tool) can be useful in fostering reflection—for example, about how one is feeling, thoughts in the moment, triggering environmental conditions—which can help in breaking behavior chains. Sometimes you can even strengthen the pause procedure by covertly instructing yourself on the goal that you want to achieve or by thinking about the benefits of not smoking. The pause itself can then become a new antecedent.

Using Stimulus Control to Increase Behavior

As noted in Table 15.1, to increase the rate of a response, a person deliberately increases and seeks out cues to perform the behavior and concentrates only on this behavior when in the situation. Competing or distracting responses must be avoided, as with the problem of procrastination (Rozental & Carlbring, 2014). Gradually, as stimulus control over the behavior in one situation is achieved, the person can extend the behavior by performing it in another, similar situation. This process of stimulus generalization means that a behavior learned in one situation can be performed in different but similar situations. The person can promote the occurrence of new antecedent cues by using reminders from others, self-reminders, or overt or covert self-instructions. The rate of a desired response is improved by increasing the times and places in which the person performs the response.

Suppose that you are working with a client who wants to increase his or her amount of daily exercise. First, more cues would be established to which the person would respond with isometric or physical activity—such as performing isometrics whenever sitting in a chair to watch television or while in the car waiting for a traffic light. Or the person might perform physical exercises each morning and evening on a special exercise mat. Other behaviors should not be performed while in these situations because a competing response could interfere with the exercise activity (Watson & Tharp, 2014). Gradually, the client could extend the exercise activities to new but similar situations—such as doing isometrics while sitting at the computer or waiting for a meeting to start. The person also could promote exercise behavior in these situations by reminders—posting an exercise chart on the wall or setting a watch or computer for predetermined reminder tones.

We previously noted the use of stimulus control to increase sleep. An example of stimulus control instructions could include: (1) go to bed or lie down to sleep only when sleepy; (2) do not read, watch television, or eat in bed; instead, use the bed only for sleeping and/or sexual activities; (3) if unable to fall asleep after 10 to 20 minutes, get out of bed and engage in some activity return to bed only when sleepy, and continue this procedure throughout the night as necessary; (4) set the alarm clock and get up at the same time every morning regardless of the amount of sleep obtained during the night; and (5) do not take naps during the day.

Although stimulus control can have powerful effects, these methods are often insufficient to modify well-entrenched behavior without the support of other strategies. Stimulus control methods usually are not sufficient for long-term self-change unless accompanied by other self-management methods that exert control over the *consequences* of the target behavior such as self-reward, which is discussed in the following section and illustrated in Learning Activity 15.2. Examples of other components often used with stimulus control include cognitive restructuring, problem-solving and stress-coping skills, breathing and muscle relaxation, and education about the problem topic. Mindfulness-oriented skills are also combined to increase reflectivity and help the person revise views of, and responses to, thoughts and urges (Ong, Shapiro, & Manber, 2008).

Model Example: Stimulus Control

This model example illustrates how stimulus control **LO2** can be used to help Isabella achieve her goal of increasing positive thoughts about her math ability. Recall that the principle of change in using stimulus control to increase a behavior is to increase the cues associated with the behavior.

Learning Activity 15.2

Stimulus Control

The purpose of this activity is to help you reduce an unwanted behavior by using stimulus control methods.

1. Specify a behavior that you find undesirable and wish to decrease. It can be an overt one, such as smoking, eating, biting your nails, or making sarcastic comments, or it can be a covert behavior, such as thinking about yourself in negative ways or thinking how great food or smoking tastes.
2. Select one or more stimulus control methods to use for behavior reduction from the list and examples given in Table 15.1. Remember, you will be reducing the number of cues or antecedent events associated with this behavior by altering the times and places in which the undesired response occurs.

3. Implement these stimulus control methods daily for 2 weeks.
4. During the 2 weeks, engage in self-monitoring of your target response. Record the type and use of your method and the amount of your target behavior, using frequency or duration methods of recording.
5. At the end of 2 weeks, review your recorded data. Did you use your selected method consistently? If you did not, what contributed to your infrequent use? If you used it consistently, did you notice any gradual reduction in the target behavior by the end of 2 weeks? What problems did you encounter in applying a stimulus control method with yourself? What did you learn about stimulus control that might help you when using it with clients?

Here's how the helper will implement this principle with Isabella:

1. The helper will establish at least one cue that Isabella can use as an antecedent for positive thoughts. The helper might suggest something like putting a piece of tape over her watch.

2. Isabella and the helper will develop a list of several positive thoughts about math. Each thought can be written on a blank card that Isabella can carry with her.

3. The helper will instruct Isabella to read or think about a thought on one card *each* time she looks at her watch. The helper will instruct her to seek out the opportunity deliberately by looking at her watch frequently and then concentrating on one of the positive thoughts.

4. When Isabella gets to the point where she automatically thinks of a positive thought after looking at her watch, other cues can be established that she can use in the same way. For instance, she can put a smiley face on her math book. Each time she gets out her math book and sees the smiley face, she can use this cue to concentrate on another positive thought.

5. Isabella can promote more stimulus control over these thoughts by using reminders. For instance, she can put a list of positive thoughts on the mirror or closet door in her room. Each time she sees the list, it serves as a reminder. Or she can ask a friend or classmate to remind her to "think positively" whenever the subject of math or math class is being discussed.

Self-Reward Overview

Self-monitoring and stimulus control procedures **L03** may be enough to maintain the desired goal behavior for many people. However, for some, **self-reward** procedures are useful to help them regulate and strengthen their behavior. Many actions are controlled by self-produced consequences as much as by external consequences.

According to Bandura (1971), there are three necessary conditions of self-reinforcement, or self-reward:

1. The individual (rather than someone else) determines the criteria for adequacy of her or his performance and for resulting reinforcement.

2. The individual (rather than someone else) controls access to the reward.

3. The individual (rather than someone else) is his or her own reinforcing agent and administers the rewards.

Notice that self-reward involves both the self-determination and the self-administration of a reward to strengthen or increase a desired response. In other words, a self-presented reward, like an externally administered reward (e.g., praise from others), is defined by the function it exerts on the target behavior. A reinforcer (self or external) is something that, when administered following a target response, tends to maintain or increase the probability of that response in the future. A major advantage of self-reward over external reward is that a person can apply this strategy independently and, gradually, internalize sustaining attitudes and confidence.

Self-rewards can be positive or negative. In positive self-reward, one presents oneself with a positive stimulus (to which one has adequate access) *after* engaging in a specified behavior. Examples include praising yourself after you have completed a long and difficult task, buying yourself a new CD or DVD after you have engaged in a specified amount of piano practice, or envisioning that you are resting in your favorite spot after you have completed your daily exercises. Negative self-reward involves the removal of a negative stimulus after execution of a target response. Taking down an uncomplimentary picture or chart from your wall after performing the target response is an example of negative self-reward.

Our discussion of self-reward as a therapeutic strategy is limited to the use of positive self-reward for several reasons. First, there has been very little research to validate the negative self-reward procedure. Second, by definition, negative self-reward involves an aversive activity. It usually is not realistic for people to keep unpleasant things in their home or to put an ugly picture on the wall. Many people will not consistently use a strategy that is perceived as aversive. Third, we do not recommend that helpers suggest strategies that seem negative given that reasonable and more positive alternatives are generally available.

Like other management strategies, self-reward has been used in a variety of applications. Degotardi and colleagues (2006), for example, explored the use of self-reward as one component of a cognitive-behavioral intervention with juvenile fibromyalgia, with results showing significant decreases in pain, somatic symptoms, anxiety, fatigue, and sleep disturbances. Notably, self-reinforcing strategies often can be based on antecedent factors that precede problematic behaviors or circumstances—potentially providing help in avoiding difficulties. Cihak and Garna (2008) illustrated this approach with developmentally disabled students with the aim of avoiding outbursts or aggression. Teaching these students self-reinforcing strategies proved effective in reducing problematic behavior and greater on-task time, and, secondarily, afforded the teacher greater opportunity to help other students because less monitoring time was needed. Breevaart, Bakker, and Demerouti (2013) examined the use of self-reward among maternity care nurses and found improved work environments, increased employee engagement, and consistent use of job resources when the self-management tool was used by staff. Likewise, Bishop (2013) evaluated a positive use of self-reward for older nurses who showed increased job engagement when reflecting the inherent job satisfaction when helping others and original reasons for entering the profession.

Kocovski and Endler (2000) found that depression and social anxiety tend to be significantly correlated with weak tendencies toward self-reward or positive self-reinforcing behavior. Negative self-attitudes and negative emotionality can serve as barriers to developing skills of self-reward as well as contribute to negative perpetuating cycles. Conversely, variables have been examined relative to their likely support of self-reward, such as the importance of explicit goals (preferably self-chosen) as part of change strategies involving self-reward (Kuhl & Baumann, 2000).

Some of the clinical effects typically attributed to the self-reinforcement procedure also may be due to certain external factors, including a client's previous reinforcement history, client goal setting, the role of client self-monitoring, surveillance by another person, external contingencies in the client's environment, and the instructional set given to the client about the self-reward procedure. The exact role that these external variables may play in self-reward is still relatively unknown. However, a helper should acknowledge and perhaps try to capitalize on some of these factors to heighten the clinical effects of a self-reward strategy.

Self-Reward Components

Self-reward involves the client's planning of appropriate rewards and conditions in which they will be used. Four components of self-reward are:

1. selection of appropriate self-rewards,

2. delivery of self-rewards,

3. timing of self-rewards, and

4. planning for self-change maintenance.

These components are described in this section and summarized in the following list. Although we discuss the components separately, keep in mind that all are integral parts of an effective self-reward procedure.

Component 1: Selection of Appropriate Self-Rewards

In helping a client to use self-reward effectively, the therapist must devote some time and planning to the selection of rewards that are appropriate for the client and for the desired target behavior. Selecting rewards can be time consuming. However, effective use of self-reward is dependent on the availability of resources or opportunities that are truly reinforcing to the client. The helper can assist the client in selecting appropriate self-rewards; however, the client should assume the major role in determining the specific contingencies.

Rewards can take many different forms. A self-reward may be verbal/symbolic, material, or imaginal. One verbal/symbolic reward is self-praise, such as thinking or telling oneself, "I genuinely did a good job here" or "I am proud of the effort I made here to do a good job." If clients are highly self-critical, then some cognitive change work may be needed to establish new patterns of reframing automatic critical evaluations, or cognitive restructuring of underlying belief systems (e.g., regarding personal inadequacy) should be undertaken. See the Cognitive Change Strategies chapter or resources such as self-affirmation interventions (Cohen & Sherman, 2014; Kost-Smith et al., 2012) to guide this additional support intervention.

A material reward is something tangible—an event (such as a movie), a purchase (such as a favored snack or accessory), or a token or point that later can be exchanged for a reinforcing event or purchase. An imaginal reinforcer is the covert visualization of a scene or situation that is pleasurable and produces good feelings. Imaginal reinforcers might include picturing yourself as a thin person after losing weight or imagining that you are water skiing on a lake that you have all to yourself.

Self-rewards also can be classified as current or potential. A current reward is something pleasurable that happens routinely or occurs daily, such as eating, talking to a friend, or reading a newspaper. A potential reward is something that would be new and different if it happened, something that a person does infrequently or anticipates doing in the future. Examples of potential rewards include going on a weekend trip or buying a luxury item (something you love but rarely buy for yourself, not necessarily something expensive). Engaging in a luxury activity—something you rarely do—can be a potential reinforcer. For a person who is very busy and constantly working, simply doing nothing might be a luxury activity that would be a potentially potent reinforcer.

In selecting appropriate self-rewards, a client should consider the availability of these various kinds of rewards. We believe that a well-balanced self-reward program involves a *variety* of types of self-rewards. A helper might encourage a client to select both verbal/symbolic and material rewards. Relying only on material rewards may ignore the important role of positive self-evaluations in a self-change program. Further, material rewards have been criticized for overuse and misuse. Imaginal reinforcers may not be as powerful

as verbal/symbolic and material ones. However, they are completely portable and can be used to supplement verbal/symbolic and material rewards when it is impossible for an individual to use these other types (Watson & Tharp, 2014).

In selecting self-rewards, a client should also consider the use of both current and potential rewards. One of the easiest ways for a client to use current rewards is to observe which daily thoughts or activities are reinforcing and then to rearrange these so that they are used in contingent rather than noncontingent ways (Watson & Tharp, 2014). However, whenever a client uses a current reward, some deprivation or self-denial is involved. For example, agreeing to read the newspaper only after cleaning the kitchen involves initially denying oneself a pleasant, everyday event to use it to reward a desired behavior. Some people do not respond well to any form of aversiveness associated with self-change or self-directed behavior. One way to prevent self-reward from becoming too much like programmed abstinence is to have the client select novel or potential reinforcers to use in addition to current ones.

There are several ways in which a helper can help a client identify and select various kinds of self-rewards. One way is simply with verbal report. The helper and client can discuss current self-reward practices and desired luxury items and activities. The client also can identify rewards by using *in vivo* observation. The client would be instructed to observe and list current consequences that seem to maintain some behaviors. Finally, the client can identify and select rewards by completing preference and reinforcement surveys. See Box 15.2 for one such example (Watson and Tharp, 2014, pp. 241–242).

The client can complete this sort of preference survey in writing or in a discussion. Clients who find it difficult to identify rewarding events might also benefit from completing a more formalized reinforcement survey, such as the Reinforcement Survey Schedule or the Children's Reinforcement Survey Schedule (Cautela, 1977). Additionally, the client can be given homework assignments to identify possible verbal/symbolic and imaginal reinforcers. For instance, the client might be asked to make a daily list for a week of positive self-thoughts or of the positive consequences of desired change. Or the client could make a list of all the things about which she or he likes to daydream or of some imagined scenes that would be pleasurable.

Sometimes a client may seem thwarted in initial attempts to use self-reward because of difficulties in identifying rewards. Watson and Tharp (2014) noted that people whose behavior consumes the reinforcer (such as smoking or eating), whose behavior is reinforced intermittently, or whose avoidance behavior is maintained by negative reinforcement may not be able to identify

BOX 15.2	Personal Rewards Preference Survey (Watson & Tharp, 2014)

1. What will be the rewards of achieving your goal?
2. What kind of praise do you like to receive, from yourself or from others?
3. What kinds of things do you like to have?
4. What are your major interests?
5. What are your hobbies?
6. What people do you like to be with?
7. What do you like to do with those people?
8. What do you do for fun?
9. What do you do to relax?
10. What do you do to get away from it all?
11. What makes you feel good?
12. What would be a nice present to receive?
13. What kinds of things are important to you?
14. What would you buy if you had an extra $20? $50? $100?
15. On what do you spend your money each week?
16. What behaviors do you perform every day? (Don't overlook the obvious or the commonplace.)
17. Are there any behaviors that you usually perform instead of the target behavior?
18. What would you hate to lose?
19. Of the things you do every day, which would you hate to give up?
20. What are your favorite daydreams and fantasies?
21. What are the most relaxing scenes you can imagine?

reinforcing consequences readily. Individuals who are locked into demanding schedules may not be able to find daily examples of reinforcers. Depressed people often report trouble identifying reinforcing events. In these cases, the helper and client have several options that can be used to overcome difficulties in selecting effective self-rewards.

A client who does not have the time or money for material rewards might use imaginal rewards. Imagining pleasant scenes following a target response is referred to as *covert positive reinforcement*. Using this procedure, the client usually imagines performing a desired behavior, and then imagines a reinforcing scene. A helper might consider use of imaginal reinforcers only when other kinds of reinforcers are not available.

A second option is to use a client's everyday activity as a self-reward. Some clinical cases have used a mundane activity, such as using the phone or opening the daily mail, as the self-reward. If a frequently occurring behavior is used as a self-reward, then it should be a desirable or at least a neutral activity. As Watson and Tharp (2014) note, clients should not use as a self-reward any high-frequency behavior that they would stop immediately if they could. Using a negative high-frequency activity as a reward may seem more like punishment than reinforcement.

No thought, event, or imagined scene is reinforcing for everyone. Often what one person finds rewarding is very different from the rewards selected by someone else. When self-rewards are used, it is important to help clients choose rewards that will work well for *them*—not for the helper, a friend, or a spouse/partner. The practitioner should consider the guidelines in Table 15.2 to

---

TABLE 15.2 Guidelines in Determining Effective Self-Rewards

1. *Individualize* the reward to the client.
2. The reward should be *accessible* and *convenient* to use after the behavior is performed.
3. *Several* rewards should be used interchangeably to prevent satiation (a reward can lose its reinforcing value because of repeated presentation).
4. Different *types* of rewards should be selected (verbal/symbolic, material, imaginal, current, potential).
5. The rewards should be *potent* but not so valuable that an individual will not use them contingently.
6. The rewards should not be *punishing* to others. Watson and Tharp (2007) suggest that if a reward involves someone else, then the other person's agreement should be obtained.
7. The rewards should be *compatible* with the desired response. For instance, a person losing weight might select rewards such as new clothing or thoughts of a new body image after weight loss. Using eating as a reward is not a good match for a weight-loss target response.
8. The rewards should be *relevant* to the client's values and circumstances as well as appropriate to her or his culture, gender, age, socioeconomic status, and other salient features (e.g., personality and personal philosophy).

help the client determine self-rewards that might be used effectively.

Component 2: Delivery of Self-Rewards

Specifying the conditions and method of delivering self-rewards is the second part of working out a self-reward strategy with a client. Effective self-reward delivery is dependent on systematic data gathering; therefore, self-monitoring is an essential first step.

Second, the client needs to identify the precise conditions under which a reward will be delivered. In other words, the client needs to state the rules of the game: *what* and *how much* has to be accomplished before administering a self-reward. Self-reward usually is more effective when clients reward themselves for small steps of progress. Performance of subgoals should be rewarded. Waiting to reward oneself for demonstration of the overall goal usually introduces too much of a delay between responses and rewards.

Finally, the client needs to indicate how much and what kind of reward will be given for performing various responses or different levels of the goals. Reinforcement usually is most effective when broken down into small units such as tokens or points that are self-administered frequently. After a certain number of points or tokens are accumulated, these units may be exchanged for a larger reinforcer. Learning Activity 15.3 walks you through a self-reward exercise with questions to consider.

Component 3: Timing of Self-Rewards

The helper needs to instruct the client about appropriate timing of self-reward. There are three ground rules for deciding when a self-reward should be administered:

1. The client should administer a self-award *after* performing the specified response, not before.

2. The client should administer a self-award *immediately* after the response. Long delays may render the procedure ineffective.

3. A self-reward should follow *actual performance,* not promises to perform.

Component 4: Planning for Self-Change Maintenance

Self-reward, like any self-change strategy, requires environmental support for long-term maintenance of change. The last component of using self-reward involves helping the client find ways to plan for self-change maintenance. First, the helper can give the client the option of enlisting the help of others in a self-reward program. Other people can share in or dispense some of the reinforcement if the client is comfortable with this idea (Watson & Tharp, 2014). Second, the client should plan to review with the helper the data collected during self-reward. The review sessions give the helper a chance to reinforce the client and to help the client make any necessary revisions in the use of the strategy. Helper expectations and approval for client progress may add to the overall effects of the self-reward strategy if the helper serves as a reinforcer to the client.

Learning Activity 15.3

Self-Reward

This activity is designed to have you engage in a self-reward process.

1. Select a target behavior that you want to increase. Write down your goal (the behavior to increase, the desired level of increase, and the conditions under which the behavior will be demonstrated).

2. Select several types of self-rewards to use and write them down. Seek to identify a variety of reinforcers that include verbal/symbolic, material (both current and potential), and imaginal. See whether your selected self-rewards meet the following criteria:
   a. Individually tailored to you?
   b. Accessible and convenient to use?
   c. Several (to prevent satiation)?
   d. Different types?
   e. Potent?
   f. Not punishing to others?
   g. Compatible with your desired goal?
   h. Relevant to your gender and culture?

3. Set up a plan for delivery of your self-reward: What type of reinforcement will be selected and how much will be administered? How much and what demonstration of the target behavior are required?

4. When do you plan to administer a self-reward?

5. How could you enlist the aid of another person?

6. Apply self-reward for a specified time period. Did your target response increase? To what extent?

7. What did you learn about self-reward that might help you in suggesting its use to diverse groups of clients?

Caveats with Applying Self-Reward Strategies

The use of rewards as a motivational and informational device is a controversial issue (Eisenberger & Cameron, 1996). Using rewards as incentives, especially material ones, has been criticized on the grounds that tangible rewards are overused, misused, and often discourage rather than encourage the client.

Before suggesting self-reward, the helper should carefully consider the individual client, the client's previous reinforcement history, and the client's desired change. Self-reward may not be appropriate for clients from cultural backgrounds in which the use of rewards is considered undesirable or immodest (Kanfer & Gaelick-Buys, 1991). When a helper and client do decide to use self-reward, two cautionary guidelines should be followed. First, material rewards should not be used solely or indiscriminately. The helper should seek ways to increase a person's intrinsic satisfaction in performance before automatically resorting to extrinsic rewards as a motivational technique. Second, the helper's role in self-reward should be limited to providing instructions about the procedure and encouragement. The client should be the one who selects the rewards and determines the criteria for delivery and timing of reinforcement. When the target behaviors and the contingencies are specified by someone other than the person using self-reward, the procedure hardly can be described accurately as a self-change operation.

Model Example: Self-Reward

This example illustrates how self-reward can be used **LO3** to help Isabella increase her positive thoughts about her ability to do well in math:

1. *Selection of self-rewards:* First, the helper helps Isabella select some appropriate rewards to use for reaching her predetermined goal. The helper encourages Isabella to identify some self-praise she can use to reward herself symbolically or verbally ("I did it" and "I can gradually see my attitude about math changing"). Isabella can give herself points for daily positive thoughts. She can accumulate and exchange the points for material rewards, including current rewards (such as engaging in a favorite daily event) and potential rewards (such as a purchase of a desired item). These are suggestions; Isabella is responsible for the actual selection. The helper suggests that Isabella identify possible rewards through observation or completion of a preference survey. The helper makes

sure that the rewards that Isabella selects are accessible and easy to use. Several rewards are selected to prevent satiation. The helper also makes sure that the rewards selected are potent, compatible with Isabella's goal, not punishing to anyone else, and relevant to Isabella.

2. *Delivery of self-rewards:* The helper helps Isabella determine guidelines for delivery of the rewards selected. Isabella might decide to give herself a point for each positive thought. This allows for reinforcement of small steps toward the overall goal. A predetermined number of daily points, such as 5, might result in delivery of a current reward, such as watching television or going over to her friend's house. A predetermined number of weekly points could mean delivery of a potential self-reward, such as going to a movie or purchasing a new item. Isabella's demonstration of her goal beyond the specified level could result in the delivery of a bonus self-reward.

3. *Timing of self-rewards:* The helper instructs Isabella to administer the reward *after* the positive thoughts or after the specified number of points is accumulated. The helper emphasizes that the rewards follow performance, not promises. The helper should encourage Isabella to engage in the rewards as soon as possible after the daily and weekly target goals are met.

4. *Planning for self-change maintenance:* The helper helps Isabella find ways to plan for self-change maintenance. One way is to schedule periodic check-ins with the helper. In addition, Isabella might select a friend who can help her share in the reward by watching TV or going shopping with her or by praising Isabella for her goal achievement.

Self-Efficacy Overview

Self-efficacy is viewed as a cognitive process that **LO3** mediates behavioral change. *Self-efficacy* refers to our judgments and subsequent beliefs about how capable we are of performing certain things under specific situations. These capabilities include, but are not limited to, overt behaviors—for example, they also comprise how capable we believe we are in managing our thoughts or feelings in specific situations as well as how capably we can undertake particular actions. If our self-efficacy beliefs are broad, then we think we can accomplish something in most situations (like being able to communicate in our native language in a variety of contexts). If our self-efficacy beliefs are situation- or task-specific, then they likely do not generalize across contexts. For example, we may believe we can be assertive or resist temptation in some situations but not in others.

Self-efficacy beliefs are critically important to self-change. Without a belief that we can be successful, people have little incentive to undertake change efforts or to persevere in the face of difficulties. Self-efficacy is fundamental to fostering motivation and perseverance through the goals that one sets and evaluations by oneself and others of progress. Self-efficacy is typically assessed within life domains (e.g., academics, specific health problems) or aspects of functioning (e.g., emotional self-efficacy) so that the beliefs and expectancies being assessed are closely relevant to the self-management task at hand.

Various forms of health-related self-efficacy are particularly prominent in the self-management practice literature. Findings demonstrated that self-perceptions of one's ability to successfully undertake specific health-promotive activities are significantly predictive of engagement in those activities and intentions to sustain them. Moreover, self-efficacy as well as one's perceptions of one's illness has been found to fully mediate the relationship between the actual severity of the illness and the person's overall sense of satisfaction with his or her health (Greco et al., 2015). This points to powerful opportunities that psychologically oriented interventions targeting perception and self-efficacy beliefs have for undertaking self-care behaviors important to slowing illness progression and increasing clinical indicators of health and also for increasing more subjective quality of life (Stretton, Latham, Carter, Lee, & Anderson, 2006). Findings of robust roles of self-efficacy and effectiveness have been found within the telehealth framework, which greatly expands capacity to support individuals who are more difficult to access (Sanford et al., 2006).

What Is Distinct about Self-Efficacy

There are some important distinctions to keep in mind. Self-efficacy beliefs foster expectations about our personal abilities to accomplish something. They are related to, but are different from, *outcome* expectations—that is, our beliefs that our actions will result in desired outcomes (Bandura, 1986). We may feel that we have the ability to accomplish a task—for example, at school or work—and thus we have high self-efficacy in this regard. But if we believe that this ability alone is not sufficient for achieving the desired outcome—such as succeeding in a change or recognition of a job well done—then we have low outcome expectations (perhaps due to beliefs that the outcome is dependent on other people, events, or forces that are not predictable or are not likely to be efficacious). Including outcome expectations and factors likely to affect the

outcome of an attempted task is clearly important to assessment. As important as self-efficacy is to fueling people's pursuits of what is important to them, so, too, is realistic appraisal of whether this is enough. It is crucial to take into consideration barriers that can thwart success regardless of the skills and beliefs that individuals can bring to the effort.

Self-efficacy is not the same as self-esteem. For example, we can have high self-efficacy beliefs about certain tasks or abilities but low overall self-esteem. Low self-esteem can be due to a lot of reasons, such as not valuing things we do well as much as things we believe we are not able to successfully accomplish, or input from others that devalues what we believe we can do well. In general, however, self-esteem is enhanced when our self-efficacy is high in domains of life that we care most about and in which we desire to exert personal control—when we feel capable of doing what is required to achieve success or when we realize that we have reached our goal. Underlying self-efficacy are currents of either optimism and hope that yield high efficacy or helplessness and despair that contribute to low efficacy.

We can have high self-efficacy in some life domains but low self-efficacy in others, believing, for example, that we are capable of being successful at work but are lousy at parenting. In general, efficacy beliefs also build on experience, whether vicarious or actual, and draw from our cognitive schemas about who we are (e.g., my experiences with and input from others about my academic ability incline me to have high or low self-efficacy about mastering an academic challenge, depending on the nature of that experience and input).

Thus, self-efficacy is not fixed but is largely learned and shaped by life experience, and it can be relearned and reshaped through focused intervention. Part of the reason why self-efficacy is so important is that it has been found to be a significant component in many issues germane to well-being, like tackling versus avoiding challenges and opportunities, degree of effort expended, persistence with the task, problem-solving, coping, performance, confidence, determination, optimism, hopefulness, and enthusiasm (cf. Cervone et al., 2011; Shumaker, Ockene, and Riekert, 2009). The list of self-efficacy research is far greater than we can present here. Thus, we encourage you to undertake your own literature search of problems, goals, or populations of particular relevance to you.

Sources of Self-Efficacy

Several sources contribute to self-efficacy and to similar concepts in the constellation of one's personality or personal constructs. Bandura (1997) points to the following factors that influence efficacy expectations. These factors, then, constitute important targets of enrichment and change through professional helping interventions.

1. environmental experiences such as modeling and vicarious learning,

2. mind-body states such as emotional arousal,

3. social persuasions—the encouraging or discouraging information that people receive and most remember, and

4. actual performance accomplishments.

We briefly describe these and link them to the underlying cognitive structures and processes that link self-efficacy beliefs to behavioral outcomes.

Modeling and Environmental Influences

A person's self-efficacy is influenced by reciprocal interactions of cognitive, affective, behavioral, relational, and environmental and/or cultural variables. Environmental influences include the extent to which one has models available to observe certain behaviors undertaken, the consequences of those behaviors, and the goals achieved. This involves vicarious or observational learning, which begins very early in life. Modeling is, as we have seen earlier in this book, a common part of helping practice. Helpers often role-play or engage in desired behaviors (e.g., assertiveness under pressure) to facilitate a client's learning and confidence. Modeling is a common part of group work and therapeutic homework assignments. Modeling by others who the individual views as relevant or similar to oneself is often ideal because this helps the client accept the belief that "If that person can do it, then I probably can as well."

One of the premises behind self-efficacy theory is that its effect is often one of mediating the relationship between background variables and outcomes. That is, factors such as one's demographic characteristics may be associated with outcomes such as school success or school failure. But their effect is largely exerted through factors that have to do with beliefs about one's ability to be successful as well as situational characteristics (like quality and encouraging role models, opportunities to build the incremental skills) that may support or thwart development of these beliefs. In a study of adolescents from different racial/ethnic backgrounds, Smith, Walker, Fields, Brookins, and Seay (1999) found that factors of ethnic identity and self-esteem were relatively weakly related to outcomes (e.g., pursuing prosocial means of goal attainment). However, the strength of their predictive pathways through the youths' positive self-efficacy beliefs was much

stronger. This finding illustrates the value of efforts to foster healthy, positive self-views such as positive ethnic identity and self-esteem. But a related target should also include the models, messages, and opportunities to foster sturdy self-efficacy expectancies.

Family of origin, culture, and environmental setting mold a person's perceived self-efficacy, which contributes to cognitive development and functioning. Bandura (1993) illustrated ways in which perceived self-efficacy can operate at multiple levels, both individual and collective. This is illustrated in an examination of factors that shape career decision self-efficacy of African American students, in this case in relationship to engineering—a profession in which minority students have tended to be under-represented (Austin, 2010). Results showed that career self-efficacy and engineering-related goal intentions were influenced by math and science confidence, ethnic identity, family relations, school factors, and economic status. Thus, while preventive and supportive interventions in service settings such as schools are critical, these results remind us of the importance of history, family, and community in change efforts.

This is echoed in findings of women's success in science education (here, specifically in male-dominated atmospheric sciences), in which perceived self-efficacy was crucial to perseverance and resilience (Charlevoix-Romine, 2009). However, strategic relationship building was also key—facilitating entry into the academic community and further development of meaningful professional relationships that provided modeling, mentoring, and encouragement. Ideally, external influences work in concert, such as teachers providing concrete academic information and supportive feedback regarding progress and performance, with family and peers providing emotional support. Although reality is often far from ideal, evidence of this kind of combined self-efficacy support holds strong promise to support self-efficacy, identity, and engagement of potentially at-risk students such as immigrant youth (Gaytan, 2010).

Note that perceived self-efficacy is also affected by a person's worldview, often reflective of one's cultural perspective. Oettingen (1995), for example, examined cultural effects on self-efficacy relative to differences based on individualism versus collectivism, power differential, masculinity, and avoidance of uncertainty. In collectivist cultures, members of core groups are likely to be a primary source of efficacy information for each individual. In contrast, in individualistic cultures, there is higher reliance on one's own evaluations and emotional reactions. Cultures or social conditions in which there are large power differentials are likely to find those with greater power as stronger sources of environmental influence as opposed to those exhibiting less power disparity. In the latter context, individuals may be more inclined to see their actions and outcomes as more closely tied to their skill and efficacy belief and less vulnerable to external impediments.

Although self-efficacy remains an important therapeutic factor, it is essential to realize that real-world factors have historically impinged and continue to impinge differently on people's actual ability to be efficacious. For some individuals, even if success in accomplishing a task is possible, this may not be sufficient for achieving desired goals because of more powerful external factors that can negatively affect actual outcomes. That said, enriching the availability of models and mentors is a powerful source of strengthening clients' skill sets as well as their beliefs and confidence in their potential to be successful.

Mind-Body States Such as Emotional Arousal

What we are feeling emotionally and the bodily sensations and phenomena accompanying differing emotions have important implications for which cognitions we are likely to access from memory and to generate in that context. If we are feeling highly anxious, for example, then we will have a different set of cognitions salient to our information processing in the moment than if we are feeling calm or proud. Thus, if we are feeling anxious in a situation, it will be difficult to cognitively access memories of when we were successful in the past or to focus on aspects of the situation that address how we might be successful. Emotional states discordant with confidence, in turn, are likely to activate a set of schemas and perceptions that are unlikely to support high self-efficacy expectations.

Thus, even if one generally has a sturdy sense of self-efficacy, one's current emotional state (such as feeling depressed, anxious, or fearful) can undermine one's ability to access beliefs and skills related to a specific task at hand, engendering uncertainty, hesitancy, and less effort or effectual performance. This is where cognitive change strategies described previously in the book, such as noticing what triggers one's negative emotions and negative self-talk, can be important aids to managing self-efficacy in context. One's ability to be aware of and manage one's emotional state (e.g., to shift from a high level of emotional arousal to a lower level, from anxiety more toward determination) is a valuable tool for managing self-efficacy beliefs and expectations.

Similarly, we are becoming increasingly aware of the ways in which our thoughts, feelings, and behaviors interact, and how these affect and are affected by many bodily systems, such as biochemical and neurological processes. Some of this work involves the information molecules,

peptides, and receptors that serve as biochemicals of emotion (Pert, 1993) and ways in which messenger molecules or neuropeptides influence self-efficacy. As we've noted, a person who has a high degree of self-confidence and higher perceptions of personal control (compared to someone with lower self-confidence) is inclined to attempt more difficult tasks, invest more energy, persevere longer in seeking solutions when faced with adversity, and refuse to blame himself or herself when failure is encountered. One hypothesis here is that the production of endogenous morphine (endorphins) in the brain is high and that the production of catecholamines (stress hormones) is low, a fact that is relevant because production of endorphins is positively correlated with confidence. Endorphins exert an analgesic effect, which spreads throughout the body, reducing sensitivity to pain and lessening automatic activities like cardiac reactivity and blood pressure (Maddux, 2009).

When we feel we are not in control, our feelings of low self-efficacy can increase the production of catecholamines (Bandura, Taylor, Williams, Mefford, & Barchas, 1985). Thus, through multiple pathways, our emotional state affects our perceived level of self-efficacy. This state, in turn, causes information molecules or neuropeptides to produce either stress hormones or brain opioids, depending on our emotional state. In addition to the cognitive change strategies noted (see Chapters 11 and 12), calming-oriented methods such as breathing, muscle relaxation, and mindfulness (see Chapter 13) may be useful in reshaping neurophysiological patterns of responding to stress.

Although self-efficacy fundamentally refers to beliefs, it (like other cognitions) is far from being all in the head. Thinking and feeling experiences (such as hope, forgiveness, optimism, and determinism) are intricately interwoven with our physiology and genetic makeup, which collectively interact with our social conditions to shape our behaviors and outcomes (Snyder & Lopez, 2007). Some clients may find it beneficial to assess their sense of emotional self-efficacy, which includes factors such as using and managing own emotions, identifying and understanding own emotions, dealing with emotions in others, and perceiving emotion through facial expressions and body language. Pool & Qualter (2012) provide an illustration of an emotional self-efficacy assessment and a brief intervention with university students in preparation of the challenges of seeking postgraduation employment.

Social Persuasions

Social persuasion refers to the encouraging or discouraging information that people receive and remember, which shapes their confidence. The consistent and reliable support of close others, as we have repeatedly seen, is crucial. Reed (2003) found, for example, that parental monitoring and support, in conjunction with bolstered self-efficacy, significantly enhanced youths' academic achievement—which served as important protective factors buffering negative effects of neighborhood characteristics such as crime and impoverishment. Bandura, Barbaranelli, Caprara, and Pastorelli (2001) found that effects of low socioeconomic status were mediated by parental expectations of and aspirations for their adolescent children and were powerful predictors of their children's perceived self-efficacy and career aspirations.

Helpers specifically orient their comments and means of engagement with clients to enhance a client's confidence or self-efficacy expectations about performing specific tasks. For example, a helping professional might foster positive self-efficacy by talking with the client about his or her past success in performing similar or related tasks, expressing optimism that those successes can be replicated. Or the helper can attempt to build confidence by reviewing self-monitoring data, emphasizing incremental improvements, and providing ongoing reminders and encouragement regarding the stepwise process of goal attainment.

Unlearning, or challenging and reconstructing internalized negative information, is frequently a component of treatment. Schomerus and colleagues (2011) illustrate the negative potential of self-stigma or negative self-evaluations, in this case relative to mental health and substance abuse. They illustrate degrees to which awareness of stereotypes about types of people or problems becomes more incorporated, because stereotypes are applied to oneself and progressively undermine self-efficacy in these domains, such as drinking refusal. Although we have outlined basic self-efficacy enhancement strategies here and cognitive change strategies in other chapters, keep in mind that there are often problem-specific interventions to enhance self-efficacy, such as those in the addictions arena (Hyde, Hankins, Deale, & Marteau, 2008).

There are complex relationships involving self-efficacy. Its significance relative to reading and health literacy is one example. Wolf and colleagues (2007) found that low levels of literacy were associated with low adherence to successful HIV medication adherence. However, this effect was mediated by self-perceptions such that those with low literacy but high self-efficacy were more successful in their goal of medication compliance. In work with self-management of diabetes, Thompson (2011) found self-efficacy to be significantly associated with both health literacy and self-management practices.

If the helper can maximize the client's perceived self-efficacy and expectancies about treatment, then the client's confidence in using the specific steps associated with the treatment protocol will increase, and that confidence will enhance the potential benefits and effectiveness of treatment. Instrumental assistance with feedback is another element of social persuasion. Education about and *partializing* a complex or intimidating task is one example—breaking the ultimate goal into component parts that are more readily achievable and diagnostic to the client regarding areas that are more difficult than others.

Although the degree of success in achieving therapeutic goals may be largely a function of a client's self-efficacy, it is important to note that factors such as a client's age, gender, social class, and cultural and ethnic background may influence the level of efficacy or confidence he or she brings to the therapeutic tasks as well as the contexts within which the client will continue to function. Interventions are increasingly reflecting awareness of personal and contextual factors. One example focuses on the mental health needs of low-income predominantly minority women living with AIDS. Here, the intervention paired a cognitive behavioral stress management package (such as strategies identified in Chapters 11–14) with an expressive supportive therapy component that encouraged expression of feelings as well as social support and group practice within a group treatment context. Women in the combined treatment group increased their levels of self-efficacy to cope with their illness and reduced their depression and anxiety after intervention and long-term follow-up (Jones et al., 2010).

Performance Accomplishments

First-hand accomplishment experience generally has the greatest influence on self-efficacy beliefs—actually doing something, understandably, stands as strong evidence for the hope of future success. This is part of why breaking down tasks to manageable scales and, piece by piece, building to a successful whole is part of cognitive behavioral techniques to revise self-efficacy appraisals and future beliefs. Note the descriptions provided in chapters related to cognitive change and to cognitive stress management such as problem-solving and stress inoculation.

The specifics of efforts will vary according to the target whether, for example, the self-efficacy beliefs are about eating behavior, gambling, smoking, exercise, success in math or some academic or work domain, ability to manage tasks of independent living, or other valued goals. The following are steps that have broad-based applicability relative to supporting incremental performance accomplishment (Watson & Tharp, 2014):

a. Pick a target or subgoal that you feel you have a strong or "maybe" chance of accomplishing—a do-able first step (later you can incrementally add more difficult targets).

b. Focus on the *process* of change—focusing on a skills development attitude rather than the final outcome—and practice, practice, practice.

c. Distinguish the present from the past, actively relegating past discouraging or failure outcomes to the past, monitoring present progress, and attending to small, incremental improvements.

Whether by dent of personality or past experience, there is huge variability in how people perform—for example, what they are willing to attempt, how long they will persist, and how varied their mastery efforts will be. At one extreme are people who are motivated, energized, and risk-taking despite the possibility of failure—partly because they do not anticipate failure, are able to interpret failure in ways that do not significantly diminish their future self-efficacy expectations, and persist more vigorously. At the other extreme are people who are characterized by depressive feelings that contribute to pessimism, a low level of energy, and negative internal dialogue, resulting in low levels of attempted performance and greater inclination to interpret failure as further evidence that they are not capable ("This is just another example that I can never do anything right"), thus deepening future low-efficacy expectations.

Most of us fall somewhere between these two extremes. And, as previously noted, we can see ourselves and behave quite efficaciously in some life domains but struggle greatly in others. In fact, evidence indicates that we can have varying degrees of perceived self-efficacy in different aspects of a single domain. This has implications for assessment and intervention. To illustrate, self-management of hypertension involves a number of factors, such as sustaining changes in diet, not smoking, adherence to medication, engaging in physical activity, and practicing weight management techniques. Each self-care behavior can be complex to change and sustain in its own right, and individuals can vary regarding their perceived efficaciousness across the behaviors, which can result in less effective behavior and compromised health outcomes (Warren-Findlow, Seymour, & Huber, 2012). Some results indicate the value of helping clients track self-efficacy across multiple factors as well as tailoring interventions to target the specific aspects of self-efficacy of greatest challenge to that client (Martin et al., 2008).

Ideally, interventions will exert some influence over environmental factors that might serve to complicate or undermine development of stronger, more positive self-efficacy beliefs related to an individual's self-management goals. However, there are limits to this ability. Some work attentive to ways that factors such as social disadvantage can undermine success has developed a "shift and persist" strategy (Chen & Miller, 2012; Chen, Miller, Lachman, Gruenewald, & Seeman, 2012). Shifting entails use of strategies aimed at adjusting oneself to features of one's environment that are problematic. This could involve reframing the meaning or implications of an external stressor in a less threatening manner or use of coping or self-calming techniques toward not allowing a stressor to evoke negative emotional reactions or negative beliefs in an individual. These authors characterize persistence as enduring adversity with strength, holding oneself steady and finding meaning in difficult situations, and maintaining optimism about the future. In addition to cognitive, affective, and coping skills, these authors emphasize the value of steady role models and reinforcement in building resilience. This clinical theory and intervention approach arose out of a focus on youth development in poverty contexts yet has broad applicability to a range of adversities that may stymie self-efficacy.

Summary

In short, perceived self-efficacy is a major determinant of whether people engage in a task, the amount of effort they exert if they do engage, and how long they will persevere with the task if they encounter adverse circumstances. Yet incremental efforts to pave the foundation of behavioral accomplishment can be central to changing negative self-efficacy beliefs or appraisals. Various intervention components from prior chapters may well be part of helpers' efficacy-related interventions.

Vicarious learning for the client may include teaching the client about the cognitive underpinnings of self-efficacy and ways in which self-schemas and cognitive processing habits can contribute either positively or negatively to self-efficacy beliefs, and undertaking targeted cognitive changes to strengthen efficacy in the relevant life domains. In some cases, the helper may model or demonstrate the behaviors or help locate other sources such as YouTube videos. In some cases, understanding problematic *emotional arousal* (such as anxiety) will be important and skills related to stress management and self-soothing may be needed. Role modeling and enactment of needed skills in session may be important for *performance accomplishment*; giving the client behavioral homework, self-monitoring, and self-rewards instructions to work on between sessions may also be important. Helpers are also important sources of *social persuasion* through encouraging and reinforcing effort and progress as well as helping clients to seek reinforcement from others, whether family members, online support groups, or others who are relevant to the clients' target behavior change or life circumstances. Thompson & Graham (2015) provide a short case illustration in the employment domain that may be of interest.

Model Example: Self-Efficacy

One of Isabella's goals—asking questions and **LO3** making reasonable requests—has four subgoals: (1) to decrease anxiety ratings associated with anticipation of failure in math class and rejection by parents; (2) to increase positive self-talk and thoughts such as "girls are capable" in math class and other competitive situations from zero to two times per week to four or five times per week over the next 2 weeks; (3) to increase attendance in math class from two or three times per week to four or five times per week during the next 2 weeks of treatment; and (4) to increase verbal participation and initiation in math class and with her parents from none or once per week to three or four times per week over the next 2 weeks during treatment. Verbal participation is defined as asking questions, answering questions posed by teachers or parents, volunteering answers or offering opinions, or going to the chalkboard.

The helper can determine the level of Isabella's self-efficacy (confidence) for each of the goal behaviors. Self-efficacy can be measured by asking Isabella to give a verbal rating of her confidence for each goal on a scale from 0 (no confidence) to 100 (a great deal of confidence). Alternatively, the helper can design a rating scale and ask Isabella to circle her rating of confidence for each goal (see Learning Activity 15.4). Three examples of self-efficacy assessment are accompanied by a metric; they are followed by other examples without the 0–100 metric to conserve space.

Self-Efficacy Assessment Related to Isabella's Goals Confidence in *decreasing anxiety* (from SUDS rating of 70 to 50) about possible failure in *math class*

0 10 20 30 40 50 60 70 80 90 100

Uncertain   Total certainty

Confidence in *increasing positive self-talk and thoughts*—"girls are capable"—to four or five times per week in *math class*

0 10 20 30 40 50 60 70 80 90 100

Uncertain   Total certainty

Confidence in *answering questions asked by parents*

0 10 20 30 40 50 60 70 80 90 100

Uncertain   Total certainty

Other Examples
- Confidence in *decreasing anxiety* (from SUDS rating of 70 to 50) about possible *rejection by parents*
- Confidence in *increasing attendance* in *math class* to four or five times per week
- Confidence in *asking* questions in *math class*
- Confidence in *answering* questions in *math class*
- Confidence in *volunteering answers* in *math class*
- Confidence in *going to the chalkboard* in *math class*
- Confidence in *asking questions of parents*
- Confidence in *offering opinions to parents*

As Isabella becomes more successful in achieving her goal behaviors, measures of her self-efficacy or confidence will increase.

Learning Activity 15.4

Self-Efficacy

In this activity you are to assess and determine your level of self-efficacy.

1. Select a goal you would like to achieve. A general goal may have to be divided into subgoals.
2. Write down your goal and/or subgoals. Make sure that your written goal and subgoals are behaviorally defined, specifying the context or circumstances in which the behavior is to occur and identifying the level or amount or change sought for any given step.
3. For each goal or subgoal that you would like to achieve, construct a scale (ranging from 0 to 100) to measure your self-efficacy (confidence) in successfully meeting the goal requirements. Consider all pertinent contexts, including each person with whom and each setting in which the goal is to be performed.
4. Assess your self-efficacy by circling the number on each scale that reflects your degree of uncertainty or certainty (confidence) in performing the (sub)goal.
5. You might wish to use the self-efficacy scales to self-monitor your confidence over a period of time as you gain more experience in performing the goal behaviors.

Applications of Self-Management with Diverse Groups and Types of Problems

Self-management has been used with an extremely [LO4] wide range of client populations and highly varied problem areas. We illustrate some specific recent research reports here. Because self-management is so broadly used, readers should search the literature and online sources for their populations or problem topics to find well-suited examples. Self-management strategies have been applied to many lifestyle and routine functioning issues such as insomnia, eating, and exercise as well as health problems, particularly chronic health conditions that require long-term monitoring and management such as diabetes, asthma, arthritis, and irritable bowel syndrome. Examples of psychosocial problems for which self-management strategies have recently been investigated include, but are not limited to, attention-deficit/hyperactivity disorder, anger, anxiety, depression, stress, and various forms of chronic mental illness. Self-management also has been used to decrease substance and alcohol abuse, to help compensate for developmental disabilities, and to improve effectiveness in classroom behavior of students with emotional or behavioral disorders.

It is important to note that self-management often is a component in addressing chronic conditions or circumstances that will require sustained engagement by clients and, often, their support networks. The need for formal helping services to support adoption of self-management strategies tends to be evident among populations with more complex and chronic challenges (e.g., psychosocial, medical, academic, labor force) and fewer internal and external resources. The following section provides illustrations across a number of populations and areas of concern.

Health Examples

Current medical practice requires that considerable responsibility for performing treatment protocols is allocated to patients and their families. People with chronic health conditions, whether physical or psychological, often must learn to administer aspects of their treatments, at times with the potential for life-altering consequences. Thus, it can be vitally important to foster self-efficacy, manage exposure and response to triggering situations, and promote self-monitoring and reinforcement.

Swerissen and colleagues (2006) tested the effectiveness of a chronic disease self-management program in four immigrant populations; the program was delivered in the native languages of the populations—Chinese, Greek, Italian, and Vietnamese. The programs involved instruction by peer leaders (trained lay people themselves with chronic health problems) and consisted of symptom management, problem-solving, managing disease-related emotions, exercise and relaxation, meditation, healthy eating, and communication skills. Relative to wait-list controls, the participants achieved better outcomes in the areas of energy, exercise, pain, and fatigue. The findings encourage use of community members serving as peer resources to bridge care access to clients whose language or cultural characteristics might otherwise present barriers to effective support.

Clinical study also is pointing to ways that cognitive factors such as one's sense of identity may come into play. Cooper, Collier, James, and Hawkey (2010) identified important themes of "reconciliation of the self" in patients striving to improve self-management of irritable bowel disease. Participants reported that being unable to predict or control the course of their condition was distressing, as was the discrepancy between functional facts of their medical condition and their sense of themselves. Social and cognitive strategies were beneficial with reframing toward a new kind of balance engaging other life priorities. Similarly, Scott and Wilson (2011) described the role of self-identity in a self-management program developed by mental health consumers that proactively sought to reframe stigmatizing views of mental health. Participants engaged in self-monitoring with a focus on revised conceptualizations and portrayals of a healthy identity, which was grounded in but reclaimed their at risk identity.

A useful clinical tool is the Perceived HIV Self-Management Scale developed by Wallston, Osborn, Wagner, and Hilker (2011). Although the focus of the clinical study was on HIV, this scale can serve as a generic template for assessing perceived self-management efficacy related to other chronic conditions. Readers, for example, may benefit from reviewing the measure and using or adapting items for use in their practice. In a similar vein, Bishop and Frain (2011) presented a self-management scale developed for persons living with multiple sclerosis. This clinical measure demonstrated sound psychometric properties in tapping five dimensions: health care provider relationship; treatment adherence/barriers; social/family support; disease knowledge/information; and health maintenance behavior. Collectively, these dimensions suggest that in addition to increasing knowledge about one's problem (e.g., multiple sclerosis), it is crucial to devote attention to cultivation of supportive relationships, acquisition of new habits or skills, and awareness of factors that can either undermine or scaffold one's self-management efforts.

Epilepsy self-management, particularly among children and young people, illuminates challenges and illustrates the need for rethinking self-management programming that may hold broad relevance. Lewis, Noyes, and Hastings (2014) undertook a literature systematic review of epilepsy self-management studies with younger populations, finding dismayingly absent or weak indicators of effectiveness. Their review of qualitative studies and focus groups demonstrated a lack of alignment between intervention theories with this illness and what children and young people found difficult with self-management of medication and the effects of epilepsy. Recommendations included involvement of children and young people in the redesign of future interventions to more fully address concerns (e.g., medication side effects, fears of injury, embarrassment, etc., and developmental factors, e.g., having to be reminded, chafing under constant parental surveillance). This critique underscores the complexity of problems with which self-management is often needed and the importance for deep understanding of one's client population to build interventions suited to their personal and contextual circumstances as well as their health conditions.

Although strategies of self-management are often approached as discrete tasks and skills, clinical evidence is revealing that the actual experience of self-management is ongoing and dynamic, with overlapping processes, tasks, and skills. Moreover, as Schulman-Green et al. (2012) describe, the processes of self-management are not wholly linear. People do not necessarily progress from initial stages, such as a focus on illness needs, to effectively activating their resources, to then successfully living with a chronic illness. The authors note there are often multiple domains of self-management, such as medical management (taking medications and attending appointments), behavioral management, such as adapting lifestyle or other behavioral activities or roles, and emotional management, including processing emotions that arise from having a chronic illness. One could add other dimensions to this such as cognitive or spiritual. In addition, individuals will have setbacks or other complicating factors arise; and people will vary in ways that their social, cognitive, or emotional characteristics or conditions come in to play. In short, there are many dimensions of diversity that will shape individuals' experiences of their health (or other) conditions as well as their comfort or success with strategies. Self-management may also involve support from a variety of helpers, such as medical personnel, counseling helpers, nutritionists, naturopaths, and others. Throughout assessment, intervention, and follow-up, it is important to have ongoing communication with clients and other providers to explore clients' self-management preferences and how they may change over time.

External Supports

Research has indicated the importance of external resources to self-management interventions—drawing upon environmental resources such as social support people and networks, spiritual connections, and opportunities to work with families or communities to develop culturally relevant approaches. Social isolation can be a significant hardship and undermining factor. This is illustrated in work, for example, with rural populations, particularly among vulnerable elders such as those who are widowed, as reflected in nutritional self-management programming efforts (Quandt, McDonald, Arcury, Bell, & Vitolins, 2000). In addition to stress reduction, social support demonstrates an enabling effect, boosting self-efficacy and strengthening the relationship of self-efficacy to the behavioral outcome of interest (Ernsting, Knoll, Schneider, & Schwarzer, 2015).

Attention also has been directed to environmental and contextual factors, including how these influence or interact with self-efficacy. Boardman and Robert (2000) found that lower neighborhood socioeconomic characteristics negatively influenced individuals' sense of self-efficacy even after controlling for individual-level SES, suggesting the power (positive and negative) of one's environment to shape one's beliefs. Racial and ethnic minority youth tend to report lower levels of academic self-efficacy and significantly greater academic disparities, including dropout rates. However, increased academic success can ameliorate sex, racial, and ethnic dropout disparities (Peguero & Shaffer, 2015), pointing to an important resilience-promotive target for schools and families. More limited self-management success was found among incarcerated individuals who had lower education and/or mental health histories and were re-entering communities, suggesting the need for more targeted and intensive interventions for these groups (Kelly, Ramaswamy, Chen, & Denny, 2015).

Cultural Variation

Sculpting interventions to be culturally relevant has been one line of innovation. Yip and colleagues (2007) illustrated a blended approach, integrating an arthritis self-management program with exercise in a Chinese population suffering from osteoarthritis. The authors tailored the program to be culturally relevant, including the omission of a more Western component of cognitive emotional therapy in light of the observation that pilot study participants did not see a focus on emotional management to be relevant to their needs. Instead, the patients indicated a desire to learn how to use exercise, including the tradition of tai chi, to control their arthritis symptoms, with the intervention group showing significant improvement on most measures compared to a control group.

Cultural adaptation is similarly illustrated in a study of chronic disease management among Native American communities. Jernigan (2010) described in detail a process of applying community-based participatory research methods to identify and adapt a chronic disease self-management program focused on diabetes. The priority of this initiative was intervention at the community level, which involved establishing trust, working with local leadership and members, and building community capacity (awareness, knowledge, health habits, engagement, and support). Innovative technology like Photovoice was used to reflect community concerns and strengths and to stimulate critical dialogue, often toward changing policies or practices that affect communities. Attention to community and cultural engagement are crucial considerations for many populations who have been marginalized and for many forms of health disparity that disproportionately affect large numbers of community members.

In addition to cultural tailoring, the success of self-management interventions also is highly dependent on social supports—often tapping members of one's community. McEwen, Pasvogel, Gallegos, and Barrera (2010) outline a culturally tailored self-management program with Mexican American adults in the United States–Mexico border region. The program positively affected a range of diabetes-related self-management behaviors, with one of the most beneficial effects being reduction of anxiety related to managing the disease. Particularly emphasized in this program was social support, including bilingual and culturally informed *promotoras* (health care workers).

Chlebowy, Hood, and LaJoie (2010) similarly document the importance of social support and cultural sensitivity in a self-management intervention with urban African American adults. They found that their participants perceived external factors such as support from family, peers, and health care providers to be important facilitators of their successful adherence to diabetes self-management plans, and they identified helpful contributions such as providing cues to action, direct assistance, knowledge, and reinforcement.

It appears that self-management strategies can be incorporated as a culturally effective intervention, especially given that self-management is time-limited, deals with the present, and focuses on pragmatic problem resolution

(Sue & Sue, 2008). Similarly, the focus on behavioral patterns as well as beliefs or orientations to promote action and not just "talk" or self-exploration would be consistent with the use of a self-management intervention. As these interventions illustrate, self-management need not be construed as a "Lone Ranger" or nonreflective method, but rather one that can sensibly build on environmental resources and cultural perspectives about self and problem-solving. Thoughtful consideration of measures is often needed. Du, Li, Lin, and Tam (2015), for example, found a measure of cultural self-efficacy to be, unexpectedly, inversely associated with collectivist orientation and positively associated with depression among a sample of Chinese immigrants. They realized that their measure captured self-efficacy of adaptation into the receiving culture but did not tap self-efficacy in preserving values and managing relationships with family and friends from the original culture—which are important to psychological well-being.

Self-management also may appeal to some clients who do not like or feel comfortable with traditional mental health services. Values and belief systems (e.g., related to self-reliance, faith, and inclusion in community) as well as characteristics of the client's environment (e.g., social, material, informational, sociopolitical) can be important dimensions of assessment to guide appropriate selfmanagement intervention planning.

Guidelines for Using Self-Management with Diverse Groups of Clients

Across the many phases and dimensions of the helping process, we have underscored the importance of attending to history, context, and diversity among clients and their circumstances. The preceding section provides examples of a research base that supports the use of self-management strategies with diverse populations yet also illustrates the value of adaptations or considerations in how these helping methods are used in collaborative practice. In this section we summarize some basic principles in using self-management approaches with diverse groups of clients with the aim of stimulating reflective intentionality. It is beyond the scope of this chapter to offer fully comprehensive and exhaustive treatment of this topic; therefore, readers are encouraged to engage in further perusal of the research and clinical literature.

As with other helping techniques, it is important to consider the client's lifestyle, behavioral patterns, and personal priorities in assessing the potential usefulness of self-management strategies. These strategies often involve a high degree of independent work and commitment to, and perseverance in, activities outside of formal helping sessions. For example, if the client seems capable of and interested in following the progress of events and sustaining a high degree of focus on his or her actions, a strategy such as self-monitoring may be effective. This may entail using a variety of self-observation and tracking tools (e.g., lists, charts, graphs, technological tools) suited to the client's personal and cognitive style. Self-monitoring may be contraindicated for clients with intellectual disabilities or attentional and executive planning challenges if the process would be experienced as frustrating or confusing, but contemporary practice with special needs populations is demonstrating creative applications.

Second, there may be benefit in adapting self-management interventions to the client's culture, circumstances, or distinctive needs. Some clients have been culturally socialized to be very private and would feel most uncomfortable in publicly displaying their self-monitoring data. For clients whose cultural identity or targeted issue is shaped by an external locus of control or views about authority or choice residing with others or with a collective, self-management may not be a good match or may need to be discussed as an option with such factors in mind. Similarly, depending on the client's history, the idea of using self-rewards may feel awkward and thus may benefit from reframing. At the very least, rewards must be tailored to be relevant and comfortable.

Third, the relevance of self-management should be considered against the client's goals and the context of the client's life. If the client is struggling with multiple problems in living, aversive external structures and discrimination, serious vulnerabilities, or overwhelming pressures, then self-management may have a limited role, if deemed appropriate at all. Consider, for example, how it might feel if you were a low-income mother with little to no social support and few resources and you were regularly abused by your live-in partner—and your helping practitioner told you to engage in some form of self-management. One or more self-management strategies, indeed, may provide this mother with some concrete relief—perhaps in better managing a persistent health problem or in helping her child better manage troubling classroom behavior. Models of active communication and collaborative planning for complex and persistent problems are increasingly being specified as core to self-management support. Goldstein, DePue, and Kazura (2009) provide a useful resource for self-management support as an ongoing process that is focused on chronic care management but has broad and flexible applicability.

Finally, it is always essential to assess the client's range of resources and to be aware of the inequitable access granted to impoverished, oppressed, and marginalized individuals within society. Barriers may arise due to personal characteristics and circumstances, such as literacy, disability, or lack of transportation, as well as to structural and systemic problems such as racism, homophobia, or similar prejudices and inequities. Kelly and colleagues (2015) found the meta-oppression experienced by racial minorities, such as inequality, stigma, and discrimination, negatively affected outcomes for self-management strategies. Understandably, these challenges present multiple real-world considerations that may need to be part of setting goals, developing action plans, building skills and supports, brokering referrals, and sustaining follow-up to improve the likelihood of success with self-management as with other helping strategies.

Self-Management as a Professional Aide for Helpers

Self-management tools are very much a part of effectiveness in the work place. Self-management in this vein often refers to employees' control or self-directedness over their own choices and behavior with limited external control by supervisors. There is overlap here with the construct of leadership because workers who employ self-management are responsible for managerial functions such as self-monitoring one's performance, taking corrective action as needed, seeking support or other resources, and having decision-making latitude. Evidence indicates that self-management skills such as self-observation, self-goal setting, and self-cueing are significantly associated with resourcefulness within the environment (more skill variety, feedback, and development opportunities) and, subsequently, to employees' daily work engagement (Breevaart, Bakker, & Demerouti, 2014).

Self-management can be significantly enhanced through training and result in significant gains in employees' self-efficacy, job performance, and less need for direct or frequent supervision (Frayne & Geringer, 2000). Skills such as self-setting goals, self-observation, visualizing oneself being efficacious, providing self-reward contingent on success, and use of constructive thought patterns are part of what is referred to as self-leadership (Granthan, Pidano, & Whitcomb, 2014). This line of theorizing argues the value of workers using these skills to develop and sustain self-directed work engagement habits suited to them and to their priorities. Beyond doing the job assigned to one by a supervisor, intentional use of these kinds of self-management strategies foster self-awareness, internally anchored motivation, and constructive coping with challenge that can be extremely helpful in the complex work world of counseling professionals.

Helpers are generally drawn to their roles on the basis of values, skill and temperament suited to the career, and a sense of personal reward and satisfaction with the work. At the same time, professional helpers are often working within contexts that contain challenges, pressures, uncertainties, fatigue, and limited control. Sustaining workers is important to a healthy workforce. This includes nurturing the internal motivations and satisfaction that initially brought helpers to their professions, as well as providing constructive feedback and mentoring. In addition to the self-management skills and sense of self-efficacy described in this chapter, evidence is pointing to the value of a sense of belonging and teamwork, where staffs are supported in decompressing, seeking scaffolding resources, and investing in positive work relationships (Bishop, 2013). These cooperative and collaborative parts of organizational life parallel the importance of external supports that we previously described and are complementary to the more self-directed work skills.

Finally, we argue the importance of self-care as an important element of professional self-management. Repeated exposure to the challenges of supporting others during difficult life circumstances can be both draining and foster development of health or lifestyle habits that compromise health or balance. Carter et al. (2013) provide a concrete illustration of this relative to chronic stress, sleep disturbance, and depression among hospice nurses. They undertook a cognitive behavioral therapy intervention that integrated cognitive change methods, relaxation techniques, stimulus control (related to sleeping behavior), health practices related to sleep, and self-monitoring. They report favorable outcomes within a group format, suggesting the value of self-care to avoid inordinate fatigue and burnout and to support long-term wellness in challenging lines of work.

CHAPTER SUMMARY

Self-management is a process in which clients direct their own behavior change by implementing selected intervention strategies or combination of strategies suited to structuring and sustaining their change goals beyond the supports of formal helping. Four strategies reviewed here are: self-monitoring; stimulus control procedures; self-reward techniques; and selfefficacy enhancement. Promoting client commitment to using self-management strategies can be enhanced by introducing these strategies later in the helping process, assessing the client's motivation for change, creating a social support system to aid the client in the use of the strategies, and maintaining contact with the client while self-management strategies are being used. The degree of success associated with each of these self-management strategies is affected by self-efficacy, a cognitive process that mediates behavioral change. These change strategies and tools can—and, we argue, *should*—be applied collaboratively with clients in the service of building on strengths and supporting empowerment and self-determination while being critically attentive to environmental factors that may be relevant targets of change as well as potential resources. Processes involved in self-regulation appear to vary across cultures and societies, and factors such as the client's cultural or collective identity and acculturation and assimilation status may affect the appropriateness of self-management or ways in which these tools and interventions are applied.

Visit CengageBrain.com for a variety of study tools and useful resources such as video examples, case studies, interactive exercises, flashcards, and quizzes.

15 | Knowledge and Skill Builder

Part One

For Learning Outcome 1, describe the use of self-monitoring and stimulus control in the following client case.

The client, Maria, is a Puerto Rican woman in her 30s who has had periods of living separately from Juan, her husband of 15 years, during their process of immigration when work has required him to travel in advance to the United States for multiple periods of time. Although they were reunited approximately 1 year ago and are now living together in the United States with the immigration process complete, Maria reports that during the past year she has had "*ataques de nervios*"—which she describes as trembling and faintness. She worries that her husband will die young and she will be left alone. Her history reveals no evidence of *early* loss or abandonment; however, she experienced a sense of loss associated with immigration to the United States in that she left family, friends, her home, and the village of her childhood behind. Also, she describes behavior that might be perceived as self-sacrificing and indicative of significant dependence on Juan. She reports being very religious and praying a lot about her anxious distress.

Maria asks for assistance in gaining some control over her "*ataques de nervios*." How would you use self-monitoring and stimulus control to help her decrease them?

What else would you focus on in addition to the use of these two strategies given Maria's cultural background and the case description?

Part Two

Learning Outcome 2 asks you to teach another person how to engage in self-monitoring. Your teaching should follow the six guidelines listed in Learning Activity 15.1: rationale; response discrimination; self-recording; data charting; data display; and data analysis. Feedback follows this Knowledge and Skill Builder section.

Part Three

Learning Outcome 3 asks you to teach another person how to use self-monitoring, stimulus control, self-reward, or self-efficacy. You may wish to refer to the steps of self-monitoring, the stimulus control principles, the components for self-reward, and the components of self-efficacy. Feedback follows this Knowledge and Skill Builder section.

Part Four

Learning Outcome 4 asks you to describe the application of a culturally relevant self-management program (self-monitoring, stimulus control, self-reward, and self-efficacy enhancement) in a given client case. Feedback follows this Knowledge and Skill Builder section.

The client, Thad, is a young African American man who recently identified himself as gay. Thad has been working with you in coming to terms with his sexual orientation. He has visited some gay bars and has participated in some gay activities, but he has not asked anyone out. He would like to go out at least once per week with a male partner. You have discussed with Thad the use of self-monitoring and self-reward as possible interventions for this goal. He is interested in these strategies.

How would you adapt and use the interventions of self-monitoring and self-reward with this particular client? How might your understanding of the self-management concepts of stimulus control and self-efficacy affect your treatment planning?

15 | Knowledge and Skill Builder **Feedback**

Part One

Self-Monitoring

1. *Treatment rationale:* In the rationale, you would emphasize how self-monitoring can provide information about the client's experience that will help in identifying appropriate strategies for intervention. You would explain to Maria that she will be recording details associated with incidents that she has labeled *"ataques de nervios" in vivo* on a daily basis for several weeks. You need to be careful to frame the rationale in a way that respects Maria's cultural values.

2. *Discrimination of a response:* Response-discrimination training would involve selecting, defining, and giving examples of the response to be monitored. You should model some examples of the defined behavior and elicit some others from the client. Specifically, you would help Maria define the nature and content of the behaviors she will be recording, such as feeling faint.

3. *Timing of self-monitoring:* Because this client is monitoring a behavior that is not highly frequent, she will engage in continuous monitoring, noting all instances in any situation. Each time she feels faint or worried she will record this information.

4. *Method of self-monitoring:* The client should be instructed to use a frequency count and record the number of times she feels faint or worried. If she is unable to discern when these start and end, then she can record with time sampling. For example, she can divide a day into equal time intervals and use the "all or none" method. If such thoughts or feelings occurred during an interval, then she would record "yes"; if they did not, then she would record "no." Or, during each interval, she could rate the approximate frequency of these behaviors on a numerical scale (e.g., 0 for *never occurring*, 1 for *occasionally*, 2 for *often*, and 3 for *very frequently*).

5. *Device for self-monitoring:* There is no one right device to assist this client with recording. She could enter tallies on a note card, a golf wrist counter, or a handheld computer to record the frequency. Alternatively, she could use a daily log sheet to keep track of interval occurrences.

6. *Charting of a response:* A simple chart might list days along the horizontal axis and frequency of behaviors along the vertical axis.

7. *Displaying of data:* For cultural or personal reasons, this client may not wish to display her self-monitoring data in a public place at home. An option would be to carry the data in her purse or backpack.

8. *Analysis of data:* The client could engage in data analysis by reviewing the data with the helper or by comparing the data with the baseline or with her goal (desired level of behavior change). The latter involves self-evaluation and may set the stage for self-reinforcement.

Stimulus Control

You can explain the use of stimulus control as another way to help Maria gain some feeling of personal control surrounding her *"ataques de nervios"* by confining them to particular places and times so that they don't occur so randomly and unpredictably. You could suggest the use of a worry spot or worry chair that she goes to at a designated time to do her worrying, and you would tell her that she is to stop worrying when she leaves this place or chair.

In addition to those two self-management interventions, it would be useful to explore Maria's feelings of loss and safety surrounding her immigration experience, the adaptations she is having to make to a different culture, and the conflicts she may be experiencing between the two cultures.

Part Two

Use Learning Activity 15.1 as a guide to assist your teaching. You also might wish to determine whether the person you taught has implemented self-monitoring accurately.

Part Three

Use the following:

Self-monitoring steps: See Learning Activity 15.1 (on page 533) and the related section of the chapter.
Principles of stimulus control: See Table 15.1 (on page 543) and the related section of the chapter.
Components of self-reward: See the Self-Reward Components beginning on page 546
Components of self-efficacy: Enhancing self-efficacy can potentially involve a wide range of strategies reviewed in other chapters (such as Chapter 11 on cognitive change strategies) as well as in this chapter. For purposes of this exercise, consider focusing on attention to past performance accomplishments and social persuasion in the sections beginning on page 553 that describe these.

Part Four

You need to determine how well the use of self-management fits with Thad's beliefs, values, worldview, and lifestyle. If Thad is receptive to the use of self-management and is oriented toward an internal rather than an external locus of control and responsibility, you can proceed. However, it is important to explore whether any external social factors may be contributing to his sense of discomfort. You may first wish to assess and work with self-efficacy, or Thad's confidence in himself and the contacts he will make with other men. Notice that

(continued)

Thad's sense of self-efficacy is related to his identity development as a gay male and as an African American. We anticipate that as Thad uses various self-management tools, his sense of self-efficacy will increase.

Self-reward can be used in conjunction with times Thad actually makes social contacts with men and goes out with a man. *Verbal symbolic rewards* used by Thad could consist of self-praise or covert verbalizations about the positive consequences of his behavior. Here are some examples: "I did it! I asked him out." "I did just what I wanted to do." "Wow! What a good time I'll have with ___."

Material rewards would be things or events that Thad indicates he prefers or enjoys, such as watching television, listening to music, or playing sports. Both current and potential rewards should be used. Of course, these activities are only possibilities; Thad has to decide whether they are reinforcing.

Imaginal rewards may include pleasant scenes or scenes related to going out: imagining oneself on a raft on a lake, imagining oneself on a football field, imagining oneself with one's partner at a movie, imagining oneself with one's partner lying on a warm beach.

Self-monitoring can be used to help Thad track the number of social contacts he has with other men.

Stimulus control can be used to help Thad increase the number of cues associated with increasing his social contacts with other men. For example, he might start in one place or with one activity where he feels most comfortable; then, gradually, he can increase his visits to other places and activities where he will find other gay men.

References

aan het Rot, M., Hogenelst, K., & Schoevers, R. A. (2012). Mood disorders in everyday life: A systematic review of experience sampling and ecological momentary assessment studies. *Clinical Psychology Review, 32*(6), 510–523.

Abenavoli, R. M., Jennings, P. A., Greenberg, M. T., Harris, A. R., & Katz, D. A. (2013). The protective effects of mindfulness against burnout among educators. *Psychology of Education Review, 37*(2), 57–69.

Abramowitz, J. S. (2013). The practice of exposure therapy: Relevance of cognitive-behavioral theory and extinction theory. *Behavior Therapy, 44*, 548–558.

Abramowitz, J. S., Deacon, B. J., & Whiteside, S. P. H. (2011). *Exposure therapy for anxiety: Principles and practice.* New York: Guilford Press.

Abudabbeh, N., & Hays, P. A. (2006). Cognitive-behavioral therapy with people of Arab heritage. In P. A. Hays & G. Y. Iwamasa (Eds.), *Culturally responsive cognitive-behavioral therapy* (pp. 141–159). Washington, DC: American Psychological Association.

Adams, J. R., & Drake, R. E. (2006). Shared decision-making and evidence-based practice. *Community Mental Health Journal, 42*, 87–105.

Adams, N., & Grieder, D. M. (2014). *Treatment planning for person-centered care: Shared decision making for whole health* (2nd ed.). San Diego, CA: Academic Press/Elsevier.

Adler, N. E., & Stewart, J. (2010). The biology of disadvantage: Socioeconomic status and health. *Annals of the New York Academy of Sciences: Special Issue, 1186*, 1–260.

Aguilera, A., Garza, M. J., & Muñoz, R. F. (2010). Group cognitive-behavioral therapy for depression in Spanish: Culture-sensitive manualized treatment in practice. *Journal of Clinical Psychology: In Session, 66*, 857–867.

Aikens, K. A., Astin, J., Pelletier, K. R., Levanovich, K., Baase, C. M., Park, Y. Y., & Bodnar, C. M. (2014).

Mindfulness goes to work: Impact of an online workplace Intervention. *Journal of Occupational and Environmental Medicine, 56*(7), 721–731.

Ainsworth, M. (1982). Attachment: Retrospect and prospect. In C. M. Parks & J. Stevenson-Hinde (Eds.), *The place of attachment in human behavior* (pp. 3–30). New York: Basic Books.

Akutsu, P. D., Tsuru, G. K., & Chu, J. P. (2004). Predictors of nonattendance of intake appointments among five Asian American client groups. *Journal of Consulting and Clinical Psychology, 72*, 891–896.

Aldarondo, E. (Ed.). (2007). *Advancing social justice through clinical practice.* Mahwah, NJ: Erlbaum.

Alghazo, R., Upton, T. D., & Cioe, N. (2011). Duty to warn versus duty to protect confidentiality: Ethical and legal considerations relative to individuals with AIDS/HIV. *Journal of Applied Rehabilitation Counseling, 42*(1), 43–49.

Amato Zech, N. A., Hoff, K. E., & Doepke, K. J. (2006). Increasing on-task behavior in the classroom: Extension of self-monitoring strategies. *Psychology in the Schools, 43*(2), 211–221.

American Counseling Association. (2014). *ACA Code of Ethics.* Alexandria, VA: Author. Retrieved from www.counseling.org

American Medical Association. (2008). *Report of the Council on Ethical and Judicial Affairs: Pediatric decision-making.* Retrieved from http://www.ama-assn.org/ama/pub/physician-resources/medical-ethics/code-medical-ethics/opinion10016.page

American Medical Association. (2010). *Report of the Council on Ethical and Judicial Affairs: Amendment to E-2.23, "HIV Testing."* Retrieved from http://www.ama-assn.org/ama/pub/physician-resources/medical-ethics/code-medical-ethics/opinion223.page

American Psychiatric Association. (1994). *Diagnostic and statistical manual of mental disorders* (4th ed.). Washington, DC: Author.

American Psychiatric Association. (2000a). *Diagnostic and statistical manual of mental disorders* (4th ed., text revision). Washington, DC: Author.

American Psychiatric Association. (2000b). Practice guidelines of the treatment of patients with eating disorders (revision). *American Journal of Psychiatry, 157*(Suppl., January), 1–31.

American Psychiatric Association. (2004). *Practice guidelines for the treatment of patients with acute stress disorder and posttraumatic stress disorder.* Arlington, VA: Author.

American Psychiatric Association. (2013). *Diagnostic and statistical manual of mental disorders* (5th ed.). Arlington, VA: Author.

American Psychological Association. (2003). Guidelines on multicultural education, training, research, practice, and organizational change for psychologists. *American Psychologist, 58,* 377–402.

American Psychological Association. (2007). Record keeping guidelines. *American Psychologist, 62,* 993–1004.

American Psychological Association. (2008). Criteria for the evaluation of quality improvement programs and the use of quality improvement data. *American Psychologist, 64,* 551–557.

American Psychological Association. (2010). *Ethical principles of psychologists and code of conduct.* Washington, DC: Author.

American Psychological Association. (2011). *APA policy statements on lesbian, gay, bisexual, and transgender concerns: Public interest directorate.* Washington, DC: Author. Retrieved from www.apa.org/about/governance/council/policy/booklet.pdf

American Psychological Association. (2012). Guidelines for psychological practice with lesbian, gay, and bisexual clients. *American Psychologist, 67,* 10–42.

American Psychological Association. (2013). *Guidelines for the practice of telepsychology.* Washington, DC: Author.

American Telemedicine Association. (2013). Practice guidelines for video-based online mental health services. Retrieved from http://www.americantelemed.org/resources/telemedicine-practice-guidelines/telemedicine-practice-guidelines#.VUOw703wvIU

Amrhein, P. C. (2004). How does motivational interviewing work? What client talk reveals. *Journal of Cognitive Psychotherapy, 18,* 323–336.

Amrhein, P. C., Miller, W. R., Yahne, C. E., Palmer, M., & Fulcher, L. (2003). Client commitment language during motivational interviewing predicts drug use concerns. *Journal of Consulting and Clinical Psychology, 71,* 862–878.

Anda, R. F., Felitti, V. J., Bremner, J. D., Walker, J. D., Whitfield, C., Petty, B. D., … Giles, W. H. (2006). The enduring effects of abuse and related adverse experiences in childhood: A convergence of evidence from neurobiology and epidemiology. *European Archives of Psychiatry and Clinical Neuroscience, 256,* 174–186.

Anderson, H. (1997). *Conversation, language, and possibilities: A postmodern approach to therapy.* New York: Basic.

Anderson, H., & Goolishian, H. (1992). The client is the expert: A not-knowing approach to therapy. In S. McNamee & K. J. Gergen (Eds.), *Therapy as social construction* (pp. 25–39). Newbury Park, CA: Sage.

Anderson, K. M., Cowger, C. D., & Snively, C. A. (2009). Assessing strengths: Identifying acts of resistance to violence and oppression. In D. Saleebey (Ed.), *The strengths perspective in social work practice* (5th ed., pp. 181–200). Boston, MA: Pearson Education.

Anderson, P. L., Price, M., Edwards, S. M., Obasaju, M. A., Schmertz, S. K., Zimand, E., & Calamaras, M. R. (2013). Virtual reality exposure therapy for social anxiety disorder: A randomized controlled trial. *Journal of Consulting and Clinical Psychology, 81*(5), 751–760.

Anderson, T., Lunnen, K. M., & Ogles, B. M. (2010). Putting models and techniques in context. In B. L. Duncan, S. D. Miller, B. E. Wampold, & M. A. Hubble (Eds.), *The heart and soul of change: Delivering what works in therapy* (2nd ed., pp. 143–166). Washington, DC: American Psychological Association.

Anker, M. G., Sparks, J. A., Duncan, B. L., Owen, J. J., & Stapnes, A. K. (2011). Footprints of couple therapy: Client reflections at follow-up. *Journal of Family Psychotherapy, 22,* 22–45.

Antony, M., & Barlow, D. (2010). *Handbook of assessment and treatment planning for psychological disorders* (2nd ed.). New York: Guilford Press.

Antoni, M. H., Lehman, J. M., Kilbourn, K. M., Boyers, A. E., Culver, J. L., Alferi, S. M., … Carver, C. S. (2001). Cognitive-behavioral stress management intervention decreases the prevalence of depression and enhances benefit finding among women under treatment for early-stage breast cancer. *Health Psychology, 20,* 20–32.

APA Presidential Task Force on Evidence-Based Practice. (2006). Evidence-based practice in psychology. *American Psychologist, 61,* 271–285.

Apodaca, T. R., Borsari, B., Jackson, K. M., Magill, M., Longabaugh, R., Mastroleo, N. R., & Barnett, N. P. (2014). Sustain talk produces poorer outcomes among mandated college student drinkers receiving a brief motivational intervention. *Psychology of Addictive Behaviors, 28,* 631–638.

Apodaca, T. R., & Longabaugh, R. (2009). Mechanisms of change in motivational interviewing: A review and preliminary evaluation of the evidence. *Addiction, 104,* 705–715.

Aponte, H. J. (1994). *Bread and spirit: Therapy with the new poor: Diversity of race, culture, and values.* New York: Norton.

Appleby, G. A., Colon, E., & Hamilton, J. (2011). *Diversity, oppression, and social functioning: Person-in-environment assessment and intervention.* Boston, MA: Allyn & Bacon.

Arch, J. J., & Craske, M. G. (2009). First-line treatment: A critical appraisal of cognitive behavioral therapy developments and alternatives. *Psychiatric Clinics of North America, 32,* 525–547.

Arcury, T. A., Quandt, S. A., McDonald, J., & Bell, R. A. (2000). Faith and health self-management of rural older adults. *Journal of Cross-Cultural Gerontology, 15,* 55–74.

Arden, J., & Linford, L. (2009). *Brain-based therapy with adults: Evidence-based treatment for everyday practice.* Hoboken, NJ: Wiley.

Arean, P. A., Raue, P., Mackin, R. S., Kanellopoulos, D., McCulloch, D., & Alexopoulous, G. S. (2010). Problem-solving therapy and supportive therapy in older adults with major depression and executive dysfunction. *American Journal of Psychiatry, 167*(11), 1391–1398.

Arkowitz, H. (2002). Toward an integrative perspective on resistance to change. *Journal of Clinical Psychology, 58,* 219–227.

Arkowitz, H., & Westra, H. A. (2004). Integrating motivational interviewing and cognitive behavioral therapy in the treatment of depression and anxiety. *Journal of Cognitive Psychotherapy, 18,* 337–350.

Artman, L., & Daniels, J. (2010). Disability and psychotherapy practice: Cultural competence and practical tips. *Professional Psychology, 41,* 442–448.

Ascoli, M., Lee, T., Warfa, N., Mairura, J., Persaud, A., & Bhui, K. (2011). Race, culture, ethnicity and personality disorder: Group Careif position paper. *World Cultural Psychiatry Research Review, 6*(1), 52–60.

Austin, A., & Craig, S. L. (2015). Transgender affirmative cognitive behavioral therapy: Clinical considerations and applications. *Professional Psychology: Research and Practice, 46,* 21–29.

Austin, C. Y. (2010). Perceived factors that influence career decision self-efficacy and engineering related goal intentions of African American high school students. *Career and Technical Education Research, 35*(3), 119–135.

Ayalon, L., Bornfeld, H., Gum, A. M., & Arean, P. A. (2009). The use of problem-solving therapy and restraint-free environment for the management of depression and agitation in long-term care. *Journal of Aging and Mental Health, 32,* 77–90.

Baams, L., Grossman, A. H., & Russell, S. T. (2015). Minority stress and mechanisms of risk for depression and suicidal ideation among lesbian, gay, and bisexual youth. *Developmental Psychology, 51,* 688-696.

Babcock, J. C, Green, C. E., & Robie, C. (2004). Does batterers' treatment work? A meta-analytic review of domestic violence treatment. *Clinical Psychology Review, 23,* 1023–1053.

Bach, P. A., Gaudiano, B., Pankey, J., Herbert, J. D., & Hayes, S. C. (2006). Acceptance, mindfulness, values, and psychosis: Applying acceptance and commitment therapy (ACT) to the chronically mentally ill. In R. A. Baer (Ed.), *Mindfulness-based treatment approaches: Clinician's guide to evidence base and applications* (pp. 93–116). New York: Academic Press.

Baer, R. A. (2003). Mindfulness training as a clinical intervention: A conceptual and empirical review. *Clinical Psychology: Science and Practice, 10,* 125–143.

Baer, R. A. (Ed.). (2006). *Mindfulness-based treatment approaches: Clinician's guide to evidence base and applications.* New York: Academic Press.

Bagby, R., Wild, N., & Turner, A. (2003). Psychological assessment in adult mental health settings. In J. R. Graham, J. A. Naglieri, & I. B. Weiner (Eds.), *Handbook of psychology: Assessment psychology* (Vol. 10, pp. 213–234). Hoboken, NJ: Wiley.

Baker, A., Mystkowski, J., Culver, N., Yi, R., Mortazavi, A., & Craske, M. G. (2010). Does habituation matter? Emotional processing theory and exposure therapy for acrophobia. *Behaviour Research and Therapy, 48,* 1139–1143.

Baker, E. K. (2007). Therapist self-care: Challenges within ourselves and within the profession. *Professional Psychology: Research and Practice, 38,* 607–608.

Baldwin, M. L., & Marcus, S. C. (2006). Perceived and measured stigma among workers with serious mental illness. *Psychiatric Services, 57,* 388–392.

Baldwin, S. A., Berkeljon, A., Atkins, D. C., Olsen, J. A., & Nielsen, S. L. (2009). Rates of change in naturalistic psychotherapy: Contrasting dose-effect and good-enough level models of change. *Journal of Consulting and Clinical Psychology, 77*, 203–211.

Baldwin, S. A., Wampold, B. E., & Imel, Z. E. (2007). Untangling the alliance-outcome correlation: Exploring the relative importance of therapist and patient variability in the alliance. *Journal of Consulting and Clinical Psychology, 75*, 842–852.

Ballou, M., & Brown, L. (Eds.). (2002). *Rethinking mental health and disorder: Feminist perspectives.* New York: Guilford Press.

Balsam, K. F., Beauchaine, T. D., Mickey, R., & Rothblum, E. D. (2005). Mental health of lesbian, gay, bisexual, and heterosexual siblings: Effects of gender, sexual orientation, and family. *Journal of Abnormal Psychology, 114*, 471–476.

Balsam, K. F., Martell, C. R., & Safren, S. A. (2006). Affirmative cognitive-behavioral therapy with lesbian, gay, and bisexual people. In P. A. Hays & G. Y. Iwamasa (Eds.), *Culturally responsive cognitive-behavioral therapy* (pp. 223–243). Washington, DC: American Psychological Association.

Bandura, A. (1971). Vicarious and self-reinforcement processes. In R. Glaser (Ed.), *The nature of reinforcement.* New York: Academic Press.

Bandura, A. (1986). *Social foundations of thought and action: A social cognitive theory.* Englewood Cliffs, NJ: Prentice Hall.

Bandura, A. (1993). Perceived self-efficacy in cognitive development and functioning. *Educational Psychologist, 28,* 117–148.

Bandura, A. (1997). *Self-efficacy: The exercise of control.* New York: W. H. Freeman.

Bandura, A., Barbaranelli, C., Caprara, G. V., & Pastorelli, C. (2001). Self-efficacy beliefs as shapers of children's aspirations and career trajectories. *Child Development, 72*(1), 187–206.

Bandura, A., Taylor, C., Williams, S. L., Mefford, I. N., & Barchas, J. D. (1985). Catecholamine secretion as function of perceived coping self-efficacy. *Journal of Consulting and Clinical Psychology, 53,* 406–415.

Barkham, M., Connell, J., Stiles, W. B., Miles, J. N. V., Margison, F., Evans, C., & Mellor-Clark, J. (2006). Dose-effect relations and responsive regulation of treatment duration: The good enough level. *Journal of Consulting and Clinical Psychology, 74, 160–167.*

Bardram, J. E., Frost, M., Szántó, K., & Marcu, G. (2012, January). The MONARCA self-assessment system: A persuasive personal monitoring system for bipolar patients. In *Proceedings of the 2nd ACM SIGHIT International Health Informatics Symposium* (pp. 21–30). New York: ACM.

Barkham, M., Hardy, G. E., & Mellor-Clark, J. (Eds.). (2010). *Developing and delivering practice-based evidence: A guide for the psychological therapies.* Chichester, West Sussex, UK: Wiley.

Barlow, D. H. (2002). *Anxiety and its disorders: The nature and treatment of anxiety and panic* (2nd ed.). New York: Guilford Press.

Barlow, D. H. (Ed.). (2014). *Clinical handbook of psychological disorders: A step-by-step treatment manual.* New York: Guilford Press.

Barnett, J. E., & Sherman, M. D. (Eds.) (2011). Psychological services for veterans and military service members and their families [Special issue]. *Professional Psychology: Research and Practice, 42*, 1–104.

Bass, B. A., & Quimby, J. L. (2006). Addressing secrets in couples counseling: An alternative approach to informed consent. *The Family Journal, 14,* 77–80.

Beauchamp, T. L., & Childress, J. F. (2013). *Principles of biomedical ethics* (7th ed.). New York: Oxford University Press.

Beck, A. T. (1993). *The Beck Anxiety Inventory.* San Antonio, TX: Psychological Corporation, Harcourt Brace.

Beck, A. T. (2005). The current state of cognitive therapy: A 40-year perspective. *Journal of the American Medical Association, 62,* 953–959.

Beck, A. T., Davis, D. D., & Freeman, A. (Eds.). (2015). *Cognitive therapy of personality disorders* (3rd ed.). New York: Guilford Press.

Beck, A. T., & Haigh, E. A. (2014). Advances in cognitive theory and therapy: The generic cognitive model. *Annual Review of Clinical Psychology, 10*, 1–24.

Beck, A. T., Steer, R. A., & Brown, G. K. (1996). *The Beck Depression Inventory II.* San Antonio, TX: Psychological Corporation, Harcourt Brace.

Beck, J. (1995). *Cognitive therapy: Basics and beyond.* New York: Guilford Press.

Beck, J. S. (2011). *Cognitive behavior therapy: Basics and beyond* (2nd ed.). New York: Guilford Press.

Becker, C. B. (2002). Integrated behavioral treatment of comorbid OCD, PTSD, and borderline personality disorder: A case study. *Cognitive and Behavioral Practice, 9*, 100–110.

Becker-Weidman, E. G., Jacobs, R. H., Reinecke, M. A., Silva, S. G., & March, J. S. (2010). Social problem-solving among adolescents treated for depression. *Behaviour Research and Therapy, 48*, 11–18.

Beidel, D. C., & Turner, S. M. (2005). *Childhood anxiety disorders: A guide to research and treatment.* New York: Routledge.

Bélanger, C., Laporte, L., Sabourin, S., & Wright, J. (2015). The effect of cognitive-behavioral group marital therapy on marital happiness and problem solving self-appraisal. *The American Journal of Family Therapy,* 43, 103–118.

Belitz, J., & Bailey, R. A. (2009). Clinical ethics for the treatment of children and adolescents: A guide for general psychiatrists. *Psychiatric Clinics of North America, 32,* 243–257.

Bell, A. C., & D'Zurilla, T. J. (2009). Problem-solving therapy for depression: A meta-analysis. *Clinical Psychology Review, 29,* 348–353.

Benish, S. G., Quintana, S., & Wampold, B. E. (2011). Culturally adapted psychotherapy and the legitimacy of myth: A direct-comparison meta-analysis. *Journal of Counseling Psychology, 58,* 279–289.

Bennett-Levy, J., Wilson, S., Nelson, J., Stirling, J., Ryan, K., Rotumah, D., … Beale, D. (2014). Can CBT be effective for Aboriginal Australians? Perspectives of Aboriginal practitioners trained in CBT. *Australian Psychologist, 49,* 1–7.

Benson, H., & Stuart, E. M. (Eds.). (1992). *The wellness book: The comprehensive guide to maintaining health and treating stress-related illness.* New York: Birch Lane.

Benson, P. (2014). Coping and psychological adjustment among mothers of children with ASD: An accelerated longitudinal study. *Journal of Autism & Developmental Disorders, 44*(8), 1793–1807.

Berg, I. K., & de Shazer, S. (1993). Making numbers talk: Language in therapy. In S. Friedman (Ed.), *The new language of change: Constructive collaboration in psychotherapy* (pp. 5–24). New York: Guilford Press.

Berg, I. K., & Miller, S. D. (1992a). Working with Asian American clients: One person at a time. *Families in Society: The Journal of Contemporary Human Services, 73*(6), 356–363.

Berg, I. K., & Miller, S. D. (1992b). *Working with the problem drinker: A solution-focused approach.* New York: Norton.

Berk, L. E. (2013). *Development through the lifespan* (6th ed.). Boston, MA: Pearson Education.

Berlin, S. (2001). *Clinical social work: A cognitive–integrative perspective.* New York: Oxford University Press.

Bernal, G., & Domenech Rodríguez, M. M. (Eds.). (2012a). *Cultural adaptations: Tools for evidence-based practice with diverse populations.* Washington, DC: American Psychological Association.

Bernal, G., & Domenech Rodríguez, M. M. (2012b). Cultural adaptation in context: Psychotherapy as a historical account of adaptations. In G. Bernal & M. M. Domenech Rodríguez (Eds.), *Cultural adaptations: Tools for evidence-based practice with diverse populations* (pp. 3–22). Washington, DC: American Psychological Association.

Bernal, G., Jiménez-Chafey, M. I., & Rodríguez, M. M. D. (2009). Cultural adaptation of treatments: A resource for considering culture in evidence-based practice. *Professional Psychology: Research and Practice, 40,* 361–368.

Bernal, G., & Sáez-Santiago, E. (2006). Culturally centered psychosocial interventions. *Journal of Community Psychology, 34,* 121–132.

Bernard, J. M., & Goodyear, R. K. (2013). *Fundamentals of clinical supervision* (5th ed.). Upper Saddle River, NJ: Pearson Education.

Bernstein, D. A., & Borkovec, T. D. (1973). *Progressive relaxation training: A manual for helping professions.* Champaign, IL: Research Press.

Bernstein, D. A., Carlson, C. R., & Schmidt, J. E. (2007). Progressive relaxation: Abbreviated methods. In P. M. Lehrer, R. L. Woolfolk, & W. E. Sime (Eds.), *Principles and practice of stress management* (3rd ed., pp. 88–122). New York: Guilford Press.

Bersoff, D. N. (2014). Protecting victims of violent patients while protecting confidentiality. *American Psychologist, 69,* 461–467.

Beutler, L. E. (2009). Making science matter in clinical practice: Redefining psychotherapy. *Clinical Psychology: Science and Practice, 16,* 301–317.

Beutler, L. E., & Castonguay, L. G. (2006). The task force on empirically based principles of therapeutic change. In L. G. Castonguay & L. E. Beutler (Eds.), *Principles of therapeutic change that work* (pp. 3–12). New York: Oxford University Press.

Beutler, L., & Clarkin, J. (1990). *Systematic treatment selection.* New York: Brunner/Mazel.

Beutler, L., Clarkin, J., & Bongar, B. (2000). *Guidelines for the systematic treatment of the depressed patient.* New York: Oxford University Press.

Beutler, L. E., Consoli, A. J., & Lane, G. (2005). Systematic treatment selection and prescriptive psychotherapy. In J. C. Norcross & M. R. Goldfried (Eds.), *Handbook of psychotherapy integration* (2nd ed., pp. 172–195). New York: Oxford University Press.

Beutler, L. E., & Harwood, T. M. (2000). *Prescriptive psychotherapy: A practical guide to systematic treatment selection.* New York: Oxford University Press.

Beutler, L. E., Harwood, T. M., Kimpara, S., Verdirame, D., & Blau, K. (2011). Coping style. In J. C. Norcross (Ed.), *Psychotherapy relationships that work: Evidence-based responsiveness* (2nd ed., pp. 336–353). New York: Oxford University Press.

Beutler, L. E., Harwood, T. M., Michelson, A., Song, X., & Holman, J. (2011). Reactance/resistance level. In J. C. Norcross (Ed.), *Psychotherapy relationships that work: Evidence-based responsiveness* (2nd ed., pp. 261–278). New York: Oxford University Press.

Bhatnagar, R., Phelps, L., Rietz, K., Juergens, T., Russell, D., Miller, N., & Ahearn, E. (2013). The effects of mindfulness training on post-traumatic stress disorder symptoms and heart rate variability in combat veterans. *The Journal of Alternative and Complementary Medicine, 19*(11), 860–861.

Bien, T. H. (2004). Quantum change and psychotherapy. *Journal of Clinical Psychology/In Session, 60,* 493–504.

BigFoot, D. S., & Schmidt, S. R. (2010). Honoring Children, Mending the Circle: Cultural adaptation of trauma-focused cognitive-behavioral therapy for American Indian and Alaska Native children. *Journal of Clinical Psychology: In Session, 66,* 847–856.

Biglan, A., Hayes, S. C., & Pistorelo, J. (2008). Acceptance and commitment: Implications for prevention science. *Prevention Science, 9*(3), 139–152.

Bigler, J. B., & Wetchler, J. L. (Eds.). (2012). *Handbook of LGBT-affirmative couple and family therapy.* New York: Taylor & Francis/Routledge.

Bijou, S. W., & Baer, D. M. (1976). *Child development I: A systematic and empirical theory.* Englewood Cliffs, NJ: Prentice Hall.

Birnie, K., Speca, M., & Carlson, L. E. (2010). Exploring self-compassion and empathy in the context of mindfulness-based stress reduction (MBSR). *Stress and Health: Journal of the International Society for the Investigation of Stress, 26,* 359–371.

Bishop, M. (2013). Work engagement of older registered nurses: The impact of a caring-based intervention. *Journal of Nursing Management, 21*(7), 941–949.

Bishop, M., & Frain, M. P. (2011). The multiple sclerosis self-management scale: Revision and psychometric analysis. *Rehabilitation Psychology, 56*(2), 150–159.

Björk, A. (2014). Stabilizing a fluid intervention: The development of motivational interviewing, 1983–2013. *Addiction Research and Theory, 22,* 313–324.

Blanco, C., Patel, S. R., Liu, L., Jiang, H., Lewis-Fernández, R., Schmidt, A. B., … Olfson, M. (2007). National trends in ethnic disparities in mental health care. *Medical Care, 45,* 1012–1019.

Bloom, M., Fischer, J., & Orme, J. (2009). *Evaluating practice: Guidelines for the accountable professional* (6th ed.). Boston, MA: Allyn & Bacon.

Bloss, E. B., Janssen, W. G., McEwen, B. S., & Morrison, J. H. (2010). Interactive effects of stress and aging on structural plasticity in the prefrontal cortex. *The Journal of Neuroscience, 30*(19), 6726–6731.

Blume, A. W., & García de la Cruz, B. (2005). Relapse prevention among diverse populations. In G. A. Marlatt & D. M. Donovan (Eds.), *Relapse prevention: Maintenance strategies in the treatment of addictive behaviors* (2nd ed., pp. 45–64). New York: Guilford Press.

Boardman, J. D., & Robert, S. A. (2000). Neighborhood socioeconomic status and perceptions of self-efficacy. *Sociological Perspectives, 43,* 117–136.

Boes, M., & van Wormer, K. (2009). Social work with lesbian, gay, bisexual, and transgendered clients. In A. R. Roberts (Ed.), *Social workers' desk reference* (2nd ed., pp. 934–938). New York: Oxford University Press.

Bohart, A. C., Elliott, R., Greenberg, L. S., & Watson, J. C. (2002). Empathy. In J. C. Norcross (Ed.), *Psychotherapy relationships that work: Therapist contributions and responsiveness to patients* (pp. 89–108). New York: Oxford University Press.

Bohart, A. C., & Tallman, K. (2010). Clients: The neglected common factor in psychotherapy. In B. L. Duncan, S. D. Miller, B. E. Wampold, & M. A. Hubble (Eds.), *The heart and soul of change: Delivering what works in therapy* (2nd ed., pp. 83–111). Washington, DC: American Psychological Association.

Bohart, A. C., & Wade, A. G. (2013). The client in psychotherapy. In M. J. Lambert (Ed.), *Bergin and Garfield's Handbook of psychotherapy and behavior change* (6th ed., pp. 219–257). Hoboken, NJ: Wiley.

Bohnenkamp, J. H., Glascoe, T., Gracey, K. A., Epstein, R. A., & Benningfield, M. M. (2015). Implementing clinical outcomes assessment in everyday school mental health practice. *Child and Adolescent Psychiatric Clinics of North America, 24,* 399–413.

Bond, G. R., Drake, R. E., & Becker, D. R. (2010). Beyond evidence-based practice: Nine ideal features of a mental health intervention. *Research on Social Work Practice, 20*, 493–501.

Bond, G. R., Drake, R. E., Mueser, K. T., & Latimer, E. (2001). Assertive community treatment for people with severe mental illness: Critical ingredients and impact on patients. *Disease Management & Health Outcomes, 9*, 141–159.

Bontempo, A., Panza, K. E., & Bloch, M. H. (2012). D-cycloserine augmentation of behavioral therapy for the treatment of anxiety disorders: A meta-analysis. *Journal of Clinical Psychiatry, 73*(4), 533–537.

Bordin, E. S. (1979). The generalizability of the psychoanalytic concept of the working alliance. *Psychotherapy: Theory, Research & Practice, 16*, 252–260.

Bordin, E. S. (1994). Theory and research on the therapeutic working alliance: New directions. In A. O. Horvath & L. S. Greenberg (Eds.), *The working alliance: Theory, research, and practice* (pp. 13–37). New York: Wiley.

Borkovec, T. D., Alcaine, O., & Behar, E. (2004). Avoidance theory of worry and generalized anxiety disorder. In R. G. Heimberg, C. L. Turk, & D. S. Mennin (Eds.), *Generalized anxiety disorder: Advances in research and practice* (pp. 77–108). New York: Guilford Press.

Bormann, J. E., Thorp, S. R., Wetherell, J. L., Golshan, S., & Lang, A. J. (2013). Meditation-based mantram intervention for veterans with posttraumatic stress disorder: A randomized trial. *Psychological Trauma: Theory, Research, Practice, and Policy, 5*(3), 259.

Borysenko, J. (1987). *Minding the body, mending the mind*. New York: Bantam.

Bowen, M. (1961). Family psychotherapy. *American Journal of Orthopsychiatry, 31,* 40–60.

Bowen, S., Chawla, N., Collins, S. E., Witkiewitz, K., Hsu, S., & Grow, J., … Marlatt, A.. (2009). Mindfulness-based relapse prevention for substance use disorders: A Pilot study. *Substance Abuse, 30*, 295–305.

Bowen, S., Chawla, N., & Marlatt, G. A. (2011). *Mindfulness-based relapse prevention for addictive behaviors: A clinician's guide*. New York: Guilford Press.

Bowen, S., Witkiewitz, K., Clifasefi, S. L., Grow, J., Chawla, N., Hsu, S. H., … Larimer, M. E. (2014). Relative efficacy of mindfulness-based relapse prevention, standard relapse prevention, and treatment as usual for substance use disorders: A randomized clinical trial. *JAMA Psychiatry, 71*(5), 547–556.

Bowen, S., Witkiewitz, K., Dillworth, T. M., Chawla, N., Simpson, T. L., & Ostafin, B. D., … Marlatt, A. (2006). Mindfulness meditation and substance use in an incarcerated population. *Psychology of Addictive Behaviors, 20*(3), 343–347.

Boyd-Franklin, N. (2013). *Black families in therapy: Understanding the African American experience*. New York: Guilford Press.

Boyer, S. L., & Bond, G. R. (1999). Does assertive community treatment reduce burnout? A comparison with traditional case management. *Mental Health Services Research, 1*, 31–45.

Boyle, P., & Rodhouse, P. (2005). *Cephalopods: Ecology and fisheries*. Oxford, UK: Blackwell Science.

Brammer, L. M., Abrego, P. J., & Shostrom, E. L. (1993). *Therapeutic psychology: Fundamentals of counseling and psychotherapy* (6th ed.). Englewood Cliffs, NJ: Prentice Hall.

Bratzke, L. C., Muehrer, R. J., Kehl, K. A., Lee, K. S., Ward, E. C., & Kwekkeboom, K. L. (2015). Self-management priority setting and decision-making in adults with multimorbidity: A narrative review of literature. *International Journal of Nursing Studies, 52*(3), 744–755.

Braveman, P., Egerter, S., & Williams, D. R. (2011). The social determinants of health: Coming of age. *Annual Review of Public Health, 32*, 381–398.

Bray, J. H. (2010). The future of psychology practice and science. *American Psychologist, 65*, 355–369.

Brazier, A., Mulkins, A., & Verhoef, M. (2006). Evaluating a yogic breathing and meditation intervention for individuals living with HIV/AIDS. *American Journal of Health Promotion, 20*(3), 192–195.

Breevaart, K., Bakker, A. B., & Demerouti, E. (2014). Daily self-management and employee work engagement. *Journal of Vocational Behavior, 84*(1), 31–38.

Brehm, J. W. (1966). *A theory of psychological reactance*. New York: Academic Press.

Brehm, S. S. (1976). *The application of social psychology to clinical practice*. Washington, DC: Hemisphere.

Brems, C. (2000). *Dealing with challenges in psychotherapy and counseling*. Belmont, CA: Cengage Learning.

Brems, C., & Johnson, M. E. (1997). Clinical implications of the co-occurrence of substance use and other psychiatric disorders. *Professional Psychology: Research and Practice, 28*, 437–447.

Bridges, N. A. (2005). *Moving beyond the comfort zone in psychotherapy*. Lanham, MD: Jason Aronson/Rowan & Littlefield.

British Association for Counselling and Psychotherapy. (2013). *Ethical framework for good practice in counselling and psychotherapy.* Leicestershire, UK: Author. Retrieved from http://www.bacp.co.uk

Brodbeck, J., Bachmann, M. S., & Znoj, H. (2013). Distinct coping strategies differentially predict urge levels and lapses in a smoking cessation attempt. *Addictive Behaviors, 38*(6), 2224–2229.

Brom, D., Pat-Yorenczyuk, R., & Ford, J. D. (Eds.). (2009). *Treating traumatized children: Risk, resilience, and recovery.* New York: Guilford Press.

Bronfenbrenner, U. (1979). *The ecology of human development.* Boston, MA: President and Fellows of Harvard College.

Bronfenbrenner, U. (2005). *Making human beings human.* Thousand Oaks, CA: Sage.

Bronfenbrenner, U., & Evans, G. W. (2000). Developmental science in the 21st century: Emerging theoretical models, research designs, and empirical findings. *Social Development, 9,* 115–125.

Brown, G. S., & Minami, T. (2010). Outcomes management, reimbursement, and the future of psychotherapy. In B. L. Duncan, S. D. Miller, B. E. Wampold, & M. A. Hubble (Eds.), *The heart and soul of change: Delivering what works in therapy* (2nd ed., pp. 267–297). Washington, DC: American Psychological Association.

Brown, L. S. (1992). Introduction. In L. S. Brown & M. Ballou (Eds.), *Personality and psychopathology: Feminist reappraisals* (pp. 111–115). New York: Guilford Press.

Brown, L. S. (2008). *Cultural competence in trauma therapy: Beyond the flashback.* Washington, DC: American Psychological Association.

Brown, L. S. (2009). Cultural competence: A new way of thinking about integration in therapy. *Journal of Psychotherapy Integration, 19,* 340–353.

Brown, L. S. (2010). *Feminist therapy.* Washington, DC: American Psychological Association.

Brown, T. A., DiNardo, P. A., & Barlow, D. H. (1994). *Anxiety disorders interview schedules for DSM-IV (ADIS-IV).* New York: Graywind.

Bryan, C., Corso, K., Neal-Walden, T., & Rudd, M. (2009). Managing suicide risk in primary care: Practice recommendations for behavioral health consultants. *Professional Psychology, 40,* 148–155.

Bryan, W. V. (2007). *Multicultural aspects of disabilities: A guide to understanding and assisting minorities in the rehabilitation process* (2nd ed.). Springfield, IL: Charles C Thomas.

Buchanan, A., Binder, R., Norko, M., & Swartz, M. (2012). Resource document on psychiatric violence risk assessment. *American Journal of Psychiatry, 169,* 1–10.

Buckner, J. D., Crosby, R. D., Silgado, J., Wonderlich, S. A., & Schmidt, N. B. (2012). Immediate antecedents of marijuana use: An analysis from ecological momentary assessment. *Journal of Behavior Therapy and Experimental Psychiatry, 43*(1), 647–655.

Bufka, L. F., & Camp, N. (2010). Brief measures for screening and measuring mental health outcomes. In M. M. Antony & D. H. Barlow (Eds.), *Handbook of assessment and treatment planning for psychological disorders* (2nd ed., pp. 62–94). New York: Guilford Press.

Burke, B. L., Arkowitz, H., & Menchola, M. (2003). The efficacy of motivational interviewing: A meta-analysis of controlled clinical trials. *Journal of Consulting and Clinical Psychology, 71,* 843–861.

Burke, B. L., Dunn, C. W., Atkins, D. C., & Phelps, J. S. (2004). The emerging evidence base for motivational interviewing: A meta-analytic and qualitative inquiry. *Journal of Cognitive Psychotherapy, 18,* 309–322.

Burke, M., Kraut, R., & Marlow, C. (2011, May). Social capital on Facebook: Differentiating uses and users. In *Proceedings of the SIGCHI Conference on Human Factors in Computing Systems* (pp. 571–580). New York: ACM.

Burns, S. T. (2010). Counseling adult clients experiencing chronic pain. *Journal of Counseling & Development, 88,* 483–490.

Busch, V., Magerl, W., Kern, U., Haas, J., Hajak, G., & Eichhammer, P. (2012). The effect of deep and slow breathing on pain perception, autonomic activity, and mood processing—An experimental study. *Pain Medicine, 13*(2), 215–228.

Butler, A. C., Chapman, J. E., Forman, E. M., & Beck, A. T. (2006). The empirical status of cognitive-behavioral therapy: A review of meta-analyses. *Clinical Psychology Review, 26,* 17–31.

Cahn, B. R., & Polich, J. (2006). Meditation states and traits: EEG, ERP, and neuroimaging studies. *Psychological Bulletin, 132*(2), 180–211.

Caldwell-Harris, C. L., & Ayçiçegi, A. (2006). When personality and culture clash: The psychological distress of allocentrics in an individualist culture and idiocentrics in a collectivist culture. *Transcultural Psychiatry, 43,* 331–361.

Calhoun, L. G., & Tedeschi, R. G. (2013). *Posttraumatic growth in clinical practice.* New York: Routledge.

Calhoun, L. G., Tedeschi, R. G., & Tedeschi, R. G. (Eds.). (2014). *Facilitating posttraumatic growth: A clinician's guide.* New York: Routledge.

Calix, A. R. (2004). *Is the ecomap a valid and reliable social work tool to measure social support?* (Unpublished master's thesis). Louisiana State University, Baton Rouge.

Campbell, C., Skovdal, M., Mupambireyi, Z., & Gregson, S. (2010). Exploring children's stigmatisation of AIDS-affected children in Zimbabwe through drawings and stories. *Social Science & Medicine, 71*(5), 975–985.

Canadian Psychological Association. (2000). *Canadian code of ethics for psychologists* (3rd ed.). Ottawa, Ontario: Author. Retrieved from http://www.cpa.ca/aboutcpa /committees/ethics/codeofethics

Canino, I., & Spurlock, J. (2000). *Culturally diverse children and adolescents: Assessment, diagnosis, and treatment* (2nd ed.). New York: Guilford Press.

Carkhuff, R. R. (1969a). *Helping and human relations. Vol. 1: Practice and research.* New York: Holt, Rinehart and Winston.

Carkhuff, R. R. (1969b). *Helping and human relations. Vol. 2: Selection and training.* New York: Holt, Rinehart and Winston.

Carkhuff, R. R. (1987). *The art of helping* (6th ed.). Amherst, MA: Human Resource Development.

Carkhuff, R. R., & Pierce, R. M. (1975). *Trainer's guide: The art of helping.* Amherst, MA: Human Resource Development.

Carkhuff, R. R., Pierce, R. M., & Cannon, J. R. (1977). *The art of helping III.* Amherst, MA: Human Resource Development.

Carlat, D. (2010). *Unhinged: The trouble with psychiatry— A doctor's revelations about a profession in crisis.* New York: Free Press.

Carlisle, L. L. (2013). Child and adolescent telemental health. In K. Myers & C. L. Turvey (Eds.), *Telemental health: Clinical, technical, and administrative foundations for evidence-based practice* (pp. 197–221). Waltham, MA: Elsevier.

Carlisle, J., & Neulicht, A. T. (2010). The necessity of professional disclosure and informed consent for rehabilitation counselors. *Journal of Applied Rehabilitation Counseling, 41*(2), 25–31.

Carlson, L. E., Beattie, T. L., Giese-Davis, J., Faris, P., Tamagawa, R., Fick, L. J., … Speca, M. (2015). Mindfulness-based cancer recovery and supportive-expressive therapy maintain telomere length relative to controls in distressed breast cancer survivors. *Cancer, 121*(3), 476–484.

Carmody, J. (2009). Evolving conceptions of mindfulness in clinical settings. *Journal of Cognitive Psychotherapy: An International Quarterly, 23,* 270–280.

Carr, E. S., & Smith, Y. (2014). The poetics of therapeutic practice: Motivational interviewing and the powers of pause. *Culture, Medicine, and Psychiatry, 38,* 83–114.

Carrington, P. (2007). Modern forms of mantra meditation. In P. M. Lehrer, R. L. Woolfolk, & W. E. Sime (Eds.), *Principles and practice of stress management* (3rd ed., pp. 363–392). New York: Guilford Press.

Carroll, A. E., DiMeglio, L. A., Stein, S., & Marero, D. G. (2011). Using a cell phone-based glucose monitoring system for adolescent diabetes management. *The Diabetes Educator, 37*(1), 59–66.

Carroll, K. M., Ball, S. A., Martino, S., Nich, C., Babuscio, T. A., Nuro, K. F., … Rounsaville, B. J. (2008). Computer-assisted delivery of cognitive-behavioral therapy for addiction: A randomized trial of CBT4CBT. *American Journal of Psychiatry, 165,* 881–888.

Carter, J. D., McIntosh, V. V., Jordan, J., Porter, R. J., Frampton, C. M., & Joyce, P. R. (2013). Psychotherapy for depression: A randomized clinical trial comparing schema therapy and cognitive behavior therapy. *Journal of Affective Disorders, 151*(2), 500–505.

Carter, P. A., Dyer, K. A., & Mikan, S. Q. (2013). Sleep disturbance, chronic stress, and depression in hospice nurses: Testing the feasibility of an intervention. *Oncology Nursing Forum, 40,* E368–E373.

Cashdan, S. (1988). *Object relations therapy: Using the relationship.* New York: Norton.

Castonguay, L. G., & Beutler, L. E. (2006a). Common and unique principles of therapeutic change: What do we know and what do we need to know? In L. E. Beutler & L. G. Castonguay (Eds.), *Principles of therapeutic change that work* (pp. 353–370). New York: Oxford University Press.

Castonguay, L. G., & Beutler, L. E. (Eds.). (2006b). *Principles of therapeutic change that work.* New York: Oxford University Press.

Cautela, J. R. (1977). *Behavior analysis forms for clinical intervention* (Vol. 2). Champaign, IL: Research Press.

Cervone, D., More, N., Orom, H., Shadel, W. G., & Scott, W. D. (2011). Self-efficacy beliefs and the architecture of personality: On knowledge, appraisal, and self-regulation. In K. D. Vohs & R. F. Baumeister (Eds.), *Handbook of self-regulation: Research, theory, and applications* (2nd ed., pp. 461–484). New York: Guilford Press.

Chamberlain, P., Patterson, G., Reid, J., Kavanagh, K., & Forgatch, M. (1984). Observation of client resistance. *Behavior Therapy, 15,* 144–155.

Chambless, D. L., Baker, M. J., Baucom, D. H., Beutler, L. E., Calhoun, K. S., Crits-Cristoph, P., … Woody,

S. R. (1998). Update on empirically validated therapies. *Clinical Psychologist, 51,* 3–16.

Chambless, D. L., & Holon, S. D. (1998). Defining empirically supported therapies. *Journal of Consulting and Clinical Psychology, 66,* 7–18.

Chang, E. C., D'Zurilla, T. J., & Sanna, L. J. (Eds.). (2004). *Social problem-solving: Theory, research, and training.* Washington, DC: American Psychological Association.

Charlevoix-Romine, D. J. (2009). Women's success in science: The role of self-efficacy and resiliency in building social capital. *Dissertation Abstracts International, 70*(2-A), 453.

Chasson, G. S., Buhlmann, U., Tolin, D. F., Rao, S. R., Reese, H. E., Rowley, T., … Wilhelm, S. (2010). Need for speed: Evaluating slopes of OCD recovery in behavior therapy enhanced with D-cycloserine. *Behaviour Research and Therapy, 48,* 675–679.

Chaudhry, S., & Li, C. (2011). Is solution-focused brief therapy culturally appropriate for Muslim American counselees? *Journal of Contemporary Psychotherapy, 41,* 109–113.

Chen, E., & Miller, G. E. (2012). "Shift-and-persist" strategies: Why low socioeconomic status isn't always bad for health. *Perspectives on Psychological Science, 7*(2), 135–158.

Chen, E., Miller, G. E., Lachman, M. E., Gruenewald, T. L., & Seeman, T. E. (2012). Protective factors for adults from low childhood socioeconomic circumstances: The benefits of shift-and-persist for allostatic load. *Psychosomatic Medicine, 74*(2), 178–186.

Chen, J., & Rizzo, J. (2010). Racial and ethnic disparities in use of psychotherapy: Evidence from national U.S. survey data. *Psychiatric Services, 61,* 364–372.

Chen, Y. (2006a). Coping with suffering: The Buddhist perspective. In P. T. P. Wong & L. C. J. Wong (Eds.), *Handbook of multicultural perspectives on stress and coping* (pp. 73–89). New York: Springer.

Chen, Y. (2006b). The way of nature as a healing power. In P. T. P. Wong & L. C. J. Wong (Eds.), *Handbook of multicultural perspectives on stress and coping* (pp. 91–103). New York: Springer.

Chernin, J. N., & Johnson, M. R. (2003). *Affirmative psychotherapy and counseling for lesbians and gay men.* Thousand Oaks, CA: Sage.

Chiesa, A., & Serretti, A. (2010). A systematic review of neurobiological and clinical features of mindfulness and meditations. *Psychological Medicine, 40*(8), 1239–1252.

Ching, S. S. Y., Martinson, I. M., & Wong, T. K. S. (2009). Reframing: Psychological adjustment of Chinese women at the beginning of the breast cancer experience. *Qualitative Health Research, 19*(3), 339–351.

Chisholm, J., & Greene, B. (2008). Women of color: Perspectives on "multiple identities" in psychological theory, research, and practice. In F. L. Denmark & M. A. Paludi (Eds.), *Psychology of women: A handbook of issues and theories* (pp. 40–69). Westport, CT: Praeger.

Chlebowy, D. O., Hood, S., & LaJoie, A. S. (2010). Facilitators and barriers to self-management of type 2 diabetes among urban African American adults: Focus group findings. *The Diabetes Educator, 36*(6), 897–905.

Choi, N. G., Hegel, M. T., Marti, C. N., Marinucci, M. L., Sirrianni, L., & Bruce, M. L. (2014). Telehealth problem-solving therapy for depressed low-income homebound older adults. *The American Journal of Geriatric Psychiatry, 22*(3), 263–271.

Christensen, A., Atkins, D. C., Berns, S., Wheeler, J., Baucom, D. H., & Simpson, L. E. (2004). Traditional versus integrative behavioral couple therapy for significantly and chronically distressed married couples. *Journal of Consulting and Clinical Psychology, 72*(2), 176–191.

Christopher, J. C., & Maris, J. A. (2010). Integrating mindfulness as self-care into counselling and psychotherapy training. *Counselling and Psychotherapy Research, 10,* 114–125.

Chu, J., Huynh, L., & Areán, P. (2012). Cultural adaptation of evidence-based practice utilizing an iterative stakeholder process and theoretical framework: Problem solving therapy for Chinese older adults. *International Journal of Geriatric Psychiatry, 27*(1), 97–106.

Chung, B., Jones, L., Jones, A., Corbett, C. E., Booker, T., Wells, K., & Collins, B. (2009). Using community arts events to enhance collective efficacy and community engagement to address depression in an African American community. *American Journal of Public Health, 99,* 237–244.

Cihak, D. F., & Garna, R. I. (2008). Noncontingent escape access to self-reinforcement to increase task engagement for students with moderate to severe disabilities. *Education and Training in Developmental Disabilities, 43*(4), 556–568.

Clark, A. J. (2010). Empathy: An integral model in the counseling process. *Journal of Counseling & Development, 88,* 348–356.

Clark, D. A., & Beck, A. T. (2010). Cognitive theory and therapy of anxiety and depression: Convergence with neurobiological findings. *Trends in Cognitive Sciences, 14*(9), 418–424.

Clarkin, J. F. (2005). Differential therapeutics. In J. C. Norcross & M. R. Goldfried (Eds.), *Handbook of psychotherapy integration* (2nd ed., pp. 343–361). New York: Oxford University Press.

Clarkin, J. F., & Levy, K. N. (2004). The influence of client variables on psychotherapy. In M. J. Lambert (Ed.), *Bergin and Garfield's handbook of psychotherapy and behavior change* (5th ed., pp. 194–226). New York: Wiley.

Cloitre, M., Cohen, L. & Koenen, K. (2006). *Treating survivors of childhood abuse: Psychotherapy for the interrupted life.* New York: Guilford Press.

Cochran, S. D., Sullivan, J. G., & Mays, V. M. (2003). Prevalence of mental disorders, psychological distress, and mental health services use among lesbian, gay, and bisexual adults in the United States. *Journal of Consulting and Clinical Psychology, 71*, 53–61.

Code of Federal Regulations. (2002). *Part 2: Confidentiality of alcohol and drug abuse patient records.* Washington, DC: U.S. Government Printing Office. Retrieved from https://www.gpo.gov/fdsys/granule /CFR-2010-title42-vol1/CFR-2010-title42-vol1-part2 /content-detail.html

Coffey, S. F., Stasiewicz, P. R., Hughes, P. M., & Brimo, M. L. (2006). Trauma-focused imaginal exposure for individuals with comorbid posttraumatic stress disorder and alcohol dependence: Revealing mechanisms of alcohol craving in a cue reactivity paradigm. *Psychology of Addictive Behaviors, 20*, 425–435.

Cohen, G. L., & Sherman, D. K. (2014). The psychology of change: Self-affirmation and social psychological intervention. *Annual Review of Psychology, 65*, 333–371.

Cohen, J. A., Mannarino, A. P., & Deblinger, E. (2006). *Treating trauma and traumatic grief in children and adolescents.* New York: Guilford Press.

Cohen, S., Janicki-Deverts, D., Chen, E., & Matthews, K. A. (2010). Childhood socioeconomic status and adult health. *Annals of the New York Academy of Sciences, 1186*, 37–55.

Comas-Díaz, L. (2006). Cultural variation in the therapeutic relationship. In C. D. Goodheart, A. E. Kazdin, & R. J. Sternberg (Eds.), *Evidence-based psychotherapy: Where practice and research meet* (pp. 81–105). Washington, DC: American Psychological Association.

Comas-Díaz, L. (2007). Ethnopolitical psychology. In E. Aldarondo (Ed.), *Advancing social justice through clinical practice* (pp. 91–118). Mahwah, NJ: Erlbaum.

Comas-Díaz, L. (2012). *Multicultural care: A clinician's guide to cultural competence.* Washington, DC: American Psychological Association.

Comas-Días, L. (2014). Multicultural psychotherapy. In F. T. L. Leong (Ed.), *APA Handbook of multicultural psychology, Volume 2, Applications and training* (pp. 419–441). Washington, DC: American Psychological Association.

Comas-Díaz, L. (2014). Multicultural theories of psychotherapy. In D. Wedding & R. J. Corsini (Eds.), *Current psychotherapies* (10th ed., pp. 533–567). Belmont, CA: Cengage Learning.

Commission on Rehabilitation Counselor Certification. (2009). *Code of professional ethics for rehabilitation counselors.* Schaumburg, IL: Author.

Cone, J. D. (2001). *Evaluating outcomes: Empirical tools for effective practice.* Washington, DC: American Psychological Association.

Connors, G. J., DiClemente, C. C., Velasquez, M. M., & Donovan, D. M. (2013). *Substance abuse treatment and the stages of change: Selecting and planning interventions* (2nd ed.). New York: Guilford Press.

Constantino, G., Malgady, R. G., & Primavera, L. H. (2009). Congruence between culturally competent treatment and cultural needs of older Latinos. *Journal of Consulting and Clinical Psychology, 77*, 941–949.

Contrada, R. J., & Baum, A. (Eds.). (2011). *The handbook of stress science: Biology, psychology, and health.* New York: Springer.

Cooper, J. M., Collier, J., James, V., & Hawkey, C. J. (2010). Beliefs about personal control and self-management in 30-40 year olds living with inflammatory bowel disease: A qualitative study. *International Journal of Nursing Studies, 47*(12), 1500–1509.

Copeland, W. E., Keeler, G., Angold, A., & Costella, E. J. (2007). Traumatic events and posttraumatic stress in childhood. *Archives of General Psychiatry, 64*, 577–584.

Copeland, L., McNamara, R., Kelson, M., & Simpson, S. (2015). Mechanisms of change within motivational interviewing in relation to health behaviors outcomes: A systematic review. *Patient Education and Counseling, 98*, 401–411.

Corcoran, J. (2000). Solution-focused family therapy with ethnic minority clients. *Crisis Intervention, 6*, 5–12.

Corcoran, J. (2005). *Building strengths and skills: A collaborative approach to working with clients.* New York: Oxford University Press.

Corcoran, J., & Pillai, V. (2009). A review of the research on solution-focused therapy. *British Journal of Social Work, 39*, 234–242.

Corey, G., & Corey, M. S. (2010). *I never knew I had a choice: Explorations in personal growth* (9th ed.). Belmont, CA: Cengage Learning.

Corey, G., Corey, M. S., & Callanan, P. (2011). *Issues and ethics in the helping professions* (8th ed.). Belmont, CA: Cengage Learning.

Corey, G., Corey, M., Corey, C., & Callanan, P. (2015). *Issues and ethics in the helping professions* (9th ed.). Belmont, CA: Cengage Learning.

Corey, M. S., & Corey, G. (2011). *Becoming a helper* (6th ed.). Belmont, CA: Cengage Learning.

Cormier, S. (2016). *Counseling strategies and interventions for professional helpers* (9th ed.). Upper Saddle River, NJ: Pearson Education.

Cormier, S., & Hackney, H. (2012). *Counseling strategies and interventions* (8th ed.). Upper Saddle River, NJ: Pearson Education.

Cosic, K., Popovic, S., Kukolja, D., Horvat, M., & Dropuljic, B. (2010). Physiology-driven adaptive virtual reality stimulation for prevention and treatment of stress related disorders. *Cyberpsychology, Behavior, and Social Networking, 13*(1), 73–78.

Council for Accreditation of Counseling and Related Educational Programs. (CACREP, 2009). *2009 CACREP Standards*. Alexandria, VA: Author. Retrieved from: www.cacrep.org

Cozolino, L. (2010). *The neuroscience of psychotherapy* (2nd ed.). New York: Norton.

Cramer, R. J., Golom, F. D., LoPresto, C. T., & Kirkley, S. M. (2008). Weighing the evidence: Empirical assessment and ethical implications of conversion therapy. *Ethics & Behavior, 18*, 93–114.

Crane, C., Barnhofer, T., Hargus, E., Amarasinghe, M., & Winder, R. (2010). The relationship between dispositional mindfulness and conditional goal setting in depressed patients. *British Journal of Clinical Psychology, 49*, 281–290.

Crane, R. (2009). *Mindfulness-based cognitive therapy*. New York: Routledge.

Craske, M. G. (2003). *Origins of phobias and anxiety disorders: Why more women than men?* New York: Elsevier.

Craske, M. G., & Barlow, D. H. (2007). Panic disorder and agoraphobia. In D. H. Barlow (Ed.), *Clinical handbook of psychological disorders: A step-by-step treatment manual* (4th ed., pp. 1–64). New York: Guilford Press.

Craske, M. G., Hermans, D., & Vansteenwegen, D. (Eds.). (2006). *Fear and learning: From basic processes to clinical implications*. Washington, DC: American Psychological Association.

Craske, M. G., Kircanski, K., Zelikowsky, M., Mystowski, J., Chowdhury, N., & Baker, A. (2008). Optimizing inhibitory learning during exposure therapy. *Behaviour Research and Therapy, 46*, 5–27.

Craske, M. G., Treanor, M., Conway, C. C., Zbozinek, T., & Vervliet, B. (2014). Maximizing exposure therapy: An inhibitory learning approach. *Behaviour Research and Therapy, 58*, 10–23.

Cronbach, L. J. (1990). *Essentials of psychological testing* (5th ed.). New York: Harper & Row.

Crimando, W. (2009). Resource brokering: Managing the referral process. In I. Marini & M. A. Stebnicki (Eds.), *The professional counselor's desk reference* (pp. 135–143). New York: Springer.

Cuijpers, P., Driessen, E., Hollon, S. D., van Oppen, P., Barth, J., & Andersson, G. (2012). The efficacy of non-directive supportive therapy for adult depression: A meta-analysis. *Clinical Psychology Review, 32*, 280–291.

Cuijpers, P., van Straten, A., & Warmerdam, L. (2007). Problem solving therapies for depression: A meta-analysis. *European Psychiatry, 22*, 9–15.

Cullari, S. (1996). *Treatment resistance: A guide for practitioners*. Boston, MA: Allyn & Bacon.

Cullen, C. (1983). Implications of functional analysis. *British Journal of Clinical Psychology, 22*, 137–138.

Cummings, N. A. (1995). Impact of managed care on employment and training: A primer for survival. *Professional Psychology: Research and Practice, 26*, 10–15.

Cunningham, P. B., Foster, S. L., & Warner, S. E. (2010). Culturally relevant family-based treatment for adolescent delinquency and substance abuse: Understanding within-session processes. *Journal of Clinical Psychology: In Session, 66*, 830–846.

Curiati, J. A., Bocchi, E., Freire, J. O., Arantes, A. C., Braga, M., Garcia, Y., … Fo, W. (2005). Meditation reduces sympathetic activation and improves the quality of life in elderly patients with optimally treated heart failure: A prospective randomized study. *Journal of Alternative and Complementary Medicine, 11*(3), 465–472.

Dahl, J., Wilson, K. G., & Nilsson, A. (2004). Acceptance and commitment therapy and the treatment of persons at risk for long-term disability resulting from stress and pain symptoms: A preliminary randomized trial. *Behavior Therapy, 35*, 785–801.

Davey, G. C. L. (Ed.). (1997). *Phobias: A handbook of theory, research and treatment.* New York: Wiley.

Davidson, P. R., & Parker, K. C. H. (2001). Eye movement desensitization and reprocessing (EMDR): A meta-analysis. *Journal of Consulting and Clinical Psychology, 69,* 305–316.

Davis, D. M., & Hayes, J. A. (2011). What are the benefits of mindfulness? A practice review of psychotherapy-related research. *Psychotherapy, 48,* 198–208.

Davis, T. E., Ollendick, T. H., & Öst, L.-G. (2009). Intensive treatment of specific phobias in children and adolescents. *Cognitive and Behavioral Practice, 16,* 294–303.

Davis, T. E., & Osborn, C. J. (2000). *The solution-focused school counselor: Shaping professional practice.* Philadelphia, PA: Accelerated Development/Taylor & Francis.

de Castro, S., & Guterman, J. T. (2008). Solution-focused therapy for families coping with suicide. *Journal of Marital and Family Therapy, 34,* 93–106.

De Jong, P., & Berg, I. K. (2013). *Interviewing for solutions* (4th ed.). Belmont, CA: Cengage Learning.

de Jongh, A., & ten Broeke, E. (2009). EMDR and anxiety disorder: Exploring the current status. *Journal of EMDR Practice and Research, 3,* 133–140.

De Los Reyes, A., & Kazdin, A. E. (2008). When the evidence says, "yes, no, and maybe so": Attending to and interpreting inconsistent findings among evidence-based interventions. *Current Directions in Psychological Science, 17,* 47–51.

de Shazer, S. (1984). The death of resistance. *Family Process, 23,* 11–17.

de Shazer, S. (1985). *Keys to solution in brief therapy.* New York: Norton.

de Shazer, S., & Berg, I. K. (1992). Doing therapy: A post-structural re-vision. *Journal of Marital and Family Therapy, 18,* 71–81.

Decety, J., & Ickes, W. (Eds.). (2009). *The social neuroscience of empathy.* Cambridge, MA: MIT.

Decety, J., & Lamm, C. (2009). Empathy versus personal distress: Recent evidence from social neuroscience. In J. Decety & W. Ickes (Eds.), *The social neuroscience of empathy* (pp. 199–214). Cambridge, MA: MIT.

Deci, E. L., & Ryan, R. M. (2012). Motivation, personality, and development within embedded social contexts: An overview of self-determination theory. In R. M. Ryan (Ed.), *The Oxford handbook of human motivation* (pp. 85–107). New York: Oxford University Press.

Decker, S. E., Nich, D., Carroll, K., & Martino, S. (2014). Development of the Therapist Empathy Scale. *Behavioural and Cognitive Psychotherapy, 42,* 339–354.

Degotardi, P. J., Klass, E. S., Rosenberg, B. S., Fox, D. G., Gallelli, K. A., & Gottlieb, B. S. (2006). Development and evaluation of a cognitive–behavioral intervention for juvenile fibromyalgia. *Journal of Pediatric Psychology, 31*(7), 714–723.

Delano-Wood, L., & Abeles, N. (2005). Late-life depression: Detection, risk-reduction, and somatic intervention. *Clinical Psychology: Science and Practice, 12,* 207–218.

DeLettre, J. L., & Sobell, L. C. (2010). Keeping psychotherapy notes separate from the patient record. *Clinical Psychology and Psychotherapy, 17,* 160–163.

Demiris, G., Oliver, D. P., Washington, K., Fruehling, L. T., Haggarty-Robbins, D., Doorenbos, A., … Berry, D. (2010). A problem solving intervention for hospice caregivers: A pilot study. *Journal of Palliative Medicine, 13*(8), 1005–1011.

Dennis, T. A., & O'Toole, L. J. (2014). Mental health on the go effects of a gamified attention-bias modification mobile application in trait-anxious adults. *Clinical Psychological Science, 2,* 576–590.

Derogatis, L. R. (1983). *SCL-90 R administration, scoring and procedures manual–II.* Towson, MD: Clinical Psychometric Research.

Derogatis, L. R. (1993). *BSI: Administration, scoring, and procedures manual* (3rd ed.). Minneapolis, MN: National Computer Systems.

DeRosa, R., & Pelcovitz, D. (2009). Group treatment for chronically traumatized adolescents: Igniting SPARCS of change. In D. Brom, R. Pat-Yorenczyuk, & J. D. Ford (Eds.), *Treating traumatized children: Risk, resilience, and recovery* (pp. 225–239). New York: Guilford Press.

Desbordes, G., Gard, T., Hoge, E. A., Hölzel, B. K., Kerr, C., Lazar, S. W., … Vago, D. R. (2014). Moving beyond mindfulness: Defining equanimity as an outcome measure in meditation and contemplative research. *Mindfulness, 6*(2), 356–372.

Devilly, G. J. (2002). Eye movement desensitization and reprocessing: A chronology of its development and scientific standing. *The Scientific Review of Mental Health Practice, 1,* 113–138.

Devlin, A. S., Borenstein, B., Finch, C., Hasan M., Iannotti, E., & Koufopoulos, J. (2013). Multicultural art in the therapy office: Community and student perceptions of the therapist, *Professional Psychology, 44,* 168–176.

DiClemente, C. C. (2003). *Addiction and change: How addictions develop and addicted people recover.* New York: Guilford Press.

Didonna, F. (2009). *Clinical handbook of mindfulness.* New York: Springer.

Diemer, J., Muhlberger, A., Pauli, P., & Zwanzger, P. (2014). Virtual reality exposure in anxiety disorders: Impact on psychophysiological reactivity. *World Journal of Biological Psychiatry, 15,* 427–442.

Dimeff, L. A., & Koerner, K. (Eds.). (2007). *Dialectical behavior therapy in clinical practice: Applications across disorders and settings.* New York: Guilford Press.

Dimidjian, S., & Hollon, S. D. (2010). How would we know if psychotherapy were harmful? *American Psychologist, 65,* 21–33.

Dimidjian, S., & Linehan, M. M. (2003). Defining an agenda for future research on the clinical application of mindfulness practice. *Clinical Psychology: Science and Practice, 10,* 166–171.

Dimidjian, S., & Linehan, M. M. (2009). Mindfulness practice. In W. O'Donohue & J. E. Fisher (Eds.), *General principles and empirically supported techniques of cognitive behavior therapy* (pp. 425–434). Hoboken, NJ: Wiley.

Dinger, U., Strack, M., Leichsenring, F., Wilmers, F., & Schauenburg, H. (2008). Therapist effects on outcome and alliance in inpatient psychotherapy. *Journal of Clinical Psychology, 64,* 344–354.

Dixon, W. A. (2000). Problem-solving appraisal and depression: Evidence for a recovery model. *Journal of Counseling & Development, 78,* 87–91.

Dobson, K. S. (Ed.). (2010). *Handbook of cognitive-behavioral therapies* (3rd ed.). New York: Guilford Press.

Donaldson, E., & Bond, F. W. (2004). Psychological acceptance and emotional intelligence in relation to workplace wellbeing. *British Journal of Guidance & Counselling, 34,* 187–203.

Donner, M. B., VandeCreek, L., Gonsiorek, J. C., & Fisher, C. B. (2008). Balancing confidentiality: Protecting privacy and protecting the public. *Professional Psychology: Research and Practice, 39,* 369–376.

Donohoe, G. (2006). Adherence to antipsychotic treatment in schizophrenia: What role does cognitive behavioral therapy play in improving outcomes? *Disease Management and Health Outcomes, 14,* 207–214.

Doweiko, H. E. (2015). *Concepts of chemical dependency* (9th ed.). Belmont, CA: Cengage Learning.

Drake, R. E., Deegan, P. E., & Rapp, C. (2010). The promise of shared decision making in mental health. *Psychiatric Rehabilitation Journal, 34,* 7–13.

Drogin, E. Y., Connell, M., Foote, W. E., & Sturme, C. A. (2010). The American Psychological Association's revised "Record Keeping Guidelines": Implications for the practitioner. *Professional Psychology: Research and Practice, 41,* 236–243.

Drum, K. B., & Littleton, H. L. (2014). Therapeutic boundaries in telepsychology: Unique issues and best practice recommendations. *Professional Psychology: Research and Practice, 45,* 309–315.

Du, H., Li, X., Lin, D., & Tam, C. C. (2015). Collectivistic orientation, acculturative stress, cultural self-efficacy, and depression: A longitudinal study among Chinese internal migrants. *Community Mental Health Journal, 51*(2), 239–248.

Duarté-Vélez, Y., Bernal, G., & Bonilla, K. (2010). Culturally adapted cognitive-behavioral therapy: Integrating sexual, spiritual, and family identities in an evidence-based treatment of a depressed Latino adolescent. *Journal of Clinical Psychology: In Session, 66,* 895–906.

Ducharme, F. (2009). Reflections from a research program on nursing interventions for family caregivers of seniors. *Canadian Journal of Nursing Research, 41*(4), 91–99.

Duncan, D. T., & Hatzenbuehler, M. L. (2014). Lesbian, gay, bisexual, and transgender hate crimes and suicidality among a population-based sample of sexual-minority adolescents in Boston. *American Journal of Public Health, 104,* 272–278.

Dutton, M. A., Bermudez, D., Matás, A., Majid, H., & Myers, N. L. (2013). Mindfulness-based stress reduction for low-income, predominantly African American women with PTSD and a history of intimate partner violence. *Cognitive and Behavioral Practice, 20,* 23–32.

D'Zurilla, T. J., & Nezu, C. M. (1999). *Problem-solving therapy: A social competence approach to clinical intervention* (2nd ed.). New York: Springer.

D'Zurilla, T. J., & Nezu, A. M. (2007). *Problem-solving therapy: A positive approach to clinical intervention* (3rd ed.). New York: Springer.

D'Zurilla, T. J., & Nezu, A. M. (2010). Problem-solving therapy. In K. S. Dobson (Ed.), *Handbook of cognitive-behavioral therapies* (3rd ed.). New York: Guilford Press.

Edelstein, B., Woodhead, E., Segal, D., Heisel, M., Bower, E., Lowery, A., & Stoner, S. (2008). Older adult psychological assessment: Current instrument status and related considerations. *Clinical Gerontologist, 31,* 1–35.

Eells, T. D., Lombart, K. G., Kendjelic, E. M., Turner, L. C., & Lucas, C. P. (2005). The quality of psychotherapy case formulations: A comparison of expert, experienced, and novice cognitive–behavioral and psychodynamic therapists. *Journal of Consulting and Clinical Psychology, 73,* 579–589.

Efran, J. S., & Cook, P. F. (2000). Linguistic ambiguity as a diagnostic tool. In R. A. Neimeyer & J. D. Raskin (Eds.), *Constructions of disorder: Meaning-making frameworks for psychotherapy* (pp. 121–144). Washington, DC: American Psychological Association.

Egan, G. (2007). *The skilled helper* (8th ed.). Belmont, CA: Thomson Brooks/Cole.

Egan, G. (2014). *The skilled helper* (10th ed.). Belmont, CA: Cengage Learning.

Eifert, G. H., & Forsyth, J. P. (2005). *Acceptance and commitment therapy for anxiety disorders: A practitioner's treatment guide to using mindfulness, acceptance, and values-based behavior change strategies.* Oakland, CA: New Harbinger.

Eisen, S. V., & Grob, M. C. (2008). Behavior and Symptom Identification Scale (BASIS-32 and BASIS-24). In A. J. Rush, M. B. First, & D. Blacker (Eds.), *Handbook of psychiatric measures* (2nd ed., pp. 77–79). Washington, DC: American Psychiatric Publishing.

Eisen, S. V., Grob, M. C., & Klein, A. A. (1986). BASIS: The development of a self-report measure for psychiatric inpatient evaluation. *The Psychiatric Hospital, 17,* 166–171.

Eisenberg, N., Smith, C. L., & Spinrad, T. L. (2011). Effortful control: Relations with emotion regulation, adjustment, and socialization in childhood. In K. D. Vohs & R. F. Baumeister (Eds.), *Handbook of self-regulation: Research, theory, and applications* (2nd ed., pp. 263–283). New York: Guilford Press.

Eisenberger, R., & Cameron, J. (1996). Detrimental effects of reward: Reality or myth? *American Psychologist, 51,* 1153–1166.

Ekman, P., & Rosenberg, E. (2005). *What the face reveals.* New York: Oxford University Press.

Eliot, S. (1994). *Group activities for counselors.* Spring Valley, CA: Inner Choice Publishing.

Ell, K., Katon, W., Xie, B., Lee, P., Kapetanovic, S., Guterman, J., & Chou, C. (2010). Collaborative care management of major depression among low-income, predominantly Hispanic subjects with diabetes: A randomized controlled trial. *Diabetes Care, 33*(4), 706–713.

Ell, K., Xie, B., Kapetanovic, S., Quinn, D., Lee, P., Wells, A., & Chou, C. (2011). One-year follow-up of collaborative depression care for low-income, predominantly Hispanic patients with cancer. *Psychiatric Services, 62*(2), 162–170.

Ellenhorn, R. (2015). Assertive community treatment: A "living-systems" alternative to hospital and residential care. *Psychiatric Annals, 45*(3), 120–125.

Elliot, A. J., & Church, M. A. (2002). Client-articulated avoidance goals in the therapy context. *Journal of Counseling Psychology, 49,* 243–254.

Elliot, A. J., McGregor, H. A., & Thrash, T. M. (2002). The need for competence. In E. L. Deci & R. M. Ryan (Eds.), *Handbook of self-determination research* (pp. 361–387). Rochester, NY: University of Rochester.

Elliott, R. (2002). The effectiveness of humanistic therapies: A meta-analysis. In D. J. Cain & J. Seeman (Eds.), *Humanistic psychotherapies: Handbook of research and practice* (pp. 57–81). Washington, DC: American Psychological Association.

Elliott, R., Bohart, A. C., Watson, J. C., & Greenberg, L. S. (2011). Empathy. In J. C. Norcross (Ed.), *Psychotherapy relationships that work: Evidence-based responsiveness* (2nd ed., pp. 132–152). New York: Oxford University Press.

Elliott, R., & Friere, E. (2008). Person-centered and experiential therapies are highly effective: Summary of the 2008 meta-analysis. *Person-Centered Quarterly, Nov.,* 1–3.

Ellis, B. J., & Boyce, W. T. (2008). Biological sensitivity to context. *Current Directions in Psychological Science, 17*(3), 183–187.

Enea, V., & Dafinoiu, I. (2009). Motivational/solution-focused intervention for reducing school truancy among adolescents. *Journal of Cognitive and Behavioral Psychotherapies, 9,* 185–198.

Engle, D. E., & Arkowitz, H. (2006). *Ambivalence in psychotherapy: Facilitating a readiness to change.* New York: Guilford Press.

Ennis, R. P., & Jolivette, K. (2012). Existing research and future directions for self-regulated strategy development with students with and at risk for emotional and behavioral disorders. *The Journal of Special Education, 48*(1), 32–45.

Epstein, L. H., Paluch, R. A., Kilanowski, C. K., & Raynor, H. A. (2004). The effect of reinforcement or stimulus control to reduce sedentary behavior in the treatment of pediatric obesity. *Health Psychology, 23*(4), 371–380.

Epstein, M. H., & Sharma, J. (1998). Behavioral and emotional rating scale: A strengths-based approach to assessment. Austin, TX: Pro-Ed.

Ergin, A., Magnus, M., Ergin, N., & He, J. (2002). Short course antiretroviral treatment in the prevention of perinatal HIV-1 transmission: A meta-analysis of randomized control trials. *Annals of Epidemiology, 12*(7), 521.

Erickson, M. H. (1954). Special techniques of brief hypnotherapy. *Journal of Clinical and Experimental Hypnosis, 2,* 109–129.

Ernsting, A., Knoll, N., Schneider, M., & Schwarzer, R. (2015). The enabling effect of social support on vaccination uptake via self-efficacy and planning. *Psychology, Health & Medicine, 20*(2), 239–246.

Eskin, M. (2013). *Problem solving therapy in the clinical practice.* Waltham, MA: Elsevier.

Evans-Chase, M. (2013). Internet-based mindfulness meditation and self-regulation: A randomized trial with juvenile justice involved youth. *OJJDP Journal of Juvenile Justice, 3,* 63–79.

Falicov, C. J. (2014). *Latino families in therapy* (2nd ed.). New York: Guilford Press.

Falsetti, S. A., Resnick, H. S., & Davis, J. L. (2008). Multiple channel exposure therapy for women with PTSD and comorbid panic attacks. *Cognitive Behaviour Therapy, 37,* 117–130.

Farber, B. A., & Doolin, E. M. (2011). Positive regard. In J. C. Norcross (Ed.), *Psychotherapy relationships that work: Evidence-based responsiveness* (2nd ed., pp. 168–186). New York: Oxford University Press.

Faryna, E. L., & Morales, E. (2000). Self-efficacy and HIV-related behaviors among multiethnic adolescents. *Cultural Diversity and Ethnic Minority Psychology, 6,* 42–56.

Fazel, S., Singh, J., Doll, H., & Grann, M. (2012). Use of risk assessment instruments to predict violence and antisocial behaviour in 73 samples involving 24,827 people: Systematic review and meta-analysis. Retrieved from http://www.bmj.com/content/345/bmj.e4692

Ferguson, K. E., & Sgambati, R. E. (2009). Relaxation. In W. O'Donohue & J. E. Fisher (Eds.), *General principles and empirically supported techniques of cognitive behavior therapy* (pp. 532–549). Hoboken, NJ: Wiley.

Feske, U., Perry, K. J., Chambless, D. L., Renneberg, B., & Goldstein, A. J. (1996). Avoidant personality disorder as a predictor for treatment outcome among generalized social phobics. *Journal of Personality Disorders, 10,* 174–184.

Fiks, A. G., & Jimenez, M. E. (2010). The promise of shared decision-making in paediatrics. *Acta Paediatrica, 99,* 1464–1466.

Fink, G. (Ed.). (2007). *Encyclopedia of stress* (2nd ed.). San Diego, CA: Academic Press.

Finn, J., & Schoech, D. (Eds.) (2008). Introduction [Special issue]. *Journal of Technology in Human Services, 26*(2–4).

First, M. B. (2010). Clinical utility in the revision of the diagnostic and statistical manual of mental disorders (DSM). *Professional Psychology, 41,* 465–473.

Fischer, J., & Corcoran, K. (2013). *Measures for clinical practice and research: A sourcebook* (5th ed., Vols. 1 and 2). New York: Oxford University Press.

Fisher, C. B., & Oransky, M. (2008). Informed consent to psychotherapy: Protecting the dignity and respecting the autonomy of patients. *Journal of Clinical Psychology: In Session, 64,* 576–588.

Fisher, G. L., & Harrison, T. C. (2013). *Substance abuse: Information for school counselors, social workers, therapists, and counselors* (5th ed.). Boston, MA: Pearson Education.

Fisher, M. A. (2008). Protecting confidentiality rights: The need for an ethical practice model. *American Psychologist, 63,* 1–13.

Fitzgerald, T. D., Hunter, P. V., Hadjistavropoulos, T., & Koocher, G. P. (2010). Ethical and legal considerations for Internet-based psychotherapy. *Cognitive Behaviour Therapy, 39,* 173–187.

Foa, E. B. (1997). Trauma and women: Course, predictors, and treatment. *Journal of Clinical Psychiatry, 58,* 25–28.

Foa, E. B., Chrestman, K. R., & Gilboa-Schechtman, E. (2009). *Prolonged exposure therapy for adolescents with PTSD: Emotional processing of traumatic experiences, therapist guide.* New York: Oxford University Press.

Foa, E., Hembree, E. A., & Rothbaum, B. O. (2007). *Prolonged exposure for PTSD: Emotional processing of traumatic experiences, therapist guide.* New York: Oxford University Press.

Foa, E. B., & Kozak, M. J. (1986). Emotional processing of fear: Exposure to corrective information. *Psychological Bulletin, 99,* 20–35.

Foa, E. B., & Kozak, M. J. (1998). Clinical applications of bioinformational theory: Understanding anxiety and its treatment. *Behavior Therapy, 29,* 675–690.

Folkman, S. (Ed.). (2011). *The Oxford handbook of stress, health, and coping.* Oxford University Press.

Follette, V. M., & Ruzek, J. I. (Eds.). (2006). *Cognitive-behavioral therapies for trauma* (2nd ed.). New York: Guilford Press.

Folstein, M. F., Folstein, S. E., & McHugh, P. R. (1975). Mini-mental state: A practical method for grading the cognitive state of patients for the clinician. *Journal of Psychiatric Research, 12*, 189–198.

Fong, M. L., & Cox, B. G. (1983). Trust as an underlying dynamic in the counseling process: How clients test trust. *Personnel and Guidance Journal, 62*, 163–166.

Fong, T., Jones, R., Rudolph, J., Yang, F., Tommet, D., Habtemariam, D., … Inouye, S. (2011). Development and validation of a brief cognitive assessment tool. *Archives of Internal Medicine, 171*, 432–437.

Ford, J. D. (2005). Treatment implications of altered neurobiology, affect regulation and information processing following child maltreatment. *Psychiatric Annals, 35*, 410–419.

Ford, J. D., Albert, D. B., & Hawke, J. (2009). Prevention and treatment interventions for traumatized children: Restoring children's capacities for self-regulation. In D. Brom, R. Pat-Yorenczyuk, & J. D. Ford (Eds.), *Treating traumatized children: Risk, resilience, and recovery* (pp. 195–209). New York: Guilford Press.

Forsyth, J. P., Fusé, T., & Acheson, D. T. (2009). Interoceptive exposure for panic disorder. In W. O'Donohue & J. E. Fisher (Eds.), *General principles and empirically supported techniques of cognitive behavior therapy* (pp. 394–406). Hoboken, NJ: Wiley.

Fowler, M. S. (2010). Treatment of late-life insomnia in female participants living in a rural community using a multi-component self-help intervention. *Dissertation Abstracts International, 71*(2-B), 1329.

Fox, M. H., & Kim, K. (2004). Understanding emerging disabilities. *Disability & Society, 19*, 323–337.

Franco, C., Mañas, I., Cangas, J., Moreno, E., & Gallego, J. (2010). Reducing teachers' psychological distress through a mindfulness training program. *Spanish Journal of Psychology, 13*(2), 655–686.

Franklin, C., Trepper, T. S., Gingerich, W. J., & McCollum, E. E. (Eds.). (2012). *Solution-focused brief therapy: A handbook of evidence-based practice.* New York: Oxford University Press.

Franklin, M. E., Ledley, D. A., & Foa, E. B. (2009). Response prevention. In W. O'Donohue & J. E. Fisher (Eds.), *General principles and empirically supported techniques of cognitive behavior therapy* (pp. 543–549). Hoboken, NJ: Wiley.

Frayne, C. A., & Geringer, J. M. (2000). Self-management training for improving job performance: A field experiment involving salespeople. *Journal of Applied Psychology, 85*(3), 361–372.

Freedland, K., Skala, J., Carney, R., Raczynski, J., Taylor, C., Mendes de Leon, C., … Veith, R. (2002). The depression interview and structured Hamilton (DISH): Rationale, development, characteristics, and clinical validity. *Psychosomatic Medicine, 64*, 897–905.

Fremouw, W., Strunk, J. M., Tyner, A., & Musick, R. (2005). Adolescent suicide assessment protocol–20. In L. Vandecreek & J. B. Allen (Eds.), *Innovations in clinical practice* (pp. 207–224). Sarasota, FL: Professional Resource.

Fremouw, W., Tyner, E. A., Strunk, J. M., & Musick, R. (2008). Suicidal adult assessment protocol–SAAP. In L. Vandercreek (Ed.), *Innovations in clinical practice.* Sarasota, FL: Professional Resource.

Fried, R. (1993). The role of respiration in stress and stress control: Toward a theory of stress as a hypoxic phenomenon. In P. M. Lehrer & R. L. Woolfolk (Eds.), *Principles and practice of stress management* (2nd ed., pp. 301–331). New York: Guilford Press.

Fuertes, J. N., Stracuzzi, T. I., Bennett, J., Scheinholtz, J., Mislowack, A., Hersh, M., & Cheng, D. (2006). Therapist multicultural competency: A study of therapy dyads. *Psychotherapy: Theory, Research, Practice, Training, 43*, 480–490.

Fulford, K. W. M., Caroll, H., & Peile, E. (2011). Values-based practice: Linking science with people. *Journal of Contemporary Psychotherapy, 41*, 145–156.

Fuller-Rowell, T. E., Evans, G. W., & Ong, A. D. (2012). Poverty and health: The mediating role of perceived discrimination. *Psychological Science, 23*(7), 734–739.

Fullerton, C. A., Busch, A. B., Normand, S. L., McGuire, T. G., & Epstein, A. M. (2011). Ten-year trends in quality of care and spending for depression: 1996 through 2005. *Archives of General Psychiatry, 68*, 1218–1226.

Gabbay, V., Oatis, M. D., Silva, R. R., & Hirsch, G. S. (2004). Epidemiological aspects of PTSD in children and adolescents. In R. R. Silva (Ed.), *Posttraumatic stress disorders in children and adolescents* (pp. 1–17). New York: Norton.

Gallagher, M. W., Thompson-Hollands, J., Bourgeois, M. L., & Bentley, K. H. (2015). Cognitive behavioral treatments for adult posttraumatic stress disorder: Current status and future directions. *Journal of Contemporary Psychotherapy, 45*, 235–243.

Gallegos, A. M., Hoerger, M., Talbot, N. L., Krasner, M. S., Knight, J. M., Moynihan, J. A., & Duberstein, P. R. (2013). Toward identifying the effects of the specific components of mindfulness-based stress reduction on biologic and emotional outcomes among older adults. *The Journal of Alternative and Complementary Medicine, 19*(10), 787–792.

Galletly, C. L., Glasman, L. R., Pinkerton, S. D., & DiFanceisco, W. (2012). New Jersey's HIV exposure law and the HIV-related attitudes, beliefs, and sexual and seropositive status disclosure behaviors of persons living with HIV. *American Journal of Public Health, 102*, 2135–2140.

Galletly, C. L., Pinkerton, S. D., & DiFranceisco, W. (2012). A quantitative study of Michigan's criminal HIV exposure law. *AIDS Care, 24*, 174–179.

Gambrill, E. (2010). Evidence-informed practice: Antidote to propaganda in the helping professions? *Research on Social Work Practice, 20*, 302–320.

Gambrill, E. D. (2012). *Critical thinking in clinical practice: Improving the quality of judgments and decisions* (3rd ed.). Hoboken, NJ: Wiley.

Gamito, P., Oliveira, J., Rosa, Pedro, Morais, D., Duarte, N., Oliveira, S., & Saraiva, T. (2010). PTSD elderly war veterans: A clinical controlled pilot study. *Cyberpsychology, Behavior, and Social Networking, 13*, 43–48.

Gammon, E. A. (2000). Examining the needs of culturally diverse rural caregivers who have adults with severe developmental disabilities living with them. *Families in Society, 81*, 174–185.

Garcia, J. G., Cartwright, B., Winston, S. M., & Borzuchowska, B. (2003). A transcultural integrative model for ethical decision making in counseling. *Journal of Counseling & Development, 81*, 268–277.

Gardiner, H. W., & Kosmitzki, C. (2011). *Lives across cultures: Cross-cultural human development* (5th ed.). Boston, MA: Pearson Education.

Garner, R. (2008). Police stress: Effects of criticism management training on health. *Applied Psychology in Criminal Justice, 4*(2), 244–259.

Garvin, C. D. (2009). Developing goals. In A. R. Roberts (Ed.), *Social workers' desk reference* (2nd ed., pp. 521–526). New York: Oxford University Press.

Gary, F. A. (2005). Stigma: Barrier to mental health care among ethnic minorities. *Issues in Mental Health Nursing, 26*, 979–999.

Gaston, G. B., & Alleyne-Green, B. (2013). The impact of African Americans' beliefs about HIV medical care on treatment adherence: A systematic review and recommendations for interventions. *AIDS and Behavior, 17*, 31–40.

Gayes, L. A., & Steele, R. G. (2014). A meta-analysis of motivational interviewing interventions for pediatric health behavior change. *Journal of Consulting and Clinical Psychology, 82*, 521–535.

Gaytan, F. X. (2010). The role of social capital and social support from adults in the academic self-efficacy, identity, and engagement of Mexican immigrant youth in New York City, *Dissertation Abstracts International, 71*(2-B), 1373.

Gazda, G., Balzer, F., Childers, W., Nealy, A., Phelps, R., & Walters, R. (2005). *Human relations development* (7th ed.). Boston, MA: Allyn & Bacon.

Gehart, D., & McCollum, E. (2008). Inviting therapeutic presence: A mindfulness-based approach. In S. Hicks & T. Bien (Eds.), *Mindfulness and the healing relationship* (pp. 176–194). New York: Guilford Press.

Geller, S. M., & Greenberg, L. S. (2002). Therapeutic presence: Therapists' experience of presence in the psychotherapy encounter. *Person-centered and Experiential Psychotherapies, 1*, 71–86.

Gelso, C. J., & Hayes, J. A. (1998). *The psychotherapy relationship*. New York: Wiley.

Gelso, C. J., & Hayes, J. A. (2002). The management of countertransference. In J. C. Norcross (Ed.), *Psychotherapy relationships that work: Therapist contributions and responsiveness to patients* (pp. 267–284). New York: Oxford University Press.

Gelso, C. J., & Hayes, J. A. (2007). *Countertransference and the therapist's inner experience: Perils and possibilities.* Mahwah, NJ: Erlbaum.

Gelso, C. J., Hill, C. E., Mohr, J., Rochlen, A., & Zack, J. (1999). Describing the face of transference: Psychodynamic therapists' recollections about transference in cases of successful long-term therapy. *Journal of Counseling Psychology, 46*, 257–267.

Gelso, C. J., Latts, M. G., Gomez, M. J., & Fassinger, R. E. (2002). Countertransference management and therapy outcome: An initial evaluation. *Journal of Clinical Psychology, 58*, 861–867.

Gelso, C. J., & Samstag, L. W. (2008). A tripartite model of the therapeutic relationship. In S. D. Brown & R. W. Lent (Eds.), *Handbook of counseling psychology* (4th ed., pp. 267–283). Hoboken, NJ: Wiley.

George, L. K., Larson, D. B., Koenig, H. G., & McCullough, M. E. (2000). Spirituality and health:

What we know, what we need to know. *Journal of Social and Clinical Psychology, 19,* 102–116.

Geppert, C. M. A. (2013). Legal and ethical issues. In B. S. McCrady & E. E. Epstein (Eds.), *Addictions: A comprehensive guidebook* (2nd ed., pp. 625–640). New York: Oxford University Press.

Germer, C. K. (2005). Mindfulness: What is it? What does it matter? In C. K. Germer, R. D. Siegel, & P. R. Fulton (Eds.), *Mindfulness and psychotherapy* (pp. 3–27). New York: Guilford Press.

Germer, C. K., & Neff, K. D. (2013). Self-compassion in clinical practice. *Journal of Clinical Psychology, 69,* 856–867.

Germer, C. K., Siegel, R. D., & Fulton, P. R. (Eds.). (2005). *Mindfulness and psychotherapy.* New York: Guilford Press.

Gerson, R., McGoldrick, M., & Petry, S. (2008). *Genograms.* New York: Norton.

Gibb, B. E., Beevers, C. G., & McGeary, J. E. (2013). Toward an integration of cognitive and genetic models of risk for depression. *Cognition & Emotion, 27*(2), 193–216.

Gingerich, S., & Mueser, K. T. (2007). Family intervention for severe mental illness. In T. Ronen & A. Freeman (Eds.), *Cognitive behavior therapy in clinical social work practice* (pp. 327–351). New York: Springer.

Gingerich, W. J., & Eisengart, S. (2000). Solution-focused brief therapy: A review of the outcome research. *Family Process, 39,* 477–498.

Gingerich, W. J., & Peterson, L. T. (2012). Effectiveness of solution-focused brief therapy: A systematic qualitative review of controlled outcome studies. *Research on Social Work Practice, 23,* 266–283.

Goldin, P. R., Ziv, M., Jazaieri, H., Werner, K., Kraemer, H., Heimberg, R. G., & Gross, J. J. (2012). Cognitive reappraisal self-efficacy mediates the effects of individual cognitive-behavioral therapy for social anxiety disorder. *Journal of Consulting and Clinical Psychology, 80*(6), 1034–1040.

Goldstein, M. G., DePue, J., & Kazura, A. N. (2009). Models of provider-patient interaction and shared decision-making. In S. A. Shumaker, J. K. Ockene, & K. A. Riekert (Eds.), *The handbook of health behavior change* (pp. 107–125). New York: Springer.

Goleman, D. (1988). *The meditative mind.* New York: Jeremy P. Tarcher/Perigee.

González, H. M., Vega, W. A., Williams, D. R., Tarraf, W., West, B. T., & Neighbors, H. W. (2010). Depression care in the United States: Too little for too few. *Archives of General Psychiatry, 67,* 37–46.

González-Prendes, A. A., & Thomas, S. A. (2009). Culturally sensitive treatment of anger in African American women: A single case study. *Clinical Case Studies, 8,* 383–402.

Good, G. E., & Robertson, J. M. (2010). To accept a pilot? Addressing men's ambivalence and altering their expectations about therapy. *Psychotherapy: Theory, Research, Practice, Training, 47,* 306–315.

Goodheart, C. D. (2011). Design for tomorrow. *American Psychologist, 66,* 339–347.

Goodman, L. A., Litwin, A., Bohlig, A., Weintraub, S. R., Green, A., Walker, J., … Ryan, N. (2007). Applying feminist therapy to community practice: Empowerment intervention for low-income women with depression. In E. Aldarondo (Ed.), *Advancing social justice through clinical practice* (pp. 265–290). Mahwah, NJ: Erlbaum.

Gorrindo, T., & Groves, J. E. (2009). Computer simulation and virtual reality in the diagnosis and treatment of psychiatric disorders. *Academic Psychiatry, 33*(5), 413–417.

Gosch, E. A., Flannery-Schroeder, E., Mauro, C. F., & Compton, S. N. (2006). Principles of cognitive–behavioral therapy for anxiety disorders in children. *Journal of Cognitive Psychotherapy, 20*(3), 247–262.

Gould, C., Edelstein, B. A., & Ciliberti, C. (2009). Older adults. In D. Segal & M. Hersen (Eds.), *Diagnostic Interviewing* (4th ed., pp. 467–494). New York: Springer.

Goyal, M., Singh, S., Sibinga, E. M., Gould, N. F., Rowland-Seymour, A., Sharma, R., … Haythornthwaite, J. A. (2014). Meditation programs for psychological stress and well-being: A systematic review and meta-analysis. *JAMA Internal Medicine, 174*(3), 357–368.

Granholm, E., Ben-Zeev, D., Fulford, D., & Swendsen, J. (2013). Ecological momentary assessment of social functioning in schizophrenia: Impact of performance appraisals and affect on social interactions. *Schizophrenia Research, 145,* 120–124.

Grant, B. F., Stinson, F. S., Dawson, D. A., Chou, S. P., Ruan, W. J., & Pickering, R. P. (2004a). Co-occurrence of 12-month alcohol and drug use disorders and personality disorders in the United States. *Archives of General Psychiatry, 61,* 361–368.

Grant, B. F., Stinson, F. S., Dawson, D. A., Chou, S. P., Dufour, M. C., Compton, W., … Kaplan, K. (2004b). Prevalence and co-occurrence of substance use disorders and independent mood and anxiety disorders. *Archives of General Psychiatry, 61,* 807–816.

Grant, J. A., Courtemanche, J., & Rainville, P. (2011). A non-elaborative mental stance and decoupling of executive and pain-related cortices predicts low pain sensitivity in Zen meditators. *Pain, 152*(1), 150–156.

Grantham, S., Pidano, A. E., & Whitcomb, J. M. (2014). Female graduate students' attitudes after leadership training. *Journal of Leadership Studies, 8*(1), 6–16.

Granvold, D. K. (2007). Working with couples. In T. Ronen & A. Freeman (Eds.), *Cognitive behavior therapy in clinical social work practice* (pp. 303–326). New York: Springer.

Grave, R. D. (2005). A multi-step cognitive behaviour therapy for eating disorders. *European Eating Disorders Review, 13,* 373–382.

Greason, P. B., & Cashwell, C. S. (2009). Mindfulness and counseling self-efficacy: The mediating role of attention and empathy. *Counselor Education and Supervision, 49,* 2–19.

Greco, A., Steca, P., Pozzi, R., Monzani, D., Malfatto, G., & Parati, G. (2015). The influence of illness severity on health satisfaction in patients with cardiovascular disease: The mediating role of illness perception and self-efficacy beliefs. *Behavioral Medicine, 41*(1), 9–17.

Green, R. (2007). Gay and lesbian couples in therapy: A social justice perspective. In E. Aldarondo (Ed.), *Advancing social justice through clinical practice* (pp. 119–150). Mahwah, NJ: Erlbaum.

Greenberg, J. S. (1996). *Comprehensive stress management.* Madison, WI: Brown and Benchmark.

Greenberg, L. S. (2011). *Emotion-focused therapy.* Washington, DC: American Psychological Association.

Greenberg, L. S., Rice, L. N., & Elliott, R. (1993). *Facilitating emotional change.* New York: Guilford Press.

Greene, B. (2009). The use and abuse of religious beliefs in dividing and conquering between socially marginalized groups: The same-sex marriage debate. *American Psychologist, 64,* 698–709.

Greene, M. P., & Blitz, L. V. (2012). The elephant is not pink: Talking about white, black, and brown to achieve excellence in clinical practice. *Clinical Social Work Journal, 40,* 203–212.

Greenson, R. (1967). *The technique and practice of psychoanalysis.* New York: International Universities.

Greeson, J. M. (2009). Mindfulness research update. *Complementary Health Practice Review, 14,* 10–18.

Gregg, J. A., Callaghan, G. M., Hayes, S. C., & Glenn-Lawson, J. L. (2007). Improving diabetes self-management through acceptance, mindfulness, and values: A random-ized controlled trial. *Journal of Consulting and Clinical Psychology, 75,* 336–343.

Grella, C. E., & Stein, J. A. (2006). Impact of program services on treatment outcomes of patients with comorbid mental and substance use disorders. *Psychiatric Services, 57,* 1007–1015.

Grepmair, L., Metterlehner, F., Lowe, T., Bachler, E., Rother, W., & Nickel, M. (2007). Promoting mindfulness in psychotherapists in training influences the treatment results of their patients: A randomized double-blind, controlled study. *Psychotherapy and Psychosomatics, 76,* 332–338.

Grillon, C. (2009). D-Cycloserine facilitation of fear extinction and exposure-based therapy might rely on lower-level automatic mechanisms. *Biological Psychiatry, 66,* 636–641.

Griner, D., & Smith, T. B. (2006). Culturally adapted mental health interventions: A meta-analytic review. *Psychotherapy: Theory, Research, Practice, Training, 43,* 531–548.

Gros, D. F., Yoder, M., Tuerk, P. W., Lozano, B. E., & Acierno, R. (2011). Exposure therapy for PTSD delivered to veterans via telehealth: Predictors of treatment completion and outcome and comparison to treatment delivered in person. *Behavior Therapy, 42,* 276–283.

Gulchak, D. J. (2008). Using a mobile handheld computer to teach a student with an emotional and behavioral disorder to self-monitor attention. *Education and Treatment of Children, 31*(4), 567–581.

Gunn, C. (2001). Chapter 2: Flight of the Appalachian bumblebee: Solution-oriented brief therapy with a young adult. *Journal of College Student Psychotherapy, 16,* 13–25.

Haley, J. (Ed.). (1967). *Advanced techniques of hypnosis and therapy: Selected papers of Milton H., Erickson, M. D.* Boston, MA: Allyn & Bacon.

Halpern, J., & Tramontin, M. (2007). *Disaster mental health.* Belmont, CA: Thomson Brooks/Cole.

Hamada, H., Martin, D., & Batty, H. P. (2006). Adapting an effective counseling model from patient-centered care to improve motivation in clinical training programs. *Medical Education Online, 11,* 1–6. Retrieved from http://www.med-ed-online.org

Hamilton, N. A., Kitzman, H., & Guyotte, S. (2006). Enhancing health and emotion: Mindfulness as a missing link between cognitive therapy and positive psychology. *Journal of Cognitive Psychotherapy, 20*(2), 123–134.

Hansen, B., Vogel, P. A., Stiles, T. C., & Götestman, K. G. (2007). Influence of co-morbid generalized anxiety disorder, panic disorder and personality disorders on the outcome of cognitive behavioural treatment of obsessive-compulsive disorder. *Cognitive Behaviour Therapy, 36*, 145–155.

Hansen, N. B., Lambert, M. J., & Forman, E. M. (2002). The psychotherapy dose-response effect and its implications for treatment delivery systems. *Clinical Psychology: Science and Practice, 9*, 329–343.

Hanson, R., & Mendius, R. (2009). *Buddha's brain: The practical neuroscience of happiness, love, and wisdom.* Oakland, CA: New Harbinger.

Hara, K. M., Westra, H. A., Aviram, A., Button, M. L., Constantino, M. J., & Antony, M. A. (2015). Therapist resistance of client resistance in cognitive-behavioral therapy for generalized anxiety disorder. *Cognitive Behaviour Therapy, 44*, 162–174.

Hardy, G., Cahill, J., & Barkham, M. (2007). Active ingredients of the therapeutic relationship that promote client change: A research perspective. In P. Gilbert & R. L. Leahy (Eds.), *The therapeutic relationship in the cognitive behavioural psychotherapies* (pp. 24–42). New York: Routledge/Taylor & Francis.

Harmon, C., Hawkins, E. J., Lambert, M. J, Slade, K., & Whipple, J. L. (2005). Improving outcomes for poorly responding clients: The use of clinical support tools and feedback to clients. *JCLP/In Session, 61*, 175–185.

Harned, M. S., Banawan, S. F., & Lynch, T. R. (2006). Dialectical behavior therapy: An emotion-focused treatment for borderline personality disorder. *Journal of Contemporary Psychotherapy, 36*, 67–75.

Harned, M. S., Korslund, K. E., Foa, E. B., & Linehan, M. M. (2012). Treating PTSD in suicidal and self-injuring women with Borderline Personality Disorder: Development and preliminary evaluation of a Dialectical Behavior Therapy prolonged exposure protocol. *Behaviour Research and Therapy, 50*, 381–386.

Harris, S. E., & Kurpius, S. E. R. (2014). Social networking and professional ethics: Client searches, informed consent, and disclosure. *Professional Psychology: Research and Practice, 45*, 11–19.

Hartman, A. (1979). The extended family as a resource for change: Ecological approach to family-centered practice. In C. B. Germain (Ed.), *Social work practice: People and environments* (pp. 239–266). New York: Columbia.

Hartman, A. (1994). Diagrammatic assessment of family relationships. In B. R. Compton & B. Galaway (Eds.), *Social work processes* (5th ed., pp. 153–165). Pacific Grove, CA: Cengage Learning.

Harvey, I. S. (2006). Self-management of a chronic illness: An exploratory study on the role of spirituality among older African American women. *Journal of Women and Aging, 18*(3), 75–88.

Harvey, I. S., & Silverman, M. (2007). The role of spirituality in the self-management of chronic illness among older Africans and Whites. *Journal of Cross-Cultural Gerontology, 22*(2), 205–220.

Hatfield, D., McCullough, L., Frantz, S. H. B., & Krieger, K. (2010). Do we know when our clients get worse? An investigation of therapists' ability to detect negative client change. *Clinical Psychology and Psychotherapy, 17*, 25–32.

Hatzenbuehler, M. L. (2009). How does sexual minority stigma "get under the skin"? A psychological mediation framework. *Psychological Bulletin, 135*, 707–730.

Hayes, J. A., Gelso, C., & Hummel, A. (2011). Managing countertransference. In J. C. Norcross (Ed.), *Psychotherapy relationships that work: Evidence-based responsiveness* (2nd ed., pp. 239–260). New York: Oxford University Press.

Hayes, S. C. (2004). Acceptance and commitment therapy, relational frame theory, and the third wave of behavioral and cognitive therapies. *Behavior Therapy, 35*, 639–665.

Hayes, S. C., Folette, V. M., & Linehan, M. M. (Eds.). (2004). *Mindfulness and acceptance: Expanding the cognitive–behavioral tradition.* New York: Guilford Press.

Hayes, S. C., Levin, M. E., Plumb-Vilardaga, J., Villatte, J. L., & Pistorello, J. (2013). Acceptance and commitment therapy and contextual behavioral science: Examining the progress of a distinctive model of behavioral and cognitive therapy. *Behavior Therapy, 44*(2), 180–198.

Hayes, S. C., & Strosahl, K. D. (Eds.). (2004). *A practical guide to acceptance and commitment therapy.* New York: Springer.

Hayes, S. C., Strosahl, K. D., Bunting, K., Twohig, M., & Wilson, K. G. (2004). What is acceptance and commitment therapy? In S. C. Hayes & K. D. Strosahl (Eds.), *A practical guide to acceptance and commitment therapy* (pp. 1–29). New York: Springer.

Hayes, S. C., Strosahl, K. D., & Wilson, K. G. (2012). *Acceptance and commitment therapy: The process and practice of mindful change* (2nd ed.). New York: Guilford Press.

Hayes, S. C., Villatte, M., Levin, M., & Hildebrandt, M. (2011). Open, aware, and active: Contextual approaches as an emerging trend in the behavioral and cognitive therapies. *Annual Review of Clinical Psychology, 7*, 141–168.

Haynes, S. N. (2006). Psychometric considerations. In M. Hersen (Ed.), *Clinician's handbook of adult behavioral assessment* (pp. 17–41). Burlington, MA: Elsevier Academic.

Haynes, S. N., Nelson, K. G., Thacher, I., & Keaweaimoku, K. (2002). Outpatient behavioral assessment and treatment target selection. In M. Hersen & L. K. Porzelius (Eds.), *Diagnosis, conceptualization, and treatment planning for adults* (pp. 35–70). Mahwah, NJ: Lawrence Erlbaum.

Haynes, S. N., O'Brien, W. H., & Kaholokula, J. K. (2011). *Behavioral assessment and case formulation.* Hoboken, NJ: Wiley.

Haynes, S. N., Smith, G. T., & Hunsley, J. D. (2011). *Scientific foundations of clinical assessment.* New York: Routledge/Taylor & Francis.

Hays, P. A. (1995). Multicultural applications of cognitive behavior therapy. *Professional Psychology, 26,* 309–315.

Hays, P. A. (2006). Cognitive-behavioral therapy with Alaska native people. In P. A. Hays & G. Y. Iwamasa (Eds.), *Culturally responsive cognitive-behavioral therapy* (pp. 47–71). Washington, DC: American Psychological Association.

Hays, P. A. (2008). *Addressing cultural complexities in practice: Assessment, diagnosis, and therapy* (2nd ed.). Washington, DC: American Psychological Association.

Hays, P. A. (2009). Integrating evidence-based practice, cognitive behavior therapy, and multicultural therapy: Ten steps for culturally competent practice. *Professional Psychology: Research and Practice, 40,* 354–360.

Hays, P. A. (2013). *Connecting across cultures: The helper's toolkit.* Thousand Oaks, CA: Sage.

Hays, P. A. (2014). An international perspective on the adaptation of CBT across cultures. *Australian Psychologist, 49,* 17–18.

Hays, P. A., & Iwamasa, G. Y. (2006). *Culturally responsive cognitive-behavioral therapy.* Washington, DC: American Psychological Association.

Hayward, R. D., & Krause, N. (2013). Trajectories of late-life change in God-mediated control. *The Journals of Gerontology Series B: Psychological Sciences and Social Sciences, 68*(1), 49–58.

Hazlett-Stevens, H., & Craske, M. G. (2003). Live (*in vivo*) exposure. In W. O'Donohue, J. E. Fisher, & S. C. Hayes (Eds.), *Cognitive behavior therapy: Applying empirically supported techniques in your practice* (pp. 223–228). Hoboken, NJ: Wiley.

Hazlett-Stevens, H., & Craske, M. G. (2009). Breathing retraining and diaphragmatic breathing. In W. T.

O'Donohue & J. E. Fisher (Eds.), *General principles and empirically supported techniques of cognitive behavior therapy* (pp. 166–172). Hoboken, NJ: Wiley.

Hazlett-Stevens, H., & Craske, M. G. (2009). Live (*in vivo*) exposure. In W. O'Donohue & J. E. Fisher (Eds.), *General principles and empirically supported techniques of cognitive behavior therapy* (pp. 407–414). Hoboken, NJ: Wiley.

Head, L. S., & Gross, A. M. (2009). Systematic desensitization. In W. O'Donohue & J. E. Fisher (Eds.), *General principles and empirically supported techniques of cognitive behavior therapy* (pp. 640–647). Hoboken, NJ: Wiley.

Heffner, J. L., Tran, G. Q., Johnson, C. S., Barrett, S. W., Blom, T. J., Thompson, R. D., & Anthenelli, R. M. (2010). Combining motivational interviewing with compliance enhancement therapy (MI-CET): Development and preliminary evaluation of a new, manual-guided psychosocial adjunct to alcohol-dependence pharmacotherapy. *Journal of Studies on Alcohol and Drugs, 71,* 61–70.

Helms, J. E. (2015). An examination of the evidence in culturally adapted evidence-based or empirically supported interventions. *Transcultural Psychiatry, 52,* 174–197.

Hembree, E. A., Cahill, S. P., & Foa, E. B. (2004). Impact of personality disorders on treatment outcome for female assault survivors with chronic posttraumatic stress disorder. *Journal of Personality Disorders, 18,* 117–127.

Henderson, D., & Thompson, C. (2011). *Counseling children* (8th ed.). Belmont, CA: Cengage Learning.

Hendricks, G. (1995). *Conscious breathing.* New York: Bantam.

Henggeler, S. W., Schoenwald, S. K., Borduin, C. M., Rowland, M. D., & Cunningham, P. B. (2009). *Multisystemic therapy for antisocial behavior in children and adolescents* (2nd ed.). New York: Guilford Press.

Henretty, J., & Levitt, H. (2010). The role of therapist self-disclosure in psychotherapy: A qualitative review. *Clinical Psychology Review, 30,* 63–77.

Hepworth, D. H., Rooney, R. H., Dewberry Rooney, G., & Strom-Gottfried, K. (2013). *Direct social work practice* (9th ed.). Belmont, CA: Cengage Learning.

Herbeck, D. M., Hser, Y., & Teruya, C. (2008). Empirically supported substance abuse treatment approaches: A survey of treatment providers' perspectives and practices. *Addictive Behaviors, 33,* 699–712.

Herlihy, B. J., Hermann, M. A., & Greden, L. R. (2014). Legal and ethical implications of using religious beliefs as the basis for refusing to counsel certain clients. *Journal of Counseling & Development, 92,* 148–153.

Hermann, M. A., & Herlihy, B. R. (2006). Legal and ethical implications of refusing to counsel homosexual clients. *Journal of Counseling & Development, 84,* 414–418.

Hermans, D., Dirikx, T., Vansteenwegenin, D., Baeyens, F., Van den Bergh, O., & Eelen, P. (2005). Reinstatement of fear responses in human aversive conditioning. *Behaviour Research and Therapy, 43,* 533–551.

Hernández, P., Carranza, M., & Almeida, R. (2010). Mental health professionals' adaptive responses to racial microaggressions: An exploratory study. *Professional Psychology: Research and Practice, 41,* 202–209.

Herring, S. J., Cruice, J. F., Bennett, G. G., Davey, A., & Foster, G. D. (2014). Using technology to promote postpartum weight loss in urban, low-income mothers: A pilot randomized controlled trial. *Journal of Nutrition Education and Behavior, 46*(6), 610–615.

Hettema, J. E., & Hendricks, P. S. (2010). Motivational interviewing for smoking cessation: A meta-analytic review. *Journal of Consulting and Clinical Psychology, 78,* 868–884.

Hettema, J., Steele, J., & Miller, W. R. (2005). Motivational interviewing. *Annual Review of Clinical Psychology, 1,* 91–111.

Hill, C. E. (2014). *Helping skills* (4th ed.). Washington, DC: American Psychological Association.

Hill, C. E. (2005). Therapist techniques, client involvement, and the therapeutic relationship: Inextricably intertwined in the therapy process. *Psychotherapy: Theory, Research, Practice, Training, 42,* 431–442.

Hill, C. E., Gelso, C. J., Chui, H., Spangler, P. T., Hummel, A., Huang, T., ... Miles, J. R. (2013). To be or not to be immediate with clients: The use and perceived effects of immediacy in psychodynamic/interpersonal psychotherapy. *Psychotherapy Research, 24,* 299–315.

Hill, C. E., & Nutt-Williams, S. E. (2000). The process of individual therapy. In S. D. Brown & R. W. Lent (Eds.), *Handbook of counseling psychology* (pp. 670–710). New York: Wiley.

Hill, D. M., Craighead, L. W., & Safer, D. L. (2011). Appetite-focused dialectical behavior therapy for the treatment of binge eating with purging: A preliminary trial. *International Journal of Eating Disorders, 44,* 249–261.

Hinton, D. W., Rivera, E. I., Hofmann, S. G., Barlow, D. G., & Otto, M. W. (2012). Adapting CBT for traumatized refugees and ethnic minority patients: Examples from culturally adapted CBT (CA-CBT). *Transcultural Psychiatry, 49,* 340–365.

Hodges, K. (1997). *Child and adolescent functional assessment scale.* Ann Arbor, MI: Functional Assessment System.

Hoffmann, M. L. (2000). *Empathy and moral development.* New York: Cambridge University Press.

Hofmann, S. G. (2014). D-cycloserine for treating anxiety disorders: Making good exposures better and bad exposures worse. *Depression and Anxiety, 31*(3), 175–177.

Hofmann, S. G., Asmundson, G. J., & Beck, A. T. (2013). The science of cognitive therapy. *Behavior Therapy, 44,* 199–212.

Hofmann, S. G., Meuret, A. E., Smits, J. A., Simon, N. M., Pollack, M. H., Eisenmenger, K., ... Otto, M. W. (2006). Augmentation of exposure therapy with D-cycloserine for social anxiety disorder. *Archives of General Psychiatry, 63,* 298–304.

Hofmann, S. G., & Otto, M. W. (2008). *Cognitive behavioral therapy for social anxiety disorder: Evidence-based and disorder-specific treatment techniques.* New York: Routledge.

Hofmann, S. G., & Smits, J. A. J. (2008). Cognitive-behavioral therapy for adult anxiety disorders: A meta-analysis of randomized placebo-controlled trials. *Journal of Clinical Psychiatry, 69,* 621–632.

Hogarth, L., Balleine, B. W., Corbit, L. H., & Killcross, S. (2013). Associative learning mechanisms under pinning the transition from recreational drug use to addiction. *Annals of the New York Academy of Sciences, 1282*(1), 12–24.

Hoge, E. A., Chen, M. M., Orr, E., Metcalf, C. A., Fischer, L. E., Pollack, M. H., ... Simon, N. M. (2013). Loving-Kindness Meditation practice associated with longer telomeres in women. *Brain, Behavior, and Immunity, 32,* 159–163.

Hoglend, P., Amlo, S., Marble, A., Bogwald, K. P., Sorbye, O., Sjaastad, M. G., & Heyerdahl, O. (2006). Analysis of the patient–therapist relationship in dynamic psychotherapy: An experimental study of transference interpretations. *American Journal of Psychiatry, 163,* 1739–1746.

Hogue, T. E. (1994). Goal attainment scaling: A measure of clinical impact and risk assessment. *Issues in Criminological and Legal Psychology, 21,* 96–102.

Hollon, S. D., Areán, P. A., Craske, M. G., Crawford, K. A., Kivlahan, D. R., Magnavita, J. J., ... Kurtzman, H. (2014). Development of clinical practice guidelines. *Annual Review of Clinical Psychology, 10,* 213–241.

Holyoake, D. D., & Golding, E. (2012). Multiculturalism and solution-focused psychotherapy: An exploration of the nonexpert role. *Asia Pacific Journal of Counselling and Psychotherapy, 3*, 72–81.

Hölzel, B. K., Lazar, S. W., Gard, T., Schuman-Olivier, Z., Vago, D. R., & Ott, U. (2011). How does mindfulness meditation work? Proposing mechanisms of action from a conceptual and neural perspective. *Perspectives on Psychological Science, 6*, 537–559.

Hood, H. K., Rogojanski, J., & Moss, T. G. (2014). Cognitive-behavioral therapy for chronic insomnia. *Current Treatment Options in Neurology, 16*(12), 321.

Hoop, J. G., DiPasquale, T., Hernandez, J. M., & Roberts, L. W. (2008). Ethics and culture in mental health care. *Ethics & Behavior, 18*, 353–372.

Hope, D. A., Heimberg, R. G., & Turk, C. L. (2010). *Managing social anxiety: A cognitive-behavioral therapy approach* (2nd ed.). New York: Oxford University Press.

Hopwood, C. J., & Bornstein, R. F. (Eds.). (2014). *Multimethod clinical assessment.* New York: Guilford Press.

Horvath, A. O., Del Re, A. C., Fluckiger, C., & Symonds, D. (2011). Alliance in individual psychotherapy. In J. C. Norcross (Ed.), *Psychotherapy relationships that work: Evidence-based responsiveness* (2nd ed., pp. 25–69). New York: Oxford University Press.

Hourani, L. L., Kizakevich, P. N., Hubal, R., Spira, J., Strange, L. B., Holiday, D. B., … McLean, A. N. (2011). Predeployment stress inoculation training for primary prevention of combat-related stress disorders. *Journal of CyberTherapy & Rehabilitation, 4*, 101–116.

Howard, K. I., Kopte, S. M., Krause, M. S., & Orlinsky, D. E. (1986). The dose-effect relationship in psychotherapy. *American Psychologist, 41,* 159–164.

Howard, K. I., Lueger, R. J., Maling, M. S., & Martinovich, Z. (1993). A phase model of psychotherapy outcome: Causal mediation of change. *Journal of Consulting and Clinical Psychology, 61*, 678–685.

Howard, K. I., Moras, K., Brill, P. L., Martinovich, Z., & Lutz, W. (1996). Evaluation of psychotherapy: Efficacy, effectiveness, and patient progress. *American Psychologist, 51,* 1059–1064.

Hsu, S. H., Grow, J., & Marlatt, G. A. (2009). Mindfulness and addiction. *Recent Developments in Alcoholism, 18*, 1–22.

Hsu, W. (2009). The facets of empowerment in solution-focused brief therapy for lower-status married women in Taiwan: An exploratory study. *Women & Therapy, 32*, 338–360.

Huey Jr., S. J., Tilley, J. L., Jones, E. O., & Smith, C. A. (2014). The contribution of cultural competence to evidence-based care for ethnically diverse populations. Annual Review of Clinical Psychology, 10, 305–338.

Hughes, P. P., & Goldstein, M. M. (2015). Privacy, security, and regulatory considerations as related to behavioral health information technology. In L. A. Marsch, S. E. Lord, & J. Dallery (Eds.), *Behavioral healthcare and technology: Using science-based innovations to transform practice* (pp. 224–238). New York: Oxford University Press.

Hülsheger, U. R., Alberts, H. J., Feinholdt, A., & Lang, J. W. (2013). Benefits of mindfulness at work: The role of mindfulness in emotion regulation, emotional exhaustion, and job satisfaction. *Journal of Applied Psychology, 98*(2), 310–325.

Hunsley, J., & Lee, C. (2014). *Introduction to clinical psychology* (2nd ed.). Hoboken, NJ: Wiley.

Hunsley, J., & Mash, E. (2007). Evidence-based assessment. *Annual Review of Clinical Psychology, 3,* 29–51.

Hunsley, J., & Mash, E. (2008). *A guide to assessments that work.* New York: Oxford University Press.

Hunsley, J., & Mash, E. J. (2010). The role of assessment in evidence-based practice. In M. M. Antony & D. H. Barlow (Eds.), *Handbook of assessment and treatment planning for psychological disorders* (2nd ed., pp. 3–22). New York: Guilford Press.

Hunter, J. A. (2010). Prolonged exposure treatment of chronic PTSD in juvenile sex offenders: Promising results from two case studies. *Child & Youth Care Forum, 39*, 367–384.

Hutchins, D., & Cole-Vaught, C. (1997). *Helping relationships and strategies* (3rd ed.). Pacific Grove, CA: Cengage Learning.

Hwang, W. (2009). The formative method for adapting psychotherapy (FMAP): A community-based developmental approach to culturally adapting therapy. *Professional Psychology: Research and Practice, 40*, 369–377.

Hwang, S. K., & Charnley, H. (2010). Making the familiar strange and making the strange familiar: Understanding Korean children's experiences of living with an autistic sibling. *Disability & Society, 25*(5), 579–592.

Hyde, J., Hankins, M., Deale, A., & Marteau, T. M. (2008). Interventions to increase self-efficacy in the context of addiction behaviours: A systematic literature review. *Journal of Health Psychology, 13*(5), 607–623.

Ince, B. Ü., Cuijpers, P., van't Hof, E., van Ballegooijen, W., Christensen, H., & Riper, H. (2013). Internet-based, culturally sensitive, problem-solving therapy for Turkish migrants with depression: Randomized controlled trial. *Journal of Medical Internet Research*, 5(10), 248–262.

Ingram, B. (2012). *Clinical case formulations* (2nd ed.). Hoboken, NJ: Wiley.

Ingram, R., Hayes, A., & Scott, W. (2000). Empirically supported treatments: A critical analysis. In C. Snyder & R. Ingram (Eds.), *Handbook of psychological change* (pp. 40–60). New York: Wiley.

Institute of Medicine. (2008). *Treatment of posttraumatic stress disorder: An assessment of the evidence.* Washington, DC: National Academies Press.

Isakson, B. L., & Jurkovic, G. J. (2013). Healing after torture: The role of moving on. *Qualitative Health Research, 23*(6), 749–761.

Ivey, A. E., & Brooks-Harris, J. E. (2005). Integrative psychotherapy with culturally diverse clients. In J. C. Norcross & M. R. Goldfried (Eds.), *Handbook of psychotherapy integration* (2nd ed., pp. 321–339). New York: Oxford University Press.

Ivey, A. E., D'Andrea, M., Ivey, M. B., & Simek-Morgan, L. (2007). *Theories of counseling and psychotherapy: A multicultural perspective* (6th ed.). Boston, MA: Pearson Education.

Ivey, A. E., Gluckstern, N. B., & Ivey, M. B. (1997). *Basic influencing skills*. North Amherst, MA: Microtraining Associates.

Ivey, A. E., Gluckstern Packard, N. B., & Ivey, M. B. (2006). *Basic attending skills* (4th ed.). North Amherst, MA: Microtraining Associates.

Ivey, A. E., & Ivey, M. B. (2000). Developmental counseling and therapy and multicultural counseling and therapy: Metatheory, contextual consciousness, and action. In D. C. Locke, J. E. Myers, & E. L. Herr (Eds.), *The handbook of counseling* (pp. 219–236). Thousand Oaks, CA: Sage.

Ivey, A. E., Ivey, M. B., & Zalaquett, C. P. (2014). *Intentional interviewing and counseling* (8th ed.). Belmont, CA: Cengage Learning.

Iwamasa, G. Y., Hsia, C., & Hinton, D. (2006). Cognitive-behavioral therapy with Asian Americans. In P. A. Hays & G. Y. Iwamasa (Eds.), *Culturally responsive cognitive-behavioral therapy* (pp. 117–140). Washington, DC: American Psychological Association.

Izycky, A., Braham, L., Williams, L., & Hogue, T. (2010). Goal attainment scaling: Usefulness of a tool to measure risk in violent mentally disordered offenders. *British Journal of Forensic Practice, 12*(2), 14–22.

Jaffee v. Redmond, WL 315841 (U.S. June 13, 1996).

Jané-Llopis, E., & Matytsina, I. (2006). Mental health and alcohol, drugs and tobacco: A review of the comorbidity between mental disorders and the use of alcohol, tobacco and illicit drugs. *Drug and Alcohol Review, 25*, 515–536.

Jaser, S. S., Fear, J. M., Reeslund, K. L., Champion, J. E., Reising, M. M., & Compas, B. E. (2008). Maternal sadness and adolescents' responses to stress in offspring of mothers with and without a history of depression. *Journal of Clinical Child and Adolescent Psychology, 37*(4), 736–746.

Jenaro, C., Flores, N., & Arias, B. (2007). Burnout and coping in human service practitioners. *Professional Psychology: Research and Practice, 38*, 80–87.

Jennings, L., & Skovholt, T. M. (1999). The cognitive, emotional, and relational characteristics of master therapists. *Journal of Counseling Psychology, 46*, 3–11.

Jennings, L., Skovholt, T. M., Goh, M., & Lian, F. (2013). Master therapists: Explorations of expertise. In M. H. Rønnestad & T. M. Skovholt (Eds.), *The developing practitioner: Growth and stagnation of therapists and counselors* (pp. 213–246). New York: Taylor & Francis/Routledge.

Jennings, L., Sovereign, A., Bottorff, N., Mussell, M. P., & Vye, C. (2005). Nine ethical values of master therapists. *Journal of Mental Health Counseling, 27*, 32–47.

Jennings, P. A., Frank, J. L., Snowberg, K. E., Coccia, M. A., & Greenberg, M. T. (2013). Improving classroom learning environments by Cultivating Awareness and Resilience in Education (CARE): Results of a randomized controlled trial. *School Psychology Quarterly, 28*(4), 374–390.

Jensen, C. D., Cushing, C. C., Aylward, B. S., Craig, J. T., Sorell, D. M., & Steele, R. G. (2011). Effectiveness of motivational interviewing interventions for adolescent substance use behavior change: A meta-analytic review. *Journal of Consulting and Clinical Psychology, 79*, 433–440.

Jernigan, V. B. B. (2010). Community-based participatory research with Native American communities: The chronic disease self-management program. *Health Promotion Practice, 11*(6), 888–899.

Jimenez, D. E., Cook, B., Bartels, S. J., & Alegría, M. (2013). Disparities in mental health service use of racial and ethnic minority elderly adults. *Journal of the American Geriatrics Society, 61*, 18–25.

Johnson, D. W. (2014). *Reaching out: Interpersonal effectiveness and self-actualization* (11th ed.). Upper Saddle River, NJ: Pearson Education.

Johnson, W. B., & Buhrke, R. A. (2006). Service delivery in a "don't ask, don't tell" world: Ethical care of gay, lesbian, and bisexual military personnel. *Professional Psychology: Research and Practice, 37*, 91–98.

Jonas, E., Graupmann, V., Kayser, D. N., Zanna, M., Traut-Mattausch, E., & Frey, D. (2009). Culture, self, and the emergence of reactance: Is there a "universal" freedom? *Journal of Experimental Social Psychology, 45*, 1068–1080.

Jones, D. L., Owens, M. I., Lydston, D., Tobin, J. N., Brondolo, E., & Weiss, S. M. (2010). Self-efficacy and distress in women with AIDS: The SMART/EST women's project. *AIDS Care, 22*(12), 1499–1508.

Jones, K. D. (2010). The unstructured clinical interview. *Journal of Counseling & Development, 88*, 220–226.

Jones-Smith, E. (2014). *Strengths-based therapy.* Thousand Oaks, CA: Sage.

Jonsson, H., & Hougaard, E. (2009). Group cognitive behavioral therapy for obsessive-compulsive disorder: A systematic review and meta-analysis. *Acta Psychiatrica Scandinavica, 119*, 98–106.

Josselson, R. (1992). *The space between us: Exploring the dimensions of human relationships.* San Francisco: Jossey-Bass.

Kabat-Zinn, J. (1990). *Full-catastrophe living: Using the wisdom of your body and mind to face stress, pain, and illness.* New York: Bantam Doubleday.

Kabat-Zinn, J. (1993). Meditation. In B. Moyers (Ed.), *Healing and the mind* (pp. 115–144). New York: Doubleday.

Kabat-Zinn, J. (1994). *Wherever you go, there you are: Mindfulness meditation in everyday life.* New York: Hyperion.

Kabat-Zinn, J. (2003). Mindfulness-based interventions in context: Past, present, and future. *Clinical Psychology: Science and Practice, 10*, 144–156.

Kabat-Zinn, J. (2005). *Coming to our senses: Healing ourselves and the world through mindfulness.* New York: Hyperion.

Kadera, S. W., Lambert, M. J., & Andrews, A. A. (1996). How much therapy is really enough? A session-by-session analysis of the psychotherapy dose-effect relationship. *Journal of Psychotherapy, Practice and Research, 5*, 132–151.

Kahn, A. P. (2006). *The encyclopedia of stress and stress-related diseases.* New York: Facts on File.

Kahn, M. (1991). *Between therapist and client: The new relationship.* New York: Freeman.

Kahneman, D., & Klein, G. (2009). Conditions for intuitive expertise: A failure to disagree. *American Psychologist, 64*, 515–526.

Kalibatseva, Z., & Leong, F. T. L. (2014). A critical review of culturally sensitive treatments for depression: Recommendations for intervention and research. *Psychological Services, 11*, 433–450.

Kalichman, S. C., Simbayi, L. C., Cloete, A., Cherry, C., Strebel, A., Kalichman, M. O., … Cain, D. (2008). HIV/AIDS risk reduction and domestic violence prevention intervention for South African men. *International Journal of Men's Health, 7*(3), 255–273.

Kaliman, P., Alvarez-Lopez, M. J., Cosín-Tomás, M., Rosenkranz, M. A., Lutz, A., & Davidson, R. J. (2014). Rapid changes in histone deacetylases and inflammatory gene expression in expert meditators. *Psychoneuroendocrinology, 40*, 96–107.

Kanfer, F. H., & Gaelick-Buys, L. (1991). Self-management methods. In F. H. Kanfer & A. P. Goldstein (Eds.), *Helping people change* (4th ed., pp. 305–360). New York: Pergamon.

Kantor, J. R. (1970). An analysis of the experimental analysis of behavior (TEAB). *Journal of the Experimental Analysis of Behavior, 13*, 101–108.

Kaplan, D. M. (2014). Ethical implications of a critical legal case for the counseling profession: *Ward v. Wilbanks. Journal of Counseling & Development, 92*, 142–146.

Kapuscinski, A. N., & Masters, K. S. (2010). The current status of measures of spirituality: A critical review of scale development. *Psychology of Religion & Spirituality, 2*(4), 191–205.

Karls, J. M., & O'Keefe, M. E. (2008). *Person-in-environment system manual* (2nd ed.). Washington, DC: National Association of Social Workers.

Karls J. M., & Wandrei, K. E. (1994). *Person-in-environment system: The PIE classification system for social functioning problems.* Washington, DC: National Association of Social Workers.

Karnieli-Miller, O., & Eisikovits, A. (2009). Physician as partner or salesman? Shared decision-making in real-time encounters. *Social Science & Medicine, 69*, 1–8.

Karno, M. P., & Longabaugh, R. (2005). Less therapist directiveness is associated with better outcomes among reactant clients. *Journal of Consulting and Clinical Psychology, 73*, 262–267.

Karno, M. P., Longabaugh, R., & Herbeck, D. (2010). What explains the relationship between the therapist structure X patient reactance interaction and drinking outcome? An examination of potential mediators. *Psychology of Addictive Behaviors, 24*, 600–607.

Karoly, P. (2005). Self-monitoring. In M. Hersen & J. Rosquist (Eds.), *Encyclopedia of behavior modification and cognitive behavior therapy* (Vol. 1, pp. 521–525). Thousand Oaks, CA: Sage.

Kasckow, J., Brown, C., Morse, J. Q., Kaerpov, I., Bensasi, S., Thomas, S. B., … Reynolds, C. (2010). Racial preference for participation in a depression prevention trial involving problem-solving therapy. *Psychiatric Services, 61*(7), 722–724.

Kasser, T. (2002). Sketches for a self-determination theory of values. In E. L. Deci & R. M. Ryan (Eds.), *Handbook of self-determination research* (pp. 123–140). Rochester, NY: University of Rochester Press.

Kauer, S. D., Reid, S. C., Crooke, A. H. D., Khor, A., Hearps, S. J. C., Jorm, A. F., …Patton, G. (2012). Self-monitoring using mobile phones in the early stages of adolescent depression: Randomized controlled trial. *Journal of Medical Internet Research, 14*(3), e67.

Kelly, P. J., Ramaswamy, M., Chen, H. F., & Denny, D. (2015). Wellness and illness self-management skills in community corrections. *Issues in Mental Health Nursing, 36*(2), 89–95.

Keeton v. Anderson-Wiley et al., 733 F. Supp. 2d 1368 (S.D.Geo. 2010).

Kehle-Forbes, S. M., Polusny, M. A., Erbes, C. R., & Gerould, H. (2014). Acceptability of prolonged exposure therapy among U.S. Iraq war veterans with PTSD symptomology. *Journal of Traumatic Stress, 27*, 483–487.

Kelly, E. W., Jr. (1995). Counselor values: A national survey. *Journal of Counseling & Development, 73*, 648–653.

Kelly, S. (2006). Cognitive-behavioral therapy with African Americans. In P. A. Hays & G. Y. Iwamasa (Eds.), *Culturally responsive cognitive-behavioral therapy* (pp. 97–116). Washington, DC: American Psychological Association.

Kemp, R., David, A., & Hayward, P. (1996). Compliance therapy: An intervention targeting insight and treatment adherence in psychotic patients. *Behavioural and Cognitive Psychotherapy, 24*, 331–350.

Kemp, S., Whittaker, J., & Tracy, E. (1997). *Person-environment practice: The social ecology of interpersonal helping.* New York: Aldine de Gruyter.

Kenney, K. R., & Kenney, M. E. (2012). Contemporary US multiple heritage couples, individuals, and families: Issues, concerns, and counseling implications. *Counselling Psychology Quarterly, 25*, 99–112.

Kessler, R. C., Demler, O., Frank, R. G., Olfson, M., Pincus, H. A., Walters, E. E., … Zaslavsky, A. M. (2005). Prevalence and treatment of mental disorders, 1990 to 2003. *New England Journal of Medicine, 352*, 2515–2523.

Kienast, T., & Foerster, J. (2008). Psychotherapy of personality disorders and concomitant substance dependence. *Current Opinion in Psychiatry, 21*(6), 619–624.

Kier, F. J., & Davenport, D. S. (2004). Unaddressed problems in the study of spirituality and health. *American Psychologist, 59*, 53–54.

Kilmer, R. P., & Gil-Rivas, V. (2010). Exploring post-traumatic growth in children impacted by Hurricane Katrina: Correlates of the phenomenon and developmental considerations. *Child Development, 81*(4), 1211–1227.

Kim, B. S. K., Hill, C. E., Gelso, C. J., Goates, M. K., Asay, P. A., & Harbin, J. M. (2003). Counselor self-disclosure, East Asian American client adherence to Asian cultural values, and counseling process. *Journal of Counseling Psychology, 50*, 324–332.

Kim, D., Wampold, B. E., & Bolt, D. M. (2006). Therapist effects in psychotherapy: A random-effects modeling of the National Institute of Mental Health Treatment of Depression Collaborative Research Program data. *Psychotherapy Research, 16*, 161–172.

Kim, J. S. (2008). Examining the effectiveness of solution-focused brief therapy: A meta-analysis. *Research on Social Work Practice, 18*, 107–116.

Kim, J. S., & Franklin, C. (2009). Solution-focused brief therapy in schools: A review of the outcome literature. *Children and Youth Services Review, 31*, 464–470.

Kim, J. S., Smock, S., Trepper, T. S., McCollum, E. E., & Franklin, C. (2010). Is solution-focused brief therapy evidence-based? *Families in Society, 91*, 300–306.

Kiosses, D. N., Arean, P. A., Teri, L., & Alexopoulos, G. S. (2010). Home-delivered problem adaptation therapy (PATH) for depressed, cognitively impaired, disabled elders: A preliminary study. *American Journal of Geriatric Psychiatry, 18*(11), 988–998.

Kiresuk, T. J., & Sherman, R. E. (1968). Goal attainment scaling: A general method for evaluating comprehensive mental health programs. *Community Mental Health Journal, 4*, 443–453.

Kiresuk, T. J., Smith, A., & Cardillo, J. E. (Eds.). (1994). *Goal attainment scaling: Applications, theory, and measurement.* Hillsdale, NJ: Erlbaum.

Kirschenbaum, H., & Jourdan, A. (2005). The current status of Carl Rogers and the Person Centered Approach. *Psychotherapy: Theory, Research, Practice, Training, 42,* 37–51.

Klein, K. J., & Knight, A. P. (2005). Innovation implementation: Overcoming the challenge. *Current Directions in Psychological Science, 14,* 243–246.

Kleinman, A. (2004). Culture and depression. *New England Journal of Medicine, 351,* 951–953.

Kliem, S., Kroger, C., & Kosfelder, J. (2010). Dialectical behavior therapy for borderline personality disorder: A meta-analysis using mixed-effects modeling. *Journal of Consulting and Clinical Psychology, 78*(6), 936–951.

Knapp, M., Hall, J., & Horgan, T. (2014). *Nonverbal communication in human interaction* (8th ed.). Boston, MA: Cengage Wadsworth.

Knapp, S., Lemoncelli, J., & VandeCreek, L. (2010). Ethical responses when patients' religious beliefs appear to harm their well-being. *Professional Psychology: Research and Practice, 41*(5), 405–412.

Knipscheer, J. W., & Kleber, R. J. (2004). A need for ethnic similarity in the therapist-patient interaction? Mediterranean migrants in Dutch mental health care. *Journal of Clinical Psychology, 60,* 543–554.

Kocet, M. M., & Herlihy, B. J. (2014). Addressing value-based conflicts within the counseling relationship: A decision-making model. *Journal of Counseling & Development, 92,* 180–186.

Kocovski, N. L., & Endler, N. S. (2000). Self-regulation: Social anxiety and depression. *Journal of Applied Biobehavioral Research, 5*(1), 80–91.

Koerner, K. (2007). Case formulation in dialectical behavior therapy for borderline personality disorder. In T. D. Eells (Ed.), *Handbook of psychotherapy case formulation* (2nd ed., pp. 317–348). New York: Guilford Press.

Koerner, K. (2012). *Doing dialectical behavior therapy: A practical guide.* New York: Guilford Press.

Kohut, H. (1971a). *The analysis of the self.* New York: International Universities.

Kohut, H. (1971b). *The restoration of the self.* New York: International Universities.

Kohut, H. (1984). *How does analysis cure?* Chicago, IL: University of Chicago Press.

Kolden, G. G., Klein, M. H., Wang, C, C., & Austin, S. B. (2011). Congruence. In J. C. Norcross (Ed.), *Psychotherapy relationships that work: Evidence-based responsiveness* (2nd ed., pp. 187–202). New York: Oxford University Press.

Koocher, G. P. (2008). Ethical challenges in mental health services to children and families. *Journal of Clinical Psychology: In Session, 64,* 601–612.

Kopta, S. M., Howard, K. I., Lowry, J. L., & Beutler, L. E. (1994). Patterns of symptomatic recovery in psychotherapy. *Journal of Consulting and Clinical Psychology, 62,* 1009–1016.

Korman, H., Bevelas, J. B., & De Jong, P. (2013). Microanalysis of formulations in solution-focused brief therapy, cognitive behavioral therapy, and motivational interviewing. *Journal of Systemic Therapies, 32,* 31–45.

Kort, J. (2008). *Gay affirmative therapy for the straight clinician: The essential guide.* New York: W. W. Norton.

Kosic, A., Mannetti, L., & Sam, D. L. (2006). Self-monitoring: A moderating role between acculturation strategies and adaptation of immigrants. *International Journal of Intercultural Relations, 30*(2), 141–157.

Kost-Smith, L. E., Pollock, S. J., Finkelstein, N. D., Cohen, G. L., Ito, T. A., Miyake, A., … Singh, C. (2012, February). Replicating a self-affirmation intervention to address gender differences: Successes and challenges. *AIP Conference Proceedings-American Institute of Physics, 1413*(1), 231.

Kottler, J. A., & Shepard, D. S. (2015). *Introduction to counseling: Voices from the field* (8th ed.). Stamford, CT: Cengage Learning.

Koven, L., Shreve-Nieger, A., & Edelstein, B. (2007). Interview of older adults. In M. Hersen & J. C. Thomas (Eds.), *Handbook of clinical interviewing with adults* (pp. 392–406). Los Angeles, CA: Sage.

Kramer, G. M., Mishkind, M. C., Luxton, D. D., & Shore, J. H. (2013). Managing risk and protecting privacy in telemental health: An overview of legal, regulatory, and risk-management issues. In K. Myers & C. L. Turvey (Eds.), *Telemental health: Clinical, technical, and administrative foundations for evidence-based practice* (pp. 83–107). Amsterdam, Netherlands: Elsevier.

Krasner, M. S., Epstein, R. M., Beckman, H., Suchman, A. L., Chapman, B., Mooney, C. J., & Quill, T. E. (2009). Association of an educational program in mindful communication with burnout, empathy, and attitudes among primary care physicians. *JAMA, 302*(12), 1284–1293.

Kraus, M. W., Cote, S., & Keltner, D. (2010). Social class, contextualism, and empathic accuracy. *Psychological Science, 21,* 1716–1723.

Krijn, M., Emmelkamp, P. M. G., Olafsson, R. P., & Biemond, R. (2004). Virtual reality exposure therapy of anxiety disorders: A review. *Clinical Psychology Review, 24*, 259–281.

Kristeller, J. L. (2007). Mindfulness meditation. In P. M. Lehrer, R. L. Woolfolk, & W. E. Sime (Eds.), *Principles and practice of stress management* (3rd ed., pp. 393–427). New York: Guilford Press.

Kuhl, J., & Baumann, N. (2000). Self-regulation and rumination: Negative affect and impaired self-accessibility. In W. J. Perrig & A. Grob (Eds.), *Control of human behavior, mental processes, and consciousness: Essays in honor of the 60th birthday of August Frammer* (pp. 283–305). Mahwah, NJ: Erlbaum.

Kumar, V. K., Cohen, C., Porter, J., & Jyothi, C. (2008). Managing obesity: Treatment approaches and psychological strategies. *Journal of Indian Psychology, 26*(1–2), 79–94.

Kuyken, W., Padesky, C. A., & Dudley, R. (2009). *Collaborative case conceptualization: Working effectively with clients in cognitive-behavioral therapy.* New York: Guilford Press.

Kvillemo, P., & Bränström, R. (2011). Experiences of a mindfulness-based stress-reduction intervention among patients with cancer. *Cancer Nursing, 34*(1), 24–31.

Laidlaw, K., Thompson, L. W., Dick-Siskin, L., & Gallagher-Thompson, D. (2003). *Cognitive behavioral therapy with older people.* West Sussex, UK: Wiley.

Lambert, M. J. (1992). Implications of outcome research for psychotherapy integration. In J. C. Norcross & M. R. Goldfried (Eds.), *Handbook of psychotherapy integration* (pp. 94–129). New York: Basic Books.

Lambert, M. J. (2010a). *Prevention of treatment failure: The use of measuring, monitoring, and feedback in clinical practice.* Washington, DC: American Psychological Association.

Lambert, M. J. (2010b). Yes, it is time for clinicians to routinely monitor treatment outcome. In B. L. Duncan, S. D. Miller, B. E. Wampold, & M. A. Hubble (Eds.), *The heart and soul of change: Delivering what works in therapy* (2nd ed., pp. 239–266). Washington, DC: American Psychological Association.

Lambert, M. J. (2013). The efficacy and effectiveness of psychotherapy. In M. J. Lambert (Ed.), *Bergin and Garfield's handbook of psychotherapy and behavior change* (6th ed., pp. 169–218). New York: Oxford University Press.

Lambert, M. J., Garfield, S. L., & Bergin, A. E. (2004). Overview, trends, and future issues. In M. J. Lambert (Ed.), *Bergin and Garfield's handbook of psychotherapy and behavior change* (5th ed., pp. 805–821). New York: Wiley.

Lambert, M. J., & Ogles, B. M. (2004). The efficacy and effectiveness of psychotherapy. In M. J. Lambert (Ed.), *Bergin and Garfield's handbook of psychotherapy and behavior change* (5th ed., pp. 139–193). New York: Wiley.

Lambert, S. F., & Lawson, G. (2013). Resilience of professional counselors following Hurricanes Katrina and Rita. *Journal of Counseling & Development, 91*, 261–268.

Lang, A. J., & Craske, M. G. (2000). Manipulations of exposure-based therapy to reduce return of fear: A replication. *Behaviour Research and Therapy, 38*, 1–12.

Lang, P. J. (1977). Imagery in therapy: An information processing analysis of fear. *Behavior Therapy, 8*, 862–886.

Lang, P. J. (1993). From emotional imagery to the organization of emotion in memory. In N. Birbaumer & A. Öhman (Eds.), *The structure of emotion* (pp. 69–92). Seattle, WA: Hogrefe & Huber.

Lang, P. J., Cuthbert, B. N., & Bradley, M. M. (1998). Measuring emotion in therapy: Imagery, activation, and feeling. *Behavior Therapy, 29*, 655–674.

Lanius, R. A., Vermetten, E., & Pain, C. (Eds.). (2010). *The impact of early life trauma on health and disease: The hidden epidemic.* Cambridge: Cambridge University Press.

LaRoche, M. J., & Christopher, M. S. (2009). Changing paradigms from empirically supported treatment to evidence-based practice: A cultural perspective. *Professional Psychology: Research and Practice, 40*, 396–402.

Lau, A. W., & Kinoshita, L. M. (2006). Cognitive-behavioral therapy with culturally diverse older adults. In P. A. Hays & G. Y. Iwamasa (Eds.), *Culturally responsive cognitive-behavioral therapy* (pp. 179–197). Washington, DC: American Psychological Association.

Lawson, D. (1994). Identifying pretreatment change. *Journal of Counseling & Development, 72*, 244–248.

Lazarus, A. A. (1989). *The practice of multimodal therapy.* Baltimore, MD: Johns Hopkins.

Lazarus, R. S., & Folkman, S. (1984). *Stress, appraisal, and coping.* New York: Springer.

Leahy, R. (1996). *Cognitive therapy: Basic principles and implications.* Northvale, NJ: Aronson.

Leahy, R. (2003). *Cognitive therapy techniques: A practitioner's guide.* New York: Guilford Press.

Leahy, R. L. (2007). Schematic mismatch in the therapeutic relationship: A social-cognitive model. In P. Gilbert & R. L. Leahy (Eds.), *The therapeutic* relationship in the cognitive behavioural psychotherapies (pp. 229–254). New York: Routledge/Taylor & Francis.

Leahy, R. L. (2010). Emotional schemas in treatment-resistant anxiety. In D. Sookman & R. L. Leahy (Eds.), *Treatment resistant anxiety disorders: Resolving impasses to symptom remission* (pp. 135–160). New York: Routledge/Taylor & Francis Group.

Leahy, R., & Holland, S. (2000). *Treatment plans and interventions for depression and anxiety disorders.* New York: Guilford Press.

Leahy, R., Holland, S., & McGinn L. K. (2011). *Treatment plans and interventions for depression and anxiety disorders* (2nd ed.). New York: Guilford Press.

Leahy, R. L., Tirch, D. D., & Napolitano, L. A. (2011). *Emotion regulation in psychotherapy: A practitioner's guide.* New York: Guilford Press.

Lê Cook, B., Barry, C. L., & Busch, S. H. (2013). Racial/ethnic disparity trends in children's mental health care access and expenditures from 2002 to 2007. *Health Services Research, 48,* 129–149.

Ledesma, D., & Kumano, J. (2009). Mindfulness-based stress reduction and cancer: A meta-analysis. *Psycho-Oncology, 18*(6), 571–579.

Lee, C. C. (2007). Conclusion: A counselor's call to action. In C. C. Lee (Ed.), *Counseling for social justice* (2nd ed., pp. 259–263). Alexandria, VA: American Counseling Association.

Lee, C. C. (Ed.). (2007). *Counseling for social justice* (2nd ed.). Alexandria, VA: American Counseling Association.

Lee, C. C. (Ed.). (2014). *Multicultural issues in counseling: New approaches to diversity.* Hoboken, NJ: John Wiley & Sons.

Lee, E. (2010). Revisioning cultural competencies in clinical social work practice. *Families in Society, 91,* 272–279.

Lee, J. J., & Miller, S. E. (2013). A self-care framework for social workers: Building a strong foundation for practice. *Families in Society: The Journal of Contemporary Social Services, 94,* 96–103.

Lee, M. Y. (2003). A solution-focused approach to cross-cultural clinical social work practice: Utilizing cultural strengths. *Families in Society, 84,* 385–395.

Lee, M. Y., & Mjelde-Mossey, L. (2004). Cultural dissonance among generations: A solution-focused approach with East Asian elders and their families. *Journal of Marital and Family Therapy, 30,* 497–513.

Lee, M. Y., Ng, S., Leung, P. P. Y., & Chan, C. L. W. (2009). *Integrative body-mind-spirit social work: An empirically based approach to assessment and treatment.* New York: Oxford University Press.

Lee, M. Y., Sebold, J., & Uken, A. (2003). *Solution-focused treatment of domestic violence offenders: Accountability for change.* New York: Oxford University Press.

Lee, M. Y., Uken, A., & Sebold, J. (2007). Role of self-determined goals in predicting recidivism in domestic violence offenders. *Research on Social Work Practice, 17,* 30–41.

Lee, M. Y., Uken, A., & Sebold, J. (2012). Solution-focused model with court-mandated domestic violence offenders. In C. Franklin, T. S. Trepper, W. J. Gingerich, & E. E. McCollum (Eds.), *Solution-focused brief therapy: A handbook of evidence-based practice* (pp. 165–182). New York: Oxford University Press.

Lee, N. K., Cameron, J., & Jenner, L. (2015). A systematic review of interventions for co-occurring substance use and borderline personality disorders. *Drug and Alcohol Review, 34,* 663–672.

Lee, Y., Chiou, P., Chang, P. & Hayter, M. (2011). A systematic review of the effectiveness of problem-solving approaches toward symptom management in cancer care. *Journal of Clinical Nursing, 20*(1–2), 73–85.

Lehman, J. S., Carr, M. H., Nichol, A. J., Ruisanchez, A., Knight, D. W., Langford, A. E., … Mermin, J. H. (2014). Prevalence and public health implications of state laws that criminalize potential HIV exposure in the United States. *AIDS and Behavior, 18,* 997–1006.

Lehmann, P., & Patton, J. D. (2012). The development of a solution-focused fidelity instrument. In C. Franklin, T. S. Trepper, W. J. Gingerich, & E. E. McCollum (Eds.), *Solution-focused brief therapy: A handbook of evidence-based practice* (pp. 39–54). New York: Oxford University Press.

Lehrer, P. M., Woolfolk, R. L., & Sime, W. E. (2007). *Principles and practices of stress management* (3rd ed.). New York: Guilford Press.

Leibert, T. W. (2006). Making change visible: The possibilities in assessing mental health counseling outcomes. *Journal of Counseling & Development, 84,* 108–118.

Leonard, N. R., Jha, A. P., Casarjian, B., Goolsarran, M., Garcia, C., Cleland, C. M., … Massey, Z. (2013). Mindfulness training improves attentional task performance in incarcerated youth: A group randomized controlled intervention trial. *Frontiers in Psychology, 4,* 792.

LePage, J. (2007). *Integrative yoga therapy manual.* Shelby, NC: Integrative Yoga Therapy.

Levis, D. J. (2009). The prolonged CS exposure therapies of implosive (flooding) therapy. In W. O'Donohue & J. E. Fisher (Eds.), *General principles and empirically supported techniques of cognitive behavior therapy* (pp. 370–380). Hoboken, NJ: Wiley.

Levis, D. J., & Krantweiss, A. R. (2003). Working with implosive (flooding) therapy: A dynamic cognitive–behavioral exposure psychotherapy treatment approach. In W. O'Donohue, J. E. Fisher, & S. C. Hayes (Eds.), *Cognitive behavior therapy: Applying empirically supported techniques in your practice* (pp. 463–470). Hoboken, NJ: Wiley.

Levitt, H., Butler, M., & Hill, T. (2006). What clients find helpful in psychotherapy: Developing principles for facilitating moment-to-moment change. *Journal of Counseling Psychology, 53*, 314–324.

Lewis, S. A., Noyes, J., & Hastings, R. P. (2015). Systematic review of epilepsy self management interventions integrated with a synthesis of children and young people's views and experiences. *Journal of Advanced Nursing, 71*(3), 478–497.

Lewis, T. F., & Osborn, C. J. (2004). Solution-focused counseling and motivational interviewing: A consideration of confluence. *Journal of Counseling & Development, 82*, 38–48.

Lewis-Esquerre, J. M., Colby, S. M., Tevyaw, T. O., Eaton, C. A., Kahler, C. W., & Monti, P. M. (2005). Validation of the timeline follow-back in the assessment of adolescent smoking. *Drug and Alcohol Dependence, 79*, 33–43.

Lilienfeld, S. O. (2007). Psychological treatments that cause harm. *Perspectives on Psychological Science, 2*, 53–70.

Lilienfeld, S. O., Ritschel, L. A., Lynn, S. J., Cautin, R. L., & Latzman, R. D. (2013). Why many clinical psychologists are resistant to evidence-based practice: Root causes and constructive remedies. *Clinical Psychology Review, 33*, 883–900.

Lindahl, K. (2003). *Practicing the sacred art of listening: The Listening Center Workshop*. Woodstock, VT: Skylight Paths.

Lindenboim, N., Comtois, K. A., & Linehan, M. M. (2007). Skills practice in dialectical behavior therapy for suicidal women meeting criteria for borderline personality disorder. *Cognitive and Behavioral Practice, 14*(2), 147–156.

Lindfors, O., Knekt, P., Heinonen, E., Härkänen, T., Virtala, E., & the Helsinki Psychotherapy Study Group. (2015). The effectiveness of short- and long-term psychotherapy on personality functioning during a 5-year follow-up. *Journal of Affective Disorders, 173*, 31–38.

Lindfors, O., Knekt, P., Virtala, E., Laaksonen, M. A., & the Helsinki Psychotherapy Study Group. (2012). The effectiveness of solution-focused therapy and short- and long-term psychodynamic psychotherapy on self-concept during a 3-year follow-up. *Journal of Nervous and Mental Disease, 200*, 946–953.

Linehan, M. M. (1993a). *Cognitive-behavioral treatment of borderline personality disorder*. New York: Guilford Press.

Linehan, M. M. (1993b). *Skills training manual for treating borderline personality disorder*. New York: Guilford Press.

Linehan, M. M. (1997). Validation and psychotherapy. In A. Bohart & L. Greenberg (Eds.), *Empathy reconsidered: New directions in psychotherapy* (pp. 353–392). Washington, DC: American Psychological Association.

Linehan, M. (2015a). *DBT skills training handouts and worksheets* (2nd ed.). New York: Guilford Press.

Linehan, M. (2015b). *DBT skills training manual* (2nd ed.). New York: Guilford Press.

Linscott, J., & DiGiuseppe, R. (1998). Cognitive assessment. In A. Bellack & M. Hersen (Eds.), *Behavioral assessment* (4th ed., pp. 104–125). Boston, MA: Allyn & Bacon.

Lipchik, E. (2002). *Beyond technique in solution-focused therapy: Working with emotions and the therapeutic relationship*. New York: Guilford Press.

Lipchik, E., Derks, J., LaCourt, M., & Nunnally, E. (2012). The evolution of solution-focused brief therapy. In C. Franklin, T. S. Trepper, W. J. Gingerich, & E. E. McCollum (Eds.), *Solution-focused brief therapy: A handbook of evidence-based practice* (pp. 3–19). New York: Oxford University Press.

Lipchik, E., & de Shazer, S. (1986). The purposeful interview. *Journal of Strategic and Systemic Therapies, 5*(1–2), 88–99.

Littell, J. H. (2010). Evidence-based practice: Evidence or orthodoxy? In B. L. Duncan, S. D. Miller, B. E. Wampold, & M. A. Hubble (Eds.), *The heart and soul of change: Delivering what works in therapy* (2nd ed., pp. 167–198). Washington, DC: American Psychological Association.

Lo, H., & Fung, K. P. (2003). Culturally competent psychotherapy. *Canadian Journal of Psychiatry, 48*, 161–170.

Locke, E. A., & Latham, G. P. (2002). Building a practically useful theory of goal setting and task motivation: A 35-year odyssey. *American Psychologist, 57*, 705–717.

Lopez, S. J., Pedrotti, J. T., & Snyder, C. R. (2014). *The scientific and practical exploration of human strengths* (3rd ed.). Thousand Oaks, CA: Sage.

Lowe, S. R., Joshi, S., Pietrzak, R. H., Galea, S., & Cerdá, M. (2015). Mental health and general wellness in the aftermath of Hurricane Ike. *Social Science & Medicine, 124,* 162–170.

Lum, D. (2004). *Social work practice and people of color: A process-stage approach* (5th ed.). Belmont, CA: Thomson Brooks/Cole.

Lum, D. (2011). *Culturally competent practice* (4th ed.). Belmont, CA: Cengage Learning.

Lundahl, B., & Burke, B. L. (2009). The effectiveness and applicability of motivational interviewing: A practice-friendly review of four meta-analyses. *Journal of Clinical Psychology: In Session, 65,* 1232–1245.

Lundahl, B. W., Kunz, C., Brownell, C., Tollefson, D., & Burke, B. L. (2010). A meta-analysis of motivational interviewing: Twenty-five years of empirical studies. *Research on Social Work Practice, 20,* 137–160.

Lundahl, B., Moleni, T., Burke, B. L., Butters, R., Tollefson, D., Butler, C., & Rollnick, S. (2013). Motivational interviewing in medical care settings: A systematic review and meta-analysis of randomized controlled trials. *Patient Education and Counseling, 93,* 157–168.

Luoma, J. B., & Hayes, S. C. (2009). Cognitive defusion. In W. O'Donohue & J. E. Fisher (Eds.), *General principles and empirically supported techniques of cognitive behavior therapy* (pp. 181–188). Hoboken, NJ: Wiley.

Lupien, S. J., McEwen, B. S., Gunnar, M. R., & Heim, C. (2009). Effects of stress throughout the lifespan on the brain, behavior, and cognition. *Nature Reviews Neuroscience, 19,* 434–445.

Lutz, A. B. (2014). *Learning solution-focused therapy: An illustrated guide.* Washington, DC: American Psychiatric Publishing.

Lutz, W., Leon, S. C., Martinovich, Z., Lyons, J. S., & Stiles, W. B. (2007). Therapist effects in outpatient psychotherapy: A three-level growth curve approach. *Journal of Counseling Psychology, 54,* 32–39.

Lutz, W., Lowry, J., Kopta, S. M., Einstein, D. A., & Howard, K. I. (2001). Prediction of dose-response relations based on patient characteristics. *Journal of Clinical Psychology, 57,* 889–900.

Lynch, T. R., & Cheavens, J. S. (2008). Dialectical behavior therapy for comorbid personality disorders. *Journal of Clinical Psychology: In Session, 64,* 154–167.

Lyons, H., Bieschke, K., Dendy, A., Worthington, R., & Georgemiller, R. (2010). Psychologists' competence to treat lesbian, gay and bisexual clients: State of the field and strategies for improvement. *Professional Psychology, 41,* 424–234.

Macdonald, A. (2007). *Solution-focused therapy: Theory, research & practice.* Thousand Oaks, CA: Sage.

Maddux, J. E. (2009). Self-efficacy: The power of believing you can. In C. R. Snyder & S. J. Lopez (Eds.), *Oxford handbook of positive psychology* (pp. 335–344). New York: Oxford University Press.

Magill, M., Gaume, J., Apodaca, T. R., Walthers, J., Mastroleo, N. R., Borsar, B., & Longabaugh, R. (2014). The technical hypothesis of motivational interviewing: A meta-analysis of MI's key causal model. *Journal of Consulting and Clinical Psychology, 82,* 973–983.

Magnezi, R., Grosberg, D., Novikov, I., Ziv, A., Shani, M., & Freedman, L. S. (2015). Characteristics of patients seeking health information online via social health networks versus general Internet sites: A comparative study. *Informatics for Health and Social Care, 40*(2), 125–138.

Mahoney, K., & Mahoney, M. J. (1976). Cognitive factors in weight reduction. In J. D. Krumboltz & C. E. Thoresen (Eds.), *Counseling methods* (pp. 99–105). New York: Holt, Rinehart and Winston.

Maimon, D., Browning, C. R., & Brooks-Gunn, J. (2010). Collective efficacy, family attachment, and urban adolescent suicide attempts. *Journal of Health and Social Behavior, 51,* 307–324.

Main, M., & Solomon, J. (1990). Procedures for identifying infants as disorganized/disoriented during the Ainsworth strange situation. In M. Greenberg, D. Cicchetti, & E. M. Cummings (Eds.), *Attachment in the preschool years: Theories, research, and interventions.* Chicago, IL: University of Chicago Press.

Malchiodi, C. A. (Ed.). (2008). *Creative interventions with traumatized children.* New York: Guilford Press.

Malouff, J. M., Thorsteinsson, E. B., & Schutte, N. S. (2007). The efficacy of problem solving therapy in reducing mental and physical health problems: A meta-analysis. *Clinical Psychology Review, 27,* 46–57.

Malow, R. M., Rosenberg, R., & Devieux, J. G. (2009). Cognitive-behavioral stress management interventions for ethnic-minority HIV-positive alcohol/drug abusers in resource limited and culturally diverse communities. *American Journal of Infectious Diseases, 5,* 48–59.

Manuel, J. K., Newville, H., Larios, S. E., & Sorensen, J. L. (2013). Confidentiality protections versus collaborative care in the treatment of substance use disorders. *Addiction Science & Clinical Practice, 8,* 1–7.

Marchand, W. R. (2012). Mindfulness-based stress reduction, mindfulness-based cognitive therapy, and Zen meditation for depression, anxiety, pain, and psychological distress. *Journal of Psychiatric Practice, 18*(4), 233–252.

Marks, I. M. (1975). Behavioural treatments of phobia and obsessive-compulsive disorders: A critical appraisal. In M. Hersen, R. M. Eisler, & P. M. Miller (Eds.), *Progress in behavior modification* (Vol. 2). New York: Academic Press.

Marks, S. (2012). Cognitive behaviour therapies in Britain: The historical context and present situation. In W. Dryden (Ed.), *Cognitive behaviour therapies* (pp. 1–24). Thousand Oaks, CA: Sage.

Marlatt, G. A., & Donovan, D. M. (Eds.). (2005). *Relapse prevention: Maintenance strategies in the treatment of addictive behaviors* (2nd ed.). New York: Guilford Press.

Marlatt, G. A., & Kristeller, J. L. (1999). Mindfulness and meditation. In W. R. Miller (Ed.), *Integrating spirituality into treatment: Resources for practitioners* (pp. 67–84). Washington, DC: American Psychological Association.

Marlatt, G. A., & Witkiewitz, K. (2005). Relapse prevention for alcohol and drug problems. In G. A. Marlatt & D. M. Donovan (Eds.), *Relapse prevention: Maintenance strategies in the treatment of addictive behaviors* (2nd ed., pp. 1–44). New York: Guilford Press.

Marson, S. M., Wei, G., & Wasserman, D. (2009). A reliability analysis of goal attainment scaling (GAS) weights. *American Journal of Evaluation, 30,* 203–216.

Martell, C. R., Safren, S. A., & Prince, S. E. (2004). *Cognitive-behavioral therapies with lesbian, gay, and bisexual clients.* New York: Guilford Press.

Martin, M. Y., Person, S., D., Kratt, P., Prayor-Petterson, H., Kim, Y., Salas, M., & Pisu, M. (2008). Relationship of health behavior theories with self-efficacy among insufficiently active hypertensive African-American women. *Patient Education and Counseling, 72*(1), 137–145.

Martinez, C. (2013). Conducting the cross-cultural clinical interview. In F. Paniagua & A.-M. Yamada (Eds.), *Handbook of multicultural mental health: Assessment and treatment of diverse populations* (2nd ed., pp. 191–204). Amsterdam, Netherlands: Elsevier.

Maruish, M. E. (2002). *Essentials of treatment planning.* New York: Wiley.

Mascaro, J. S., Rilling, J. K., Negi, L. T., & Raison, C. L. (2013). Compassion meditation enhances empathic accuracy and related neural activity. *Social Cognitive and Affective Neuroscience, 8,* 48–55.

Mash, E. J., & Barkley, R. A. (Eds.). (2006). *Treatment of childhood disorders.* New York: Guilford Press.

Mason, W. H., Chandler, M. C., & Grasso, B. C. (1995). Solution based techniques applied to addictions: A clinic's experience in shifting paradigms. *Alcoholism Treatment Quarterly, 13*(4), 39–49.

Matchim, Y., Armer, J. M., & Stewart, B. R. (2011). Effects of mindfulness-based stress reduction (MBSR) on health among breast cancer survivors. *Western Journal of Nursing Research, 33*(8), 996–1016.

Matthews, J. R. (2014). Introduction. *Professional Psychology: Research and Practice, 45,* 1–2.

Maxie, A. C., Arnold, D. H., & Stephenson, M. (2006). Do therapists address ethnic and racial differences in cross-cultural psychotherapy? *Psychotherapy: Theory, Research, Practice, Training, 43,* 85–98.

McCann, R. A., Armstrong, C. M., Skopp, N. A., Edwards-Stewart, A., Smolenski, D. J., June, J. D., … Reger, G. M. (2014). Virtual reality exposure therapy for the treatment of anxiety disorders: An evaluation of research quality. *Journal of Anxiety Disorders, 28*(6), 625–631.

McDonald, J. D., & Gonzalez, J. (2006). Cognitive-behavioral therapy with American Indians. In P. A. Hays & G. Y. Iwamasa (Eds.), *Culturally responsive cognitive-behavioral therapy* (pp. 23–45). Washington, DC: American Psychological Association.

McEwen, B. S. (2012). Brain on stress: How the social environment gets under the skin. *Proceedings of the National Academy of Sciences, 109*(Suppl. 2), 17180–17185.

McEwen, B. S., & Gianaros, P. J. (2010). Central role of the brain in stress and adaptation: Links to socioeconomic status, health, and disease. *Annals of the New York Academy of Sciences, 1186,* 190–222.

McEwen, M. M., Pasvogel, A., Gallegos, G., & Barrera, L. (2010). Type 2 diabetes self-management social support intervention at the U.S.-Mexico border. *Public Health Nursing, 27*(4), 310–319.

McGee, D., Del Vento, A., & Bavelas, J. B. (2005). An interactional model of questions as therapeutic interventions. *Journal of Marital and Family Therapy, 31,* 371–384.

McGill, D. W. (1992). The cultural story in multicultural family therapy. *Families in Society, 73,* 339–349.

McGoldrick, M. (2011). *The genogram journey.* New York: Norton.

McGoldrick, M., Gerson, R., & Shellenberger, S. (1999). *Genograms: Assessment and intervention.* New York: Norton.

McGuigan, F. J., & Lehrer, P. M. (2007). Progressive relaxation: Origins, principles, and clinical applications. In P. M. Lehrer, R. L. Woolfolk, & W. E. Sime (Eds.), *Principles and practice of stress management* (3rd ed., pp. 57–87). New York: Guilford Press.

McKay, M., Wood, C., & Brantley, J. (2007). *The dialectical behavior therapy skills workbook.* Oakland, CA: New Harbinger.

McKergow, M., & Korman, H. (2009). Inbetween—Neither inside nor outside: The radical simplicity of solution-focused brief therapy. *Journal of Systemic Therapies, 28,* 34–49.

McMain, S., Sayrs, J. H. R., Dimeff, L. A., & Linehan, M. M. (2007). Dialectical behavior therapy for individuals with borderline personality disorder and substance dependence. In L. A. Dimeff & K. Koerner (Eds.), *Dialectical behavior therapy in clinical practice* (pp. 145–173). New York: Guilford Press.

McMillan, D., & Morley, S. (2010). Single case quantitative methods for practice-based evidence. In M. Barkham, G. E. Hardy, & J. Mellor-Clark (Eds.), *Developing and delivering practice-based evidence: A guide for the psychological therapies* (pp. 109–138). Chichester, West Sussex, UK: Wiley.

McNally, R. J. (2007). Mechanisms of exposure therapy: How neuroscience can improve psychological treatments for anxiety disorders. *Clinical Psychological Review, 27,* 750–759.

McQuade, J., & Gromova, E. (2015). An examination of treatment outcomes at state licensed mental health clinics. *Journal of Contemporary Psychotherapy, 45,* 177–183.

Meador, K. G., & Koenig, H. G. (2000). Spirituality and religion in psychiatric practice: Parameters and implications. *Psychiatric Annals, 30,* 549–555.

Meador, B., & Rogers, C. (1984). Person-centered therapy. In R. J. Corsini (Ed.), *Current psychotherapies* (pp. 142–195). Itasca, IL: Peacock.

Mellody, P. (2003). *The intimacy factor.* New York: HarperCollins.

Mee-Lee, D., & Gastfriend, D. R. (2008). Patient placement criteria. In M. Galanter & H. D. Kleber (Eds.), *Textbook of substance abuse treatment* (4th ed., pp. 79–91). Washington, DC: American Psychiatric Publishing.

Mee-Lee, D., Shulman, G. D., Fishman, M., Gastfriend, D. R., & Miller, M. M. (Eds.). (2013). *The ASAM Criteria: Treatment criteria for addictive, substance-related, and co-occurring conditions* (3rd ed.). Carson City, NV: The Change Companies®.

Meehan, M., Razzaque, S., Insko, B., Whitton, M., & Brooks, F. P. (2005). Review of four studies on the use of physiological reaction as a measure of presence in stressful virtual environments. *Applied Psychophysiology and Biofeedback, 30,* 239–258.

Meer, D., & VandeCreek, L. (2002). Cultural considerations in release of information. *Ethics and Behavior, 12,* 143–156.

Mehlum, L., Tørmoen, A. J., Ramberg, M., Haga, E., Diep, L. M., Laberg, S., … Grøholt, B. (2014). Dialectical behavior therapy for adolescents with repeated suicidal and self-harming behavior: A randomized trial. *Journal of the American Academy of Child & Adolescent Psychiatry, 53,* 1082–1091.

Meichenbaum, D. H. (1993). Stress inoculation training: A 20-year update. In P. M. Lehrer & R. L. Woolfolk (Eds.), *Principles and practice of stress management* (2nd ed., pp. 373–406). New York: Guilford Press.

Meichenbaum, D. H. (2007). Stress inoculation training: A preventative and treatment approach. In P. M. Lehrer, R. L. Woolfolk, & W. E., Sime (Eds.), *Principles and practices of stress management* (3rd ed., pp. 497–516). New York: Guilford Press.

Meichenbaum, D. H. (2009). Stress inoculation training. In W. T. O'Donohue & J. E. Fisher (Eds.), *General principles and empirically supported techniques of cognitive behavior therapy* (pp. 627–630). Hoboken, NJ: Wiley.

Mennin, D., & Farach, F. (2007). Emotion and evolving treatments for adult psychopathology. *Clinical Psychology: Science and Practice, 14,* 329–352.

Mental Illness Education Project. (Producer). (2000). *Dual diagnosis: An integrated model for the treatment of people with co-occurring psychiatric and substance disorders. A lecture by Kenneth Minkoff, M.D.* (Video available from Mental Illness Education Project Videos, 22-D Hollywood Ave., Hohokus, NJ 07423).

Merideth, P. (2007, February). The five C's of confidentiality and how to deal with them. *Psychiatry, 4*(2) 28–29.

Mermelstein, D. (2010, July 29). The ever curious cellist. *The Wall Street Journal,* p. D8.

Metcalf, C. A., & Dimidjian, S. (2014). Extensions and mechanisms of mindfulness-based cognitive therapy: A review of the evidence. *Australian Psychologist, 49*(5), 271–279.

Meuret, A. E., Rosenfield, D., Seidel, A., Bhaskara, L., & Hofmann, S. G. (2010). Respiratory and cognitive mediators of treatment change of panic disorders: Evidence for intervention specificity. *Journal of Consulting and Clinical Psychology, 78(5),* 691–704.

Meuret, A. E., Wolitsky-Taylor, K. B., Twolig, M. P., & Craske, M. G. (2012). Coping skills and exposure therapy in Panic Disorder and Agoraphobia: Latest advances and future directions. *Behavior Therapy, 43,* 271–284.

Meuret, A. E., Wilhelm, F. H., Ritz, T., & Roth, W. T. (2008). Feedback of end-tidal pCO2 as a therapeutic approach for panic disorder. *Journal of Psychiatric Research, 42,* 560–568.

Meyer, D. D., & Cottone, R. R. (2013). Solution-focused therapy as a culturally acknowledging approach with American Indians. *Journal of Multicultural Counseling and Development, 41,* 47–55.

Michalak, J., Klappheck, M. A., & Kosfelder, J. (2004). Personal goals of psychotherapy patients: The intensity and the "why" of goal-motivated behavior and their implications for the therapeutic process. *Psychotherapy Research, 14,* 193–209.

Mihura, J. L., & Graceffo, R. A. (2014). Multimethod assessment and treatment planning. In C. J. Hopwood & R. F. Bornstein (Eds.), *Multimethod clinical assessment* (pp. 285–318). New York: Guilford Press.

Miller, B. (2007). What creates and sustains commitment to the practice of psychotherapy? *Psychiatric Services, 58,* 174–176.

Miller, C. (2002). Flooding. In M. Hersen & W. Sledge (Eds.), *Encyclopedia of psychotherapy* (Vol. 1, pp. 809–813). New York: Elsevier Science.

Miller, C. K., Headings, A., Peyrot, M., & Nagarja, H. (2012). Goal difficulty and goal commitment affect adoption of a lower glycemic index diet in adults with type 2 diabetes. *Patient Education and Counseling, 86,* 84–90.

Miller, G. (1997). Systems and solutions: The discourses of brief therapy. *Contemporary Family Therapy, 19*(1), 5–22.

Miller, J., & Garran, A. M. (2008). *Racism in the United States: Implications for the helping professions.* Belmont, CA: Thomson Brooks/Cole.

Miller, J. J., Fletcher, K., & Kabat-Zinn, J. (1995). Three-year follow-up and clinical implications of a mindfulness meditation-based stress reduction intervention in the treatment of anxiety disorders. *General Hospital Psychiatry, 17,* 192–200.

Miller, S. D. (1992). The symptoms of solution. *Journal of Strategic and Systemic Therapies, 11,* 1–11.

Miller, S. D. (1994). The solution conspiracy: A mystery in three installments. *Journal of Systemic Therapies, 13,* 18–37.

Miller, S. D., Duncan, B. L., Sorrell, R., & Brown, G. S. (2005). The Partners for Change Outcome Management System. *Journal of Clinical Psychology/In Session, 61,* 199–208.

Miller, T. W., Veltkamp, L. J., Lane, T., Bilyeu, J., & Elzie, N. (2002). Care pathway guidelines for assessment and counseling for domestic violence. *The Family Journal: Counseling and Therapy for Couples and Families, 10,* 41–48.

Miller, W. R. (Ed.). (1999). *Enhancing motivation for change in substance abuse treatment,* Treatment Improvement Protocol Series 35 (DHHS Publication No. SMA 99-3354). Rockville, MD: U.S. Department of Health and Human Services.

Miller, W. R. (2000). Rediscovering fire: Small interventions, large effects. *Psychology of Addictive Behaviors, 14,* 6–18.

Miller, W. R. (2004). The phenomenon of quantum change. *Journal of Clinical Psychology/In Session, 60,* 453–460.

Miller, W. R., Benefield, R. G., & Tonigan, J. S. (1993). Enhancing motivation for change in problem drinking: A controlled comparison of two therapist styles. *Journal of Consulting and Clinical Psychology, 61,* 455–461.

Miller, W. R., & C'de Baca, J. (2001). *Quantum change: When epiphanies and sudden insights transform ordinary lives.* New York: Guilford Press.

Miller, W. R., & Moyers, T. B. (2006). Eight stages in learning motivational interviewing. *Journal of Teaching in the Addictions, 5,* 3–17.

Miller, W. R., & Moyers, T. B. (2015). The forest and the trees: Relational and specific factors in addiction treatment. *Addiction, 110,* 401–413.

Miller, W. R., Moyers, T. B., Amrhein, P., & Rollnick S. (2006, July). A consensus statement on defining change talk. *MINT Bulletin, 13*(2), 6–7.

Miller, W. R., Moyers, T. B., Ernst, D., & Amrhein, P. (2003). *Manual for the motivational interviewing skill code (MISC).* Center on Alcoholism, Substance Abuse and Addiction (CASAA), University of New Mexico. Retrieved from http://casaa.unm.edu/download/misc.pdf

Miller, W. R., & Rollnick, S. (1991). *Motivational interviewing: Preparing people to change addictive behavior.* New York: Guilford Press.

Miller, W. R., & Rollnick, S. (2002). *Motivational interviewing: Preparing people for change* (2nd ed.). New York: Guilford Press.

Miller, W. R., & Rollnick, S. (2004). Talking oneself into change: Motivational interviewing, stages of change, and therapeutic process. *Journal of Cognitive Psychotherapy, 18,* 299–308.

Miller, W. R., & Rollnick, S. (2009). Ten things that motivational interviewing is not. *Behavioural and Cognitive Psychotherapy, 37,* 129–140.

Miller, W. R., & Rollnick, S. (2013). *Motivational interviewing: Helping people change* (3rd ed.). New York: Guilford Press.

Miller, W. R., & Rose, G. S. (2015). Motivational interviewing and decisional balance: Contrasting responses to client ambivalence. *Behavioural and Cognitive Psychotherapy, 43,* 129–141.

Miller, W. R., Yahne, C. E., Moyers, T. B., Martinez, J., & Pirritano, M. (2004). A randomized trial of methods to help clinicians learn motivational interviewing. *Journal of Consulting and Clinical Psychology, 72,* 1050–1062.

Miller, W. R., Zweben, J., & Johnson, W. R. (2005). Evidence-based treatment: Why, what, where, when, and how? *Journal of Substance Abuse Treatment, 29,* 267–276.

Milligan, K., Badali, P., & Spiroiu, F. (2015). Using Integra Mindfulness Martial Arts to address self-regulation challenges in youth with learning disabilities: A qualitative exploration. *Journal of Child and Family Studies, 24,* 562-575.

Milner, C. E., & Belicki, K. (2010). Assessment and treatment of insomnia in adults: A guide for clinicians. *Journal of Counseling & Development, 88,* 236–244.

Milstein, G., Manierre, A., & Yali, A. M. (2010). Psychological care for persons of diverse religions: A collaborative continuum. *Professional Psychology: Research and Practice, 41*(5), 382–390.

Mineka, S., & Zinbarg, R. (2006). A contemporary learning theory perspective on the etiology of anxiety disorders: It's not what you thought it was. *American Psychologist, 61,* 10–26.

Miranda, J., Azocar, F., Organista, K. C., Valdes, D. E., & Arean, P. (2003). Treatment of depression in disadvantaged medical patients. *Psychiatric Services, 54,* 219–225.

Miron, A. M., & Brehm, J. W. (2006). Reactance theory—40 years later. *Zeitschrift für Sozialpsychologie, 37,* 9–18.

Mischel, W. (1973). *Personality and assessment* (2nd ed.). New York: Wiley.

Mitchell, R. W. (2007). *Documentation in counseling records* (3rd ed.). Alexandria, VA: American Counseling Association.

Mockus, D. S., Macera, C. A., Wingard, D. L., Peddecord, M., Thomas, R. G., & Wilfley, D. E. (2011). Dietary self-monitoring and its impact on weight loss in overweight children. *International Journal of Pediatric Obesity, 6*(3–4), 197–205.

Mofidi, M., DeVellis, R. F., Blazer, D. G., DeVellis, B. M., Panter, A. T., & Jordan, J. M. (2006). Spirituality and depressive symptoms in a racially diverse US sample of community-dwelling adults. *Journal of Nervous and Mental Disease, 194*(12), 975–977.

Mona, L. R., Romesser-Scehnet, J. M., Cameron, R. P., & Cardenas, V. (2006). Cognitive-behavioral therapy and people with disabilities. In P. A. Hays & G. Y. Iwamasa (Eds.), *Culturally responsive cognitive-behavioral therapy* (pp. 199–222). Washington, DC: American Psychological Association.

Monahan, J., Steadman, H., Silver, E., Appelbaum, P., Robbins, P., Mulvey, E., … Banks,S. (2001). *Rethinking risk assessment of mental disorders and violence.* New York: Oxford University Press.

Morales, E., & Norcross, J. C. (2010). Evidence-based practices with ethnic minorities: Strange bedfellows no more. *Journal of Clinical Psychology: In Session, 66,* 821–829.

Morimoto, S. S., Kanellopoulos, D., Manning, K. J., & Alexopoulos, G. S. (2015). Diagnosis and treatment of depression and cognitive impairment in late life. *Annals of the New York Academy of Sciences, 1345*(1), 36–46.

Morris, M. E., & Aguilera, A. (2012). Mobile, social, and wearable computing and the evolution of psychological practice. *Professional Psychology: Research and Practice, 43*(6), 622–626.

Morrison, J. (2014). *The first interview* (4th ed.). New York: Guilford Press.

Moscript, T. (2011). Risk and resilience: Impact of early trauma on psychological and physiological functioning. In G. Appleby, E. Colon, & J. Hamilton (Eds.), *Diversity, oppression, and social functioning: Person-in-environment assessment and intervention* (3rd ed., pp. 47–60). Boston, MA: Pearson Education.

Mourya, M., Mahajan, A. S., Singh, N. P., & Jain, A. K. (2009). Effect of slow-and fast-breathing exercises on autonomic functions in patients with essential hypertension. *The Journal of Alternative and Complementary Medicine, 15*(7), 711–717.

Moyers, T. B. (2004). History and happenstance: How motivational interviewing got its start. *Journal of Cognitive Psychotherapy, 18,* 291–298.

Moyers, T. B. (2014). The relationship in motivational interviewing. *Psychotherapy, 51,* 358–363.

Moyers, T. B., & Miller, W. R. (2013). Is low therapist empathy toxic? *Psychology of Addictive Behaviors, 27,* 878–884.

Moyers, T. B., Martin, T., Houck, J. M., Christopher, P. J., & Tonigan, J. S. (2009). From in-session behaviours to drinking outcomes: A causal chain for motivational interviewing. *Journal of Consulting and Clinical Psychology, 77,* 1113–1124.

Moyers, T. B., Miller, W. R., & Hendrickson, S. M. L. (2005). How does motivational interviewing work? Therapist interpersonal skill predicts client involvement within motivational interviewing sessions. *Journal of Consulting and Clinical Psychology, 73,* 590–598.

Moyers, T. B., & Rollnick, S. (2002). A motivational interviewing perspective on resistance in psychotherapy. *Journal of Clinical Psychology, 58,* 185–193.

Mrazek, M. D., Franklin, M. S., Phillips, D. T., Baird, B., & Schooler, J. W. (2013). Mindfulness training improves working memory capacity and GRE performance while reducing mind wandering. *Psychological Science, 24*(5), 776–781.

Muccino, G. (Director). (2006). *The pursuit of happyness* [Motion picture]. United States: Columbia Pictures.

Mueser, K. T., Noordsy, D. L., Drake, R. E., & Fox, L. (2003). *Integrated treatment for dual disorders: A guide to effective practice.* New York: Guilford Press.

Muran, J. C., & Barber, J. P. (Eds.). (2010). *The therapeutic alliance: An evidence-based guide to practice.* New York: Guilford Press.

Muroff, J. (2007). Cultural diversity and cognitive behavior therapy. In T. Ronen & A. Freeman (Eds.), *Cognitive behavior therapy in clinical social work practice* (pp. 109–146). New York: Springer.

Myers, S. B., Sweeney, A. C., Popick, V., Wesley, K., Bordfeld, A., & Fingerhut, R. (2012). Self-care practices and perceived stress levels among psychology graduate students. *Training and Education in Professional Psychology, 6,* 55–66.

Mystkowski, J. L., Craske, M. G., & Echiverri, A. M. (2002). Treatment context and return of fear in spider phobia. *Behavior Therapy, 33,* 399–416.

Nadal, K. L., Griffin, K. E., Wong, Y., Hamit, S., & Rasmus, M. (2014). The impact of racial microaggressions on mental health: Counseling implications for clients of color. *Journal of Counseling & Development, 92,* 57–66.

Nadort, M., van Dyck, R., Smit, J. H., Giesen-Bloo, J., Eikelenboom, M., Wensing, M., … Arntz, A. (2009). Three preparatory studies for promoting implementation of outpatient schema therapy for borderline personality disorder in general mental health care. *Behaviour Research and Therapy, 47*(11), 938–945.

Naeem, F., Waheed, W., Gobbi, M., Ayub, M., & Kingdon, D. (2011). Preliminary evaluation of culturally sensitive CBT for depression in Pakistan: Findings from Developing Culturally-sensitive CBT Project (DCCP). *Behavioural and Cognitive Psychotherapy, 39*(02), 165–173.

Nagy, T. F. (2005). Competence. *Journal of Aggression, Maltreatment and Trauma, 11*(1–2), 27–49.

Najavits, L. M. (2002). *Seeking safety: A treatment manual for PTSD and substance abuse.* New York: Guilford Press.

Nakamura, Y. (2010). Nursing intervention to enhance acceptance of pregnancy in first-time mothers: Focusing on the comfortable experiences of pregnant women. *Japan Journal of Nursing Science, 7*(1), 29–36.

National Association of Social Workers. (2001). *NASW standard of cultural competence for social work practice.* Washington, DC: NASW Press.

National Association of Social Workers. (2008). *Code of ethics.* Washington, DC: Author.

National Association of Social Workers. (2009). *Professional self-care and social work.* Washington, DC: Author. Policy statement approved by NASW Delegate Assembly. Retrieved from www.socialworkers.org/nasw/memberlink/2009/supportfiles/ProfesionalSelf-Care.pdf

National Center for Infants, Toddlers, and Families. (2005). *Diagnostic classification of mental health and developmental disorders of infancy and early childhood.* Washington, DC: Author.

Neacsiu, A. D., & Linehan, M. M. (2014). Borderline personality disorder. In D. H. Barlow (Ed.), *Clinical handbook of psychological disorders* (5th ed., pp. 394–461). New York: Guilford Press.

Neacsiu, A. D., Ward-Ciesielski, E. F., & Linehan, M. M. (2012). Emerging approaches to counseling intervention approaches: Dialectical behavior therapy. *The Counseling Psychologist, 40,* 1003–1032.

Neal-Barnett, A. (2003). *Soothe your nerves: The Black woman's guide to understanding and overcoming anxiety, panic, and fear.* New York: Fireside.

Neff, K. D. (2003a). Self-compassion: An alternative conceptualization of a healthy attitude toward oneself. *Self and Identity, 2,* 85–101.

Neff, K. D. (2003b). The development and validation of a scale to measure self-compassion. *Self and Identity, 2,* 223–250.

Neff, K. D., Kirkpatrick, K. L., & Rude, S. S. (2007). Self-compassion and adaptive psychological functioning. *Journal of Research in Personality, 41,* 139–154.

Neff, K. D., & McGehee, P. (2010). Self-compassion and psychological resilience among adolescents and young adults. *Self and Identity, 9,* 225–240.

Neff, K. D., & Pommier, E. (2013). The relationship between self-compassion and other-focused concern among college undergraduates, community adults, and practicing meditators. *Self and Identity, 12,* 160–176.

Neighbors, H. W., Trierweiler, S. J., Ford, B. C., & Muroff, J. R. (2003). Racial differences in DSM diagnosis using a semi-structured instrument: The importance of clinical judgment in the diagnosis of African Americans. *Journal of Health and Social Behavior, 43,* 237–256.

Neimeyer, R. A. (1998). *Lessons of loss: A guide to coping.* New York: McGraw-Hill.

Nelson, D., Hewell, V., Roberts, L., Kersey, E., & Avey, J. (2012, Fall/Winter). Telebehavioral health delivery of clinical supervision trainings in rural Alaska: An emerging best practices model for rural practitioners. *Rural Mental Health, 36*(2), 10–15.

Nelson, G., Aubry, T., & Lafrance, A. (2007). A review of the literature on the effectiveness of housing and support, assertive community treatment, and intensive case management interventions for persons with mental illness who have been homeless. *American Journal of Orthopsychiatry, 77,* 350–361.

Nelson, R. O. (1977). Methodological issues in assessment via self-monitoring. In J. D. Cone & R. P. Hawkins (Eds.), *Behavioral assessment: New directions in clinical psychology* (pp. 217–254). New York: Brunner/Mazel.

Nepo, M. (2012). *Seven thousand ways to listen.* New York: Free Press.

Neufeld, J., Rasmussen, H., Lopez, S., Ryder, J., Magyar-Moe, J., Ford, A.,…Bouwkamp, J. (2006). The engagement model of person-environment interaction. *The Counseling Psychologist, 34,* 245–259.

Neufeldt, S. A., Pinterits, E. J., Moleiro, C. M., Lee, T. L., Yang, P. H., Brodie, R. E., & Orliss, M. J. (2006). How do graduate student therapists incorporate diversity factors in case conceptualization? *Psychotherapy: Theory, Research, Practice, Training, 43,* 464–479.

Newman, C. F. (2002). A cognitive perspective on resistance in psychotherapy. *Journal of Clinical Psychology, 58,* 165–174.

Newman, C. F. (2013). *Core competencies in cognitive behavior therapy: Becoming a highly competent and effective cognitive-behavioral therapist.* New York: Routledge.

Newman, M. G., Consoli, A., & Taylor, C. B. (1997). Computers in assessment and cognitive behavioral treatment of clinical disorders: Anxiety as a case in point. *Behavior Therapy, 28,* 211–235.

Newman, M. G., Kenardy, J., Herman, S., & Taylor, C. B. (1997). Comparison of palmtop-computer-assisted brief cognitive-behavioral treatment to cognitive behavioral treatment for panic disorder. *Journal of Consulting and Clinical Psychology, 65,* 178–183.

Newman, M. G., Przeworski, A., Consoli, A. J., & Taylor, C. B. (2014). A randomized controlled trial of ecological momentary intervention plus brief group therapy for generalized anxiety disorder. *Psychotherapy, 51*(2), 198–206.

Newman, M. G., Szkodny, L. E., Llera, S. J., & Przeworski, A. (2011). A review of technology-assisted self-help and minimal contact therapy for anxiety and depression: Is human contact necessary for therapeutic efficacy? *Clinical Psychology Review, 31,* 89–103.

Nezu, A. M. (2005). Beyond cultural competence: Human diversity and the appositeness of asseverative goals. *Clinical Psychology: Science and Practice, 12,* 19–24.

Nezu, A. M., & Nezu, C. M. (2010). Cognitive-behavioral case formulation and treatment design. In R. A. DiTomasso, B. A. Golden, & H. J. Morris (Eds.), *Handbook of cognitive-behavioral approaches in primary care* (pp. 201–222). New York: Springer.

Nezu, A. M., Nezu, C. M., & Cos, T. A. (2007). Case formulation for the behavioral and cognitive therapies: A problem-solving perspective. In T. D. Eells (Ed.), *Handbook of psychotherapy case formulation* (2nd ed., pp. 349–378). New York: Guilford Press.

Nezu, A. M, Nezu, C. M., & D'Zurilla, T. J. (2007). *Solving life's problems: A 5-step guide to enhanced well-being.* New York: Springer.

Nezu, A. M, Nezu, C. M., & D'Zurilla, T. J. (2010). Problem-solving therapy. In N. Kazantzis, M. A. Reinecke, & A. Freeman (Eds.), *Cognitive and behavioral theories in clinical practice.* New York: Guilford Press.

Nezu, A. M., Nezu, C. M., & D'Zurilla, T. (2013). *Problem-solving therapy: A treatment manual.* Springer.

Nezu, A. M., Nezu, C. M., & Lombardo, E. (2004). *Cognitive–behavioral case formulation and treatment design: A problem-solving approach.* New York: Springer.

Ng, C. T. C., & James, S. (2013). Counselor empathy or "Having a heart to help?" An ethnographic investigation of Chinese clients' experience of counseling. *The Humanistic Psychologist, 41*(4), 339–349.

Nichols, M. P. (2009). *The lost art of listening* (2nd ed.). New York: Guilford Press.

Nicolas, G., Arntz, D. L., Hirsch, B., & Schmiedigen, A. (2009). Cultural adaptation of a group treatment for Haitian American adolescents. *Professional Psychology: Research and Practice, 40*, 378–384.

Nielsen, S. L., Ridley, C. R., & Johnson, W. B. (2000). Religiously sensitive rational emotive therapy: Theory, techniques, and brief excerpts from a case. *Professional Psychology: Research and Practice, 31*, 21–28.

Nilsen, W. J., & Pavel, M. (2015). Behavioral health information technology adoption in the context of a changing healthcare landscape. In L. A. Marsch, S. E. Lord, & J. Dallery (Eds.), *Behavioral healthcare and technology: Using science-based innovations to transform practice* (pp. 305–316). New York: Oxford University Press.

Nissen-Lie, H. A., Monsen, J. T., & Ronnestad, M. H. (2010). Therapist predictors of early patient-rated working alliance: A multilevel approach. *Psychotherapy Research, 20*, 627–646.

Nissen-Lie, H. A., Havik, O. E., Hoglend, P. A., Monsen, J. T., & Ronnestad, M. H. (2013). The contribution of the quality of therapists' personal lives to the development of the working alliance. *Journal of Counseling Psychology, 60*, 483–495.

Nixon, M., & Young, J. Z. (2003). *The brains and lives of cephalopods.* New York: Oxford University Press.

Norcross, J. C. (2010). The therapeutic relationship. In B. L. Duncan, S. D. Miller, B. E. Wampold, & M. A. Hubble (Eds.), *The heart and soul of change: Delivering what works in therapy* (2nd ed., pp. 113–141). Washington, DC: American Psychological Association.

Norcross, J. C. (Ed.). (2011). *Psychotherapy relationships that work: Evidence-based responsiveness* (2nd ed.). New York: Oxford University Press.

Norcross, J. C., & Guy, J. D., Jr. (2007). *Leaving it at the office: A guide to psychotherapist self-care.* New York: Guilford Press.

Norcross, J. C., Koocher, G. P., Fala, N. C., & Wexler, H. K. (2010). What does not work? Expert consensus on discredited treatments in the addictions. *Journal of Addiction Medicine, 4*, 174–180.

Norcross, J. C., Koocher, G. P., & Garofalo, A. (2006). Discredited psychological treatments and tests: A Delphi poll. *Professional Psychology: Research and Practice, 37*, 515–522.

Norcross, J. C., Krebs, P. M., & Prochaska, J. O. (2011). Stages of change. In J. C. Norcross (Ed.), *Psychotherapy relationships that work: Evidence-based responsiveness* (2nd ed., pp. 279–300). New York: Oxford University Press.

Norcross, J. C., Krebs, P. M., & Prochaska, J. O. (2011). Stages of change. *Journal of Clinical Psychology: In Session, 67*, 143–154.

Norcross, J. C., Pfund, R. A., & Prochaska, J. O. (2013). Psychotherapy in 2022: A Delphi poll on its future. *Professional Psychology: Research and Practice, 44*, 363–370.

Norcross, J. C., & Wampold, B. E. (2011). Evidence-based therapy relationships: Research conclusions and clinical practices. In J. C. Norcross (Ed.), *Psychotherapy relationships that work: Evidence-based responsiveness* (2nd ed., pp. 423–430). New York: Oxford University Press.

Norton, P. J. & Price, E. C. (2007). A meta-analytic review of adult cognitive-behavioral treatment outcome across the anxiety disorders. *Journal of Nervous and Mental Disease, 195*, 521–531.

Nunnally, E. (1993). Solution focused therapy. In R. A. Wells &V. J. Giannetti (Eds.), *Casebook of the brief psychotherapies* (pp. 271–286). New York: Plenum.

Nurius, P. S., & Hoy-Ellis, C. P. (2013). Stress effects and health. In C. Franklin (Ed.), *Encyclopedia of social work online.* New York: NASW & Oxford University Press.

Nurius, P. S., & Macy, R. J. (2007). Cognitive behavioral therapies. In K. M. Sowers & C. N. Dulmus (Eds.), *Comprehensive handbook of social work and social welfare,* Vol. 2: *Human behavior in the social environment.* New York: Wiley.

Nutt Williams, E., Hayes, J., & Fauth, J. (2008). Therapist self-awareness: Interdisciplinary connections and future directions. In S. D. Brown & R. W. Lent (Eds.), *Handbook of counseling psychology* (4th ed., pp. 303–319). Hoboken, NJ: Wiley.

Nylund, D., & Corsiglia, V. (1994). Becoming solution-forced in brief therapy: Remembering something important we already knew. *Journal of Systemic Therapies, 13*, 5–12.

O'Donohue, W., & Fisher, J. E. (2012). *Cognitive behavior therapy: Core principles for practice.* Hoboken, NJ: John Wiley & Sons.

O'Halloran, P. D., Blackstock, F., Shields, N., Holland, A., Iles, R., Kingsley, M., … Taylor, N. F. (2014).

Motivational interviewing to increase physical activity in people with chronic health conditions: A systematic review and meta-analysis. *Clinical Rehabilitation, 28,* 1159–1171.

O'Hanlon, B., & Weiner-Davis, M. (2003). *In search of solutions: A new direction in psychotherapy* (rev. ed.). New York: Norton.

O'Hearn, A., & Pollard, R. Q., Jr. (2008). Modifying dialectical behavior therapy for deaf individuals. *Cognitive and Behavioral Practice, 15,* 400–414.

O'Leary, P. J. (2009). Men who were sexually abused in childhood: Coping strategies and comparisons in psychological functioning. *Child Abuse & Neglect, 33*(7), 471–479.

Oettingen, G. (1995). Cross-cultural perspectives on self-efficacy. In A. Bandura (Ed.), *Self-efficacy in changing societies* (pp. 149–176). New York: Cambridge University Press.

Oko, J. (2006). Evaluating alternative approaches to social work: A critical review of the strengths perspective. *Families in Society, 87,* 601–611.

Okun, B. F., & Kantrowitz, R. E. (2008). *Effective helping: Interviewing and counseling techniques* (7th ed.). Belmont, CA: Thomson Brooks/Cole.

Okun, B. F., & Suyemoto, K. L. (2013). *Conceptualization and treatment planning for effective helping.* Belmont, CA: Cengage Learning.

Olfson, M., & Marcus, S. C. (2010). National trends in outpatient psychotherapy. *American Journal of Psychiatry, 167,* 1456–1463.

Olkin, R. (2009). Disability-affirmative therapy. In I. Marini & M. A. Stebnicki (Eds.), *The professional counselor's desk reference* (pp. 355–369). New York: Springer.

Ollendick, T. H., & Davis III, T. E. (2013). One-session treatment for specific phobias: A review of Öst's single-session exposure with children and adolescents. *Cognitive Behaviour Therapy, 42,* 275–283.

Ollendick, T. H., Öst, L. G., Reuterskiöld, L., Costa, N., Cederlund, R., Sirbu, C., … Jarrett, M. A. (2009). One-session treatment of specific phobias in youth: A randomized clinical trial in the United States and Sweden. *Journal of Consulting and Clinical Psychology, 77,* 504–516.

Ong, J. C., Shapiro, S. L., & Manber, R. (2008). Combining mindfulness meditation with cognitive-behavior therapy for insomnia: A treatment-development study. *Behavior Therapy, 39*(2), 171–182.

Onken, L. S., & Shoham, V. (2015). Technology and the stage model of behavioral intervention development.

In L. A. Marsch, S. E. Lord, & J. Dallery (Eds.), *Behavioral healthcare and technology: Using science-based innovations to transform practice* (pp. 3–12). New York: Oxford University Press.

Opris, D., Pintea, S., García-Palacios, A., Botella, C., Szamosközi, S., & David, D. (2012). Virtual reality exposure therapy in anxiety disorders: A quantitative meta-analysis. *Depression and Anxiety, 29*(2), 85–93.

Organista, K. C. (2006). Cognitive-behavioral therapy with Latinos and Latinas. In P. A, Hays & G. Y., Iwamasa (Eds.), *Culturally responsive cognitive-behavioral therapy* (pp. 73–96). Washington, DC: American Psychological Association.

Organista, K., Dwyer, E. V., & Azocar, F. (1993). Cognitive behavioral therapy with Latino outpatients. *The Behavior Therapist, 16,* 229–232.

Orlinsky, D. E., & Rønnestad, M. H. (2005). Career development: Correlates of evolving expertise. In D. E. Orlinsky, M. H. Rønnestad, & the Collaborative Research Network of the Society for Psychotherapy Research, *How psychotherapists develop: A study of therapeutic work and professional growth* (pp. 131–142). Washington, DC: American Psychological Association.

Orlinsky, D. E., Rønnestad, M. H., & The Collaborative Research Network for the Society for Psychotherapy Research. (2005). *How Psychotherapists develop: A study of therapeutic work and professional growth.* Washington, DC: American Psychological Association.

Ornstein, E. D., & Ganzer, C. (2005). Relational social work: A model for the future. *Families in Society, 86,* 565–572.

Orsillo, S. M., & Batten, S. V. (2005). ACT in the treatment of PTSD. *Behavioral Modification, 29,* 95–129.

Osborn, C. J. (2004). Seven salutary suggestions for counselor stamina. *Journal of Counseling & Development, 82,* 319–328.

Osborn, C. J., & Kelly, B. L. (2010). No surprises: Practices for conducting supervisee evaluations. In J. R. Culbreth & L. L. Brown (Eds.), *State of the art in clinical supervision* (pp. 19–44). New York: Routledge/Taylor & Francis.

Osborn, C. J., West, J. D., Kindsvatter, A., & Paez, S. B. (2008). Treatment planning as collaborative care map construction: Reframing clinical practice to promote client involvement. *Journal of Contemporary Psychotherapy, 38,* 169–176.

Osher, F. C., & Kofoed, L. L. (1989). Treatment of patients with psychiatric and psychoactive substance abuse disorders. *Hospital and Community Psychiatry, 40,* 1025–1030.

Öst, L.-G. (1997). Rapid treatment of specific phobias. In G. C. L. Davey (Ed.), *Phobias: A handbook of theory, research and treatment* (pp. 227–247). Oxford: Wiley.

Öst, L. G. (2008). Efficacy of third wave of behavioral therapies: A systematic review of meta-analysis. *Behavior Research and Therapy, 46,* 296–321.

Öst, L. G. (2014). The efficacy of Acceptance and Commitment Therapy: An updated systematic review and meta-analysis. *Behaviour Research and Therapy, 61,* 105–121.

Ostaseski, F. (1994, December). Stories of lives lived and now ending. *The Sun, 228,* 10–13.

Ott, J. J. (2004). Mindfulness meditation: A path of transformation and healing. *Journal of Psychosocial Nursing and Mental Health Services, 42*(7), 22 29.

Overholser, J. C. (2010). Clinical expertise: A preliminary attempt to clarify its core elements. *Journal of Contemporary Psychotherapy, 40,* 131–139.

Owen, J., Devdas, L., & Rodolfa, E. (2007). University counseling center off-campus referrals: An exploratory investigation. *Journal of College Student Psychotherapy, 22,* 13–29.

Owen, J., Duncan, B., Reese, R. J., Anker, M., & Sparks, J. (2014). Accounting for therapist variability in couple therapy outcomes: What really matters? *Journal of Sex & Marital Therapy, 40,* 488–502.

Owen, J., Leach, M. M., Wampold, B., & Rodolfa, E. (2011). Client and therapist variability in clients' perceptions of their therapists' multicultural competencies. *Journal of Counseling Psychology, 58,* 1–9.

Owen, J., Tao, K. W., Imel, Z. E., Wampold, B. E., & Rodolfa, E. (2014). Addressing racial and ethnic microaggressions in therapy. *Professional Psychology, 45,* 283–290.

Oxhandler, H. K., & Pargament, K. I. (2014). Social work practitioners' integration of clients' religion and spirituality in practice: A literature review. *Social Work, 59*(3), 271–279.

Pachankis, J. E., & Goldfried, M. R. (2013). Clinical issues in working with lesbian, gay, and bisexual clients. *Psychology of Sexual Orientation and Gender Diversity, 1*(S), 45–58.

Pan, D., Huey, S. J., Jr., & Hernandez, D. (2012). Culturally-adapted versus standard exposure treatment for phobic Asian Americans: Treatment efficacy, moderators, and predictors. *Cultural Diversity and Ethnic Minority Psychology, 17,* 11–22.

Paniagua, F. A. (2005). *Assessing and treating culturally diverse clients: A practical guide* (3rd ed.). Thousand Oaks, CA: Sage.

Paniagua, F. (2013). Culture-bound syndromes, cultural variations, and psychopathology. In F. Paniagua, F., & Yamada, A.-M. (Eds.), *Handbook of multicultural mental health* (pp. 25–47). Amsterdam, Netherlands: Elsevier.

Paniagua, F., & Yamada, A.-M. (Eds.). (2013). *Handbook of multicultural mental health.* Amsterdam, Netherlands: Elsevier.

Paradis, C. M., Cukor, D., & Friedman, S. (2006). Cognitive-behavioral therapy with Orthodox Jews. In P. A. Hays & G. Y. Iwamasa (Eds.), *Culturally responsive cognitive-behavioral therapy* (pp. 161–175). Washington, DC: American Psychological Association.

Parrish, C. L., Radomsky, A. S., & Dugas, M. J. (2008). Anxiety-control strategies: Is there room for neutralization in successful exposure treatment? *Clinical Psychology Review, 28,* 1400–1412.

Parson, T. D., & Rizzo, A. A. (2008). Affective outcomes of virtual reality exposure therapy for anxiety and specific phobias: A meta-analysis. *Journal of Behavior Therapy and Experimental Psychiatry, 39,* 250–261.

Pascoe, E. A., & Richman, L. S. (2009). Perceived discrimination and health: A meta-analytic review. *Psychological Bulletin, 135*(4), 531–554.

Patel, C. (1993). Yoga-based therapy. In P. M. Lehrer & R. L. Woolfolk (Eds.), *Principles and practice of stress management* (2nd ed., pp. 89–137). New York: Guilford Press.

Patsiopoulos, A. T., & Buchanan, M. J. (2011). The practice of self-compassion in counseling: A narrative inquiry. *Professional Psychology: Research and Practice, 42,* 301–307.

Patterson, G. R., & Forgatch, M. S. (1985). Therapist behavior as a determinant for client noncompliance: A paradox for the behavior modifier. *Journal of Consulting and Clinical Psychology, 53,* 846–851.

Paulson, B., Truscott, D., & Stuart, J. (1999). Clients' perceptions of helpful experiences in counseling. *Journal of Counseling Psychology, 46,* 317–324.

Paunovic, N., & Ost, L. G. (2001). Cognitive-behavior therapy vs. exposure therapy in the treatment of PTSD in refugees. *Behaviour Research and Therapy, 39,* 1183–1197.

Peden, A. R., Rayens, M. K., & Hall, L. A. (2005). A community-based depression prevention intervention with low-income single mothers. *Journal of the American Psychiatric Nurses Association, 11,* 18–25.

Pedro-Carroll, J. L. (2005). Fostering resilience in the aftermath of divorce: The role of evidence-based programs for children. *Family Court Review, 43*(1), 52–64.

Peguero, A. A., & Shaffer, K. A. (2015). Academic self-efficacy, dropping out, and the significance of inequality. *Sociological Spectrum, 35*(1), 46–64.

Perez-Ara, M. A., Quero, S., Botella, C., Banos, R., Andreu-Mateu, S., Garcia-Palacios, A., & Breton-Lopez, J. (2010). Virtual reality interoceptive exposure for the treatment of panic disorder and agoraphobia. *Annual Review of CyberTherapy and Telemedicine, 8*, 61–64.

Persons, J. B. (2008). *The case formulation approach to cognitive-behavior therapy.* New York: Guilford Press.

Persons, J. B., Beckner, V. L., & Tompkins, M. A. (2013). Testing case formulation hypotheses in psychotherapy: Two case examples. *Cognitive and Behavioral Practice, 20*, 399–409.

Persons, J. B., & Tompkins, M. A. (2007). Cognitive-behavioral case formulation. In T. D. Eells (Ed.), *Handbook of psychotherapy case formulation* (2nd ed., pp. 290–316). New York: Guilford Press.

Pert, C. (1993). The chemical communicators. Interview by B. Moyers with C. Pert, in *Healing and the mind* (pp. 177–193). New York: Doubleday.

Peterson, C., & Seligman, M. (2004). *Character strengths and virtues: A handbook and classification.* Washington, DC: American Psychological Association.

Petrila, J. (2009). Congress restores the Americans with Disabilities Act to its original intent. *Psychiatric Services, 60*, 878–879.

Pfeifer, J. H., & Dapretto, M. (2009). "Mirror, mirror, in my mind": Empathy, interpersonal competence, and the mirror neuron system. In J. Decety & W. Ickes (Eds.), *The social neuroscience of empathy* (pp. 183–198). Cambridge, MA: MIT.

Piasecki, T. M., Hufford, M. R., Solhan, M., & Trull, T. J. (2007). Assessing clients in their natural environments with electronic diaries: Rationale, benefits, limitations, and barriers. *Psychological Assessment, 19*, 25–43.

Piet, J., & Hougaard, E. (2011). The effect of mindfulness-based cognitive therapy for prevention of relapse in recurrent major depressive disorder: A systematic review and meta-analysis. *Clinical Psychology Review, 31*, 1032–1040.

Pigeon, W. R. (2010). Treatment of adult insomnia with cognitive-behavioral therapy. *Journal of Clinical Psychology, 66*, 1148–1160.

Pinquart, M., Duberstein, P. R., & Lyness, J. M. (2007). Effects of psychotherapy and other behavioral interventions on clinically depressed older adults: A meta-analysis. *Aging & Mental Health, 11*, 645–657.

Pirlott, A. G., Kisbu-Sakarya, Y., DeFrancesco, C. A., Elliot, D. L., & MacKinnon, D. P. (2012). Mechanisms of motivational interviewing in health promotion: A Bayesian mediation analysis. *International Journal of Behavioral Nutrition and Physical Activity, 9*, 1–11.

Pistorello, J., Fruzzetti, A. E., MacLane, C., Gallop, R., & Iverson, K. M. (2012). Dialectical behavior therapy (DBT) applied to college students: A randomized clinical trial. *Journal of Consulting and Clinical Psychology, 80*, 982–994.

Platt, M., & Allard, C. B. (Eds.) (2011). Military sexual trauma [Special issue]. *Journal of Trauma & Dissociation, 12*(3), 213–346.

Pomerantz, A. M. (2005). Increasingly informed consent: Discussing distinct aspects of psychotherapy at different points in time. *Ethics and Behavior, 15*, 351–360.

Ponterotto, J. G., Suzuki, L. A., Casas, J. M., & Alexan, C. M. (Eds.). (2010). *Handbook of multicultural counseling* (3rd ed.). Thousand Oaks, CA: Sage.

Pool, L. D., & Qualter, P. (2012). Improving emotional intelligence and emotional self-efficacy through a teaching intervention for university students. *Learning and Individual Differences, 22*(3), 306–312.

Pope, K. S., & Vasquez, M. (2011). *Ethics in psychotherapy and counseling* (4th ed.). Hoboken, NJ: Wiley.

Powers, M. B., Vörding, M. B. Z. V. S., & Emmelkamp, P. M. G. (2009). Acceptance and commitment therapy: A meta-analytic review. *Psychotherapy and Psychosomatics, 78*, 73–80.

Prochaska, J. (1999). How do people change, and how can we change to help many more people? In M. Hubble, B. Duncan, & S. Miller (Eds.), *The heart and soul of change* (pp. 227–258). Washington, DC: American Psychological Association.

Prochaska, J. O., & DiClemente, C. C. (1982). Transtheoretical therapy: Toward a more integrative model of change. *Psychotherapy: Theory, Research and Practice, 19*, 276–288.

Prochaska, J., DiClemente, C., & Norcross, J. (1992). In search of how people change: Applications to addictive behaviors. *American Psychologist, 47*, 1102–1114.

Prochaska, J. O., & Norcross, J. C. (2010). *Systems of psychotherapy: A transtheoretical analysis* (7th ed.). Belmont, CA: Cengage Learning.

Prochaska, J. O., & Norcross, J. C. (2014). *Systems of psychotherapy: A transtheoretical analysis* (8th ed.). Belmont, CA: Cengage Learning.

Putterbaugh, D. (2015, June). Self-care in the world of empirically supported treatments. *Counseling Today, 57*(12), 53–55.

Quandt, S. A., McDonald, J., Arcury, T. A., Bell, R. A., & Vitolins, M. Z. (2000). Nutritional self-management of elderly widows in rural communities. *Gerontologist, 40,* 86–96.

Quinn, J. M., Pascoe, A., Wood, W., & Neal, D. T. (2010). Can't control yourself? Monitor those bad habits. *Personality and Social Psychology Bulletin, 36*(4), 499–511.

Rachman, S. (1980). Emotional processing. *Behaviour Research and Therapy, 18,* 51–60.

Rachman, S., & Lopatka, C. (1986). Do fears summate? III. *Behaviour Research and Therapy, 24,* 653–660.

Radeke, J. T., & Mahoney, M. J. (2000). Comparing the personal lives of psychotherapists and research psychologists. *Professional Psychology: Research and Practice, 31,* 82–84.

Rafaeli, E., Bernstein, D. P., & Young, J. (2010). *Schema therapy: Distinctive features.* New York: Routledge.

Ramos, C., & Leal, I. P. (2013). Posttraumatic growth in the aftermath of trauma: A literature review about related factors and application contexts. *Psychology, Community & Health, 2,* 43–54.

Raskin, N., & Rogers, C. (1995). Person-centered therapy. In R. J. Corsini & D. Wedding (Eds.), *Current Psychotherapies* (5th ed., pp. 128–161). Itasca, IL: Peacock.

Raskin, N., Rogers, C., & Witty, M. (2014). Client-centered therapy. In D. Wedding & R. J. Corsini, (Eds.), *Current psychotherapies* (10th ed., pp. 95–150). Belmont, CA: Cengage Learning.

Rath, T. (2007). *StrengthsFinder 2.0.* Washington, DC: Gallup.

Razza, R. A., Bergen-Cico, D., & Raymond, K. (2013). Enhancing preschoolers' self-regulation via mindful yoga. *Journal of Child and Family Studies, 24,* 1–14.

Ready, D., J., Geradi, R. J., Backscheider, A. G., Mascaro, N., & Rothbaum, B. O. (2010). Comparing virtual reality exposure therapy to present-centered therapy with 11 U.S. Vietnam veterans with PTSD. *Cyberpsychology, Behavior, and Social Networking, 13*(1), 49–54.

Rebeta, J. L. (2015). Diversity, culture and personality disorders. In A. T. Beck, D. D. Davis, & A. Freeman (Eds.), *Cognitive therapy of personality disorders* (3rd ed., pp. 140–151). New York: Guilford Press.

Rector, N. A. (2013). Acceptance and commitment therapy: Empirical considerations. *Behavior Therapy, 44*(2), 213–217.

Reed, G. M. (2010). Toward ICD-11: Improving the clinical utility of WHO's international classification of mental disorders. *Professional Psychology, 41,* 457–464.

Reed, M. C. (2003). The relation of neighborhood variables, parental monitoring, and school self-efficacy on academic achievement among urban African American girls. *Dissertation Abstracts International: Section B: The Sciences and Engineering, 64*(6-B), 2987.

Rehm, L. P., & Adams, J. H. (2009). Self-management. In W. T. O'Donohue & J. E. Fisher (Eds.), *General principles and empirically supported techniques of cognitive behavior therapy* (pp. 564–570). New York: Wiley.

Rennie, D. L. (1994). Clients' deference in psychotherapy. *Journal of Counseling Psychology, 41,* 427–437.

Renshaw, K. D. (Ed.). (2011). Working with the new generation of service members/veterans from Operations Enduring and Iraqi Freedom [Special series]. *Cognitive and Behavioral Practice, 18,* 82–148.

Reynolds, S. K., Wolbert, R., Abney-Cunningham, G., & Patterson, K. (2007). Dialectical behavior therapy for assertive community treatment teams. In L. A. Dimeff & K. Koerner (Eds.), *Dialectical behavior therapy in clinical practice: Applications across disorders and settings* (pp. 298–325). New York: Guilford Press.

Reupert, A. (2006). The counsellor's self in therapy: An inevitable presence. *International Journal for the Advancement of Counselling, 28,* 95–105.

Reynolds, C. F., Thomas, S. B., Morse, J. Q., Anderson, S. J., Albert, S., Dew, M. A., ... Quinn, S. C. (2014). Early intervention to preempt major depression among older black and white adults. *Psychiatric Services, 65*(6), 765–773.

Ricci-Cabello, I., Ruiz-Pérez, I., Rojas-García, A., Pastor, G., Rodríguez-Barranco, M., & Gonçalves, D. C. (2014). Characteristics and effectiveness of diabetes self-management educational programs targeted to racial/ethnic minority groups: A systematic review, meta-analysis and meta-regression. *BMC Endocrine Disorders, 14,* 60. Retrieved from http://www.biomedcentral.com/1472-6823/14/60

Rice, V. H. (Ed.). (2012). *Handbook of stress, coping, and health: Implications for nursing research, theory, and practice.* Thousand Oaks, CA: Sage.

Richard, D. C. S., & Lauterbach, D. L. (Eds.). (2007). *Handbook of exposure therapies.* Boston, MA: Academic Press.

Richards, M. M. (2009). Electronic medical records: Confidentiality issues in the time of HIPAA. *Professional Psychology: Research and Practice, 40,* 550–556.

Richards, P. S., & Worthington Jr., E. L. (2010). The need for evidence-based, spiritually oriented psychotherapies. *Professional Psychology: Research and Practice, 41*(5), 363–370.

Richardson, B., & Stone, G. L. (1981). Effects of cognitive adjunct procedure within a microtraining situation. *Journal of Counseling Psychology, 28,* 168–175.

Ridley, C. R. (2005). *Overcoming unintentional racism in counseling and therapy: A practitioner's guide to intentional intervention* (2nd ed.). Thousand Oaks, CA: Sage.

Ridley, C. R., & Kelly, S. M. (2007). Multicultural considerations in case formulation. In T. D. Eells (Ed.), *Handbook of psychotherapy case formulation* (2nd ed., pp. 33–64). New York: Guilford Press.

Ridley, C., & Lingle, D. W. (1996). Cultural empathy in multicultural counseling: A multidimensional process model. In P. B. Pedersen, J. G. Draguns, W. J. Lonner, & J. E. Trimble (Eds.), *Counseling across cultures* (4th ed., pp. 21–46). Thousand Oaks, CA: Sage.

Riolli, L., Savicki, V., & Spain, E. (2010). Positive emotions in traumatic conditions: Mediation of appraisal and mood for military personnel. *Military Psychology, 22*(2), 207–223.

Ritterband, L. M., Thorndike, F. P., Gonder-Frederick, L. A., Magee, J. C., Bailey, E. T., Saylor, D. K., & Morin, C. M. (2010). Efficacy of an Internet-based behavioral intervention for adults with insomnia. *Archives of General Psychiatry, 66*(7), 692–698.

Rizvi, S. L., Steffel, L. M., & Carson-Wong, A. (2013). An overview of dialectical behavior therapy for professional psychologists. *Professional Psychology: Research and Practice, 44*(2), 73–80.

Roberts, A. C., & Nishimoto, R. (2006). Barriers to engaging and retaining African-American post-partum women in drug treatment. *Journal of Drug Issues, 36,* 53–76.

Roberts, L. (2008, June 30). Work-based learning and the wisdom of elders. *Behavioral Healthcare.* Retrieved from http://www.behavioral.net/article/work-based -learning-and-wisdom-elders

roberts potts, r. (2012). Dear Uncle Ronnie. In D. Savage, & T. Miller (Eds.), *It gets better: Coming out, overcoming bullying, and creating a life worth living* (pp. 181–184). New York: Plume/Penguin Group.

Robjant, K., & Fazel, M. (2010). The emerging evidence for narrative exposure therapy: A review. *Clinical Psychology Review, 30,* 1030–1039.

Robles, B. (2009). A synopsis of the Health Insurance Portability and Accountability Act. In I. Marini & M. A. Stebnicki (Eds.), *The professional counselor's desk reference* (pp. 69–77). New York: Springer.

Rochkovski, O. (2006). Houses are a necessary illusion: Uncovering family process through asking families to draw a plan of their homes. *Australian and New Zealand Journal of Family Therapy, 27,* 10–15.

Rocque, B. (2010). Mediating self-hood: Exploring the construction and maintenance of identity by mothers of children labeled with autism spectrum disorder. *Disability & Society, 25*(4), 485–497.

Rodrigues, H., Figueira, I., Lopes, A., Gonçalves, R., Mendlowicz, M. V., Coutinho, E. S. F., & Ventura, P. (2014). Does D-cycloserine enhance exposure therapy for anxiety disorders in humans? A meta-analysis. *Plos One, 9*(7) Retrieved from http://search.ebscohost.com /login.aspx?direct=true&db=psyh&AN=2014-30996 -001&site=ehost-live

Roemer, L., & Orsillo, S. M. (2009). *Mindfulness- and acceptance-based behavioral therapies in practice.* New York: Guilford Press.

Rodriguez, B. I., & Craske, M. G. (1993). The effects of distraction during exposure to phobic stimuli. *Behaviour Research and Therapy, 31,* 549–558.

Rogers, C. (1942). *Counseling and psychotherapy.* Boston, MA: Houghton Mifflin.

Rogers, C. (1951). *Client-centered therapy.* Boston, MA: Houghton Mifflin.

Rogers, C. (1957). The necessary and sufficient conditions of therapeutic personality change. *Journal of Consulting Psychology, 21,* 95–103.

Rogers, C. (1977). *Carl Rogers on personal power.* New York: Delacorte Press.

Rogers, C., Gendlin, E., Kiesler, D., & Truax, C. (1967). *The therapeutic relationship and its impact: A study of psychotherapy with schizophrenics.* Madison, WI: University of Wisconsin.

Rogers, E. M. (1995). *Diffusion of innovations* (4th ed.). New York: Free Press.

Rogerson, M. D., Gottlieb, M. C., Handelsman, M. M., Knapp, S., & Younggren, J. (2011). Nonrational processes in ethical decision making. *American Psychologist, 66,* 614–623.

Rollnick, S., Miller, W. R., & Butler, C. C. (2008). *Motivational interviewing in health care: Helping patients change behavior.* New York: Guilford Press.

Ronen, T. (2007). Cognitive behavior therapy with children and adolescents. In T. Ronen & A. Freeman (Eds.), *Cognitive behavior therapy in clinical social work practice* (pp. 189–211). New York: Springer.

Ronen, T., & Freeman, A. (Eds.). (2007). *Cognitive behavior therapy in clinical social work practice.* New York: Springer.

Rønnestad, M. H., & Skovholt, T. M. (2003). The journey of the counselor and therapist: Research findings and perspectives on professional development. *Journal of Career Development, 30,* 5–44.

Rønnestad, M. H., & Skovholt, T. M. (2013). *The developing practitioner: Growth and stagnation of therapists and counselors.* New York: Taylor & Francis/Routledge.

Root, M. P. (1992). Reconstructing the impact of trauma on personality. In L. S. Brown & M. Ballou (Eds.), *Personality and psychopathology: Feminist reappraisals* (pp. 229–265). New York: Guilford Press.

Roseborough, D. J. (2006). Coming out stories framed as faith narratives, or stories of spiritual growth. *Pastoral Psychology, 55,* 47–59.

Rosen, C. S., Greenbaum, M. A., Schnurr, P. P., Holmes, T. H., Brennan, P. L., & Friedman, M. J. (2013). Do benzodiazepines reduce the effectiveness of exposure therapy for posttraumatic stress disorder? *Journal of Clinical Psychiatry, 74,* 1241–1248.

Rosen, D., Morse, J. Q., & Reynolds, C. F. (2010). Adapting problem-solving therapy for depressed older adults in methadone maintenance treatment. *Journal of Substance Abuse Treatment, 40*(2), 132–141.

Rosen, D. D., Rebeta, J. L., & Rothschild, S. Z. (2014). Culturally competent adaptation of cognitive-behavioural therapy for psychosis: Cases of Orthodox Jewish patients with messianic delusions. *Mental Health, Religion & Culture, 17*(7), 703–713.

Rosenberger, E. W., & Hayes, J. A. (2002). Therapist as subject: A review of the empirical countertransference literature. *Journal of Counseling & Development, 80,* 264–270.

Rosengren, D. B. (2009). *Building motivational interviewing skills: A practitioner workbook.* New York: Guilford Press.

Roth, B., & Calle-Mesa, L. (2006). Mindfulness-based stress reduction (MBSR) with Spanish- and English-speaking inner-city medical patients. In R. A. Baer (Ed.), *Mindfulness-based treatment approaches* (pp. 263–284). New York: Academic Press.

Roth, D. A., Foa, E. B., & Franklin, M. E. (2003). Response prevention. In W. O'Donohue, J. E. Fisher, & S. C. Hayes (Eds.), *Cognitive behavior therapy: Applying empirically supported techniques in your practice* (pp. 341–348). Hoboken, NJ: Wiley.

Roysircar, G., Sandhu, D. S., & Bibbins, Sr., V. (2003). *Multicultural competencies: A guidebook of practices.* Alexandria, VA: Association for Multicultural Counseling and Development.

Rozental, A., & Carlbring, P. (2014). Understanding and treating procrastination: A review of a common self-regulatory failure. *Psychology, 5*(13), 1488–1502.

Ruf, M., Schauer, M., Neuner, F., Catani, C., Schaue, E., & Elbert, T. (2010). Narrative exposure therapy for 7–16 year olds: A randomized controlled trial with traumatized refugee children. *Journal of Traumatic Stress, 23,* 437–445.

Ruiz, F. J. (2012). Acceptance and commitment therapy versus traditional cognitive behavioral therapy: A systematic review and meta-analysis of current empirical evidence. *International Journal of Psychology and Psychological Therapy, 12*(3), 333–358.

Safran, J., & Muran, J. (2000). *Negotiating the therapeutic alliance: A relational treatment guide.* New York: Guilford Press.

Safran, J., & Muran, J. (2006). Has the concept of the therapeutic alliance outlived its usefulness? *Psychotherapy, 43,* 286–291.

Safran, J., Muran, J., & Eubanks-Carter, C. (2011). Repairing alliance ruptures. In J. C. Norcross (Ed.), *Psychotherapy relationships that work: Evidence-based responsiveness* (2nd ed., pp. 224–238). New York: Oxford University Press.

Safran, J., Muran, J., Wallner Samstag, L., & Stevens, C. (2002). Repairing alliance ruptures. In J. C. Norcross (Ed.), *Psychotherapy relationships that work: Therapist contributions and responsiveness to patients.* (pp. 235–254). New York: Oxford University Press.

Saleebey, D. (Ed.). (2013). *The strengths perspective in social work practice* (6th ed.). Upper Saddle River, NJ: Pearson Education.

Saltzman, W. R., Babayan, T., Lester, P., Beardslee, W. R., & Pynoos, R. S. (2009). Family-based treatment for child traumatic stress: A review and report on current innovations. In D. Brom, R. Pat-Yorenczyuk, & J. D. Ford (Eds.), *Treating traumatized children: Risk, resilience, and recovery* (pp. 240–254). New York: Guilford Press.

Salyers, M. P., & Bond, G. R. (2009). Innovations and adaptations of Assertive Community Treatment.

American Journal of Psychiatric Rehabilitation, 12, 185–190.

Sanchez, L. M., & Turner, S. M. (2003). Practicing psychology in the era of managed care: Implications for practice and training. *American Psychologist, 58,* 116–129.

Sanchez-Meca, J., Rosa-Alcazar, A. I., Marin-Martinez, F., & Gomez-Conesa, A. (2010). Psychological treatment of panic disorder with or without agoraphobia: A meta-analysis. *Clinical Psychology Review, 30,* 37–50.

Sanford, J. A., Griffiths, P. C., Richardson, P., Hargraves, K., Butterfield, T., & Hoenig, H. (2006). The effects of in-home rehabilitation on task self-efficacy in mobility-impaired adults: A randomized clinical trial. *Journal of the American Geriatrics Society, 54*(11), 1641–1648.

Satink, T., Cup, E. H., de Swart, B. J., & Nijhuis-van der Sanden, M. W. (2014). How is self-management perceived by community living people after a stroke? A focus group study. *Disability & Rehabilitation, 37*(3), 223–230.

Saunders, S. M., Miller, M. L., & Bright, M. M. (2010). Spiritually conscious psychological care. *Professional Psychology: Research and Practice, 41,* 355–362.

Savage, D., & Miller, T. (2012). *It gets better: Coming out, overcoming bullying, and creating a life worth living.* New York: Plume/Penguin Group.

Sayers, S. L., & Tomcho, T. J. (2006). Behavioral interviewing. In M. Hersen (Ed.), *Clinician's handbook of adult behavioral assessment* (pp. 63–84). Burlington, MA: Elsevier Academic.

Schaie, K. W., & Carstensen, L. L. (2006). Social structures, aging, and self-regulation in the elderly. New York: Springer.

Schare, M. L., & Wyatt, K. P. (2013). On the evolving nature of exposure therapy. *Behavior Therapy, 37,* 243–256.

Scheid, T. L. (2005). Stigma as a barrier to employment: Mental disability and the Americans with Disabilities Act. *International Journal of Law and Psychiatry, 28,* 670–690.

Schneider, K. J. (2011). Existential-humanistic psychotherapies. In S. B. Messer & A. S. Gurman (Eds.), *Essential psychotherapies: Theory and practice* (3rd ed., pp. 261–294). New York: Guilford Press.

Schoenbeck, S. (2010). Living your values. *Spirituality and Health, Nov.–Dec.,* pp. 62–65.

Schomburg, L. M., & Prieto, A. R. (2011). Trainee multicultural case conceptualization ability and couples therapy. *Journal of Marital & Family Therapy, 37,* 223–235.

Schomerus, G., Corrigan, P. W., Klauer, T., Kuwert, Ph., Freyberger, H. J., Lucht, M. (2011). Self-stigma in alcohol dependence: Consequences for drinking-refusal self-efficacy. *Drug and Alcohol Dependence, 114*(1), 12–17.

Schulman-Green, D., Jaser, S., Martin, F., Alonzo, A., Grey, M., McCorkle, R., … Whittemore, R. (2012). Processes of self-management in chronic illness. *Journal of Nursing Scholarship, 44*(2), 136–144.

Schunk, D. H., & Zimmerman, B. J. (2008*). Motivation and self-regulated learning: Theory, research, and applications.* New York: Erlbaum.

Schüz, B., Bower, J., & Ferguson, S. G. (2015). Stimulus control and affect in dietary behaviours. An intensive longitudinal study. *Appetite, 87,* 310–317.

Scott, A., & Wilson, L. (2011). Valued identities and deficit identities: Wellness recovery action planning and self-management in mental health. *Nursing Inquiry, 18,* 40–49.

Seabury, B. A., Seabury, B., & Garvin, C. D. (2011). *Foundations of interpersonal practice in social work.* Thousand Oaks, CA: Sage.

Sedlmeier, P., Eberth, J., Schwarz, M., Zimmermann, D., Haarig, F., Jaeger, S., & Kunze, S. (2012). The psychological effects of meditation: A meta-analysis. *Psychological Bulletin, 138*(6), 1139–1171.

Sedney, M., Baker, J., & Gross, E. (1994). "The story" of a death: Therapeutic considerations with bereaved families. *Journal of Marital and Family Therapy, 20,* 287–296.

Segal, D., & Hersen, M. (2009). *Diagnostic interviewing* (4th ed.). New York: Springer.

Segal, Z. V., Williams, J. M., & Teasdale, J. D. (2013). *Mindfulness-based cognitive therapy for depression (*2nd ed.*).* New York: Guilford Press.

Selekman, M. D. (1993). *Pathways to change: Brief therapy solutions with difficult adolescents.* New York: Guilford Press.

Seligman, M. E. P., & Csikszentmihalyi, M. (2000). Positive psychology: An introduction. *American Psychologist, 55,* 5–14.

Serino, S., Triberti, S., Villani, D., Cipresso, P., Gaggioli, A., & Riva, G. (2014). Toward a validation of cyber-interventions for stress disorders based on stress inoculation training: A systematic review. *Virtual Reality, 18*(1), 73–87.

Sexton, T. L., & Kelley, S. D. (2010). Finding the common core: Evidence-based practices, clinically relevant evidence, and core mechanisms of change.

Administration and Policy in Mental Health and Mental Health Services Research, 37, 81–88.

Shallcross, L. (2010, July). Confronting the threat of suicide. *Counseling Today, 28*–35.

Shapiro, F. (2001). *Eye movement desensitation and reprocessing: Basic principles, protocols, and procedures* (2nd ed.). New York: Guilford Press.

Shapiro, S. L., & Carlson, L. E. (2009). *The art and science of mindfulness.* Washington, DC: American Psychological Association.

Shaw, L. R., Chan, F., Lam, C. S., & McDougall, A. G. (2004). Professional disclosure practices of rehabilitation counselors. *Rehabilitation Counseling Bulletin, 48,* 38–50.

Shelton, K., & Delgado-Romero, E. A. (2013). Sexual orientation microaggressions: The experience of lesbian, gay, bisexual, and queer clients in psychotherapy. *Psychology of Sexual Orientation and Gender Diversity, 1*(S), 59–70.

Sherry, A., Adelman, A., Whilde, M. R., & Quick, D. (2010). Competing selves: Negotiating the intersection of spiritual and sexual identities. *Professional Psychology: Research and Practice, 41,* 112–119.

Shiffman, S., Stone, A. A., & Huffard, M. R. (2008). Ecological momentary assessment. *Annual Review of Clinical Psychology, 4,* 1–32.

Shilkret, C. J. (2008). Long-term therapy in the age of managed care: The case of Don. *Smith College Studies in Social Work, 78,* 287–300.

Shilts, L., & Thomas, K. A. (2005). Becoming solution-focused: Some beginning thoughts. *Journal of Family Psychotherapy, 16*(1–2), 189–197.

Shonkoff, J. P., Boyce, W. T., & McEwen, B. S. (2009). Neuroscience, molecular biology, and the childhood roots of health disparities. *JAMA, 301*(21), 2252–2259.

Shumaker, D., & Medoff, D. (2013). Ethical and legal considerations when obtaining informed consent for treating minors of high-conflict divorced or separated parents. *The Family Journal, 21,* 318–327.

Shumaker, S. A., Ockene, J. K., & Riekert, K. A. (Eds.). (2009). *The handbook of health behavior change.* New York: Springer.

Siegel, D. J. (2010). *The mindful therapist.* New York: Norton.

Siegel, R. D. (2010). *The mindfulness solution: Everyday practices for everyday problems.* New York: Guilford Press.

Silberschatz, G. (Ed.). (2005). *Transformative relationships: The control-mastery theory of psychotherapy.* New York: Brunner-Routledge.

Silenzio, V. M. B., Pena, J. B., Duberstein, P. R., Cerel, J., & Knox, K. L. (2007). Sexual orientation and risk factors for suicidal ideation and suicide attempts among adolescents and young adults. *American Journal of Public Health, 97,* 2017–2019.

Silverman, W. K., & Albano, A. M. (1996). *Anxiety disorders interview schedule for children.* New York: Oxford University Press.

Simon, C. E., Crowther, M., & Higgerson, H. (2007). The stage-specific role of spirituality among African American Christian women throughout the breast cancer experience. *Cultural Diversity & Ethnic Minority Psychology, 13,* 26–34.

Simone, D. H., McCarthy, P., & Skay, C. (1998). An investigation of client and counselor variables that influence likelihood of counselor self-disclosure. *Journal of Counseling & Development, 76,* 174–182.

Simos, G., & Hofmann, S. G. (2013). *CBT for anxiety disorders: A practitioner's handbook.* Hoboken, NJ: Wiley.

Simpson, D. (2009). Adolescents with OCD: An integration of the transtheoretical model with exposure and response prevention. *Best Practices in Mental Health, 5,* 14–28.

Simpson, H. B., Zuckoff, A., Page, J. R., Franklin, M. E., & Foa, E. B. (2008). Adding motivational interviewing to exposure and ritual prevention for obsessive-compulsive disorder: An open pilot trial. *Cognitive Behaviour Therapy, 37,* 38–49.

Singh, N. N., Lancioni, G. E., Manikam, R., Winton, A. S. W., Singh, A. N. A., Singh, J., & Singh, A. D. A. (2011). A mindfulness-based strategy for self-management of aggressive behavior in adolescents with autism. *Research in Autism Spectrum Disorders, 5*(3), 1153–1158.

Skovholt, T. M. (2001). *The resilient practitioner: Burnout prevention and self-care strategies for counselors, therapists, teachers, and health professionals.* Boston, MA: Allyn & Bacon.

Skovholt, T. M., & Jennings, L. (2004). *Master therapists: Exploring expertise in therapy and counseling.* Boston, MA: Allyn & Bacon.

Skovholt, T. M., & Starkey, M. T. (2010). The three legs of the practitioner's learning stool: Practice, research/theory, and personal life. *Journal of Contemporary Psychotherapy, 40,* 125–130.

Skovholt, T. M., & Trotter-Mathison, M. (2011). *The resilient practitioner: Burnout prevention and self-care strategies for counselors, therapists, teachers, and health professionals* (2nd ed.). New York: Routledge/Taylor & Francis.

Skovholt, T. M., & Trotter-Mathison, M. (2013). Therapist professional resilience. In M. H. Rønnestad & T. M. Skovholt (Eds.), *The developing practitioner: Growth and stagnation of therapists and counselors* (pp. 247–264). New York: Taylor & Francis/Routledge.

Slagle, D. M., & Gray, M. J. (2007). The utility of motivational interviewing as an adjunct to exposure therapy in the treatment of anxiety disorders. *Professional Psychology: Research and Practice, 38*, 329–337.

Slatcher, R. B., Chi, P., Li, X., Zhao, J., Zhao, G., Ren, X., … Stanton, B. (2015). Associations between coping and diurnal cortisol among children affected by parental HIV/AIDS. *Health Psychology, 34*, 802–810.

Slater, M., & Wilbur, S. (1997). A framework for immersive virtual environments (FIVE): Speculations on the role of presence in virtual environments. *Presence: Teleoperators and Virtual Environments, 6*(6), 1–20. Retrieved from http://publicationslist.org/data/melslater/ref-232/pres5.pdf

Smedley, B. D., Stith, A. Y., & Nelson, A. R. (Eds.). (2003). *Unequal treatment: Confronting racial and ethnic disparities in health care*. Washington, DC: National Academies Press.

Smith, D., & Fitzpatrick, M. (1995). Patient–therapist boundary issues. *Professional Psychology, 26*, 499–506.

Smith, E. P., Walker, K., Fields, L., Brookins, C. C., & Seay, R. C. (1999). Ethnic identity and its relationship to self-esteem, perceived efficacy, and prosocial attitudes in early adolescence. *Journal of Adolescence, 22*, 867–880.

Smith, T. B., Rodriguez, M. D., & Bernal, G. (2011). Culture. *Journal of Clinical Psychology, 67*, 166–175.

Smith, T. B., Rodriguez, M. D., & Bernal, G. (2011). Culture. In J. C. Norcross (Ed.), *Psychotherapy relationships that work: Evidence-based responsiveness* (2nd ed., pp. 316–335). New York: Oxford University Press.

Smolar, A. I. (2003). When we give: Reflections on intangible gifts from therapist to patient. *American Journal of Psychotherapy, 57*, 300–323.

Snyder, C. R., & Lopez, S. J. (2007). *Positive psychology: The scientific and practical explorations of human strengths*. Thousand Oaks, CA: Sage.

Sobell, L. C., & Sobell, M. B. (2008). Timeline followback. In A. J. Rush, M. B. First, & D. Blacker (Eds.), *Handbook of psychiatric measures* (2nd ed., pp. 466–468). Washington, DC: American Psychiatric Publishing.

Soler, J., Valdepérez, A., Feliu-Soler, A., Pascual, J. C., Portella, M. J., Martín-Blanco, A., … Pérez, V. (2012). Effects of the dialectical behavioral therapy-mindfulness module on attention in patients with borderline personality disorder. *Behaviour Research and Therapy, 50*(2), 150–157.

Sommers-Flanagan, J., & Sommers-Flanagan, R. (2014). *Clinical interviewing* (5th ed.). New York: Wiley.

Sonderegger, R., & Barrett, P. M. (2004). Assessment and treatment of ethnically diverse children and adolescents. In P. M. Barrett & T. H. Ollendick (Eds.), *Handbook of interventions that work with children and adolescents: Prevention and treatment* (pp. 89–111). New York: Wiley.

Sparks, J. A., Duncan, B. L., Cohen, D., & Antonuccio, D. O. (2010). Psychiatric drugs and common factors: An evaluation of risks and benefits for clinical practice. In B. L. Duncan, S. D. Miller, B. E. Wampold, & M. A. Hubble (Eds.). *The heart and soul of change: Delivering what works in therapy* (2nd ed., pp. 199–235). Washington, DC: American Psychological Association.

Spiegler, M. D., & Guevremont, D. C. (2010). *Contemporary behavior therapy* (5th ed.). Belmont, CA: Wadsworth.

Spira, J. L., Johnston, S., McLay, R., Popovic, S., Russoniello, C., & Wood, D. (2010). Expert panel: Future directions of technological advances in prevention, assessment, and treatment for military deployment mental health. *Cyberpsychology, Behavior, and Social Networking, 13*(1), 109–117.

Spring, B., Duncan, J. M., Janke, E. A., Kozak, A. T., McFadden, H. G., DeMott, A., … Hedeker, D. (2013). Integrating technology into standard weight loss treatment: A randomized controlled trial. *JAMA Internal Medicine, 173*(2), 105–111.

Springer, D. W., Lynch, C., & Rubin, A. (2000). Effects of a solution-focused mutual aid group for Hispanic children of incarcerated parents. *Child and Adolescent Social Work Journal, 17*, 431–442.

St Lawrence, J. S., Brasfield, T. L., Jefferson, K. W., Alleyne, E., O'Bannon III, R. E., & Shirley, A. (1995). Cognitive-behavioral intervention to reduce African American adolescents' risk for HIV infection. *Journal of Consulting and Clinical Psychology, 63*(2), 221–237.

Stahler, O. J., Fairclough, D. L., Philipps, S., Mulhern, R. K., Dolgin, M. J., Noll, R. B., … Butler, R. W. (2005). Using problem-solving skills training to reduce negative affectivity in mothers of children with newly diagnosed cancer: Report of a multi-site randomized trial. *Journal of Consulting and Clinical Psychology, 73*, 272–283.

Stanley, E. A., Schaldach, J. M., Kiyonaga, A., & Jha, A. P. (2011). Mindfulness-based mind fitness training:

A case study of a high-stress predeployment military cohort. *Cognitive and Behavioral Practice, 18*, 566–576.

Standard, R. P., Sandhu, D. S., & Painter, L. C. (2000). Assessment of spirituality in counseling. *Journal of Counseling & Development, 78*, 204–210.

Stebnicki, M. A. (2009). Empathy fatigue in the counseling profession. In I. Marini & M. A. Stebnicki (Eds.), *The professional counselor's desk reference* (pp. 801–812). New York: Springer.

Steenkamp, M. M., Litz, B. T., Gray, M. J., Lebowitz, L., Nash, W., Conoscenti, L., … Lang, A. (2011). A brief exposure-based intervention for service members with PTSD. *Cognitive and Behavioral Practice, 18*, 98–107.

Steinhubl, S. R., Wineinger, N. E., Patel, S., Boeldt, D. L., Mackellar, G., Porter, V., … Topol, E. J. (2015). Cardiovascular and nervous system changes during meditation. *Frontiers in Human Neuroscience, 9*(145). First published online. doi: 10.3389/fnhum.2015.00145

Stepp, S. D., Epler, A. J., Jahng, S., & Trull, T. J. (2008). The effect of dialectical behaviour therapy skills use on borderline personality disorder features. *Journal of Personality Disorders, 22*(6), 549–563.

Stiffman, A. R., Orme, J. G., Evans, D. A., Feldman, R. A., & Keeney, P. A. (1984). A brief measure of children's behavior problems: The Behavior Rating Index for Children. *Measurement and Evaluation in Counseling and Development, 16*, 83–90.

Stobbe, J., Wierdsma, A. I., Kok, R. B., Kroon, H., Roosenschoon, B., Depla, M., & Mulder, C. L. (2014). The effectiveness of assertive community treatment for elderly patients with severe mental illness: A randomized controlled trial. *BMC Psychiatry, 14*. Retrieved from www.biomedcentral.com/1471-244X/14/42

Stoley, P., Awad, M., Byrne, K., DeForge, R., Clements, S., Glenny, C., & The Day Hospital Goal Attainment Scaling Interest Group of the Regional Geriatric Programs of Ontario. (2012). A multi-site study of the feasibility and clinical utility of Goal Attainment Scaling in geriatric day hospitals. *Disability & Rehabilitation, 34*, 1716–1726.

Strasser, A. (2015). Trauma-focused cognitive behavioral therapy: An evidence based practice applicable with minority children. *Gallaudet Chronicles of Psychology, 3*(1), 38–42.

Straus, S. E., Richardson, W. S., Glasziou, P., & Haynes, R. B. (2010). *Evidence-based medicine: How to practice and teach it* (4th ed.). Edinburgh, Scotland: Elsevier.

Stretton, C. M., Latham, N. K., Carter, K. N., Lee, A. C., & Anderson, C. S. (2006). Determinants of physical health in frail older people: The importance of self-efficacy. *Clinical Rehabilitation, 20*(4), 357–366.

Stroebe, W. (2008). *Dieting, overweight, and obesity: Self-regulation in a food-rich environment.* Washington, DC: American Psychological Association.

Strong, S. R. (1968). Counseling: An interpersonal influence process. *Journal of Counseling Psychology, 15*, 215–224.

Strong, S. R., Welsh, J., Corcoran, J., & Hoyt, W. (1992). Social psychology and counseling psychology: The history, products, and promise of an interface. *Journal of Counseling Psychology, 39*, 139–157.

Strong, T. (2000). Six orienting ideas for collaborative counselors. *The European Journal of Psychotherapy, Counselling and Health, 3*, 25–42.

Strong, T. (2002). Constructive curiosities. *Journal of Systemic Therapies, 21*(1), 77–90.

Strong, T., & Zeman, D. (2010). Dialogic considerations of confrontation as a counseling activity: An examination of Allen Ivey's use of confronting as a microskill. *Journal of Counseling & Development, 88*, 332–339.

Strosahl, K. D., Hayes, S. C., Wilson, K. G., & Gifford, E. V. (2004). An ACT primer: Core therapy processes, intervention strategies, and therapist competencies. In S. C. Hayes & K. D. Strosahl (Eds.), *A practical guide to acceptance and commitment therapy* (pp. 31–58). New York: Springer.

Substance Abuse and Mental Health Services Administration. (2013). *Results from the 2012 National Survey on Drug Use and Health: Mental Health Findings* (NSDUH Series H-47, HHS Publication No. (SMA) 13-4805). Rockville, MD: Author.

Sue, D. W. (2001). Multidimensional facets of cultural competence. *The Counseling Psychologist, 29*, 790–821.

Sue, D. W. (Ed.). (2010). *Microaggressions and marginality.* Hoboken, NJ: Wiley.

Sue, D. W. (2010). *Microaggressions in everyday life: Race, gender, and sexual orientation.* Hoboken, NJ: Wiley.

Sue, D. W., Arredondo, P., & McDavis, R. J. (1992). Multicultural counseling competencies and standards: A call to the profession. *Journal of Counseling & Development, 70*, 477–486.

Sue, D. W., Bernier, J. E., Durran, A., Feinberg, L., Pedersen, P., Smith, E. J., & Vasquez-Nuttall, E. (1982). Position paper: Cross-cultural counseling competencies. *The Counseling Psychologist, 10*, 45–52.

Sue, D. W., Capodilupo, C. M., Torino, G. C., Bucceri, J. M., Holder, A. M. B., Nadal, K. L., & Esquilin,

M. (2007). Racial microaggressions in everyday life: Implications for clinical practice. *American Psychologist, 62,* 271–286.

Sue, D. W., & Sue, D. (2008). *Counseling the culturally diverse: Theory and practice* (5th ed.). New York: Wiley.

Sue, D. W., & Sue, D. (2013). *Counseling the culturally diverse: Theory and practice* (6th ed.). New York: Wiley.

Sullivan, J. (2004). *Living large: Transformative work at the intersection of ethics and spirituality.* Laurel, MD: Tai Sophia.

Summerfeldt, L. J., Kloosterman, P. H., & Antony, M. M. (2010). Structured and semistructured diagnostic interviews. In M. Antony & D. Barlow (Eds.), *Handbook of assessment and treatment planning for psychological disorders* (2nd ed., pp. 95–137). New York: Guilford Press.

Summers, N. (2012). *Fundamentals of case management practice* (4th ed.). Belmont, CA: Wadsworth.

Suppiger, A., In-Albon, T., Hendriksen, S., Hermann, E., Margraf, J., & Schneider, S. (2009). Acceptance of structured diagnostic interviews for mental disorders in clinical practice and research settings. *Behavior Therapy, 40,* 272–279.

Swerissen, H., Belfrage, J., Weeks, A., Jordan, L., Walker, C., Furler, J., … Peterson. C. (2006). A randomised control trial of a self-management program for people with a chronic illness from Vietnamese, Chinese, Italian and Greek backgrounds. *Patient Education and Counseling, 64*(1–3), 360–368.

Swift, J. K., Callahan, J. L., & Vollmer, B. M. (2011). Preferences. *Journal of Clinical Psychology, 67,* 155–165.

Tan, S-Y., & Brad, W. (2005). Spiritually oriented cognitive-behavioral therapy. In L. Sperry & E. P. Shafranske (Eds.), *Spiritually oriented psychotherapy* (p. 77–103). Washington, DC: American Psychological Association.

Tan, J. O. A., Passerini, G. E., & Stewart, A. (2007). Consent and confidentiality in clinical work with young people. *Clinical Child Psychiatry and Psychiatry, 12,* 191–210.

Tanaka-Matsumi, J., Seiden, D. Y., & Lam, K. N. (1996). The culturally informed functional assessment (CIFA) interview: A strategy for cross-cultural behavioral practice. *Cognitive and Behavioral Practice, 3,* 215–233.

Tang, J. (2014). *Examining cognitive behavioral therapy with Asian American patients in an acute psychiatric partial hospital setting.* Counseling Psychology Dissertations, Northeastern University.

Tarasoff v. Regents of the University of California et al., 551 P.2d 334. (1976).

Tarvydas, V. M. (2012). Ethics and ethics decision making. In D. R. Maki & V. M. Tarvydas (Eds.), *The professional practice of rehabilitation counseling* (pp. 339–370). New York: Springer.

Tavee, J., & Stone, L. (2010). Healing the mind: Meditation and multiple sclerosis. *Neurology, 75*(13), 1130–1131.

Taylor, S. (2004). Efficacy and outcome predictors for three PTSD treatments: Exposure therapy, EMDR, and relaxation training. In S. Taylor (Ed.), *Advances in the treatment of posttraumatic stress disorder: Cognitive behavioral perspectives* (pp. 13–37). New York: Springer.

Taylor, E. H. (2006). The weaknesses of the strengths model: Mental illness as a case in point. *Best Practices in Mental Health, 2,* 1–30.

Taylor, L., McMinn, M. R., Bufford, R. K., & Chang, K. B. T. (2010). Psychologists' attitudes and ethical concerns regarding the use of social networking web sites. *Professional Psychology: Research and Practice, 41,* 153–159.

Teasdale, J. D., Moore, R. G., Hayhurst, H., Pope, M., Williams, S., & Segal, Z. V. (2002). Metacognitive awareness and prevention of relapse in depression: Empirical evidence. *Journal of Consulting and Clinical Psychology, 70*(2), 275–287.

Tenhula, W. N., Nezu, A. M., Nezu, C. M., Stewart, M. O., Miller, S. A., Steele, J., & Karlin, B. E. (2014). Moving forward: A problem-solving training program to foster veteran resilience. *Professional Psychology: Research and Practice, 45*(6), 416–424.

Teyber, E., & McClure, F. (2011). *Interpersonal process in therapy* (6th ed.). Belmont, CA: Cengage Learning.

Theokas, C., & Lerner, R. M. (2006). Observed ecological assets in families, schools and neighborhoods: Conceptualization, measurement and relations with positive and negative developmental outcomes. *Applied Developmental Science, 10,* 61–74.

Thoma, N. C., & McKay, D. (Eds.). *Working with emotion in cognitive-behavioral therapy: Techniques for clinical practice.* New York: Guilford Press.

Thomas, V. L., & Gostin, L. O. (2009). The Americans with Disabilities Act: Shattered aspirations and new hope. *Journal of the American Medical Association, 301,* 95–97.

Thompson, A. (2011). The relationship among health literacy, self-efficacy, and self-management of individuals with diabetes. *Dissertation Abstracts International, 71*(7-B), 4181.

Thompson, M. N., & Graham, S. R. (2015). Self-efficacy beliefs. In P. J. Hartung, M. L. Savickas, & W. B. Walsh (Eds.), *APA handbook of career intervention, Volume 2: Applications* (pp. 171–182). Washington, DC.

Thyer, B. A. (2009). Evidence-based practice, science, and social work: An overview. In A. R. Roberts (Ed.), *Social workers' desk reference* (2nd ed., pp. 1115–1119). New York: Oxford University Press.

Thyer, B., & Myers, L. (2000). Approaches to behavior change. In P. Allen-Meares & C. Garvin (Eds.), *Handbook of social work direct practice* (pp. 197–216). Thousand Oaks, CA: Sage.

Thyer, B. A., & Myers, L. L. (2011). The quest for evidence-based practice: A view from the United States. *Journal of Social Work, 11*, 8–25.

Thyer, B. A., & Pignotti, M. (2011). Evidence-based practices do not exist. *Clinical Social Work Journal, 39*, 328–333.

Tishby, O., & Wiseman, H. (2014). Types of countertransference dynamics: An exploration of their impact on the client-therapist relationship. *Psychotherapy Research, 24*, 360–375.

Tjeltveit, A. C., & Gottlieb, M. C. (2010). Avoiding the road to ethical disaster: Overcoming vulnerabilities and developing resilience. *Psychotherapy: Theory, Research, Practice, Training, 47*, 98–110.

Tompkins, K. A., Swift, J. K., & Callahan, J. L. (2013). Working with clients by incorporating their preferences. *Psychotherapy, 50*, 279–283.

Torrey, W. C., & Drake, R. E. (2010). Practicing shared decision making in the outpatient psychiatric care of adults with severe mental illnesses: Redesigning care for the future. *Community Mental Health Journal, 46*, 433–440.

Treadway, M. T., & Lazar, S. W. (2009). The neurobiology of mindfulness. *Clinical Handbook of Mindfulness, 2*, 45–57.

Trepper, T. S., McCollum, E. E., De Jong, P., Korman, H., Gingerich, W., & Franklin, C. (2012). *Solution-focused brief therapy treatment.* In C. Franklin, T. S. Trepper, W. J. Gingerich, & E. E. McCollum (Eds.), *Solution-focused brief therapy: A handbook of evidence-based practice* (pp. 20–36). New York: Oxford University Press.

Truax, C. B., & Mitchell, K. M. (1971). Research on certain therapist interpersonal skills in relation to process and outcome. In A. Bergin & S. Garfield (Eds.), *Handbook of psychotherapy and behavior change: An empirical analysis.* (pp. 299–344). New York: Wiley.

Tryon, G. S., & Winograd, G. (2011). Goal consensus and collaboration. In J. C. Norcross (Ed.), *Psychotherapy relationships that work: Evidence-based responsiveness* (2nd ed., pp. 153–167). New York: Oxford University Press.

Tryon, W. W. (2005). Possible mechanisms for why desensitization and exposure therapy work. *Clinical Psychology Review, 25*, 67–95.

Tsao, J. C., & Craske, M. G. (2000). Timing of treatment and return of fear: Effects of massed, uniform- and expanding-spaced exposure schedules. *Behavior Therapy, 31*, 479–497.

Turner, A., Anderson, J. K., Wallace, L. M., & Bourne, C. (2015). An evaluation of a self-management program for patients with long-term conditions. *Patient Education and Counseling, 98*(2), 213–219.

Turner, J. A., Edwards, L. M., Eicken, I. M., Yokoyama, K., Castro, J. R., Tran, A. N., & Haggins, K. L. (2005). Intern self-care: An exploratory study into strategy use and effectiveness. *Professional Psychology: Research and Practice, 36*, 674–680.

Turner-Stokes, L. (2010). Goal attainment scaling: A direct comparison of alternative rating methods. *Clinical Rehabilitation, 24*, 66–73.

Turvey, C. L., & Myers, K. (2013). Introduction. In K. Myers & C. L. Turvey (Eds.), *Telemental health: Clinical, technical, and administrative foundations for evidence-based practice* (pp. 3–9). Amsterdam, Netherlands: Elsevier.

Twohig, M. P., & Peterson, K. A. (2009). Distress tolerance. In W. O'Donohue & J. E. Fisher (Eds.), *General principles and empirically supported techniques of cognitive behavior therapy* (pp. 265–271). Hoboken, NJ: Wiley.

Underwood, P. W. (2012). Social support: The promise and the reality. In V. H. Rice (Ed.), *Handbook of stress, coping, and health: Implications for nursing research, theory, and practice* (2nd ed., pp. 355–380). Thousand Oaks, CA: Sage.

Ungar, M. (2011). *Counseling in challenging contexts.* Belmont, CA: Cengage Learning.

United States Department of Veterans Affairs. (2014). PTSD: National center for PTSD. *Mobile app: Mindfulness coach.* Retrieved from http://www.ptsd.va.gov/public/materials/apps/mobileapp_mindfulness_coach.asp

U.S. Census Bureau. (2011, March). *Overview of race and Hispanic origin: 2010.* Retrieved from http://www.census.gov/prod/cen2010/briefs/c2010br-02.pdf

U.S. Department of Health and Human Services. (2001). *Mental health: Culture, race, and ethnicity—A supplement to mental health: A report of the surgeon general—Executive summary*. Rockville, MD: Author.

U.S. Department of Health and Human Services, Office of Minority Health. (2013, April). *National standards for culturally and linguistically appropriate services in health and health care (CLAS)*. Washington, DC: Author. Retrieved from www.thinkculturalhealth.hhs.gov

U.S. Department of Veterans Affairs and Department of Defense. (2004). *VA/DoD clinical practice guidelines for the management of post-traumatic stress*. Washington, DC: Author.

Valiente-Barroso, C. (2014). Brain plasticity associated with meditation experience: Neurofunctional approach and structural findings. *International Journal of Brain and Cognitive Sciences, 3*(1), 6–24.

Vallejo, Z. (2009). Adaptation of a mindfulness-based stress reduction program for addiction relapse prevention. *The Humanist Psychologist, 37*, 192–206.

VanBuskirk, K. A., & Wetherell, J. L. (2014). Motivational interviewing with primary care populations: A systematic review and meta-analysis. *Journal of Behavioral Medicine, 37*, 768–780

VandenBos, G. R. (2007). *APA Dictionary of Psychology*. Washington, DC: American Psychological Association.

van Dixhoorn, J. (2007). Whole-body breathing: A systems perspective on respiratory retraining. In P. M. Lehrer, R. L. Woolfolk, & W. E. Sime (Eds.), *Principles and practice of stress management* (3rd ed., pp. 291–332). New York: Guilford Press.

Van Horn, P., & Lieberman, A. F. (2009). Using dyadic therapies to treat traumatized young children. In D. Brom, R. Pat-Yorenczyuk, & J. D. Ford (Eds.), *Treating traumatized children: Risk, resilience, and recovery* (pp. 210–224). New York: Guilford Press.

Vasilaki, E. I., Hosier, S. G., & Cox, W. M. (2006). The efficacy of motivational interviewing as a brief intervention for excessive drinking: A meta-analytic review. *Alcohol and Alcoholism, 41*, 328–335.

Vera, M., Vila, D., & Alegria, M. (2003). Cognitive-behavioral therapy: Concepts, issues, and strategies for practice with racial/ethnic minorities. In G. Bernal, J. E. Trimble, A. K. Berlew, & F. T. Leong (Eds.), *Handbook of racial and ethnic minority psychology* (pp. 1–15). Thousand Oaks, CA: Sage.

Vervliet, B., Craske, M. G., & Hermans, D. (2013). Fear extinction and relapse: State of the art. *Annual Review of Clinical Psychology, 9*, 215–248.

Vicary, D., & Andrews, H. (2000). Developing a culturally appropriate psychotherapeutic approach with indigenous Australians. *Australian Psychologist, 35*, 181–185.

Vilardaga, R., Bricker, J. B., & McDonell, M. G. (2014). The promise of mobile technologies and single case designs for the study of individuals in their natural environment. *Journal of Contextual Behavioral Science, 3*(2), 148–153.

Villani, D., Grassi, A., Cognetta, C., Toniolo, D., Cipresso, P., & Riva, G. (2013). Self-help stress management training through mobile phones: An experience with oncology nurses. *Psychological Services, 10*(3), 315–322.

Viner, R. M., Christie, D., Taylor, V., & Hey, S. (2003). Motivational/solution-focused intervention improves HbA_{1c} in adolescents with Type 1 diabetes: A pilot study. *Diabetic Medicine, 20*, 739–742.

Virnig, B., Huang, Z., Lurie, N., Musgrave, D., McBean, A. M., & Dowd, B. (2004). Does Medicare managed care provide equal treatment for mental illness across races? *Archives of General Psychiatry, 61*, 201–205.

Vittengl, J. R., Clark, L. A., Dunn, T. W., & Jarrett, R. B. (2007). Reducing relapse and recurrence in unipolar depression: A comparative meta-analysis of cognitive-behavioral therapy's effects. *Journal of Consulting and Clinical Psychology, 75*, 475–488.

Vocisano, C., Klein, D., Arnow, B., Rivera, C., Blalock, J., Rothbaum, B., … Thase, M. E. (2004). Therapist variables that predict symptom change in psychotherapy with chronically depressed outpatients. *Psychotherapy: Theory, Research, Practice, and Training, 41*, 255–265.

Vohs, K. D., & Baumeister, R. F. (Eds.). (2011). *Handbook of self-regulation: Research, theory, and applications* (2nd ed.). New York: Guilford Press.

Vohs, K. D., & Finkel, E. J. (2006). *Self and relationships: Connecting intrapersonal and interpersonal processes*. New York: Guilford Press.

Wachtel, P. L. (2010). Beyond "ESTs": Problematic assumptions in the pursuit of evidence-based practice. *Psychoanalytic Psychology, 27*, 251–272.

Wade, S. L., Walz, N. C., Carey, J., McMullen, K. M., Cass, J., Mark, E., & Yeates, K. O. (2012). A randomized trial of teen online problem solving: Efficacy in improving caregiver outcomes after brain injury. *Health Psychology, 31*(6), 767–776.

Wagner, C. C., & Ingersoll, K. S., with Contributors. (2013). *Motivational interviewing in groups*. New York: Guilford Press.

Wald, J. (2008). Interoceptive exposure as a prelude to trauma-related exposure therapy in a case of posttraumatic stress disorder with substantial comorbidity. *Journal of Cognitive Psychotherapy, 22*, 331–345.

Walfish, S., McCalister, B., O'Donnell, P., & Lambert, M. J. (2012). An investigation of self-assessment bias in mental health providers. *Psychological Reports, 110*(2), 639–644.

Walker, J. A., & Prince, T. (2010). Training considerations and suggested counseling interventions for LGBT individuals. *Journal of LGBT Issues in Counseling, 4*, 2–17.

Wallace, J. E., & Brinkerhoff, M. B. (1991). The measurement of burnout revisited. *Journal of Social Service Research, 14*, 85–111.

Walsh, C. A., Olson, J. L., Ploeg, J., Lohfeld, L., & MacMillan, H. L. (2011). Elder abuse and oppression: Voices of marginalized elders. *Journal of Elder Abuse & Neglect, 23*, 17–42.

Walsh, W. B., Craik, K., & Price, R. (Eds.). (2000). *Person-environment psychology: New directions and perspectives* (2nd ed.). Mahwah, NJ: Lawrence Erlbaum.

Wallston, K. A., Osborn, C. Y., Wagner, L. J., & Hilker, K. A. (2011). The Perceived Medical Condition Self-Management Scale applied to persons with HIV/AIDS, *Journal of Health Psychology, 16*(1), 109–115.

Walter, J. L., & Peller, J. E. (2000). *Recreating brief therapy: Preferences and possibilities.* New York: Norton.

Walters, K. L., Mohammed, S. A., Evans-Campbell, T., Beltrán, R. E., Chae, D. H., & Duran, B. (2011). Bodies don't just tell stories, they tell histories. *Du Bois Review: Social Science Research on Race, 8*(1), 179–189.

Wampold, B. E. (2001). *The great psychotherapy debate: Models, methods, and findings.* Mahwah, NJ: Erlbaum.

Wampold, B. E. (2007). Psychotherapy: The humanistic (and effective) treatment. *American Psychologist, 62*, 857–873.

Wampold, B. E. (2010). The research evidence for common factors models: A historically situated perspective. In B. L. Duncan, S. D. Miller, B. E. Wampold, & M. A. Hubble (Eds.), *The heart and soul of change: Delivering what works in therapy* (2nd ed., pp. 49–81). Washington, DC: American Psychological Association.

Wampold, B. E., & Brown, G. S. (2005). Estimating variability in outcomes attributable to therapists: A naturalistic study of outcomes in managed care. *Journal of Consulting and Clinical Psychology, 73*, 914–923.

Wampold, B. E., Goodheart, C. D., & Levant, R. F. (2007). Clarification and elaboration on evidence-based practice in psychology. *American Psychologist, 62*, 616–618.

Wang, C. J., & Huang, D. J. (2013). The HIPAA conundrum in the era of mobile health and communications. *JAMA, 310*(11), 1121–1122.

Ward v. Wilbanks et al., No. 09-CV-11237 (E. D. Mich. July 26, 2010).

Warren-Findlow, J., Seymour, R. B., & Huber, L. R. B. (2012). The association between self-efficacy and hypertension self-care activities among African American adults. *Journal of Community Health, 37*(1), 15–24.

Watson, D. L., & Tharp, R. G. (2007). *Self-directed behavior: Self modification for personal adjustment* (9th ed.). Pacific Grove, CA: Thomson Wadsworth.

Watson, D. L., & Tharp, R. G. (2014). *Self-directed behavior: Self modification for personal adjustment* (10th ed.). Pacific Grove, CA: Thomson Wadsworth.

Watson, J. C., & Greenberg, L. S. (2011). Empathic resonance: A neuroscience perspective. In J. Decety & W. Ickes (Eds.), *The social neuroscience of empathy* (pp. 125–138). Cambridge, MA: MIT.

Watson, J. C., Steckley P. L., & McMullen, E. J. (2014). The role of empathy in promoting change. *Psychotherapy Research, 24*(3), 286–298.

Weber, J. G. (2011). *Individual and family stress and crisis.* Thousand Oaks, CA: Sage.

Weiner-Davis, M., de Shazer, S., & Gingerich, W. J. (1987). Building on pretreatment change to construct the therapeutic solution: An exploratory study. *Journal of Marital and Family Therapy, 13, 359–363.*

Weiss, J. (2002). Control-mastery theory. *Encyclopedia of Psychotherapy, I,* 1–5.

Weisz, J. R., & Kazdin, A. E. (Eds.). (2010). *Evidence-based psychotherapies for children and adolescents.* New York: Guilford Press.

Weisz, J. R., McCarty, C. A., & Valeri, S. M. (2006). Effects of psychotherapy for depression in children and adolescents: A meta-analysis. *Psychological Bulletin, 132,* 132–149.

Welch, S. S., Rizvi, S., & Dimidjian, S. (2006). Mindfulness in dialectical behavior therapy (DBT) for borderline personality disorder. In R. A. Baer (Ed.), *Mindfulness-based treatment approaches: Clinician's guide to evidence base and applications* (pp. 117–139). New York: Academic Press.

Welfel, E. R. (2016). *Ethics in counseling and psychotherapy: Standards, research, and emerging issues* (6th ed.). Boston, MA: Cengage Learning.

Welfel, E. R., & Patterson, L. E. (2005). *The counseling process* (6th ed.). Pacific Grove, CA: Cengage Learning e.

Wells, R. E., Yeh, G. Y., Kerr, C. E., Wolkin, J., Davis, R. B., Tan, Y., ... Kong, J. (2013). Meditation's impact on default mode network and hippocampus in mild cognitive impairment: A pilot study. *Neuroscience Letters, 556,* 15–19.

Werth, J. L., Hastings, S. L., & Riding-Malon, R. (2010). Ethical challenges of practicing in rural areas. *Journal of Clinical Psychology: In Session, 66,* 537–548.

Werth, J. L., Jr., Welfel, E. R., & Benjamin, G. A. H. (2009). *The duty to protect: Ethical, legal, and professional considerations for mental health professionals.* Washington, DC: American Psychological Association.

Werthwein, R. A. (2009). A situational approach to smoking cessation: Using the straight up S3 intervention to promote cessation among African Americans. *Dissertation Abstracts International, 69*(11-B), 7155.

West, R. T. (2005). Time for a change: Putting the Transtheoretical (Stages of Change) Model to rest. *Addiction, 100,* 1036–1039.

Westen, D., Novotny, C. M., & Thompson-Brenner, H. (2005). EBP ≠ EST: Reply to Crits-Christoph et al. (2005) and Weisz et al. (2005). *Psychological Bulletin, 131,* 427–433.

Westra, H. A. (2012). *Motivational interviewing in the treatment of anxiety.* New York: Guilford Press.

Westra, H. A., & Arkowitz, H. (2010). Combining motivational interviewing and cognitive-behavioral therapy to increase treatment efficacy for generalized anxiety disorder. In D. Sookman & R. L. Leahy (Eds.), *Treatment resistant anxiety disorders: Resolving impasses to symptom remission* (pp. 199–231). New York: Routledge/ Taylor & Francis Group.

Westra, H. A., & Arkowitz, H. (2011). Introduction to the Special Series: Integrating motivational interviewing with cognitive behavioral therapy for a range of mental health problems. *Cognitive and Behavioral Practice, 18,* 1–4.

Westra, H. A., & Aviram, A. (2015). Integrating motivational interviewing into the treatment of anxiety. In H. Arkowitz, W. R. Miller, & S. Rollnick (Eds.), *Motivational interviewing in the treatment of psychological problems* (2nd ed., pp. 83–109). New York: Guilford Press.

Westra, H. A., & Dozois, D. J. A. (2006). Preparing clients for cognitive-behavioral therapy: A randomized pilot study of motivational interviewing for anxiety. *Cognitive Therapy and Research, 30,* 481–498.

Whaley, A. L., & Davis, K. E. (2007). Cultural competence and evidence-based practice in mental health services: A complementary perspective. *American Psychologist, 62,* 563–574.

Wharton, A. S. (1993). The affective consequences of service work: Managing emotions on the job. *Work and Occupations, 20,* 205–232.

White, M. (2007). *Maps of narrative practice.* New York: Norton.

White Kress, V., Eriksen, K., Rayle, A., & Ford, S. (2005). The *DSM-IV TR* and culture: Considerations for counselors. *Journal of Counseling & Development, 83,* 97–104.

Wickman, S. A., & Campbell, C. (2003). An analysis of how Carl Rogers enacted client-centered conversation with Gloria. *Journal of Counseling & Development, 81,* 178–184.

Wiederhold, B. K., & Wiederhold, M. D. (2008). Virtual reality for posttraumatic stress disorder and stress inoculation training. *CyberTherapy and Rehabilitation, 1*(1), 23–35.

Wiederhold, M. D., Salva, A. M., Sotomayor, T., Coiro, C., & Wiederhold, B. K. (2009). Next generation stress inoculation training for life saving skills using prosthetics. *Annual Review of CyberTherapy and Telemedicine, 7,* 116–121.

Williams, A. L., Selwyn, P. A., Liberti, L., Molde, S., Njike, V. Y., Mccorkle, R., ... Katz, D. L.. (2005). A randomized controlled trial of meditation and massage effects on quality of life in people with late-stage disease: A pilot study. *Journal of Palliative Medicine, 8*(5), 939–952.

Williams, D. R., & Sternthal, M. J. (2007). Spirituality, religion, and health: Evidence and research directions. *Medical Journal of Australia, 186,* S47–S60.

Williams, M. T., Malcoun, E., Sawyer, B. A., Davis, D. M., Noun, L. B., & Bruce, S. L. (2014). Cultural adaptations of prolonged exposure therapy for treatment and prevention of Posttraumatic Stress Disorder in African Americans. *Behavioral Sciences, 4,* 102–124.

Wilson, T., Baker, S. E., Freeman, M. R., Garbrecht, M. R., Ragsdale, F. R., Wilson, D. A., & Malone, C. (2013). Relaxation breathing improves human glycemic response. *The Journal of Alternative and Complementary Medicine, 19*(7), 633–636.

Winnicott, D. W. (1958). *The maturational processes and the facilitating environment.* New York: International Universities.

Wise, E. H., Hersh, M. A., & Gibson, C. M. (2012). Ethics, self-care and well-being for psychologists:

Reenvisioning the stress-distress continuum. *Professional Psychology: Research and Practice, 43*, 487–494.

Wisniewski, L., & Kelly, E. (2003). The application of dialectical behavioral therapy to the treatment of eating disorders. *Cognitive and Behavioral Practice, 10*, 131–138.

Wisniewski, L., Safer, D., & Chen, E. (2007). Dialectical behavior therapy and eating disorders. In L. A. Dimeff, & K. Koerner (Eds.), *Dialectical behavior therapy in clinical practice: Applications across disorders and settings* (pp. 174–221). New York: Guilford Press.

Witkiewitz, K., & Bowen, S. (2010). Depression, craving, and substance use following a randomized trial of mindfulness-based relapse prevention. *Journal of Consulting and Clinical Psychology, 78*, 362–374.

Witkiewitz, K., & Marlatt, G. A. (2004). Relapse prevention for alcohol and drug problems: That was Zen, this is Tao. *American Psychologist, 59*, 224–235.

Witkiewitz, K., Marlatt, G. A., & Walker, D. (2005). Mindfulness-based relapse prevention for alcohol and substance use disorders. *Journal of Cognitive Psychotherapy, 19*(3), 211–228.

Wolf, M. S., Davis, T. C., Osborn, C. Y., Skripkauskas, S., Bennett, C. L., & Makoul, G. (2007). Literacy, self-efficacy, and HIV medication adherence. *Patient Education and Counseling, 65*(2), 253–260.

Wolitzky, D. L. (2011). Contemporary Freudian psychoanalytic psychotherapy. In S. B. Messer & A. S. Gurman (Eds.), *Essential psychotherapies: Theory and practice* (3rd ed., pp. 33–71). New York: Guilford Press.

Wolitzky-Taylor, K. B., Horowitz, J. D., Powers, M. B., & Telch, M. J. (2008). Psychological approaches in the treatment of specific phobias: A meta-analysis. *Clinical Psychology Review, 28*, 1021–1037.

Wollburg, E., & Braukhaus, C. (2010). Goal setting in psychotherapy: The relevance of approach and avoidance goals for treatment outcome. *Psychotherapy Research, 20*, 488–494.

Wolowitz, D., & Papelian, J. (2007, Spring). Minor secrets, major headaches: Psychotherapeutic confidentiality after Berg. *Bar Journal* [publication of the New Hampshire Bar Association], *48*(1), 24–28. Retrieved from http://www.nhbar.org/publications/display-journal-issue.asp?id=359

Wolpe, J. (1958). *Psychotherapy by reciprocal inhibition.* Stanford, CA: Stanford University Press.

Wolpe, J. (1990). *The practice of behavior therapy* (4th ed.). New York: Pergamon.

Wong, P. T. P., & Wong, L. C. (Eds.). (2006). *Handbook of multicultural perspectives on stress and coping.* New York: Springer.

Wongtongkam, N., Ward, P. R., Day, A., & Winefield, A. H. (2014). A trial of mindfulness meditation to reduce anger and violence in Thai youth. *International Journal of Mental Health and Addiction, 12*(2), 169–180.

Wood, D. P., Wiederhold, B. K., & Spira, J. (2010). Lessons learned from 350 virtual-reality sessions with warriors diagnosed with combat-related posttraumatic stress disorder, *Cyberpsychology, Behavior, and Social Networking, 13*, 3–11.

Wood, J. V., Perunovic, W. Q. E., & Lee, J. W. (2009). Positive self-statements: Power for some, peril for others. *Psychological Science, 20*(7), 860–866.

Worthington Jr., E. L., Hook, J. N., Davis, D. E., & McDaniel, M. A. (2011). Religion and spirituality. In J. C. Norcross (Ed.), *Relationships that work* (2nd ed.). New York: Oxford University Press.

Worthington, R. L., Soth-McNett, A. M., & Moreno, M. V. (2007). Multicultural counseling competencies research: A 20-year content analysis. *Journal of Counseling Psychology, 54*, 351–361.

Xu, J., Vik, A., Groote, I. R., Lagopoulos, J., Holen, A., Ellingsen, Ø., … Davanger, S. (2014). Nondirective meditation activates default mode network and areas associated with memory retrieval and emotional processing. *Frontiers in Human Neuroscience, 8*(86), 1–10.

Yager, J. (2001). E-mail as a therapeutic adjunct in the outpatient treatment of anorexia nervosa: Illustrative case material and discussion of the issues. *The International Journal of Eating Disorders, 29*, 125–138.

Yakovenko, I., Quigley, L., Hemmelgarn, B. R., Hodgins, D. C., & Ronksley, P. (2015). The efficacy of motivational interviewing for disordered gambling: Systematic review and meta-analysis. *Addictive Behaviors, 43*, 72–82.

Yalom, I. D. (2009). *Staring at the sun: Overcoming the terror of death.* San Francisco, CA: Jossey Bass.

Yates, A. J. (1975). *Theory and practice in behavior therapy* (pp. 152–182). New York: Wiley.

Yip, Y. B., Sit, J. W., Fung, K. K. Y., Wong, D. Y. S., Chong, S. Y. C., Chung, L. H., & Ng, T. P. (2007). Impact of an arthritis self-management programme with an added exercise component for osteoathritic knee sufferers on improving pain, functional outcomes, and use of health care services: An experimental study. *Patient Education and Counseling, 65*(1), 113–121.

Yoman, J. (2008). A primer on functional analysis. *Cognitive and Behavioral Practice, 15*, 325–340.

Young, A., & Flower, L. (2001). Patients as partners: Patients as problem-solvers. *Health Communication, 14,* 69–97.

Young, J. E., Weinberger, A., & Beck, A. T. (2001). Depression. In D. H. Barlow (Ed.), *Clinical handbook of psychological disorders: A step-by-step treatment manual* (3rd ed.). New York: Guilford Press.

Young, J. E., & Brown, G. (2001). *Young schema questionnaire*: Special edition. New York: Schema Therapy Institute.

Young, J. E., Klosko, J. S., & Weishaar, M. E. (2003). *Schema therapy: A practitioner's guide.* New York: Guilford Press.

Young, J. E., Rych, J. I., Weinberger, A. D., & Beck, A. T. (2014). Cognitive therapy for depression. In D. H. Barlow (Ed.), *Clinical handbook of psychological disorders* (5th ed., pp. 275–331). New York: Guilford Press.

Young, M. (2013). *Learning the art of helping* (5th ed.). Upper Saddle River, NJ: Pearson Education.

Younggren, J. N., & Harris, E. A. (2008). Can you keep a secret? Confidentiality in psychotherapy. *Journal of Clinical Psychology: In Session, 64,* 589–600.

Zahn, M. R., & Zahn B. S. (2007). Mature adults: Working with the depressed aging patients. In T. Ronen & A. Freeman (Eds.), *Cognitive behavior therapy in clinical social work practice.* New York: Springer.

Zalaquett, C. P., Fuerth, K. M., Stein, C., Ivey, A. E., & Ivey, M. B. (2008). Reframing the DSM-IV-TR from a multicultural/social justice perspective. *Journal of Counseling & Development, 86,* 364–371.

Zanarini, M., Frankenburg, F., & Vujanovic, A. (2002). The interrater and test-retest reliability of the revised diagnostic interview for borderlines (DIB-R). *Journal of Personality Disorders, 16,* 270–276.

Zane, N., Hall, G. C., Sue, S., Young, K., & Nunez, J. (2004). Research on psychotherapy with culturally diverse populations. In M. J. Lambert (Ed.), *Handbook of psychotherapy and behavior change* (5th ed., pp. 767–804). New York: Wiley.

Zayfert, C. & Becker, C. B. (2007). *Cognitive-behavioral therapy for PTSD: A case formulation approach.* New York: Guilford Press.

Zoellner, L. A., Abramowitz, J. S., & Moore, S. A. (2003). Flooding. In W. O'Donohue, J. E. Fisher, & S. C. Hayes (Eds.), *Cognitive behavior therapy: Applying empirically supported techniques in your practice* (pp. 160–166). Hoboken, NJ: Wiley.

Zoellner, L. A., Abramowitz, J. S., Moore, S. A., & Slagle, D. M. (2009). Flooding. In W. O'Donohue & J. E. Fisher (Eds.), *General principles and empirically supported techniques of cognitive behavior therapy* (pp. 300–308). Hoboken, NJ: Wiley.

Zoogman, S., Goldberg, S. B., Hoyt, W. T., & Miller, L. (2014). Mindfulness interventions with youth: A meta-analysis. *Mindfulness, 6*(2), 290–302.

Zuckerman E. (2010). *Clinician's thesaurus* (7th ed.). New York: Guilford Press.

Zuckoff, A., Swartz, H. A., & Grote, N. K. (2015). Motivational interviewing as a prelude to psychotherapy of depressed women. In H. Arkowitz, W. R. Miller, & S. Rollnick (Eds.), *Motivational interviewing in the treatment of psychological problems* (2nd ed., pp. 137–169). New York: Guilford Press.

Zur, O. (2009). Psychotherapist self-disclosure and transparency in the Internet age. *Professional Psychology: Research and Practice, 40,* 22–26.

Zur, O., Williams, M. H., Lehavot, K., & Knapp, S. (2009). Psychotherapist self-disclosure and transparency in the internet age. *Professional Psychology, 40,* 22–30.

Zvolensky, M. J., Bernstein, A., & Vujanovic, A. A. (Eds.). (2011). *Distress tolerance: Theory, research, and clinical applications.* New York: Guilford Press.

Name Index

A

Aan Het Rot, M., 542
Abeles, N., 408
Abenavoli, R. M., 483
Abney-Cunningham, G., 25
Abramowitz, J. S., 494, 495, 496, 497, 507, 512, 513, 522, 523
Abrego, P. J., 79, 160, 162
Abudabbeh, N., 408
Acheson, D. T., 509, 516
Acierno, R., 521
Adams, J. R., 38, 325
Adams, N., 254
Adelman, A., 43
Adler, N. E., 430
Aguilera, A., 436, 537
Ahearn, E., 484
Aikens, K. A., 483
Ainsworth, M., 180
Akutsu, P. D., 324
Albano, A. M., 198
Albert, D. B., 521
Albert, S., 440
Alberts, H. J., 483
Alcaine, O., 480
Aldarondo, E., 407
Alegria, M., 44, 407
Alexan, C. M., 407
Alexopoulos, G. S., 380, 408, 440
Alferi, S. M., 443
Alghazo, R., 59, 71
Alleyne-Green, B., 407
Almeida, R., 11
Alonzo, A., 558
Alvarez-Lopez, M. J., 474

Amarasinghe, M., 265
Amato Zech, N. A., 539
Amlo, S., 94
Amrhein, P. C., 25, 345, 346, 363, 364, 367, 484
Anda, R. F., 429, 520
Anderson, C. S., 551
Anderson, H., 52, 354
Anderson, J. K., 529
Anderson, K. M., 184
Anderson, P. L., 522
Anderson, S. J., 440
Anderson, T., 253
Andersson, G., 341
Andreu-Mateu, S., 522
Andrews, A. A., 316
Andrews, H., 52
Angold, A., 520
Anker, M. G., 93, 99, 100, 280, 308
Anthenelli, R. M., 338
Antoni, M. H., 443
Antonuccio, D. O., 317
Antony, M. A., 340
Antony, M. M., 186, 198
Apodaca, T. R., 345, 360, 362
Aponte, H. J., 39
Appelbaum, P., 199
Appleby, G. A., 182
Arantes, A. C., 483
Arch, J. J., 516
Arcury, T. A., 558
Arden, J., 107, 108, 179
Areán, P. A., 16, 19, 407, 440, 441
Arias, B., 11, 12
Arkowitz, H., 337, 338, 339, 344, 345, 346

Armer, J. M., 483
Armstrong, C. M., 522
Arnold, D. H., 319
Arnow, B., 77
Arntz, A., 400
Arntz, D. L., 22
Arredondo, P., 54
Artman, L., 131
Asay, P. A., 154
Asmundson, G. J., 380
Astin, J., 483
Atkins, D. C., 316, 413
Aubry, T., 26
Austin, A., 408
Austin, C. Y., 552
Austin, S. B., 87
Avey, J., 54, 55
Aviram, A., 340, 359, 378
Ayalon, L., 440
Ayçiçegi, A., 306
Ayub, M., 408
Azocar, F., 407, 408

B

Baams, L., 430
Baase, C. M., 483
Babayan, T., 521
Babcock, J. C., 406
Babuscio, T. A., 63
Bach, P. A., 480
Bachler, E., 88
Bachmann, M. S., 542
Backscheider, A. G., 521
Badali, P., 483
Baer, D. M., 189

June, J. D., 522
Jurkovic, G. J., 386
Jyothi, C., 542

K

Kabat-Zinn, J., 7, 134, 413, 475, 479, 480
Kadera, S. W., 316
Kaerpov, I., 440
Kahler, C. W., 286
Kahn, A. P., 425
Kahn, M., 82, 94, 95
Kahneman, D., 10
Kaholokula, J. K., 177, 178, 186, 188, 189, 190, 191, 192, 193, 219, 225, 226, 228, 282, 285, 288
Kalibatseva, Z., 44
Kalichman, M. O., 386
Kalichman, S. C., 386
Kaliman, P., 474
Kanellopoulos, D., 380, 408, 440
Kanfer, F. H., 550
Kantor, J. R., 189
Kantrowitz, R. E., 56
Kapetanovic, S., 441
Kaplan, D. M., 41, 70, 253
Kaplan, K., 60
Kapuscinski, A. N., 432
Karlin, B. E., 438
Karls, J. M., 182, 183, 205
Karnieli-Miller, O., 268
Karno, M. P., 140, 345, 361
Karoly, P., 534
Kasckow, J., 440
Kasser, T., 39
Katon, W., 441
Katz, D. A., 483
Katz, D. L., 483
Kauer, S. D., 539
Kavanagh, K., 337
Kayser, D. N., 337
Kazdin, A. E., 24, 520
Kazura, A. N., 560
Keeler, G., 520
Keeney, P. A., 284
Kehl, K. A., 529
Kehle-Forbes, S. M., 519, 521
Kelley, S. D., 20
Kelly, B. L., 311

Kelly, E. W., 27, 41
Kelly, P. J., 538, 560
Kelly, S. M., 321, 408
Kelson, M., 345
Keltner, D., 80
Kemp, R., 338
Kemp, S., 224
Kendjelic, E. M., 310, 311
Kenney, K. R., 48, 53
Kenney, M. E., 48, 53
Kern, U., 461
Kerr, C. E., 473, 474
Kersey, E., 54, 55
Kessler, R. C., 323
Khor, A., 539
Kienast, T., 400
Kier, F. J., 432
Kiesler, D., 79
Kilanowski, C. K., 542
Kilbourn, K. M., 443
Killcross, S., 541
Kilmer, R. P., 386
Kim, B. S. K., 154
Kim, D., 308
Kim, J. S., 342, 343, 350
Kim, K., 44
Kim, Y., 555
Kimpara, S., 306, 307, 312, 315, 337, 339, 340, 341
Kindsvatter, A., 268
Kingdon, D., 408
Kingsley, M., 344
Kinoshita, L. M., 408
Kiosses, D. N., 440
Kircanski, K., 495, 496, 497, 500, 515, 516, 517
Kiresuk, T. J., 275, 283, 288
Kirkley, S. M., 41
Kirkpatrick, K. L., 315
Kirschenbaum, H., 79
Kisbu-Sakarya, Y., 345, 346, 360
Kitzman, H., 475
Kivlahan, D. R., 16, 19
Kiyonaga, A., 450
Kizakevich, P. N., 450
Klappheck, M. A., 257
Klass, E. S., 546
Klauer, T., 554
Kleber, R. J., 23

Klein, A. A., 284
Klein, D., 77
Klein, G., 10
Klein, K. J., 24
Klein, M. H., 87
Kleinman, A., 197
Kliem, S., 440
Kloosterman, P. H., 198
Klosko, J. S., 398, 400
Knapp, M., 108, 109, 115, 116
Knapp, S., 71, 149, 151, 152, 432
Knekt, P., 342, 344
Knight, A. P., 24
Knight, D. W., 60
Knight, J. M., 483
Knipscheer, J. W., 23
Knoll, N., 558
Knox, K. L., 43
Kocet, M. M., 42
Kocovski, N. L., 546
Koenen, K., 520
Koenig, H. G., 431, 432
Koerner, K., 24, 267, 414
Kofoed, L. L., 265
Kohut, H., 81, 82, 86, 94
Kok, R. B., 26
Kolden, G. G., 87
Kolden, G. G., 87
Kong, J., 474
Koocher, G. P., 17, 58, 64
Kopta, S. M., 303, 316
Korman, H., 343, 347, 348, 349, 350, 355
Korslund, K. E., 493
Kort, J., 17, 43
Kosfelder, J., 257, 440
Kosic, A., 534
Kosmitzki, C., 180
Kost-Smith, L. E., 547
Kottler, J. A., 37
Koufopoulos, J., 151
Koven, L., 199, 216
Kozak, A. T., 539
Kozak, M. J., 495
Kraemer, H., 381
Kramer, G. M., 63, 64
Krantweiss, A. R., 514
Krasner, M. S., 483
Kratt, P., 555
Kraus, M. W., 80

Subject Index

Unintentional racism, 52–53, 54
Unique personhood, 324
Utilization, of resistance, in SFT, 348–349

Validating responses, 82–85
Validation
    of client's experience, empathy and, 81–85
    cultural empathy and, 85
    in dialectical behavior therapy, 27, 82–85
    invalidating environments, 82
    Learning Activity, 84
    six levels of, 83–85
Validity
    content, 185
    in evidence-based assessment, 185
    incremental, 185
Values
    conflicting, between clients and helpers, 40–42, 70
    cultural, and confidentiality, 61–62
    cultural self-awareness, 222–223
    defined, 39
    ethical, of helpers, 56–57
    ethical bracketing of, 42
    personal, 39, 42
Values-based practice
    commitment to, 39–45
    guiding principles of, 40
    LGBTQ clients and, 42–44
    with other cultural groups, 44–45
    race and, 44

summary of, 45
Verbal communication, nonverbal behavior and, 108
Veterans, exposure therapy and, 521–522
Victim blaming, avoiding, 52–53
Video teleconferencing (VTC), 64
Violence
    risk assessment for, 199–200
    to self, 200–201
Virtual reality exposure therapy (VRET), 508–509, 510, 522
Vision of client improvement, 252
Visitor-type relationships, 349, 353

Walden v. Centers for Disease Control and Prevention, 41
Ward v. Wilbanks et al., 42
Warmth, 89
Wise mind, 480
Working alliance, 90–93
    client feedback and, 90
    defined, 76
    empirical support for, 90
    helper skills and, 91
    Learning Activity, 91
    parts of, 90
    trust in, 91
Worldview, 54

Youth Outcome Questionnaire (YOQ), 280

Zen, 7